Laurie Brady

CURRICULUM DEVELOPMENT

CURRICULUM DEVELOPMENT
THEORY INTO PRACTICE

Fourth Edition

Daniel Tanner
Rutgers University

Laurel Tanner
Temple University

Upper Saddle River, New Jersey
Columbus, Ohio

Library of Congress Cataloging-in-Publication Data

Tanner, Daniel.
    Curriculum development: theory into practice / Daniel Tanner, Laurel Tanner.—4th ed.
        p.   cm.
    Includes bibliographical references and index.
    ISBN 0-13-086473-0
    1. Education—United States—Curricula—History.   2. Curriculum planning—United States.
    I. Tanner, Laurel.   II. Title.
LB1570.T23 2007
375'.001—dc22

2005026920

Vice President and Executive Publisher: Jeffery W. Johnston
Executive Editor: Debra A. Stollenwerk
Assistant Development Editor: Elisa Rogers
Production Editor: Alexandrina Benedicto Wolf
Production Coordination and Text Design: Thistle Hill Publishing Services, LLC
Design Coordinator: Diane Lorenzo
Cover Designer: Jeff Vanki
Production Manager: Susan W. Hannahs
Senior Marketing Manager: Darcy Betts Prybella
Marketing Coordinator: Bryan Mounts

This book was set in Garamond by Integra Software Services. It was printed and bound by
Hamilton Printing Company. The cover was printed by Phoenix Color Corp.

Pearson Prentice Hall™ is a trademark of Pearson Education, Inc.
Pearson® is a registered trademark of Pearson plc
Prentice Hall® is a registered trademark of Pearson Education, Inc.
Merrill® is a registered trademark of Pearson Education, Inc.

Pearson Education Ltd.
Pearson Education Singapore Pte. Ltd.
Pearson Education Canada, Ltd.
Pearson Education—Japan

Pearson Education Australia Pty. Limited
Pearson Education North Asia Ltd.
Pearson Educación de Mexico, S.A. de C.V.
Pearson Education Malaysia Pte. Ltd.

10 9 8 7 6 5 4 3 2
ISBN: 0-13-086473-0

For Lloyd C. Chilton

Addressing the problem of creating a "rational *curriculum,*" Herbert Spencer (1860) wrote, "in education, then, this is the question of questions." Indeed, the question of questions is as old as civilization itself. But it was Spencer who ushered in the modern era for education when he held that, "To prepare us for complete living is the function which education has to discharge." Yet not until the early decades of the twentieth century did curriculum making emerge fully as a field of specialized university study. The harbinger for this development was the idea of progress, which drove the progressive-humanitarian movement in education and society.

We have witnessed many new developments and continued controversies concerning the curriculum since the publication of the third edition of *Curriculum Development: Theory into Practice.* Indeed, since the publication of the first edition, we have seen a series of demands on both the curriculum and the schools. In successive periods, the call has been for "change," then "innovation," then "restructuring" and, most recently, "reform." At first glance, it might appear that these successive demands were merely repetitive slogans, essentially of the same ilk, seemingly in validation of Mark Twain's Law of Periodical Repetition and the notion that history repeats itself. But there are some significant differences attached to these demands. In some cases, the matter was simply one of adopting certain fads and fashions, only to discard them eventually for new ones. However, restructuring and reform have been accompanied by establishing special-interest schools while avoiding the need to strengthen and renew our unitary school structure and commitment to serve all children in the cosmopolitan school with a comprehensive curriculum. The concept of reform also carries the connotation of correction of faults (or of evils and abuses, as in politics). Then there is the dangerous penchant for crying "crisis" in promoting drastic measures for reform.

The most powerful force in life is renewal. Throughout this text we have endeavored to address the ideas, developments, problems, and issues in the curriculum field from the perspective of renewal. And the means to renewal—the path to progress—lies with problem solutions. In examining or proposing a prescription for reform, the approach typically taken begins with objectives. But we cannot really know the objectives until the problem is identified and defined. In effect, one must start not with objectives, but with a problem situation from which the problem(s) must be defined and diagnosed, drawing upon the best available evidence from the knowledge base of the relevant field.

The fourth edition of *Curriculum Development* reveals how the curriculum field has been built upon a vast and rich body of knowledge, and how progress is made through the uses of the best available evidence rather than following the dominant sociopolitical tide or fashion of the times and repeating the mistakes of the past.

This edition is divided into four parts. Part I focuses on the emergence and transformation of the school curriculum to serve the democratic prospect, tracing how American educational leaders adapted and transformed European ideas in building a uniquely unitary system of education and a unique outlook on curriculum. Turning points are identified leading to the development of the modern curriculum.

Part II examines changing conceptions of curriculum, revealing how traditional concepts such as subject matter and course of study came to be rejected in favor of seeing curriculum as a process for transforming knowledge into the working power of intelligence. The concept of the hidden curriculum, which bears a negative and even deleterious meaning, is replaced by the *collateral* curriculum through which so many enduring interests are developed as the teacher teaches by indirection as well as by direction. Chapter 6 presents the development of the curriculum paradigm over the course of the twentieth century beginning with John Dewey's *Sources of a Science of Education.* The curriculum paradigm begins with the identification and examination of a problem situation. Through the application of the curriculum paradigm, educators have a compass for determining why certain movements succeed while others fail (predictably). In essence, if a movement is to succeed, the structure and function of the curriculum must be in harmony with the nature and needs of the learner and with the highest, widest, and deepest principles of American democracy. This is not a vague or impractical ideal, but one that is manifest by means of educational opportunity and access to curriculum in every dimension. Chapters 7 and 8 explore the sources and forces for curriculum renewal—society, the learner, and the world of knowledge—in connection with the curriculum paradigm. Chapter 9 examines and evaluates the conflicting educational theories through which ideological differences and disputations are drawn and impact virtually every substantive decision affecting curricular ends and means.

Part III is centered on curriculum design, development, and evaluation. Drawing from the biological principle that structure determines function, or the architectural principle that form follows function, the chapters point to the means for taking a macro-approach in place of the penchant to pursue a micro- or segmental approach in addressing the structure and function of the school and college curriculum. The idea and practice of general education are treated fully in chapters 10 and 11. The emergence of the problem-focused, integrated core curriculum is contrasted with the core curriculum composed of segmental or disjointed subjects. The idea of general education for building unity through diversity is contrasted with the conflict of cultures and special interests that impact contemporary life. Various curriculum designs are presented, ranging from the disciplinary design for specialized knowledge to correlation, lamination, fusion, broad fields, combined fields, and the integrated, problem-focused core curriculum for general education. The construction and function of units of work are given special attention in curriculum building. The need for creating an articulated curriculum is addressed by revealing how the curriculum must meet the criteria of scope, sequence and balance.

Chapter 12 provides an in-depth assessment of the major national proposals and legislation for curriculum reform and renewal over the course of the past century, encompassing their impact for progress along with setbacks for retrenchment. Nationalizing influences are examined, including the emergence of the contemporary high-stakes testing pandemic, which has led to the widespread practice of teaching-to-the-test with emphasis given to established-convergent learning as opposed to emergent learning. Chapter 13 attacks the problems of youth who do not complete a higher education for a gainful career. Chapter 14 is devoted to the problems of interpreting educational research in terms of making constructive applications

of research findings to educational policy and practice. Special attention is given to detecting and preventing research bias and exposing the widespread practices of proving the project and amassing one-sided data to fit a political agenda. The latter research has been fashioned to undermine (unsuccessfully) the belief in education on the part of the public—a belief that is fundamental to what may be called the American Creed. The longstanding dualism and conflict between the adherents of qualitative and quantitative research is resolved by embracing the principle that all good research is governed conceptually and methodologically by ideas and practices of the highest possible quality.

This principle carries through part IV of the text, which makes the case for the teacher, supervisor and administrator as being intelligent consumers of research. Part IV is devoted to the roles of professional educators at every level—school, district, state and federal—in curriculum development, and their responsibility to understand and harness the forces and sources for school improvement. Throughout the text, curriculum development is treated as a problem-solving process, and the need for using the best available evidence in the process of determining practice and making progress is emphasized. We call special attention to a cross-reference at the end of selected chapters in which the reader is referred to the Best Practices Checklist at the end of the book. The checklist may be used to determine whether a school is operating at the imitative-maintenance level, the mediative-adaptive level, or the generative-creative level. Through the use of the criteria in the Best Practices Checklist, teachers and administrators will be able to effect needed measures for substantive school improvement.

Each chapter is followed by a list of problems for investigation and discussion—not for the purpose of reviewing the treatment of each chapter, but to extend the student's thinking on the implications of the ideas and issues that have bearings for professional practice.

Acknowledgments

We appreciate those whose interest and supporting ideas have contributed to this edition and earlier editions. Our wide-ranging discussions with the late Ralph W. Tyler were invaluable in testing our ideas and gaining insight on the modern evolution of the curriculum field. Others who have contributed to our thinking and who have provided helpful suggestions deserve acknowledgement: Lynn M. Burlbaw, Dennis C. Buss, Joseph J. Chambliss, Cheryl J. Craig, Larry Cuban, Linda Darling-Hammond, Angela S. Fanelli, Barry J. Galasso, James C. Hayden, Peter S. Hlebowitsh, Virgil M. Johnson, Craig B. Kridel, Marcella Kysilka, Frances Schoonmaker, Edmund C. Short, William Shubert, Lauren A. Sosniak, and Cui Yunhuo.

We are also grateful to the following reviewers of this edition: Judith A. Bazler, Monmouth University; India Broyles, University of Southern Maine; Dennis C. Buss, Rider University; Donna M. Carney, Edinboro University of Pennsylvania; Elizabeth Davenport, Florida A&M University; Leena Furtado, California State University, Dominguez Hills; James G. Henderson, Kent State University; and Robert C. Morris, State University of West Georgia.

Over the years, grants from the Rutgers Research Foundation aided with the investigation of several topics related to this and earlier editions. The resources and staff of the Alexander Library of Rutgers University were invaluable in this project and in our work on each of the earlier editions. Appreciation is extended to Marion Ann Keller, who did the word processing with care and cheer. We are grateful to Debra A. Stollenwerk, Executive Editor at Prentice Hall, who supported both this edition and the third edition, and made invaluable suggestions along the way. Lloyd C. Chilton, former Executive Editor at Macmillan, gave his full support for the first two editions, and graciously and generously offered invaluable guidance and assistance whenever called upon throughout the development of all four editions.

Daniel Tanner
Laurel Tanner

CONTENTS

Chapter 6	A PARADIGM FOR THE CURRICULUM FIELD: COMPASS FOR CURRICULUM RENEWAL	124

Chapter 7	SOURCES AND FORCES FOR CURRICULUM RENEWAL: SOCIETY AND THE WORLD OF KNOWLEDGE	148

Chapter 11 DETERMINING THE STRUCTURE OF THE CURRICULUM: DESIGN FOR SYNTHESIS   251

Chapter 12 PROPOSALS FOR REFORM: CURRICULAR PRIORITIES AND POLARITIES   279

Chapter 15   WHO MAKES THE CURRICULUM?   385

Chapter 16   CURRICULUM IMPROVEMENT: ROLE OF THE TEACHER   405

PART I

PERSPECTIVES AND PROSPECTS

Where anything is growing, one former
is worth a thousand reformers.

— Horace Mann

CHAPTER 1

BEGINNINGS
FROM IDEALS TO REALITIES

The dynamic and exciting possibilities of schools for helping children along the road to successful lives are contained in one word: curriculum. *Success* in this context means the realization of individual potentialities and participation in constructive social relationships. The idea to keep in mind is that the curriculum is concerned with what is taught and how it is taught, in organic relationship to the learner and society. A more detailed definition of curriculum is given later, but the point here is that the conception of curriculum unifies what schools set out to be learned and ways that students can be connected with it in their own lives. The unified conception grew out of the work of John Dewey in his famous Laboratory School at the University of Chicago (1897–1904). During the twentieth century, famous theorists who were also gifted practitioners, such as Ralph Tyler (1949) and Hilda Taba (1962), constructed procedures for teachers and supervisors to follow in curriculum development that were based on Dewey's conception. Sharing an emphasis on the relationship between curriculum and instruction, their approaches came to define the essence of reliable and authentic procedures for many modern school staffs. These procedures have been refined by others, including the present authors, building on this heritage.

Whether we are developing a medical school program or an elementary school program, the principles of curriculum *and* instruction should be followed, emphasized Tyler (1986). The advice was firmly grounded in years of research and experience in working with curricular groups. But what, specifically, does relating curriculum and instruction mean as you work on the curriculum? Tyler would answer, as he did to a group of curriculum leaders: "Curriculum and instruction have to do with what children can learn, how can they learn it, how can

they be aided to continue that learning, and how we know that what we are doing is worthwhile and is a sensible way of doing it" (p. 73). Tyler's talk was given in the 1980s but there is a distinctively contemporary feel. We are always asking the same questions, or should be asking them, as we seek to improve the curriculum.

Tyler's contributions to the curriculum field were many, and to this day leaders in evaluation and measurement make use of many of his key ideas. The point of importance is that Tyler's ideas also descended from others'. "A Jeffersonian insistence on the importance of education in a democracy is his basic theme," observed a colleague about Tyler (Cronbach, 1986, p. 48), going on to note that Tyler's steps in evaluation follow Dewey's steps in thinking. Tyler's work, like that of other curriculum theorists and practitioners, flows out of curriculum developments that began with the founding of our public school system and extends to the present. We are speaking of nothing less than the development of our professional field.

The pillars of the curriculum field were real people involved in real events. Their failed as well as successful efforts are a kind of collective biography, the flesh-and-blood story of a professional field. It is truly fascinating because it is our own story. Better yet, it can be useful to curriculum developers: teachers, supervisors, and administrators. It helps us build on the successes and avoid the failures. It really is impossible, we believe, to separate the development of the field from its guiding principles. By following principles worked out by those who came before us and by applying best practices (approaches generally agreed upon by experts in the field), we gain and maintain our professional identity. The first three chapters of this book are a kind of professional biography. As you will see, from the earliest days of American nationhood, there are triumphs and there are failures, which, in the biography of a person, might be called missteps.

The Battle to Improve and Democratize the Curriculum

We begin with the biggest triumph to this day: the establishment of a publicly supported, publicly controlled secular school system. This institution opened up enormous opportunity for the realization of human possibilities through improved access to the curriculum. Of course, the curriculum would have to be worth having access to. It was a problem that came up very early, for improving the work of teachers and what was taught gave impetus to public support. The need to acquaint teachers (even those isolated from educational centers) with current educational thought was powerfully argued by Connecticut's superintendent of public instruction, Henry Barnard, and led to the publication of the *Connecticut Common School Journal,* which he edited from 1838 to 1842. It is to the everlasting credit of the leaders in the battle for state-supported and state-controlled public schools that they saw access and improvement as inseparable problems.

Much recent literature is about improving access. Yet it is what we have been about, almost from the very beginning. In the early years after the founding of the republic, access to the curriculum was denied to slaves and American Indians, often to girls as well. There has been much progress in improving access to schooling. Although the United States was the first nation to champion the cause of universal secondary education, this came about only after a long and hard struggle. As recently as 1940, almost 80 percent of adults over 25 years of age had less than 12 years of schooling. By the twenty-first century, 88 percent of adults over 25 had completed at least high school (National Center for Education Statistics [NCES], 2001).

There is no doubt that we have made progress. Today more previously excluded groups have access to the curriculum than ever before, women and minorities among them. Indeed, females have higher rates of high school completion and some college than males (NCES, p. 23).

Access to the curriculum varies stunningly in the world. In many parts of the world, females are still denied access to schooling on religious and other grounds. The United States has led the world in access to education in accord with democratic principles and the national interest (Stanley, 2001). Yet the problem of access is complicated and unfinished. For example, the practice of assigning students to separate tracks continues to deny access of lower-track students to a curriculum focused on problem solving rather than memorization (Webb, Nemer, Chizhik, & Segrue, 1998). Students not bound for college often leave high school without adequate preparation for the world of work. Truly, democracy is a work in progress.

But to return to the beginning, the task of establishing our public school system was met with seemingly insurmountable opposition.

Profiles in Courage

We owe an inestimable debt to those heroes of the early curriculum wars. They pushed forward, often in the face of great hostility, to forge the great school systems developed from 1779 to 1865. They were able to move ahead with improving teaching and introducing modern studies into the curriculum. To secure common public schools was "an unceasing struggle" (Butts & Cremin, 1953, p. 242). Most of the controversy concerned public support of schools available to all. The battle for schools took place during a time of fervent individualism and weak government. Historian Carl Kaestle tells us, "It is easy to underestimate the resistance to state school systems" (1983, p. 136).

Without the surveys on school conditions, meetings with parents and teachers and speeches in favor of state school systems—all by the leaders who seemed to be everywhere at once, in rural kitchens, town meetings, and the halls of the legislature—the public school system would have been much longer in coming. It was a battle of endurance. In some states, for every step forward there was a step backward. The leaders may have been depressed, but they did not give up. The resilience of Henry Barnard, for example, was remarkable, when the Connecticut legislature abolished his position "in an evil hour" (Monroe, 1893).

Horace Mann and Henry Barnard, executive secretaries of their state school boards, were the principal leaders in the early public school movement. (They literally gave their lives for the schools.) There were other gifted leaders, less well known, who furthered Mann's work in other parts of the country. Indeed, John Pierce of Michigan surpassed Mann by including a state university as the apex of his system of public education.

It is hard to imagine that something so familiar as a tax-supported public school was once the kind of political issue that, like abortion and gun control today, split people into battling camps. But such was the case with the public school controversy in mid-nineteenth-century America. It is not that the battle lines were distinctly drawn. Parents who needed their children's earnings joined forces with persons who thought it unfair that people without children should have their property taxed to educate other people's children. Leaders of the public school movement from upper-middle-class families joined forces with laboring classes and finally won the battle.

Jefferson's Footsteps

Actually, education policies for extending educational opportunity were right in the Jeffersonian tradition; that is, they had been enunciated by Jefferson. We are all familiar with Jefferson's words of wisdom about the relationship between education and freedom: "If a nation expects to be ignorant and free in a state of civilization," he wrote in 1816, "it expects what never was and never will be" (Lee, 1961, pp. 18–19). Jefferson's interest in public education began earlier, with the birth of our nation. In 1776, in a report to the Virginia legislature about changes in the government necessary for independence, Jefferson called for a public school system. The bill was turned down, but the idea was in the air and people later would see its wisdom.

As one might expect from the man who wrote the Declaration of Independence, Jefferson's interest in education went beyond its necessity for representative government. Educational opportunities were essential for giving each person the chance to advance to the limits of his or her powers, and thus for human happiness.

Jefferson as Educational Philosopher. Jefferson is one of our most important educational philosophers. In his discussions on education, our responsibilities as curriculum workers are remarkably evident: to develop an intelligent citizenry and to provide educational opportunities that guarantee each individual the chance for optimal development. These two goals of public education have not changed. What has changed, however, are the ways of achieving them. According to Lawrence A. Cremin, the noted educational historian, "we can portray the entire course of American educational history as the gradual realization of the Jeffersonian ideal" (1965, p. 40). Since the

founding of our public school system, this has been our charge.

Because the state's responsibility is realized through the curriculum, it follows that the course of educational history is largely (or should be) concerned with curriculum improvements aimed at Jefferson's ideal. We are speaking of nothing less than the development of the curriculum field.

It was in the Jeffersonian spirit that the common-school reformers such as Barnard, Mann, and a host of others labored. The public saw the wisdom of the policies. Much was also in the timing; the leaders who accomplished such a difficult feat of establishing public schools were on the side of history. In the words of Butts and Cremin, "the tide of democracy was running, ever more strongly in their direction" (1953, p. 185).

The Giants and What We Can Still Learn from Them

The names Jefferson, Barnard, and Mann often inspire a feeling of awe for their moral and intellectual stature. We admire them for their brilliance and leadership in shaping American political and educational traditions, and sometimes we are a little bit amazed that they were there at the right time.

The work of Jefferson, Barnard, and Mann is spectacular, so much so that we may be blinded to their specific contributions. As John Dewey, himself a giant, wrote, "there were giants in those days," and he pointed out the need to avoid "a vague indiscriminate adulation of the Founding Fathers" (Dewey, 1940, p. 3). Hero worship or, for that matter, intransigent cynicism could create indifference to what they contributed "and to what we still may learn from them."

Of the outstanding persons closely connected with the founding of the republic, Jefferson was the most concerned with public education. Benjamin Franklin could add curriculum reform to his outstanding list of achievements. Discontented with the ornamental education from the old world, Franklin emphasized the practical. His proposal for an academy, discussed later, was years ahead of its time. Although Jefferson was certainly utilitarian, and proud of it, he envisioned education in terms of the preservation of liberty. Jefferson's proposal for a common-school system in his own state is well known. Less appreciated is his Congressional report on the government of the western territory, which furnished the basic elements of the Ordinances of 1785 and 1787. As a scholar on Jefferson put it, "the Ordinances, like Jefferson himself, further wedded the democratic state to the public school" (Lee, 1961, p. 8). Thus the foundation was laid and the seeds were planted for a public education system.

But the system itself was still to be formed. Enter Mann and Barnard. Although they are seldom recognized as founding fathers, they certainly meet the criteria: They built the nation, educationally speaking, and their influence persists.

The methods used by key leaders in forging educational reform are not things dead and gone. They are ideas that continue to grow and strengthen as we go about the business of curriculum improvement, which always will be unfinished.

Laying the Groundwork (The Necessity of a Precursor)

All great reforms have one thing in common: they are the combined effort of many. No leader or educator can do anything alone. The time must be right, and the groundwork must be laid in advance; that is, others must be of similar mind to give support in common cause. And so it was with Horace Mann. In no way could he have accomplished what he did as an educational former unless preparation had been in the making. The person who did more than any other to prepare the way for Mann was James G. Carter, a teacher who after a number of years began to write on educational subjects.

James G. Carter: The Paul Revere of Curriculum.
In the 1820s, in essays that were widely circulated and reprinted and enormously influential, Carter awakened the public to the poor quality of the free schools and the need for immediate improvement if the tradition of free schools was to continue in Massachusetts. He remarked upon the ability of the settlers to see ahead and create free schools, which he attributed to the desire for equality. Massachusetts had been a model for the other New England colonies in establishing free schools, but it was no longer a model. School legislation enacted in 1789 changed all that. Under the law, towns had the power to create school districts, but under this decentralized system, local opposition to taxation for education combined with public apathy, was gradually leading to a decline in the quality of the public schools. When Carter began his reform campaign through publications in support

of public education, the point had been reached where, as Butts and Cremin noted, the public schools were "often deserted by almost everyone who could afford private education. With little state control, local districts managed schools in the interests of local economy, and in doing so, often ignored even the barest standards of instruction" (1953, p. 146).

What Had to Be Reformed

The heading for this section is somewhat deceptive. In the 1820s nearly everything was wrong with the Massachusetts public schools. If one were to ask, for example, whether there were publicly supported secondary schools, the answer would be no. As Carter pointed out in his calls to action, the Latin grammar (secondary) schools to which people had once felt a strong attachment were passing away, albeit for good reason: Their classical curriculum was unsuited to the practical needs of the changing times. However, there were no publicly supported secondary schools to take their place. Academies with modern curricular offerings were available to those who could afford the tuition, books, and board, but their advantages were far beyond the reach of most people. "What would our ancestors have thought of their posterity?" asked Carter (1824a, p. 8), with reference to those who nearly 200 years before, despite their concern with staying alive in a new settlement, provided by law for the support of secondary schools in all towns of 100 families. Private academies may have had a function but it was not a public function. The people still needed secondary schools accessible to children of all social classes.

Elementary Education

The best that could be said about the elementary school in the 1820s was that it existed, although sick and weak. Yet democracy was too much in the bones of the people of Massachusetts to give up their schools. The people were paying a price for the district system and local control of schools. Carter drew attention to two glaring costs: untrained teachers and poor textbooks. Having nothing else to fall back on, the incompetent teachers taught just as they had been taught—rote and recitation, supported by the rod. The method of teaching by question and answer made it possible for pupils to *seem* to have learned a great many important facts, but the pupils did not understand the memorized facts. They had connected the question and its answer with some outside association, and they were able to parrot passages with verbal accuracy, thus impressing and delighting those to whom the words had a correct meaning. But a more thorough examination showed their meaning for the pupil to be as much a mystery as the hocus pocus of a magician.

The relation of teacher to text was much the same as child to text. "Indeed, so superficial has the education of most instructors of common schools been," wrote Carter, "that a book is to them a new subject. The particular form and words, in which the principles of any branch of learning have been expressed, and the principles themselves, are with them identical; and if the words are varied, the principles are not recognized" (p. 63). Teachers had much influence in the selection of textbooks and, as might be expected, they preferred the same books they were taught as pupils.

But there had been enormous achievements in science, which resulted in new educational methods. The old books did not reflect the method of inductive science as a way of learning. The old methods would not help children develop knowledge from observation and experience. Granted, the books had been revised to keep pace with scientific discoveries, but they were still written to conform to traditional methods. And most primary school teachers tended to confine the curriculum to mechanical skills associated with reading, writing, and arithmetic.

Ultimately, the methods used by the teacher limited the teacher's effectiveness. One problem is of particular interest because it continues to stand in the way of access to knowledge: the failure of the classroom teacher to work with the "teacher in the text"— the author of the book. In *The District School as It Was* (1833), Warren Burton described his experience as a schoolboy in Massachusetts. The approach to teaching grammar was parsing: pupils recited the parts of speech in each line of prose or poetry. Wrote Burton,

> The fact is neither we nor the teacher entered into the writer's meaning. . . . [T]he particular sense of the passages was not examined. We could not do it perhaps, from the want of maturity of mind; the teacher did not, because he had never been accustomed to anything of the kind in his own education. And it never occurred to him that he could deviate from the track, or improve upon the methods of those who taught him (p. 41).

Carter was a giant on the educational reform scene. Although certainly not as famous as Mann or Barnard, his criticisms and proposals came early and, as we have noted, paved the way for those who followed. As a way of remedying the shortcomings in the free schools, Carter proposed that the state reassert control of education. He followed up this proposal with another, a teacher training institution to better prepare teachers and generate a badly needed feeling of professionalism among teachers. This state-supported and state-controlled institution would have an experimental school for children. Carter's argument is powerful and eloquent. "Our ancestors ventured," he said, "to do what the world has never done before, in a perfect manner, when they established free schools. Let us do what they have never so well done yet, and establish an institution for the exclusive purpose of preparing instructors for them. This is only a second part, a development or consummation of the plan of our fathers" (1826, p. 46).

The bill was defeated by one vote, but never a person to be defeated himself, Carter continued his agitation for normal schools. In 1839 his campaign bore fruit. (By then the Massachusetts Board of Education and its secretary, Horace Mann, had taken office and joined in the effort.) The public normal school—a first in the United States—opened at Lexington, Massachusetts, in July. Another soon followed at Barre. It was the culmination of the agitation he had begun more than a decade before.

How did this whistle-blower and constructive change maker accomplish so much for education? Already mentioned is publication; Carter was a teacher and a writer on public education. But he also succeeded in getting himself elected to the legislature and drew up the bill creating the Massachusetts State Board of Education. Thus he was involved in shaping the course of action on his proposals.

Common Sense Reform

There were a great number of reform movements in New England in this period. While some were intellectual movements—transcendentalism is the leading example—most were specifically directed at particular evils and made concrete proposals for reform. Abolition and women's rights and, of course, education are examples.

"Horace Mann of Massachusetts and Henry Barnard of Connecticut pioneered in the improvement of schools with an approach that could hardly have been more down-to-earth," wrote Daniel Boorstin, the historian, in his *The Americans: The National Experience* (1965, p. 44). What was their approach? In short, it was to inform the public about school conditions and make suggestions about improving the conditions. But the process was anything but short, and these two reformers asked much of themselves. Barnard traveled up and down the state gathering information about the schools. He probably conducted the first school survey in the United States. Its scope was wide, ranging from instructional procedures to school buildings. Barnard reported that 200 different books were being used in the few main subjects in the curriculum, "making confusion worse confounded" (quoted in Jenkins & Warner, 1937, p. 27). School conditions were reported in detail: "of 40 schoolhouses in a certain county, only one had any means of ventilation . . . and the average size of a school building (each housing about 30 children) was $18\frac{1}{2}$ feet long, $7\frac{1}{2}$ feet wide, and 7 feet high" (Boorstin, p. 44). Barnard and Mann made annual reports to their state boards of education. Mann's reports to the Massachusetts Board of Education (1837–1848) were especially widely read. Ever fresh and filled with the promise of the future, they are part of our curriculum legacy. Mann's observations about the relation of instructional approaches to the purposes of the public school could have been made today as a response to home schooling advocates. Mann argued that teaching children in groups is important not just for practical and financial reasons but also for social purposes. Cremin (1957) put Mann's contention beautifully: "Only in a heterogeneous group of students could the unifying and socializing goals of the common school be accomplished" (p. 16).

Besides keeping the lay public and profession acquainted with conditions, Mann and Barnard did another down-to-earth thing: they founded institutions. Teacher education and inservice education began in their administrations. Barnard's teachers institutes were probably the first organized vehicles for continuing professional development of teachers.

The reform movement was cosmopolitan. "The currents of reform did not seep below the Mason-Dixon line," wrote Commager, "but they flowed across the Atlantic like some gulf stream" (1960, p. 15). Mann and Barnard traveled to Europe so as to avail the public in their states with the latest and best educational practices. The trips were always made at their own expense.

A Continuing Threat: A Separate Curriculum for Poor Children

Throughout the nineteenth century the elementary school curriculum would expand. Starting with the so-called Three Rs, curricular offerings would multi-

ply and differentiate. Reading, for example, was subdivided into grammar, declamation, and literature. Increasing social demands on individuals' skills led to an increase in the importance of writing although most of the emphasis was on penmanship and spelling. Additions to the elementary curriculum during this period included geography, history, nature study, and the fine and industrial arts. Toward the end of the century, cooking for girls and industrial arts for boys (for pedagogical rather than vocational reasons) began to come into the curriculum. Music and drawing gained admission, although they were often regarded by the public as fads and frills. Every new subject was introduced for a reason, and sometimes for several reasons, discussed later. The point is that there was development and there was progress. Curriculum development was a reality.

However, there was a point of crisis with implications for today: a situation in the curriculum that we are not entirely done with. In the 1820s the schools were at a crossroads. There would be either a common (public) school system with a common curriculum for rich or poor alike or a special system for poor children. There was danger that the free schools might degenerate into, as Carter put it, "mechanized seminaries," such as those seen in Europe, for educating the poor, while private institutions would provide an improved curriculum for the well-to-do (1824b, p. 20). In fact, this was already happening in the cities. What was beginning to take shape was the continuing conflict between the pursuit of efficiency and having the best for all the children of all the people.

The Pursuit of Efficiency

Monitorial Instruction

The instructional approach that Carter feared would destroy the democratizing function of the school was already here. The monitorial or Lancastrian system was a plan for educating poor children. It was imported from London and involved one teacher teaching a packaged lesson to some pupils called monitors who, in turn, taught others. In London, Joseph Lancaster's huge school, with more than a thousand pupils, literally taught itself under the general supervision of one master. The plan excited wide interest, and such schools were established throughout London. The excitement quickly spread to visitors. In 1805, the school in London was visited by a member of the New York Free School Society and the system was adopted in the Society's schools. For a short time (1815–1830) the method was in vogue, operating in American cities before the fight for state-supported schools open to the children of rich and poor alike was won.

Monitorial instruction competed with another new method of instruction, also imported from Europe. The Pestalozzian method was based on the idea that knowledge is developed from observation and experience. Naturally, monitorial instruction did not last long in competition. Yet what Carter called "mechanized seminaries" may still be found whenever and wherever people equate efficiency and economy with instruction.

Individuals of power may support an innovation without the power of knowledge. They may succeed in committing others to the idea, at least for a while. In 1818, Governor DeWitt Clinton of New York did just that, devoting his eloquence to the support of monitorial instruction.

> I can confidently recommend it as an invaluable improvement, which, by a wonderful combination of economy in expense, and rapidity of instruction, has created a new era in education. The system operates with the same efficiency in education as labor-saving machinery does in the useful arts (cited in Wickersham, 1886, p. 283).

Limitations of a Mechanical View of Education

Joseph Lancaster had a limited and mechanical view of education: drill. This is clear from Lancaster's explanation of what he perceived to be the advantages of his method. "Each boy can spell one hundred words in a morning. If one hundred scholars can do that two hundred mornings yearly, the following will be the total of their efforts at improvement" (Graves, 1914, p. 57). He then declared that this would result in an annual achievement of two million words spelled. He approached arithmetic from the same perspective: the number of sums done in a given period of time, not the computational skills learned through application. The point is that the monitorial system was not genuine instruction but mechanistic. Lancaster seems to have been ignorant of the psychologically based teaching method of reformers in Europe at the time. Johann Pestalozzi, for example, sought to instruct children by experience and observation. Pestalozzi's perspective was radically different from that of Lancaster, although the aim of both was

human welfare. (Pestalozzi's contributions to the curriculum are discussed shortly.)

It is just as true today as it was in Lancaster's time that attempts to teach large classes as cheaply as possible are bound to result in mechanical instruction. This is as true at the university as at the elementary, middle, junior high, and high school levels. When classes are small, university teachers are more likely to help their students develop methods of observation and thinking than when the classes are very large lecture sections. Under the latter condition, assessment of students' achievement is likely to take the form of multiple-choice tests rather than asking students to write a paper on a consequential problem or issue. The principle is clear. Class size controls the nature of instruction and form of assessment.

Dewey made the point clearly in a paper given in 1902 when he was at the University of Chicago, where he founded an elementary school in 1896 to serve as a testing ground for his theories. Dewey stood for the idea of education as the effort to provide a situation conducive to the child's complete development. Classes were large in the public schools at the time, especially in the big cities, and ran from 35 to 60 children in a room. But, said Dewey, it was in "the face-to-face contact of teacher and child . . . that the real course of study, whatever be laid down on paper, is actually found." A large class, in Dewey's words,

> can hardly be said to be an ideal condition, even from the standpoint of uniform progress in reading, writing, and arithmetic, and the symbols of geography and history; but it certainly is better adapted to securing these results than that of the symmetrical and complete development of all the powers, physical, mental, moral, aesthetic of each individual child. . . . How do we have the face to continue to speak at all of the complete development of the individual as the supreme end of educational effort? Excepting here and there with the genius who seems to rise above all conditions, the school environment and machinery (school organization and administration) almost compel the more mechanical features of school-work to lord it over the more vital aims (Dewey, 1902a, pp. 24–25).

Although we no longer have monitorial instruction, and classes of 50 are uncommon in the public schools, we still have what Dewey called "machinery constructed for turning out another kind of goods" (p. 24), a scheme for administration and teaching that lends itself to a curriculum based on rote and recitation and a limited contact between child and child and child with teacher. Class size is only one of the conditions that determine whether the teacher's work is mechanical or thoughtful. Others include how the curriculum is developed and how teachers are prepared and supervised.

Direct Instruction: The Past Comes Calling

One might argue that monitorial instruction created a tradition of mechanical instruction in the large cities and that since that time, the emphasis in urban education has been on keeping pupils under surveillance and on task with little or no opportunity for discussion. This would be a rash judgment, but it is certain that a number of present programs have these same basic elements. An example is "direct instruction," an approach that gained a foothold in the 1970s for working with educationally disadvantaged pupils. The emphasis of direct instruction is on back-to-basics through drill and recitation, which means children's ability to answer questions at a low cognitive level.

The origins of intensive direct instruction can be traced to the 1960s as a compensatory education program for educationally disadvantaged preschoolers, aimed at having them enter first grade on a par with their more privileged age-mates. "Intensive direct instruction," as it was called then by the program's developers, Bereiter and Englemann (1966), was a kind of educational force-feeding. They described it as a "general bombardment approach" (p. 56). Games and rest periods were not a part of their program, but cold correction procedures such as "a slap or a good shaking" were. For 4-year-olds "who pout or refuse to respond," isolation in "a small, poorly lighted closet should serve quite well" (pp. 87–88).

Obviously, this would not constitute good advice to teachers today, nor did it then. Moreover, wise parents want schools for their own children where the teacher explains well and children are treated kindly. The trouble is that the dangers of a dual system of education—one to develop reasoning ability and the other, a mechanical system for the poor—have not been checked. The "highly structured setting of the Direct Instruction approach," for example, is still being promoted as a means of helping educationally disadvantaged children catch up with "affluent children" who "know more and are equipped to learn faster" (Englemann, 1999, p. 77). As noted by Keller, a teachers' guide was published that "grew out of the work

begun by maverick researcher Siegfried Englemann in the 1960s . . . which lays out in detail what teachers should say and do in lessons" (2002, p. 27). The teacher is, in effect, reduced to a technician. There is no room for professional discretion, which is an enormous problem with scripted lessons. What we have is rote teaching for rote learning. Both teacher and student operate at a low cognitive level.

Englemann maintained that his approach will help poor children catch up. Yet it would not be tolerated by parents in schools serving advantaged children, where the curriculum is more likely to be geared to higher level objectives. A rule of thumb is Dewey's oft-cited thought from *The School and Society:* "What the best and wisest parent wants for his own child, that must the community want for all of its children. Any other ideal for our schools is narrow and unlovely; acted upon, it destroys our democracy" (1900a, p. 7).

Emergence of a New Curriculum System

A Standard American Language

One of the most important developments toward a system based on building the best for all was the study of English in American schools. This development dates from the middle of the eighteenth century, when new kinds of schools arose to meet the intellectual and commercial needs of a rapidly changing society. English became universally studied in elementary and secondary schools in the quest for building a unified nation. In a pronunciation-conscious egalitarian society, correct speech had to be accessible to everyone. Precision in language and uniform rules for all were important for breaking down class distinctions. Enter Noah Webster, who like the other founding fathers was there at the right time. He understood clearly what we, ourselves, have had to relearn from time to time: a uniform language without class distinctions depends on the schools. Webster was, in the words of Boorstin, "the most influential American writer on language" (1958, p. 284). His *American Spelling Book* was published in 1789. The word chosen by Boorstin to describe the popularity of the speller is "colossal," a word that is well deserved, for it sold more than 60 million copies by the end of the nineteenth century. This, Boorstin wrote, was "a symptom and a symbol of the mobility of American society" (p. 284).

The need for a curriculum built upon the best in language and thought for all children continues to this day.

Sectional Differences

From 1830 until the Civil War the keynote of curriculum proposals was expansion. The reasons behind demands for the new subjects are important for they have become woven into the fabric of curriculum thought. Democratic ideals were, of course, closely linked with demands for the new subjects in the curriculum. Thus one finds demands for history, geography, and government as "preparation for citizenship." The growing interest in science during the period led to demands for natural science and natural history as well.

Granted these developments, most people still regarded the main job of the new common (public) schools as providing the people with minimum knowledge centered on the basics of reading, writing, and arithmetic. But, as Cremin noted, there were enormous differences among the various sections of the nation. In New England and the cities, new subjects were gradually incorporated in the required curriculum. In areas where opponents of tax-supported public schools still reigned supreme, the curriculum reflected their victory: "the curriculum tended to remain even more rigidly within the confines of the older R's" (Cremin, 1951, p. 188).

The Textbook and an Up-to-Date Curriculum

Amateurs made the initial contributions to American science; take Benjamin Franklin as a leading example. One might add other leaders in the Revolutionary era; Daniel Rittenhouse in astronomy and Joseph Priestly in chemistry are just two. These persons, who were businessmen, ministers, and planters, delighted in discovery. Interest in the natural world continued to accelerate. Huge amounts of information were classified, and scientific fields became more specialized. Professional science began in America in the early decades of the nineteenth century (operating alongside amateur science), and science received increasing attention in the curriculum. America was building its own curriculum. Noah Webster's groundbreaking work promoted new interest in English as the American language, making it increasingly possible for instruction in knowledge held by all citizens.

These developments led to a huge multiplication in the number and kinds of textbooks in the first three decades of the nineteenth century. In comparing the number of available textbooks in the years 1804 and 1832, a writer observed that "a number of works have been published in branches of study which were then [1804] unknown in our schools" (quoted in Cremin, 1951, p. 188). The new subjects would undergo great changes as they developed.

Geography is a fascinating example. In its early version, geography consisted of little beyond locating places and boundaries. This would change as the curriculum was influenced by industrialization as geography became a study of our relation to the physical environment. Toward the end of the nineteenth century, John Dewey and the teachers in his famous laboratory school pioneered in humanizing geography in the elementary curriculum (L. Tanner, 1997, pp. 64–90).

Textbooks are, of course, based on a plan of instruction, and many of the early nineteenth-century textbooks were based on the catechetical plan. (Many later textbooks made no great improvement in this approach.) Curriculum improvement requires improvement in instruction based on the learners' understanding and motivation. Thus although studies expanded within the first decades of the nineteenth century, the approaches followed by teachers often led to little more than superficial acquaintance with the new subjects. This would change, and it continues to change as teachers follow best practices.

Going Beyond the Minimum

With the leadership of Horace Mann, Massachusetts had by 1850 developed a progressive system of public schools, an example set before the eyes of other states. The list of required school subjects in Massachusetts included reading, writing, arithmetic, orthography, English grammar, and geography. However, as Mann pointed out to his board, these requirements were "the *minimum* but not the maximum. Any town may enlarge the course of studies to be pursued in its schools as much as it may choose" (quoted in Cremin, 1951, p. 188). Accordingly, the curriculum in some towns included subjects such as history and bookkeeping, and vocal music was offered in Boston.

Curriculum expansion had not yet occurred in many other areas, however. Until 1849, Ohio required only that reading, writing, and arithmetic be taught. In that year, English grammar and geography were added.

Curriculum expansion depended greatly on the availability of textbooks and other materials on the new subject. A problem confronted by pioneer schools in the West was that textbooks were published mainly in the East.

At present, the principle of minimum curriculum requirements is still followed by the states. One result is that students in poorer school districts do not have the same full range of educational opportunities offered in districts serving more advantaged populations. Over the years, courts have wrestled with this issue in nearly half the states. For example, New Jersey revised its school-financing formula in order to provide broader curricular offerings for students in the poorest urban districts (school financing, 1990). Kentucky required schools to meet seven goals, including systematic study in the arts and preparation for advanced education in academic and vocational fields (Worth & Hartocollis, 2002). Were he here today, Dewey would be pleased. The arts not only had a place in his laboratory school curriculum, but they were so closely interwoven with the other curriculum areas that they could not have been extricated. Take, for example, the development of historical insights. As children studied industrial development, they experienced the process. Dewey's interest in art continued to grow with his stature as a philosopher. As Philip Jackson (1998) points out, Dewey recognized that experiences in the arts can help us live our lives more fully. The curriculum can put Dewey's view to work.

The question of the minimal responsibility of a state to educate its children is "more philosophical than fiscal" (Worth & Hartocollis, 2002, p. 24). However, the point that Horace Mann made so long ago still applies. Minimums should not be regarded as maximums, and all districts should continually seek to provide wider access to knowledge for all children. In effect, the effort should be directed at optimizing educational opportunity rather than setting minimum standards.

Ideas as Instruments of Curriculum Change

Conceptions of learning and intelligence generally parallel trends of thought regarding humankind, nature, and the world. So it was with the new voice of science that in the seventeenth and eighteenth centuries led to dissatisfaction with the view of human nature as innately sinful. The new worldview held that people were what they were for natural and discoverable reasons. Human nature meant great possibilities. The groundwork was being laid for educational theories based on environmentalism. John Locke (1632–1704), the English philosopher who also had a background in medicine, argued that human nature is in part the outcome of the influence of the environment on the child. Locke believed that knowledge was attained empirically, through the method of inductive science, and he was a great promoter of the empirical approach to learning. According to Locke, the individual learned through perceptions of the world provided by the senses. But the individual gave form to his or her key perceptions through a process of reflection. And according to Locke, children learned through play.

Environmentalism, Empiricism, and Method. Environmentalism and empiricism were profoundly important influences on method. One learns through one's senses: sight, touch, hearing, smell, and taste. Was it not obvious, then, that this would be the most fruitful approach to classroom learning? Even before Locke, Francis Bacon (1561–1626) advanced the idea that learning would be most effective if the teacher started with careful observation of nature and developed the powers of induction rather than mere rote and recitation. It was precisely this idea that Colonel Francis W. Parker would apply in the Quincy, Massachusetts, public schools two and a half centuries later. The Quincy system was regarded as revolutionary even then (1875).

Realism in Education. Even before Locke, the educational reformer and Moravian bishop Comenius (1592–1670) systematized the idea of developing the powers of induction into a method. The teacher should begin with the observation of simple phenomena, leading to the complex. Moreover (and this *was* revolutionary) learning aids—pictures and actual objects—should be used for developing children's sense experience.

In Germany, realism in education became a reality when educators established schools (Realschulen) where emphasis was put on the use of actual objects and excursions to acquire firsthand knowledge of life. In Switzerland, Jean Jacques Rousseau (1712–1778) popularized interest in the idea of sense realism when he argued for the free expression of children's natural impulses and the substitution of play and observation of nature for books and the classical (linguistic) studies. In England, a number of proposals for educational reform were made, based on sense realism.

Of these, the infant school was the most famous and successful.

Achievements as Instruments of Curriculum Change

Just as achievements in science led to new conceptions of human nature and new methods of inquiry, so they also led to stunning practical achievements. Within a year of the Declaration of Independence, James Watt's steam engine made its appearance. A new technological age had begun. The practical accomplishments made possible by applying science to the development of new tools and machines were nothing less than spectacular. They pointed to the potential of secular knowledge for improving the conditions of living and for controlling the power of nature for human welfare.

Little wonder, then, that there were demands for a more practical education. New schools (academies) appeared, and proposals were made for reforming the curriculum along the lines of sense realism. One of the most interesting of these proposals, and a portent for secondary education, was Benjamin Franklin's plan for the academy.

Franklin's Academy. Franklin envisioned a new kind of school—the academy—that would provide a useful education. In his *Proposals Relating to the Education of Youth in Pennsylvania* (1749), Franklin supported his arguments for an education that was secular and practical rather than religious and classical by citing the European empiricists and sense realists. His proposal called for a uniquely modern secondary school, in sharp contradiction to the tradition-bound Latin grammar school brought over from Europe. Franklin knew well that a secular education, with the study of English rather than Latin, would be opposed by classicists and religionists. Ultimately this happened and led to the school's demise.

Throughout Franklin's curriculum proposal, practical educational experiences were stressed. The use of the English language was a primary goal. Art also was included as an aid to creative expression. Practical mathematics (particularly accounting) was another core study. Franklin devoted special attention to the social studies, which included modern history, geography, social history, political history, religious and moral history, and political science. French, German, and Spanish were offered for prospective merchants and Latin and Greek for students preparing for the ministry.

In Franklin's proposal, actual experience with machines was important in developing insights into the contributions of science to commerce, manufacture, and civilization itself. Similarly, practical experiences in agriculture were an important part of the study of natural history. In line with the realist view of the importance of concrete teaching aids, Franklin envisioned a plentiful supply of maps, globes, and scientific apparatus.

It was Franklin's hope to develop an education for practical living that was as respectable as an education grounded in religion and the classics and more valuable. But Franklin was a hundred years ahead of his time. Because of the heavy hand of the Latinists in the academy, the English school was neglected in favor of the Latin school. (Indeed, the Latin teachers plotted the demise of the English school in the academy.) In 1789, Franklin demanded that the English school be separated from the Latin school and the corporation be dissolved. He had enough years of experience with the institution to pronounce a failure the first attempt to combine the values of a classical and a modern education. The classicists had won the first battle, but they had not won the war. Gradually they lost ground. (To this day, however, they have not admitted defeat.) Franklin's academy was not a failure, for it gave impetus to the academy movement and a modern curriculum that ultimately led to the universalization of secondary education through the emergence of the public high school.

In sum, when such influential theorists as John Locke and Jean Jacques Rousseau began to insist that human nature is the function of the influences that saturate an individual's environment, for good or for evil, environmentalism was born. This idea not only came to have a profound effect on the curriculum, but also gave support to what was to become a passionate American belief in the educability of the people. Thus there were new opportunities for women who sought higher education. An illustration of this development in Pennsylvania was reported by Wickersham (1886).

Nothing is more remarkable in the educational policy inaugurated in 1838 than the place accorded to female education. From all the State had done for higher education previously, it could hardly be learned that such beings as women or girls were to be found within the borders of the state. . . . It seems to have been generally unknown either that girls could be educated beyond the simple arts of Reading, Writing or Arithmetic, or that they were entitled to any higher education. The credit of the discovery that girls should have an equal place with boys in a system of public instruction, higher as well as lower, belongs to the Legislature of 1838. It was a great discovery (pp. 389–390).

Environmentalism had begun to deeply affect educational policy. Environmentalism and learning from experience and observation were two main beliefs in what would, over the course of a century, become the basis for promoting universal educational opportunity and for modernizing the curriculum in tune with the nature of the learner and with the democratic prospect.

The Vision of Human Development

To look back on the years after the Civil War is to see the power of a tremendously influential idea on American education: evolution. The idea that species (including humans) are not changeless but had evolved as the result of environmental changes and adaptive changes, had to be faced by professional philosophers and either rejected outright or worked into their philosophies. (It should be noted that teachers of philosophy were almost always clergymen.)

Idealism and the Child's Self. The philosophy of idealism, of which there were many forms, was a response to the theory of evolution. The basic idea was that the real nature of the universe was spiritual, not material, and exists because of a universal mind: God's. Likewise, the most important thing about the human is the spiritual self or personality, not the physical being. Just as the universe is undergoing an evolutionary process of growth and development, so the individual's personality and spiritual nature is going through a similar process of growth and change. Thus it is important to respect the child's self and personality and provide the best conditions possible so that the child's (spiritual) nature can develop and unfold.

The Social Nature of Knowledge. Some idealists began to develop a social outlook, arguing that knowledge is the outcome not of an individual mind but of a community of minds. They stressed the growth of human experience and the fact that the individual cannot exist in isolation from society. Idealism was probably the most influential philosophy taught in colleges and universities in the late nineteenth century. John Dewey drew selectively

from these views for their emphasis on child growth and the social nature of learning, discarding such dualisms as mind versus matter, ideas versus experience, and the individual versus society. He was also sharply critical of the notion that the child's personality could ever unfold of itself (1902b). Dewey went on to forge a very different philosophy by orchestrating the American pragmatic spirit and the method of intelligence wrought by science with the democratic prospect.

European Influences on the Elementary School

The phrase *the method* has been used from time to time by educators, its meaning depending on the teaching approach then in fashion. In the early nineteenth century in Europe, "the method" meant Swiss educator Johann Pestalozzi's object-lesson approach. In 1861 object teaching was adopted in the schools in Oswego, New York, and a city normal school was created to train teachers in the new method. In the 1890s, a wave of pedagogical excitement was created in the United States by Herbart's formula for classroom instruction. "The method" referred to the teaching steps developed by Herbart's followers and brought to the United States by Americans who had studied in Germany.

Pestalozzi (1746–1827), Johann Friedrich Herbart (1776–1841), and Friedrich Fröebel (1782–1852) had a great influence on nineteenth-century education in America, but it was their practical ideas that attracted teachers. The principles behind the practices were not always well understood by teachers, with the result that "the method" often bore little resemblance to its original form. What was practical found its way first into American classrooms. Ideas that seemed unworkable or out of tune with the functions of public schooling were discarded by reformers. For example, Pestalozzi's naturalistic idea that the purpose of education was to free the child and at the same time shape him seemed conflicting to Horace Mann. But Mann was strongly attracted to the Pestalozzian principle that children should be treated kindly and with respect, which Mann believed was essential for teaching self-discipline and for creating a good society (Cremin, 1961, pp. 11–12).

In 1900 Dewey wrote that his laboratory school was attempting "to carry into effect certain principles which Fröebel was perhaps the first to consciously set forth" (Cremin, 1961, pp. 11–12). Among these principles was children's play (activity) as an educational method. But Dewey rejected the idea of Fröebel's disciples that the materials used in the activity should be artificial and symbolic. Dewey contended that the materials and the activities "must be as 'real,' as direct and straightforward, as opportunity permits" (Dewey, 1900b). In the kindergarten of Dewey's school, work centered on learnings related to home and neighborhood life.

Pestalozzi's Influence on the Curriculum

The nineteenth century was a decisive period in American curriculum development, and the ideas and practices of Pestalozzi deserved much credit. In the twenty-first century, Pestalozzian ideas continue to influence American education through their further development by others, particularly Dewey. An illustration is the Pestalozzian conception of education as a developmental process, starting from the familiar and plain and moving toward the understanding and application of abstract ideas. This seems to anticipate Dewey's pedagogical principles as he worked them out in his laboratory school at the University of Chicago (1896–1904). Dewey wrote: "The first pedagogical question is, How, out of the crude native experience which the child already has, the complete and systematic knowledge of the adult consciousness is gradually and systematically worked out" (1897a, p. 364). For Dewey, as for Pestalozzi before him, the answer was to build on the child's real experiences; experience was the starting point of the curriculum.

Object Teaching.   For Pestalozzi the sense impressions obtained from the object lessons were the experiences. Object teaching required, first of all, an object—a flower, fruit, toy, tool, or animal (or a model or picture of the object). Through the use of the senses, the child gained ideas about the object. Through sense perception, the child developed concepts and basic ideas and translated them into appropriate words. The objectives of object teaching were to develop alertness, accuracy of perception, concepts and generalizations, and vocabulary. Although object teaching had serious limitations, such as the failure to reveal the interrelatedness of objects in the activity, these goals fit in strikingly well with the objectives of elementary education today. Unfortunately, however, teachers in the nineteenth century described the goals of object teaching in terms of faculty psychology (to cultivate the faculty of reasoning, as if reasoning were a separate and mechanistic function, for example) rather than for the development of a scientific frame of mind. This was because faculty psychology was the generally accepted pedagogical psychology of the times.

Criticisms of Object Teaching.   As object teaching became formalized into a method, a growing number of criticisms were associated with it. In too many instances, lessons were unrelated because there was no overall plan. Also, what began as a science lesson on fruit or flowers might end up as a lesson on religion. Another unfortunate ending could be (and often was) a senseless vocabulary lesson. Finally, some teachers would insist that appropriate responses were wrong when they were not couched in the teacher's terminology. Obviously, for the most part these problems were not implicit in the method itself; they were abuses of the method and, hence, problems of teacher education.

Impact on Educational Thinking.   Despite the abuses, criticisms, and limitations, object teaching was a tremendously important reform. It revolutionized teaching. The prevailing educational method had been hearing individual recitations, but now the teacher had to stand before a class, ask the right questions, and get children to use their senses and their minds. It broadened and improved the curriculum. Oral language work entered the primary grades, and in the upper elementary grades, oral and written language work replaced somewhat the narrow emphasis on English grammar. Object teaching did much to introduce science as a subject. Arithmetic also underwent changes: from words about numbers to concrete number ideas. Yet, an inherent limitation of object teaching was its focus on objects as finished products. The most profound revolution in teaching was to find its expression in Dewey's laboratory school, where the materials under study were subjected to the test of life experience. Hence, geography was revolutionized. The new "home geography" began with the study of local terrain. This required observation outdoors. The concept of learning as inquiry, the uses of visual aids, and the field trip were all here to stay.

Herbart's Influence on the Curriculum

Toward the end of the nineteenth century, object teaching, which had become a fad, began to give way to a new method: five instructional steps to be followed in order. The instructional procedure grew out of the theories of the eminent German psychologist Johann Friedrich Herbart.

The Formal Steps of Instruction. Herbart was the first educational writer to emphasize instruction as a process. According to Herbart, the teacher must present new ideas in a way that associates them with ideas that are already part of the pupil's experience. This meant, of course, that the teacher had to know of the child's previous knowledge and interest. In keeping this psychology in mind, the teacher would follow what became known as the *five formal steps of teaching and learning*. The steps were as follows:

1. *Preparation,* in which the previous learning experiences are called to the pupil's attention
2. *Presentation,* in which the new information is given out
3. *Association,* in showing the relationship between the new facts and the old
4. *Generalization,* in making up rules or general principles that express the meaning of the lesson
5. *Application,* in giving the general principles meaning by using them in practical situations or applying them to specific examples

For about 15 years, spanning into the early twentieth century, more and more teachers organized their lessons along the five steps. "Without question," wrote Elsbree, "these five simply stated steps exercised more influence on teaching practice between 1890 and 1905 than all other psychological and philosophical creations combined" (1938, p. 407). It is easy to see why a method that presented new ideas in a way that connected them with the learner's experience was welcomed so eagerly by American educational theorists. This was a time when memorization and recitation were the main methods of teaching.

Certainly the method made it possible for teachers to provide instruction that was more meaningful to students. Yet most teachers followed it rigidly rather than creatively. In their defense, the pattern was rigid to begin with. It was based on a mechanistic theory of mind. "The mechanistic theory," as Bredo (2002) points out, "saw complex ideas as assembled out of elementary ideas" (p. 11). This was the psychology of associationism, which argues that the mind is built up from ideas that are linked together. Thus a teacher must relate new subject matter in the learner's mind to his or her former ideas. This was a strictly mechanical process. A serious limitation inherent in the theory was its uniformity in all subjects for all pupils. But a new psychology was in the wings, which not only influenced Dewey but was influenced by Dewey.

Stemming from Darwin, William James (1890) of Harvard argued that although the mind is influenced by environment it also acts upon the environment in creative ways. The learner is not a passive reflector of his or her world but a doer who helps change the world. Bredo (2002) contrasts James's psychology with that of behaviorists whose methods aim at controlling others. According to Bredo, James's and Dewey's emphasis was "democratic, unlike Watson's or Skinner's behavioristic approaches which were oriented toward developing a science for controlling others" (p. 25). The idea of the child as active rather than passive—one who has the potential of altering his or her environment—streamed into American educational theory. It was up to educators to develop this potential. The influence of evolution on the conception of education was as powerful as its influence on biology. About biology, Steve Jones, the geneticist, writes: "Nowadays no biologist could work without Darwin's theory. Evolution is the grammar of their science" (2000, p. xxix). Likewise, every good teacher is concerned, or should be, with helping students act on choices intelligently. As Cremin (1961) pointed out, Dewey "wanted schools to inculcate habits that would enable individuals to control their surroundings rather than merely adapting to them" (p. 123).

Yet the Herbartian's concern with the problem of method was a good thing for teaching. Herbart's ideas on the unity of knowledge also drew educators' attention to the need for curriculum synthesis before the turn of the century.

Fröebel's Influence on the Curriculum

Dewey adopted (and adapted) Fröebel's idea that play is the method of development and learning in his experimental school. Mention must be made of two other Fröebelian principles that Dewey and his faculty tried to carry out in the curriculum. The first was Fröebel's idea of group activity as a means of developing in children a sense of community and mutual interdependence or, put more simply, good social relations. The second idea was to use the activities to reproduce on the child's level the occupations of the mature society. Dewey wove this idea into the civilization theme on which his curriculum was based. But Dewey took Fröebel's ideal much further in seeing learning as developmental: the evolution of human occupations and society and the increasing control of nature for human purposes. Although the idea of occupations was Fröebel's, Dewey developed it in a far more profound way. Where Fröebel saw education as a kind of unfolding from within, Dewey viewed growth as stemming from the interaction of the organism with the environment.

Of course, Fröebel is most famous for his concept of a less formal school environment where children could learn through play. He called the school the *kindergarten,* a garden where children could grow. His emphasis on manipulating objects, exploration, and self-expression led to a realization of the importance of activity in learning.

The first successful experiment with public school kindergartens was in St. Louis in 1873. The class was taught by Susan Blow, who had taken a course in kindergarten methods. The experiment was so successful that she organized a training school to educate coworkers. As graduates were produced, the kindergarten grew in St. Louis. The movement quickly took root, and by the end of World War I the kindergarten had been accepted as the first rung of the American educational ladder. Nevertheless, a whole century later, a number of states still do not require school systems to offer kindergarten.

Criticism of the "New Education"

There is no question that the thought and writings of Pestalozzi, Fröebel, and Herbart influenced the public school curriculum in the late nineteenth century. As one might expect, the influence on practice varied from one locale to another. But where it was adopted, the new education met with opposition, the critics calling for a return to an education that had been largely eclipsed years before. Such was the case in Detroit in the 1890s. The reforms resulting from the application of the principles of Herbart and Fröebel were criticized by groups who wanted to return to the three Rs, a fundamental curriculum that had long since disappeared. Two attacks against the progressive principles will illustrate the nature of this opposition.

The first attack was on a change in the subject matter of arithmetic. The critics objected to the practical problems, because the great value of arithmetic was, according to them, in the mental discipline it afforded.

The second attack was leveled against a proposal by an assistant superintendent to use a daily newspaper for teaching reading, history, and geography. The principal supported her proposal on the grounds that the life of the surrounding adult community must be taken into account more directly in the curriculum. She interested the *Detroit Evening News* in her idea, with the result that the paper submitted a proposal to the school board to supply a newspaper that was reduced in size, with editorial comment committed for use in the schools. The board charged that this was a fad and vetoed the idea. They also reinstated the old kind of arithmetic.

In the 1896–1897 school year, Detroit Superintendent William E. Robinson responded to the board's criticism. Educational methods are always in a state of transition, he said, because educators are continually searching for better methods. Detroit, like every other city that had improved its methods to keep up with the requirements of the times, had been accused of introducing fads, but Detroit seemed not to realize that the changes were no longer considered radical and indeed had been incorporated into the curriculum for some time. Robinson noted that it was difficult to respond to the criticisms because the critics never defined what was meant by "fads and frills." Robinson stated the outlook of the "new education" as clearly as it could be put:

> If by "fads" they mean drawing, music, physical culture and elementary science, then I say that these subjects have been a part of the course of study in Detroit for the past twenty-five years, and it seems rather late in the day to defend their introduction. If they mean that intelligent teaching of those subjects is a fad, then I confess that the schools are afflicted with this "fad" disease. A teacher who is able to teach reading so that a child can pick up any reading matter within his vocabulary and read it intelligently, instead of pronouncing mechanically the words on the page of the reader, is without doubt a "faddist." If they mean that it is better to recite in concert the various capes and bays and gulfs of North America than to have a knowledge of the construction of the continent of North America and give an intelligent expression of the effect of this construction on the occupations of the inhabitants with the

commercial results, and from this knowledge of mathematics to estimate its size and distances, and to this add what he had learned of its history, then I will have to admit that much time is spent on fruitless ornamentation. . . .

If it is better to cram the mind with a lot of facts that are absolutely worthless when the child is thrown upon his own resources, than to lead him step by step to think for himself, to find out for himself that all subjects are dependent and related, and to become self-reliant, then the children of our schools are to be pitied for their visionary training. . . .

Robinson retired in 1897, but his 11-year administration was marked by continual curriculum extension and expansion, the introduction of the kindergarten, and provision for the deaf and blind. As Moehlman noted, "the encouragement of the 'new education,' resulting from the stimulating influence of Herbart and Fröebel, had taken root in the east and worked west rapidly" (p. 152).

By 1900 the eight-year elementary school curriculum in Detroit included 17 subjects: reading, writing, composition, literature, grammar, arithmetic, geography, history, spelling, government, drawing, music, physical culture, natural science, domestic science, domestic art and manual training (industrial arts). The growth of the curriculum from the ungraded school of the three Rs in the 1840s was, in little more than a half century, nothing short of remarkable.

Love at First Sight: The High School

The first public high school was established for boys by the Boston School Committee in 1821. It was so successful that in 1826 a high school for girls was founded. Democracy was on the march; in 1827, mainly through the spadework of James G. Carter, Massachusetts passed legislation under which all towns of 500 families were required to establish and support public high schools. Gradually the high school idea spread. Its growth underwent dramatic acceleration in the closing years of the nineteenth century, and through the first two decades of the twentieth century. It had become clear that the high school decidedly was part of the public school system. It just made sense. How could a public school system trying to provide equality of opportunity for all have secondary schools open only to those who could pay?

The high school was open to children of all social classes, and it did away with the threat of a dual system of education embodied by the academy. Perhaps not surprisingly, the frontier states were particularly well disposed toward the coeducation high school. According to Brubacher (1966), "free land had made the people there too egalitarian" to look favorably upon a dual school system in which elementary and secondary schools were differentiated by an individual's social future. "These people, like democracy-loving people everywhere, took the high school to their bosoms" (p. 410). One look at the curriculum of the academy, the high school's ancestor, tells why: Most academies had two programs, one for youngsters rounding out their education and the other for those planning on college. The academy ideal would be within reach of all through the public high school.

The problem was to get the children, many of whom viewed the curriculum as an impossible challenge, in the door. But the high school could be flexible in order to attract them, at least until the report of the Committee of Ten in 1893. There was no theoretical framework for curriculum development beyond the purposes of meeting student and societal needs and the promise of democracy. The approach to curriculum change was, as put by Kandel (1930), "venturesome and daring . . . inviting and forward-looking . . . fumbling and empirical" (pp. 460–461).

An example of how this change took place is the high school in Galesburg, Illinois. In 1885, Galesburg High School had a program that consisted mainly of the classics and foreign languages and was designed for college-preparatory students. William Steele, the superintendent, noted that the school's function was so narrow that "its very existence was at times threatened" (1911, p. 184). In 1885, Galesburg High School recognized its responsibility to the many and added a more practical program for students who expected to complete their education in the high school. The subjects substituted for the Latin (classical) program were physiology, bookkeeping, English history, Constitution of the United States, chemistry, history of literature, and political economy. The instruction was organized into departments: Latin, mathematics, English, and science. In 1895, the curriculum was revised again and Galesburg High School offered three programs: the *Latin,* for college-preparatory students; the *commercial,* for those wanting to prepare themselves for business; and the *scientific,* for those who did not plan to enter college but wanted a broader education than the elementary school provided. What was later to become known as a *comprehensive* high school was taking shape.

In 1895 Galesburg High School took a radical step. All subjects were made elective. On entering the high school, the student, with the advice of the parents and eighth-grade teacher, chose the subjects he or she wanted to study for a semester. The value of each subject was first explained to the youngster.

The purpose of the Galesburg policy was to reduce the dropout rate. Forty percent of entering ninth-graders were dropping out in their first year. More than half of these were leaving school because they were failing their work in some subject. They knew that failure in any subject meant that they would never graduate from the school. As Steele recounted,

> This did not seem to be a sufficient reason for discouraging a youngster in his effort to get an education. A wise parent would not treat his own child in that way. He would make all the more effort to find some line of work that the child could follow advantageously. A school should treat its pupils as a wise parent does his child. . . .
>
> It was thought by the Board that nothing could be more absurd than to think of education as consisting of a knowledge of certain subjects. . . . It was certainly a recognition of this absurdity when the high schools first divided their curriculum into two or more courses (programs) of study (p. 203).

The diploma, however, was not deceptive. A certain number of credits was assigned to each subject, and when a required number had been reached, the student was awarded a diploma on which was listed each subject that had been completed and the number of credits assigned. "The door to honorable graduation was never closed on the student by the school" (p. 204). Within two years after the elective policy was adopted, the school building had to be more than doubled in capacity to accommodate the youngsters applying for admission. (In that period, there was almost no increase in the enrollment in the elementary school.)

From 1885 to 1911, the high school in Galesburg grew by more than 500 percent, increasing at nearly 10 times the rate of either the elementary school or the population. The broadened curriculum—including public speaking, vocational subjects, and student activities such as clubs, literary contests, and musical organizations—were all factors in the growth. But, according to Steele, the critical factor was the school's objective: "to make it a place where every one, no matter what type of mind he might have, would find something that appealed to him and into which he could throw his energies and thus discover what kind of person he was" (p. 201).

It would be misleading to imply that all high schools followed the radical policy of Galesburg High School in offering a more comprehensive curriculum. Nevertheless, most large high schools had begun to adapt their programs to the needs of changing student populations. (Small high schools had one curriculum, geared to the college bound.) High schools increased enormously during this period, as did the number of youngsters who took the opportunities. No sooner were high school buildings erected than they were deemed inadequate to accommodate the throngs. As indicated, one reason was that the principle of curricular uniformity (a single program for those preparing for college) had given way in many high schools to curricular flexibility. Another was the rapid development of cities and towns and the development of railroads (later, "electric roads" or "interurbans"), which helped bring people together and stimulated a desire for greater educational opportunity.

Growing Pains

Americans had taken to the high school idea with enthusiasm. All very well, it might be said, but this assumes that teachers were prepared to give instruction in well-recognized subjects. It also assumes that school staffs were large enough to do the job. In too many cases this just was not so. There were many very small high schools with very small instructional staffs. In some four-year high schools the entire curriculum was taught by two, three, or four teachers. A study of the conditions in the high schools of the state of Washington by two University of Washington professors in 1917 found a "large proportion" of teachers in very small high schools "attempting to give instruction in subjects for which they have insufficient preparation" (Koos & Woody, 1919, pp. 236–237). "Our facts constitute a protest against the needless multiplication of very small high schools," they wrote, and "the policy of encouraging the multiplication of small and feeble institutions in disregard of proximity to population centers" is "nothing less than the encouragement of an inefficient school system" (p. 238).

Influenced by business values, efficiency (and its converse, inefficiency) was the leading concern of many reformers in the first two decades of the twentieth century. For example, as discussed later, there was much interest in the content of the curriculum as it related to the needs of life. Efficiency aside, when it comes to curricular advantage large schools have it over small schools. The number of small schools was rapidly becoming a highly charged issue. Since 1900 education leaders had been aware of the advantages of school consolidation and district reorganization for improved educational services, facilities, and resources. By the middle of the twentieth century the number of school districts was rapidly decreasing and the average size increasing. Some might call it efficiency but by whatever name the result was a more diversified and enriched curriculum, and advancement in educational opportunity for an increasingly cosmopolitan population.

Improving Teaching in High Schools

In America the ideas put forth by educational reformers found the most fertile soil in the elementary school. By the last quarter of the nineteenth century ideas and examples of methods of teaching brought over from Europe by Mann and Barnard in the 1840s had become "old hat" in progressive systems like Detroit's. The elementary school was the locus of experimentation—Dewey's school (1886–1904) was the leading example—resulting in a new and enduring set of principles for teachers (L. Tanner, 1997). Many of these ideas applied equally well to secondary schools. There are at least three reasons why the elementary school held center stage in the theater of reform. First, for most children elementary school was it; they did not get past elementary school. Rich and varied curricular experiences had to happen in elementary school, if they were to happen at all. Second, the new methods of teaching found by Americans in Europe, Prussia in particular, were at the elementary level. (Prussia had a long tradition of universal elementary education.) Fröebel himself considered his ideas appropriate for young children—upper elementary, at most. Third, college entrance requirements that determined the major part of the secondary program discouraged experimental programs at the high school level. The elementary school may have held center stage, but the secondary school was waiting in the wings. In fact, high school teaching was under the microscope, being examined critically by some researchers. In his book *How Teachers Taught* (1984), Cuban reviewed studies of high school instruction before 1900. His conclusion: Administrators and teachers were "harnessed" to the belief "that children learned best through repetition and memorization" (p. 31). There were exceptions: science, history, and later, the arts, industrial arts, and vocational studies.

During the early twentieth century, there was evidence of reform at the secondary level. It was less meteoric than at the elementary level and drew on some of the same ideas. At the University of Wisconsin, for example, a high school was established in 1912—it had been on the drawing board since 1909—for preparing teachers *and* for demonstrating best practices in secondary education (Miller, 1919). A number of other universities also maintained demonstration high schools. The University of Wisconsin High School and The Ohio State University schools demonstrated such ideas as Dewey's problem-solving method, in which students are engaged in finding ways to solve a common problem. Developing such habits of self-responsibility was seen as essential in a democracy and received increasing attention by secondary educators as the twentieth century wore on.

Perspective

Although it is often thought that curriculum reform followed the founding of the public school system, this is not entirely the case. Agitation for better teachers and an improved, expanded curriculum led to the establishment of the public school system.

By 1840 the pieces for curriculum development were all in place: supervision, teacher education, and inservice education. (At least they had been invented.) They did not get there by accident. The story of how they got there is absolutely fascinating and conveys a sense of the creativity and utter determination of the founders. It also provides a sense of the purposes of our field in a democratic society.

For more than two centuries the ideal of democracy has been the basis for improving educational opportunity. That ideal was given substance for curriculum workers by Thomas Jefferson. In the ideals for America set forth by Jefferson, the responsibilities of curriculum workers are given vivid life: to develop intelligent citizenship and to provide each individual with educational opportunities for optimal development. It is safe to say that never before or since have civic responsibilities been stated more simply and clearly. Nor have they changed in more than two centuries. Like those before us, we call upon our creativity to find new ways of meeting them. It has been observed that the entire history of our field has been the continuing effort to realize the Jefferson ideal.

Along the way educators developed a body of best creative practices for curriculum development. Interesting and courageous contributors along the way include Horace Mann, Henry Barnard, and James G. Carter, who are recognized as early leaders, and John Dewey, America's leading philosopher. But always Thomas Jefferson remains the father of them all.

In his study of the key persons of the American Revolution, Bailyn (2003) writes that "these were truly creative people" (p. ix) and remarks on their boldness "in transcending the world they were born into" (p. 6). He might well have been speaking of the generation who strove to realize the development of free, secular public education. Like the American founders, they created patterns uniquely different from the world of their birth. For example, nowhere in the world was there an institution providing public secondary education for all adolescents; the American high school was an original. (Not until after World War II was secondary education available to all in England.)

There can be little doubt that state supervision of public schools and the founding of normal schools were given a boost by the general atmosphere of reform from 1830 to 1860. The reform movement of Horace Mann's generation involved more than one societal institution. Some of the reformers were concerned with slavery, others with women's rights, for example. Some were concerned with more than one reform effort. Mann, who fought for state support and control and played an active role in founding the normal school, went to Congress. There he launched a campaign against slavery. If it had not been for his educational contributions, his career in Congress would have received relatively greater attention. Perhaps the most important aspect of Mann's view of the curriculum is that he saw its purposes as common to all. It would be devoted to what we call general education.

Never were Americans served better than by the great educational reforms of this period. Carter, Mann, and Barnard had the whole of education to reform and new institutions to build, and they did so in a remarkably brief period. Barnard worked prodigiously with his survey of schools in Connecticut. Going up and down the state, he became known as "that young man with the notebook." The people learned what their schools were really like. Carter wrote essays on education, recalling the public to the remarkable invention of their ancestors: free public

schools that had been allowed to decay in favor of private tuition academies. Granted that the academies had broad curricula that included practical as well as cultural subjects, but who could afford them? Only a small percentage of the age group could, Carter pointed out, trying to rouse the public from its inertia and finally, after a decade, succeeding. For Mann there was just one answer to the problem of academies, which were taking money from the public schools and, more importantly, removing affluent children from public school classrooms, denying other children joint association. Mann's concern was well placed. Research would later document the importance of the background of fellow students for achievement. But Mann also had deeper reasons. The health of the republic depended on preventing social discord by bringing people together. The answer was to improve the public schools so that parents would no longer send their children to academies. Mann's efforts to do so are part of our curriculum heritage and may be found in his 12 reports (1837–1848) to the Massachusetts Board of Education. Mann, Carter, and Barnard achieved their purpose; the public school had become an institution of American life. Not that they ever doubted it would. They knew that history was on their side.

They had achieved success. And most important for us all, "Under Mann's aggressive leadership Massachusetts in many ways taught the nation the ideals of popular education" (Cremin, 1961, p. 12). Yet the story does not end with Mann, and this is where we come in. We know that just being able to attend school is no guarantee of access to the curriculum. Although access has improved markedly for previously excluded groups, curriculum workers still must be vigilant against undemocratic proposals masked as reforms. An early example is monitorial instruction, which, as Carter pointed out, was viewed by some as an acceptable substitute for public schools. Those "mechanized seminaries," as Carter called them, already existed in Europe.

We never adopted mechanized seminaries, except in a brief period before the battle for public schools was won, but narrow managerial schemes are proposed repeatedly (for other people's children) under the guise of reforms. In Mann's reports to the Massachusetts Board of Education, one finds ideas about teaching that are amazing for his time and, indeed, timeless. Mann relentlessly attacked rote learning and conceived of learning as an active process in which the learner does the "effective work." By this it is meant self-direction, and the key to self-direction is motivation. From the moment the desire is felt, the child learns to work independently (that is, without being prodded from some outside source). Mann was one of the first advocates of individualized instruction, arguing that children differ in affect, ability, and interest and that lessons should be adapted to those differences. The fact that Mann wrote about these things in no way indicates that they were universally accepted. There was strong opposition to some of his ideas; gentle discipline instead of harsh discipline comes to mind.

Americans immediately took to the high school. In fact it was such a hit that high schools sprang up almost like mushrooms. By the end of the nineteenth century, it was clear that small, weak schools had become a problem. The effort to put a "people's college" within easy reach of all had led to inadequate curricula. After all, a good school requires teachers who are knowledgeable and skillful in their teaching fields. This was hardly likely when the same faculty—sometimes only two or three—taught every subject in the curriculum. The problem could be and was handled by school consolidation, yet the problem of out-of-field teaching continues. Interest in curriculum research at the secondary level lagged behind the elementary school for several reasons; most notably, for most students school ended with elementary school. Improving teaching at the secondary level drew on some of the same ideas as at the elementary level; for example, engaging students in finding ways to solve common problems. But practices in curriculum development flow from the realism and idealism of Jefferson.

PROBLEMS FOR STUDY AND DISCUSSION

1. Does the following statement present a fair portrayal of Horace Mann and Henry Barnard? Explain.

   Horace Mann, Henry Barnard and other promoters of a gentle pedagogy eagerly publicized the romantic ideals emanating from Europe, which assailed memorization, textbooks, physical discipline and the usual features of the neighborhood school [William J. Reese, "The Origins of Progressive Education." *History of Education Quarterly*, Vol. 41 (Spring 2001), p. 10].

2. According to Cremin: "As with the battle for freedom itself, victories are never final and somehow today's educators find themselves fighting the same battles Mann was supposed to have won over a century ago. Popular apathy and dissatisfaction, rising private school enrollments, sectarianism, objections to school taxes, a shortage of qualified teachers, disagreements over what a good teacher is . . . and cries for harsher discipline—all of these problems have been raised anew" [Lawrence A. Cremin (ed.), *The Republic and the School: Horace Mann on the Education of Free Men*. New York: Teachers College Press, 1957, p. 27].

   In your view, is Cremin's statement, made midtwentieth century, valid today? Explain. If your answer was affirmative, which of these problems bear on curriculum improvement? Why?

3. Darwin led to an important new outlook in education that stressed knowledge as the outcome of active human experience. What evidence do you see of this idea in instructional approaches today? Where do you see it lacking?

4. This chapter emphasizes the importance of treating curriculum and instruction in a unified fashion. Some writers have suggested that they be treated as separate entities. Do you see problems with this view? Explain.

5. Why did the public school reformers build new secondary schools instead of reforming the Latin grammar school?

6. Mann believed that heterogeneous groups of students were important for social unification in the young republic. Today, the republic is older but Mann's view that the school must provide for the realization of social goals still stands. Moreover, research points to the importance of group ability composition for student achievement.

   Classroom studies of group composition and learning generally show that, when students actively participate in group collaboration, low-ability students learn best in groups with high-ability students, high-ability students perform well in any group composition, and medium-ability students learn the most in relatively homogeneous groups [Noreen M. Webb, Karian M. Nemer, Alexander W. Chizhik, & Brenda

Segrue, "Equity Issues in Collaborative Group Assessment: Group Composition and Performance." *American Educational Research Journal,* Winter 1998, pp. 607–651.]

Which measures would you recommend, as a curriculum worker concerned with improving access to the curriculum?

7. As early as 1826, James G. Carter proposed a teacher education institution with an experimental school for children. Do you think this was a good idea? Why? What examples of such schools can you find today?

8. Draw up a list of the approaches used by early school leaders as they sought public support— and achieved remarkable success. Which would be useful today as teachers face problems that require attention from the public as well as the profession?

9. It is commonly believed that efforts for the reform of education in America date from the founding of the public school system. How would you criticize this position?

10. In what ways does a mechanical view of instruction conflict with Jeffersonian principles and the ideals of Horace Mann?

11. In your experience, do schools provide broader curricular offerings than the minimum requirements set by the state? Explain.

CHAPTER 2

NEW DIRECTIONS AND TURNING POINTS IN THE CURRICULUM

The achievements and ideas of the early leaders laid the groundwork for creative curriculum thought. Dewey's ideas on teaching children self-direction and social responsibility, for example, can be traced to Mann. Developments in the curriculum speeded up as Francis Parker applied Pestalozzian ideas, which he had observed in Europe, in an American school system. Parker's ideas involved functionalism, that is, teaching skills through actual use, a novel idea in 1875 and a best practice today for those who seek to improve the curriculum for children and youth. In 1896, Dewey's famous laboratory school was established at the University of Chicago. The purpose of Dewey's school was, in Dewey's words, "to discover in administration, selection of subject matter, methods of learning, teaching, and discipline, how a school could become a cooperative community while developing in individuals their own capacities and satisfying their own needs" (Mayhew & Edwards, 1936, p. xvi). Dewey's school produced many lessons for today (L. Tanner, 1997).

Not only were these events of great interest toward the end of the nineteenth century, but they also are of interest today, for they turned out to be turning points in the development of the curriculum and thought about the curriculum.

Some of these ideas seem obvious, but they were not always so until tested in practice. Take Tyler's concern, discussed in the previous chapter, about "whether what we are doing is worthwhile." Not everything can be taught, and therefore we must ask what is of most worth. This question was a turning point in curriculum thought. The essay by the philosopher Herbert Spencer (1820–1903), *What Knowledge Is of Most Worth?* (1860), had considerable influence on curriculum thinking. Since its publication we have never stopped asking Spencerian questions. As Frances Schoonmaker (2001) points out, the question of most

worth "invites and extends dialogue rather than limiting and closing it" (p. 28). Granted this; for curriculum workers the dialogue is not engaged in for its own sake. It has a down-to-earth purpose: curriculum evaluation and improvement. Asking "whether what we are doing is worthwhile" is one version of Spencer's question. Not all of the turning points in the curriculum signaled progress. Some, such as the report of the Committee of Ten on Secondary School Studies (1893) and the report of the Committee of Fifteen on Elementary Education (1895), are generally considered conservative and perhaps regressive. The history of the curriculum has had its ups and downs, but the idea of progress has been the engine for the transformation of the curriculum in a democratic society.

This chapter considers the great events and the great ideas of the nineteenth century that proved to be influential in the evolution of the curriculum. Among the turning points examined are Spencer's ideas on education, Parker's work in the Quincy, Massachusetts, schools, the work of the National Education Association's Committee of Ten and Committee of Fifteen, the laboratory school at the University of Chicago and, finally, the founding of high school standards and accreditation associations to establish criteria for college entrance.

What Knowledge Is of Most Worth?

A field can take an amazing new course after the appearance of one publication. An example with which most people are familiar is Darwin's *Origin of Species,* which marked a titanic turning point in the development of science and had a resounding impact on social science, philosophy, and theology. Although Spencer's essay is, probably unknown to most people outside the field of education, curriculum took just as startling a new course after the publication of *What Knowledge Is of Most Worth?* His essay was published in the United States in 1860. Spencer insisted that because of the importance of the knowledge of natural sciences to human welfare and social progress, the sciences must have a prominent place in the curriculum. He was but one of many English and American writers who argued that a curriculum confined to study of the classics was not adequate preparation for living.

Science Enters the Curriculum

It will be remembered that the methods of science led to changes in the methods of education. The idea that children should be taught to corroborate what they learn from their own investigation was a Pestalozzian method and strikingly parallels the scientific method. Pestalozzi and his followers opposed the prevailing education on the ground that it was not the way people acquired knowledge of the world and was, therefore, unpsychological. The moment that dissatisfaction arose with a closed approach to natural phenomena, the die was cast: Science would enter the curriculum. The conflict between the classicists, who thought that the mind was formed through mastery of subjects such as grammar and logic, which were thought to state the actual rules of mental operation, and the progressives, who urged that science should be brought into the schools, continued until the middle of the nineteenth century. Although science was to gain a prominent place in the curriculum, the conflict between the humanities or classics on one side and science on the other raged throughout the twentieth century.

In the nineteenth century, prominent scientists wrote treatises on education, methodically pointing out the reasons for giving science due recognition in the curriculum. Recommending science to curriculum makers in England (the home of the Industrial Revolution) occupied the attention of Thomas Henry Huxley, a champion of Darwin's theory of evolution. Huxley pointed out that it was a highly improvident policy for a great country like England with enormous commercial interests to fail to offer instruction in chemistry and physics, on which its industrial greatness and world leadership depended. The growing industrial competition in international trade eventually caused England to accede to this view. Knowing about this episode helps us understand our own time.

In the twenty-first century, the place of science in American schools continues to gain significance for similar reasons.

It was Herbert Spencer who made the representative argument for science in the curriculum. In his famous essay, he stated that the purpose of education was "to prepare for complete living" and that the only way of determining the worth of an educational program was first to classify, in order of importance, the leading activities of life and then to evaluate the curriculum on the basis of the extent to which it offered this preparation. Spencer's classification of life activities was ordered as follows:

1. Those ministering directly to self-preservation
2. Those securing the necessities of life (ministering indirectly to self-preservation)
3. Those that aid in the rearing and discipline of offspring
4. Those involved in maintaining one's political and social relations
5. Those that occupy the leisure part of life, gratifying tastes and feelings (1860, p. 32).

In applying his own test, Spencer held that science was the knowledge of most worth in educating for self-preservation, yet it received the least attention in the curriculum. Spencer was one of the most respected and admired, even revered, philosophers of his time and had a large following in America. "I believe there is no other man whose thoughts are so valuable for our needs as yours are," wrote Edward L. Youmans, editor of *Popular Science Monthly,* to Spencer in 1863 (Cremin, 1961, p. 91). As a result of the publication of Spencer's essay and the discussion that followed, the study of science gained a new stature and was more rapidly introduced into all levels of the curriculum.

Spencer's Effect on Curriculum Theory

Spencer's influence on the curriculum would have been profound simply on the basis of his advocacy of science. This was the immediate effect of his essay. But the larger and probably more important effect has been on curriculum theory. Spencer's question paved the way to theory development. What knowledge is of most worth? We know that schools cannot teach everything, and somehow the society and school faculty must determine "worth." The problem of worth is both practical and philosophical. Ralph Tyler (1949) dealt with the problem in his famous rationale for planning a program of instruction. Tyler's guide for determining the greatest worth would be the school's objectives.

Determining Worth.

But Tyler was well aware that the objectives themselves "are matters of choice, and they must be therefore the considered value judgments of those responsible for the school" (p. 4). Tyler quickly got down to business in his rationale. The faculty must have a philosophy for guidance in the making of judgments. Data must also be available to decision makers if judgments about objectives are to be wise. Neither philosophy nor information stands by itself as a sufficient basis for arriving at objectives. When Tyler spoke of *considered* value judgments," he was saying that the value (worth) assigned to a topic or subject should be determined by knowledge and information about important problems of the day, for example, as well as the school's philosophy.

No Permanent Answer.

Equally important in curriculum development is the need to ask Spencer's question continually. "When Spencer asked, 'What knowledge is of most worth?' he posed a question which must always be considered and reconsidered," observes Oliver, who goes on to point out that what might have been of great worth at one time gives way to a new worth with the advancement of knowledge (1969, p. 250). Indeed, virtually every national report on school reform has addressed this question implicitly if not explicitly. A chief problem has been that in periods of perceived crisis, the schools find themselves vulnerable to narrow sociopolitical demands for shifting curriculum priorities, giving emphasis to one side of the curriculum at the expense of an equally worthy side (D. Tanner, 1986, 2000).

Arriving at Consensus.

It is one thing to theorize that "most worth" should be determined on the basis of philosophy and the best available evidence. It is quite another, however, for the theory to be put into practice. Curriculum is the responsibility of various groups, often with conflicting ideas and ideals. A guiding principle offered by Clark (1988) is genuine participation. Faculty members, parents, and students should not be asked condescendingly for input. They should be "mobilized to participate actively in the developmental processes and decision making of the school. Not only do they participate eagerly, but their participation is authentic" (pp. 191–192).

Clark offers as an example the development of a high school core curriculum. A study committee of parents, teachers, and district curriculum staff spent a year developing recommendations under the leadership of a principal. Community groups conducted hearings, and each faculty member worked intensively to develop recommendations. The developmental process involved task forces of teachers representing all areas of the curriculum working with district curriculum specialists. The point of importance is that the process took time (three years) and required interactions among the individuals who participated in the development of the curriculum as well as in decision making on related concerns. Conflicts became secondary to the goal. Moreover, as Clark points out, the participants did not regard the work as something to be finished, but as outcomes requiring follow-up. All participants were seen as members of an "active" school (p. 193). Clark speaks from his experience as an educational leader.

Researchers have shown considerable interest in the concept of curriculum deliberation, the process by which persons representing groups with differing ideals arrive at consensus about the curriculum. Deliberation can take place in many settings and under many institutional arrangements. It has been found that the curriculum conference is a particularly useful way of arriving at consensus. A curriculum conference is a well-planned, prepared situation in which participants meet to work on matters of common concern with regard to the curriculum and to determine and improve the curriculum. Clearly this is different from a standing curriculum committee meeting or special workshop. The curriculum conference requires a great deal of planning or "prestructuring," in which "a preliminary study takes place to write a report that contains information from multiple data sources about . . . subject matter, learners and teachers. But existing curricula are also analyzed" (Frey, 1982). The report highlights the best available evidence as well as differences in viewpoints. (Here the material may be useful in sorting evidence from opinion.) The report reflects on the tentative conclusions about the curriculum's design and function. At this point the report becomes what is, willy-nilly, a proposal. Participants are expected to read the material before the conference.

In a study about curriculum conferences as means of arriving at consensus, Mulder and Thijsen (1990) found that participants who had large differences of opinion before the conference approached high levels of agreement during the conference. But the same participants held different opinions several weeks after the conference, compared with the decisions reached during the conference. Thus one is forced to raise the possibility that the agreement was superficial and a matter of expediency or reached through subtle social pressure. The report that the participants read in advance of the conference was probably well intended. It was assumed that they came new to the curriculum issue and that they needed material that would make it easier to grasp. Nevertheless, there is a price to be paid when time is short and when the decision-making process does not involve participants in the preliminary study. When participants meet only once, and many have glanced at papers while someone else is talking, their initial presumptions are likely to remain unchanged.

The insight to be gained from this study is that consensus should not be a curriculum group's greatest concern; the paramount concern is building a sound basis for decisions, and this requires full and open communication.

Until Spencer's essay, most educators did not even think in terms of "most worth." Making choices is more difficult than anyone seems to admit. Curriculum development and decision making should be seen as part of a problem-solving process.

Progressive Education as a Movement

Like many young educators of his day, Francis W. Parker (1831–1902) studied pedagogy in Germany. He was greatly impressed by Pestalozzi's emphasis on study of the physical world and Herbart's principle of curriculum correlation. Parker was also inspired by the educational ideas of Fröebel, in particular the importance of the pupil's activity and the social aspect of education. Particularly attractive to Parker was Fröebel's principle of learning through social participation rather than the learner as an isolated individual. Thanks to Parker, these ideas landed, spread out, and altered the American educational landscape. In his elementary school work, Parker extended these ideas to include a whole language approach in the curriculum. Interestingly, Fröebel's ideas were suppressed in Germany. German educational tradition stressed passive obedience to authority. Fröebel found fertile soil in the democratic United States.

What is the turning point with which we are concerned? Here it was the application of progressive methods of instruction in Quincy, Massachusetts. If progressive education had a beginning as a movement, it was surely with Parker's work in Quincy. Indeed, Dewey (who made the most creative contribution to American education) called Parker the father of progressive education. According to Pearson (2000), Parker and Horace Mann were "giants" in the early reform of reading instruction. Both opposed the alphabetic approach to teaching reading—a "learn the parts before the whole" approach (p. 153). Did this opposition lead to lasting change? We are getting ahead of our story.

An Appalling (and Eye-Opening) Discovery

The educational moment that proved to be a turning point in the curriculum began in 1875 when Parker was named superintendent of schools in Quincy. His charge was to examine and improve education in Quincy. Two years before, on public examination day, the Quincy School Committee had made an appalling discovery. The graduates of the grammar schools were unable to spell, write, or speak effectively. When asked by the committee members to read from an unfamiliar book, they were bewildered and lost. They had been trained only for examination and could not read with fluency or comprehension. Furthermore, questions about their studies revealed that the children had no understanding of the thinking process. All they could do was parrot memorized responses to memorized questions prepared in advance by their teacher.

Buttressed with his study of elementary school methods in Germany, Parker had his opportunity to apply them as superintendent. Unlike many superintendents of today, he carried out curriculum development responsibilities personally. Parker understood his charge clearly: to help the children of Quincy to develop the power of expression.

Parker's Pedagogy

Because Parker believed that methods of teaching should be patterned on the child's natural way of learning, he adopted the word method of teaching reading. This, after all, was the way children learned to speak the language. Grammar was thrown out of the school and talking and writing were put in.

Conversation, which was one of the innovations in Quincy schools, was cultivated as an art. "What did you do last evening?" or "What did you see on your way to school this morning?" were questions being answered by children who previously had been mouthing words by rote, without understanding the ideas they represented. All writing was related to children's activities, experiences, and feelings. Spelling was taught through this meaningful kind of writing.

Parker was opposed to teaching geography via the disconnected morass of facts and statistics in textbooks. Instead, the children took field trips around Quincy and made mud models and sketches of the landscape. These methods were revolutionary at a time when in most schools pupils were expected to remain in the same position throughout the day (in rows of seats bolted to the floor) without turning their heads.

The novel approaches of the "Quincy system," as it came to be known, attracted national attention. Children were learning to read, write, spell, and think simultaneously and holistically. As Parker said, they were learning to "talk" with their pens, as they had learned to talk with their tongues: by using them (Campbell, 1967, p. 82).

The reaction to these methods was mixed. There were those who called Parker a charlatan, as they would have called anyone who tried to teach children how to think before they had thoroughly memorized the implements (facts) for thinking. In the main, however, his methods were widely acclaimed in both the general press and professional literature. Typical was the statement of B. G. Northrup, secretary of the Connecticut State Board of Education: "In Quincy, the children write better *throughout all the schools of the town* than is the case in *all* the schools of any other town within my knowledge in our country" (1880, p. 131).

A London journal, however, was unimpressed, finding the developments in Quincy to be nothing more than Fröebel's theories put into action (Campbell, 1967, p. 88). A comment frequently heard in educational circles was that Parker's ideas were not original. This was true; they had been tried in various places in this country and abroad, and Parker was the first to say so. But he had brought them together as a set of ideas and given them flesh and blood in one New England town. Moreover, Parker was the first to attempt to systematize and adopt the "new education" in a whole district.

Parker viewed the developments in Quincy more as a "spirit of study," a *search* for the natural methods of teaching, than as a system or a method. Quincy was an educational breakthrough, Parker said, because it rejected traditional education and penetrated the "very thick crust of conservatism and conceit" (p. 88).

Parker's Ideas Today

Parker's work in Quincy opened the way for classroom learning environments in which children's uses of reading and writing are inseparable. By the 1960s, most elementary teachers had abandoned the traditional credo that reading and writing must be taught separately. Language experience approaches in which children learned to read from the stories they dictated about their experiences (oral language transposed to experience charts) were often the main part of reading instruction.

Even so, the traditional fractured curriculum was a stubborn foe. In the 1970s and 1980s legislative mandates seriously undermined both functional learning and curriculum synthesis. Policy makers became enamored of minimum competency testing as a means of supervising instruction from afar (as from some state capital). As Jensen and Roser (1990) observed, reading and writing were reduced "to collections of separate skills that, even when mastered, do not add up to literacy" (p. 10). Who could have believed that a century after Parker's work in Quincy, reading would revert once again to a mindless activity, in this case, blank-filling on worksheets?

Things changed in the 1990s. Indeed, Parker's principle was literally reinvented. "Learning to read and write are interrelated processes that develop in concert with oral language," wrote one reading expert (Strickland, 1990). Whole language is based on the idea that "language, including reading, is best taught and learned when it is put to work in the service of other purposes, activities, and learning efforts," points out Pearson (2000, p. 180). This was language in use, and it was "natural" learning, as Stahl and Miller noted (1989, p.88). Parker would have applauded the use of the term. But his pleasure would have been short-lived, just as whole language appeared to be short-lived. "At century's end," wrote Pearson, "just when it appeared as if whole language, supported by its intellectual cousins (process writing, literature-based reading and integrated curriculum), was about to assume the position of conventional wisdom for the field, the movement was challenged seriously" (2000, p. 184). The pendulum had swung back toward an isolated skills approach. Among the reasons suggested by Pearson was that reading had become a policy agenda item (for both major political parties) and, in consequence, pressure was increasing on educators in all fields, particularly reading, to use test scores as the indication of student performance.

Politics

BAD IDEA

Nevertheless, the death of whole language (by whatever name, in whatever era) is exaggerated. Once Parker's idea entered the literature it never left. Many theorists continue to emphasize that the "art of language" is a unity, created out of ideas and experiences in our own lives and the lives of others. Good teachers work on this principle.

The Report of the Committee of Ten

We begin our discussion of the report of the Committee of Ten (1893) of the National Education Association (NEA) with a point of central importance. When the high school idea was born in the 1820s, it was not intended to be a college preparatory institution. The Boston School Committee established a school to provide "the young men who are not intended for a collegiate course of studies, and who have enjoyed the usual advantages of the public school with the means of completing a good English education, and of fitting themselves for all the departments of commercial life" (Grizzell, 1923, p. 42). A high school for girls appeared five years later in 1826. But secondary education could not be completely democratic until it took on the college preparatory function of the academy as well as preparing students for the world of work. This happened early, and the dual purpose secondary school rapidly became the normal order of things in the American community. In fact, the high school was revered and inseparable from the community, in no small way because it provided all of the advantages of the academy for moving up the socioeconomic ladder.

The Impact of Universities

All would have been fine, except that the high school was not exactly independent where its curriculum was concerned. In fact it was paying a hefty price for its relationship with the colleges and universities to which a tiny minority of students aspired. A word about that relationship here: The state colleges and universities west of the Alleghenies admitted the graduates of selected high schools without examination. After 1870, all that the high school graduate in Michigan had to do to be admitted to the University of Michigan was to present his certificate of graduation from an approved secondary school. The foundation was being laid for an accreditation plan. By the end of the nineteenth century, several major associations of colleges and secondary schools had been founded in the United States. The advantages accruing to high school students were enormous.

But not unexpectedly, colleges and universities began to play an increasingly significant role in the development of high school curriculums. This influence was advantageous but also created problems. College pressures on high schools became organized. In the East in particular, courses that high schools ought to offer were spelled out in detail (including bibliographies).

The Problem of Articulation. No doubt high schools were uneven in the variety and quality of their courses, but the high school had not been originally intended to be a college preparatory institution. Nevertheless, the growing interest in high schools focused on the articulation of high school and college. From 1870 until the report of the Committee of Ten in 1893, this issue overshadowed other problems of secondary education. According to Wesley, the college preparatory function of the high school "gained almost a monopoly of the thought and attention devoted to high schools" at conventions of the National Education Association during this period (1957, p. 67). From 1888 to 1890, only 14.4% of those enrolled in high school were preparing for college. Thus the curriculum for more than 85% of the students was being ignored in favor of discussing the program for less than 15% (Commissioner of Education, 1893).

The Secondary Curriculum—Battle Lines to the Present

Despite the tiny proportion of students involved, as the nineteenth century progressed the college preparatory function took on increased importance. This by no means should be taken to indicate agreement on the purpose of the high school. Indeed, the variety of purposes that the high school tried to serve seemed inevitably to conflict. Some saw the high school as a college preparatory institution and others as a place where non-college-bound students could prepare for life in society. When only a small percentage of the population even attended high school, these conflicts were not urgent. But when secondary education began to expand in the last decades of the nineteenth century, these problems became pressing. Although some were demanding a more practical education, others were continuing to argue for mental discipline and a curriculum with heavy emphasis on the classics. What was happening is well expressed by Butts and Cremin: "The lines of battle were being formed that were to last for a hundred years to the present" (1953, p. 134).

Today those calling for practical learning opportunities seem to be losing the battle. The question that ought to concern every curriculum worker is why academic and practical goals should have to be placed in opposition. They need not be, and according to parents they ought not be. This was the finding in Goodlad's large-scale study of schooling (1984). In a chapter titled "We Want It All," Goodlad reported that parents of high school students gave "very important" ratings to four goals of schools: academic, vocational, social and civic, and personal (pp. 33–60; Rose & Gallup, 2005, p.45).

In the closing decades of the twentieth century, vocational education opportunities (under which Goodlad included both learning how to choose an occupation that matches one's skills and developing specialized knowledge leading to economic independence) declined. As more states required students to take more academic courses for a diploma, school shops closed. The further shrinking of vocational education was on the federal policy agenda for education. In 2003, the Bush administration announced plans to end financial support to vocational education and reallocate the funds "to help students pass the state tests mandated by the No Child Left Behind Act," this as one writer observed, "Even as unemployment rises" (Winerip, 2003). The decision seemed imprudent, simply from the standpoint of common sense. Further, research shows "a link between school characteristics and students' success when they enter the labor market" and "the place of vocational education in the curriculum is a key factor in the transition process" (Hallinan, 2001, p. 26).

President Eliot's Concerns

President Charles W. Eliot of Harvard had curriculum in mind when he called for school reform in 1888. His concerns had been brewing for some time. Influenced by Spencer's work, Eliot (1869) proposed a "new education," based on the sciences (pure and applied), mathematics, and modern European languages. According to Cremin (1961), Spencer's answer that science is of most worth "was obviously influential in the formulation of the Committee of Ten, which gave parity to natural sciences in the secondary school program" (pp. 92–93). As a university administrator, Eliot (who was a powerful figure in the NEA) had another curriculum-related concern that probably led to the

appointment of the Committee of Ten. Eliot was concerned about the rising age of entering freshmen at Harvard, a problem also at other American colleges. As he saw it, the problem lay in both the organization and the curricula of elementary and secondary education.

The ten-year elementary curriculum was long and narrow and was followed by an enormously crowded secondary program, usually of four years. In 1888, Eliot gave a speech titled "Can School Programs Be Shortened and Enriched?" before the NEA's Department of Superintendence. Eliot, who had an extensive acquaintance with the curriculum problems of the schools, believed that the answer to the question was yes.

Eliot was especially concerned with arithmetic, particularly the undue amount of time devoted to reviews in the upper elementary grades. He proposed that the number of grades in the elementary school be reduced from ten to eight. He suggested that the program in arithmetic, which was taking up to one sixth of the school time for ten years, be contracted to six years, making room for algebra and geometry in the seventh and eighth grades. He held that the amount of time devoted to the study of grammar was too long and should be limited by culling out the memorization of rules and precepts and, instead, teaching the use of English through practice. Eliot suggested that beginning in the primary grades children be taught natural science by means of demonstrations and laboratory experiences rather than only from books. Elementary physics, also taught by laboratory methods, would be introduced in the upper-elementary grades.

Eliot argued that the idea that democratic theory implied an identical curriculum for every child and uniform tests for promotion was "fallacious and ruinous. Democratic theory," he said,

> does not undertake to fly in the face of nature by asserting that all children . . . are alike and should be treated alike. Everybody knows that children are infinitely diverse. . . . Every child is a unique personality. . . . Hence, in the public schools of a democracy the aim should be to give the utmost possible amount of individual instruction, to grade according to capacity . . . and to promote not by battalions, but in the most irregular way possible. (National Education Association, 1893, pp. 617–625)

Eliot's speech stimulated much discussion over the next few years and calls for education reform. The result was the appointment by the NEA of three committees: the Committee of Ten on Secondary School Studies, the

Committee of Fifteen on Elementary Education, and the Committee on College Entrance Requirements. Of these, the Committee of Ten was the most influential.

Composition of the Committee of Ten. College professors predominated the composition of the committees; indeed, the Committee of Ten included five college presidents. It is obvious from the major recommendations of the committee that the report was dominated by the more conservative beliefs and ideas of the colleges and universities of the 1890s. For example, the report reflected a belief in the value of the classical subjects for mental training.

Determining the Course of Secondary Education

The report of the Committee of Ten was enormously influential on the secondary curriculum for a generation after its publication in 1893. One of the ways in which it was influential concerns the rise of national committees for guidance on curriculum problems. Since the Committee of Ten, the recommendations of groups of eminent persons have influenced educational policy. The 1980s and 1990s witnessed a veritable foray of such reports on educational reform, effecting nationalizing influences on the school curriculum. The most notorious of these documents, *A Nation at Risk,* was issued in 1983 by the National Commission on Excellence in Education, appointed by the U.S. Secretary of Education.

The procedure usually operates in this fashion: National task forces or committees are appointed and meet to deliberate on the problems assigned to them, for example, the decline of U.S. preeminence in global industrial markets. After the discussions, one or two committee members write up the agreements, and the report is circulated among the other committee members for their verification. By the time the recommendations are implemented, the group of experts has scattered to the four winds. Eminent persons who decide what to include or remove from the curriculum are seldom around to take responsibility for the outcomes.

A Paradoxical Report. The report of the Committee of Ten cast the mold for secondary education for years to come, but the report itself was strikingly paradoxical. The report states without equivocation that "secondary schools do not exist for the purpose of preparing boys and girls for colleges" (National

Education Association, 1894, p. 51). Yet despite this recognition, the report proceeds to recommend curricular offerings geared almost entirely toward college preparation, although high school was a terminal institution for the overwhelming proportion of students.

What actually was behind this recommendation? Was it in the spirit of democracy or a conservative spirit? Did the committee sincerely believe that the traditional college preparatory subjects were best for those who sought from the high school some kind of vocational preparation? These questions have been endlessly debated by students of curriculum. We know that some of the people on the committee believed that study of the classics (such as Latin) developed mental power and was therefore eminently practical. The committee based its curriculum recommendations on the doctrine of mental discipline. Concluding its recommendations on the regrouping of subjects, the report contended: "[E]very youth who entered college would have spent four years in studying a few subjects thoroughly; and, on the theory that all the subjects are to be considered equivalent in educational rank for the purposes of admission to college, it would make no difference which subjects he had chosen from the programme—he would have had four years of strong and effective mental training" (p. 53).

Students could elect a curriculum from one of four programs: Classical, Latin Scientific, Modern Languages, or English. (See Figure 2.1.) Election from a variety of subjects, however, was not recognized.

Following the recommendations of the Committee of Ten led to problems. According to Brubacher (1966), "Insistence on this kind of curriculum resulted in a high dropout rate among high school students" (p. 422). In some sense, at least, the report was unremittingly conservative. Although it was a response to calls for reform, it both reaffirmed and restored the traditional doctrine of mental discipline. Similarly, 90 years later, the writers of *A Nation at Risk* harkened back to the alleged benefits of a failed curriculum of university-based academic disciplines that had been implemented in the schools during the years of the Cold War and space race. "The writers of *A Nation at Risk* are, one feels, not far removed in spirit from the members of the Committee of Ten," noted one observer (Reid, 1988, p. 127).

Yet for all of its conservative recommendations, the report of the Committee of Ten was devoted to the concept of a common curriculum for all youth. When the report was attacked for this stand, Eliot defended the committee's position, arguing that the

Figure 2.1 Range of Curricular Offerings (High School) as Proposed by the Committee of Ten on Secondary School Studies, 1893.

1st Secondary School Year	2nd Secondary School Year

Latin .... 5 p.
English Literature, 2 p.⎫
English Composition, 2 p.⎬ 4 p.
German [or French] .... 5 p.
Algebra .... 4 p.
History of Italy, Spain, and France ... 3 p.
Applied Geography (European
    political–continental and
    oceanic flora and fauna) .... 4 p.
 	
                              25 p.
	Latin .... 4 p.
	Greek .... 5 p.
	English Literature, 2 p.⎫
	English Composition, 2 p.⎬ 4 p.
	German, continued .... 4 p.
	French, begun .... 5 p.
	Algebra,* 2 p.⎫
	Geometry, 2 p.⎬ 4 p.
	Botany or Zoology .... 4 p.
	English History to 1688 .... 3 p.
	
	                              33 p.
	
	*Option of bookkeeping and commercial arithmetic.

3rd Secondary School Year	4th Secondary School Year

Latin .... 4 p.
Greek .... 4 p.
English Literature, 2 p.⎫
English Composition, 1 p.⎬ 4 p.
Rhetoric, 1 p.⎭
German .... 4 p.
French .... 4 p.
Algebra,* 2 p.⎫
Geometry, 2 p.⎬ 4 p.
Physics .... 4 p.
History, English and American ...... 3 p.
Astronomy, 3 p. 1st ½ yr. ⎫
Meterology, 3 p. 2nd ½ yr.⎬ 3 p.
 	
                              34 p.
 	
*Option of bookkeeping and commercial arithmetic.
	Latin .... 4 p.
	Greek .... 4 p.
	English Literature, 2 p.⎫
	English Composition, 1 p.⎬ 4 p.
	English Grammar, 1 p.⎭
	German .... 4 p.
	French .... 4 p.
	Trigonometry ⎫
	Higher Algebra ⎬ 2 p.
	Chemistry .... 4 p.
	History, (intensive) and Civil
	    Government .... 3 p.
	Geology or Physiography,⎫
	    4 p. 1st ½ yr. ⎬ 4 p.
	Anatomy, Physiology, and ⎬
	    Hygiene, 4 p. 2nd ½ yr.⎭
	                              33 p.

Source: Committee of Ten. *Report of the Committee of Ten on Secondary School Studies* (Washington, DC: National Education Association, 1893), p. 4.

European system of classifying children into "future peasants, mechanics, trades-people, merchants, and professional people" (1905, p. 330) was unacceptable in a democratic society.

The Aftermath: The Colleges Get What They Want.
The Committee of Ten not only prioritized the school subjects but also defined the content of each subject in detail. Their report was enormously influential, "a gospel" for the writers of the high school curriculum

(Nelson & Calfee, 1998, p. 10; Sizer, 1964, p. xi). Thus, although there might be initial euphoria if one's subject happened to be identified as a major subject by the committee, the recommendations could be chafing, in fact downright irritating. This is precisely what happened in the case of English. As pointed out by Nelson and Calfee (and shown in Figure 2.1), English was defined as one subject with two main aspects, both stressing written language, "the study of literature and training in the expression of thought"

(p. 10). On the face of it this seems reasonable. As Nelson and Calfee point out, it did not turn out that way. In terms of time allocated to each component, the curricular stress "was weighted toward literature, the study of works of 'good' authors" (p. 10). For the colleges, the report of the committee seemed to be working very well with regard to instruction in literature. In many high schools, teachers had adapted their instruction to the pleasure of the colleges. They followed the literary criticism approach of colleges and universities, and their students were reading the works that were recommended. The colleges and universities were dictating high school instruction in English to the nth degree. As Nancy Nelson and Robert Calfee, authorities in the field of English, tell us: "Schools had extensively annotated texts and reading guides for students to use in their analyses of works of 'great' authors, and a uniform list of titles had been established" (p. 10).

As might be expected, the situation was unacceptable for many high school faculty. They could get no professional satisfaction from a literature curriculum composed of works already selected for them and a writing curriculum composed of essays concerning that same literature. Nelson and Calfee explain what happened:

> Numbers of high school teachers, particularly in the East, opposed the set curriculum imposed on them, and created organizations to voice objections. In fact, the National Council of Teachers of English (NCTE) was formed later (in 1911) largely as a means of concerted action on the part of high school teachers to resist this kind of curriculum and to give more attention to students' interests and experiences in their reading and writing. (pp. 10–11)

For years many high school teachers and experts in secondary education would hold objectionable the dictating of curriculum requirements by colleges and universities. They questioned the old mental discipline theory that certain courses had innate powers of preparing students for college and they felt, justifiably, that they were being tamped down in their efforts to develop a curriculum that would meet the needs and interests of all secondary school students. Eventually research studies, discussed later, put the old mental discipline idea at rest but never buried it completely. Today the relation between colleges and universities and high schools retains some atmospheric similarities with the aftermath of the report of the Committee of Ten. Growing numbers of students are enrolled in the Advanced Placement courses that colleges and universities total up to determine the rigor of their high school work. The numbers have escalated along with competition for admission to prestigious colleges. More than a century after the report of the Committee of Ten, the focus of many high schools is on college standing. Thus, as Hallinan (2001) points out, the needs of all students to "learn about careers and pathways to occupational goals go by the board or at least get short shrift" (p. 25).

While some high school students are concerned with being admitted to a prestigious college, others would gladly be admitted to a college. Still others hope that the door will be open if they decide to pursue post-secondary education. According to Brubacher, the "Committee of Ten looked forward to the day when colleges would be accessible to all secondary students who had creditably accomplished their work no matter what group of subjects they had studied" (1966, p. 414). Certainly, the committee tried to equate the value of subjects. The report stated that "all the subjects between which choice is allowed should be approximately equivalent to each other in seriousness, dignity, and efficacy" (National Education Association, 1894, p. 43).

The Legacy of the Committee of Ten

The committee's hope that the high school curriculum ought to permit any student to go to college has come to be increasingly realized. In the early twenty-first century, many state colleges and universities provided the opportunity for all high school graduates to attend college, even those who did not follow a prescribed college preparatory course. Access to higher education also increased for students with a graduate equivalency diploma (GED) and for those without a diploma who had reached the age of 18. In California, for example, every 18-year-old is guaranteed admission to a state-supported community college. The national emphasis has been on open-access higher education, but this has not been accompanied by a modern reconstruction of the secondary school curriculum to serve the cosmopolitan student population.

As the nineteenth century came to a close, the college was also experiencing a remarkable development. Its curriculum was being adapted more and more to preparation for various vocations along with the traditional classical courses. In 1902 Dewey observed that "things seem to be taking their own course" where the question of preparation for college versus preparation for community life was concerned. He wrote prophetically that when

> the high school has worked out on its own account the broadening of its own curriculum, I believe we shall find that the high school and the college have arrived at a common point. The college course will be so broad and varied that it will be entirely feasible to take any judicious group of studies from any well organized and well managed high school, and accept them as preparation for college. It has been the narrowness of the traditional college curriculum on the one side and the inadequacy of the content of high school work on the other, which have caused a large part of our mutual embarrassments. (1902a, pp. 65–66)

College Domination. Generally speaking, Dewey's prophecy has arrived. The college curriculum has undergone a vast revolution. Indeed, colleges and universities today are vocational institutions. Adolescents, even late bloomers, can go to college and study from among a very wide range of offerings. What Dewey could not foresee a mere decade after the report of the Committee of Ten was that the report would reinforce the trend toward college domination of the high school curriculum. Thus the high school, which was not originally intended to become a college preparatory institution, was transformed into one, at least in the eyes of the committee and many school faculties. It became increasingly difficult for the high school to work out effective programs for noncollege preparatory students. The report of the Committee of Ten was a turning point: reactionary in some ways, progressive in others.

The Report of the Committee of Fifteen

Agitators for educational reform do not always achieve what they hope for once they have set the reform machinery in motion. In fact, the final result may well be the opposite of what they had hoped for. A case in point was the report of the Committee of Fifteen. As noted, Harvard's Charles Eliot was opposed to dealing with children en masse and schooling them as flocks. He also favored the teaching of science by means of laboratory experiences instead of merely from books. Eliot knew full well that science is far more than a body of knowledge. It is also a way of thinking. It asks us to allow the facts in even when they may not conform to preconceptions. It advises us to formulate

alternative hypotheses and test which are best supported by the evidence. Eliot knew that this kind of thinking is a necessary tool for a democracy.

However, the Committee of Fifteen (1895) protested strongly against the scientific method in elementary science teaching.

> It is important not to hasten the use of a strictly scientific method on the part of the child. . . . He is rather in the imitation stage of mind than in that of criticism. He will not reach the comparative or critical method until the era of higher education. (*Educational Review*, p. 270)

In light of this conclusion, one hour of "oral lessons" in natural science (which included hygiene) was recommended.

The committee's approach to the development of the child was mechanical. Schoolwork was distributed into eight separate years, each with its own definite subjects to be covered. The committee was cool to the concept of curriculum synthesis. "Rigid isolation of the elements of each branch" was considered essential in elementary learning (p. 275). The committee's outlook almost compelled the teacher of a given grade to take an isolated view of her work rather than be guided by the ideal of the child's whole development. The number of children in a room, which in the graded schools of the time often ran as high as 60 was an added condition that, in Dewey's words, "compel them to be led in flocks, if not in hordes" (1902a, p. 26).

Class size was not dealt with by the Committee of Fifteen. But, as every teacher knows, the curriculum is profoundly influenced by school conditions. Large classes make it less likely for teachers to plan lessons that stress individual inquiry and judgment and provide for the individual child's needs. What teachers know from experience is now confirmed by research. Studies have found "that in smaller classes there is more individualized support for learning" (Blatchford, Moriarty, Edmonds, & Martin, 2002, p. 102). As it happened, the committee emphasized a curriculum broken up into isolated parts that did not require individual inquiry. Had the committee included observation and experimentation in science instruction and treated each child as unique, there would have been conflict with at least two existing conditions: a large number of children in a room, which limited the contact of teacher with child and of child with child, and the teacher's outlook, which was confined to one year of the child's development. The committee's report merely reinforced existing conditions.

Reinforcing the Status Quo

Eliot had proposed that the number of elementary grades be reduced from ten to eight. This recommendation was endorsed in the report of the Committee of Fifteen, as was his plan to substitute the study of algebra for arithmetic in the seventh and eighth grades. (See Figure 2.2.) At the outset of the report, the committee stated that grammar, literature, arithmetic, geography, and history are the subjects in the elementary

Figure 2.2   The Elementary School Curriculum as Proposed by the Committee of Fifteen, 1895.

Branches	1st Year	2nd Year	3rd Year	4th Year	5th Year	6th Year	7th Year	8th Year
Reading	10 lessons a week	5 lessons a week						
Writing	10 lessons a week	5 lessons a week	3 lessons a week					
Spelling lists				4 lessons a week				
English Grammar	Oral, with composition lessons				5 lessons a week with textbook			
Latin								5 lessons
Arithmetic	Oral, sixty minutes a week		5 lessons a week with textbook					
Algebra							5 lessons a week	
Geography	Oral, sixty minutes a week		*5 lessons a week with textbook				3 lessons a week	
National Science and Hygiene	Sixty minutes a week							
U.S. History							5 lessons a week	
U.S. Constitution								*5 les.
General History	Oral, 60 minutes a week							
Physical Culture	Sixty minutes a week							
Vocal Music	Sixty minutes a week divided into 4 lessons							
Drawing	Sixty minutes a week							
Manual Training or Sewing and Cookery							One-half day each	
No. of Lessons	20 + 7 daily exer.	20 + 7 daily exer.	20 + 5 daily exer.	24 + 7 daily exer.	27 + 5 daily exer.	27 + 5 daily exer.	23 + 6 daily exer.	23 + 6 daily exer.
Total Hours of Recitations	12	12	11	13	16¼	16¼	17½	17½
Length of Recitations	15 min.	15 min.	20 min.	20 min.	25 min.	25 min.	30 min.	30 min.

*Begins in second half of year.

Source: Committee of Fifteen. "Report of the Sub-Committee on the Correlation of Studies in Elementary Education." *Educational Review,* 9 (March 1895), p. 284.

school with the greatest value for training the mind. This was the philosophy of William T. Harris, who wrote most of the report and was the highly influential school superintendent and educational philosopher of the time. Throughout the report, the committee held the line against newer subjects, allotting them relatively little time in the school program.

There were some vigorous expressions of dissent by committee members on such points as "oral lessons" in science (telling by the teacher) and the failure to include observation and experimentation in science instruction. But Harris and other conservatives won out, despite the mounting evidence on the need for hands-on experience in children's mental and social development.

The Final Result

In the paper he presented at the 1893 NEA meeting, Eliot suggested a reduction in the time devoted to grammar and arithmetic so that the elementary school program could be diversified and enriched. The result of the committee's deliberations, however, was to give these subjects even higher priority than they had before. Indeed, grammar now topped what had become the official list of the common branches. It may be said that the effect of the report of the Committee of Fifteen on the elementary curriculum was to entrench and intensify the problems that Eliot had sought to solve.

On the matter of curriculum synthesis, the report of the Committee of Fifteen was a turning point for the worse. The problem of curriculum segmentation and isolation continues to this day.

Dewey's Laboratory School at Chicago

On the occasion of Dewey's ninetieth birthday, Oliver Franks, the British ambassador to the United States, wrote:

> For fifty years Dr. Dewey has urged us to relate the school to life and above all to the life of the child. Wherever British children today are active, purposeful, and happy in school there is little doubt that they owe something to the active, purposeful, and long life of a great American philosopher (Highlights of Dewey's life, 1949, p. S-2).

The tribute was one of many from leaders in education, government, and the arts from all over the world. In *The New Leader* magazine, which had run

many of Dewey's articles, Dewey was honored for his contributions to the fields of education, psychology, ethics, art, and political science. Although Dewey wrote on a range of problems, it was education that had, as *The New Leader* noted, virtually been revolutionized by his ideas. And not only in the United States, but abroad as well.

If that revolution had a beginning, it was surely in the experimental school founded by Dewey at the University of Chicago in 1896. Like any laboratory, the purpose of the school was to test theoretical ideas and advance the body of knowledge in a field—in this case, education. The ideas to be tested were Dewey's philosophical and psychological principles, or as Dewey put it, his "philosophical interpretation of psychology"(Mayhew & Edwards, 1936, p. 464). Dewey believed that thinking (and knowledge) developed as children attempted to solve problems that originated in active situations. For Dewey, this (or any) theoretical principle is of little value unless tested.

The Curriculum Problem: What Dewey Hoped to Discover

With regard to the curriculum, Dewey and the teachers in the laboratory school hoped to identify the direct, present experiences of children from which more organized and technical knowledge would grow as children progressed through school.

The solution of this curriculum problem was, in Dewey's words, "extremely difficult," and he wrote many years later that "we did not reach it; it has not yet been reached and in its fullness will never be reached" (p. 468). But the problem was posed and that in itself was a lasting contribution. And the records, notes, and plans of the school indicate that Dewey and the laboratory school teachers probably went a greater distance toward the solution than Dewey recognized (L. Tanner, 1997).

Differences with Harris. Dewey's laboratory school was founded a year after the Report of the Committee of Fifteen and was a study in contrast. For Harris, the conservative leader in education who wrote the report, a school subject is an entity unto itself, external to the pupil and mastered through effort rather than interest. It was up to the teacher to take the systematic knowledge of adult consciousness, which had been hammered out through centuries, and do the best he or she could with it. The child must enter on the "fruits of civilization" in their mature form (1898, p. 36). Dewey took issue with this view. As he pointed out in an article titled "The Psychological Aspect of the School Curriculum" (1897a), a school subject is both a logical whole (a system of facts, methods and principles) and a form of living personal experience.

"Geography," said Dewey, "is not only a set of facts and principles, which may be classified and discussed by themselves; it is also a way in which some individual feels and thinks the world. It must be the latter before it can be the former (p. 361). Dewey was to elaborate on this principle a few years later in *The Child and the Curriculum* (1902b).

In an article published in 1897, Dewey went on to state that

> [w]ith the child, instruction must take the standpoint not of accomplished results, but of the crude beginnings. We must discover what there is lying within the child's present sphere of experience (or within the scope of experiences which he can easily get) which deserves to be called geographical. It is not a question of *how* to teach the child geography, but first of all the question of *what* geography is for the child. (p. 361)

Dewey emphasized his substantial disagreement "with the view taken by Dr. Harris in the Report of the Committee of Fifteen regarding the comparative worthlessness of the psychological basis" (p. 357). Dewey argued that "the primary point of concern in education is beyond question with the subject as a special mode of personal experience, rather than with the subject as a body of wrought-out facts and scientifically tested principles" (p. 361).

Harris's view of instruction was the opposite, and it had become educational policy through the report of the Committee of Fifteen. Dewey found this view dangerously deficient. "The crying evil in instruction today," he wrote, "is that the subject-matter of the curriculum, both as a whole and in its various stages, is selected and determined on the objective or logical basis instead of upon the psychological" (p. 363).

Subject Matter as Experience. At the heart of Dewey's approach to curriculum development was his theory of knowledge. Learning and education are social in nature because there is always human interaction involved: the influence of some people on others. The sets of facts, concepts, ideas and generalizations that we label geography, mathematics, science, and so on are nothing more or less than selections from past social life and "represent the answers found for social needs" (1900c, pp. 222–223).

It is all too easy to regard these sets of facts, concepts, ideas and generalizations as external to the learner, to be mastered by encouragement and devices by the teacher. But Dewey believed that the maximum benefit for the child was when systematic knowledge grows out of experiences and interests that the child already has. The instructional problem is how to bring about this growth. The first thing to be determined is the kind of experience appropriate for the child at a given time: what kind of experiences get a hold on the youngster, what he is capable of doing and can do to the greatest advantage and with the least waste of time. These interests and experiences offer a key to the selection and organization of subject matter.

Subject Matter as Purpose. What a ridiculous thing to insist that there is a fixed body of knowledge that is forever set off and labeled physics, geography, or history, said Dewey. "Exactly the same objective reality will be one or the other or none of these three, according to the interest and intellectual standpoint from which it is viewed" (1897a, p. 362). For example, a square mile of territory, when viewed from one interest, would be labeled trigonometry, from another standpoint we would label the facts regarding it geography, and from still another interest, it would become historical knowledge. "There is absolutely nothing in the fact, as an objective fact, which places it under one head," pointed out Dewey. "Only as we ask what purpose or end some individual has in view do we find a basis for selecting and arranging the facts under the label of any particular study" (p. 362).

Dewey and the laboratory school teachers hoped to determine how, out of the child's interest and purpose, a subject as a form of experience gradually differentiated itself from other experiences and developed into the systematic knowledge of the adult.

The Curriculum

The curriculum in the school conducted by Dewey consisted of the child's side (activities) and the teacher's side (logically organized bodies of subject matter: science, mathematics, history, language, literature, the arts, and physical culture). It was a developmental curriculum in every sense of the word.

Reasons for Activities. Behind the activities was Dewey's conception of the psychological nature of the child. Dewey argued that children are inherently active with strong impulses to investigate, to share with others what they have found out, to construct practical things, and to create. Dewey developed this psychological concept into a curriculum principle: The child's impulses are an enormously important educational resource, and opportunities should be provided to children to develop the impulses through engagement in activities.

Dewey also saw activities as a means of achieving curriculum synthesis. A constructive activity (cooking, carpentry, or sewing) provides the opportunity for learning about materials and processes. "Animal, vegetable life, soil, climate, etc. are studied not as mere *objects* (a psychological unreality) but as factors in action," wrote Dewey in his plan for the school (1895, p. 10).

The activities had three important functions:

1. They led to the sets of useful facts and principles known as science, history, literature—bodies of systematized knowledge.
2. They were the means of curriculum synthesis and revealing the social significance of knowledge.
3. They were means of using and developing the child's inherent impulses so as to enhance the growth of the child.

Interrelating the Dimensions. The development of the curriculum in the laboratory school depended on teachers' keeping the dimensions clearly in mind. In order to do this, they organized their plans by subheadings, "From the Child's Standpoint" and "From the Teacher's Standpoint." The teachers' plans were published every Friday in the *University [of Chicago] Record*. In reading the plans, one notes that the teacher's standpoint is first. Ideas and concepts are classified by subject, followed by the child's standpoint—the activities in which children engage in learning the concepts and how social life developed.

What is of importance is that teachers began with the subject field and planned the activities that called for progressively more complex interrelated understandings. They did *not* begin with the activities and try to extrapolate ideas from the subject field.

Generalists and Specialists. So weighty was the intellectual load on the teacher that Dewey dropped the idea of having one teacher teach the children in all studies. Instead the school assumed a recognized role for teacher specialists as well as generalists. Dewey's reason is worth quoting:

> One of the reasons for this modification of the original plan was the difficulty of getting scientific facts presented that were facts and truths. It has been assumed that any phenomenon that interested a child was good enough, and that if he were aroused and made alert that was all that could be expected. It is, however, just as necessary that what he gets should be truth and should not be subordinated to anything else. . . . The difficulty of getting scientific work presented except by those who were specialists has led to the change in regard to other subjects as well. (Mayhew & Edwards, 1936, pp. 35–36)

Although one person was responsible for coordinating each child's program, the children learned to take their questions to the teachers who were specialists in whatever area to which a problem belonged in.

Curriculum Coherence. Dewey found that specialization need not lead to compartmentalization. "The undue separation which often follows teaching by specialists," he wrote, "is not inherent in the method, but is the result of lack of supervision, cooperation and control by a unified plan" (1897b, p. 75). The laboratory school had such a plan: a civilizational theme. Beginning with activities familiar to 4- and 5-year-olds because they were activities of the home, the developing curriculum led to the study of related occupations in early civilization. Following the way of social evolution, it traced human progress through discovery and invention to the occupations and organization of contemporary society.

The study of occupations provided opportunities for developing the child's increasing ability to conceptualize, to bring out a special idea. For instance, farming as studied by 6-year-olds simply showed what some people do and how they serve others. Seven-year-olds reviewed this material, but the emphasis was on the evolving needs in human history that required this occupation and the way it has affected present social life.

Dewey and his laboratory school faculty, and members of the university faculty in pedagogy, chose occupations as an organizing theme, although there are other possible organizing themes, Dewey noted. What is of critical importance, Dewey found, is that teachers confer constantly to achieve a coherent curriculum. The laboratory school appears to have pioneered in collaborative decision making and teacher reflection. Dewey recounted that "fellows and members of the faculty of the pedagogical department, graduate-student assistants, and the regular teaching staff of the school all met weekly with the directors to discuss the reports of the school in relation to theoretical principles and to revise future plans accordingly" (Mayhew & Edwards, 1936, p. 370).

The laboratory school experimented with and discarded many activities in subject matter fields, which was its purpose. The teachers' work proceeded in accord with a clearly defined framework: the occupations that make for society, and Dewey's concept of progression from activities to formal studies. As Wirth points out in his discussion of the laboratory school, there was a well-considered curriculum design (1966, p. 198).

One can see readily from the records of the laboratory school, the photographs of student activities, and the examples of student work that remain, that the curriculum was based on psychological knowledge about children and on logically organized and useful facts, concepts, ideas, and generalizations and principles from the major fields of knowledge. It appears to have been a curriculum of high quality in which the children engaged in knowledge applications to the real world.

The Dewey School, as it became known, introduced educators and parents to the possibilities of what a curriculum can be. As Dewey reminds us, the curriculum is always in the making: it is never made (Mayhew & Edwards, 1936, p. 464).

High School Accreditation for College Admission

After the Civil War, school and college people became increasingly concerned with a fundamental question: What are the best criteria for determining admission to college? The concern stemmed from a chaotic situation. Procedures were inadequately defined and carelessly applied. Sometimes they depended on the relationship between a certain college and a certain teacher. The variety of acceptable high school programs and the diversity of college entrance requirements led educators to become interested in the problem of high school accreditation for college admissions. Setting up an accreditation plan called for common action that would be beneficial to both schools and colleges, not to mention students. The effort to formalize the cooperation and establish it permanently led to the establishment of regional accrediting associations before the turn of the century. These have been of enduring value.

Standards and Accreditation

Accreditation began in the American West, where the state university was considered part (the third level) of the public school system. And so it was that in 1869–1870, the University of Michigan admitted graduates from selected high schools without examination, on the principal's recommendation and on the submission of a certificate of courses and grades. Committees of university faculty visited the schools to evaluate them and determine whether their graduates would be eligible for acceptance into the university.

What did the school visitors look at? The visiting committees emphasized such criteria as the number of qualified faculty, the size of classes, and the facilities and resources in judging the academic fitness of the high schools. But of particular importance is that they also evaluated the curriculum. For example, Krug (1964) tells of a report on a rejected high school that recommended changes in the course of study and textbooks (pp. 151–152). However, for the most part, the procedure impelled the colleges to eliminate their highly specified and widely differing entrance requirements and examinations.

In examining the reports, Krug found frequent criticisms of the attitudes of school boards. Some school people "appreciated this as a help in getting what they wanted." As one superintendent told Michigan's president, James B. Angell, the accreditation system "had strengthened the high schools of the state by providing support against lukewarm board members" (p. 152). The accreditation system also worked against the not uncommon practice of faculty and administrative appointment by political influence.

Other state universities established similar admissions policies. Indiana University's accrediting plan, adopted in 1873, provided for accreditation of high schools by the state board of education. The practice was well regarded and was soon found in other parts of the country.

Regional Associations of Colleges and Secondary Schools. Bringing the state systems together regionally and permanently was the next logical step. In 1895, the North Central Association of Colleges and Secondary Schools was established. In 1902, this association worked out standards to be applied in judging the fitness of secondary schools for accreditation. Using the term *unit* to represent a year of secondary school study in a subject, the North Central Association defined acceptable high schools as those requiring 15 units for graduation. Detailed requirements were specified for subjects that were acceptable to colleges in terms of entrance units.

In addition to the North Central Association, five other regional associations were formed. In order of their founding, they are: The New England Association (1885), the Middle States Association (1887), the Southern Association (1895), the Northwest Association (1917), and the Western Association (1924).

The College Entrance Examination Board. In 1900 another institution of continuing influence came into being. The College Entrance Examination Board was founded for the purpose of constructing and administering examinations for high school students applying for admission to college. Once again, the purpose was standardization and the solution of a very practical problem: Teachers and principals no longer had to prepare students "going to different colleges in different amounts and different books of Latin, Greek and other subjects" (Krug, p. 150). This had not been as much of a problem when only a tiny proportion of the age group attended college.

The College Entrance Examination Board was an East Coast invention. The founding college members were Barnard, Bryn Mawr, Columbia, Cornell, Johns Hopkins, New York University, University of Pennsylvania, Rutgers, Swarthmore, Union, and Vassar. (Harvard joined later.) One reason for the board's founding was that as public high schools grew in number, the link between high school preparation and college requirements lessened. Students far from the East Coast could not sit for the college's own examinations, and admissions officers lacked enough information to evaluate unknown applicants from unknown schools. The Eastern member colleges allowed applicants to take the College Board examinations in place of their own examinations. Most colleges continued to rely on high school accreditation in admitting applicants.

The time came, however, when the number of qualified high school graduates increased to the point where colleges had more qualified applicants than they could admit. The Scholastic Aptitude Test (SAT), intended to provide colleges with a way to evaluate an applicant's ability to learn, was administered by the College Board beginning in 1926 with a limited population. Renamed the Scholastic Assessment Test in 1993 in belated but masked recognition of the limited validity of the test as a measure of aptitude, the

SAT has grown enormously over the years and has come to garner great media attention, especially when declining scores could be cited. The American College Testing Program (ACT) was established later (1959) to serve a function similar to the SAT. It is used mainly in north central states.

New Criteria for Good Secondary Schools

The creation of the College Entrance Examination Board allowed the newly established regional accrediting associations to work toward the improvement of secondary schools generally, rather than focusing mainly on standards thought to be most applicable for college preparation. But for many years the accreditation standards tended to be defined along quantitative lines, having tenuous relationship to the actual quality of the school.

Then in 1932 the six regional associations embarked on an effort to form and test new criteria along such dimensions as the school's philosophy, student population, curriculum, community, faculty, guidance services, student activities program, instructional resources and facilities, and other educational factors. As a result of these efforts, principles were established in recognition that schools must, within broadly defined limits, vary their programs according to the particular needs of their own communities and student populations. Criteria were developed for identifying characteristics and functions of "good" secondary schools. These criteria were stated in manuals that have been continually revised over the years (National Study of School Evaluation, 2002).

Local school staffs are required to complete a comprehensive self-appraisal of the educational program, followed by an evaluation conducted by a visiting committee of educators from other schools and colleges. The local school then receives a report concerning its strengths and areas of needed improvement in connection with the accreditation status.

Of enormous importance is the approach of the National Study of School Evaluation, which places emphasis on continuous growth and improvement rather than on the meeting of minimum quantitative standards. Self-appraisal, outside expert judgment, objective evidence, and practices in comparable schools with successful programs are identified as important aspects of accreditation.

Representatives of the six voluntary regional accrediting associations comprising the National Study of School Evaluation have attempted to influence a change "from maintaining minimum standards to the striving for excellence in all aspects of a school's work" (1987, p. 9). It has been an uphill battle. State mandates and nationalizing influences have weakened the effects of regional accrediting organizations. Since the report of the National Commission on Excellence in Education (1983), legislatures and state departments of education have taken a regulatory approach to improving the quality of schools. The number of academic courses required for graduation from high school has been increased; schools think that they need to require three years of this course and two of that. The regulatory changes have ignored the need to provide students with learning opportunities of the hands-on variety, which many students prefer and which help ignite the spark of learning.

Indeed, regulation has continued to stamp out curricular differences and opportunities. Such differences had become a source of increasing frustration to university administrators, who believed that students would be better prepared if they all took the same courses. For example, in 1991, the City University of New York proposed that high-school students be required to take a set of traditional academic courses geared to examinations of the Regents of the State of New York (Lewis, p. 18). By 2003 students were required to take five Regents examinations in order to graduate (Goodnough, 2003). Meeting student needs requires thinking beyond state examinations, which schools are not encouraged by state and national policies to do.

The Eight-Year Study, which was conducted in the 1930s, examined 30 schools and nearly 3,000 students enrolled in 300 colleges to determine the effect of traditional academic school admission requirements on the success of college students. The study found that what was needed was a good high school with a well integrated curriculum, as opposed to the traditional list of academic courses, and students would succeed in college (Aikin, 1942a). The approach to accreditation of the National Study of School Evaluation is supported by this study. The Eight-Year Study is discussed in chapter 4 and other sections of this text.

American postsecondary education is enormously diverse. Differences in mission among higher education institutions mean that there is no single best approach to determining qualifications for admission: there is a college suited for almost anyone who aspires to further education.

Perspective

For better or worse (in some cases, both) we are surrounded by the effects of nineteenth-century turning points in education. It was Herbert Spencer, the English philosopher, who put the question in its most memorable form: What knowledge is of most worth? (Spencer's answer was science in its applications to life needs.) The question is enormously important for determining the educational goals to be given attention. Today, the question of most worth is losing out to the frenzy of student test preparation. Yet, according to Goodlad, public expectation continues to be high "for educational attention to all four of the traditional purposes of schooling in our democracy: the personal, social and vocational as well as the academic" (2003, p. 25). Teachers and curriculum personnel need to ask Spencer's question themselves. The question has no final answer. The curriculum is necessarily unfinished and unfinishable.

Francis Parker was a giant in the early reform of reading instruction, and his idea of teaching skills through use stands as a best practice in education. Actually, reading specialists and early childhood educators continue to rediscover (indeed, reinvent) Parker's Quincy system—in between periods of back-to-basics retrenchment. Parker demonstrated in a public school system (Quincy, Massachusetts) before the twentieth century that children can have a more meaningful educational experience if reading, writing, and oral language are taught holistically. (It is Parker who invented what is today called "the reading-writing connection" by experts in reading.) This is not to imply that Parker's principle was without opposition. There were always critics and attempts to reduce reading to an assortment of isolated skills. In the late 1980s and 1990s Parker's method was reinvented under the label of the whole language approach, but by 2000 the pendulum-swing to curriculum change seemed to be in full force. Those seeking a return to a phonics-first position seemed to be winning the day. Nevertheless, the idea that learning to read and write are interrelated processes is here to stay. Good teachers will not wait for the pendulum to swing their way again.

Parker's emphasis throughout the curriculum in Quincy (and later, at the Cook County Normal School in Chicago) was on observing, describing, and understanding phenomena appropriate to the child's experience. When these abilities had begun to develop, conventional school subjects were introduced. It's of little wonder that Dewey referred to Parker as "the father of progressive education." Dewey himself built on Parker's developmental concept in working out the curriculum in his own school.

To this day, educators try to integrate the traditional subject curriculum. This curriculum became fully entrenched by the reports of the Committee of Ten on Secondary School Studies and the Committee of Fifteen on Elementary School Studies issued toward the close of the nineteenth century. The Committee of Ten was created in response to demands for uniform college entrance requirements. The high school was not originally intended to be a college preparatory institution. Although most students did not go to college, the larger effect of the committee's recommendations was to turn the high school into a college preparatory institution. (This was not surprising because the committee included five college presidents.) The only subjects discussed by the committee were those required for college entrance. The subjects were to be taught the same way whether or not a student was college bound.

At the close of the nineteenth century, the high school curriculum ignored the needs of adolescents. Many students dropped out, pointing to the need for a more useful curriculum. The report of the Committee of Ten was a big setback in this regard. Was the document simply an expression of conservative caution and self-interest? It is all too easy to dismiss it as such. But we know that the ideal of equality—of both status and opportunity—has shaped institutions including public schools. The idea of a dual educational system, such as that found in European countries, was repugnant to committee members, particularly Charles W. Eliot, president of Harvard University. The committee called for a common curriculum because they believed that all high school students should have an opportunity to go to college.

Yet the committee's report was based on the premise that there is only one right answer to the question of "most worth," There are many "most worths" depending on the needs of students and society. This fact has been clearly recognized by the regional accrediting associations established before the close of the nineteenth century. In the 1930s, the six regional associations formed a national committee that established principles that recognized the need for schools to vary their programs according to the particular needs of their communities and student populations. The National Study of School Evaluation has continued to publish guides for school improvement planning intended to serve the needs of various types of high schools and programs. In 1900 the College Entrance Examination Board was established, and it continues to be the leading agency in college admission testing and has served its purpose well. However, there is the continuing problem of the high school curriculum being driven by the external influences of the colleges and college admissions testing. It is a more direct shortcut to showing educational results, and much cheaper as well to teach the test than to improve the school learning environment and the qualities of the learning experiences. This makes standardized testing appealing to public officials, and fast results also make ready copy for the mass media. As a result, the testing industry has undergone enormous growth and influence.

The regional accrediting associations are institutions of great value in recognizing the need for appropriate resources and facilities to support a full and rich curriculum. The diversification of American life has promoted the comprehensiveness of the curriculum in schools and colleges. What Dewey predicted has come to pass, despite the pressures for standardization and uniformity.

One of the great turning points for American education was the establishment of the Dewey school at the University of Chicago in 1896. It was demonstrated that the nature of the learner, the structure and function of knowledge, and the ideals of a free society can be wrought harmoniously in the life and program of the school. Dewey and the teachers attempted to build up the child's experience so that it would eventually grow to encompass systematized knowledge. Dewey found that curriculum coherence can be achieved by basing instructional strategies on an organizational framework.

The nineteenth century was a remarkably productive time for education. Famous philosophers such as Spencer and Dewey turned their attention to education. Best practices that stand to this day emerged. It was a time of great optimism for a better future. Educators and society had gained a foothold on the ladder of curriculum improvement. The challenge of the twentieth century was to build on these beginnings. The challenge existed in every field, not just education. But in every field education was the key to unlock the door to opportunity.

PROBLEMS FOR STUDY AND DISCUSSION

1. Why was Dewey's laboratory school a turning point in curriculum thought and educational improvement?

2. Dewey and the teachers in his school attempted to establish their school as a form of community life. They believed that schools could prepare children for social living only if the school were a small cooperative society. "The idea involved a radical departure from the notion that the school is just a place in which to learn lessons and acquire certain forms of skills," Dewey recounted years later. "It assimilated study and learning within the school to the education which takes place when out-of-school living goes on in a rich and significant social medium." [Dewey, J. (1936). "The Chicago experiment." In K. C. Mayhew and A. C. Edwards. *The Dewey school.* New York: Appleton-Century, p. 466.] Do the curriculum and school organization today reflect the concept that the school is just a place to acquire academic skills or that school is a small cooperative community? Give examples.

3. Do you believe that Dewey's idea in question 2 was a positive contribution? Why or why not?

4. In discussing Ralph Tyler's basic work in curriculum development, John Goodlad notes: "The question of what knowledge is of most worth becomes an integral part of curriculum planning." [Goodlad, J. I. (1979). *What schools are for.* Bloomington, IN: Phi Delta Kappa Educational Foundation, p. 43.] From your own experience, do teachers and administrators ask Spencer's question? Do you think that it is important for them to do so? Why or why not?

5. What illustrations can you give of Parker's reforms in the curriculum today?

6. In what ways did the Committee of Ten reduce the independence of the high school curriculum?

7. Compare the Report of the Committee of Ten with the report of the NEA Commission on the Reorganization of Secondary Education, *Cardinal Principles of Secondary Education* (1918), in terms of (a) the problems addressed and (b) curricular opportunities for different groups of students. In your opinion, were these reports well grounded in their diagnoses and prescriptions? Explain.

8. The *Evaluative Criteria* for secondary schools states the following expectations for faculty involvement in curriculum development:

   The faculty, under the leadership of the building administrators, is actually involved in curriculum development procedures; curriculum evaluation and revision procedures; the selection of instructional materials; and the resolution of curriculum/instruction-related problems. [National Study of School Evaluation. (1987). *Evaluative criteria,* 6th ed. Falls Church, VA: National Study, p. 59.]

   Evaluate your own school on the above expectations indicating the extent to which each expectation is being met.

9. In a democratic society, public schools should be responsive to public expectations for education. According to John Goodlad, whose study of schooling was cited in this chapter, there is a "continuing public expectation for educational attention to all four of the traditional purposes of schooling in our democracy: the personal, social, and vocational as well as the academic." [Goodlad, J. I. (2003, April 23). A nation in wait. *Education Week,* 22, 32, 25.]

   Take stock of your school with respect to the four educational goals. Are all being given attention, or is the focus on one or two? Explain.

10. What is your appraisal of the proposal of the Committee of Fifteen as a curriculum for today's schools?

11. According to P. David Pearson, a sound approach to instructional improvement

    retains the practices that have proved useful from each era, but transforms and extends them, rendering them more effective, more useful, and more supportive of teachers and students. And it may represent our only alternative to the pendulum-swing view of our pedagogical history. [Pearson, P. D. (2000). Reading in the twentieth century. In T. L. Good (Ed.), *American education: Yesterday, today, and tomorrow.* (Ninety-ninth Yearbook of the National Society for the Study of Education, Part 2, p. 153). Chicago: University of Chicago Press.]

    In your view, which of the nineteenth-century turning points discussed in this chapter should be retained and extended? Support your response.

CHAPTER 3

CENTURY OF THE CURRICULUM

Like all other professions our work crosses the borders of time. Curriculum developments spill over from one day to the next, and even one century to the next. When the twenty-first century dawned, the nation continued to build upon the challenges of the twentieth century. The old century is still with us. Educators are heirs to a rich body of best practices—problems, too, of course, but the point is that the foundations for the curriculum were made over the course of the twentieth century. In this chapter, we claim our heritage.

The previous chapters addressed the development of the American single-track ladder of education, whose unitary character seemed to emerge stronger than before with each NEA committee. (Take the Committee of Ten, for example: Despite its vulnerability to criticism as a conservative instrument of the colleges and universities, its recommendations implied adherence to a unitary education system and opportunities that flow from such a system.) The single-track ladder of education started with elementary schools and was continued by secondary schools that led to colleges and universities. A distinctively democratic education structure had been created with a curriculum to match; that is, a common fund of knowledge for all. Its success would depend on the best available knowledge being made available to all. This encompassed not only what was taught, but also how and under what conditions. With the opening of the twentieth century, progressive educators became increasingly concerned over the appalling conditions of school overcrowding and inadequate resources accompanying urbanization.

Charles W. Eliot saw keenly how industrial changes in the last half of the nineteenth century had profoundly affected the public provision of education. The population had been rushing into cities. "This rush into urban life has had a very ill effect on schools," said Eliot (1900, p. 197).

> It has tended to make schools large machines. The grading of classes in a large school had to be inflexible and the product had to be uniform like that of a flour mill. That meant that the quick children were held back and the slow driven forward, to the great disadvantage of both. It meant marking time. It meant bad air and crowded rooms with fifty or seventy pupils to a teacher. These are impossible conditions for good teaching. (p. 198)

Crowding was a problem both in school and out, introducing new risks to children's health. Eliot acknowledged that some of the conditions in the schools had been improved by the turn of the century. More attention had been given to good air and proper heat and light, and more flexibility had been given to programs and curriculum choice. But, he said, much more remained to be done to solve the problems in urban education.

In subsequent decades, public education in large cities underwent a great transformation. In the 1930s, for example, the most progressive developments in American education were found in cities—New York and Houston are illustrations. Houston's integrated curriculum was based on the Deweyan principle that intelligence must guide action and reflects a clear conception of the role of education in the development of the democratic process. "A public school system," wrote Edison Ellsworth Oberholtzer, a curriculum expert in Houston, "must be concerned primarily with the general good. The curriculum development staff aimed to develop the integrated curriculum in such a way that it would be of greatest service to the entire school interests of the city" (1937, p. 5).

Today, despite the great progress in promoting child welfare in the twentieth century, the problem of children living in high-poverty neighborhoods continues to plague the nation. In the 1990s, public housing projects were demolished and many persons who were living in urban slums had to move. There was a shift: The population of high-poverty neighborhoods spread out in some cities—Detroit, Chicago, and Cleveland, for instance—and moved into the older suburbs of these cities (Pear, 2003, p. 26). Thus there is still poverty in the inner city, but now there is more in the suburbs. The poverty has not gone away; it has just moved. What it means is that more areas have to deal with poverty. Those problems are pretty much the same, whether in the city or suburbs, not to mention poverty in rural America.

And since the War on Poverty programs of the 1960s, educators have learned much about how to help children growing up under conditions that negatively shape their lives. An integrated program of interventions including curriculum improvement, safe housing, access to health care, and ties to the world of work can "break the cycle of disadvantage," but a concerted attack remains to be undertaken (Schorr, 1989).

As in Charles Eliot's day, educators are attempting to open the door to America's mainstream through the curriculum. But there is one striking difference: Educators know a great deal more. Research and experience have taught us much since 1900, and the problem now is to use and build on what we have learned.

Unfortunately, and this is a big problem, the body of research and experience is often ignored. A new fad in education comes along, occupying educators' attention and taking space in education journals. Examples in the 1990s were cooperative learning and whole language, the integration of reading and writing. Both were sound ideas but were carried to extremes that threatened to destroy their value. Those supporting the principles and practices involved in cooperative learning, for example, had trouble supporting the unsupportable idea that individuals should never work alone. This notion was conveyed in the literature at the end of the twentieth century (Johnson & Johnson, 1999). It is not the way cooperative learning was conceived and practiced at the beginning of the twentieth century. In Dewey's experimental school, children worked on independent projects as well as in groups. Teachers used a variety of approaches, seeking to determine which were most likely to foster children's development as problem solvers, both individually and collaboratively.

How Fads Impede Progress

As noted, the practice of cooperative-collaborative learning was given its theoretical formulation by Dewey at the University of Chicago in the 1890s. Parker introduced the integration of reading and writing in Quincy, Massachusetts, in 1875. Yet, as MacGinitie (1991) points out, both ideas were treated as new in the 1990s. Treating old ideas as new cuts them off from their theoretical underpinnings and impedes curriculum improvement. The graveyard of education fads is crowded. Fads often were stimulated by sound concepts but the concepts were misunderstood, distorted and misapplied and eventually abandoned in disappointment by teachers and administrators. The newest approach is often labeled a *reform,* a counterreaction intended to undo the excesses of the previous reform. If we are to have real curriculum improvement, curriculum development must be directed at problem solutions through the use of the best available evidence consistent with research findings and experience.

The twentieth century is the century of the curriculum. It is the century of Thorndike and of Dewey, of Newlon and of Rugg, of Bobbitt and of Charters, of Flexner and of Hutchins, of Tyler and of Taba, of Caswell and of Schwab, of Goodlad and many others. More ideas about curriculum improvement appeared during the twentieth century than in all previous centuries. (In fact, the study of curriculum as an academic specialization began in the 1920s.) We turn now to a discussion of these ideas and the problems they were meant to solve.

Achieving Transfer of Learning

Everyone agrees that what is learned in school should transfer to new situations, both in and out of school. But when interested citizens and educators talk about what should be included in the school curriculum, there is strong disagreement about the probability of transfer. It has long been argued that the study of the traditional academic disciplines and classical languages is the best kind of education and will provide for mental discipline and transfer of learning. When the evidence fails to reveal these claimed benefits, instead of seeking ways of integrating these studies and relating them to the life of the learner and to social reality, there is the tendency to look to extreme learner-centered approaches and to negate systematically organized knowledge. These viewpoints are not merely extremes, they are dangerous dualisms, the kind that Dewey sought to eliminate in his laboratory school. Most curriculum workers reject them. They believe that transfer frequently fails to occur but that transfer can be accomplished. They seek to improve the curriculum so as to optimize the transfer effects (Eggebrecht et al., 1996).

Certainly conventional education affords some transfer. Even through conventional methods, youngsters learn to read and most are able to bring their reading skills to bear in ordinary situations. As adults, they are able to apply their arithmetic skills to ordinary situations. This type of transfer is taken for granted. Educators are concerned with the kind of transfer that involves reflective thought in applying what has been learned in one situation to other contexts, the learning of other things and the solution of unanticipated problems. An example of the former (skill transfer) would be for high school students to use the process skills from mathematics in solving chemistry problems or as consumers as a matter of course. Students in chemistry classes typically have difficulties with basic mathematical procedures, much less higher mathematics (Menis, 1987). An example of the latter—namely, reflective transfer—might be students' ability to use concepts from chemistry in considering ecological problems.

Research and experience over the past century hold that transfer is more likely when the curriculum is deliberately planned to foster transfer (Perkins & Salomon, 1988). Yet every curriculum worker is sure to encounter the older, discredited theories on transfer and must know why they should be rejected. Moreover, this knowledge can help in considering curriculum alternatives as well as judging current curricula and methods. Many current practices in the schools were adopted under the influence of the long-discredited theory that certain studies improve the mind (mental discipline) and improve one's ability to master other subjects (transfer).

Thorndike's Monumental Study

One of the most portentous pieces of research for the curriculum field was conducted by Edward L. Thorndike in the early 1920s. In a huge study involving 8,564 students, Thorndike sought to measure the relative disciplinary value of various high school subjects by assessing gains in "general intelligence" that could be attributed to the study of one subject or group of subjects instead of another. For instance, he compared the gains in intelligence test scores of pupils who studied English, history, geometry, and Latin with those who studied English, history, geometry, and shopwork. He was trying to measure the relative disciplinary value of Latin and shopwork. Thorndike found that no one study (be it Latin or anything else) is more likely than any other study to result in a general improvement of the mind. Thorndike concluded:

> By any reasonable interpretation of the results, the intellectual values of studies should be determined largely by the special information, habits, interests, attitudes, and ideals which they demonstrably produce. The expectation of any large difference in general improvement of the mind from one study rather than another seems doomed to disappointment. The chief reason why good thinkers seem superficially to have been made such by having taken certain school studies is that good thinkers have taken such studies, becoming better by the inherent tendency of the good to gain more than the poor from any study. When the good thinkers studied Greek and Latin, these studies seemed to make good thinking. Now that the good thinkers study Physics and Trigonometry, these seem to make good thinkers. If the abler pupils should all study Physical Education and Dramatic Art, these subjects would seem to make good thinkers. These were, indeed, a large fraction of the program of studies for the best thinkers the world has produced, the Athenian Greeks. (1924, pp. 1–22, 98)

What Thorndike was saying was that those who had the most to start with gained the most regardless of the particular studies they pursued and that there is no hierarchy of subjects for mental discipline. He also argued that learning is specific rather than a matter of sharpening one's intellectual faculties via the discipline of certain subjects, Latin in particular.

Demolishing Mental Discipline

Thorndike's research was part of a chain of events that demolished the theory of mental discipline as a basis for curriculum development. It will be recalled from the discussion in chapter 1 that educational theorists enthusiastically picked up Herbartian educational psychology, which stressed that new subject matter must be related in the pupil's mind to his or her previous learning. Thus, the "psychology" of mental discipline was abandoned in favor of Herbartian psychology. This happened in the United States by 1885. (In Europe, Herbartian psychology had taken hold 20 years earlier.) Another early link in the chain was William James of

Harvard, who proposed in *The Principles of Psychology,* published in 1890, that psychology is a natural science. This left many in the intellectual world thunderstruck, because the study of the mind had always been the domain of philosophers. James said that the study of the mind must be based on the study of behavior, that it was fallacious to conceive of the mind as composed of separate faculties as did the faculty psychologists.

James was the founder of the school of objective psychology. His ideas were pursued, developed, and applied by Edward Thorndike of Teachers College, Columbia University (Mayer, 2001, pp. 40–41). Other erosive influences on the doctrine of the inherent disciplinary value of the classical studies were the application of the evolutionary idea to society, child interests, the need for practical knowledge, and the necessity for the secondary school to meet the needs of an increasingly heterogeneous population.

Research on Transfer

Thorndike began challenging the doctrine of transfer shortly after the turn of the century. His first frontal attack was a study conducted with Woodworth in 1901, which showed that improvement in one mental function seldom brings about commensurate improvement in another function, regardless of similarity. Transfer could occur but not because of the disciplinary value of any classical study; it would occur only if the old and new activities had common or related content or methods of study (Thorndike, 1906).

Curriculum developers concluded from Thorndike's research that the best way to prepare a student for an activity or goal was to have the student take a direct route: the study of the subject or the practice of the activity itself.

A host of studies conducted during the 1920s, 1930s, and 1940s confirmed Thorndike's findings, which demolished the disciplinary doctrine. Thorndike's study was repeated in 1927. Broyler, Thorndike, and Woodward reported that the findings of their study concurred with the earlier study; both studies "agree in disagreeing with the traditional doctrine that Latin, algebra and geometry are the prime disciplinary subjects of high school" (p. 382). Thorndike's study was repeated again in 1945 by Wesman, whose investigation

> failed to reveal superior transfer to intelligence for any one of the achievement areas or subjects measured (Latin, German, French, mathematics, natural science, social studies, contemporary affairs) and indicated the desirability of direct engagement in meaningful mental processes rather than dependence on transfer from school subjects. (pp. 391–393)

But probably the most stunning attack (aside from Thorndike's 1924 study) on the idea that certain subjects have superior transfer to intelligence was delivered by the Progressive Education Association's Eight-Year Study (1933–1941). As is shown in the discussion on the Eight-Year Study in chapter 4, the study proved that success in college does not depend on credits earned in high school in prescribed academic subjects.

Effects of Thorndike's Studies

Thorndike's findings on transfer had an enormous effect on education. The findings were cited as justification for eliminating classical studies such as Latin and ancient history from the curriculum. Thorndike's findings produced two other striking effects. First, because Spencerian questions could no longer be answered on the basis of the alleged disciplinary value of given subjects, there had to be other means of determining the relative values of studies. Concern over finding such means was an important factor in the appointment by the NEA in 1911 of a Committee on Economy of Time in Education, charged with identifying the "minimum essentials" of the curriculum. There can be little doubt that Thorndike's emphasis on teaching specific knowledge and skills influenced the committee's decision to pursue a mechanistic approach to curriculum development. However, Thorndike's work lent justification to the inclusion of modern, practical, and technical studies in the curriculum taught as nearly as possible in the context in which they were to be used. Nevertheless, the effort to bring the modern and career-oriented studies into an honorable place in the school curriculum has been a continuing struggle. In the early 1970s, some educational policy makers—most notably the U.S. commissioner of Education—reasserted the "equal status" of vocational and academic subjects (Marland, 1971, p. 35). But from the 1980s through the early 2000s, governors and legislatures were enacting programs for "excellence in education," which in several states involved reducing the number of units that high school students were permitted to take in elective courses and programs, including vocational education, and instituting new requirements for graduation. These programs were based on the policy established by President Ronald Reagan and continued by succeeding administrations (of Bush, Clinton, and Bush), promoting an agenda in the name of academic excellence to meet "world-class standards." The policy was established after the publication of the Report of the National Commission on Excellence in Education (1983).

Is Mental Discipline Really Dead?

The answer to the above question is, of course, "yes." The dramatic story of its demise is 100 years old. The education policies just discussed are based on a theory that is as outmoded as the idea that blood is manufactured in the liver, which physicians believed until the seventeenth century (Nuland, 1988, p. 122). And in a way, they are just as dangerous. As Goodlad (2002) points out, there can be little assurance that scores on mandated standardized tests transfer to problem-solving skills and preparation for earning a living. In fact, the idea borders on the absurd. We have long been aware that there are deficiencies in knowledge transfer even in the same field. Many graduates of science programs, for example, have difficulty explaining scientific phenomena that they have personally experienced (Gardner, 1991). The problem of basing policy on discredited theory demonstrates in bold strokes that a curriculum that meets the demands of our democracy depends not just on research and expertise but equally on the political contexts within which education decisions are made. It is not just research that will help curriculum workers develop good programs; rather, policy makers must base policies on the best available evidence. In the years since the *A Nation at Risk* report was released, the best evidence has been too often ignored by policy makers who uncritically followed the report (Bracey, 2003).

Changing Conceptions of Learning and Transfer

It is easy to be seduced by an approach to learning that promises wide general transfer. This is because educational theorists look to and hope for wide transfer. In the 1950s and 1960s there was much interest in the intellectual processes of learning. This was given impetus by the space race with the Soviet Union. Discovery or insight was formalized into the inquiry-discovery method. Budding elementary school scientists (it was hoped) would learn how to make discoveries that would one day contribute to national

supremacy in space. Be that as it may, the conception of learning itself as problem-solving activity was sound and a desirable alternative to the view of the learner as a responding mechanism, which had dominated educational psychology during the early twentieth century (Mayer, 2001, p. 65).

Inquiry-discovery teaching seemed to provide wide transfer. The promise was in the method itself: Inquiry-discovery and learning how to learn (ways of learning) as taught via subjects such as mathematics and science could be applied by students in new situations. According to Jerome S. Bruner, it was "indeed a fact that massive general transfer can be achieved by appropriate learning even to the degree that learning properly under optimum conditions leads one to 'learn how to learn'" (1960, p. 6). Obviously, Bruner was not calling for a return to the doctrine of mental discipline. Yet he held that each academic discipline is undergirded by a structure of academic knowledge, and by revealing this structure, massive learning transfer would occur.

A Failed Promise. The idea of the structure of knowledge failed to effect the promised transfer of learning. First, most subjects had nothing resembling a single structure or organizing principle. Even in fields such as physics and mathematics, there was little agreement among university scholars on a single structure. Organizing principles change in accordance with one's purpose in studying a given subject. Thus, the idea of structure was a fiction. Second, the notion of holding abstract knowledge apart from practical knowledge worked against the possible transfer of learning. Third, if each discipline has its own independent structure, then each must be treated as a separate cocoon in the curriculum.

Bruner and Dewey: Important Differences. Initially, educational theorists were struck by apparent similarities between Bruner's ideas and those of Dewey. Learning how to learn and inquiry-discovery stem in no small way from Dewey's reflective thinking. Yet there are important differences. On the one hand, Bruner was addressing himself to ways of learning *within individual disciplines* such as physics and mathematics. He insisted that these would transfer to other kinds of problems faced by the student. Dewey, on the other hand, was referring to interdisciplinary and applied knowledge for social problem solving as a task for which the school must prepare the rising generation. Here Dewey's idea was similar to that of Thorndike, who suggested that the best way to learn something was by the most direct route possible: to practice the process itself. Dewey went much further. Whereas Thorndike held that we must match learning situations specifically for transfer, Dewey held that knowledge must be made generalizable for transfer.

Increasing the Possibility of Transfer

According to Richard S. Prawat (1989), promoting knowledge, transfer, and skill in students "is a major—many would say *the* major—goal of education" (p. 1). And, as Hilda Taba emphasized, "Since no program, no matter how thorough, can teach everything, the task of all education is to cause a maximum amount of transfer" (1962, p. 21). In summarizing the recent research on transfer, Prawat concluded that in order to facilitate transfer, "teachers need a firm grasp of the most important ideas in each of the subject matter areas they teach," and further, "[t]hey should have at their command detailed information about the developmental course of children's thinking in those content areas" (p. 34). Concerning key ideas, as Bruner stated in 1960, "[t]he basic ideas that lie at the heart of all science and mathematics and the basic themes that give form to life and literature are as simple as they are powerful" (p. 12). More recently, learning theorists have come to recognize that transfer is also enhanced when pupils understand why they are engaging in a given activity or learning task. As in the 1960s, science curricula of the early 2000s stress inquiry, but there are important differences. The purpose of the 1960s curriculum efforts was to have learners "discover or illustrate a scientific concept or principle . . . devoid of application and connection to society," whereas the recent programs "focus on exploring questions and problems that learners can potentially find meaningful and related to their lives" (Krajcik, Manlok, & Hug, 2001, pp. 224–225). Clearly, lessons were learned by curriculum makers who initially failed to make the inquiry meaningful to learners. Teaching for transfer to students' lives is incorporated in current learning theory and thus in today's science programs. The point is that transfer increases when learners are deliberately made aware that what they are learning might be useful in other situations.

Unfortunately, early in the twentieth century Thorndike's findings were used to buttress the theory

of stimulus-response (S-R) psychology rather than seeing it as evidence of the need for subject matter that is designed to be highly generalized for applicability or transfer to a wide range of situations. The consequence was a doctrine of narrow specificity that was manifested in the scientism of Franklin Bobbitt and found its legacy in the psychology of behaviorism. As Anderson and Gates observed in 1950, "During the heyday of behaviorism, psychology neglected or disregarded the intellectual processes and their role in learning" (pp. 14–15). Unfortunately, behaviorism would have a new heyday in the 1970s. The emphasis in many schools was on atomizing the curriculum into minuscule objectives. There were voices of dissent, for example, that of Lee Cronbach (1977), who reminded educators once again that developmental objectives, when the teacher states how he or she would like the learner to function after instruction, are more generalized and more concerned with transfer than are narrow behavioristic objectives. Developing problem-solving skills has a similar transfer objective. As Cornbleth (1982) rightly notes, there is simply no way to list all the occasions for transfer. But, suitable levels of accomplishment can be specified as Ralph Tyler and his staff did in the Eight-Year Study.

Scientism in Curriculum Development

Thorndike argued that there must be elements in situations outside of school that are identical with the elements taught in school if students are to apply school learning to these out-of-school situations. Thorndike's studies had an immediate effect on curriculum development. For example, in order to select arithmetic topics, some curriculum developers began looking at the quantitative problems encountered by adults. They also examined adults' newspapers and other reading materials in order to develop reading and spelling objectives and the materials used in the teaching of reading and spelling. Tyler gives us a description:

> Shortly after Thorndike developed the idea of identical elements, curriculum objectives were broken down into tiny specific things to be learned. In Thorndike's psychology of arithmetic, more than 2000 objectives for elementary school arithmetic were listed in such detail that 1 + 2 = 3 is a separate learning objective from 2 + 1 = 3. Fortunately this

practice was discontinued when Charles Judd and his students showed that students could learn to use general principles to guide them and could learn a few dozen general principles in a subject which they could adapt to the hundreds of specific matters they encountered. (1988, p. 271)

As Tyler points out, after 1925, curriculum developers formulated generalized educational objectives. However, in the 1960s and 1970s the practice of breaking down curriculum objectives into minute things to be learned was revived in the so-called behavioral (behavioristic) objectives movement.

Business Ideology and the Curriculum

In the years before World War I, some educational reformers decided that modern business was admirably suited as a model for the schools (Zilversmit, 1993). For nearly a century, the attraction has remained. We see "a nation that still worships successful businessmen," observed a writer on how education is influenced by business ideology (Segal, 1996, p. 44). According to Segal, business has traditionally sought "simplistic—but always financially profitable—solutions to complex problems" (p. 44), which explains its continuing appeal to reformers in institutions such as government and education. In this section we will see how the worship of business ideology by one group of reformers began to influence curriculum development nearly a century ago.

At the time, there was great national excitement over a new system of industrial control known as scientific management. Franklin Bobbitt, a member of the faculty in educational administration at the University of Chicago, argued that school systems could operate more efficiently and economically if they would borrow the principles of scientific management. The principles of management being applied in business and industry were particularly applicable to a "backward" institution such as education, held Bobbitt. The analogy between the two institutions, education and industry, was obvious; "education is a shaping process as much as the manufacture of steel rails," said Bobbitt (1913, p. 11). Bobbitt's theme was that education must follow the example of industry and focus on the product. Standards for that product must be established and scales of measurement used to see "whether the product rises to standard." Educators must realize that

it is possible to set up definite standards for the various educational products. The ability to add at

a speed of 65 combinations per minute, with an accuracy of 94 per cent is as definite a specification as can be set up for any aspect of the work of the steel plant. (p. 13)

Educators as Mechanics

Bobbitt's argument for the need for educational standards elicited no appreciable objections from the nation's educational leaders. But his proposal for establishing these standards was to become a matter of continuing controversy as standards for educational products or outcomes were to be set by the business and industrial world. It was the role of men of practical affairs to decide what they wanted and the role of educators to determine how it could be produced and to produce it without question. Thus, educators would no longer be concerned with the what of the curriculum but only with the how. As Callahan commented in his classic study of the influence of industry on public school administration: "Doubtless many educators who had devoted years of study and thought to the aims and purposes of education were surprised to learn that they had misunderstood their function. They were to be mechanics, not philosophers" (1962, p. 84).

How would the needs and desires of practical people become known? The kinds of educational products they needed would be determined via the survey method. But the surveys would not be conducted by school people. Scientific educational management as efficient as that found in the business world required that the surveys be conducted by those in business. In this way, education would be turned to the needs of business. With scientifically determined job specifications, scales of measurement, and standards of attainment, said Bobbitt, "we shall have [for] the first time a scientific curriculum for education worthy of our age of science." A few years later, when his attention turned from school administration to curriculum making, Bobbitt himself used the survey method for defining curricular aims and content.

Business Leadership. At the time Bobbitt published his ideas on the role of business people in determining educational objectives, people of influence were advancing a theory of business leadership for the society as a whole. Among them was Arthur Twining Hadley, president of Yale University, who, in his book *Standards of Morality* (1907), proposed that business people assume a larger role in the solution of contemporary social problems in return for protection of their vested interests. Bobbitt's argument that business people should set educational standards was a not unexpected outcome of the theory of business leadership.

Although easily explainable, the importance of Bobbitt's advocacy of a business-led education system should not be underestimated. Two policies that appear to stem directly from this advocacy continue to operate to this day: First, business values and procedures are the model for educational administration, with the result that educational decisions tend to be made on economic rather than educational grounds. Second, education (and government) has turned to business and industry for the solution of pedagogical problems. An illustration of this from the 1960s is performance contracting, in which some school districts turned to industry for learning systems to improve pupil performance in reading and arithmetic as measured by standardized achievement tests. Performance contracting not only failed to produce the results that were promised, but the practices also proved to be counterproductive. This was disappointing yet hardly unexpected. What remains a puzzle is why countless educators continue to believe that business can do everything better, including education (Segal, 1996; D. Tanner, 1973, 2000).

In the early 2000s, Philadelphia turned over some of the city's elementary and middle schools to for-profit companies (Walsh, 2002). Other cities have also entered into such contracts. The schools have been those serving the most disadvantaged pupil populations. According to Segal (1996), the "crusade" of such companies "to mesh corporate profits with educational reform is a logical extension of the traditional business-education partnership" (p. 44).

The Inefficient Curriculum.   Not the least of the effects of the national infatuation with efficiency in Bobbitt's day was a barrage of criticism directed at the public school curriculum. The curriculum was characterized by some critics as impractical and ineffective (failing to prepare for a living) and therefore a waste of the taxpayers' money. It was characterized by others as failing to prepare pupils in academic work and moral training. Still a third group criticized the school for its failure to hold pupils. This problem was regarded as a direct reflection of the curriculum and a source of educational waste. A fourth criticism was more of an ultimatum; some reform economists demanded that the schools either show measured results of their outcomes in terms

of social betterment or have their budgets reduced. In short, what was being called for by the critics was a more efficient curriculum, although what this meant certainly varied with the interests of the critics. Nevertheless, almost all the critics agreed about one thing: The schools were extravagant with public funds. Curriculum efficiency meant economy. This could be achieved by having pupils study *only* what they needed (the basics), and nothing more. This way of thinking formed the backdrop for the operations of the Committee on Economy of Time created in 1911 by the NEA's Department of Superintendence.

The Committee on Economy of Time

Let us examine the reasons for the committee's charge to define the minimum essentials of the curriculum. Research had exploded the myth that certain subjects had value for mental discipline, so there was urgent need for a new answer to Spencer's question, "What knowledge is of most worth?" This would require new approaches to curriculum development. Second, friends of education as well as enemies were demanding that the selection of curriculum content be based on quantitative evidence instead of opinion. The quantitative method was being applied to the solution of all educational problems, including the definition of the standard units in a course of study. Last but not least was a growing body of research that seemed to show that the amount of time spent on a given subject had little influence on the results. The pioneering study (which was ignored by educators when first reported) had been conducted in 1897 by Rice, who concluded that more than 15 minutes per day for spelling was utterly wasteful.

The temper of the times was clear, as expressed in a speech by Leonard Ayres of the Russell Sage Foundation to the Harvard Teachers Association in 1912. "'How much?' and 'how many?' and 'with what result?' are going to displace guess work, imagination, and oratory as criteria for shaping educational policies," said Ayres (p. 309).

Curriculum Making by Common Denominator. The first phase of the committee's work was to find out what was being taught (and, where achievement data were available, what was being learned) in representative school districts and make recommendations based on the findings. The result was curriculum making by common denominator. To illustrate, in his report on arithmetic, Walter Jessup (1915) of Iowa State College noted that there was wide variation among the cities in the amount of time given to arithmetic. He recommended that the time devoted to arithmetic in the various grades not exceed the median time expenditure throughout the country. The first grade, for example, should not exceed 75 minutes per week as that was the median time expended in first grades (p. 129).

There was absolutely no theoretical basis for the idea that the median time spent on a given subject should become the standard. Yet this was what the committee found desirable for spelling, arithmetic, and handwriting.

This is not to imply that the committee's four major reports (published as the yearbooks of the National Society for the Study of Education in 1915, 1917, 1918, and 1919) contributed nothing of value to educators. This would be manifestly unfair and misleading. What was being taught in other school systems was of intense interest to superintendents, and the surveys reported in the NSSE yearbooks were widely circulated and discussed. However, prevailing practice was hardly a sound basis for curriculum improvement.

Determining What Should Be Taught. The second phase of the committee's work was to make recommendations concerning the content of the curriculum. All of the recommendations were based on the principle of social utility. The approach used for determining what should be taught was to find out what people who are living and working successfully need to be able to do and just what information and skills they need in order to live and work successfully. The committee relied heavily on the method of collective judgment or consensus. Library books, for instance, were recommended on the basis of the number of times each book appeared on supplementary reading lists in 50 American cities. History content was selected by analyzing books, encyclopedias, newspapers, and periodicals to see which persons, places, and dates were most frequently mentioned.

A Conservative Response. It was the committee's initial decision to derive a curriculum from current practice, rather than the committee's inadequate methodology, that was to plague the curriculum maker in succeeding years. As Cremin put it,

the Committee had ended by defining the goals of education in terms of life as it was, and hence by proposing a curriculum that would accommodate youngsters to existing conditions with little emphasis on improving them. This was hardly the progressive or Deweyan ideal, however much it was construed as such in some circles. (1961, p. 196)

The Doctrine of Specific Objectives

The principal method for curriculum construction embraced by the Committee on Economy of Time had the appearance of being scientific, and educators were striving for the academic respectability associated with the new age of science. Therefore, one would expect that this method would attract adherents. This is exactly what happened. As with the movement for scientific management in industry at the time, many educators proceeded to confuse quantitative measurement with science. Franklin Bobbitt, W. W. Charters, Charles C. Peters, and David Snedden, all professors of education, trod in the steps of the committee.

Curriculum Development as Job Analysis. "Let us discover what the activities are which make up man's life and we have the objectives of education," wrote Bobbitt (p. 49) in *The Elementary School Journal* in 1914. It was Bobbitt's theory that the curriculum that prepared the learner for these specific activities was the curriculum that prepared the learner for life. Because educational objectives were activities and activities were learned through performance, activity analysis discovered both the objectives of the curriculum and the curriculum itself. The method of activity analysis is also known as job analysis. As implied by the name, the method concerns the analysis of the specific activities in the performance of a given job, such as operating a machine. Bobbitt and Charters applied this method to curriculum construction, the implication being that whatever the schools taught could be reduced to 20,000 or 30,000 specific mechanical skills or behaviors.

Activity or Job Analysis and Behaviorism. In addition to appearing businesslike and efficient, the new method was also highly compatible with the mechanistic psychology, behaviorism, which described human behavior in connectionist terms of S-R (stimulus-response) bonds. Habit formation and uniformity of response are the predominant concepts in both doctrines. Significantly, Charters (1927) wrote of the desirability of automatic responses on the part of the learner "when given situations recur frequently" (p. 24). Indeed, behaviorism provided a theoretical basis for job analysis as a curriculum-making technique. Many educators, even Kilpatrick (1918), a student of Dewey's who emphasized that activity must be at one with the child's goals, began describing education in connectionist terms. Peters (1930) actually defined education as "the acquisition of a large aggregate of 'hair-trigger sets' for responding to the particular problems that will confront the educand in the future" (p. 33).

The ideal of humans behaving like automatons was the antithesis of the Deweyan ideal. Dewey, like Lester Ward before him, saw the improvement of individual and social welfare through the expanding power of human intelligence. But as another famous educational philosopher, Boyd Bode (1927), observed, behaviorism is "a psychology that explains intelligence by explaining it away" (p. 191). Behaviorism also contributed to the divorce of education theory from the goal of social reform and the democractic prospect.

A Dangerous Deficiency. Obviously, only the lowest training objectives concern repetitive tasks. In society, many of the most important objectives, such as the ability to make adequate decisions on civic responsibility, health, or family life involve varying and unforeseeable conditions. Curriculum objectives such as these involve the transfer of learning for problem solving, rather than the repetition of identical operations. This points to a dangerous deficiency in activity or job analysis as a means for curriculum development; it is fixed on the lowest level of objectives: those requiring mechanical responses. Objectives that require higher-level thinking processes are avoided because they do not fit in a theory that trains people to act mechanically. Activity or job analysis simply cannot be made to cover the entire gamut of curriculum objectives.

Educational Engineering. In his book *How to Make a Curriculum,* published in 1924, Bobbitt developed the basic premises and methodology of the Committee on Economy of Time into a well-organized curriculum theory. Bobbitt compared the curriculum maker to an engineer. It was the task of the educational engineer to use educational surveying instruments to locate the specific objectives in the various subject fields. Education, said Bobbitt,

should "prepare for the fifty years of adulthood, not for the twenty years of childhood and youth" (p. 4). It was the task of the curriculum maker to define the major fields of adult experience and analyze them into smaller and smaller units in determining the specific activities to be performed. The specific activities, similar to job specifications in industry, comprised the content of the various subjects.

Significantly, curriculum making by activity or job analysis in no way conflicted with the traditional subject organization of the curriculum. The "scientific" curriculum was the old subject curriculum with a new authority.

Bobbitt and Charters: The Crucial Difference. Although Bobbitt and Charters were of one mind concerning the nature of subject matter, their ideas on the source for curriculum objectives differed. Whereas Bobbitt's scheme was to "discover" curriculum objectives by "scientific analysis," Charters (1924) held that the philosopher sets up the aim and the analyst provides only the technique for working the aim down "into the terms of a curriculum."

This difference is significant. Bobbitt maintained that we can determine what people *should* do by identifying the things they *do* do. Charters, warning against this, saw activity analysis as a means for implementing previously selected objectives. It was Bobbitt's scheme that prevailed. The idea that curriculum objectives can be discovered by scientific means, much as one takes a census, was basic to the new notion of curriculum making.

Walking in Bobbitt's Footsteps. Peters and Snedden were educational sociologists who walked in Bobbitt's footsteps, endorsing without question the idea that the curriculum should consist of thousands of minute objectives to be obtained by consensus. Snedden's (1921) "sociological determination of objectives in education" divided educational objectives into two categories, production and consumption (the ability to do and the ability to appreciate). The result was to further compartmentalize vocation and culture. This again was the antithesis of the Deweyan goal, which was to demolish the barriers between the social classes and between vocational education and education for leisure.

Clearly the effect of job analysis was to atomize subject matter in the mind of both teacher and learner. This doctrine was diametrically opposed to the movement to humanize subject matter through curricular synthesis. The curriculum field was to be characterized by such conflicting currents and movements throughout the twentieth century.

Behavioristic Objectives: The Second Time Around.   During the 1960s interest in specific (behavioristic) objectives was revived. The same approach—analyzing subject matter into atomistic performance objectives—was used. In both instances, behaviorism was the educational psychology of the day. And there was at both times a dominant faith among educators that technology would solve all educational problems, including those in the realm of curriculum and method. This faith was intensified in the late 1970s when the popular press reduced the outcomes of education to the mechanics of basic skills.

Nevertheless, there is an important difference between these two movements that occurred a half century apart. Bobbitt's doctrine was reformist in spirit; it was based on the theory of utilitarianism. Although the curriculum produced by Bobbitt's method turned out to be the traditional curriculum with a new authority (that of "science"), his objective nonetheless was to make a curriculum that would prepare the learner to perform real-life activities. The behavioristic objectives movement of the 1960s and early 1970s did not subject the curriculum to a reappraisal. The assumption was that content would not be changed, only divided into minute behaviors. These were, in most instances, not behaviors at all in the sense of changes in relation to one's environment but verbalisms at a mechanical level. The following "behavioral" objective is illustrative: "Given a diagram of the human body illustrating one or more human body systems (including skeletal, muscular, digestive, circulatory, and respiratory systems), [the student will] be able to name the body systems shown" (Dillman & Rahmlow, 1972, p. 51).

The result of both activity analysis as a method for curriculum making and its reinvention in the late 1960s and 1970s was a narrow-minded curriculum focused on lower cognitive processes. Both movements were static as far as the curriculum was concerned in that they viewed the curriculum as the means for adapting the learner to existing conditions. Breaking down the curriculum into minute segments has another damaging result: It leads away from an understanding of the unity of all knowledge. Obviously, a disintegrated curriculum and reductionist conception of the learner also are not likely to lead to transfer of learning.

Scientism, Technology, and the Curriculum

The scientism of Bobbitt and Charters was essentially rooted in technology. (It will be recalled that Bobbitt compared the curriculum maker to an engineer.) As has been shown, efficiency, an aim in the factory where the process is mechanical, was adopted as a goal for all aspects of education including curriculum making. The job analysis approach to curriculum development was the factory system imposed on the curriculum. It was nonphilosophical, treating curriculum making as mainly a technological problem. The difference between this group, who labeled its curriculum theories "scientific," and those who argued that education decisions should be based on carefully tested hypotheses, open to continual verification and correction, is fundamental. Included in the latter group were Dewey, Bode, and Rugg.

Child Development Knowledge and the Curriculum

The relation between child development theory and curriculum theory is fascinating. It is the story of two parallel fields that needed desperately to get together, if the best education possible was to be made available for children and youth. Actually, they did get together at one point, early in the development of both fields. The curriculum that Dewey and the teachers in his laboratory school worked out was grounded on concepts of growth and change. Dewey formulated stages of growth that were entirely concerned with how to transform school subjects in the most productive way and with, of course, the least resistance (Dewey, 1900c; L. Tanner, 1997).

According to Goffin (2001), an expert in early childhood education, "psychological theories strive to be descriptive and value-free" but "educational theories are intentionally prescriptive and value-laden" (p. 154). Thus she sees "an education-versus developmental issue" (p. 154). For Dewey, such dualisms were anathema. He began with the question of what children should be learning and developed his psychology accordingly. There is no doubt that growth theory is tied to curriculum in the title of his 1900 article, "The Psychology of the Elementary Curriculum."

What happened, however, was that the union between child development and curriculum development was short-lived. (It would be no exaggeration to say that it began and ended with Dewey.)

Child Study

Child development as a field began in the 1890s, in a movement with great pedagogical popularity: child study. Although labeled a fad by some and steeped in sentimentality by others, the child-study movement gained academic respectability after 1900 when it became associated with experimental psychology. But even in its early stages, child study had an impact on curriculum and method, particularly in kindergarten. Early studies conducted by Hall, Bryan, and Hancock, for example, revealed that movement involving the large muscles should be free in young children. For this reason, and because of possible danger to the children's eyesight, the handwork in kindergarten that required delicate coordination and precision was dropped from the curriculum.

It is important to note that leaders in the child-study movement saw it as an instrument for education reform as well as a means for gaining new knowledge about children. As G. Stanley Hall, who started the movement, said, the method and curriculum of the school would have to change if practice were to be in accordance with the new knowledge.

In its infancy, child study was closely tied to the school. Not only did teachers gather the data for those engaged in research, but teachers themselves also became deeply involved in the process of child watching. What they themselves learned as they observed the children, questioned them, collected and compiled miscellaneous facts about them, wrote their biographies, checked their sight and hearing, and weighed and measured them for science was that each child was indeed unique. Whether this new insight was translated into action in the form of new ways of working with children was another question.

Classroom Application

Child study was both systematic and unsystematic, and much worthless as well as worthwhile information was accumulated. Quality of research, however, was not the primary problem for those trying to reform the schools. There was, after all, plenty of good research on which there was a consensus. The question was how could the findings be applied in the classroom? Their concern was borne out by what happened (or failed to happen) to the findings of child study. An excellent illustration is the method of freely chosen activities that was confirmed by child study in the early years of the movement. The idea that the child should choose his or her own activities had been promoted by Parker, and he was delighted when it was sanctioned by research. But it was not until well into the second decade of the twentieth century that the idea worked its way into the elementary classroom (via, of course, the kindergarten).

As child study gained academic status in the university, it lost its identification with educational concerns. The questions being asked by researchers were less often the questions asked by educators. When they happened to be the same, by coincidence, the answers took longer to affect school practice because child study and education had become parallel developments. This continues to pose problems for today's teachers and children. Nearly all teacher education programs, at least at the elementary-school level, require courses in child development. But knowing the principles of child development does not automatically result in the selection of instructional methods most likely to improve learning. With child development and teaching methods assigned to separate departments administratively and conceptually, knowledge of the principles of child development has not been linked to teaching enough to significantly transform the methods of teaching.

Child study, or child development, as it is now generally known, has continued to influence educational practice, but the delay in implementing findings continues to be a genuine concern. The findings of child study do not, of course, answer the paramount curriculum question; although researchers have, on the whole, determined what children are able to learn at various ages, they cannot declare what children should learn. The fact that it can be demonstrated that children can learn certain things or that their learning of certain things can be accelerated appreciably does not solve the problem of curriculum choices and priorities.

Theory of Curriculum Development

G. Stanley Hall advanced the radical thesis that the curriculum and methods of teaching be determined by the needs of the child as revealed through child study. The content of the curriculum was to be based on data from child development as determined by questionnaire and inventory. Hall (1891) wanted the curriculum to be individualized from the moment the child entered the school. To this end, he stressed the importance of ascertaining what children actually knew on entering school and developing the child's program in accordance with this knowledge.

In a real sense, Hall's work provided the capstone for the works of Rousseau, Pestalozzi, and, to some extent, Parker, because it supplied a scientific basis for child-centeredness. Unlike Hall, however, Parker saw the public school as a great force for the improvement of society.

Insofar as Hall's theory of curriculum development had authoritative underpinnings (experimental psychology), it was a radical-progressive idea. Oddly, however, his rationale for the individualization of education was conservative: It was in support of the doctrine of laissez-faire, for the purpose of individualization was to identify the gifted child, give him or her encouragement, and expend less energy on the dull child. Wrote Curti (1935) about Hall's influence:

> Although Hall opened up new fields and emphasized new aspects of human life his influence was largely directed to the support of individualism and laissez-faire. This was the effect of the cult of child study, which tended to make the curriculum child-centered, and to single out for particular attention the gifted child. (pp. 426–427)

A Laissez-Faire Curriculum. The point Curti was making was that a child-centered curriculum is a laissez-faire curriculum; it does not direct itself to social needs and concerns. This was actually a contrapositive force in the progressive movement, both in the very early stages of the movement and in the 1920s. As Dewey stressed, education reform cannot be conceived apart from social reform; the two are deeply interwoven. As Fass (1989) points out, our experience with school reform over the century has "linked the reform of the schools directly to the reform of the society as John Dewey had intended" (p. 14). But a child-centered curriculum appealed to many privileged parents who wanted their children to enjoy school without being introduced to unsettling social ideas.

When carried to its ultimate extreme, a child-centered laissez-faire curriculum is no organized curriculum at all. In the 1920s, the child-centered curriculum was built, in some places, entirely on the momentary interests of children. By stressing individual values at the expense of social values and by discounting the role of the school in social change, Hall cast the die for the romanticist education of the 1920s, a move that some progressive educators regarded as disastrous and tried their utmost to stop.

In developing his own curriculum theory based on laissez-faire, Hall turned his back on the mounting and often frightening problems being faced by a rapidly changing society. When the progressive movement in education finally gathered momentum, it did so, in the words of Cremin, "as part of a vast humanitarian effort to apply the promise of American life—the ideal of government by, of, and for the people—to the puzzling new urban-industrial civilization that came into being during the latter half of the nineteenth century" (1961, p. viii).

Educational Opportunity and Social Progress: The Biological Connection

Despite the social philosophies of Hall and William T. Harris, laissez-faire was on the decline. (Harris, whom we met in the previous chapter, believed that it was the purpose of education to serve existing social and economic conditions. He also thought that the idea of pupil self-discipline was antithetical to the social purpose of the school, which was to train the child to accept authority.)

A new curricular age was dawning. "The recognition of the shortcomings of our individualistic social philosophy has made many people look at our schools from an entirely new point of view," wrote William D. Lewis, principal of Philadelphia's William Penn High School, in 1914. "If they emerge from the high school with an indifferent, selfish, *laissez-faire* philosophy, they will become either the unthinking victims or the plunderers of our devil-take-the-hindmost social order" (p. 6).

American progressivists, attributing many of the pervading social ills to a long-standing condition of "rugged individualism" or laissez-faire, sought to attack these social ills through enlightened social action. The new progressive social philosophy was to generate a veritable revolution in the role and function of the high school.

Planning for a Better Human Condition

The outlook of the education progressivists toward evolutionary improvement was that progress is possible but certainly not inevitable. Progress is most likely to occur when humans *plan* for what they consider to be a better human condition and focus their energies on achieving these goals.

The Ideas of Lester Ward. The new point of view had been in the making since 1883 when Lester F. Ward, in his now classic *Dynamic Sociology,* attacked the weaknesses of laissez-faire and proposed instead a planned society. In other words, progress is controlled not by the laws of evolution but by the human control of nature. Education has a leading role in making a better life.

The Forgotten Founder. Curiously, Ward is almost forgotten. But Ward was the creator of some of our most fundamental conceptions about the curriculum, ideas that were further developed by Dewey. Ward was a founder of the field of sociology but spent most of his life as a government paleontologist. At the age of 65 he became a professor of sociology at Brown University. What makes Ward so fascinating and important was that he applied biological knowledge to the problem of social reform.

The measure of progress as defined in the field of biology—control over the environment—is found in Ward's writings (1883). A century later, Francisco Ayala, the evolutionary biologist, tells us that *Homo sapiens* is marked off from other animals by "extreme advance in the ability to perceive and react to the environment . . . complex social organization, control over the environment, *the ability to envision future states and to work toward them,* and values and ethics are developments made possible by the human's greatly developed capacity to obtain and process information about the state of the environment" (1982, p. 122).

Ward's ideas are not only still useful but also can be found in contemporary ideas. In effect, Ward had anticipated the emergence of the field of sociobiology by almost a century.

Education: An Environmental Quality. In *Dynamic Sociology,* Ward's emphasis is on humans' ability to deliberately plan alterations in their environment. Ward explained the basic difference between biological, unconscious evolution (genesis) and deliberate, conscious evolution (telesis). Late on the evolutionary scale, the capacity for telic progress had come out of the meandering processes of biological evolution. Although the human capacity for thought evolved genetically, it is up to humans to take advantage of the opportunities it offers to improve their lives. Telic progress is a planned, conscious process that requires the development and application of intelligence. The means is education,

which is a "quality of the environment" (p. 631), and it is in government's interest to make it as widely available as possible.

The ability to consciously change the natural and social environment—the criterion of progress in evolutionary biology today—is that of Ward's telesis. As the present authors have noted,

> [i]n Ward's writings we find the biological basis for educational opportunity, and for the development of intelligence as the most important purpose of the curriculum: The human, unlike other organisms, has knowingly adapted its social environment and with reflective intelligence will effect social progress. This will be done through education, which develops the ability to study situations and work out solutions. . . . That there *is* a scientific basis for educational opportunity is often forgotten, probably because Ward has been forgotten. Educational opportunity is usually supported by its advocates on ideological grounds rather than on biological grounds. It has both. It is the science—the telic conception—that makes Ward's argument different from earlier arguments. (1987, pp. 540–541)

As Henry Steele Commager (1967) pointed out about Ward's place in history, "No earlier American educator—neither Jefferson nor Horace Mann nor Henry Barnard—had based his educational program so firmly on scientific foundations or had faced so clearly its logical implications or consequences" (pp. xxxvi–xxxvii).

With clarity unlike others in his time, Ward (1886) saw the influence of environment on talent and intellectual ability. "Like plants and animals," he wrote, humans have "latent capacities which for their development simply require opportunity" (p. 349).

Progress, Intelligence, and the Curriculum

The curriculum was vital to telic progress, and Ward gave it a great deal of thought. He knew that unless the curriculum fostered the development of intelligence, education could not be a means of social reform. As it was, education tended to be superficial and disconnected from the natural world. What was needed was a curriculum "which continually knits the physical being to his environment and does not ultimately depend upon memory or upon tradition" (1883, p. 602).

Ward's ideas about the curriculum were sound, but they needed to be transformed instrumentally into ways to guide teachers. How does one teach children to apply their intelligence, and how is intelligence developed? Dewey (1910, 1916) provided the approach: a problem-solving method for the school that corresponded to the scientific method. Dewey's problem-solving method or method of intelligence made Ward's more general concepts about the curriculum operational. The connection between Ward's idea that human progress is achieved by applied human intelligence and Dewey's problem-solving method or method of intelligence is direct. If progress is to be achieved by applied human intelligence instead of by waiting for nature's slow processes, there has to be a way, and Dewey supplied it. For Dewey, thinking is problem solving and his paradigm has come to be called variously *problem solving, critical thinking, reflective thinking, functional thinking, scientific thinking,* the *complete act of thought,* and the *method of intelligence.*

Knowledge Availability: The Critical Factor.
Dewey built on a second feature of Ward's philosophy: the idea that knowledge should be equally available to all members of society. Ward argued for this passionately because he was so certain that unless knowledge were democratized, the possibilities for social progress and democracy were nil. Ward believed that the huge gap between the ignorant and the intelligent was caused by the "unequal distribution" of knowledge (1883, p. 602).

But how is knowledge distributed? Dewey viewed the problem this way: Educational opportunity is shared knowledge and concerns, and progress is achieved through breaking the class barriers to sharing. Thus, the problem was one of learning together as well as what is to be learned. Today, as in Ward's and then Dewey's time, to conduct education programs so that students cannot learn together not only betrays the democratic dream but also reduces the possibilities for telic progress.

Ward's Argument Today.   Ward's own argument that knowledge must be equally available still stands on its own. More important, it reappears in contemporary forms (although Ward himself is rarely given credit, or even mentioned). The principle of equal educational opportunity involves more than the right to go to school; it is deeply concerned with the curriculum, with what Goodlad calls "access to knowl-edge" (1984, pp. 130–166). Goodlad's classic study of schools found large differences from school to school in children's opportunities for knowledge. In arguments well supported both by his own research and by principles from the curriculum literature, Goodlad argued for change and improvement.

With the argument so well stated, the problem then becomes one of changing practice. Teacher education is important, but so is support where resources are inadequate. According to a specialist in rural education, for example, "formulas that rely on property wealth to fund school routinely deprive rural children of the equitable and adequate education they deserve—and that they are guaranteed under most state constitutions" (Tompkins, 2003, p. 44).

Similarly, those who fight the censorship of curriculum materials are embracing the principle of access to knowledge so that students have the opportunity to investigate significant social ideas and problems. Such opportunities are essential for developing the critical thinking skills required for participation in telic progress. Those engaged in dropout-prevention programs in schools are following Ward's advice from 1886 that opportunities must be "actively thrust" on individuals (p. 345).

Unlike advocates of eugenics (improving intelligence through controlled mating and parentage), Ward (1909) believed "that the human brain is adequate today—and always has been adequate—for any purposes which it may be called upon to perform" (p. 221). The great need, argued Ward, was not to increase humankind's hereditary genius, but to develop human intelligence through education.

In looking at our history, it is clear that Ward's environmentalism won out in the end. Developments in curriculum and educational policy throughout the twentieth century reveal that environmentalism became the dominant influence in American education. As we have stated elsewhere:

> Environmentalism was not a mere abstract idea. American educators took their cues from a society that clearly believed (since the Revolution) that environment shapes human destiny, and they proceeded to expand educational programs and opportunities on a scale unprecedented anywhere else in the world. They were relentless in their efforts as environmentalism, rather than eugenics or hereditary social privilege, became the great twentieth-century credo for American education (L. N. Tanner & D. Tanner, 1987, p. 539).

Democracy and Education

By linking school and society in a new way, Ward irrevocably linked democracy and education, for at the heart of dynamic democracy lay the ability to make intelligent decisions, and this required training in citizenship as well as a certain atmosphere or way of life in the school itself. It was unrealistic, for instance, to suppose that pupils could learn to think independently in a situation that required unthinking obedience. Thus, it was quite naturally concluded that in order to produce good citizenship, the schools themselves would have to become laboratories for citizenship where school problems were being solved.

A decade after Ward's *Dynamic Sociology* was published, Francis Parker pointed to the common school as the key to human progress and fused the philosophies and fortunes of democracy and education. In a chapter in *Talks on Pedagogics* (1894) titled "Democracy and Education," Parker wrote that the democratic principle of mutual responsibility—the idea that each member of society contributes to the good of all—must be translated into educational goals that reflect the enormous responsibility of citizenship. But more important even than the formalized curriculum was the social power of the school to break down the clannishness and prejudices of people from all parts of the world who were learning together in the school. "The common school," wrote Parker, "is the embryonic democracy" (p. 423).

Dewey Forges the Link

In 1916, Dewey's *Democracy and Education* was published. This remarkable work forged the definitive link between democracy as a social process for achieving people's highest goals and education as the democratic way of preparing people to make intelligent decisions about social change. Like Parker, Dewey saw the school as a democracy in microcosm. And like Parker, Dewey viewed education as a social process and a social function. But, cautioned Dewey, "the conception of education as a social process and function has no definite meaning until we define the kind of society we have in mind" (p. 112).

Unless our ideal of society is clear, the definition of education as a social function would fit as appropriately in a dictatorship as in a democracy. And even in a democracy, the social aim of education could become perverted into a narrow nationalistic aim. This happened twice in the second half of the twentieth century: In the late 1950s and early 1960s the science and mathematics curricula were given priority to meet the nationalistic goal of supremacy in the Cold War and space race, and from the 1980s into the 2000s when graduation requirements for high school students were increased in these fields in order to regain leadership and dominance in global industrial markets. In both instances, the public schools were held scapegoat for shortcomings in our political, industrial, and military sectors (D. Tanner, 2000; Goodlad, 2003).

To Dewey, the democratic ideal of education was "a freeing of individual capacity in a progressive growth directed to social aims" (Dewey, 1916, p. 115). Education was growth but it had a distinctly social as well as individual purpose.

Could not the desire for social change produced by education result in civil disorder, if not revolution? It could not, according to Dewey's definition of democracy. Dewey anticipated that question, which he must have felt would trouble educators as well as the lay public. He answered it this way:

> A society which makes provision for participation in its good of all its members on equal terms and which secures flexible readjustment of its institutions through interaction of the different forms of associated life is in so far democratic. Such a society must have a type of education which gives individuals a personal interest in social relationships and control, and the habits of mind which secure social changes without introducing disorder. (p. 115)

Although Dewey made the definitive statement on democracy and education that formed the bedrock of progressive educational theory, the connection between an enlightened citizenry, social change, and the school was being made by education practitioners and theorists well in advance of 1916. Indeed, Dewey himself advanced the educational goal of the development of social consciousness and conceptualized the school as "an embryonic society" (pp. 16–18) (using almost the same words as Parker) in 1899 in three lectures to parents at the University of Chicago. These lectures were published as *The School and Society* and have never gone out of print.

Unity through Diversity. In 1909, historian Ellwood P. Cubberley pointed out that well before 1900 the school had experienced a shift in purpose and direction. Said Cubberley: "The task is thrown more and more upon the school of instilling into all a social and political consciousness that will lead to unity amid diversity, and to united action for the preservation and betterment of our democratic institutions" (p. 55). Our forebears saw clearly that every nation must have a common culture in order to thrive. Our uniqueness resided in the strength to be drawn from a polyglot populace sharing the ideals of American democracy.

Diversity Versus Unity.   To see unity and diversity as conflicting forces was to raise ominous problems for school and society to this very day. In the 1990s, a battle over the social studies curriculum broke out that, as one observer put it, was "fundamentally a battle over the idea of America" (Berger, 1991, p. 1). The curriculum debate was essentially over the principle that the curriculum should emphasize themes that unite Americans. In a number of cities and states, educators reviewing history and social studies curricula were recommending that far greater emphasis be put on the roles of nonwhite cultures in American society (Perry & Winne, 2001). In the 1990s, many educators were wrestling with the question of how to impart a greater sense of America's cultural diversity without misconstruing the Western intellectual roots of the Founding Fathers and the major roles played by the European immigrants who laid the foundation for government and other institutions in America.

Many teachers began to put more emphasis on the contributions of non-European immigrant groups to America, such as the role of Chinese-American laborers in developing the American West. And more students were studying varying interpretations of such themes in America's history (Sleeter, 1995). Some educators expressed concern, however, over emphasizing "ethnic and racial themes at the expense of the unifying ideals that precariously hold our highly differentiated society together" (Schlessinger, cited in Verhovek, 1991, p. A14; Schlessinger, 1998).

The issues in the battle concerned multicultural education: one of the most emotional curriculum issues confronted by education since the 1990s.

Dewey's Conception of Democracy.   In *Democracy and Education,* Dewey orchestrated the theory of American democracy into a philosophy of education. No less important is Dewey's definition of democracy as a social process, as a constellation of *experience* and not simply a form of government. "Since the process of experience is capable of being educative, faith in democracy is all one with faith in experience and education," wrote Dewey in 1939 (p. 229). But what does this mean in practical terms? Obviously, Dewey anticipated the question.

> If one asks what is meant by experience in this connection my reply is that it is that free interaction of individual human beings with surrounding conditions, especially the human surroundings, which develops and satisfies need and desire by increasing knowledge of things as they are. Knowledge of conditions as they are is the only solid ground for communication and sharing; all other communication means the subjection of some persons to the personal opinions of other persons. (p. 229)

Democracy is social, but is also personal. It is "a way of personal life controlled not merely by faith in human nature in general but by faith in the capacity of human beings for intelligent judgment and action if proper conditions are furnished" (p. 227). Here is where the school comes in. Curriculum is vitally important, of course, but so is the way that decisions about curriculum and school governance are made. If education is to be truly democratic, democratic values must imbue the entire school (Gutmann, 1999). Unfortunately, in the last few decades, secondary education has been steadily moving away from this direction (Rury, 2002; Wraga, 1994).

The Revolution in Secondary Education

Ideally, the high school curriculum would be diversified without tracking. Actually, until the early 1990s the American public high school curriculum was more diversified than many people believed. A study conducted in 1991 for Congress on the status of vocational education found that students planning on college took "a substantial number" (Wirt, p. 427) of vocational education courses. And only 24% of all the students who took vocational education courses were planning "to go to work full-time after high school" (p. 427). Students were being provided with more opportunities than they now have to use knowledge for practical purposes, whether vocational or avocational.

A Flexible School Structure: The Comprehensive High School

The diversification as revealed by the student transcripts was possible only because of the existence of a flexible school structure: the comprehensive high school. A peculiarly American invention, the comprehensive high school is friendly to the breadth of student participation in programs that interest them. This flexibility was clearly the intention of its creators at the opening of the twentieth century.

It is notable that there has been "an erosion of distinctions between curricular tracks" (Stevenson, Kochanek, & Schneider, 1998, p. 211). However, as the distinctions have eroded, many high schools have become academic high schools. There are fewer opportunities for all students to follow their educational and occupational aspirations, and high test scores have become the badge of self-worth. In his excellent analysis of recent developments, Rury (2002) poses this question: "If the high school is to become little more than a preparatory school, and post-secondary institutions are the means to allocating individuals to their occupational destinations, in what sense does the high school retain its democratic and egalitarian purposes?" (p. 323). There is a great cost to students and society when education policies are developed without examining our vast experience with education reforms. Such experience points to the great value of work in the studio arts, industrial arts, and vocational areas. They were a means of meeting the needs and values of adolescents beyond the core studies if they were to stay in school. Many things have changed in the world since the comprehensive high school structure emerged early in the twentieth century, but one thing has not changed. Students still have interests and they are not all the same. The democratic high school still must provide opportunities for all to develop their talents and interests. This is the answer to Rury's question, and it is the challenge for educators today, just as it always has been. However, it is certainly more difficult when policies are not made in the interests of children (Anderson, 1988; L. Tanner, 2000).

Educational Theory and the Adolescent Years

The theoretical basis for curriculum change in the first two decades of the century had two main strands. The first strand was social reformism. In 1900 in *The School and Society,* Dewey described the school as an "embryonic community" that would improve the society by making it "worthy, lovely and harmonious" (1900a, p. 44). As Cremin wrote, "what was new in Dewey's analysis is his social reformism. The school is recalled from isolation to the center of the struggle for a better life" (1961, p. 119). In 1916, Dewey defined democracy in educational terms in *Democracy and Education*. By then, he had become widely recognized as the leading spokesman for progressive education. According to Cremin, the work "orchestrated the many diverse strands of pedagogical progressivism into a single inclusive theory and gave them unity and direction. Its very existence lent new vigor to the drive for educational reform" (p. 121).

The second major strand was child development, which turned the spotlight of teaching on the student. According to psychologist G. Stanley Hall, effective education must consider the student's needs, nature, and development. In this regard, Hall's work, *Adolescence,* which appeared in 1904, was a milestone. It put the pedagogical spotlight on the period that occurs between 13 and 18 and stimulated inquiries into the psychological significance of adolescence. These studies had a profound effect on school organization, educational aims, subject matter, and methods in secondary education. As Brown and Theobald (1998) point out, "then, just as now, people looked to the secondary school as the social institution that must . . . successfully shepherd young people into adulthood" (p. 109).

Today, under the principles of the new educational theory, subjects should be included in the curriculum only if they have value for the genuine needs and growth of the student. To build the curriculum on the basis of mere tradition or deferred values was to invite the failure of the student and the failure of the school. These principles also provided a basis for revising or dropping existing subjects. In connection with the latter, the new societal emphasis on efficiency and economy had a buttressing effect. Those subjects that were dropped usually were the least popular and therefore the most expensive to offer. Greek was dropped from the curriculum in many high schools for this reason.

At this writing, increased graduation requirements in academic subjects and the closing of school shops and studios have curtailed opportunities for many students to do something in school that they like and are good at. Yet we have a history of meeting such needs; it is in our curricular psyche, so to speak, and the curriculum structure is flexible. The high school curriculum is a far cry from the report of the Committee of Ten, which ignored the needs of youth. Granted that the report predated the publication of Hall's *Adolescence* by several years, education and school board members had already recognized the need to take into account the young person's nature, needs, and interests in keeping him or her in school, coupled with the expanding social need for a better educated populace.

The Junior High School

The junior high school was foreshadowed by the recommendations of the Committee of Ten to introduce secondary school subjects in the seventh and eighth grades. It was also a response to a substantially different problem: Compulsory education laws generally prescribed school attendance only until the child was 14 years of age. With the 8–4 plan of school organization, the break between the eight-year elementary and high school came at the wrong time. It was easier for many budding adolescents, particularly those of uncertain purpose, to terminate their education with graduation from elementary school than to enter a distant and unfamiliar building and take new and strange subjects beyond the basics under several new and strange teachers. A three-year junior high school extending from grades seven through nine, particularly if the program provided the opportunity for election of courses in accordance with pupils' interests and aptitudes, would retain many pupils through the period when most dropping out took place.

It was also argued by its proponents that the junior high school was supported by the findings of G. Stanley Hall and others and that early adolescence is a period of powerfully developing interests. A varied curriculum was needed that was exploratory and enriching in purpose. Those who objected to the junior high school argued that curriculum reform could be accomplished within the existing 8–4 organizational framework. Although administrative changes, per se, are no guarantee of an improved program, it can be said with certainty that junior high schools showed more activity in curriculum reform and significantly greater student retention than did the conventional 8–4 plan. Junior high schools *could* be more experimental because they were not a part of the high school (which had its requirements dictated by the colleges). Hence, shifting the ninth grade to the junior high school would diminish the college dominance over the ninth-grade curriculum. At the same time, the problem of holding budding adolescents together with young children in the eight-year elementary school would be solved by reducing the elementary school to six years.

In addition to beginning secondary education earlier and starting each pupil on studies leading to a suitable goal, junior high schools were to provide training for those who would soon enter the world of work. The first junior high schools (originally called intermediate schools) were established in Berkeley, California, and Columbus, Ohio, in 1909 and in Los Angeles in 1910. The fact that by 1930 there were approximately 4,000 junior high schools attests to the remarkable popularity of the new school. The 6–3–3 plan was well on its way toward replacing the old 8–4 system (Cubberley, 1947, pp. 554–555).

The Curriculum. The curriculum principle of variety characterized junior high schools. In the more progressive schools, pupils changed curricula and dropped courses freely. This created a concern on the part of many teachers and principals that the curriculum for some, at least, was disjointed. A related question was how long a course was to run to be worthwhile. The curriculum was frankly exploratory, but it was uncertain whether the material could be reorganized into courses as short as two months or even two weeks with promise of satisfactory results. The values of some studies could be realized only if courses and programs continued longer than most students were likely to remain in school. Yet continuity was needed if education were to have an integrating rather than a disintegrating effect. Thus, curriculum development was also based on a second principle, that of continuity in learning.

Most educators subscribed to the principle that the junior high school program should become increasingly differentiated as the pupil continued in school. At the beginning there would be common learnings or general education consisting of what all citizens should know. The time devoted to common learnings would gradually decrease as pupils pursued options into differentiated curricula in accordance with their different interests and goals.

This reopened the question of what is a common, integrating education. It also posed the question of whether it was not undemocratic to differentiate pupils on the basis of future vocations at the age of 12 or 13. It was also feared that those pupils who should have extended education would be attracted into trade courses by short-term goals. According to Thomas H. Briggs (1920), who was instrumental in the development of the junior high school and who had served on the Commission on the Reorganization of Secondary Education (1918), there was small chance that irrevocable errors of choice would be made at this early stage, as long as mistakes were rectified through a flexible curriculum when pupils changed their life aims.

Still, it was difficult in some schools to transfer into a new program under the practice of curriculum tracking. And democracy demanded an open-ended educational system that permitted all individuals to proceed with their education as far as their capabilities, interests, and ambitions carried them. This was most likely to happen when education was of a broad nature for as long as possible. Even when "academic," "industrial," and "commercial" curricula were housed in the same junior high school, pupils were not likely to be exposed in any significant degree to knowledge that ought to be common to all.

Exploratory Courses.   Although there was astonishing variation in practice, many junior high schools offered general exploratory courses in major fields of learning. The basic idea behind courses in general science, general mathematics, general history, general social studies, and language arts was to reveal to each pupil the possibilities of a general field of knowledge and aid in the intelligent election of those subjects attracting his or her interest. In line with educational theory, exploratory courses were to be life-related through the elimination of artificial barriers among the various specializations within each field and through the application of broad principles to everyday experience.

The general exploratory courses were also regarded as an essential part of a general education. But the unique feature of exploratory courses was their guidance function; this was a way of discovering each pupil's interests and aptitudes so that he or she could be given intelligent guidance.

In practice, however, the general courses proved to be disappointing and invited much criticism. In retrospect, this appears to be a consequence of the failure to translate general aims into a more integrated curriculum and into specific teaching practices rather than a failure of the concept of exploratory learning, per se. Put another way, the idea of revealing to pupils the basic principles of the major fields of learning through unified courses had never been tested.

Criticism of Junior High Schools.   In the 1960s there was a rising chorus of criticism aimed at the junior high school by persons advocating a different plan of organization and a different curriculum for young adolescents. One criticism was that the junior high school had not lived up to its commitment to provide a program attuned to the nature and needs of young adolescents. As Kindred and his associates pointed out in 1968, nationalizing influences since the late 1950s had brought a disturbing change: "the thrust downward of the senior high school program with its emphasis upon subject matter specialization" (p. 29).

Supporters of the middle school plan of school organization argued that the junior high school had a conventional subject matter curriculum; that is, its curriculum was organized vertically by subject areas and did not provide for horizontal articulation. This kind of curriculum was unsuitable for 10- to 14-year-olds. Supporters stressed that the middle school was an opportunity to develop interdisciplinary block-time programs. These were especially appropriate for easing youngsters' transition from a self-contained to a departmentalized program. Different ways could be found to organize the curriculum to meet personal-social needs. This could be done unhampered by the stresses inherent in a school that was continually made aware that the ninth grade is part of the high school program (and record). Actually, block-time core studies were widely instituted in junior high schools (Wright, 1949, 1950, 1952, 1958, 1962, 1963).

According to Kindred and his associates, the real reason for adoption of the middle school was that it was a simple solution to the problem of overcrowded buildings. Space could be freed in elementary and high schools by creating "schools in the middle"; two grades could be taken from each unit and put in the middle school. "This reason . . . and a desire for better racial balance, has been responsible for its adoption rather than the educational program to be conducted in the middle school" (p. 35).

In 1968, there were 7,437 American public junior high schools, including grades seven and eight or grades seven through nine. Data were not available for middle schools. By 2000, there were 11,205 middle schools, with grade spans beginning with four, five, or six and ending with grade six, seven, or eight. There were only 3,608 junior high schools (National Center for Education Statistics, 2001). Whatever their motives, middle school advocates had clearly been successful in changing the grades and ages included in the unit of schooling for young adolescents.

Clearly, changing a school's grade span does not, in itself, lead to program reform. As Epstein (1990) concluded in her study of middle-grade schools,

what happens in a school or classroom is more important than the name on the school door. . . . The hard work of developing excellent programs is not accomplished merely by changing grade spans or constructing smaller buildings, but by attending to practices that are responsive to the needs of early adolescents. (p. 444)

What really counts, then, in middle-grade schools is whether they follow recommended practices for young adolescents such as exploratory, enrichment, and special-interest education, that is, giving students opportunities to explore, gain enrichment, and develop special interests in a range of fields. Another recommendation is to develop block-of-time programs that afford the opportunity to build the needed coherence and units for meaningful learning (Elmore & Wisenbaker, 2000, p. 280). In this connection, it should be noted that an integrated curriculum plan does more than attempt to establish some sort of contact between and among different subject fields. As Leonard (1947) pointed out in the mid-twentieth century it "endeavors to establish new threads of relationships by cutting across subject lines" (p. 293). These are the "big ideas" that were discussed earlier in this chapter on transfer of learning.

According to Epstein, also recommended are interdisciplinary teams of teachers and common planning time for the teams. Nevertheless, team teaching is not a curriculum design. It is only an organizational tactic designed to improve what teachers are already doing. Some middle school teams emphasize the pupil guidance function. The teachers on the team represent individual subjects such as mathematics, science, English, and social studies, and teams are organized by grade level. The teams themselves may be interdisciplinary, but the curriculum is likely to be the conventional subject curriculum.

Curriculum correlation and other best middle school practices are fostered by regular planning meetings. As recently as the 1990s, when the middle school idea was well established this was still a problem in many schools. A national study of middle-grade practices by researchers at Johns Hopkins University found that only about a third of the schools that used interdisciplinary teams gave the teams at least two hours of scheduled common planning time weekly. The study concluded that "the majority of teams do not have the common planning time they need to become truly effective" (MacIver, 1990, p. 460).

Ten years later, according to one middle-school expert, trends at work in America hampered attempts to follow best practices. Among the trends were "accountability pressure" and "increased high stakes testing" (Elmore, 2000, p. 291). In response to that pressure: "Schedules were departmentalized, and bells rang every 50 minutes. Most middle schools more closely resembled junior highs than true middle schools" (p. 291).

It gives pause for thought that many of the advantages claimed for middle school in the 1960s were given for the junior high school earlier in the twentieth century. Junior highs, it was said, offered more opportunities than the self-contained classroom and the departmentalized high school for exploratory education, guidance, interdisciplinary teaching, and horizontal plans of curriculum articulation. By the 1960s, it was felt by critics of junior high schools that they had not met these opportunities. Today, the opportunities are harder to come by. Teachers and administrators are finding it an uphill battle to implement best practices in middle-grade schools. In the words of Elmore, "the issue of education has become increasingly politicized" (p. 291).

Exemplary Schools: The Great Divide.   Yet the curriculum in some middle-grade schools does seek to develop skills in reading and communication through interdisciplinary units that deal with the real world and learning really seems to be fun (Moss & Fuller, 2000). Where are these schools? A national study reported by Becker (1990) found that schools giving attention to higher-order thinking tend to be those serving upper-middle-class families. This was the case for junior and senior high schools as well. Such schools are providing more students with more electives, more academic opportunities, and "an intellectually richer academic life" (p. 457). It is our experience that the tremendous difference in curricular opportunities still exists in the 2000s. It is crucial to create such opportunities for all children and adolescents. As discussed in the first chapter, offering the best possible curriculum for all is the only acceptable objective in a democracy. As will be discussed later in the text, much depends on leadership. A good middle school principal is a leader focused on problem solutions.

The junior high school was an early twentieth century development. In the early twenty-first century, it is clear that the attainment of the reformers' ideal has been wanting in many aspects. Despite the criticisms leveled at this institution, it did open the gates to secondary education at a time when so many adolescents were ending their formal schooling with the eight-year elementary school. At the same time, it gave recognition to early adolescence as a crucial period of development. It provided for a more diversified curriculum and also served as an experimental base for block-time core classes. Unfortunately, the junior high was diverted from its mission as the raising of standardized test scores became a primary concern. Designing a curriculum to meet the needs of early adolescents has been put on the back burner and the curriculum has been frozen in its separate-subject state in the process. Yet today it has become increasingly important to help students meet such developmental tasks as desiring and acquiring social responsibility and independence of thought. These are cross-disciplinary and interdisciplinary in nature. Interdisciplinary teams of teachers are a step in the right direction, but only a step. There is much work to be done on the curriculum, and a number of schools and school districts have initiated experimental programs (Elmore, 2000).

Changing Times for Secondary Education

Times change, and so do ways of thinking. In the space of a generation after the report of the Committee of Ten in 1893, Americans had gotten rid of the nineteenth-century habit of thinking of high school as only for the select few. The Committee of Ten was out of date. It had based its report on an outmoded theory of mental discipline, the idea that a few school subjects, mainly languages and mathematics, can develop mental powers that transfer either to college or a job. For Americans, who are practical people, this made no sense. As will be remembered, psychological studies early in the century, by Thorndike, for example, supported what was common sense.

The Committee of Ten had advised in its report to the NEA that the high school be viewed as a selective institution. It had not foreseen the rising tide of democracy that would change the educational climate. As Cremin (1955) observed, the report by members of the Commission on Reorganization of Secondary Education which advised the NEA in 1918

that every young person be provided with high school up to the age of 18 was a true revolution. In a quarter of a century we had moved from selectivity to universality.

Americans in general believed that this was a good thing. The problem was now that the old theory for selecting school subjects had been disproven; where to find a new one? As Brubacher (1966) points out, commission members did not have to look far. A new theory was "ready to hand" (p. 422) in the practicality and idealism of John Dewey, whose well-read *Democracy and Education* (1916) had been published two years earlier. Thus the commission drew up cardinal principles in which school subjects were selected for their potential, in Dewey's words, "to further new experiences which may, in some respects at least, surpass the achievements embodied in existing knowledge and works of art" (1916, p. 214). This was a far cry from choosing subjects for their alleged powers to discipline the mind.

Problems Faced by Secondary Education

The first two decades of the twentieth century were given over by secondary educators to the urgent business of reshaping the curriculum along the lines of an utterly different educational and social philosophy. In so doing they were faced with enormous problems, both theoretical and practical—some seeming to defy solution.

With secondary education pushed down to the seventh grade, many teachers in the junior high school sought to imitate the senior high school in a setting of departmental specialization. The practice of tracking in junior high schools left students unlikely to change their programs; they were cut off from associations with pupils pursuing different aims and life goals. In a real sense, this was predestination: the antithesis of the educational opportunity that educators had been trying to improve by increasing the holding power of the school. (As mentioned, the latter was the raison d'être of the junior high school as stressed in the Cardinal Principles report of 1918.)

This problem was far more common in the high school. Curriculum tracking often had led to social isolation, even where the various curricula were offered under the same roof. In such instances, students were unlikely to be aroused by new interests and unlikely to revise their ambitions. Equally important was the loss of opportunity to identify and develop common interests and common ideals.

Theoretical Issues.   The main problem with which educators wrestled was how to provide in the high school a distinct curriculum for each individual that would meet personal goals and also broad social needs. This raised several theoretical issues: Which courses were most likely to meet democratic social objectives, or should all courses be revised to this end? Which courses should be required of all students? How should the problem of what appeared to be an innate dualism between vocational and so-called cultural courses, with their unfortunate social concomitants, be resolved? Even within the same subject there were apparently opposing aspects. Science, for example, had both applied and theoretical sides.

Should subjects be taught differently according to pupils' needs? The Committee of Ten (1893) had answered this question with a resounding "no." The committee had viewed preparation for college as the best preparation for life. But thinking on this question had undergone radical change. Indeed, many had swung to the opposite extreme, holding that preparation for "life"—economic efficiency and public service—was the best preparation for college (Yocum, 1913). Some educators believed that this was equally epigrammatic but just as baseless as the dictum of the Committee of Ten.

Dewey's Integral Vision.   In 1901, Dewey addressed a conference of secondary educators in Chicago on these problems. It was time, he said, for separate vocational high schools to become integral parts of the city high schools (1902c, p. 21). As for the conflict in studies, this could be approached in two ways: (1) by viewing the curriculum in the context of the needs of the individual and (2) by viewing what appear to be opposing elements as complementary and essential parts of a whole. Training in a vocation, unless that training were moored in its cultural context, was narrowing. "Just as in life the technological pursuits reach out and affect society on all sides, so in the school corresponding studies need to be imbedded in a broad and deep matrix," said Dewey. The converse was also true; those studies regarded as preparing for college were "relatively dead and meaningless unless surrounded with a context of obvious meanings," such as through studies in industrial arts (p. 25). In other words, their applications to human activities should be made apparent.

Dewey also spoke of another concern of secondary school educators: curriculum fragmentation because of increasing specialization. Isolation was needed for the unhindered development of a specialization, he said. But the time had come when it was necessary to pull the connecting elements of the specializations together into a meaningful whole. "The sole object of the separation is to serve as a means to the end of more effective interaction," he pointed out (p. 16). What subjects should be required of all students? Here Dewey stressed the importance of those subjects that "deal directly with the problems of health, citizenship, and the means of communication through the vernacular" (p. 8). The principle to follow in curriculum reorganization, Dewey said, was to view all the school studies in light of their place in human activities. Expansion of the curriculum should also follow this principle.

Dewey's criteria for curriculum development provided a theoretical vehicle for educators to use in their attempted escape from college domination. Educational reformers also followed Dewey's lead in developing specific principles for reorganizing the secondary school curriculum. A succession of books based on Dewey's view followed. According to Albert Yocum (1913), professor of education at the University of Pennsylvania, preparation for a vocation was being confused with preparation for life. This had produced "two almost equally unhappy extremes: a professional specialization which ignores general training and culture and an academic specialization which refuses to relate itself to life." This, he said, was a crisis that could be resolved only by "the paralleling of general education and specialization, and the relating of each as fully as possible to life" (p. 25).

Yocum pointed out that in their eagerness to individualize education, school people were inadvertently encouraging premature specialization. They were also excluding from the curriculum "much that all students should possess in common, whether as part of a common culture or as a means to the direct preparation for a common life from which a common culture can result" (p. 28).

The Commission on the Reorganization of Secondary Education

These ideas had gained currency in 1913 when the National Education Association appointed a committee to develop fundamental principles for the reorganization of secondary education. The report of the Commission on the Reorganization of Secondary Education was five years in the making. Its impact on educational policy has yet to be equaled.

Determining Secondary Education. "Secondary education should be determined by the needs of the society to be served, the character of the individuals to be educated, and the knowledge of educational theory and practice available," wrote the commission (1918, p. 7), indicating the bases for curriculum development. All three—the society, the nature of the secondary school population, and educational theory—had undergone changes requiring extensive modification of secondary education.

But the overriding objective of the secondary school was to give flesh and blood reality to the ideal of democracy, declared the commission. Democratic education "should develop in each individual the knowledge, interests, ideals, habits, and powers whereby he will find his place and use that place to shape both himself and society toward ever nobler ends" (p. 9). This was the dominant theme of the report and, by no coincidence, the theme of Dewey's *Democracy and Education* (Butts, 1978, p. 220).

Cardinal Principles of Secondary Education

The commission named seven principal objectives, the "Cardinal Principles," of education: health, command of fundamental processes (reading, writing, arithmetic, and oral and written expression), worthy home membership, vocation, citizenship, worthy use of leisure, and ethical character. These objectives could best be met in a unified organization embracing all curricula: the comprehensive high school, a school with no counterpart anywhere in the world.

Far from being isolated, the objectives were actually closely interrelated. Their interrelation must be reflected in the curriculum throughout the period of secondary education if the student were to be prepared for effective functioning in a democratic society. An illustration was the relation between vocational and citizenship education (social studies) in the high school curriculum. Favored in the report was "the infusion of vocation with the spirit of service" and "the vitalization of culture by the world's work" (p. 16).

The report addressed itself squarely to the formidable problems of secondary education, finding every subject in need of reorganization so that it could contribute more effectively to the seven Cardinal Principles. Indeed, the place of each subject in the curriculum depended on the value of its contribution.

Specialization and Unification. "With increasing specialization in any society comes a corresponding necessity for unification. So in the secondary school, increased attention to specialization calls for more purposeful plans for unification," stated the report (p. 23), paraphrasing Dewey's words of nearly two decades earlier. Unification would be accomplished mainly through *constants,* those courses required of all students. These were to be determined by the objectives of health, command of fundamental processes, worthy home membership, citizenship, and ethical character.

Unification was, of course, a fundamental purpose of education in a democracy. In addition to the comprehensive organization of the school itself and the curriculum in general education, unification could be attained through the mingling of students from all walks of life as they participated in social activities, school government, and athletics.

In addition to constants, the secondary school should provide *curriculum variables* (specialized courses determined by the student's goals) and *free electives* to be taken in accordance with interests, generally to meet the objective of the worthy use of leisure time (although electives could also be taken in accordance with vocational needs or interests other than avocational).

The commission advanced two important principles in connection with specialization and unification: (1) the more the time for curriculum variables, the more purposefully should be the time spent on constants as a vehicle for unification; and (2) the more differentiated the curriculum, the more important is the students' social mingling.

A Developmental Focus. The idea that individual development is a continuous process was being emphasized in educational theory. An abrupt break between elementary and secondary education was therefore undesirable. On this basis, the commission endorsed the division of secondary education into junior and senior periods, each ordinarily three years in length and each with discrete purposes.

The junior high school should offer the pupil an opportunity to follow his or her interests, to explore his or her abilities and aptitudes. Seventh-graders should not be required to select a specialization but, rather, should have some experience with a variety of vocations—agricultural, commercial, and industrial—plus homemaking for girls and, for some pupils, some work in a modern foreign language. The foregoing should be organized into short units so that every pupil could take several units. The commission stressed that the work "should be of real educational value, in addition to its exploratory value" (p. 24).

Both junior and senior high schools should be of the comprehensive type to provide students with a sound basis for a wise curriculum choice in addition to serving as organs of unification.

Curriculum Differentiation and Course Content.
On the one hand, the commission endorsed the idea of teaching subjects differently in accordance with the needs and interests of pupils. On the other hand, curriculum differentiation did not mean that the content of every course should be determined by the dominant element in the curriculum. Such a practice, warned the report, "would ignore other objectives of education just as important as that of vocational efficiency" (p. 22).

Immediate Versus Deferred Values.   As a reaction against formalism, some educators advocated that pupils study only that which was of immediate interest or value to them. Here the commission drew the line. "This extreme," they declared, "is neither necessary nor desirable. They [the pupils] should be helped to acquire the habits, insights, and ideals that will enable them to meet the duties and responsibilities of later life" (p. 17). However, they should be encouraged to respond to present duties and responsibilities as well, as a foundation for future behavior.

Overage Elementary Pupils.   In a section of the report dealing with the articulation of secondary education with elementary education, it was recommended that overage pupils who are retained in the elementary school when they can no longer benefit from it be admitted to the secondary school. "Experience has shown," argued the commission, "that the secondary school can provide special instruction for overage pupils more successfully than the elementary school can" (p. 19). Experience continues to support promotion policies that give attention to social and emotional factors as well as achievement levels.

A Sense of Years to Come.   It can be said in retrospect that the authors of the Cardinal Principles had not only an accurate grasp of the pedagogic present but also a remarkable sense of years to come. In no small way, they determined the shape of the secondary school. They had a vision of secondary education for all youth. That vision was fulfilled over the course of the twentieth century.

Prophetically, the report declared that in the interests of democracy higher education could no longer be the province of the privileged (p. 20). Just as secondary schools should admit those who can no longer be served adequately by the elementary school, so should institutions of higher learning admit those whose needs are no longer met by the secondary school, maintained the commission. This reform did not begin to emerge in any significant way until after midcentury when public junior and community colleges in some states began enrolling persons over age 18 who had not graduated from high school. Another nontraditional path to postsecondary education has been the high school equivalency credential. Today, hundreds of thousands take the tests of general educational development (GED) and are awarded high school equivalency certificates. Thousands of these persons prepare for the tests independently.

The Cardinal Principles were more than a declaration of independence by the high school from college domination. As Arthur Wirth (1972) has pointed out, the report's insistent message was that the high school should meet the needs of all youth not just those who were college bound. The commission members had in mind a design to adjust the curriculum to changing times and a movement toward social democracy. But probably even they failed to realize the magnitude of their contribution to the field of curriculum development. Since its publication, the report has provided the framework for the continual development of the secondary school curriculum.

This is not to say that the comprehensive high school has been free of criticism. Far from it. Let us examine some of the leading criticisms. Almost immediately, the commission's report was vigorously assailed in David Snedden's book *Vocational Education* (1920). Snedden, a vocational educator, opposed the proposal to include vocational education in a comprehensive high school. He argued that it was possible to provide effective training for vocations only in specialized schools. Snedden minced no words about his view of the Commission. It was "confused" (p. 96) and its proposals, "vague, if not mystical" (p. 103). Study about vocations had been confused with true vocational education, held Snedden, who contended that the comprehensive high school idea reflected an academic snobbishness. "Toward all current problems, intricate and baffling, of vocational education the committee (that is, the Commission) maintains a serene scholastic aloofness, possibly the same slightly contemptuous indifference which characterized the attitude of our scholastic forebears toward manual labor in general" (p. 104).

Snedden's criticism is indeed fascinating in light of interpretations of the report by some revisionist historians. According to Lazerson and Grub (1974), for example, the comprehensive high school proposal was an elitist plot to isolate vocational students from mainstream secondary schooling and maintain the appearance of equality. There is no denying that outcomes in many urban high schools differed from the commission's stated intentions. In the 1980s Goodlad (1984), Oakes (1985), Tyler (1988), and countless others pointed out that tracking was the practice in many high schools and where it existed it made equal access to the curriculum impossible. Rigid tracking is a form of placement with little chance to move from program to program (Lucas, 1999). The commission's stated intention in the report was just the opposite: "Flexibility of organization and administration" including (the commission's words were "secured by") "possible transfer from curriculum to curriculum" (p. 22). Somehow, in many schools, students were locked into programs or felt that they were, which amounts to the same thing.

The 1980s barrage of criticism set in motion a powerful detracking movement (LeTendre, Hofer, & Shimitzu, 2003). According to a study by Lucas (1999), formal tracking programs "have been dismantled, and . . . the organizational form no longer persists at the secondary level" (p. 134). Other researchers, however, have found something different: "curricular or organizational differentiation of students is widespread and persists in elementary grades through the end of high school (LeTendre, Hofer, & Shimitzu, 2003, p. 45).

A Cliff-Hanger for Democracy. The commission on the Reorganization of Secondary Education in 1918 expressed its downright opposition to segregated vocational programs, which were under serious consideration. In Illinois, for instance, a proposal put before the legislature and favored by many industrialists could have split the entire school system in two for young people over age 14. Dewey (1913) attacked the proposal as undemocratic. The separation of general education from vocational education would be used to "mark off to the interests of employers a separate class of laborers" and was "the greatest evil now threatening democracy in education" (p. 374).

Dewey's proposal and subsequent influences on the comprehensive high school idea were discussed extensively and acrimoniously by Snedden (1920) in his book on vocational education (pp. 397–410).

So Dewey won out, but the point of importance is that a comprehensive plan was radical indeed, at a time when many bankers and industrialists were supporting a measure that would have established a system of schools absolutely separate from the regular schools and with a completely different curriculum.

Another Cliff-Hanger. In the 1940s and 1950s, James B. Conant, a highly respected scientist and university president whose writings on educational policy were enormously influential, recommended the continuation and strengthening of comprehensive secondary education as the best assurance of a "classless" and free society (Conant & Spaulding, 1940; Conant, 1959b). There can be little doubt that his writings helped defuse attacks on the comprehensive high school in the years after World War II and throughout the Cold War.

Conant saw clearly that the challenges of providing high-quality academic and vocational programs for all students in a comprehensive setting were enormous, but he believed that it must be done. Throughout the twentieth century, access to knowledge improved for previously excluded groups. Indeed, it has improved since Conant's day and continues to improve in our own. Since Goodlad's study of schooling in 1984 and Oakes's 1985 book on tracking, more American schools have abandoned their programs of tracking. Detracking, however, has not necessarily led to a diversified curriculum. Changing graduation requirements and more high-stakes testing have left students with fewer curricular options in many schools.

Perspective

The comprehensive or cosmopolitan high school was born under a lucky star. For one thing, Americans were more comfortable with all children under the same roof rather than in separate schools with separate curricula. For another, most towns could afford only one school. This permitted social mingling but did not, of course, guarantee it. Differentiated curriculums could keep students as apart as if they lived on different planets. The Commission on Reorganization of Secondary Education (1918) recognized the unifying function of education as essential to democracy and recommended that it be met in three ways: (1) through subjects that were particularly valuable for this purpose, especially the social studies and literature; (2) school organization and administration that fosters the social mingling of students; and (3) student participation in activities in which they should have a great deal of shared responsibility, such as athletic events, school government, and social activities.

The comprehensive school's luck held throughout the century. It had highly respected champions—John Dewey in 1913 and James Conant in the 1950s—when the going got rough and it might have been derailed. Both fought for the democratic ideal in curriculum. For Dewey, democracy was more than a form of government but a way of living together and growing as individuals and a society. For Conant, our liberty depended on these things.

Problems were different in large cities that had a history of separate vocational schools. Bringing students together was more difficult, but at least the system would not be broken in two, thanks to Dewey's intervention in 1913 and the *Cardinal Principles* report of 1918. By the end of the century, tracking of students was breaking down, but the curriculum would not be truly diversified unless students could elect courses and programs that met their interests. Many schools had become virtually academic high schools. Tracking is undesirable, but sameness is no more democratic. The comprehensive framework, however, is still there and flexible.

Throughout the century, the conflicting currents of efficiency and human growth and development

competed for the curriculum. Efficiency as the basis for curriculum development and the adulation of business and industry reached a fever pitch in the early decades. But there were skeptics. For example, in a paper delivered before the Massachusetts Education Association in 1912, Leonard Ayres, a leader in educational administration, spoke enthusiastically about the commonalities between education and industry. As a result of changes in industrial activity, "each workman lays as many bricks in one hour as he formerly laid in three" (p. 302). The ideas and processes reshaping education, he said, are "similar to those that are reshaping the processes of industry." The question was not whether "the new method" (which Ayres called "scientific") should be adopted, but rather, "How shall we utilize it?" (p. 302). But a discussant, Edward Hartwell of the Massachusetts Board of Education, had serious reservations. "It seems to me," he said, "that the essential problems of education are problems of growth and development" (1912, p. 317). We should avoid as inapplicable "criteria by which the efficiency of the builders and operators of dead machines is properly judged." If there was any doubt about the depth of his concern, it was dispelled by his concluding statement:

> My plea is that we should discriminate in our investigations of educational matters between methods and criteria that are applicable to living mechanisms and their activities and those which pertain to the realm of the inventor, the engineer, and the manufacturer. (p. 317)

The conflicting currents between efficiency and having the best for all the children of all the people were traced in the first three chapters. (Hartwell, interestingly enough, was a statistician.)

In urban schools, problems at the close of the twentieth century were much as they were at the opening of the century. Many urban schools have inadequate resources for learning and are unattractive, if not unsafe, places. It is harder to develop in students the desire to go on learning, which, as Dewey pointed out, is the most important objective of all. As Charles Eliot recognized, curriculum improvement is crucial in creating opportunities for children in poverty. Today, poverty is also a problem in rural areas and in older suburban communities as well as in major cities.

Early in the century, Thorndike's research refuted the accepted doctrines for offering certain subjects in the school curriculum, setting into action a chain of events that has continued to influence the curriculum (not always in wise ways). For centuries, certain classical subjects were included in the curriculum because they were believed to develop the mind and disciplined habits of thinking. One outcome of Thorndike's studies was that such subjects could no longer be justified on the basis that they developed the mind. Another was that educators had to find other ways of determining the relative value of subjects. This led to the appointment of NEA's Committee on Economy of Time in Education, which followed a mechanistic approach to curriculum development in identifying the "minimum essentials" of the curriculum. Thorndike had interpreted his research to mean that elements in the school curriculum should be identical with opportunities for their use by learners (or adults) outside of school. This idea was applied in strikingly different ways. It led to the reductionist activity-analysis approach to curriculum making of Bobbitt and Charters but also to such more holistic learning activities as students defining a local community problem and generating actual solutions. This practice is followed in some schools today in helping young people learn to participate intelligently in a democratic society.

All educators want to improve the probability of transfer of learning, both to school learning and life outside the school. The curriculum must be deliberately planned to foster transfer. We know that a fragmented curriculum decreases the likelihood of transfer and that broad generalizations and knowledge applications that transcend disciplines increase the possibility of transfer. We have come to recognize that transfer is enhanced when students understand why they are engaging in a certain activity or learning task. Today, science curriculum materials stress inquiry, but there are important differences with the 1960s. The purpose of the curriculum efforts of the 1960s was to have learners "discover" scientific concepts without application or relation to society, but now curricula focus on exploration of problems and questions that learners can relate to as meaningful in their own lives. Clearly, lessons were learned by curriculum developers who initially failed to make the inquiry meaningful to learners.

Whether called middle schools or junior high schools, schools for middle-grade children have not lived up to their opportunity and responsibility for providing a coherent curriculum along with exploratory studies for older children and young adolescents. The curriculum often is laid out in separate subjects. In fact, efforts to develop integrated curricula have had a setback in many schools where teachers focus defensively on preparing students for standardized tests. Yet exemplary (and enjoyable) middle school programs do exist, revealing that the curriculum can be challenging, meaningful, and enjoyable.

Lester Ward's ideas concerning education and progress have been lasting and significant. Only humans have the capacity for telic progress, which is deliberate progress requiring the development and application of intelligence. According to Ward, who was a botanist and founder of sociology in America, this is the most important purpose of the curriculum and it is in the interest of government to provide the educational opportunity that will ultimately cause social progress. Intellectual ability is the outcome of opportunity. The curriculum should link the individual with the environment—the real world—and not depend on either memory or empty traditions. The application of the learner's intelligence can speed up the slow evolutionary processes of human progress.

Dewey's problem-solving method or method of intelligence built on Ward's more general ideas about the curriculum and made them operational. Dewey also built on a second feature of Ward's philosophy: the principle that knowledge should be equally available. According to Dewey, educational opportunity means shared knowledge and concerns; the problem is one of learning together as well as what is learned. Late in the century, the emphasis on multiculturalism placed even greater demands on the unifying functions of democratic education. Today, multicultural education is still an emphasis. But after the attacks on America on September 11, 2001, various cultural groups gathered together under the comforting and always welcoming umbrella of democracy and the emphasis was, as in earlier times, on becoming a unified society. But intercultural education needs to be rediscovered by building unity through diversity.

In a sense nothing had changed where our responsibilities are concerned. In new times, educators continue to look for new ideas and initiatives for meeting the old idea of unification. The search is unending. This is what Ralph Tyler called an "unfinished task" in education.

PROBLEMS FOR STUDY AND DISCUSSION

1. In 1918 the Commission on Reorganization of Secondary Education addressed aspects of students' social development not dealt with in the academic curriculum. According to Brown and Theobald (1998), "much of the contemporary extracurriculum has drifted far afield of these original intentions" (p. 120). They explain:

   > Competitive interscholastic sports allow only the best players, as judged by adults, to participate. The same is often true of drama productions, musical groups, debate teams, even science and mathematics groups, which have a competitive orientation. Student-initiated and student-run activities are a rarity. . . . Rather than becoming a training ground for democracy, initiative, and well-roundedness, extracurricular programs have become a training ground for expertise—competitively honed and adult-controlled. (p. 120)

   Examine the student guides of several high schools. Do you think the above statement is fair? Why or why not? If so, how would you bring the extracurriculum back in line with the original intention of being integral to the curriculum rather than being "extra"?

2. As the influence of the business philosophy is described in this chapter, do you find that it is still present in American education? What is your view as to its main influence on the curriculum?

3. Is social unification (interculturalism) still a valid function for today's curriculum, or should ethnicity be emphasized (multiculturalism) above any shared heritage? Explain.

4. What principles and examples can you give teachers to help them develop in children the desire to go on learning?

5. This chapter pointed out that in the 1930s curriculum supervisors helped teachers in developing integrated curricula. In your view, is this kind of help needed by teachers today? Why or why not? In your experience, would such help be available for teachers who need and request it? Explain.

6. Leonard Ayres and Edward Hartwell, both educational administrators, held different views about criteria for curriculum development and evaluation. Which view, if either, is a dominant emphasis on curriculum development today? Justify your answer.

7. Some urban school boards have turned over the management of certain schools to private, for-profit companies. Are such actions supported by research and experience? Support your response.

8. You are a curriculum supervisor. How would you respond to the argument that Latin should be included in the curriculum because it disciplines the mind and facilitates the development of disciplined habits of thinking and transfer to English?

9. The Commission on the Reorganization of Secondary Education viewed the social studies and the humanities as studies contributing to social solidarity; they should, therefore, be taken by all students. What is the implication of this principle for grouping? Many high schools permit students to elect courses in these fields rather than require the same courses to be taken by all students. Does this weaken the social unification function of the curriculum? Why or why not?

10. What are the implications of Ward's and Dewey's conceptions of educational opportunity for curriculum development?

11. Examine the curriculum guides of several high schools and middle-grade schools. What evidence do you find of efforts to develop interdisciplinary curriculums?

12. In connection with the preceding question, visit one or more of the schools. What evidence do you find of interdisciplinary teaching and integrated learning (where interdisciplinary teams, for example, are helping students make links between concepts in various subject areas)?

13. In 1920 Snedden described Dewey's proposals for vocational education as vague and impractical. Snedden strongly implied that Dewey had vocational education confused with education about vocations. Examine Dewey's chapter on vocational education in *Democracy and Education* (1916). Do you think Snedden's criticism was justifiable? Support your response.

14. Is the principle that citizenship tasks taught by the school should be genuine and involve practice supported by research? Explain. To what extent is citizenship education made genuine or real to students in your school?

CHAPTER 4

EVOLUTION OF THE MODERN CURRICULUM

"Please send price and ordering information for your 26th Yearbook which you may know that Ralph W. Tyler has described as one of the five most significant curriculum events of the 20th century," wrote Charles Perrone, a librarian at Burlington County College in New Jersey to the National Society for the Study of Education (C. Perrone, personal communication, July 7, 1988). The librarian did not say what the four other events were. His interest was in the Twenty-sixth Yearbook (1927), which, luckily for him (and us), was reprinted in 1969.

According to Tyler (1971), the most significant events (besides the Twenty-sixth Yearbook) were: (1) Thorndike's investigations of transfer of learning, (2) Dewey's laboratory school at the University of Chicago, (3) analysis of activities to determine curriculum content, which Tyler traced to programs for training skilled workers for war-related jobs in 1917–1918, and (4) the Eight-Year Study, discussed later in this chapter.

Our interest here is in the Twenty-sixth Yearbook, which represented a stunning leap forward in achieving a unified theory in the curriculum field. The story begins with the fall of mental discipline as a curriculum theory, which had left a great void. Into the void jumped activity analysis, child centeredness, ways of investigating learning, studies of children and adolescents, and, last but not least, democracy, or the "power to share effectively in social life" (Dewey, 1916, p. 418), each claiming to be the paramount basis for curriculum development. The void was filled but not with a unified theory. Instead, various curriculum reform efforts were undertaken, based on incomplete and often conflicting criteria for determining what knowledge is of most worth.

The diversity of reform efforts might have made consensus seem impossible. But rather than decrying the confusion and conflict that characterized curriculum making, our forebears decided to do something about it. The ultimate result was a theoretically based system for curriculum development that has guided educators to this day. Of course, this did not happen overnight, but over decades, by generations of educational theorists. We also learned a great deal about who should be involved in curriculum development and how. This chapter is concerned with principles that are still basic to curriculum development and how a curriculum comes alive.

Theoretical Steps Forward

It is unnecessary to stress anything as familiar as the importance of a unified theory to successful curriculum development. As in other professions, the services of the curriculum specialist must rest on the mastery of a common body of knowledge and skills. In the 1920s curriculum development was in the early stages of becoming a professional field and was called *curriculum making*. It was Harold Rugg, a professor at Columbia's Teachers College, who had the idea to bring together the disjointed and opposing viewpoints and, as much as possible, unify them. If there was a hero in the curriculum making movement, it was surely Harold Rugg.

The Twenty-sixth Yearbook

In 1924 Rugg and a group of curriculum professors associated with the National Society for the Study of Education (NSSE) received a grant to prepare a yearbook for the society on the theme of curriculum making. Thus began the monumental work of NSSE's Committee on Curriculum Making, chaired by Rugg. For two years the committee of 12 reviewed trends, studied outcomes, and endeavored, in Rugg's words, "to map out new paths" (1927b, p. x). They met regularly in what Rugg described as "prolonged round-table conferences over similarities and divergences in educational theory" (p. xii). Their report was published in 1927 in two volumes as NSSE's Twenty-sixth Yearbook. The Twenty-sixth Yearbook is regarded today as a landmark in the evolution of curriculum theory.

Seeking Consensus.   The Committee on Curriculum Making sent a questionnaire to selected American school systems to determine their involvement in curriculum development. Based on the returns, it seemed clear that curriculum revision was widespread in the 1920s and that a nationwide movement for curriculum revision was under way. In elementary and secondary schools and even in colleges, dissatisfaction with the existing program was growing. Hundreds of school systems were revising curricula. The problem was, as Counts (1927) pointed out in his chapter on high schools, change was not being "directed intelligently." It was just happening (p. 161). Courses were dropped from and added to the curriculum in the dark, so to speak, without evaluation and an overall design.

The problem of design was compounded by the problem of theory. Theory had been largely neglected. According to Rugg (1927a), the development of educational theory required

> the vigorous impact of opposed schools of thought upon each other. The development of education theory has been much hampered in our day by the lack of intellectual controversy. School men have been more concerned with educational practice, with administration, than with hard thinking concerning the direction in which education is moving and ought to move. Administration is ousting analysis. (p. 1)

Rugg recounted that many years earlier the National Herbart Society had served as a way for people to come together and exchange views. The meetings of the Herbartians were genuine open forums. Much of contemporary educational theory, he said, was the result of their early meetings and publications. This was evident from the first few yearbooks of the Herbart Society (National Herbart Society Yearbooks 1–5, 1895–1899; reprinted by Arno Press and the *New York Times,* 1969). For example, members presented their theoretical positions on how to integrate the curriculum. But with the phenomenal

multiplication of teacher associations and other educational associations and institutions, said Rugg, "our national societies have become 'listening' organizations. Discussion has waned. Intellectual resistance has dwindled" (1927a, p. 1).

Rugg was wrestling with the kind of questions that beset us today. This very problem—the importance of organizational unity in countering poorly conceived curriculum changes—was dealt with by Robert Anderson (1988) in the Eighty-seventh Yearbook of the National Society for the Study of Education. (The National Herbart Society was the ancestor of the National Society for the Study of Education.)

New Approach to Curriculum Making.   The Committee on Curriculum Making found that curriculum development was being approached by methods that were lamentably inadequate. In the words of Rugg and Counts (1927),

> [t]he responsibility for curriculum making is commonly borne by committees composed of teachers and administrators who are already overburdened with work. As a consequence, the existing program is always taken as the point of departure, and attention is centered on the addition of new materials or the subtraction of old materials from the established school subjects. (p. 427)

In effect, there was virtually no movement toward fundamental reconstruction of the school curriculum.

Having described the situation regarding curriculum development in most schools, the committee made recommendations based on practices and experience in the more progressive cities. These practices, or steps to be taken, had been observed by committee members. First in importance in the committee's view was the development of a "thoroughly professional and research attitude" (p. 429) toward the problem of curriculum improvement on the part of those in charge: the superintendent, supervisory staff, board of education, and teachers. Effective curriculum development was impossible without recognition of the professional nature of the task.

Second, funds must be provided for a continuous and comprehensive program of curriculum development. Its effectiveness was contingent on the establishment of a central and autonomous department of curriculum. The heart of the instructional work, which the committee noted usually constitutes the major portion of school administration, would be the department of the curriculum.

The third suggestion was the appointment of professionally prepared curriculum development specialists, whose responsibilities would be carried out under the leadership of an assistant superintendent or curriculum director. The committee's survey had found that in most districts there was no individual with expertise in curriculum development who was responsible for the total program of curriculum development.

Fourth, the administrator in charge of curriculum improvement should be provided with adequate facilities and resources. The department should be located in a central building with the other administrators, and a professional library was of the essence.

The fifth suggestion or step concerned the actual work of curriculum making. Most of the work of preparing courses of study would be done by committees of principals and teachers. The fifth step was to organize the committees. Here the NSSE Committee on Curriculum Making interjected a word of advice based on the experience of Denver, Winnetka, and other systems: Funds must be appropriated to release those doing the work of curriculum making from all classroom responsibilities. This was an absolutely essential condition, argued Rugg and Counts (1927), for doing the "laborious work of assembling and organizing materials, preparing, criticizing and revising outlines, selecting books, phrasing objectives and illustrating methods of teaching." To ensure that it was done professionally, teachers who are released from the classroom "should be chosen for professional rather than for political reasons" (pp. 441–442).

Finally, the number of committees should be small. There should be a coordinating committee, including the curriculum director or assistant superintendent, who can see the curriculum whole and not as disjointed, independent subject specializations and domains. Another critically important suggestion was to merge the separate subject committees to form broad fields of interrelated subjects: for example, a committee on the social studies rather than on history, civics, geography, economics, and so on.

Curriculum continuity, the committee maintained, could be achieved by having a single committee for each broad curriculum field, which would consider the entire program from the 1st through the twelfth grade. "Individuals responsible for visualizing the whole scheme must constantly be integrating the work of these smaller groups. By no other method,"

concluded Rugg and Counts, "can we secure the unification of related activities and materials and the continuity and development which our current school system so sadly lacks" (pp. 442–443). This need remains paramount to this day in connection with the curriculum at all levels, from the elementary school through the college.

Theory Development: Reaching Consensus. The Committee on Curriculum Making achieved unexpected consensus on questions involving philosophical differences. Much of the debate revolved around the issue of child growth versus social needs as the starting point for curriculum construction. The group finally agreed that both views were important and interrelated, and both were incorporated in the final statement (Rugg, 1927a). The committee, under the leadership of Harold Rugg, had made a clear beginning in the search for a curriculum paradigm, as discussed in detail in chapter 6.

The committee stressed that the key to curriculum making lay in the application of scientific principles. Looking at the process itself, there were essentially three tasks to determine: the objectives of education, the modes and materials of instruction, and the organization (appropriate grade placement) of learning experiences. The goals of education and the content of the curriculum would emerge from studies of American society and individual development. But above all, "care should be exercised to validate proposal changes experimentally" (p. 23).

According to Tyler (1971), the curriculum development process as outlined by Rugg and Counts presented some limitations "from the failure to recognize that preparing lists of activities and materials is only part of the task which also includes developing interest in using them on the part of teachers and overcoming the passive attitudes of pupils toward school work" (p. 36). Tyler explained that unless a teacher actually discovers and believes that the instructional program is grievously lacking, he or she will not invest time and energy to use a different one effectively. Those engaged in the leading curriculum improvement projects of the 1930s learned this lesson and found ways of devising and evaluating alternative curriculum designs and learning outcomes.

In looking back on the contributions of the NSSE Committee on Curriculum Making, Walker (1975) pointed out that the "Twenty-sixth Yearbook is an admirable piece of work, deserving of more attention and appreciation than it receives," and, unlike most recent work, it "kept everyone's eye pretty much on the ball of curricula and curriculum making" (p. 279). The work of the NSSE Committee on Curriculum Making was indeed admirable; it focused on the problem, and it was more: It established principles of curriculum development for a newly emerging field of university study and systematic professional practice. To be sure, conflicting viewpoints continued to divide members of the infant field (Schoonmaker, 2001). But they now had a set of principles against which to screen new proposals and evaluate old ones.

The Society for Curriculum Study

The Society for Curriculum Study grew out of the efforts of pioneer Henry Harap in the field of curriculum. It started in 1928 with Harap's efforts to find a means of exchanging ideas on curriculum making. By 1932 the group had become known as the Society for Curriculum Study (D. Tanner, 1991). As the decade progressed, instructional supervision came to be recognized as an integral part of curriculum improvement. In 1941 the society merged with the NEA's Department of Supervision and Directors of Instruction to become the Association for Supervision and Curriculum Development, and the relationship between supervision and curriculum development was signalized.

The Society for Curriculum Study viewed its function as continuing the work of the Rugg committee. In 1936, the society embarked on a joint project with the Department of Supervision and Directors of Instruction to produce a summary of then-current curriculum thought and practice. Such a book, they believed, might be useful to school officials and teachers. Like the Rugg committee, the Harap committee put forward a point of view and proposed an approach to curriculum development.

The Harap committee took the position that "it is the function of the school to improve living in a democratic society" (Harap, 1937, p. vii). What this meant was that school life, and particularly the curriculum, must have a social focus. "Problems of our common life, suitable to the experience and maturity of each group, should make up the major portion of the curriculum," said the committee (p. 49). The curriculum would be evaluated in terms of students' ability and desire to react with increasing intelligence to lifelike problem situations. The good society was never static but encouraged human achievements and

was evidenced by a society undergoing progressive change. The good life was social—what seemed promising for the society as a whole was paramount. "As a consequence," concluded the committee, "the school should be society centered rather than child centered" (p. 54).

To be sure, this was a theoretical step, but unfortunately the Harap committee seemed to have fallen into the trap of either-or thinking by setting democratic social aims against learner centeredness, rather than seeing the two as interdependent. In the light of world and national events in the 1930s, however, it is not difficult to see why the Harap committee took the position that the curriculum should emphasize activities that would prepare children to be involved in sharing the responsibility and power that was the heart of democracy. These goals were, of course, not new.

Democracy, Despotism, and the Curriculum. Dictatorships had come to power in Germany, Italy, the Soviet Union, and Spain. All were based on the idea that it is the leader's job to regiment the people and lead them for the good of the state. The promises and political preachings of the dictators captured the imaginations of disenchanted Europeans, who paid the price of having their political liberties completely suppressed. The horror of the Holocaust, in which millions of Jews and other minority scapegoats and political dissidents lost their lives, still shocks the world, but the fact that it happened in Germany, one of the world's leading centers of university scholarship, made American educators uneasy. Americans began to feel that their democracy was being threatened. Added to this, America was experiencing the worst economic depression in modern times. These problems were uppermost in the minds of the Harap committee members.

Authoritarianism versus Democracy in the Classroom. One does not have to live in a dictatorship to be a dictator. As the committee pointed out, a teacher can either function as a leader or "be a little dictator in the classroom." Teaching children the skills of democratic living required that neither they nor their teachers feel that they work in a dictatorship. "Where does dictatorship leave off and leadership begin, and how can the distinction be reflected by the curriculum and methods of learning?" (Harap, 1937, p. 28). This question was destined to be asked by educators again and again in succeeding decades. As

Tyler (1988) pointed out, educating for democratic citizenship is "the most generally accepted goal of American education"; further, the question of "what young people should learn in order to participate intelligently in this changing society must be faced anew by each new generation" (p. 268).

Units of Work.   The Harap committee proposed that the curriculum be composed of a series of learning units. The term *unit*, as the committee pointed out, had gained acceptance since William Kilpatrick had popularized the project method two decades earlier. According to Harap (1937), the concept of the learning unit could be traced to Kilpatrick's attempt to unify the traditional curriculum, which was broken up into small, unrelated pieces (pp. 76–77). As we have pointed out, however, the idea of giving unity to the curriculum through the learner's experience was advanced by Dewey much earlier and was applied in his laboratory school.

According to the Harap committee, a learning unit, also known as a unit of work, was based on a real situation. These situations gave the learning units coherence. Units were not kept within the confines of a single subject field. Take, for example, the learner's question of how his or her family obtains food. As Harap argued, "To keep a child's inquiry concerning his food supply within the limits of geography is manifestly absurd. Even if one set out deliberately to do so, it could not be accomplished" (p. 78). Many units drew on all school subjects. For instance, the study of water supply originating in the social studies involved map study, graphic representation, science, mathematics, government, and history. Today such a problem might originate in the broad field of ecology.

Units of work were viewed by the Harap committee as the smallest subdivision of the curriculum. The committee selected eight "areas of living," or groups of related activities for learning units: living in the home, leisure, citizenship, organized group life, consumption, production, communication, and transportation.

The conventional subjects were viewed as merely accessory in a "functional curriculum" (p. 97). In other words, concepts from fields of knowledge were used as needed in the study of comprehensive areas of living. However, remedial classes in reading and arithmetic could be offered to treat deficiencies in these areas, and separate subjects could be studied as electives.

Even though the Harap committee called its proposal society centered, it was based on the recognition that children go through stages of development.

Educational programs must be geared to these levels. The activities for a given class depended on the maturity of the learners. Moreover, "the choice of the pupils themselves will determine exactly what enterprises should be undertaken in any grade" (p. 110). There is no doubt that the Harap proposal drew on knowledge about the child, realizing that interests must be considered if children are to learn. The Harap committee's conception of the appropriate curriculum encompassed the psychological as well as the social point of view.

Fundamental Characteristics of Modern Curriculum Development.   The Harap committee identified concepts on which modern curriculum development is based. The individual events may be different for each of us as we seek to improve the curriculum, but we still should proceed on the following:

1. No professional staff has to start from scratch. For more than a century, researchers and practitioners have studied curriculum problems and reported their findings. An enormous number of studies is to be found. Even better, summaries of findings on major curriculum problems (transfer of learning, for example) are readily available in the search for the best available evidence.

2. Curriculum development is a continuous process. Change is the most constant characteristic of our society, and the rising generation must be able to understand and deal intelligently with the issues of a changing society. The world of knowledge changes continuously; the advancement of knowledge requires that curriculum development be continuous.

3. Curriculum development activities should result in resources that are adaptable to the special needs of particular groups of students. Teachers should be encouraged to adapt the materials they have developed collaboratively to their own students and to use other resources and lessons of their own.

4. A major change in curriculum requires broad-based involvement and support. No one group, be it teachers or administrators, should carry out the work independently. Teachers, principals, supervisors, parents, students, and other community members should be involved in making major decisions concerning basic principles, objectives, scope, and organization.

5. A constantly improving education to meet the needs of students and a democratic society requires

the personal commitment of the teacher. Teachers must believe that a curriculum problem is serious, not just hear that it is. This is most likely to happen if they identify the problem.

6. Planning for curriculum improvement requires adequate resources: financial and material, time, and expertise. Every school district should have a curriculum development program, but its nature depends greatly on the commitment of resources. Financial limitations must be faced, but what the Harap committee counseled long ago is still true: "more money can usually be secured if the public is convinced that the proposal will materially improve the prospect of pupil growth" (p. 116). It also should be remembered that much can be accomplished with a knowledgeable and committed existing staff.

7. Proposed solutions to problems should be based on the best available evidence rather than popular trends. Proposed solutions to curriculum problems should be tried out for a time. (The professional staff should not impose their answer.) The curriculum should be evaluated continuously in terms of its effects on students, teachers, and the community. (Curriculum evaluation is often, and wrongly, equated with testing.)

8. A good curriculum development program is characterized by enthusiasm and commitment. "No great accomplishment," the Harap committee observed, "comes in any field without people who *care*, without leaders who have faith in their principles and who have a certain fervor in seeing that these principles have a fair trial" (p. 117).

Modern curriculum development owes much to the Society for Curriculum Study but perhaps even more to Rugg and his committee, who sought to unify opposing views and contributed to the development of a curriculum paradigm.

The Landmark Schools: They Touch Our Lives

The lives of students continue to be touched by the contributions of curriculum pioneers. As Cremin (1961) pointed out, there were many strands of progressive education, and each represented at first an idea in one person's mind. Some of these strands became woven into the modern curriculum. Two program strands in particular deserve to be discussed here because the ideas behind them became principles on which modern curriculum development is based. One was developed in an experimental private school, the Lincoln School of Teachers College, Columbia University, and the other in a suburban public school system, the Winnetka, Illinois, schools.

The Lincoln School

The Lincoln School was the creation of a curriculum reformer par excellence, Abraham Flexner, whose name is generally associated with reform in medical education. The origins of the school can be traced to Flexner's brilliant and monumental essay "The Modern School" (1916) in which Flexner wrote that the purpose of education was to develop in children "the power to handle themselves in our own world" (p. 98). This power depended on an understanding of the physical and social world. The former required the ability to observe and interpret phenomena; the latter required an understanding of contemporary industry, science, and politics.

Flexner believed that useless subjects should be eliminated from the curriculum (p. 98). Claims for a place in the curriculum because of their historical or cultural value alone were not sufficient for including traditional subjects. The curriculum should include purposeful subjects. The objective of the modern school was intellectual power, which, Flexner believed, would most likely be developed by realistic education.

The curriculum of the modern school would be organized around activities in four basic fields: science, industry, aesthetics, and civics, but science would be the central field. Flexner also stressed the importance of making cross-connections among the four fundamental fields.

Flexner saw the modern school as a center for scientific curriculum making, a laboratory school. The teachers would develop and test educational materials and methods as they proceeded with curriculum reconstruction in accord with Flexner's principles. Their findings would serve as guidelines for curriculum development in other schools.

Things moved quickly where Flexner was concerned. In 1917 his Modern School opened as the Lincoln School of Teachers College, Columbia University. The school was funded by the General Education Board (which had been created by John D. Rockefeller in 1902 as an instrument of educational philanthropy and to promote the idea and practice of general education). Flexner had been a member of the board since 1913. The purpose of Lincoln was to bring about curriculum reform. The General Education Board was not set up for administering a school, so they decided that a highly regarded institution should supervise what appeared to be a radical project. It selected Teachers College. A study at Teachers College found that this decision resulted in critical problems for Lincoln (Buttenwieser, 1969). They are discussed shortly.

Lincoln was established as a laboratory school, just as Dewey's school had been two decades earlier, but in this case the venture was supported by Rockefeller funds. According to Buttenwieser, Lincoln's purpose was to change the character of American education just as Johns Hopkins had changed the nature of medical studies.

At Lincoln, attention was to be directed particularly to the problem of curriculum synthesis within and between the major fields of knowledge. As Gehrke (1991) observed many years later, this has continued to be an enormous practical problem to this day.

Units of Work. The curriculum of the elementary division of the Lincoln School was organized around the unit of work. Operationally, however, the separate subject was still omnipotent. This was evident in the evaluation process; the final step of the unit was a summary of subject areas covered, and reporting to parents was by subjects.

Hypothetically at least, the idea for a unit originated with the children. The child-centered school of thought held that nothing should be learned that does not arise from the child's interests or "felt needs." But in reality, units often were teacher initiated or chosen cooperatively by teacher and class. When pupils showed little inclination to hunt for a worthwhile problem, the teacher had to compensate and assign one (theory notwithstanding). Details for the units, even teacher-assigned ones, were generally not planned in advance.

The new education held that subject matter and skills were most effectively learned when there was a real need for them. Theoretically, there was no place in the new curriculum for isolated subject matter and drill. Did Lincoln teachers dispense with subject matter and skill development except as the need arose? Put another way, were all skills—reading, for instance—taught via the unit of work? This decision, like all curriculum decisions at Lincoln, was individual. Some teachers relied completely on the unit as both the vehicle and the criterion for worthwhile learning.

Thus, which arithmetical operations they taught depended on the children's need to use these processes to solve a problem about which they had become curious. Other teachers scheduled separate periods for instruction and practice in skill development. Second-grade teachers Katharine Keelor and Pauline Miner, for example, set aside 35 minutes per day for formal reading instruction, including an individualized silent reading program for able readers (Zirbes, 1925).

On completion, units of work were broken down into subject-matter components to determine what kinds of content had grown out of the various activities. This was an essential part of summarizing and assessing the educational effectiveness of the unit. As an example, one teacher's summary of a fourth-grade unit on foods indicates that the pupils had done work in the following subjects: reading, composition, geography, history, science and household arts, fine arts, and arithmetic. The specific topics covered were listed under each subject; in history, for example, students had studied primitive ways of getting food. In composition, they had written poems on orchards, farms, and gardens and a book on the jelly business. In geography, they had studied the effects of climate, altitude, and latitude on growing fruit (Tippett, 1927).

Significantly, reporting to parents was based on pupil progress in the traditional subjects, although the report card also had a section dealing with habits and attitudes. The latter included specific behaviors under the headings of appreciations, initiative, cooperation, responsibility, work habits, consideration of others, honesty and trustworthiness, personal habits, and health habits.

It will be recalled from the discussion in chapter 2 that the program in Dewey's laboratory school was based on his theory of curriculum. Dewey (1902b) wrote about the child: "He goes to school and various studies divide and fractionalize the world for him" (p. 6). But Dewey did not advocate that the subjects be discontinued. In children's activities and trips were the sources of the major fields of knowledge. In Dewey's curriculum theory the subjects were given an experiential nature that served to integrate the child's world. As Mayhew and Edwards, who taught in Dewey's school, wrote, when the children reached adolescence, the faculty found that their perspective slowly changed "from the psychological approach of the learner or mere observer of facts to the logical one of the adult, who observes to an end and classifies what he has observed with the purpose of its further use" (1936, p. 223).

But Lincoln was not guided by a coherent curriculum theory. According to Buttenwieser (1969), one reason was that Teachers College was unable to provide effective leadership. The Teachers College faculty represented widely divergent outlooks.

Nevertheless, during the first decade of Lincoln's existence, excellent curriculums were accomplished. Harold Rugg developed an entire social studies curriculum, focusing on social problems and the interrelationships of several subject fields. A new approach to mathematics that focused on everyday, useful problems was developed by two Lincoln teachers. Another Lincoln contribution, as previously discussed and as reported by Buttenwieser, was the "unit of work" concept. Indeed, Buttenwieser's study reported that the Elementary Division at Lincoln invented the learning unit. Nevertheless, as Wraga (1996) points out, the unit idea—an effort to provide the child with a coherent learning experience, concerned with a real problem and having a purpose accepted by the child as his or her own—is an outgrowth of the cooperative problem-solving activities that Dewey and his colleagues initiated in the laboratory school at Chicago.

Invention or not, the units and other curriculums produced at Lincoln were widely disseminated, and they probably served as models for organizing the curriculum in many of the nation's public schools. The units are still useful models of a way of organizing the curriculum, and collections are available in leading libraries for teacher education today (Tippett, 1927; Cremin, 1961, pp. 283–287).

Curriculum Integration in the High School. One of the purposes for establishing Lincoln School was to develop models for curriculum integration. The Rugg social studies materials, developed in the 1920s at the junior high school level, helped to realize this promise. Curriculum synthesis was achieved through problem-focused study of American social, political, and economic institutions. The impact of Rugg's social studies series of texts was national (he was the first to integrate the social sciences into the social studies). But more importantly, it was the breadth of Rugg's conception of the social studies that provided the foundation for curriculum reorganization at Lincoln. As Nelson (1978) writes, "Not only the social sciences, but English, the physical and biological sciences, even mathematics, would be restructured under the broad umbrella of social studies, the central vehicle of curriculum essentials" (p. 122). In 1927,

plans were made at Lincoln to develop integrated courses at the secondary school level.

The General Course. The model for curriculum synthesis that evolved was the block-time core or "general course," an effort to integrate social studies, English, and the fine arts (except in the ninth grade where the core was social studies and science). By 1935, about half of student time was spent in the core course for general education, the balance being allocated to required and elective courses in mathematics, science, modern foreign languages, music, physical education, home economics, and the fine and industrial arts. Ultimately, the core courses that developed were as follows:

1. Seventh grade: Man and His Environment
2. Eighth grade: Early American Life
3. Ninth grade: Living in a Machine Age
4. Tenth and eleventh grade: Ancient and Modern Cultures (two-year sequence)
5. Twelfth grade: Youth in America Today (vocations, the individual, family, citizen)

The integrated program had two major objectives: the development of the individual to full capacity and participation of the school in the progressive improvement of an industrial democracy. Here the influence of Harold Rugg and George Counts is evident: The secondary school was to participate in the process of social reconstruction.

Problems of Democracy: Firsthand Experience. Problems and projects served as organizing centers for the curriculum in the core courses. The high school staff at Lincoln attempted to include socioeconomic realities in the curriculum, particularly during the Great Depression of the 1930s. It was felt that firsthand experience with the problems of our society would be the best way to generate interest and concern on the part of youth and, not incidentally, to lay the groundwork for imaginative solutions when youth reached adulthood.

It was further believed that an intimate acquaintance with the problems of democracy was essential for personal development. Youth would find a purpose in life. Moreover, youth would discover that personal satisfactions harmonize with societal needs. Without purpose an integrated personality was an impossibility. A major goal of child-centered schools was personality integration; the term *integration* as used by educational philosophers during the 1920s and 1930s referred to personality. It was contended that a curriculum integrated through units or projects was the best, indeed the only, path to the larger goal of personality integration.

Field Study. It is every social studies teacher's dream to provide students with extensive travel-study opportunities. At the Lincoln School the dream became a reality in 1937. A sizable grant from the Alfred P. Sloan Foundation made it possible to take large groups on trips to study the socioeconomic realities of American life, at the time of the Great Depression, as part of the core curriculum. As preparation for Living in a Machine Age, 50 ninth graders lived for eight days in the homes of rural New England farmers to study a less mechanized society than their own. As part of their study of "economic and social planning in a democracy," 50 twelfth graders toured the Tennessee Valley Authority and various other federal reconstruction projects and cooperative enterprises in Georgia and Maryland undertaken during the Great Depression. Fifteen eleventh graders were selected to go to Pennsylvania and West Virginia to do a field study about the poverty-stricken communities that were affected by the massive technological unemployment in the coal and steel industries.

An attempt was made to evaluate the educational outcomes of the eleventh-grade field-study experience. The investigation, conducted with the assistance of the Progressive Education Association's evaluation staff, found "evidence of an astounding development on the part of fifteen boys and girls in a relatively short time" (Baker, 1938). The group that went on the trip made significantly greater academic gains than the group that remained at home and, not surprisingly, revealed greater sensitivity toward the social issues involved (Raths, 1938).

Curriculum Research. Development of the core concept in a laboratory school was an unparalleled opportunity to gain theoretical knowledge in the curriculum field. Although it was believed that the core course was a more effective approach to learning than were the traditional subject courses, no one was really certain of this.

Mention should be made here of the kinds of curriculum studies conducted at Lincoln. In 1927, Otis W. Caldwell, director of the school, described three types of curriculum studies in progress: a retrospective-descriptive study of a third-grade unit on boats, a study to determine what map facts were used by adults as a basis for curriculum construction in the social studies, and a similar study in biology.

One must not get the idea that the Lincoln staff and its mother institution were unmindful of the need for studies that would produce an objective account of results. Although there was not a consensus that such studies were needed or even possible, curriculum evaluation was a persistent concern for Rugg, Shumaker, Bonser, and undoubtedly other members of the Teachers College faculty (Bonser, 1927).

The Problem of Curriculum Evaluation. In 1934, in an appraisal of student achievement, L. Thomas Hopkins, Lincoln's curriculum specialist, and James E. Mendenhall, a professor of social studies at Teachers College, reported that there was a need for a new type of achievement test to determine the results of the new curriculum of the school. Like most laboratory schools, Lincoln had demonstrated clearly that its students did not suffer in terms of achievement, as measured by standardized tests. But studies were needed to measure the additional kinds of learnings and benefits purportedly afforded students by the new curriculum (Hopkins & Mendenhall, 1934).

Teachers College had a long-abiding faith that evidence supporting the school's program would ultimately be produced. Although the Lincoln staff did not undertake such concerted research, the systematic research on the idea and practice of correlation and synthesis through the core curriculum was to be conducted on a massive scale nationally in the Eight-Year Study (1933–1941) in which the Lincoln School participated.

The year 1941 marked the beginning of the end for the Lincoln School. Faced with huge operating deficits during the Great Depression, Teachers College drew from the Lincoln School's endowment. With the endowment being depleted, Teachers College decided to merge Lincoln with the Horace Mann School, a subject-centered demonstration school also connected with the college. Following a long and bitter legal battle with parents and alumni, in 1947, the courts dealt the final blow to the Lincoln School, upholding a decision by the Teachers College trustees and administration to close the school and transfer the funds from the sale of land and buildings to the Horace Mann-Lincoln Institute. The decision of college trustees to close the Lincoln School was couched under the allegation that it "had not functioned to the fullest extent of its potentialities for experimentation" (*Teachers College Record*, 1947).

Curriculum Theory and Design.   In the view of Hollis L. Caswell (1976), in a letter to the authors of this text, the Lincoln School curriculum "possessed substantial unity and rested upon a reasonably easily perceived theoretical base" (Caswell, personal communication, May 29, 1976). (In 1938 Caswell established and chaired at Teachers College the first Department of Curriculum and Teaching in the United States.) Moreover, in the words of Caswell, "Rugg's search for a 'new synthesis of knowledge' was a definite, clear-cut approach to curriculum reorganization based on a well-defined theory."

The justification for closing the Lincoln School seems questionable in light of the impressive curriculum designs and evaluation records created by the faculty and staff (Barnes & Young, 1932; Baxter & Young, 1933; Lincoln School Staff, 1927). In his study, Buttenwieser (1969) indicates that the fate of Lincoln was really sealed at the beginning when the General Education Board chose Teachers College to administer the school. Teachers College appeared primarily interested in psychological experimentation and testing, whereas Flexner and the board were concerned with curriculum reform. Interestingly, both Flexner and Caldwell (the school's first director) predicted that one day the college would undercut Lincoln's purpose by transferring Lincoln's endowment resources into its own purposes.

According to Rugg and Shumaker, who in 1928 examined the programs of more than 100 so-called progressive schools, not many had abolished school subjects and not a single one had abandoned the subject organization in the upper elementary grades and the high school. Even at the Lincoln School, categorized by Rugg and Shumaker as a child-centered institution, the elementary curriculum was based on units that recognized the various subject fields.

In the 1920s, the experimentalists developed new curriculum structures and arrangements (e. g., correlation and broad fields). They applied the findings of child development to the organization, placement, and articulation of studies.

In Winnetka, Illinois, Superintendent Carleton Washburne and his staff conducted grade-placement investigations to determine when children could most effectively learn to read. They conducted similar studies on arithmetical operations, spelling words, and basic facts in history and geography. Following this approach to its logical conclusion, the Winnetka system attempted to adapt its curriculum to the needs of individual children. The method used—the forerunner of programmed instruction and mastery learning—is examined in the paragraphs that follow.

The Two-Part Curriculum.   In 1927, Carleton Washburne wrote: "Our observation has been that schools which attempt to develop all their knowledge-and-skill subjects from childlike activities often do a 'sloppy' job in giving the children mastery of the tool subjects and sometimes distort the so-called 'childlike' activities in an attempt to bring in knowledge and skills" (p. 227). Washburne also was seeking a scheme for answering any criticisms that the basic skills would be neglected in an integrated curriculum. The Winnetka curriculum was divided into two distinct parts: the *tool subjects*, also called *common essentials*, and activities. The tool subjects—arithmetic, reading, the language arts, and, at first, the social studies—were subdivided into units of achievement. (Ultimately, the social studies were placed in the activities curriculum.)

Individual Instruction.   Children were allowed to work on an achievement-skills unit as long as needed for mastery. They worked independently, using self-instructive, self-corrective materials developed by the Winnetka staff. After each self-test, the child was given a check test by the teacher. Class assignments and recitations were abolished. All elementary grades in Winnetka were organized on this basis.

What came to be known as the Winnetka Plan was the first systemwide attempt to individualize the subject curriculum. It was based on the idea that the best way to improve the curriculum was to reorganize it so that each child could master it at his or her own rate. Pupil assignments were based on curriculum studies conducted by Washburne and his staff, who wrote teaching materials for reading, arithmetic, spelling, history, geography, and science. The idea was based on a plan for individual instruction developed in 1913 by Frederic L. Burk at the San Francisco State Teachers College laboratory school.

Curriculum Investigations.   A major point of interest is that when Washburne began his work at Winnetka in 1919, textbooks and the school curriculum (which tended to follow textbooks) were arbitrarily graded. In arithmetic, for example, some schools in the

United States taught long division in the third grade whereas others introduced it in the fourth or fifth grade. Washburne and his associates conducted investigations involving more than 500 cities to determine at what mental age children could most effectively learn the various arithmetical operations. They found that the mental age necessary for each arithmetical operation was considerably higher than the age at which it was usually taught in school.

The findings from this study formed the basis for arithmetic assignments made to individual pupils in the Winnetka elementary schools and influenced the content of textbooks throughout North America; there was, for the first time, an attempt to gear the order of arithmetic topics to the developmental abilities of the child. Ultimately, however, Washburne was to be disappointed in the application of research findings to the teaching of arithmetic. Textbooks, after all, were still written in terms of the mental age of the average child, although research indicated it was the mental age of the individual that was the key to his or her learning effectively. Wrote Washburne in 1963: "Tradition and inertia (and lack of knowledge as to how to individualize instruction) have made practice lag behind scientific findings in this (as in all fields)" (p. 38).

The Continuing Theoretical Problems.   Two grave theoretical problems with Washburne's scheme continue to concern modern educators. The first is whether the "common essentials" were really nothing more or less than a convenience system. At the time, William Kilpatrick (1925) pointed out that there was no agreement among educators on what constituted "*the* common essentials." "Not 'the common essentials' but 'some common essentials' that lend themselves to self-teaching assignment—these constitute the content of the first part of the Winnetka scheme," he contended (p. 281). This issue is as critical today as it was when Kilpatrick raised it in 1925.

The second issue concerns individualized instruction as programmed instruction. Often we hear the terms *individualized instruction, programmed instruction, self-paced instruction*, and *computer-assisted instruction* used interchangeably. Many proponents of programmed instruction believe erroneously that to use self-paced programs is automatically to individualize instruction. In actuality, the only factor individualized is the rate of correct items completed. The really provocative issue, as Kilpatrick had pointed

out, was that the subjects identified as essential were those that were most easily subjected to itemized programming and testing. Certain operations—calculation in mathematics, for example—may lend themselves to mechanical teaching more than do other subjects, such as social studies. Even the skills involved in calculation are only mechanical tasks until they become operational tools in the processes of critical thinking for problem solving.

If we follow Dewey, critical thinking is motivated by a problem. It must be a real problem, the pupil's own problem. Neither a simulated problem nor a practice problem intended to help pupils perform well on reasoning items on tests would qualify, for as Dewey noted (1916), such problems "are his *only* as a pupil, not as a human being" (p. 183). For Dewey, things happen as a result of inquiry. The course of events has been influenced.

The following illustrates Dewey's view of thinking as a developing process that involves seeing a real problem through:

> Children in one third grade class were uneasy about the number of sledding accidents in their town involving children and cars. A survey of community recreation facilities revealed that there was no safe place for children to use their sleds, causing many sledding accidents each winter. The class planned and made a snow slide on the side of a hill and developed rules and regulations for its safe use. (L. Tanner, 1988, p. 72)

The only way that children will learn to solve real problems is by using firsthand experience. The point of importance, however, is that there are many desirable educational experiences and outcomes that do not lend themselves to a system of self-paced instruction. This was shown in the Winnetka Plan.

Curriculum Adaptation.   The Winnetka Plan was a notable example of curriculum adaptation, the idea that the school could best be improved by rearranging the existing curriculum in accord with the findings of child development. In this connection, nothing conveys the interest of educators in curriculum adaptation more clearly than the title of the Twenty-fourth Yearbook of the National Society for the Study of Education, published in 1925: *Adapting the Schools to Individual Differences.*

Curriculum adaptation continues to be the most common approach to curriculum development. That the curriculum will be encapsulated in separate subjects is still generally accepted. Yet there have been changes in learning theory across the twentieth century. They merit our attention and help us see where Winnetka fit into the scheme of things—and where we are now. As Mayer (2001) points out, in the early twentieth century, schools followed a "one size fits all approach" (p. 54). Individual differences were ignored, and many students failed because they could not keep up with the class. The proposed solution to the problem was adapting the instructional pace to individual differences. This was Washburne's contribution (Zilversmit, 1993). Not that he invented it, but he applied it in a school system and it was where he shone: his star in the progressive constellation.

The idea retained enormous popularity for much of the century. One could care about children and still leave the subject organization intact. According to Zilversmit, this was one key reason why the Winnetka school board was attracted to Washburne. He was progressive but did not forget the essentials. One should also keep in mind that although the subject curriculum remained intact, there were vast differences between the way things were done in Winnetka and nearby communities. Elgin, Illinois, schools for example, followed a traditional one-size-fits-all approach and pupils had few opportunities to work on projects that interested them, which Winnetka children could do in the activities part of the program.

Adapting the pace assumed a number of different labels. What became known as *mastery learning, outcome-based education,* and *second-chance systems* (Fitzpatrick, 1991, p. 21) were essentially variations on the Winnetka Plan, with all of the same problems of Washburne's system of individual instruction, and more. They were based on the concept of "equality of outcomes" as a goal of education rather than optimization of opportunity.

In the 1970s, Washburne's approach was given a theoretical formulation by Benjamin Bloom. According to Bloom (1976), virtually all children can learn what schools have to teach through a rich and stimulating learning environment, well-designed instruction, remedial help when needed, and the time they need to master the material (p. 4).

Bloom's idea is sound and constructive but easily misapplied. The difficulty comes in putting Bloom's idea into practice. The focus in many districts is on learner outcomes and assessing the outcomes, rather than on skilled teaching and providing remedial help as needed. Time is often viewed as a fully expendable and limitless resource. "What matters is not *when* the student achieves the outcome but, rather, *whether* the student eventually achieves success" (Fitzpatrick, 1991, p. 21). This statement by an assistant superintendent for instruction in a high school district may appear on the surface to be sensible, but what happens to a student who is locked into an unproductive curriculum and learning environment? Will more time solve the problem, or will the student, in frustration, give up in failure or drop out?

Going Full Circle: Back to Dewey.   As the century closed, a shift occurred in the way of thinking about individual differences. The new emphasis (really a very old one) was on what Mayer calls "cognitive process instruction" but might be more usefully viewed by teachers as problem solving or, as Dewey put it, "acting intelligently" (1916, p. 103). The idea is that the ability to learn is made up of a number of cognitive processes, such as how to find the important part in a passage, and such processes can be taught for those who lack them. Successful students learn them on their own. According to Mayer, "such strategies are seldom taught directly to students" (p. 55). What must not be omitted from the discussion are the factors of interest and motivation. It is easier to find the important passage in a paragraph if one is trying to solve a problem of interest. We do this on our own, when reading instructions on using a new appliance, for example.

The challenge of individual differences is still that they be met by a rich and varied curriculum geared toward meeting the varied needs and interests of individuals. But the need to know how to solve problems is a constant—for everyone. It is essential throughout one's life. Dewey's acting intelligently is a transfer-oriented outcome of schooling.

Let us return to Winnetka before going on to the next section on curriculum research. As in Washburne's time, school subjects continue to provide the framework for curriculum development in most school systems. The focus is on modifying instructional strategies rather than changing the design and function of the curriculum. By changing the design—for example, including more unit teaching, as in the Lincoln School—it is more possible to meet individual differences. Students can have more opportunities to work on aspects and projects that interest them, a key to problem solving and learning.

Curriculum Research

Interwoven in the fascinating story of the development of the curriculum field is the thread of professionalism. (The word *profession* comes from the Latin, meaning "a public declaration or vow.") One of the hallmarks of a profession concerns research: Professionals have a responsibility to base decisions on the best available knowledge. But educators receive surprisingly little information about their obligation to look to research for help in making decisions. The assumption is that they learn about this professional responsibility as they complete teacher or administrator certification requirements. But the assumption is not always correct, and the responsibility must be made more explicit. Ralph Tyler (1987) called on those preparing teachers and administrators to address this need systematically. "I believe the student should early in the study of education understand the effect of relevant research findings in limiting the consideration of curriculum alternatives to those that are consistent with what is known about learning and other relevant factors in education," declared Tyler (p. 604).

This tradition of research-based practice is part of the evolution of the modern curriculum. The tradition is not always followed. Educational leaders frequently find that it is difficult to change beliefs with mere facts.

According to Tyler, "The purpose of research is to get a more generalized understanding of a phenomenon," and the responsibility of policy makers and school personnel is "to seek to get an understanding of research" in attempting to meet the needs of particular schools (Evangelof, 1989, p. A18). Tyler's point is that it is the school's responsibility to use research in addressing local problems. Researchers should not use their general findings to impose programs on particular schools. It is not their responsibility. "While researchers and school personnel have common interests, they do not have common responsibilities" (p. A18). The relation between researchers and school persons is addressed in this section.

Research from Relevant Fields

Research in fields other than curriculum development, such as educational psychology, child development, and sociology, do not answer the ultimate curriculum questions, such as "What knowledge is of most worth?" but may be useful in making decisions about what should be taught and how it is taught. A good illustration is Thorndike's research on transfer of learning, which was discussed in chapter 3. Thorndike was not a curriculum specialist; in fact, curriculum as a formal field of study had not yet emerged when he conducted his monumental studies. But Thorndike's findings influenced curriculum thought and justified opening the classroom doors to fields such as vocational-technical studies, social studies, laboratory sciences, and studio arts.

Similarly, Benjamin Bloom's research has greatly increased our understanding of the relationship between teacher behavior and student learning. Bloom viewed the classroom as an ecological system consisting of factors or variables that directly influence students' achievement in school. As Bloom (1980) pointed out, by focusing on alterable variables (such as styles of interactions with students), teachers can improve student learning greatly.

According to Bloom, "When these interactions of teachers with their students are altered, there are significant improvements in student learning" (p. 382). For example, one variable is the quality of teachers' explanations; students who have difficulty in learning do better when teachers provide strong explanations and directions. Supervisors have used the variables in providing teachers with feedback about what they are (or are not) doing and what they can do to change. Moreover, and more important perhaps, the variables provide ways of analyzing teachers' classroom problems. As pointed out, Bloom's view that all children can learn also has influenced the curriculum, although his challenge most often has been applied to the curriculum in mechanistic ways (p. 384).

Bloom and his associates developed a classification of cognitive processes in a hierarchical order. Higher-level cognitive outcomes of the curriculum are defined as those involving the development of thinking processes rather than simply recall. The cognitive taxonomy has been used by many teachers as a means for designing instructional activities encompassing a wider range of cognitive learnings.

Much of modern curriculum thought rests on the Deweyan view that children play an active role in their own intellectual development and its outcomes. Sociologist James Coleman's landmark study, *Equality of Opportunity* (1966), described this feeling of self-responsibility as fate control. Coleman found that the achievement of children who perceive a causal relationship between what happens to them and their own behavior was significantly higher than those who perceive that what happens to them is the result of luck or other forces outside themselves or beyond their control. This finding attracted great educational interest and influenced the curriculum by revealing the potential benefits of heterogeneous classes and the deleterious effects of social isolation of economically disadvantaged children.

The point of this section can be summed up in these words by Dewey: "The scientific content of education consists of whatever subject-matter, selected from other fields, enables the educator, whether administrator or teacher, to see and think more clearly and deeply about whatever he is doing" (1929, p. 75).

Vocabulary Research

One of the most influential kinds of research on practice has been vocabulary research: efforts to assess children's word knowledge for the purpose of determining the grade placement of textbooks. Washburne's work on this problem at Winnetka has already been discussed. Washburne was deeply concerned and worked hard to base curriculum material on scientific research. According to Clifford (1978), much of the education research conducted in the first decades of the twentieth century was directed at vocabulary and readability studies.

Hundreds of such studies were conducted. Edward L. Thorndike was an early leader in vocabulary investigation. His publications on language in particular from 1908 to 1949 numbered about 75 (Clifford, 1978). According to Clifford, vocabulary research supported the curriculum reforms of the progressives who sought to make classroom experiences more meaningful. It was thought that teachers with more information about vocabulary and readability would be better equipped to develop units of study engaging students in the use of a wider variety of printed materials. And vocabulary research "was part of a much larger campaign against a false psychology of mental discipline, against the scholar's arrogances and the teacher's self-deceptions" (p. 183). In the words of McDonald (1964), "Thorndike slew the dragon of mental discipline" (p. 6). Other researchers in the progressive era were determined that the dragon stay dead.

Developmental psychology, which came to the fore in the 1920s and 1930s, was a great support in

this endeavor. As Pearson (2000) argues: "The motive in developing readability formulas was to present children with texts that matched their interests and developmental capacities rather than baffle them with abridged versions of adult texts" (p. 156). He recounts how the first readability formula, which made its appearance in 1923, was followed by 80 more, and that the formulas were critical in the commercial production of reading materials until the 1980s. They did not survive the literature-based reading and whole language movements of the 1980s and 1990s, although there was evidence of their recovery at the century's end (Pearson, 2000, p. 156).

Readability is, of course, a concern in selecting texts and other commercial reading materials. Nevertheless, in their penchant for quantification, there was the tendency for researchers to overlook the most powerful factor in readability and vocabulary building: interesting ideas. In effect, readability formulas, word counts, and vocabulary lists mean little if the material is devoid of interesting ideas.

Obviously, studies concerned with factors bearing on curriculum development are far too numerous to permit adequate discussion in the space available, but some of the major studies in the twentieth century will be considered.

The Eight-Year Study

The most important and comprehensive curriculum experiment ever carried on in the United States was the Eight-Year Study, sponsored by the Progressive Education Association (PEA) in the 1930s. The study grew out of the realization of secondary school educators that they would never be able to establish an experimental basis for curriculum revision unless they were granted the freedom to do so by the colleges. College entrance requirements determined the major part of the secondary curriculum; these requirements had frozen the curriculum into 16 Carnegie units.

In 1930 the PEA took the first step by establishing a commission to deal with the problem of the relation between school and college. In 1931, after a year's study, the commission issued a report on the shortcomings of the secondary school. Most of these shortcomings could be attributed at least indirectly to the unsatisfactory relation between school and college that made fundamental reconstruction an impossibility. The curriculum was unrelated to the real concerns of youth. It had neither the purpose nor the direction needed for unity and continuity.

Schools did not know their students and failed to be concerned about what happened to them after graduation (or dropping out). The content and organization of the curriculum prevented the student from developing his or her own educational power. Nearly always the curriculum was laid out in isolated fragments as work for the students to do. They passed through the curriculum with neither an awareness nor an understanding of the forces shaping human destiny and were left unprepared for community life. Anthropologically speaking, the schools were failing as inductors of the young into society.

The commission doubted whether success in college depended on the study of certain subjects for a prescribed length of time. The time had come to test this assumption and plan a better education for secondary schoolers.

The Experiment. The commission gained the cooperation of more than 300 colleges and universities in 1932, and a small number of secondary schools (to be chosen by the commission's directing committee) were to be released from the restrictions of college entrance requirements. The waiver from the usual subject and unit requirements would extend over a five-year period beginning with the class entering college in 1936. The colleges were assured by the commission that "only schools of the highest character and established reputation would be selected." This was not the primary concern of the commission, however, in selecting the schools. It was, rather, that the schools chosen had to be willing to experiment in a progressive direction.

Apparently, not all of the selected schools actually lived up to these expectations. Twenty-one years later, Wilford Aikin (1953), director of the study, said that were he to do it again, any school "failing to carry on significant curriculum developments" would "be dropped early in the study" (p. 11).

The 30 Schools. The commission chose 30 schools that seemed both willing and able to conduct exploratory studies and make creative changes in the secondary school curriculum. Schools began to change their curriculums in the fall of 1933. The commission did not prescribe a curriculum to be tested. Each school determined what changes should be made in the curriculum in view of the special needs of its students and the community. The schools were half public and half private, located from Los Angeles to Boston and from Madison, Wisconsin, to Tulsa, Oklahoma. However, most of the students in the study were from the public schools. The schools ranged from large city high schools with large groups of minority students to small private schools. Six of the participating schools were laboratory schools connected with universities.

Functions of Evaluation. Evaluation was an ongoing process from the beginning of the experiment. It had to be. To begin with, data concerning the progress of the college-bound students had to be obtained for the colleges. And then there were the new programs; the participating schools needed to be able to identify the strengths and weaknesses of the programs to make improvements on the basis of evidence. Last, but not least, the clarification of objectives demanded by a program of evaluation was needed to give direction to curriculum change. A number of the schools had vague objectives that had to be clarified if they were to serve as guides for curriculum development and the construction of evaluation instruments.

The evaluation was conducted with total independence from the PEA. One of the most monumental tasks of the evaluation committee, headed by Ralph Tyler of the University of Chicago, was to help the participating schools develop instruments to evaluate student progress in terms of objectives that dealt with thinking processes. The only tests available were for measuring achievement in the traditional subject curriculum. Interschool evaluation committees were formed for the objectives that were most commonly stressed by the 30 schools, such as the development of effective ways of thinking, increased sensitivity to social problems, and effective work habits and skills. Each committee's task was to define an objective in terms of the behaviors sought and to identify ways of obtaining evidence about these kinds of behavior. These methods—tests, questionnaires, interviews, and the like—became the basis for evaluative instruments developed by Tyler's staff. The instruments were used in appraising student progress.

College Follow-up Study. The second phase of the evaluation program took place in the colleges under the direction of college staff. Each graduate of the 30 schools was matched with another student in the same college who had graduated from a school not in the Eight-Year Study and, thus, had met the usual college entrance requirements. The students were matched on the basis of age, sex, race, scholastic aptitude scores, home and community background, and interests. The matching was done by the colleges. Through personal interviews and information from college records and college personnel, the college staff of the Eight-Year Study became well acquainted with each student. A total of 1,475 matched pairs of students were studied.

The Findings.   Established beyond question by the study was the fact that the graduates of the 30 schools were not handicapped in college by their experimental high school programs. In fact, graduates of the 30 schools had higher grade point averages, received more academic honors, and were found to be more precise, systematic, and objective thinkers and more intellectually curious than their matchees. Furthermore, they were more actively concerned about what was happening in the world, earned more nonacademic honors each year in college, and were more resourceful in meeting new situations.

Interestingly enough, those students graduating from the six schools judged to be the most experimental (departed most from tradition)

> were strikingly more successful than their matchees. Differences in their favor were much greater than the differences between the total Thirty Schools and their comparison group. Conversely, there were no large or consistent differences between the least experimental graduates and their comparison group. (Chamberlin, Chamberlin, Drought, & Scott, 1942, p. 209)

It was clear that, at least as far as the 30 schools were concerned, the more experimental the school, the greater was the success of students in college. It was also evident that success in college does not depend on the study of a prescribed sequence of subjects in high school.

Curriculum Development in the 30 Schools. "My teachers and I do not know what to do with this freedom. It challenges and frightens us. I fear that we have come to love our chains" (Aikin, 1942a). This remark made by one principal a short time after the 30 schools were selected probably reflected the feelings of many in the experiment. Here, in a real sense, was the predicament of progressivism in the 1930s. As Dewey had warned, it was time to stop being a movement of protest and to start the search for a new curriculum. Thus, it was one thing to sit back and blame the problems of the high school

curriculum on the stranglehold of the colleges. It was quite another thing to build something better when that stranglehold was removed. This was progressivism's moment of truth, and the Eight-Year Study more than met the challenge.

Curriculum Consultants.   The 30 schools were guided in their efforts to make significant curriculum changes by specialists in the field of curriculum. As indicated earlier, the policy of the directing committee was to encourage and assist each school in developing its own plans rather than deciding what curriculum changes should be made.

As mentioned previously, the Commission on the Relation of School and College issued a report indicating areas needing improvement by secondary schools. These suggestions provided a starting point for many of the schools, but this was hardly enough to help the schools find a sense of direction. Those that asked for help were provided curriculum consultants. Years later, Aikin (who served as a curriculum consultant as well as director of the study) said that "many of the Thirty Schools were ready for such assistance long before it was available to them. Had that been done earlier and in greater abundance, the contribution of the Eight-Year Study to secondary education would have been greater than it was" (1953, p. 14).

The curriculum staff of the Eight-Year Study attempted to keep each school informed of developments in the other schools, made class visits, taught demonstration lessons, and conducted workshops or curriculum clinics. Each member of the staff visited each school once for the purpose of getting mutually acquainted. After that, visits were made only by invitation. According to Aikin, those schools that took the most advantage of staff assistance made the most significant curriculum changes (1953, p. 12).

Enter: The Workshop.   One of the most important approaches for helping teachers deal with their curriculum problems is the workshop. The workshop is actually a contribution of the Eight-Year Study (L. Tanner, 1986). The first workshop was organized in the summer of 1936 by Ralph Tyler, director of evaluation for the Eight-Year Study, in response to demands by teachers from the 30 schools. The teachers were feeling confused about how to approach the task of developing a curriculum. They came to the Tyler-led six-week institute at The Ohio State University with definite problems on which they wished to work. The term *workshop* was then coined. The participants received assistance from various faculty members and the results were so useful that more workshops were organized. There can be little doubt that the workshops contributed to the experiment's outcomes. As time passed, workshops became a common inservice education approach. Within a generation or two, however, supervisors had lost sight of the key factor in the success of the original workshop: The teachers themselves had identified the problems they wanted to work on and the ones on which they needed assistance.

Curriculum Synthesis.   Although each school went its own way in making changes in the curriculum, three goals were sought by all schools:

1. To identify ways of breaking down the barriers between subjects so that the real meaning of fields of knowledge could be made apparent to the student
2. To encourage student self-direction
3. To provide individual guidance

Schools in the study attempted to bring the curriculum closer to the real concerns of youth by designing correlated and fusion courses, broad-fields courses, culture-epoch courses, career-centered courses, and problem-focused core curricula. (In some schools, the problems of job training and employment were studied in core curricula based on adolescent needs.) As Vars (1991) points out, "The evolving concept of core curriculum was tested in the famous Eight-Year Study of the Progressive Education Association" (pp. 14–15). The concept proved successful. Examining the five volumes which describe the study (Aikin, 1942a; Aikin, 1942b; Chamberlin, Chamberlin, Drought, & Scott, 1942; Giles, McCutcheon, & Zechiel, 1942; Smith, & Tyler, 1942), it would be hard to come to a different conclusion. As Wraga (2001) points out, the students in schools with the core curriculum organization "were engaged in intellectual work at a level of sophistication to which many college classrooms aspire even today" (p. 37). Wraga based his conclusion primarily on the volumes by Aikin (1942a) and Smith and Tyler that dealt with evaluation.

Developers of core curricula encountered certain problems. Giles, McCutcheon, and Zechiel (1942) reported that schools experimenting with fusion courses such as mathematics-science found that the scope of a course was determined by the logical organization of one of the fields. Consequently, in some cases one field tended to dominate the other, thereby mitigating the principle of unification (p. 35).

Forced to find organizing centers other than systematized bodies of knowledge, teachers and curriculum consultants turned to problem-centered core curriculums. Subject matter from various fields was brought in as needed for the understanding and solution of problems.

The culture-epoch approach, where subject matter was controlled by broad themes, was used by the Horace Mann School of Teachers College, Columbia University, to unify the curriculum. This was a broad approach to unification, far broader than fused studies such as mathematics-science or English-social studies because a culture-epoch could be dealt with in terms of its literature, science, technology, art, music, economic system, social system, or political system. A criticism frequently associated with this approach to curriculum synthesis was that although the senior year was usually devoted to a study of contemporary American problems, the entire first three years (grades 9 through 11) were devoted to a study of the past. The impact of the Eight-Year Study suffered due to its untimely release around the time of the outbreak of World War II, when high schools sought to speed up the curriculum to meet the emergency manpower demands of the military.

The core curriculum is discussed in considerable detail in chapter 10. However, mention should be made here of the fact that in 1950, just eight years after the study, only one of the schools in the experiment had continued to develop a problem-focused core curriculum (Redefer, 1950, p. 34). One might well ponder the reasons why this was so when the results of the study so strikingly favored the continued development of this approach to curriculum reorganization. One answer could be the Cold War and McCarthyism, which began in the late 1940s and led to the censorship of virtually any aspect of the curriculum adjudged to be controversial. Problem-centered core curricula required the free and open examination of the issues that marked our economic and political life. This was not easy in an era of censorship of ideas and guilt by association. Even the NEA's Educational Policies Commission took the position in 1949 that members of the Communist Party should not be employed as teachers. Little wonder, then, that many teachers were unwilling to subject the economic system to scrutiny for fear of being labeled *red*. The social forces of the day exerted a far stronger influence on the curriculum than the findings of the Eight-Year Study.

A second and related factor was the drive for the discipline-centered curriculum through the national curriculum projects in the wake of the Cold War and space race, with priority given to the sciences and mathematics. This nationalistic drive served to put the idea and practice of the integrated core curriculum and general education into a virtual eclipse for decades. A number of studies have since buttressed the Eight-Year Study's findings (Tanner & Tanner, 1990, pp. 233–234). The 1990s and early 2000s witnessed the rediscovery of the need for an integrated core curriculum.

The Concept That Never Died. The Eight-Year Study was not a continuing force after the experiment. As mentioned, the study was a casualty of World War II; the findings were released in 1942 when war headlines blotted out such matters as curriculum experimentation. After the war the criticism of progressive education that began in the late 1930s gained in intensity. This, combined with the Cold War, strengthened education conservatism. The international situation caused a return to more authoritarian and traditional programs. Discipline-centered reforms were viewed as the answer to the crisis in national security. Interdisciplinary curricula became a casualty of that crisis (Bruner, 1960).

However, as noted, the concept of interdisciplinarity never died, and the need for curriculum articulation and synthesis through problem-focused studies is resurgent in a free society. The times today are different, of course, but as in the 1930s the timing of curriculum integration efforts with critical societal problems is more than coincidental. In the twenty-first century American society faces the need to deal with poverty, ethnic conflict, public health, youth unemployment, economic dislocations, social disaffection, drugs and narcotics, child welfare, the homeless, violent crime, and environmental protection, not to mention the related problems on a global scale along with war and peace.

To study real-life problems is, inevitably, to break down the barriers between the academic disciplines. And some schools and colleges are rediscovering the problem-focused core course.

Despite the fact that there was a smothering wave of conservatism in the years immediately following the Eight-Year Study, the study is alive and well in the education literature. Even during the era of discipline-centered curriculum reforms, the study was never really out of the literature. Its fascination remains, leading one to ponder why, with our modern statistical techniques, we do not undertake comparable comprehensive and large-scale experimentation in education.

The Activity Curriculum

As noted, elementary-school curriculum research during the 1920s was slanted toward curriculum adaptation. In Winnetka, for example, studies were conducted to determine the optimum time for beginning instruction in reading and fundamental arithmetic processes. These investigations were mainly concerned with fitting the conventional subjects to the child rather than with evaluating new forms of curriculum organization. Undeniably, making the traditional curriculum serve the child better was a revolution in and of itself (and one that passed many schools by).

The Activity Movement. The idea of the child's doing—learning through activity—is part of our curriculum legacy. Beginning in the 1920s, this idea assumed the proportions of a movement. The activity movement in the progressive education era was a reaction to the formal school, where all learning was to be conducted in utter silence and the learner was to remain motionless unless given permission to move. This clearly worked against the nature of the growing, developing child. Hence, it was understandable that activity was defined in terms of gross, overt movement. Overlooked was the idea that learning in itself is an active process; it can (and often does) go on without overt signs.

Activity programs were, on the whole, expressions of child-centered education; most proponents of activity conceived of education as a process that transcended codified knowledge. The objective was child growth through experiences, active experience that was visible to the naked eye. For many, however, activity was an end, rather than a means. Indeed, some even ascribed magical properties to child activity.

By 1930, the terms *activity movement, activity program,* and *activity curriculum* had become the commonplace in pedagogical parlance. Used freely and sometimes interchangeably with these terms were *units, unit of work, central theme,* and *center of interest.*

As might be expected, some schools tried to build the curriculum entirely around child activity. Most of these efforts were to be found in the primary grades. In the Francis W. Parker School, for example, there were no subjects in either the first or second grade; the curriculum at these levels was based on centers of interest, which were never the same two years consecutively.

Where public school enthusiasts jumped abruptly from a subject-matter format to a total program of activities, they tended to resume the traditional pattern for teaching the three Rs. Activities generally were continued in social studies and the creative arts. Although a curriculum organized in toto on the basis of activities seemed well suited to the gifted and the above-average, it did not appear (as revealed by achievement test scores) to provide sufficient opportunity for the mastery of basic skills for the less able. On this basis, according to some leaders in the field, the time allocated for activities was reduced, and reading, spelling, and arithmetic were taught again as separate subjects (Mossman, 1934).

By the 1930s, the activity movement had moved away from activity for its own sake and was beginning to include the objectives of individual, social, and intellectual development through purposeful activity, as expressed in the writings of John Dewey.

There was a need to test the relative worth of activity and subject matter curriculum organization. Obviously, in order to evaluate the outcomes of activity programs, there had to be agreement on what an activity program was. In a reminiscence years later, Ralph Tyler, who was involved in evaluating activity programs in the 1930s and 1940s, described the problems of defining an activity program (1991, pp. 4–5).

Research on the Activity Curriculum. The education literature of the 1930s contains scores of studies designed to assess the relative value of activity and subject-centered curricula. A number of school systems conducted experimental studies of their own programs. The overwhelming majority of studies used standardized achievement tests that were developed in terms of subject-centered curricula. Some studies did attempt to evaluate gains in terms of both subject matter and activity goals. Unfortunately, these were in the decided minority. In most studies, investigators concluded that the activity curriculums led to little or no loss in the mastery of basic skills and subject-matter knowledge and substantial gains over a subject organization in goals involving thought processes and responsible independence.

The New York City Experiment. The most comprehensive and well designed of these investigations was a New York City experiment involving 75,000 children and 2,500 teachers over a six-year period. In 1935, the Board of Education of New York City launched an experimental program with progressive educational methods. Typical schools, designated as activity schools, were encouraged to develop curriculums based on units and projects originating from pupil interest rather than traditional textbook learning. Although 70 schools initiated experimental programs, it was not feasible to conduct a careful evaluation on such a large scale. Most of the research involved eight activity schools, each matched with a control school. The schools were matched for neighborhood, average intelligence, and socioeconomic status of pupils.

The research program was aimed at measuring growth in a wide variety of educational outcomes, both tangible and intangible. Tests of study skills, social attitudes, "work spirit," and individual adjustment were developed by J. Wayne Wrightstone, then a research associate at Teachers College, Columbia University. Evaluation procedures included both tests and classroom observations.

Activity children surpassed control children in growth in critical thinking, initiative, leadership, and other objectives of activity curriculums. Control pupils gained somewhat more in some academic subjects (notably arithmetic) although the differences were small and statistically insignificant. Unquestionably, the objectives of the activity program had been achieved. In their final report on the experiment, Jersild, Thorndike, and Goldman (1941) concluded:

> While the control children seem to have a slight but statistically unreliable advantage as far as achievement in academic subject matter is concerned, the activity children surpass the controls in the frequency with which they exercise such presumably wholesome activities as leadership, experimentation, self-initiated enterprises, participation in oral discussion, and the like. The activity children have more experiences and show more tangible accomplishments in the field of arts and crafts. The activity children, as already noted, tend to be superior in tests that call for intellectual operations. [These were the Wrightstone tests of working skills, explaining facts, applying generalizations, critical thinking, and current events.] (p. 308)

Discipline and Curriculum Organization. Of great interest is the fact that children in the activity program also tended to surpass the control children in discipline. This is contrary to the opinion held by many teachers (and parents) that children in traditional programs show better discipline and "respect for school authority." In the first three of the five semesters in which the children were observed, the control children exhibited fewer behavioral problems, whereas the activity children showed better discipline than the controls in the last two semesters. As Jersild, Thorndike, and Goldman (1939) emphasized:

> The greater degree of freedom and self-direction afforded by the activity program has not been a signal for poor discipline and disorder on the part of the pupils. Rather, according to the findings in connection with the "work spirit" category, as well as according to the independent testimony of observers who have visited many classes and have gone into the same classes day after day, the pupils have risen to the occasion in a highly satisfactory way. (p. 206)

Wrightstone's Study. Wrightstone (1935) conducted another important study in which he focused on outcomes that were emphasized by progressive educators, such as being able to interpret facts, apply generalizations, work independently, and organize materials. Using matched pairs of elementary and secondary pupils from three pairs of public schools, he found that in no case (other than the quantity of recitation in classrooms) did the subject-centered schools show a statistically significant superiority over the experimental schools. Schools with various kinds of reorganized curricula demonstrated a significant superiority in recall of physics and chemistry facts, literature acquaintance, and working-skills ability. In reporting the results of his study, Wrightstone concluded that his findings were "tentative proof of the validity of the educational theory and principles upon which the newer-type practices in the selected schools are established" (p. 116).

Decline of Interest in Activity Organization. Despite these encouraging findings, interest in the activity organization of the elementary curriculum, as revealed by the educational literature, had faded by the mid-1940s. This is a striking parallel with the core curriculum. In both cases, research findings were highly encouraging, but the interest of educators dropped off nonetheless. Research findings were not used as a basis for curriculum decision making. Nevertheless, purposeful activity requiring freedom of movement and discussion is today deemed essential for the development of cooperation and critical thinking and for otherwise expanding intellectual horizons and productive social behavior.

The Decline of Curriculum Experimentation

"What we sorely need," wrote John Goodlad in 1966, "is a rejuvenation of the experimental quest" (p. 110). Goodlad was questioning the discipline-centered curriculum reform projects of the late 1950s and 1960s. The major goal of the projects was to have students develop the modes of inquiry in a discipline so as to think like scholar-specialists. These goals and the means for reaching them were established in advance by university scholar-specialists. The discipline-centered projects were federally supported in a nationalistic response to the Cold War and space race. The materials were trial taught and refined, but as Goodlad pointed out at the time, "[r]arely, if at all, are two sets of means contrasted with each other and compared as to their effectiveness in achieving a given objective" (p. 108). In effect, the scientists and mathematicians leading these projects had avoided the scientific method(s) and resorted to promotional tactics and claims.

Actually, application of the scientific method(s) to curriculum problems had begun to decline much earlier. In 1950, Caswell pointed out that most of the references cited in recent reviews of curriculum research were general discussions. Very few presented rigorous studies of well-defined problems (p. 439). He contrasted this against the 1930s, when hundreds of studies using methods of scientific inquiry were conducted.

Demonstrations Versus Experiments. Goodlad was not to have his wish. Whereas the purpose of experimental testing of new programs is to determine the effects, tests of social and educational programs over subsequent years, extending through the 1970s and 1980s, were usually intended to provide accountability data concerning the supplying of services. They were demonstration projects, not experiments. Demonstration of a program implies that its value has been established. This, however, was rarely the case. As Stake (1991) points out, "Evaluation is invoked for many purposes, many of them with little concern about the production of information. Evaluation studies are prescribed to legitimize authority and to protect program operations from criticism" (p. 80).

A field test of a program should address both the program's procedures and effects. If evaluation policies are to be sound, including those of the U.S. Department of Education, systematic consideration must be given to the above (Boruch, 1991, p. 153).

The One-Size-Fits-All Reform Curriculum. In the 1960s, evaluation specialists, like others involved in the War on Poverty, were energized by the charge to improve educational opportunities for the disadvantaged. Attempting to find which practices work best, some evaluation specialists sought a universally accepted or one best set of instructional procedures and a single reform curriculum. Others cautioned against sweeping generalization and standard curriculum design. Recognizing that local circumstances and programs differ, they urged that evaluators turn their attention to assisting practitioners to experiment and adapt evaluations from the large studies to their own situations (Stake, 1991, pp. 67–68). This did not happen.

Educational opinion in the late 1960s and early 1970s was "do your own thing." Radical romantic reformers were mainly concerned with "freeing" children to learn. Lawrence Cremin (1973) described the open classroom movement as "ahistorical and atheoretical" (p. 5). It did not, he said "pose educational problems with the profundity of the earlier progressive movement and it did not advance constructive suggestions for reform" (Ryan, 1978, p. 113).

Radical reformers showed little or no interest in testing their ideas. Their impact was mainly in the sector of alternative schools, which were not used for experimentation. Although the curriculum in these schools differed little from the curriculum in conventional schools, calls began to be heard for an authoritarian pedagogy.

The schools were criticized for not doing their job, which prompted reactions for a return to the basics. Educators, under the iron hand of state legislators, defined sets of narrow objectives for which teachers and administrators were to be held accountable through statewide minimum-

competency testing. Recounting the stroy, Stake points out that:

> Under the pressure for accountability, much of the appetite for understanding was overwhelmed by a craving for protection. Educators implored measurement specialists to develop a methodology that pointed to the shortcomings of students. By 1980, student assessment rather than program evaluation was the major player in the school improvement movement. (1991, pp. 74–75)

The Endurance of Curiosity. But local schools could not remain inattentive to their own curriculum and morale problems. Indeed, as Stake continues, "Within some schools, classrooms, and networks of educators, curiosity endured. What additional knowledge might improve things? Pretty clearly there was a confidence in local knowledge, situational knowledge and teacher based knowledge" (p. 75). What Stake was describing was the democratic-participative approach to problem solving based on the scientific method. In the early 1990s, when Stake made his observation, the educational climate had changed. There was a whole constellation of changes focusing on teacher professionalism. The climate was one of enlarging teachers' roles as curriculum developers, assessors of classroom progress and researchers into classroom and school problems (Cochran-Smith & Lytle, 1999). The first two roles are irrevocably linked. They harken back to Tyler's view of the purpose of evaluation: to provide information to teachers for the purpose of curriculum improvement (Tyler, 1949).

By the close of the century, the educational "weather" had changed again. Standardized achievement testing was narrowing the curriculum and many teachers, feeling too threatened to do otherwise, were teaching to the test. (A major goal of testing had become supervision of teachers.) All this was a far cry from what Tyler had envisioned. As D'Agostino (2000) writes, "Tyler believed the main role of tests was to help teachers evaluate and improve their curriculum" (p. 323). Whatever the climate, this is still a best practice in education.

Using Best Practices: Goodlad's Study of Schooling

What is all too easy to forget is that educators have a heritage of research and evaluation from which to draw: benchmarks on which to evaluate the curriculum. This is another kind of curriculum research, one used by Goodlad in his comprehensive national study of schooling. Goodlad looked at schools in terms of the best practices that have emanated over the years in the research literature; for example, the importance of discussion and other activities requiring student participation in preparing students for effective citizenship. The Goodlad study found too much "teacher-talk" (pp. 230–232). Goodlad also looked at the problem of ability grouping in terms of the literature, which finds that teachers of homogeneously grouped low-achievers do not expect students to succeed, and that the teachers transmit their low expectations to the students (pp. 153–157). Goodlad's report sharply criticized the practice of grouping students into fast- and slow-ability groups in core subjects.

Goodlad's study was a landmark because it compared what was going on in the schools with what should be going on. The point is that the professional staff of a school can do what Goodlad did, on a much smaller scale, of course. Dependable criteria exist in the literature for evaluating a school and developing an agenda for curriculum improvement.

The Mythical Average School

In the closing decades of the century, some published reports began by accepting the proposition that schools in general are worse than they used to be. They implied a judgment about individual schools based on studies of the "current condition of American education" (D. Tanner, 1993, pp. 288–297). Beside the fact that there is no evidence to support the generalization about a systemwide crisis, such studies may actually prevent individual schools from addressing their own genuine problems. There are problems in every school, but they may not be the problems identified in national reports on the condition of education (Posner, 1992, p. 25).

There is no such thing as a typical school; schools, like persons, are individuals. "It is possible to make valid judgments about American secondary education but only *school by school*," wrote James B. Conant in 1959 (p. 16). Many years have elapsed since the publication of Conant's famous report, *The American High School Today*, but his point remains valid. In Conant's time, like our own, there was a rising chorus of criticism about the quality of education, but he remained firm in his insistence that the typical high school simply does not exist. Therefore, he

insisted, it is unscientific to pass judgment on secondary schooling as a whole.

Large-scale studies, such as the National Assessment of Educational Progress and reports of the National Center for Educational Statistics on the conditions of education, can point to large-scale national problems, but it is up to the local district and school to determine whether a given problem exists in their own school. If it does, they can face it openly, rather than shoving it under the rug, knowing that other school systems also have the problem. In fact, hiding the problem is the worst possible course, for at least two reasons: first, because regarding a problem as nonexistent allows the problem to continue; and second, as the ancient saying goes, "truth will out"—what really happened will show for all to see.

This can be shattering to school staffs and the community. A recent example, concerning high school dropouts, occurred in Houston. A state audit determined that "more than half of the 5,500 students who left high school should have been declared dropouts but were not" (Schemo, 2003, p. A1). The audit resulted in a recommendation that the ranking of 14 of the 16 middle and high schools be lowered "from the best to the worst" (p. A1). As the report points out, the undercounting of school dropouts indicates "how the focus on school accountability" can "sometimes go wrong, driving administrators to alter data or push students likely to mar a school's profile—through poor attendance or low test scores—out the back door" (Schemo, 2003, A1).

Accountability and responsibility are not synonymous. The professional's responsibility is to seek problem-solutions. In the case of preventing and dealing with dropouts, there are many possible solutions, starting with curriculum improvement (McPartland, Balfanz, Jordan, & Legters, 2002; Nelson, 1988).

The Future of Curriculum Research

We have traveled far since the first use of research results in the curriculum-improvement process. The idea of improving the curriculum through research once led virtually every major school system to have as part of its central office staff some kind of research unit. Small school systems can seek the help of schools of education in universities, which all have research responsibilities (some of which are written into the institution's legislative charter).

A cooperative, ongoing school/university program should be in operation for this purpose.

In this and the previous chapters we have presented some of the most important examples of curriculum research in the twentieth century. Yet it is just a sampling of the research in various areas of the curriculum and teaching. The research division of the National Education Association, the John Dewey Society, the Society for Curriculum Study, and the National Society for the Study of Education all were early leaders in conducting curriculum research. In recent years, the American Federation of Teachers has devoted special attention to the study of curriculum problems. If the future is built on the best work already done, the impact of research on practice will be more marked.

But the "if" is a big one. A better and brighter future depends on whether educational policies and practices are based on the best available evidence. In recent years national education policies have had a crisis orientation. They have often been politically motivated rather than based on convincing proof. Lest we forget, each teacher and administrator also makes the policies that he or she follows in their own work. They can advance the impact of research by basing practice on the best that is known.

Perspective

With mental discipline demolished, American educators badly needed a replacement: a theoretical basis for curriculum development. It's not that there was any shortage of candidates. Of those vying to fill the void, democracy has today emerged stronger than ever. It was Dewey who gave democracy its educational formulation. For Dewey, democracy is more than a form of government; it is a sound process enabling people to shape things in furtherance of higher aims.

The Twenty-sixth Yearbook of the National Society for the Study of Education was one of the most important educational events in the twentieth century. We owe much to the Committee on Curriculum Making under Harold Rugg's leadership, for its members were able to merge conflicting perspectives into a new perspective. Over the years that perspective developed into an instrumentation for curriculum development that continues to be used in one form or another in the twenty-first century.

Fortunately, in curriculum development we need not start from scratch. Our forebears laid down a set of principles for us to follow. These ideas and steps to be taken were based on practices and experience in the more progressive cities and have stood the test of time. Curriculum development is a professional task, and its effectiveness depends on the establishment of a central department of curriculum and the appointment of an individual (assistant superintendent or curriculum director) with expertise and responsibility for the total program of curriculum development. Most of the work of preparing materials and activities is done by teachers and principals organized into a small number of committees and coordinated by the curriculum director, who can see the curriculum whole. Curriculum continuity is achieved by having committees that consider not only entire fields from first through the twelfth grade, but the interrelationships of the fields in creating a totally integrated plan. As Dewey found in his laboratory school, a coherent curriculum is no accident. It is achieved through careful design, continuous evaluation, supervision, cooperation, and basing instruction on a unified plan. Teachers involved in curriculum work should be released from classroom duties and should be chosen for professional rather than political reasons.

Tyler added another evolutionary dimension to curriculum work: the understanding that developing materials and activities is only part of the work of curriculum development. Teachers must develop an interest in using them, and students' passive or negative attitudes toward school work must be overcome.

The development of our field is a fascinating story, told through the achievements of individuals and groups. The Society for Curriculum Study developed a set of principles, building on the work of the Rugg committee. Curriculum development is a continuous process because the world of knowledge is undergoing continuous change and the rising generation must be able to understand and deal intelligently with the issues of a changing society. Curriculum development should result in materials that are adaptable to the needs of particular groups of students. A major change in curriculum requires broad-based involvement; no single group, be it teachers or supervisors, should carry out the work independently. An improved curriculum to meet the needs of children and a democratic society requires the teacher's personal commitment. Teachers must believe that a curriculum problem is serious, and this is most likely to happen when the teachers identify the problem. The nature of the school district's curriculum development program depends greatly on the financial resources available, but more money can usually be obtained if the public is convinced that the proposal will make children's lives better and richer. The solution to a curriculum problem should be evaluated over time. Members of the school staff should never assume they have the answer. The curriculum should be evaluated in terms of its effects on students, teachers, and the community. Learning units that are truly unitary give the curriculum coherence, because units are not confined to a single subject field. A good curriculum development program is characterized by enthusiasm—there can be no real accomplishment in any field without people who care.

All of the foregoing principles, ideas, and practices evolved well before midcentury. As in Washburne's time in Winnetka, school subjects continue to provide the framework for curriculum development in most school systems. The focus is on modifying instructional strategies rather than changing the design and function of the curriculum. By changing the design—for example, including more unit teaching as in the Lincoln School—it is possible to build curricular coherence and meet individual needs. There are more opportunities for students to work on projects that interest them. Such opportunities are key in motivation and learning to solve problems.

Lincoln remains an inspiration. The units of work developed in elementary classrooms at the Lincoln School remain exemplary models of curriculum integration. They may still be located in leading education libraries. At the secondary school level, the model that developed was the core course. Its major purposes were individual and democratic social development. Nelson Rockefeller, who became the governor of New York and later vice president of the United States, was a graduate of the Lincoln School. In a television interview many years later he said that his education at Lincoln fostered in him the spirit of social consciousness and public service. From Lincoln we learn that the key to a coherent learning experience links ideas to reality. The curriculum choices we make should be guided by and be consistent with what is known about learning. *Should* is the key word here, for the principle is not always followed in practice. In landmark curriculum studies, such as the Eight-Year Study, some of the most sophisticated evaluation instruments were developed. The researchers did not depend on existing tests designed to evaluate conventional curriculums. Indeed, much can be learned today from the evaluation instruments developed in the Eight-Year Study. Unfortunately, we have not drawn from these instruments, as schools are pressured to make good showings on standardized tests of limited predictive validity. At the same time we have allowed the tests to drive the curriculum rather than using tests and comprehensive evaluation techniques to serve the cause of curriculum improvement. Dependable criteria exist in the literature for evaluating a school and developing a program of curriculum improvement. There is no such thing as an average school.

Today, a major goal of testing has become the supervision of teachers. This is a far cry from Tyler's view of the purpose of testing, which was to provide information to teachers for the purpose of curriculum improvement through problem solving (Tyler, 1949). Whatever the educational climate, problem solving is still a best practice in education.

PROBLEMS FOR STUDY AND DISCUSSION

1. Tyler's list of the most significant curriculum events of the twentieth century was made in 1988. Do you think that it should be amended (additions or deletions)? Why and in what respects?

2. As discussed in this chapter, workshops were an inservice education approach contributed by the Eight-Year Study. Teachers identified the problems on which they wanted to work. Do you think this is a good idea? Explain.

3. In connection with problem 2, in your experience, are workshops today built around teacher-identified problems? Give examples.

4. In the Eight-Year Study, assessments were concerned with transfer-oriented student outcomes. This was because they were specifically developed for the objectives most stressed by the 30 schools, such as the development of effective ways of thinking, increased sensitivity to social problems, and effective work habits and skills.

Teachers identified the objectives, and consequently test developers were concerned with rich outcomes. How do today's "high stakes" tests differ from the vision of curriculum and evaluation in the Eight-Year Study?

5. In connection with problem 4, is contemporary policy on testing and evaluation (a) consonant with, (b) in violation of, or (c) unrelated to the principles developed by the Society for Curriculum Study? Explain.

6. As discussed in this chapter, the Committee on Curriculum Making was concerned with the problem of achieving curriculum continuity and synthesis. Examine the curriculum in your own school district and identify efforts to improve the continuity and integration of the curriculum. Is there a single committee for each curriculum area that considers the entire program from the first through the twelfth grade? What roles are played by administrators and supervisors to promote the articulation and continuity about which Rugg and Counts were so concerned in the 1920s?

7. According to an expert on the impact of testing
   . . . the statewide mandated competency tests turn nearly a half century of curriculum and evaluation theory and practice on its head. Instead of testing and measurement being used in the service of educational objectives, curriculum and instruction, the new tests put objectives, curriculum, and instruction in the service of measurement. [Airasian, 1994, p. 96.]

Do you see this as an important contemporary issue? Why or why not?

8. As discussed in this chapter, when units of work were completed at the Lincoln School, they were broken down to determine their subject matter components. Compare this approach to curriculum integration with Dewey's laboratory school. (See chapter 2). Frame your response in terms of (1) the starting point for integration, and (2) the role of children's interests. What problems did the Lincoln teachers encounter in getting a unit started? In your view were they satisfactorily resolved? Why?

9. In your view, are the objectives of contemporary educators who attempt to develop interdisciplinary units fundamentally the same as those of curriculum pioneers in the 1920s and 1930s? Explain.

10. Some veteran teachers serving on curriculum improvement teams or projects can remember earlier projects in which they participated. Often these projects had similar purposes, such as the development of interdisciplinary thematic approaches to teaching the humanities. Often these teachers have strong feelings about what was most and least worthwhile. Do you believe that these teachers can provide the team with curriculum lessons from the past about the pitfalls and potentialities of local curriculum development efforts? Explain. Should a deliberate effort be made to include as participants in local curriculum development efforts teachers who well remember previous efforts? Why?

11. According to Stephen J. Thornton, the social studies as an elementary school subject first emerged in the 1930s. It was based on the study of social functions that meet human needs. It drew upon history, sociology, economics, and so on, integrating them in the study of these social functions. The social studies are periodically attacked as anti-intellectual and had fallen "afoul of right-wing censorship by mid-century. Nevertheless," points out Thornton, "no wholesale return to the academic subjects as the organizational basis for the curriculum developed." [Thornton, 2001, p. 195.]
    How do you account for the survival of the curricular form of the social studies?

12. According to Edmund C. Short, "While the people dealing with curriculum practice may know what they need more knowledge about, the researchers capable of generating the knowledge often do not hear the practitioners' questions and are removed enough from practice that they do not generate similar questions on their own" (Short, 1991, pp. 363–364). Two possible solutions to this dilemma are offered by Short: (1) teachers and supervisors could conduct research into real curriculum problems, and (2) the two groups—university researchers and school practitioners—could be brought more closely together. What real curriculum problems would you like to see investigated?

PART II

THE EMERGENT CURRICULUM FIELD

All other problems are solved when the problem of curriculum is solved.

—Mark Van Doren

CHAPTER 5

CHANGING CONCEPTIONS OF CURRICULUM

Mark Van Doren (1959) observed that "the curriculum is not something which it is fashionable to ponder; and as for being rational about it, few oddities are more suspect" (p. 108). In making this observation, Van Doren was reiterating a concern voiced by Herbert Spencer a century earlier.

In his essay, "What Knowledge Is of Most Worth?" (1860), Spencer proposed that this was "the question of questions" in education. "Before there can be a rational *curriculum*," held Spencer, "we must settle which things it most concerns us to know" (p. 29).

That curriculum as a systematic field of study is of recent development may seem outlandish when one considers that there is no such institution as a school, college, or university without a curriculum. Yet in the eyes of the student, the process of formal education is viewed merely as subjects or courses to be taken. And although teachers and professors devote considerable attention to the adoption and revision of subject matter as encapsulated in courses or subjects, they give relatively little attention to the interaction and interdependence of the elements that comprise the concept that has come to be called *curriculum*.

The rise of virtually all civilized societies has been accompanied by educational prescriptions and programs for the acculturation of successive generations. The concept of curriculum is implicit even in the earliest educational prescriptions and programs of civilized societies. Aristotle was concerned with curriculum when he wrote, "As things are . . . mankind are by no means agreed about the things to be taught. . . . Again about the means there is no agreement" (*Politica*). Yet the actual term *curriculum* is a relatively modern term, dating from the nineteenth century, according to *The Oxford English Dictionary,* whereas the term *pedagogy* dates back to the early seventeenth century.

It can be contended that virtually every institution of society has a curriculum: the family, church, business, industry, library, museum, newspaper, and radio and television stations (including the commercials that teach people to want what they do not need). Aside from the miseducative functions of some of these institutions, and aside from the fact that most such institutions do not ordinarily use the concept *curriculum* to denote the nature of their operations, the school (and the college and university) performs a constellation of educative functions that is not matched by any other institution. Chief among these is the systematic organization and interpretation of the culture's knowledge and skills needed for the growth of the rising generation.

When the term *educational institution* is used, one immediately thinks of the school, college, or university, although other institutions do indeed perform educational functions. The school, college, and university contain libraries of their own, and they may also use other kinds of libraries. But the library does not contain the school, college, or university. The library is charged with the storage, retrieval, and dissemination of codified scholarship and other material and media, but only the school, college, and university are concertedly responsible for the systematic reconstruction of the necessary knowledge paradigms and skills. This orchestral function of the school encompasses a program of systematic instruction and evaluation unmatched by any other institution.

The question of whether institutions other than the school, college, or university do indeed have a curriculum becomes irrelevant when the unique educative and curricular functions of the school, college, and university are recognized. It is possible to develop literacy in individuals and small populations without the curriculum of schooling, but no society has attained literacy without the curriculum of schooling. It is not by accident that the term *curriculum* has come to be so closely identified with the school, college, and university and not with any other institution of society. It is therefore puzzling that contemporary curricularists have tended to define curriculum as though it were independent of the knowledge paradigms of the cumulative cultural experience. We shall meet this problem again.

According to Cremin, sustained concern with curriculum emerged in this country during the early decades of the progressive period of the twentieth century and "with the rapid growth of professional training for educators during the progressive period, the burgeoning literature of curriculum-making became the substance of a distinct field of study. . . . " Hence it can be said that curriculum has a long past but a short history.

A Matter of Definition

As in the case of most newly emerging distinct fields of study, considerable effort is directed at finding curriculum's appropriate definition, ascertaining its parameters, and seeking a measure of recognition commensurate with its bordering fields of scholarship. Newly emerging fields are also characterized by sharply conflicting schools of thought, which reflect the dramatic conceptual changes of the field.

The concept *curriculum* has undergone marked changes during the twentieth century without any consensus having been reached on an appropriate definition. The term itself derives from Latin, referring to a race course. This may seem far removed from the ways the term has evolved, but in a sense a curriculum in modern times typically is conducted within parameters of time and the meeting of established criteria, including conditions and standards for conduct and completion. Students may justifiably feel that they are engaged in running a race course in their studies and examinations. Today, most textbooks on curriculum and many works on educational theory offer some definition of curriculum. Many contemporary curricularists regard the matter of definition as highly significant, even crucial, for conceptual and operational progress. Whether the matter of definition holds such great significance is examined in the concluding section of this chapter. But

regardless of this issue, an analysis of differing definitions of curriculum reveals to the student the profound changes that have occurred during the twentieth century concerning the role of the school in our society, conceptions of the learner, and the nature of knowledge.

Moreover, these factors in the educative process (namely, the nature of knowledge, the nature of the learner, and the wider social conditions) are conceived differently, and often on conflicting terms, by educators holding differing educational ideologies or philosophies. A traditionalist, then, would be at odds with a progressivist on the definition and function of the curriculum. This chapter examines the conflicting conceptions and functions of the curriculum as reflected in conflicting educational ideologies or philosophies. The issues raised in this chapter are developed in greater detail throughout part II of this text and especially in chapters 7 and 8.

A Proposed Modern Definition of Curriculum

The evolution of the concept of curriculum is treated in detail in this chapter according to contrasting and oppositional traditionalist and progressivist outlooks. The authors of this text propose a modern, progressivist conception of curriculum, taking into account the interactions of (1) the nature of the learner, (2) the world of knowledge, and (3) society. This requires that education must be a dynamic process of individual and social growth. Curriculum is the means and ends through which education is made instrumental. Although John Dewey wrote more profoundly on the curriculum and education than any other educator over the course of the first half of the twentieth century, he never actually offered a definition of curriculum. However, he defined education as "that reconstruction or reorganization of experience which adds to the meaning of experience, and which increases ability to direct the course of subsequent experience (1916, pp. 89–90). In effect, education has no end beyond itself. From Dewey's definition of education, the present authors propose the definition of curriculum as *that reconstruction of knowledge and experience that enables the learner to grow in exercising intelligent control of subsequent knowledge and experience.*

In this definition the concept of curriculum is generative, not passive or inert as in a published course of study. It encompasses not only formal subject matter, but also the processes through which the learner becomes increasingly knowledge/able. Most definitions of curriculum, whether traditionalist or modern, sever curriculum from instruction and from the learning process through which the learner becomes increasingly knowledge/able. Our proposed definition regards knowledge as dynamic in that it must be transformed into the working power of intelligence by means of the learning process—and all this is encompassed in the modern meaning of curriculum.

The proposed definition of curriculum is presented again in the concluding section of this chapter, following a detailed examination of how and why the concept of curriculum has evolved so dramatically over time.

Traditionalist Conceptions and Functions of Curriculum

Curriculum as Subject-Matter Content

Make learning relevant

To many people, curriculum is seen simply as the subject-matter content of a course or course of study. To the professional educator, this conception poses problems because it indicates that curriculum, as subject matter, must invariably be organized as subjects. In reality there are many ways to design and structure a curriculum beyond subjects. The curriculum can be correlated; organized as interdisciplinary units of work or as problems and themes that integrate several subjects, broad fields, or combined fields of study; projects and activities beyond given subjects; and so on. (A detailed analysis of curriculum design and function is presented in part III of this text.)

The term *content*, often used by professional educators as well as lay people, poses a related problem, for it implies that curriculum is *contained* within the discrete boundaries of a subject, and so contained it is merely inert matter or inert subject matter. As discussed later, experimentalist-progressive educators held that to be a curriculum the program of studies must be actualized or made operational in the life of the learner. The research base to support this view is very powerful in connecting the concept of curriculum with the nature of the learner and the life of the learner in society (Aikin, 1942; Jackson, 1992). As discussed later, to the experimentalist-progressive, content is inert and contained, whereas

it must be released and transformed into the working power of intelligence if it is to become curriculum.

Curriculum as the Cumulative Tradition of Organized Knowledge

During the early years of the twentieth century, most educators held to the traditional concept of curriculum as the body of subjects or subject matters set out by teachers for students to cover. Adding to the confusion, such terms as *course of study* and *syllabus* were being used synonymously with curriculum.

To the traditionalist (perennialist and essentialist), curriculum must be conceived as the cumulative tradition of organized knowledge to be imparted to each rising generation.

Aside from suffering from archaic notions of mind and experience, the perennialist (or classical humanist) devalues the dynamic nature of knowledge, the modern scientific studies, and the practical applications of knowledge. The fundamental premise is that the best exemplars of the past, the so-called permanent studies, are valid for the present and for all time. "Knowledge is truth. The truth is everywhere the same. Hence education should be everywhere the same," declared Hutchins (1936, p. 66). Perennialists and essentialists embrace the long-refuted doctrine of mental discipline (faculty psychology) and reject any consideration of the interests and needs of the learner, or the treatment of contemporary problems in the curriculum, on the ground that such concerns are temporal and only detract from the school's mission of cultivating the mind.

The emerging demands for social reform during the early decades of the twentieth century—coupled with developments in psychiatry, medicine, and the various behavioral sciences—led to a more integrated conception of human nature. Progressive educators, buttressed by research findings on the transfer of learning, demolished the old conception of mind as a separate entity and challenged the notion that certain studies possess uniquely inherent powers for the cultivation of the intellect (mental discipline).

As discussed later, the advances in our knowledge of human behavior and the learning process, coupled with the growing recognition of the need for modern studies in the curriculum and the need for the vast extension of educational opportunity in and for a free society, all augured a modern conception of curriculum. Nevertheless, the reader would be remiss in concluding that the perennialist conceptions of education and curriculum are artifacts of a bygone age that might better be relegated to a museum, for perennialist expositions on the curriculum have garnered considerable attention to this day. Because the perennialist shares with the essentialist the premise that the school curriculum must be properly delimited to basic education on which the traditional academic studies are built, as opposed to elective options (vocational, exploratory, enrichment studies), perennialism shares in any resurgence gained by essentialism. The continuing influence of essentialism and perennialism on the school curriculum is reflected in the resurgent call for "back to basics."

Although the colleges have no difficulty in warding off perennialist criticisms, the schools are vulnerable. In eras of social retrenchment, essentialism gains wide currency as the means of reducing the curriculum for economy and "efficiency," and essentialism is a handmaiden of perennialism.

In 1907, the essentialist William C. Bagley wrote that the curriculum and the work of the teacher "must represent a storehouse of organized race experience, conserved against the time when knowledge shall be needed in the constructive solution of new and untried problems." Although, as discussed later, many progressives also recognize the importance of the codified experience of the human race, their conception of such experience extends far beyond that of the essentialist, who delimits it primarily to certain organized bodies of academic knowledge. Moreover, where the essentialist tends to see such knowledge largely as something to be acquired and stored for some future use, the progressivist is concerned with the significance of such knowledge in the life of the learner.

Curriculum as Disciplinary Knowledge

A Curriculum Manifesto. The doctrine of structure-of-the-discipline emerged from the report of a national conference of scientists and other university scholars held at Woods Hole on Cape Cod in the fall of 1950, financed by the National Science Foundation, the U.S. Office of Education, the Air Force, and the RAND Corporation. The purpose of the Woods Hole Conference, as it came to be known, was to fashion a rationale for curriculum reform to meet "the long-range crisis in national security" of the Cold War and space race (Bruner, 1960, p. 1). The conference was chaired by the psychologist Jerome Bruner, who also wrote the conference report, *The Process of Education* (1960),

a small book that almost immediately became a veritable curriculum manifesto for the schools. The report provided the rationale for the national discipline-centered projects in school sciences and mathematics, already in progress and sponsored largely by the National Science Foundation and other federal agencies.

A tenet of the rationale was that constituent academic disciplines such as in the sciences and mathematics are each built on a structure that reveals how the knowledge is related within the discipline. According to Bruner, the structure-of-the-discipline is embodied by the fundamental ideas, concepts, and generalizations that define the discipline. Thus "the curriculum of a subject should be determined by the most fundamental understanding that can be achieved of the underlying principles that give structure to that subject" (Bruner, p. 31), and that structure would best be determined by scholars at the forefront of their disciplines (p. 8).

The specialized nature of university scholarship resulted in a like model imposed on the schools. University scholars held that the school curriculum should be formulated according to the "structures of the disciplines." This notion soon became a doctrine that dominated the curriculum field for more than a decade, from the late 1950s through much of the 1960s. Specialists in the social studies, the visual and performing arts, and the language arts sought to emulate the physical sciences and mathematics in the elusive search for disciplinary structure. Leading curriculum theorists, such as Joseph Schwab, seized on *disciplinarity*, to coin a term, as the ruling doctrine for curriculum development at all levels. "To identify the disciplines which constitute contemporary knowledge is to identify the various materials which constitute the resources of education and its obligations," held Schwab (1964, p. 7).

Problems of Curriculum Fragmentation. Some scholars went even further than Schwab in arguing for the disciplines as the sole source of the curriculum. Phenix (1962) declared that "[t]he curriculum should consist entirely of knowledge which comes from the disciplines" (p. 64).

The disciplinary doctrine resulted in a multiplicity of disciplines vying for a distinct place in the curriculum at the elementary and secondary levels. Moreover, there was disagreement, even among scholars in the same areas of specialized knowledge, as to the elements that constitute the structure-of-the-discipline.

Although disciplinarity is a valuable mode for organizing certain specialized areas of knowledge in order to facilitate scholarly communication and, at the university level, to advance such knowledge, its appropriateness as *the* ruling principle for curriculum development came into question. Other modes of organizing knowledge for the curriculum can be justified in terms of life relevance, the nature of the learner, and the demands of society.

The advocate of disciplinarity may share with the perennialist and the essentialist the conception of curriculum as the cumulative tradition of organized knowledge and the devaluation of practical knowledge, but here is where the cause for common ground ends. Unlike the perennialist view, the disciplinary conception regards knowledge as dynamic and places the methods of science central to the development of knowledge. Whereas the perennialist and essentialist regard the mind as a vessel to be filled or a muscle to be exercised, the advocate of disciplinarity regards disciplinary inquiry as the key to intellective development.

Although the disciplines doctrine rejects the traditional conception of knowledge as fixed or permanent and regards knowledge as the product of a process known as disciplined inquiry, it confines such inquiry to the boundaries of the established disciplines. The fact that many problems transcend the individual disciplines and call for interdisciplinary approaches is virtually ignored or rejected by proponents of the disciplines doctrine.

What about the nature, needs, and interests of the learner? Concern for the nature of the learner is dismissed as the learner is to be viewed ideally as a miniature version of the university scholar on the forefront of his or her discipline. According to Phenix (1962), "There is no place in the curriculum for ideas which are regarded as suitable for teaching because of the supposed nature, needs, and interests of the learner, but which do not belong within the regular structure of the disciplines" (p. 64).

One of the rare educators to raise questions concerning the validity and viability of disciplinary structure for defining and designing the school curriculum was Hollis Caswell. Soon after publication of Bruner's *The Process of Education*, Caswell (1962) commented on some troublesome aspects of disciplinary structure. "In the first place," wrote Caswell, "specialists in the academic disciplines do not seem too certain just what is the structure of knowledge with which they deal" (p. 107). Caswell went on to point out that Bruner was

calling for university scholar-specialists to lead the way, "the same kind as those who dominated secondary education for a hundred years and to whose work he refers who would lead us out of the wilderness into a more ordered, rational, and meaningful plan of education for elementary and secondary schools" (p. 109). Referring to Bruner's examples of how disciplinary structure would define the school curriculum, Caswell stated, "I found not one illustration that seemed to relate to problems of day-to-day living of ordinary citizens" (p. 109).

Violation of the Curriculum Paradigm.   Over the course of the national discipline-centered curriculum reforms, most educators were unable to establish the structure-of-the-discipline in any definitive and instrumental sense for their field. At one point some universities had actually offered a course on "the-structure-of-the-disciplines" (Schwab, 1974, p. 162). But the concept of disciplinary structure became irrelevant to the practical concerns of educators in connecting curriculum to the life of the learner and society.

However, over the course of the national discipline-centered curriculum reforms, the idea and practice of general education for an enlightened democratic citizenship was cast aside in favor of specialized, puristic knowledge. The learner was to be cast in the image of the scholar-specialist on the forefront of the discipline (Bruner, pp. 27–28). In effect, the disciplinary doctrine violated the curriculum paradigm in virtually every way, and it should have been predictable that the entire program was destined for failure. But the language of *The Process of Education* was seductive. The federal grants for discipline-centered school reforms were of unprecedented magnitude. And the groundswell in the wake of the Cold War and space race was irresistible.

What was perhaps most surprising was the readiness of schools of teacher education to embrace and promote the disciplines doctrine and the national disciplinary curriculum-reform projects. In the late 1960s, Ralph Tyler commented to the authors of this text, "Well, you've read *The Emperor's New Clothes*." The disciplines doctrine was to collapse by the early 1970s as a result of neglecting the practical needs of society, ignoring and even violating the nature of the learner and dismissing practical knowledge in the life of the learner, and producing myriad disciplinary domains competing for a place in the school curriculum.

Curriculum as an Instructional Plan or Course of Study

One of the most longstanding conceptions of curriculum is that of an instructional plan or, synonymously, a course of study. The most systematic application of this concept of curriculum was made through the disciplinary curriculum reforms during the height of the Cold War and space race. Although the method claimed for the implementation of the discipline-centered curriculum was to be that of inquiry learning, the method of inquiry (or discovery) became little more than a slogan, especially when many of those responsible for creating the disciplinary curriculum packages sought to make them "teacher proof"—a contradiction in terms, to say the least. Furthermore, the "inquiry" was directed at specialized disciplinary knowledge to the deliberate exclusion of practical knowledge geared to the learner's development and life experience, and to the wider social situation.

Woodring (1964) noted that, to some extent, the disciplinary movement represented a return to the older tradition that dominated the schools before the progressive revolution in that it conceived of curriculum as subject matter organized as separate academic disciplines (p. 5). As discussed earlier, the disciplinary movement departed from the older tradition in many significant ways, but the conception of curriculum embraced by this movement was nonetheless a return to the notion of curriculum as a course of study and independent subjects defined as academic disciplines.

Taba (1962) rejected the progressive concept of curriculum (e.g., "the life and program of the school") for being so broad as to be nonfunctional and proposed that a "curriculum is a plan for learning."

Problem of Dualism.   One of the difficulties with the concept of curriculum as an instructional plan or course of study is that it does not distinguish between a curriculum and a lesson plan or unit plan or syllabus for an individual course. But perhaps the most significant issue is that such definitions imply that the *processes* by which such plans or syllabi are put into action are outside the curriculum. As discussed later, many contemporary curriculum writers maintain that instruction is indeed separate from curriculum. This notion of separation is reflected in Macdonald's definition of curriculum as "those planning endeavors which take place prior to instruction" (1965, p. 6).

The problem of dualism between curriculum and instruction arises in all definitions in which curriculum is regarded as a plan. Hirst (1974) defines curriculum as "a plan of activities deliberately organized so that pupils will attain, by learning, certain educational ends or objectives" (p. 132). Although Hirst sees a curriculum arising only in a teaching situation, his definition is that of a *plan* for teaching and learning activities and not of the experience itself. An almost identical definition, which raises the same difficulties, is offered by Saylor and Alexander (1974): "[W]e define curriculum as a plan for providing sets of learning opportunities to achieve broad goals and related specific objectives for an identifiable population served by a single school center" (p. 6).

The conception of curriculum as a plan or written course of study, set apart from instruction or the means of activating and conducting the learning process, not only is dysfunctional, but it also reinforces the contemporary dogma that the determination of the school curriculum is made as a matter of policy outside the classroom, or even the school, and it is the responsibility of the teacher to "deliver" the curriculum by the process of instruction. Thus external tests formulated by state or federal policy are seen as defining the subject matter, whereas teachers instruct for the test and/or deliver the curriculum.

Although Eisner (1994), sees curriculum "as a series of planned events that are intended to have educational consequences," he proceeds to address the conduct and operational consequences that are *implicit* to any curriculum in action, thereby indicating that the concept of curriculum is actually a plan in action (p. 95). The concepts of hidden or covert curriculum, implicit curriculum, and collateral curriculum are addressed later in this chapter.

The concept of curriculum as a plan is advanced by Oliva (2001), who defines curriculum as "a plan or program for all experiences which the learner encounters under the direction of the school" (p. 7). As discussed later, such definitions do not account for what commonly happens to the best-laid plans or programs when they are implemented. An incidental but educationally significant question might be raised concerning Oliva's choice of the word *encounter* in defining the curriculum, for encounter is commonly used as a meeting or engagement in conflict. This may accurately portray the all-too-common relationship between the student and the curriculum as oppositional. But as Dewey stated in a lecture to parents: in traditional education, instead of productive interaction "[w]e get the case of the child vs. the curriculum" (1902).

Curriculum as Measured Instructional Outcomes (Products): A Technological Production Model

The new instructional technology and the growing trend toward standardized-achievement testing have given impetus to conceiving of the curriculum in terms of test results. With schools and teachers being evaluated according to student scores on standardized tests, there has been an increasing tendency for teachers to teach to the test. Hence the test not only provides the quantitative data on the outcomes of instruction, but it also exerts a powerful influence on instructional processes and largely determines the curriculum. In effect the curriculum is seen as the quantitatively measured outcomes of instruction. Such a conception of curriculum reduces the schooling process to a technological system of production.

The origin of the notion of curriculum as a production system can be traced to the efforts in education during the early decades of the twentieth century to apply industrial "scientific management" to education (Callahan, 1962). These efforts were exemplified in the method of job analysis. In recent years, the notion of curriculum as a production system has been embodied in the doctrine of specific "behavioral" objectives, behaviorism and the theory of operant conditioning, developments in instructional technology (including systems analysis), performance contracting, and accountability.

Activity Analysis. Although activity analysis incorporated the progressive idea of linking the curriculum to life experience, it departed from the progressive rationale by reducing curriculum to an analysis of adult activity and thereby overlooked the authentic life of the learner. The operation of job analysis or activity analysis was designed to secure educational objectives in an efficient way, corresponding to the analysis of activities involved in the performance of jobs in the world of industry and business. Because education is concerned with processes that extend beyond job performance, the term *activity analysis* came to be more popular among curriculum developers during the early decades of this century.

Developed by Franklin Bobbitt and W. W. Charters, the method of activity analysis came to be cloaked as the scientific way to build a curriculum. According to Bobbitt (1924), life consists of the performance of specific activities. If education is preparation for life, then it must prepare for these specific activities. These activities, however numerous, are definite and particularized, and they can be taught; therefore, these activities will be the objectives of the curriculum. "The curriculum will then be that series of experiences which children and youth must have by way of attaining these objectives," reasoned Bobbitt, who proceeded to define curriculum as "*that series of things which children and youth must do and experience* by way of developing abilities to do the things well that make up the affairs of adult life; and to be in all respects what adults should be" (p. 42). The school, according to Bobbitt, simply deals with those objectives that are not sufficiently attained through undirected experience.

Aside from certain problems inherent in activity analysis—such as its static orientation toward society, the virtually unlimited number of objectives possible, its notion of the child as merely an adult in the making, its misuse of the term *scientific*, and so on—this method was derived by Bobbitt and Charters from analyses of the production models of business and industry. To Bobbitt (1924), curriculum making is the job of the "educational engineer," (p. 2); to Charters (1922), "[i]n its simplest forms it involves the analysis of definite operations, to which the term job analysis is applied, as in the analysis of the operations involved in running a machine" (p. 350). This mechanistic model shows its legacy in various education doctrines and proposals in contemporary education, such as behavioristic objectives and accountability.

The Persistent Problem of Dualism. Despite the sharply contrasting and conflicting differences between those who see curriculum as a plan, or as subject-matter content, or as measured outcomes of instruction, these definitional conceptions all share the notion of dualism between curriculum and instruction, between ends and means. However logical such a distinction may appear in theory, it leads to serious conceptual and practical difficulties. To separate curriculum from instruction, or to separate subject matter from method, is to make the same error as in separating knowledge from that which renders our actions intelligent. Thus, to see the curriculum merely as ends is like conceiving of getting to a destination without having to take the trip.

The mechanistic process-product dualism is most explicitly set forth in behavioristic psychology as measured by behavioristic objectives. With regard to the behaviorist's doctrine that all behavior is inevitably controlled, we might well heed the wry admonition of the late Nobel Laureate Isaac Bashevis Singer, who stated in a TV interview shortly before his death in 1991 that "[w]e must believe in free will; we have no choice."

The rise of cognitive psychology over the past half century, emphasizing higher-order thinking (as did Dewey early in the twentieth century), resulted in the corresponding decline of behaviorism, as pointed out in other sections of this text. Nevertheless, the residue of behaviorism continues to plague the schools through mechanistic teaching methods and materials, including workbooks and worksheets, and repetitive practices of "drill-skill-kill" and memorization-regurgitation. Further, the conception of curriculum as measured instructional outcomes ("products") is buttressed by the pandemic of external examinations through which the schools are evaluated, coupled with the growing practice of teaching to the test.

Those who believe that behaviorism has long gone into full eclipse need to be reminded that as long as teachers use mechanical worksheets and gear their lessons and tests to rote learning, behaviorism will remain alive and learning will remain largely convergent rather than emergent. One of the persistent problems of education is failure to recognize that the extent to which learning outcomes are more and more narrowly specified and restricted for measurement, the lower the capability of the learner to generalize and apply knowledge to new or unforeseen situations or emergent conditions.

Accountability as Production Outcomes ("Products"). At various times, under the banner of accountability, the schools have been pressured to adopt the techniques of industrial plant management in assessing their efficiency through quantitative input-output measures. Addressing school principals, an officer of the Ford Foundation stated:

> Similar to the plant manager in a large industrial corporation, the principal is the key person responsible for the productivity of the organization. The school, like the industrial plant, represents a process. Raw material goes in and a product comes out. The change that occurs between

input, that is the entering pupil, and output, the departing pupil, . . . measures the school. (1968, pp. 6–7)

A former U.S. associate commissioner of education argued that the schools be made accountable through performance contracting: "In the same way that planning . . . and performance warranties determine industrial production and its worth to consumers, so should we be able to engineer, organize, refine, and manage the educational system" (Lessinger, 1971, p. 14). Under such accountability curriculum is reduced to a component of a production process called educational engineering, and the efficiency of the process is assessed in terms of quantifiable performance specifications, warranties, and outcomes.

Educational and curricular problems are not the same as engineering and production problems of a factory. This does not mean that curricular processes and learning outcomes cannot be assessed but rather that the ways and means of such assessment cannot be likened to the quality controls and efficiency measurement specifications of the industrial plant. The human equation is infinitely more complex in an institution, the school, that is concerned with the rising generation—the generation that is our society's own future.

Nevertheless, educators continue to be pressured into adopting the relatively simplistic paradigms of business, industry, and the military. Although performance contracting for accountability collapsed after the questionable technique of teaching to the test was exposed, such contracting with the private sector received an incredible resurrection from President George H. W. Bush's "Education Strategy" unveiled in early 1991 under the title *America 2000*. In virtually all instances, the contractual arrangements were directed at inner-city schools having low scores on the state-mandated tests and serving, to paraphrase Dewey, "other people's children" (1900a, p. 7). Three U.S. presidents in succession—George H. W. Bush, Bill Clinton, and George W. Bush—endorsed *America 2000* and the call for a national system of examinations through American achievement tests in the five (academic) core areas that, obviously, define the school curriculum, or the curriculum that really "counts."

Further impetus was given to teaching to the test under the federal No Child Left Behind Act of 2001. The business-industrial production model of schooling has been dominant in school administration for over a century, and has been promoted as a model of accountability and production efficiency for the public schools to this day. This view has survived and prevailed regardless of evidence showing that the school curriculum cannot be construed simply as a production process and measured as products analogous to the industrial world (Callahan, 1962; Tanner, D., 2000b; Weiss, 1989).

Curriculum as Cultural Reproduction

Growing out of the college-student protest movement of the 1960s and early 1970s, and its countercultural rhetoric, the new academic left gained a strong presence in education faculties in colleges and universities during the 1980s. Functioning as a kind of academic federation of critical theorists, revisionists, neo-Marxists, deconstructionists, anarchists, and radical reconstructionists, the new academic left portrayed the school curriculum as cultural reproduction: a selection of studies or subject matters designed to maintain the existing social order. As the educational historian Freeman Butts (1978) observed, the new academic left, or neoradicals, were portraying the public schools as mere instruments of oppression by American capitalism on behalf of the privileged classes (p. 372). And the teacher was portrayed largely as an unwitting accomplice to the massive social inequities and oppression perpetuated by the social system. The new academic left proceeded to hold the school as a powerless or, at best, a marginal institution for effecting social change (Bowles & Gintis, 1976, pp. 8–11), leading one to question why those identified with the new academic left were devoting their careers to heaving polemical grenades at the public schools (Giroux, 1983).

The Hidden Curriculum. The "discovery" of the *hidden curriculum* in the education literature provided ready grist for the radical left in portraying the school as covertly operating a hidden curriculum alongside the formal curriculum, through which the real power and social controls in the dominant society are exercised.

Ignoring the positive attributes of the so-called hidden curriculum—such as learning by indirection, or learning to cope effectively with school regularities that have payoff in life—critical theorists seized upon the concept of the hidden curriculum as the chief means through which the function of schooling in capitalist society is cultural reproduction. Entire chapters could be found devoted to the hidden curriculum in the literature of the critical theorists who portrayed it as "an agency of social control, one that functions to provide differential forms of schooling to different classes of students" (Giroux, 1983, p. 47). To critical theorists, the notion of hidden curriculum provided new opportunity to formulate a pedagogy of opposition and resistance (Giroux, 1983, p. 62). To Giroux (1988), "the hidden curriculum in schools works in a subtly discriminating way to discredit the dreams, experiences, and knowledges associated with students from specific class, racial, and gender groupings" (p. 182).

Critical theorists overlook the fact that no society, democratic or otherwise, would allow the schools to function in opposition to the ideals and institutions of society. Further, critical theorists have never made inroads in working with the schools. Their writings have been largely directed for their own consumption in academe.

No mention is made by contemporary critical theorists that the ideology of contestation and resistance was fundamental to the radical college-student left implicit in the term *counterculture* and in the countercultural literature of the late 1960s and early 1970s, which sounded its trumpet call as "the great refusal" (Roszak, 1969, p. 41).

A key problem of the call of the critical theorists for turning the function of curriculum to resistance and opposition is one that plagued the educational reconstructionists during the 1930s: the problem of indoctrination.

Progressivist Conceptions and Functions of Curriculum

The influence of progressive education during the first half of the twentieth century brought about a profound change in the conception of curriculum. The need for a radically new conception of curriculum was the inevitable result of a number of forces: changes in the conceptions of knowledge, particularly scientific knowledge; changes in the knowledge of the learning process as a result of the child-study movement; and the need to link formal school studies with the life of the learner and the changing demands of the larger social scene. Nevertheless, in the process of rejecting traditional conceptions of curriculum, progressive educators were far from universal agreement as to how curriculum should be defined. Moreover, traditional conceptions of curriculum have remained influential to this day.

To the progressivists, a body of school subjects, subject matters, syllabi, course of study, list of courses, or documented program of studies are inert and do not a curriculum make until the material becomes actualized by the learner. Hence curriculum is far more than a representation of the cumulative tradition of knowledge. To some progressivists, curriculum was seen as the embodiment of the best elements of the experience of culture in the process of acculturation. For other progressivists, buttressed by advances in educational psychology and the movement for democratic social reform, curriculum was to be conceived as more dynamically experiential.

Curriculum as Knowledge Selection/Organization from the Experience of the Culture

Although the conception of curriculum as the cumulative tradition of knowledge, as exemplified by perennialist and essentialist educators, is an essential part of the human race experience, it is only a limited part of such experience. Such experience embodies not only the cumulative tradition of knowledge but also the total culture of a society, the common elements that make a society more than a mere aggregation of individuals. Dewey's mandate for recognizing the vital importance of transferring and reconstructing the cultural experience through the curriculum is reflected in the definition of curriculum offered by Smith, Stanley, and Shores. After pointing out that in all literate societies the institution known as the school is charged with the specialized function of teaching certain things, Smith, Stanley, and Shores (1957) offer this definition of curriculum: "A sequence of potential experiences is set up in the school for the purpose of disciplining children and youth in group ways of thinking and acting. This set of experiences is referred to as the *curriculum*" (p. 3).

Despite the apparent legitimacy of such an anthropological definition, its exclusive focus on acculturation treats schooling, in Dewey's words, "as if the education of the immature which fills them with the spirit of the social group to which they belong, were a sort of catching up of the child with the aptitudes and resources of the adult group." Progressive communities "endeavor to shape the experiences of the young so that instead

of reproducing current habits, better habits shall be formed, and thus the future adult society be an improvement on their own" continued Dewey (1916, p. 92). To Dewey, by virtue of educating the rising generation, the school is serving to develop the potentials of the future society (p. 92). Although Dewey recognized the importance of encompassing in curriculum the codified experience of the culture, to Dewey such experience is not an endpoint but a turning point in the continuous reconstruction of knowledge and society.

In their anthropological definition, Smith, Stanley, and Shores stressed that in a democratic society curriculum is far more than *cultural reproduction* (a favorite term used by the radical left in attacking the public schools). A democratic society values independent thinking in the context of the widest sense of social responsibility.

In the same vein, Lawton (1975), a British educator, views curriculum as "a selection from the culture of society." He goes on to state that "[c]ertain aspects of our way of life, certain kinds of knowledge, certain attitudes and values are regarded as so important that their transmission to the next generation is not left to chance," and so society entrusts the *selection* to professional educators in institutions known as schools (pp. 6–7). Although this definition is far more comprehensive than the traditional conception of curriculum as the established bodies of knowledge or the courses of study, it raises the question of whether the curriculum represents merely a *selection* from the culture, or, more provocatively, a *reconstruction* of knowledge and experience for the improvement of the culture. There is indeed a vast difference between curriculum as conceived merely for cultural transmission to the next generation or for cultural improvement.

Clearly stressing the significance of the role of the school in a democratic society, Lawton is not characterizing curriculum as merely cultural reproduction, although his definition might be so construed by a critical theorist.

As the universities were begetting more knowledge at what seemed to be an incessantly accelerated pace, these institutions and the lower schools were faced with the dilemma of how this knowledge should be assimilated into the curriculum. The immediate response was the accretion of subjects in the existing curriculum, the revision of course content, and, to a somewhat lesser extent, the displacement of some studies. Paradoxically, the specialization of knowledge was both a cause of and a response to the knowledge explosion.

The increasing specialization of knowledge made the curriculum more remote from pervading personal and social needs and problems. During the early decades of the twentieth century, emerging social reforms and the new demands for education reforms called for a closer relationship between the curriculum and life. Newer and wider conceptions of curriculum were the inevitable result.

Curriculum as Modes of Thought

In *How We Think* (1910, 1933), Dewey noted how the traditional concept of curriculum as a collection of different subject matters or disciplines, each logically organized as to "content" within its own boundaries, tended to impose a misconception of logical method on the teacher, while fragmenting knowledge and isolating it from the life of the learner. Dewey (1933) saw reflective thinking as the unifying process in curriculum: the mode of thought so vital to productive citizenship in a free society. Dewey clearly stressed that this was not to be confused with disciplinary inquiry, which is abstract, specialized, and remote from practical applications in the affairs of living (pp. 62, 81). Yet proponents of the disciplines doctrine were to identify disciplinary inquiry as Deweyan.

Unaccountably, a number of leading educators failed to recognize the difference between disciplinary inquiry and Dewey's conception of reflective thinking. Bentley Glass (1970), a leading figure in the discipline-centered curriculum reforms, viewed disciplinary inquiry as stemming from the ideas of Dewey (pp. 29–30). Hilda Taba (1962) likened the inquiry-discovery method as explicated by Jerome Bruner, the chief spokesman for disciplinary inquiry, with Dewey's ideas on the relation of action to thought (pp. 214–215). The idea of inquiry-discovery embraced in the discipline-centered curriculum reforms struck a blow at the traditional notion of separation between content and process and at the traditional pedagogical methodology of memorization-regurgitation. The necessary unity between content and process, or subject matter and method, had indeed been expounded by Dewey. To Dewey (1915a), learning is learning to think, but the child's style of thinking is qualitatively different from that of the adult scholar (pp. 102–115). Dewey (1933) also warned that the "so-called disciplinary studies" raise the

"danger of the isolation of intellectual activity from the ordinary affairs of life" (p. 62).

Reflective Thinking.   Although Dewey did not confine his conception of curriculum to modes of thought, he saw reflective thinking as the means through which curriculum elements are unified. To Dewey, reflection is not merely confined within specialized domains of knowledge but is extended to social problem solving. Thought is not divorced from action but is tested by application. Dewey (1916) identified the following as essentials of reflection:

> They are first that the pupil have a genuine situation of experience—that there be a continuous activity in which he is interested for its own sake; secondly, that a genuine problem develop within this situation as a stimulus to thought; third, that he possess the information and make the observations needed to deal with it; fourth, that suggested solutions occur to him which he shall be responsible for developing in an orderly way; fifth, that he may have the opportunity and occasion to test his ideas by application, to make their meaning clear and to discover for himself their validity. (p. 102)

Unfortunately, many educators have misinterpreted Dewey by alleging that his essentials of reflection were intended as hard and fast—as the actual step-by-step means, and the only means, by which problems are solved scientifically—as *the* scientific method. But Dewey's opening statement in *How We Think* (1933) says: "No one can tell another person in any definite way how he *should* think any more than how he ought to breathe or to have his blood circulate" (p. 3). Dewey went on to stress that the different ways of thinking can be described in their general features and that some ways of thinking are better than others; he then explained why reflective thinking is the better way. But Dewey (1933) was careful to point out that the phases or steps in reflective thinking are not rigid or uniform. "No set rules can be laid down on such matters," he wrote (p. 116).

Dewey (1916) attacked the separation between thought and action, thinking and doing, subject matter and method, content and process, ends and means. Reflective thinking, then, would resolve the dualism between curriculum and instruction (pp. 179–192). Explicit in Dewey's rationale for reflective thinking is the testing of conclusions through application. Some definitions of curriculum as modes of thought treat these modes as thought severed from action in the pupil's own life situation. This is particularly characteristic of the disciplines doctrine, which imposes the mature scholar-specialist's mode of thought on the immature learner and ignores modes of thought that are relevant to social problem solving from the vantage point of the pupil. Thus, Dewey viewed curriculum as more than the transmission of established modes of thought and the validating of so-called truths within disciplinary boundaries.

Curriculum as Experience

Although the progressivists were united in criticizing the discontinuity between traditional subject matter and the learner, and the divorce of the school studies from the realities and demands of life, they were divided as to the conception and function of curriculum. "The scheme of a curriculum must take account of the adaptation of studies to the needs of existing community life; it must select with the intention of improving the life we live in common so that the future shall be better than the past," wrote Dewey (1916, p. 225).

Dewey stressed the need to develop and conceive of the various studies as exemplifying the reflectively formulated human experience. "They embody the cumulative outcome of the efforts, the strivings, and the successes of the human race generation after generation," declared Dewey (1902b, p. 12). Similarly, the child is to be conceived of as "fluent, embryonic, vital," with the curriculum serving to develop the child's present experience to a richer maturity. "Abandon the notion of subject-matter as something fixed and ready-made in itself, outside the child's experience; cease thinking of the child's experience as something hard and fast . . . and we realize that the child and the curriculum are simply two limits which define a single process. Just as two points define a straight line," wrote Dewey (1902b, pp. 11, 12).

Curriculum as Guided Learning Experience.   In growing recognition that the impact of school (and college) as a learning-living environment is enormously powerful and pervasive, progressive educators from the 1920s through well past mid-twentieth century were defining curriculum as all the experiences provided the learner under the guidance of the school (or college). A definition by Bonser in 1920 regards the curriculum as "the experiences in which pupils are expected to engage in school, and

the general order of sequence in which these experiences are to come" (p. 1).

A definition offered by Caswell and Campbell in 1935 states that the curriculum is "composed of all the experiences children have under the guidance of teachers" (p. 66). A report on the Eight-Year Study, published in 1942, concluded that "the curriculum is now seen as the total experience with which the school deals in educating young people" (Giles, McCutchen, & Zechiel, p. 293).

These emerging definitions were a sharp break from the traditional conception of curriculum. The recognition that what pupils learn is not limited to the formal course of study but is affected, directly and indirectly, by the total school environment, called for a broad definition of curriculum as guided school experience. The implication was that "everything that influences the learner must be considered during the process of curriculum making" (Caswell & Campbell, p. 66).

But the very breadth of such definitions presents no clues as to the kinds of experiences that properly should be provided by the school and those that can be secured through other agencies and from the wider society. A problem with these definitions is that even under the guidance of the school and the teacher, learners encounter undesirable as well as desirable experiences. Thus, these definitions fail to make this important distinction. Furthermore, these broad definitions appear to treat learning experiences as objectives in themselves, with no mention being made of the needed outcomes of such experiences.

Nevertheless, curriculum writers continued to proffer similarly broad definitions. In 1946, Spears noted that "the concept of curriculum had broken loose from its academic moorings and moved on out into the total program of activities that was to serve the individual learner while under the guidance of the school" (p. 116). The definition offered by Tyler in 1957, conceived of curriculum as "all of the learning of students which is planned by and directed by the school to attain its educational goals" (p. 79). Tyler went on to point out that this inclusive definition encompasses educational objectives, all planned learning experiences (including extraclass and learning activities at home insofar as they are planned and directed by the school to attain its aims), and the appraisal of student learning. At the time, Tyler was addressing a national conference on testing problems, and so it seemed appropriate to include the assessment of student learning in his conception of curriculum. The inclusion of goals and learning outcomes implies continuity between ends and means. However, Tyler's definition, like the aforementioned definitions that see curriculum as planned learning experiences, gives no indication of how school learning experiences differ from those that are not under the purview of the school. The definition offered by Alberty and Alberty in 1962, which described curriculum as "all of the activities that are provided for students by the school," also fails to indicate the uniqueness of the learning experiences provided by the school although they pointed out that "[i]t is by means of these activities that the school hopes to bring about changes in the behavior of students in terms of its philosophy and goals" (p. 155).

Curriculum as Guided Living: The Planned Learning Environment in Action.   Another example of a broad definition, offered by Rugg in 1947, is that the curriculum is "[t]he life and program of the school . . . an enterprise in guided living . . . the curriculum becomes the very stream of dynamic activities that constitute the life of young people and their elders" (p. 650).

Although Rugg's definition calls for continuity between school studies and life, it fails to differentiate between school functions and those of other social institutions. For example, the family might also be described as an "enterprise in guided living."

Nevertheless, the broadened conception of curriculum as guided living or as the planned learning environment was to have profound implications for what previously was regarded as extracurricular in the school and college. With a mounting body of research revealing that extracurricular activities, and even patterns of informal student association in school and college life (including college dormitory life), have powerful influences on educational growth, educators were impelled to see the educational institution as a uniquely comprehensive environment for linking codified knowledge to the life and growth of the learner.

Changing Conceptions

Changes in the conception of curriculum are reflected in three succeeding editions of the *Dictionary of Education*. The 1959 edition of the *Dictionary of Education* offered the following three definitions of curriculum:

(1) a systematic group of courses or sequences of subjects required for graduation or certification in a major field of study, for example, *social studies curriculum, physical education curriculum*; (2) a general over-all plan of the content or specific materials of instruction that the school should offer the student by way of qualifying him for graduation or certification or for entrance into a professional or vocational field; (3) a group of courses and planned experiences which a student has under the guidance of the school or college. (Good, p. 149)

With the exception of the latter part of the third definition, which sees curriculum as "planned learning experiences," these definitions reflect the traditional conceptions of curriculum that were dominant until the 1930s. The last edition of the *Dictionary of Education* broadened the conception of curriculum significantly by adding to the earlier definitions the statement that curriculum "may refer to what is intended, as planned courses and other activities or intended opportunities or experiences, or to what was actualized for the learner, as in actual educational treatment or all experiences of the learner under the direction of the school" (Good, 1973, p. 157).

Although the latter definition may be criticized as too vague and broad, just as the other definitions in the *Dictionary of Education* may be criticized as too narrow and traditional, these different definitions reflect the conflicting and changing conceptions of curriculum during the twentieth century. The traditional conceptions of curriculum were no longer deemed appropriate for a progressive society.

Most significantly, the concept of curriculum as guided learning experience conceives of the teaching learning process as integral to curriculum. The dominant view among contemporary curriculum theorists regards curriculum and instruction as separate and distinct realms. The implication of this dualistic view are discussed later in this chapter.

Similar changes have been manifested on the other side of the Atlantic. The *Dictionary of Education* (1996) published in Britain (Lawton & Gordon) contrasts the "narrow" definition of curriculum—"programme for instruction"—against the wider definition that encompasses "all the learning that takes place in a school or other educational institution, planned and unplanned." The *Dictionary* offers a third definition as "a selection from the culture of a society" (p. 81).

The first definition suffers from what was discussed earlier, namely the failure to distinguish curriculum from a syllabus, a written course of study or plan that, by itself, is inert. The second definition is comprehensive and functional, but it fails to indicate the nature, organization, and treatment of knowledge so as to empower the learner toward becoming increasingly knowledge/able (able to make intelligent use of knowledge). The third definition is anthropological, and, although it is modern, also neglects to indicate the educative criteria for making and treating the cultural selections.

Extraclass Activities

The conception of curriculum as an all-school learning experience and as guided living necessitated a breakdown in the traditional, rigid separation between classroom course work and other school-sponsored learning activities. In fact, the growing acceptance of the broader conception of curriculum led to the rejection of the term *extracurriculum*, which had been used in reference to school activities deemed outside the curriculum. Such terms as *cocurricular activities* and *allied activities* began to be used, but even these were unsatisfactory because they indicated that such activities were conjoint to rather than integral to the curriculum.

Nevertheless, the practice was not to allow extra class activities to carry credits toward graduation. However, with the broadening of the curriculum, the lines between some of these activities and classroom course work became less distinct. Many schools began to organize such activities as band, orchestra, chorus, journalism, photography, filmmaking, drama, dance, and the like into formal courses carrying academic credits. A similar transformation occurred in our colleges and universities. (Today, some universities offer doctorates in filmmaking and drama, for example.)

Great impetus was given to student activity programs in progressive schools during the 1930s in growing recognition that such activities help children and youth to learn to live together and also contribute to so-called academic coursework. Field trips extended into field projects. Camping and outdoor education sponsored by the schools included not only nature study but also conservation and community service activities. An entire issue of the *Phi Delta Kappan* in 1938 was devoted to camping and outdoor education. "In all probability, the educationist of the year 2000 A.D. will look back on us and wonder why we, the school people of 1938, failed to include the camp as an integral unit of our educational system" (Schorling, p. 114). Perhaps the most outstanding early school-camp and outdoor-education programs for elementary and secondary school students were developed in California in San Diego County. In its visionary scenario for American education for the post–World War II years, the NEA's Educational Policies Commission viewed community service as integral to the educative mission of the school (1944, 1952). Community-service activities were incorporated in the problem-focused, block-time, core curriculum in progressive secondary schools. Faunce and Bossing (1958) describe how students and the core teacher in a small community traced a health problem to the water supply and enlisted the state department of health and the local government to undertake a water-system project to correct the problem (p. 321).

By the late 1950s, the curriculum retrenchment of essentialism, followed by the "pursuit of academic excellence" through the discipline-centered curriculum of the Cold War and space race, resulted in a sharp curtailment of extraclass activities and the elimination of most problem-focused core programs. To the essentialists and perennialists, extraclass activities were seen as trivial and beyond the school's purview of intellectual training. Community-service activities were caricatured by Bestor (1956) as "busywork in good causes," and the problem-focused, integrative core curriculum was seen by Bestor as producing nothing but "complete intellectual chaos" (pp. 59, 203).

Research Findings.   Emerging empirical research was showing powerfully positive relationships between participation in school activities and college aspiration and achievement. An investigation of two heterogeneous populations of high school students yielded findings that led the researcher to the following conclusions:

> Specifically, distinctive patterns of extracurricular involvement were associated with high levels of aspiration and subsequent college attainment, controlling for various measures of family socioeconomic status, ability, grade performance (in high school), and peer status. Students whose extracurricular pursuits included both athletic and service-leadership roles had not only the highest level of aspirations but also the greatest chance of fulfilling those aspirations after graduating. . . . These findings seem to suggest that the experiences provided by participation in service and leadership activities helped the student develop resources and capacities which facilitated his adjustment to the greater academic and independence demands of college. (Spady, 1971, pp. 384–385)

Despite the emergences of an inclusive conception of curriculum embracing school (and college) as a designed learning environment and way of associated living, researchers continued to use the term *extracurriculum* instead of student activity programs or extraclass activities. Nevertheless, in the *Handbook of Research in Curriculum* (1992), Berk concluded that well-controlled studies were revealing that "extracurricular participation has positive implications for many aspects of individual development, including academic performance, educational aspirations, school retention, prosocial personality characteristics, political attitudes and behavior, self-esteem, current psychological well-being and satisfaction, and future extracurricular and community participation" (p. 1031). Further, for example, the number of social studies courses taken in high school appears to have no affect on actual political activity; however, adolescent participation in school political activities does carry into young adulthood, such as campaign participation and tendency to vote and to discuss political issues (p. 1029). Berk concluded that although education and the general public appreciate the value of student activity programs, such activities are seen by school boards as being in competition with the academic curriculum (p. 1036). Berk noted that despite the widely appreciated positive influence of student activities on students, this has been "entirely overlooked in recent national reports on the quality and condition of American education" (p. 1036).

Berk (1992) holds that student activity programs are primarily the province of secondary education and that younger children are probably not mature enough to support a differentiated extracurricular program (p. 1002). There is no evidence to support such a conclusion. The middle school and upper-elementary grades are fertile grounds for pupil activity programs. Witness the power of 4-H clubs in garnering children's interests and participation, for example. In China, the authors of this text visited "Children's Palaces" where schoolchildren of all ages participated in comprehensive after-school activity programs in music, dance, the visual arts, and so on, with focused enthusiasm. Ideally, such programs should be part and parcel of in-school offerings in view of their considerable benefits for children's social and cognitive growth.

The College Experience. In his report on the college experience for the Carnegie Foundation, Boyer (1987) wrote extensively on the significance of participation in student activities apart from intercollegiate sports, which engage only a very small number of students. The quality of student involvement in activities is directly linked to the effectiveness of the undergraduate experiences. Involved students stay enrolled, observed Boyer, and activities add greatly to the intellectual life of the college community by enlarging what students are learning in their formal courses (p. 193).

Obviously, participation in student activity programs should effect an even more powerful influence in secondary school, during the formative years of adolescence, as compared with the college years. Yet the research literature on student activities in college tends to be even more unequivocally favorable than that pertaining to the secondary school. This may reflect the popular fashion of university researchers to engage in fault-finding and skepticism regarding the school experience, whereas they tend to look favorably at the college experience, which, after all, is reflective of the vineyard in which they labor.

At the college level, there is increasing recognition that informal student activities and interactions may have at least as powerful an influence on the lives of students as the formal course of study. Large-scale analyses of the research literature over a 20-year period concerning the impact of college on students led to the conclusion: "The educational impact of a college's faculty is enhanced when their contacts with students extend beyond the formal classroom to informal nonclassroom settings" (Pascarella & Terenzini, 1991, p. 620). This influence went beyond the student background characteristic and was found to be linked with such positive outcomes as "perceptions of intellectual growth during college, increases in intellectual orientation, liberalization of social and political values, growth in autonomy and independence, increases in interpersonal skills, gains in general maturity and personal development, educational aspirations and attainment, orientation toward scholarly careers, and women's interest in and choice of sex-atypical (male-dominant) careers" (p. 621). These outcomes were also evident from student peer interactions, revealing a strong influence on growth in intellectual development and orientation, academic and social self-concept, general maturity and personal development, and educational aspirations and attainment.

In another study of the research literature on the impact of the college experience on students, Astin reported similar findings revealing that the educational development of the undergraduate is strongly connected to the degree to which the student is actively engaged or involved in the extraclass college experience. General education outcomes are enhanced not only when students devote a lot of time to study, but also "when they socialize with diverse student peers, when they serve as tutors for each other, and when they engage each other in discussions of contemporary issues." Astin (1993) concluded that in view of the findings, it was clear that faculty need to rethink radically their approach to curriculum in that they focus excessively on course "content" in their identification with their own disciplines. Instead, there would be much greater payoffs in learning outcomes by placing more emphasis on pedagogy and the interpersonal and environmental context of college life (pp. 425–427). In effect, Astin was alluding to the power of the hidden curriculum, or what the authors of this text call the *collateral curriculum* in educational development. If the collateral curriculum exerts such a powerful influence on the college student's educational development, then it must surely be at least equally influential on the youngsters at the secondary and elementary levels. In effect, extraclass activities cannot be regarded as merely extracurricular because they have a pervasive bearing on educational development including academic achievement. The nature and significance of the collateral curriculum are discussed in some detail toward the close of this chapter.

Significantly, in 1993 President Clinton chose Rutgers University to announce his program of national service for college students because Rutgers had in place the Civic Education and Community Service Program, which involves more than 600 students; students can choose nontraditional ways to obtain academic credit. Such programs are not new, although most do not involve academic credit. The Columbia College Citizenship Council at Columbia University has engaged undergraduates in organized community service since its founding in 1957. During the mid-1960s, students in the Citizenship Council worked with the City University of New York's pioneering College Discovery and Development Program, a citywide effort to discover and develop the college potential of at-risk youngsters beginning at the end of the ninth grade (Tanner, D., & Lachica, 1962). The City University program was a forerunner of the federal Upward Bound program. Today, the City University and Columbia projects are administered separately, but they have been in continuous operation for more than four decades.

The reader should recall that the report of the Educational Policies Commission dating back to 1944 had described how secondary schools can institute community service programs as integral to the curriculum. In *High School: A Report on Secondary Education in America* (1983), Ernest Boyer of the

Carnegie Foundation pointed to the powerfully positive influences of student activities in socialization and academic success, and he recommended that every student be required to complete a community service activity (p. 209).

Recognizing the connection between participation in student activities in high school and college success, leading colleges have been regarding such participation as a key criterion for admission. High school students and their guidance counselors are fully aware of this. The problem, however, is whether the student participates in extraclass activities mainly to buttress the chances for college admission or because of a genuine need for the fulfillment of enrichment, exploratory, and special-interest experiences beyond the confines of the established coursework.

Collateral Lessons. The inescapable connection between student activities and the formal coursework came to be recognized by the U.S. Supreme Court in a 1988 decision in which students had protested the principal's excision of two pages from the school newspaper. The court ruled that the work on the newspaper was indeed curricular in that it was under teacher supervision and carried academic credit. Consequently, reasoned the court, the students were not entitled to full protection of the First Amendment. The dissenting opinion of the court pointed to the danger of school authorities exercising flagrant censorship over student ideas. For the students involved in this case, the real lesson seemed to be that they are on a waiting list for their rights to express their ideas on extant issues (Hazelwood School District v. Kuhlmeier, 108 U.S. 562).

Because the success of the formal course of study is not independent of student activities and the wider life of the school, effective curriculum planning requires that student activities be conceived and conducted as integral to curriculum and not as "extracurricular." In the case of the Supreme Court decision upholding the power of the school administration to censor the school newspaper, the collateral or hidden lesson for students is that constitutional rights do not apply to them, and that such rights are merely abstractions from an abstract document. As discussed later in this chapter, it should not be surprising, then, when it is found that students develop antidemocratic attitudes from their experience in school and society.

Educators have come to recognize increasingly what the experimentalist-progressives discovered early in the twentieth century, namely the powerful effects of participation in student activities on learning outcomes, cognitive as well as affective, regardless of whether such participation carries academic credit. Even though participation may not carry academic credit, it cannot be treated effectively as outside the real curriculum.

The Curriculum-Instruction Dualism

The contention that curriculum and instruction are separate realms has gained widespread acceptance among contemporary curriculum theorists. The emergence of this dualistic view, as mentioned earlier in this chapter, stems from several developments, not the least of which is the burgeoning body of research on instruction and the technology of instruction. Such research has become so specialized that much of it is focused on the analysis of teaching as severed from subject matter and from the learning that occurs as a result of teaching. Hence the behaviorists are not alone in ascribing to the curriculum-instruction dualism.

Content and Process. The traditional notion of curriculum as content and instruction as process has been embraced by educators over many years. As held by Broudy, Smith, and Burnett (1964), "curriculum consists primarily of certain content organized into categories of instruction . . . modes of teaching are not, strictly speaking, a part of curriculum" (p. 79). In effect, curriculum is merely content or subject matter having an existence independent of the processes through which the knowledge is produced. Such dualistic conceptions of curriculum and instruction regard knowledge as independent of the processes through which the learner becomes knowledgeable. Yet knowledge is at the same time a product of inquiry and the raw material for fueling, shaping, and controlling inquiry. To ascribe a separate existence to knowledge, an existence independent of the ways and means through which knowledge is developed and through which people become knowledgeable, is like separating the act of swimming from water.

The divorce between content and method is reflected to this day in the test-driven curriculum, the treatment of subject matter as ends rather than raw material, and the isolation of studies from life experience.

Skill and Meaning. Virtually every teacher has observed children who are able to read aloud but unable to explain the meaning of what they have just finished reading. In effect their performance in the act of reading demonstrates that the *skill* of reading can be attained in the absence of meaning. Without meaning there can be no transformation of the skill and the material that is read into the working power of intelligence.

Curiously, the research literature on reading uses such terminology as "reading of content materials" and "content textbooks," and some of the leading textbooks on the teaching of reading bear such titles as *Content Area Reading* (Vacca & Vacca, 2002), indicating that reading is also taught as a skill apart from "content" or ideas. Reading is a process of communication of ideas. As a thought process, it is inseparable from what it is that is being communicated. The material that is to be read remains inert until it becomes meaningfully actualized by the reader.

In the same vein, subject matter is just subject matter, and a plan for learning is just a plan for learning. The material is inert until it is put into operation and tested on the anvil of experience. This is why experimentalist-progressives rejected the traditional conceptions of curriculum and struggled to bring a fuller, richer, and more functional meaning to curriculum.

Ends-Means Dualism. Although contemporary curriculum writers differ markedly in their definitions of curriculum, we have seen how an ends-means dualism is inherent in many of these definitions. A dualistic doctrine has come to be embraced that severs curriculum from instruction. The doctrine of dualism violates Dewey's thesis of the intrinsic continuity of ends and means. According to Dewey (1916), "an end which grows up within an activity as plan for its direction is always both ends and means . . . every divorce of end from means diminishes by that much the significance of the activity" (p. 124).

To conceive of knowledge as merely results that are separate from the actions and events that produced the results robs any activity of its meaning. "An aim implies an orderly and ordered activity, one in which the order consists in the progressive completing of a process," wrote Dewey (1916), and when one is shooting at a target, "not the target but *hitting* the target is the end in view" (pp. 119, 123). To conceive of ends and means as separate or discontinuous is to separate artificially functions that are organically interdependent.

There is no point in shooting without a target to shoot at, nor is there any sense in devising targets without conceiving of the act of hitting the targets.

In a similar vein, to separate science from its bodies of organized knowledge and its methods of inquiry would be destructive to science. Thus, to sever curriculum from instruction not only is of doubtful use and validity in the practical world of the school but also creates ruptures and stumbling blocks in curriculum research and development. For example, as plans were being made for the national curriculum-reform projects during the second half of the 1950s, it soon became apparent that curriculum reform required much more than course-content revision. The traditional notion of science as organized subject matter had to be rejected in view of the realization that science also is a way of thinking and involves certain systematic methods of inquiry. It thus became necessary to conceive of subject matter and method as inseparable.

Indeed scientific progress has required dramatic changes in the conceptions of science. As Einstein (1950) put the matter, "the realm of physics has so expanded that it seems to be limited only by the limitations of the method itself" (p. 98). This observation should give curriculum theorists food for thought concerning the long-held dualism between content and method, or curriculum and instruction. Knowledge has come to be seen as a way of knowing and searching, and not as an end product or body of subject matter separate from the methods through which it was developed and through which it is made comprehensible and applicable.

When contemporary curriculum scholars dissect curriculum from instruction, they are embracing a dualism leading to educational discontinuity and isolation. The classic philosophical systems embraced many dualisms, such as the separation of mind from activity. Dewey pointed out in 1899 that the then current question of separating subject matter and method "is a survival of the medieval philosophic dualism" (in Archambault, 1964, p. 132). Contemporary educators who separate curriculum from instruction are, in a similar vein, separating knowledge from the activities known as teaching and learning. One of the consequences is that a considerable portion of the research on classroom instruction has been conducted with a focus on teacher-pupil verbal interaction without any connection whatsoever with the organized knowledge known as subject matter and resultant outcomes in pupil growth.

Research on Teaching

Administratively, the consequences of the separation of curriculum and instruction finds the study of teaching relegated to one group of specialists, the assessment of learning outcomes to another group of specialists, the determination of what should be taught to the educational policy makers external to the school, and the "delivery" of instruction to the teacher. Such jurisdictional separations reduce the professional role of the teacher and supervisor, and they result in mechanical and disjointed prescriptions. In the field of supervision, for example, schools of education offer course work in the supervision of instruction, and school districts have supervisors of instruction as though the matter of curriculum is settled by state-mandated subjects and external testing.

In separating instruction from curriculum, a growing number of educational researchers have developed a specialty of analyzing the act of teaching. Through these efforts, a considerable number of systems for analyzing teaching have been produced. Dunkin and Biddle (1974) observe, "In spite of the sharp increase in studies of classroom events, most recent research has focused on the *activities* rather than the *effects* of teaching," and much of the research on learning has been directed only at special kinds of learning and such research "does not meet the challenge provided by the sheer complexity of the classroom setting and of the learning tasks pursued there" (pp. 15–16, 22–23).

An examination of the last two editions of the *Handbook of Research on Teaching* reveal a perpetuation of this problem and the acknowledgment that only a beginning has been made in linking teacher behavior to student achievement and to other outcomes (Richardson, ed., 2001; Wittrock, ed., 1986). Researchers tend to focus on that which is most amenable to measurement, not necessarily that which is most significant in education. The need to study the effects of different classroom and school learning environments and resources remains an unmet challenge.

What is the point of studying teaching unless such study is related to student growth? Is such study undertaken merely to provide teachers with alternative and prescriptive models of teaching? After discussing some of the "evils in education that flow from the isolation of method from subject matter," Dewey (1916) observed that "[n]othing has brought pedagogical theory into greater disrepute than the belief that it is identified with the handing out to teachers recipes and models to be followed in teaching" (p. 199).

Search for a Theory of Instruction.   In *Toward a Theory of Instruction* (1966), Bruner reaches the following conclusion:

> Finally, a theory of instruction seeks to take account of the fact that a curriculum reflects not only the nature of knowledge itself but also the nature of the knower and the knowledge-getting process. It is an enterprise par excellence where the line between subject matter and method grows necessarily indistinct. . . . Knowledge is a process, not a product. (p. 72)

If Bruner's thesis is valid, then a search for a theory of instruction apart from a theory of curriculum would seem fruitless. Although Bruner appears to recognize this, he proposes several elements or features for a so-called theory of instruction, which appear to be largely behavioristic (i.e., narrow sequencing of material, specifying and pacing rewards and punishments, and so on), without attempting to attack the problem of a theory of curriculum. This is not to fault Bruner for failing to produce a theory of curriculum but rather to point out the contradiction in seeking a theory of instruction apart from a theory of curriculum and, at the same time, vaingloriously declaring that instruction and curriculum are necessarily indistinct.

The terms *teaching* and *instruction* are generally used interchangeably. It is revealing that although Dewey did not directly ascribe different meanings to these terms, he tended to use the term *teaching* in a broader sense as a vitally shared experience in the art of communication. In contrast, he tended to use the term *instruction* in a narrower framework, such as in criticizing traditional education as proceeding "by instruction taken in a literal sense, a building into mind from without." In acknowledging the contributions of Herbart to teaching method, Dewey (1916) pointed out that Herbart's "philosophy is eloquent about the duty of the teacher in instructing pupils . . . it slurs over the fact that the environment involves a personal sharing in common experiences. . . . It takes, in brief, everything educational into account save its essence" (pp. 81, 84).

The Hidden Curriculum and the Collateral Curriculum

In recent years, the literature in education has given increasing attention to the hidden curriculum, or the discrepancy between what is intended and what is actually experienced (Erickson & Shutz, 1992, pp. 474–475). The tendency has been to couch the hidden curriculum negatively, although its power may indeed be positive (pp. 474–475). As treated by Jackson (1968) and Dreeben (1968), classroom and school life provide not only a formal or "official" curriculum, but also a "hidden" curriculum through which students learn certain social norms—punctuality, taking one's turn (patience), conformity, good work habits, and so on—behaviors that may have a payoff not only in school, but also for successful socialization throughout life. Of course, there can be a negative side to the hidden curriculum, such as when students learn to dislike mathematics, or when pupil obedience outweighs initiative.

However, the notion of the hidden curriculum was seized upon by critical theorists and others of the radical left to validate their thesis that the school is a chief agency for inculcating the attributes for social control over the rising generation (Apple, 1990, pp. 49, 80–81). In *Democracy and Education* (1916), Dewey had turned the notion of social control and social efficiency on its head by pointing out how the school in a democracy must develop the powers of the rising generation to be in control rather than under control of their destinies through the exercise of the method of intelligence, while social efficiency is measured by universal educational opportunity (pp. 142, 176). But critical theorists have taken primarily a negative and even somewhat sinister view of the hidden curriculum as a covert function for imposing external social controls and mechanisms for social efficiencies to fit the dominant corporate interests of society. Giroux (1983) urged fellow critical theorists to study the full workings of the hidden curriculum so that they might find ways to counter the dominating classroom practices so as "to minimize the impact of the hidden curriculum while simultaneously helping teachers and students develop radical classroom practices that work in the interest of emancipatory rather than dominating concerns" (p. 60). "Furthermore," stated Giroux (1988), "we are provided with little understanding of how the hidden curriculum in schools works in a subtly discriminating way to discredit the dreams, experiences, and knowledge associated with students from specific class, racial, and gender groupings" (p. 182).

The Collateral Curriculum

Recognizing that much of the controversy on the hidden curriculum has become unproductive, in the third edition of this text (1995), the authors proposed the use of the term *collateral curriculum* rather than hidden curriculum, following Dewey's use of the term *collateral learning*. However, the term *collateral* is not at all synonymous with *hidden*. In fact, the concept of collateral curriculum encompasses far richer and more inclusive meanings than hidden curriculum. We have discussed the powerful impact of school and college life on students beyond the formal course work. Hence the design and conduct of the school and college as learning communities cannot be separated from the formal course work as far as intellectual and social growth of the learner are concerned. Consequently, it appears to be more productive to use the term *collateral* curriculum rather than hidden curriculum if educators are to unleash the fullest positive potential of education.

Collateral Learning.   In focusing narrowly on the information and skills to be learned through the formal course of study, teachers tend to overlook the importance of collateral learning. Pupils may receive a grade of A in a literature course, but if they have learned to dislike good literature it is doubtful that they will be impelled to read such literature on their own. In this case the collateral learning will have a more powerful and enduring impact on the learner's present and future behavior than the target subject matter. Indeed, most of the factual information learned in school is readily forgotten soon after the examination, whereas collateral learning as connected with attitudes, appreciations, and values can be far more enduring. "Perhaps the greatest of all pedagogical fallacies is the notion that a person learns only the particular thing he is studying at the time," observed Dewey (1938), who went on to stress how "collateral learning in the way of formation of enduring attitudes, of likes and dislikes, may be and often is much more important than the spelling lesson or lesson in geography or history that is learned." And, added Dewey, "The most important attitude that can be formed is that of desire to go on learning" (p. 48). If the curriculum weakens this impetus, it will have failed to realize its most important meaning and mission.

Those involved in conducting the Eight-Year Study were well aware of the collateral curriculum in addressing the significance of learning outcomes as evidenced by growth in interests, attitudes, appreciations, and intellectual curiosity. Ingenious evaluation instruments were developed to assess these outcomes, which, to this day, more than a half century later, are rarely treated in curriculum evaluation (Smith, Tyler, & Evaluation Staff, 1942; Chamberlin, Chamberlin, Drought, & Scott, 1942). One of the lessons from the Eight-Year Study is that collateral learning must not be regarded as something outside the curriculum or as merely an incidental and accidental outcome of the curriculum. Desirable collateral learning is much more likely to occur if it is treated as integral to the planned and guided learning experiences that comprise the curriculum.

Similarly, extraclass activities should not be considered as outside the curriculum. As discussed earlier, such activities can exert powerful influences on the learner. If the curriculum is so conceived as to correlate such activities with those more directly connected with the formal course of study, the possibilities for realizing the desired learning outcomes of the curriculum are enhanced enormously.

As noted, the concept of hidden curriculum has been used by education critics to describe mainly unintended and negative outcomes from school settings, such as learning to dislike mathematics or learning to be docile. It has also been used to describe intended and positive outcomes that are provided for implicitly rather than as an explicit part of the curriculum, such as those pertaining to socialization. The broadening of the conception of curriculum to encompass all of the learning experiences provided by the school attests to the recognition of the importance of what heretofore was treated as of peripheral significance or as nonexistent. One may learn about the social significance of cooperation or minority rights in the abstract in the social studies class, but whether such learning has become part of the developmental process of the learner is evidenced by actual behavior in the laboratory, shop, or playing field.

Dreeben (1968) has pointed out that in addition to the learnings that occur as a result of the formal course of study, students learn to accept certain social norms and to act in accordance with them. He observes that, ironically, some of the bureaucratic properties of school organization, which have been regarded negatively in some of the literature on schooling, such as those which call for the submergence of self-interest and the breakdown of certain parochial divisions, also have positive functions. According to Dreeben, "it should also be remembered that the same norms seem to contribute also to a sense of tolerance, fairness, consideration, and trustfulness, and to the expectation among members of the populace that they possess a legitimate claim to participate in all areas of public life and that none shall be entitled to special treatment of whatever kind—expectations whose prevalence today underlie some of the more radical social changes that have taken place in American history" (pp. 147–148).

Further Illustrations and Implications of the Collateral Curriculum. A few rather common examples will help illustrate the power of the collateral curriculum. When Shakespeare is studied as literature, many students learn to dislike Shakespeare. When Shakespeare is studied as theater and is *performed*, students are more likely to appreciate and even enjoy Shakespeare; they also learn about Shakespeare's work authentically—in the medium for which the work was intended—from the stage, not the page.

As another example, when seventh graders memorize the various formulas using π in solving problems on the dimensions of a circle, they make frequent errors in calculation. Several months later, when taking a multiple-choice achievement test, they proceed to calculate laboriously the answers to each item without realizing that calculation may not even be necessary. Under the time pressures of the test, they are more likely to make absurd errors, such as coming up with a diameter that is, say, little more than half the circumference. And because they are taking so much time to do their calculations, they must rush through the other test items that may require calculation as well as cogitation to the extent that they suffer a penalty for lack of time. Many of the students learn that they dislike mathematics.

In contrast, when the students discover the meaning of π (and its significance in history) through the use of string, ruler, and all sorts of circular objects, and proceed to formulate "lawful" statements in their own words concerning the relationships between the various dimensions of the circular objects, they learn collaterally what a formula is and why formulas are so indispensable in solving mathematical and scientific problems. When taking a multiple-choice achievement test several months later, they are often able to select the correct answers for the circumference, diameter, and radius of a circle without having

to do calculations. (Or, if they should need to do some calculations, they are able to move ahead with the test more confidently.) But the most telling outcome is that mathematics is more meaningful and is more likely to be appreciated and even enjoyed when approached thoughtfully rather than mechanistically.

It can be seen that the collateral curriculum resides in learning to understand, appreciate, and even enjoy mathematics (or Shakespeare), or learning to dislike mathematics (or Shakespeare).

As another example, students are studying a unit on the Middle Ages and the event of bubonic plague. They then go on to study Chaucer, the Anglo-French wars, and so on. Chronology determines the topic. In a contrasting classroom and school, when students are studying the devastating effects of the bubonic plague on Europe, the curriculum is made unitary by studying science as well as politics in history and relating the Black Death of 1347 to twentieth-century epidemics, including influenza, tuberculosis (the "white plague"), and AIDS. In the former illustration, the curriculum is governed by a factual order of events and dates that are painstakingly memorized for the test and painlessly forgotten. And the curriculum is likely to be boring. In the latter case, the curriculum is governed by *ideas* that relate to the life of the learner in the widest social context. Capitalizing on students' interests, the teacher of history will work with the teacher of literature and science on an interrelated curriculum so that, for example, students may be reading biographies of scientists while studying history.

Doctrine of Specificity. As noted earlier in this chapter, definitions of curriculum by behaviorists and others who incorporate in their definitions the measurement of outcomes in terms of specifiable objectives fail to allow for some of the most significant powers of curriculum engagement, namely collateral learning through the collateral curriculum. Although not a behaviorist, as cited earlier in this chapter, Hirst (1974) defines curriculum as "a plan of activities deliberately organized so that pupils will attain, by learning, certain educational ends or objectives. . . . I see a curriculum arising only in a teaching situation, where a set of objectives is clearly specifiable" (p. 132).

Traditional definitions fail to account for what Dewey (1938, p. 48) referred to as "collateral learning" or the collateral curriculum. The collateral curriculum may often be far more powerful than the intended curriculum. For example, after completing their geography lessons with wall maps, young children may point to the ceiling when asked the direction of north and to the floor when asked the direction of south. And they may be unable to transfer their map work in geography to conceptualizing the geography of their locale and to the practical uses of simple maps. Under such circumstances, the intended curriculum is dysfunctional and miseducative. It is also not uncommon for the collateral curriculum to have effects that are far more powerful in a positive direction than the intended curriculum.

Further, the teaching-learning process is conducted mainly in *emergent* situations in which actual events and consequences do not follow the specifiable objectives and instead take unpredictable turns. In contrast, the *established-convergent* situation is expected to be perfectly predictable and specifiable, such as in the factory-production line where quality control is measured by uniformity of product, and efficiency by measure of output over input (Tanner, D., 2000b, p. 198). In the emergent situation, human variability and differences allow for improvement. The emergent situation is almost invariably more interesting than the established-convergent situation. The former allows for fruitful mistakes. The latter values the specifiable and predictable—anathema to human nature and, especially, the nature of the child and adolescent.

Virtually every state mandates the teaching of U.S. history and government or civics, including the Constitution and Bill of Rights, on the ground that it will foster good citizenship. During the late 1950s and early 1960s the Purdue Opinion Panel under H. H. Remmers found that although the Constitution and Bill of Rights were universally required to be studied in history and social studies, adolescents might have been learning the factual material for the test, but they were unable to relate the facts to their own lives and to the wider social issues. As a consequence, a very high proportion of the adolescents were found to be embracing antidemocratic and authoritarian attitudes in direct violation of the Constitution and Bill of Rights.

Replications of Remmers's studies a quarter of a century later revealed that the same conditions were still prevalent despite the fact that the Purdue research was conducted in an era of rank McCarthyism, whereas we like to think of our contemporary era as more enlightened (Galasso, 1986; Johnson, 1986; Flathmann, 1987). Such findings reveal that it is not sufficient to mandate certain studies in the curriculum, but that the attitudes, understandings, and values that adolescents bring with them to school cannot be ignored or compartmentalized as outside the curriculum. The social life of the school may enhance democratic attitudes or perpetuate antidemocratic attitudes, and the mandated study of the Bill of Rights, treated in splendid academic isolation, becomes "purely academic" or "merely academic." As such, it has no bearing on the life and times of adolescents.

Clearly, then, if educators recognize the significance of learning experience and outcomes, positively and negatively, then they will see the need to take the fullest possible account of them in curriculum development and evaluation. Hence they will not be working unwittingly with a hidden curriculum; instead, they will be taking into account the collateral learning that gives full measure to that thing we call curriculum.

As mentioned, the experimentalist-progressive educators who designed and evaluated the Eight-Year Study were well aware of the significance of the collateral curriculum, and so there was no need to mull over a hidden curriculum. For example, they investigated not only the learnings that grew out of the literary works in the syllabi, but also the nature and extent of voluntary, recreational reading in which students were engaged. Obviously, when students are encouraged to use the school library at all hours for recreational reading, browsing, and working on projects of their own making as well as on assignments, the school curriculum takes on a wider and richer meaning and function.

The experimentalist-progressives who sought a definition of curriculum as "the life and program of the school," or as "all the experiences a learner has under the auspices of the school," appear well justified in their efforts despite the problem of ambiguity and vulnerability to assault by the essentialists who viewed this as license to call "anything the cat dragged in" as having a legitimate place in the curriculum.

A Unitary Conception of Curriculum

The emergence of the curriculum field as a distinct subject of study has given rise to many conflicting conceptions of curriculum. The reader may justifiably conclude that no single definition can satisfy all parties concerned, because, after all, the different definitions reflect the different schools of thought in the curriculum field—as well as changing conceptions of organized knowledge, the learner, the educative process, and the larger social situation. If this is the case, then, is agreement on definition so essential to conceptual progress, as many curricularists believe? Is it possible to have a general basis for consensus in a field without agreement on definition? In this concluding section, the foregoing questions are addressed in connection with the importance of consensus for conceptual progress in the curriculum field.

Codified Knowledge and Becoming Knowledge/able

Over the years curricularists have sought an adequate definition of curriculum. We have seen how the con-

ception of curriculum has changed dramatically over time, reflecting the advances in organized knowledge, advances in our understanding of the learner, and changing expectations concerning the reciprocal roles of school and society. How these factors are seen is dependent on the philosophy of the educator. Hence we have seen how a traditionalist defines curriculum differently than an experimentalist-progressive.

As shown in Table 5.1, curriculum has been variously defined as (1) the cumulative tradition of organized knowledge, (2) the instructional plan or course of study, (3) measured instructional outcomes (technological production system), (4) cultural reproduction, (5) knowledge selection/organization from the culture, (6) modes of thought, and (7) guided living/planned

Table 5.1   Conflicting Conceptions of Curriculum.

Conception of Curriculum	Controlling Mode	Function
Traditionalist		
Cumulative tradition of organized knowledge	Academic subject matter "Permanent" studies (classics) "Essential" studies/skills Established disciplines	Subject-matter mastery Cultural inheritance Mental discipline Knowledge transmission
Disciplinary knowledge	Disciplinary inquiry	Specialized knowledge production in academic disciplines
Instructional plan/course of study	Stated intentions for instruction (context and methods)	(Eclectic)
Measured instructional outcomes ("products")	Fixed standards by subjects External testing Technological production (input/output measures) Behavioristic objectives	Efficiency Accountability Controlled behavior Subject-matter mastery Outcomes predictability
Progressivist		
Knowledge selection/ organization from the culture	Cultural norms for individual and social growth Curriculum synthesis	Cultural assimilation and improvement Democratic citizenship
Modes of thought (as citizen)	Reflective thinking Problem method Curriculum synthesis	Personal-social growth Democratic citizenship
Guided experience/planned learning environment	Community life Felt needs Reflective thinking Problem method Curriculum synthesis Behavioral goals and outcomes	Effective living Self-realization Personal-social growth Democratic citizenship
Reconstruction of knowledge and experience	Cultural experience integral to life Reflective thinking Problem method Curriculum synthesis	Personal control of knowledge and experience Personal-social growth Democratic citizenship

learning environment. As discussed throughout this chapter, each definition reflects a particular and often conflicting perspective—and fails to engender a full meaning of curriculum. Some definitions are so narrow that they convey a restricted and only partial meaning of curriculum, at least with regard to how the concept has been treated in the practical world of the educational institution. Other definitions are so broad that they fail to distinguish between the function of the school or university from that of any other agency having some sort of educative function, whether central or peripheral to its mission.

The meaning of curriculum has changed so significantly over the years and reflects so many conflicting schools of thought that it is highly unlikely that any universally accepted definition can be reached. Nevertheless, curricularists may utilize a definition to describe the orientation of their work in the field. The present authors contend that the school or university is unique in its organization and treatment of knowledge and experience in attempting to meet its educative function. No other institution of society compares with the school or university in the systematic reconstruction of knowledge and experience for educative purposes. Furthermore, the dynamic nature of knowledge and experience invalidates the notion of knowledge or learning as terminal achievements or ends. If knowledge and experience are dynamic, then education should have no end beyond itself. Obviously the concept of curriculum takes on a special meaning in a democratic society as opposed to a totalitarian society. Of course, all civilized societies regard curriculum as the medium through which codified knowledge is so treated as to enable the rising generation to become increasingly knowledge/able. In a democratic society, being knowledge/able puts the individual *in* control of experience as opposed to being put *under* control. This brings us to a more comprehensive and unified concept of curriculum.

A Proposed Definition

The most profound and systematic analysis of the curriculum and its social significance was made by the American philosopher John Dewey (1859–1952). In his lectures to parents of children attending his laboratory school at the University of Chicago before the turn of the century (published in 1899 in *The School and Society*), Dewey called for a new conception, organization, and treatment of curriculum in accord with the dynamic nature of knowledge and the changing

social conditions auguring the democratic prospect. Consequently, the mission of the school and its curriculum must be seen in these terms: "All that society has accomplished for itself is put, through the agency of the school, at the disposal of its future members. All its better thoughts of itself it hopes to realize through the new possibilities thus open to its future self" (p. 7).

In effect, the school curriculum is presumably designed not only to inculcate each member of the rising generation in the best elements of knowledge, systematically organized or codified since the dawn of civilization, but also to enable each member of the rising generation to use that knowledge to improve the life of the individual and the life of society. (And all this through a system of universal public education spanning 12 short years.)

We close this chapter with the definition of curriculum proposed at the chapter's opening, a definition derived from Dewey's definition of education. Although Dewey never explicitly defined the curriculum, his exhaustive writings on curriculum did provide definitive meaning to the concept. Indeed his definition of education renders such a definitive meaning. For Dewey viewed education as a *generative* process—that is, a process through which the learner extends and deepens the capability of exercising intelligent control over changing conditions of life. In his orchestral work, *Democracy and Education* (1916), Dewey not only forged a systematic theory of education in a free society, but also devoted a series of chapters to the nature of knowledge and subject matter, and to the various areas of the curriculum and how they must be treated in their interdependence. He offered a definition of education as "that reconstruction or reorganization of experience which adds to the meaning of experience, and which increases ability to direct the course of subsequent experience" (1916, pp. 89–90). Under this definition, curriculum cannot be "delivered." Curriculum requires the reconstruction, reorganization, and transformation of knowledge into the working power of intelligence on the part of the teacher and learner.

From such a definition of education, the authors of this text offer the following definition of curriculum: *that reconstruction of knowledge and experience that enables the learner to grow in exercising intelligent control of subsequent knowledge and experience* (see Table 5.1). Through the medium of that thing we call curriculum, the learner is to grow in knowledge/ ability—or in the social power and insight required of the good person leading the good life in the good society.

Perspective

Educational institutions are constantly engaged in curriculum decisions without giving corresponding attention to curriculum as a subject of thought. As education begets new knowledge at a seemingly accelerated pace, the response has been to parcel such knowledge into increasingly specialized domains. However, the specialization and segmentation of knowledge have made the curriculum more remote from life at a time of a rising demand to make the curriculum more responsive to emerging societal needs and problems.

During the early decades of the twentieth century, the long-standing conception of curriculum as the cumulative tradition of organized knowledge came to be challenged.

Traditionalists continued to see the curriculum as a distillation of the cumulative tradition of organized knowledge, or as synonymous with the course of study. Pressures to promote educational efficiency and accountability gave impetus to the test-driven curriculum, with curriculum seen in terms of instructional ends or measurable (test) results or products. Progressivists sought a more comprehensive and functional conception of curriculum as a planned learning environment or as the guided experiences provided under the auspices of the school. They were keenly aware that experiences in the wider life of the school often have a more powerful and lasting impact on what is learned than the formal course of study. In effect they began to recognize the power of collateral learning and the need to take deliberate account of such experience as integral to curriculum.

The great variety of conflicting definitions of curriculum emerging in the twentieth century reflected differences in the vantage points from which curriculum is studied, conflicting educational philosophies, changing societal influences and demands on education, and the enormous difficulty in seeking to define such a complex concept, which, like knowledge itself, is limited only by the boundaries and tools of thought.

Each of the types of definitions of curriculum enumerated presents serious difficulties. When curriculum is conceived as guided experience, we are left with no clues as to how such experience in school differs from guided experience provided by other societal institutions and processes. Although it can be argued that there should be no sharp lines of demarcation between school and life, the school would not exist if it did not provide unique and authentic learning experiences—experiences that could not be provided adequately in any other way.

Most of the other types of definitions of curriculum raise the specter of dualism: between thought and action, between subject matter and instruction, between ends and means. It is as if to separate the act of talking from the language that is spoken. Knowledge is severed from the processes by which it is created, transmitted, and transformed. However theoretically derived, such separations are fictional constructs that cannot be taken as representing the real, practical world of curriculum and the school. In order to avoid drowning in a sea of complexities, humans create systems or ways of analyzing phenomena, but the trouble begins when they take their own fictional constructs and assume that these constructs are true in the larger ecological picture. In thinking about curriculum, various curriculum writers have sought to dissect it so that each specialist is given a piece of the action. For example, in separating curriculum from instruction, we have researchers who study instruction apart from whatever it is that is being taught and learned. Although such separations may enhance specialized scholarship, they tend to become self-serving exercises that cloud rather than illuminate curricular problems.

The conceptions of curriculum as used by experimentalist-progressives were more encompassing and functional in giving recognition to the wider nature of knowledge and the learning process, as well as the school as a specially designed environment for learning. Yet their proposed definitions remained somewhat vague in not being connected with the conception of knowledge as codified or systematized, and necessarily coupled with the processes through which one becomes knowledge/able. John Dewey defined education as "that reconstruction or reorganization of experience which adds to the meaning of experience, and which increases ability to direct the course of subsequent experience." Dewey's definition clearly sees education as an open process to transform experience into the working power of intelligence. Extending Dewey's definition of education, the authors of this text offer the following definition of curriculum: *that reconstruction of knowledge and experience that enables the learner to grow in exercising intelligent control of subsequent knowledge and experience.*

Educators have no way of knowing the exact nature of the subsequent experience of the learner in life. But if the process of education and that thing we call curriculum are successful here and now, the learner will be enabled to grow in social power and insight throughout life.

In the definition of curriculum proposed by the authors of this text, the curriculum is seen as a unity in which the reconstruction of knowledge is integrally related to the learner's ability to increase his or her control of knowledge and experience. If the school conceives of curriculum in this way, the curriculum will be unified rather than fragmented, and personal-social problems and needs will not be considered intrusions on the work of the school.

PROBLEMS FOR STUDY AND DISCUSSION

1. How do you account for the wide differences among contemporary curriculum writers in defining curriculum?
2. What are your views on the issue concerning the dualism between curriculum and instruction, or between subject matter and method?
3. In searching for a theory of instruction, Bruner acknowledges that "a curriculum reflects not only the nature of knowledge itself but also the nature of the knower and the knowledge-getting process," and he concludes that "knowledge is a process, not a product." [Jerome S. Bruner, *Toward a Theory of Instruction* (Cambridge, MA: Harvard University Press, 1966), p. 72.]
   In view of Bruner's statement, does it makes sense to seek a theory of instruction apart from a theory of curriculum? Explain.
4. What significance for curriculum lies in Einstein's observation that "the realm of physics has so expanded that it seems to be limited only by the method itself"? [Albert Einstein, *Out of My Later Years* (New York: Philosophical Library, 1950), p. 98.]
5. What is your assessment of the definition of curriculum proposed by the authors of this text?
6. Would you say that the curriculum in your school is test driven? Why or why not? What are the consequences of the test-driven curriculum?
7. What is the significance of collateral learning and the collateral curriculum? The authors of this text point out that if collateral learning and the collateral curriculum are taken into account, much of what lies in what has been called the hidden curriculum would be revealed. (It would no longer be hidden.) Do you agree? Explain.
8. As a high school student, did you participate in any school activities (collateral learning/collateral curriculum) outside the formal course of study that exerted a positive or negative influence on your attitudes, interests, appreciations, values, or academic achievement? As a college student? Explain.
9. In what ways is the concept of curriculum given special meaning and treatment in connection with the school or college, as contrasted against other major social institutions?
10. The term *curriculum delivery* is in common usage in the education literature. What does this expression signify for the role of the teacher? If the curriculum is to be "delivered," who makes the curriculum? What is implied by this expression for the concept of *knowledge* and the process through which the learner is to become *knowledge/able*?

CHAPTER 6

A Paradigm for the Curriculum Field
Compass for Curriculum Renewal

The maturity of a field of scholarship is characterized by a struggle to find unity; the formative years are characterized by fragmentation and disputation. The struggle for unity is not aimed at building conformity or eliminating diversity, but at enhancing comprehensibility. In this effort, the specifics of analysis yield to the interrelations of synthesis. Specification yields to generalization. The practical world of experience becomes more comprehensible and manageable.

In this chapter a compass or paradigm is presented to provide the keys to curriculum renewal and to explain why so many curriculum reforms are destined for failure from the start. We have used the term *paradigm* as synonymous with compass, indicating that paradigms provide direction for professional practitioners in their work. The reader should not be put off by the paradigm concept, for it actually is a simplified representation of the consensual elements that govern the practice of any profession. Virtually every professional field is governed by systems of principles, exemplars, models, and procedural techniques that advance the knowledge and practice of the field. Taken together, these systems of principles, exemplars, and techniques are referred to as paradigms. Professional fields also use these paradigms in the preparation of future practitioners.

Put simply, a curriculum reform effort is destined for failure if the design and function of the curriculum violates the nature of the learner and violates the democratic prospect. These then are three fundamental factors in the educational process that must be seen in complementary or harmonic relationship: (1) the nature and needs of the learner; (2) the kind of society professed, upheld, and sought (e.g., democratic); and (3) the structure and function of the curriculum. The three fundamental factors are key elements of the curriculum paradigm. In this chapter, the struggle to build a paradigm for curriculum development is examined with a view toward advancing professional practice, as opposed to following whatever sociopolitical tide may be dominant at a particular time.

The Route Toward a Paradigm for the Curriculum Field

Since the appearance of Thomas Kuhn's *The Structure of Scientific Revolutions* (1962, 1970, 1996), there has been a growing body of literature on the significance of paradigms in scholarly inquiry. Unfortunately, some of the literature has treated the paradigm concept in esoteric and excessively complex ways. Kuhn and others have held that the social sciences remain in a preparadigm stage, in contrast to the natural sciences and mathematics. This may indeed be the case, but it nevertheless does not diminish the significance of the efforts and accomplishments in seeking to develop problem-solving models to advance our knowledge in the social sciences, including the field of education and the curriculum.

With regard to the obsession with agreement on definitions in the social sciences, Kuhn contends that verbal definitions have little meaning by themselves until consensus about past and present decomplishments is attained, other than serving as pedagogic aids (1996, pp. 160–161). The concepts to which they point gain full significance only in the context of the interactions of phenomena, methodology, and paradigm applications (p. 142).

In describing how those concerned with natural phenomena adopt the simplest conceptual scheme into which the complex elements of raw experience can be fitted and arranged, James B. Conant, an eminent scientist, educator, and statesman, endorsed the view that "it is meaningless to inquire into the absolute correctness of a conceptual scheme as a mirror of reality" (1964a, pp. 14–15). Conant went on to show how, even in the sciences, the same term will acquire radically different meanings according to the context in which it is used.

Kuhn describes paradigms as the entire constellation of beliefs, values, and techniques shared by a given scientific community and employed by that community as models or exemplars for denoting concrete puzzle solutions that are the basis for the solution of other puzzles or problems. "The study of paradigms," notes Kuhn, "is what mainly prepares the student for membership in the particular scientific community with which he will later practice" (1970, p. 11). A paradigm or set of paradigms constitutes what members of scientific communities share in accounting for the relative fullness of their professional communication and the relative unanimity of their professional judgments. A paradigm is not a mere compromise or eclectic representation, but a consensual model or exemplar for problem solutions. It is a synthesis of modes of thought and methodology of a field that makes progress possible through substantive problem solving.

The preparadigm period in any community of scholars is marked by "deep debates over legitimate methods, problems, and standards of solution, though these serve rather to define schools than to produce agreement" (1970, p. 47). The conflicting schools vie with one another for allegiance and disappear only when paradigms are developed.

From Kuhn's analysis, it appears that the social sciences, including the curriculum field, are struggling to emerge from the preparadigm period. Bochner (1969) is more sanguine about this emergence. In a chapter called "Psychology and Pedagogy," he relates how the conflicting schools were largely outgrown by the 1930s as it became increasingly difficult not to recognize that different schools and systematic positions were all making significant contributions (p. 75). The advancement of cognitive psychology and the corresponding decline of behaviorism, for example, provides connections with the democratic prospect for which higher-order thinking is required of all citizens. Although psychology does not answer the curriculum questions (e.g., developing higher-order thinking in consumer education, or in the study of literature), it serves as a scientific source for the curricularist to draw upon in developing a curriculum based upon the best available evidence concerning the nature of the learner and the learning process.

Conflicting Schools of Thought and Shifting Grounds

Contending that the social sciences are in a preparadigmatic stage, Kuhn points out that the social sciences are beset by many conflicting schools and lack the paradigms needed to synthesize past achievements with present activity and to provide for further progress through ongoing concrete problem solutions. Hence social scientists either tend to hold allegiance to various schools that often behave like warring factions or, at the other extreme, they shift their ground all too easily in accordance with the dominant trends in the field or the demands of the wider social situation. The consequence is that old ground is constantly being reworked or that novel tides and superficial fashions are taken for progress.

Kuhn contends that progress in the social sciences is impeded by the tendency of social scientists to put more energy into factional disputation than into efforts toward synthesizing knowledge for the purpose of solving substantive problems, the tendency to ride the dominant tide of the times, and the tendency to shift their ground in research for the sake of expedience. Examples of such events are all too numerous. Myrdal (1969) has given this problem concerted attention in *Objectivity in Social Research*. Some of our most eminent social scientists contribute to this problem. Take, for example, Jerome Bruner's influential pronouncement (1960, pp. 10, 17–32) in one era that the chief educational problem stems from our neglect of the top quarter of our students (our future intellectual leaders), whereas in a subsequent era he fixed the chief problem on our neglect of children at the bottom (1971, pp. 18–21). In one era, Bruner offered us the disciplinary curriculum prescription; in a subsequent era he discarded this prescription in favor of social relevance of the curriculum.

Coupled with the tendency for curriculum shifts to reflect the dominant shifts in the sociopolitical tides are the disputations in the social sciences and education reflecting differences of specialization and sociopolitical/philosophical orientation. Taken together, these conditions make conceptual progress and improved practice very difficult. For example, leading figures such as B. F. Skinner (1971) would not recognize that behaviorism fails to represent the totality of human nature and that advances in the psychology of learning by mid-twentieth century was clearly in the direction of the more holistic cognitive psychology.

Contemporary behaviorists have sought some accommodation with cognitive-developmental psychology, which had virtually eclipsed behaviorism since the mid-twentieth century as a result of advancements in the study of human behavior. Nevertheless, many aspects of behaviorism are incompatible with the holistic cognitive-developmental psychology, so that eclectic combinations are often contradictory. Ironically, the schools remain mired in many respects in the mold of the drill-skill repertoires of behaviorism with the cheap pedagogical instruments of worksheets, workbooks, and mechanistic testing. The school continues to suffer this incompatibility. The contradictory shifts in valuations, the conflicting schools of thought, and the vulnerability of the social sciences to research bias give cause for the need for consensual commitment to the best available evidence as the key to sound educational policy and practice. In this chapter the efforts and successes in developing a curriculum paradigm by experimentalist-progressive educators is examined with a view toward improving professional practice in the real world of the school and in advancing the education profession by building upon the best available evidence.

Systematic Curriculum Development

The rise of experimentalist thought during the early decades of the twentieth century called for the assessment of educational practices through more rigorous intellectual forms. Dewey pointed out that although traditional schools could set great store in standardized tests and measurements, progressive schools were faced with the more complex task of organizing and assessing qualitative processes and results that are not entirely amenable to quantitative measures. "If he [the educator] can organize his qualitative processes and results into some connected intellectual form," wrote Dewey in 1928, "he is really advancing scientific method much more than if, ignoring what is actually most important, he devotes his energies to such unimportant by-products as may now be measured" (1928a, p. 200).

Dewey went on to stress that if we want schools to perpetuate the present order, attempts to determine educational objectives and select subject matter through wide collections and accurate measurements of data may be perfectly appropriate. However, if the schools are to educate with social change in view, a quite different method and content are required for education science. Here it is necessary to employ comprehensive and acute methods not only for ascertaining progress and failure in learning, and in assessing the appropriateness of the ways of organizing the curriculum, but also for detecting the causes of the observed effects. To Dewey, this requires a far more highly skilled kind of research than the mere notation of the results of mechanically applied tests.

Even in mathematics and physics, observed Dewey (1929a), quantitative data are secondary to qualitative ideas and, in the absence of guiding principles and rationale, what is taken for scholarly activity is really a kind of scrap collecting. Dewey was not contending that qualitative research is better than quantitative research. To repeat, his point was that all research must be built upon sound qualitative ideas. In effect, he resolved the dualism between quantitative and nonquantitative research (pp. 64–67). Unfortunately, the dualism has been perpetuated in the educational research community to this day, as evidenced by the formal establishment of a special group on qualitative research in the American Educational Research Association and the number of papers debating the merits of one research methodology over the other.

Dewey (1928a) also stressed the need for educational practice to be guided by theoretical ideas that in turn are tested and advanced on the anvil of practice. He warned that many of the progressive schools of that day were so enmeshed with protest against traditional forms of education that their activities centered on deviation, innovation, and removal of restrictions with the consequence that they neglected their responsibility for building up the theoretical side of education (pp. 199–200, 204). Today, many charter schools, alternative schools, and special-interest schools are being established mainly on political grounds rather than being built upon sound theoretical principles derived from the best available research evidence on curriculum, teaching, and learning. Indeed, there is a vast body of research on education on which the curriculum paradigm has been built over the course of the twentieth century. Dewey and other experimentalists laid the groundwork for the paradigm by framing the critical questions, by focusing on educational practice, by taking an aggregate approach in studying social conditions, by drawing from the human sciences as screens for testing educational practice, and in using philosophy for formulating working hypotheses for practical purposes and evaluation, as opposed to mere speculation and esoteric academicism.

The Sources of a Science of Education

What is it that marks a field as scientific? In posing this question in *The Sources of a Science of Education* (1929c), Dewey pointed out that such a question leads to a shift away from the notion of uniform objective traits in subject matter and toward the *ways* or *methods* of dealing with subject matter or problems—the systematic methods of inquiry that enable us to understand and control knowledge more intelligently, less haphazardly (pp. 7–9). Such inquiry helps solve problems, suggests new problems for solution, refines old procedures, and creates new and better ones. In posing the question as to the sources of a science of education, continued Dewey, we must ask the following (enumerated by the authors of this text):

1. What are the ways by means of which the function of education in all its branches and phases—selection of material for the curriculum, methods of instruction and discipline, organization and administration of schools—can be conducted with systematic increase of intelligent control and understanding?

2. What are the materials upon which we should draw in order that educational activities may become in a less degree products of routine, tradition, accident, and transitory accidental influences?

3. From what sources shall we draw so that there shall be steady and cumulative growth of intelligent, communicable insight and power of direction? (pp. 9–10)

   Dewey then added the following questions (enumerated and paraphrased by the authors of this text):

4. What are the ultimate problems to be drawn from concrete experience (educational practice) for investigation by means of working hypotheses of comprehensive and practical application? (pp. 33, 54, 56)

5. What educational values and objectives are to be determined or derived from the educational process, and how are they to be evaluated and met? (pp. 73–76)

In his *Basic Principles of Curriculum and Instruction* (1949), Ralph W. Tyler, who served as director of research for the Eight-Year Study, used these same questions and key elements of the model for curriculum development as followed in the Eight-Year Study. Here Tyler also drew extensively from Dewey's *The Sources of a Science of Education* (1929).

The isomorphism between Tyler's four questions (see Table 6.1 on p. 131). and Dewey's five questions, discussed earlier, is unmistakable. The reader is advised to contrast the two sets of questions, keeping in mind that whereas Tyler begins logically with the identification of objectives, Dewey pragmatically raises the question of determining and evaluating the objectives from the problems attendant to the educational situation and its outcomes. Hence inquiry begins with the problem situation, not with the objectives.

Educational Practice. Dewey (1929a) went on to stress that educational *practices* are the sole source of the ultimate problems to be investigated and are also the final test of value of research conclusions. "Concrete educational experience is the primary source of all inquiry and reflection because it sets the problems, and tests, modifies, confirms or refutes the conclusions of intellectual investigations," wrote Dewey (p. 56). This necessitates sympathetic contact between the researcher and the teacher. Education then determines the knowledge sources of the various human sciences (biology, psychology, sociology, and so on); but such knowledge does not become scientific, as far as education is concerned, until it serves educational purposes. This is accomplished when it enables us to solve problems that arise in education (pp. 39–42).

The Human Sciences and Social Conditions. Regarding psychology and the social sciences as screens, Dewey (1929a) warned against making a sharp distinction between *what* is learned and *how* we learn it. Such a distinction concludes in the tendency to assign the determination of the process of learning to psychology and of subject matter to social science, with the result that we deal with segments rather than continuities of the learning process. "That a person can learn efficiently to read and yet not form a taste for reading good literature, or without having curiosities aroused that will lead him to apply his ability to read, to explore fields outside of what is conventionally termed good reading matter, are sad facts of experience" (pp. 62–63). With regard to the relationship between the social sciences and social conditions, Dewey criticized the tendency to separate the psychological processes of skill acquisition from the social conditions and needs through which the skill is applied. He also criticized the dominant psychology of the times for being mechanistic and neglecting the most important factor in education, namely, the longitudinal or span-of-growth factor.

In connection with the study of social conditions as a source for determining the curriculum, Dewey (1929a) leveled this criticism at the pseudo-science of activity analysis:

> The shortest cut to get something that looks scientific is to make a statistical study of existing practices and desires, with the supposition that their accurate determination will settle the subject matter to be taught, thus taking curriculum-forming out of the air, putting it on a solid factual basis. This signifies, in effect and in logic, that the kind of education which the social environment gives unconsciously and in connection with all its defects, perversions and distortions, is the kind of education the schools give consciously. Such an idea is almost enough to cause one to turn back to the theories of classicists who would confine the important subject matter of instruction to the best of the products of the past, in disregard of the present and prospective social conditions. (pp. 72–73).

Philosophy. Turning to philosophy as a source, Dewey criticized the notion that philosophy is concerned with determining ends, whereas the science of education is concerned with determining means. According to Dewey (1929), philosophy serves a regulative function and is significant to the extent to which it provides working hypotheses of comprehensive application. "But if a philosophy starts to reason out its conclusions without definite and constant regard to the concrete experiences that define the problem for thought," cautioned Dewey, "it becomes speculative in a way that justifies contempt" (p. 56).

Unfortunately, this has been the case all too often. As will be discussed in chapter 9, there has been a tendency in recent times for many educational philosophers to remove themselves from the practical concerns and problems of schooling and to become engaged in self-serving esoteric academicism. In the case of the critical theorists, neo-Marxists, and others of the new left in academia, the focus has been on negation: portraying the school as a tool of the existing power elite for cultural reproduction, social control, or maintenance of the existing social order (Bowles & Gintis, 1976; Giroux, 1983). Their professional work has been centered on attacking the public schools rather than on working constructively on ways to improve conditions and to test hypotheses for problem solutions. As related in part I of this text, experimentalist-progressives throughout the twentieth century sought to forge a democratic vision for the American public schools and to address the practical problems of promoting educational opportunity, academic freedom, curriculum unity and diversity, curriculum modernization and enrichment, creation of a productive environment for learning, and linking school life with social needs. Such problems require continual attention in a free society. Democracy requires a shared vision and belief in the potentials of school and society, and democracy as a philosophy serves as our compass. To remove educational philosophy from the practical problems of our schools is to surrender the educational cause and make philosophy irrelevant.

Educational Objectives. Finally, Dewey (1929) emphasized that educational objectives must be determined from the educational function. He was careful to point out that this does not mean that only educators should determine objectives, but rather that the educative process is the means whereby truly educative objectives can be formulated, tested, and met. In activity analysis, nationalized testing, or any scheme in which educational objectives are determined from outside the educational function or process, the educational cause is surrendered. In Dewey's words, "the *educative process* in its integrity and continuity should determine them. . . . For education is itself a process of discovering what values are worth while and are to be pursued as objectives" (p. 74). The incessant external pressures on schools to censor certain materials, to avoid controversial issues, to indoctrinate for certain ends, or to minister to narrow nationalistic and special interests are all examples of forces that impinge on the educative process and make it noneducative or miseducative. Such pressures stem from conditions that are outside the educative process and run counter to the concept of education as enlightenment.

Sources of Educational Objectives

Dewey (1902b, pp. 4–8) noted that the fundamental factors in the educative process are (1) the learner ("the immature, undeveloped being"); (2) society ("certain social aims; meanings, values incarnate with the matured experience of the adult"); and (3) organized subject matter ("the specialization and divisions of the curriculum"). Dewey warned that the tendency is for these factors to be treated "in their separateness, to insist upon one at the expense of the other, to make antagonists of them" with the result that, instead of seeing them in organic interaction, each becomes the basis for a warring sect with its own set of independent truths.

When this happens a really serious practical problem—that of interaction—is transformed into an unreal, and hence insoluble, theoretical problem. Instead of seeing the educative process steadily and as a whole, we see conflicting terms. We get the case of the child versus the curriculum; of the individual nature versus social culture. Below all other divisions in pedagogic opinion lies this opposition (1902b, pp. 4–5).

In modern times, many educators have switched their allegiance in succeeding periods from discipline-centered studies to learner-centered curricula; from curricula for social relevance to curricula for development of basic skills. Instead of seeking to determine how the various sources can contribute coherently to the task of education, each source is regarded as the basis for allegiance or opposition. Each source becomes a sect for its own doctrines. "The educative process is the due interaction of these forces," observed Dewey (1902b), and "such a conception of each in relation to the other as facilitates completest and freest interaction is the essence of educational theory" (p. 4).

Dewey's rationale as explicated in *The Sources of a Science of Education* (1929a) and in his other writings, and particularly his identification and analysis of the three sources of educational objectives, were subjected to considerable refinement and elaboration over the ensuing decades.

In 1931, referring to the prodigious amount of activity in curriculum change, ranging from miscellaneous tinkering to radical reconstruction, Bode observed that the ensuing welter of diverse and conflicting curricular aims stems from three sources or points of view: (1) the standpoint of the subject-matter specialist, (2) the standpoint of the practical man, and (3) the interests of the learner. Although Bode's second source may appear at first glance to be different from any of Dewey's sources, it actually corresponds to Dewey's second source, namely, "certain social aims; meanings, values incarnate with the matured experience of the adult" (pp. 543–544). Bode warned of the pitfalls inherent in these sources or determinants in the absence of consideration of what constitutes a good life in a good society. Education should be a means for acquiring an outlook on life rather than receiving a ready-made outlook, contended Bode. In tune with Dewey, Bode pointed out that the schools in a democracy cannot impose an official creed on the learner, but must enable the learner to develop a philosophy

of life or social outlook through genuine educative participation.

Search for Consensus. As we have pointed out, a field can be said to come of age when its practitioners share a sense of community as exemplified by a paradigm or set of paradigms that governs their work and accounts for the relative fullness of their professional communication and consensus of judgment. Recall from our discussion in chapter 4 that the search for such consensus was vividly expressed in the monumental, two-volume, twenty-sixth yearbook of the National Society for the Study of Education, under the chairmanship of Harold Rugg (1927a). This was the society's first yearbook devoted to curriculum. The second volume of the yearbook contained 58 numbered paragraphs representing points of consensus in a composite statement. The first group of paragraphs was addressed to the resolution of the conflict between the nature and interests of the learner and the demands of adult life, and the selection and organization of subject matter—in essence, the three fundamental factors explicated by Dewey. Regarding the relationship between the first two factors, the report emphasized that there should be no conflict between proper education and preparation for later life. Reaffirming the experimentalist commitment, the report stated, "[t]he ultimate test (of either principle) is the effectiveness with which subsequent situations are met by the individual so educated" (p. 13). In a supplementary statement as to whether education should be focused on the present life of the learner or the life of the adult, George S. Counts wrote, "The end of education is to be found in neither the one period nor the other, but rather in the growth of the power of the learner to cope with his environment" (1927, p. 74).

Addressing the matter of selection and organization of subject matter, the composite statement acknowledged the importance of thoroughly systematized, codified, and specialized knowledge "developed through a long social evolution," but concluded that the curriculum should be developed "from the starting point of the needs of the learner, irrespective of the content and boundaries of existing subjects" (p. 22).

Although the twenty-sixth yearbook represented a search for consensus, the yearbook chairman, Harold Rugg, acknowledged differences in the schools of thought in the curriculum field, and he attributed some of these differences to the lack of a common professional vocabulary, obviously reflecting the immaturity of the field (p. 3). The curriculum field had not yet come of age; nevertheless the yearbook was testimony to the emergence of a notable group of professionals who were able to focus their concerns on the key factors of the curriculum field and the profound issues of the educational situation.

As noted by Cremin (1971), the curriculum field was emerging as a specialized area of professional activity during the 1920s (pp. 207–220). The sense of professional community in the curriculum field was to draw impetus with the establishment of the Society for Curriculum Study during the early years of the Great Depression (the society was to merge in 1942 with the NEA's Department of Supervision and Directors of Instruction to become the Association for Supervision and Curriculum Development). After the establishment of the first department of curriculum at Teachers College, Columbia University, under Hollis Caswell in 1938, leading schools of education throughout North America and elsewhere instituted similar departments. At the same time, a notable body of research literature was becoming evident about curriculum—a field that was coming of age.

The Curriculum Paradigm

The need for a scientific foundation for education was becoming clearly evident to Dewey and his fellow experimentalists in order to advance educational practice, as opposed to allowing the determining factors in education to be set by "tradition, imitative reproduction, and response to various external pressures wherein the strongest force wins out," to use Dewey's own words (1929a, pp. 14–15). In effect, a scientific basis for education would create teachers who would no longer seek simple recipes and whose success would be measured by examination results and regimental order in the classroom.

As mentioned, Dewey was explicit in stressing that the scientific base was not to be confused with empiricism or quantitative measurement, but it would create and unleash richly conceptual and imaginative avenues for finding problem solutions through systematic inquiry. Although Dewey noted that there is a distinction between art and science, there should be no opposition between the two. As in medicine or architecture, professional practice is indeed an art that is scientifically grounded. So be it in education.

Paradigms are not concocted out of a hat, but from the world of practice. Dewey had formulated his

three fundamental factors in the educative process from the work in his laboratory school at the University of Chicago. These, coupled with Dewey's *Sources of a Science of Education* (1929a), became the basis for the development of a paradigm for curriculum development in the Eight-Year Study (1932–1940), perhaps the largest-scale longitudinal study, comparing matched pairs of students, ever undertaken on the curriculum. As discussed in chapter 4, the Eight-Year Study grew out of the need to free the secondary-school curriculum from college-preparatory dominance so that an experimental basis for curriculum development could be established.

Curriculum Development as Inquiry and Problem Solving

If education is to advance in knowledge and practice, then it must employ the methods of scientific inquiry as opposed to tradition, imitation, dictate, narrow interests, and external political pressures, contended Dewey. Dewey variously referred to the methods of scientific inquiry as scientific method, reflective thinking, method of intelligence, hypothetical thinking, and the problem method. In explicating scientific method as phases in a chain of systematic inquiry, Dewey (1933) was careful to point out that the phases are not rigidly sequential or steplike (pp. 106–118).

As shown in Table 6.1, Dewey's phases of scientific inquiry or reflective thinking for problem solving were to be restated by leading curricularists in their efforts to promote systematic approaches to curriculum development throughout the twentieth century. This was to be coupled with the systematic study of the fundamental factors in the educative process or sources of educational objectives: (1) the nature of the learner; (2) our highest and most inclusive social ideals, values, and needs; and (3) the selection and organization of knowledge in the creation of curriculum. Taken together, the problem method and the fundamental factors were to be fashioned as a paradigm to advance curriculum development as a professional field.

To guide the program of curriculum development and evaluation, the staff of the Eight-Year Study developed a paradigm, which was later published under the authorship of Giles, McCutchen, and Zechiel in 1942 in their curriculum report after completion of the study. The report, *Exploring the Curriculum,* described how curriculum development and evaluation for the Eight-Year Study required

Table 6.1 Educational Improvement (and Curriculum Development) as a Problem-Solving Process.

Dewey, 1916	Dewey, 1933	Glies, McCutchen, and Zechiel, 1942	Taba, 1945, 1962	Tyler, 1949
Situation of significant experience	Suggestions stemming from a perplexing situation (pre-reflective)	Identifying objectives	Diagnosis of needs	What educational purposes should be sought?
Identification of problem(s) deriving from the situation	Intellectualization of the difficulty into a problem to be solved	Selecting the means for attaining these objectives	Formulation of objectives	What educational experiences can be provided that are likely to attain these purposes?
Observations and information bearing on the problem(s)	Use of leading ideas/*hypotheses* to initiate and guide investigation	Organizing these means	Selection of content	How can these educational experiences be effectively organized?
Formulations of suggested solutions (hypotheses)	Mental elaboration of ideas, evidence, and possibilities	Evaluating the outcomes	Organization of content	How can we determine whether these purposes are being attained?
Applications and validation of suggested solutions	Testing *hypotheses* by action		Selection of learning experiences	
	Deriving and implementing solutions, resulting in a cleared-up, unified situation and the advancement of knowledge and practice		Organization of learning experiences	
			Evaluation	

Source: Adapted from Daniel Tanner, "Curriculum History," in Harold E. Mitzel (ed.), *Encyclopedia of Educational Research*, 5th ed., Vol. 1 (New York: Macmillan/Free Press, 1982), p. 417.

131

attention to four fundamental questions pertaining to (1) identifying objectives, (2) selecting the means for attaining these objectives, (3) organizing these means, and (4) evaluating the outcomes. (These questions have a correspondence with Dewey's essentials of reflection or inquiry, as shown in Table 6.1.) In keeping with Dewey's conception of continuity and interdependence between aims and means, Giles, McCutchen, and Zechiel presented a model for curriculum development, shown in Figure 6.1, in which the four fundamental questions or problem areas are represented as interdependent determinants: objectives, subject matter, methods and organizations, and evaluation. Recognizing that these determinants arise from an educational situation, and are necessarily interdependent, they avoided portraying them as linear steps.

There are many ways of illustrating how aims or objectives derive from existing situations. For example, a given school might find that a dramatic change in the ethnic makeup of its pupil population has been accompanied by various forms of overt conflict between and among the pupil reference groups. An examination of the existing curriculum

Figure 6.1 Interrelationship of Determinants in Curriculum Development.

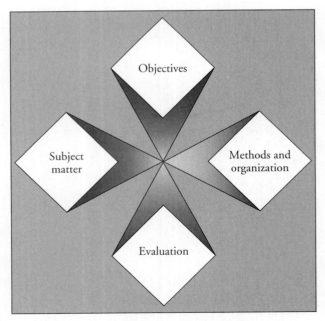

Source: Adapted from H. H. Giles, S. P. McCutchen, and A. N. Zechiel, *Exploring the Curriculum* (New York: Harper, 1942), p. 2.

may reveal that no provisions are made for the study of intergroup conflict. After diagnosing the situation, the faculty might revise its program in social studies, or it may make more substantive curricular changes. In the latter instance, a problem-focused unified studies curriculum might be developed in which history, the social studies, and literature are synthesized. Through the unified studies curriculum, students would investigate the causes, effects, and possible solutions of intergroup conflict in school and society, along with other pervading problems. Key educational aims derived from this situation might be to develop understandings, skills, and obligations for applying democratic ideals as a guide for everyday living and to develop competencies in and commitment to reflective thinking as the means for solving social problems. Various behavioral objectives might be identified in connection with these larger educational aims (not to be construed in the narrow-minded behavioristic sense). In evaluating the outcomes of the curriculum, a variety of techniques and instruments might be employed, such as attitude scales, pupil questionnaires, classroom interaction studies, anecdotal records, and achievement tests. Thus, not only do the objectives derive from the educational situation, but also changes in curricular content, methods of teaching, and organization of subject matter become necessary in attempting to deal with the situation effectively. Moreover, special techniques and instruments for evaluation may be required.

Three Fundamental Approaches to Sources. In connection with the Eight-Year Study, the following three approaches or sources were identified in the process of curricular organization and analysis: (1) the social-demands approach, (2) the adolescent-needs approach, and (3) the specialized subject-matter approach. These approaches clearly correspond to Dewey's three sources, namely, the learner, society, and organized subject matter (Giles, McCutchen, & Zechiel, 1942, pp. 22–48). In 1945, Hilda Taba elaborated on the significance of these three sources of data in curriculum planning: (1) studies of society, (2) studies of learners, and (3) studies of subject-matter content (pp. 85–92).

Although the various elements of the curriculum paradigm for the Eight-Year Study were discussed rather extensively in *Exploring the Curriculum* (Giles et al., 1942), it was to be orchestrated more fully as a paradigm by Ralph W. Tyler in 1949.

In his monumental text on secondary education, Alexander Inglis (1918), a leading member of the Commission on the Reorganization of Secondary Education, which produced the *Cardinal Principles of Secondary Education* (1918), offered three primary criteria for meeting the educative function: (1) "the psychological demands of the learning process as determined by the mental development and previous experiences of the pupils" (nature of the learner and the learning process), (2) "the demands and activities of life in which the students will utilize the various elements of their education," and (3) "the entire organization of (curricular) materials and methods" (pp. 712–713). Inglis stressed that the traditional curriculum as logically organized subjects will have to undergo radical reorganization in the light of the nature of the learner and the emerging conditions of modern life. In effect, the three fundamental determinants or sources for curriculum development identified by Inglis in 1918 corresponded to Dewey's three sources and to the factors or determinants identified by the Commission on the Reorganization of Secondary Education. As shown in Table 6.2, the same three sources were

Table 6.2 Fundamental Factors, Sources, or Determinants for Curriculum Development.

Dewey, 1902	Commission on the Reorganization of Secondary Education, 1918	Inglis, 1918	Rugg (Ch.), Committee on Curriculum Making, 1927
Learner (developing, immature individual)	Learner (character of)	Learner (nature of) and learning process	Learner (nature and interests of)
Society (social aims, meanings, values from the matured experience of the adult)	Society (needs of)	Life (demands of)	Adult life (demands of)
Reflectively formulated, systematized, life-related knowledge (subject matter)	Subject matter and methods (knowledge applications to life activities)	Curriculum (selection and organization of materials and methods)	Curriculum (selection and organization of the)

Bode, 1931	Giles, McCutchen, and Zechiel, Eight-Year Study, 1942	Taba, 1945	Tyler, 1949
Learner (interests of) Practical man (standpoint of)	Adolescent needs Social demands	Learners (studies of) Society (studies of)	Learners (studies of) Contemporary life outside the school (studies of)
Logical, systematized subject matter	Specialized subject matter	Subject matter (studies of)	Subject specialists (suggestions from or relevance of subject matter for the nonspecialist)

explicated by the Committee on Curriculum Making in 1927 (chaired by Harold Rugg), by Boyd Bode in 1931, in the Eight-Year Study (1932–1940; Giles et al., 1942), by Hilda Taba in 1945, and by Ralph Tyler in 1949.

Dewey's influence on the Commission on the Reorganization of Secondary Education is clearly indicated in the commission's report, *Cardinal Principles of Secondary Education* (1918). In its opening pages, the report identified the key factors or determinants for education as (1) the character and nature of the learners to be served, (2) the needs of society, and (3) the organization of subject matter and methods to reveal the applications of knowledge to life activities.

Table 6.2 reveals how leading scholars throughout the first half of the twentieth century identified the identical three factors, sources, or determinants for curriculum development. As discussed earlier, Dewey had warned in 1902 that when there is failure to consider these fundamental factors, or when they are treated separately, or when one is advanced at the expense of the others, or when antagonists are made of them, the educational process goes awry as insoluble problems are piled one on another. From Tables 6.1 and 6.2 we see the consensual elements and structure for systematically advancing research and practice in the curriculum field. In effect the structural elements for the curriculum paradigm were clearly identified and used in the Eight-Year Study. The paradigm served as a compass for treating the fundamental factors in vital interaction, rather than in opposition. The paradigm clearly provided the elements for making wiser curriculum decisions based on the best available evidence and served to advance knowledge in the field derived through scientific inquiry or the problem method.

The "Tyler Rationale"

Based on Dewey's work, as explicated in *The Sources of a Science of Education* (1929), and the work of Giles, McCutchen, and Zechiel (1942) on the Eight-Year Study, Tyler presented a full elaboration of the paradigm for curriculum development in *Basic Principles of Curriculum and Instruction* (1949). Developed as a syllabus for a basic curriculum course at the University of Chicago, Tyler's handbook has been widely used in curriculum courses and widely discussed in the curriculum literature from midcentury to the present day. Although various modifications

have been proposed, Tyler's explication of the curriculum paradigm has not been fundamentally changed.

As discussed, the connection of Tyler's model with the work of Dewey and the model that guided the Eight-Year Study is unmistakable. Yet to this day Tyler's *Basic Principles* is commonly referred to as *the Tyler rationale* and as one man's version of how a curriculum should be developed (Kliebard, 1986). Although there are many ways to derive a curriculum (e.g., from tradition, external influences, trial and error, authoritative dictate, imitation, etc.), the experimentalist curriculum paradigm stemming from the work of John Dewey, the Commission on the Reorganization of Secondary Education (1918), Alexander Inglis (1918), Harold Rugg et al. (1927), the Eight-Year Study (Giles et al., 1942), Ralph Tyler (1949), Hilda Taba (1945), and others, has put the curriculum field on a more scientific and professional footing. Moreover, as discussed in various sections of this text, many of the reductionist curriculum reforms externally and politically imposed on the schools throughout the twentieth century and to this day might have been doomed to failure from the beginning had the reform proposals been tested against the paradigm. Many of these reforms violated the nature of the learner, conflicted with our democratic social ideals under the pressure of vested interests and narrow nationalistic interests (e.g., the Cold War and space race), created unsound priorities and hierarchies of subject matters that set one side of the curriculum against another (e.g., the sciences and mathematics over the arts, the "essentials" over the "nonessentials"), and led to the fragmentation of the curriculum and its isolation from life experience.

The experimentalist curriculum paradigm not only has been used for school curriculum development, but also for curriculum development in higher education, particularly in professional schools such as social work, engineering, and medicine. For example, perhaps the most provocative, comprehensive, influential, and long-term program to reform medical education since midcentury was the one undertaken at Western Reserve University (now Case Western Reserve), which drew upon the curriculum paradigm (Williams, 1980).

Four Fundamental Questions. The "rationale" proposed by Tyler (1949, p. 1) for analyzing and developing the curriculum begins with a mandate for seeking answers to the following four fundamental questions (Table 6.1):

1. What educational purposes should the school seek to attain?

2. What educational experiences can be provided that are likely to attain these purposes?

3. How can these educational experiences be effectively organized?

4. How can we determine whether these purposes are being attained?

In essence, Tyler's questions represent the four-step sequence of (1) identifying objectives, (2) selecting the means for the attainment of these objectives, (3) organizing these means, and (4) evaluating the outcomes. A striking feature of Tyler's questions is that they relate to Dewey's essentials of reflection. However, Dewey repeatedly emphasized that aims derive from existing situations—from the resources and difficulties of these situations—and he noted that theories about the proper ends of our activities often violate this principle by assuming that ends are established outside our activities, with the consequence that they limit intelligence because they are externally derived or imposed (1916, pp. 121–122).

Interdependent Functions. If we conceive of aims as properly deriving from the existing situation, rather than being externally derived or imposed, the function of identifying aims must be interdependent with other functions in curriculum development. Consequently, Tyler's linear sequence of questions appears to be faulty because it fails to show this necessary interdependence. However, in the concluding paragraph to his syllabus, Tyler cautioned against following the questions or problems in linear order, and he held that the point(s) of attack must be determined after taking all factors into consideration (p. 128).

A more satisfactory model was developed by Giles, McCutchen, and Zechiel in their curriculum report on the Eight-Year Study, published in 1942. After raising essentially the same four questions that appeared in the Tyler rationale several years later, Giles, McCutchen, and Zechiel (1942) presented a schematic representation for curriculum development, shown in Figure 6.1, in which four functions are represented as interdependent rather than as linear steps.

A number of curricularists have treated the four questions as linear steps. Taba (1962, p. 12), for example, further divided them into a seven-step sequence, as follows and as shown in Table 6.1.

Step 1: Diagnosis of needs

Step 2: Formulation of objectives

Step 3: Selection of content

Step 4: Organization of content

Step 5: Selection of learning experiences

Step 6: Organization of learning experiences

Step 7: Determination of what to evaluate and of the ways and means of doing it

However logical Tyler's or Taba's sequence may appear, there is an educational situation already in existence, operating with implicit if not explicit objectives, and other curriculum determinants. If there is any starting point, it derives from that situation and should be focused on a diagnosis of the problems arising from that situation. The diagnosis involves evaluation from the very start, and evaluation should be continuous and not merely a final step. In other words, a four-step or seven-step sequence may be suitably logical for analytical purposes, but in the real world of curriculum development the processes must be treated in ecological relationship, beginning with the situation itself and its attendant problems.

In essence, then, the four functions in curriculum development (identifying objectives, selecting the means for the attainment of these objectives, organizing these means, and evaluating the outcomes) are interdependent functions rather than rigidly sequential steps. Although Figure 6.1 shows these functions as interdependent, it does not indicate the bases on which decisions regarding these functions are made. Decisions on the selection of educational objectives, selection and organization of subject matter, organization of instructional methods and learning experiences, and utilization of systematic evaluation procedures should be based on the best available evidence and guided philosophically. As discussed earlier, Dewey had pointed to the regulative function of philosophy in curriculum development and its significance of providing working hypotheses of comprehensive application. Tyler (1949) was well aware of the use of philosophy and, in virtually the same words as Bode (1931), noted that "philosophy attempts to define the nature of a good life and a good society" (p. 34). However, Tyler viewed philosophy, along with psychology, as a mere screen for selecting objectives. Dewey considered philosophy as more of a compass, and he viewed all of the "human sciences" as screens through which knowledge can be drawn to serve educational purposes. It appears that Tyler's identification of the "psychology of learning" as a screen for educational objectives and his omission of other human sciences was an oversight. Otherwise, he would likely have made a case for the pertinence of psychology over the other human (behavioral) sciences.

Sources of Objectives. In answer to the question "What educational purposes should the school seek to attain?" Tyler (1949) identified the following three sources: (1) studies of the learners themselves, (2) studies of contemporary life outside the school, and (3) suggestions from subject specialists (pp. 4–5; see Table 6.2). In the curriculum literature, Tyler is generally credited with having identified these key sources of educational objectives. However, as discussed earlier, these same sources had been formulated by Dewey in 1902 and had served as a basis for curriculum theory and development throughout the first half of the century. But Dewey had warned that these sources must be treated as interactive; otherwise, in their separateness they become the basis of warring sects: the learner versus subject matter, needs of the learner versus social demands, and so on. Kliebard (1969) has pointed out that where Dewey creatively reformulated these sources relative to the educative process, Tyler simply opted for an eclectic approach of laying them out side by side. Although Tyler took the position that no single source provides an adequate basis for educational objectives and curriculum development, he tended to treat them separately rather than as interactive sources. According to Tyler, "Each of these sources has certain values to commend it. Each source should be given some consideration in planning any comprehensive curriculum program" (p. 5). If these sources are treated as mere components rather than as organically interacting factors in curriculum development, their treatment often tends to become mechanical and the task of curriculum development tends to be regarded as merely technological, as evidenced by the earlier efforts in activity analysis and the more recent work on behavioristic objectives. Moreover, the so-called sources are not merely sources as such but also are influences that affect not only educational objectives but also the structure and content of the curriculum per se.

In connection with Tyler's third source, suggestions from subject specialists, Tyler cautions that the question to be directed at specialists should be, "What can your subject contribute to the education of young people who are not going to be specialists in your field?" (p. 26). Tyler goes into considerable detail in differentiating between specialized education and general education and in discussing the advantages of devising organizing structures other than the traditional subject divisions or disciplines. Here he notes the value of broad fields and core approaches for integrating knowledge and making it more life-relevant. Yet such efforts for developing curriculum synthesis have been made by generalists rather than specialists. Indeed, the era of the discipline-centered curriculum reforms of the 1960s was marked by a war among the disciplines as each discipline vied for priority in the curriculum. Moreover, the specialists rejected the function of general education and opted instead for disciplinary courses designed as though each student were to become a scholar-specialist in each of the numerous disciplines.

How the pieces fit together is the key concern of the curricularist. In this sense, the curricularist is not merely a specialist in the field of curriculum theory and development but also a generalist in that his or her concern goes beyond the separate specialized subject matters. The curricularist is concerned with interrelationships in the macrocurriculum and interdependence of elements comprising totality of the curriculum. Oddly, Tyler identified only the subject specialist in his scheme, although his syllabus was obviously directed at the curricularist as generalist. Consequently, the concept of organized subject matter as one of the sources, as explicated by Dewey and others, appears to be more satisfactory when treated integratively rather than segmentally.

Interaction of Determinants and Sources

If we regard philosophy as performing a regulative function, then it appears appropriate to incorporate it in the model showing the interrelationship of the determinants in curriculum development. Similarly, if we heed Dewey's admonition that objectives and other determinants must be derived from and tested in the educative process, the educative process should be incorporated in this model. Dewey regarded this as a crucial matter because otherwise sources external to the educational process tend to impinge on the curriculum with the result that the school becomes vulnerable to narrow and vested miseducative interests. This is commonly manifested in externally imposed and self-imposed censorship of the curriculum, the avoidance of controversial problems in the curriculum, the tendency toward indoctrination as a curricular function, and the delimitation of the curriculum to the safe function of skill development and the transmission of facts and information.

Figure 6.2 shows the interrelationships of determinants in curriculum development with philosophy as regulator in the context of the educative process. This schematic representation resolves the difficulties stemming from a linear conception of curriculum development. In a linear conception, one ordinarily assumes that objectives are always the starting point, but objectives always arise from a situation. In education, they should arise from the educative process and should be tested by that process. When objectives are regarded as the starting point, they tend to be derived from outside the educative process and are imposed on that process. Similarly, the selection and organization of subject matter, the methods of instruction, and the techniques and procedures of evaluation cannot be treated apart from objectives and as separate entities. They are organically interactive and interdependent.

What one learns in history or science or literature is inseparable from how one learns the so-called subject matter. Evaluation is shortsighted and narrow-minded if it deals only with the retention of facts and information and not with the ways in which the learner is able to reconstruct knowledge in a variety of novel problem situations.

In a similar vein, the sources of curriculum objectives should be viewed as interactive. The three sources, namely the learner, society, and organized subject matter—identified by Dewey, used in the Eight-Year Study, and further explicated in the Tyler rationale—should also be regarded as curricular *influences*. For example, changes in society exert certain demands on the school, which need to be interpreted by educators in the light of the educative process. Otherwise, the externally imposed demands may undermine the educative process. We have already alluded to certain problems encountered by schools, such as externally imposed censorship, self-censorship in response to the general public climate,

Figure 6.2   Interrelationship of Determinants with Philosophy in Curriculum Development.

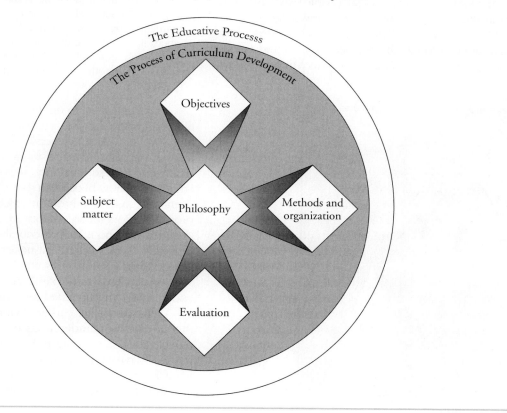

the elimination of controversial material in the curriculum, the constriction of the curriculum to skill development, the perversion of the educative process to one of indoctrination or to narrow nationalistic interests, and so on. Similarly, changes in the wider world of knowledge influence the curriculum. But again, it is the responsibility of educators to interpret these changes in terms of appropriate subject matter and in consideration of the nature of the learner and democratic social ideals. All of these should be regulated by educational philosophy and tested by the educative process.

The curricular sources and influences are portrayed as interactive in Figure 6.3. Included is an added category that might be called the wider world of organized knowledge or codified knowledge from which the curriculum is derived. It is from the wider world of knowledge from which educational institutions create the curriculum including subject-matter divisions for teaching and learning. As discussed in chapter 5, the creation of such divisions and specialization is convenient for organizing knowledge into subject matters for systematic instruction, but serious difficulties arise when the separate domains of specialized subject matter have to be resynthesized if they are to be useful in social problem solving and even in the development of new knowledge.

It is also seen in Figure 6.3 how the curriculum is developed through the various sources and forces in interaction. In building the curriculum, decisions must be made not only in the selection of subject matter but also in determining the context for the subject matter, including the structure or framework for the courses of study (i.e., discipline-centered or interdisciplinary studies), the modes of instruction, and the function of the curriculum in terms of the relationship of the courses of study to the life of the learner, the wider world of knowledge, and the larger society.

How these sources are drawn on and the nature and extent of their influence in building the curriculum should be guided by philosophy. In the absence of a guiding philosophy, the curriculum tends to be a product of ad hoc decisions, typically stemming from a combination of traditional practices and more immediate expediencies or even pressures from outside the educational situation.

Reassessment of the Curriculum Paradigm

Thomas Kuhn (1970) has pointed out that on the matter of disagreement on values for theory choice, the differences cannot be resolved by empirical proof.

> What one must understand is the manner in which a particular set of shared values interacts with the particular experiences shared by a community of specialists to ensure that most members of the group will ultimately find one set of arguments rather than another decisive. That process is persuasion. (p. 200)

Kuhn goes on to discuss how practice in a scientific field (and here we are using the term *scientific* in the Deweyan sense) depends on the ability, acquired from exemplars or models, to group situations into similarity sets. These similarity sets may well be rather crude, but they become a basis for persuasion and eventual consensus through which the field can make progress. "Counter-arguments are, in any case, always available, and no rules prescribe how the balance must be struck," states Kuhn, but nevertheless, "as argument piles on argument and as challenge after challenge is successfully met, only blind stubbornness can at the end account for continued resistance" (p. 204).

As mentioned earlier, Tyler's reconstruction of the curriculum paradigm has been subjected to great debate to this day. Certain weaknesses in Tyler's model have been identified and modifications have been suggested by the authors of this text in an effort to refine the model and to clarify points of

Figure 6.3   Curricular Sources and Influences.

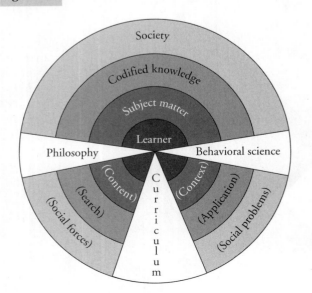

misunderstanding. Although different writers have criticized Tyler's version, their proposals, for the most part, have followed the same general model explicated by Tyler. Even those writers who have dismissed Tyler's version entirely have tended to follow this same general model in their own proposals. Thus it appears that the model is indeed a basis for consensus in the curriculum field and can be considered a paradigm for the field. In this section, some of the more recent criticisms and proposals of curricularists are examined in the light of a paradigm for the curriculum field.

Tyler's Version of the Curriculum Paradigm: Criticism and Modification

Perhaps the most common criticism leveled at Tyler's model is that it treats curriculum development as though it were a linear and almost a technological production process. This problem is easily overcome by treating the sources and determinants in curriculum development as organically interactive, as was done in the Eight-Year Study and as represented in Figures 6.2 and 6.3.

   The paradigm refined by Tyler has been criticized by Kliebard (1969) as suitable "for those who conceive of the curriculum as a complex machinery for transforming the crude raw material that children bring with them to school into a finished and useful product" (pp. 5–6). Indeed, Tyler's model has been misused by the behaviorists in this fashion. But virtually the same model was used by experimentalists in the Eight-Year Study. The point is that the paradigm is not inherently a mechanical production model, but a problem-solving model based upon the method of intelligence.

   Throughout his syllabus, Tyler repeatedly cautions against any singular approach as universally valid. His discussion of learning experiences, particularly in the development of reflective thinking ability, can hardly be interpreted as a production process to transform raw materials into a finished product. Moreover, his conception of behavioral objectives is comprehensive and consistent with the experimentalist view of the learner as an autonomously thinking individual, and it is at odds with the behaviorist description of the learner as a response system. Unfortunately, Tyler's definition of education as a "process of changing the behavior patterns of people" may appear to be behavioristic. However, his statement of rationale reveals a far more comprehensive and sophisticated conception of education.

It should be realized that the origins of behavioral objectives were not behavioristic but stemmed from the ingenious efforts in the Eight-Year Study to evaluate student progress through evidence of learning outcomes that would be more comprehensive and enduring. The conception of Tyler who was director of evaluation for the study, had a conception of behavior that clearly was in this vein and was not rooted in behaviorism. This work on behavioral goals was extended significantly in the efforts to develop programs in general education in the secondary school and college after World War II. Will French (1957) and others undertook a systematic study of behavioral goals of general education in the high school and proceeded to identify illustrative behaviors for evaluation. For example, under the goal of intellectual self-realization, evidence is sought of the student's ability to work independently (e.g., planning and carrying out a research report or project), to seek evidence on all sides of problems, to evaluate evidence (e.g., distinguishing fact from opinion, recognizing bias), to formulate and test hypotheses in seeking problem solutions, and so on. Similar evaluation efforts were undertaken at the college level by Dressel and Mayhew (1954) for the American Council on Education with considerable success. However, what was originally a progressive and holistic concept came to be seized on by the behaviorists who proceeded to whittle the concept of behavioral objectives down into minutiae of mechanistic and disjointed responses suited to programmed instruction, workbooks, and worksheets for the schools. In an era of curricular reductionism and essentialism, behaviorism became enormously appealing in that it fitted the production-efficiency model of schooling (reduced inputs/high output specifications).

   As director of the Cooperative Study in General Education under the sponsorship of the American Council on Education after World War II, Tyler made a seminal contribution in developing instruments for the promotion and assessment of higher-order thinking at the college level, just as he did in his work as a university examiner at the College of the University of Chicago and at the secondary school level as director of the evaluation staff for the Eight-Year Study before World War II. On balance, Tyler's contributions to the curriculum field were very much in the Deweyan experimentalist tradition.

   As noted, many curricularists have faulted the logical linearity of the Tyler rationale. Such criticism may be well justified in the sense that it has been followed in linear sequence by many curricularists, but this does not invalidate the rationale as a viable model or paradigm. Indeed, in the final section of his syllabus, Tyler explains that his analysis is presented to provide the student with a rational picture of the field. But Tyler pointed out that in the actual work of curriculum development in the school or college, no such sequence is to be followed (p. 128).

Alternative Proposals.   Schwab (1970) criticized the continuing restatement of the Tyler rationale in the curriculum literature; yet Schwab's analysis actually uses the various curricular sources and determinants explicated by Tyler (pp. 20, 38). It will be recalled that Schwab had been one of the leading advocates of the disciplinary doctrine that governed the curriculum mobilization reforms of the late 1950s and the decade of the 1960s (era of the Cold War and space race). Toward the end of the 1960s, the disciplinary doctrine, led by university scholar-specialists, was in a state of collapse as a result of the student protest movement and the demand for curricular relevance coupled with the mounting evidence revealing the failure of the national discipline-centered projects to live up to the grandiose claims for the "new math," "new physics," "new chemistry," and so on, for the schools.

Once a leading proponent of the disciplinary doctrine, Schwab (1964) had contended that "[t]o identify the disciplines which constitute contemporary knowledge is to identify the various materials which constitute the resources of education and its obligations (p. 7).

With the collapse of the national discipline-centered curriculum projects, Schwab described the curriculum field as being in a state of crisis. One cause of this crisis, acknowledged Schwab in a remarkable turnabout, was the domination by subject-matter specialists and the general absence of curricularists and other educationists in the discipline-centered reforms. Schwab (1970) stressed the need to take account of all sources for deliberation: teachers, supervisors, administrators, curricularists, philosophers, specialists in the subject-matter fields, and specialists in the various behavioral sciences (p. 19).

Without acknowledging his own role as a leading proponent of the disciplines doctrine, Schwab (1969) addressed the weaknesses inherent in disciplinarity as the ruling mode of curriculum design and function:

> . . . of greatest importance to our purposes here, this mode precludes any systematic use of arts which aim to discover the relations which exist or which

can be induced among various subject areas—the arts which make possible recognition and repair of divorces. . . .

> Prevasive specialism unexamined creates in students the illusion from which we all suffer to some degree—the illusion that subject matters as now distinguished are inevitable products of natural divisions. (pp. 240–241)

Schwab (1970) then turned to the numerous and conflicting orientations to the curriculum. "One curriculum effort is grounded in concern only for the individual, another in concern only for groups, others in concern only for cultures, or communities, or societies, or minds, or the extant bodies of knowledge," observed Schwab (p. 23). Each orientation, continued Schwab, concerns a different subject matter, and each orientation is grounded in a theory borrowed from one of the behavioral sciences. "No curriculum, grounded in but one of these subjects, can possibly be adequate or defensible," he maintained (p.23). Schwab then pointed to the need to take account of all the human sciences in any defensible curriculum. It will be recalled that Dewey (1929a) had made this point in *The Sources of a Science of Education* and that these knowledge sources must serve educational purposes.

Schwab (1970) contended that the crisis in the curriculum field was a result of undue reliance on theory. A renascence of the field would come about only if energies are diverted from theoretic pursuits to three other modes of operation: the practical, the quasi-practical, and the eclectic (pp. 1–14). The practical mode is concerned with the diagnosis of problems or ills of the curriculum and leads to decisions for action. Here Schwab appeared to be recognizing Dewey's admonition concerning the emptiness of theory when divorced from practical considerations, along with the limitations of university scholar-specialists and their specialized disciplinary orientation to curriculum construction (1916, pp. 156–159). Schwab had come around to recognizing the consequences of what Weinberg had warned against: the divorce between the discipline-centered university and the mission-oriented society (1967, p. 145).

The recognition of the necessary function of the curriculum to facilitate communication and action, as expounded by Vaihinger (1935), was being rediscovered in modern times. However, the eclectic approach, such as the prescription offered by Schwab (and like all eclectic approaches), tends to be an admixture of elements rather than providing for the needed curriculum synthesis. As discussed earlier, a number of progressive educators during the first half of the twentieth century sought to identify areas of consensus in the curriculum field so as to develop a model or paradigm for the scientific and practical advancement of education. Whereas the eclectic construction is one of compromise, the function of a paradigm is one of synthesis.

Schwab (1970) went to considerable length to show what can be gained from the practical mode. This mode is indeed appealing and sensible. Not many educators would hold that we need not address practical problems. However, the experimentalist, the perennialist, the essentialist, the reconstructionist, and the eclectic will each have a different view as to the nature of the practical problem and the means by which the problem is to be treated. Schwab's assumption that all orientations will yield readily to the power of the best available evidence appears to be naive. The very diagnosis of practical problems, the determination of the priorities among myriad practical problems to be attacked, the means for attacking these problems, the interpretation of the findings, and the application of the results will be influenced by theory. In the long run, human progress is determined by our practical decision making based on the *theoretical* criterion of the best available evidence. Except in the most obvious and routine matters, knowledge is never final but is treated as tentative. Practical decisions are made according to the best available evidence, pending the emergence of yet better evidence. Indeed human progress has derived from the continual advancement of evidence-based knowledge, a fundamental tenet of Dewey's experimentalist theory.

Other Criticisms.   As discussed earlier, a significant number of curricularists have not recognized the continuity and impetus of ideas and practical applications that led to the emergence of the experimentalist paradigm for the curriculum field during the first half of the twentieth century. Drawing on Kuhn's thesis that the hard sciences are the true exemplars of paradigm-guided inquiry, Jickling (1988) has contended that scientific inquiry is an objectionable model for the curriculum field. In reply to Kuhn's critique of the social sciences as sciences, Paul Samuelson, Nobel laureate in economics, quipped that economics is "neither astrology nor theology" (1983, p. 14). We might add that such is the case for the curriculum field and indeed for all fields of social science.

Despite the differences in philosophy (e.g., liberalism or conservatism), there are sets of tools and parameters, models and exemplars, that define the field and guide inquiry by professionals. This should not be construed to mean that the levels of predictability and understanding of social phenomena are to be compared with those attained in the physical sciences or even in the biological sciences. Social behavior, fortunately, will always be too complex for that. But this does not lessen the significance of the paradigms of scientific inquiry that guide the social sciences as scholarly communities.

In his contention that the curriculum field has no paradigm base for systematic inquiry, Jickling (1988) proceeded to cite the earlier writings of Robin Barrow (1983). However, after reading the present authors' historical tracings concerning the emergence of a curriculum paradigm, Barrow took issue with Jickling and concluded that "the 'model' or 'paradigm' ought to be recognized as fundamental to curriculum" (1988, p. 62).

Misinterpretations and Distortions.   As discussed earlier, Schwab's criticism of theory when it is treated apart from the reality of the practical world of curriculum is consistent with Dewey's view. In Schwab's analysis (1970), the various sources and determinants in the curriculum paradigm are inescapably treated. His criticisms and conclusions bear a striking resemblance to Dewey's analysis in *Sources of a Science of Education* (1929). The paradigm stemming from Dewey's *Sources of Science of Education* and the Tyler rationale served Schwab well in the formulation of his proposals for the curriculum field.

The crisis in the curriculum field that Schwab addressed had resulted from the reliance on a *single* source, namely, the university scholar-specialists in curriculum reform. The discipline-centered reforms deliberately turned away from the practical applications of knowledge, the problems of society, and the nature of the learner. Had the paradigm stemming from Dewey's *Sources of a Science of Education,* the work of Alexander Inglis, the Eight-Year Study, and the Tyler version been followed, the curriculum reforms would not have been one sided and the crisis would have been averted. The paradigm is immanently practical in that it shows how the sources and determinants must be treated in balance and in vital interrelationship. In the opening comments to his syllabus, Tyler (1949) cautions that no single source is adequate to provide a basis for wise and comprehensive decisions. Schwab reaches the same conclusion.

Consequently, most of the criticisms leveled at the Tyler rationale can be resolved by modifying the paradigm to show the necessary interrelationship of determinants and sources in curriculum development. Other criticisms appear to stem from a misreading of the paradigm—for example, the allegation that it is mechanistic and suited mainly to behavioristic approaches. We have seen how the paradigm has been useful to curricularists representing virtually any discipline or professional field undergoing curriculum renewal. That the Tyler syllabus is simply one man's version of how a curriculum should be developed and that this version is a production model, is not borne out by the fact that the paradigm on which Tyler's syllabus was based has been used by curricularists in wide-ranging situations. Furthermore, we have seen how the paradigm is not simply one man's invention. It was developed as a distillation of the key sources and determinants in curriculum development from theory and practice spanning the course of a half century. Kliebard (1977) has sought to formulate the central question of curriculum and the problems attendant to that question, namely, what should be taught; this, in turn, leads to problems of curriculum differentiation, the modes and effects of teaching what has been selected, and how the various parts of the curriculum should be interrelated in order to create the whole. In his analysis, Kliebard draws from the heritage of the field since the turn of the twentieth century and particularly from the work of Dewey. Despite his criticisms of Tyler, Kliebard's question and the attendant problems are well within the paradigm explicated by Tyler.

Tyler's orchestration of the paradigm has been criticized as an oversimplified conception of the complex process of curriculum development. Of course, curriculum development is a highly complex process. But the function of a model or paradigm is to make complex phenomena comprehensible and manageable. In seeking clarity, situations are grouped into similarity sets, which are represented in some kind of equilibrium. The effort toward clarity results in a simplification and rather crude representation of reality. Yet the very simplification makes it possible to test theory in practice, though the paradigm itself should not be treated or assessed as a literal representation of reality. Most of the criticisms leveled at the Tyler rationale have stemmed from such misreadings of the paradigm. This paradigm can be continually refined and modified. It is not an immutable monument, but simply a way of enhancing communication and enabling practitioners to test theory in the real world of curriculum development.

Conversion to another model or paradigm awaits another revolution in the curriculum field. Until that revolution is forthcoming, the existing model or paradigm will remain in use and will be studied by serious students of curriculum.

Why Reforms Succeed or Fail

In her study of the national programs for school reform, past and present, Barbara Presseisen (1985) of the Regional Educational Laboratory on Research for Better Schools used the curriculum paradigm as presented in the 1980 edition of *Curriculum Development* by the authors of this text. In her study, appropriately titled *Unlearned Lessons,* Presseisen found that most of the reforms were largely misguided in failing to derive lessons from the past and in violating the fundamental factors in the paradigm. A more detailed study by Peter Hlebowitsh (1987), tracing the national educational reform efforts since mid-twentieth century, also found that failures were vividly connected with violations of the curriculum paradigm, such as ignoring or distorting the nature of the learner, bending the curriculum to narrow nationalistic purposes at the expense of the cosmopolitan democratic interest, avoiding systematic research for problem solutions, and neglecting to build on the vast body of research and best practices in the curriculum field.

The testing of the curriculum paradigm by Presseisen, Hlebowitsh, and others has served to reveal its practicality and validity. Surely it will be refined and modified as new knowledge emerges in the curriculum field. But educational reformers would do well to test their schemes against the paradigm and with the benefit of the great store of research and experience in curriculum development, past and present. Otherwise, we shall continue to witness successive periods of educational and curriculum reform by reaction and counterreaction at great loss to the rising generation and to our society.

Paradigm as Key to Synthesis and Progress

The notion of a paradigm for the curriculum field should be seen not as esoteric or particularly complex, but as serving as a practical model for gauging and directing our professional work so as to ensure progress. If the nature of the learner is ignored or distorted in the process of developing and implementing the curriculum, then the process will invariably go awry.

Another determinant is the kind of society we stand for (and the social ideals embraced). Hence the nature of the learner will be conceived differently in a democratic society than in a totalitarian society. In a free society, there is the expectation that the curriculum will foster independent (critical) thinking in the context of democratic social responsibility (e.g., respecting the rights of others). In a totalitarian society, indoctrination is legitimized in the curriculum to ensure the subordination of the individual in service to the superior interests of the nationalistic state. Hence the very structure and function of the curriculum cannot be considered apart from these determinants and how these determinants interact (the learner, society, and the selection, organization, design, and function of the curriculum). Unfortunately, it has not been uncommon for the curriculum to conflict with the nature of the learner and with our democratic social ideals. We shall return to this problem throughout this text.

In short, the paradigm represents the knowledgeability of a field, in the form of models or exemplars, for revealing concrete problems and for solving these problems. The collapse of the disciplinary doctrine points to the inadequacy of any narrow approach to curriculum reform and reveals the need for a curriculum paradigm or set of paradigms rather than simply seeking compromise among incompatible elements. The paradigm enables the community of scholars and practitioners to put new prescriptions to the test of all that a field has accomplished. Thus it helps the members of the given community to anticipate problems and to avoid the temporal tides of vogue reforms, shortsighted panaceas, and misguided reforms.

The Three Fundamental Factors

Many educational achievements that are taken for granted today were gained through great struggle and creative effort in a humanitarian movement to make democracy work. Many of these advances have been addressed in part I and many others are treated throughout this text. Every major educational advance, retreat, or failure has been linked to the needed interdependence of three fundamental factors: (1) the kind of society envisaged politically, socially, and economically (namely American democracy); (2) the nature and needs of the learner; and (3) the structure and function of the curriculum. For example, over the course of the past century, the United States led the way among democratic nations toward attaining universal secondary

education and open-access higher education. Of course, problems of educational equity persist. The point is that hard-won social reforms, such as educational equity, require continuous vigilance in the face of changing social conditions and oppositional forces. Yet the belief in education is a principal part of the American Creed, and no politician can erase this belief. The question is whether the more privileged in society want the same level of educational opportunity for other people's children that they want for their own.

Distortion and Ignorance of General Education

As another example, the idea for a core curriculum for general education (to create a common universe of discourse, understanding, and competence so as to develop autonomously thinking, socially responsible citizens of a free society) emerged over the course of the first half of the twentieth century in our secondary schools and colleges. The idea and practice of general education requires the building and strengthening of vital connections between school and society, the learner and the curriculum. Unfortunately, many school administrators are unaware of the vast literature on general education and are inclined to confuse the term *general education* with the formless general-curriculum track, which is neither college preparation nor vocational in function. Unfortunately the practice of separating students into college-preparatory, vocational, and general curriculum tracks is practiced in too many high schools. In the truly comprehensive high school having a truly working core of general education, shared by all students, and having a diversified curriculum with flexible options for elective programs in college-preparatory and vocational studies—along with exploratory, enrichment and special-interest studies—the practice of curriculum tracking is totally unnecessary.

The National External Testing Pandemic.
Another wide-reaching distortion of general education or the core curriculum is reflected in the national external testing pandemic which gained impetus from two national reports on educational reform, namely *A Nation at Risk* (National Commission on Excellence in Education, 1983), and *America 2000* (1991). Whereas the original idea of a core curriculum for general education required a highly integrated,

life-related curriculum for American democracy, the national external testing pandemic has been based on test results in standard academic studies, subject by subject. (Most recently, art has been added as an afterthought, but the art tested is not studio art, but art as a verbal/academic subject.)

The testing pandemic has mitigated notable efforts in curriculum design and articulation for a core curriculum in general education, and instead it instituted a segmental and disjointed set of "standards" as measured by national and state test scores. Although improvements have been made in the tests over time, the pedagogical response has been "teaching to the test" while students want to know what will be on the test and how can they attain higher test scores, as opposed to the process of education as a stimulating and challenging shared endeavor.

The idea and practice of general education is addressed in great detail in chapter 9, but our brief discussion here is simply to illustrate how reforms can be counterproductive by violating the curriculum paradigm. Both *A Nation at Risk* (1983) and *America 2000* (1991) were based on faulty premises. This was also the case at the height of the Cold War and space race with the issuance of *The Process of Education* (1960). In *The Process of Education* the nature of the learner was distorted in the image of the university scholar-specialist. The school curriculum was reconfigured so as to be built on the separate academic disciplines with priority given to mathematics and the sciences to meet the exigencies of the Cold War and space race. The democratic prospect and general education were virtually ignored in the curriculum. The school curriculum was turned to theoretical knowledge to the neglect of knowledge applications to the life of the learner and nature of the learner. The emphasis was given to the alleged "structure" of the separate academic disciplines. From the curriculum paradigm it was predictable that the national discipline-centered reforms were destined to failure, as discussed in detail in chapter 10.

The chief premise of *A Nation at Risk* (1983) was that the public schools (not the colleges and universities, or corporate America) were to blame for the alleged decline of U.S. hegemony over global industrial markets, resulting in the economic rise of Japan and Germany in industrial productivity. The opening words of *America 2000* (1991) were: "Eight years after the National Commission on Excellence in Education declared us a 'Nation at Risk,' we haven't turned things around in education" (p. 15).

Again, from the curriculum paradigm it was predictable that all three national reports were destined for failure for subordinating the nature of the learner to narrow nationalistic interests, to the neglect of the democratizing function of the school and the curriculum. Essentially these reports neglected or distorted the three fundamental factors in the educative process, as formulated in the curriculum paradigm.

Further, the political leaders who were responsible for these national reports were never held accountable for their misguided allegations and claims. For example, the first goal listed for American education in *America 2000* was that by 2000, "All children in America will start school ready to learn" (p. 19). How this could be envisaged in nine short years without concerted and massive social reconstruction remains a mystery to this day. Nevertheless, the schools have been caught in the expanding web of external, high-stakes national and statewide testing as called for in *America 2000*, while the promised education transformation has (predictably) failed to occur.

Finally, whereas the democratizing model for the school was cosmopolitan in student population and comprehensive in curriculum, in recent years the focus has been on specialized schools to meet the needs of special populations (alternative schools, school of choice, specialized schools, school vouchers, and so on), reflecting the wider social fragmentation.

In the face of these setbacks, there remain the powerful correctives of evidence-based research explaining why misguided reforms fail and pointing to constructive efforts toward concerted education renewal. Our history reveals that this has been the basis upon which social and education progress is made.

If the twentieth century was the Age of Synthesis, as some scholars maintain, curricularists will have to think less about the alleged knowledge explosion and more about the problems explosion. A concerted focus on substantive problems will require a movement toward synthesis in the curriculum field. Far more energy has been expended in the curriculum field for resurrecting old disputations and inventing new causes for disputation rather than for substantive problem solving. The curriculum field has a rich heritage of achievements that can lend perspective to the contemporary educational situation and thereby serve as a basis for consensus and progress.

Paradigm-Based Fields and the Value of the Textbook

Kuhn (1970) goes to some lengths to discuss the importance of the textbook as a pedagogical tool in fields that are paradigm-based, such as the natural sciences. "These textbooks expound the body of accepted theory, illustrate many or all of its successful applications, and compare these applications with exemplary observations and experiments" (p. 10). Not until the last stages in the education of a scientist, observes Kuhn, is the textbook supplemented or replaced by the actual scientific literature on which the textbook has systematically organized the knowledge of the field. "Given the confidence in their paradigms, which makes the educational technique possible," continues Kuhn, "few scientists would wish to change it." Accordingly, "one cannot help but notice that in general it has been immensely effective," he concludes (p. 165). Kuhn is not contending that the textbook is the only proper pedagogical device or that it is immune from abuse. Instead he points to it as a key means of initiation to the systematic organization of knowledge and paradigms in mature fields of scholarship. Kuhn contrasts the role of the textbook in the natural sciences with other fields, including the social sciences, in which textbooks play a less decisive role. In the social sciences and education, most notably during the late 1960s and early 1970s when "relevance" was the ruling slogan, it was not uncommon for college professors to use popular literature on au courant topics as substitutes for textbooks and the systematic treatment of organized knowledge and practice in their fields. Best-sellers such as *Crisis in the Classroom,* written by the journalist Charles Silberman (1970), were being used with other popular readings in the place of textbooks in courses ranging from curriculum to educational administration and educational sociology, with the result that some college students were required to read identical material in different courses. (As a journalist, following the publication of *Crisis in the Classroom* Silberman turned his peripatetic interest to another topic, and authored a book on criminal violence and the justice system. He was "finished" with education.)

Although it is difficult to imagine a student of chemistry, physics, biological science, engineering, medicine, mathematics, or law without having the benefit of textbooks, it is not uncommon to find some faculty in the social sciences boasting that they have discarded the use of textbooks. A sociology professor, for example, boasts that she has been teaching sociology to undergraduates for 10 years without textbooks (Rogers, 1987). Most significantly, the censors start with school textbooks. Computer-programmed instructional materials are rarely censored, mainly because they tend to be geared to established-convergent learning. Good textbooks are rich in ideas for emergent learning, which opens them to censorship (Tanner, D., 1999, pp. 133–134).

There is no question that it is helpful and often necessary to supplement the textbook with current materials and primary source materials, but if there is a systematic knowledge base in a field, a good text should serve as a key vehicle for helping the student develop in understanding and competence through the systematic exposure to the knowledge base. The use of au courant materials to promote temporarily fashionable topics and practices, and neglecting to benefit from and build on the vast body of professional knowledge and practice, finds both neophytes and veteran practitioners repeatedly rediscovering the wheel and repeating errors. Thus we find that many rediscovered best practices—such as writing across the curriculum, higher-order thinking, heterogeneous grouping or student inclusion, and curriculum articulation and synthesis—are being promoted without benefit of the vast and rich knowledge base of the curriculum field (Tanner, D., 1989).

Perspective

Throughout the twentieth century to this very day, education opinion and practice have been sharply divided as to whether the dominant source and influence for curriculum development should be the body of organized scholarship (the specializations and divisions of academic knowledge), the learner (the immature, developing being), or society (contemporary adult life). Instead of seeing these sources and influences as organically interactive, each becomes a rallying point for a warring sect. Each era of societal crisis witnesses a clamor to make one source and influence dominant over the other. The result is that curriculum development becomes a piecemeal enterprise and the curriculum suffers from imbalance and fragmentation.

It has been shown how the curriculum becomes vulnerable to narrow and even miseducative interests when objectives are derived from sources that are external to the educative process. Objectives must be derived from and tested through the educative process. When theory is similarly treated, that is, when it is derived from and tested in the educative process, it makes immediate practice useful in a far wider range of contexts and under far deeper conditions. Theory then provides the hypotheses to be tested in efforts to solve practical problems. Practice in the absence of theory has limited applicability to wider and novel conditions. In this vein, theory is in the end the most practical of all things. But when theorizing is not tested in the educative process, it becomes self-serving and is not theory; instead, it becomes mere speculation or dogmatic assertion. One group asserts that the curriculum should be delimited to the established academic disciplines; another group sees it being properly concentrated on facts and skills; another group maintains that the curriculum should derive from the interests and needs of the learner; yet another group contends that it must be attuned to the demands of adult life. Nothing is resolved and nothing is solved. Each sect has its day as the schools shift from one extreme to another in response to shifting external crises and demands.

The curriculum field came to be identified as a distinct area of study by mid-twentieth century with the emergence of a model or paradigm intended to represent a consensual basis for systematic curriculum development. The model or paradigm serves to account for the various sources and determinants in curriculum development and is based on the reflective formulation and testing of alternatives for the solution of practical problems. The conceptual origins of the paradigm span the entire first half of the twentieth century, stemming from Dewey's experimentalist theory. This problem-solving model or paradigm has been subsequently modified and refined, though it continues to be a source of debate among leading contemporary curricularists. Alternative proposals have been made, but such proposals appear to be derived from factors that are accounted for in this extant model or paradigm. In this sense, the model or paradigm has served as a basis for communication in the curriculum field. It also has been followed to some extent in working on problem solutions in the curriculum field, such as those attacked in the Eight-Year Study. Because some have used the paradigm mechanically, it has been criticized as mechanistic. But the paradigm has also been used in an organically interactive way. Crises in the curriculum field have arisen when a single source or determinant is allowed

to overpower all of the other sources and determinants. The paradigm helps practitioners recognize the need to consider the necessary interrelationships of all sources and determinants if the curriculum is to be balanced and coherent, and if problem solutions are to be addressed.

In the absence of a paradigm or set of paradigms to synthesize past achievements with contemporary activity, and to provide the means for making progress through ongoing problem solutions, the curriculum field has been buffeted by shifting demands and trends. In one era the call is for disciplinarity. The reaction to the excesses of disciplinarity then gives rise to a call for relevance. The reaction to the excesses of relevance is succeeded by a call for back to the basics. Each successive call for reform is a reaction to the excesses of its preceding reform movement. The result is movement but not progress. Innovations are adopted, discarded, and reinvented like changing fashions. Rather than being conceived and implemented for substantive problem solving, they more often represent cosmetic changes or the inconsequential manipulation of managerial arrangements.

It has been shown that the curriculum paradigm has been eminently useful in setting the criteria for evaluating the efficacy of educational reform proposals and in ascertaining the causes of failure of various reform efforts. If the curriculum is to be consonant with the ideals of American democracy, it must be structured to meet the function of general education, and not merely basic education at one end of the educational ladder and specialized education at the other. This requires a synthesis of the curriculum so as to address our most pervasive social problems in a technological age. A free society requires an enlightened citizenry capable of higher-order thinking in solving personal-social problems in the context of social responsibility. Throughout the twentieth century, many of the national reform efforts for American education were doomed from the start because they neglected or distorted the nature of the learner, subverted the democratic interest to narrow nationalistic or special interests, imposed aims on the schools that were outside the educational situation, and failed to develop an integrated curriculum structure to meet the unified and diversified functions required of a cosmopolitan society.

No model or paradigm rightly serves to eliminate debate or differences in theoretical orientation. Progress depends on such differences provided that they are tested reflectively in the field of practice. The model or paradigm provides a basis for evidence-based testing. It is not a literal representation of the world of curriculum development, but an economical and simplified scheme for dealing practicably with the complex process of curriculum development.

It synthesizes past achievements with current practice. It cannot be dismissed lightly unless something that is more comprehensive and convincing can take its place.

PROBLEMS FOR STUDY AND DISCUSSION

1. According to Bode, "We believe that our curricula should be revised, but we do not know where or how to begin. Our susceptibility to educational fads has become notorious." [Boyd Bode, *Modern Educational Theories* (New York: Macmillan, 1927), p. 232.]

   Although Bode made this comment in 1927, would you say it is valid for the educational situation today? Explain.

2. With regard to curriculum development, what is the significance of the statement that "theory is in the end the most practical of all things"?

3. It has been observed that "*expertise* consists in such an analytic comprehension of a special realm of facts that the power to see that realm in the perspective of totality is lost." [Harold J. Laski, "The Limitations of the Expert," in U.S. Senate Committee on Government Operations, *Specialists and Generalists* (Washington, DC: U.S. Government Printing Office, 1968), p. 55. (Originally published in 1930.)]

   What is the significance of this statement concerning the roles of various persons other than the subject specialist in curriculum development?

4. "The user of the house," wrote Aristotle, "will even be a better judge than the builder." ["Specialization and the General Ability to Judge," from *Politica*, Book III, Chapter 11.] What role, if any, should the student have in curriculum development and evaluation?

5. Mark Van Doren observed that although the college (or school) is meaningless without a curriculum, the problem of what should be studied and how this should be interrelated and fitted together is not accepted as a real problem. "All other (educational) problems are solved when the problem of the curriculum is solved." [Mark Van Doren, *Liberal Education* (Boston: Beacon, 1959), p. 108.]

   From your own experience, do teachers and administrators devote adequate time to the interrelationships of studies and the problem of developing a balanced, coherent total curriculum for the school? Explain. Is the curriculum problem the most significant educational problem? Explain.

6. What is your assessment of the Tyler rationale? Do you see the need for modifying it in any way? Explain.

7. In the curriculum literature, considerable attention has been devoted to three fundamental factors that have served as sources for educational objectives and other curricular decisions. These factors are (1) the learner, (2) society (social aims and conditions, and meanings and values from matured experience of adult life), and (3) organized subject matter.

   How do you account for the tendency of these factors to be treated as separate and even antagonistic to one another in connection with the curriculum? Give examples of how this has affected the curriculum.

8. What illustrations can you give of situations in which noneducative and even miseducative influences are exerted on the curriculum from sources external to the school? What is your assessment of statewide and national external testing and the practice of teaching to the test?

CHAPTER 7

SOURCES AND FORCES FOR CURRICULUM RENEWAL
SOCIETY AND THE WORLD OF KNOWLEDGE

The modern history of curriculum reform, indeed education reform, reveals the repeated failure to recognize and treat the three fundamental factors in the educative process in vital interdependence: (1) the nature of the learner, (2) social conditions and democratic ideals, and (3) the selection and organization of knowledge or subject matter in the development and implementation of the curriculum. Instead, at various times the fundamental factors have been treated independently of one another or even antagonistically. Thus we have the pupil-centered curriculum versus the society-relevant curriculum. We have witnessed how narrow nationalistic interests, from the "crisis" of the Cold War and space race to the "crisis" of the "Japanese challenge," have created priorities favoring certain subjects at the expense of a balanced and articulated curriculum (e.g., the sciences and mathematics over the humanities, the arts, and the practical studies). We have seen how, at various times, the college-bound population has been favored over all others. Then, during periods of economic and social retrenchment there is the predictable curriculum retrenchment of "back to basics."

It should be obvious that educational reform efforts are destined to fail when the fundamental factors are treated separately or in opposition to one another. Moreover, when reforms are fueled by successive waves of reaction and counterreaction, special interests tend to be served at the expense of the wider social interest of democracy.

The need for recognizing the vital interdependence of the fundamental factors in the educative process has been neglected in the schools, especially at times of narrowly directed sociopolitical pressures and influences. But surprisingly, this neglect has been a common shortcoming among educational theorists despite the rich legacy handed down by experimentalist-progressive educators throughout the first half of the twentieth century. Further, many of the national reports on educational (school) reform inflict damage on the rising generation through the influence of misguided reforms in advancing narrow priorities and prescriptions that set the fundamental factors in the educative process in opposition to one another. Denis Lawton, a British sociologist and curricularist, has wisely cautioned that the school curriculum cannot justifiably be developed on the basis of any one of the three determinants without creating insurmountable problems (1978, pp. 2–4). Recall from the preceding chapter that this warning was offered by Dewey back in 1902.

Many authors of textbooks on curriculum unfortunately have chosen to treat the three fundamental factors in the educative process as three separate and oppositional theories—again without learning the lesson from the experimentalist paradigm.

There has also been a tendency, even among those who have sought to build on the experimentalist legacy, to treat the three fundamental factors or determinants as *sources* of data for curriculum development while neglecting to recognize and treat them also as *influences* on educational aims and the curriculum.

The focus of this chapter and the following chapter is on the needed recognition of the vital interdependence of society, the world of codified knowledge, and the learner as both sources and influences for curriculum design and development.

Society as Curricular Source and Influence

The celebration of the anniversary of the Declaration of Independence often is occasion for the media to recall the phrase in the Declaration on the "unalienable rights to Life, Liberty and the pursuit of Happiness." Hence we find a feature article appearing in the Sunday *New York Times* on the eve of the 227th anniversary of the Declaration raising the issue that, "While most Americans can agree on definitions of life and liberty, the Declaration's first two inalienable [sic] rights, happiness is another matter" (Leland, 2002, p. 1WK). In typical fashion, the journalist goes on to trivialize the American pursuit of happiness as manifested in the ravenous American consumer culture exemplified by the shopping mall, the pursuit of a new car, a washer/dryer, a new set of golf clubs, and prescriptions for Viagra and antidepressant drugs.

Of course, none of the above was in existence at the time when the founding fathers, as children of the Enlightenment, conceived of the Declaration. But this is not the issue. To the founding fathers, the pursuit of Happiness was not manifested in material consumption, but in the individual's right to pursue complete living in a free society. To Herbert Spencer (1860) complete living meant finding a congenial calling or vocation, an enriching avocation (worthy use of leisure time), effective parenthood—including education, health, and good housing—the highest production and enjoyment of the arts, and all that makes for the enlightened citizen leading the good life in a free society (pp. 32–70).

In *Education and the Cult of Efficiency,* Callahan (1962, pp. 34–39) recounts the case of a Mr. Schmidt whose job in the early 1900s at Bethlehem Steel was loading slabs of pig iron weighing 92 pounds into railroad cars. The nation's leading efficiency expert of the time, Frederick Taylor, who was contracted by the steel company, found that Schmidt and his fellow workers managed to load an average of 12.5 tons per man in a 10-hour workday. Schmidt had been observed at the end of the day, trotting home where he was finishing construction on his little house. So it seemed obvious to Taylor that the men were not working to full capacity. The problem then was to determine Schmidt's real capacity for loading pig iron. By offering a small wage inducement, it was found that Schmidt's lifting load was increased from 12.5 tons to 48 tons per day, although Schmidt weighed only 130 pounds. Yet Schmidt still managed to trot home afterward to continue working on his little house. Clearly, Schmidt was engaged in the "pursuit of Happiness." Unfortunately, Schmidt did not benefit from the subsequent social reforms leading to an 8-hour workday, a 40-hour workweek, minimum wage, workmens' compensation, health insurance, safety regulations, union membership, free public schools, and so on. But it cannot be disputed that Mr. Schmidt, in working on his house, was engaged in the pursuit of Happiness, which probably was one of the compelling reasons why he and his family had migrated from Germany to the United States in the first place. The founding fathers fully understood the meaning of the pursuit of Happiness.

Contemporary Life Needs

According to Ralph W. Tyler (1949), the school must employ some system for analyzing and selecting from contemporary life learning objectives appropriate to the school's clientele (pp. 16–25). Although this point may appear to be a common-sense principle, great controversy has raged over the system and criteria to be employed and the extent to which the curriculum should be based on contemporary life. Furthermore, any realistic and useful analysis of society as a *source* of data should include society as a powerful *influence* on the school's objectives and curriculum.

When Herbert Spencer posed the question in 1860 "What knowledge is of most worth?" he answered his own question by pointing to science as the most important subject matter for preparing children and youth for complete living. According to Spencer, science is the key to complete living: for preservation of health, earning a living, effective parenthood, good citizenship, the highest production and enjoyment of the arts, and intellectual and moral discipline (pp. 32–70).

Spencer's view that the function of the school should be focused on effective living, and that the knowledge key to successful life in society is science, came as a disturbing blow to the custodians of the classics who had enjoyed a long and unyielding grip on the school and college curriculum. Not only did Spencer attack the classical studies for being irrelevant to modern living, but he also challenged the claim that such studies are best for disciplining the mind by contending that the sciences are far superior for this task. Dewey (1916) was to criticize Spencer more than half a century later for having failed to recognize that unless science as subject matter is methodologically transformed so as to be applied to life needs and problems, it may be treated in the curriculum as just another inert body of information (pp. 258–259). Nevertheless, Spencer's thesis gave impetus to the idea that the aims and functions of education must be relevant to effective living in modern society rather than merely being designed to transmit the cultural heritage, an idea that was embraced by American progressive educators in their efforts to reform education during the early decades of the twentieth century.

However, the study of contemporary life as a basis for educational objectives and curriculum construction came to be undertaken in some quarters in a mechanistic and static way. The scientific management movement in industry during the early decades of the twentieth century influenced such educators as Bobbitt (1924) and Charters (1923) to adapt the technique of job analysis or activity analysis to curriculum construction. The fundamental assumption underlying this technique—namely, that each area of life activity is reducible to perfectly specifiable components and tasks—ignores the fact that many activities in democratic societies require independence of judgment and the use of free intelligence under incessantly changing conditions. In a free society the school is expected to do more than prepare the rising generation to become acceptable cogs in society's machinery, no matter how satisfactory that machinery may be at a given time. The widespread use of narrowly conceived behavioristic objectives, workbooks, and computer "worksheets" in fashioning the curriculum during the latter half of the twentieth century likewise ignored the fact that life activities are dynamic, not static, and require a high order of free intelligence for social insight and problem solving.

Social Problem Solving. The attempt to focus the curriculum on social problem solving gained considerable momentum through the efforts of progressive educators during the Great Depression. Reviewing the emerging curricula in the secondary schools during the 1930s, Mackenzie (1942) offered these observations:

> Current problems facing the American people, alternative solutions to social difficulties, and the viewing of future possibilities are common centers of attention. The immediate community is surveyed and studied. Community needs are analyzed and programs of action developed. . . . Students not only read about problems in these areas; they actually work out solutions. Parents are brought in frequently to participate and aid in the development of solutions to persistent problems of life outside the school. Situations more directly under the school are attacked by students and teachers. . . .
>
> Whether one views the recent curriculum developments in general education from the standpoint of stated purposes, course organization, scope of the required program, units of work, or actual learning experiences, there are unmistakable evidences of a recognition of a social goal and responsibility as well as a concern for the full development of the individual for effective democratic living. (pp. 85–86)

Progressive schools of that era commonly designed their curricula in general education to focus on such life-problem areas as personal and community health, conservation of natural resources, intercultural relations, world peace, consumer education, technology, housing, vocations and employment, economic relations, and so on. One of the most creative and successful efforts in this direction was the *Building America* series of monthly pictorial paperback and annual hardback books for junior high schools, published from 1936 through 1942 and reaching sales of over a million copies monthly (Newman, 1960; Tanner, D., 2002). Harold Rugg's textbooks for junior and senior high schools also were widely used and followed a frame of reference on the evolution of modern American democracy with a focus on pervasive problems and issues confronting contemporary society. Both *Building America* and the Rugg textbooks were to come under attack by ultrarightist groups and went into eclipse by the early 1940s (Tanner, D., 1999; Robinson, 1983). The heterogeneously grouped problems-of-democracy course, once widely offered in the high schools, largely disappeared during the national discipline-centered curriculum reforms despite the strong endorsement of the course by James Conant in his report on the American high school (1959b).

Educational and social conservatives have long been opposed to introducing unsettling ideas and issues into the school curriculum. Instead, they have held that the schools would do well to be concerned with the "essentials" or basic education for the masses.

Efforts to derive objectives and construct the curriculum through studies of contemporary life have been attacked over the years by traditionalists. In *The Restoration of Learning,* Arthur Bestor (1956) devoted an entire chapter to "The Menace of Excessive Contemporaneity," in which he contended that the study of contemporary problems detracts the school from its essential mission of developing intellectual discipline (pp. 125–138). He went on to argue that when the school addresses contemporary problems and issues, it makes itself vulnerable to pressure groups and thereby waives its academic immunity.

However, if the school avoids all treatment of contemporary problems and issues, it is abrogating the very principle of academic freedom that Bestor seeks to protect. Avoidance of a principle serves only to undermine, and not to protect, the principle. Furthermore, when the school divorces itself from contemporary problems and issues it is failing to meet its responsibility to students as citizens. Because the future has its roots in the present, and because the rising generation represents the future society, the school that holds itself oblivious to problems and issues in contemporary life is denying its students learning experiences that are essential to the building of a better society.

The demand for curricular "relevance" during the late 1960s and early 1970s witnessed a reemergence of efforts to open the curriculum to the treatment of pervading social problems. However, where the earlier efforts were directed at total curricular reconstruction and synthesis, as exemplified by the problem-focused, integrated-core curriculum, the later response was to make allowance for these needs by adding new and specialized courses to the existing programs of studies and to increase the elective options through a kind of warehouse curriculum. The new fragmentation of the curriculum, noted a British theoretical physicist, is a reflection of the general condition of fragmentation in society (Bohm, 1971, p. 10).

By the closing years of the twentieth century, various professional associations were rediscovering the need for curriculum synthesis in order to relate the school curriculum to wider social conditions. For example, the American Association for the Advancement of Science shifted its focus from disciplinary knowledge and the gifted and talented to the problem of identifying a common core of understandings, appreciations, and capabilities in science, mathematics, and technology to be developed by all members of a free society by the time they complete their schooling (1989, p 19). The National Council for the Social Studies joined with the American Historical Association as a commission to formulate guidelines for developing a coherent curriculum core for effective citizenship and a rich cultural life for the twenty-first century (1989). However, with the dearth of problem-focused curriculum materials in the social studies available to teachers and students in the 1990s, Ralph Nader's Center for Study of Responsive Law sought to help fill the vacuum by issuing in 1992 an action-oriented text or sourcebook, *Civics for*

Democracy: A Journey for Teachers and Students (Isaac). Unfortunately, it seemed doubtful that the schools were ready for such a dynamic approach as offered in *Civics for Democracy*.

Today, burgeoning social problems at home and abroad would seem to augur for a renewal of problem-focused studies in the curriculum in general education or the core curriculum at the middle-school and secondary levels. But where the chief emphasis for general education and the core curriculum was once on curriculum articulation and synthesis, external testing programs at state and national levels were addressing the core curriculum as separate, independent subjects. Nevertheless, the need to connect the curriculum to the life of the learner is undeniable in American democracy. And this requires concerted efforts to build an articulated curriculum in general education. To focus the curriculum on "purely academic" subjects and to expect the rising generation to derive "real" social learning from raw experience is to abrogate the comprehensive and cosmopolitan function of the school in a free society. The school has a special mission to equip the rising generation with the skills and ideals for building a better society and not merely to preserve the status quo. This means that the schools have a responsibility to counter the perverse effects of society on youth and to ensure that work experience for in-school youth be monitored by the school to see to it that it is educative and not exploitative. Referring to the special mission of the school, Dewey (1916) wrote:

> Every society gets encumbered with what is trivial . . . with what is positively perverse. The school has the duty of omitting such things from the environment which it supplies, and thereby doing what it can to counteract their influence in the ordinary social environment. By selecting the best for its exclusive use, it strives to reinforce the power of this best. As a society becomes more enlightened, it realizes that it is responsible *not* to transmit and conserve the whole of its existing achievements, but only such as to make for a better future society. The school is its chief agency for the accomplishment of this end. (p. 24)

Thus, society is both a source and an influence whereby the school develops its objectives and curriculum. In an enlightened society, the school is endowed with the mission of drawing from the social environment the best elements that give promise of enabling the rising generation to build a better society.

Societal Demands and Pressures

"No educational system can escape from the political community in which it operates," observed Robert Hutchins (1968), who went on to declare that "[t]he system must reflect what the political community wants it to do. The system can set out formally to change the community only if the community includes change of this kind among its aims" (p. ix).

Free societies look to the school as a key agency of social improvement and recognize the need to protect academic freedom. However, at times of national crisis, there is the tendency to regard the school more narrowly as an instrument of national purpose. Examples since midcentury are the censorship of instructional materials under the influence of McCarthyism during the early years of the Cold War, the narrow curricular focus of the National Defense Education Act of 1958 and of the projects sponsored by the National Science Foundation during the Cold War and post-Sputnik era, and the efforts to exploit for nationalistic purposes the most academically talented children and youth during this same era. Beginning with the mid-1960s, the United States drastically changed its education priorities by turning toward children and youth in poverty. But President Lyndon Johnson's War on Poverty could not compete with the war in Vietnam.

When in one era the schools were blamed for neglecting the academically talented, in a succeeding era the schools were blamed for having failed the disadvantaged. When education had been seen as the key instrument of national supremacy in the era of the Cold War and space race, it had come to be blamed in a succeeding era for the alleged decline of the United States and the rise of Japan and Germany in dominating the global industrial marketplace, according to two national reports issued by the U.S. Department of Education, *A Nation at Risk* (1983) and *America 2000* (1991). In these two nationalistic assaults on the public schools, no blame was leveled at the military-industrial complex and government for the misallocation of resources and misguided priorities. And no credit was given the public schools for the nation's number-one global ranking in knowledge production. As was the case at the height of the space race, the call for global economic mobilization was for curriculum priority in the sciences and mathematics (to which was added computer literacy), national achievement testing, and special programs for the academically gifted and talented.

Despite the continuing influences in these directions today, the need for a more balanced and coherent core curriculum in the schools and colleges, coupled with the need for educational and social equity and remediation, could not be denied in the face of the rising fragmentation and conflict among the multitude of cultures. The key question was whether cosmopolitanism would be served in the spirit of democracy, by fostering a sense of unity through diversity, or whether U.S. diversity will be the basis for cultural division and conflict. United States history reveals that no institution has been more pivotal than the public schools. U.S. history also reveals that the public tends to recoil against extreme measures and seeks a balanced and comprehensive role for American schools. As John Goodlad (1984) found in his study of schooling, "We want it all," to which might be added, "And why not?"

Community, School, and Multiculturalism

Concerted efforts to develop the school as a community center were undertaken early in the twentieth century, as evidenced by the issuance of two yearbook volumes in 1911 by the National Society for the Study of Education, *The City School as a Community Center,* Part I, and *The Rural School as a Community Center,* Part II. In 1953 the society issued *The Community School,* Part II (M. F. Seay, chair).

Through the first half of the twentieth century, progressive educators sought to develop the notion of the community school, with the aim of building closer ties between the school and the community, by having the school serve the comprehensive educational needs of all residents of its area, whether children or adults, and by linking the curriculum to community needs. However, the late 1960s and early 1970s witnessed the use of the term *community school* in American major inner cities as a militant demand for control of elementary schools by the dominant group in the immediate neighborhood served by the school. Ironically, where the earlier concept of community school sought greater unity among the diverse elements of the region served by the school, later it came to be associated with political conflict over the control of the local school by special interest groups. By the end of the 1990s, the abuses and scandals attendant to local control eventuated in its elimination and a move toward more centralized responsibility for the administration of inner-city schools. Obviously, the meaning of community in community school had undergone a radical reversal from the 1930s to the 1960s and extending to the present day. Today, the word *community* often refers to a special-interest group or particular ethnic or religious group—as set apart and, often, in isolation or in conflict with other groups (Schlesinger, 1998).

Whereas the advancement of intercultural education was a leading priority in school and society early in the twentieth century, as exemplified in the work of the Society for Intercultural Education in New York City, today the shift has been to multicultural education. The metaphor for intercultural education was not the "melting pot," but was embodied in *e pluribus unum*, "from many, one"—the building of unity through diversity. The idea and practice of general education or the core curriculum in the school and college, as advanced by experimentalist-progressive educators over the course of the first half of the twentieth century, grew out of the recognition of the need to create a commitment to the common cause of American democracy and cosmopolitanism while giving recognition to cultural diversity.

Those who regard the contemporary magnitude of immigration as insurmountable to the creation of a sense of common culture for American democracy should take note of the U.S. census data revealing that the proportion of foreign born in the U.S. population in the early decades of the twentieth century was far higher than it is today, resulting in enormous pressures on the schools of American cities not only for the education of immigrant children and American-born children of foreign-born parents, but also for immigrant adults in night-school literacy classes.

The sense of unity through diversity was identified by Gunnar Myrdal (1941) as the *American Creed*. As noted elsewhere in this text, Myrdal pointed out that the principal element in the American Creed is the belief in education. On the opening page of his classic study of the Negro in America, Myrdal observed that amidst the impression of chaos, and unrest in American life, there is this seeming paradox of common belief:

> Americans of all national origins, classes, regions, creeds, and colors, have something in common: a social *ethos*, a political creed. It is difficult to avoid the judgment that this "American Creed" is the cement in the structure of this great and disparate nation. . . .
>
> America, compared to every other country in Western civilization, large or small, has the *most*

explicitly expressed system of general ideals in human relations. . . . To be sure, the political creed of America is not very satisfactorily effectuated in actual social life. But as principles which *ought* to rule, the Creed has been made conscious to everyone in American society. (20th Anniversary Edition, 1962, p. 3)

Picking up on the idea and ideals of the American Creed, Schlesinger (1998) warns that the American experiment "in creating a common identity for people of diverse races, religions, languages, cultures" is threatened by the tribalisms of multiculturalism (p. 124). Schlesinger points to the current global situation in which nations are being torn apart by ethnic, racial, and religious differences (pp. 13–14). He devotes an entire chapter to the schools and criticizes bilingual education for promoting segregation and self-ghettoization, dooming children to second-class citizenship. He holds that the positive claims for bilingual education are unsupported and that it shuts doors to the larger world (pp. 113–114).

The research literature on the effects of bilingual education is remarkably weak and sketchy (Willig & Ramirez, 1993). Ironically, the case for bilingual education stems from the Supreme Court ruling (Lau v. Nichols, 1974) in which a group of Chinese parents in San Francisco sued for more English instruction for their children in the public schools. The court ruled that the schools must provide assistance for language-minority students. Many states proceeded to legislate bilingual education programs, with the consequence that bilingual education became targeted largely for Hispanic children from lower-income families. To Schlesinger (1998), bilingual education has become an educational establishment with a vested interest in building a political lobby in retaining a Hispanic constituency (p. 113).

Society as Curricular Source and Influence: Changing Functions of Schooling

The function of the school and the model of curriculum embraced at a particular time reflect the demands and expectations of the larger society. As discussed previously, changing sociopolitical forces have exerted changing demands and expectations on the school. In various eras, the tendency is for the school to respond to whatever pressures are most dominant. Although the school in a pluralistic society embracing democratic ideals is expected to be responsive to the demands and expectations of society, there is the tendency in eras of crisis to react with imbalanced prescriptions. Instead of viewing these functions as interactive and symbiotic, and seeking ways of developing them within a unified and coherent curriculum structure, they are viewed as incompatible alternatives. Should the curriculum focus on preserving and transmitting the cultural heritage, or should its emphasis be on developing fundamental skills? Should the curriculum be geared to fostering personal growth, or should its focus be on achieving social growth? Should the main emphasis of the curriculum be on promoting the disciplines of academic scholarship, or should it be geared to social correction? These are some of the dichotomies raised when different functions of the school and its curriculum are seen as conflicting alternatives. The solution is not in finding an eclectic middle ground, but in seeking curriculum articulation and synthesis (see chapter 9 and part III).

Although the ways of organizing the curriculum are discussed in detail in part III, a brief review of several conceptions of the function of the school will serve to illustrate how these conceptions are set off against one another to reflect philosophical polarities and societal priorities.

Fundamental Skills

In his monumental work, *Science in History* (1971), a noted British scientist and science historian, J. D. Bernal, described how the rising industrialism in England during the early nineteenth century made it necessary to provide instruction in the three Rs for children of the working classes. According to Bernal,

> the new working class needed enough acquaintance with the three R's to do their jobs properly, and provision for teaching them was reluctantly provided on the cheapest possible basis. But there was all the more reason for seeing that the education of the masses did not go too far, and that it introduced no unsettling ideas. (p. 1149)

In the United States, the waves of immigrants during the first three decades of the twentieth century brought special focus to education for literacy. This educational function was broadened to include Americanization for these millions of new citizens. However, American progressive educators were concerned that the schools would yield to the Old World conservatism and to the demands of the corporate sector that education of children be limited to the three Rs. Attempts by progressive educators to enrich the curriculum were attacked as "frills." For their own children, the privileged sought a rich and balanced curriculum. Criticizing these antidemocratic influences, Dewey (1917) wrote:

> He who is poorly acquainted with the history of the efforts to improve elementary education in our large cities does not know that the chief protest against progress is likely to come from successful business men. They have clamored for the three R's as the essential and exclusive material of primary education—knowing well enough that their own children would be able to get the things they protest against. Thus they have attacked as fads and frills every enrichment of the curriculum which did not lend itself to narrow economic ends. Let us stick to business, to the essentials, has been their plea, and by business they meant enough of the routine skills in letters and figures to make those leaving the elementary school at about the fifth or sixth grade useful in *their* business, irrespective of whether pupils left school with an equipment for advance and with the ambition to try to secure better social and economic conditions for their children than they themselves had enjoyed. (p. 332)

Although American society and schools have long since passed the days of child labor and exploitation, back-to-basics has been a recurrent movement throughout the twentieth century and to this day. In examining the views of the de-schoolers and school blamers, along with the simplistic prescription of back to basics, one must wonder whether those who consciously portray the school as ineffectual are unconsciously fearful that a rich curriculum will convey too many unsettling ideas for the rising generation.

Skill Mastery as Preparation.   Education conservatives embrace the fundamental-skills model of curriculum for the elementary level of schooling on the ground that the mastery of the three Rs is essential for successful later learning in the academic disciplines. "On the elementary level," declares Mortimer Smith (1970), "the task of the school is to provide those sets of symbols and sets of facts that are necessary preliminary to all later learning and understanding" (p. 443). (Smith was co-founder, with Arthur Bestor, of the Council for Basic Education, a national organization to promote basic education.)

Mortimer Adler's widely read book, *The Paideia Proposal: An Educational Manifesto* (1982), called for

12 years of basic schooling for all, without any electives except for foreign languages. The curriculum would be composed of the basic academic subjects with some concessions for the arts. (The word *paideia* was taken from ancient Greece, meaning "rearing the child.") Great emphasis is given to coaching and drilling, and didactic teaching. This is capped in the upper grades by Socratic questioning on literary works adjudged to be of high literary merit.

Although progressive educators recognize the importance of the fundamental skills, they see these skills not merely as preparatory for later learning but as relevant to the child's present life. Moreover, they do not regard the function of elementary schooling as being limited to mastery of the three Rs but see the elementary-school curriculum fulfilling a wide range of functions, from cognitive development to socialization. In this connection, they recognize that the fundamental skills are not learned for their own sake but must be developed in a wide range of life contexts. Hence, they see these skills and understandings being developed through a comprehensive curriculum including learning activities in the social studies, sciences, the arts, industrial arts, health, and so on.

New Media: Old Basics. The advent of the computer was expected to promote a breakthrough in the teaching of basic skills as well as in overall academic achievement, especially for lower-achieving, at-risk pupils at the elementary-school level. From the time of the War on Poverty to this day, as reflected in the National Right to Read program, vast federal funds have been expended to integrate the computer into the curriculum rather than to use the computer as a vehicle for integrating the curriculum. The promised revolution failed to materialize as the computer came to be used, as far as remedial instruction is concerned, as an electronic workbook following a repertoire of programmed instruction. The new technology was used segmentally and could not substitute for the kinds of aggregate rich stimulation for effective concept formation and cognitive and social development. In a related way, wildly extravagant claims were made for television back in the 1950s and 1960s in effecting an educational revolution comparable to the effects on education following the invention of movable type (Stoddard, 1957, p. 27). Nevertheless, television in the classroom might have had a significant impact had it been used as a "window to the world," as in the case of the British Broadcasting Corporation's programming for the schools. Unfortunately, in the United States, school television has been used largely as a "talking face" in imitation of conventional, didactic instruction. Ironically, the "revolutionary" new media have been used primarily for conventional instruction even beyond basic education. It is equally ironic that essentialists as a rule have tended to look skeptically at the new media as well as audiovisual aids, in general on the grounds that they detract the learner from advancing in the development of abstract learning (Bestor, 1956, pp. 108–109). Such an assertion is, of course, totally unfounded. Visual imagery and three-dimensional models have been essential in scientific work, such as in the discovery of DNA, the design of buildings, bridges, medical instruments, and every kind of tool in the creation of civilization, not to mention the great significance of the visual arts.

Recurrent Emphasis. The call of "back to basics" is bellowed by tax conservatives not only in periodic cycles of social and economic retrenchment, but even at times of national mobilization. From the Cold War to the battle for global economic dominance, the call has been for giving priority to the academic disciplines, especially the sciences and mathematics (Bruner, 1960), and for what has been called the "New Basics"—which appear to be the academic subjects coupled with computer literacy—to which is added nationalized and statewide testing, testing, and more testing (National Commission on Excellence, 1983; *America 2000*, 1991).

Typically, education reform cycles have tended to be by reaction and counterreaction, with little or no attempt to evaluate systematically which knowledge has actually been gained so as to effect substantive progress. Most reforms have been fairly short lived, but the disciplines doctrine of the Cold War extended over two decades, and the current reform wave for turning the schools to global economic mobilization through the New Basics and nationalized testing stems back to two federal reports: *A Nation at Risk* (1983) and *America 2000* (1991). For the most part, the nationalized testing pandemic has revealed what educators have known for many years. Children in poverty do poorly on the tests, whereas children from advantaged environments do well on the tests. However, the nationalized testing pandemic is not accompanied by corresponding financial support to schools in an effort to attack the problem of inequality of educational opportunity, but has been used to penalize the lower-scoring schools through reduction of funding and the creation of alternative schools, schools of choice, charter schools, and school vouchers. It is far cheaper to create other kinds of schools than to provide the wide-scale support needed for the public school system at large and especially for inner-city public schools. The No Child Left Behind Act of 2001, signed by President George W. Bush, embraced many of these regressive elements and punitive sanctions directed at public schools serving the most severely underprivileged children (U.S. Department of Education, 2002).

Literacy. As discussed in chapter 5, although the concept of literacy originally was associated with the Americanization of immigrants during the first three decades of the twentieth century by learning the rudiments of reading and writing, *literacy* has come to be used widely by essentialists in their attacks on the schools for neglecting the essentials in the curriculum. The national best-seller by Edward D. Hirsch, *Cultural Literacy: What Every American Needs to Know* (1987), revivified the term *literacy* along with the notion that mastery of lists of factual information, as evidenced on multiple-choice tests, defined the educated person. In a similar vein, Ravitch and Finn of the U.S. Department of Education drew on the periodic report cards on the nation's schools in the National Assessment of Educational Progress, administered by Educational Testing Service, to expose what 17-year olds do not know (in their 1987 book *What Do Our 17-Year Olds Know?*). Soon the term *literacy* was being attached to virtually every academic subject, resulting in a multitude of literacies (e.g., scientific literacy, mathematical literacy, economic literacy, cultural literacy, computer literacy, and so on). There appeared to be a general failure to recognize that such segmental uses of the term only exacerbated the fragmentation of the curriculum.

Testing as a Nationalizing Influence on the Curriculum

Educational policy makers at the state and national levels have been using standardized tests increasingly to buttress their political agenda for school reform. In so doing, the test data are commonly misinterpreted and distorted. The media and the public have been led to believe that tests such as the Scholastic Aptitude Test (SAT) and the tests used in the National Assessment of Educational Progress and the International Study of Educational Achievement are valid national indicators of academic achievement, when in fact they have severe limitations and have been widely misused (Madaus, 1992; Carson, Huelskamp, & Woodall, 1993).

The key mechanism for assessing "excellence" in President George H. W. Bush's *America 2000* (1991) was to be manifested in the American Achievement Tests to be made available nationally and to be used in ascertaining the progress toward achieving the national educational goals for the year 2000 (e.g., "U.S. students will be first in the world in science and mathematics achievement"). *America 2000* was the outgrowth of the 1989 Education Summit meeting of the nation's governors and President Bush, a meeting at which Bill Clinton played a key leadership role. On his election as president, Clinton endorsed the development of the American Achievement Tests.

As in the case with statewide assessment testing, and with the Preliminary Scholastic Aptitude Test (PSAT) and SAT, teachers have come under enormous pressure to teach to the test. In fact, the practice has become so widespread that it is advocated and regarded by many school administrators as a "best practice." (The National Association of Secondary School Principals has been marketing such a package to its membership in connection with the SAT over many years.) To the extent that teaching to the test is practiced, the test becomes the curriculum or, at least, shapes the curriculum.

Considering the powerful influence of testing on the curriculum, it is surprising that the *Handbook of Research on Curriculum* (1992) does not have more entries on testing. Writing in the handbook, Madaus and Kellaghan cite data showing that the space devoted to testing in the *Education Index* has exploded to such a proportion in recent years that it far exceeds the space devoted to curriculum. Madaus and Kellaghan also point out that although policy makers cannot mandate what goes on in the classroom, they have been using testing programs as an accountability device, coupled with important rewards or sanctions for school administrators and teachers, to the extent that the curriculum eventually conforms to the test (pp. 126, 137).

High-Stakes Tests. Tests have come to be widely used for high-stakes social decision making. As Madaus (1999) points out, high-stakes tests are being used to make such decisions having important social consequences such as (1) graduation, promotion, or placement of students; (2) evaluation or rewarding of teachers or administrators; (3) allocation of resources to schools or school districts; and (4) school or school system certification. Further, "Policymakers have mandated that the results be used *automatically* to make such decisions" (p. 77).

Madaus offers several general principles relating to the power of testing in influencing the curriculum, two of which have wide and profound social implications:

> The more any quantitative social indicator is used for social decision making, the more likely it will be to distort and corrupt the social processes it is intended to monitor. . . . (p. 79)
>
> When test results are used for important social decisions, the changes in the system brought about by such a use tend to be both substantial and corrupting. . . . (p. 79)
>
> When test-results are the sole or even partial arbiter of future educational or life choices, society tends to treat the results as the major goal of schooling rather than as a useful but fallible indicator of achievement. (p. 87)

Each year, the U.S. Department of Education issues *The Nation's Report Card*, from the test results of the National Assessment of Educational Progress (NAEP). Student achievement is measured in various academic subjects at grades 4, 8, and 12—conforming to the grades recommended for national testing in *America 2000*—with state-by-state comparisons made of the results. In her study of NAEP's history and influence on educational policy, Epstein (1996), concluded that

> NAEP has been transformed into a high stakes assessment that uses state comparisons and national standards that were set by an independent, elite governing board to generate education reform activities in the states. As a federal policy, using a high stakes assessment as a reform strategy may or may not raise students' real academic achievement levels, but there is no question that used as an instrument of reform the National Assessment will become a powerful nationalizing influence on the curriculum in the nation's schools. (p. 40)

Reinforcing the Segmental Subject Curriculum. Targeted on the separate academic subjects, NAEP has hardened the traditional segmental subject curriculum, and any weaknesses revealed by the annually released test results have garnered considerable media attention.

Of course, some of the most significant learning experiences cannot be evaluated through paper-and-pencil tests, especially in the multiple-choice format. Aside from classroom affective outcomes, there are experiences in the laboratory, shop, and studio that require other forms of evaluation. Oral communication, including the expression of collaboration, dissenting ideas, demonstration, and project work, are other examples of significant learning experiences that cannot be assessed through such tests.

Standardized test results have been used in national reports on educational reform as "evidence" of the failure of American public education and to justify radical and unwarranted policy changes affecting the structure and function of the schools when, in fact, the same test findings might better justify the conclusion that the nation's schools have been making significant progress in serving increasingly heterogeneous populations, as shown in the Sandia report (Carson, Huelskamp, & Woodall, 1993). The suppression of the Sandia Report by the U.S. Department of Education is a notorious example of what can happen when the findings of a study financed by a federal agency run counter to established federal political policy (Tanner, D., 1993).

Cultural Heritage

As noted in chapter 5, the perennialist sees the chief task of education as the preservation and transmission of the cultural heritage. The schism between cultural or liberal education and education for life in contemporary society stems from the centuries-old notion that the humanistic studies embody the "treasuries of truth" to be protected by a "high priesthood" for the privileged classes (Dewey, 1915a, p. 25). Although many modern-day perennialists advocate the humanistic studies for all, the traditional social distinction attached to such studies has been reflected in a curriculum schism that holds the liberal studies above the practical in intellective worth. Indicative of the schisms in American society, as Dewey (1916) noted, is the "separation and mutual contempt of the 'practical' man and the man of theory and culture" (p. 159). When culture is taken as merely an internal refinement of mind as opposed to social efficiency, and when the latter is interpreted narrowly as skills divorced from the spirit and meaning of social action, warned Dewey, two separate educational aims emerge that are "fatal to democracy" (pp. 142–143).

Cultural Transmission and Social Power.
Addressing the implications of this schism (between the cultural and practical) for general education, Conant (1949) made this observation at mid-twentieth century:

> Roughly speaking, the basic argument about general education turns on the degree to which the literary and philosophic traditions of the western world, as interpreted by scholars and connoisseurs before World War I, should be the basis of the education of *all* American youth. The watershed between two fundamentally opposed positions can be located by raising the question: For what purpose do we have a system of public education? If the answer is to develop effective citizens of a free democratic country, then we seem to be facing in one direction. If the answer is to develop the student's rational powers and immerse him in the stream of our cultural heritage, then we appear to be facing in the opposite direction. By and large, the first position represents the modern approach to education; the latter the more conventional view. Those who look down one valley regard conventional "book learning" as only one element in the landscape; those who look down the other believe that developing the "life of the mind" is the primary aim of civilization and this can be accomplished only by steeping youth in our literary and philosophical heritage. (pp. 74–75)

Conant went on to stress that we will have to discard the "cultural presuppositions" that undergirded education in an earlier era in view of the fact that "the social setting of maturing youths as well as grown men and women is vastly different in this country . . . from anything the world has ever seen before." Allies of the humanities must ruthlessly reexamine their premises and must make their studies "really relevant to the present scene," warned Conant (pp. 79, 83, 92).

Nevertheless, the cultural presuppositions for traditional liberal education remain more than a museum piece. Despite the revolutionary transformation of the undergraduate curriculum in the twentieth century through the modern and practical studies, the failure to build a coherent core curriculum in general education in the face of knowledge specialism and fragmentation gives cause for perennialists to vent their timeworn call for a return to the "timeless" liberal arts. Moreover, old traditions die hard. The belief that liberal education marks a truly cultural education, as opposed to practical studies, continues to garner snob appeal on the part of so many liberal arts graduates (who must face the practical reality of going on to graduate and professional studies if they are to earn a living). The phenomenon of Allan Bloom's *Closing of the American Mind* holding the number-one position over many weeks on national lists of best-sellers during 1987 revealed that a belligerent perennialist attack on the university for neglecting the traditional liberal arts was vastly appealing to American readers.

Traditionalists see the school as well as the college as appropriately being concerned, predominantly if not solely, with the transmission of the cultural heritage, built on a foundation of facts and skills in the elementary grades. Mortimer Adler's *Paideia Proposal* (1982) exemplifies this view.

In an essay on education, Einstein (1950) observed that "[s]ometimes one sees in the school simply the instrument for transferring a certain maximum quantity of knowledge to the growing generation," and he proceeded to warn that such knowledge is dead. Accordingly, contended Einstein, "the aim must be the training of independently acting and thinking individuals who see in the service of the community their highest life problem" (p. 32).

The dualism between cultural heritage and social power as educational aims, noted Dewey (1916), is taken as intrinsic and absolute when it is actually historical and cultural. "The problem of education in a democratic society is to do away with the dualism," wrote Dewey. This problem continues to haunt education to this day.

Knowledge Production: Disciplinarity

As we have noted, the era of the Cold War and space race was marked by an unprecedented curriculum-reform effort in the United States that sought to create a new generation of knowledge producers in emulation of the specialized university scholar. The pursuit of academic excellence embodied in the knowledge production-disciplinary model of curriculum was seen as serving nationalistic interests at a time when U.S. leaders feared Americans were in danger of falling behind the Soviets in scientific-technological-military developments. University scholars in the academic disciplines led the curriculum reforms during this era with the support of enormous federal funds.

These reforms were governed by a neo-essentialist doctrine of disciplinarity that saw curriculum content at the elementary and secondary levels being derived from and molded to the established academic disciplines of university scholarship. Although leading essentialists at first applauded these curriculum reforms, many of them began to have second thoughts regarding the priority given to the sciences and mathematics, and to the decline of history in favor of the contemporary social science disciplines in the curriculum.

By the end of the 1960s, the dominance of the knowledge production-disciplinary model came to be challenged as a result of the clamor for curriculum relevance on the part of high school and college youth, rising social disaffection and protest, and a growing awareness that American quality of life was eroding and that education and knowledge must be geared to social problem solving if the American dream is to be fulfilled.

Knowledge production remains a chief function of the university, and the disciplinary structure of the curriculum reflects the departmental organization of specialized knowledge of the university defining majors in the undergraduate curriculum and areas of graduate study. Leading colleges have sought to provide for a curriculum core for general education which may be organized thematically, as broad fields (e.g., natural science, biological sciences, humanities, social sciences, and so on), or in a variety of correlated and interdisciplinary designs. With knowledge specialism as king in the university, it is difficult to find faculty who are willing to devote time and effort, if not a career, to the idea and practice of general education.

The impact and consequences of the knowledge production-disciplinary model when applied to the school curriculum are treated in detail in part III.

Individual-Social Growth

The function of education for individual and social growth is orchestrated in the writings of John Dewey. Although some of Dewey's educational and social theories have been discussed in earlier chapters, and are treated in detail in chapter 9, along with their curricular implications, a brief mention of his theory of education as individual and social growth is presented here to contrast it with traditional conceptions of the function of education. According to Dewey (1948):

> Education has been traditionally thought of as preparation: as learning, acquiring certain things because they will later be useful. The end is remote, and education is getting ready, is a preliminary to something more important to happen later on. Childhood is only a preparation for adult life, and adult life for another life. . . .
>
> If at whatever period we choose to take a person, he is still in the process of growth, then

education is not, save as a by-product, a preparation for something coming later. . . . The best thing that can be said about any special process of education . . . is that it renders its subject capable of further education. . . . Acquisition of skill, possession of knowledge, attainment of culture are not ends: they are marks of growth and means to its continuing. (p. 184–185)

Democracy and Social Progress.   The vital connection between individual growth and the social growth of a democracy is stressed by Dewey (1948) in describing the purpose of democratic social institutions.

> That purpose is to set free and to develop the capacities of human individuals without respect to race, sex, class or economic status. And this is all one with saying that the test of their value is the extent to which they educate every individual into the full stature of his possibility. Democracy has many meanings, but if it has a moral meaning, it is found in resolving that the supreme test of all political institutions and social arrangements shall be the contribution they make to the all-around growth of every member of society. (p. 186)

Dewey (1948) saw the means to such growth as deriving from a curriculum model of personal-social problem solving through the method of intelligence. He warned of the dangers inherent in confining this method to scientific and technological advancement while neglecting the political-social-moral sphere. "Not only has the improvement in the method of knowing remained so far mainly limited to technical and economic matters, but this progress has brought with it serious new moral disturbances," wrote Dewey. He went on, "I need only cite the late war, the problem of capital and labor, the relation of economic classes, the fact that while the new science has achieved wonders . . . it has also produced and spread occasions for diseases and weaknesses." (p. 125)

Ironically, Dewey's views were distorted by many of his attackers who caricatured his message as a call for "life adjustment" (Rickover, 1959, p. 136). It was Dewey who stated that "the social definition of education as getting adjusted to civilization, makes of it a forced and external process, and results in subordinating the freedom of the individual to a preconceived social and political status" (1897). According to Dewey, "education is the fundamental method of social progress and reform," but he warned that the only sure method of social reconstruction is when individual activity has a responsible sharing of the social consciousness. "I believe that education is a regulation of the process of coming to share in the social consciousness," wrote Dewey (1897c).

Although both the individual-social growth function and the knowledge production-disciplinary function focus on inquiry-discovery as educational method, the former tends to be geared to solving pervading social problems (ecology, racial conflict, poverty), whereas the latter is more concerned with the problems that are of significance to specialized scholars on the forefront of their disciplines.

As we entered the twenty-first century, efforts toward educational improvement appeared to take the form of peripatetic responses to the demands of special-interest groups in a social situation marked by fragmentation and conflict. The call for education as a regulation of the process of coming to share in the democratic social consciousness seemed to be drowned out by social confusion and multicultural conflict.

Skills Versus Growth. As discussed earlier, changing societal priorities and expectations have wrought marked shifts in the direction of education in recent decades. Because educational objectives are conceived at different levels (from the wider society to the local school system and to the individual classroom), and because they represent a broad spectrum of expectations (from the most general ideal to the most specific objective), it is useful to make some distinctions. Thus, when education is seen by the larger society as fostering democratic citizenship, ethical character, worthy use of leisure time, or mental health, such broad expectations of the school may be considered *ideals*. At a more specific level, education may be seen as developing in pupils a command of the fundamental processes; the ability to purchase and use goods and services wisely; the appreciation of beauty in literature, art, music, and nature; the development of salable skills; and the ability to think critically—such expectations may be referred to as educational *aims*. Finally, at an even more specific point of reference, educators identify such measurable expectations as the ability to identify and define problems; to make relevant hypotheses; to select and analyze data pertinent to the solution of problems; and to formulate valid conclusions, solutions, and generalizations. Such specific expectations may be referred to as *behavioral objectives* (not to be confused with *behavioristic objectives*).

Tyler has noted that where behavioral objectives were conceived in evaluating the Eight-Year Study to assess such abilities of pupils as "applying principles to concrete situations" and "interpreting experimental data," in recent years behavioral (actually behavioristic) objectives in education have been patterned after the industrial and military world of training and management by objectives, with the result that these objectives have been so narrowly specific as to lose sight of the wider nature of the human learner and the purposes of education. Referring to the tendency on the part of a number of education leaders to fashion behavioral objectives with excessive specificity and narrowness, Tyler (1973) observed that "they failed to distinguish between (1) the learning of highly specific skills for limited job performance and (2) the more generalized understanding, problem-solving skills and other kinds of behavior patterns that thoughtful teachers and educators seek to help students develop" (p. 57). In this sense, the former are not really behavioral objectives, but *behavioristic* objectives. Obviously, educators who see the function of the school as patterned properly according to the skills model, for example, will differ markedly in the formulation of educational ideals, aims, and behavioral objectives from those educators who opt for the growth model. Table 7.1 illustrates how these two contrasting models result in sharply different educational ideals, aims, and objectives.

Although the data in Table 7.1 are focused on cognitive abilities, it should be stressed that educational ideals, aims, and behavioral objectives may also encompass affective learning such as attitudes, appreciations, and values. Thus, for example, the ideal of democratic citizenship embraces the value of open-mindedness (as an educational aim), and may be evidenced (as a behavioral objective) in the learner's commitment to seeking and testing pertinent data representing all sides of an issue or problem.

As another illustration of how attitudes and appreciations may be encompassed in the growth model, let us assume that an educational aim calls for developing in the learner a love of good literature. A behavioral objective consonant with this aim is seeking to ascertain the extent to which the learner, as a result of curricular experiences, is impelled to read good literature for his or her own enjoyment.

Under the individual-social growth function, skills are recognized not as ends in themselves but as instrumental to the development of the ability to think reflectively. The ideal is the democratic (autonomously thinking, socially responsible) citizen. In connection with the skills function, the mastery of skills tends to be considered an adequate end in itself.

Table 7.1   Contrasting Functions of the School with Regard to Ideals, Aims, and Objectives.

Purpose	Function	
	Skills (behavioristic)	**Growth (behavioral)**
Ideal	Performance of specified skills	Democratic (enlightened) citizen
Aim	Subject-matter mastery	Reflective thinking
Objective (examples)	Conjugates correctly at least 90 percent of any regular "ie" verb in Spanish Changes percents to decimals with accuracy to three decimal places Given a list of 35 chemical elements, recalls and writes the valences of at least 30 of them Calculates the area of a circle correctly	Recognizes existence of a problem Makes relevant hypotheses Selects pertinent data Applies data to solution(s) Forms tentative solution(s) Tests validity of solution(s) through application Reaches valid conclusion(s) Makes applications to new problem situations
Method	Coaching drills (error-oriented) Established-convergent	Problem solving/hypothetical thinking (idea-oriented)
Evaluative resource activity (example)	Worksheet exercises Workbooks Programmed instruction Standardized achievement tests Teaching to the test Recitation	Emergent Projects (individual/group) in school laboratories, studios, shops, and in the field Practical applications Student portfolios Field trips Supervised field experience Critical-thinking tests (comprehensive)

Significantly, the problem method, student school-community projects, and student portfolios (Table 7.1) were used with great success in the more experimental schools in the Eight-Year Study. The portfolio idea was virtually forgotten until it was revived by Ernest Boyer in his report on the American high school (1983), in recognition that conventional testing instruments fail to represent and assess much of the most significant classroom learning experiences. More recently, Educational Testing Service (ETS) has sought to co-opt the student portfolio among the "new forms of assessment" being developed. Nevertheless, there was no danger that the ETS standardized achievement tests would be playing a diminished role in American education.

Returning to the individual-social growth function (Table 7.1), the students are engaged in addressing authentic problems in school and society—problems that are authentic to the life and growth of the learner. Unfortunately, opposition to the problem method arises because it often engages the learner with unsettled and unsettling ideas that may be unacceptable to special-interest groups. The easy way out is to focus the school years on facts and skills and relegate authentic problem solving to the college years as some educators have suggested (Bell, 1968, p. 181). A free society requires that all of its members have a common cause and shared concerns and that problems be revealed rather than concealed for the enlightenment of the rising generation.

The problem method is inherently optimistic in opening up the possibilities for improved conditions and progress. Curiously, although acknowledging that cognitive and developmental psychologists universally recognize the great educative power in engaging students in authentic problem solving, Prawat (1993) has characterized problem solving as "defining the world in negative terms, as a series of obstacles to be overcome." He proposes that the focus be "less on problems and more on possibilities in a given situation" through what he terms "idea-based social constructivism" (pp. 5–14). However, Prawat not only has mischaracterized authentic or practical problem solving as pessimistic, while overlooking the fact that it is indeed idea based, but he has also created an artificial dualism between problems and possibilities. Authentic or practical problem solving is inherently rich in possibilities because it is an open system of inquiry and seeks solutions based on the best available evidence. The danger of focusing the curriculum on possibilities as opposed to problem solutions is that of indoctrination, for the possibilities are not put through the systematic test of problem solving.

The significance of personal-social problem solving in generating the powers of independent thinking in the context of democratic social responsibility gains renewed recognition at times of social disaffection and conflict. Paradoxically, when the growth function of the school should provide learning experiences to enhance intercultural understandings and cooperation, as opposed to multicultural separation and conflict, the curriculum emphasis in the social studies in recent years has been on multicultural education.

The Panel on Youth of the President's Science Advisory Committee, under the chairmanship of James S. Coleman (1974), pointed out that the schools have traditionally focused on narrow skills at the self-centered or individualistic level. The committee emphasized that it is also important for the schools to develop learning environments to enhance "mutually responsible and mutually rewarding involvement with others that constitutes social maturity" (p. 3). Unfortunately, the ensuing testing pandemic has mitigated such cooperative, cosmopolitan, intercultural learning activity.

Any effort to conduct research on the effects of schooling, or to devise testing programs to assess learning outcomes, must take into account the various comprehensive functions of schooling and their interactions.

As discussed earlier, the public, education policy makers, and the media have embraced the notion that standardized achievement tests are the most valid indicators in assessing academic achievement of individuals and populations, along with measuring the effects of schooling. The political response, then, is for school administrators to have teachers align the curriculum to the tests so as to raise the test scores in their districts. Such tactics may well serve the political agenda, but

they do not serve as valid indicators of educational improvement. Aside from the exceedingly low predictive validity of standardized tests in connection with academic achievement, and aside from the fact that such tests measure only a small fraction of the kinds of learning that actually occur in the school, teaching to the test, or "curriculum alignment," has deleterious effects on the teaching-learning process and the curriculum. Much can be done to improve these tests by gearing them to knowledge applications and critical-thinking processes. Standardized achievement tests have inherent limitations that must be recognized by the profession, policy makers, and the public.

The World of Knowledge as Curricular Source and Influence

An extended discussion concerning the relationship between the world of knowledge and the curriculum is provided in chapter 8. It shows how the search for and application of knowledge go on in the larger society in a wide range of contexts that transcend the subject-matter boundaries or disciplines of specialized scholarship. Emphasis is given to the vital mediative role played by the school in relating organized scholarship to life experience. In performing this mediative role, the school curriculum cannot be limited to disciplinary knowledge or specialized subject matter but must be concerned with the interrelationships and applications of knowledge in a wide variety of contexts.

Subject Matter Specialists

Although the curriculum of the school and college must be influenced profoundly by the wider world of knowledge, Tyler (1949) viewed subject specialists as the key source of educational objectives as far as organized knowledge is concerned (pp. 25–33). Disciplinary knowledge has been an outgrowth of specialized university scholarship and has served as a most effective means of generating problem solutions within the disciplines. However, efforts to make disciplinarity the single ruling theory for curriculum development, from the elementary school through the university, reached a crisis by the end of the 1960s when it was realized that knowledge applications for social problem solving required interdisciplinary and social-problems approaches in curriculum development. Disciplinary knowledge has a central and vital place in specialized education, but the school and even the college must also be concerned with general education and exploratory and enrichment education.

The influence of subject-matter specialists has been so pervasive that the curriculum often is conceived as merely a total list of separate subject matters with courses designed within the confines of each subject-matter domain. The enormous expansion of national and statewide achievement testing, subject by subject, has served to harden the lines separating the subjects. Curriculum revision thus becomes a matter of accretion and deletion of courses and course content within each of these separate subject domains. Whitehead (1929) addressed this problem when he urged educators "to eradicate the fatal disconnection of subjects which kills the vitality of our modern curriculum" (p. 10).

Although Tyler (1949) recognized the problem of curriculum fragmentation as a result of knowledge specialization, and although he urged that knowledge specialists ask, "What can this subject contribute to the education of young people who are not to specialize in it?" he assumed that this problem can be solved by the specialists themselves (pp. 27–33). When knowledge specialists address this question, along with the question of how their knowledge can contribute to the solving of larger societal problems, they must be willing and able to pursue cross-disciplinary and interdisciplinary approaches. For example, ecological problems such as energy conservation are not confined to a single discipline but require a synthesis of many areas of knowledge: economics, politics, geography, chemistry, physics, engineering, biology, public health, and the like. The same situation applies to curriculum construction when the curriculum is to serve the need for the development of social power and insight for the rising generation, rather than for the training of specialists. In the absence of the perspective of the generalist, the specialist has little inclination to address these larger problems. This brings us to the necessary role of the generalist in school and society. An extended discussion of the discipline-centered curriculum (knowledge specialization) is presented in chapter 11.

Curriculum Generalists

The problem of the specialist's and generalist's roles has been so pervasive in government, education, and society that a subcommittee of the U.S. Senate Committee on Government Operations published a selection of readings in 1968 titled *Specialists and Generalists,* from which the following quote from an essay by Whitehead (1925) is extracted:

Another great fact confronting the modern world is the discovery of the method of training professionals, who specialize in particular regions of thought and thereby progressively add to the sum of knowledge within their respective limitations of the subject. . . .

This situation has its dangers. It produces minds in grooves. Each profession makes progress, but it is progress in its own groove. Now to be mentally in a groove is to live in contemplating a given set of abstractions. The groove prevents straying across country, and the abstraction abstracts from something to which no further attention is paid. But there is no groove of abstractions which is adequate for the comprehension of human life. Thus in the modern world, the celibacy of the medieval learned class has been replaced by a celibacy of the intellect which is divorced from the concrete contemplation of the complete facts. . . .

The dangers arising from this aspect of professionalism are great, particularly in our democratic societies. The directive force of reason is weakened. The leading intellects lack balance. They see this set of circumstances, or that set; but not both sets together. . . . In short, the specialized functions of the community are performed better and more progressively, but the generalized direction lacks vision. The progressiveness in detail only adds to the danger produced by the feebleness of coordination.

This criticism of modern life applies throughout, in whatever sense you construe the meaning of a community. It holds if you apply it to a nation, a city, a district, an institution, a family, or even to an individual. . . .

Wisdom is the fruit of a balanced development. It is this balanced growth of individuality which it should be the aim of education to secure. . . .

My own criticism of our traditional educational methods is that they are far too much occupied with intellectual analysis, and with the acquirement of formalized information. What I mean is, that we neglect to strengthen habits of concrete appreciation of the individual facts in their full interplay of emergent values, and that we merely emphasize abstract formulations which ignore this aspect of the interplay of diverse values.

In every country the problem of the balance of the general and specialist education is under consideration. . . . I know that among practical educationalists, there is considerable dissatisfaction with the existing practice. Also, the adaptation of the whole system to the needs of a democratic community is very far from being solved. I do not think that the secret of the solution lies in terms of the antithesis between thoroughness in special knowledge and general knowledge of a slighter character. The make-weight which balances the thoroughness of the specialist intellectual training should be of a radically different kind from purely intellectual analytical knowledge (pp. 47-48).

Whitehead's call for a radically different kind of make-weight for general knowledge in contrast to specialized knowledge has profound implications for curriculum development. In this task, general education—that is, the universe of discourse, understanding, and competence that enlightened citizens of a free society must share in common—cannot be construed as an amalgam of the existing subjects or disciplines of knowledge. A new structure for interdisciplinary studies that is focused on social-problem solving, and guided by some image of the good person leading the good life in the good society, becomes necessary. (A discussion of alternative ways of organizing subject matter and structuring the curriculum is presented in chapter 10.)

Micro- and Macrocurricular Problems. When addressing problems of general education, educators are concerned with macrocurricular problems—problems that transcend the knowledge compartments of the specialized disciplines. In contrast, the subject matter specialists tend to be concerned with microcurricular problems, or those kinds of questions that come within the province of their own disciplines. The problem of specialization that Whitehead addressed in 1925 has become even more acute as a result of the advances in specialized knowledge and the neglect of organizing and utilizing knowledge more broadly for solving pervading societal problems in a democracy.

A number of contemporary educators, including knowledge specialists, have recognized the need for the generalist in attacking the problem of curriculum fragmentation and in developing a more coherent curriculum that is relevant to life problems. In pointing to the dangers of the discipline-centered curriculum reforms of the 1950s and 1960s—with their emphasis on purity, abstraction, and fragmentation—and their neglect of social problem

solving, a nuclear physicist observes that "education at the elementary level of a field is too important to be left entirely to the professionals in that field, especially if the professionals are themselves too narrowly specialized in outlook." He concludes that "[s]pecialization is 'blessed' in the sense that only the specialist knows *what* he is talking about; yet, if only the specialist knows what he is talking about, only the generalist knows *why* he should talk at all" (Weinberg, 1967, pp. 154–155, 161).

Caswell (1966) put the matter very directly in addressing the problem of curriculum articulation, stressing the role of curriculum generalists who are able to see across the subject divisions and boundaries with a view of the total educational offering of the school or college. In Caswell's words,

> They must be able to build a whole of educational experience that is larger than the sum of its parts because of the mutual support and interrelationship of the parts. Only general curriculum workers are in a position to discharge this responsibility. Others must of course contribute, but no one else has the freedom from vested interest to look impartially at the competing claims of various groups of specialists and to balance these interests in terms of the best service to students and society. (p. 8)

What priorities should be given to the various studies? How should these studies interrelate with one another? How should these studies relate to the life of the learner and the problems of the larger society? How can the curriculum best be designed to serve the function of individual-social growth? These are only some of the questions that educators do not seek to answer unless they are oriented as generalists and are able to come to grips with some philosophical questions. As Cremin (1966) pointed out,

> someone must look at the curriculum whole and raise insistent questions of priority and relationship. Education is more than a succession of units, courses, and programs, however excellent; and to refuse to look at curricula in their entirety is to relegate to intraschool politics a series of decisions that ought to call into play the most fundamental philosophical principles. (p. 58)

Such decisions call into play philosophical questions of no less import than those that undergird specialized subject matters and, therefore, cannot be thought of as matters to be dealt with by administrators alone through mere organizational arrangements of the curriculum.

Mediative Role of the School

In pointing to the educative influences of various societal institutions other than the school, essentialists and perennialists, including some leading educators who occupied key positions in the U.S. Department of Education, have advocated that the school curriculum be limited to the established academic studies that are appropriate for cultivating the qualities of mind, as opposed to addressing social problems (Ravitch, 2000). The implication is that the child and adolescent are to come to school with only their intellect and leave everything else at home.

The schools of a free society are expected to play a mediative role in connection with the influences of other social institutions on the child and adolescent. Often such influences are miseducative and propagandistic, as in the case of television advertising, not to mention the obsession with crime, violence, and escapism through the video tube. The thought provoking character of the curriculum derives from reflective consideration of experiences outside the school. The educative effectiveness of the school hinges on this mediative role of the school. Of course, other societal institutions, such as the museum, art gallery, and concert hall provide educative experiences for which there are no substitutes. The fact that a sizable proportion of children and adolescents have never visited a museum or art gallery, or attended a professional symphonic concert, cannot be ignored by the school. Even if all youngsters engaged in such experiences, the school can play an important mediative role in relating the knowledge sources outside the school to the school curriculum and vice versa. If the school is to be effective in its educative mission, it cannot ignore the way youngsters use their leisure time. For example, success in the teaching of reading is related to the learner's interest in reading for pleasure outside of school.

It is tempting to simplify the role of the school by confining its curriculum to the essentials or to the traditional academic disciplines. Learners also live outside the school, and they bring this life experience to the school. Whether learners bring their school experience to their life experience outside of school hinges on this mediative role of the school. To ignore this role is to ignore the essential mission of the school in a free society.

"There is only one road to democracy: education," states Benjamin Barber, "And in a democracy, there is only one essential task for the educator: teaching liberty" (1992, p. 15). The task is engendered in the macrocurricular function of general education, which unites school experience to life beyond the school in a free society.

Perspective

The key sources and influences that must be taken into account in developing the objectives and curriculum of the school are (1) the kind of society valued (e.g., in and for a democratic civic culture); (2) the wider world of knowledge as subjected to knowledge selection, codification, and organization for systematic study by the rising generation; and (3) the nature of the learner. In this chapter, emphasis was given to the vital interdependence of these sources and influences. The chapter that follows gives extended discussion to the nature of the learner as curricular source and influence. The vital interdependence of the above three sources and influences is mitigated by the growing fragmentation of the school and college curriculum reflecting the general condition of fragmentation in society. The effects of this fragmentation, and even conflict, on the learner is quite obvious and is often manifested in the problem of the learner versus the curriculum.

The function of the school and the model of curriculum followed tend to reflect the demands and expectations of the larger society. In different epochs, shifting demands and expectations have impelled the school to change its dominant function. Some of these major functions have been (1) the development of fundamental skills, (2) the transmission and preservation of the cultural heritage, (3) knowledge-production/disciplinarity, and (4) individual-social growth. Not only do the larger sociopolitical forces exert a profound influence on the goals and functions of the school, but they also influence the direction, interpretation, and application of educational research.

Specialization and fragmentation in the larger world of knowledge have had their concomitant effects on the curriculum of the school and college. The influence of the subject matter specialist has been so pervasive that the curriculum tends to be conceived as a total list of separate subject matters. As a result, the dominant focus in curriculum development in recent years has been on microcurricular problems to the neglect of macrocurricular problems, the latter referring to problems that transcend the knowledge compartments of the separate subject matters or disciplines. Insufficient attention has been given to the needed interrelationship of studies and the relevance of school studies to the life of the learner and the problems of the larger society. If the curriculum is to have relevance for social problem solving, a new synthesis will be required, and the role of the curriculum generalist will need greater recognition.

Moral education can no longer be regarded as mere moralistic preachments to maintain the status quo of the social order. Democratic social ideals require that the rising generation be equipped with the power of reason in attacking social inequities and iniquities, and thereby to make possible a better society. The schools of a free society are the chief agency for developing in the rising generation the power of reason so as to bring about the needed social transformation.

The history of the curriculum reveals repetitive periods of reform and counterreform reflecting the shifts in sociopolitical tides. Educators must be able to draw on the larger social situation for curriculum improvement. Concomitantly, they must examine external demands and pressures critically and constructively with a view toward solving problems stemming from the educational situation. Otherwise, the curriculum will be bent to whatever special interests are dominant at a particular time. Programs will be adopted that treat mere symptoms, only to be discarded in a succeeding epoch. It is the responsibility of educators to ensure that the schools serve the widest public interest so as to be true to the principles of democracy.

PROBLEMS FOR STUDY AND DISCUSSION

1. What illustrations can you give of how sociopolitical forces have influenced the curriculum? How have these forces influenced the kinds of educational research undertaken and the interpretation of this research?

2. Cremin contended that "someone must look at the curriculum whole and raise insistent questions of priority and relationship," and "to refuse to look at curricula in their entirety is to relegate to intraschool politics a series of decisions that ought to call into play the most fundamental philosophical principles." [Lawrence A. Cremin, *The Genius of American Education* (New York: Random House-Vintage, 1965), p. 58.]

   Do you agree with Cremin? Why or why not? To what extent have curricular changes in your own school been guided by philosophical principles? Explain.

3. Examine some of the statements of educational goals and some of the major curriculum proposals prior to 1955 and compare these with statements and proposals from the 1980s to today with regard to the treatment of "democracy" [e.g., Educational Policies Commission, *Education for ALL American Youth—A Further Look* (Washington, DC: National Education Association, 1952); National Commission on Excellence in Education, *A Nation at Risk* (Washington, DC: U.S. Department of Education,

   1983); and *America 2000* (Washington, DC: U.S. Department of Education, 1991). What differences do you find? How do you account for these differences?

4. In consideration of the changing functions of schooling discussed in this chapter, which function do you believe to be most appropriate for the schools of our society? Explain.

5. What crucial differences do you find between the idea and practice of multicultural education today, and intercultural education as conceived and treated by progressive educators through the early decades of the twentieth century? Arthur Schlesinger, points to the great historic success of the American Creed of building unity through diversity—the unity of democratic civic culture. However, he holds that the very assimilating and unifying culture embodied in the American Creed is being undermined by the "ideologues of ethnicity" who promote militant multiculturalism [*The Disuniting of America: Reflections on a Multicultural Society* (1998), pp. 137, 150]. What are your views on this issue?

6. The concept of social control has been used by critical theorists and others in describing the function of the school by means of the "hidden curriculum." They see the schools working with other more powerful social institutions so as "to

generate structural inequalities of power and access to resources. . . . Through their curricular, pedagogical, and evaluative activities in day-to-day life in classrooms, schools play a significant role in preserving if not generating these inequalities" (Apple, 1990, p. 64). Do you believe that in general teachers, consciously or otherwise, are actually engaged in promoting inequality? Explain.

Experimentalist-progressive educators, following Dewey, viewed social control positively as a means of empowerment in "the rights and responsibilities of the individual in gaining knowledge and personally testing beliefs, no matter by which authorities they were vouched for" (Dewey, 1916, p. 344). In your opinion, which interpretation of social control predominates in the contemporary educational literature describing the role and function of American schools and teachers? Explain.

7. How do you account for the eclipse of the once ubiquitous problems-of-democracy course in the secondary schools? Do you believe that such a course is needed today? Explain. What forces would mitigate efforts to restore such a course today?

8. Children spend more time at home watching television than the time they spend in school. How do you account for the failure of television to meet the great expectations for its place as a medium of learning in the school? How do you account for the wide use of the computer in the school as a kind of electronic workbook?

9. How do you account for the recurrent curricular retrenchment of "back to basics," despite the repeated failure of curricular fundamentalism? What points of conflict have arisen regarding the functions of the school curriculum (e.g., basic skills, cultural heritage, knowledge production, individual-social growth)?

10. U.S. schools are now recognized as the most heavily driven by external testing. To what extent is the curriculum of your school driven by external testing? Is teaching to the test a common practice in your school? Explain. What is your assessment of this practice?

CHAPTER 8

THE NATURE OF THE LEARNER AS CURRICULAR SOURCE AND INFLUENCE

It will be recalled that in his version of the curriculum paradigm, Ralph Tyler (1949) identified the use of philosophy and psychology as some screens for selecting educational objectives and curricular approaches (pp. 33–43). But the questions remain: Which philosophy? Which psychology? Obviously, the essentialist and perennialist (traditionalist) will select a very different psychology than the experimentalist. The conflicting educational philosophies are contrasted in detail in chapter 9, but suffice to say that the philosophy and ideals we have for education do not derive from the pieces of evidence obtained from psychology but govern the direction and uses to which psychology is put. Moreover, personal philosophy and ideals govern the ways in which the learner is viewed as a source of educational objectives and as an influence on the curriculum. Obviously, educators' conceptions of the nature of the learner, and their idealization of the good person leading the good life in the good society, have a direct bearing on how they formulate educational objectives and the curriculum.

Conflicting Conceptions of the Learner

With regard to the use of psychology as a screen for education objectives and curriculum development, Tyler (1949) pointed out that every teacher and curriculum developer must operate on some kind of theory of learning and that it is useful to have the learning theory formulated in concrete terms to assess its tenability for the curriculum (pp. 41–42). Among the many warring sects of psychology, three conflicting conceptions of the learner have had the most direct influence on teaching and the curriculum: (1) the learner as a mind to be disciplined (faculty psychology); (2) the learner as an organism to be conditioned so as to respond in externally controlled and predictable ways (behaviorism); and (3) the learner as an autonomously thinking, socially responsible individual who is capable of controlling his or her own destiny by means of the method of intelligence or problem method (cognitive/developmental psychology).

Faculty Psychology and Mental Discipline

Emerging late in the eighteenth century and growing in influence over the course of the nineteenth century, faculty psychology conceived of mind as separate and distinct from the physical body, endowed by independent powers governing reason, feeling, and volition. Under its doctrine of mental discipline, faculty psychology held that the powers of mind were to be developed and strengthened by means of exercise, like a muscle. Repetitive tasks, such as drill, memorization, and recitation by regurgitation were considered beneficial, and certain studies—especially the classics—were most valued for disciplining the mental faculties and for effecting the powers of transfer of learning to other studies. Or mind might be seen as a container into which the most valuable facts and elements of knowledge are to be poured. Learning was seen as necessarily distasteful.

Charles Dickens opens his reformist novel *Hard Times* (1854) with a harsh classroom scene to match the harsh life wrought by the industrial revolution. On the opening page, the schoolmaster, Mr. Gradgrind, is declaring his demand for "nothing but Facts," and that "You can only form the minds of reasoning animals upon Facts" (p. 1). Dickens describes the schoolroom with the pupils seated as an "inclined plane of little vessels then and there arranged in order, ready to have imperial gallons of facts poured into them until they were full to the brim" (p. 2).

Persistent Doctrine Despite Research Findings.
Although the doctrine of mental discipline and transfer of learning (along with faculty psychology) was virtually displaced by the research of Thorndike (1924) and others, it continued to have its adherents, namely essentialists and perennialists, throughout the twentieth century and into contemporary times. In attacking progressive education as "anti-intellectualist," Hofstadter (1963) argued that the experimental evidence has not refuted the notion of mental discipline and learning transfer, and he saw validity in Bruner's thesis that massive general transfer can be achieved under circumstances in which the learner learns how to learn (1960, p. 350). However, Bruner's thesis is based on a model of the learner who is capable of thinking by means of a process of inquiry-discovery (pp. 37–38, 58–59). Although parallels have been drawn between this process of inquiry-discovery and Dewey's reflective thinking, Bruner confined such learning to the style of the mature scholar-specialist on the forefront of an academic discipline, whereas Dewey viewed reflective thinking as a process of individual-social problem solving that transcends subject matter boundaries. Moreover, where Bruner's thesis that "intellectual activity anywhere is the same" (p. 33) presupposes that the learner is to be regarded as a miniature adult scholar, Dewey (1902b) held that the child is a child, qualitatively different from the adult in cognitive style, interests, and needs (p. 5–6). Bruner's thesis, which served as a basis for the rationale that guided the discipline-centered curriculum reforms of the 1950s and 1960s, allowed the curriculum developers to ignore the nature of the learner as a source of educational objectives and as an influence on the curriculum, because the immature learner was to be created in the image of the university scholar-specialist.

In his widely read *Paideia Proposal: An Educational Manifesto* (1982), Mortimer Adler, a leading perennialist, declared that, "The cooperative art of the teacher depends on the teacher's understanding of how the mind learns by the exercise of its own powers, and on his or her use of this understanding to help the minds of others to learn" (p. 61). The doctrine holding mind as a virtually disembodied organ, possessing independent faculties for exercise, was satirized by Ambrose Bierce in his *Devil's Dictionary* (1875) where he defined mind as "n. A mysterious form of matter secreted by the brain. It's chief activity consists in the endeavor to ascertain its own nature, the futility of the attempt being due to the fact that it

has nothing but itself to know itself with" (in E. R. Hopkins, Ed., 1967, p. 196).

In her attack on progressive educational reform over the course of the twentieth century, Ravitch (2000) followed Hofstadter's rejection of Thorndike's research on mental discipline and transfer of training, and proceeded to omit aspects of Thorndike's findings that were central to his conclusions.

Considering the time frame, President Jeremiah Day of Yale University might be forgiven for embracing faculty psychology and mental discipline in his faculty report of 1829 prescribing a fixed curriculum of intellectual studies as opposed to introducing modern and useful studies:

> The two great points to be gained in intellectual culture, are the *discipline* and the *furniture* of the mind; expanding its promise and storing it with knowledge. The former of these is, perhaps, the more important of the two. A commanding object, therefore, in a collegiate course, should be, to call into daily and rigorous exercise the faculties of the student.

However, Theodore Sizer (1984), a former dean of the Harvard School of Education, who somehow garnered a reputation as a progressive educational reformer during the late twentieth century and early twenty-first century, might not so easily be forgiven in holding that the job of education today is to help people "to exercise their minds" and for echoing Day's call for a school curriculum that strengthens the "discipline and furniture of the student's mind" (pp. 84, 89–90). Although enormous advancements have been made in understanding mind in terms of growth in human development, perennialists continue to conceive of mind as a muscle to be exercised or a vessel to be filled with knowledge for use in some remote future.

Behaviorism: The Learner as an Organism to be Conditioned. Behaviorism grew vastly appealing to the schools with growing popularity of workbooks and worksheets through the 1930s and 1940s, followed by programmed texts and teaching machines (1960s) and the contemporary uses of the computer as an electronic workbook. To the behaviorist, "teaching is simply the arrangement of contingencies of reinforcement" (Skinner, 1968, p. 5). Behaviorist theory is derived from experimental work with lower organisms, namely, laboratory rats and pigeons. "In shaping the behavior of a pigeon, success depends on how the requirements for reinforcement are set," declared Skinner, and he went on to advise, "In deciding what behavior to reinforce at any given time, the basic rule is 'Don't lose your pigeon'" (p. 158). When applied to human learning, behaviorist theory tends to be focused on the lower cognitive processes with motives being controlled through conditioning by rewards and punishments. The mechanistic model of the learner assumed by behaviorist theory leads to a curriculum that is programmed step by step in small units, focused on immediately observable and measurable learning "products." The process is one of specificity, not generalizability; the emphasis is on convergent learning, not emergent learning and higher-order thinking, as in the case of cognitive psychology and experimentalist philosophy.

Dewey and his fellow experimentalists took sharp issue with behaviorism as well as with faculty psychology and the doctrine of mental discipline. Dewey (1922) rejected the claim that behaviorism is scientifically based and the notion of fixity and certainty in the behavior of lower organisms as being victims of an outgrown psychology. "He is a victim of a popular zoology of the bird, bee, and beaver, which was largely framed to the greater glory of God," wrote Dewey, who then pointed out that such mechanical responses or "instincts in the animals are less infallible and definite than is supposed, and also that the human being differs from the lower animals in precisely the fact that his native activities lack the complex ready-made organization of the animals' original abilities" (p. 107).

Freedom of Intelligence. Dewey (1916) contended that educational aims in a democracy must be governed and derived through learning activities that enable the learner to have foresight of results, rather than having such aims dictated by the teacher and met through a serial aggregate of imposed tasks.

> To talk about an educational aim when approximately each act of a pupil is dictated by the teacher, when the only order in the sequence of his acts is that which comes from the assignment of lessons and the giving of directions by another, is to talk nonsense. It is equally fatal to an aim to permit capricious or discontinuous action in the name of spontaneous self-expression . . . aim means foresight in advance of the end or possible termination. If bees anticipated the consequences of their activity, if they perceived their end in

imaginative foresight, they would have the primary element in an aim. Hence it is nonsense to talk about the aim of education—or any other undertaking—where conditions do not permit of foresight of results . . . (pp. 118–119)

Externally imposed aims limit intelligence, holds Dewey. "They limit intelligence because, given ready-made, they must be imposed by some authority external to intelligence, leaving to the latter nothing but a mechanical choice of means" (p. 122).

In this connection, the behaviorist opts for a model of the learner, and the culture, as being derived from greater, not less, control. "What is needed is more control, not less, and this is itself an engineering problem of the first importance," contended Skinner (1971, p. 171). Indicative of the influence of behaviorism in educational theory and practice was the growing use of the term *educational engineering,* along with attempts to shape the curriculum and the learner according to narrowly conceived and externally imposed behavioristic objectives (Sizer, 1983, pp. 679–683).

The Learner as an Autonomously Thinking, Socially Responsible Individual

The growing scientific advances in cognitive psychology has impelled behaviorists to seeks ways of linkage or convergence with cognitive theory. This may work out to some extent where behaviorists and cognitivists view the brain as a kind of computer, but the study of "mind" encompasses thinking, emotions, attitudes, motivations, learning, abilities, understandings—in short, and especially, how humans gain and use knowledge in their world. Cognitive theory, obviously, has profound significance for education.

The rise of pragmatism and experimentalism through the twentieth century gave cause for a fully comprehensive theory of learning. The work of Thorndike and Woodworth (1901), and Thorndike (1924), and others in demolishing the doctrines of mental discipline and transfer of learning opened the doors of the school and colleges to the sciences, social sciences, arts, vocational studies, and so on. Great advances were made in the teaching of reading and throughout the school curriculum. Pragmatic philosophy under William James (1958), John Dewey (1916), and others advanced the testing of ideas according to their consequences. In orchestrating pragmatism into experimentalism, Dewey advanced the method of intelligence for hypothetical thinking and problem solving, processes necessary for enlightened citizenship in a democratic society. For Dewey, thinking and acting according to the best available evidence (the method of intelligence) is the means to growth in social power and insight and becoming an educated person. Further, evidence-based decision making has been the road to progress for almost all major institutions in democratic societies.

Group Dynamics and Cooperative Learning.

From the late 1930s through the mid-1950s, the research on group dynamics from the field of social psychology attracted considerable interest among educators, including curricularists. The leading researcher in the study of group processes was Kurt Lewin (1890–1947), who also built the foundation for action research. Lewin, a leading Gestaltist at the University of Berlin, developed his field theory in the United States through the study of human behavior in the total or naturalistic social situation. As a refugee from Nazi Germany who worked out of "America's heartland" at the University of Iowa, Lewin had an abiding faith in the democratic prospect. He and his associates conducted ingenious experiments in naturalistic situations assessing group productivity comparing democratic against authoritarian and laissez-faire classroom conditions. The findings clearly supported Lewin's democratic faith. In a typical Lewinian action-research experiment, he attacked the problem of farm mothers failing to follow the prescribed instructions on the nutrition of their first child, despite one-to-one sessions with a nutritionist at the University hospital in Iowa City, and despite their being given printed materials on discharge from the hospital. Lewin set up an experiment comparing the individual treatment to having the farm mothers meet in small discussion groups with the nutritionist, for the purpose of reaching a consensual decision at the end of the group session. The findings revealed that the group-decision and longer-term method was far superior to the one-on-one instruction, both in immediate and longer-term effects, as well as being far more economical (1952, pp. 467–473).

From the work of Lewin and his associates, educators began giving systematic attention to group processes and cooperative learning in the classroom and to human relations on a broader level. Hilda Taba (1955) was one of the curriculum leaders in this work during the mid-twentieth century. However, some educators tended to overlook the negative side of group process in which the pressure for conformity reigns and there is little or no tolerance for divergent thinking.

The rediscovery of cooperative learning with the opening of the twenty-first century has yielded positive findings and promising prospects for participative-group approaches, but the research and program implementation have been undertaken without building on the pioneering work of yesteryear and without considering the lessons to be learned from the negative side of group process.

Categorizing and Evaluating Learning Outcomes

Cognitive Processes

The ways of categorizing and evaluating cognitive outcomes of a curriculum, especially with regard to higher-order thinking, received special attention just before and after World War II. The need to evaluate longer-term learning outcomes of a curriculum was given special attention is the Eight-Year Study (1932–1941) under the direction of Ralph W. Tyler (Smith & Tyler, 1942). Similar efforts were advanced at leading colleges seeking to improve their curriculums in general education. In the Eight-Year Study, Tyler and his associates devised ingenious instruments for evaluating higher-order thinking and the ability to apply knowledge intelligently when confronting unanticipated situations and problems. The instruments included the assessment not only of cognitive outcomes, but of attitudinal ones as well. The criteria for measuring the outcomes were expressed in terms of behavioral goals, such as rendering evidence of the following capabilities: to identify propaganda; to separate fact from opinion; to work independently and without supervision when it is appropriate to do so; to enjoy the process of learning, not just the finished product; to appreciate by act and statement other cultures and the cultural contributions of immigrants (French et al., 1957).

Tyler and other experimentalists were well aware that most of the factual knowledge learned in the classroom is quickly forgotten after the examination, so they sought to evaluate comprehensively the kinds of learning that have longer-range consequences in the life of the learner. Great emphasis was given to higher-order thinking and the processes of engaging in the method of intelligence (critical thinking and problem solving).

The behaviorists, in contrast, conceived of behavior as being shaped not by the method of intelligence, but by conditioning based upon highly specific contingencies of reinforcement. The process is one of specificity, not generalizability as in the case of the experimentalists.

At the college level, comprehensive examinations were developed to replace or to supplement instructor-made, end-of-course examinations. Test items were designed to evaluate such outcomes as the ability "to evaluate the authenticity of given sources of information appropriate to a given problem," and "to formulate or recognize hypotheses based on given data or situations" (Dressel & Mayhew, 1954, p. 108). Leading colleges had established an independent board of examiners to develop and administer comprehensive examinations and to conduct institutional evaluation of the undergraduate curriculum in general education.

In their comprehensive study of evaluation for general education, Dressel and Mayhew identified the following critical thinking abilities for problem solving (essentially an extension of Dewey's problem method or method of intelligence).

A Tentative List of Problem-Solving Aspects of Critical Thinking

1. Ability to recognize the existence of a problem
2. Ability to define the problem
3. Ability to select information pertinent to the solution of the problem
4. Ability to recognize assumptions bearing on the problem
5. Ability to make relevant hypotheses
6. Ability to draw conclusions validly from assumptions, hypotheses, and pertinent information
7. Ability to judge the validity of the processes leading to the conclusion
8. Ability to evaluate a conclusion in terms of the application (pp. 177–178)

Cognitive Taxonomy.   In 1956, a committee of college and university examiners published a handbook for classifying educational objectives for the cognitive domain under the title, *Taxonomy of Educational Objectives* (B. Bloom). The "taxonomy" came to be used widely by colleges and secondary schools engaged in the development of test items and examinations for higher-order thinking. The classification of the cognitive processes is shown in Table 8.1 in what is intended to be a hierarchical order, from simple to complex levels of thinking: (1) knowledge,

(2) comprehension, (3) application, (4) analysis, (5) synthesis, (6) evaluation, (7) problem solving, and (8) creation. Categories 7 and 8 were added by Tanner and Tanner in the first edition (1975) and in subsequent editions of *Curriculum Development: Theory into Practice*. Not until 2001 did Bloom's associates add the categories of problem solving and creation to the taxonomy (Anderson & Krathwohl).

The widespread and continued use of the *Taxonomy of Educational Objectives* over many decades occasioned the issuance of a yearbook by the National Society for the Study of Education in 1994 presenting "a critical analysis and evaluation of a recognized classic in American education" (Preface, p. vii). In the yearbook, Kreitzer and Madaus acknowledged the wide impact of the taxonomy over many decades and raised questions concerning the validity of the hierarchical structure of the taxonomy and the rigidity in which it has been used by some educators (pp. 64–78).

Although this schema is intended as a taxonomy, it cannot be considered as such in a truly scientific sense, for even Bloom and his associates acknowledge that the determination of the cognitive levels is somewhat arbitrary and that any number of approaches can be employed in identifying and classifying cognitive categories. Furthermore, although the taxonomy lists the cognitive processes in a hierarchical order, the processes do not follow such an order in actual learning situations. For example, it is not uncommon for learners to engage in the application of knowledge before they proceed with an in-depth analysis of the knowledge. Hence, a student may build an electromagnet before he or she decides to analyze the principles of electromagnetism, or the student may build a model steam-propelled boat before analyzing its working principles. In both instances, principles are being put into applications prior to analyzing the principles. As another example, the learner may engage in the cognitive process of synthesis, say in the use of language to communicate certain unique ideas (e.g., a poem), and afterward engage in an analysis of the structural elements and relationships of the communication.

The Spiral Curriculum.   Putting the matter more simply and perhaps more profoundly, young children seek synthesis before they can engage in the process of analysis. Yet in the taxonomy, analysis precedes synthesis. In actuality, for example, the child has no problem in grasping the concept of "house" or of

Table 8.1 Classification of Cognitive Categories.

1.00 *Knowledge*
  1.10 Knowledge of specifics
  1.11 Knowledge of terminology
  1.12 Knowledge of specific acts

1.20 *Knowledge of Ways and Means of Dealing with Specifics*
  1.21 Knowledge of conventions
  1.22 Knowledge of trends and sequences
  1.23 Knowledge of classifications and categories
  1.24 Knowledge of criteria
  1.25 Knowledge of methodology

1.30 *Knowledge of Universals and Abstractions in a Field*
  1.31 Knowledge of principles and generalizations
  1.32 Knowledge of theories and structures

2.00 *Comprehension*
  2.10 Translation
  2.20 Interpretation
  2.30 Extrapolation

3.00 *Application*

4.00 *Analysis*
  4.10 Analysis of elements
  4.20 Analysis of relationships
  4.30 Analysis of organizational principles

5.00 *Synthesis*
  5.10 Production of a unique communication
  5.20 Production of a plan or proposed set of operations
  5.30 Derivation of a set of abstract relations

6.00 *Evaluation*
  6.10 Judgments in terms of internal evidence
  6.20 Judgments in terms of external criteria

*7.00 *Problem Solving*
  7.10 Defining the problem
  7.20 Formulating hypotheses
  7.30 Testing the hypotheses

*8.00 *Creation*
  8.10 Formulation of a unique idea, product, or process

*Categories not in the original, added by Tanner and Tanner in the first edition of *Curriculum Development: Theory into Practice* (1975) and in subsequent editions. See also L. W. Anderson & D. R. Krathwohl (Eds.), (2001). *A Taxonomy for Learning, Teaching and Assessing: A Revision of Bloom's Taxonomy of Education Objectives.* New York: Longman.

Source: Condensed from B. Bloom, J. T. Hastings, and B. F. Madaus. *Handbook on Formative and Summative Evaluation of Student Learning* (New York: McGraw-Hill, 1971, pp. 271–273).

"doctor" or of "doggie." As the child develops cognitively and socially, the child's understanding of these concepts deepens and widens with experience. Analytical and other forms of thinking come into play, as the learner advances, but all along the way the learner (hopefully) is constantly resynthesizing the concept or idea or experience at deeper, wider,

higher, and richer levels. Even an architect must continually grow in his/her concept of "house." Indeed, this process of growth must pervade the entire curriculum as a spiral process.

Following Dewey, this spiral process might well be called the *spiral curriculum*. Toward the close of *How We Think* (1933), Dewey wrote, "There is no end to this spiral process: foreign subject matter transformed through thinking into a familiar possession becomes a resource for judging and assimilating additional foreign subject matter" (p. 291).

Knowledge and Information. Despite its limitations, the cognitive taxonomy can serve as a valuable device for enabling teachers to design instructional activities encompassing a wider range of cognitive learnings. Classroom recitation, pupil assignments, and teacher-made tests typically focus mainly on the recall of specifics and the ways and means of dealing with specifics. As shown in Table 8.1, such learning is classified at the lowest cognitive level. One reason why teachers tend to place so much emphasis on teaching and testing for lower cognitive learning is that they find such material easiest to evaluate. The cognitive taxonomy can be useful in helping teachers gauge instruction so as to encompass a fuller spectrum of cognitive learning styles.

Although the cognitive taxonomy categorizes the retention of information as knowledge, students often find themselves memorizing and regurgitating such information without comprehending the material and without the ability to apply the information to different situations. All too often information is treated in education as an end product or commodity rather than being used as working power. The error of equating information with knowledge is pointed out by Dewey (1916).

> Probably the most conspicuous connotation of the word knowledge for most persons today is just the body of facts and truths ascertained by others; the material found in the rows and rows of atlases, cyclopedias, histories, biographies, books of travel, scientific treatises, on the shelves of libraries.
>
> The imposing stupendous bulk of this material has unconsciously influenced men's notions of the nature of knowledge itself. The statements, the propositions, in which knowledge, the issue of active concern with problems, is deposited are taken to be themselves knowledge. The record of knowledge, independent of its place as an outcome of inquiry and a resource in further inquiry, is taken to *be* knowledge. The mind of man is taken captive by the spoils of its prior victories; the spoils, not the weapons and the acts of waging the battle against the unknown, are used to fix the meaning of knowledge, of fact, and truth.
>
> If this identification of knowledge with propositions stating information has fastened itself upon logicians and philosophers, it is not surprising that the same ideal has almost dominated instruction. (p. 220)

As discussed later, the cognitive processes are inseparable in life from the affective processes (interests, attitudes, appreciations, and values). Our treatment of these processes in terms of contrasting schema or classifications is done for analytical purposes only.

Affective Processes

In life, the affective processes—interests, attitudes, appreciations, and values—are inseparable from the cognitive processes. Yet some contemporary educators paint a stereotypic portrait of the research scientist as one who is engaged "in the cool neutrality of experimental inquiry" (Greene, 1973, p. 137). Almost any account of the trials and tribulations of the scientist engaged in research on a significant problem reveals that the scientist's technical work is given force and direction through his or her imagination and motives (Watson, 1969). Although the technical aspects of science differ significantly from the technical aspects of art, the dedicated scientist, no less than the dedicated artist, is passionately engaged in his or her work. On a more mundane level, whether the learner is approaching a social problem or a scientific problem, one cannot speak of being open to data on all sides of a problem or of being able to recognize bias on which data are formulated and selected, or of using one's intuition in developing a hypothesis and testing possible solutions, without having one's interests, attitudes, appreciations, and values engaged.

Untenable Dualism. In short, how we think is virtually directed by an organic interaction of cognitive and affective processes. Yet some educators erroneously view these processes as though they were two virtually separate domains or functions. A former U.S. commissioner of Education makes this highly questionable distinction:

> The cognitive function of instruction is directed to the achievement and communication of knowledge, both the factual knowledge of the sciences and the formal relationships of logic and mathematics—knowledge as both specific data and generalized structure. It is discipline in the ways of knowing, involving perception, the inductive, deductive, and intuitive processes, and the techniques of analysis and generalization. It involves both the immediate grasp of sensory objects and the abstractive processes by which the intellect constructs its ideas and fashions its ideals.

The affective function of instruction pertains to the practical life—to the emotions, the passions, the dispositions, the motives, the moral and aesthetic sensibilities, the capacity for feeling, concern, attachment or detachment, sympathy, empathy, and appreciation. (McMurrin, 1967, p. 41)

This statement is a schizoid portrayal of human nature.

The learner is divided into two separate faculties for purposes of instruction. Modern behavioral science does not reveal such a separation. To assume that perception, intuition, and various systematic modes of thought are within the province of the cognitive domain and are independent of affective processes represents a mechanical conception of human nature not unlike that promulgated by the faculty psychologists of some generations past. Moreover, to hold that the affective function, not the cognitive function, pertains to the practical life leaves us with the notion that our practical life is governed independently of our ways of knowing. To face this kind of practical life would make human progress an impossibility. As Dewey (1933) pointed out, "[m]ethods that, in developing abstract intellectual abilities, weaken habits of practical or concrete thinking fall as much short of the educational ideal as do the methods that, in cultivating ability to plan, to invent, to arrange, to forecast, fail to secure some delight in thinking, irrespective of practical consequences." Furthermore, the fact that one is knowledgeable about the different forms of thought is no guarantee that one will be a good thinker. Good thinking depends on the attitudes, values, and motivations that animate one's character (p. 228).

Critical thinking and problem solving require a penetrating curiosity, an openness to considering all pertinent data in seeking the best available evidence, and the use of the imagination in visualizing possible solutions to be put to the test of application. Obviously, these attributes do not accrue independently of attitudes, motivations, appreciations, and a value system.

The effective teacher knows that it is not enough for students to learn their lessons. However successful a teacher may be in developing the student's ability to make technical analyses of classical literary works or of scientific phenomena, the educational process cannot be considered successful if it leaves the pupil with a dislike for such material. Similarly, as a result of his or her learning experiences, a student may come to be committed to a value (e.g., women should receive equal pay for equal work), but if, in the commitment to such a value, the student deliberately avoids consideration of views alien to his or her own, then this commitment, however righteous, is dogmatically based rather than being a product of reason.

The curriculum must be made to function holistically so that cognitive and affective processes are organically interrelated. To increase the focus of the curriculum on the affective processes as an antidote to a narrowly cognitive-based curriculum suffers from the danger of creating a new imbalance to counter the old. The problem is not one of finding proper antidotes but rather of developing the interdependence between the cognitive and affective processes. Just as the traditional curriculum suffered from treating knowledge as though it were a kind of fixed and ready-made subject matter to be imposed upon the learner, a one-sided emphasis on affective processes deprives the learner of the working power that comes when knowledge is the material for reflective thinking.

Psychomotor Processes

Integrally related to the cognitive and affective processes are the psychomotor processes. Outside of the work undertaken by neurologists, physiologists, psychologists, and educators in connection with neuromuscular disorders, relatively little systematic investigation has been undertaken to ascertain how various educational programs can contribute to the effective development of psychomotor processes among normal children and youth. The most systematic work in this area has been conducted in the field of physical education, health, dance, and athletics, with the emergence of kinesiology or the study of human movement. In recent years, increasing attention has been given to psychomotor processes in the field of industrial education in connection with the learning of techniques involving complex manipulative skills.

As discussed later in this chapter, the work of Jean Piaget points to the essential relationship between the experiences of the infant and young child in manipulating objects and the development of perception and intelligence. Although most psychomotor tasks are inherent in the human organism and are developed naturally under normal conditions, there is a need to build on this natural development various skills of a more complex nature for the effective performance of a wide variety of life tasks ranging from swimming to the development of manipulative skills in typing, playing a musical instrument, or operating a piece of industrial machinery. Other examples are perceptual abilities involving visual, auditory, tactile discrimination, and coordinated action; physical abilities; skilled movements; and expressive-interpretive movements.

The higher psychomotor processes do not operate independently of the cognitive and affective processes. For example, whether one is concerned with the learning of handwriting, learning to send and receive Morse code, improving one's swimming style, learning a new art technique, performing an industrial operation requiring skilled manipulative technique, playing the piano, developing expressive and interpretive movement in modern dance, or learning a surgical technique, the cognitive and affective processes are interdependent with the psychomotor processes.

Developmental Stage Theory

Stages of Intellectual Development

Traditional educational practice has been based largely on the notion that the child's mental structure is the same as that of the adult and that the child merely lacks the adult's range and depth of knowledge and experience. Under this assumption, curriculum construction was regarded as properly the adult's logical formulation of organized subject matter to be imposed unilaterally on the child (as a miniature adult). As we have seen, a modern statement of this view is made by Bruner, who, as chief theoretician for the discipline-centered curriculum reforms of the space age, proposed that the child's intellectual activity is essentially the same as that of the adult scholar and that any differences are a matter of degree, not of kind (Bruner, 1960, p. 14).

Qualitative Differences.   The research of Jean Piaget over several decades points to the identification of significant qualitative differences between the cognitive processes of the child and the adult. Piaget (1950) theorized that intellective capability undergoes qualitative developmental changes linked to the child's maturation. In this connection, Piaget identified four developmental stages: (1) the *sensory-motor* stage (first 2 years), when the child learns to control perception and motor responses in dealing with

physical objects and language; (2) the *preoperational* or *representational* stage (to about age 6 or 7), in which the child learns to extract concepts from experience and later to make perceptual and intuitive judgments; (3) the stage of *concrete operations* (between ages 7 and 11), in which the child learns to solve physical problems by anticipating consequences perceptually; and (4) the stage of *formal operations* (late childhood or early adolescence), in which the youngster learns to think hypothetically and to theorize and experiment (pp. 87–158).

According to Piaget, each developmental stage is a necessary condition for subsequent intellective development and these stages cannot be telescoped or accelerated appreciably, although there is some overlapping. The failure of traditional education, observed Piaget (1970), lies in its treatment of the child "as a small adult, as a being who reasons and feels just as we do while merely lacking our knowledge and experience," and "since the child viewed in this way was no more than an ignorant adult, the educator's task was not so much as to form its mind as simply to furnish it; the subject matter provided from outside was thought to be exercise enough in itself" (pp. 159–160). When confronted with Bruner's thesis that "intellectual activity anywhere is the same," Piaget was quoted as saying, "I never understand Jerome Bruner and I don't think he ever understood me" (*New York Times*, 19, 1972, p. 49).

Roots in Dewey.   Although developmental stage theory is almost universally and exclusively credited to Piaget, its roots originate with Dewey's observations of children in his laboratory school at the University of Chicago. Within three years following the school's opening in 1896, Dewey warned in 1899 that the child is not capable of engaging in technical scientific inquiry. "There is no distinction between experimental science for little children and the work done in the carpenter shop," noted Dewey, and "such work as they can do in physics or chemistry is not for the purpose of making technical generalizations or even arriving at abstract truths. Children simply like to do things and watch to see what will happen" (p. 44). Dewey later proposed three stages following the stage of infancy in intellectual development. The first stage, in earliest childhood, is manifested by a curiosity that leads the child into everything and to manipulate objects until they cease to reveal new properties, but this curiosity is not the same as reflective thinking. The second stage occurs through social interaction when the child learns that he or she can learn from others. At this second stage, the child's incessant "whys" are not demands for technical or scientific explanations but for more and bigger facts or ideas. Yet the child is seeking more than a mere heap of information or disconnected facts (1910, pp. 31–32). Dewey's third stage is manifest as the youngster's curiosity is no longer satisfied with immediate answers to spontaneous questions. Instead the learner seeks more remote relationships and, through reflective thinking, a "distant end controls a sequence of inquiries and observations and binds them together as a means to an end" (1933, p. 39).

Educational Implications of Developmental Stages.   The educational implication of the theories of Dewey and Piaget is not that the child's intellective development will unfold of its own accord under any conditions, but that appropriate environment conditions in the school and home must be provided in connection with each developmental stage. Differences in the school or home environment will produce differences in the quality of the child's performance at each developmental stage and subsequent stages.

To deny adolescents the stimulation of hypothetical thinking is no less an error than to impose this style of thinking on the young child. For the young child, a group project such as that involving the construction of objects can be an invaluable experience in developing the child's perceptions and impulses toward trying things out and in developing his or her capabilities for social cooperation. The vital role of such cooperation in the intellectual development of the learner and in laying the groundwork for reflective thinking was noted by Piaget (1970), who pointed out that "it is such cooperation that is most apt to encourage real exchange of thought and discussion, which is to say, all the forms of behavior capable of developing the critical attitude of mind, objectivity and discursive reflection." Moreover, instead of "submission to external constraint," the collaboration and self-discipline derived through such classroom activity is "morality in action, just as 'active' work is intelligence as act" (1970, p. 180). Obviously, it takes a highly skilled and sensitive teacher to design and organize appropriate learning environments and to select and arrange suitable curricular materials for children and youth at various developmental stages.

Erikson's Developmental Stage Theory

Erik Erikson, a disciple of Sigmund, Freud, extended Freud's psychodynamic theory so as to stress the significance of sociocultural factors in development. Although Erikson's early stages of development are similar to Freud's, his later stages are less concerned with internal conflicts and are directed at the resolution of biosocial-psychological crises in human development. Clearly the school must play a vital role in Erikson's developmental stage theory, for the school is uniquely endowed with the mission of socializing the rising generation and engaging children and youth in a systematic learning environment so as to develop their fullest potentials. Obviously, failure in home life and school life will hinder the full and wholesome development of the individual.

Erikson's developmental stages (1950) are summarized as follows:

1. **Oral-sensory stage,** during which the infant is entirely dependent on the parents for nurturance and protection, through which the infant develops a basic sense of trust (or insecurity and mistrust).

2. **Muscular-anal stage,** during which the young child masters control of elimination and gains a rudimentary sense of autonomy.

3. **Locomotor-genital stage,** during which the child learns to channel sexual urges into socially acceptable behavior and gains initiative.

4. **Latency stage,** during which the child enters school and moves beyond the family into society, thereby developing a sense of industry and competence (as opposed to failure and inferiority).

5. **Pubescent/adolescent stage,** during which the adolescent faces an identity crisis ("Who am I?" "What are my life goals?"), copes with problems of developing sexuality, and learns to control psychosocial impulses (identity versus role confusion).

6. **Young adulthood stage,** during which the individual develops a clearer sense of identity, progresses toward career goals, and develops meaningful relationships with members of the opposite sex as well as wider and more mature social relationships (intimacy versus isolation).

7. **Adulthood stage,** during which productive/generative working relationships are fully developed (as opposed to stagnation) in one's career and social life.

8. **Maturity-stage,** during which the individual achieves a sense of ego integrity and wisdom, as opposed to despair and futility.

Needs and Developmental Tasks

There has been a great deal of confusion and debate over the uses of the term *needs* and the extent to which the curriculum should be based on pupil needs. "Needs" have been used in the education literature as curricular aims, such as the "ten imperative needs of youth" proposed by the Educational Policies Commission at mid-twentieth century, as well as in selecting subject matter and learning experiences (1952, p. 216).

Over the years, educational psychologists have developed various statements of needs that generally fit into Maslow's categories of (1) physiological needs, such as physical health; (2) social needs, such as belonging, security, competence, and status; and (3) ego-integrative needs, such as self-esteem, enlightenment, autonomy, aesthetic-creative self-actualization, and overall personality integration (1970, pp. 35–51).

Havighurst attempted to orchestrate needs into biosocial-psychological tasks that he referred to as the developmental tasks of life. A developmental task is defined as "a task which arises at or about a certain period in the life of the individual, successful achievement of which leads to his happiness and to success with later tasks, while failure leads to unhappiness to the individual, disapproval by society, and difficulty with later tasks" (1972, p. 2). Table 8.2 presents a list of developmental tasks beyond those that occur in infancy.

Educational Implications of Developmental Tasks.   The implications of developmental tasks for the school and curriculum should be apparent to educators. For example, the developmental tasks in early childhood of forming concepts and learning language to describe social and physical reality and getting ready to read are not provided for adequately in many disadvantaged homes, raising special problems for the pupil and the teacher. At the adolescent level, the failure of the school to provide

---

Table 8.2   Developmental Tasks of Childhood, Adolescence.

Early Childhood
1. Forming concepts and learning language to describe social and physical reality
2. Getting ready to read
3. Learning to distinguish right and wrong and beginning to develop a conscience

Middle Childhood
1. Learning physical skills necessary for ordinary games
2. Building wholesome attitudes toward oneself as a growing organism
3. Learning to get along with age-mates
4. Learning an appropriate masculine or feminine social role
5. Developing fundamental skills in reading, writing, and calculating
6. Developing concepts necessary for everyday living
7. Developing conscience, morality, and a scale of values
8. Achieving personal independence
9. Developing attitudes (democratic) toward social groups and institutions

Adolescence
1. Achieving new and more mature relations with age-mates of both sexes
2. Achieving a masculine or feminine social role
3. Accepting one's physique and using the body effectively
4. Achieving emotional independence of parents and other adults
5. Preparing for marriage and family life
6. Preparing for an economic career
7. Acquiring a set of values and an ethical system as a guide to behavior
8. Desiring and achieving socially responsible behavior

Source: Condensed from Robert J. Havighurst, *Developmental Tasks and Education,* 3rd ed. (New York: McKay, 1972).

vocational curricula to prepare youngsters for gainful employment (along with the failure of society to find places for adolescents in the world of work) prevents them from meeting the developmental task of preparing for a career.

Little attention has been given to the necessary interaction and interdependence of developmental tasks. An adolescent who is denied the means of preparing for a career and, as a result, cannot find gainful employment will encounter severe problems with other developmental tasks, such as achieving emotional independence of parents and other adults, achieving new and more mature relations with age-mates of both sexes, achieving a masculine or feminine social role, preparing for marriage and family life, acquiring a set of values and an ethical system as a guide to behavior, and desiring and achieving socially responsible behavior. Surveying the conditions in our major cities with regard to inadequate vocational curricula in the high schools and unemployment among the majority of boys who were school dropouts, Conant described the situation in 1961 as "social dynamite" (p. 2). In 1968, after surveying the wreckage of the epidemic of urban riots, the National Commission on Civil Disorders reported that most of the rioters were older teenagers and young adults and recommended that vocational programs in the high schools, which were reaching only a small fraction of youth, be greatly expanded and strengthened (p. 74). Subsequent reports have reiterated the importance of the acculturation of the adolescent in society by relating education to the world of work through actual work experience (*Panel on Youth*, 1974). However, these reports have given less attention to the need to ensure that such work experience is educative in the fullest sense. For example, how can the school enable adolescents to gain insight into the existing deficiencies and inequities in the world of work and the possibilities for effecting improvements and solutions?

When adolescents are denied the means of achieving socially responsible behavior, the result often is socially undesirable and irresponsible behavior. Increasing recognition is being given to the socializing and vocational-education function of the college in preparing college youth to meet the developmental tasks of life. However, a majority of our youth do not go on to college and, for them, the high school is the key social institution in laying the groundwork for these life tasks. More

systematic efforts must be given to designing the high school curriculum to enable adolescents to meet the biosocial-psychological tasks that provide the basis for life success.

The failure to meet the biosocial-psychological needs of adolescents has been a chronic problem in the United States, as evidenced by the huge populations of unemployed youth become engaged in antisocial activity. But the problem of social isolation and alienation is manifested in adolescent life within school as well as out of school. Adolescence is a time of life through which emotions are greatly exaggerated, even to the "crisis" level, especially when teenagers are denied such social needs as belonging, security, competence, and status; ego-integrative needs as self-esteem and overall personality integration (Maslow, 1970); and such developmental tasks as getting along and achieving more mature relations along with age-mates, and developing a set of values and an ethical system and achieving socially responsible behavior (Havighurst, 1972).

Although extreme school violence is very rare, the nation was shocked during the late 1990s by a series of tragic events involving the use of guns. The most notorious incident occurred at Columbine High School in Littleton, Colorado, when in the spring of 1998 two male students, self-described and described by their fellow students as "The Outcasts," filled with rage, shot and killed 12 students and a teacher and wounded 24 other students before killing themselves. The two boys left videotape messages of their plans for the massacre and the rage they shared, particularly against varsity athletes (the "jocks") who had hazed, bullied, and beaten them (*New York Times*, December 14, 1999, p. A22). The incident understandably left indelible scars on the school although, ironically, years later a number of championship football seasons was credited with bringing the entire student body together (*New York Times*, September 20, 2003, p. D5). Although schools throughout the nation, including Columbine, instituted strict rules against bullying and hazing, the response was mainly the employment of security guards, installation of surveillance cameras, periodic searches of student lockers, and the trial and sentencing of young teenage killers as adult criminals. Most seriously lacking was the concerted study of the causes and prevention of social disaffection, violence, and the alienation of adolescents in school and outside of school.

Organic Interdependence of Tasks and Processes

Stressed repeatedly throughout this section of the chapter is the necessary interdependence of the various cognitive, affective, and biosocial developmental processes. Figure 8.1 presents a three-dimensional schema showing this interdependence. Represented on one plane are the various levels of cognitive development. On a second plane are the affective processes, needs, developmental tasks, and moral stages. The third plane represents the various developmental stages.

Each category on a given plane should be thought of as organically interactive not only with the other categories on the same plane but also with those on the two other planes. Thus, for example, the act of creation is actually a wedding of cognitive, affective, and the various other biosocial-psychological processes. Similarly, value systems not only are connected organically to moral development but, if they are founded on reason, rather than bias and impulses, such systems also are developed and modified through the continuous evaluation of knowledge and experience. Consequently, the human organism is seen not as a set of mechanical responses but as a being capable of continuous growth through the reconstruction of experience.

The organic interdependence of affective and cognitive processes is supported by research that consistently shows a causal link between affect and achievement. Concludes Bloom, "[t]he relatively high relation between cognitive behaviors and affective characteristics under most school conditions suggests that instruction must take these into consideration in determining what is necessary to develop both high cognitive learning outcomes as well as more positive affective characteristics" (1976, p. 106).

If the school ascribes to a growth function, the organic interdependence of the various tasks and processes (Figure 8.1) must be taken into account. If, for example, the older child and adolescent are denied experiences in the formal operations of hypothetical thinking on social problems, and the testing of ideas in action situations, then cognitive development and other aspects of affective-biosocial development will be hindered. To study ecology, literature, history, social studies, composition, or drama without examining moral questions is to rob education of its authentic mission in free society. The study of moral questions in the absence of reflectively formulated data is equally bankrupt. The fact that students are engaged in a heated debate is no indication of an enlightening learning experience.

Spectrum of Human Intelligences

"The notion that intelligence is a personal endowment or personal attainment is the great conceit of the intellectual class," commented Dewey, in holding that we were only beginning to tap the intelligence of the masses. Dewey went on to differentiate between the specialized intelligences that make for expertise in the sciences, arts, and other areas, and the wider social intelligence required of a democracy (1927, pp. 209, 211).

Figure 8.1   Interaction of Cognitive, Affective, and Biosocial Developmental Processes.

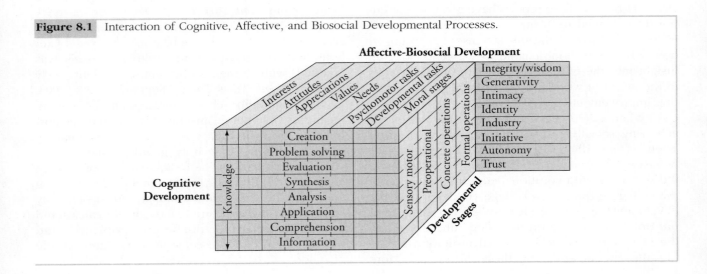

Contemporary investigations into cognitive development have led to a view of intelligence as multifaceted, in recognition that people have different cognitive strengths and styles. Howard Gardner (1987) has identified seven types of intelligence: (1) linguistic, (2) logical-mathematical, (3) musical, (4) bodily-kinesthetic, (5) spatial, (6) interpersonal, and (7) intrapersonal. Gardner's pluralistic concept of intelligence may not be as radical as he claims, that is if one realizes that we have long recognized the different talents of different people and multiple talents of individuals. Moreover, every advanced society requires that these talents be developed and made effective in a social matrix of interdependence. The especially dynamic quality of a free, diverse society requires the unleashing of the pluralistic talents and intelligence through a system of popular education that provides multiple opportunities for success.

One might argue that Gardner gives insufficient attention to the kind of hands-on, practical, inventive intelligence that has produced all sorts of mechanical and electronic devices and processes. One might argue that the visual arts require more than spatial intelligence. Indeed, one might proceed to modify or elaborate on Gardner's seven types of intelligence without taking issue with the thesis of multiple intelligence.

Gardner applies his theory of multiple intelligences to the school curriculum. In calling for a diversified curriculum to unleash the multiple latent talents of children, Gardner seems to be attuned to the reforms advocated by experimentalist-progressives throughout the twentieth century. However, whereas these progressivists also sought a core curriculum being focused on the common concerns, interests, and capabilities that make for a productive and democratic citizenry, Gardner has dismissed the significance of the core as "the uniform view" for the "uniform school." He goes on to propose that school personnel include "assessment specialists" and a "curriculum broker" to "match students' profiles, goals, and interests to particular curricula and to particular styles of learning." Although Gardner acknowledges the problem of "premature billeting," he fails to give sufficient consideration to the problem of ghettoizing the curriculum and to the fact that so many talents develop throughout the school years (and throughout life) to the extent that children and adolescents are constantly changing their career goals and avocational interests. In view of his call for the early identification of these seven intelligences in children, and the corresponding curriculum channeling, Gardner seems to imply that these intelligences are inherent or native. To Dewey,

> *effective* intelligence is not an original, innate endowment. No matter what the differences are in native intelligence (allowing for the moment that intelligence can be native), the actuality of mind is dependent upon the education which social conditions effect. (1927, p. 209)

The proposal that the secondary school curriculum be composed of *constants* (the core of studies shared by all) and *variables* (the diverse studies that provide for enrichment, exploratory, special interests, and specialized learning experiences) as embodied in the 1918 report of the Commission on the Reorganization of Secondary Education—and which gave impetus to the comprehensive high school—served to combine the concept of multiple interests and talents with multiple opportunities. The comprehensive high school has its corresponding model in the land-grant university. The advocacy for creating schools of choice in recent years, with each school focused on a specialized area (such as the sciences and technology, the arts, and so on), beginning at the elementary level, raises ominous questions as to using the schools for social separation and isolation of youngsters according to special interests.

Dewey's Fourfold Developmental Learning Activities

From his observation in his laboratory school at the University of Chicago, Dewey identified four compelling impulses, interests, or "instincts," that must find expression through the school curriculum (1900a, pp. 43–62). We prefer to refer to the four impulses as the "fourfold developmental learning activities." The activities are interdependent and tied to the growth and development of the child and indeed throughout life. The four compelling impulses, interests, or activities identified by Dewey are (1) social, (2) investigative, (3) constructive, and (4) artistic.

It is puzzling that Dewey did not include physical activity as one of the impulses or interests, especially in view of the significance he gave to the design of the classroom (including the furniture) and school to meet the needs of the growing learner for bodily movement and activity. Dewey went further in demolishing the mind-body dualism and the emphasis given in

Figure 8.2   The Fivefold Developmental Learning Activities

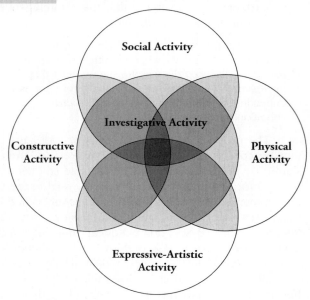

Investigative Activity.   Children and adolescents like to look into things, in finding things out, in seeing how things "work." Manifested first at an informal, rudimentary, and exploratory level for the child, investigative activity provides the child with new information and ideas and stimulates the imagination. Later, the processes of inquiry become more formalized and focused as the learner grows in the processes requiring critical and hypothetical thinking for problem solving. Hence the processes of inquiry eventually mold concrete and practical experience with the theoretical, connecting the "what is" to the "what if" and to the possibilities of "what could be." The investigative activity is not merely technical and confined to the sciences, but also cultivates the method of intelligence in all matters of democratic citizenship. The investigative activity is intelligence at work.

Constructive Activity.   Children and adolescents like to make things with a variety of materials and the use of tools. From rudimentary and crude beginnings, the learner grows in the capacity to use models and plans and even to design plans in building something. In effect, the constructive activity should engage the social and investigative activity as well as the artistic activity. The traditional schoolroom allows little place for constructing or building things, and one might well ponder the extent to which Dewey's criticism of the traditional classroom of his day applies to the classroom of today.

> There is very little place in the traditional schoolroom for the child to work. The workshop, the laboratory, the materials, the tools with which the child may construct, create, and actively inquire, and even the requisite space, have been for the most part lacking. The things that have to do with these processes have not even a definitely recognized place in education. They are what the educational authorities who write editorials in the daily papers generally term "fads" and "frills." (1900a, p. 32)

Dewey went on to fault the physical design of the traditional classroom and furniture as being conceived for passivity and listening, and not for active engagement. In Dewey's words,

> . . . everything is arranged for handling as large numbers of children as possible; for dealing with children in masse, as an aggregate of units, involving, again, that they be treated passively. . . . (1900a, p. 32)

traditional schools to physical quietude and passivity. Consequently we have added physical activity as one of the impulses or interests of the learner. The interdependence of the "fivefold activities of developmental learning" is depicted in the Venn diagram (Figure 8.2).

Social Activity.   The social activity is manifested in play, conversation, and communication. The most powerful educational resource is language as social expression. Children, indeed all of us, like to talk about things and people: the relationships between things and people, and between people and people, or human concerns. As a living-learning environment, the school cannot ignore or suppress the social activity of language. Through the curriculum, the school must find the means of selecting, organizing, and focusing on learning experiences for the expression and growth of the social activity of language in productive ways. In the traditional school, children and adolescents are required to engage in the routines of recitation apart from their social experience and concerns. "There is all the difference in the world between having something to say and having to say something," observed Dewey (1900, p. 56). No wonder then that pupil responses tend to be short and even given in incomplete sentences—in contrast to their use of language outside of school or in expressing social concerns, or when they are engaged in investigating a genuine problem, or constructing a project, or designing and creating a mural, or performing a play.

On the same basis is explicable the uniformity of method and curriculum. If everything is on a "listening" basis, you can have uniformity of material and method. (1900a, p. 32–33)

Under these conditions, education is treated as a production process, with outcomes being measured as "products," instead of education being conceived and treated as a growth process with outcomes being measured according to the individual's growth in deriving meaning from experience and in exercising intelligent control of experience.

Artistic Activity.   Growing out of the communicating (social) and constructive functions is artistic or aesthetic activity. According to Dewey, "Make the construction adequate, make it full, free, and flexible, give it a social motive, something to tell, and you have a work of art" (1900a, p. 44).

Unfortunately, although artistic activity is given some time in the classroom and school schedule at the elementary level, little time is allocated at the secondary level unless the student elects a specialized studio art class. The point is that the studio arts tend to be diminished to the point of virtual disappearance in the curriculum in general education in the upper grades as pressure is exerted for increased time for the advanced "academic" subjects.

Dewey viewed the compelling activities or interests as interdependent and generative; that is, by finding expression through the school curriculum, the activities endow the learner with power to grow in the ability to direct experience with intelligence. "Now, keeping in mind these fourfold interests," wrote Dewey, "the interest in conversation or communication; in inquiry, or finding out things; in making things or construction; and in artistic expression—we may say they are the natural resources, the uninvested capital upon the exercise of which depends the active growth of the child" (1900a, pp. 47–48).

Physical Activity.   Some discussion has been given to the significance of physical activity (psychomotor) in human development and to the inadequacy of the classroom and overcrowded school environment with its emphasis on passivity and the suppression of physical activity. As Dewey pointed out, learning is not purely intellectual or cognitive; to derive meaning from cognitive learning the learner must be actively engaged. Dewey addressed this problem of externally imposed discipline as the "consequence of the abnormality of the situation in which bodily activity is divorced from

the perception of meaning" (1916, p. 165). In effect, we have identified each of the compelling interests of the learner as activity, whether social, investigative, constructive, or artistic.

In addition, organized physical activity conducted by the school can have powerfully positive educative consequences for health, lifelong recreational interests, social interaction and growth, aesthetic interests, and so on. Teachers are all too familiar with the consequences of externally imposed restrictions and penalties on pupils requiring them to be quiet and even passive, and suppressing their active tendencies. Restlessness and even unruliness, rather than actively shared responsibility, are the result. The problem is not merely to provide pupils with opportunities to relieve tensions, but also to provide the means for actualizing their impulses positively, releasing a constellation of activity for wholehearted engagement in the learning process and through the entire curriculum spectrum.

Moral Education

A characteristic concern of traditional education has been to instill children and youth with the moral virtues through lists of moralistic homilies and commandments, ranging from obedience to constituted authority to honesty and fair play. Such verbal moralizing in terms of virtues and vices not only has been shown to have little effect on the moral character of the pupil, but it also regards morals as something apart from knowledge and growth in intelligence.

Many contemporary educators who reject the traditional precepts of moralistic education choose to see morality as something beyond intelligence. "*Why* aim for intelligence more than personal sensitivity or aesthetic awareness or openness to others or the growth of feeling?" asks Maxine Greene (1973, p. 182). Such a question conceives of intelligence and morality too narrowly and creates a schism between the two. Is the truly intelligent individual not aesthetically aware? Is he or she closed-minded or insensitive to the ideas and feelings of others? If we conceive of intelligence merely as command of a high degree of technical knowledge or having a high I.Q., a case can be made for viewing morality as something beyond intelligence. But if we conceive of intelligence and knowledge as organically connected with conduct, such intelligence and knowledge bind individual growth to social growth. Morals that are not shaped and directed by intelligence tend to be reduced to mere lists of slogans or catechetical commandments. According to Dewey,

[M]orals is [sic] often thought to be an affair with which ordinary knowledge has nothing to do. Moral knowledge is thought to be a thing apart, and conscience is thought of as something radically different from consciousness. . . . Moral education in school is practically hopeless when we set up the development of character as a supreme end, and at the same time treat the acquiring of knowledge and the development of understanding, which of necessity occupy the chief part of school time, as having nothing to do with character. (1916, p. 411)

Dewey pointed out that if the school studies are taken merely as knowledge acquisition, they have only a narrow technical worth, but when they are engaged in "under conditions where their social significance is realized, they feed moral interests and develop moral insight." He also noted that "the great danger which threatens school work is the absence of conditions which make possible a permeating social spirit," and he held that "all education which develops power to share effectively in social life is moral" (1916, pp. 414–416, 418).

Stages of Moral Development. A number of efforts have been made to examine systematically moral behavior as a developmental or growth process. A systematic scheme was developed by Kohlberg, who identified three levels and six stages of moral development. Kohlberg held, "There is a general factor of maturity of moral judgment much like the general factor of intelligence in cognitive tasks" (1970, pp. 71–72).

Thus, at the preconventional level, the child moves from the stage of obeying authority simply to avoid punishment or to gain rewards, to the stage of acting mainly to satisfy himself or herself. At the conventional level, the individual moves from the stage of conforming in order to gain approval or to avoid disapproval, to a stage of "doing one's duty" in maintaining the existing social order for its own sake. Finally, at the postconventional level, the individual moves from an orientation of morality of contract, in which the rights of others are respected and honored, to an orientation of choice and conscience—based on universal ethical principles, such as those pertaining to justice, reciprocity and equality of human rights, and respect for the dignity of man.

Kohlberg reported that his experimental studies with youngsters in the junior high school demonstrated that when pupils who are at various moral stages are engaged by their teachers in an examination of moral conflict situations, a significant proportion of youngsters from the lower stages moved up at least one stage in his schema of moral development. However, Kohlberg acknowledged that such developmental progress is not a matter of special lessons but requires that the total school be imbued with justice as a living matter.

The decline of social controls, the emergence of the do-your-own-thing ethic, and the rising problems of social disorder and corruption have led to a resurgent interest in moral education. Unless moral education is connected to action and is governed by the principle of reason, it will be reduced to moralistic homilies, sentimentalism, or indoctrination. Traditionally, moral values have been associated with maintenance of a tranquil social order. From the educational standpoint, moral values acquire a far more profound meaning. If moral education is focused on democratic ideals of equality of opportunity, equality of human rights, and the dignity of humanity, it must necessarily come to grips with existing social iniquities and inequities. The preservation of privilege at the expense of human deprivation and suffering becomes open to examination and question through education. Social ideals are tested on the anvil of social reality. This kind of moral education, contrasted against the traditional preachments for moral and "spiritual" values, is unsettling to the status quo. As long as the power of reason prevails, the likely outcome is social improvement. In a free society, the school is the chief agency for instilling the rising generation with the power of reason.

Constructivism

The 99th Yearbook of the National Society for the Study of Education (NSSE, Part I, 2000) is titled *Constructivism in Education*. In the introductory chapter, the editor describes constructivism as "a currently fashionable magic word in the western intellectual firmament" (Phillips, p. 1). The key thesis of constructivism is that knowledge is made rather than "found" or "discovered." Accordingly, knowledge is actively constructed, whether by the researcher or by the learner. Seen as "ways of knowing," and in view of a great significance attributed to constructivism in education, it is both puzzling and revealing that the word *constructivism* was not even listed in the index of the 1985 NSSE Yearbook, *Learning and Teaching the Ways of Knowing* (part II, Eisner). Puzzling because of its extensive treatment in the literature of academe throughout the 1990s to today; revealing because it represents how vulnerable academe is to shifting fashions and even to political correctness. This is especially the case for social thought (sociology and philosophy in particular, and also psychology).

Elements of constructivism are widely accepted, such as the need for the learner to be actively engaged in the process of learning. In this vein, Dewey and Piaget are identified as constructivists (Phillips, 2000, pp. 13–15), although neither used the term itself in any systematic way.

It is generally recognized that the individual academic disciplines do not exist as such in nature; hence the need for interdisciplinary inquiry in areas of scientific research, such as the research on DNA, which has required the collaboration of cell biologists, biochemists, and physicists. Of no less significance is the need for curriculum integration for children and adolescents who, given the knowledge compartments and isolation of knowledge in the separate school subjects, are unable to make the knowledge connections for productive life in the real world.

Radical Cultural/Social Constructivism and the World of Science

The above aspects of constructivism may seem eminently sensible to most educators, but great disputation has been generated by radical cultural or social constructivism, the roots of which are found in the writings of von Glasersfeld (1995), Vygotsky (1978), and the Edinburgh School of sociologists (Bloor, 1976). Radical cultural or social constructivists have targeted science for attack in particular. They refuse to recognize that science is the quest for knowledge in seeking problem solutions based upon the testable findings from systematic inquiry (observation and experimentation) into the physical and natural world—findings must meet the criteria of reliability (replication) and validity—and the processes of inquiry must be unremittingly committed to the quest for the best available evidence. Instead, radical constructivists hold that science is to be seen just as a discourse devised by a particular specialized, interpretive community operating under particular social conditions and influenced by political opinion, economic incentive, and ideological climate. The response to this conception or misconception of science is seen by scientists themselves as a point of view that "leaves no ground whatever for distinguishing reliable knowledge from superstition" (Gross & Levitt, 1994, p. 45). Whatever an individual's intellectual or anti-intellectual

orientation, one is destined for a rude consequence when sitting down without the support of a chair. The laws of gravity will prevail regardless of intellectual orientation, bias, or cultural affiliation—even for the radical cultural/social constructivist.

Science Works.   It would appear that the two-culture divide between radical cultural/social constructivism and science would paralyze the world of academe, but science prevails in a democracy because science works. It holds to no a priori truths and champions academic freedom by its commitment to the method of intelligence, employing multiple-working hypotheses in seeking problem solutions, and to the quest for the best available evidence in guiding inquiry in the pursuit and uses of knowledge.

One of the great ironies historically is that the attacks on science during the Age of Enlightenment came from the political and religious right, whereas today the attacks come to no small extent from the radical left. From the time of the Enlightenment to today, science has opened the way to freedom of inquiry and to dispelling ignorance, superstition, dogma, and dictate by authority. In modern times antiscience sentiments were rampant in the college student protest movement of the 1960s and early 1970s (Roszak, 1972), indicating to some observers that yesteryear's college student radicals are tenured radical professors today in the social sciences and humanities (Kimball, 1991).

Although the radical left have raised quite a storm in reviving the two-culture split in academe, their convoluted rhetoric has limited their influence beyond academe. Their language became a target for parody when in 1996 a New York University mathematical physicist was able to publish a feature article in *Social Text*—a leading radical journal, using key terms and expressions of postmodernist and social constructivist style, and deliberately using nonsensical language (Sokal & Bricmont, 1997). The nonsensical title of the article featured on the cover of the journal was "Toward a Transformative Hermeneutics of Quantum Gravity."

Finally, the linkage of Dewey with constructivism must be qualified. While Dewey advanced the need for school children to engage in activities involving construction, investigation, social interaction, and artistic expression, he championed the methods of science or the method of intelligence as the key mode for building an enlightened citizenry for life in a democratic society (1933, pp. 171–178, 195–202). As Dewey contended, despite the triumphs of science in advancing civilization, the need to harness the methods of science for inquiry throughout the school and college curriculum, and indeed in life in society, remains a critical challenge to American democracy (1939, pp. 154–184). In this connection, Dewey's work in largely unfinished (Tanner, D., 1983a, pp. 34–38).

The Collateral Curriculum and the Hidden Curriculum

As discussed in chapter 5, contemporary writers on curriculum have treated the concept of the hidden curriculum as a newly discovered phenomenon, whereas experimentalist-progressive educators have long given attention to the significance of the curriculum in effecting unanticipated learning outcomes. Whereas contemporary curricularists and school critics have tended to treat the hidden curriculum mainly as a detrimental influence, experimentalist-progressives recognized the enormous productive powers of what they have variously termed the *collateral curriculum,* the *informal curriculum,* and the *incidental curriculum.* As a consequence, they gave concerted attention to designing the classroom and school as a living learning environment so as to optimize the possibilities for stimulating pupils to develop enduring interests and appreciations that go beyond the formal curriculum and examinations. (They even went so far as to redesign the classroom furniture so as to stimulate student engagement in the curriculum.)

Excessive Quantification

The excessive concern for specificity in setting educational objectives and assessing learning outcomes through worksheets, standardized achievement tests, and teacher-made tests focused on recall and narrow skills all reflect the undue emphasis given to the lower cognitive levels when education is seen as a production process as opposed to a growth process. Moreover, these practices are based on the questionable assumption that pupils learn only the particular thing that educators have targeted for them. Yet certain unanticipated collateral learnings may be far more significant to the pupil than the targeted material. In addressing this problem, Dewey noted that much of the knowledge and technical material that is supposed to be amassed in school, and on which the pupil is tested, eventually is forgotten and has to be learned over again in changed form, or actually has to be unlearned, if he or she is to make progress

intellectually. But collateral learning—enduring attitudes toward what is learned and toward learning itself—may count for much more in one's future because such learning governs whether or not one will have the desire to go on learning (1938, p. 48).

An exclusive emphasis on quantifiable objectives and outcomes delimits the possibilities for important qualitative outcomes. Teachers commonly find that pupils develop interests in pursuing ideas or probing into material in far greater depth and breadth than the particular lesson was intended to take them. Yet unless teachers make provisions for the further pursuit of such collateral learning, such as through individual and group projects, the impetus for self-impelled learning will be lost and the prescribed lessons will take on a mechanical character.

Fruitful Mistakes. Another related educational problem connected with the obsession with narrowly specific objectives and quantitative measurements of outcomes is the failure to appreciate that in life some of the most significant learning occurs through fruitful mistakes. Too often mistakes in schoolwork are counted as penalties rather than treated as opportunities for effective learning. Correct answers memorized and regurgitated for the examination have little bearing on developing the pupil's desire and capability for continued learning, whereas the pupil who is investigating significant problems and is allowed to learn through mistakes will be better equipped to deal intelligently with future problems. The whole notion of hypothetical thinking is based on a recognition that the solutions to problems are not always self-evident and that solutions often are derived by pursuing divergent paths. Longer-term projects in the classroom, seminar, laboratory, shop, and studio environments—designed to stimulate pupils to think divergently in formulating and investigating problems—can provide opportunities for valuable kinds of collateral learnings and can enhance the pupil's desire and capability for continued learning.

Error-Oriented versus Idea-Oriented Curriculum. Such practices as teaching to the test ("curriculum alignment"), along with recitation and the employment of worksheets and tests for memorization-regurgitation, or "drill-skill-kill" exercises, reflect an error-oriented curriculum as opposed to an idea-oriented curriculum. The outcome of the error-oriented curriculum clearly tends to be manifested in boredom and negative attitudes toward learning. Exercises and assignments are to be "gotten over" as "chores" as painlessly as possible. The collateral or unintended learning outcomes understandably tend to be negative.

In contrast, when learning experiences are idea-oriented so as to engage students in inquiry into substantive concerns, and into problems and issues that are of vital significance to them, and when adequate curriculum resources are available for such inquiry, then the learning becomes generative. The focus is shifted from specificity to possibility. Unforeseen and more enduring learning outcomes of a positive nature, then, are more likely to emerge from both the formal and collateral curriculum.

Collateral learning is not accidental learning. It derives from a planned curriculum that engages students in emergent learning situations, ensuring that the curriculum is not delimited to established-convergent experiences. In effect, the hidden curriculum could not really be hidden when human variability rather than predictability is valued.

Perspective

A number of sources and influences whereby the school develops its objectives and curriculum were discussed in this chapter, namely, (1) society, (2) the world of knowledge, and (3) the nature of the learner. The vital interdependence of these sources and influences was examined. For example, the growing fragmentation of the school and college curriculum reflects the general condition of fragmentation in society.

The function of the school and the model of curriculum followed tend to reflect the demands and expectations of the larger society. In different epochs, shifting demands and expectations have impelled the school to change its dominant function. Some of these major functions have been (1) the development of fundamental skills, (2) the transmission and preservation of the cultural heritage, (3) knowledge-production disciplinarity, and (4) individual-social growth. Not only do the larger sociopolitical forces exert a profound influence on the goals and functions of the school, but they also influence the direction, interpretation, and application of educational research.

Specialization and fragmentation in the larger world of knowledge have had their concomitant effects on the curriculum of the school and college. The influence of the subject-matter specialist has been so pervasive that the curriculum tends to be conceived as a total list of separate subject matters. As a result, the dominant focus in curriculum development in recent years has been on microcurricular problems to the neglect of macrocurricular problems—the latter referring to those problems that transcend the knowledge compartments of the separate subject matters or disciplines. Insufficient attention has been given to the interrelationship of studies and the relevance of school studies to the life of the learner and the problems of the larger society. If the curriculum is to have relevance for social problem solving, a new synthesis will be required, and the role of the curriculum generalist will need greater recognition.

Education has been narrowly interpreted as a process of changing the behavior patterns of people. Such a narrow interpretation conceives of the learner as a mere cog in the machinery of the technological society. In contrast is the interpretation of education as that reconstruction or reorganization of experience that adds to the meaning of experience and that increases ability to direct the course of subsequent experience. This interpretation views the learner as an autonomously thinking, socially responsible individual who has control of his or her own destiny. The two radically different interpretations of education and conceptions of the learner vitally affect the uses educators make of psychology in the design and operation of the instructional program. The broader vision of education and the learner requires a broader vision of the curriculum and of the society. In this broader vision, cognitive goals cannot be considered apart from affective processes and moral principles, and such goals must be directed at competence in reflective thinking for the development of social power and insight.

Moral education can no longer be regarded as mere moralistic preachments to maintain the status quo of the social order. Democratic social ideals require that the rising generation be equipped with the power of reason in attacking social inequities and iniquities, and thereby to make possible a better society. The schools of a free society are the chief agency for developing in the rising generation the power of reason so as to bring about the needed social transformation.

The history of the curriculum reveals repetitive periods of reform and counterreform reflecting the shifts in sociopolitical tides. Educators must be able to draw on the larger social situation for curriculum improvement. Concomitantly, they must examine external demands and pressures critically and constructively with a view toward solving problems stemming from the educational situation. Otherwise, the curriculum will be bent to whatever special interests are dominant at a particular time. Programs will be adopted that treat mere symptoms, only to be discarded in a succeeding epoch. It is the responsibility of educators to ensure that the schools serve the widest public interest so as to be true to the principles of democracy.

PROBLEMS FOR STUDY AND DISCUSSION

1. What illustrations can you give of how socio-political forces have influenced the curriculum? How have these forces influenced the kinds of educational research undertaken and the interpretation of this research?

2. Cremin contended that "someone must look at the curriculum whole and raise insistent questions of priority and relationship," and "to refuse to look at curricula in their entirety is to relegate to intraschool politics a series of decisions that ought to call into play the most fundamental philosophical principles." [Lawrence A. Cremin, *The Genius of American Education* (New York: Random House-Vintage, 1966), p. 58.]

   Do you agree with Cremin? Why or why not? To what extent have curricular changes in your own school been guided by philosophical principles? Explain.

3. Tyler defined education as "a process of changing the behavior patterns of people." [Ralph W. Tyler, *Basic Principles of Curriculum and Instruction* (Chicago: University of Chicago Press, 1949), pp. 5–6.] In contrast, Dewey defined education as "that reconstruction or reorganization of experience which adds to the meaning of experience and which increases ability to direct the course of subsequent experience." [John Dewey, *Democracy and Education* (New York: Macmillan, 1916), pp. 89–90.]

   How do these two definitions reflect different conceptions of the learner and the function of the curriculum? How would you define education?

4. Describe any collateral learning experiences on the part of yourself or your pupils that turned out to be far more significant educationally than the target subject matter.

5. Bruner has contended that "there is a continuity between what a scholar does on the forefront of his discipline and what a child does in approaching it for the first time." [Jerome S. Bruner, *The Process of Education* (Cambridge, MA: Harvard University Press, 1960), p. 28.]

   How does this statement conflict with Piaget's theory of intellectual development? What are the implications of these two conflicting views for curriculum development?

6. What is the significance of developmental tasks for curriculum development? Moral stages?

7. What would the school curriculum look like if it were built upon Dewey's fourfold functions of developmental education? How would it differ from the conventional curriculum today?

8. Examine some of the statements of educational goals and some of the major curriculum proposals prior to 1955 and compare these with statements and proposals in recent times with regard to the treatment of "democracy." [e.g., Educational Policies Commission, *Education for ALL American Youth—A Further Look* (Washington, DC: National Education Association, 1952); National Commission on Excellence in Education, *A Nation at Risk* (Washington, DC: U.S. Department of Education, 1983); and *America 2000* (Washington, DC: U.S. Department of Education, 1991)]. What differences do you find? How do you account for these differences?

9. In consideration of the changing functions of schooling discussed in this chapter, which function do you believe to be most appropriate for the schools of our society? Explain.

10. Using the cognitive categories in Table 8.1, examine some teacher-made tests in terms of the proportion of items devoted to the various categories. To what extent do the items require comprehension, application, synthesis, and evaluation, as compared to recall of information and specific-skill operations? What implications do such considerations have for the curriculum?

11. How does Dewey's description of the traditional classroom of the early 1900s compare with classrooms of today?

12. What is the curricular significance of the "fivefold developmental learning activities"?

CHAPTER 9

CURRICULAR SOURCES AND INFLUENCES
CONFLICTING EDUCATIONAL THEORIES

"If we are willing to conceive education as the process of forming fundamental dispositions, intellectual and emotional, toward nature and fellow men," wrote Dewey, "philosophy may even be defined as *the general theory of education*." And, accordingly, "the business of schooling tends to become a routine empirical affair unless its aims and methods are animated by such a broad and sympathetic survey of its place in contemporary life as it is the business of philosophy to provide" (1916, pp. 383–384).

One cannot penetrate very deeply into any significant curricular problem or issue without encountering philosophical considerations. The term *philosophy* is often used by teachers and administrators to convey their common-sense outlook on educational and curriculum matters. However, educational philosophy emerges from concrete and systematic consideration of the uncertainties and most significant aspects of the educational condition. It not only animates and assesses aims, values, and means, but also provides generalized meaning for the widest range of conditions. Educational philosophy is not the external imposition of prefabricated ideas on a given situation that have radically different origins; rather, it is a formulation of theoretical ideas derived from systematic consideration of the educational condition, whereas "[e]ducation is the laboratory in which philosophic distinctions become concrete and are tested" (Dewey, 1916, p. 384).

In most treatments concerning the conflicting schools of educational philosophy or theory, curriculum is subordinated to a host of other considerations. In this chapter the various schools of thought are examined in terms of curriculum as the focal point.

Need for a Guiding Philosophy

In Tyler's conceptual scheme for the curriculum, philosophy is employed chiefly "to screen the heterogeneous collection of objectives thus far obtained so as to eliminate the unimportant and the contradictory ones" (1949, p. 33). Tyler's conception of philosophy as a mere "screen" for selecting educational objectives appears to make its function mainly mechanical and somewhat external to the educative process.

Bode recognized the function of philosophy as a source of illuminating educational aims and practice when he wrote, "if the younger generation is to achieve 'participation' in our social life the emphasis in curriculum construction and in teaching must be placed on social outlook, on reflective consideration of what constitutes a good life in the social order" (1931, p. 548). In the absence of reflective consideration of what constitutes the good person leading the good life in the good society, the curriculum tends to be regarded as a mechanical means of developing the necessary skills of young people in conformance with the pervading demands of the larger social scene. Under such circumstances, the school does not need to bring into question the existing social situation, nor does it need to enable pupils to examine through reflective thinking possible alternative solutions to social problems. Instead, the school merely is expected to do the bidding of whatever powers and forces are most dominant in the larger society at any given time. Current history reveals vivid illustrations of this condition. For example, the era of discipline-centered curriculum reforms, extending from the mid-1950s to the late 1960s, in which the curriculum was retooled to serve the nation's Cold War interests while the problems of poverty and social disaffection were largely ignored;

the era unleashed by a federal report *A Nation at Risk* (1983), called for school reforms to meet the nation's alleged need for techno-industrial mobilization in the wake of the Japanese and German challenge to U.S. dominance in the global economic marketplace; and the era of the external national and statewide testing pandemic following the federal report *America 2000* (1991), which called for national academic standards by means of a neo-essentialist curriculum in the "new basics" to bring U.S. students to be first in the world in science and mathematics, to prepare all children to start school ready to learn, and to bring all students to a level of literacy for competition in the global economy and for effective citizenship—all this by the year 2000. As discussed earlier, the reforms advocated in *America 2000* have carried well into the new century.

Philosophy and Objectives

It is a common practice for the school to have a formal statement of philosophy and objectives developed by its faculty and administration for circulation to parents, students, and the general public. At the secondary level, such a statement may appear in the student handbook. Accreditation procedures commonly require each secondary school to develop a statement of philosophy and objectives, and it typically includes a number of items holding to the fostering of democratic values, the recognition of individual differences, the school's commitment to community needs, and other general statements. Obviously, such statements are meaningless if they are inconsistent with or contradictory to actual educational practice.

Educational Practice May Contradict Stated Philosophy. Unfortunately, it is the exceptional school faculty and administration that seek to test the curriculum and administrative practices against the school's statement of philosophy. It is not at all unusual to find faculties that have developed elaborate lists of objectives for the curriculum when these objectives have little or no connection with, or actually may be contradictory to, the overall statement of philosophy established for the school. For example, a school's statement of philosophy might include an aim upholding democratic principles and fostering democratic values. Unless the school is able to translate such ideals into effective practice, the ideals are nonfunctional and the school actually may be

working against its own professed ideals. Thus, a school's statement of philosophy and aims might include the development of reflective thinking skills in pupils, whereas the actual curriculum is geared to pupil indoctrination, or to narrow-minded behavioristic objectives, and significant problems of controversy are ignored or avoided in the curriculum. In contrast, another school's faculty might decide that one of the ways of fostering democratic values is to develop students' abilities in reflective thinking as applied to social problems and issues. Examples of behavioral objectives that might be identified and assessed in connection with this goal are that students are able to recognize the existence of a problem or issue, are committed to examining all sides of an issue and to seeking pertinent data from different sides, are able to distinguish fact from opinion, are able to recognize bias in determining the pertinence of data to the solution of the problem, are able to formulate workable hypotheses for the solution of the problem, are able to test these hypotheses through appropriate methods and procedures, are able to verify the conclusions or solutions reached by testing them in a variety of situations pertinent to their own lives, and so on.

No Substitute for Theory.   The point to be made is that objectives and educational practices must be governed by a theory of what the school seeks to achieve. Objectives are not a substitute for such a theory. Moreover, in the absence of a theory of what the school seeks to achieve, or when mere lip service is given to the school's statement of philosophy and goals, the school becomes vulnerable to all sorts of whims and doctrines. And objectives are employed chiefly for training in facts and narrow skills, and in the fitting of the learner as a mere cog in the mechanism of school and society. As Bode pointed out, "[t]he purpose of education is not to fit the individual for a place in society, but to enable him to make his own place. . . . We put shoes on a child to protect his health and not to bind his feet" (1927, p. 237).

Under the banner of educational reform, narrow nationalistic pressures have been imposed on the public schools, accompanied by false and misleading allegations and demands, often leaving the schools with problems of misguided curriculum priorities, curriculum imbalance, and insufficient consideration of the need to articulate the curriculum with the nature of the learner and with the democratic social outlook. Without a guiding philosophy that is put to the test of everyday practice, the school is without a compass or without a rudder, and school administrators and faculty are without a vision of the democratic prospect.

Conflicting Educational Philosophies

The foregoing discussion has pointed out how the school needs a philosophy to guide its ends and means. Philosophy serves as both a source and an influence for educational objectives and curriculum development. However, there are many diverse and conflicting philosophies of education that may be classified according to various degrees of conservative and progressive polarity.

Theodore Brameld is often credited with having developed a system of categorizing educational philosophies or theories—namely, essentialism, perennialism, progressivism, and reconstructionism. However, these terms were widely used long before Brameld's categorization. For example, Dewey's powerful case for experimentalist theory and the experimental method in *Democracy and Education* (1916) found many progressive educators eventually referring to themselves as experimentalists. In 1931 John L. Childs of Teachers College, Columbia University, wrote a book, *Education and the Philosophy of Experimentalism*, in which he systematically stated the case for experimentalism. The first major figure to lead the cause for essentialism and who referred to himself as an essentialist early in the twentieth century was William C. Bagley, also of Teachers College. In *Foundations for American Education* (1947), Harold Rugg, who had been Bagley's first Ph.D. student at the University of Illinois, describes Bagley's essentialism, which was far more moderate in tone and substance than the essentialism that was to follow after mid-twentieth century (see Bagley, 1934, *Education and Emergent Man*). In the same work, Rugg uses the term *perennialism* (p. 614) in noting that Mortimer Adler, a leading exponent of that philosophy, had indicated his preference for the term over *scholasticism*, derived from the church schoolmen of the Middle Ages and premised on the ideas of St. Thomas Aquinas (1225–1247). Adler's preference can be understood in the recognition that scholasticism is ecclesiastical in origin, whereas perennialism is secular.

Nevertheless, Brameld did examine the various philosophies systematically. The authors of this text have chosen to use these classificatory terms and have added certain categories and subcategories to

help clarify some of the emerging differences and points of confusion. The categories used are clearly descriptive in delineating the fundamental differences concerning the nature of knowledge, the structure and function of the curriculum, and the nature of the learner.

Table 9.1 presents a synoptic view of several major conflicting philosophies of education representing a wide range of conflicting educational pathways and destinies. The purpose here is not to present a systematic and exhaustive treatment of each of these philosophies but rather to illustrate briefly how they serve as sources and influences for contemporary educational aims and curricular decisions.

Teachers are so caught up with the need to develop effective classroom practices that they understandably look on educational theory as a field of esoteric specialization removed from the practical concerns of the school. Although theory will not provide simplistic answers to such questions as "What do I do on Monday?" it does provide a basis for ascertaining whether one's practices are consonant with one's beliefs and for understanding the implications of alternative educational pathways and destinies. As "the endeavor to attain as unified, consistent, and complete an outlook upon experience as possible" (Dewey, 1916, p. 378), philosophy gives meaning and direction to our actions. In the absence of philosophy, the teacher is vulnerable to externally imposed prescriptions, often mechanically treated, and to whatever schemes are dominant and fashionable at any given time. This does not mean that philosophy is a shield against change. "Any person who is open-minded and sensitive to new perceptions, and who has concentration and responsibility in connecting them has, in so far, a philosophic disposition," noted Dewey (p. 380).

The Conservative Vision

The conservative sees the curriculum as being properly concentrated on the cultural inheritance: the tried, the tested, and the true studies. The chief task of education is to conserve the best of our past and, in this way, the present will be adequately dealt with. The traditional studies are seen as the best means of cultivating the intellect, and it is the power of the intellect that enables humanity to cope successfully with the present. Efforts to build or reconstruct the curriculum to make it relevant to contemporary

Table 9.1 Synoptic View of Conflicting Educational Philosophies.

Philosophy	Controlling Aim	Curriculum	Method	Ideal of Learner
Perennialism	Cultivation of the rational powers; academic excellence	Basic education/ liberal arts; Great Books of the Western World	Mental discipline; drill teaching; literary discussion/ Socratic questioning	Rational being guided by first principles; mind elevated above biological universe
Essentialism	Academic excellence; cultivation of the intellect	Basic education/ fundamental academic disciplines	Mental discipline; mastery of academic subject matter; drill/coaching; disciplinary inquiry	Rational being in command of essential facts and skills that undergird the intellective disciplines
Experimentalism	Reflective thinking for social problem solving; democratic citizenship; growth	Comprehensive, unified, problem-focused studies, in democratic classroom/ school setting	Social problem solving through reflective thinking (scientific method) and democratic processes	Autonomously thinking, socially responsible democratic citizen; organism in biological continuity with nature
Reconstructionism	Building an ideal democratic social order (a practical Utopia)	Social problems, corrective programs scientifically determined for collective action	Critical analysis of societal flaws and programmatic needs for corrective action	Rebel committed to and involved in constructive social redirection and renewal
Romantic naturalism	Individual freedom to develop one's potentials	Learning activities based on child's felt needs	Laissez-faire; free learning environment for artistic self-expression; spontaneous activity	Unfolding flower
Existentialism	Inner search for meaning of one's own existence	Themes on the human condition; learning activities free of rational constraints, designed to free the individual to find one's own being	Introspection (examining one's own feelings, impulses, thoughts) in a free learning environment	Flower in search of the meaning of its own existence

problems or to the interests of the learner are misguided and detract education from its only truly legitimate mission: cultivation of the intellect.

Conservatives differ significantly in their curricular prescriptions. For example, the perennialist sees the best thinking of the past exemplified in the great literary works of the ages. The essentialist sees it exemplified in the traditional "intellective" or academic disciplines. Both see such studies being properly built on a solid foundation in the three Rs provided in the elementary grades. Both view mind as an entity to be developed and strengthened through exercise and, for this purpose, abstract studies are valued over direct experience. Retrospection is valued over action.

That the overwhelming evidence from cognitive and developmental psychology has discredited such a notion of mind is of no matter to the perennialist or essentialist. Mind is mind, and it is the paramount province of the educational institution to be engaged in developing the intellect through the "intellectual studies."

Perennialism

The perennialist believes that because people are uniquely endowed with the rational faculty, education must be aimed exclusively at the cultivation of the intellectual virtues. In contrast to the experimentalist, who recognizes the continuity between the human being and the biological universe, the perennialist sees mind as transcending biological nature. Education must pursue the perennial truths and not be misdirected toward meeting contemporary needs that are only temporal. According to Robert M. Hutchins, education must "draw out the elements of our common human nature [that] are the same in any time or place," and any notion of educating a person to live in any particular time or place is "foreign to the true concept of education" (1936, p. 66).

Permanent Studies.   For the perennialist, the cultivation of the intellectual virtues is accomplished only through the "permanent" studies that constitute our intellectual inheritance. These virtues are embodied in the Great Books of the Western World that "cover every department of knowledge," wrote Hutchins, who saw the foundation for the Great Books as consisting of grammar, which "disciplines the mind and develops the logical faculty, . . . the rules of reading, rhetoric and logic," and mathematics, which provides for "correctness in thinking" (1936, pp. 81–84). The

perennialist's conception of the ideal education is presented succinctly in this statement by Hutchins:

> The ideal education is not an *ad hoc* education, not an education directed to immediate needs; it is not a specialized education, or a preprofessional education; it is not a utilitarian education. It is an education calculated to develop the mind.
>
> I have old-fashioned prejudices in favor of the three R's and the liberal arts, in favor of trying to understand the greatest works that the human race has produced. I believe that these are the permanent necessities, the intellectual tools that are needed to understand the ideas and the ideals of our world. (1963, p. 18)

An identical curricular prescription is offered by Adler (1939), who sees education as properly delimited to the basics at the elementary level. It is then to be realized in the college by means of the cultivation of the rational powers through the liberal arts, capped by the Great Books of ancient, medieval, and modern times, which "are a repository of knowledge and wisdom, a tradition of culture which must initiate each new generation" (pp. 62–63). The Great Books are timeless because they deal with the permanent ideas and problems of humanity, argues the perennialist. Some perennialists would add the classical languages and perhaps a modern language such as French to this list. Vocational or practical studies have no place in the school curriculum because such studies are temporal and do not cultivate the intellectual virtues. The same is said for physical education and the study of contemporary affairs. "Our erroneous notion of progress has thrown the classics and the liberal arts out of the curriculum, over-emphasized the empirical sciences, and made education the servant of any contemporary movements in society," argued Hutchins (1936, p. 65).

Because the perennialist is concerned with "perennial truths" or "immutable values" that can only be derived through "pure reason," the perennialist categorically dismisses any empirical data from the behavioral sciences that reveal, for example, that the so-called perennial studies are not more effective than other studies in disciplining the intellect. Similarly, the perennialist dismisses the research findings on the importance of affective influences in learning. As far as student interests are concerned, they are irrelevant to the determination of the curriculum because students are immature and unable to judge what is best for themselves. Whether the students dislike the permanent studies also is irrelevant (Hutchins, 1936, p. 86). "The primary aim of the educational system in a democratic country is to draw out the common humanity of those committed to its charge. This requires careful avoidance of that attractive trap, the *ad hoc*, that which may be immediately interesting, but which is transitory, or that which is thought to have some practical value under the circumstances of the time . . . ," wrote Hutchins (1972, p. 209).

Opposition to Electives.   In the quest for curricular relevance, many secondary schools and colleges have resorted to ad hoc changes in course offerings and the expansion of elective options without undertaking a fundamental assessment and redesign of the total curriculum. The perennialist is not calling for such assessment and redesign from the standpoint of the pervading problems and needs of the learner and society; instead, a return to the permanent studies is the answer, on the ground that such studies are never transitory but are of value in any time or place. Although the perennialist maintains that the vocational studies are valueless not only on the grounds that they are not intellective but also because such studies readily become obsolescent as a result of technological change. It is the skilled technical graduate, and not the liberal arts graduate, whose services are in greatest demand in the technological society.

Perennialist prescriptions for education, particularly for the lower levels of schooling, portray the mind as a kind of vessel to be filled with facts and truths, or muscle to be strengthened by memoriter exercise. "Elementary education can do nothing better for a child than store his memory with things deserving to be there," declared Mark Van Doren, and, "[h]e will be grateful for them when he grows up, even if he kicks now" (1959, p. 94).

Traditional Dualisms.   Inherent in perennialist thinking are the traditional dualisms of mind versus body, cultural studies versus vocational studies, permanent studies versus contemporary studies, intellect versus emotion, knowledge versus experience, and so on. Anchored in perennialist thought is the metaphysical notion, developed by Plato and Aristotle, that rational knowledge is derived from a higher source than experience. The advent of experimental science demolished this notion. Yet, as Dewey noted, we are left with a curriculum that clings to the artifacts of the old education, a curriculum that is an inorganic composite of inconsistent, dualistic, and antagonistic tenets.

> Certain studies and methods are retained on the supposition that they have the sanction of peculiar liberality, the chief content of the term liberal being uselessness for practical ends. . . . The result is a system in which both "cultural" and "utilitarian" subjects exist in an inorganic composite where the former are not by dominant purpose socially serviceable and the latter not liberative of imagination of thinking power.
>
> Only superstition makes us believe that the two are necessarily hostile so that a subject is illiberal because it is useful and cultural because it is useless. (1916, pp. 301–302)

A chief problem with perennialism is its fundamental premise that the sole purpose of education should be the cultivation of the intellect, and that only certain studies have this power. According to Hutchins, "Grammar disciplines the mind and develops the logical faculty. . . . Correctness in thinking may be more directly and impressively taught through mathematics than in any other way," and the permanent studies "cultivate the intellectual virtues" (1936, pp. 62, 82, 84). The perennialist position embraces the long-refuted doctrine of mental discipline (faculty psychology) and rejects any consideration of the interests and needs of the learner, or the treatment of contemporary problems in the curriculum, on the ground that such concerns are temporal and only detract from the school's mission of cultivating the mind.

The emerging demands for social reform during the early decades of the twentieth century—coupled with developments in psychiatry, medicine, and various behavioral sciences—led to a more integrated conception of human nature. Progressive educators, buttressed by research findings on the transfer of learning, demolished the old conception of mind as a separate entity and challenged the notion that certain studies possess uniquely inherent powers for the cultivation of the intellect (mental discipline).

Significance in Higher Education.   Although perennialism has long lost the place of dominance it once held in higher education, its leading proponents have been persistently visible and opportunistic. When Robert M. Hutchins (1899–1977) became president and chancellor of the University of Chicago in 1929, he sought to establish an undergraduate core curriculum based on the Great Books of the Western

World. However, the faculty opted for a broad-fields curriculum in general education that provided for the natural sciences, social sciences, and humanities—each as integrative areas. Under Hutchins's administration, many progressive innovations were instituted for general education. The undergraduate college was established to spearhead the curriculum in general education. A nucleus of experimentalist-progressives who had been working on the evaluation of educational outcomes in general education at The Ohio State University were recruited to Chicago to develop a system of comprehensive examinations and an independent board of examiners so as to evaluate longer-term learning outcomes through the curriculum in general education. Under the influence of Hutchins, the university dropped intercollegiate football and other varsity sports, along with its Big Ten membership.

Although Hutchins envisioned the undergraduate college as a four-year program combining the last two years of high school with the freshman and sophomore undergraduate years, with the curriculum devoted entirely to general education, the plan proved unworkable despite the claims made for its viability (Tanner, D., 1983b, p. 21; Ford Foundation, 1957). Nevertheless, the Chicago program in general education gained wide attention and exerted considerable influence in American higher education. One of the great ironies of Hutchins's tenure at Chicago was that, unbeknown to Hutchins, the world's first self-sustaining nuclear chain reaction was achieved by a University of Chicago team conducting their experimental work under the stands of the university's football stadium during World War II, proving that such a reaction was possible for the creation of a nuclear bomb.

Following his tenure at Chicago (1929–1951), Hutchins devoted himself to the cause of academic freedom at a time of the Cold War and the rise of McCarthyism. In his later years, he was impelled to change his perspective and became a defender of America's public schools.

Ironically, although the perennialists have long been severe critics of many features of American education and have opposed Dewey's progressive education, the rise of the radical romanticists during the late 1960s and early 1970s found some of the leading perennialists defending our system of education and reappraising Dewey's theories in a far more favorable light and defending him from misrepresentation (Barzun, 1971, pp. 1–8; Hutchins, 1972,

pp. 200, 226). The extremist nature of the criticisms leveled at the schools by the radical romanticists during this period led some leading perennialists to stand up in defense of American public education. Noting that for the first time in American history the value of universal, free, compulsory education was being questioned, Hutchins observed that "nobody has a kind word for the public school, the institution that only the other day was looked upon as the foundation of our freedom, the guaranty of our future, the cause of our prosperity and power, the bastion of our security, and the source of our enlightenment" (Hutchins, 1973, pp. 12–13). Hutchins went on to point out that radical criticism of public education had reached the stage of overkill with its call for abolishing compulsory education, eliminating the formal curriculum and catering to the evanescent whims of children, using public funds to establish alternative school systems, and even for abolishing the public schools altogether. To Hutchins, such decisions would only promote social segregation and the kind of individualism that is a danger to democracy.

Many perennialists view higher education as properly the province of an academically elite class and look on mass higher education as a kind of education inflation that has lessened the value of education by replacing the intellective literacy studies with all sorts of "relevant" contemporary studies. However, in the emergent age of science and technology, it was not possible for the traditional literary studies to retain their exalted reign over the curriculum in higher education.

At the same time, the fragmented and competing special interests of the undergraduate student population have found college students and faculty challenging the sanctity of the Great Books or canon of Western civilization as the appropriate core for liberal or general education. From the 1960s through much of the 1980s, college faculties had yielded to the demands for relevance in the undergraduate curriculum to the extent that any semblance to a core curriculum in general education was replaced by distribution electives involving hundreds of courses. In effect, each student could pursue one's own pattern of coursework to meet one's special interests. College faculties were more concerned with knowledge specialism and their departmentalized knowledge biases, so they readily acceded to the student demands for relevance, through electives. At the same time, the specialization requirements (for the student's major field) remained largely intact.

Nevertheless, it is one thing to call for a return to a classical literary curriculum and quite another to design an interdisciplinary core of studies revealing the interdependence of knowledge and addressing the common and pervasive problems of a free society in a scientific/technological age. During an extended period from the late 1970s into the 1990s, leading colleges and universities were grappling with the problem of curriculum fragmentation and were rediscovering the need to develop a common core for general education. Although it was clear that there would be no return to the perennialist curriculum of liberal education, it was not clear that the colleges were ready to drop their competing interests and act progressively to develop an articulated curriculum for general education.

Resurgent Controversy. The perennialist-essentialist cause was given considerable impetus during the tenure of William J. Bennett as chair of the National Endowment for the Humanities followed by his position as U.S. secretary of Education (1985–1988) in the Reagan administration at the height of the back-to-basics retrenchment. From the time when a chief federal officer for education was first appointed (Henry Barnard, 1867), virtually every person in that office was a progressive educator, or at least became a progressivist during their tenure, with one notable exception: William Bennett. Bennett's tenure was marked by repeated attacks on the schools for allegedly neglecting the basics. His proposals for reforming the curriculum of the elementary school and high school were centered on a core of basics giving emphasis to literary works of Western civilization (1988, 1987). As long as Bennett focused his attacks on the public schools, he seemed to be on safe ground, in that pubic school leaders seem to prefer acquiescence to confrontation. But when he attacked the undergraduate college curriculum at some of our prominent universities, he found himself a target of powerful counterattacks by influential university leaders. The situation became so rancorous that it impelled the presidents of Harvard and Stanford to make a joint appearance in May 1987 to denounce Bennett's charges (*Chronicle of Higher Education*, May 27, 1987, pp. 17, 21). As a consequence, with an election year impending, President Reagan reassigned Bennett to head the federal program for drug control where his efforts, understandably, were seen as less successful. Bennett's successor at the National Endowment for the Humanities, Lynne V. Cheney, continued in the same vein as Bennett in extolling *McGuffey's Readers* and the work of the Committee of Ten (1892), and in attacking the schools for neglecting the traditional humanities (n.d., pp. 7, 15).

During 1987 and 1988 a book by Allan Bloom of the University of Chicago, *The Closing of the American Mind*, became a national best-seller and a text for conservative attacks on higher education for having acquiesced to student demands for relevance and for having abandoned the traditional reliance on the Great Books of Western culture as the bedrock of the liberal arts curriculum. Although Bloom's criticisms, leveled against the fragmentation of the curriculum as a result of the competing disciplines seemed well grounded, his sweeping diatribes against mass education appeared ill considered. For example, he could title a chapter, "Our Ignorance" and declare in his concluding chapter that "[a]ll that is human, all that is of concern to us, lies outside natural science" (p. 356). Here Bloom appeared to be hallowing his own ignorance of how science has contributed not only to our understanding and control of the material world, but also to the democratic prospect in revealing the unrealized potentials of humanity.

The dynamic conditions of modern industrial societies require a dynamic and not a static curriculum. It is easy to put the onus on mass education. However, the notion that the curriculum should be limited to the so-called estate of timeless knowledge came to be shattered by the inevitable force of changing knowledge.

That many of our college students have turned to sensation over reason cannot be explained away as simply the result of mass education or the demise of the perennial curriculum. These students also reject the method of intelligence wrought by science and choose to blame science and technology for the evil uses to which so-called rational knowledge is put. They mistakenly place the blame on the rational methods of science rather than on the political forces that have turned the products of science and technology to ill use.

Perennialism Popularized. Perhaps the most successful and surely the most durable popularizer of perennialism has been Mortimer J. Adler, a disciple of Hutchins at the University of Chicago who went on to serve as associate editor of the anointed One Hundred Great Books of the Western World for almost half a century. Facetiously called "the Lawrence Welk of philosophy," Adler conducted Socratic dialogues in seminar discussions of the "Great Ideas" from the Great Books were shown on public television during the late 1980s. The limitations of the Socratic method may well have been apparent to discerning viewers in that it inevitably leads to convergence on the "master's" established conclusions. (This contrasts sharply against Dewey's reflective thinking.)

The back-to-basics retrenchment of the 1970s and 1980s proved opportune for Adler to endorse the essentialist school-reform menu of basics with drill and coaching exercises, leading up to perennialist literary study and Socratic questioning on ideas rooted in the classics, as presented in his *Paideia Proposal: An Educational Manifesto* (1982). Adler dedicated his book to Horace Mann, John Dewey, and Robert Hutchins. Yet throughout Adler's career he was a leading critic of Dewey. Indeed Dewey's writings clearly run counter to Adler's perennialist prescriptions, as embodied in *The Paideia*, along with Adler's conception of mind as a vessel or muscle, and Adler's doctrine that the One Hundred Great Books are the true repositories of permanent knowledge. To Adler, "Youth itself is the most serious impediment—in fact, youth is an insuperable obstacle to being an educated person" (1982, p. 9). To Dewey, childhood and youth are not obstacles, but genuine phases of growth and development, for, in Dewey's words, "immaturity designates a positive force or ability—the *power* to grow" (1916, p. 50).

The stereotype of the truly educated individual steeped in the traditional literary classics of Western civilization and in possession of an encyclopedic mind had been promoted as never before on the leading network TV quiz show of the latter 1950s. It so happened that the indomitable winner week after week was an ordinary-looking young man from New York who did have an encyclopedic mind. However, when a young instructor of literature at Columbia was chosen as challenger and was found to be enormously more appealing to the national audience, the reigning winner was induced by the TV producers to give the wrong answer and yield to the more attractive opponent. The opponent was Charles Van Doren, the son of the distinguished Columbia literary scholar Mark Van Doren. Week after week, the young Van Doren came up with the correct answer. In a guest appearance on another show for his network, Van Doren topped the *Ed Sullivan Show* in audience ratings, a feat accomplished only once before, by Elvis Presley. With his appearance on the quiz show, Van Doren was threatening to topple the shows of the

two rival networks. Van Doren's portrait appeared on the cover of *Time*. Thousands of marriage proposals to the young bachelor poured into the network offices each week. After four months of defending his title, Van Doren finally lost to a challenger. Not only had he broken TV's record for quiz-show winnings, but he now had an agent to handle the avalanche of TV offers.

Newspaper and magazine articles were extolling the virtues of a classical education as epitomized by Van Doren's demonstrated mnemonic powers. The media pointed to Van Doren, a graduate of St. John's College of Annapolis, Maryland, as a beneficiary of a purely classical curriculum, devoted entirely to the canons of Western civilization: the One Hundred Great Books. *Time* chronicled the Van Doren family's intellectual literary heritage. As the son of Mark and nephew of Carl, both of whom had made their mark as literary scholars of first rank, young Charles was following "a family tradition of literary excellence based on forthright thinking." As quoted in *Time*, "[t]he Van Dorens represent a tradition of people that is almost dead now, like Thoreau and Emerson. They have their roots in the 19th century. They are content and confident in themselves." The *Time* chronicle took note that "[t]he Van Doren tradition of self-reliance crossed the Atlantic in the 1650s when Pieter van Doren arrived in Peter Stuyvesant's Manhattan from Gravezand, Holland" (1957, p. 46).

However, the bubble was to burst with a thud when it was revealed that Charles Van Doren's initial steps to TV success had been staged. When it was also discovered that Van Doren had been fed the clues to the correct answers prior to each show, the ensuing scandal led to congressional hearings and investigations of fraud and deceit on the part of the TV networks. Not until three decades later did network quiz shows begin to reappear, and they never regained the mass audience appeal they once commanded. Charles Van Doren, who had been heralded as "Columbia's most cherished hero since Sid Luckman was tossing [football] passes at Baker Field," left Columbia to join Mortimer Adler's Institute for Philosophic Research and subsequently worked on Adler's operations on the Great Books for Encyclopaedia Britannica and as a member of the Paideia Group, which produced *The Paideia Proposal*. To this day, many people identify the highly educated person as one who is in possession of encyclopedic knowledge.

Essentialism

Where the perennialist views the liberal arts and Great Books as embodying the timeless intellectual virtues and perpetuating the cultural heritage, the essentialist sees this heritage being directed at modern needs through the fundamental academic disciplines of English (grammar, literature, and composition), mathematics, science, history, and modern foreign languages. These subjects, logically organized, are essential to the development of our mental capacities. The performing arts, industrial arts, vocational studies, physical education, and other areas of the curriculum are regarded as frills. Perhaps the most comprehensive case for essentialism was developed by the historian Arthur Bestor in *The Restoration of Learning* (1956). To Bestor, the mission of the school is "intellectual training," and this is to be accomplished through a curriculum concentrated on "the fundamental intellectual disciplines . . . disciplined study in five great areas: (1) command of the mother tongue and the systematic study of grammar, literature, writing; (2) mathematics; (3) sciences; (4) history; and (5) foreign language" (p. 120). To the essentialist, certain so-called academic areas of systematized knowledge best represent the race experience that is to be transmitted to children and youth.

Training of the Intellect.   Essentialists contend that the school's "full-time task lies" in "equipping students with intellectual powers," and that the "concern with the personal problems of adolescents has grown so excessive as to push into the background what should be the school's central concern, the intellectual development of its students" (Bestor, 1956, p. 120). The school is seen as being sidetracked from its central task of intellectual training when it ministers to personal-social needs of youth by embracing such tasks as developing saleable skills, health and physical fitness, democratic citizenship, consumer competence, and worthy use of leisure time (p. 117–119).

Essentialism shares with perennialism the position that the curriculum must be centered on intellective training and that the path to intellective power is to be found only to certain academic studies. Although the essentialist, unlike the perennialist, recognizes the place of the modern laboratory sciences in the curriculum, the essentialist places the modern social sciences, vocational education, physical education, art, music, and other "nonacademic" studies at the lowest priority levels in the curriculum. "The first duty of the school, if it values

its own educational integrity," declares Bestor, "is to provide a standard program of intellectual training in the fundamental disciplines" (p. 364). Pupil interests and needs are of limited concern as a basis for determining the curriculum. According to Bestor, "To such an extreme have many educationalists gone that they seem anxious to satisfy all imaginable needs except those of the mind" (p. 120).

Essentialists regard efforts to integrate or synthesize the studies below the college level as misguided. They hold that integration or synthesis arrives only after the student "has marshalled the array of separate intellectual powers" derived from each of the fundamental academic disciplines. Thus, the task of the school is to distinguish the elements that make up these disciplines and, "[t]hese various elements having been distinguished, the secondary school has as its primary task the systematic exploration of them, through study of the separate organized disciplines" (pp. 60, 62, 63).

The essentialist shares the same views as the perennialist with regard to the school's focus on mental discipline and the irrelevance of pupil interests. According to Admiral Hyman Rickover, a leading essentialist during the Cold War:

> For all children, the educational process must be one of collecting factual knowledge to the limit of their absorptive capacity. Recreation, manual or clerical training, etiquette, and similar know-how have little effect on the mind itself and it is with the mind that the school must solely concern itself. The poorer a child's natural endowments, the more does he need to have his mind trained. . . . To acquire such knowledge, fact upon fact, takes time and effort. Nothing can really make it "fun". (1958, p. 61)

Here the essentialist shares with the perennialist Aristotle's notion that "youths are not to be instructed with a view to their amusement, for learning is no amusement, but is accompanied with pain" (*Politics, Great Books*, 1952, p. 544).

Like the perennialist, the essentialist conceives of the mind as a vessel or container. Individual differences are marked off according to mental capacities, and education is simply a matter of filling and stretching each mind with the same curricular brew to the utmost of each mind's capacity. "After thirty years or more in the business," writes an educator, "I think I know something about individual differences. There are jugs of different capacity, and there are powers of different capacity, too. What I am talking about here is the nature of the wine and its availability to all" (Cornog, 1963, p. 3). However, where the perennialist sees the proper curricular brew as consisting of the liberal arts and Great Books, which embody the timeless intellectual virtues and perpetuate the cultural heritage, the essentialist holds that intellectual excellence is exemplified by the logically organized, fundamental academic disciplines. Both the perennialist and the essentialist see the role of the elementary school as concentrated simply on providing mastery of the basic skills and facts that are necessary preliminary to subsequent learning.

Educational Meritocracy. Many essentialists advocate the establishment of high academic standards through a system of uniform and rigorous examinations. In calling for such examinations to be administered as pupils move from elementary to secondary school and at the completion of compulsory schooling, the historian Arthur Bestor sees the examinations being used to sort out pupils for "the standard program of disciplined intellectual training"—to "furnish part of the data upon which the school administrator can begin the delicate process of advising the square pegs not to head for the round holes"—and to dramatize that the continuance of educational opportunity is "a privilege bestowed upon the meritorious and the energetic" (Bestor, 1956, p. 354).

After stating the case for the standardized test as the chief instrument to be used in the search for talent, John Gardner, president of the Carnegie Corporation, viewed the school as a stringent sorting-out process whereby the less able youngsters discover their limitations.

> But as education becomes increasingly effective in pulling [sic] the bright youngsters to the top, it becomes an increasingly rugged sorting-out process for everyone concerned. This is true today and it will be very much more so in the future. The schools are the golden avenue of opportunity for able youngsters; but by the same token they are the arena in which less able youngsters discover their limitations. This thought rarely occurred to the generations of Americans who dreamed of universal education. They saw the beauty of a system in which every young person could go as far as his ability and ambition would take him, without obstacles of money, social standing, religion, or race. They didn't reflect on the pain involved for those who lacked the necessary ability. Yet pain there is and must be. (1962, p. 68)

In sharp contrast is Dewey's view that education must focus on the development of potentialities and not on the setting of limitations. The quantitative measurement of mind is a fiction, maintained Dewey, and, "[h]ow one person's abilities compare in quantity with those of another is none of the teacher's business. It is irrelevant to his work" (1916, p. 203). Quantitative measures cannot be made for motivation and changing aspirations; nor can such measures predict intellectual development and changing opportunities. Further, history is replete with evidence that the "best and the brightest" do not necessarily possess a monopoly on the wisdom or ethical character. Turning again to the practice of using standardized tests for the search of academic talent, a physician friend and neighbor of the authors of this text commented at a dinner party that she felt sympathy for students today who must submit to so many competitive tests. "I can save lives, but I can't pass standardized tests," she confided.

Liberal Arts Professors as School Blamers. From mid-twentieth century in contemporary times, some of the most vehement attacks against the public schools have come from faculties of arts and sciences. The problems reached such proportions that it led to a report issued in 1954 by a committee of the American Academy of Arts and Sciences, which was quoted extensively by James Conant (1959a, pp. 63–64). It is worth reproducing here the sections of the report selected by Conant because the problem has continued to the present day in varying degrees of intensity. The vehemence of the attacks should be puzzling in view of the fact that it is not matched by comparable attacks leveled against the college student body who overwhelmingly are graduates of the public high schools. Conant quotes the opening sentence and the closing paragraph of the report as follows (Conant, 1959a, p. 63):

> There exists among a considerable number of the defenders of the liberal arts a shocking ignorance of the social problems with which the modern school is confronted. Consequently, these professors attack many of the most well-meant endeavors of our public schools on the basis of inadequate and fallacious criteria.

The report went on to point out that if the curriculum prescribed by the liberal arts professors were to be followed, "our whole national life would be in danger of collapse." Quoting further from the report:

> To repeat: though criticism is needed, there is no salvation in the present fashionable tendency to

attack the public school system by the use of incommensurate criteria, forgetting completely that this school system—whatever its obvious defects—has been for about a hundred years the most important instrument in the amalgamation of millions of poor immigrants and native citizens. As a matter of fact, this great achievement has been made possible largely by the use of methods severely criticized by outsiders. Without an attempt at understanding the complexity of a school system which at the same time should fulfill the demands of equality and of quality, of justice and differentiation, of democracy and of an elite within this democracy—and without understanding the difficult task of relating developments in education to broad changes in our social cultural pattern—without such endeavors on all sides, there can be no productive discussion. (Jones, Keppel, & Ulich, 1954)

Conant then offered this amendment to the closing words of the report: "Without an understanding of the complexities of public education resulting from the diversities of American communities, there can be no productive discussion of the shortcomings of our tax-supported schools"—to which he added:

College professors of the liberal arts and many of their friends often discuss school problems as though schools operated in the stratosphere—that is, in a social vacuum. To be sure, it is a convenient fiction to assume all children enter school with the same interests, abilities, preconceived ideas, and return to homes that are culturally identical. It is even more convenient to assume that a community has no interest in a school except as an instrument for developing intellectual power. (pp. 64–65)

As a distinguished educator, scientist, and statesman, Conant was probably the last of the college presidents who carried out the long-standing tradition of college presidents in advancing and defending American public education and its role as a key institution of advancing democracy. After Conant, the college presidents generally joined the liberal arts professors in attacking the schools or they assumed a posture of seeming indifference while they could go on to boast that their freshman classes were the best ever in promise and performance.

Neo-essentialism. The essentialist position—with its strong emphasis on basic education and academic excellence through science, mathematics, and modern foreign languages, and its call for developing our nation's intellective resources through ability grouping

and rigorous scholarship standards—was in tune with the tenor of the Cold War. During the early years of this period, essentialists exerted a considerable influence on the elementary and secondary school curriculum with great impetus being given to standardized testing. However, the federal support of national curriculum reform projects, led by university scholar-specialists, eventuated in the emergence of neo-essentialism, with the disciplines doctrine as the dominant influence on the curriculum during the era of the Cold War and space race.

The disciplines doctrine was launched in a report by Jerome Bruner issued in 1960 after a meeting sponsored by the National Academy of Sciences in response to the Cold War. The National Science Foundation had begun to support school curriculum projects in the sciences and mathematics beginning in the early 1950s, but what was lacking was a rationale to undergird these projects. The rationale was provided by Bruner's report, which embraced the doctrine that the individual disciplines in the sciences and mathematics each have structures that give form to curriculum construction from the elementary school upward. The disciplinary doctrine advanced by Bruner reflected the traditional mind-set of university scholars whose interests in their respective specialized disciplines are centered on knowledge purity and abstraction. University scholars in the myriad social sciences almost immediately embraced the disciplinary doctrine, although the lion's share of the funding for the national disciplinary projects was allocated to the sciences and mathematics. In perspective, the entire effort reveals what happens when university scholar-specialists are given full power (voice and funding) for national curriculum reform in the elementary and secondary schools.

The national discipline-centered projects and the disciplinary doctrine dominated school curriculum reform for almost two decades, but their failure should have been predictable from the start. The notion of "structure of the discipline" proved to be elusive to the extent that it was never validated. The disciplinary curriculum projects violated the nature of the learner, neglected the practical applications and uses of knowledge in the life of the learner and in civic life, led to the isolation and fragmentation of the curriculum, and gave almost exclusive emphasis to puristic and abstract knowledge in the specialized academic disciplines.

The disciplinary doctrine continues to serve in higher education, where knowledge specialism is followed and pursued. But even in higher education, the function of general education for a free society requires the integration of knowledge in the form of a common core. Further, the most advanced forms of research and scholarship require cross-disciplinary and interdisciplinary collaboration and inquiry, for nature does not follow the boundaries of subjects or disciplines.

By the close of the 1960s, disciplinarity as the single ruling doctrine for curriculum reform was shattered by the demand for relevance. Essentialism appeared to be hopelessly out of date. The call was for humanizing the schools. Suddenly such themes as alternative education, values education, moral education, and death education were appearing in the educational literature and in the curriculum. In the secondary school, minicourses on diverse topics were being offered. At the elementary level, the open classroom was in vogue. At the secondary and collegiate levels, the concept of general education was all but forgotten. Instead of undertaking the difficult task of developing a balanced and coherent curriculum, the response of educators was a kind of default: simply allow for more free and distributed elective options and introduce more au courant courses.

Each excessive action inevitably eventuates in an equal and opposite excessive reaction. Essentialism was to have its place in the sun once again.

Back to Basics. By the mid-1970s, the old essentialism was in a state of renascence with the rallying cry of back to basics being heard once again throughout the land. The National Assessment of Educational Progress, which had been inaugurated a decade earlier, was now being followed by statewide programs of minimum-competence testing.

Essentialists see competency-based education as being concentrated on the fundamental skills. They are opposed to those who would employ it in terms of the meaning and importance of competency in life-role activities, such as in consumer education or political citizenship.

Many essentialists are opposed to the comprehensive secondary school. They not only see the high school curriculum appropriately concentrated on the traditional academic subjects, but they also favor separate academic high schools for those of higher scholastic ability. The American essentialist influence has had its counterpart in Britain, where it had been focused on opposing the government policy of developing comprehensive schools in place of the tradi-

tional tripartite and selective system. In response to a 1965 government "white paper" calling for a policy of developing comprehensive schools in Britain, a group of essentialists began issuing a series of "black papers," which appeared almost annually from 1969 into the 1980s. In addition to opposing open education and the government-mandated development of comprehensive secondary schools, the black papers embraced a back-to-basics prescription and the use of tests for "the national monitoring of basic standards for all children at the ages of 7, 11, and 14 or 15" (Cox & Boyson, 1977).

All kinds of sweeping allegations are found in the Black Papers, such as "[i]n mathematics, the obsession with the need for understanding before learning, usually citing poor Piaget as proof, is the major cause of low standards" (p. 24). (The assumption is that understanding is not real learning or that one must learn before one can understand.) Like their American compeers, British essentialists rest much of the blame for allegedly lower standards on John Dewey. In response to a government report showing that standards have not fallen, the report was quickly dismissed and Dewey was blamed in these words: "During the past forty years, as the 'progressive' philosophy of education adumbrated by John Dewey has gained ground in British and American schools, the teaching of English has probably been more adversely affected than any branch of the curriculum" (p. 30).

In the United States, the back-to-basics retrenchment was to extend throughout the 1970s and 1980s, buttressed by statewide minimum-competency testing and national standardized tests of academic achievement. Even the professional education associations seemed to join the tide backward to the essentials. For example, a publication issued by the National Association of Secondary School Principals titled *Reducing the Curriculum* (1982) presented itself as a blueprint for cutbacks and recommended that priorities be established, with "essential" courses being given number-one priority, and "desirable" courses be given number-two priority. Soon the studio arts and industrial arts were being eliminated from the curriculum. The adage "Beware of what you want, for you might get it" seemed to hold true with respect to the Council for Basic Education, an organization founded by Arthur Bestor for the purpose of promoting basic education and eliminating the curriculum "frills." The curriculum fundamentalism had become so extreme that in 1975 the council added the arts to its canon of officially accredited basic subjects, and in

1979 it actually issued papers defending the place of the arts in basic education (Barzun & Saunders, 1979). The council subsequently moved toward a more centrist position on the school curriculum, where it remains to this day.

Cultural Literacy: The New Essentialist Catchword. One of the national best-sellers of 1987 was *Cultural Literacy: What Every American Needs to Know*, which contained a clever marketing gimmick in the form of nearly 5,000 factual items in the back of the book that "every American needs to know." The items, obviously drawn up arbitrarily and giving rather short shrift to the sciences, were promoted by the author as defining the cultural knowledge base for the schools and the nation. To the unwary public, the items offered as "knowledge" were nothing less than information in the form of isolated facts. The use of the term *literacy* was soon seized on by virtually every special-interest group for each subject area of the curriculum in promoting prescriptions for their own brand of literacy: mathematical literacy, scientific literacy, technological literacy, computer literacy, economic literacy, political literacy, artistic literacy, and so on (Tanner, D., 1989). In embracing the item, the essentialists had forgotten the humble historic origins of literacy that had emerged early in the twentieth century to mark a rudimentary capability in English for the waves of immigrants reaching our shores.

To Hirsch and many essentialists, a fact-based curriculum is fundamental to any further learning. It seemed that Dickens's Mr. Gradgrind in *Hard Times* had come back to life in the curricular hard times during the educational retrenchment of the 1980s.

Basics "Old" and "New." By the early 1990s it was becoming increasingly evident that the fundamentalist curriculum retrenchment, along with the statewide minimum-competency testing and the national achievement testing programs, had resulted in lowering the achievement of our student populations (Madaus, 1992). Progressive ideas such as whole language, writing across the curriculum, teaching for higher-order thinking, teaching mathematics and science through hands-on experience, student projects and portfolios, and so on were being rediscovered as though they were new inventions. Nevertheless, certain reports on national education policy, such as the one issued by the U.S. secretary of Labor's Commission on Achieving Necessary Skills (1992),

proposed that beginning in middle school, a record be kept of every youngster's performance standard in qualifying for a "Certificate of Initial Mastery" in each performance competency so as to leave school with the essential skills sought by employers. The endorsement of a new national testing program (American Achievement Tests) by the Bush, Clinton, and Bush administrations, stemming from the National Education Goals in *America 2000* (1991), was testimony to the enduring appeal of curriculum reductionism as a simple solution to the complex problems of education.

Essentialism predictably is resurrected during periods of economic retrenchment and conservative social influence. Few educators would hold that the fundamental processes should not have a fundamental place in the curriculum. The progressivist sees the fundamental processes as tool processes and sees education as the means of improving the social condition rather than merely fitting individuals in the basic competencies required of the existing social machinery. Whereas the essentialist sees the essential subjects as the complete core of the curriculum, the experimentalist-progressive sees the essentials as providing the tools upon which to build a comprehensive, articulated curriculum of interdisciplinary studies for general education and extended macrocurricular studies (exploratory, enrichment, special-interest, and specialized studies).

The external testing pandemic of today has ensured the continued dominance of essentialism over the school curriculum. As noted, the so-called new basics in *America 2000* are almost indistinguishable from the predecessor basics or traditional basics with the exception of the addition of computer literacy. Although significant efforts have been made in recent years to relate the basics to useful knowledge and practical applications, such as in mathematics, the applications rarely connect with social problems and issues. Alfred North Whitehead, one of the leading theoretical mathematicians of the twentieth century, envisioned the inclusion of social statistics in the mainstream of the school mathematics curriculum (1929a, pp. 12–14). However, this remains to be accomplished. Literature cannot be taught without connecting with social problems and issues, but the correlation between literature and social studies has been limited in most high schools under the departmental structure. Further, the external testing instruments, delimited to the most part by subject boundaries and the multiple-choice format for electronic scoring, mitigate such connections, not to mention the political avoidance of serious controversy in the test items by the testing agencies.

Eclecticism

Many teachers and administrators appear to function intuitively or expediently in response to whatever trends may be dominant. They do not base their choices or test their choices in terms of a systematic philosophy or theory of education. "We may fasten together many different beliefs, not fusing them into a harmonious pattern but keeping them as separate pieces, ready to shift about into different positions, checkerlike, as the need arises," states Brameld in describing the eclectic approach. He sees eclecticism in the curriculum as "smatterings of many things without purpose or design" (Brameld, 1971, pp. 59, 62).

Although this may well be an accurate portrayal of how many educators function and an accurate description of the condition of the school and college curriculum, those who ascribe to the eclectic view contend that their choices are more deliberate. The eclectic borrows from various philosophies in the belief that each philosophy has something of value and that no one philosophy is sufficiently complete or suited to varying conditions. But because eclecticism finds many elements from the traditional philosophies appropriate for contemporary times, its outlook tends to be conservative.

Selecting the "best" from each of all possible worlds is deceptively seductive. The best for one eclectic may be the worst for another. Because the different philosophies are conflicting, the eclectic selection involves compromise rather than resolution. For example, how does one resolve the conflict between the behaviorist's conception of the learner and the humanist's conception, not to mention the conflicting curricular prescriptions? On some such issues, even compromise is not practicable. Because eclectic representations differ so markedly from one another, eclecticism is not a philosophy per se, but a synthetic formulation compounded from differing systems. (Consequently, eclecticism is not represented in Table 9.1.)

Perhaps the most thoughtfully formulated eclectic statement on the curriculum is the Harvard Committee Report, *General Education in a Free Society*. Its eclectic spirit is revealed in such statements as the following: "[e]ducation can therefore be wholly devoted neither to tradition or experiment. . . . It must uphold at the same time tradition and experiment. . . though common aims must bind together the whole educational system, there exists no one body of knowledge, no single system of instructional equally valid for every part of it" (1945, pp. 51, 79).

Another example of an eclectic curricular prescription that exerted a powerful influence on American education was the Conant report on the high school (1959b). In this work, Conant embraced the democratizing function of the comprehensive secondary school, with its heterogeneous pupil population. At the same time he advocated the use of standardized tests for ability grouping, and special counseling and sorting of the academically talented, to meet nationalistic interests in the space race and in the Cold War battle for global leadership. (The experimentalist would regard the use of education for narrow nationalistic interests as inimical to democracy and as a contradiction of what education should be.)

Another example of an eclectic proposal for school reform, *High School: A Report on Secondary Education in America* by Ernest L. Boyer, was issued in 1983 under the auspices of the Carnegie Foundation for the Advancement of Teaching. Boyer's report, as in the case of Conant's report of a quarter of a century earlier, avoided the accusatory and condemnatory language characteristic of so many reports on school reform during the 1970s and 1980s. Although Boyer embraced a number of progressive ideas and practices, such as the need for curriculum integration through common learnings or general education and the abandonment of the Carnegie unit in inventorying academic credits, he proceeded to propose a standard list of courses and credits by academic units required for graduation, units virtually identical to Carnegie units. As did Conant, Boyer addressed the democratizing function of the American high school. But unlike Conant, Boyer did not support the comprehensive high school. Although he touched on the problems of dropouts and youth unemployment, he focused on the weaknesses of existing programs of vocational education without showing how they might be strengthened. He seemed willing to scrap the comprehensive high school in favor of a general academic high school geared primarily to serving the precollege population. For the academic elite in the sciences and mathematics, Boyer proposed the establishment of a national network of federally supported residential academies.

The weakness of the eclectic approach lies in the inconsistencies and contradictions that are inevitable when conflicting philosophical elements are drawn together, or when the eclectic simply decides not to deal with such elements, however significant they may be. Omission or avoidance is not a substitute for resolution or even compromise.

The Progressive Vision

The progressive sees humanity in an evolving universe. Hence knowledge is not static or timeless but dynamic. Education must be viewed as a process of growth and not merely a process of cultural transmission. Mind is viewed in biological continuity with nature, not a thing apart. The nature and interests of the learner and social conditions, as well as the race experience, must be considered in developing a balanced and coherent curriculum.

The natural sciences, which have brought about a revolution in our conception of ourselves and of the universe, are based on the method of intelligence. Applied to the human condition, the method of intelligence has enabled us to exercise greater control over our own destiny. It has served to free humanity from dogmatic authority, superstition, blind fear, and prejudice, thereby serving as the key tool of democracy. A society that aspires to democratic ideals must employ democratic means if such ideals are to become a reality. The curriculum must be based on the method of intelligence if an enlightened citizenry is to emerge. The method of intelligence is not something apart from attitudes, feelings, and emotions, but enables us to better understand and constructively direct our affective dispositions.

The progressive vision has been defracted into several widely differing and even conflicting images. The most systematic and consistent progressive educational theory is experimentalism. It is not by accident that experimentalist theory emerged from the democratic currents of American life and thought in the twentieth century. Virtually all other educational theories or philosophies in Western civilization stem from European origins.

Some progressivists are impatient with the open-mindedness of the experimentalist vision. They think the school needs to play a more direct function in reconstructing society for a democratic social order. In a sense, their theory of reconstructionism may be more radical than progressive. Other progressives have avoided entirely the social message of the progressive

vision by embracing only the humanitarian precepts of child-centeredness. In so doing, they have tended to romanticize the nature of the learner, with the result that their vision is more romantic than progressive. As discussed later in this chapter, the romanticist view of the learner has also been embraced by many radical critics of American education.

Experimentalism

In a remarkable book, *Dynamic Sociology, or Applied Social Science*, published in 1883, Lester Ward systematically explicated the idea of progress and the belief in the educability of the people as essential to a progressive democratic society. Ward held that the dynamic evolutionary forces in the natural world require a dynamic conception of knowledge. But where evolution in nature is a meandering process, human progress requires the release of intelligence through popular education to improve the human condition.

Ward prophetically pointed out that this would require a dynamic and articulated curriculum, a curriculum that did not yet exist. For Ward, the curriculum must meet the test of relative *generality* and relative *practicality*. Ward proposed three universal curricula. The first universal curriculum for the school should be aimed at general and practical knowledge. The second universal curriculum should provide for even greater generality and practicality and embrace many interdependent branches. The third universal curriculum should be directed at advanced studies, elected by the student with teacher guidance, for life pursuits (specialization). These ideas came to be expressed in a rudimentary way through the concept of curriculum constants and variables in the *Cardinal Principles* report of 1918. However, Ward's prophecy called for a macrocurricular design and function that was not to be given full and systematic attention for almost half a century until experimentalist educators directed their efforts to the idea and practice of general education as the keystone for specialized education, enrichment education, exploratory education, and special-interest education in the context of the cosmopolitan, comprehensive high school.

To social reformers who contended that the solution to social inequity resides in the redistribution of wealth, Ward pointed out that "[t]hey are working at the roof instead of at the foundation of the structure which they desire to erect." The foundation, Ward held, rests with the diffusion of knowledge through universal education, whereby intelligence would be released for individual and social improvement (pp. 497, 597). Ward's riposte of 1883 seemed just as apropos to contemporary radical critics who have portrayed the public schools as either a marginal institution or one that is designed to limit social opportunity. For their own children, of course, they have great belief in the positive power of education (see Ravitch [1987] for a criticism of radical-left revisionism).

Ward's passionate belief in the power of the environment and his faith in the school as a planned environment for releasing intelligence for a progressive and democratic society was to find expression in Dewey's experimentalist philosophy. "He anticipated John Dewey," wrote Commager, "and supplied him with a scientific basis for much of his educational philosophy" (1967, p. 258). Unfortunately, Ward never gained the recognition he deserved during his lifetime, and even to this day (Tanner, L. N., & Tanner, D., 1987, pp. 537–547).

Dewey's experimentalist philosophy also took roots from the pragmatism of two contemporaries of Ward's, mathematician Charles Peirce (1839–1914) and psychologist William James (1842–1910). As did Ward, they rejected the doctrine of absolute or a priori truths of the traditionalists and held that truth derives from the scientific investigation of ideas through the test of consequences. "Science is dynamic. Whatever it touches is transformed," observed Ward (1883, p. 497).

As shown in Table 9.1, experimentalist views on the curriculum and on educational aims are in vivid contrast to the conservative theories of essentialism and perennialism, and to the radical theories of reconstructionism, romantic naturalism, and existentialism.

To the experimentalist, absolute philosophies, with their fixed truths, appeal to authority and privilege because they promote dogmas that are not to be tested by scientific inquiry. Hence the suffix -*ism* is inimical to experimentalist thinking, for *ism* implies a certain closed-minded belief. The experimentalist commitment is to the testing of ideas and the holding of beliefs as tentative pending verification through the method of intelligence. Dewey put the matter in these words in addressing the reconstructionists:

> . . . those who are looking ahead to a new movement in education adapted to the existing need for a new social order, should think in terms of Education itself rather than in terms of some 'ism about education,

even such an 'ism as "progressivism." For in spite of itself any movement that thinks and acts in terms of an 'ism becomes so involved in reaction against other 'isms that it is unwittingly controlled by them. For it then forms its principles by reaction against them instead of a comprehensive constructive survey of actual needs, problems, and possibilities (Dewey, 1938, pp. vi–vii).

In this chapter, *ism* is used to denote the contrasting and conflicting theoretical systems. It is acknowledged that *ism* in the sense of a fixed doctrine does not apply to experimentalist theory, because the experimental method of inquiry and action is promised on the best available evidence.

Search for Unity and the Democratic Prospect. In pointing out how experimentalism, as orchestrated by John Dewey, was inescapably the expression of the uniquely American experience, James Conant wrote, "I had the feeling that, like the Austro-Hungarian Empire of the nineteenth century, if John Dewey hadn't existed he would have had to be invented" (1959a, p. 94).

As orchestrator of experimentalist thought, Dewey held that a democracy requires a citizenry committed to and capable of reflective thinking in solving pervasive social problems. Dewey rejected the traditional philosophies and their dualistic, oppositional tenets: mind versus body, intellectual versus character development, knowing versus doing, intellect versus emotion, theoretical versus practical knowledge, logical versus psychological knowledge, scientific versus humanistic studies, mind versus matter, nature versus nurture, ends versus means. He pointed out the need to view the person as a whole being in continuity with the biological universe. Where Dewey rejected the traditional educational theories for their reliance on external imposition and authoritarian methods, he opposed the romantic progressivists for viewing the child as a naturally unfolding being whose fruition is best realized through spontaneous activity and self-fulfillment in an environment without social direction. "Freedom means essentially the part played by thinking—which is personal—in learning: it means intellectual initiative, independence in observation, judicious invention, foresight of consequences, and ingenuity of adaptation to them," wrote Dewey (1916, p. 352).

Dewey contended that the curriculum should not be a mere conglomeration of divided and specialized subject matters but should be reflectively formulated, coherently designed, and meaningfully attuned to the improvement of existing community life. He observed that the traditional educational philosophies had failed to come to grips with "the deepest problems of common humanity," had overlooked the fact that the curriculum "is humanized in the degree in which it connects with the common interests of men as men," and had created conditions in the curriculum that "infect the education called liberal with illiberality." According to Dewey, "A curriculum which acknowledges the social responsibilities of education must present situations where problems are relevant to the problems of living together, and where observation and information are calculated to develop social insight and interest" (1916, pp. 225–226).

Reflective Thinking. Dewey held that the processes of instruction should be based on the processes of reflection. Traditional education, with its "method of imposition from the side of the teacher and reception, absorption, from the side of the pupil," observed Dewey, "may be compared to inscribing records upon a passive phonographic disc to result in giving back what has been inscribed when the proper button is pressed in recitation or examination" (Dewey, 1934, p. 212). He viewed traditional practices as inimical to the development of the enlightened democratic citizen.

As discussed earlier, Dewey deplored the mechanical and specialized treatment of science as something separate from social problems and moral direction. To Dewey, science should serve in the interests of humanity. Its methods in education have a clear moral purpose: to combat bias and ignorance, to act by reason rather than by authority or superstition, to free intelligence and to provide intellectual control over conduct, and to judge truly. Human progress is not served when scientific judgments are separated from moral judgments, believed Dewey. Witness the misuses of science to destroy rather than to improve civilization, or the harmful effects in our history when moral standards are established and imposed by unreasoning authority or through superstition.

Dewey criticized the old ideal that held that the pursuit of knowledge for its own sake is good in itself. To Dewey, intelligence and knowledge must be directed at foreseeing the consequences of existing social conditions and taking sides in behalf of the consequences that are preferred (1929b, p. 144).

In 1964, the Nobel physicist Max Born put the matter in these words:

> In the operation of science and its ethics a change has taken place that makes it impossible to maintain the old ideal of the pursuit of knowledge for its own sake which my generation believed in. We were convinced that this could never lead to any evil since the search for truth was good in itself. That was a beautiful dream from which we were awakened by world events. (1964, p. 2)

Born was not expressing his disillusionment with science and rational intelligence, but was pointing to the need for science and rationality to be directed at the human condition. More than half a century earlier, Dewey had warned the scientists that because science was divorced from concern with the social and moral ideals for which it is used, its discoveries are used for aims that are "survivors of a prescientific age, that is, of barbarism." He added, "Even where science has received its most attentive recognition, it has remained a servant of ends imposed from alien traditions" (1910, p. 127).

Quantification in Education. Dewey repeatedly took issue with those who sought to reduce education to quantifiable measurements as though such reductionism made education scientific. He noted that quantitative measures in education through IQ and standardized achievement testing, as well as in determining objectives, were being promoted on the grounds of educational efficiency; but such efficiency was conceived in terms of perpetuating the present order. For Dewey the function of education is to unleash human potentials, not to set limitations, so that the existing order can be transformed into a better one (1928c, p. 200). The outcome of scientific methods is not uniformity and standardization of procedure but the liberation of individuals by enabling them to see new problems, devise new procedures, thereby making for diversification rather than for set uniformity (Dewey, 1929a, p. 12).

Addressing the same problem, Bode took issue with those who view education as being properly reduced to the attainment and assessment of quantifiable skills as though such a function removed education from the wider social concerns and made education neutral. To Bode, such efforts limited education to fitting individuals as cogs in the existing social mechanism and reflected the aristocratic tradition. "The irony of the situation is that these highly modern persons are a century or two behind the times," wrote Bode. "There is no such thing as being neutral" (1927, p. 234).

Dewey has been attacked by essentialists for the excesses taken in humanizing the curriculum, but he has also been attacked by humanists for the excesses taken in reducing the curriculum to that which is most amenable to quantifiable and standardized measures. Despite the clear stance taken by Dewey against simplistic and mechanistic approaches to complex education problems, the blame for such approaches is sometimes rested on Dewey. For example, Eisner asked, "Why do the schools, so often, pursue simplistic, mechanical solutions to complex educational problems?" Eisner fixed the blame on Dewey and Thorndike (1985, pp. 8, 10). Not until the third edition of *The Educational Imagination* (1994) did Eisner excise his attack on Dewey in linking him with Thorndike in fixing the blame for the mechanistic state of the curriculum. In earlier editions, Eisner concluded that Franklin Bobbitt's curriculum work in activity analysis stemmed from the tradition established by Dewey and Thorndike. How Dewey could be so linked with Thorndike and Bobbitt, when he clearly and repeatedly criticized the mechanistic approaches developed by these men, is indeed puzzling. But as we have seen, Dewey has been anathema for educators at opposite poles of the educational spectrum, whether perennialist or humanist. As discussed later, by the late 1980s many of those who had attacked Dewey came to see him as a true seer for education and the democratic prospect.

Democratic Ideal.   Dewey's democratic educational theory also continues to be a subject of misinterpretation. For example, Broudy caricatures Dewey's democratic ideal as an effort to restore our society to the spirit of the New England town meeting. But it was Dewey who pointed out:

> The old principles do not fit contemporary life as it is lived, however well they may have expressed the vital interests of the times in which they arose. . . .
> The older publics, in being local communities, largely homogeneous with one another, were also, as the phrase goes, static. (1927, pp. 135, 139)

Dewey emphasized repeatedly that if democracy is to come into its own, it will require a kind of knowledge and insight that does not yet exist. One of the necessary conditions relevant to our time is that the scientific attitude be adopted in human affairs so that science and technology are used as servants of a humane life and for an enlightened social order rather than being used for private power and profit and public intimidation (1929, p. 155).

Demand for Relevance.   Following a rash of riots in ghettos and violent protest on college campuses during the 1960s, college and high school students began demanding curriculum relevance. The discipline-centered curriculum at the secondary level was regarded as irrelevant to the social situation. However, the call was not to reconstruct the curriculum along the lines of experimentalist thinking but to pursue radical alternatives. Aside from the appearance of some alternative schools and the implementation of certain administrative innovations to humanize education, the response of most secondary schools and colleges was manifested in ad hoc changes, such as the expansion of elective options and the allowance of some academic credit for work experience. At the elementary level, open education came into vogue. But instead of being implemented as a means of curriculum reconstruction, open education was often adopted as an administrative rearrangement for teaching the fundamental skills under the theme of individualized instruction.

Yet the late 1960s and early 1970s witnessed an unprecedented interest in the attacks on schools leveled by the radical left, attacks that were publicized widely in the mass media. In his essay "John Dewey and His Betrayers," Sidney Hook noted that whereas in the past the severest criticisms of American public education came from the traditionalists who opposed the alleged inroads of progressive education on the curriculum, the new wave of attacks "comes from those who regard themselves as libertarians and humanists and who profess themselves inspired to a considerable degree by the thought of John Dewey" (1973, p. 111). Hook accused the radical left of being intellectually irresponsible in disregarding and distorting Dewey's writings.

Where the radical left advocated "incidental" education and even the elimination of the public school, Dewey had looked to public education as the key means of social insight and progress. To Dewey, freedom is not the lack of control and direction, or the right of everyone to do his or her own thing, but rather "the basic freedom is that of freedom of *mind* and of whatever degree of freedom of action and experience is necessary to produce freedom of intelligence" (1946, p. 61).

Reconstructionism

To many progressive educators, experimentalist ideas are too neutral and do not provide sweeping educational reforms. Progressivists who sought a more direct ideology for correcting social ills and building a better society embraced reconstructionism.

Education for Social Reconstruction.   The reconstructionist views the school as a chief means for building a new social order. Although reconstructionist ideas are found in the historic stream of utopian writings, the Great Depression witnessed a call to harness the school for social reconstruction. In a series of addresses delivered in 1932 to various education associations, George S. Counts called for progressive educators to address the great crises of the times, fashion a new vision of human destiny based on social welfare, and challenge the schools to the task of giving the rising generation the means toward realizing such a vision (1932). Although Counts acknowledged that the school is but one of the many formative social agencies, he held that this should not deter progressive educators from channeling the powers of the school toward social reconstruction. Nor should educators fear that such a role of the school will result in ideological impositions on the learner, for any kind of powerful education is indeed a kind of imposition, contended Counts.

As noted, Dewey warned the reconstructionists that their cause in directing the curriculum at prescriptive social correction raised the danger of ideological imposition or indoctrination—anathema to democracy. At the 1934 NEA conference, Dewey pointed out that it would be revolution enough if educators were to recognize social changes and act on that recognition in the schools (Dewey, 1934, p. 745).

Counts's reconstructionism was to take on a militant advocacy that went far beyond his vision and intent. During the Great Depression, educators with Marxist leanings, such as Theodore Brameld, called on teachers to "influence their students, subtly if necessary, frankly if possible, toward acceptance of . . . the collectivist ideal" (1935, p. 55). Decades later, Brameld was to repeat his call for teachers "to strengthen control of the schools by and for the goal-seeking interests of the majority of mankind," which are "the fountainhead of utopian potentials" (1971, p. 519).

Implementing experimentalist ideas in the curriculum would, in itself, constitute a revolutionary transformation; it would defeat censorship and open the curriculum to the reflective examination of alternative ideologies, however controversial, and it would seek to develop autonomously thinking, socially responsible citizens.

The pluralistic character and centrist tendencies of American society need not be viewed pessimistically as barriers to social correction and improvement. As a foreign observer noted before midcentury, if an ordinary American faces a problem without having any specific clues for its solution, one of the recommendations he or she is likely to resort to is "education"—for "the belief in 'education' is a part of, or a principal conclusion from the American creed" (Myrdal, 1944, 1962). Americans look to education as a key institution for social improvement. Their tendency to lend an open ear to every attack on the schools that comes along during periods of social crisis stems from their great expectations of the role of the school in correcting social problems and not from their lack of faith in education. At the same time, the American public has resisted radical proposals for its schools, whether it be the abandonment of the comprehensive secondary school in favor of the dual European model or the use of the school for imposing reconstructionist ideology on children and youth. Radical educational reforms have been left to the alternative schools, which are on the periphery of the mainstream of American education.

Utopian Visions.   Although reconstructionism embraces democracy as the appropriate goal of education, experimentalists see the educational means of reconstructionism as inculcating prescribed beliefs in the learner. To the experimentalist this is indoctrination, and democratic ends cannot be attained by indoctrination. There is all the difference in the world between prescribing beliefs and in identifying problem areas for reflective consideration of issues and solutions on the part of the learner (Bode, 1935, p. 22; Dewey, 1937, p. 235).

History is replete with utopian schemes for education and society. However noble and admirable may be the utopian visions of reconstructionism, the history of utopian schemes, noted Mumford, reveals an unmistakable absolutism:

> Strangely, though the word *freedom* is sometimes included in the description of utopia—indeed, one nineteenth-century utopia was called Freeland—the pervasive character of all utopias is their totalitarian absolutism, the reduction of variety and choice, and the effort to escape from such natural conditions or

historical traditions as would support variety and make choice possible. These uniformities and compulsions constitute utopia's inner tie to the megamachine (1970, p. 210).

Whatever their techniques for realizing their ends, "almost all utopias emphasize regularity, uniformity, authoritarianism, isolation, and autocracy," contended Mumford, for the strategies for creating the coming world invariably are placed in the hands of a narrow elite who are the "accredited ministers of progress" (pp. 210–211). The prescriptions of reconstructionism are concerned with promoting the welfare of the masses in a democratically regulated utopian society. The reconstructionist prescriptions do not preclude indoctrination, and indoctrination is ideological imposition on the learner. As such it raises the question of whether reconstructionism embraces a kind of political absolutism that Mumford was concerned about.

The Indoctrination Controversy. The call for reconstructionism can best be understood by the horrendous conditions of unemployment, poverty, hunger, social dislocation, and disaffection that combined to create a suffering humanity in the Great Depression of the 1930s. Under the tenor of the times, Counts's message in *Dare the School Build a New Social Order?* (1932) electrified educators and stimulated great debate, but reconstructionism was to have virtually little impact on the schools as the nation underwent social and economic reforms for recovery under the administration of Franklin Roosevelt. Yet a national survey of social attitudes of high school teachers, conducted in 1936 under the auspices of the John Dewey Society, as reported in the society's first yearbook (Hartmann, 1937), found many teachers sharing Counts's views on curricular issues. For example, 65% of teachers disagreed with the statement that "Persons who wished to bring about a 'New Social Order' make poorer teachers than those who adhere strictly to their own specialty"; 83% disagreed with the statement that "It is pedagogically unprofitable to discuss serious social problems with adolescent youngsters"; and 62% disagreed with "A classroom teacher should make every effort to prevent his pupils from discovering his position on controversial issues." Responses to some of the social and public issues in the survey reflected the critical condition of the state of national emergency resulting from the economic and social collapse of the Great Depression. Hence 87% of the teacher respondents

could express their disagreement with the statement, "There is no such thing as a "class struggle" in American life today" (pp. 182–189).

On balance, the survey revealed that teachers shared many experimentalist-progressive ideas and opinions, and even reconstructionist views, contrary to the stereotypical portrayal of the teacher as essentialist and conservative.

The indoctrination controversy raised by Counts found the board of the Progressive Education Association divided into two camps: one calling for the association to take a stand on critical social issues; the other calling for a humane and caring curriculum rather than a curriculum to raise the social conscience of the rising generation. This division was debated at a board meeting, as recalled by a board member, while men were fighting each other for scraps of food from the garbage cans in the alley of the hotel where the board was meeting (Redefer, 1949, p. 189).

Looking back on George S. Counts over a half century after publication of *Dare the School*, the noted philosopher Sidney Hook, a close colleague of Counts's, expressed his belief that Counts "at heart" was opposed to indoctrination and largely shared and advocated experimentalist ideas in the advancement of American democracy (telephone interview and letter in Tanner, D., 1991, pp. 36–38, rev. ed., 2002). Interestingly, Counts's *Dare the School*, first published in 1932, was reissued almost half a century later and remains in print (1978).

Pluralistic and Centrist Character of American Society. Unlike the new academic left in the discussion that follows, the reconstructionists of the Great Depression and the post–World War II years did direct their efforts toward school problems including school improvement. However, their influence was tempered by the indoctrination issue and the pluralistic and centrist character of American society, which buffers any militant attempt toward doctrinal agreement for collective social reconstruction, just as it buffers or resists any extremist political platform.

The New Academic-Left Radicalism

Out of the radical student protest of the 1960s generation emerged the new academic left, who became the "tenured left" in the universities (Diggins, 1992;

Kimball, 1991). Whereas the reconstructionists were concerned with the need to forge connections with the underprivileged and to engage the schools and other social institutions in working toward a democratic transformation, the critical theorists and others of the new academic left in schools of education focused on exposing the function of the hidden curriculum as a conspiratorial vehicle for imposing on the rising generation subtle modes of social control, domination, and subjugation.

Dewey Decimated

Turning to European sources for their ideologies, the new academic left proceeded to identify themselves as critical theorists, deconstructionists, revisionists, postmodernists, reconceptualists, and neo-Marxists. They faulted the schools for their impotence on the one hand and for exercising a powerful repressive role in maintaining the existing social order on the other hand. When not portraying the role of the school as inconsequential, they were portraying the teacher as an unwitting accomplice to a hidden scheme (in the hidden curriculum) for promoting "cultural reproduction" or "social control"—as opposed to "emancipation of the masses." With regard to Dewey, on the one hand they would attack him for his liberal ideology and for having provided the groundwork that led to the existing state of affairs in the public schools (Bowles & Gintis, 1976); on the other hand, they would see the work of Dewey and his fellow experimentalists as having but little impact on the schools (Apple, 1990, p. 176). In making their case, they did not hesitate to revise the historical record so as to buttress their assault on the schools and on progressive educators who did not fit into the radical fold. For example, Bowles and Gintis contended that "Proponents of the use of tests for educational tracking found support in John Dewey's writings" (Bowles & Gintis, 1976, p. 197). However, in *Democracy and Education* (1916), Dewey actually attacked the efforts to measure differences in mental abilities in these words: "How one person's abilities compare in quantity with those of another is none of the teacher's business. It is irrelevant to his work" (p. 172). Jencks portrayed the public school as a "marginal institution" (1972, p. 262), and Illich called for the "deschooling" of society (1971) and verified Spring's thesis that "the primary purpose of the school system is social control for a corporate state" (1972, in Spring, p. x). Spring ended his book with

these words: "The only possible solution is ending the power of the school" (p. 172).

Crises of Negativism and Contradiction

Regardless of which position was taken on the power, importance, or impotence of the public school, the new academic left shared a profound negativism toward the public schools and even sought righteous justification in distancing themselves from the problems of school people. As Hlebowitsh points out, "radical commentators have written much about how schools fail . . . , but they have also left us with little in the way of solutions that might work within the social and political realities of our schools" (1992, p. 46). Those of the academic left in schools of education seemed to forget that the role of professional schools is to prepare professional practitioners and to advance professional practice. Instead, they patterned themselves after their compeers in the liberal arts who followed a long tradition of school blaming, as Conant had pointed out (1949, p. 146).

Curiously, in their attacks on the comprehensive high school and their call for equity by reducing the curriculum to academic subjects, the new academic left were in league with the essentialists. Instead of working to promote a common core for general education, within the context of diversified studies (without tracking) for a cosmopolitan pupil population, the academic left, like the essentialists, called for the return of the high school to a one-track academic curriculum.

By the late 1980s, the wider university community began to object to the ideological imposition of political correctness and the ethical problem of indoctrination in academe. The new academic left were also facing problems with internal theoretical contradictions (Kimball, 1991). Their destructive stance of negation left them without any program for constructive practical action for the schools. At the same time, the new academic left were beset by fractious multiculturalist elements within their ranks. Widely divided, they were never able to develop a philosophy or coherent program of action, not to mention a following beyond their own ranks in academe. The crisis was capped by the forced suppression of student protests in Beijing, China, in May 1989 and the collapse of the Soviet Union and Marxist ideology.

Dewey Rehabilitated. In the face of the growing ideological crisis on the American college campus, the academic left turned to Dewey. In doing so, they had to rehabilitate Dewey. Whereas they had once debased him as a liberal, he was now a radical liberal or reconstructionist. In 1983 Aronowitz and Giroux attacked Dewey's instrumentalism as having "resulted in a curriculum that, far from widening the base of the citizenry in the classical sense of the term, resulted in the educational complement to the specialization and degradation of the labor force in factories and offices" (p. 50). Only three years later, Giroux would write that "radicals and conservatives alike have ignored John Dewey's vision of public schools as democratic spheres, as places where the skills of democracy can be practiced, debated, and analyzed" (1988, p. 114). Appropriating Dewey to their camp, the academic left turned to Richard Rorty's scholarship on Dewey and to Robert Westbrook's *John Dewey and American Democracy* (1991) (Tanner, D., 1993).

Antipathy Toward Science, the Enlightenment, and the Idea of Progress.   Progressivists embraced the idea of progress and the Enlightenment for advancing reason, science, and democracy, whereas critical theorists, postmodernists, and others of the new academic left took a regressive interpretation of history. They devalue science and the Enlightenment as a "delusion," as a force of man's domination of man by man (Diggins, 1992, pp. 22, 349), and as just another way of knowing contrived by European and American white men (Wilson, 1998, p. 58). With regard to the hostility toward science by the radical academic left and their rejection of the Enlightenment, Gross and Levitt see it as enigmatic and irrational that educators could mock the contribution of science in enabling civilization to progress from ignorance to insight, liberation, and the advancement of knowledge (1994, p. 3). Pointing to the many inconsistent and idiosyncratic strands of the new radical academic left, composed in the main of humanists and faculty identified with cultural studies, Gross and Levitt note that the new left do not share a consistent doctrine or well-defined center. "What enables them to coexist congenially, in spite of gross logical inconsistencies, is a shared sense of injury, resentment, and indignation against modern science" (p. 5). To Gross and Levitt, there is something medieval and superstitious in their rejection of science, despite their "hypermodern language" (p. 3).

Education and the American Creed.   Although the origins of the Enlightenment were European, it was largely through Thomas Jefferson that the Enlightenment took early root in America, for Jefferson promoted education as the chief means of advancing humanity and advanced the support of the field of education by government. "Belief in education became a part of the American Creed and has since then retained its hold upon the mind of the nation," wrote Myrdal. "In this field, America early assumed world leadership and has held it up to the present time" (1961, p. 1182). It can be said that whereas the Enlightenment was conceived in Europe, through popular education it was delivered in America.

The great legacy for advancing democracy by belief in the idea of progress through popular education is so ingrained in the American Creed that no opposition is sufficiently powerful to stop it. In the words of Jefferson just two years before his death: "And when this progress will stop no one can say" (quoted in Nisbet, 1980, p. 198).

The Romantic Vision

Romantic Naturalism

The quest for progressive educational reforms during the early decades of the twentieth century witnessed the emergence of child-centered doctrines. In rejecting the traditional conception of child as a miniature adult, and in battling against the coercive, authoritarian methods of traditional education, the romantic progressivists embraced the notion of the child as a flower to unfold naturally into fruition. This unfoldment and fruition could best be realized by capitalizing on the natural propensities of the child. The pervasive idea of the child's natural development led to the notion that the school must be an environment in which the child's spontaneity, felt needs, and activity are seen as positive energies for effective learning.

Science and Sentiment.   Although the child-study movement in education had begun as an effort to induce educational reform through the scientific study of the child, it came to be dominated by sentiment rather than by science. At the 1900 annual meeting of the National Education Association, an officer of the Child-Study Division of the NEA carried the case for sentiment over science by declaring, "Better is it to know nothing of the plant's structure and functions, but to love in order to gain knowledge. Better still that love and knowledge should kiss each other" (Bailey, 1900, p. 585).

Undoubtedly, the efforts of the romantic progressivists to kindle in teachers more affectionate and empathic attitudes toward children were well justified in view of the authoritarian educational practices of the times. Their belief in the centrality of child life in the curriculum led them to regard child interests and spontaneous activity indulgently as achievements rather than as means toward intellective and social growth. Dewey repeatedly admonished the romantic progressivists for this failure. To Dewey, their view "fails to see that even the most pleasing and beautiful exhibitions are but signs, and that they begin to spoil and rot the moment they are treated as achievements." When such activities are continually initiated but do not arrive at a higher level, we have a situation as bad as the continual repression of initiative in conformity with authority, contended Dewey. "It is as if the child were forever tasting and never eating; always having his palate tickled upon the emotional side, but never getting the organic satisfaction that comes only with digestion of food and transformation of it into working power" (1902b, p. 16).

Radical School Reform.   In their zeal for radical educational reform, many contemporary critics have embraced the tenets of romantic naturalism, although they rarely acknowledge that their ideas have an earlier record in modern history. The reaction against the pursuit of academic excellence beginning in the mid-1960s brought forth a rash of best-selling books exposing the schools for every conceivable failure and evil and proposing a variety of formulas for freeing pupils to learn. It was a time when many college students were embracing activism and self-sensation and rejecting reflection and self-discipline. "Doing your own thing"—the situation ethic of the ghetto street—became fashionable on the college campus.

A. S. Neill's *Summerhill*, published in 1960, became a best-seller in the United States several years later when the atmosphere was ripe for romantic educational ideas. Recounting the precepts on which his school has operated since its founding in England in 1921, Neill revealed his romantic notion of the child's innate goodness and the need for the school to provide freedom for the child to flower forth.

Well, we set out to make a school in which we should allow children to be themselves. In order to do this, we had to renounce all discipline, all direction, all suggestion, all moral training. . . . All it required was what we had—a complete belief in the child as a good, not an evil being. For almost forty years, this belief in the goodness of the child has never wavered; it rather has become a final faith.

My view is that a child is innately wise and realistic. If left to himself without adult suggestions of any kind, he will develop as far as he is capable of developing. (p. 4)

Although Neill denied the need for a formal curriculum, he explained that the offering of traditional academic subjects at Summerhill is a necessary concession to the university entrance examinations. "Books are the least important apparatus in a school," announced Neill. "Most of the school work that adolescents do is simply a waste of time, of energy, of patience. It robs youth of its right to play and play and play" (p. 5).

Neill's *Summerhill* was read widely in the United States, but few of his readers and followers were aware that the Summerhill School failed to attract and serve a significant constituency in England. The total enrollment at Summerhill has ranged only from 45 to 60 pupils, with the majority of the youngsters from American families residing temporarily in England.

Although Neill belonged to an earlier generation of romantic progressivists, the new wave of romanticists and romantic anarchists carried the same echo, telling the American public that the child's natural capacity for education is destroyed by the schools. "The purpose of elementary pedagogy, through age twelve, should be to delay socialization, to protect children's free growth," declared Paul Goodman. He went on to advocate, "We must drastically cut back formal schooling because the present extended tutelage is against nature and arrests growth" (1970, p. 86).

The persistent indictment of middle-class values permeates much of the radical-reformist literature (Engler, 1973). The schools are often portrayed as socialization instruments for perpetuating all of the evils associated with the profit-making system. Jonathan Kozol went so far as to link the atrocities in Vietnam with the learning inculcated by the schools as early as the elementary grades (1975), overlooking the fact that the colleges and high schools were a chief source of protest against the war. Kozol later turned to education in Castro's Cuba as an appropriate model. He portrayed education in Cuba as humanizing, whereas education for the poor in the

United States is exploitative and debilitating. He went on to describe how 100,000 Cuban children, half of them below the age of 14, were sent to the fields and mountains to teach the nation to read and write (1978). The romantic portrayal of child as the parent of humanity is a common element in the literature on radical school reform. To a considerable extent the radical school reform effort of the 1960s was more of a literary movement than an educational movement. The literature on radical school reform was well represented on the nation's lists of best-sellers, and it was widely discussed in the media and in teacher-education classes. Its impact on the schools was mainly in the sector of alternative schools and through some cosmetic adjustments of mainstream education. Although the rationale for alternative schooling during the 1960s was to provide child-centered approaches to education, the alternative schools of the late 1970s and 1980s were centered largely on academic achievement, with particular emphasis on the basics. More recently, alternative schools have been centered on serving the special-interest needs of special-interest groups or concentrated on specialized academic functions, such as science and technology or the arts. In recent years, Jonathan Kozol emerged as a passionate defender of American public schools and opponent of school vouchers and alternative schools. His concern for at-risk children remained unshaken, but now he looked to the potentials for school regeneration (1991).

Conception of the Learner.   Even at the college level, the innate goodness of youth is proclaimed. Theodore Roszak, theoretician for the counterculture of the 1960s and early 1970s, portrayed the student as a wildflower that must not be crushed by the world of scientific rationality.

> The young, miserably educated as they are, bring with them almost nothing but healthy instincts. The project of building a sophisticated framework of thought atop those instincts is like trying to graft an oak tree upon a wildflower. How to sustain the oak tree? More important, how to avoid crushing the wildflower? And yet such is the project that confronts those of us who are concerned with radical social change. For the young have become one of the very few social levers dissent has to work with. This is that "significant soil" in which the Great Refusal has begun to take root. If we reject it in frustration for the youthful follies that also sprout here, where then do we turn? (1969)

In answering his own question, Roszak went beyond the romantic naturalist's simple prescription of allowing the learner to blossom into full flower by removing constraints and enriching the environment. Roszak's answer was that we must turn away from the rationality of science and toward nonintellective consciousness, as exemplified in the tranquil inner contemplativeness of the Eastern religions, in order to proclaim a new, vast, marvelous heaven and earth. In a later work, Roszak viewed the true source of spiritual regeneration in the transcendent "rhapsodic ideal" of the Romantic poets (1972). Like the existentialists and the radical critics of rationality and science, Roszak confused the scientific outlook and methods of science with the evil political uses to which science is put. They romanticized the magic of nonintellective consciousness and ignored the fact that antirationality and antiscience have their own tyrannies.

Turning again to the romanticist's view of the young child, we find it proclaimed that the schools and the adult world destroy the creative capacity of children.

> Nobody starts off stupid. You only have to watch babies and infants, and think seriously about what all of them learn and do, to see that, except for the most grossly retarded, they show a style of life, and a desire and ability to learn that in an older person we might well call genius. Hardly an adult in a thousand, or ten thousand, could in any three years of his life learn as much, grow as much in his understanding of the world around him, as every infant learns and grows in his first three years. But what happens, as we get older, to this extraordinary capacity for learning and intellectual growth?
>
> What happens is that it is destroyed, and more than by any other one thing, by the process that we misname education—a process that goes on in most homes and schools. We adults destroy most of the intellectual and creative capacity of children by the things we do to them or make them do. (Holt, 1964, p. 167)

In portraying the child as good and the school as evil, romantic critics conveniently ignore the body of research on child development. To expect the individual to grow and develop cognitively throughout life at the same rate and in the same way as during the first three years of life would deny one the qualitative changes that are manifest as one progresses through the developmental stages. If we could envision such a fantastic phenomenon, we would see the child as simply developing into an even bigger and better child: a child monster.

Furthermore, the fact that the young child learns his or her native language so readily and "naturally" without a formal curriculum is not a valid basis for assuming that all learning can be realized in the same way if only educators allow the child's genius to find its own fruition. The development of oral language, although still a mystery, may be psychobiologically rooted, believes Chomsky, in a way essentially different from other forms of cognitive learning (1968). Thus, learning to speak one's native language does not require the systematic organization of knowledge and experience requisite for learning mathematics, chemistry, drafting, or carpentry. Language is the medium of social communication. It finds expression and growth in every dimension of meaning and purposeful action. In a rich and stimulating social environment, oral language learning becomes fluid and generative. This should give us pause to consider how in the traditional error-oriented classroom of rote and recitation, children will tend to avoid speaking in paragraphs and asking why and what-if questions for fear of revealing their ignorance.

Rousseau. The romantic portrayal of the child as innately good and the adult world as a conspiracy of evil parallels Jean-Jacques Rousseau's romantic vision of education as expressed in his iconoclastic *Émile,* published in 1762. "God makes all things good; man meddles with them and they become evil," wrote Rousseau (1911, p. 5). Other Rousseauian aphorisms are:

We can do much, but the chief thing is to prevent anything being done.

Reverse the usual practice and you will almost always do right.

Young teacher, I am setting before you a difficult task, the art of controlling without precepts, and doing everything without doing anything at all.

Let the child do nothing because he is told; nothing is good for him but what he recognizes as good.

Yet Rousseau tempered his romantic view of child with a call for "well-regulated liberty," and he recognized that the child's cognitive capabilities undergo qualitative changes as he or she undergoes new developmental stages. Thus, curiosity must be "rightly directed" according to "the means of development for the age which we are dealing," Rousseau contended. Nor is the curriculum without focus and

direction. "The real object of our study is man and his environment," wrote Rousseau. He emphasized that as the child approaches adolescence, "much skill and discretion are required to lead him toward theoretical studies." In teaching the pupil to observe the phenomena of nature, the teacher's responsibility is to "[p]ut the problems before him and let him solve them himself. . . . Let him not be taught science, let him discover it" (pp. 9, 56, 58, 84, 130, 141).

Curriculum.   Contemporary romanticists go so far as to deny the idea of curriculum on the grounds that knowledge is so subject to change it is senseless to plan what it is that the child should be taught.

The notion of a curriculum, as an essential body of knowledge, would be absurd even if children remembered everything we "taught" them. We don't and can't agree on what knowledge is essential. . . .

The idea of the curriculum would not be valid even if we could agree what ought to be in it. For knowledge changes. Much of what a child learns in school will be found, or thought, before many years, to be untrue. . . . Since we can't know what knowledge will be most needed in the future, it is senseless to try to teach it in advance. . . .

Learning is not everything, and certainly one piece of learning is as good as another (Holt, 1964, pp. 175–177).

According to Paul Goodman, "The effort to channel the process of growing up according to a preconceived curriculum and method discourages and wastes many of the best human powers to learn and cope." What, then, should the teacher and the school provide in the absence of a curriculum? Goodman's answer is that "[i]ncidental education, taking part in the ongoing activities of society, must again be made the chief means of learning and teaching" (1970, pp. 85–86). Goodman even claimed, "Very many of our youth, both poor and middle class, might be better off if the system did not exist, even if they had no formal schooling at all" (1964, p. 39). However, he later qualified this view by acknowledging that academic schools should continue to serve the academically talented, "and such schools are better off unencumbered by the sullen uninterested bodies of the others" (1970, p. 88). Although romanticists typically profess egalitarian principles, and many have a penchant for claiming to find genius in the disadvantaged slow learner, Goodman revealed his educational elitism by advocating that secondary schooling be confined to the academically talented youth, and the others should be left to gain whatever "incidental education" that might be found in the ongoing activities of society. Oddly, Goodman saw the larger society as corrupt and repressive, and yet he somehow viewed it as providing a more meaningful education than formal schooling for most of our youth who only clog the schools with their "uninterested bodies" (1970, p. 88). A similarly elitist view was propounded by Edgar Friedenberg, another radical romanticist (1967, pp. 250–251, 257). Ivan Illich (1971) advocated that all schools be abolished, and he romanticized the powers of society and the growing information technology as capable of fulfilling the educational needs of children and youth.

In contrast, other romanticists advocate radical changes in the school by doing away with the notion of a planned curriculum and centering all learning activities on the child's present felt needs. They envision the school as a giant smorgasbord of learning activities, with the child free to pick out whatever pursuits he or she wants.

> We cannot know, at any moment, what particular bit of knowledge or understanding a child needs most, will most strengthen and best fit his model of reality. Only he can do this. He may not do it very well, but he can do it a hundred times better than we can. The most we can do is try to help, by letting him know roughly what is available and when he can look for it. Choosing what he wants to learn and what he does not is something he must do for himself. . . . In short, the school should be a great smorgasbord of intellectual, artistic, creative, and athletic activities, from which each child could take whatever he wanted, and as much as he wanted, or as little. (Holt, 1964, pp. 179–180)

In attacking the dogmatisms of traditional education, the romanticists would impose a new set of dogmatisms on the teacher and the school. Do away with curriculum and allow the child to find fulfillment through his or her immediate interests, teachers are told. Recounting his own teaching experiences in a traditional school, even a more moderate romanticist writes, "I had little impact on the school and ultimately quit. Still I gradually found ways of teaching that were not based on compulsion but on participation; not on grades or tests or curriculum, but on pursuing what interested the children" (Kohl, 1969, p. 14).

The romantic radical finds no meeting ground with the organized knowledge of humanity. Curriculum planning is an imposition on the teacher and pupil. Presentism is the key doctrine of

relevance. Free verbal interaction and overt activity in the classroom replace systematic reflection and are taken for freedom. The teacher's role is indirect, that of a guide and facilitator who must get out of the way of children. "What we need to do, and all we need to do," contends Holt, "is bring as much of the world as we can into the school and the classroom; give the children as much help and guidance as they need and ask for, listen respectfully when they feel like talking; and then get out of the way. We can trust them to do the rest" (1967, p. 189).

When put into operation through private alternative schools, romanticist ideology soon faces a crisis of reality. As in the case of other forms of protest schools, the very few that manage to survive wind up with curricula that are not substantively different from the curricula of conventional schools (Duke, 1978). Consequently, alternative schools have not been useful for experimentation (Coleman, 1974, p. 86).

As mentioned, to a considerable extent the radical romanticism of the 1960s was a literary movement, with many of the books on educational reform directed at the general public and making national best-seller lists. When the tide shifted away from radical school reform, some of the authors left for more fertile fields, and others did a virtual about-face by embracing the conservative backlash of back to basics. Kozol turned to basic education or literacy (1985) and later became a leading defender of public education and advocate of children in poverty (1991). Whereas Postman cowrote *Teaching as a Subversive Activity* in 1969, he wrote *Teaching as a Conserving Activity* in 1979. As in professional sports, one could simply join the opposition team and change uniforms.

Romantic Naturalism and Experimentalism. The contemporary educational romanticists almost invariably promote their ideas as though they were newly discovered. Only rarely is mention made of the rootings of their ideas. Sadly, when a romanticist acknowledges that these ideas have earlier rootings, the acknowledgment is given to Dewey: "Like Dewey, Neill stressed free animal expression, learning by doing, and very democratic community processes," propounded Goodman, revealing that he either never read or understood Dewey (1964, p. 55). Time and again Dewey criticized the romantic progressivists who believed that pupils should not be exposed to a curriculum plan or suggestion from the teacher on the ground that it would be "an unwarranted trespass upon their sacred intellectual individuality." Dewey called such a position "really stupid. . . [because] it misconceives the conditions for independent thinking" (1946, pp. 37–38). He stressed that spontaneous pupil activity only undermines freedom because it subjects immature children to uncontrolled, haphazard influences, with the result that learning activities are superficial and lacking in intelligently directed thought. "Direct immediate discharge or expression of an impulsive tendency is fatal to thinking," argued Dewey. "Genuine freedom, in short, is intellectual, it rests in the trained *power of thought*. . . . To cultivate unhindered unreflective external activity is to foster enslavement, for it leaves the person at the mercy of appetite, sense, and circumstance" (1933, pp. 87, 90).

The Inner Vision

Existentialism

The search for the meaning of human existence in an indifferent universe, the quest for personal significance in an age of impersonal technology, and the need for individual awareness in an age of the mechanical masses led to the resurrection of existentialist thought during the second half of the twentieth century. Rooted in the works of the nineteenth-century Danish philosopher-theologian Søren Kierkegaard, existentialist ideas were extended greatly in the writings of such men as Nietzsche, Heidegger, Jaspers, Camus, Buber, and Sartre. Kierkegaard contended that humanity can find reality not through the grand designs of rational thought, but through the passion of faith. Faith and the meaning of existence are not things that can be imposed on the individual by some outside authority. Our highest interest is our own existence, held Kierkegaard, and our interest in our existence constitutes our reality.

The plight of the lonely individual in an uncaring universe became an overwhelming theme in literature during the years since midcentury. This concern and the search for authentic personal identity also became central in the writings of a number of theorists in the field of psychotherapy during this period. In an era of mechanical impersonalization and depersonalization, alienation, disappearance of religious control and influence, and disillusionment with science, the idea of finding meaning through subjective introspection rather than through objective rational thought became

vastly appealing to certain segments of the college generation. Seeing themselves freed from rational constraints, they could challenge the repressions and inadequacies of our social institutions through a metaphysical revolt. Rather than losing oneself in the drug scene or in occultism, or even in the esoteric mysticism of Roszak's counterculture, one could find oneself in the private estheticism of existential thought.

Because the universe is indifferent to humanity, the individual must assign to himself or herself the meaning of one's own existence, believes the existentialist. Humanity cannot find such meaning in religious dogma, social philosophies, or science. People are absolutely worthless in the cosmos, so the individual must find his or her own absolute worth. By finding the meaning of one's own existence, one is free to choose what he or she is and becomes, and one can find the authentic self through the full awakening of spontaneous human powers. The self-encounter rather than the group-encounter is stressed. If this appears to some to be excessively self-centered and individualistic, the existentialist argues that this condition applies to each of us and so it becomes reciprocal between individuals, or, in Buber's words, between "I" and "Thou." One's own need to be free must be reciprocal; it must recognize the need for another person to be free.

Freedom and Rational Thought. In setting limits on rational thought, in seeking to be free of the excess baggage of intelligence, the existentialist is acting to restrict rather than to free intelligence. Thus their quest for freedom is marred by the very limits existentialists set on rational thought, limits that serve the cause of anti-intellectualism. In Dewey's words,

> It is a curious state of mind which finds pleasure in setting forth the "limits of science." For the intrinsic limit of knowledge is simply ignorance; and the point in extolling ignorance is not clear except when expressed by those who profit by keeping others in ignorance. There is of course an extrinsic limit of science. But that limitation lies in the ineptitude of those who put it to use; its removal lies in rectification of its use, not in abuse of the thing used. (1962, p. 98)

To denigrate rational thought because the uses to which science is put are abusive of human beings is to misplace the blame, argued Dewey. "The eye sees many foul things and the arm and the hand do many cruel things. Yet the fanatic who would pluck out the eye and cut off the arm is recognized for what he is" (p. 97).

In rejecting the rational mode of science, existentialists tend to caricature science as being coldly neutral, and they see scientific thought as being devoid of morality. In this connection they confuse scientific thought with the political misuses to which the products of science and technology are put. "The best available evidence has nothing to do with morality or human fulfillment," argued Maxine Greene. "We need only recall the testing that led to the A-bomb and the H-bomb, to extermination camps, to nerve gas, to napalm" (1973, p. 103). Political reasoning, not scientific reasoning, led to the uses of nuclear energy for bombs rather than for building a better humanity. When Greene alleges that science is not moral or beneficent, witness "the Nazis' final solution of 'the Jewish problem': the application of scientific knowledge to mass extermination" (p. 129), Greene confuses scientific thought with political decision making. The fact that an evil act can be planned and executed rationally does not mean that such an act is the logical outcome of rational thought. The problem of how to exterminate a people is not a problem of science any more than is the problem of how to assassinate a president. To pose such a problem in the first place is indicative of irrational forces at work. The conception of an evil act does not originate with the motives of science but derives from personal, social, or political motives. Moreover, the fact that an evil act can be planned and executed rationally fails to make a case in favor of irrationality or nonrational thought. What kind of case could be made to show that human history would have been better through irrational or nonrational thought rather than rational thought? (Tanner, D., 1983a, pp. 34–38). Human history has been a battle between irrational and rational thought. When Greene holds that "[t]he best available evidence has nothing to do with morality or human fulfillment" (p. 129), the implication is that we should not guide our thoughts and actions according to "the best available evidence." If one is thinking scientifically, one must know the *problem* to which the best available evidence is being put. If the problem is how to eliminate disease, starvation, environmental pollution, poverty, crime, and so on, is there a better prospect for solution or remediation than making use of the best available evidence? The persistence of these problems is not

the result of rational thought but of people's failure to wage an attack on these problems through rational ends and means.

Greene contends that science is an inadequate model for the existentialist because "scientific thinking is concerned with objectification and excludes the intuitive awareness and self-encounters required of philosophy," and she goes on to declare, "When the existentialist speaks of knowing, he speaks of passionately engaging and of vouching for his ideas with his life. The cool neutrality of experimental inquiry is usually alien to such a man" (1973, p. 137). Here Greene confuses science with cold empiricism. To emasculate philosophy from science is to have no science. Science is philosophy. The key scientific ideas do not stem from empiricism. The record of history reveals that scientists, no less than any group, have vouched for their ideas with their lives. The historic record is not very kind to the leading existentialists in their relationship to totalitarianism (Lilla, 2001; Lottman, 1982; Judt, 1992).

It is fallacious to assume that the existentialist thinker, the artist, and the poet are passionately engaged, whereas scientific inquiry is coldly neutral and devoid of passion. As Bronowski pointed out, creation—whether in art or in science—engages the whole being. "A gifted man cannot handle bacteria or equations without taking fire from what he does and having his emotions engaged" (1958, p.58). Einstein discussed the profound faith with which scientists must be imbued in their aspiration toward truth and understanding. "I cannot conceive of a genuine scientist without such profound faith," he wrote, as he likened the profound reverence for rationality to a spirit of religiosity:

> [W]hoever has undergone the intense experience of successful advances made in this domain [science], is moved by profound reverence for the rationality made manifest in existence. By way of the understanding he achieves a far-reaching emancipation from the shackles of personal hopes and desires, and thereby attains a humble attitude of mind towards the grandeur of reason incarnate in existence, and which in its profoundest depths, is inaccessible to man. This attitude, however, appears to me to be religious, in the highest sense of the word. . . .
>
> The further the spiritual evolution of mankind advances, the more certain it seems to me that the path to genuine religiosity does not lie through the fear of life, and the fear of death, and blind faith, but through striving after rational knowledge. (1950, pp. 29–30)

The existentialist seeks to engage in introspection beyond reason because he or she cannot find through reason the answer to the ultimate question of the meaning of one's existence. "Whatever its ultimate meaning, the universe into which we have been thrown cannot satisfy our reason; let us have the courage to admit it once and for all," wrote Marcel (1949, p. 92). If people turn away from reason, can they really be free, or will they merely become shackled by the illusions of their own creation? This is the pitfall in the existentialist dream. Turning again to Dewey,

> For the neglect of sciences that deal specifically with facts of the natural and social environment leads to a side-tracking of moral forces into an unreal privacy of an unreal self. . . . Each sign of disregard for the moral potentialities of science drafts the conscience of mankind away from concern with the interactions of man and nature which must be mastered if freedom is to be reality. It diverts intelligence to anxious preoccupation with the unrealities of a purely inner life. (1922, pp. 10–11)

But to Greene, Dewey failed to deal with the existentialist "experience of nothingness" and ennui, "a pervasive boredom of which Dewey [in his healthy mindedness] seemed to know little" (1973, p. 130). It would appear, then, that the existentialists were offering educators a philosophy of futility and despair, masquerading as hyperradicalism. Their profound negativism found them allied with the multicultural admixture of the academic left. But as far as the role of the school is concerned, their programmatic prescriptions took the form of radical romanticism. The healthy child and adolescent intuitively knows that there is nothing in the "experience of nothingness."

Existentialism and the Curriculum. To the existentialist, the route to knowledge is personal; education should help the individual find the meaning of one's own existence. Because the child is born into "a world of meaninglessness, that is, a world that does not have meaning already woven into and embedded in it," he or she can extract "possibilities without exacting reciprocal tribute of human compliance." The school, therefore, must be an environment in which "the full exercise of the spontaneous human self is the avenue to authenticity as a person." Educators must extricate the child from "the crushing overload of social controls," and "the school must direct its attention to the release of the human self, to the involvement of the child in personal decision and

moral judgment to a far greater degree than he knows at present" (Morris, 1970, pp. 258, 260).

To awaken the child existentially, the curriculum should provide considerable time for private introspection and the study of moral questions concerning humanity's predicament. Neither the standard curriculum of essential subject matters nor the experimentalist focus on the development of trained intelligence through social problem solving is adequate to the task of enabling the pupil to find oneself. This does not mean that all organized subject matter must be discarded, but rather that the pupil must be allowed the widest possible latitude in determining the portions of organized subject matter that are authentic to one's own being. Moreover, the subject matter should not be focused on objective or practical knowledge but on the individual predicament. The sciences and vocational studies are of least significance. The social studies should deal with the meaning of individual freedom rather than citizenship, social institutions, or codified knowledge. Obviously, literature, poetry, art, and music can be significant sources for enabling students to confront the human condition. The goal is self-development and self-fulfillment.

Knowledge is not transmitted but offered to the pupil, and the teacher engages in dialogue with the pupil to encourage thinking for oneself and to make knowledge personal. Some existentialists, such as Kneller, would abolish the school altogether and have each youngster go to a teacher for an "I" and "Thou" dialogue (1971, p. 264). Such an arrangement is reminiscent of Rousseau's *Émile* and of the proposals of some contemporary radical romanticists who see organized schooling as thwarting the child's powers for spontaneous self-realization.

When efforts are made to put existentialist ideas into practice in an actual school (invariably it is a small private school with a relatively homogeneous pupil population), the ideas and functions tend to resemble many features associated with romantic naturalism. For example, a description of one existential school calls for "the absence of authoritarian hierarchical structures, required courses, assigned groups, prescribed number of classroom hours, grades, evaluations," with emphasis given to "learning through self-motivation and self-regulation . . . equal status of all pursuits . . . evaluation through self-criticism . . . teaching based on interest . . . spontaneous formation of learning groups, centered on common interests . . . teacher retention based on student demand" (Rosenberg, 1973, pp. 479–480). As in A. S. Neill's Summerhill School, young children— 4-year-olds—have an equal vote with faculty at the general school meetings, although it is admitted that they rarely attend these meetings. The descriptions of the school are pregnant with sentimental idealization of the child.

Existentialists may argue justifiably that such a school is not a valid representation of existential education, but the point is that whatever has been presented as an existential school in operation appears unwittingly to have succumbed to practices that the romantic naturalist would applaud. Aside from the enormous practical problems of existential schooling is the question of how it is possible for a child to find the meaning of his or her existence—to develop a philosophy of life—when education is focused on spontaneous self-realization. "It is certainly as futile to expect a child to evolve a universe out of his own mere mind as it is for a philosopher to attempt that task," observed Dewey (1902b, p. 18). This leads to the philosophical problem of how the personal measures for individual self-direction and self-fulfillment will become unselfishly directed toward the goal of remaking a civilization. Somehow this quest for self-fulfillment will become transformed to the social task of rebuilding a civilization, contends Kneller as he offers this quote of Camus: "There is a whole civilization to be remade" (1971, p. 264). The question is whether the existentialist's private vision can lead to the realization of the public promise.

Perspective

"The most important educational problem today is the problem of direction," wrote Bode (1927, p. 40). The problem of educational ends and means is of signal consideration in any philosophy or theory of education. Many teachers and administrators regard educational philosophizing as a kind of academic exercise remote from the real world of the school. This may indeed be the case when philosophical positions are derived from *outside* the educational situation and then imposed *on* the educational situation. When the educational situation is the source and testing ground of philosophical ideas, such ideas become crucial to the direction and means of education and to educational progress. For example, a school's statement of philosophy may be premised on democratic principles, but if these principles are not tested in practice they are meaningless.

Schools commonly have a statement of philosophy, formulated by the faculty and administration, although the statement is rarely systematically formulated from and tested against actual practice. Without such testing, the school curriculum is vulnerable to whatever external demands and pressures are most pervasive at any given time. Because the external demands and pressures are constantly being recycled, the school often tends to yield to them on a superficial level of adopting certain prepackaged programs and theories along with their labels and slogans. The up-to-date school is the trendy school, rather than the school that is engaged in curricular problem solving by testing alternative ideas in the light of practice. To say that a given practice works is not saying much. It may work in terms of maintaining the status quo or in terms of regressing to some ideal alien to democracy, such as indoctrination. Educational theories and practices must be tested against alternative theories and practices if progress is to be made.

Dewey regarded philosophy as the general theory of education, for he viewed education as the process of forming fundamental dispositions toward nature and fellow humans, and he saw education as the laboratory in which philosophic distinctions become concrete and are tested. However, educational decisions and practices often have been derived in the absence of a guiding philosophy. Insufficient attention has been given to basing such decisions on reflective consideration of the good person leading the good life in the good social order. Under these circumstances, the school becomes vulnerable to whatever influences are most pervasive at a particular time, and the response is a kind of mechanical tinkering with the curriculum. Because few proponents of conflicting educational theories have sought to see education as the laboratory in which philosophical distinctions become concrete and are tested, each theory becomes a matter of theological allegiance, and curriculum change becomes a mechanical response to external imposition.

Hutchins observed, "The failure of educational philosophy reflects the failure of our philosophy in general. It is not the schools that make their purposes, but the people that control them" (1973, p. 14). Yet, despite these shortcomings, no other society has made education so accessible to its people as the United States, and no other society has managed to provide within a unitary educational system such a diversified and comprehensive curriculum for such a pluralistic population. In this sense, education in the United States is indeed a laboratory in which philosophical distinctions become concrete and are tested. It was not by chance that the United States gave birth to experimentalist theory.

Looking back over the course of the life and writings of John Dewey, one can well understand how he came to be venerated and reviled—like most individuals in history who proved in the end to be almost always in the right.

PROBLEMS FOR STUDY AND DISCUSSION

1. How do you account for the constant recycling of educational reform movements in which the same themes, such as back to basics, reappear at periodic intervals?

2. Make an approximation of the number of articles appearing under the topic of "democracy" in the latest annual edition of *Education Index*. Compare this with (1) any year between the end of World War II and midcentury and (2) any year during the 1970s. What conclusions can you draw regarding the concern with this topic in the contrasting eras?

3. Do you agree with the following statement? Why or why not?

   It is necessary to bear in mind that education cannot be divorced from social theory, from a conception or standard of social organization. This proposition is not enjoying wide favor at present. There are many educators nowadays who have scant patience with what they call philosophizing. To them the problems of education are all problems to be worked out with a yardstick and statistical curves. . . . No account is taken of the fact that the individual must either be fitted to become a cog in the social mechanism, or else must be educated according to some notion of how this mechanism should be changed. To suppose that the work of education can be carried on effectively without reference to the larger issue is plain self-deception. There is no such thing as being neutral. [Boyd H. Bode, *Modern Educational Theories* (New York: Macmillan, 1927), p. 234.]

4. According to Hutchins, "Knowledge is truth. The truth is everywhere the same." [Robert M. Hutchins, *The Higher Learning in America* (New Haven, CT: Yale University Press, 1936), p. 66.] According to Bruner, "intellectual activity anywhere is the same." [Jerome S. Bruner, *The Process of Education* (Cambridge, MA: Harvard University Press, 1960), p. 14.]

   What are the implications of these statements for curriculum development?

5. Dewey identified these fundamental factors in the educative process: (1) the learner, (2) society, and (3) organized subject matter, and he noted that the tendency is to treat these factors "in their separateness, to insist upon one at the expense of the other, to make antagonists of them." [John Dewey, *The Child and the Curriculum* (Chicago: University of Chicago Press, 1902b), pp. 4–8.]

   How is this antagonism reflected in the views of the essentialist and the romantic naturalist? How do these views compare with your own?

6. The following are two contrasting statements on the curriculum. What are your reactions to these statements?

   For all children, the educational process must be one of collecting factual knowledge to the limit of their absorptive capacity. Recreation, manual or clerical training, etiquette, and similar know-how have little effect on the mind itself and it is with the mind that the school must solely concern itself. The poorer a child's natural endowments, the more does he need to have his mind trained. . . . To acquire such knowledge, fact upon fact, takes time and effort. Nothing can really make it "fun." [Hyman G. Rickover, "European vs. American Secondary Schools," *Phi Delta Kappan*, 40 (November 1958), p. 61.]

   Learning is not everything, and certainly one piece of learning is as good as another. . . . In short, the school should be a great smorgasbord of intellectual, artistic, creative, and athletic activities, from which each child could take whatever he wanted, and as much as he wanted, or as little. [John Holt, *How Children Fail* (New York: Dell, 1964), pp. 177, 180.]

7. According to Dewey, "the basic freedom is that of freedom of mind and of whatever degree of freedom of action and experience is necessary to produce freedom of intelligence." [John Dewey,

Problems of Men (New York: Philosophical Library, 1946), p. 61.]

How does Dewey's conception of freedom contrast with that of the romantic naturalist? What are the curricular implications of these contrasting views of freedom?

8. Does the following statement present a fair portrayal of scientific thinking? Explain.

> For the existentialist, science cannot serve as model or paradigm, largely because scientific thinking is concerned with objectification and excludes the intuitive awareness and the self-encounters required of philosophy. When the existentialist speaks of knowing, he speaks of passionately engaging and of vouching for his ideas with his life. The cool neutrality of experimental inquiry is usually alien to such a man. . . . [Maxine Greene, *Teacher as Stranger* (Belmont, CA: Wadsworth, 1973), p. 137.]

9. In a national best-seller, a humanities professor wrote: "All that is human, all that is of concern to us, lies outside natural science." [Allan Bloom, *The Closing of the American Mind* (New York: Simon & Schuster, 1987), p. 356.] How does such a statement reflect on the two cultures or divorce between the humanities and sciences? Why was this divorce of such great concern to Dewey and later to C. P. Snow? [John Dewey, *Freedom and Culture* (New York: Putnam, 1939), p. 154; C. P. Snow, *Two Cultures and the Scientific Revolution* (New York: Cambridge University Press, 1959).]

10. Does your school have a formal statement of philosophy? If so, does the life and curriculum of your school reflect the statement of philosophy in action? Why or why not? What changes would you like to see in the life and curriculum of your school?

PART III

CURRICULUM DESIGN, DEVELOPMENT, AND EVALUATION

Our question . . . which is the question of the nation and the ages, is *how can general education be so adapted to different ages and, above all, differing abilities and outlooks, that it can appeal deeply to each, yet remain in goal and essential teaching the same for all?* The answer to this question, it seems not too much to say, is the key to anything like complete democracy.

—Harvard Committee on General Education in a Free Society

CHAPTER 10

THE SEARCH FOR A CORE CURRICULUM
GENERAL EDUCATION IN A FREE SOCIETY

"In the nation, 'general education' is at last in vogue. Its principles bid fair to become the operative educational theory of the remainder of this century." So wrote F. Champion Ward, dean of the College of the University of Chicago, in a 1950 faculty report on general education (p. 8). Ward's optimism concerning the prospects for general education was widely shared by educators at midcentury. Instead of becoming "the operative educational theory of the remainder of this century," general education yielded to the forces of departmental specialism and special-interest constituencies in the undergraduate population. As far as the schools were concerned, the pressures of the Cold War and space race led to a neo-essentialism of federally funded discipline-centered curriculum reforms with priority given to the sciences and mathematics.

A quarter of a century after Ward's pronouncement, general education appeared to be in vogue once again in American colleges. The response to the campus turmoil of the 1960s had impelled faculties in colleges and secondary schools to reduce requirements, to multiply options, and to devise a host of special-interest electives. The curriculum had come to be referred to as a cafeteria or warehouse curriculum, and it was being described as in a state of anarchy. University scholars, concerned mainly with specialized knowledge, had been all too ready to abandon responsibility for developing a balanced and coherent core curriculum for general education. The struggle for rights seemed to give way to a battle for special interests on the part of competing groups, and the school and college curriculum began to reflect the growing fragmentation of society. In the curriculum literature the terms *general education* and *democracy* received little discussion in contrast to the literature of mid-twentieth century.

In response to the student demand for relevance, a number of significant efforts had been made to develop interdisciplinary courses in the colleges and secondary schools during the 1960s and early 1970s. Again, these courses were mainly offered as electives among the myriad special-interest courses available. By the mid-1970s, it was becoming clear that the undergraduate curriculum required reconstruction for general education. During the latter part of the 1970s, the term *general education* was appearing once again not only in professional journals but in newspaper and magazine articles describing the latest efforts to reconstruct the undergraduate curriculum at leading colleges. On occasion, general education was even front-page news (*New York Times*, Feb. 26, 1978). The words of Ward at mid-twentieth century seemed to be echoing in the halls of academia as we entered the last quarter of the century. An article in the *Saturday Review* on curriculum reforms at Harvard opined that if the reforms are successful, "they will exert a powerful influence on higher education for the balance of the century" (Schiefelbein, 1978, p. 12). The reforms at the undergraduate level, calling for curriculum reconstruction for general education, contrasted sharply with the curriculum retrenchment in elementary and secondary schools under the back-to-basics and competency-based banners.

From the close of the twentieth century to the present day, the colleges have been struggling to find some degree of consensus on a core curriculum for general education in the wake of pressures from the divided interests of the academic left and multiculturalism. At the same time, perennialists were renewing their case for a classical core of Western literary studies—all in the midst of an academic culture that values specialized knowledge production above all else. The typical but tentative solution was one of compromise, with the colleges reducing the vast number of electives under the rubric of general education options and establishing criteria for elective courses designated as acceptable for general education. Although the numbers of such electives were sharply reduced, the practice of distribution requirements or controlled electives by designated categories (e.g., humanities, natural science, social sciences, gender studies, and so on) found students continuing to divide themselves according to their special interests. The need for a coherent core curriculum for general education for a free society remained ever urgent, especially in an era of social fragmentation and conflict.

As far as the school curriculum was concerned—despite unifying efforts such as whole language, writing across the curriculum, and higher-order thinking—the focus was on a multitude of separate literacies (cultural literacy, mathematics literacy, scientific literacy, technological literacy, aesthetic literacy, economic literacy, political literacy, computer literacy, and so on).

All but forgotten throughout the last half of the twentieth century was that the very idea and practice of general education grew out of the experimentalist-progressive efforts for universal secondary education and the democratization of the high school, along with a progressive parallel movement in higher education in recognition of the limits of traditional liberal education. The great divide between liberal education and general education, as James Conant pointed out, marked the difference between the old literary education, as interpreted by scholars and connoisseurs before World War I, and the modern requirements of an enlightened citizenry in a free society. "The watershed between [the] two fundamentally opposed positions," Conant contended, "can be located by raising the question: For what purpose do we have a system of public education?" (1949, pp. 74–75).

Knowledge, Education, and Life

"What nutrition and reproduction are to physiological life, education is to social life," observed Dewey (1916, p. 11). Education not only is the means through which a culture is transmitted but also the means through which it is transformed. A primitive society is able to accomplish its educational functions without schools and formal curricula because the gap between what the rising generation needs to know and do in order to take over the tasks of the established generation can be bridged by direct shared experience. But in the modern, literate, technological society, the growing complexity of knowledge and life is such that society looks to the school and something that has come to be called the curriculum as necessary for enabling the rising generation to gain the needed insight and power to build a better society.

The changing nature of knowledge, changing conceptions of the learner, and changing demands of social life have called for a changing conception and function of curriculum. In this chapter, the relationship between knowledge and the curriculum is examined in the light of problems relating to the expansion of knowledge, the growing specialization and fragmentation of knowledge, and the search for synthesis in order to meet the unifying function of general education in a free society.

Early in the twentieth century, the German philosopher Hans Vaihinger described how human beings have developed knowledge systems or thought edifices in order to keep from drowning in an ever-expanding sea of knowledge and information. Manifest in what has come to be called *curriculum*, these knowledge systems or thought edifices were developed to meet the practical need for making the world more comprehensible and also to serve to facilitate the development of new knowledge. But Vaihinger pointed out that these systematic representations are fictional constructs and, although they are necessary, scholars make the error of treating them as if the real world were organized in this fashion. The consequence is that these isolated, compartmentalized constructs are treated as accomplishments in themselves and thus undermine the very purpose for which they were conceived: to facilitate communication and action (1924).

Education and Life

Dewey noted that one of the weightiest problems of education is the isolation of the curriculum from life experience (1916, p. 10). Alfred North Whitehead, the noted British philosopher and mathematician, also addressed this problem. Calling on educators "to eradicate the fatal disconnection of subjects which kills the vitality of our modern curriculum," Whitehead advocated the study of "[l]ife in all its manifestations" as the subject matter for education. After reviewing a list of isolated subjects that comprise the curriculum, Whitehead observed, "The best that can be said of it is, that it is a rapid table of contents which a deity might run over in his mind while he was thinking of creating a world, and had not yet determined how to put it together" (1929a, p. 10–11).

Dewey and Whitehead went to great lengths to show the need for curriculum synthesis and to show how the curriculum might be made relevant to life experience.

Unique Functions of the School. Of course, significant educational functions are performed by agencies other than the school and university: public libraries, museums, the mass media, the military, civic and professional organizations, business, industrial enterprises, and so on. The school and university are conceived by modern societies as laboratories for the testing of ideas in ways that are not otherwise possible. This requires the continual and systematic reconstruction of knowledge as represented in what has come to be called the *curriculum*. The school and university, unlike any other institution of society, are engaged in this systematic process. The university is conceived not merely for the preservation and transmission of knowledge, but also for the development of new knowledge with the expectation that this will make for a better society. And because the school, more than any other social institution, is responsible for the formal education of the rising generation, the school is society's chief agency for shaping society's future. As special places to perform these unique functions, including the function of enlightened criticism of society, the free society creates special protections for the school and university, under the principle of academic freedom, to ensure the possibilities of its own improvement.

This is not an easy task, particularly for the school, which is always under pressure to confine itself to the narrowest and least controversial functions—namely, skill development and knowledge transmission, the latter often being construed as information rather than knowledge. At the university level, the multiplicity of knowledge edifices and compartments of specialized knowledge often are taken as the spoils of inquiry rather than as the means of facilitating the solving of pervading life problems. Not only are the specialized knowledge compartments isolated from one another, but also when they are treated as self-serving domains they become remote from life experience. The problem of curriculum congestion, isolation, and

remoteness has been a persistent one, and it has become more acute with the incessant expansion and increasing specialization of knowledge.

As laboratories for the testing of ideas, the schools also are expected to enable educators to learn more about the learner and, hence, to continually improve the teaching-learning process. Although this function is not explicitly recognized in many schools, administrators and teachers in more successful schools are cognizant of the necessary role of the school in performing this function.

Knowledge and the Curriculum

The advancement of society is predicated on its capacity to resolve practical problems: wide-ranging problems encompassing such varied concerns as water, food, energy, health, population growth and migration, ethnic relations, international relations, transportation, communication, housing, recreation, poverty, crime, employment, and so on. Thus society, of necessity, is mission oriented. Its renewal and prosperity derive from its capability of applying its knowledge to the resolution of practical problems. A host of institutions are created to accomplish this mission. The most global of these institutions, other than government itself, is the educational institution, for it not only is concerned with the development of knowledge but also with making each rising generation more knowledgeable than its predecessor, making possible a better future society.

As mentioned earlier, the educational institution, in its effort to meet the practical need of making the world more comprehensible, has organized knowledge (and the ways of dealing with knowledge) into thought edifices and categories, which comprise the curriculum. Although intended to serve this practical need, these edifices and compartments have come to represent myriad knowledge specializations, especially in the university. This has led to the compartmentalization and fragmentation of knowledge and the further separation of knowledge from life problems. Pointing to the self-serving tendencies of specialized scholars working in separate knowledge domains, Weinberg has criticized the resulting knowledge fragmentation in our universities and has noted how this fragmentation has invaded even our elementary classroom (1967, p. 117). Although in this connection Weinberg was referring to the impact of the discipline-centered curriculum reforms of the Cold War and space race, the problem of curriculum fragmentation and remoteness from life experience remains a per-sistent one. Weinberg calls for a renewed effort to develop the relatedness of the knowledge domains so that knowledge will be made relevant to the mission of society in addressing its pervading problems. Obviously, this requires the reconstruction and resyn-thesis of the curriculum if the educational institution is to meet its public purpose.

Eclosion and Synthesis: The Unfolding of Knowledge

In his study of the history of knowledge, the mathe-matician Salomon Bochner (1969) challenges the notion that we are living in an age of knowledge explosion. The development of systematic knowledge is seen by Bochner as the product of two contraposed though not necessarily oppositional forces: eclosion and synthesis. Eclosion represents a bursting forth of new knowledge characterized by fluidity, penetra-tion, and proliferation; synthesis is characterized as a reaction to eclosion in which areas of knowledge mature, become highly systematic and verifiable, and, therefore, less prone to being upset by new develop-ments or disputations. Bochner calls the period of the half century around 1800 the Age of Eclosion and sees the twentieth century as the Age of Synthesis.

The influence of Darwin's *Voyage of the Beagle* (1839) and *Origin of Species* (1859) exerted a revolu-tionary impact not only on the natural sciences, but also on philosophy, theology, and social science. Pasteur's unceasing work in advancing the germ theory of disease around 1865, despite enormous opposition from the medical profession, was indeed a revolution, laying the foundation of scientific med-icine and creating the new field of bacteriology, as well as influencing the development of such fields as immunology, antisepsis, sanitation, and biochemistry. However revolutionary were the scientific break-throughs of the twentieth century, the new knowl-edge did not produce the overthrow or require a veritable upheaval of existing systematized knowl-edge. For example, the revolutionary work of Einstein was accommodated into physics and philosophy. The revolutionary work of Freud was accommodated into medicine, psychology, and education (despite contin-uing disputations to this day).

During the Age of Eclosion, when the amount of systematic knowledge was relatively small, new knowl-edge of any significance was likely to exert fundamen-tal changes and disputations and also give rise to the

major organizational areas of knowledge. In the Age of Synthesis, the mature network of knowledge insights tends to accommodate new developments without major disruptions to the established areas of knowl-edge. Thus, despite the alleged knowledge explosion of the twentieth century, the mature domains of schol-arship have assimilated the new knowledge without having to undergo the severe reformulations that were characteristic of the Age of Eclosion.

Efforts toward the synthesis of knowledge are no less creative than the earlier developments characteristic of the Age of Eclosion. To resolve diffi-culties and dualisms, to harmonize oppositions, and to internalize contrarieties requires a profound creativity no less significant than the spectacular developments in knowledge breakthroughs charac-teristic of the Age of Eclosion. Although this can be demonstrated more clearly in the physical sciences than in the social sciences or humanities, even in the latter fields it is becoming increasingly evident that various systematic positions and frameworks are making valuable contributions.

Knowledge Specialization and Fragmentation. Nevertheless, the Age of Synthesis has been accom-panied by an age of knowledge specialization that creates new problems of knowledge fragmentation. The knowledge specialization is not a product of the Age of Synthesis but rather a result of the growth of the knowledge industry and the sociology of its insti-tutions. In the words of the biologist Bentley Glass,

> It is well recognized that many, if not most, scienti-fic breakthroughs come about when the techniques and concepts of quite different scientific fields are brought together in an original synthesis of insight and imagination. Yet it seems unavoidable that the increasing narrowness of specialization tends to reduce the possibility that this will happen. (1970, p. 72)

Glass went on to discuss how our university scholars seek to enhance their reputation by digging out minuscule facts and information, whereas a lower premium is given to publishing comprehensive books and reviews that reveal the interrelationships of knowledge and its domains. The Nobel laureate Eugene Wigner recounted how his own field has become so specialized that he could not understand half the reports in *Physical Review Abstracts*. "Perhaps it is partly the jargon—the technical expressions. It hurts me," stated Wigner, "and I'm afraid it will hurt physics" (in Walsh, 1973, p. 533). Weinberg (1967) proposed that the university "accord the generalist of broad outlook the status and prestige it now confers upon the specialist of narrow outlook," and he proposed that "the university reestablish its relevance to the interdisciplinary real world" (pp. 161, 163). Indeed we find that despite the obsession with specialization in the university, the need for synthesis is exemplified in the emergence of new cross-disciplinary and interdisciplinary fields such as biophysics, sociobiology, ecology, and integrated studies in the broad field of humanities.

The Search for Synthesis

Perhaps the major curriculum problem for the twenty-first century stems more from a problems explosion than a knowledge explosion. Today, the scientific establishment and the general public are impelled to become less concerned with the exponential rate of growth of knowledge than with the uses to which knowledge is put in the face of exploding societal problems. By the closing decade of the twentieth century, the public had been led to believe that the age of space would usher in a future of unlimited knowledge frontiers to be conquered. But instead of turning people outward, the age of space seemed to focus our concerns back to Earth as we realized that the capability of going to the moon or Mars is in no way an escape from the problems on Earth. Perhaps the most profound comment made by our astronauts on their first visit to the moon was how beautiful Earth is when viewed from this distant vantage point! Meanwhile, there was a growing realization that the quality of life, indeed our very survival, was not so much dependent on coping with a knowledge explosion but on our capacity to deal with a problems explosion. A new awareness of our finite resources gave us cause to consider the problems of environmental deterioration, overpopulation, energy use, migration, health, poverty, food production, and so on, with the likelihood of economic and social stagnation unless we turn our intelligence to the wise use of resources.

The Macrocurriculum and the Microcurriculum

The early decades of the twentieth century witnessed a growing awareness of problems created by course proliferation, knowledge fragmentation, and the isolation and remoteness of studies from life. Coupled with the development of new knowledge concerning the nature of the child and adolescent, the need for a reconstruction of the curriculum became apparent to progressive educators. They proceeded to develop new curricular frameworks and designs leading to correlation, fusion, broad fields, and integrated core approaches.

These efforts, which would appear to lend credence to Bochner's thesis regarding the twentieth century as the Age of Synthesis, represented an unprecedented concern for addressing macrocurricular problems, not merely microcurricular problems. The whole was seen as more than the sum of its parts. Curriculum development required attention to the interactions of the constituent subject matters and relevance of these subject matters to the life of the learner. Segmental approaches to curriculum development within each subject-matter area had resulted in the fragmentation and isolation of knowledge and learning.

Attention to macrocurricular problems resulted in efforts to develop vertical and horizontal curriculum articulation—the former referring to developing coherence *within* given fields of study over the various grade levels or years of schooling, the latter to developing the interrelationships *between* and *among* fields of study at either a given level or over various levels of schooling. The segmental approach was no longer adequate to the task of curriculum development, contended progressive educators who sought an ecological approach. The concern for general education—or that part of the curriculum designed to provide for a common universe of discourse, understanding, and competence—during the first half of the twentieth century represented a macrocurricular concern and resulted in the creation of various new curricular designs and frameworks, ranging from correlational to interdisciplinary approaches. Nevertheless, the specialization of knowledge, the segmental organizational structure of the university and the secondary school, the influence of tax conservatives and essentialists, narrow national priorities concerned with military defense, and the difficult task of grappling with macrocurricular problems all served as countervailing influences to curriculum synthesis. The problem of synthesis remains a profound and persistent one.

To Facilitate Communication and Action. However logically the curriculum categories may be construed, they need to be justified on psychological and practical grounds. Furthermore, the categories should be recognized as fictional constructs, designed to facilitate communication and action. The test of their validity lies in how effectively they do this.

The traditional approach has been to conceive of general education as composed of three broad areas of knowledge: natural science, social science, and the humanities. However, even those comprehensive divisions necessarily disappear under practical conditions. For example, the concern for the environment gives rise to the study of ecology, a study that bridges the natural sciences and social sciences. Only tradition separates the humanities from the natural sciences, for if the humanities exemplify the great human achievements and moral concerns, how can the humanists exclude science and technology? Yet as Monod pointed out, modern societies have accepted the treasures and powers of science without accepting science as a source of truth that demands a thorough revision of ethical premises. "Armed with all the powers, enjoying all the riches they owe to science, our societies are still trying to live by and teach systems of values already blasted at the root by science itself" (1972, p. 176). The consequence has been a widening split or inner division in our culture, leading to two cultures in conflict (Dewey, 1922, pp. 11–13; Snow, 1959). Although the world of academia has contributed to this dualism, it is uniquely endowed to develop the needed synthesis; more than any other institution, its chief function is the reconstruction of knowledge for the improvement of society (Tanner, D., 1983a).

The Macrocurriculum: Complementary Functions

It will be recalled from the discussion in chapter 9 that Lester Ward, who systematically explicated the idea of progress as a principal belief for progressive education and American democracy, envisioned an articulated threefold curriculum emerging in the twentieth century. The threefold universal curriculum envisioned by Ward would have to meet the test of relative generality or universality and practicality (1883, pp. 621–622).

Ward's threefold universal curriculum was to take root in the form of three macrocurricular aims (or functions) as advanced in the *Cardinal Principles* report of 1918 (Commission on the Reorganization of Secondary Education) and the text by Alexander Inglis, also published in 1918. Inglis had served as a key member of the commission that produced the *Cardinal Principles* report. In the text by Inglis, three interdependent macrocurricular aims of function were identified for the newly emerging comprehensive high school: (1) the sociocivic aim of democratic citizenship, (2) the economic-vocational aim, and (3) the individual-avocational aim. The sociocivic aim was to be provided through the curriculum constants, whereas the other aims were to be met through curriculum variables: elective programs for vocational education and free electives for individual-avocational interests (Inglis, 1918, pp. 667–668). In similar style and substance, the *Cardinal Principles* report and Inglis's text described the comprehensive high school as the universal secondary school and outlined the curriculum needed to meet the changing social conditions.

Figure 10.1 depicts the interdependence of these three comprehensive aims. In the words of Inglis:

> "Since every individual is at once a citizen, a worker, and a relatively independent personality, and since those three phases of activity cannot be divorced, it follows that a fundamental principle in the organization of curriculums is the conception that each of the three aims mentioned must be recognized in due proportion and that no curriculum which ignores or minimizes any one of those aims can be acceptable." (Inglis, p. 668)

The sociocivic aim was not limited to the social studies, but it was to meet the comprehensive function of general education or learnings shared by all members of a free society. Inglis called for the restructuring of the curriculum and teaching methods more appropriately attuned to the nature of the learner and the democratic prospect, as opposed to the traditionally compartmentalized or segmental subject curriculum (p. 712).

Structure and Function.   Inglis's call for such a restructured curriculum for a common learning reached fruition in the 1930s with the development of the core curriculum focused on pervading social problems, issues, conflict and themes relating to life in a free society (Smith, Stanley, & Shores, 1957, pp. 314–319).

Unfortunately, the core curriculum has come to be seen in secondary and higher education as composed of those subjects required of all students. In many cases the subjects may be selected from course

Figure 10.1 The Three Interdependent Aims of the Macrocurriculum.

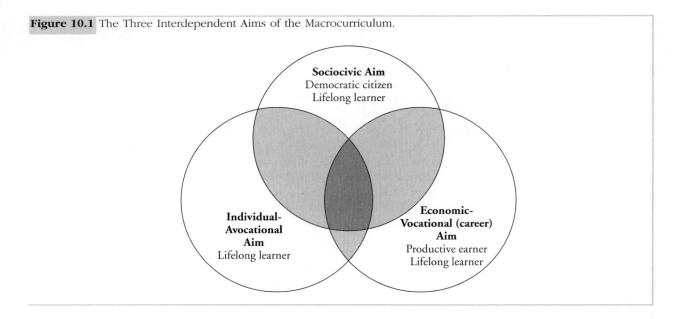

listings under various subject categories, further mitigating the fundamental principles of the core idea: the engagement in the study of concerns, problems, and issues shared by all members of a free society to be conducted in the heterogenerously grouped classroom.

Before returning to this problem, it is useful to expand Inglis's threefold macrocurricular aims or functions so as to see the modern curriculum more explicitly. Figure 10.2 depicts five interdependent and comprehensive macrocurricular functions, namely (1) general education, (2) specialized education, (3) exploratory education, (4) enrichment education, and (5) special-interest education.

General education may be regarded as that part of the curriculum designed to provide for a common universe of discourse, understanding, and competence. General education is ordinarily referred to as the *common core*, or that part of the curriculum in school or college that is required of all students. The function of general education corresponds with the sociocivic aim as proposed by Inglis (Figure 10.1). In turn, the function of specialized education corresponds with the economic-vocational aim, also proposed by Inglis.

Because disciplinary knowledge is a product of knowledge specialization, and because so many of the knowledge specialties lay claim to being disciplines, the disciplinary mode has been regarded by many educators as more suitable for specialized education than for general education. Specialized education is

ordinarily regarded as representing the student's major field or his or her preprofessional, professional, prevocational, and vocational studies. Exploratory education is intended to enable the student to investigate and extend inquiry into areas that the student might consider as a possible field for specialization or career preparation.

Enrichment education is intended to supplement, broaden, and deepen the learner's educative experience. Exploratory and special-interest enrichment education may be provided through the free or controlled election of formal courses, as well as through participation in the student activities program. The interdependence of the five macrocurricular functions may be illustrated in the case where a student having a special interest in student publications, and who joins the staff of the student newspaper, may subsequently decide on a career in journalism; or a student enrolled in a studio-arts course for enrichment may develop a special interest or lifelong avocational pursuit of music or the visual arts. As another example, a student pursuing elective studies for exploratory purposes may find his or her calling in a related career.

The complementarity of the five macrocurricular functions cannot be overemphasized. General education should facilitate and illuminate all other curriculum functions. Exploratory and enrichment education often influence a student's decisions regarding specialized education, and so on. Curriculum balance and coherence require that these functions be taken

Figure 10.2 The Five Complementary Functions of the Macrocurriculum.

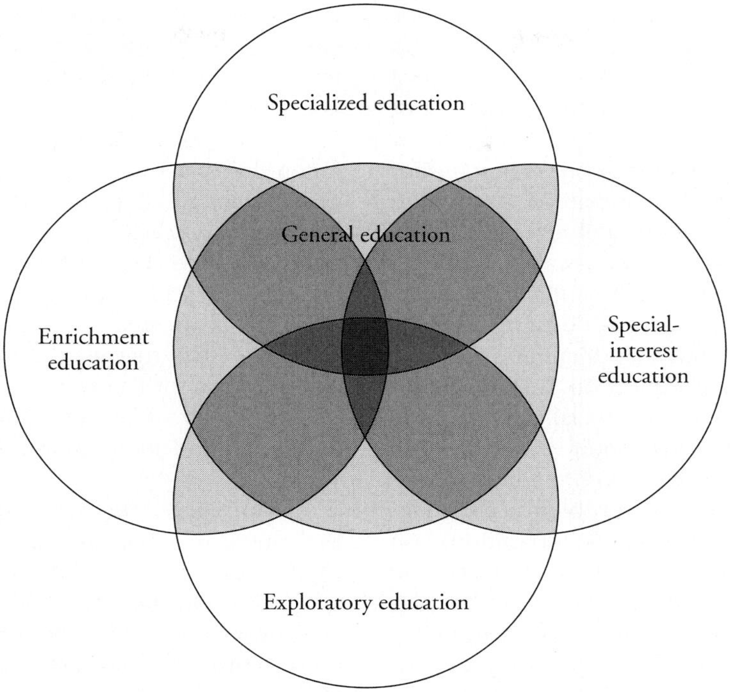

Source: Adapted from Daniel Tanner, *Secondary Education: Perspectives and Prospects.* New York: Macmillan, 1972, p. 319; and Daniel Tanner and Laurel Tanner, *Supervision in Education: Problems and Practices.* New York: Macmillan, 1987, p. 428.

into account in ecological relationship. The lines between and among the five macrocurricular functions must be fluid and functional. This is the imperative of the macrocurriculum.

General Education for a Free Society

The very idea and practice of general education grew out of the experimentalist-progressive efforts for universal secondary education and the democratization of the high school, along with a progressive parallel movement in higher education in recognition of the limits of traditional liberal education.

The universalization of secondary education and the forces for open-access higher education led to a great and growing heterogeneity of the student population in school and college, a heterogeneity that mirrored the diversity of society at large. The accompanying diversification of the curriculum in school and college reflected not only the growth of knowledge and

the changing conceptions of knowledge but also the heterogeneous character of the student populations.

The notion of liberal education as the province of a privileged class came to be recognized as untenable in modern democratic society. Liberal education bore an aristocratic invidium that was rooted historically in ancient Greece, where society was divided into freemen and slaves. The aristocratic and leisure class of freemen could pursue the cultural or liberal studies, whereas the utilitarian needs of the social order were carried out by slaves. The belief that liberal education is properly the exclusive province of the privileged class, along with the idea that it is superior to and should be divorced from the practical studies, had been perpetuated for centuries. Because the privileged were free to cultivate their intellect in contemplation of the good life, those studies that were above practical concerns, namely the liberal arts, were deemed to be most suitable for such cultivation.

Modern democratic society holds to the ideal that all individuals are free and that all have a share in the productive work of society. The traditional concept of the liberal arts suffered not only from a social exclusiveness but also from a knowledge exclusiveness favoring the literary studies. Science and technology not only helped destroy slavery and drudgery, but also required a broader conception of the knowledge that all citizens of a free society must share in common. Thus, the term *general education* emerged in place of liberal education. General education, then, is regarded as "that part of a student's whole education which looks first of all to his life as a responsible human being and citizen" (Harvard Committee Report, 1945, p. 51). It is that part of the curriculum that is designed to provide for a common universe of discourse, understanding, and competence. In essence, general education is intended to develop autonomously thinking, socially responsible citizens of a free society. This requires a curriculum that is not concerned exclusively with the human heritage but also with the pervading problems of humanity. General education necessitates an outlook on knowledge that is essentially different from the knowledge world of specialized education. The difference in outlook on knowledge also requires a different organization and treatment of knowledge for general education, as contrasted with specialized education.

To this day, even those contemporary educators who are allies of general education in the college tend to look on the function of the secondary school curriculum principally as preparation for college. Obviously, this works against the development of an authentic curriculum of general education along with diversified studies for the adolescent population, and it reduces the curriculum function for the elementary school to basic education or literacies. Clearly, a larger vision of the curriculum was required of educators at all levels.

General Education and the Phases of Schooling

The Comprehensive High School

Some of the most avid allies of general education at the college level are prone to disregard the importance of general education in the schools where they see education as being properly concentrated on facts and skills. Stating the case for general education in the undergraduate years, Daniel Bell viewed the college experience as "the testing years—the testing of oneself and one's values" with the college being an environment "of broad intellectual adventure, the place where one can resist, momentarily, the harness that society now seeks to impose at an earlier and earlier stage on its youth," whereas the function of the secondary school is that of "concentrating on facts and skills" (1968, p. 181). In choosing to see the secondary school as mere preparation for college, Bell ignored the fact that the majority of youth do not go on to attain a college education. For them the end of secondary schooling signals the end of their formal education. Are they to be denied the opportunity of general education and the testing of their values? Are they not expected to share fully the rights and responsibilities that accrue to all members of a free society? And for those who do go on to college, are the secondary school years merely to be a tooling up for the "broad intellectual adventure" of the college years?

Throughout the twentieth century and to this day the American secondary school has waged a struggle to develop its own authentic curriculum in general education. On the one hand, there are those college educators who have chosen to see the secondary school curriculum as concentrated on facts and skills to tool up pupils for college. Then there are those college educators who see the secondary school curriculum as properly being limited to the academic disciplines that correspond to the liberal arts studies of the college (Bestor, 1956; Bennett, 1987). Because the secondary school is concerned with the developing adolescent, and because its student population is so diverse, it cannot simply be limited to a precollege function. The struggle of the secondary school to develop its own authentic curriculum has been long and hard. The cosmopolitan character of its pupil population not only requires a curriculum that is diversified but also a curriculum that enables all of the youth of all of the people to share in a common universe of discourse, understanding, and competence—in short, to become independently thinking and socially responsible members of a free society. This is the purpose of general education.

An American Invention.   The comprehensive high school has been rightly called "a peculiarly American phenomenon" (Gardner in Conant, 1959b, p. 18). Early in this century the United States chose not to pattern its system of secondary education after the dualistic system of European nations in which the terminal student and the student who is destined for the university attend separate schools. Such separations are marked not only by differences in ability and achievement but also by differences in social class. With the establishment of cooperative federal-state programs for vocational education in 1917, some educators and many industrialists advocated separate specialized vocational schools after the European pattern. When the dust was settled, the prevailing sentiment favored a unitary school that, in the words of the 1918 report of the NEA Commission on the Reorganization of Secondary Education, would serve as "the prototype of a democracy in which various groups must have a degree of self-consciousness as groups and yet be federated into a larger whole through the recognition of common interests and ideals" (p. 26).

Thus evolved a unitary, multipurpose school—the comprehensive high school—that was designed to provide (1) a general education for all youth as citizens of a democratic society, (2) specialized programs for vocational proficiency for those youngsters planning to enter the world of work after high school, (3) the specialized program of academic preparation for college, (4) exploratory studies and experiences to enable adolescents to investigate new sources of learning, (5) enrichment studies and experiences to widen and deepen the sources of learning for all adolescents, and (6) special-interest studies to meet individual interests apart from specialized studies (see Figure 10.2).

Although these functions often have been more of an ideal than a reality, over the years the idea of the comprehensive high school has prevailed in the face of constant criticism. The criticism has come from widely divergent sources. For example, during the height of the space race, Admiral Rickover expressed his view that educational efficiency must prevail over "democratic" education:

> One cannot argue the issue of comprehensive schooling versus separate secondary education on a philosophical basis. But one can argue it on the basis whether the country really has a choice as between efficient education—that is, separate schools above the elementary levels—and pure "democratic" education which insists on the inefficient time-wasting comprehensive high school. In my opinion, we no longer have that choice. We must opt for efficiency. (1963, p. 89)

It may have been easy for a U.S. admiral to choose efficiency over democracy, but the public was not swayed to abandon their unitary school

system. Nevertheless, not only did traditionalist academicians such as Bestor (1956) and Hofstadter (1963, pp. 334–338) continue to make the case for the traditional academic high school, but even some radical romanticists of the 1960s, whose attacks on American schools appeared to be cloaked in an egalitarian humanism, revealed their masked elitism in advocating that the high school continue to serve the academically able youth whereas the less able youth would be better off out of school (Goodman, 1964, pp. 39, 88; Friedenberg, 1967, pp. 250–251, 257).

The Democratizing Function.   The ranks of educators supporting the comprehensive school and general education were growing thin under the new onslaught of education criticism, the new thrust for specialized vocational and academic high schools, and the nationalizing influences that had led to a new curriculum hierarchy under the banner of disciplinarity. Among the few national figures supporting the comprehensive ideal was James B. Conant. Despite his narrow prescriptions for gearing the high school to the exigencies of the Cold War, Conant's faith in the democratizing function of the comprehensive high school remained unshaken. As president of Harvard over two decades, extending from the Great Depression to midcentury, he had presided over reforms that led to a cosmopolitan student population. During this transformation, Harvard students who came from the nation's comprehensive high schools were demolishing the myth that the best preparation for college is provided by the specialized academic high schools.

Citing a study on admissions policy by a Harvard faculty committee, Harvard psychologist Jerome Bruner pointed out that "Harvard students enrolled from public high schools carry away more honors than students of like aptitude enrolled from the great independent preparatory schools of the Eastern seaboard" (1960, p. 71). In his recognition of such findings at Harvard and at other leading universities, Conant became convinced that the comprehensive high school not only could meet the test of academic excellence but also was the key educational institution for advancing the democratic ideal of a unity based on diversity. Observing in 1970 that some of the more progressive European nations were adopting the comprehensive model, Conant expressed perplexity as to why Americans were not more fully supportive of the institution that was their very own creation.

I am an advocate of the comprehensive school, yet I must admit that the future of this institution is far from certain in the United States. It is strange that the enthusiasm for an American invention is so limited in this country just at the time when other nations are beginning to explore application of the basic idea. . . . Are the high schools of the United States to be so designed as to be effective means of forwarding the idea of a unity based on diversity in a democratic community, or is the comprehensive concept to be given at best only lip service? Far more than the nature of our schools is involved in the answer to this question. The entire structure of our nation may be at stake—possibly even its survival as an open society of free men. (in Eurich, 1970, pp. 73, 80)

In his autobiography, *My Several Lives* (1970b), Conant remarked, "If someone had told me when I was a chemist that in my old age I would devote a considerable amount of time and energy to examining the public high schools of the United States, I should have branded him as demented" (p. 613). In this same work, Conant selected only four of his many major addresses for inclusion in their entirety in an appendix. One of them was a 1952 speech, "Unity and Diversity in Secondary Education," stating the case for the comprehensive high school and general education. As discussed in chapter 12, the reports of various national committees on youth education, through the last quarter of the twentieth century to this day, expressed virtually no support for the comprehensive high school and made little mention of the theory and practice of general education. At the same time, as discussed later, the comprehensive high school was being widely adopted in Britain, Sweden, and certain European countries as the means of advancing educational opportunity and democratizing the educational system through a unitary school structure.

Moreover, from the 1980s to current times, various reports on educational reform were conceiving the high school as properly limited to a general academic curriculum (Sizer, 1984; Boyer, 1983; Goodlad, 1984; Powell, Farrar, & Cohen, 1985; U.S. Department of Education, 1991). If the comprehensive high school was mentioned at all, it was dismissed or criticized as the vehicle for student tracking (Oakes, 1985). At the same time, some educators were lending credence to this notion by fixing the blame back to the *Cardinal Principles* report of 1918 when, in fact, the 1918 report of the Commission on the

Reorganization of Secondary Education had clearly and repeatedly opposed tracking (Oakes, 1985, pp. 33–35). It envisioned a universal curriculum of constants (general education) coupled with curriculum variables selected to meet the exploratory and specialized needs (vocational and academic) of a cosmopolitan student population. The commission report of 1918 held that vocational studies should not be a barrier to higher education. The report pointed to the pitfalls of tracking and social segregation and predestination by means of specialized or special-type schools as opposed to the comprehensive high school.

Curiously, critics of the comprehensive high school during the 1980s and 1990s were strangely silent or even favorably disposed toward special-type or alternative schools that were being promoted and established in various sections of the nation (Boyer, 1983, pp. 245–246). Under the banner of "choice," the Reagan and both Bush administrations had promoted alternative schools and had engaged the U.S. secretary of Education in that effort. The director of the federally funded National Center on Effective Secondary Schools questioned the primacy of the comprehensive high school and summarized the case being made for alternative or special-type schools to serve the "increased diversity in learning styles, career aspirations, and social values" (Newmann, 1988, p. 1). It seemed that the growing fragmentation of American society was to be mirrored by a splitting up of the school system to serve the special interests of different populations. Although the general public was not ready to split up the schools and abandon the comprehensive concept and function of the American high school, the events leading the opening of the twenty-first century gave credence to Conant's concerns about the future of this uniquely American institution.

Conant was aware that if the comprehensive high school is to be the "effective means of forwarding the idea of a unity based on diversity in a democratic community," such a quest for unity must be reflected in the curriculum. The diversity of the pupil population in the comprehensive high school requires a diversified curriculum, but the ideal of unity based on diversity in a democracy also requires that the curriculum provide a common ground whereon the rising generation can examine problems that are shared by all members of society. This is the task of general education. Moreover, the very nature of the problems confronted by all members of a democratic society requires that attention be given to curriculum synthesis, because these problems do not fit into the established disciplines or the knowledge categories that comprise the subject curriculum.

Despite the extensive literature, dating from the *Cardinal Principles* report of 1918 to the writings of James Conant, explaining the means of providing for a diversified curriculum without tracking, there remains a curious confusion on the issue of tracking. Unfortunately, recent studies of the issue generally overlook the seminal historic literature and tend to confuse rather than clarify the issue (LeTendre, Hofer, & Shimizu, 2003, pp. 45–89).

European Developments.   As noted, Conant had expressed concern over the growing attacks on the American comprehensive high school at a time when other advanced democratic nations were adopting the comprehensive model. As a notable example, in the 1950s, the Swedish government provided for a 10-year study in which Stockholm was divided in half, comparing one sector having comprehensive schools with the other sector, which followed the old system of divided-selective schools. When it was found that the comprehensive system met the traditional standards at most levels and actually raised them at some, the entire nation became committed to the comprehensive model (Husén & Boalt, 1968; Benn & Chitty, 1997, p. 43). Clearly, the increased holding power of the comprehensive model resulted in the vast expansion of educational opportunity. Inclusion as contrasted against selection in secondary education can only advance the process of democratization (Husén, 1989, p. 346).

In the foreword to a study of the history of the comprehensive school in Britain (Benn & Chitty, 1997), Brian Simon points out that whereas in 1965 90% of students of secondary school age were enrolled in divided tripartite schools based on selection at age 11, by 1997 over 90% of the students were in comprehensive secondary schools (Simon, 1976, p. viii). Despite the efforts of conservative governments to dismantle the comprehensive system, and despite the "persistent and unprincipled" attacks against the comprehensive schools, the British people supported the historic transformation. Yet, the British government has supported the creation of alternative schools directly financed by the state "with the aim of outflanking the comprehensive system" (Simon, p. viii). Similar developments have been occurring in the United States with regard to policies advocating

alternative schools and the uses of public funds in support of such schools (U.S. Department of Education, *America 2000*, 1991, pp. 25–26).

As with the American experience, the advent of the comprehensive secondary school in Britain and Sweden has required concerted attention to the design and function of a curriculum for general education along with a diversified curriculum (Benn & Chitty, 1997, pp. 464–466). The unparalleled historical cosmopolitanism of the American secondary school population, coupled with the rise of multiculturalism over interculturalism, has complicated the prospects for building a sense of unity through diversity through a coherent curriculum in general education. Nevertheless, the need for such an integrated curriculum is as profound as ever and cannot be ignored in a free society.

The House Plan and School Within a School Plan. Smaller class sizes have been associated with smaller schools, especially at the elementary level, but there is no reason why smaller school units and classes cannot be provided in the comprehensive high school. Under the house plan, the comprehensive high school provides for a designated faculty for general education and guidance within each house (Aikin, 1942b). The advantages that accrue to the smaller classes (Nye, Hedges, & Konstantanopolis, 2000) would be coupled with an articulated curriculum in general education in a cosmopolitan setting encompassing specialized, exploratory, enrichment and special-interest curricular options that are not available in small schools.

In effect, every student in the high school is assigned to a particular house with a nuclear faculty. The large comprehensive high school is thus subdivided into smaller units while retaining the benefits of specialized resources, facilities, student services, and faculty specialists required of a comprehensive curriculum. The school within a school plan may be similar to the house plan, or it may enroll a particular segment of the school population assigned to work with a particular group of faculty in an experimental or innovative curriculum (Tanner, D., & Lachica, 1967).

In major cities where large high schools serve a high proportion of minority populations from areas plagued by social problems, there has been a trend to establish small school units, often called "academies" offering special-interest curricula for a more personalized education. Unfortunately, the large inner-city high school is often confused with the comprehensive high school (Darling-Hammond, Ancess, & Ort, 2002) when, in fact, the typical large-city high school is not comprehensive. It may be a specialized vocational or academic high school, although it is typically a general academic high school offering some nonvocational shop classes, limited classes in office practice, no cooperative supervised work-study programs in trades and industries and distributive occupations or health occupations, and no tech-prep program bridging the upper grades of the high school with the community college. The smaller school units seem to produce significantly better outcomes in comparison to the large failing inner-city high school, but the latter should not be confused with the comprehensive high school.

The Junior High School

The establishment and growth of the junior high school was given great impetus by the 1918 Commission on the Reorganization of Secondary Education in recognition of the inadequacies of the 8-year elementary school to serve the needs of young adolescents for developing "the common knowledge, common ideals, and common interests essential to American democracy" in a nation where "racial stocks are widely divided, various forms of social heredity come into conflict, differing religious beliefs do not always make for unification, and the members of different vocations often fail to recognize the interests that they have in common with others" (p. 22).

It was recognized that the task of general education in the comprehensive high school applies fully to the junior high school. Yet, because the needs, interests, and other characteristics of the young adolescent differ significantly from those of the older adolescent, and from the child, the junior high school was not regarded as a miniature senior high school nor as an extension of elementary schooling.

In addition to the need for a unified as well as a diversified curriculum, the commission stressed the need for young adolescents to engage in a rich variety of exploratory electives. Further, the commission pointed to the dangers to democracy resulting from the alarmingly low holding power of the school system. In the words of the commission's report:

> At present only about one-third of the pupils who enter the first year of the elementary school reach the four-year high school, and only about one in nine is graduated. Of those who enter the seventh school year, only one-half to two-thirds reach the first year of the four-year high school. Of those who enter the four-year high school about one-third leave before the beginning of the second year, about one-half are gone before the beginning of the third year, and fewer than one-third are graduated. These facts can no longer be safely ignored. (p. 8)

Notable Accomplishments. The phenomenal growth and widespread acceptance of the junior high school during the first half of the twentieth century removed the ninth grade from the college preparatory influence. Prior to the development of the junior high school, the colleges traditionally evaluated the four years of high school studies as a basis for college admission. By incorporating the ninth grade into the junior high school, opportunities were opened to redesign the curriculum at this level for the early adolescent, despite the fact that many colleges continued to view the ninth grade as part of the college preparatory program.

Also, by incorporating grades seven and eight into its structure, the junior high school was able to provide youngsters at this level with a wider range of curricular experiences than was offered by the traditional 8-year elementary school, which tended to concentrate its curriculum on skill development in the fundamental processes. With young adolescents entering the stage of formal operations in their cognitive development, in which they are developing their capabilities for hypothetical thinking and more sophisticated problem solving, the junior high school appeared to offer promising opportunities for designing a curriculum that was particularly suited to this age group. Moreover, the junior high school was equipped with facilities and resources not ordinarily available in the elementary school, such as libraries, laboratories, shops, gymnasiums, art and music studios, and so on. It also attracted more male teachers to grades seven and eight.

As documented by a series of revealing national surveys by Grace Wright for the U.S. Office of Education (1949, 1952, 1958, 1963), the junior high school pioneered in the development of new curricular designs such as through block-time, correlated, and integrated core classes for general education. Unfortunately, the Cold War and space race found the school curriculum being turned over to the university scholar-specialists wedded to their separate disciplines, with the consequence that the curriculum became centered on a hierarchy of disconnected disciplines and puristic specialized knowledge in violation of the nature of the learner and in neglect of the idea and practice of general education (Tanner, D., 1971; Weinberg, 1967).

Pressures of the Cold War pushed many junior high schools to pattern their curricula after the senior high school, particularly with regard to the academic studies. Grouping pupils by ability in all academic subjects became a widespread practice. As noted, the priority given the academic studies was accompanied by a neglect of the general education function, not to mention the exploratory and enrichment functions of the curriculum. In many respects, the junior high school assumed a function of sifting and sorting youngsters in preparation for the senior high school. In accommodating itself to the pressures of the times, the junior high school curriculum was showing signs of losing the recognizable curriculum authenticity it had managed to gain throughout its formative years.

The call to humanize the schools during the second half of the 1960s and early 1970s witnessed increasing attacks on the junior high school. In his report for the Carnegie Corporation, Silberman attacked the junior high school along with the senior high school as being slow to reform and for being repressive and authoritarian. "And the junior high school, by almost unanimous agreement," declared Silberman, "is the wasteland—one is tempted to say cesspool—of American education" (Silberman, 1970, p. 324). Silberman, however, failed to identify the source of "almost unanimous agreement," and he made no specific recommendations for the junior high school.

Although the junior high school has received more than its share of criticism, its effort to develop curriculum authenticity is evidenced by the fact that through the decades of its development and expansion, the junior high school, more commonly than the senior high school, instituted block-time, core, and broad-fields approaches to curriculum organization for purposes of general education (Wright, 1949, 1952, 1958, 1963). These approaches to curriculum organization are discussed later in this chapter.

The Middle School

From the 1960s to contemporary times, increasing numbers of educators looked to the emerging middle school as being particularly well suited to the task of bridging the childhood phase of elementary schooling with the adolescent phase of secondary schooling.

Advocates of the middle school contended that the junior high had become an imitation of the high school. They also held that because youngsters were reaching puberty about a year earlier than previous generations, ninth-graders now were capable of adjusting to the senior high school and, at the same time, the middle school would be more appropriately geared to the educational needs of youngsters as they mature from late childhood into early adolescence.

Surely the legitimacy of these assumptions and claims is well grounded (Johnson, 1980). However, the middle school revival gained impetus as a result of demographic changes in which the adolescent population was in a state of decline, whereas the childhood population was increasing. In effect, school boards were converting junior high school buildings to middle schools in order to take the pressure off the elementary schools.

Middle schools most commonly incorporate grades six through eight, placing the ninth grade back into the high school, where it had been during the early twentieth century prior to the emergence of the junior high school. With more than 4 out of every 10 secondary-school students going on to college, the reestablishment of the 4-year high school has placed added emphasis on the ninth grade as being integral to the college preparatory program. This places additional constraints on the curriculum in the ninth grade, although it also can be argued that the pursuit of academic excellence during the Cold War and space race had already impelled the junior high school to imitate the senior high school in concentrating its reforms on the academic side of the curriculum. Nevertheless, the incorporation of the ninth grade into the high school makes the ninth-grader who plans to go on to college cognizant of the fact that the colleges will evaluate the four years of the student's high school work in determining admission.

Struggle for Authentic Identity.   The professional identification of the middle school has been with the National Association of Secondary School Principals (Council on Middle Level Education, *An Agenda for Excellence*, n.d.). This identification reflects the rise of the middle school being accompanied by the corresponding decline of the junior high school. It is revealing that a publication by the National Association of Secondary School Principals (1985) devoted to trends and practices in middle-level education actually "lifted" the functions and goals of middle-level education entirely from a foundational book on the junior high school (Gruhn & Douglass, 1956). In effect, the functions and goals of the middle school were regarded as identical to those of the junior high school as articulated before the mid-twentieth century. To this day, the middle school has had a problem of establishing an authentic identity of its own, as opposed to being simply a school in the middle. In fact, a publication by the National Middle School Association (Alexander & McEwin, 1989) was titled *Schools in the Middle*, and a recent report on middle schools by the National Center for Education Statistics was issued under the title *In the Middle* (2000). The problem of identity of the middle school was reflected in the title of an article in *Education Week*, "Muddle in the Middle" (Bradley, 1998, pp. 38–42).

Although the junior high school never became really freed from the college preparatory function of secondary schooling, the middle school is not so encumbered because it is not a reorganized secondary school. Proponents of the middle school point out that it is specifically designed to make available to youngsters a far wider range of learning options than would be provided in the self-contained classroom of the elementary school without adopting the strictly departmentalized structure of the high school. The middle school curriculum may be so organized as to include such features as block-time and unified studies, team teaching, flexible scheduling, and special offerings and facilities that are less likely to be available in the elementary school, such as industrial arts, homemaking, typing, laboratory science, library work, physical education, and so on. Through independent study and exploratory options, many middle schools aim to provide greater opportunity for pupil self-direction and responsibility than is possible in the self-contained classroom of the elementary school. Perhaps the weakest aspects of the middle school have been the lack of concerted attention given to the development of a coherent curriculum in general education and the lack of resource facilities such as well-stocked and well-equipped libraries, shops, studios, and laboratories. There is also the question as to the appropriateness of mixing eighth-graders of age 13 with fifth- or sixth-grade children of age 10 or 11 in the same school.

Many school districts have established middle schools to deal with administrative problems such as the need to alleviate crowded conditions in existing schools and the need to desegregate the pupil populations; quite often the middle school is housed in a building that was formerly an elementary school.

(The dramatic growth of the junior high school also can be attributed to administrative convenience, namely, that it was more economically feasible for a school district to build such a school than to construct additional elementary and high schools to accommodate the rising enrollments.) Under such circumstances, the school district is inclined to neglect the need for the middle school to develop its own authentic curriculum for the population group it serves, with the result that it becomes merely an in-between school.

In general, the facilities and resources of the junior high school have been more extensive than these of the middle school, along with the higher percentage of male teachers and the provisions for more advanced studies and specialized faculty in the junior high school. The junior high school has also served a larger and more cosmopolitan pupil population.

When school districts establish middle schools for purposes of desegregation, they also need to recognize that by virtue of creating a school with a more cosmopolitan population than is characteristic of the neighborhood elementary school, concerted attention must be given to designing the curriculum in general education in view of the democratizing function. To ignore this opportunity and responsibility is philosophically indefensible in the schools of a society that holds to the democratic ideal. Yet many secondary schools have neglected to design the curriculum to meet this function, despite the fact that they are plagued by racial polarization and conflict as reflected in society at large.

The Elementary School

During the first half of the twentieth century, the dominant pattern of instructional organization in the elementary school was the self-contained classroom, in which a teacher is assigned the responsibility for instruction in virtually all areas of the curriculum with a class of children at a given grade level. It was believed that not only did the self-contained approach allow the teacher to know the children more intimately but also that it would provide for curriculum integration. However, the traditional practice was for self-contained classroom teachers to follow a daily schedule in moving from one subject of study to another. Consequently, the subjects tended to be treated separately with daily slots for arithmetic, reading, grammar, spelling, writing, social studies, science, and so on. The focus of the traditional self-contained classroom tended to be on the development of fundamental skills, with relatively little attention being given to the wider goals of general education.

Modified Teaching Arrangements.   In growing recognition of the enormous demands being placed on the self-contained classroom teacher, many elementary schools were providing this teacher with some form of special assistance through a helping teacher who gave consultant help, or through special teachers who assumed direct responsibility for instruction in certain subjects. As the pressures mounted to provide for more specialized instruction, such as the teaching of foreign languages at the elementary level, an increasing proportion of schools provided special teachers for instruction in this area and in such other areas of the curriculum as music, art, physical education, and reading—and the regular teacher continued to be responsible for the major portion of the curriculum. Some form of partial departmentalization of instruction in the upper elementary grades was not uncommon. Some schools adopted a dual-progress plan in which pupils in the upper elementary school spent about a half a day in the self-contained classroom and the remainder of the day in departmentalized studies on a nongraded basis. However, many elementary educators had reservations concerning departmentalization and favored some form of team teaching along with the use of teacher aides or paraprofessionals instead. When team teaching was employed, the arrangements more typically were on a collegial rather than hierarchical basis.

Nongraded School.   During the 1960s, an increasing proportion of elementary schools were adopting nongraded organizational plans at the primary level. The purpose of nongraded arrangements was to facilitate continuous pupil progress by allowing children to advance at their own rates in the various subjects, particularly reading and mathematics.

Although the proponents of nongrading claimed that it provided for pupil differences and fostered a longitudinal concept of curriculum, or vertical curriculum articulation, the nongraded approach presented its own difficulties. For example, many nongraded schools had replaced the so-called graded lockstep with mechanical criteria for establishing the level of pupil placement in their studies, namely, standardized achievement test scores. Moreover, although it was claimed that the nongraded approach

allowed for greater attention being given to vertical curriculum articulation, it also tended to work against horizontal curriculum articulation or the interrelationships among the various studies that constitute the total curriculum.

Finally, the claim that nongraded arrangements provide for superior pupil achievement over graded patterns has not been substantiated by research. The superiority of a particular administrative pattern— whether nongraded, multigraded, departmentalized, or self-contained—has not been borne out in terms of pupil achievement, probably because the teacher variable is more powerful than the administrative variable. Moreover, if the curriculum is narrowed to a skill-drill function, such a function may be performed in a wide variety of organizational or administrative arrangements. To the extent that the organizational or administrative pattern effects substantive changes in the learning environment, including teacher-pupil interactions, it will likely produce changes in learning outcomes. Hence there is a need to study learning in terms of the ecology of the school and classroom (Tanner & Tanner, 1987, pp. 121–163, 190, 505).

Open Classroom.   During the early 1970s, the center of gravity in the call for educational reform at the elementary level shifted to an informal organizational approach that was most commonly called the open classroom or open school. Patterned after the reforms that were being made in primary schools in England, the open classroom was heralded as an answer to the avalanche of criticisms that had fallen on American schools during the latter 1960s. The open classroom was seen as the means of humanizing the elementary schools in answer to the accusations that the schools were repressive.

In England, the open classroom idea was associated with the integrated curriculum in recognition that subject-matter boundaries and separate time slots for different subject matters and learning activities are not suited to the nature of young children. In many respects the efforts to reform the English primary schools along these lines during the late 1960s and early 1970s closely resembled the American progressive-educational reforms of the early twentieth century, although the American reform efforts were more directly steeped in democratic social ideology.

Although these contemporary educational reforms in England were being hailed as a model for American educational reform in the 1970s, many American schools adopted the open classroom mainly as an organizational arrangement for individualized, differentiated, and specialized learning activities. Relatively little attention was being given to developing curriculum integration through the open classroom.

The collapse of the open classroom in the United States, despite widespread promotion (Silberman, 1970, pp. 207–322), can be attributed to the failure to provide for curriculum articulation from age level to age level and among the various subjects, the misapplication of informal education for older children, the gross distortion of the idea itself in holding that schools without classroom walls would provide for curriculum articulation and teacher communication, teacher dissatisfaction with the noise levels in open-space schools, and general lack of teacher commitment and time for curriculum planning for articulation (Snyder, Bolin, & Zumwalt, 1992, pp. 422–425). The promotion of schools without walls also was promised on the naive notion that such schools would operate with greater efficiency and economy, whereas in reality the architecture turned out to be more costly than the traditional egg-crate classroom designs.

Individualized Instruction Arrangements and Mastery Learning. In response to the curriculum-retrenchment demands of the latter half of the 1970s, the open classroom came under attack both in this country and in England. The concept of individualized instruction was adapted to the skill function of schooling with the elementary curriculum focused on the three Rs. Workbooks, worksheets, and programmed materials were reappearing in elementary classrooms, along with inventories of behavioristic objectives. Individualized instructional programs—such as Individually Guided Education (IGE), developed during the mid-1960s through funds from the managerial efficiency–oriented Kettering Foundation—began to be adopted on a wider scale in the elementary schools. Sweeping claims were made for these programs, usually in terms of pre- and posttest scores of achievement in reading and arithmetic. Where control schools were used, the comparison populations were nonrandomly selected or were not matched according to criteria such as aptitude, achievement, socioeconomic background, and teacher ability. Proving the project appeared to be the overriding consideration, rather than investigating alternative approaches to curriculum design for the improvement of learning (Elmore & Sykes, 1992, p. 200; Snyder, Bolin, & Zumwalt, 1992, pp. 414–415).

The mastery-learning concept gained widespread interest and application during the late 1970s. Although it is contended that mastery-learning strategies are appropriate at all levels of education, they have been most widely employed at the elementary level, particularly in connection with the skill function of schooling. Under the assumption that "individual differences in school learning under very favorable conditions will approach a vanishing point," mastery learning relies heavily on the completion of discrete learning tasks with continuous feedback and corrective measures for the individual pupil through diagnostic-progress tests, programmed materials, workbooks, quizzes, and so on (Bloom, 1976, pp. 4–5). Obviously, the more rudimentary skills are most amenable to such measures. Consequently, schools that seek to implement mastery-learning strategies tend to narrow the curriculum focus to reading and mathematics. The extent to which the repertoire of continuous feedback, correction, and repeated testing constitutes a kind of teaching to the test under mastery learning has received little attention. It should not be surprising if such a repertoire, combined with the added time element of mastery learning, did not result in the self-fulfilling validation of the mastery concept. To compare experimental groups with control groups under such circumstances may be like running against a wooden-legged competitor. Virtually no systematic studies have been undertaken to compare the mastery-learning strategy in the skill function of schooling with alternative strategies in the growth function of schooling. Because the latter entails far more than skill development, the evaluative criteria necessitate the inclusion of such learning outcomes as divergent thinking, learning transfer, hypothetical thinking on personal and social problems, affective changes, and a host of the other macro-learning outcomes in addition to proficiency in the fundamental skills.

Alternative Schools or Schools of Choice. As noted, the 1918 Commission on the Reorganization of Secondary Education had pointed to the social divisiveness of special-type schools and the inflexibility of the curriculum in comparison to the comprehensive school where students can change their programs of study without severance of school relationship. Almost three-quarters of a century later, President George H. W. Bush was offering a national education strategy in *America 2000* promoting schools of "choice" on the ground that it "will create the competitive climate that stimulates excellence" (p. 53). In linking competition with "excellence," Bush's education strategy called for the reallocation of public funds to private schools just so long as these schools are deemed to "serve the public" (pp. 14, 31). More than 20 years earlier, in his autobiography, James Conant reflected on the issue of public funds for private schools. "The greater the proportion of our youth who attend independent schools, the greater the threat to our democratic unity," stated Conant. "Therefore, to use taxpayers' money to assist such a move is, for me, to suggest that American society use its own hands to destroy itself" (1970, p. 464).

Although President Bill Clinton, who succeeded Bush, almost immediately expressed his opposition to the use of public funds for private schools, he supported "schools of choice." Clinton's successor, George W. Bush, strongly endorsed his father's position as expounded in *America 2000*. With strong support from the federal level, public school systems in many regions designated special-type schools as "schools of choice" or as "magnet schools" from the elementary through the secondary levels. In some instances, parents were forced to choose whether their child, getting ready to enter kindergarten, should enroll, for example, in a magnet school for science and technology or a magnet school for fine, visual, and performing arts. Waiting lists were not uncommon when parental choice resulted in oversubscribing the school for science and technology (favored because it typically had the best equipment, facilities, and most highly qualified teachers). It was not uncommon for school districts to administer entrance examinations for kindergarten enrollment, with the practice of delaying admission for those with low scores—a policy of educational malpractice in view of the need for universal preschool and kindergarten access for the socialization of children in a democracy. The need for wholesome socialization in young children should be paramount, rather than high-pressure cognitive learning. Effective socialization in early childhood is a powerful foundation not only for social growth, but also for cognitive development (Shepard & Graue, 1993, pp. 293–305). Then there is the problem of the lack of validity of such tests (p. 304).

Further, the notion that the potentialities for cognitive development are generally established during early childhood not only lacks research support, but contemporary research on human development also reveals that intelligence is developed from rich environmental stimulation and experience throughout the lifespan (Bruer, 1999).

An analysis of 70 longitudinal studies examining academic/cognitive and social/behavioral measures administered in preschool or kindergarten and the first two grades revealed significant rank-order changes and concluded, "Instability or change may be the rule rather than the exception" (LaParo & Planta, 2000, p. 476).

Special-Type Schools. Aside from the obviously unscientific basis for separating young children into special-type schools, there is the pervasive question of social separation in the schools of a cosmopolitan society. Such separation was rejected even at the secondary level back in 1918 by the Commission on the Reorganization of Secondary Education on the ground that it works against the democratic interest. This might well have given pause for thoughtful educators to wonder whether the young nation was beginning to suffer from a hardening of the arteries. However, the general public remained opposed to school vouchers and were not about to abandon their belief in education. One only had to examine the enrollment statistics revealing the increased holding power of the high school and expanded access to higher education throughout the twentieth century, as envisioned prophetically by the members of the 1918 Commission on the Reorganization of Secondary Education.

Nevertheless, the development in recent years of myriad small, special-interest high schools in some of the major cities, organized around ethnocentric programs and basic skills for minority groups, raises ominous questions regarding cultural isolation and segregation. With the curriculum geared to basic academic skills and a narrow special theme for a small, special-interest population, these schools do not require the rich libraries, laboratories, studios, and shops needed for a comprehensive or cosmopolitan high school.

Many major-city school districts have been responding to the problem of multicultural differences and conflict in inner cities by creating separate schools for separate cultural constituencies. Conspicuously absent were concerted efforts to develop intercultural programs from the elementary level through the high school. Such efforts, undertaken by progressive educators before mid-twentieth century (Kilpatrick & Van Til, 1947), appeared just as urgent under the contemporary conditions of social fragmentation and conflict. The establishment of special-interest schools to serve special-interest constituencies seemed to reflect the conflicting culture (Schlesinger, 1998). It appeared that the time was ripe for rediscovering the idea and practice of general education and bringing renewal to the uniquely American institution known as the comprehensive high school.

Accelerated Schools

A disturbing observation made by more thoughtful teachers is the phenomenon of higher-achieving students seeking to find out what will be on the test (what specifically they will be held accountable for). When an examination is impending, such students have little patience with the teacher who departs from the target material with enrichment goals and activities. However, lower-achieving students tend not to press the teacher for what will be on the examinations. They exhibit great interest in ideas, problems, and issues that touch their lives. Enrichment goals and activities are not only highly motivating, but they also unleash unexpected talents and abilities. In effect, the higher-achieving students seem to exhibit a demand for lower-cognitive material ("what's on the test"), whereas lower-achieving students seem to respond better to higher-cognitive material.

This seeming paradox may be explained by the fact that higher-achieving students are successful on their examinations, whereas lower-achieving students meet with relatively little success. Hence, the former will be motivated to seek the path of least resistance by focusing on the facts and skills for the examinations, whether or not the material is interesting, challenging, and relevant to their lives; in contrast, the lower-achieving students, having had little success with examinations, remain unmotivated. Unfortunately, as teachers seek to induce higher-achieving students to engage in learning activities and to use materials for higher-order thinking, the typical classroom repertoire for lower-achieving students is on facts and drills. The point is that all children and youth are interested in ideas that touch their lives, and it is through idea-oriented teaching that facts become meaningful and skills become truly instrumental or useful. However, instead of idea-oriented teaching and learning, the focus, especially for lower-achieving students, is on error-oriented teaching and learning. (The student seeks to avoid errors in the belief that the teacher's job is to expose student errors.) The consequence is that students will restrict their ideas in essay writing, will refrain from asking questions for fear of revealing their ignorance, and will tend to respond mechanically with short answers to teacher questions.

In an effort to address these problems for lower-achieving, at-risk children, Henry Levin and his colleagues have instituted total-school programs at the elementary and middle levels under the premise that what works with gifted children also works effectively for all children. This premise is derived from John Dewey's poignant statement in the opening paragraph of *The School and Society* (1899): "What the best and wisest parent wants for his own child, that must the community want for all of its children. Any other ideal for our schools is narrow and unlovely; acted upon, it destroys our democracy" (p. 7). Although Levin and his associates promoted the effort under the banner of accelerated schools (Levin, 1990), the project actually has been directed not at compressing or speeding up the curriculum, but on deepening and widening it through the integration of studies, engaging children in higher-order thinking and active learning, enriching the learning resources (and eliminating worksheets), engaging teachers in decision-making authority and responsibility for curriculum development, engaging parents in working with the professional staff, and developing a shared sense of vision for the school as a community and belief in the potentials of all children. Emphasis is given to democratic processes and cooperative teacher-pupil planning.

Although some might prefer to see carefully designed experimental controls for the project, it should be borne in mind that virtually all of the elements in the project have a long-standing research base for best practices stemming from the experimentalist-progressive tradition. In view of the standing pressure to demonstrate results on standardized academic achievement tests, the focus of the project has been largely on academic studies, although the studies are organized and treated in integrated ways. Nevertheless, the academic curriculum is not a complete curriculum. The studio arts, industrial arts, and other so-called nonacademic studies have powerfully positive effects on cognitive and social development for both academic success and life success. One naturally finds open collaboration, cooperation, and initiative in the shop class and studio-arts class, but not so much in the math class (Sizer, 1984, pp. 146–148; Goodlad, 1984, p. 222; Young, 1966; Whitener, 1974). Consequently, accelerated schools would do well to provide for a more comprehensive curriculum.

General Education and Knowledge Specialism

Educators are often prone to distinguish general education from the knowledge world of specialized scholarship in terms of subject matter rather than in terms of outlook on knowledge and life, along with method of organizing and treating knowledge. Specialized-puristic scholarship requires a different outlook on knowledge and its organization than does general education. Before discussing the various ways of organizing knowledge in the curriculum, a brief examination of this difference in outlook on knowledge is presented.

The Scholar-Specialist and the Citizen

Acknowledging that there are various motives that lead one to the temple of specialized scholarship, including the drive to satisfy personal ambition and to revel in a sense of superior intellectual power, Einstein pointed out that there are other powerful motives of quite a different character.

> I believe with Schopenhauer that one of the strongest motives that lead men to art and science is escape from everyday life with its painful crudity and hopeless dreariness, from the fetters of one's own ever shifting desires. A finely tempered nature longs to escape from personal life into the world of objective perception and thought.... With this negative motive there goes a personal one. Man tries to make for himself in the fashion that suits him best a simplified and intelligible picture of the world; he then tries to some extent to substitute this cosmos of his for the world of experience, and thus to overcome it.... He makes this cosmos and its construction the pivot of his emotional life, in order to find in this way the peace and security which he cannot find in the narrow whirlpool of personal experience. (1934, pp. 20–21)

It cannot be denied that the work of such scholar-specialists has changed the world profoundly and that the change has been of immeasurable benefit. But the puristic knowledge edifices of the scholar-specialist represent only one side of knowledge. The ordinary citizen also tries to make for himself a simplified and intelligible picture of the world, but not as a substitute for the world of experience. Instead, his or her motive is to cope more effectively with the complexities and demands of life. In this quest it is not enough to prepare oneself for an occupation, but one must also develop a vision of the good person leading the good life in the good society. In a free society, the citizen is expected to develop the ability to think reflectively, to communicate thought, to make intelligent judgments, to discriminate wisely among values in coming to grips with problems and issues that are common to all citizens. General education in a free society, then, is intended to develop the independently thinking, socially responsible citizen.

The enlightened citizen in a free society is expected to govern his or her actions and come to grips with the problems of life experience through rational thought. But this is not the specialized rational thought of puristic scholarship that serves a private aestheticism. However, many individuals have sought to make for themselves a simplified picture of the world not through rational means but through the dogmas of the occult and superstition. It is ironic that the occult and astrology have been so appealing to some elements of the college generation, for one assumes that the seats of higher learning are steeped in rational thought. If this rational thought is narrowly conceived to serve a private aestheticism it, too, fails to come to grips with the pervading problems of the times.

Addressing the plight of the lost individual in the impersonal technological society, Dewey warned that the divorce of science from moral and social concerns "diverts intelligence to anxious preoccupation with the unrealities of a purely inner life," leaving the masses to "swarm to the occult for assistance" while the cultivated smile contemptuously. "They might smile, as the saying goes, out of the other side of their mouths," continued Dewey, "if they realized how recourse to the occult exhibits the practical logic of their own beliefs. For both rest upon a separation of moral ideas and feelings from knowable facts of life, man and the world." And, in the absence of the needed integration to illumine social intelligence, added Dewey, "we shall be deprived of the aid of past experience to cope with the most acute and deep problems of life" (1922, pp. 11–13).

Dewey's concern that the failure to employ the methods of science and the tools of technology for the amelioration of social problems and general enlightenment appears to be manifest today in the widespread fascination, even among the college population, with escapism, superstition, and sensation-seeking experience through the occult, Asian mysticism, and drugs and narcotics. Catastrophe and the supernatural have become sure-fire profit-making themes for novels, television, and film. The gurus of the counterculture of the 1960s and 1970s found the college generation in the humanities most susceptible to their otherworldly message. The two cultures split between the science and humanities, so evident in the curriculum, became manifest in the college generation and in society at large (Tanner, D., 1983a, pp. 34–38).

General education is aimed at providing the integration needed to illumine social intelligence so that people can cope with the most acute and deep problems of life. To yield to unintelligent forces is to submit to superstition, blind authority, fear, and escapism. Unfortunately, general education had fallen into neglect in the secondary schools and colleges at a time when its mission was never more urgent.

Two Cultures

Dewey called attention to a widening split or inner division in American culture as a result of the narrow influence of science and its technological consequences in determining the relations that human beings sustain to one another in the absence of employing science for moral direction. Such a split in modern culture, he warned, portends the demise not only of democracy but also of all civilized values (1939, p. 154).

Twenty years later, C. P. Snow struck a tender nerve in intellectual circles in a Cambridge University lecture, "The Two Cultures," when he pointed to the widening split in Western society between two polar groups, literary intellectuals and scientists. Snow contended that the widening gulf of mutual comprehension between the two groups had resulted in a practical and intellectual loss to society. He attributed the culture divide to two conditions that had emerged in the Western world, but most acutely in England: educational specialization and the crystallized social divisions. "There is only one way out of this: it is, of course, by rethinking our education," stated Snow (1959, p. 19). After referring to the narrowness of the Oxford and Cambridge scholarship examinations in fostering knowledge specialization, Snow attacked both the narrowness of educational specialization and the restriction of education to a tiny elite as being disastrous to a society that must perform the practical tasks of the world.

Practical and Moral Concerns. "Intellectuals, in particular literary intellectuals, are natural Luddites," declared Snow as he traced the historic tendency of the academicians to hold themselves aloof from the practical and moral concerns of the industrial and scientific revolutions (1959, pp. 23–29). Even in the field of science, noted Snow, wide gaps have been created between pure and applied science.

> Pure scientists have by and large been dimwitted about engineers and applied science. . . . They wouldn't recognize that many of the problems were as intellectually exacting as pure problems, and that many of the solutions were as satisfying and beautiful. Their instinct—perhaps sharpened in this country by the passion to find a new snobbism wherever possible, and to invent one if it doesn't exist—was to take it for granted that applied science was an occupation for second-rate minds. I say this more sharply because thirty years ago I took precisely that line myself. . . . We prided ourselves that the science we were doing could not, in any conceivable circumstances, have any practical use. The more firmly one could make that claim, the more superior one felt. (1959, pp. 33–34)

Snow went on to contend that if we are to meet the cultural and practical future, we cannot begin by thinking only of the intellectual life or only of the social life, but we must break the existing pattern of separate educational cultures, the narrow specializations that produce such separation, and the narrow elitism of advanced education. And, he continued,

> Closing the gap between our cultures is a necessity in the most abstract intellectual sense, as well as in the most practical. When those two senses have grown apart, then no society is going to be able to think with wisdom. For the sake of the intellectual life . . . for the sake of the western society living precariously rich among the poor, for the sake of the poor who needn't be poor if there is intelligence in the world, it is obligatory for us and the Americans and the whole West to look at our education with fresh eyes. (pp. 53–54)

The Widening Gap. Studies seeking to list or rank America's "leading intellectuals" or to identify the "intellectual elite" are notorious for favoring literary figures and for neglecting scientists. One such study by a sociologist created the list of 70 "elite intellectuals" based upon citations in 22 selected "intellectual" journals. Not a single scientist made the list (Kadushin, 1974). A recent listing of the top 100 international public intellectuals, both living and dead, included only three scientists but not Albert Einstein or Charles Darwin (Posner, 2001). Both lists were dominated by literary figures, although the more recent listing included public figures of limited scholarly productivity, as might be expected from a list drawn from "media mentions." Obviously, in both of the studies cited, the bias was rooted in the very selection of the sources ("intellectual journals" and "media mentions"); nevertheless C. P. Snow's two-culture thesis and the neglect of science remains a continuing bias and poverty of understanding of how science as a mode of thought has been a foundation stone for social progress and democracy.

Education as Unifier. Although Snow had criticized education for leading the Western world to two cultures, he also viewed education as the key means of bringing about unification and synthesis. Addressing this problem 14 years earlier, the Harvard Report pointed to the unfortunate consequences of creating divisions between the liberal and the illiberal in terms of the humanities and the sciences. It also stressed the need to recognize that although specialism is necessary, its tendency to divide people from one another requires that education in a democracy develop the understandings that all citizens must share in common as members of a joint culture. Accordingly, the curriculum must be so developed as to represent, in the words of the Harvard Committee on General Education in a Free Society:

> a scheme of relationship between subjects which shall be similar for all students yet capable of being differently carried out for different students. Within it there must be place for both special and general education: for those subjects which divide man from man according to their particular functions and for those which unite man and man in their common humanity and citizenship. This scheme, further, should provide a continuing bond of training and outlook not only between all members of the high school but also between the great majority who stop at high school and the minority who go on to college, such that their education should not differ in kind but only in degree. (1945, pp. 32–33)

Although secondary and higher education have been vastly extended since the time of the Harvard Report, the search for curriculum unity yielded to further knowledge specialization and fragmentation through the disciplinary priorities of the 1950s and 1960s. Moreover, the demand for curriculum relevance during the 1960s and early 1970s, the back-to-basics retrenchment of the 1970s and 1980s, and the multitude of literacies and the special interests of

multiculturalism of today (as opposed to intercultural education) all fragmented the curriculum in different ways. The situation of contemporary times finds groups split apart from one another in seeking their own special-interest studies and activities. The legitimacy of special-interest education cannot be denied, but to ignore the need for curriculum coherence is to allow the curriculum to reflect the divisions that set people apart and against one another in social life.

The Problem of Curriculum Organization

At the secondary and college levels, the total curriculum may be classified according to five broad functions: (1) general education or those learnings that all educated members of a free society share, (2) exploratory education, (3) enrichment education, (4) specialized education—including college-preparatory, prevocational or preprofessional, and vocational or professional studies, and (5) special-interest education. Exploratory and enrichment education encompass formal studies typically provided through controlled electives. Special-interest studies are usually provided through free electives and also through student activities such as publications, band, orchestra, intramural and varsity athletics, student government, and clubs.

At the elementary level, the curriculum may be conceived as encompassing the function of general education and the function of exploratory and enrichment education. Although the fundamental skills are essential to general education, the traditional elementary school concentrates on these skills as though they were appropriate ends in themselves, rather than the tools for wider and richer learning. The traditional assumption has been that the child must first master the fundamental skills and facts before he or she can use these skills and facts in understanding his or her environment. The tendency in traditional educational practice is to fail to recognize that skills, concepts, and patterns of thinking are developed concomitantly as children seek to enlarge and deepen their comprehension of the environment. The consequence is that the skills and facts are not translated into the working power of general education.

Educators often are prone to distinguish general education from specialized education in terms of subject matter rather than in terms of outlook along with method of organizing and treating knowledge. Thus far in this chapter, the discussion has centered on the difference in outlook. Furthermore, there is the tendency on the part of teachers and students to regard the curriculum simply as a body of subjects and subject matter. There is an inadequate understanding of the various ways in which the subject matters can be organized and treated in the framework of the total school curriculum.

The Subject Curriculum and General Education

The arrangement of studies into subjects is the oldest approach to curriculum organization, dating back to the medieval *trivium* and *quadrivium*. The subject approach also remains the most widely accepted organization of curriculum. The durability and pervasiveness of the subject curriculum may be attributed to many factors, but perhaps most important is that it serves as a convenient institutional means of systematizing knowledge for instruction, inventorying knowledge for academic credits, annexing new knowledge in the curriculum, and accommodating the curriculum to the growing specialization of knowledge.

Operational Convenience. Administratively, the subject curriculum is operationally convenient. At the elementary level, teachers can be made to feel that they are treating the ground to be covered as they move from subject to subject in their daily and weekly class schedules. Textbooks, workbooks, and curriculum packages tend to be organized to fit the established subject categories that comprise the curriculum of the elementary and secondary schools.

At the secondary and college levels, knowledge is conveniently categorized and departmentalized according to subjects and subjects fields, and courses can be added, deleted, modified, combined, and split into myriad subspecialties without disturbing the existing curriculum framework. The courses can be scheduled easily, and credits can be allocated, inventoried, and assessed uniformly and conveniently. If pupils demand relevance in the curriculum, courses can be added without changing the existing courses. In the high school, for example, the English department can add courses in African American literature or filmmaking, or the social

studies department can add courses in African American history or sociology without changing the curriculum structure of the department or school. Subjects can be kept up to date by periodically adopting new textbooks and plugging in new course packages.

In the high school, credits are inventoried with uniform convenience through the Carnegie unit. Almost from the time that the Carnegie Foundation proposed the standard unit of measurement for high school credits (1909), the Carnegie unit was imposed on the high schools. With the endorsement of the College Entrance Examination Board, the Carnegie unit became the quantitative measure for assessing credits for college admission. (One Carnegie unit is gained with the completion of a minimum of 120 clock hours in a subject during a school year, with 16 units required for graduation.)

Although the Carnegie unit has been of great convenience to college admissions officers, it is not well suited to the diversified curriculum of a modern comprehensive high school. The Carnegie unit has been criticized for helping make the class schedule inflexible and for impeding the development of a more functional curriculum. Although an increasing number of high schools began to abandon the Carnegie unit during the early 1970s in an effort to provide for greater curriculum flexibility and to provide greater recognition for the so-called nonacademic studies, most of these schools have substituted a system of accounting for credits that could be translated quite easily into Carnegie units. In short, the subject curriculum is most conveniently suited to the Carnegie unit or any other system of quantitative accounting of high school credits. Although the Carnegie unit has been the target of criticism over the years for having imposed a mechanical inflexibility on the high school curriculum, the Carnegie unit did not create the traditional structure of curriculum organization and the inertia that preserves it. The subject curriculum and the system of amassing credits, subject by subject, toward graduation are easily understood by parents and students and can be assessed with utmost convenience for college admissions.

Systematization and Specialization of Knowledge. Whether the problem is one of accommodating new knowledge or of providing some room for courant topics, the subject curriculum is most convenient administratively. As already mentioned, the new knowledge or au courant material can be encapsulated into new courses without affecting the existing courses and the organizational structure of the curriculum. New knowledge and new ways of treating knowledge breed new specializations in the university, and these specializations can be accommodated into the subject curriculum most easily by adding specialized courses to the existing course offerings. Our larger universities typically offer courses numbering into the thousands even at the undergraduate level, whereas the larger high schools commonly offer hundreds of courses in imitation of the world of higher learning. The number of new subjects, subject matters, and courses is governed mainly by the practical limitations of the high school or university rather than by the nature of knowledge itself.

Although the so-called knowledge explosion has given rise to new disciplines and subdisciplines in the university, along with new specializations, the multiplication of subject matters and courses also has been a product of specialized scholarship independent of substantive changes in knowledge. Thus, for example, a given department of English or literature will have a faculty specialist in Elizabethan literature, or a history department will have a specialist on the Civil War, who will offer courses in the given area of specialty. As mentioned earlier, the desire and demand to make studies au courant also leads to a multiplicity of new subject matters and courses.

Specialized Knowledge and General Education. Although specialization provides for greater depth of knowledge treatment, this is accomplished at the expense of breadth. Knowledge becomes strongly compartmentalized and the faculty become isolated from one another according to their subject specialties.

The development of knowledge not only is partly a product of specialization but also breeds further specialization. In turn, there is the need for the preparation of more specialists. Although specialization finds its justification in the university and society, many pervading problems in society—the energy crisis, the growing cancer epidemic, or rising crime and social conflict—require interdisciplinary approaches to their solution.

Moreover, the design of a curriculum is necessarily different when the aim is to develop a specialist as contrasted with the aim of developing the whole person as an effective citizen in a free society. In the words of the Harvard Report:

> We are living in an age of specialism. . . . Each of these specialties makes an increasing demand on the time and interest of the student. Specialism is the means for advancement in our mobile social structure; yet we must envisage the fact that a society controlled wholly by specialists is not a wisely ordered society. We cannot, however, turn away from specialism. The problem is how to save general education and its values within a system where specialism is necessary. (1945, p. 53)

The subject curriculum lends itself readily to specialized knowledge in that it defines the boundaries of an area of knowledge, for the most part in conformance to the departmental structure of the college and faculty alliances and territorial jurisdictions. This mitigates concerted recognition of the need to develop a curriculum for general education in the college as well as in the secondary school. The reward system favoring knowledge specialization in the college exacerbates the problem. It should be remembered also that teachers in the secondary schools are largely products of college departments with affiliation to departmentalized knowledge edifices.

External Testing. The subject curriculum is an enormous convenience for the entire industry of external testing. As mentioned, the subject curriculum defines the boundaries or parameters of the requisite departments of knowledge, making it far easier to find the knowledge specialists for constructing the test items, subject by subject. It is far more complex, conceptually and operationally, to construct examinations that cross subject boundaries and that are designed to assess growth in interdisciplinary knowledge and the uses of knowledge in real life. At both the state and national levels, the external tests, subject by subject, are commonly intended to represent achievement in "core knowledge," but the idea of "core knowledge" implies knowledge integration for productive living and lifelong learning in a free society. By their nature, the separate knowledge departments tend to go their separate and specialized ways.

Modifications and Alternatives to the Core Curriculum. Throughout the twentieth century and extending to this day, significant efforts have been made in modifying and even in creating alternatives to the subject curriculum to meet the function of general education through a more articulated design at both the school and college levels. These encompass such designs as correlation, fusion, broad fields, combined fields, and other constructs including the integrated, problem-focused core curriculum. New designs for curriculum synthesis, such as the problem-focused core curriculum, required not only reconstructing the very structure and content of the curriculum, but also the employment of critical thinking and methods of inquiry for problem solving. Alternative curriculum designs, critical thinking, and problem solving are discussed in detail in the next chapter.

Perspective

A main current of American educational thought at mid-twentieth century was that through general education a unity out of diversity could be created. The expansion of studies to accommodate the growing specialization of knowledge portended a growing fragmentation in education and society. The task of general education was not conceived in opposition to the imminent force of specialization but rather as a means of providing for a common universe of discourse, understanding, and competence among the diverse elements of a free society. The notion of liberal education had come to be associated historically with education for a privileged class, whereas general education was to be the province of all citizens of a free society. Moreover, where liberal education was focused primarily on the human heritage, general education was conceived as an outlook on knowledge encompassing not only the human heritage but also the changing conditions and demands of life in a modern democratic society.

General education, then, was conceived to provide each rising generation with the social power and insight necessary for intelligently attacking the problems of a common humanity. Where specialized knowledge and life callings were separating people from one another, general education was aimed at revealing humanity's interdependence in a modern democracy. The outlook on knowledge embraced by general education required new ways of organizing the curriculum. In the face of the growing specialization and fragmentation of knowledge, this was no mean task.

The twentieth century was marked by notable efforts and accomplishments in developing a coherent core curriculum for general education in the secondary school and college to meet the unifying needs of American democracy. As the powerful engine of inclusion, as opposed to the traditions of a selective and divided system of secondary schooling, which finds limits rather than possibilities for the rising generation, the idea and practice of general education took on special significance in the American high school. Through the cosmopolitan comprehensive high school, adolescents could benefit from a diversified curriculum (Figures 10.1 and 10.2) without tracking, and it was not mandatory to pursue a traditional college preparatory curriculum to gain entrance to college. In effect, the comprehensive high school advanced open-access higher education.

The universalization of secondary education and open-access higher education had created a great and growing heterogeneity of the student populations in the high school and college. This impelled leading educators to call for and devise interdisciplinary and more integrated approaches to the design of the curriculum to meet the macrocurricular function of general education for a free society. Despite the notable accomplishments of these efforts, powerful contravening forces were at work. The forces for knowledge specialization in the university, coupled with the growing social fragmentation and divided interests in society, have countered the prospects for any movement for the renewal of general education in the secondary school and college for the twenty-first century. Further, at various times the school curriculum has been turned to nationalistic mobilization, stretching from the priorities of the Cold War and space race to the more recent priorities for upholding the nation's dominance over the global economic sphere for the twenty-first century. The more recent reform priorities have subjected the schools to a pandemic of external testing in the name of "standards" as determined for each of the academic subjects. In the face of the growing social diversity, fragmentation and conflict, the need for a coherent core curriculum for general education for a free society remains ever urgent. In the interests of the democratic prospect, it is predictable that the idea and practice of general education will regain recognition and vitality. (Refer to the Best Practices Checklist on pages 481–499.)

PROBLEMS FOR STUDY AND DISCUSSION

1. In responding to the demand for curriculum relevance during the 1960s, many secondary schools and colleges liberalized the elective options and added a host of elective courses on special contemporary topics. This approach, which remains in practice, has been called the warehouse or cafeteria model of curriculum building. Some educators have called this the junkyard model, not so much in disparagement but in reference to the fact that the learner is left to choose whatever he can find from among a diverse collection of scraps. What is your assessment of this model? Most high schools and colleges have settled on distribution requirements to ensure that students pursue a range of studies from different subject fields for purposes of general education. What limitations and problems tend to accrue to this approach?

2. Most high schools and colleges have settled on distribution requirements whereby students can elect courses within designated subject-field categories—such as science, social science, and humanities—to meet the requirements for general education. One "advantage" of distribution requirements is that faculty are relieved of the onerous responsibility of designing a coherent curriculum in general education. What limitations and disadvantages accrue to distribution requirements?

3. The mid-twentieth century was marked by an outpouring of books and journal articles on general education. It was also a period of enormous activity in curriculum building and in experimental programs for general education in the secondary school and college at an intensity not seen since the Great Depression. How do you account for the relative lack of attention and priority given to general education today?

4. Examine the student handbooks and curriculum guides of several high schools, middle schools, and junior high schools. What evidence do you find of any concerted attention being given to general education?

5. Compare the catalogues of the College of the University of Chicago with that of the University of Wisconsin-Green Bay with respect to the contrasting approaches to general education. How do these approaches compare with the general education program as offered by your own college? Which approach, if any, do you prefer? Explain.

6. From your knowledge and experience at the elementary and middle school levels, along with the related literature, what evidence can you find indicating concern and activity in building an integrated core curriculum in common learnings or general education? Would you say that most elementary-level teachers in the self-contained classroom tend to allocate time for teaching the basic subjects separately, or do they integrate these subject through comprehensive units of work and pupil projects? Explain and illustrate.

7. What is the significance of the two-cultures split in academia? What were its origins and what have been the consequences for the school, the college, and society.

8. Reflecting on the time-worn dualism between the humanities and the sciences, John Dewey held that it serves to "infect the education called liberal with illiberality" (1916, p. 228). The dualism seems to infer that what is liberal must then be useless. How does this dualism relate to the curriculum divide between academic and vocational studies, between academic studies and the practical arts, between academic studies and the studio arts, between the humanities and the sciences? What are the implications, as you see them, for the curriculum and the learner?

9. How do you account for the spectacular rise and sudden demise of the open classroom?

10. Why do so many adolescents continue to prefer their community comprehensive high school over the specialized or special-interest high school? The comprehensive high school has been criticized for its large size and consequent impersonal atmosphere. The house plan was successfully developed as a means of providing a faculty within a faculty, whereby each house faculty would be responsible for the core curriculum and guidance for an identified student population. This was devised to provide adolescents with a more intimate learning environment for general education, while also providing them with the comprehensive curricular offerings and specialized faculty and facilities that cannot be

provided in the small high school. What information can you find on the house plan? Are you able to find any schools operating with the house plan? What do you think of the house plan and its prospects for today?

11. What is the significance of the macrocurriculum? To what extent do school faculty and administrators consciously consider the macrocurricular designs and functions when undertaking curriculum revision? Explain.

CHAPTER 11

DETERMINING THE STRUCTURE OF THE CURRICULUM
DESIGN FOR SYNTHESIS

A fundamental principle in biology holds that structure determines function. In architecture, the principle is that form follows function. This principle is of no less significance for the curriculum. As discussed in chapter 9, toward the close of the nineteenth century, Lester Ward envisioned the development of a unified curriculum, common to all, emerging in the twentieth century. It will be recalled that Ward recognized that the idea for a unified core of studies required a curriculum structure very different from the traditional separate-subject curriculum, but he never ventured a proposed design.

Although the term *core* had been used sporadically at the close of the nineteenth century and early part of the twentieth century, experimentalist educators during the 1920s, and especially during the Great Depression of the 1930s, developed systematic approaches to building the curriculum in general education as a core focused on pervading social problems or trends. In effect, core came to be identified with the interdisciplinary study of social problems or themes of relevance to American democracy and required of all students. The methodology of the core curriculum embraced problem solving by means of hypothetical or critical thinking, cooperative teacher-student planning, the uses of a rich range of resource materials beyond the textbook, and engagement in a wide range of student projects.

Today, core has come to be regarded as merely the subjects required of all students. In the same vein, national and state tests for establishing measures of accountability and standards have been built on the segmental subjects that comprise the designated core studies. The testing pandemic of contemporary times has reinforced the segmental subject curriculum as the dominant structure. Nevertheless, the need for generalizable and useful knowledge remains persistent, and various modifications of the subject curriculum have emerged and continue to be employed, sometimes deliberately and sometimes intuitively, such as teachers getting together, formally or informally, to correlate literature and social studies, or science and mathematics, or science and society, and so on.

This chapter examines alternative structures of curriculum organization to meet the function of general education. For contrast, the integrated problem-focused core curriculum is discussed, coupled with the related efforts to provide for curriculum articulation by attending to the need for adequate scope, sequence, and balance; by means of the spiral curriculum; and through unit teaching and learning.

Alternative Patterns of Curriculum Organization

When educators are engaged in the revision of course content within a discipline or subject field, they are dealing with microcurricular problems. When they are designing total programs in general education or specialized education, or when they are seeking to develop interrelationships between general education and specialized education, they are concerned with macrocurricular problems. Similarly, when they are attempting to develop more effective approaches to horizontal and vertical curriculum articulation, they are concerned with a macrocurricular problem.

There are several major schemes or constructs for organizing knowledge within the subject curriculum. Subject matter may be organized in terms of (1) disciplinarity, (2) lamination, (3) correlation, (4) fusion, and (5) broad fields.

In recognition that discipline-centered approaches are artifacts of knowledge purity, abstraction, and specialism, and therefore are not suited to the function of general education, other constructs have been developed (lamination, correlation, fusion, and broad fields). Although these constructs or approaches to organizing subject matter differ significantly from one another, they nevertheless retain the essential characteristics of the subject curriculum.

The term *core* is ordinarily used by schools and colleges to denote the body of courses required of all students or the broad fields from which courses are to be selected to meet the common curricular requirements for general education, as contrasted against specialized, exploratory, enrichment, and special-interest education.

A radical departure from the subject curriculum is the core curriculum organized according to personal and social problems of a universal nature. The personal-social problems core represents curriculum synthesis to the extent that the traditional subject divisions become virtually indistinct. Consequently, the personal-social problems core is a distinct mode of curriculum organization for general education.

Core as Distribution Electives

Under this arrangement, commonly provided at the college level and to a somewhat lesser extent in the secondary school, students are allowed to meet the requirement in general education by selecting from lists of courses under such broad-fields categories as science, social science, humanities, and so on. As discussed later, this approach should not be confused with a broad-fields curriculum for general education whereby entire branches of knowledge are systematically integrated or combined into such broad fields as natural science, biological science, ecology, physical science, social science, humanities, and so on— and are required of all students.

The student election of courses as listed under broad-field categories can leave each student with a different complement of courses, mitigating the principle of providing for a truly common core of studies to meet the idea and practice of general education. In effect, under this arrangement of allowing students to select from lists of courses under broad-fields categories, the faculty is virtually absolved of responsibility for developing a coherent curriculum design to meet the function of general education.

Throughout the past decade, colleges and universities, awakened to the problem of course proliferation,

revealed a renewed interest in the idea and practice of general education. Many colleges pared down the number of elective courses through which students were allowed to meet the general education requirements. The colleges were recognizing that the students were electing courses on the basis of scheduling convenience, special interests, or special attractions other than meeting the function of general education. Where the college faculties did not proceed to design interdisciplinary courses for general education, they at least established criteria that courses had to meet in order to be designated as appropriate for the function of general education.

The problem of course proliferation and curriculum congestion is not only the result of knowledge specialism in the discipline-centered university, but also of the special interests of a divided student population. The chief problem of the school, the college, and of American society at large is not how to separate groups according to their differences, but how to develop a sense of unity through diversity. Distributive elective requirements, however formulated, cannot meet the need for a common and coherent curriculum in general education.

Core as Academic Disciplines

The disciplinary construct is the purest form of organizing knowledge in the subject curriculum. Although the disciplinary rationale and the problems connected with organizing the curriculum strictly according to disciplines are treated in detail in this chapter, a brief discussion of this approach is presented here in connection with general education.

Many educators who had opposed the traditional treatment of knowledge as being fixed or static and as something to be "mastered" by memorization and regurgitation found the thesis of "knowledge as search" vastly appealing as presented in the disciplinary rationale. Taba went so far as to liken Bruner's discovery method to Dewey's conception of learning (1962, pp. 214–215). However, it is one thing to follow the inquiry mode of a discipline, such as physics or mathematics, and quite another to employ an inquiry mode in addressing a societal problem, such as the energy crisis or multicultural conflict. Dewey's reflective thinking was focused clearly on the latter type of problem solving, which requires an integrative treatment of knowledge and its applications. Whereas the peculiar disciplinary mode that attaches to a given discipline may be indispensable to certain forms of knowledge production in the world of the university scholar-specialist, it has presented enormous difficulties for the general education of the learner. Because general education in a free society is concerned with the enlightened citizen who is capable of personal-social problem solving, and because such problem solving requires an integrative treatment of knowledge, educators have been impelled to look to constructs other than disciplinarity in organizing the various subject matters of the curriculum.

Fragmentation and Synthesis. Whereas the scholar-specialist's work is confined to one small segment of his or her discipline, the disciplinary rationale holds that the developing learner grasp the structure and mode of inquiry for each of the major disciplines. Aside from the question as to whether the developing learner can be expected to accomplish such an enormous feat, there is the question as to how specialized disciplinary scholarship can satisfy a general education function. This is a persistent problem not only in the secondary school but also in higher education.

As discussed, many high schools and colleges have abandoned their efforts to develop a coherent curriculum in general education and instead have opted for distribution requirements. Thus, for example, the college freshman who plans on becoming an economist may find himself or herself attempting to meet the distribution requirement in science by enrolling in a first course in chemistry alongside other students who plan on becoming chemists. The underlying premise for distribution requirements is that college graduates should have a broad background of knowledge. Problems arise for the learner because each first course in a given discipline is construed to prepare the student for the second course, and the second course for the third, and so on, as though every student is to become a knowledge specialist in the given discipline.

With regard to the social sciences, for example, a disciplinary advocate contended that the needed approach is to "bring the frontiers of social science knowledge into the curriculum by respecting and protecting the integrity of each discipline," and he viewed the central problem of curriculum development in these words: "How can we identify those analytical tools of the various social sciences which can then be related to the students' experience at all levels from grade one to the Ph.D.?" (Senesh, 1971, p. 126).

To this day, university scholar-specialists see the secondary school curriculum as appropriately geared to the academic disciplines, such as through the discrete social sciences (sociology, economics, anthropology, linguistics, psychology, and political science) as opposed to the more integrative social studies. That undergraduates find great dissatisfaction with introductory courses that are construed as first steps of a long sequence leading to the Ph.D. has been ignored by disciplinary advocates who have sought to impose such a formula on the child beginning with the first grade. Furthermore, advocates of the disciplinary construct have chosen to ignore the need to design the curriculum so as to illumine the interrelationships among the various domains of disciplinary knowledge. Somehow the student is expected to make his or her own synthesis and transfer—something that happens with disturbing infrequency.

Curriculum Congestion. The disciplinary rationale recognizes that the expansion of knowledge cannot be accommodated through curriculum accretion or by endlessly adding more and more subject matter to the course of study. Instead an effort is made to represent each discipline as a mode of inquiry with a focus on those key concepts and central ideas that form its so-called structure. Yet the notion of structure has been elusive, with different scholars coming up with vastly different approaches to organizing disciplinary subject matter.

Moreover, the disciplinary construct presents its own problem of curriculum congestion. When carried to its logical conclusion, such as reducing the social studies into its component disciplines and representing each component discipline in the elementary and secondary-school curriculum, the result is an impossible congestion of the curriculum. Figure 11.1 illustrates such an arrangement. Within each discipline are any number of courses. Under the disciplinary approach, each discipline is regarded as a discrete entity. But because the real world is not organized as disciplines, various transdisciplinary studies emerge to deal with the knowledge interfaces between and among the disciplines. Thus we have not merely geography, but also physical geography, economic geography, and so on. Taken in its fullest sense, geography is a broad field rather than a discipline. Anthropology not only has many interfaces with sociology, psychology, and history, but also with biology. Because of its many necessary interfaces between the social and biological sciences, efforts to find the

Figure 11.1   Disciplinarity: The Social Sciences and History.

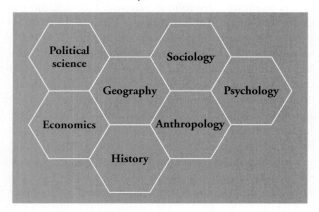

structure of a discipline of anthropology require an artificial reductionism of the field into subspecialties having fewer interconnections with the cultural world. Similar difficulties accrue to each of the so-called social-science disciplines and to history. When we speak of history, we may be dealing with political history, social history, art history, the history of science, and so on.

Disciplinarity accounts for specialized scholarship at the expense of the interrelationships of the knowledge domains and the practical applications of knowledge. Attention to such relationships and applications requires curriculum synthesis. Curriculum synthesis takes into account not only the learner, society, and the wider world of knowledge but also the problem of curricular proliferation and congestion. There is simply no time in the school day, nor, for that matter, in the college student's course schedule, to account for each and every discipline or knowledge specialty.

As Alfred North Whitehead observed, "Lack of time is the rock upon which the fairest educational schemes are wrecked. It has wrecked that scheme which our fathers constructed to meet the growing demand for the introduction of modern ideas. They simply increased the number of subjects taught" (1947, p. 176).

Other Limitations of Disciplinarity.   The learner, society, and the wider world of knowledge are important sources of consideration in curriculum development. The discipline-centered approach is focused on the structure of, and inquiry into, each

discrete discipline. The learner is regarded as a budding scholar-specialist. Disciplinary knowledge for its own sake takes precedence over the interests of the learner and the problems of society.

Proponents of the disciplinary rationale have tended to denigrate applied knowledge in favor of abstract knowledge. In so doing, they have slighted the treatment of knowledge for purposes of general education or what may be termed the sociocivic function of education in a democracy. Although the National Council for the Social Studies has long recognized the centrality of the sociocivic function in education, many social scientists have purported that their disciplines are scientific and neutral and have regarded this function as "sociocivically repulsive" (Scriven, 1964, p. 97). In short, educators who are concerned with general education and the sociocivic function of education in a democracy recognize the limitations of the disciplinary construct and the need for other constructs in addressing knowledge in terms of pervading personal-social problems, whereas most disciplinary advocates have either ignored or opposed this curriculum function (as if the social sciences were akin to pure mathematics).

Although a legitimate case may be made for the disciplinary construct in developing the future scholar-specialist, it has not been a viable curriculum construct for general education. Even in the case of the scholar-specialist, the disciplinary construct has revealed serious limitations. For example, the disciplines, when taken by themselves, are inadequate to the task of dealing with such problems as environmental pollution, population growth, food resources, public health, unemployment, housing, and so on. Interdisciplinary, problem-focused approaches are necessary even at the advanced levels of university scholarship for both knowledge production and application in society.

Core as Correlated Subjects

Correlation represents an effort to develop certain common relationships between or among two or more subjects and still retain the usual subject divisions (Figure 11.2). In other words, correlation is an attempt to counter the isolation and compartmentalization of subjects without radically reconstructing the subject curriculum. For example, the teacher of English may work together with the teacher of history or social studies by having students write compositions or read literary works that relate to historical periods or to contemporary social problems.

Figure 11.2 Correlation.

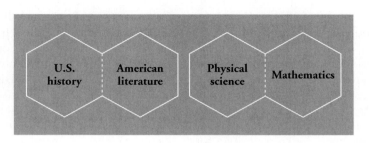

Thus, the work in literature might be organized to relate to the work in the social studies through (1) a chronological-historical approach, (2) a thematic approach, or (3) a problems approach. Following the chronological-historical approach, students in the English class might be assigned to read such material as Franklin's autobiography or selected essays of Jefferson at the same time that they are studying the American Revolutionary period in the history class. Similarly, they might read Benet's *John Brown's Body* or Crane's *Red Badge of Courage* or selected speeches of Lincoln while they are investigating the Civil War period in the history class. They might read Steinbeck's *The Grapes of Wrath* at the time that they are studying the Great Depression of the 1930s in the history class, and so on.

In an effort to overcome the limitations of the chronological-historical approach, the English teacher may organize the material thematically, that is, according to such themes as man's inhumanity to man or self-identity in a mass-technological society, paralleling the treatment of related material in the social studies class.

Or the assigned work in the English class might be focused on social problems as related to the social studies class by examining the literature of social protest, or investigating literary censorship or schoolbook censorship, and so on. Obviously, the problems approach requires a far greater amount of course revision than the chronological-historical approach, as well as considerable sophistication on the part of the teacher.

Literature also might be correlated with art and music through broad themes that have evolved historically. A less common approach is to correlate the subject matter from two fields according to genre. The composer Virgil Thomson made this recommendation some years ago:

Poetry and music are two sides of the coin of vocal expression, which includes vocal music, declaimed poetry, and all that lies between them. . . . Here a revision of the study of poetic literature as well as that of music is indicated, which would take account of the coin between the two faces. (1938, p. 310)

The correlation of physical science and mathematics also serves to bridge the subject matters of two subject fields. Correlation also may be developed between two separate subjects in the same subject field, such as geography and history. Because the subjects and subject fields retain their separate identities, correlation does not provide for true curriculum synthesis. Nevertheless, it is a significant attempt to articulate the subject matters of two or more subjects, disciplines, or subject fields. At the college level, correlated approaches often are referred to as cross-disciplinary studies. Because each discipline retains its distinguishing identity in the correlated approach, the treatment of the subject matter is not truly interdisciplinary.

Teaching Arrangements. There are many teaching arrangements in correlating subject matters. A single teacher who is responsible for two or more courses and attempts to relate these subjects to one another, such as geography and history, is seeking curriculum correlation. Or two teachers who have the same students at different times of the day may attempt to correlate subjects or subject fields without altering the class schedules.

A further step is to schedule the two classes at the same time so that the two teachers may combine their classes on occasion for team teaching. A more systematic teach-teaching arrangement is to have both teachers meet with combined classes in a block time or double period. The teachers may divide their classes occasionally or regularly according to the treatment of topics or the activities assigned the pupils. Or a single teacher, having competence in two subject fields, may be responsible for working with a single class group in a block time of two consecutive periods.

Of course, the block-time arrangement does not guarantee curriculum correlation. Block-time teaching may simply be an administrative arrangement to allow students to spend more time with a teacher with whom they can identify for counseling purposes. The block-time teacher might then be responsible for working with a single group in English and social studies, for example, along with serving as the group's homeroom teacher. The teacher may make no attempt at correlating English and social studies. The two subject fields are simply laminated in a single block of time.

Obviously, the extent of correlation attained depends on the commitment of teachers to the concept, their ability to develop common threads between subjects, and their ability to work together effectively when team-teaching arrangements are prescribed. Block-time teaching also may be designed to provide for curriculum fusion and even for curriculum synthesis.

Core as Laminated Subjects

In many instances when related studies are brought together under a broad-field subject, the subject matter is not treated as an interrelated field, but rather as composed of several self-contained units. Under such conditions, the organization and treatment of the subject matter is simply laminated. For example, a course in the industrial arts might be organized so as to cycle from woodworking to metalworking, to electronics, to graphic arts, and so on—as contrasted against a broad-fields course in which the various industrial arts are interrelated or orchestrated. In a similar fashion, the home economics course in the middle school or junior high school might cycle from foods and nutrition, to clothing and textiles, to family life, with each phase being treated as a separate unit. The old-fashioned biology course was simply a lamination of botany followed by zoology. Today, the course represents a true fusion of botany and zoology, and it may even be organized with a particular orientation, such as through a molecular, biochemical, or ecological approach.

The elementary teacher in the self-contained classroom may seek to treat the various studies as interrelated, or as discrete subjects with a specific time allocation for each in minutes in the daily schedule, such as arithmetic from 8:30 to 9:10 A.M. The block-time teacher in the middle school or junior high school might seek to integrate or correlate the social studies and literature, or might simply allocate one half of the double-period block to each, and proceed to teach the social studies and literature as separate subjects. In the latter case, the social studies and literature are simply laminated into a double-period time block. Under such circumstances, as mentioned earlier, the block-time arrangement allows the teacher to work daily with fewer students, but the mere lamination of subjects does little if anything for curriculum articulation.

Core as Fused Subjects

In contrast to correlation, which provides for the development of relationships between two or more subjects or subject fields that nevertheless remain essentially intact, fusion represents the merging of related subjects into a new subject. For example, the newer earth science courses emerged from a fusion of certain areas of physical science and geography. The combining of various history courses into the single subject of world history is another example of fusion. Fusion most commonly is undertaken within the same subject field, although it may involve the merger of subject matter from two or more fields.

Pointing to the need for new curriculum designs for general education as distinct from the traditional subject-matter constructs for specialized education, Whitehead (1929a) proposed various ways of correlating and fusing different subjects, such as correlating mathematics with geography, and fusing mathematics with social study by means of social statistics (pp. 10–18).

Although Whitehead did not propose a title for the fused studies, they might well be called statistical social analysis. Today it is not uncommon to find college courses with such titles as mathematical sociology, biostatistics, and computers in society. Notable among the many approaches to fusion at the college level is the merger of biology and physics into biophysics. This fusion has produced a synthesis and treatment of subject matter quite distinct from that which is developed in the separate subjects of biology and physics. Another example is the newly emergent field of sociobiology (Wilson, 1999).

The evolvement of fusion can be illustrated with the case of biology (see Figure 11.3). At the high school

Figure 11.3   Fusion.

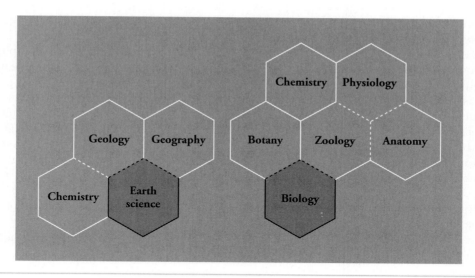

level before the turn of the twentieth century, separate courses were offered in botany, zoology, anatomy, and physiology. These courses were listed along with other sciences as illustrations of "good" secondary school programs of studies by the Committee of Ten in 1894 (National Education Association, 1894, pp. 41, 46–47). During the early decades of the twentieth century, these separate subjects were fused into the single subject of biology, and biology became a general education subject in high school. However, for many years the high school biology course represented a lamination of botany and zoology rather than a true fusion of subject matter. Today, biology is not merely a lamination or conglomeration of separate subjects but a fusion of the variegated and interactive aspects of the life sciences. In recent years the Biological Sciences Curriculum Study group has shown signs of seeking to make the BSCS course in high school biology relevant to pervading societal problems. Modern biological science comprises many disciplines and subdisciplines, so that if the variegated subject matter of biology is developed as a unified synthesis, it can be said to represent a broad-fields approach rather than simply a fusion approach.

Obviously, whatever the rubric might be, the key to curriculum fusion lies in the interrelatedness of the subject matter and its treatment. If the teacher merely treats the material as separate subject matters under the rubric of a new course title, the material is merely laminated and not fused.

Broad Fields

In the broad-fields approach, the attempt is made to develop some degree of synthesis or unity for an entire branch of knowledge. There are a great variety of designations for broad-fields subjects, such as social studies, American studies, general science, physical science, English language arts, fine arts, industrial arts, and others.

The broad-fields approach may also encompass two or more branches of knowledge. Examples are the natural science course, offered by some colleges as part of the curriculum in general education, which treats the physical and biological sciences within an interdisciplinary framework, and the humanities course in the college or high school, which is designed to reveal the interrelationships of accomplishments by civilizations throughout history in literature (drama, poetry, novel), the fine arts (music, painting, sculpture, architecture, and related arts), dance, and philosophy.

The subject of general science in the elementary school, middle school, and junior high school is also intended to be a broad-fields synthesis, although it is often treated as a sampling of laminated subject matters from different areas of science. Recognizing the limitations of disciplinary subjects, a 1970 report by the Commission on M.I.T Education called for the inclusion of general science courses in restructuring the curriculum in general education on the ground that there is a "need for subjects which cut across department boundaries to examine broad philosophical issues underlying science or engineering" (p. 23).

Although the recommendations of the 1970 report were not adopted at the time, in recent years, M.I.T. had made significant efforts toward improving the articulation of the curriculum for general education.

Many high schools will use a broad-fields designation, such as social studies, merely as a rubric for a variety of courses ranging from U.S. history to economics, but these are not broad-fields courses. As indicated, the broad-fields approach represents an effort to develop a unity among the various disciplines and subjects that constitute a branch of knowledge.

The first concerted proposal to develop the social studies and history as an articulated broad field was undertaken in 1916 by a committee of the Commission on the Reorganization of Secondary Education. The monumental report of the 1932 Commission on the Social Studies of the American Historical Association and the 1989 report of the National Commission on the Social Studies in the Schools also addressed the continuing problem of developing a coherently articulated field amidst myriad segmental academic specializations or disciplines. In the foreword of the 1989 report, the noted historian Charles Beard is quoted from one of the volumes of the report of the 1932 Commission, which opened with these words: "Such is the unity of all things that the first sentence on instruction in the social studies in the schools strikes into a seamless web too large for any human eye" (p. 1).

The separate subjects or disciplines that comprise the social studies do not reveal the seamless web, despite the fact that no social phenomenon or problem of any great significance can be confined to a single discipline. The continuing tension between knowledge specialism in the discipline-centered university and the need for knowledge synthesis to meet the function of general education in the secondary school and college remain a crucial problem to this day—a problem that has great ramifications not only for the educational institution, but also for the prospects of a free society.

Although the broad-fields approach is most commonly a synthesis of an entire branch of knowledge, it may even go so far as to synthesize two or more branches of knowledge into a new field. Ecology represents such a synthesis. As shown in Figure 11.4, ecology is a synthesis of knowledge from the biological, physical, and social sciences along with agriculture. To the extent that the study of ecology is organized according to social problems for general education, it is no longer a broad-field subject, but reaches full synthesis as a problem-focused area of the core curriculum.

Figure 11.4 The Broad Field of Ecology.

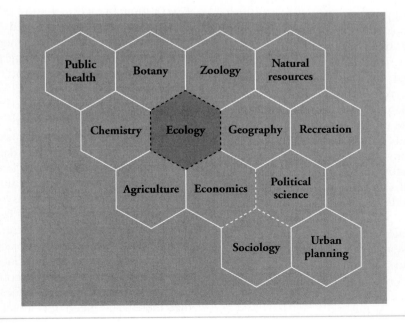

The broad fields are not a survey approach, which tends to be a sampling of disparate elements within a laminated framework. The broad-fields approach not only provides an opportunity to develop the interrelationships of subject matters that otherwise would be fragmented but also avoids the unmanageable multiplicity of disjointed courses that congest the curriculum.

Colleges, as well as elementary and secondary schools, have organized broad-fields studies in an effort to develop a measure of coherence in the curriculum, particularly for purposes of general education. A notable example is the curriculum plan for general education as evolved at the University of Chicago during the 1940s; it consisted of unified courses required of all students in the broad fields of the social sciences, humanities, and natural sciences. Instead of organizing the courses according to the constituent disciplines of a field, the approach was to develop each course as a synthesis of knowledge in the field. Thus, the social sciences were organized as a two-year sequence of Social Science 1, 2, and 3. Social Science 1 was focused on the "great issues" of American democracy; Social Science 2 was organized according to the theme of industrial society, the individual, and culture; and Social Sciences 3 dealt with the value problem of freedom and control. Each course included "great readings," which were drawn not only from classical works but also from contemporary writers. The two-year sequence of humanities consisted of Humanities 1, 2, and 3. Humanities 1 was designed to develop relationships of poetic literature, the visual arts, and music in terms of such topics as art and nature, elements and form, tradition, and contemporary trends. Humanities 2 was focused on interpretation of various modes of literary expression: history, rhetoric, drama and fiction, and philosophy. Humanities 3 included contemporary works in poetry, drama and fiction, art, and music. The natural sciences sequence was divided equally between the physical and biological sciences. Although considerable emphasis was given to the reading of original papers spanning the centuries of scientific investigation, the sequence included laboratory work. Finally, the curriculum in general education was capped by a one-year sequence called Observation, Interpretation, and Integration—designed to provide an integrating schema for the total curriculum in general education.

Although the broad-fields curriculum developed at the University of Chicago may be criticized for being too tradition-oriented in placing great emphasis on literary sources and historical treatment, the broad fields may be so organized as to focus on contemporary material, such as in the modern physical and biological sciences, or social sciences. And although the curriculum in general education at Chicago has undergone marked changes to this day, it has been described by Daniel Bell as the "most thoroughgoing experiment in general education of any college in the United States" (1968, p. 26).

Many colleges have taken a far more progressive approach to curriculum construction in general education by organizing the subject matter around contemporary problems and investigations and by providing for considerable laboratory, studio, and field experience. The Chicago plan nevertheless represents one of the most significant efforts in higher education to develop a coherent curriculum in general education through the broad-fields approach. Over the years, the Chicago plan has undergone modifications, such as building the general education curriculum on yearlong sequences in each of four broad fields—the humanities, social sciences, physical sciences, and biological sciences—with students being allowed to choose from among several variants in the sequence within each field. For example, in the social sciences the student may select a sequence based on one of three themes: Freedom and the Political Order; Self, Culture, and Society; or Liberty, Equality, and Fraternity in Contemporary America. Other variations have been implemented in recent years, but the quest for a coherent curriculum in general education continues to be the central priority at Chicago.

Combined Fields. Earlier in this chapter, block-time teaching was discussed as a means of correlating the subject matter from two subject fields such as English and social studies. However, the block-time arrangements may be designed to go beyond correlation by breaking down the subject-matter boundaries into a unified or combined-studies framework. Instead of merely juxtaposing English and social studies in the school schedule and placing these subjects under the jurisdiction of a teacher who correlates certain subject matters from the two distinctive fields, the combined-fields approach may be designed so as to provide for greater synthesis of subject matter from the two broad fields.

The project Science, Technology, and Society represents a concerted effort to combine what otherwise might be treated as separate fields. The purpose is to break down or eliminate the subject-matter boundaries to reveal the vital interconnections between science and technology and the implications for society (Tanner, D., 1990, pp. 195–197). In effect, fields that otherwise would be isolated are interrelated.

Obviously, developing a significant degree of synthesis between two broad fields requires a far greater extent of curriculum reconstitution than correlation. Because secondary school teachers tend to be prepared as specialists in a given subject or subject field, and because there is a lack of ready-made resource materials designed for a combined-fields approach, the combined-studies teacher is faced with a difficult challenge of treating the fields as an interrelated area of study. Team teaching may be helpful in this regard, but if each teacher sees himself or herself as a specialist who is responsible mainly for instruction in one of the two combined fields, the effort will be little more than correlation.

The Humanities.   After the late 1960s most of the larger secondary schools instituted variously designed courses in the humanities. This development signified a belated response to the curriculum imbalance created by the priorities of the Cold War era and was aided by the creation of the National Endowment for the Humanities as a result of the passage of the National Foundation on the Arts and the Humanities Act of 1965.

The concept of humanities presents an enormous challenge in developing curriculum synthesis among studies that encompass so many areas of human achievement and experience. However, the humanities have been so variously conceived and construed that no general patterns have emerged to represent the humanities in the secondary schools. There is wide disagreement among educators as to what the humanities signify. Some see the humanities more traditionally as "the great human achievements" as exemplified by the masterworks of literature, the arts, and philosophy through the ages (see Figure 11.5). Oddly, proponents of this view have excluded the sciences from the humanities. One only has to think about the invention of printing or the meaning of evolution to realize how profoundly humanity has been affected by science and technology. Moreover, the ranks of the great philosophers of the nineteenth and twentieth centuries are well represented by scientists, for science is a vital branch of modern philosophy.

Although the neglect of science may be traced back to the Renaissance humanists, how can twenty-first century intelligentsia exclude science from the

Figure 11.5   The Broad Field of Humanities.

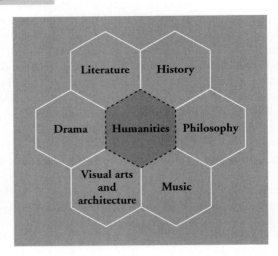

humanistic studies? Somehow they see the humanities and not the sciences as being concerned with values. The separation of the sciences from moral concerns has placed humanity in the impossible condition of living in two unrelated worlds and has kept mankind from using science in waging a full attack on the most acute and deepest problems of life.

Many who call themselves humanists have caricatured the sciences as coldly cognitive or as constituting merely a knowledge realm of empirics, whereas aesthetics are assigned to a different knowledge realm and philosophy to yet another knowledge realm (Greene, 1973, pp. 99–115; Phenix, 1964, p. 28). "A civilization cannot hold its activities apart, or put on science like a suit of clothes—a workday suit which is not good enough for Sunday," wrote Bronowski. "When we discard the test of fact in what a star is, we discard it in what a man is" (1956, pp. 55, 59). Not only do many humanists fail to recognize that scientists can find science "paralyzingly beautiful," the words used by Oppenheimer in describing Einstein's early papers (1971, p. 11), but they also deny the possibilities for the aesthetic appreciation of science by the nonscientist.

Humanists commonly separate the studio arts and performing arts from the humanities. They see the treatment of the arts in the humanities as appreciation—to develop the connoisseur—not as *doing*. This separation is reflected in the creation of separate federal endowments: the National Endowment for the Humanities and the National Endowment for the Arts. It has also led to the fragmentation of the curriculum, with the humanities acquiring an academic flavor whereas the studio arts, performing arts, and industrial arts are regarded as nonacademic frills. Harold Taylor argued the case for organizing and treating the humanities to attain total curriculum synthesis and not as another set of compartmentalized studies in the fragmented subject curriculum.

> I question the whole idea of the humanities as a special area of the curriculum designed to take care of human values which, presumably, the rest of the curriculum can then safely ignore while it goes on ladling out its generous supply of facts. The humanities are not culture-containers, or value-containers, or courses in the higher things. In one sense there is no such thing as the humanities, unless we are willing to accept the idea that science is not a humanistic discipline and that facts have nothing to do with values. . . .
>
> We may, of course, use the words arts, science, history, philosophy, sociology, and literature to describe certain bodies of knowledge which are grouped together by convention, and we can separate the arts and the humanities from the natural and social sciences simply by naming them as separate items and assembling materials under the proper subject-matter headings. But it is crucial to remember that in doing this scholars and educators are organizing knowledge in order to distribute it and that the names of the subjects do not correspond to the areas of experience out of which they were first created. . . .
>
> My proposal is, therefore, that we return to the root of the matter, in the quality and variety of experience available to the race, and that we consider education in the humanities not as a problem of developing a separate set of courses in a separate section of the curriculum, but as the creation of a spirit of inquiry and aesthetic interest throughout the whole curriculum and the entire environment of the school or college. (1968, pp. 21, 23, 25)

Unfortunately, the trend has been otherwise, and all too often the humanities courses in the secondary schools are imitative of the college courses, centering on the Great Books or serving as surveys of Western civilization, art history, and philosophy. With only a small minority of students enrolled, the humanities in the high school have not been serving a general education function. It is easier to praise the humanities than to design the curriculum so that it is permeated with the humanistic spirit of uniting humanity in the interests of a free society.

As noted, many who regard themselves as humanists portray the humanities as revealing the great human achievements, whereas science is seen as concerned merely with achievements relating to technical knowledge. One might be amused (or appalled) to find that a federally financed study to identify the nation's leading intellectuals rejected scientists from consideration on the ground that science is "value neutral" and "does not deal with meaning and significance" (Kadushin, 1974; see also Posner, 2001). The profound ignorance reflected in such reasoning is all too widely shared by those who call themselves humanists. From Galileo to Darwin to Einstein, scientific achievement has shaken humanity at its very roots. To reveal how the sciences are inescapably connected with the humanities, and how the reflective methods of scientific thinking can serve to illumine the wider social intelligence, remains one of the most profound goals of general education in a free society.

The Integrated, Problem-Focused Core Curriculum

In the preceding pages, various structural arrangements for the subject curriculum were discussed. Figure 11.6 presents a synoptic scheme of these alternative constructs for the subject curriculum as well as two other forms of curriculum organization:

Figure 11.6   Structuring the Curriculum.

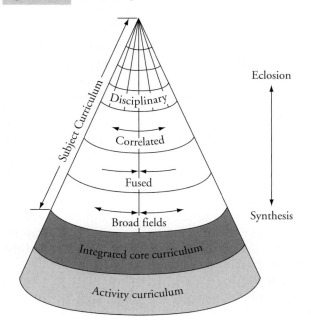

the integrated core curriculum and the activity curriculum. As shown in Figure 11.6, the separate disciplines are located at the peak of the curriculum cone and represent eclosion of knowledge in the curriculum. At the base of the cone are the integrated core curriculum and the activity curriculum, representing the synthesis of knowledge in the sense that these structural arrangements are designed to completely dissolve the traditional subject boundaries in an effort to relate the curriculum to the life of the learner. In other words, the structure of the curriculum is related to function. Thus, disciplinary knowledge serves a different function than interdisciplinary knowledge and, therefore, has a different structure for the organization and treatment of knowledge. Whereas the disciplinary structure for organized knowledge serves the function of academic specialism, the function of general education requires knowledge synthesis and application to the life of the learner as a citizen of a free society.

Distinctive Structure and Treatment. In earlier chapters some description was made of the core curriculum organized according to pervading social problems and themes, as developed in the progressive schools before mid-twentieth century. Trump and Vars viewed the integrated problem-focused core as a "quantum leap" beyond various approaches to provide for more unified studies. "Instead of correlating and fusing the separate subjects, core is based directly on problems and concerns of young people as they grow up in contemporary society" (1976, p. 223).

The problem-focused core curriculum might replace all or part of the subject curriculum in general education with the purpose of creating a universe of inquiry, discourse, and understanding among youngsters of different backgrounds and aspirations who, as citizens of a free society, are obliged to share certain common responsibilities and problems. The core is also intended to make the curriculum relevant to the learner's personal life. The core curriculum is organized according to the problems and needs of students who demand personal and social understanding and action. Consequently, the divisions of subject matter that are characteristic of the subject curriculum are dissolved, because the problems are not confined to singular disciplines, subjects, or subject fields that constitute the separate bodies of organized knowledge.

At the time of the Eight-Year Study, it was not uncommon for some schools having a problem-focused core to offer it in combination with subject-centered courses in mathematics and science as part of the general-education requirements on the ground that the problem-focused core did not always provide systematic treatment of these fields. However, this depended on the shared expertise of the core faculty team and the availability of appropriate materials. Interestingly, those schools in the Eight-Year Study that were most advanced in developing the problem-focused core curriculum in place of the subject curriculum for general education found that their graduates produced notably superior academic records in college over the graduates of the other schools in the study, as well as over the graduates who had followed the traditional academic college-preparatory curriculum (Aikin, 1942).

The problem-focused core might be of two approaches or types. In one type the core faculty preplans the problem areas and learning activities, whereas in the other type the problems and activities are developed cooperatively by the students and teacher. The first type may be referred to as the preplanned core, and the second type may be called the open core.

The Preplanned Problems Core. Under this type of core, the faculty is responsible for preplanning the content, resources, and activities that are organized around key social problem areas and issues, arranged in an articulated sequence through the various grade levels. These problem areas encompass significant personal-social concerns common to all youngsters. Although the problem areas, resource materials, and learning activities are preplanned by the core faculty, in many core programs of this type the students are provided some latitude in selecting from a number of problem areas and are encouraged to add to, modify, or even eliminate certain problem areas.

It has been noted that the core curriculum "places considerable emphasis upon the deliberate study of the moral content of the culture—especially as this content bears upon the resolution of the social issues that divide the people and thereby prevent effective social action" (Smith, Stanley, & Shores, 1957, p. 315). Problems for investigation may relate to a wide range of concerns, such as racial conflict, ecology, the energy crisis, the population explosion, world food supply and global hunger, censorship in the mass media, propaganda analysis, academic freedom, personal and public health, the aged, consumer economics, war and peace, drugs and narcotics, multicultural conflict and intercultural understanding, community planning, personal and social values, occupations, housing and slums, human rights, and many others.

Figure 11.7 is a schematic representation of how a given problem area, the energy crisis, may be conceptualized and mapped for a unit of work in which specific problems for investigation could be developed. (This particular problem area seems to reach crisis proportions periodically, only to be forgotten until the next political episode.) The core class might be organized into committees for intensive investigation of problems in a particular problem area. For example, one student committee might concentrate on public policy concerning population growth, distribution, and control. Another student committee might focus its investigations on the prospects for and problems with alternative energy sources, such as solar radiation, nuclear energy, and so on. Yet another committee may examine the energy problem in terms of its effects on the environment. Each of the various student committees may be responsible for preparing a comprehensive written report on a problem as well as engaging in related projects (such as the building of a model plan or conducting a community survey). Progress reports and tentative findings of each committee may be presented periodically to the entire class for discussion and for eliciting suggestions for further investigation. Panel presentations, demonstrations, exhibits, guest resource persons, field

Figure 11.7   Mapping a Unit on the Energy Crisis.

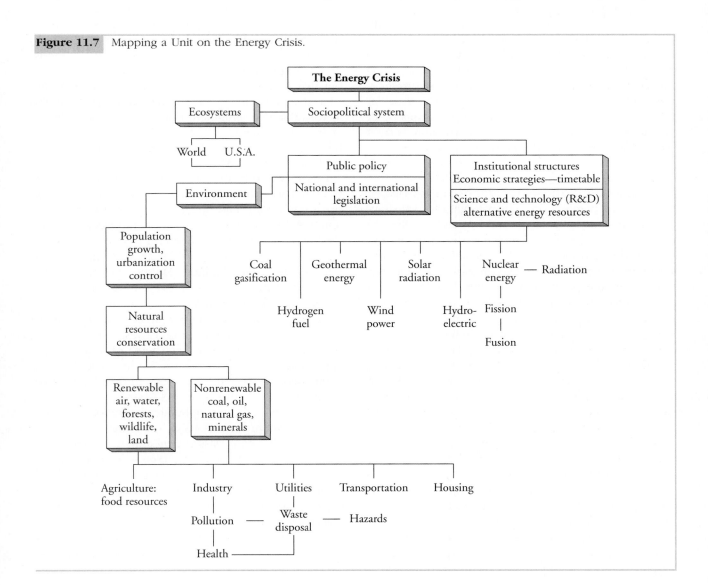

studies, and extensive library work are commonly employed.

Because no standard textbooks or prepackaged curriculum materials are available commercially, the faculty work in teams to develop resource units for each problem area. The resource unit is a comprehensive guide for the core teacher and students, including a statement of objectives and rationale; a description of the problem area and its scope, including related topics; an identification of specific problems and issues for investigation, including key concepts, skills, and generalizations; suggested learning activities and projects; a description of teaching-learning resources and materials, including bibliographical sources; and guidelines for evaluation activities.

Because the problem areas transcend the traditional subject divisions and encompass a wide range of pupil activities, extensive library resources are required and the core teacher must be able to draw on community resources. Team-teaching arrangements enable the core faculty to share their particular talents and expertise. Before this text discusses other characteristics common to the core curriculum, a brief discussion of the second type of core, the open core, is presented.

The Open Core.   The second type of core is based on teacher-pupil planned activities without a formal structure of preplanned problems and learning activities. In other words, there is no preplanned curriculum, and the students and their teacher cooperatively formulate the problem areas to be studied during the school year. This allows the pupils to have considerable freedom and responsibility for curriculum determination. Nevertheless, the typical practice is to have the youngsters assess the proposed problems in terms of a number of criteria, such as the following: Is the problem a significant one for all pupils? Are there sufficient resource materials and data available for the intelligent investigation of the problem? Is the problem one that can be treated effectively in terms of the capabilities of the pupils and the time available during the term or year? What priority should be given to this problem in relation to other problems in terms of time allocation during the school year?

Because the rationale of the open core is to make the curriculum highly relevant to the lives of the pupils, the problems are almost completely centered on the concerns of adolescents rather than on the demands of adult society. Possible gaps in content, scope, and sequence of studies are willingly sacrificed in an effort to make the curriculum relevant to pupil problems, needs, and interests. Obviously, a great deal of teacher-pupil planning is required and the teacher must be highly resourceful. The absence of a predetermined curriculum requires a very rich collection of library and other resource materials geared to pupil interests. Relatively few schools employ the open-core approach.

Common Characteristics of the Problem-Focused Core Curriculum.   Both types of core are focused on general education and, in the secondary school, the core may exist alongside specialized and special-interest and exploratory studies that are organized according to disciplines and traditional subject lines.

Because the core problems are those deemed relevant to the values and ideals of a democratic society, efforts are made to employ democratic methods and procedures in the classroom. It has been pointed out that it is a chief function of the core curriculum "that the democratic value system is not only taught as a standard of judgment but that it is also deliberately criticized and reconstructed so as to bring it into line with the social realities of today" (Smith, Stanley, & Shores, 1957, p. 315). Thus, not only are concerted efforts made to foster pupil respect for the opinions of others and to develop a commitment to the testing of one's values and ideas according to reflective thinking, but also the societal shortcomings are examined with a view toward their constructive resolution. The unifying method is that of problem solving through reflective thinking. During the progressive era, many core programs followed modified versions of Dewey's problem method in guiding students in their investigations and to foster open-minded approaches to problems and issues. Although the core curriculum has many attributes of a workshop approach, it is far more rigorous in the sense that it is committed to problem solving through reflective thinking.

In view of the general education rationale of the core curriculum and its focus on democratic values and ideals, the core class is deliberately grouped heterogeneously. Because the problems being investigated are comprehensive and deemed to be of universal significance, and because the pupils are encouraged to help one another, it is believed that a wide range of ability levels can be accommodated in the core class.

In replacing all or most of the conventional subjects in general education, the core is scheduled as a block of time encompassing at least two class periods that, in turn, are combined with the homeroom. The larger block of time enables the pupils to engage in intensive projects including community fieldwork. It also allows the core teacher to spend more time with fewer pupils. In this regard, the teacher is expected to serve in a guidance capacity. Obviously, both types of core place great emphasis on cooperative teacher-pupil planning.

Assessment of the Problem-Focused Core Curriculum. Earlier chapters discussed the success of the core curriculum found in many of the schools involved in the Eight-Year Study. Although block-time programs are commonly found in middle schools and junior high schools, only a small fraction of these programs are based on the core rationale as described in the preceding pages.

The core idea never gained the widespread acceptance that was expected of it by progressive educators. Yet the implementation of core programs in the secondary school was sufficient to justify several national surveys on the structure and practices pertaining to the core curriculum, conducted by the U.S. Office of Education from 1949 through the 1950s (Wright, 1950, 1952, 1962, 1963). In these surveys, the block-time, problem-focused core was still visible, especially in junior high schools. In a Maryland school district, for example, a problem-focused core developed for grades 7 through 12 included such problem areas as the environment, consumerism, intercultural relations, technology, living in one world, and health and safety.

One of the most widely adopted practices in the high school over many decades was to require a problems of democracy course in the senior year, required of all students. Growing out of the call for linking the curriculum to the democratic prospect, as explicated by the Commission on the Reorganization of Secondary Education in its report of 1918, the problems of democracy course was given renewed impetus by James B. Conant in his 1959 report on the American high school, issued at the height of the Cold War and space race (1959b pp. 75–76). Nevertheless, this course, taken by itself, was clearly insufficient to meet the democratizing function of general education. In the face of the great national thrust toward discipline-centered curriculum projects, giving priority to the sciences and mathematics, the problems of democracy course was unable to hold its once prominent place in the school curriculum.

The problem-focused core curriculum, indeed general education as a movement, was countered if not virtually eclipsed by the hysteria of the Cold War and space race of the 1950s and 1960s, the back-to-basics retrenchment of the 1970s and 1980s, and the multitude of literacies of the early 1990s coupled with the national education goals expressed in *America 2000* and *Goals 2000*. As in the era of the Cold War and space race, the national education goals for 2000 gave priority to the sciences and mathematics to meet nationalistic interests (this time, for technoindustrial mobilization in response to the alleged American lag in the competition for global industrial markets). Not only have recent studies provided extensive evidence that the schools have been falsely blamed for a host of alleged failures, but also that the educational priorities have been misplaced (Carson, Huelskamp, & Woodall, 1993; Tanner, D., 1993). Moreover, when nationalistic interests drive the curriculum, the consequence not only is curricular imbalance, but also the approach taken is specialized and discipline centered as opposed to an integrated curriculum for general education.

Over the years, there have been many other countervailing influences. Teachers are products of departmentalized discipline-centered curricula in the colleges and universities, and so they tend to be oriented toward the subject curriculum. Secondary-school faculties tend to imitate the colleges in their departmentalized structure. Indeed, the colleges have allowed their own curricula in general education to erode in favor of specialism and special-interest studies.

Textbooks and other curriculum materials are geared to the subject curriculum, and this serves a great convenience for teachers. Without extensive resource materials the core class is unable to attack problems in any great breadth and depth of treatment. The core curriculum requires enormous teacher resourcefulness because pupils are given great latitude and considerable responsibility in their learning activities. The core curriculum requires teachers to have considerable breadth and depth of background in general education. Team-teaching arrangements are not always provided to enable core teachers to share their special capabilities.

Another serious problem was the unrealistic expectation that teachers should develop their own curriculum materials when resources are lacking. Recent estimates by publishers indicate that instructional materials account for approximately 1.25% of the school budget. The core approach requires a far greater investment in instructional materials than does the subject curriculum. Core classes rarely have been provided with the needed resources.

The core idea was also severely undermined during the era of the Cold War and McCarthyism. The vitality of the core curriculum stems from its commitment to open-minded inquiry into pervading personal-social problems and issues. During that era, many teachers, lacking administrative and community support, were reluctant to allow their pupils to broach highly controversial sociopolitical problems and issues. Even today the censorship of instructional materials is widespread. The problem is so great that the American Library Association has established the Intellectual Freedom Committee, which publishes a bimonthly newsletter giving a dateline accounting of incidents of school censorship.

Without freedom to investigate controversial questions of personal-social significance, the core curriculum is denied its raison d'être. The failure of the piecemeal responses to student demands for curriculum relevance seems to call for a new curriculum synthesis in general education. Whether the problem-focused core curriculum will be reinvented in some new form remains to be seen.

Nevertheless, the idea of the problem-focused or thematically integrated core curriculum continues to live along with the idea and practice of general education in the secondary school and college (Means, 1992). From time to time, one finds the problem-focused core being rediscovered. As discussed in chapter 12, from the 1980s to the present, a host of reports on the secondary school and college have called for renewed attention to the idea and practice of general education. In his study of the college curriculum, Ernest Boyer, president of the Carnegie Foundation for the Advancement of Teaching, called for an integrated, life-connected core curriculum required of all undergraduates (1987, pp. 90–92). It is puzzling, however, that he made no such proposal in his study of the high school (1983).

As discussed later in this chapter, the widespread practice of developing and using units of work from the elementary level through the high school has most commonly been organized thematically, although it has also been organized according to life problems of concern to children and youth. But whatever the specific approach taken, the need for an integrated curriculum in general education remains one of the most persistent problems in American education, and it will always be of concern as long as popular education for a free society remains paramount in ideals and actions.

Persistent Life Situations.   One of the most interesting efforts in the curriculum field around mid-twentieth century was a curriculum proposal built on persistent life situations. Developed by Florence Stratemeyer and her associates at Teachers College, the proposal was based on a principle from research on learning transfer: School learning is more likely to be carried over into life outside of school if the school studies are directed at life situations. The proposal also took account of the nature of the developing learner by identifying life situations for study from early childhood through adolescence and into adulthood. Stratemeyer and her associates stressed the importance for teachers to differentiate between superficial situations and significant ones, and they proceeded to formulate lists of persistent life situations for possible study under such categories as intellectual power, health, intergroup relations, natural phenomena, technological resources, and aesthetic expression and appreciation. Nevertheless, they did not offer a preplanned curriculum design on the ground "that the intrinsic motivation provided by specific concerns of individuals and groups will, in the long run, result in a more effective selection of learnings than will any preplanned structure" (Stratemeyer, Forkner, McKim, & Passow, 1957).

One of the chief difficulties with the proposal was that persistent life situations are so numerous that one can easily lose sight of the integrative elements for curriculum design. In contrast, preplanned molar problems or themes, as in the problem-focused or thematic core curriculum, lend themselves quite naturally to curriculum integration. For example, the problem of maintaining and protecting personal and public health, under conditions of ecological assault, subsumes any number of persistent life situations. Yet the situations are addressed holistically in relation to the integrative molar problem or theme. Moreover, the problem-focused core approach was clearly more provocative, as attested by the extent to which it came under the direct assault of the censors during an era of ordeal for academic freedom.

The Activity Curriculum and the Open Classroom

The activity curriculum was discussed in some detail in part I. The activity curriculum was developed early in this century in progressive elementary schools in an attempt to treat learning as an active process that is consonant with the child's propensities to shape materials, to share experiences, to find things out, and to express himself or herself artistically. The term *experience curriculum* came to be used synonymously with the activity curriculum. Traditional subject boundaries were discarded, and the curriculum was centered largely on areas of child interest, with the skills in the fundamental processes being developed from the larger areas of activity, rather than from a separate focus on the three Rs.

The impetus for the activity curriculum grew out of the new knowledge concerning child growth and development in recognition that children require active engagement and socialization for effective learning. The curriculum of the Dewey Laboratory School, for example, was based largely on four impulses: (1) the social impulse, (2) the constructive impulse, (3) the impulse to investigate and experiment, and (4) the expressive or artistic impulse (Mayhew & Edwards, 1936, pp. 40–41). (Today, these might better be termed *developmental functions* or *activities* rather than *impulses*.) A fifth function, *physical* activity might be added (Tanner, D., 2005, pp. 36–37). The curriculum of the Dewey School was powerfully grounded in a democratic social rationale through the study of occupations revealing human interdependence and social progress. The basics were treated as fundamental processes or tool studies for the ideational and hands-on work of the children.

The activity curriculum was widely developed in progressive schools at the primary level during the first three decades of the twentieth century, but in many cases, unlike the curriculum in the Dewey School, the activity curriculum was not grounded in a deliberate social rationale. Although attention was given to the impulses or motives/potentials cited previously, the activities often were treated as ends in themselves, as though an active classroom, in and of itself, is indicative of purposeful learning.

The failure to recognize the shortcomings of such a romanticist approach found radical educators of the late 1960s and early 1970s promoting open schools and open classrooms in which children would be free to engage in learning activities based on their expressed interests, obviating the need for an organized curriculum. In an era of radical student activism and protest on college campuses, the time seemed ripe for radical-romanticist reform down to the elementary school. Alternative elementary schools were established as a foray of books on radical school reform made the best-seller lists. For example, a leading proponent of the open classroom described it as a setting to enable pupils "to make choices and pursue what interests them" and that, for the teacher, "the things that work best for him are the unplanned ones, the ones that arise spontaneously because of a student's suggestion or a sudden perception" (Kohl, 1969, pp. 20, 40). He pointed out that the open classroom is in a constant state of flux and takes its direction according to what happens to be engaging the attention of the pupils and their teachers at the moment. "It is hard to distinguish between apparent chaos and creative disorder," wrote Kohl (p. 39).

Holt, too, presented the open classroom as an environment in which pupil activities derive from their interests, and he maintained that the task of the teacher is to make the pupil feel "that whatever he is interested in is OK, a perfectly good place to look at and begin to explore the world, as good as any other, indeed better than any other" (1972, p. 91). According to Holt, curriculum planning is a kind of adult intervention on the learner and "the more we intervene in children's lives, however intelligently, kindly, or imaginatively, the less time we leave them to find and develop their own ways to meet their true needs. The more we try to teach them, the less they can teach us" (p. 66). From our curriculum history it should have been anticipated that children left to their own devices do not a curriculum make, but make chaos and disorder.

Unit Teaching and Learning

As discussed in part 1, progressive educators during the early decades of the twentieth century sought a unitary design and treatment of the curriculum by organizing studies into units of work. Today, it is common for textbooks at all levels and subjects to be organized as units; however, the use of the term *unit* for textbooks may simply be to designate chapters and chapter groupings by topics rather than to represent units of work as originally intended. In effect, the unit of work was to extend the studies beyond the textbook through the use of a wide variety of resources and activities.

Units of work were developed throughout the elementary and secondary levels by faculty members working in teams. For the core curriculum at the secondary school level, the unitary work in the more progressive schools was developed through the study of problems of youth and of society. Teaching-resource units were developed by and for the faculty who also developed learning-resource units for the students. The latter, which included all kinds of materials bearing on the unit of work, were often housed in files in the school library.

Criteria for Selecting and Developing Units of Work.   The faculty of the Lincoln School at Teachers College carefully developed criteria from actual practice to be used in selecting and developing units of work. Some of these criteria are summarized as follows:

1. The unit of work must be selected from real-life situations and must be considered worthwhile by the child because the child feels that he has helped select it and because he finds in it many opportunities to satisfy his needs.

2. The unit of work must afford many opportunities for real purposing and real projects, and it will be something the child can carry into normal activity.

3. The unit of work must stimulate many kinds of activities and so provide for individual differences.

4. The unit of work must make individual growth possible.

5. The succession of units of work must provide for continuous group growth from one level to the next.

6. Each unit of work must furnish leads into other related units of work and must stimulate in the child the desire for a continued widening of interests and understandings.

7. Each unit of work must meet the demands of society and must help clarify social meanings.

8. Each unit of work must be accompanied by progress in the use of such tool subjects as contribute to that unit (Barnes & Young, 1932, pp. 31–40).

Significantly, instead of regarding the basics as independent subjects and ends, they are treated as fundamental tools (means) or fundamental processes for developing higher-order thinking including problem-solving and knowledge applications in the

life and growth of the learner. A criterion that should be added to this listing, in view of its implicit expression in the writings of the staff of the Lincoln School, is that *sufficient time, expertise and material resources must be made available for the effective development and implementation of the unit of work.*

Taba enumerated eight systematic steps for planning a unit of work: (1) diagnosing needs, (2) formulating objectives, (3) selecting content, (4) organizing content, (5) selecting learning experiences, (6) organizing learning experiences, (7) evaluating, and (8) checking for balance and sequence (1962, pp. 347–349). The linear sequence offered by Taba may not be the most practicable and valid approach in the sense that evaluation should be continuous (formatively) as well as being conducted at the culmination of the unit (summatively). In the same vein, scope, sequence, and balance must be taken into account from the beginning to the culmination of the unit of work.

Although units of work, as developed by progressive educators, were intended to cut across subject lines and link the courses of study to practical applications and meanings in the life of the learner, they were often used merely to designate the topics to be covered within each of the traditional subjects. In other words, with insufficient understanding, recognition, and effort being given to alternative designs or patterns of curriculum organization, units of work tended to conform to the textbook for the given course or subject. In sharp contrast, let us now examine historic exemplars of authentic units of work.

Exemplar of a Problem-Focused Unit of Work. Although there has been a great proliferation of successful units of work developed over the course of a century from the elementary through the high school level, a few exemplars are presented here because of their historical significance and because they reveal how resources may be used in connection with unit planning, teaching, and learning.

One of the earliest modern and systematic uses of the unit of work or unit teaching was developed by Ellsworth Collings, a county superintendent of schools in rural Missouri (1923). Collings, a former graduate student of William Kilpatrick, referred to his work as a project curriculum, and indeed the curriculum developed under his leadership included many projects, but it should be noted that the unit of work is more encompassing than a project and typically includes a number of related projects. Collings had designated three typical one-room schools for intensive study of the efficacy of unit teaching; one school was the experimental school, and the two others were control schools. Collings began his study in 1917. The three selected schools were matched for size of enrollment, pupil age levels (from 6 to 16), standardized test scores, resources, social and economic status of families, and other variables. The chief occupation was general farming, with parents having approximately a fifth-grade education. In none of the three school districts was there a community organization of any kind. The teachers in the three schools were in their early 20s and had completed two years of study at the state university or state normal schools, although the experimental school teachers had received most of their preparation at the state university.

A remarkable aspect of the undertaking by Collings was the painstaking detail of his research, published in book length by Macmillan in 1923. The pupils were selected as matched pairs in achievement at the beginning, and four years later at the end of the experiment comparisons were made using national standardized achievement tests and other measures. The pupils and their parents were also evaluated on attitudes toward school and education, and other factors.

Before the study was undertaken, all three schools followed a traditional curriculum. Throughout the study, the control schools continued the traditional curriculum with specific time slots for basic skills, the study of history, geography, and government, and other subjects. In contrast, block-time teaching was provided in the Experimental School for projects and units of work and excursions.

Although the pupils in the Experimental School engaged in many units of work and projects, a particular unit of work is singled out here to illustrate how the unit of work may have a direct effect on community life, and how a community problem can be a source for the school curriculum. The unit selected was on community diseases. The pupils surveyed the area served by their school and found that 78% of the families reported at least one case of influenza within the previous two years. It should be noted that an outbreak of influenza A, which had begun in an army post in Kansas in 1918, resulted in one million deaths in the United States and 30 million worldwide by the time the pandemic ended in 1919 (Swenson, 1988, pp. 183–185). Of the other diseases, the pupils found that almost one fourth of the families reported at least

one case of typhoid within the previous two years. The students plotted their findings graphically for a report to be presented at a community meeting. The children decided to focus their unit of work on typhoid because it led all other diseases other than influenza and because they felt that their work on typhoid might have a more direct positive influence in the community.

The pupils obtained bulletins on the causes of typhoid from the University of Missouri Cooperative Extension Service (every land-grant university operates such a service) and other references on the disease. Their survey revealed that many families were not aware that typhoid was spread by the housefly. A house-to-house survey by the pupils revealed that many homes were lacking screens on windows and doors and that flies were swarming around manure piles, rubbish piles, and garbage cans and in weeds around the houses. The pupils prepared a report and made lantern slides for presentation at a community meeting (Wednesday at 7 P.M. on December 3, 1918). The children served refreshments at the end of the meeting. A follow-up survey by the students revealed a marked increase in the screening of homes and in the removal of sources harboring houseflies around the homes.

The outcomes of the curriculum were far in favor of the Experimental School pupils over the Control School pupils on virtually every measure connecting to the school curriculum: achievement in conventional subjects; attitudes toward school and education; phases of conduct in life outside the school (e.g., reading for pleasure at home, engaging in instrumental music and club activities; eating fruits and vegetables daily). The percentage of children stricken with a disease during the year declined for both the Experimental School and the two Control Schools, although it declined more dramatically for the Experimental School. The percentage of parents visiting the school during the year increased to 92 for the Experimental School in comparison to 10 for the Control Schools. Similarly dramatic differences favoring the Experimental School over the Control Schools were evidenced in the percentages of voters approving school improvement levies, raising teacher salaries, and building a rural high school. And whereas only 8% of the eighth-grade graduates from the Control Schools entered high school, the overwhelming majority of the graduates from the Experimental School continued on to high school.

This unit of work developed by Ellsworth Collings in a rural school reveals how children attacking a significant community problem can serve as a powerful influence for community improvement and democracy in action. Today, many high schools and colleges offer credit for ancillary community service activities, and many high school students participate to buttress their record for admission to selective colleges. But the unit of work implemented by Ellsworth Collings had ramifications throughout the school curriculum and at virtually all age levels of the students and throughout the community. The work was indeed pioneering. It is puzzling, to say the least, that it is virtually forgotten in the annals of curriculum studies.

In their problem-focused units of work, the students in the Experimental School were engaged in varying degrees according to age levels, in critical thinking for problem solving, following Dewey's problem method and what was to be identified systematically, a half-century later, as the problem-solving aspects of critical thinking:

1. Ability to recognize the existence of a problem

2. Ability to define the problem

3. Ability to select information pertinent to the selection of the problem

4. Ability to recognize assumptions bearing on the problem

5. Ability to make relevant hypotheses

6. Ability to draw conclusions validly from assumptions hypotheses, and pertinent information

7. Ability to judge the validity of the processes leading to the conclusion

8. Ability to evaluate a conclusion in terms of its application (Dressel & Mayhew, 1954, pp. 177–178).

What is so significant about the contributions of Ellsworth Collings is that the units of work connected problem solving or the method of intelligence from the school and into community education and action. In the truest sense of the term, this was a community school.

Exemplar of a Thematic Unit of Work.   A highly developed and successful unit of work was Children and Architecture, developed for the sixth grade at the Lincoln School of Teachers College at Columbia University and implemented in 1930. The purpose was not directed at the study of architecture as a specialized

field, but to investigate the human side of architecture, its relationship to everyday life, and as an expression of civilizations. In developing and implementing the unit, the teacher obtained the cooperation of the Metropolitan Museum of Art and other museums, art studios, and other agencies in New York City. Also enlisted in the effort was the school library staff and faculty in the fine and industrial arts and theater. The class made many excursions not only to museums and landmark buildings, but also to sites under construction. They evaluated schools of architecture not only historically, but also in relation to aesthetic and functional design in connection with the contemporary urban environment. In the industrial arts, they made blueprints and designed models of buildings, constructed models of bridge structures and tested them for stress, and made plaster casts of historical building ornaments. The unit provided extensive opportunities for photography, essay writing, poetry, and student engagement in many individual and group projects. Achievement gains on pre- and poststandardized tests in the traditional subjects far exceeded expected gains. The unit on architecture was developed in such detail that it was published book length under the authorship of the 6th-grade teacher and a research assistant (Barnes & Young, l932). Obviously, such a unit could well be developed for students in the middle school, junior high school, or senior high school. Although the unit on architecture at the Lincoln School was developed thematically ("Architecture as a Continuous Evaluation"), it provided numerous opportunities for inquiry into problems and controversies (Barnes & Young, Preface).

Material Resources for Units of Work: The Building America Series.   Unit teaching ordinarily requires considerable work on the part of the teacher in selecting and organizing resource materials beyond the textbook. Because textbooks often are out of date, it is necessary nevertheless for teachers to use contemporary source materials and subject matter beyond the textbook reflecting the teacher's professional judgment and knowledgeability. A nearly forgotten project of historic significance designed to provide teachers and students at the junior and senior high school levels with curricular materials focused on pervasive social problems was conceived and developed during the depths of the Great Depression. The project was proposed in 1933 and initiated in 1935 by the Society for Curriculum Study, which later merged with the Association for Supervision and Curriculum Development. The project, known as *Building America*, was under the editorship of Paul R. Hanna of Stanford University. The editorial board was composed mostly of founding members of the John Dewey Society, including Hanna, who were leaders in the curriculum field. The series, published mostly by Americana, was designed as oversized pictorial paperbacks issued monthly with annual hardback editions extending from 1935 to 1948. Each issue was focused on a particular social problem or theme incorporating several related problems, typically organized around questions for investigation and discussion, and included a detailed bibliography. Although the approach was to study pervading contemporary problems, the historical background was treated in detail with documentary analysis. In effect, each issue could be used by teachers and students as teaching-learning units. The photography was remarkable and might best be described as neorealistic, a form that was to emerge after World War II in European cinema. The issues typically included appropriate historical drawings, editorial cartoons, charts, and graphs.

From 1935 through 1948, 91 issues of *Building America* were published with such titles as *Civil Liberties, Women, Advertising, Health, Food, Our Constitution, Our Water Resources, Our Land Resources, Russia, We Consumers, War or Peace, Crime, Social Security, Youth Faces the World, Community Planning, Libraries, Art and the American Craftsman, Electronics, American Democracy in Wartime, Veterans,* and *Planning for the Postwar World*. The titles of the issues do not do justice to the dynamic and candid treatment of the controversial issues, the academic integrity of the series, and its respect for the intelligence of the student. The issue on *Power* investigated the Tennessee Valley Authority, Boulder Dam, and other projects at a time when most of rural America was without electricity. Issues of the *Building America* series gave extensive treatment to such events as the Scopes trial, on the teaching of evolution, and the barring of a concert performance by Marian Anderson in Constitution Hall in Washington, DC, by the Daughters of the American Revolution because of her race, and how the concert was held outdoors in front of the Lincoln Memorial.

The wave of Cold War hysteria following World War II gave rise to censorship of curricular materials and raised suspicions of any serious treatment of controversial problems and issues in the schools. The *Building America* series had been spectacularly popular, with paperback sales averaging over a million copies a month and with thousands of copies of the annual hardback editions. The series also became widely popular for adult education. However, despite the endorsement of the *Building America* series by national and state education agencies, including the California State Board of Education and the California Curriculum Commission, the series became a target for attack by the conservative press, ultra-right-wing groups, and the California Joint Legislative Committee on Un-American Activities. Sales of the series plummeted, and in 1948 the last issue of *Building America* was published. Looking at *Building America* today, one finds that it encompassed virtually every major social movement spanning the twentieth century and extending to contemporary times—from civil rights to women in society, from war and peace to ecology, from totalitarianism to democracy, from public health to consumerism, from community planning to crime, and so on. *Building America* is invaluable as a primary source for understanding the wave of school censorship in the early years of the Cold War (Tanner, D., 2002; Newman, 1960).

The Unit of Work: A Continuing Endeavor. Significantly, some authors of curriculum resources, including texts, whether by intention or otherwise will follow a unit approach without identifying it as such. Two outstanding examples will illustrate. *Civics for Democracy: A Journey for Teachers and Students* (Isaac, 1992), developed for the Center for Study of Responsive Law, is organized around the major social movements through the twentieth century to contemporary times. It is action oriented in identifying possible projects to be undertaken by students, and it is richly documented as a combined text and sourcebook.

Another exemplar is *The Nature of Recreation* (Wurman, Levy, & Katz, 1972), developed for the American Federation of Arts and the Group for Environmental Education. Although many units of work used today cover such problem areas as ecology, multiculturalism, the Holocaust, consumerism, and so on, *The Nature of Recreation* is discussed here because of the unique presentation in handbook format through which students extending over an extraordinarily wide range of age and grade levels, from the upper elementary through the high school, could engage in the systematic investigation of common problems and needs with a view toward prescribing solutions. The handbook was developed in honor of Frederick Law Olmsted, a pioneer in landscape architecture whose works ranged from the design of Central Park in

New York City to his proposal for the creation of a national park in the Yosemite Valley in California.

The handbook begins by engaging each student in taking checklist inventories of almost 100 recreational activities on "What did you do last year?" and "What would you like to have done?" The responses of the class could then be compared with the results of a national survey presented in the handbook. The students proceed with working on sections of the handbook on recreational needs and performance criteria: inactive/active, individual/group, young/old, specific/nonspecific, small/large, linear/nonlinear, flat/sloped, time and weather/climate, preservation and construction, and so on. Photographs and drawings are richly provided along with data to be used as each student diagnoses problems and formulates possible solutions. Checklists and time/distance maps are provided for students to locate the availability of their recreational resources and to prescribe the resources needed. Each student selects one resource for intensive analysis of conditions and possibilities, and proposes a program. The handbook includes an extended bibliography on recreation, the man-made environment, and leisure. It should be noted that the worthy use of leisure time has been a universal problem of contemporary living. Anyone opposed to the study of recreation on grounds that it is frivolous and not an "academic" subject should contrast the time children and adolescents (and adults) spend watching television against reading a book for recreation. Then there is the biological-social need for recreation as recreation.

Toward an Articulated Curriculum

The development of the problem-focused core and thematic core curriculum was a signal advancement for curriculum renewal and articulation and for connecting the school curriculum to the life of the learner and to the wider society in serving the democratic prospect. As discussed, the development of teaching-learning units of work has been a hallmark of efforts to develop an articulated curriculum. Yet in a fully articulated curriculum, the units of work must fit together with all other curricular approaches so as to provide for comprehensive and harmonious scope, sequence, and balance. Further, the curriculum must provide for connections between and among the various studies (horizontal articulation) and connections

from grade level to grade level in what Dewey envisioned as the spiral curriculum.

The Spiral Curriculum

In *Experience and Education* (1938), Dewey pointed to the need to reorganize the curriculum so that it is consciously and progressively articulated and so that the learning experiences are continually expanded and deepened in intellectually related ways. Regarding the learner, connectedness in growth must be the watchword, for knowledge is not a fixed possession. It is the responsibility of educators to so design the curriculum that new ideas growing out of present experience become the ground for wider and richer experiences and new problems that engage the learner in an active quest for new ideas. "The process is a continual spiral," wrote Dewey (p. 97). The concept of the spiral curriculum is embodied in Dewey's definition of education and in the definition of curriculum offered by the authors of this text: "that reconstruction of knowledge and experience which enables the learner to grow in exercising intelligent control of subsequent knowledge and experience" (see chapter 5).

In developing meaning from experience, children seek conceptual connections holistically (synthesis). The child readily grasps the concept of "tree." One does not start with photosynthesis. But the meaning of "tree" grows as long as one is engaged in learning. It has no end. Unfortunately, much organized subject matter is sequenced from part to whole rather than from whole to part and back to whole at a continually richer, deeper, and wider level.

Jerome Bruner is generally credited with the concept of the spiral curriculum. In *The Process of Education* (1960), Harvard psychologist Bruner promoted the idea of the spiral curriculum without having cited Dewey. Bruner's conception of the spiral curriculum almost immediately became a slogan among curricularists. However, there was a failure to recognize that Dewey's spiral curriculum takes its starting point from the learner's experience and reveals the interrelatedness of all areas of knowledge that comprise the school curriculum. In sharp contrast, Bruner's spiral curriculum takes its starting point from each separate discipline as conceived by the scholar-specialists on the forefront of that discipline. "We might ask, as a criterion for any subject taught in primary school, whether, when fully developed, it is worth an adult's knowing, and whether having known it as a child makes the person a better adult," wrote Bruner (p. 52).

From the Deweyan perspective, the statement might read, "We might ask, as a criterion for any subject whether it is worth a child's knowing, and whether having known it as a child makes the child a better person."

Bruner's conception of the child as miniature adult scholar-specialist was advanced in the entirely unfounded dictum, "The schoolboy learning physics *is* a physicist, and it is easier for him to learn physics behaving like a physicist than doing something else" (p. 14). Under the Brunerian dictum, the schoolboy was to be a miniature scholar-specialist in each and every discipline.

This notion raised further complications aside from the distorted conception of the nature of the learner. In advancing his conception of the spiral curriculum, Bruner held that the curriculum for each discipline or subject "should be determined by the most fundamental understanding that can be achieved of the underlying principles that give structure to that subject" (p. 31). In effect, each discipline or subject is to be treated as an articulated domain of specialized knowledge production, virtually independent of the other disciplines or subjects in the school curriculum, because "different disciplines have widely different conceptual schemes" (Schwab, 1962, p. 197). Under such a doctrine, the disciplines are directed at the function of specialized education to the neglect of the macrocurricular function of general education. No concerted attention is to be given to horizontal curriculum articulation (interdisciplinary knowledge and the interrelationships between and among the various subjects that comprise the school curriculum). Focused exclusively on each discipline unto itself, puristic and abstract knowledge is promoted to the neglect of practical knowledge applications in the life of the learner and in the life of the wider society. Such was the case with the national discipline-centered reforms of the era of the Cold War and space race that gave the schools the "new math," "new physics," and so on. That the billion-dollar effort failed should have been no surprise, considering that it violated the curriculum paradigm in distorting the nature of the learner, in turning the curriculum to meet narrow nationalistic interests, in neglecting the cosmopolitan democratic interest, and in neglecting applied knowledge (chapter 6). What should be surprising is how readily educators, including curricularists, jumped on the discipline-centered bandwagon with only a few dissenting voices (Tanner, D., 1971; Kline, 1973). It should be remembered that the Cold

War and space race had created an atmosphere of near hysteria. Bruner's *Process of Education* was the report of a federally funded conference to develop a school-reform rationale to meet the alleged crisis of national security. The puristic, discipline-centered knowledge specialists of the university readily filled the void when grant monies became available through the prestigious National Science Foundation. The spiral curriculum as conceived by Bruner found each discipline spiraling in separate realms and in different directions, creating a new fragmentation of the curriculum.

Scope, Sequence, and Balance: Vertical and Horizontal Articulation

The Deweyan concept of the spiral curriculum relates not only to the vertical integration or deepening of knowledge but also to the horizontal integration or widening of knowledge. When educators seek to improve the coherence of studies within a given discipline or subject field, they are attending to the vertical articulation or sequence of the curriculum. When they seek to develop the interrelationships between and among different disciplines or subject fields, they are concerned with the horizontal articulation along with the balance and scope of the curriculum.

Thus, when educators attempt to improve the coherence between 9th-grade general science and 10th-grade biology, 10th-grade biology and 11th-grade chemistry, and 11th-grade chemistry and 12th-grade physics, they are concerned with vertical curriculum articulation. In contrast, when they attempt to develop interrelationships between 7th-grade general science and 7th-grade mathematics, or between English and social studies at a given grade level, they are concerned with horizontal curriculum articulation. In a similar vein, the 9th-grade science teacher may work with the 9th-grade social studies teacher toward developing horizontal curriculum articulation by relating the two subjects in terms of the social implications of science. In developing vertical or horizontal curriculum articulation, the different subject fields or disciplines may retain their own autonomy as separate subjects, or the separate subject lines may become less distinct or even made to disappear. Curriculum synthesis is attained to the extent to which the subject lines are no longer distinguishable.

Because teachers are products of discipline-centered universities, and because the textbooks and course packages reflect the university scholar-specialist's view of his or her knowledge domain, they tend to ignore the need for curriculum articulation and synthesis not only on the horizontal plane but also on the vertical plane. Consequently, the scope of each course of study tends to be confined to a segment of the discipline or subject field of which it is a part. The sequence of courses within a discipline or subject field tends to be organized in linear fashion regardless of whether the sequence is psychologically sound. In fact, the sequence may be arranged more for administrative convenience or tradition than to follow the logic of the subject matter. As an example, modern biology requires the use of chemistry, but chemistry almost always follows biology in the high school curriculum. English literature may (arbitrarily) precede American literature, with both subjects being organized chronologically.

The isolation of teachers according to departments and subject specialties also works against curriculum articulation and synthesis. The mathematics teacher in the ninth grade may rarely, if ever, find occasion to work with the science teacher at the same grade level and at other grade levels for purposes of curriculum articulation. Departmental allegiances and lines are such that curriculum development in the high school and college is confined to individual departments that represent the disciplines and subject fields as though they were autonomous domains of knowledge. The task of curriculum integration is left to the learner, who somehow is expected to transfer his or her learnings from one knowledge domain to another. Meanwhile, teachers continually complain that pupils do not transfer their learnings between the various subjects of the school curriculum. Yet the teachers themselves rarely give concerted attention to the problem of curriculum fragmentation and isolation that works against learning transfer.

Although the concept of balance is readily understood, more often than not the curriculum suffers from imbalance. Shifting curriculum priorities by reaction and counterreaction in successive periods of educational reform have contributed to this problem. Historically, such dualisms favoring the academic studies over the practical, the cultural over the useful, and the study of the past over the present have worked against a balanced curriculum. At the same time, we have witnessed shifts in national priorities, such as favoring the sciences and mathematics to meet nationalistic "crises" ranging from the Cold War and space race to the contemporary challenge

in competition for global industrial markets. Or, during times of social and economic retrenchment, there is the call for curriculum reductionism—back to basics and the corresponding neglect of a full, rich, and balanced curriculum for all children and youth. A balanced curriculum might be likened to balanced nutrition. Both are necessary for optimum growth and development: physically, intellectually, socially, or emotionally.

Figure 11.8 is a diagrammatic representation of scope, sequence, and balance in the curriculum. The horizontal plane represents the extent of articulation among the various studies offered at a given grade or age level. The vertical plane represents the extent of sequential articulation within a given field of study over time. The scope of the curriculum may be seen as encompassing both the vertical and horizontal planes. The balance of the curriculum may be seen as the extent to which the various offerings of studies taken together are sufficiently diversified, yet interrelated, complete, and equally honored.

Balance refers to the extent to which the curriculum is in harmonious proportion. Scope refers to the full sweep, area, or range of the curriculum. Sequence refers to the continuity of the curriculum. In effect, efforts to improve the balance, scope, and sequence of the school or college curriculum are directed at bringing the studies into harmonious proportion, fullest range, and systematic continuity.

Figure 11.8   Curriculum Articulation: Toward an Articulated Curriculum.

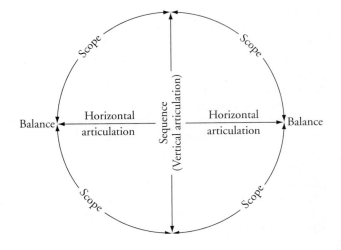

Prospects

Despite the curricular conservatism of the proposals for school reform in the closing of the twentieth century and opening years of the twenty-first century, the indications were clear that the need for a coherent curriculum in general education in the school and college was gaining recognition once again. Not since the progressive education efforts during the first half of the twentieth century had such attention been given to writing across the curriculum, critical thinking, and comprehensive evaluation of student achievement through the uses of student portfolios, projects, and community service activities. However, on closer examination there were indications that many of these contemporary efforts—writing across the curriculum, for example, and higher-order thinking—were being developed and inserted as segmental programs rather than serving as unifying processes for the macrocurricular function of general education. Nevertheless, there were clear signs that at long last the scientific community was becoming increasingly aware of the limitations of the discipline-centered curriculum and was embarking on programs to point the way toward breaking down the traditional subject boundaries and revealing the interconnections among the sciences, mathematics, and technology and the wider social implications.

Reconstructing the Curriculum

In looking to education for the new century, renewed efforts toward curriculum synthesis were occurring in the sciences. Significantly, the thrust was not for knowledge specialism but for a knowledgeable citizenry. The National Science Teachers Association had embarked on a federally funded program, "Scope, Sequence, and Coordination of Secondary School Science" and produced *The Core Content, A Guide for Curriculum Designers* (1992).

Perhaps the most systematic and comprehensive program in this direction was undertaken under the auspices of the American Association for the Advancement of Science, known as Project 2061. The underlying rationale rejected the notion that more and more subject matter was required. Instead, the curriculum must be reconstructed "to reduce the sheer amount of material covered; to weaken or eliminate rigid subject-matter boundaries; to pay more attention to the connections among science, mathematics, and technology; to present the scientific endeavor as a social enterprise that strongly influences—and is influenced by—human

thought and action" (1989, p. 5). It was stressed that such efforts should encompass all grades and all studies in the curriculum. The approach taken should build on the curiosity and creativity of students. Instead of starting with emphasis on answers to be learned, the teaching-learning process should start with questions about interesting phenomena. Students should become actively engaged in investigation and knowledge application. Project 2061 has embarked on developing alternative curriculum models with the goal of wide use based on the success of these models.

Unfortunately, the concept of scientific literacy, rather than general education, was chosen as the conceptual goal of Project 2061; unfortunate simply because of the great proliferation of literacies and the curriculum fragmentation resulting from each special-interest group seeking to promote its own literacy in the school curriculum. Although most of the panels for Project 2061 (biological and health sciences, physical and informational sciences and engineering, mathematics, and technology) developed rationales consistent with the overarching goals of Project 2061, the panel on social and behavior sciences reflected a disciplinary bias with a focus on abstract concepts rather than life problems and knowledge applications for democratic citizenship. It was clear that any concerted effort to reconstruct the curriculum for general education requires university scholars to put aside their microscopic lenses of specialism and look more ecologically at the curriculum.

The inescapable need for a sense of coherence and synthesis in the curriculum is reflected in Figure 11.9. At first glance it seems that the subjects in the curriculum are related in a kind of symmetry. However, such symmetry begins to take shape only when the subjects are interrelated as broad fields (e.g., natural science, humanities, language arts and communications, and social studies and history) or when they are correlated and fused into more functional combinations. As discussed in chapter 10 and illustrated in Figure 11.9, full synthesis derives when the knowledge categories become subsumed through the study of life problems.

High schools commonly offer hundreds of courses, but the mandates for a core of traditional academic subjects to meet graduation and college-entrance requirements limit student options for exploratory, enrichment, and special-interest studies beyond college preparatory studies. Often, the core requirements may be met through electives from within the traditional academic subject categories. The problem is

Figure 11.9 Curriculum Eclosion and Synthesis.

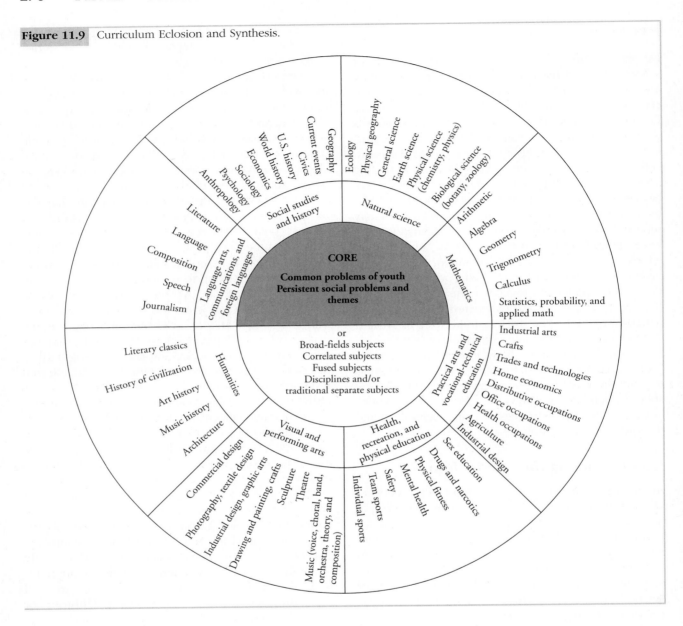

how to meet the need for a diversified curriculum while providing for a core curriculum for a common universe of discourse, understanding, and competence in the secondary school and college.

Whether the problem-focused core curriculum will be reinvented as proposed by some leading educators (Boyer, 1987) remains to be seen, but it is clear that no subject—whether in literature, science, history or social studies—could neglect the pervading problems of society as long as the democratic prospect is viable.

Perspective

Notable efforts have been made in school and college to devise new curriculum structures to provide for a greater measure of relationship and synthesis among areas of knowledge. The traditional subject curriculum was reorganized in terms of (1) disciplinarity, (2) correlation, (3) fusion, and (4) broad fields. Although the disciplinary approach rejected the traditional conception of subject matter as something given or fixed, it nevertheless conceived of knowledge as belonging to and developing from the specialized domains of university scholarship. This specialized outlook on knowledge is not well suited to the task of general education.

Other modes of organizing knowledge (correlation, fusion, and broad fields) have been designed to build greater relationships among the organized studies within the framework of the subject curriculum. But the subject curriculum, nevertheless, calls for a logical organization of studies with limited relevance to the life problems and life experience of the learner. In response to this need, progressive educators sought a new curriculum synthesis. The result was the integrated problem-focused core curriculum as an alternative to the traditional subject curriculum. In the integrated problem-focused core approach, subject-matter boundaries were largely dissolved as the curriculum was organized according to pervading problems of personal and social significance. Unlike the disciplinary approach, which treated each knowledge domain as following a distinct mode of inquiry, the problem-focused core approach was based on the premise that inquiry into pervading problems of personal-social significance requires not only a unity of knowledge but also a unified mode of inquiry or method of intelligence shared by all enlightened citizens of a free society. Experimentalist educators saw not only the need for a more unified structure for the curriculum, but also the method of intelligence as the unifying method for general education. The growing specialization of knowledge, the increasing fragmentation of society, the inertia of education tradition, the dearth of appropriate curriculum materials, and the opposition to the treatment of controversial problems, all prevented this core idea from gaining general acceptance.

Various time periods have witnessed rising demands to relate the curriculum to significant societal problems. Efforts have been made in the secondary school and university to provide for interdisciplinary and problem-focused studies. However, the main thrust of these efforts has been to meet the special interests of diverse groups of students by providing for a greater variety of elective options. Instead of seeking a curriculum synthesis for purposes of general education, the response has been to make ad hoc modifications of the curriculum in accordance with special demands. Nevertheless, the regenerated interest in interdisciplinary studies indicated that the need for curriculum coherence and synthesis cannot be ignored in the long run. At the secondary and college levels, efforts have been made to provide academic credit for a variety of community experiences. Nevertheless, these efforts have lacked a corresponding attempt to develop curriculum coherence and to foster the democratic ideal through general education. Buffeted and eroded by the centripetal and diverse forces of specialism and special interests, general education seems all but forgotten in educational theory and practice.

The great democratizing vision through general education cannot be denied, although the years of crisis mentality have taken their toll. Some of the efforts toward educational improvement reflected a revitalized concern for this larger vision of American education, particularly at the college level. However, the schools have been mired in a proliferation of separate literacies: mathematical, scientific, technological, cultural, political, economic, artistic, and so on. The various professional associations have been directing their efforts at promoting curriculum reform within their own literacy domains. However, unlike the discipline-centered curriculum reforms that were geared to knowledge specialization, purity, and abstraction, the literacies were directed at the kinds of knowledge-competencies deemed fundamental to all who complete a high school education. Whereas the idea and practice of general education conveyed a search and commitment for curriculum unity in an age of specialism, the term *literacy* conveyed a kind of elemental level of competence in a multitude of separate categories of the curriculum. The separation or disjunctures appear to fit the prevailing external testing pandemic of the curriculum, subject by subject.

The need for building the curriculum holistically by giving systematic attention to scope, sequence, and balance is greater than ever at a time when the forces of specialism and divided interests are so prevalent.

The problem of a divided curriculum and a divided society does not augur well for American democracy. In order to draw strength from diversity, a shared democratic vision and mission are necessary, and this must be reflected in the structure and function of the curriculum.

At times, educators may avoid questions concerning the function of education in helping create the good person leading the good life in the good society, but in the long run these questions cannot be denied. The great divisions and conflicts in modern society have impelled educators once again to seek ways of making the curriculum relevant to life problems. In the crowning decade of the twentieth century and with the opening of the new century, the idea and practice of general education were being rediscovered in colleges and universities. Notable efforts were being made to develop a sense of unity and coherence in the curriculum. In sharp contrast, curriculum change at the elementary and secondary levels appeared to be dominated by the traditional subject divisions and competency testing. Judging by the wider course of events, however, the idea and practice of general education of all levels could not be permanently, denied.

PROBLEMS FOR STUDY AND DISCUSSION

1. In view of the following statement by Dewey, written in 1902, what measures do you recommend for building the needed "harmony" in the curriculum?

   > The problem of the multiplication of studies and the consequent congestion of the curriculum, and the conflict of various studies for a recognized place in the curriculum; the fact that one cannot get in without crowding something else out; the effort to arrange a compromise in various courses of study by throwing the entire burden of election upon the student so that he shall make his own course of study—this problem is only a reflex of the lack of unity in social activities themselves, and the necessity of reaching more harmony in our scheme of life. . . .
   >
   > The body of knowledge is indeed one; it is a spiritual organism. To attempt to chop off a member here and amputate an organ there is the veriest impossibility. The problem is not one of elimination, but of organization; of simplification not through denial and rejection, but through harmony. [John Dewey, *The Educational Situation* (Chicago: University of Chicago Press, 1902a), pp. 85–86, 89.]

2. What is the significance of the spiral curriculum? How does Bruner's version differ from Dewey's conception?

3. Compare some high school student handbooks in terms of the core course requirements for graduation. To what extent do the requirements specify subject categories under which students may elect courses to meet the core requirements for graduation (distribution requirements)? Can you find evidence of efforts to develop a coherent core curriculum?

   Examine the undergraduate catalog of the college you are attending with a view toward seeking answers to the above question. What are your findings and opinions relative to the issues raised in this chapter?

4. How do you account for persistent rediscovery of the idea and practice of general education in the secondary school and college throughout the twentieth century? What forces have worked against curriculum synthesis for general education in the secondary school and college? Why is it that distribution-elective course requirements inevitably fail to meet the function of general education as a common universe of discourse, understanding, and competence required for effective living in a free society?

5. There is a biological principle that structure determines function, and an architectural principle that form follows function. How does this relate to the structure and function of the curriculum?

6. Is the separation between the humanities and sciences justified? What have been the consequences of such separation?

7. To what extent have you been required to formulate hypotheses in your college courses? Give examples by listing some of the hypotheses for the various courses.

8. What do you think of the proposal for the school mathematics curriculum made by the great mathematician Alfred North Whitehead? If implemented, what implications would the proposal have for curriculum articulation horizontally (across subjects)?

9. Why have the traditional academic disciplines been inadequate to the task of general education?

10. What contemporary societal problems would be appropriate for a problem-focused core curriculum? What would be the prospects for implementing such a curriculum today?

CHAPTER 12

PROPOSALS FOR REFORM
CURRICULAR PRIORITIES AND POLARITIES

If one can imagine a miracle and suppose that all adult thoughtful Russians overnight deserted the standard of Marx and rallied to the ideas of Lincoln, shall we say, there would still be the task of re-educating all the children and youth between five and twenty-five in a new philosophy.

So wrote James Conant at mid-twentieth century in *Education in a Divided World,* subtitled *The Function of the Public Schools in Our Unique Society* (1949, p. 22). Nobody, not even the experts in international affairs, imagined that if and when the collapse of the Soviet Union and Marxism were to occur, it would do so without warning. Yet in May 1988 Soviet Premier Mikhail Gorbachev ordered the cancellation of the final secondary school history examinations on the ground that a more candid and accurate interpretation of Soviet and world history was needed. Gorbachev also ordered the rewriting of history textbooks to reflect the new openness (*glasnost*) in Soviet society (*New York Times*, May 31, 1988, pp. A2, 14). This action should have been seen as momentous, a harbinger of events of world-shaking proportions. Apparently, Gorbachev knew that any social transformation toward democracy could not succeed without transforming the school curriculum. However, the political and economic crisis leading to the Soviet coup of 1990 portended that the struggle for democracy would be long and arduous in a nation that had no democratic tradition.

If democratic social ends are to be realized, democratic educational means must be effected. This was Conant's point when he wrote at mid-twentieth century concerning the inextricable linkage between the public schools as expressions of democratic ideals and democracy as a system of government and social life. Hence, a free society requires freedom of inquiry, the lessening of social distinction between occupational groups, and the increasing extension of educational opportunity for the youth of each successive generation.

Looking back, one realizes that virtually the entire second half of the twentieth century was devoted to the Cold War and its impact on the school curriculum. This was succeeded by demands on the public schools for techno-industrial mobilization and the call to advance the nation's hegemony in global affairs for the twenty-first century.

Nevertheless, the twentieth century was marked by signal accomplishments in advancing educational opportunity by means of a unitary and comprehensive school structure, the advancement of the idea and practice of general education to meet the democratic prospect, and the provision for a diversified curriculum to meet the needs of a cosmopolitan student population.

Conant believed that the concrete expression of our democratic ideals resides in our system of public education and through the comprehensive high school, in which there is a vital flow between general education and vocational education (1949, pp. 5–6, 64, 70, 151).

In reviewing the national reports on educational reform over the course of the twentieth century and to the present day, it seems clear that the extent and intensity of the forays criticizing American public education in these reports and in the popular press have no parallel in any other nation. These kinds of national reports have continued into the twenty-first century in that they reflect our polyglot society, conflict of cultures, special interests at the expense of the wider social interest, political opportunism, and shifting nationalistic priorities. With all the cacophony, if one were to find harmony it would be in the abiding belief in education on the part of the American people. In examining the various sources of criticism, however, one is likely to overlook the source identified by Conant in the social elitism of "intellectual circles." As far as the intelligentsia are concerned, Conant commented, he was not one to disparage the values inherent in a life dedicated to study and aestheticism. "But," continued Conant, "the inadequacy of outlook of the average intellectual when face to face with the realities of the United States is nowhere more tragically reflected than in certain recent books and articles about education" (p. 50).

The forays of misguided and perverse attacks being leveled against American public education from intellectual circles and the mass media at mid-twentieth century reached ever higher levels of crescendo at every perceived political crisis during the second half of the twentieth century. The situation became so extreme that even Robert M. Hutchins, a leading perennialist, devoted an extended essay to the defense of America's public schools. In describing the antischool campaign as having reached a stage of "overkill," Hutchins pointed out that "nobody has a kind word for the institution that was the other day the foundation of our freedom" (1972, p. 155). The situation described by Hutchins has plagued American public schools to this day.

Any significant proposal for educational improvement or reform must have significant bearings on the curriculum. The focus of this chapter is on the major national educational reports, proposals, and programs since the opening of the twentieth century, and their consequences for the curriculum. In this connection, the tension between the forces for knowledge specialism and those for knowledge synthesis are examined from the perspective of the idea and function of general education in a free society.

Proposals for General Education: The Democratic Vision and the Practical Need

For a pyramidal society putting a severe strain on obedience, the safest and best education is one that wears away the energy of youth in mental gymnastics, directs the glance toward the past, cultivates the memory rather than the reason, gives polish rather than power, encourages acquiescence rather than inquiry, and teaches to versify rather than to think.

These were the words of the American sociologist Edward A. Ross in 1901 (p. 17). Ross held that whereas the concept of social efficiency in the old pyramidal society found only a privileged class enjoying the fullest measure of social and educational advantage, social efficiency in a democracy required that the pyramid be inverted so as to release the intelligence of the ordinary citizen by extending educational opportunity to all. The old function of external control would have to give way to a secular civic and moral education, prophesied Ross, and this would require a new structure and function of the curriculum. "Just what shape this new education will take, no one can say," continued Ross, "but it will not be merely one more branch of study like ethics or civics" (p. 177).

Although Ross did not have a name for "this new education," it was to find its expression in the twentieth century in the idea and practice of general education. The challenge of general education lay not only in creating a unified curriculum design for a common learning in a diverse society, but also in creating a design in an age of knowledge specialism, social conflict, and divided interests.

Democracy's High School

No document of the twentieth century was more influential in shaping the structure and function of the American educational system than the report of the NEA Commission on the Reorganization of Secondary Education, *Cardinal Principles of Secondary Education* (1918). No document has been such a durable target of attack over so many decades by both the conservative right and radical left.

The *Cardinal Principles* report laid the framework and rationale for a unitary school structure through the comprehensive (cosmopolitan) high school at a time when American industrialists had been seeking a divided school system along the lines of European systems. The report promoted coeducation and universal secondary education (to age 18) at a time when only one third of the children entering first grade continued on to the ninth grade. The report prophetically envisioned the community college movement and advocated open-access higher education through the junior college, and it held that "higher institutions of learning are not justified in maintaining entrance requirements and examinations of a character that handicaps the secondary school in discharging its proper functions in a democracy." Again, in the words of the report, "The conception that higher education should be limited to the few is destined to disappear in the interests of democracy" (pp. 19–20).

The *Cardinal Principles* report gave recognition to adolescence as a stage of rapid social development. "The physical, intellectual, emotional, and ethical characteristics of young people are still but vaguely comprehended," noted the report, and it advocated the serious study of social and educational needs of youth in teacher education (p. 32). As discussed later, national reports on education reform issued decades later and even in contemporary times were to regard adolescence as virtually a pathological stage in human development. A 1993 article in the *New York Times* was titled "Adolescence Isn't a Terminal Disease" (Dec. 21, p. C12).

Embracing Dewey's concept of social efficiency in a democracy (1916, pp. 138, 141, 144–145), in sharp contrast to social efficiency in undemocratic societies, the *Cardinal Principles* report called for the fullest release of human potential through the widest extension of educational opportunity. Hence, the individual not only would develop the knowledge, interests, and ideals to find a productive role in society, but also would "use that place to shape both himself and society toward ever nobler ends" (p. 9).

Unification and Specialization.   The curriculum of the comprehensive or cosmopolitan high school would meet both the specializing and unifying functions of education—specialization for productive vocations and unification for effective democratic citizenship. At the same time, the specialization function would be flexible to allow ready transfer among the curricular programs. The unification function would be provided through the curriculum *constants* (the common or universal studies) along with the joint association in school life of students who had widely different social backgrounds and widely different educational and vocational goals. The specialization function would be provided through curriculum *variables* (elective programs) to meet vocational or special educational goals and also to cultivate individual or personal and avocational interests (worthy use of leisure).

In effect, the report was advocating a no-track high school with diversified studies of elective programs (variables) and a common core (constants) to meet the sociocivic aim of general education. In pointing to the necessary connection between vocation and democratic citizenship, the report stressed that "this commission enters its protest against any and all plans, however well intended, which are in danger of divorcing vocation and socio-civic education" (p. 16).

As Conant was to discover, the ideas in the *Cardinal Principles* report, along with those of Alexander Inglis in *Principles of Secondary Education* (1918) and the writings of John Dewey, fit the new problems of the times "as a key fits a lock" (Conant, 1959, p. 93). Inglis had been a key member of the commission that wrote the *Cardinal Principles* report, and his text was published in the same year that the report was issued by the U.S. Bureau of Education. (Revisionist and other educational historians have failed to recognize the influence of Inglis and often refer to the *Cardinal Principles* report as "Mr. Kingsley's Report," (Kliebard, 1986, p. 112) after Clarence Kingsley, a Brooklyn mathematics teacher who had been elected chairman of the commission but who left little in his own writings that would connect him in style and substance with the report.)

Departmentalized Subjects and Curriculum Isolation.   Both Inglis and the *Cardinal Principles* report addressed the problem of curriculum isolation as a result of the subject-centered curriculum and departmentalization, a problem that remains to this day. As Inglis pointed out,

> In the past the materials of high-school subjects of study have been organized and taught according to the demands of the studies as logically organized fields of knowledge. In the reorganization of secondary education problems of subject organization and teaching methods must be approached from a different point of attack. . . . In some cases the entire organization of materials and methods must be changed. (p. 712)

Inglis proposed that the studies be organized and treated to be in accord with the nature of the learner in order to develop the working power of intelligence to meet the demands of life.

In the same vein, the *Cardinal Principles* report noted,

> If the only basis upon which a high school is organized is that of the subjects of study, each department being devoted to some particular subject, there will result an over-valuation of the importance of subjects as such, and the tendency will be for each teacher to regard his function as merely that of leading the pupils to master a particular subject, rather than that of using the subjects of study and the activities of the school as means for achieving the objectives of education. (p. 27)

Ironically, the notion of subject-matter mastery and mastery learning were to be revived in recent years when unprecedented efforts were being given to standardized achievement testing under the production model of schooling. In contrast, the *Cardinal Principles* report rejected the notion of mastery of the basics, or the mastery of a subject, but conceived of education not in the measurement of endpoints but measures of growth. Hence, the basics were described as fundamental processes or as tools for learning.

Global and Intercultural Education. Much of what was written in the *Cardinal Principles* report remains remarkably current. The task of curriculum synthesis to meet the function of general education remains a challenge to the middle and secondary school, and to the college as well. At a time of heightened social divisions in society, alternative schools are being established to separate groups according to special interests. The concept of unity through diversity has been eroded under the pressures of divided interests. The educational and social significance of the comprehensive objectives of the report are no less vital today than when they were formulated (health, command of the fundamental processes, worthy home membership, vocation, democratic citizenship, worthy use of leisure, and ethical character).

The vision of the report might best be summed up in the mission it held for the comprehensive high school as "the prototype of a democracy in which various groups must have a degree of self-consciousness as groups and yet be federated into a larger whole through the recognition of common interests and ideals" (p. 26). Perhaps no description of contemporary America more appropriately portrays the present scene than as presented in the *Cardinal Principles* report:

> In America, racial stocks are widely diversified, various forms of social heredity come into conflict, differing religious beliefs do not always make for unification, and the members of different vocations often fail to recognize the interests that they have in common with others. The school is the one agency that may be controlled definitely and consciously by democracy for the purpose of unifying its people. (p. 22)
>
> As a people we should . . . deal more sympathetically and intelligently with the immigrant coming to our shores, and have a basis for a wiser and more sympathetic approach to international problems. . . .

This means a study of specific nations, their achievements and possibilities, not ignoring their limitations. Such a study of dissimilar contributions in the light of the ideal of human brotherhood should help establish a genuine internationalism, free from sentimentality, founded on fact, and actually operative in the affairs of nations. (pp. 14–15)

In his study of general education in the high school, published in 1957, Will French noted that the comprehensive purposes and functions of secondary education had reached almost universal acceptance among professional and lay groups in determining what the curriculum should be (p. 22). At mid-twentieth century, Butts and Cremin assessed the gains made as a result of the influence of the *Cardinal Principles* report and concluded that "no retreat was possible or desirable" (1953, p. 505).

Countervailing Influences. The era of the Cold War and space race, followed by the thrust for U.S. global political and economic hegemony through the turn of the twenty-first century, coupled with the alternative school movement, brought an unprecedented assault against the comprehensive high school. Academicians on both the conservative right and radical left were joined in a strange alliance in attacking the comprehensive high school and in advocating a one-track academic high school. Indeed, this was the high school of the nineteenth century. The academic left would not recognize that the comprehensive high school as envisioned in the *Cardinal Principles* report is a no-track high school with diversified studies centered on a common core. Those on the academic right resented the egalitarianism of the report. "The report is breathless with the idealism of the Progressive era," wrote Richard Hofstadter, "with the hope of making the world safe for democracy and bringing a full measure of opportunity to every child" (1970, p. 336). In the same vein, Oakes wrote of the comprehensive high school and of the language of the *Cardinal Principles* report in disparagement. "Before long this new kind of education had become thoroughly cloaked in the jargon of democracy," wrote Oakes (1985, p. 34). The idealism of the *Cardinal Principles* might be a target for ridicule, but it is difficult to dismiss it when one considers that the security and well-being of the peoples of the world hinge on the extent to which the world is safe for democracy, and the foundations of American democracy rest on "bringing a full measure of opportunity to every child."

Dismissing the democratizing accomplishments of progressive education over the course of the past century, Diane Ravitch, an assistant secretary of Education in the Reagan administration under William Bennett, echoed Hofstadter in portraying almost any departure from the traditional academic curriculum by progressivists as the mark of anti-intellectualism (2000, p. 16). Ravitch simply ignored the great historic struggle of progressive educators to defend and promote academic freedom to advance critical thinking and the method of intelligence in the curriculum and to support the extension of educational opportunity for all children and youth. These efforts and achievements are not artifacts of history, but remain current to this day. In the foreword to his book on the divisive effects of multiculturalism and in his argument for an intercultural society, Arthur Schlesinger, Jr., states:

> Our public schools in particular have been the primary instrument of forming an American identity. . . . What students are taught in schools affects the way they will thereafter see and treat other Americans, the way they will thereafter conceive the purpose of the republic. The debate about the curriculum is a debate about what it means to be an American. (1998, pp. 21–22)

ALL American Children and *ALL* American Youth

Despite World War II, which had put school improvement and the extension of educational opportunity on hold for the duration, visionary educators recognized that the end of the war and the midcentury period of postwar reconstruction would signal a turning point of momentous proportions for American education. Throughout the Great Depression the Educational Policies Commission (EPC) of the National Education Association had promoted the needs of children and youth in connection with the social and educational agenda of Franklin D. Roosevelt's New Deal, from the school hot-lunch program and preschool programs to youth education for productive employment. Now, looking past World War II, the Educational Policies Commission undertook the task of creating a document that would describe in some detail how the democratic vision of educational opportunity might be implemented. In a unique format, the commission told the story of how the schools of the mythical community of Farmville and the mythical

community of American City were organized and functioning in the mythical state of Columbia. The purpose was not to provide a blueprint or to fantasize a Utopian scheme, but to illustrate how democratic policies and principles might be carried out through the application of the best professional practices in building "the kinds of schools which America needs and must have" (1944, p. vi).

The two key documents embodying these proposals were *Education for ALL American Children*, issued in 1948, and *Education for ALL American Youth,* published in 1944 and revised eight years later under the subtitle *A Further Look.*

Both documents focused on the democratizing function of the school and the curriculum, as evidenced by this statement concerning the elementary curriculum:

> Let the elementary school curriculum derive its goals from the domains and values of the social scene. Let its methods conform to the demands and values of human growth and development. The good elementary school is not concerned exclusively either with the nature of society or with the nature of childhood. The good elementary school is developmental, with a social criterion, concerning democratic values. (p. vi)

The curriculum was to be designed in terms of children's needs and democratic values rather than through mechanical subject designations. Many of the curriculum illustrations presented in *Education for ALL American Children* were built on the concept of the integrated curriculum or integrated day. The concept of community school was emphasized and was seen as the means of linking the school and community to the ideals of democratic living. *Education for ALL American Children* was received with relatively little debate, possibly because its formulations reflected ideas and practices widely accepted for elementary education in that era.

Early Childhood Education. The proposal of the Educational Policies Commission that the elementary school encompass the nursery school years was far-reaching at a time when only a minority of school districts were providing kindergarten. In fact the Educational Policies Commission as far back as 1938 had advocated that a primary or junior school—combining the nursery school (children at 2 and a half to 3 years of age), kindergarten, and first two elementary grades—be made an important unit of the public school system without segregating children in separate buildings. Such a design, stressed the commission, would be in accord with the modern findings of child development, as well as meeting a vital social need (1938, p. 6).

It was not until President Lyndon Johnson's War on Poverty during the latter 1960s that a national effort was made for preschool education. However, this effort, known as Head Start, was directed at children in poverty and thereby isolated these children within the program. Moreover, being administered separately from the public school system, the Head Start teachers were typically lacking in professional qualifications and there was a lack of coordination with the elementary school, with the consequence that the expected longer-term effects in cognitive and social development were disappointing (McDill, McDill, & Sprehe, 1969, pp. 19–23). Looking back, it is clear that the proposal of the Educational Policies Commission for integrating the nursery school years into the public elementary school was far reaching not only for its day, but also to this day.

The Secondary School Core Curriculum. The EPC's report, *Education for ALL American Youth*, was a comprehensive proposal for reconstructing the curriculum of the secondary school in directions markedly different from existing practice. Instead of a prescribed list of separate courses to cover each of the areas of general education, the report proposed a core curriculum or common-learnings program that was designed to provide for the fullest integration of learning experiences. The design for common learnings closely paralleled the integrated core curriculum developed by the more experimental schools of the Eight-Year Study. In the setting of the comprehensive secondary school, the heterogeneously grouped class in common learnings was conceived to provide for the study of broad problems that all members of a free society share in common. Conventional subject boundaries would be dissolved in an effort to develop the necessary interrelationships of knowledge in addressing such problems.

The common-learnings sequence was to extend from grades 7 through 14 (including the 2 years of junior college) in a continuous daily block of time. The curriculum in common learnings was to be preplanned by the faculty, and the entire curriculum would be made relevant to the "imperative needs of youth," which included democratic citizenship, health, family and societal living, consumer economics, scientific understandings, aesthetics, leisure,

vocational proficiency, and ethical values. Learning activities were intended to help youth develop in their (1) ability to think rationally and to respect truth arrived at by rational processes, (2) respect for others and ability to work cooperatively, (3) insight into ethical values and principles, (4) ability to use their time wisely, and (5) ability to plan their own affairs, as individuals and groups, and to carry out their plans efficiently.

Figure 12.1 shows the relationship of the common learnings to the other areas of the curriculum. As proposed by the commission, pupils in grades seven through nine devote half of the school day to common learnings (constants), one third to personal interests or exploratory learnings (variables), and the remaining one sixth to health and physical education. In grade 10 the students begin to pursue some specialized learnings, including vocational and college-preparatory work, and the common learnings constitute half of their program of studies. In grades 11 and 12 the common learnings constitute one third of the school day, and the specialized studies are expanded to match the amount of time devoted to common learnings. In grades 10 through 12, one sixth of the school day is devoted to individual-interest studies. Students are not tracked according to specialized programs. These programs are highly flexible and are related to the common learnings. The time allocated to health and physical education remains constant throughout all grades. The study of personal health is correlated with the treatment of community-health problems in common learnings. The common-learnings faculty is responsible for pupil guidance among other duties; however, specialized guidance services also are provided.

Beyond the integrated core of common learnings, students would have access to diversified programs in vocational education, advanced academic studies, and electives for exploratory, enrichment, and special-interest needs. As advocated in the *Cardinal Principles* report, there would be no tracking in the comprehensive secondary school. The lines between and among the specialized programs would be fluid and the classes in common learnings would be grouped heterogeneously. Interestingly, the advanced academic studies or college preparatory curriculum are categorized under vocational preparation in the sense that they meet the specialization function of the curriculum and in recognition that college-bound students are concerned with career goals and the selection of their major field in college.

Figure 12.1 The Curriculum in American City.

Periods per day	GRADES							
	Early Seconday School			High School			Community College	
	7	8	9	10	11	12	13	14
1	**Personal Interests** (Exploration of personal abilities and individual interests, discovery of interests in art, music, science, languages, sports, crafts, home and family problems, and leisure activities.)			**Individual Interests** (Elected by the student, under guidance, in fields of avocational, cultural, or intellectual interest.)				
2				**Vocational Preparation** (Includes education for industrial, commercial, home-making, service, and other occupations leading to employment, apprenticeship, or homemaking at the end of Grade XII, XIII, or XIV; education for technical and semiprofessional occupations in community college; and the study of sciences, mathematics, social studies, literature, and foreign language in preparation for advanced study in community college, four year college, or university. May include a period of productive work under employment conditions, supervised by the school staff. Related to the study of economics and industrial and labor relations in "Common Learnings.")				
3				**Science** (Methods, principles, and facts needed by all students.)				
4	**Common Learnings** (A continuous course for all, planned to help students grow in competence as citizens of the community and the nation; in understanding of economic processes and of their roles as producers and consumers; in living together in family, school, and community; in appreciation of literature and the arts; and in use of the English language. Guidance of individual students is a chief responsibility of "Common Learnings" teachers.)							
5								
6	**Health and Physical Education** (Includes instruction in personal health and hygiene; health examinations and follow-up; games, sports, and other activities to promote physical fitness. Related to study of community health in "Common Learnings.")							

Heavy line marks the division between "differential studies" (above) and "common studies" (below).

Sources: Educational Policies Commission, *Education for ALL American Youth—A Further Look* (Washington, DC: National Education Association, 1952), p.233; *Planning for American Youth,* rev. ed. (Washington, DC: National Education Association, 1951), p. 48.

Nevertheless, it might be equally useful to conceive of these studies as outgrowths of general education.

Unitary Structure and Comprehensive Functions. The report of the Educational Policies Commission envisioned a unified school structure encompassing nursery school through grade 14 or the community college. In effect, vocational preparation would be provided through the upper grades of the high school and extending into the community college.

Not until the early 1990s were formal provisions developed for coordinating the junior and senior year of the high school with the two years of the community college in a two-plus-two program of vocational-technical education. The concept of the two-plus-two program was received by school leaders with great expectations, but it was never funded with the change of administrations at the federal level.

Clearly, the commission's proposal was decades ahead of its times with regard to the structure and function of the educational system and the structure and function of the curriculum.

Indeed, the commission's proposal for the comprehensive secondary school reaffirmed and reformulated the educational objectives in the 1918 *Cardinal Principles* report in terms of "the ten imperative needs of youth":

1. To develop salable skills for intelligent and productive participation in economic life

2. To develop and maintain good health and physical fitness

3. To understand the rights and duties of democratic citizenship

4. To understand the significance of and conditions conducive to successful family life

5. To know how to purchase and use goods and services intelligently

6. To understand the methods of science and its influence on human life

7. To develop appreciation of beauty in literature, art, music, and nature

8. To use leisure time wisely

9. To develop respect for others, to grow in ethical values and principles, and to live and work cooperatively with others

10. To develop the ability to think rationally, to develop their thoughts clearly, and to read and listen with understanding (pp. 225–226)

Among the noted members of the commission, when the revised edition of *Education for ALL American Youth* was issued, were James Conant, chairman; Dwight D. Eisenhower, who at the time was president of Columbia University; and Arthur H. Compton, Nobel laureate in physics. (Compton had set up the secret project at the University of Chicago during World War II in which the first controlled nuclear chain reaction was made, leading to the development of the atom bomb.) Despite its illustrious membership, the commission was no match for the conservative assault that was to be launched against *Education for ALL American Youth* in the wake of the Cold War and space race.

The Conservative Assault. Although *Education for ALL American Youth* was widely read and discussed by educators, the Cold War climate coupled with tax conservatism prevented the report from having the impact on school reform that was expected of it by progressive educators. Indeed, the report became the target of attack for supporting the comprehensive high school, for its proposed comprehensive goals and functions of the curriculum, and for its rationale for curriculum articulation and synthesis for common learnings or general education.

In testifying at congressional national defense and education hearings in 1962, Admiral Hyman Rickover called *Education for ALL American Youth* "one of the most influential studies of the function of the high school," and he proceeded to attack it for endorsing the comprehensive high school, for promoting "this strange conglomerate" of common learnings that is to be studied by all pupils together, and for proposing a curriculum that is "not concerned with academic studies" (1963, pp. 161–162).

In criticizing the notion of curriculum synthesis through common learnings, Arthur Bestor contended that "the stage of integration or synthesis arrives—for the mature man and for the student alike—after, but only after, he has marshaled the array of separate intellectual powers that he knows are required." Accordingly, proposed Bestor, "the fundamental secondary school program should consist of continuous and systematic work in the five great areas of mathematics, science, history, English, and foreign languages, and a sound minimum roster of courses for the secondary school would consist of at least five years of graded work in each of these fields" (1956, pp. 60, 326). He called for the elimination of social studies in favor of five years of history, the homogeneous grouping of students at all grade levels according to measures on standardized achievement tests, and the disallowance of credits for nonacademic electives. If an integrated course is offered at all, it should come at the senior year and be limited to those youngsters who do not continue their formal education beyond high school, whereas college-bound students should wait until the college years for integrated studies, advised Bestor.

The Harvard Report on General Education

Looking to the shape of education for the years beyond midcentury, the Harvard Committee on General Education in a Free Society viewed general education as the means of building unity from diversity. "The root idea of general education is as a balance and counterpoise to the forces which divide group from group within the high school and the high school from the college," states the report. And, although recognizing the need for curriculum diversity in the high school, the Harvard Report also called for a principle of curriculum unity through an interdependence of studies in general education on the ground that it is through such studies that "the civilizing work of preparing for American life takes place" (1945, p. 14).

Seeking to reconcile the conflicting differences between modern and traditional educational ideologies, the Harvard Report made a number of curriculum proposals that were generally constructive though hardly extraordinary. The major recommendations for the secondary school are summarized as follows:

1. At least half of the student's program should be devoted to general education; although all students need not pursue exactly the same courses, their general education should embrace common aims and ideals.

2. The general education program should be distributed throughout the entire four years of high school.

3. The minimum of eight units of general education should consist of three units of English, three units of science and mathematics, and two units of social studies.

4. Students planning to attend college should pursue further studies in one or more of the preceding areas in high school whereas, for the others, additional work in general education may be pursued

in art, music, English, American life, and general science.

5. Noncollege-bound students should be able to devote approximately one third of their studies to specialized education, including vocational and business education. Such specialized studies should not be wholly vocational in intent but should bear a relationship and spirit similar to studies in general education, as does further work in mathematics or languages for those preparing for college.

Although the Harvard Report acknowledged that the fine arts serve an important function in general education by enhancing the cultural heritage, developing aesthetic appreciations, and providing opportunities for performance experiences, it did not call for required courses in this area. In a similar vein, the report cited the importance of shop work in the general education of all students, including the college bound, but left this as an elective subject. Physical education was included as an important area of general education, whereas health education was regarded as a legitimate responsibility of the school in those areas where the family and community do not meet such needs. Regarding student activities, the report appropriately viewed these as an extension of classroom activities and not as an entity apart from the educational program.

Although the Harvard Report noted that the organization of the curriculum into rigid autonomous units results in students being unable to transfer their learnings from subject to subject, it nevertheless opted for a subject curriculum and called on teachers to develop the needed interrelationships among areas of knowledge. Schools might well experiment with a variety of approaches to general education, within a framework of common ideals and purposes, noted the report.

Search for Unity.   The report was widely read and discussed by college educators, but it gave little cause for stir among secondary school educators because its recommendations for the secondary school were well within the realm of existing educational practice. In calling for greater interdependence between general education and specialized education, the Harvard Committee noted that it had sought to present

a scheme which accepts the claims of a common culture, citizenship, and standard of human good, yet also the competing claims of diverse interests, gifts, and hopes. Certainly some such scheme cannot be absent from American education if it is to produce at one and the same time sound people and a sound society. (p. 102)

Yet in the era of discipline-centered curriculum reforms, which was to follow a decade later, the need for such a scheme was forgotten. Whatever criticisms may be leveled at the Harvard Report for its eclectic orientation, it supported the comprehensive high school and envisioned the curriculum in general education as building the common bonds among the diverse interests of a polyglot society. It also recognized the need for making the formal studies more concretely applicable to the life of the learner. "We have stressed the importance of the trait of relevance, and we have urged that, while in school, the pupil should be helped to see beyond conceptual frameworks and make concrete applications," declared the report (p. 176).

The continued growing fragmentation and conflict in society today finds educators giving little attention to the unification possibilities of general education. How to create a spirit of unity through the great diversity of American society and the great differences in individual interests, talents, and aspirations finds educators suffering a widespread ignorance, according to the Harvard Report. In the words of the Harvard Report in addressing what it called "the question of the nation and age":

It is, *how can general education be so adapted to different ages and, above all, differing abilities and outlooks, that it can appeal deeply to each, yet remain in goal and essential teaching the same for all?* The answer to this question, it seems not too much to say, is the key to anything like complete democracy. (emphasis in the original, p. 93)

Unfortunately, in our age of divided and conflicting cultural interests and knowledge specializations, educators have given relatively little attention to curriculum unification. Nevertheless, from the time of its issuance to this day, whenever there has been a resurgent interest in general education in higher education, the Harvard Report is dusted off and reexamined for its eloquent testimony to the theory of general education in a free society.

Resurgent Essentialism

The great expansion of American public education over an extended period of post–World War II recovery was countered by a new wave of tax conservatism

and the call to take the school curriculum back to basics. In a systematic explication of the essentialist position, Arthur Bestor, a history professor at the University of Illinois, offered his "Program for Redeeming the Unfulfilled Promise of American Education" in his widely read book, *The Restoration of Learning* (1956). Although the book was one man's version, it garnered wide support in academia and the media. As noted, Bestor's proposal was to delimit the school curriculum to mathematics, science, history, English, and foreign languages. The social studies would be eliminated in favor of history. No academic credits would be allowed for any nonacademic coursework. No public funds should be expended for facilities and resources to support "gladiatorial" sports. Efforts by educationists to increase the holding power of the high school are "warranted neither by the statutes nor by common sense" and lead to "an enormous waste of educational resources." We ought not be concerned with the total number of dropouts, but whether we are losing students of high caliber. Bestor did not even list art and music in the appendix of the book. He deplored the idea and practice of general education as opposed to liberal education (pp. 402–403). Sputnik I gave Bestor renewed attention in the national media for a brief period, but his essentialism was to be completely eclipsed by the neoessentialist disciplinary curriculum reforms in the sciences and mathematics financed by the National Science Foundation and other federal agencies from the mid-1950s through the 1960s.

Conant's Report on the High School

While serving as U.S. high commissioner to West Germany and as first U.S. ambassador to the Federal Republic of Germany spanning a major period of the post–World War II reconstruction of that nation, James Conant developed a renewed interest in the American comprehensive high school. On ending his distinguished diplomatic career, he agreed to conduct a study of the comprehensive high school for the Carnegie Corporation. Soon after embarking on his study, Sputnik I was launched and with it came a wave of heightened assaults against American schools, particularly the comprehensive high school, by influential critics who made good copy for the media in the wake of the Soviet satellite.

Issued in 1959 and addressed to school boards, Conant's report, *The American High School Today*, was enormously influential. The most significant aspect of Conant's report was his support of the comprehensive high school. At a time when the comprehensive high school was being attacked at congressional hearings, Conant remained a staunch advocate of this type of school. In supporting the comprehensive high school, Conant presented data showing that students in such schools can attain levels of academic achievement at least on a par with those students who attend the more specialized academic high schools.

At no time since its invention did the comprehensive high school undergo attacks so severe as to threaten its existence. At congressional hearings during 1958, the comprehensive high school was assaulted by a number of influential figures who advocated that Americans scrap this institution in favor of the divided European system (U.S. Senate Committee on Labor and Public Welfare, 85th Congress). It is no exaggeration to say that Conant's prestige—coupled with the tenor, timing, and practical format of his report—saved the comprehensive high school. Unlike the highly progressive report issued seven years earlier by the Educational Policies Commission under his chairmanship, Conant's 1959 report was eclectic. In view of the climate of the times, Conant's eclectic prescriptions buffered the main assaults against the comprehensive high school.

Sustaining the Comprehensive Curriculum. In his study, Conant found that the enrollment in many high schools was too small to offer a sufficiently diversified curriculum along with the needed specialized faculty, resources, and facilities (libraries, laboratories, shops, studios, etc.). To offer a full and rich curriculum with a qualified faculty, the graduating class should number at least 100.

Conant's recommended program in general education was based on the traditional subject curriculum and the Carnegie unit. He prescribed a curriculum that he deemed representative of the best in current practice rather than of the most promising experimental approaches or idealizations of what might be done in the high schools. In the academic subjects required for graduation, students would be grouped by ability, subject by subject, but would not be tracked. Hence, a student might be in a high-ability class in English and in a middle-ability class in mathematics. Diversified programs for the development of marketable (vocational) proficiency should be offered in line with the federal-state funding, but students should

not be tracked or labeled *vocational* or *college preparatory*. However, an academic inventory should be made to ensure that the highest ability students pursue the advanced academic studies including advanced-placement courses. Although the body of research from the time of the Eight-Year Study has revealed that the traditional pattern of academic subjects cannot be supported as best preparation for college success, Conant's proposals for the college bound, and especially for the academically talented, endorsed the notion perpetuated by most colleges that there is indeed a best pattern.

Turning again to the proposals for the subjects required of all, Conant recommended that the time devoted to English composition during the four years should occupy about half the total time devoted to the study of English, and that each student should be required to write an average of one theme a week, to be evaluated by the teacher. In view of this, teachers of English should be assigned no more than 100 students. Although art and music were not required, it was recommended that all students be "urged" to include art and music in their elective programs. In the courses required of all, the grading standards should be flexible so that a passing grade may be given to students provided they have worked to full capacity. At the same time, appropriate remedial support should be provided.

The movement for small, alternative, special-interest secondary schools in the inner cities in recent years has left these schools lacking in the needed critical mass as identified by Conant (1959). Almost half a century after Conant, the National Association of Scholars (NAS) issued a report addressed to governors, *An Open Letter: Recommendations for Reforming the American High School* (2005). The letter held that high schools need a minimum enrollment of 500 to be able to provide a rich and diversified curriculum and for a highly qualified and stable faculty (more characteristic of larger high schools). A principal recommendation was that the high school provide for career-oriented (technical-vocational) programs of study which could lead to college, as well as college preparatory studies and a core curriculum for all. In effect, NAS had rediscovered the American comprehensive high school without cognizance of Conant's national study of 1959.

Democratizing Function. In the face of his prescriptions for the academically talented, Conant believed that the democratizing function of the comprehensive high school would be met by housing a heterogeneous population, by avoiding tracking of students according to college preparatory and vocational programs, and by providing a diversified curriculum including vocational education to meet the needs of youth who are not college bound. In effect, the main democratizing function would be provided through the joint association of students in school activities, in heterogeneously grouped home-rooms, in certain heterogeneously grouped elective courses, and especially through a heterogeneously grouped course called Problems of Democracy, required of all seniors. The idea for such a course was hardly new. In fact, the original idea for a course on problems of democracy can be traced to the Committee on Social Studies of the 1918 Commission on the Reorganization of Secondary Education, which issued the *Cardinal Principles* report. Conant envisioned the democratizing function as reaching full fruition in this senior course.

Conant's endorsement of the Problems of Democracy course induced many high schools to continue to offer such a course or to develop one. However, it was to undergo near total eclipse under the weight of the national discipline-centered curriculum reforms of the space race. Clearly, Conant expected too much from this single course as the makeweight for the democratizing function of the curriculum. Yet in the 1990s, a period of social fragmentation and conflict, the modest provision of a problems of democracy course appears to be a major step toward meeting a crucial need in general education. Although Conant's eloquent words describing the nature and function of this single course may well be overstated, they do testify to the function of the total curriculum in general education in a free society:

> This course should develop not only an understanding of the American form of government and of the economic basis of our free society, but also mutual respect and understanding between different types of students. Current topics should be included; free discussion of controversial issues should be encouraged. This approach is one significant way in which our schools distinguish themselves from those in totalitarian nations. This course, as well as well-organized homerooms and certain student activities, can contribute a great deal to the development of future citizens of our democracy who will be intelligent voters, stand firm under trying national conditions, and

> not be beguiled by the oratory of those who appeal to special interests. (pp. 75–76)

Clearly, it is hard to fathom how Conant could expect a single 12th-grade course, along with homerooms and student activities, to accomplish such a profound mission. If a single social-problem-focused course, heterogeneously grouped, "can contribute a great deal to the development of future citizens of our democracy who will be intelligent voters, stand firm under trying national conditions, and not be beguiled by the oratory of those who appeal to special interests," one is impelled to wonder how much could be accomplished if such a function permeated the total curriculum in general education. After all, this was the stated goal of general education as conceived in the earlier reports endorsed by Conant. Furthermore, what about the dropouts who do not have the opportunity to take this 12th-grade course in American problems? In capping his proposals for a subject curriculum and ability grouping in the academic subjects with such a problem-focused course in the senior year of high school, Conant appeared to be implying that such a singular course would atone for whatever deficiencies accrue to his curriculum prescriptions for the entire four years of high school. In this connection one cannot avoid the conclusion that Conant expected too much from too little too late.

Yet, looking back a half century later on Conant's advocacy of the senior Problems of Democracy course, one is impelled to find merit in even such a modest proposal in the face of the multicultural fragmentation and conflict that pervades across the nation, coupled with the problems of poverty, health, unemployed youth, slums, crime, global conflict, human rights, and national security. Citizenship in a civil society requires a shared awareness and concern for common problems and needed solutions. Ideally, problems of democracy should be integral to the core curriculum for general education, but Conant's proposal was at least a step in a needed direction.

Conant's recommendations came to be so widely adopted that it seems likely that had he advocated the abandonment of the comprehensive high school, this institution might well have been dealt a mortal blow. Never before in its short history had it been under such concerted attack. Conant's support of this institution could not have come at a more propitious moment in history.

Conant's Report on the Junior High School

Conant followed up his report on the high school with one on the junior high school, also commissioned by the Carnegie Corporation. Issued in 1960, the report on the junior high school was brief and its recommendations closely paralleled the report he had issued a year earlier on the high school. Conant acknowledged that the junior high grades provide the transition from the child-centered elementary school to the more subject-centered high school, and that because special competence is required of teachers working with this age group, this school should not be viewed as a training ground for high school teachers. Yet his curriculum proposals tended to view the junior high school as a pupil training ground for the senior high school.

Some of the major recommendations are summarized as follows:

1. All pupils in grades seven, eight, and nine should be required to take English, social studies, mathematics, and science. Heavy emphasis should be given to reading skills and composition in English, and the social studies should include an emphasis on history and geography. All pupils should also take physical education and some work in art and music. All boys should have some industrial arts, and girls should take homemaking. Ninth-grade science may include biology or a special laboratory course in physical science.

2. Students should be grouped in the academic courses, subject by subject, according to their ability levels.

3. To facilitate the transition to the junior high school, block-time teaching should be provided in grade seven. Although the block-time teacher in most cases would be responsible for instruction in social studies and English, the purpose is not necessarily to break down subject boundaries or to orient the curriculum to the problems of young adolescents but rather to enable the teacher to work daily with fewer individuals and to spend more time with them in an instructional and guidance capacity.

4. Some, if not all, students should begin the study of a modern foreign language on a conversational basis in grade seven with a bilingual teacher.

5. Able pupils should be identified early and should start algebra in grade eight so that they may be ready for college-freshman mathematics through an advanced-placement course in the 12th grade.

6. Systemwide coordination of the curriculum should be provided in each subject field, grades K–12 (vertical articulation).

7. Specialized guidance and testing services should be provided.

8. Student activities should be regarded as part of the total school program.

Implications. Conant's prescriptions for the junior high school might well be faulted for giving insufficient attention to the democratizing function of this institution and of its curriculum in general education. Significantly, block-time teaching was proposed not for curriculum correlation or integration but to ease the transfer of children from the elementary school to the junior high school. Yet this recommendation undoubtedly helped many junior high schools preserve block-time classes at a time when the curriculum reforms were in the direction of disciplinary studies.

Perhaps of greatest significance was Conant's failure to see the junior high school as an institution having its own curriculum and philosophy in tune with the nature of young adolescents. His vision of the junior high school was mainly conceived as a preparatory institution for the high school years. As in the case of his report on the high school, Conant pointed out that his recommendations were "purposely conservative," reflecting what he saw as the best in established practice, and that any imaginative developments for improving the curriculum would have to "await the test of time" (p. 45).

As time would have it, the ensuing middle school movement would shift the ninth-grade from the junior high school back into the traditional four-year senior high school. It should be recalled that the establishment of the junior high school early in the twentieth century was not only intended to meet the needs of emerging adolescents who were inappropriately mixed with young children in the traditional eight-year elementary school, but also to free the ninth grade from college preparatory dominance and to encourage curriculum experimentation with block-time classes and elective options for exploratory, enrichment, and special-interest studies.

Slums and Suburbs

Following his 1959 report on the high school and his 1960 report on the junior high school, Conant issued his report on schools in metropolitan areas in 1961 under the title *Slums and Suburbs*. Here he provided a vivid contrast between the schools in affluent suburbs against those in inner cities. "In the suburb there is likely to be a spacious modern school staffed by as many as 70 professionals per 1,000 pupils," noted Conant, whereas "in the slum one finds a crowded, often dilapidated and unattractive school staffed by 40 or fewer professionals per 1,000 pupils." Conant prophetically and repeatedly warned that "social dynamite is building up in our large cities in the form of unemployed, out-of-school youth" (1961, pp. 3, 146).

Acknowledging that the practice of ability grouping of students in the academic courses required for graduation could conceivably result in de facto segregated classes in racially mixed schools, Conant held that this could be prevented by providing for a large middle group in which there would be considerable student mixing, along with fairly small high-achieving and remedial class groupings. At the same time, students should be assigned to such groupings subject by subject in the required academic courses, and tracking should be avoided. Hence, a student in a vocational program might well be in a social studies class with a future lawyer.

Although Conant's curricular prescriptions generally followed his earlier reports, he made a powerful case for the need of the nation to address both the great disparities in resources and facilities for children and youth in the schools of metropolitan areas and the toll taken in wasted lives and social disorganization in cities. He pointed out that aside from the alarming rate of dropouts from these schools, even when students attained a high school diploma they were faced with unemployment because they lacked the salable skills that could have been developed in the federal-state funded programs in vocational education (office practice, trades and industries, distributive occupations, health occupations, cooperative-supervised work placement, and so on).

In his impassioned plea for the nation to address the conditions of slum schools, Conant stressed that this would require an improvement in the lives of the families who inhabit the slums. Finally, "without a drastic change in the employment prospects for urban Negro youth, relatively little can be accomplished." Conant ended his report with a call for the nation to face up to the problems of slums and slum schools, and to face up to the dangerous social situation "before it is too late" (p. 147).

Conant's warnings of "social dynamite" garnered some media attention, but the new thrust for education was to be directed at excellence in the academic disciplines, led by university scholar-specialists with federal funding for curriculum reform in the sciences and mathematics in the wake of the Cold War and space race. Not until the riots of 1967 in central cities did the nation turn to the problem of social dynamite and the plight of inner-city schools.

The Discipline-Centered Curriculum and the Decline of General Education

In the knowledge-production world of the departmentalized university, the knowledge categories are separated from one another as disciplines for purposes of specialized scholarship. However, the discipline-centered approach for the education of the scholar-specialist neglects the macrocurricular function of general education. The disciplinary approach for the budding scholar-specialist also neglects the nature of the immature learner whose interests and cognitive styles are qualitatively different from the specialist. In failing to meet the function of general education, the discipline-centered approach neglects the practical applications of knowledge in the life of the learner and of the wider society. Hence, any effort at curriculum reform for schools must be built on the interconnections of knowledge in relation to the nature of the learner and to social conditions.

An extended discussion of the discipline-centered curriculum is presented here in view of the continuing influence of the discipline-centered university on the school curriculum. In our discussion, it is useful to understand why the national discipline-centered projects in response to the Cold War and space race came to exert such a pervasive influence over such an extended period of time only to fail, and why educators were remiss in recognizing the neo-essentialism in the disciplinary doctrine and the inherent shortcomings of a discipline-centered curriculum. The implications of these events are of profound significance for contemporary efforts toward curriculum articulation and synthesis.

The Discipline-Centered University and the Mission-Oriented Society

Through the centuries, humans have developed thought edifices in which logical forms of knowledge have been categorized for further knowledge production and use. These knowledge categories, whether organized as disciplines or as subject fields, serve as the frames of reference through which educational institutions formulate their curricula for the purposes of transmitting the cultural experience to the rising generation and for enabling each new generation to meet the emergent needs of a changing society.

However, several serious problems arise as a result of the ways in which the knowledge categories are regarded and treated. The incessant expansion of knowledge requires that the knowledge categories undergo continuous transformation and resynthesis. Moreover, although knowledge expands, the time available for its study remains limited for each generation. Instead of subjecting the knowledge categories to continuous transformation and resynthesis, the traditional tendency has been to accommodate the new knowledge in the curriculum through the ad hoc processes of accretion, deletion, modification, and compression.

As Hans Vaihinger pointed out early in the twentieth century, humans create "fictional constructs" that are necessary for organizing knowledge systematically, but they look on these logical constructs as ends in themselves and as an independent value for knowledge, rather than using them for the purpose for which they were organized in the first place: to serve the practical need for communication and action (1924, p. 170). The failure to recognize these constructs as useful fictions resulted in the treatment of knowledge in the curriculum apart from its necessary application to life problems. Under the banner of the fictional construct, "structure of the discipline," the practical applications of knowledge were sacrificed in favor of the theoretical and abstract elements of the knowledge categories. However, in life situations the knowledge categories are not isolated and segmented; life problems require cross-disciplinary and interdisciplinary approaches for their solution. Even in the research milieu of advanced university scholarship, scientists and social scientists must engage in cross-disciplinary and interdisciplinary efforts in order to solve many kinds of problems.

Limitations of Disciplinarity. To meet the mission-oriented needs of society, the university organizes professional schools, colleges, and institutions in such wide-ranging fields as public health, medicine, engineering, agriculture and environmental science, architecture, social work, education, and so on because the discipline-oriented departments are not geared to meet these action-relevant needs.

Yet the world of academia has an ingrained tradition of maintaining the purity of knowledge. Theory is held aloof from practical or utilitarian matters. Although this tradition is rooted partly in the ancient notion that mind is above worldly affairs, it also grew out of a historic need to safeguard academia from external imposition and persecution. Hence, the social seclusion of the world of scholarship led to the university being caricatured as an ivy-covered ivory tower. Although this image is not a viable one in a scientific-technological age, the tradition of maintaining the purity of knowledge has persisted in many quarters of academia. Dewey noted that, like feminine chastity, the established tradition of maintaining the purity of knowledge in the university has required all kinds of external safeguards to hedge it about (1939, p. 152).

The limitations of disciplinarity have long been recognized, yet such limitations were largely forgotten as the knowledge purists led the new wave of curriculum reform. The sciences and mathematics became the appropriate models for structuring subject matter in every knowledge domain. Addressing the problem of the growing purity, abstraction, and specialization in university scholarship, a great twentieth-century mathematician, John von Neumann, described the dangerous trends in the field of mathematics in these words:

> As a mathematical discipline travels far from its empirical source, or still more, if it is a second and third generation only indirectly inspired by ideas coming from reality, it is beset with very grave dangers. It becomes more and more pure aestheticizing, more and more purely "L'art pour l'art." This need not be bad if the field is surrounded by correlated subjects which have closer empirical connections or if the discipline is under the influence of men with an exceptionally well developed taste. But there is a grave danger that the subject will develop along the line of least resistance, that the stream, so far from its source, will separate into a multitude of insignificant branches. . . . In other words, at a great distance from its empirical source, or after much

"abstract" inbreeding, a mathematical subject is in danger of degeneration. At the inception the style is usually classical; when it shows signs of becoming baroque, then the danger signal is up. (1947, p. 196)

Alvin Weinberg, a nuclear physicist and director of the Oak Ridge National Laboratory, holds that much scholarship in the basic sciences has moved too far from the neighboring sciences and has become baroque. He contends that scientific scholarship should be adjudged according to its "social merit or relevance to human welfare and the values of man" and, accordingly, "that field has the most scientific merit which contributes most heavily to and illuminates most brightly its neighboring scientific disciplines" (1967, pp. 74–75). To Weinberg, the unity of science is developed not within separate domains of specialized scholarship but through the interrelationship of these domains and, consequently, "the most valid criteria for assessing scientific fields come from without rather than from within the scientific discipline that is being treated" (pp. 75–82).

The incongruence between the mission-oriented society and the discipline-oriented university is described by Weinberg:

Our society is mission-oriented. Its mission is resolution of problems arising from social, technical, and psychological conflicts and pressures. Since these problems are not generated within any single intellectual discipline, their resolution is not to be found within a single discipline. . . . In society the nonspecializer and synthesizer is king.

The university by contrast is discipline-oriented. Its viewpoint is the sum of the viewpoints of the separate, traditional disciplines that constitute it. The problems it deals with are, by and large, problems generated and solved within the disciplines themselves. The university's standards of excellence are set by and within the disciplines. What deepens our understanding of a discipline is excellent. In the university the specialist and analyst is king. (p. 145)

Other difficulties arise when the systematic knowledge in the various knowledge categories is regarded as suitable for the learner without having to undergo a transformation to psychologize it for the learner, the assumption being that the immature learner can perceive and use such knowledge in the manner of the advanced scholar who helped create it. The knowledge-world of the advanced scholar-specialist not only is essentially different from that of the immature learner but also is essentially different from that of the adult citizen whose callings are not within the domains of specialized scholarship.

Promoted as a doctrine rather than as a theory to be tested, disciplinarity dominated the curriculum scene from the 1950s through the 1960s. It became the ruling doctrine for curriculum reform. Although disciplinarity remains a dominant mode of curricular organization for specialized university scholarship, and although it continues to exert a significant influence on the curriculum at the preuniversity and lower levels of schooling, it is no longer the ruling doctrine for curriculum development. Yet the world of knowledge specialization exerts a continuing influence toward organizing the curriculum according to the disciplines of university scholarship. This problem continues to be of such great concern that a 2004 issue of a publication of the American Educational Research Association was devoted to the theme of "Disciplinary Knowledge and Quality Education" (Leonardo, pp. 3–5). It is puzzling that not a single citation was made concerning the most influential work historically in setting the nation's school curriculum on a discipline-centered course, namely Jerome Bruner's *Process of Education* (1960), a report of a national conference in response to the space race crisis in national security.

A Curriculum Manifesto

Less than a year after the launch of Sputnik I, a conference composed predominantly of scientists, mathematicians, and psychologists convened at Woods Hole on Cape Cod in Massachusetts by the National Academy of Sciences. Providing financial support and planning assistance for the conference were such agencies as the National Science Foundation (NSF), the Air Force, the RAND Corporation, the U.S. Office of Education, the American Association for the Advancement of Science, and the Carnegie Corporation. The conference was designed to explore the possibilities for improving education in science in the elementary and secondary schools at a time when they were under severe attack for the nation's alleged lag behind the Soviets in the space race. The Cold War had already led to the establishment of several national curriculum projects under NSF funding, but these projects were not wedded by a curriculum rationale and their efforts to produce new course packages were still at the preliminary stages.

The outcome of the Woods Hole conference, *The Process of Education,* written by conference chairman Jerome Bruner, served as the manifesto for curriculum reform in the elementary and secondary schools over the ensuing decade.

Decline of General Education and the Democratic Ideal

The link between *The Process of Education* and the crisis of the space race is reflected in the opening paragraph, which calls attention to the "widespread renewal of concern for the quality and intellectual aims of education . . . accentuated by what is almost certain to be a long-range crisis in national security" (1960, p. 1). The report declares: "The top quarter of public school students, from which we must draw intellectual leadership in the next generation, is perhaps the group most neglected by our schools in the recent past" (p. 10).

A decade later, responding to a different sociopolitical crisis, Bruner did an about-face by accusing the public schools of concentrating on "the more intelligent kids" and neglecting "the children at the bottom" (in Hall, 1970, p. 51). This reversal reflects on how education priorities can be turned about as a result of sociopolitical influences and illustrates how leading educators are prone to see priorities as polarities.

In one epoch, democracy is to be saved by focusing on the academically gifted, but in a succeeding era it is to be saved by giving priority to the low achiever or disadvantaged learner. Instead of realizing that a democratic society requires that educational opportunity be optimized for all children and youth and that the curriculum must be reconstructed in a balanced way to address the needs shared by the widest membership of society, narrow priorities are established to the neglect of the cosmopolitan-universal needs.

Nationalistic Interests. Dewey warned early in twentieth century that "[o]ne of the fundamental problems of education in and for a democratic society is set by the conflict of a nationalistic and a wider social aim," and he pointed to the European experience, and particularly the German experience, in which "the new idea of the importance of education for human welfare and progress was captured by national interests and harnessed to do a work whose social

aim was definitely narrow and exclusive" (1916, p. 113). The schools were expected to meet a narrow social aim that was to be interpreted not in terms of developing an enlightened and progressive humanity but in terms of meeting the civic function of preparing the citizen for service to the state. As stated by Dewey:

> So far as Europe was concerned, the historic situation identified the movement for a state-supported education with the nationalistic movement in political life—a fact of incalculable significance for subsequent movements. Under the influence of German thought in particular, education became a civic function and the civic function was identified with the realization of the national state. The "state" was substituted for humanity; cosmopolitanism gave way to nationalism. To form the citizen, not the "man" became the aim of education. . . . When the actual practice was such that the school system, from the elementary grades though the university faculties, supplied the patriotic citizen and soldier and the future state official and administrator and furnished the means for military, industrial, and political defense and expansion, it was impossible for theory not to emphasize the aim of social efficiency. And with the immense importance attached to the nationalistic state, surrounded by other competing and more or less hostile states, it was equally impossible to interpret social efficiency in terms of a vague cosmopolitan humanitarianism. Since the maintenance of a particular national sovereignty required subordination of individuals to the superior interests of the state both in military defense and in struggles for international supremacy in commerce, social efficiency was understood to imply a like subordination. (1916, pp. 109–110)

Within seven months following the launch of Sputnik I, the United States embarked on its first official education mission to the U.S.S.R. The report of the mission, *Soviet Commitment to Education,* described the Soviet education system in glowing terms, with education being "a kind of grand passion" (1959, p. 1). Throughout the report, the implications were drawn that we must take lessons from Soviet schools. "We cannot afford to be apathetic about educational developments in the U.S.S.R.," concluded the report. "Clearly the Soviet Union is bent on overtaking and surpassing us as a world power, and it proposes to use education as one of the primary means of obtaining this objective" (1959, p. 116). The myth of Soviet supremacy in the sciences, mathematics, and technology was being perpetuated, and it was America's schools that were at fault and needed to be fixed in the face of the space-race crisis. No leading politician, intellectual, industrialist, or journalist of that day would describe Soviet society as a "backward, poverty-stricken society" as they were to do over the years after the Soviet collapse (Schoenfeld, 2004, p. 15). Nobody was to report on the dire straits of Soviet schools, especially in rural areas where schools often lacked adequate plumbing and other essential facilities and resources.

During the Cold War and space race, the democratic social aim of American education yielded to the narrow nationalistic aim as the federal government looked to curriculum reform as the means of meeting the crisis. The contribution of university scholars in the creation of the most advanced weapons systems had led the nation's political leadership to look to the university scholars for devising curricula in science and mathematics for the elementary and secondary schools to meet the Cold War crisis. The alleged superiority of Soviet education, with its heavy emphasis on science and mathematics and its exploitation of academically talented children and youth, was to be matched and surpassed by the American pursuit of academic excellence. Hence, the Woods Hole conference focused on the education of the academically talented coupled with a priority to be given to science and mathematics in the curriculum.

The view of knowledge for curriculum building was to be that of university scholar-specialists on the forefront of their disciplines. The discipline-oriented university scholars were given a new mission-oriented task. Nevertheless, the discipline-oriented university scholars comprising the membership of the Woods Hole conference developed a rationale for modeling curriculum reform in the schools along the more abstract and specialized lines of university scholarship in which knowledge is pursued and treated in its "purity."

The Structure of the Disciplines Doctrine

At the time of the Woods Hole conference, a veritable army of applied scientists and mathematicians in the universities were engaged in applied research projects deemed essential to national security and funded by prestigious federal agencies. As pointed out by Morris Kline, director of a leading research institute on applied mathematics, when the government turned to the universities to enlist scholars for

the national curriculum-reform programs to be directed at the lower levels of schooling, those scholars who were engaged in the more remote and puristic pursuits and who had been left behind now were able to seize control of the curriculum reforms (1973, p. 135). University scholars who were not oriented toward applied or practical research, and who had been bypassed over the years in connection with federally supported scientific research, suddenly found that huge grants were available for national curriculum-reform projects through the National Science Foundation. The consequence was that the curriculum reforms over almost two decades were dominated by the puristic structure-of-the-disciplines doctrine.

Bandwagon Effect. The physical sciences and mathematics occupied the highest rungs of the disciplinary hierarchy on the grounds that they are built upon conceptual schemes most amenable to quantification and prediction and, therefore, their disciplinary structures would most readily be validated. Although the validation of the disciplinary doctrine was never established, scholars in biology, the social sciences, and even in the visual arts and language embraced the doctrine.

It may seem strange that the disciplinary doctrine should have evoked such a bandwagon effect, especially when it could not be validated even in mathematics and the physical sciences, but academicians, like people in general, tend to move with the fashions and especially with the grant monies. At that time, many leaders in some of the so-called nonacademic fields, such as the fine arts, began to subscribe to the disciplinary doctrine so as to make their fields more essential to the school curriculum by eliminating the studio experiences and claiming their fields as academic disciplines. In so doing, they were robbing the arts of their essential attributes and functions for general education and significance in daily life. To this day, proponents of the discipline-centered curriculum must be reckoned with not only in the sciences and social sciences, but also in the arts. In their efforts to create discipline-based art education, they delimit the studio arts and emphasize art as an academic study through art history, criticism, and aestheticism or connoisseurship (National Society for the Study of Education, 1965, part. II, pp. 121–122; 1992, part II, pp. 42–43, 74–75, 114–115, 188).

The structure-of-the-disciplines doctrine as proposed by Bruner not only served as the key idea governing the national course-content improvement projects but also came to exert the dominant influence on curriculum theorists. Schwab warned educationists that unless they take into account the structures of the disciplines, "our plans are likely to miscarry and our materials, to misteach," and "there will be failure of learning or gross mislearning by our students" (1962, p. 197).

Schwab's notion that "different disciplines have widely different conceptual schemes" and his contention that seeking conceptual schemes that cut across disciplines is a fruitless exercise (p. 203) are clearly contradicted by the treatment of knowledge in Schwab's own field of biology, for example, where the advance of knowledge has required new fusions between established domains of knowledge, leading to the creation of such fields as biochemistry, biophysics, and sociobiology. Schwab not only overlooked the necessary fusions of disciplines and fields in the world of scholarly research, but he also ignored the necessary interrelationships among these areas of knowledge when they are brought to bear on all kinds of practical problems in society, whether in medicine, energy resources, ecology, or other fields. For example, ecology is not limited to the biological sciences but involves knowledge from the physical sciences, geography, economics, political science, engineering, agriculture, and, indeed, any area of knowledge that relates to the environment—including the arts and architecture.

Moreover, many leading scientists do not agree with Schwab's contention that even within the field of science the conceptual schemes are so widely different that it is fruitless to find any unity of knowledge. The Nobel laureate Albert Szent-Gyorgi observed that the "unification of knowledge is the greatest achievement of science," and he proposed that "what I would like to see taught in school is this new subject—nature, not physics and chemistry" (1970, p. 3).

The university scholars who developed the discipline-centered projects for the schools made sweeping claims for their work and did not submit to impartial evaluations. In those rare instances when controlled research was conducted, the scholars violated the tenets of scientific research by setting up conditions so as to prove the project. It seemed hypocritical that these were the scholars who had claimed that a basic objective of their discipline-centered projects was to instill in students the methods of scientific inquiry.

For almost two decades, the national discipline-centered projects dominated the school curriculum by the weight of academic authority, federal funding, endorsement of powerful national agencies and associations (e.g., the private foundations, National Science Foundation, U.S. Office of Education, and the professional education associations and journals)—all in an atmosphere of space-race crisis. Few educators were willing to point out that the discipline-centered projects conflicted with the nature of the learner, promoted knowledge purity and abstraction at the expense of practical application and relevance to the life of the learner, emphasized knowledge specialism to the neglect of general education and democratic citizenship, and failed to address the deepest social problems. In short, the disciplinary doctrine and the national discipline-centered reform effort had violated the curriculum paradigm, and consequently they were doomed to failure from the start (see chapter 6).

Knowledge Purity and Abstraction. To the university scholar-specialists, practical applications of knowledge only contaminated the discipline, for such application requires the crossing of disciplinary boundaries and even the elimination of boundaries.

The puristic orientation of the curriculum reforms in the sciences and mathematics was the subject of a scathing indictment by the physicist Alvin Weinberg:

> These two tendencies—toward purity and fragmentation as opposed to application and interdisciplinarity . . . seem to me to portend trouble in the relation between the university and society. First, I speak about the great curriculum reforms, especially in the sciences. These reforms started in the high schools but have now been extended, particularly in mathematics, downward to the grade schools, and in many instances upward to the colleges. . . . Insofar as many of the new curricula have been captured by university scientists and mathematicians of narrowly puristic outlook, insofar as some of the curricula reflect deplorable fragmentation and abstraction, especially of mathematics, I consider them to be dangerous. . . . The professional purists, representing the spirit of the fragmented, research-oriented university, took over the curriculum reforms, and by their diligence and aggressiveness, created puristic monsters. (1967, pp. 153–154)

The separation between pure and applied knowledge and the compartmentalization of knowledge into mutually exclusive disciplines and subjects reflect the self-serving logic of academia where matters of concern are purely academic and removed from the test of intelligent action. "Education is the acquisition of the art of the utilization of knowledge," noted Whitehead, and "ideas which are not utilized are positively harmful." Whitehead further described education as "a preparation for battling with the immediate experiences of life, a preparation by which to qualify each immediate moment with relevant ideas and appropriate actions," and he defined education as "the guidance of the individual towards a comprehension of the art of life; and by the art of life I mean the most complete achievement of varied activity expressing the potentialities of that living creature in the face of its actual environment" (1929a, pp. 4, 6, 58, 61).

The tendency for the disciplinary studies to isolate intellectual activity from ordinary life was a matter of great concern for Dewey, who warned:

> In the case of the so-called disciplinary or preeminently logical studies, there is danger of the isolation of intellectual activity from the ordinary affairs of life. Teacher and student alike tend to set up a chasm between logical thought, as something abstract and remote, and the specific and concrete demands of everyday events. The abstract tends to become so aloof, so far away from application, so as to be cut loose from practical and moral bearing. (1933, p. 62)

When knowledge is cut off from use—from its applicability to the world—in giving meaning to what is baffling in the world, there is danger that it will become "an object of aesthetic contemplation," Dewey noted. "There is much emotional satisfaction to be had from a survey of the symmetry and order of possessed knowledge, and the satisfaction is a legitimate one. But this contemplative attitude is aesthetic, not intellectual" (1916, p. 397). Thirty-one years after Dewey's warning, a leader in building the modern foundations of mathematics and computer theory, John von Neumann, pointed to the "very grave dangers" of mathematics becoming "more and more pure aestheticizing, more and more purely 'l'art pour l'art,'" as it becomes less and less "inspired by the ideas coming from 'reality'" (1947, p. 196). This is not to deny the aesthetic qualities of a discipline, but when the discipline becomes so puristic and esoteric that its relationship to the life of the learner is denied, when it has no bearings on the development of social power and insight in enabling the learner to cope

more effectively with the environment, then its educational function becomes severely limiting.

Whitehead, who was Bertrand Russell's collaborator in producing one of the greatest mathematical treatises of all time, wrote concerning the need for education to be useful: "Pedants sneer at an education which is useful. But if education is not useful, what is it? Is it a talent to be hidden away in a napkin? Of course education should be useful, whatever your aim in life" (1929a, p. 3).

The proposition that the fundamental ideas that constitute the structure of a discipline will lead to massive general transfer of learning failed to prove valid principally because general transfer requires wide applicability of what is comprehended. To see the disciplines of knowledge as mutually exclusive domains that are divorced from practical application in the life of the learner is to work against massive general transfer.

Distorted Conception of the Learner

Although Bruner's report of the Woods Hole conference (1960) stressed the importance of stimulating the young learner to use intuition as opposed to rote learning, and thereby develop inquiry into the significance and connectedness of what is learned, the report cast the child as a miniature scholar-specialist whose intellectual activity is not qualitatively different from that of the scholar on the frontier of knowledge. In Bruner's words, "intellectual activity anywhere is the same, whether at the frontier of knowledge or in a third-grade classroom" (1960, p. 14).

Bruner bent the developmental stage theory of Jean Piaget to make it fit the Brunerian thesis that "intellectual activity anywhere is the same." The fact that Piaget's work reveals that young children are incapable of hypothetical thinking and that they do not reach this stage of intellective development until late childhood or early adolescence was ignored by Bruner and his fellow academicians.

Stages of Intellective Growth. Even if university scholarship and the curriculum of the university were confined to the established disciplines of knowledge, the knowledge world of the immature learner is qualitatively different from that of the mature scholar-specialist in the university. As Whitehead observed, "The craving for expansion, for activity, inherent in youth is disgusted by a dry imposition of disciplined knowledge. The discipline, when it comes, should satisfy a natural craving for the wisdom which adds value to bare experience" (1929a, p. 50). Whitehead recognized that the learner's mental growth is developmental and that it undergoes qualitative changes through the maturational process, and he identified this growth in terms of stages of development, not unlike those identified by Dewey and later by Piaget.

Discussing the "stages of mental growth," Whitehead attacked the notion of undifferentiated intellective development as a patently false psychology:

> The pupil's progress is often conceived as a uniform steady advance undifferentiated by change of type or alteration of pace . . . I hold that this conception of education is based upon a false psychology of the process of mental development which has gravely hindered the effectiveness of our methods. (1929a, p. 27)

From observations of children in his laboratory school, Dewey made these observations concerning mental development and the curriculum:

> According to the older view mind was mind, and that was the whole story. Mind was the same throughout . . . fitted out with the same assortment of faculties whether in child or adult. . . . The only important difference that was recognized was one of quantity, of amount. The boy was a little man and his mind was a little mind—in everything but the size the same as that of the adult. (1915, p. 102)

Dewey described how this fallacious premise undergirded the traditional curriculum in which the subject matter was formulated from the vantage point of the adult mentality, except that the material was reduced in quantity and simplified for the "little men" of childhood. However, mind is not so fixed, contended Dewey, but is a growing process, and although this growth is a continuity, it is marked by qualitative changes. Thus, qualitative differences in the curriculum are required so that the learning material is appropriate to the changing stages or phases of human development.

> If once more we are in earnest with the idea of mind as growth, this growth carrying with it typical features distinctive of its various stages, it is clear that an educational transformation is again indicated. It is clear that the selection and grading of material in the course of study must be done with reference to proper nutrition of the dominant directions of activity in a given period, not with reference to

chopped-up sections of a ready universe of knowledge. (1915, p. 104)

Instead of asking whether a given subject matter is worth a child's knowing, Bruner proposed that "[w]e might ask, as a criterion for any subject taught in primary school, whether, when fully developed, it is worth an adult's knowing" (1960, p. 52). Thus, the curriculum is not conceived in terms of its appropriateness for the child as child, but for a child who is a miniature adult and who is to become a full-sized adult by dealing with a scaled-down version of the logically formulated subject matter of adult scholarship. The authenticity and integrity of childhood is sacrificed by seeing the child as merely a future adult scholar.

Teacher-Proof Curricula

Some leading spokesmen for the major curriculum-reform projects in the sciences advocated teacher-proof curricula. They envisioned the development of ideal curriculum packages of uniform quality control—packages that would be somewhat resistant to teacher tampering or to variation in individual teacher's style, orientation, or competence.

Responding to the notion of teacher-proof curricula and to the character of the curriculum reforms then taking place in the United States, a noted British educator made these remarks at an international curriculum conference:

> I have no time whatever for any system which recruits high-powered thinkers to contrive and foist a curriculum on the schools. This cannot work unless we believe that the teacher of the future is to be a low-grade technician working under someone else's instructions rather than a professional making his own diagnoses and prescribing his own treatments. (Clegg, 1968, p. 9)

Declining Enrollments in Science

The mandate for the national discipline-centered curriculum was to mobilize the schools in turning out more scientists to meet the space-race priorities for national security (Bruner, 1960, p. 1; American Institute of Physics, 1960, pp. 17–18). It was expected that the discipline-centered projects would double the proportion of students completing at least one course of high school physics. Instead the numbers underwent a sharp decline. And over a period when college enrollments were doubling, the proportion of college students majoring in physics also underwent a sharp decline (*Carnegie Quarterly*, 1970, p. 5; Ellis, 1967, p. 77; Watley & Nichols, 1969, pp. 2, 4–18).

Although these unanticipated enrollment declines may well have been influenced by changing social attitudes on the part of high school and college students in an era of rising social disaffection and social consciousness, many knowledgeable observers attributed the enrollment declines to the curriculum reforms as exemplified by the PSSC physics course. An editorial in *Science*, the journal of the American Association for the Advancement of Science, expressed concern that the enrollment declines indicated a reaction on the part of youth to the excessive pressures exerted on them in high school through the stringent requirements of the new curricula, particularly the PSSC physics course (Abelson, 1967). An article in *Carnegie Quarterly* also criticized the PSSC course for treating physics as the physicist sees it, with the result that the subject matter is too abstract and frightens away adolescents, who carry their fears of the subject over into college (1970). Similar criticisms were leveled at the new high school chemistry projects even by college professors. Addressing his colleagues, a noted chemistry professor maintained that the curriculum reforms were pressuring adolescents "to do too much, too fast, too soon" and that, in adopting these reforms, educators had committed "a crime against a generation" (King, 1967, p. 474).

The Myth of a Monolithic Structure

With the curriculum reforms at the secondary level being pushed down to the elementary level as the result of the influence of university scholars, it was only a matter of time before these scholars would be impelled to examine the curricula in their own fields at the college level. During the second half of the 1960s, a commission of the American Institute of Biological Sciences sought to identify the common content elements to be used as a basis for developing an ideal undergraduate course of study in biology. The commission reasoned that the best approach would be to identify the common content elements found in the core course work in biology at selected universities that were adjudged to be influential in the field and noted for their teaching programs in biology.

In-depth studies were made of the content of the courses, and it was found that only 7% of the course content was shared (Commission on Undergraduate Education, 1967, p. 21). The commission concluded that there is no single ideal curriculum and it abandoned the notion that there is a common body of content that could serve as a basis for constructing an ideal biology curriculum. Finally, the commission noted that college and university professors would not be amenable to the idea of an ideal curriculum because their orientations differ widely. Ironically, the university scholars who sought to impose ideal curricula on the elementary and secondary schools, formulated according to the structure-of-a-discipline doctrine, avoided any corresponding effort to impose such a model of curriculum reform on their own institutions.

The search for the structure-of-a-discipline was beginning to fade. If such structure could not be found in the highly empirical physical sciences, not to mention the biological sciences, then how could it be found in the social sciences? Even in economics, the most empirical of the social sciences, a Galbraith, Friedman, and Samuelson will come up with entirely different and even conflicting prescriptions for attacking such problems as inflation, unemployment, and poverty. Such prescriptions could not be objectively derived from a quantitative analysis of factual knowledge in the discipline of economics but would be shaped by one's sociopolitical philosophy. Yet, the main thrust of curriculum reform in the social sciences during the disciplinary movement was in imitation of the physical sciences and the search for structure-of-a-discipline.

That one's philosophical and sociopolitical orientation determines how the social sciences are interpreted and used can easily be demonstrated in the practice of changing economic advisers whenever an opposition party wins the U.S. presidential election. It seems only inevitable that efforts to find a monolithic disciplinary structure were bound to fail in economics and other social sciences, as well as in the less empirical areas of language and the fine arts. Yet scholar-specialists in these fields sought to imitate the "hard" sciences in seeking claim to a disciplinary structure to be imposed on the school curriculum. Like the emperor's new clothes in the fable by Hans Christian Andersen, if the university scholar specialists saw the structure-of-the-discipline, so too did the educationists. It must be realized that the disciplinary doctrine did promote the disciplinary bias of specialized university scholarship, even if it was inappropriate for the school curriculum and also for the college curriculum in general education.

Aftermath of the New Math

A growing protest also was becoming evident through the 1960s and early 1970s against the narrow bias of the major mathematics projects in focusing on the abstract side of the subject as opposed to the applications of mathematics to the physical world. As far back as 1962, a memorandum signed by 48 mathematicians warned of the danger that the new mathematics projects were representing mainly the theoretical and abstract aspects of mathematics and, in so doing, were ignoring the needs of youngsters who seek to "understand the world around us" (Ahlvors et al.).

Purity Versus Application. The noted mathematician Richard Courant held that the splitting of mathematics toward a pure versus an applied variety posed a most serious threat of one-sidedness to education, and he contended that the relationships of mathematics to other realms of knowledge are necessary to keep mathematics alive and prevent it from drying into a dead skeleton (1962, pp. 297–320). Writing in the journal of the American Association for the Advancement of Science, another mathematician observed that "one can only conclude that much of modern mathematics is not related to science but rather appears to be more closely related to the famous scholastic arguing of the Middle Ages" (Hemming, 1965, p. 474).

The curriculum reforms in mathematics not only had focused on the theoretical and abstract side of the discipline but also had sought to compress into the existing school curriculum an unrealistic amount of college-level mathematics. A 1963 conference on school mathematics, sponsored by the National Science Foundation and chaired by Jerome Bruner, advocated "that a student who has worked through the full thirteen years of mathematics in grades K through 12 should have a level of training comparable to three years of top-level college training today" (1963, pp. 2–3).

Looking back on the curriculum reforms in mathematics, Morris Kline held that the university mathematicians were presumptuous in imposing on the schools a narrow vision of mathematical knowledge, and he criticized them for not taking account of the enormous complexity of pedagogical problems.

> The mathematics professors did not hesitate to take on a task that calls for considerable pedagogical acumen. One can say that they were presumptuous. They acted as though pedagogy was only a detail, whereas if they had really learned anything at all from their studies, they would have known that almost any problem involving human beings is enormously complex. The problems of pedagogy are indeed more difficult than the problems of mathematics, but the professors had extreme confidence in themselves. (1973, p. 129)

Intelligence and Wisdom. Kline made the point that people commonly assume that the mathematics professor is the epitome of intelligence and hence can be expected to exercise the utmost wisdom in prescribing solutions to problems. Wisdom is much more than intelligence, stressed Klein, for wisdom includes such qualities as "judgment, the capacity to learn from experience, the perception of values, the understanding of human beings, and the capacity to use knowledge for the solution of human problems." Although probability indicates that the qualities of wisdom are distributed no more among mathematicians than among any other groups of people selected at random, observed Kline, the narrowness of mathematics and the fact that mathematics per se is not concerned with the complex problems of the world may leave mathematicians without their share of the world's distribution of wisdom. In pointing to pure mathematics as a remote refuge, Klein offered this quotation by Bertrand Russell:

> "Remote from human passions, remote even from the pitiful facts of nature, the generations have created an ordered cosmos, where pure thought can dwell as in its natural home and where one, at least, of our nobler impulses can escape from the dreary exile of the actual world." (1973, p. 133)

Although the isolation of intellectual activity from life affairs is peculiarly characteristic of pure mathematics, scholars in other domains of knowledge specialization are tempted to find a similar refuge. In pointing to the tendency for specialized scholars to hold their disciplinary studies so aloof from life demands that they often tend to be inept when they rode into matters outside their own specialties, Dewey made these observations:

> The gullibility of specialized scholars when out of their own lines, their extravagant habits of inference and speech, their ineptness in reaching conclusions in practical matters, their egotistical engrossment in their own subjects, are extreme examples of the bad effects of severing studies completely from their ordinary connections in life. (1933, p. 62)

Search for Balance and Synthesis. In the year following the collapse of the new math, some efforts were being made to balance the relationship between abstraction and useful applications in the mathematics curriculum, although these efforts were not matched by the level of financial support and professional commitment provided for the earlier reform movement. A counterreaction to the discipline-centered curriculum and the demand for curriculum relevance arose, only to be followed by a counter-counterreaction of curriculum retrenchment through back to basics. With the turn of the twenty-first century a number of curriculum projects at the elementary and middle-school levels were designed to relate mathematics not only to the sciences, but also to the life of the learner. Some of these projects have made significant inroads in connecting mathematics to its practical uses in modern life. However, much remains to be accomplished in connecting mathematics to social problems, as envisioned by Whitehead in his call for the application of mathematics in the study of society and in the sciences to meet the function of general education (1929a, pp. 12–13). But here, Whitehead was well aware of the problems of waste under a system of external testing (p. 21). Today, our system of national external testing, subject by subject, is anathema to curriculum integration to meet the function of general education.

Citizenship Rediscovered

The disciplinary doctrine had led to a rejection of the social studies and the sociocivic function of the curriculum in favor of the social sciences as discrete domains of specialized scholarship. Throughout the twentieth century, the sociocivic function emerged as one of the central functions of education in this country. Now it was to be totally rejected. After all, the scholar-specialists in the graduate schools who are on the forefront of their disciplines in political science, economics, sociology, and so on are not concerned with citizenship education but with preparing budding political scientists, economists, and other social scientists. The general education function of the curriculum had come to be rejected as specialized knowledge in the form of disciplinarity took precedence. For example, the executive director of the American Political Science Association declared that the long-standing tradition of citizenship education is misguided and is a misconception of political science. Accordingly, "political science cannot be conceived

as a branch of civics [for i]t is an intellectual discipline, a body of knowledge about the political behavior of human beings" (Kirkpatrick & Kirkpatrick, 1962, p. 103). Clearly, there was a failure to recognize that political behavior, like human behavior in general, is influenced psychologically, culturally, socially, economically, and morally.

The protest against Vietnam and the urban convulsions of the late 1960s (the riots, burning, and looting in the ghettos of some cities during the summer of 1967), followed by the Watergate scandal, caused a reexamination of the sociocivic function of education. Fearing that the Watergate course of events had left a residue of disillusionment and cynicism in the rising generation, the U.S. Office of Education launched its Citizenship Education Program in 1976. Such professional organizations as the American Political Science Association turned to legitimizing, once again, the sociocivic function of education through its Committee on Pre-college Education.

The National Task Force on Citizenship Education, sponsored by the Danforth and Kettering foundations, issued its report in 1977 calling for the schools to assume the major task of citizenship education in view of the erosion of the educational roles of the home, community, and other institutions. Among the 21 recommendations were those involving the idea that citizenship education should be broadened and should provide for (1) the treatment of constitutional rights and liberties, the environment, ethical values, interdependence of peoples, and human rights and responsibilities; (2) the development of skills of participation in civic life and commitment to values compatible with democratic principles; (3) heterogeneous grouping of students in all schoolwork related to civic competence; (4) the involvement of the entire school faculty in teaching citizenship education; and (5) a democratic school environment (pp. 9–12).

This report might have given educators cause for wondering why it did not appear at the height of McCarthyism, but even after the fall of Senator McCarthy the Cold War curriculum prevailed along with the continued assaults on academic freedom and the censorship of curriculum materials, as documented in back issues of the *Newsletter on Intellectual Freedom* of the American Library Association. The superpatriots who wanted the schools to indoctrinate for patriotism would not recognize that democratic citizenship abhors indoctrination and requires the capacity and commitment of the citizenry to think and act reflectively on problems and issues. Even to avoid reflective consideration of such problems and issues is to avoid the function of democratic citizenship. In so doing, a kind of citizenship education other than democratic citizenship education will fill the void, whether by intent or default.

Looking to the course to be taken for the curriculum in the twenty-first century, the National Council for the Social Studies joined with the American Historical Association and other agencies as the National Commission on Social Studies in the Schools that issued its report calling for a curriculum focused on democratic citizenship (1989, p. 3). Unfortunately, advocates of each of the social science disciplines wrote separately on the need for students to understand the leading concepts and theories of each discipline, rather than revealing the interdisciplinary problems to be addressed for democratic citizenship and general education.

Although the colleges have acted over recent years to incorporate community service as a requirement for undergraduates, and to use such service as a criterion for admission, the school curriculum has come to treat democratic citizenship more in terms of service and patriotism rather than in political participation beyond service (Westheimer & Kahne, 2003). The collapse of the Soviet Union and the rise of international terrorism have given cause for the renewal of citizenship for American democracy not only in the social studies and history, but also in the curriculum in general education. The problem of general education remains most critical for the democratic prospect to this day. Despite the monumental failure of the disciplines doctrine, university academicians would not abandon it. The nature of academic specialization and departmentalization, coupled with the nationalizing external testing in the separate subjects or disciplines in the twenty-first century, give continued reinforcement to the disciplines doctrine and the segmental curriculum. Nevertheless, the problem of general education will not go away as long as the commitment to the democratic prospect and an enlightened civil society is in continued renewal.

Emergence of Alternative Approaches to Disciplinarity

In apparent recognition that there is no monolithic structure of the subject matter of physics, a committee of the American Institute of Physics recommended that alternative types of physics courses be developed to make the subject more relevant to adolescent interests and to the problems of humanity. This led to the creation of Harvard Project Physics, a course designed to reveal the humanistic attributes of physics. However, the treatment of physics in terms of practical and technological applications to societal problems remained limited in the Harvard Project Physics course.

Studies undertaken during the development of the Harvard Project Physics course revealed that teachers' personalities and value systems are more strongly related to students' achievement in physics and their attitudes toward the subject than are the extent of teachers' preparation in physics and mathematics and their knowledge of physics.

The developers of Harvard Project Physics had hoped that the humanistic approach would help make physics a general education subject in high school, but the task of connecting the study of physics with social concerns remains to be accomplished.

Many of the science projects at the elementary level were influenced initially by the PSSC rationale and claimed to model the pupil's investigation of science after the fashion of the professional scientist. Claims were made that children were engaging in such scientific processes as formulating hypotheses, controlling variables, interpreting data, and experimenting. Their actual activities appeared to be more accurately described as observing, measuring, inferring, predicting, and communicating.

Efforts to build the subject matter according to the structure-of-a-discipline doctrine gave way to process-oriented approaches. In many projects, the content was organized into diverse units that served as focal points of pupil activity rather than being organized according to the structure of a discipline. An increasing number of emerging projects were organized as combined science studies.

The Curriculum, the Learner, and Society

Eventually, the BSCS group began to develop materials that relate biology to adolescent and social problems. Reports by the BSCS group beginning in the early 1970s said that the new biology programs would bridge the many interfaces of science and society. One such report by the BSCS director fittingly describes the intended directions of the curriculum reforms, appropriately directed at transforming "The Unreal School in the Real World":

Artificial subject-matter barriers that divide curricular content will tend to disappear, and students will be concerned more and more with solutions to problems where a great variety of disciplines interact. The study of pollution, for example, cannot be contained solely within the discipline of biology or chemistry, but involves all of the natural sciences as well as economics, political science, history, geography, and even art and aesthetics. With subject matter lines breaking down, the education of teachers will not be so much in the disciplines as in societal concerns. . . . (Mayer, 1974, p. 5)

This statement might well have been taken not only from the contemporary literature, but also from the literature on the core curriculum of the progressive era. Nevertheless, it signaled the recognized place that was to be accorded ecology in the interdisciplinary curriculum for the twenty-first century.

"The Remaking of American Education." It will be recalled that the Carnegie Corporation had joined with various federal agencies in financing the Woods Hole conference that gave us the disciplinary doctrine for curriculum reform in response to the crisis of the Cold War and space race. But this time the Carnegie Corporation turned not to an educator but to a journalist, Charles E. Silberman, a member of the board of editors of *Fortune*.

Silberman, who only four years earlier had championed the disciplinary curriculum reforms in a *Fortune* article under the title "The Remaking of American Education" (1961, pp. 125, 131) now pronounced these reforms a failure in his Carnegie report, which was published in 1970 under the title *Crisis in the Classroom* (carrying the promising if not presumptuous subtitle "The Remaking of American Education"). The book immediately became a national best-seller. In 1966 Silberman had extolled the disciplinary reforms as creating "a mass educational system successfully dedicated to the pursuit of intellectual excellence" (p. 122). By 1970, Silberman characterized these reforms as "adult dictation," and he wrote that whereas the university scholars "knew what they wanted children to learn; they did not think to ask what children wanted to learn." Overlooking his own misguided pronouncements of an earlier era, Silberman declared that "the effort was doomed to failure" because it had neglected pupil needs and because the university scholars had acted naively and arrogantly, having had little first-hand experience in the elementary and secondary

classroom, and having designed teacher-proof materials as though teachers were mere technicians. Silberman also criticized the curriculum-reform movement for its "academic provincialism" in being directed at the separate disciplines without seeing the curriculum as a whole (pp. 180–183). He then accused the university scholars of having committed an even more fatal error:

The most fatal error of all, however, was the failure to ask the questions that the giants of the progressive movement always kept at the center of their concern, however inadequate some of their answers may have been: What is education for? What kind of human beings and what kind of society do we want to produce? What methods of instruction and classroom organization, as well as subject matter, do we need to produce these results? What knowledge is of most worth? (p. 182)

The Open Classroom. In 1963, the Central Advisory Council for Education (England) was commissioned by the minister of education to make a study of primary education and the transition to secondary education. Soon after the report, *Children and Their Primary Schools*, was released in 1967, it came to be known as the Plowden report, after the name of the council's chairman, and it attracted considerable attention among American educators and educational critics.

The Plowden report noted that progressive educational ideas had been slow in being adopted into practice and that although the ideas of Dewey, Whitehead, and others were available in the literature, few teachers had given much time to the study of this literature even in their college days.

"The informal English schools demonstrate in practice what Dewey argued in theory," noted Silberman, in *Crisis in the Classroom*, and he concluded that "informal education can work as well in the United States as in England" (pp. 222–266). Silberman devoted an entire chapter, "It Can Happen Here," to show how the English model of informal primary education would help put all levels of American elementary education on the needed course. What Silberman seemed to be saying in his Carnegie report is that America did not need a Silberman report but a Plowden report.

Some American educators rushed to adopt the open classroom as though the English had discovered a new educational panacea. The open-classroom idea, as developed in English primary schools, came to be used to denote such a wide range of adaptations and such differing conceptual stances in American schools as to cause considerable confusion. In many cases the main thrust was on more efficient use of space and staffing arrangements than on the improvement of learning.

Finally, where the open-classroom concept, as developed in the Dewey school around the turn of the century, was designed to provide for curriculum integration and to foster a democratic social outlook, many schools that claimed to have adopted the open classroom gave little or no consideration to such integration and social goals.

The "Youth Problem"

The 1970s witnessed the issuance of three national reports on the high school and adolescent education. It was clear by the tone and substance of these reports that the agendas were a reaction to the social protest and disruption on the college campuses that filtered down into the high schools during the late 1960s and the early 1970s. The tensions led to resignations of presidents of some of the leading universities, such as Clark Kerr of the University of California at Berkeley and Nathan Pusey of Harvard.

The three national reports on the high school and adolescent education were issued by the National Commission on the Reform of Secondary Education (Kettering Foundation, 1973), the National Panel on High School and Adolescent Education (U.S. Office of Education, 1976), and the Panel on Youth of the President's Science Advisory Committee (1974). All three reports faulted the comprehensive high school for its increased "holding power" over adolescents. Historically, the increased holding power of the American high school had been considered one of the signal accomplishments of American education. Now, in an era of retrenchment, conservative forces were seeking a retreat from the historic mission for universalization of secondary education and the support of a unitary school structure, capped by the comprehensive high school as the vehicle for the vast extension of educational opportunity.

Fortunately, the American public was not ready to abandon its belief in education. Unfortunately, the national reports of that era virtually dismissed the democratizing function of the comprehensive high school and the curriculum in general education as the means of fostering a sense of unity through diversity.

Unity Through Diversity.   Recall (chapter 5) that the experimentalists had long championed student activities as integral and not ancillary to the mission of the school and college curriculum. In his 1978 president's report, Derek Bok of Harvard cited the sociologist James Coleman in noting that many telling democratizing capacities are not so much developed from the formal curriculum than from the experiences through joint association with persons from different backgrounds, cultures, and interests. Bok stressed the significance of bringing students of every race, religion, and economic group into joint association through student activities and campus life at Harvard so as "to develop a tolerance and appreciation of human diversity with all its variety of values, backgrounds, and points of view" (*Harvard Magazine*). Unfortunately, unlike James Conant, Bok connected this not with school life in the comprehensive high school, but with college life on the sequestered Harvard campus. And, ironically, it was none other than James Coleman who had chaired President Nixon's Panel on Youth, which in its report of 1974 attacked the comprehensive high school and called for reducing the high school to more strictly academic functions, creating alternative special-interest high schools, and devising mechanisms for curtailing the formal schooling of disadvantaged youth through work training. It appeared that whereas social diversity was regarded as a powerfully positive democratizing force in the college, it was seen as a negative force in the high school that should not be diverted from its singular college preparatory mission. Finally, none of the reports addressed the critical problem of adolescent acculturation in school and society.

The 1970s were a time when the colleges were beginning once again to address the need for a coherent core curriculum for general education, whereas the schools were still mired in the retreat to basics, minimum-competency testing, and production-efficiency assessment. The efforts of the colleges to revivify the curriculum in general education were to ebb and flow throughout the remainder of the twentieth century and into the twenty-first century.

Education for Techno-Industrial Mobilization

With the end of the Cold War, the new foray of national reports and attacks on the public schools turned to techno-industrial mobilization to meet the threat of global economic competition. After decades of Cold War and the creation of a vast weapons economy, U.S. leaders seemed to have suddenly awakened to the prospect that Japan and West Germany were poised to overtake and surpass the United States in dominating the global economic marketplace. As history would have it, once again the public schools were to be the nation's scapegoat.

"Nation at Risk"

In past eras, any major sociopolitical shift was accompanied by the call for a marked change in the priorities and directions of the school curriculum. But this time the shift from Cold War mobilization to techno-industrial mobilization found the proposed curricular remedies, with a few variations, remarkably similar to those that followed the launching of Sputnik I.

In a single year (1983) three national reports called for curriculum priority in the sciences and mathematics through federal funding, raising the requirements in the sciences and mathematics for college entrance, giving increased emphasis to modern foreign languages and computer literacy, using nationwide standardized tests to certify the transition through levels of schooling, raising graduation requirements in the four academic "basics" and adding the "new basic" of computer science, increasing academic learning time and reducing electives, eliminating "nonessential" subjects, instituting ability grouping and special programs for the academically talented, increasing the amount of homework and establishing a longer school day and school year, establishing a federal mechanism for the assessment of student achievement for national, state, and local evaluation and comparison, and raising the standards for teaching.

The report of the National Science Board (NSB) of the National Science Foundation, *Educating Americans for the 21st Century* (1983), held that "[t]he National Science Foundation, which has recognized expertise in leading curriculum development, should again take the leadership role in promoting curriculum evaluation and development for mathematics, science and technology" (p. 46).

Here the NSB report conveniently overlooked the reasons for massive failure of the NSF-funded national curriculum-reform projects that produced the "new math" and "new science" in response to the crisis of the Cold War and space race. In appallingly unscientific fashion, the NSB report sought to make the case for the nation's inferior position against other industrial nations in school achievement by comparing test results for the mass of American 18-year-olds with the small elite of compeers in other nations. The report documented this alleged inferiority of U.S. schools with reference to a source that actually warned against such a misinterpretation. The source cited was an article in which the director of the International Assessment for the Evaluation of Educational Achievement stressed that the top U.S. students score as well as the corresponding population in other nations, but in the comprehensive high school system of the United States there is much greater educational yield because there is more opportunity to develop the potentials of both the academically talented and the less able than in the traditional selective systems of Europe (Husén, 1983, p. 456).

Fixing the Blame. By far the report that garnered the widest treatment in the media and has served as the launching pad for attacks on public schools and for proposed remedies carried the alarming title *A Nation at Risk: The Imperative for Educational Reform.* Issued in 1983 by the National Commission on Excellence in Education, a commission appointed by the U.S. secretary of Education and chaired by the president-elect of the University of California, the report began: "Our nation is at risk." This declaration of alarm was followed by the ominous statement that "[i]f an unfriendly foreign power had attempted to impose on America the mediocre educational performance that exists today, we might well have viewed it as an act of war" (p. 5).

Fixing the blame on the public schools, rather than on government, industry, the scientific establishment, and the universities, the report declared that "[t]he citizen is dismayed at a steady 15-year decline in industrial productivity as one American industry after another falls to world competition" (p. 18). The report distorted the data from the International Evaluation of Educational Achievement by listing as the first "indicator of risk" the allegedly low scores by U.S. students on the tests in comparison with students in other nations. Not until the closing pages of the report was it acknowledged that American schools have been a major vehicle for social and educational opportunity, that the proportion of the American college-age population enrolled in college far exceeds that of other industrial nations, and that international test-score comparisons had revealed that when matched with the best of other nations, U.S. students do indeed compare favorably. Unfortunately, U.S. political leadership and the mass media chose to give credence only to the condemnatory passages of the report.

Leading its list of recommendations under "Content," the report recommended a minimum program for high school graduation consisting of the following requirements in the "Five New Basics": four years of English, three years of mathematics, three years of science, three years of social studies, and one half year of computer science. For the college-bound, two years of foreign language in the high school were recommended in addition to work taken in foreign language earlier. Clearly, except for computer science, the Five New Basics were the Old Basics clothed in the call to redirect the mission of the schools toward regaining the nation's technological leadership and dominance in global industrial markets.

Among the findings in *A Nation at Risk* were that expenditures for school textbooks and curricular materials had declined by 50% over the previous 17 years, and that the budget for textbooks and related materials now accounted for only 0.7% of the operating costs of schools whereas the recommended level ranged from 5 to 10%.

Considering that the impetus for *A Nation at Risk* was in America's decline in the global industrial marketplace, it is puzzling that the National Commission on Excellence had little to say about vocational-technical education other than deploring the "migration" of students from vocational and college preparatory programs to "general track" courses in large numbers.

Conveniently overlooked by all was the fact that the original charge to the National Commission on Excellence was that of "assessing the quality of teaching and learning in U.S. public and private schools, colleges, and universities." Instead, the commission chose not to look at the colleges, universities, and private schools.

The real risk to the United States was that *A Nation at Risk* failed to look at the nation's seething problems of youth unemployment, social disaffection, and conflict—and failed to address the need to modernize the overcrowded and underfinanced schools, the need for a more coherent curriculum in general education, and the need to reconstruct programs in vocational education.

The Business-Industrial Connection.   Among the many puzzling and contradictory elements common to the national reports on education reform issued during the 1980s was the endorsement given the enlistment of the business-industrial sector in increasing the managerial efficiency of public schools. From the 1980s through 2005 the business sector was characterized as dominated by the "creed of greed" reflecting illegal financial machinations and unethical corporate practices, often at the expense of corporate productivity, not to mention the public interest. Once again, the fault of the nation's declining power in global economic competition was not to be fixed on the nation's business-industrial sector, political leadership, or universities—but on the public schools.

Finally, although many of the reports called for the schools to promote good citizenship, there was virtually no mention of *democratic* citizenship and the vital significance of general education at a time when society was becoming increasingly fragmented and divisive.

The *Action for Excellence* report, issued in 1983 by the Task Force on Education for Economic Growth of the Education Commission of the States, echoed most of the allegations and prescriptions offered in *A Nation at Risk*. In declaring the United States in a state of emergency and in linking the schools with the nation's declining position in the global economic marketplace, the task force recommended that the schools be mobilized through a partnership with industry to develop the skilled human capital needed to regain preeminent position.

Reducing the Curriculum

In contrast to the tone and substance of the reports on school reform issued by national commissions, panels, and task forces, several publications appeared during the 1980s in which the case was made for casting the function of the school in a far more restrictive perspective, and with it the nature and function of the curriculum. Although the back-to-basics retrenchment and minimum-competency testing had failed to deliver what was promised, the advocacy of essentialism continued unabated throughout the 1980s and even gained added momentum during the latter part of that decade in no small measure through the advocacy of William J. Bennett as U.S. secretary of Education and the publication of E. D. Hirsch's best-selling *Cultural Literacy* in 1987.

Basic Schooling

Mortimer Adler's *Paideia Proposal: An Educational Manifesto* (1982) made the case for a single-track essentialist curriculum to be followed in the 12 years of basic schooling. Writing on behalf of the Paideia Group—whose membership included many leading essentialist-perennialists—in a project supported by the MacArthur Foundation, Adler delimited the curriculum to the areas of (1) language, literature, and the fine arts; (2) mathematics and natural science; and (3) history, geography, and social studies. In somewhat of a concession for Adler, the essential studies would include some activity in the studio arts and would be supplemented by some "auxiliary studies" consisting of physical education including health, "manual" activities (typing, cooking, sewing, and shop classes of a nonvocational nature), capped by a survey of occupations. Vocational training would be provided in the community college or on the job itself.

The essential studies would be treated through "three distinct modes of teaching and learning," namely (1) didactic instruction, lecture, and recitation through textbooks and other aids for the acquisition of organized knowledge; (2) coaching and drilling exercises in reading, writing, speaking, listening, calculating, and so on for the development of intellectual skills (skills of learning); and (3) Socratic questioning and response for the enlarged understanding of ideas and values through the discussion of literary works and other works of art and involvement in artistic activity. There would be no electives other than a choice of a foreign language.

Adler's schema garnered a wide readership, and the advocacy of coaching as a method began to permeate the education literature without a critical examination of the limitations of coaching and drilling exercises as dull and repetitive. Few educators challenged Adler's perennialist configuration of mind (as a muscle), being strengthened by proceeding from acquisition of information and skills through repetitive drills and exercises, with the teacher functioning as an athletic coach, and finally "raising the mind from a lesser or weaker understanding to a stronger and more fuller one" by means of Socratic questioning (p. 53). And, surprisingly, school people did not question the validity of Adler's doctrine holding the Socratic method as the epitome of intellective engagement, a method of prescientific convergent thinking in contrast to emergent thinking in the formulation and testing of hypotheses.

As far as the nature of the adolescent learner is concerned, it is to be explained by explaining it away. Adler wrote that "youth is an insuperable obstacle to being an educated person" (p. 9) without explaining how it is possible to become educated without having to live the life of youth.

"Less Is More": Essentialist Schools

The aphorism "less is more" (or "more means worse") was echoed in the arguments by essentialists in Britain during the 1970s as an expression of their opposition to the democratizing efforts of the government to create comprehensive secondary schools. A decade later, it was being echoed by Theodore Sizer, former headmaster of Philips Academy in Massachusetts in *Horace's Compromise: The Dilemma of the American High School* (1984), written under the auspices of the National Association of Secondary School Principals and the National Association of Independent Schools in a project supported by several private foundations. "Horace" is a beleaguered middle-aged teacher of English in a suburban high school who is incessantly compromising his work and concealing his bitterness. As a member of Mortimer Adler's Paideia Group, Sizer drew many of his curricular prescriptions and rationale from the *Paideia Proposal*. "High schools cannot be comprehensive and should not try to be comprehensive," declared Sizer, for the job of the high school is to help students "exercise their minds," and it is through the essential studies that the "discipline and furniture" of the mind are provided. "Compulsory attendance," contended Sizer, "should cease when a young citizen demonstrates mastery of the minima, and most young citizens should master these minima before senior high school" (pp. 84, 88, 89, 216).

Sizer characterized the American high school as a supermarket; yet he criticized the high schools for mandating most of the courses taken, namely from the five areas of English, social studies, mathematics, science, and physical education. He called for the elimination of vocational education, yet in his selection of an example of an ideal setting for learning, he described a teaching situation in a high school vocational class in electronics in which the students were vitally engaged in hands-on collaborative learning with lessons relating to the physical sciences and mathematics.

"A political philosophy, essentially that associated with American constitutionalism, is the bedrock of enlightened democratic citizenship," declared Sizer. Only a few pages earlier he had dismissed the constitutional principle of state-church separation, which gave the nation the secular public school, when he offered that "by pretending there is a wall between religious issues and their schools, public school people remove themselves from the argument about the ways that religion must properly exist in their schools"—to which he added, "[p]erhaps the most absurd current hullabaloo is over prayer in schools" (pp. 128, 133).

Without citing earlier work by progressive educators with block-time classes and the correlation and integration of studies, Sizer proposed that such designs would make it economically feasible for the teacher to work with 80 students daily instead of 120 as is commonly the case.

Sizer's book, *Horace's Compromise*, was identified as the first report from a study of high schools. The second report, also under the same sponsorship, was published a year later (1985) bearing the title *The Shopping Mall High School*. Whereas Sizer only a year earlier had characterized the American high school as a supermarket, it was now caricatured as a shopping mall. Oddly, both reports were presumably drawn from the same data source. It was claimed in the second report that the studies were based on a rough national representation of high schools, with the schools "grouped in geographical clusters." With the researchers located in Boston, it turned out that over 35% of the student populations in the national representations were enrolled in high schools in and around Boston, and over 77% of the national representation were enrolled in schools located in the areas of Boston, San Diego, and Denver (Powell, Farrar, & Cohen, 1985, pp. 325–331). How this could even be construed as a rough representation of American high schools defied the imagination, not to mention the credibility of the research. When James Conant studied the American high school over a quarter of a century earlier, he wisely noted that it is not possible to draw a scientific sampling of schools and student populations that are so massively diverse and geographically separated. Instead, he identified criteria for well-functioning schools and developed his recommendations from data drawn from those schools.

Narrowing the Vision and Mission. Although *The Shopping Mall High School* correctly viewed schools as faced with the challenge of making serious educational demands on students and making it possible for almost all to succeed, the authors viewed these efforts as largely incompatible. The authors concluded that educators need to recognize that schools cannot do everything well for everyone and that they might better focus on intellective purpose and the development of students' intellective capacities through the academic disciplines.

Clearly the authors of the second report had set out to validate Sizer's first report of the study of high schools, and their conclusions and recommendations simply echoed Sizer. The very orientation, design, and tone of the reports from a study of high schools might well have given cause for the National Association of Secondary School Principals to sponsor a study of the more successful comprehensive high schools. However, the education literature and the media were not hospitable to the comprehensive or cosmopolitan high school at a time when the fashion was toward curriculum reductionism and the creation of alternative schools with a narrowly defined academic curriculum. Most of the principals in that organization were at schools of the comprehensive type. Significantly, despite the attacks on the comprehensive high school and efforts to create a dual system through separate vocational schools, along with the advocacy of returning the high school to a traditional academic curriculum, adolescents in most communities other than major cities have sought to attend the comprehensive high school when it is seen as their community high school.

Despite the evidence revealing that academic high schools, as opposed to comprehensive high schools, do not deliver the achievement benefits claimed for them, the school-reform literature relentlessly continued to promote the academic high school and the academic curriculum. A systematic study of academic high schools of the selective type (high-ability students) corroborated earlier studies in finding that "there is no support whatsoever for any positive benefits associated with attending higher-ability schools." In fact, it was found that some of the outcomes of attending such schools were in a negative direction, such as in selecting less-demanding coursework, developing lower self-concepts and lower educational and occupational aspirations (Marsh, 1991, pp. 445–480). It seems that in a more naturalistic, mixed-ability high school, students with high academic ability develop a more realistic picture of themselves—not to mention the democratizing benefits and richer curricular offerings that accrue to students at all levels of ability from attending a comprehensive high school.

A Further Look at the Schools

Considering the bludgeoning taken by the schools in the forays of studies and reports on school reform, and considering the blatant contradictions inherent in the reform proposals as well as the epochal shifts to undo the damages of each wave of reform, one might well understand when school people simply tend to go with the tide of the times. One might well sympathize with school people who are hesitant to open the pages of yet another study or report proposals, for fear of being assaulted once again. In reading the opening sentences of John Goodlad's *A Place Called School* (1984), one might well have gotten the impression that it was yet another study and set of proposals in the ilk of the school blamers:

> American schools are in trouble. In fact, the problems of schooling are of such crippling proportions that many schools may not survive. It is possible that the entire public education system is nearing collapse. (p. 1)

"A Study of Schooling." Despite the dire pronouncement, *A Place Called School* proved rich in useful insights and data on schooling and the curriculum. As the key report of a comprehensive project called *A Study of Schooling* under the direction of John Goodlad, the findings from classroom observations and questionnaires were drawn from 38 schools in 13 communities in 7 sections of the nation. Acknowledging that a truly representative sample of the nation's schools would be an impossibility, Goodlad held that the schools in his study nevertheless had a high degree of variability and representation. He drew on a vast array of source material in his study, which was sponsored through grants from several private foundations and the U.S. Department of Education.

Following almost two decades of back to basics, one could not take issue with Goodlad's findings that the emotional tone of the classroom tends to be flat, that there is a predominance of "frontal teaching" (dominance by the teacher) and the use of worksheets and quizzes with emphasis on repetitive and mechanistic reinforcement of basic skills, and that student recitation is largely regurgitative. Goodlad appropriately criticized the common practice of student ability grouping and tracking, pointing out that classes "containing a heterogeneous mixture of students achieving at all levels were more like high than low track classes in regard to what students were studying, how teachers were teaching, and how teachers and students were interacting" (p. 159). He pointed to the need for classrooms to be more cooperative-collaborative in tone and climate and to give increased emphasis to reflective thinking rather than rote learning and mechanical skills. He warned of the dangers in the trend toward highly specific curricular mandates and interventions by the states.

Goodlad pointed to the need for building curriculum balance and coherence for general education, drawing considerably from the Harvard Report (1945). He went so far as to prescribe the high school curriculum in general education as being drawn from the five "knowledge domains" as follows: up to 18% in literature and language (English and other), up to 18% in mathematics and science, and up to 15% each for the social studies, arts, and vocations. Up to 10% would be in physical education. The balance (approximately 10%) would be in special-interest studies (guided electives). However, he did not explore in any depth how greater curriculum synthesis might be developed through alternative designs to the traditional subject curriculum. As in the more experimental schools of the Eight-Year Study, the problem-focused, integrated core curriculum was successful in providing adolescents with rich opportunities for taking initiative in their learning activities, developing intellectual curiosity and responsible self-direction, extending their capabilities for cooperation and collaboration, and, in short, developing the kinds of interests, capabilities, and commitments that have enormous consequences for life enrichment and success.

Early Childhood as Opportunity, Adolescence as Problem. By far the most puzzling and disturbing proposal by Goodlad was for the radical restructuring of the public school system. Instead of 1 year of kindergarten and 12 years of formal schooling, beginning at age 5 and ending at age 18, he proposed beginning school at age 4 and ending at age 16. He contended that this would reduce the "extraordinary costs in developing curricula," would provide for massive early entrance to college and into the occupations and professions, and thereby "provide a longer period of payment into social security, helping to bail out this sinking benefit of retirement" (p. 346).

Aside from the questionable reasoning for funding the social security program by cutting back on the last two years of secondary schooling is the extraordinary cost to the individual and society in providing productive employment for waves of 16-year-olds who do not go on to college. Moreover, they and their compeers would be denied the psychosocial developmental experiences, so vital for adolescents, from joint association in the latter years of high school. Efforts to reduce the age of college entrance by two years were attempted during the early 1950s under grants from the Ford Foundation. Even though the early admissions population was a selected elite in comparison to their compeers in college, they encountered significantly more adjustment problems and evidenced a high dropout rate. Even those who completed college opined overwhelmingly that they had reservations about such acceleration (1957, pp. 62, 88). The existing structure of 12 years of schooling does not preclude acceleration through advanced placement and early graduation through additional course load and examinations.

For those not going on to college, Goodlad is less certain—perhaps they would enter into a program combining work, study, and service under some form of government-business-industry partnership. Here Goodlad seemed to echo the national reports on school reform of the 1970s. Goodlad's stereotypical characterization of adolescents as trivial minded and prone to socially troublesome behavior seemed to justify delimiting the high school to those who are more amenable to academic studies. "Indeed, one does wonder about the appropriateness of secondary schools," continued Goodlad, "both for the youths who graduate and for those who drop out of the eleventh and twelfth grades," as he went on to propose the "drastic solution" of cutting off the last two years of high school (p. 325). "The extraordinary costs in developing curricula, in teacher frustration, in policing schools, and in monitoring absenteeism will be reduced," reasoned Goodlad. His proposal to begin schooling two years earlier surely had merits, but the question remained as to why the benefit to young children should be paid for by adolescents. Comparative national studies reveal that there is indeed much benefit to be derived from preschool education in terms of socialization, whereas there is considerable evidence to show that it is of dubious value for cognitive acceleration. The myth that adolescence is too late and that the die is cast in early childhood emerged from the efforts to seek a short-cut solution in the War on Poverty of the late 1960s and early 1970s. This myth was perpetuated largely through the misinterpretation and distortion of research literature (Bloom, 1984). The consequence was that early childhood programs, such as Head Start, were developed extensively with federal funds whereas programs for adolescents were of the patchwork variety. To this day there is a lack of concerted effort to redesign the high school curriculum with a view toward constructing a rich and stimulating learning environment for adolescents.

Historically, the twentieth century ushered in the first comprehensive and systematic studies of adolescence as a distinctive period of human development (Hall, 1905). With the opening of the twenty-first century, it seemed that adolescence was pushed aside in favor of early childhood education. But a society that neglects a large segment of its adolescent population does so at its own peril. And our society is paying the price.

Carnegie Foundation Report on the High School

In view of the long-standing neglect of the need to reconstruct the high school curriculum in recognition of adolescence as a crucial stage of human development, the issuance of *High School: A Report on Secondary Education in America* (1983) by Ernest Boyer, president of the Carnegie Foundation, seemed long overdue.

At the outset, Boyer stated that his report was specifically aimed at "searching for ways to strengthen the academic quality of the public school." And although he claimed that the "purpose was to examine a cross-section of American public schools," only 15 public high schools were actually visited for study (pp. xii–xiii). Boyer's report drew heavily from Goodlad's Study of Schooling, which involved data from only 12 high schools.

A Subject Curriculum. Boyer made a strong case for curriculum coherence by relating the curriculum to "our interdependent, interconnected, complex world." In seeming contradiction, instead of calling for new designs for curriculum correlation and synthesis, he held to the "integrity of the disciplines" and called on teachers of the separate subjects to somehow "bring a new interdisciplinary vision into the classroom" by making the necessary "connections between the disciplines" (pp. 114–117). The high school curriculum, according to Boyer, should be a single academic track with two thirds of the units composed of a core of common learning: five units of language (including two of foreign language and one-half unit in arts), two and one-half units of history and one unit of civics, two units of science, and two of mathematics. In addition, half-unit courses would be required in technology, health, a seminar on work, and a senior independent project.

Of Boyer's five units of language, only two and one-half are in English (basic English, literature, and speech), and two are in foreign language. The foreign-language requirement is baffling in view of the massive failure of the drive to develop second-language fluency for all through the National Defense Education Act (1958), when enormous federal funds were expended for this purpose in the absence of recognizing that without the opportunity to communicate in a second language in daily life students are left with only another empty curriculum requirement.

Despite acknowledging the appalling problem of youth unemployment and the expressed interest of many adolescents in vocational education, Boyer viewed the high school as properly becoming more academically oriented, with the last two years being devoted to elective clusters for career exploration and the pursuit of advanced academic subjects. Instead of calling for the strengthening of the comprehensive high school, he recommended magnet schools in large cities for gifted and talented students in the arts or sciences and a national network of residential academies in science and mathematics. Finally, all students would complete a community service requirement through volunteer work during evenings, weekends, or summers.

Proposal for an Integrated, Life-Related Core Curriculum in College. Boyer's endorsement of the traditional subject curriculum in his core of common learning for the high school is particularly baffling because it has been known for many years that it is unrealistic not only for young adolescents to make the knowledge connections when the studies are segmented, but it is also the case for college students. On completing his report on the high school, Boyer turned to a study of the college. In *College: The Undergraduate Experience in America* (1987), Boyer devoted an entire chapter to his proposal for an integrated core to meet the function of general education—vividly similar in purpose and function to the integrated core developed for students in the more

progressive high schools of the Eight-Year Study of almost a half century earlier.

After appropriately pointing to the disjunctures in the undergraduate curriculum as a result of the competing interests of departmentalization, Boyer held that "the core program must be seen ultimately as relating the curriculum consequentially to life" and,

> To achieve these ends, we suggest as one possible approach *the integrated core*. By the integrated core we mean a program of general education that introduces students not only to essential knowledge, but also to connections across the disciplines, and, in the end, to the application of knowledge to life beyond the campus. The integrated core concerns itself with the universal experiences that are common to all people, with those shared activities without which human relationships are diminished and the quality of life reduced. (p. 91)

In many respects, Boyer appeared to have a wider and more integrated vision for the college curriculum, whereas his vision for the high school curriculum was far more traditional. Although he quoted the president of Yale as acknowledging that "[t]he high schools in this country are always at the mercy of the colleges" (p. 252), Boyer did not explore how the high schools might be freed from this subjugation.

America 2000/Goals 2000

In an address at the White House in the spring of 1991 attended by the nation's governors, President George H.W. Bush announced his program, *America 2000*, for the "revolutionary" transformation of schools. Two years earlier President Bush had convened the Education Summit with the nation's governors from which the six national education goals were adopted with the pledge that the goals would be met by 2000. In response to the Education Summit, Congress established the National Council on Education Standards and Testing and the National Education Goals Panel, which was created to report annually to Congress on the progress toward the goals. The six national education goals to be attained by 2000, as stated in *America 2000, Sourcebook*, were: (1) all children will start school ready to learn; (2) the high school graduation rate will be at least 90 percent; (3) U.S. students will leave grades 4, 8, and 12 having demonstrated competency in the five core subjects of English, mathematics, science, history, and geography; and all students will learn to use their minds well, so they may be prepared for further learning and productive employment in the modern economy; (4) U.S. students will be first in the world in science and mathematics achievement; (5) every adult will be literate and possess the knowledge and skills necessary to compete in a global economy and exercise the rights and responsibilities of citizenship; and (6) every school will be free of drugs and violence and will offer a disciplined environment conducive to learning (U.S. Department of Education, 1991, p. 19).

Almost immediately after taking office, under the rubric of Goals 2000, President Bill Clinton endorsed virtually all of the elements in *America 2000* with the exception of Bush's call for school vouchers. As governor of Arkansas Clinton had taken a leadership role at the Education Summit and in the development of the national education goals. Clearly, the first goal of school readiness could not possibly be met without massive social reconstruction to eliminate poverty and social conflict, not to mention the acculturation problems of new waves of immigrant families from underdeveloped, diverse nations. And even if the nation embarked immediately on such a program, 2000 was only a few short years ahead.

Thoughtful educators might also have cause for concern that renewed impetus was being given to the test-driven curriculum and to the announced plan to assess student achievement in meeting "new World Class Standards" through "American Achievement Tests," with priority given to the sciences and mathematics. Once again, it was held that the United States has the world's best system of higher education whereas the system of elementary and secondary education puts the "nation at risk" (p. 9, 53). No explanation was given to how it is possible for such a disjuncture to exist when American high school graduates have no problem competing against the best and brightest students of other nations who attend U.S. colleges and universities, and when the United States provides access to higher education for a larger proportion of its population than any other nation. Once again, in defining the essential studies, the five traditional academic subjects were listed, to the omission of the arts and social studies (other than geography and history). The immediate response to *Goals 2000* was for the various professional associations to establish achievement standards for their subject fields. Although the efforts were clearly

directed at general education, insufficient attention was being given to what each subject domain can contribute to other areas of knowledge so as to create a coherent, balanced, and articulated curriculum for general education. Finally, the gnawing problem of children and youth in poverty who cannot leave their problems at home when they go to school, and of youth who are unable to find a productive role in society, remained the unfinished business of the nation.

The Sandia Study

We have seen how American public education has been buffeted by incessant and contradictory attacks and pressures for reform and counterreform by successive shifts in political priorities from the White House to the state house, by a penchant for the mass media to look for bad news about the schools, for university social scientists to take on a profound negativism toward the schools, and for the public schools to serve as the scapegoat for shortcomings in the political, military, and business sector. There is a saying that in the end, "the facts will kick."

Following the issuance of *America 2000,* a number of new studies gave evidence that the allegations leveled at American public education and the priorities set for the reform of the school system in *America 2000, A Nation at Risk,* and in other policy documents reflected much misinformation and were seriously misdirected.

A comprehensive study, *Perspectives on Education in America,* conducted by the Sandia National Laboratories for the U.S. Department of Energy, was effectively prevented from issuance as a federal document, suppressed by the U.S. Department of Education, and delayed from publication by any means for more than two years because so many of the principal findings ran counter to the allegations and priorities in *America 2000* and *Goals 2000* (Carson, Huelscamp, & Woodall, 1993; Tanner, D., 1993a). Drawing data from such accredited sources as the National Center for Education Statistics, National Science Foundation, U.S. Department of Education, U.S. Department of Labor, U.S. Bureau of the Census, College Entrance Examination Board, National Assessment of Educational Progress, and various international agencies, the Sandia study revealed that, among other favorable findings, changes in SAT scores were the result of demographic changes, and that when today's test takers are matched against the test-taking population of the late 1970s, the SAT scores were actually rising; that the U.S. led the world in the proportion of its population earning the bachelor's degree in all fields, and in science and engineering in particular; that despite declines in the college-age population, the number of doctorates in the physical sciences and engineering was at an all-time high; and that the United States was underinvested in elementary and secondary education, contrary to the data presented in *America 2000*. The study also revealed that dramatic and accelerating demographic changes have been taking place in schools as a result of increases in immigration, representing more than 150 languages, and that almost one third of the pupils were minorities, principally from Latin America and Asia.

With regard to the goal of U.S. students being first in the world in science and mathematics, the Sandia study found that if comparisons were made of those completing their scientific studies, the evidence already pointed to the United States being first in the world. The Sandia study stressed that educational priorities need to be directed toward improving the education of minority and inner-city children and youth. Whereas *America 2000* claimed systemwide failure of public schools, the Sandia data referred to this as "crisis commentary" that is "simply not true" (p. 172). The findings of the Sandia Study are discussed in greater detail in chapter 14, "Evaluation for Curriculum Improvement."

A number of other studies by international agencies in the 1990s revealed that U.S. public education ranked highest or among the highest in educational yield, but the United States failed to make the top 10 among the world's industrial nations in indices of health and child welfare (United Nations Development Program, 1992). It was also found that although U.S. schools ranked high on various measures of academic achievement, the United States ranked low in access to early childhood education (prekindergarten) in comparison to other advanced industrial nations, as well as in access to vocational education in the secondary school.

It appeared that the United States clearly needed a reformulation of the prescriptions and priorities in *Goals 2000,* an end to the crisis rhetoric, and a concerted commitment on the part of the political and educational leadership to build on the comprehensive, cosmopolitan, and humanitarian qualities of schools.

No Child Left Behind

Although the No Child Left Behind Act is not a policy report or research study, but an act of Congress signed into law by President George W. Bush in 2001, it is discussed briefly here because many of its features are connected to *America 2000*. The act was labeled by President Bush as his agenda for education reform, and it was directed at closing the achievement gap between disadvantaged and advantaged children and youth. As called for in *America 2000*, accountability and achievement were to be determined by external testing, with the states required to make annual reading and mathematics assessments for all children. In addition, sample populations in each state were to be tested annually for grades four and eight in reading and mathematics through the National Assessment of Educational Progress (administered by Educational Testing Service).

Although federal funds were to be provided to help schools serving disadvantaged students to raise achievement levels, the punitive aspects of the legislation were severe. Unless the schools make adequate annual progress for three consecutive years, federal funds could be used to transfer disadvantaged students to higher-performing public or private schools. The act further stipulated that funding will be provided for charter schools and the expansion of school choice. Whereas the long-established American tradition was for federal funds to be directed at supporting and strengthening the public schools, the funds could now be taken away from the public schools and reallocated to nonpublic schools.

The act mainly overlooked the fact that the highest performing schools are not likely to sustain annual gains in test scores simply because their scores are highest and the range for improvement is obviously and realistically limited. Further, demographic shifts in student populations commonly result in significant changes in test scores, regardless of the status of the school.

Other features of No Child Left Behind provide for strengthening the math and science curriculum K–12, establishing a comprehensive research-based reading program K–12, providing higher quality teachers for all pupils, and supporting character education.

With the focus on external testing, No Child Left Behind delimits the curriculum to the basics and mitigates a full and rich curriculum, especially for disadvantaged children and youth, while impelling teachers to teach to the test. In perspective, it would seem that if no child is to be left behind, legislation on school improvement will need to be accompanied by concerted programs for universal preschool education, vocational education, health care, parent education, housing, and gainful employment.

Perspective

"Ours is an age of crisis," declared Silberman, but every age is an age of crisis. In the curriculum field, as in other areas of human activity, a crisis mentality tends to breed narrow-minded prescriptions and to lead to extreme actions that sooner or later result in a call for counterreaction.

The priority accorded the sciences and mathematics as a result of the crisis psychosis of the Cold War and space race resulted in a new curriculum hierarchy and imbalance, and led to the compression of college-level studies down into the high school curriculum. Moreover, the focus on the separate disciplines of knowledge aggravated the problem of curriculum fragmentation. Instead of seeing the school curriculum as an ecological whole, it was regarded simply as the sum of its parts. Thus, although the reform efforts were hailed as a veritable curriculum revolution, the strategy taken was one of developing disciplinary curriculum packages to be adopted by the schools independently of the relationships of a given knowledge package to other areas of knowledge in the school curriculum. Some of the leading spokespeople for the major science projects actually maintained that teacher-proof curricula were needed, as though the teacher is merely a low-grade technician whose job it is to plug himself or herself into the self-propelled curriculum package.

No doubt the school curriculum needs reconstruction, for it is deeply ingrained with factual information and narrow skills remote from the life of the learner. However, the disciplinary view of knowledge is so centripetal, and each knowledge domain becomes so turned back on itself, that it loses its connections with other knowledge domains and with the ordinary but vital problems of life. Moreover, whatever justification could be offered for the disciplinary mode of scholarship in the university is insufficient for imposing the same model on the elementary and secondary schools.

Disciplinarity remains a powerful force in the realm of specialized university scholarship and it continues to influence the school curriculum. However, the curriculum of the school and college encompasses far more than specialized and departmentalized knowledge. The sum of the separate disciplines cannot make a whole curriculum. Because educators are working with real people in action-relevant contexts, curriculum development requires systematic consideration of (1) the nature and interests of the learner, (2) the problems of society, (3) the interdependence of knowledge, (4) the continuity between theoretical and applied knowledge, (5) the authentic function of general education as compared with that of specialized education, and (6) involvement of the whole school community, and not merely the scholar-specialist. Such considerations require interdisciplinary and social-problem approaches to curricular organization. Inquiry into such problems is different from inquiry into abstract and specialized knowledge. The paradigm of the curriculum field (discussed in detail in chapter 3) reemerged once again in the last quarter of the twentieth century.

What is so puzzling, however, is that the disciplinary doctrine gained adherents among the fraternity of educationists, including curriculum theorists, and that it dominated the curriculum field for so long a period. The crisis of the space race and the unprecedented level of funding of discipline-centered curriculum projects clearly contributed to the long-held dominance of the disciplinary doctrine. The voices of opposition to such a narrow doctrine and to the turning of the curriculum to meet narrow nationalistic interests were rarely heard.

In the face of these nationalizing influences on the curriculum, some efforts were being made in recent years to build a common core of learning in the school and college. Some were contending that such a core was especially needed as a counterpoint to the alleged exponential explosion of specialized knowledge. However, it was becoming increasingly evident in the twenty-first century that the pervading need was how to marshal knowledge for an effective attack on the exploding problems of society, and how to develop the needed curriculum synthesis for creating a sense of unity through our great social diversity. A variety of designs was being developed to provide for a more interrelated curriculum through faculty teams, block-time or modular-flexible scheduling, student portfolios, and thematic or problem-focused courses in ecology, civics for democracy, consumer education, and so on. Such efforts, however successful, were being made in the face of increasing statewide and national testing programs and other nationalizing influences affecting the curriculum.

The quest for a balanced and coherent curriculum, consonant with the ideals of a free society, reappears at regular intervals because it cannot be denied indefinitely. In an age of knowledge specialism and social fragmentation and conflict, the need for a unified core curriculum for general education was never more significant. The march of democracy in world affairs gives evidence that those who sought to advance the idea and practice of general education in the school and college were on the side of history. (Refer to the Best Practices Checklist on pages 481–499.)

PROBLEMS FOR STUDY AND DISCUSSION

1. With the end of World War II, the president of Harvard, James Conant, (1945) stated that he looked forward to a united front in education tied together by the basic aims of general education in the secondary school and college. He concluded with these words:

   Armed with *General Education for a Free Society* in one hand and *Education for ALL American Youth* in the other, I should hope to answer all critics of the future of our American schools! (p. 33)

   Why did the "united front" between the secondary school and college fail to materialize? What is the situation today? What events have led to the decline of general education in the secondary school and college? In the face of its decline, why has general education undergone renewed concern over the course of time to this day?

2. It might be said that the land-grant university and the comprehensive high school have much in common in offering a diversified curriculum uniting theoretical and practical studies, in serving heterogeneous populations, and in leading the way to coeducation on a universal scale.

   How do you explain the establishment of the land-grant university after the Civil War, whereas it was not until the twentieth century and the proposal of the Commission on the Reorganization of Secondary Education (1918) when the comprehensive high school began to take root?

3. How do you account for the failure of those responsible for the discipline-centered curriculum reforms to take into account (1) the relationship of a given curriculum project to other new projects being adopted by the schools and (2) the relationship of the new curriculum project to the total curriculum of the school? What is the situation today with regard to curriculum-reform projects?

4. Many of those who advocated teacher-proof curricula were at the same time calling for inquiry-focused teaching. Do you see a contradiction between teacher-proof curricula and inquiry-focused teaching? Explain.

5. What role should teachers play in curriculum development? Justify your answer.

6. What trends do you see today in the direction of curriculum change? In your opinion, what kinds of changes are needed? Explain.

7. How do you account for the lack of strong opposition to the disciplinary movement by educationists over a period of two decades? Is there strong opposition to the dominant curriculum movement today? Explain.

8. What is your assessment of the charges leveled at the public schools in *America 2000*?

9. How do you account for the division of the school curriculum into "academic" and "nonacademic" subjects, whereas no such division exists in the college or university? What are the educational and social consequences of such a curriculum division in the schools?

10. From his study of grouping practices in the schools, Goodlad (1984) found that heterogeneously grouped classes reflect a more productive learning atmosphere than homogeneous classes. Consequently, he recommended that in the common core of studies at all levels of schooling, students should be assigned to classes randomly so as to ensure

heterogeneity [John Goodlad, *A Place Called School*, pp. 297–298]. Considering the intended function of general education, what is the underlying rationale for heterogeneous grouping? Do you agree with Goodlad? Explain.

11. If you were asked to submit a plan for redesigning the curriculum for your school, what would be the major features and recommendations in your plan? What arguments would you raise in support of your plan?

CHAPTER 13

THE CURRICULUM AND THE WORLD OF WORK

"It is a strange state of affairs in an industrial democracy when those very subjects are held in disrepute which are at the heart of the national economy and those students by implication condemned who will become its operators," declared the Harvard Report (1945, p. 27).

Educational theory has been marked by a wall of separation stemming from the time of ancient Greece when the life of labor was regarded as servile and the life of leisure was conceived ideally as the rational life. This dualistic conception reflected the division of society itself: a life of contemplative appreciation for the free man and a life of servile labor for the slave. Carried to its logical conclusion, the two sides of life represented unintelligent practice on the one hand and unpractical intelligence on the other (Dewey, 1958, p. 93).

According to the Harvard Report, "Modern democratic society clearly does not regard labor as odious or disgraceful; on the contrary, in this country, at least, it regards leisure with suspicion and expects its 'gentlemen' to engage in work" (p. 52). The notion of the contemporary worker being engaged in unintelligent practice not only is inimical to the democratic ideal but also denies the modern technological society of a vital source of reflective direction of its activities. Indeed, the evils that have come to be associated with technology reflect such a denial by viewing people merely as mechanical components in the industrial process. Workers are regarded as appendages of the machine rather than the machine being the appendage of people. The consequence is that society is denied the quality of workmanship that is vital to its own improvement, and the worker sees the fruits of labor only in terms of material reward. Work is regarded as something to put up with, with the result that the personal-social equation is submerged and the quality of life is made to suffer.

American education has been marked by a long struggle to reveal the cultural possibilities of work and to equip the citizen to give intelligent direction to life. Yet a strange state of affairs exists in American education. Many educators see social power and insight stemming only from the academic side of the curriculum, and they deny the possibilities of such power and insight deriving from vocational education. Wittingly or unwittingly, they have perpetuated an oppositional conception of curriculum that works against a democratic social order. This educational opposition separates education from vocation as though the making of a living can be separated from living, and as though the thinking person and working person cannot be one and the same.

The Democratic Ideal: A Unitary School Structure

Dewey wrote in 1916:

> Every expansive era in the history of mankind has coincided with the operation of factors which have tended to eliminate distance between peoples and classes previously hemmed off from one another. . . . A democracy is more than a form of government; it is primarily a mode of associated living, of conjoint communicated experience. (pp. 100–101)

At the time when Dewey wrote *Democracy and Education*, the high school enrolled only a small fraction of the adolescent age group. In fact, a far smaller proportion of the age cohort was enrolled in high school in that day than is enrolled in college today. Yet, over the first two decades of the twentieth century, the high school population multiplied by more than threefold whereas the actual population of the adolescent age group increased by less than 20%. Although universal secondary education was not to become a reality until decades later, the rising enrollments, coupled with the expanding requirements of industrialism and technology, were accompanied by a surge of demand for vocational studies in the curriculum. Other leading industrial nations had established a dual system of schooling, with separate vocational schools for the working classes and academic schools for the more privileged classes. One of the key issues of the day was whether the United States should pattern its system of schooling after the dual European model or whether it should seek a new comprehensive model. Indeed, in various sections of the United States, separate vocational schools had already been established.

A second related issue pertained to the purposes and function of vocational education. On the one hand were those who promoted vocational education to meet the industrial demands for trained workers and to compete with the industrial productivity of other nations. On the other hand were the progressive educators, who envisioned vocational education as a means of providing for the "liberation of a greater diversity of personal capacities which characterize a democracy" and who saw this being accomplished within a comprehensive school setting that would provide for "a mode of associated living, of conjoint, communicated experience" (Dewey, 1916, p. 101).

Nationalistic and Vested Interests Versus the Democratic Interest

National support for vocational education was provided at the college level more than half a century before it was instituted at the secondary level of schooling. The Morrill Act of 1862, signed by President Abraham Lincoln, provided land grants that led to the establishment of a national network of land-grant colleges and universities. The Morrill Act stipulated that the leading purposes of these colleges "shall be, without excluding other scientific and classical studies . . . to teach such branches of learning as are related to agriculture and the mechanic arts . . . in order to promote the liberal and practical education of the industrial classes in the several pursuits and professions of life" (Commager, 1968a, pp. 412–413). These land-grant institutions or "people's colleges" were to become the great state universities that enrolled students from all segments of society.

The Battle for a Unitary System.   The structure of American education was approaching a critical turning point. On the one hand were those industrial groups and educators who advocated the splitting of the school system along the lines of the dual European model. On the other hand were those who viewed a dual system as promulgating social cleavage and stratification; they urged that the United States, in the interests of its democratic ideals, choose a unified system of comprehensive schooling. No model for such a unified system existed anywhere else in the world, and proponents of comprehensive schooling contended that the United States must develop its own unique pattern if it were to be true to its democratic ideals. Writing in *The New Republic* in 1915, Dewey attacked legislative proposals in Illinois and elsewhere that called for the establishment of a dual education system as leading to a segregation and stratification of social classes.

> The segregation proposed is to divide the children of the more well-to-do and cultured families of the community from those children who will presumably earn their living by working for wages in manual and commercial employments. . . . Many of us have been disturbed at the increasing tendency toward stratification of classes in this country. We have wondered if those European prophets were correct who have insistently foretold that the development of fixed classes in this country was only a question of time. Few would have dreamed that the day was already at hand when responsible and influential persons would urge that the public school system should recognize the separation as an accomplished fact, and adapt to it its machinery of administrative control, its courses of study and its methods of instruction in the public school. (p. 283)

Dewey also argued that by providing for vocational education within a unified system, the vocational and academic studies would receive constant reciprocal stimulation and permeation, and different pupils would be in constant personal association. Under a dual system, he warned, the old curriculum would be left frozen in its narrow form in one type of school, whereas vocational education in the other type of school would be reduced to narrow training to create a source of manpower for exploitation in the interests of industrial efficiency.

Most major pieces of federal educational legislation during the twentieth century have been enacted in response to international or domestic crises. Just two months before the entry of the United States into

World War I, President Woodrow Wilson signed into law the Smith-Hughes Act of 1917, which provided federal funds to be matched by state allocations for vocational education of less-than-college level in agriculture, trades and industries, and home economics for persons over 14 years of age. In the face of the war-preparedness climate that pervaded the times (and spurred the passage of this legislation), the National Education Association promptly warned against the establishment of a dual system of education along the lines of European education systems (1918, p. 26).

The Battle for Democratic Interest.   A year prior to the passage of the Smith-Hughes Act, Dewey had warned in *Democracy and Education* of the danger of turning education to fit narrow nationalistic interests, as had been the case in Germany. Dewey called for a kind of vocational education that was consonant with the democratic ideal of developing social power and insight for the rising generation. Pointing out that "the intellectual *possibilities* of industry have multiplied," Dewey stressed that industrial conditions were making industry less and less an educative resource for the great masses and, consequently, the "burden of realizing the intellectual possibilities inhering with work is thus thrown back on the school." He warned of the danger of making the school an adjunct to manufacture and commerce. "Education would then become an instrument of perpetuating unchanged the existing industrial order of society, instead of operating as a means of its transformation," declared Dewey (1916, pp. 367, 369).

Dewey envisioned this transformation being signified when every member of society "shall be occupied in something which makes the lives of others more worth living," and he pointed out that such a society "denotes a state of affairs in which the interest of each in his work is uncoerced and intelligent: based upon its congeniality to his own aptitudes." He noted that although education cannot effect such a change apart from a corresponding redirection of industrial and political conditions, "it does mean that we may produce in schools a projection in type of the society we should like to realize," making it possible to "gradually modify the larger and more recalcitrant features of adult society" (1916, pp. 369–370).

Dewey vigorously opposed the splitting of the educational system along the lines of European schooling. "To split the system," he wrote, "is to treat the schools as an agency for transferring the older

division of labor and leisure, culture and service, mind and body, directed and directive class, into a society nominally democratic" (1916, p. 372). Not only did he point to the danger of splitting the educational system along two curriculum tracks but he also attacked the traditional dualistic notion, perpetuated particularly by the literary intelligentsia, setting cultural and vocational education in opposition. In this connection, Dewey noted the inherent contradiction in the prevalent attitude on the part of the college educated who would deny vocational education to those who do not go on to college while they themselves reap the benefits of vocational education in the higher institutions.

> By a peculiar superstition, education which has to do chiefly with preparation for the pursuit of conspicuous idleness, for teaching, and for literary callings, and for leadership, has been regarded as non-vocational and even as peculiarly cultural . . . many a teacher and author writes and argues in behalf of a cultural and humane education against the encroachments of a specialized practical education, without recognizing that his own education, which he calls liberal, has been mainly training for his own particular calling. He has simply got into the habit of regarding his own business as essentially cultural and of overlooking the cultural possibilities of other employments. (1916, pp. 365–366)

Dewey attacked those who would establish a separate system of schooling as seeking merely to turn out more efficient workers for the existing industrial order, rather than developing human beings who are equipped to reconstruct the existing scheme. Dewey's opposition to a dual school system was shared by many educators and, as mentioned earlier, led to the passage of an NEA resolution to this effect in 1918. In that same year the NEA's Commission on the Reorganization of Secondary Education supported vocational education in the context of the comprehensive high school that would serve as "the prototype of democracy" (p. 26).

As discussed in chapter 12, if any single document marked the historic turning point of commitment to the comprehensive high school as opposed to the dual European model of secondary education, it was the *Cardinal Principles* report (1918) of the Commission on the Reorganization of Secondary Education. As James Conant pointed out, "this document was taken as the starting point for almost all forward-looking reforms in public high schools for forty years" (1964b, pp. 19–20).

Revisionists and other critics from the radical left have chosen not to recognize that Dewey and the members of the Commission on the Reorganization of Secondary Education had taken their stance in advancing the comprehensive high school and in holding that the adoption of a dual system of schooling, as in Europe, would perpetuate the social stratification that was characteristic of the European nations. They failed to recognize how close the United States was to adopting the dual European model, for the comprehensive high school had no counterpart anywhere in the world (Hofstadter, 1970, pp. 334–337).

Lawrence Cremin, Pulitzer prize-winning historian, described the *Cardinal Principles* report as "a statement which literally ushered in a whole new age—an age that embraced an educational revolution." Cremin described the transformation of the high school as conceived by the *Cardinal Principles* report:

> From an institution conceived for the few, the high
> school became an institution conceived for all. From
> an adjunct to the college, the high school became
> the pivotal point in the public school system, one
> which carried forward objectives yet unfinished
> by the elementary school and opened new vistas
> leading on to the college.... Such was the grand
> design of this Commission, one which, in weaving
> a multitude of new and pressing demands into
> an integral view of the school, was able to face
> squarely toward the future and thereby to usher
> in a whole new age in American secondary
> education. (1955, p. 307)

The Struggle for a Recognized Place in the Curriculum

Through the Smith-Hughes Act of 1917, a federal-state partnership for vocational education was established, and the various programs came to be operated within the structure of a unitary school system. Nevertheless, the level of support remained relatively modest in view of the kinds of facilities and resources that were needed for effective vocational education in a technological society. Moreover, the programs as provided by the 1917 legislation were categorical rather than comprehensive, being limited to production agriculture, trades and industries, and home economics.

Although the unitary type of high school predominated in various sections of the nation, most of the high schools offered only a limited range of vocational programs and were not truly comprehensive. The curriculum of the high school remained biased largely in favor of the college preparatory function, and only a small fraction of the majority of youngsters who did not go on to college were being reached by federally supported programs of vocational education.

Bypassing the Schools

The Great Depression had created a vast army of out-of-school, out-of-work youth. Various federal programs were created to deal with this problem, but these efforts were largely in the form of stopgap measures of limited educational effectiveness. Many of the programs were administered independently of the schools. Although a comprehensive design for vocational education in the setting of the comprehensive high school was needed, legislation in 1929 and 1935 simply provided additional funds for the expansion of the existing programs as stipulated under the Smith-Hughes Act of 1917. This was a time when college graduates in the liberal arts, lacking salable skills, also were faced with unemployment.

The tendency of the federal government to bypass the schools in many of its emergency programs raised the fear in the minds of some educators that a dual system of education might be created. A 1938 report of the Educational Policies Commission pointed to the danger that in bypassing the schools the federal government might be sowing the seeds for a dual educational system. This report called for the consolidation of educational programs within the structure of the unitary school system, from the nursery school through the high school and community college. Three years later, the commission reiterated its stance and criticized the failure of the schools to provide adequately for vocational education. "There will be no 'out-of-school unemployed youth' for federal agencies to educate, when schools everywhere extend their responsibilities to all young people until they are satisfactorily established in adult vocations" (1941, pp. 32–33).

Almost a quarter of a century later—at a time of general economic prosperity, but when mounting unemployment among youth had created "social dynamite" in the urban poverty sectors—the federal government turned again to nonschool emergency agencies such as the Office of Economic Opportunity and its Job Corps program to provide for job training outside the school system. Once again, these efforts proved to be largely ineffective. The needed reassessment and reconstruction of vocational education in the context of the comprehensive high school was never more urgent.

From Postwar Visions to Cold War Counterforces

World War II had given cause for various groups of educators to examine the prospects of the comprehensive high school and vocational education for the coming era of postwar reconstruction. Two notable reports, the Harvard Report and a report by the Educational Policies Commission, were issued in this connection.

Postwar Visions. Although the Harvard Report of 1945, issued with the end of World War II, focused on general education in school and college, it strongly endorsed the role and function of vocational education in the context of the comprehensive high school. Pointing to the need to endue the various studies in the curriculum "with a respect commensurate to their equally necessary part in American life," the Harvard Report recommended that for students who are ending their formal education with high school approximately one third of their time might be devoted to vocational education. Concerning the relationship between general and specialized (vocational) education, the report stated, "These two sides of education should be thought of as connected, the special forever flowing out of the general and forever returning and enriching it" (pp. 28, 102, 103).

As we have seen, in *Education for ALL American Youth* (1944, revised 1952), the NEA's Educational Policies Commission envisioned a model educational system in which students in the setting of the comprehensive high school would have access to a full range of programs extending through grades 13 and 14 (the community college) for successful entry to the world of work (pp. 264–286).

The time devoted to vocational education would total one sixth in grade 10, one third in grades 11 and 13, and one half in the community college, which would be administered integrally to the school district (grades 13 and 14). The significance of this far-reaching proposal to meld the upper division of the high school with the community college for vocational/career education can be appreciated only in the light of the fact that it was not until the early 1990s that federal legislation supported this articulated structuring of the curriculum of the high school and community college. This came to be called the two-plus-two or tech/prep program.

The model proposed by the Educational Policies Commission (1944, 1952) called for supervised work experience as integral to the curriculum. The curriculum in vocational education would be broadly based and geared realistically to community conditions so as to minimize the possibilities for technological unemployment. The high schools also would offer opportunities for further specialized studies through part-time and evening classes for out-of-school youth, whereas the community college would play a key role in preparing students for technical and semiprofessional occupations through formal studies and supervised work experience. Through effective counseling and a comprehensive curriculum in the high school, the gates of higher learning would be kept open to all who might benefit from further education. Students would not be tracked according to curricula, and the various programs would be kept flexible and interrelated, taking into account the needs of those students who enter the world of work directly from high school, those who will go on to the community college, and those who plan to pursue education beyond the community college.

Significantly, as part of general education, all students would be engaged in community service projects. However, unlike the community-service programs for high school and college students proposed and implemented in recent years, the programs described in *Education for ALL American Youth* would be fully articulated with the curriculum—such as students undertaking a systematic study of community health problems and making the data available to community officials.

The Comprehensive High School in Cold War Crisis

From the military sector and the halls of Congress to the halls of academia, the Cold War call was to turn American education to serving narrow nationalistic interests. The issue of splitting the educational system was raised once again. To meet the Soviet threat in the battle for global supremacy and in the space race, a dual educational system would be required. The comprehensive high school had never been so severely threatened since its establishment. Conant's defense of the comprehensive high school at this juncture in history was to prove decisive.

Cold War Criticisms

Unlike the Harvard Report, which generated little controversy, *Education for ALL American Youth* came under severe attack during the Cold War. Taking a cue from the ancient dualism between thinking man and working man, Arthur Bestor, a leading essentialist, contended that "liberal education is the education by which a man achieves freedom [and] self-reliance," whereas vocational programs "breed servile dependence." Not only did Bestor fail to explain how a person can be free when not prepared to earn a living, but he also viewed vocational studies as mere training in tricks of the trade. "The West was not settled by men and women who had taken courses in how to be a pioneer," he continued, as if to imply that the West was settled by historians, philologists, and literati (1956, pp. 38, 67–68, 79–80). Bestor attacked *Education for ALL American Youth* and its proposals for vocational education as subverting the school's goal of intellectual training in favor of "life adjustment." Vocational courses should carry no academic credit, contended Bestor, and should not in general be open to students under the age of 17.

The Comprehensive High School as Scapegoat

Within three months after the launching of Sputnik I, congressional hearings were being held to determine the school reforms needed for national defense. Such nationally visible figures as Admiral Hyman Rickover (father of the nuclear submarine) and Wernher von Braun, the German-educated missile expert who had played a key role in developing the V-1 and V-2 rockets that the Germans launched against civilian populations in Britain during World War II, were called to testify at the hearings. Now that von Braun was working for the U.S. missile program, he was treated in the American media as an almost heroic figure. Hollywood romanticized his life in a film *I Aimed at the Stars*, leading some viewers to quip that the correct title should have been *I Aimed at the Stars, But Hit London Instead.*

Testifying before a committee of the U.S. Senate in January 1958, von Braun offered the solution to the chief shortcoming of America's school system. Referring to his own education as European rather

than German, von Braun offered that we rid schools of the "ballast" by adopting the "European" system (when he seemed to be describing the system in Nazi Germany).

> There is a lot more ruthlessness over there in just washing out the less competent. It is, you might say, a survival-of-the-fittest type of training: whoever does not live up to the standards is simply eliminated . . . the less able will be dropped with a lot less regard to their own personal interests.
>
> Thus the European school systems . . . are loaded with much less ballast. . . . As a result, the teachers of these schools need not bother with the less gifted. (U.S. Senate Committee on Labor hearings, 1958, p. 65)

Finally, von Braun endorsed Rickover's proposal for the creation of a federal commission to serve as an "inspection agency, to establish standards of educational requirements for graduates of high schools" (p. 67). (As history would have it, the crisis of techno-industrial competition with Japan and Germany was to impel Congress to pass legislation in 1991 that led to the creation of the National Council on Education Standards and Testing in addition to the National Assessment of Educational Programs and other federally supported testing programs for the schools [Epstein, 1996].)

Appearing before the Senate committee on the same day as von Braun was Lee DuBridge, a noted physicist and member of the President's Science Advisory Committee. After testifying that special federal support should be targeted for the school curriculum in the sciences and mathematics, DuBridge cited the need for the teacher "to recognize and encourage special talent [and who] must be an effective friend and counselor to students and especially to those who are unusually gifted and ambitious." As far as the less-able student is concerned, DuBridge declared,

> The right of a student to an education is a right which persists as far as his intellectual capabilities and his ambition should take him. This might be to the sixth grade, in the case of the unfortunate individual, and might be through the doctor of philosophy for those who are better favored by genetics or environment (p. 67).

Unfortunately, the senators did not ask DuBridge or von Braun what society should do with those unfortunate individuals who are dropped from school when they reach the sixth grade because they are less favored by genetics or environment. Even assuming that American schools were able to unload their "ballast," to use von Braun's expression, we must ask not only what will society do with these youngsters, but also what will they do to society.

Whereas von Braun, DuBridge, and Rickover unhesitatingly blamed the public schools for America's alleged missile gap, they found no fault with America's scientific-industrial-military complex, nor with the colleges and universities.

As cited in chapter 10, Rickover contended that we no longer had a choice between "democratic" education in the "time-wasting" comprehensive high school and efficient education by means of the dual system. "We must opt for efficiency," he declared (1963, p. 89).

The sentiments of such figures as Rickover and von Braun were shared by a legion of academicians who were quick to seize on the Cold War and space race to vent the essentialist-perennialist assault against the egalitarianism of the comprehensive high school. The Council for Basic Education, founded by Bestor in 1956, drew most of its membership from academia and capitalized on the crisis mentality of the times (Hayden, 1992). In his Pulitzer prize–winning work, *Anti-intellectualism in American Life,* Richard Hofstadter (1970) fixed the *Cardinal Principles* report and the vocationalism of the comprehensive high school as chief sources of blame for promoting mass education over the quality education of a selective system. "European education pointed to the outmoded past; science and democracy looked to the future," wrote Hofstadter in his portrayal of the progressivist vision. But now the progressivist ideas were in for a rude awakening, for "[t]his way of thought has been jolted by scientific competition with the Soviet Union." Hofstadter held the Soviet secondary school system as a model of "a demanding academic curriculum to large numbers" (pp. 351–352). Hofstadter conveniently ignored the readily available evidence on the pervasive shortcomings of the Soviet system, such as the limited access to secondary schooling for older adolescents. (Not until 1975 did the Soviets require 10 years of schooling for all youth.) Some of the other known shortcomings pointed to the restrictions imposed on academic scholarship by political authorities, the uses of the curriculum for the political indoctrination of children and youth, the educational favoritism accorded children of party officials, the limited access to higher education for the children of workers, the restrictions attendant to a system of channeling educational access to manpower needs through a dual schooling structure, the antiquated educational methods that pervaded the system, and the appallingly substandard school facilities and resources in many areas.

Whereas during the 1950s the nuclear age was heralded as auguring a future of unlimited energy and the space age a future of unlimited boundaries, the opening of the twenty-first century found the nation faced with the unemployment of nuclear and aerospace engineers and the problems of how to safely dispose of nuclear warheads and waste from nuclear power plants, and how to cope more effectively with ecological problems.

In Defense of the Comprehensive High School

Although Conant's 1959 Carnegie report on the American high school had focused to a great extent on the college preparatory population and the pursuit of academic excellence at a time of Soviet competition, he nevertheless made many significant recommendations concerning vocational education. Conant pointed out that in those cities having separate specialized academic and vocational high schools, the other high schools were left without federally supported programs of vocational education.

Conant stressed that "the comprehensive high school is characteristic of our society and further that it has come into being because of our economic history and our devotion to the ideals of equality of opportunity and equality of status" (p. 8). He pointed out that the land-grant universities had developed diversified curricula and had dissolved the distinctions that had marked traditional higher education, with the result that these institutions have come to be recognized as a symbol of equality of status and a means to the realization of this ideal. He envisioned the comprehensive high school in a similar vein, enhancing equality of status of all honest pursuits. He noted that in the large Eastern cities selective academic high schools were to be found, whereas such schools had not spread to the Middle West and Far West. Conant noted that such schools tended to be found in areas where there is no large and powerful state university, and he observed that this phenomenon was probably not accidental. He also commented that these schools in certain ways resemble the preuniversity schools of Europe. Conant expressed his belief that the homogeneous nature of the population enrolled in selective academic high schools denied students the democratizing social advantages that accrue to attending the comprehensive high school. Similarly, the separate vocational high school perpetuated social separation.

Conant noted that in his survey of comprehensive high schools he was able to find programs that were highly successful in preparing youngsters for skilled employment in industry, and that in some communities youngsters who had completed programs in trades and industries had gone on to the community college for advanced preparation in tool design, a career field of great opportunity. He also supported programs of supervised work experience and recommended that high schools participate in the federal programs of vocational education in accordance with the needs of their student populations and the employment situation. He held that students should not be tracked according to vocational and college preparatory programs but should be allowed to pursue studies in the various areas of the school curriculum in accordance with their interests and capabilities, although he did recommend ability grouping in the general education courses along with selective criteria for admission to advanced academic studies. Conant expressed his belief that high school youngsters should have an ultimate vocational goal. Even if they change their minds during high school or in later years, such a goal attaches greater significance to their studies. Finally, in upholding his conviction of the social benefits to be gained through the comprehensive high school over the specialized high school, Conant concluded: "I believe it is important for the future of American democracy to have as close a relationship as possible in high school between the future professional man, the future craftsman, the future manager of industry, the future labor leader, the future salesman, and the future engineer" (p. 127). In his follow-up report (1967), Conant reiterated this statement in bold print and concluded that high schools' facilities and resources still required vigorous strengthening.

Conant's defense of the comprehensive high school, in a report that became a kind of quasi-official manual for school boards and administrators throughout the nation, turned the tide away from a dual educational system. The comprehensive high school had survived the Cold War crisis.

Era of Social Crisis

The plight of out-of-school, unemployed youth and the smoldering conditions of inner cities were largely ignored during the 1950s when national priorities in education were focused on the academically talented and on the improvement of those academic studies that were deemed essential to the nation's Cold War needs. The high schools seemed relatively unconcerned about the occupational preparation and placement of youngsters who were seeking a place in the world of work and instead gave priority to improving the academic disciplines and the college preparatory program and to the college placement of academically promising students. Although the danger signals were in evidence in urban areas, the schools encountered difficulties in turning from the old crisis of the Cold War to the new crisis of social disaffection and unemployment that was plaguing disadvantaged youth.

"Social Dynamite"

As discussed in chapter 11, in 1961 Conant's *Slums and Suburbs* appeared, a report on urban education based on his observations made during his Carnegie studies. "I am convinced that we are allowing social dynamite to accumulate in our large cities," declared Conant, as he estimated that in some slums most of the population between the ages of 16 and 21 was out of school and out of work (pp. 2–18).

Conant noted that the larger cities lacked truly comprehensive high schools and that we were belatedly recognizing that a caste system finds its sharpest manifestation in an educational system. Regarding the need for vocational education, Conant pointed out that even those youngsters in the slum areas who gained high school diplomas were likely to face unemployment without effective vocational education. He wisely understood that high school and even college students undergo changes in career aspirations, and he recognized the need for a smooth transition from full-time schooling or college to full-time employment (p. 40). A high school or college graduate with marketable skills will invariably be able to use those skills regardless of subsequent career changes.

Needed Reforms. "It is far more difficult in many communities to obtain admission to an apprentice program that involves union approval than to get into the most selective medical school in the nation," continued Conant (pp. 46–47). He reported that he found schools with effective vocational programs where students completing such programs also were adequately prepared to go on to college. He recommended that vocational programs be made available in grades 11 and 12, and possibly earlier, and that such studies constitute up to half the student's time. Moreover, the schools should assume a more direct responsibility for job placement and follow-up of their graduates and dropouts.

"The critics of American education, so it seems to me, are under an obligation to be both concrete with their proposals and to be clear as to the premises from which they start their arguments"; regarding our slum schools, "we need to know the facts, and when these facts indicate a dangerous social situation the American people should be prepared to take prompt action before it is too late," Conant concluded (pp. 136, 137).

Conant's assessment and his recommendations were attacked by many intelligentsia, both black and white, as a middle-class prescription to be imposed on disadvantaged Black youth so as to have them conform to the work ethic of American society (Smiley, 1967, p. 140). These critics of vocational education tended to overlook the fact that Black and Hispanic youth were not adequately represented in the existing high school programs of vocational education as well as in the skilled occupations, that the skilled occupations are requiring ever higher qualifications for entry, that vocational education of a high quality is the means of developing these qualifications, and that entry into skilled occupations would open the way to increased social power on the part of all youth who do not go on to college.

Efforts to Expand and Improve Vocational Education. The mounting youth unemployment and social disaffection in the central cities impelled President John F. Kennedy in 1961 to request the secretary of Health, Education, and Welfare (HEW) to assess the impact of the various national vocational education acts. A panel appointed by the HEW secretary issued its report in 1963. The panel found "that graduates of high school vocational programs are less likely to be unemployed than other high school graduates, the vocational graduates do in fact work in the occupations for which they prepare, and that vocational education increases their subsequent earnings" (Panel, 1963, p. xvi). The panel also reported

that despite commitment to the comprehensive high school, the vocational programs were limited in scope and were serving only 13% of the 15-to-19 age group. Furthermore, vocational home economics was found to account for most of the enrollment.

The panel cited the failure of existing federal legislation to provide adequate support for occupational clusters, along with the failure of vocational programs to reach youth in the largest cities as well as those rural youth who will migrate to urban areas in search of employment. The report also stressed that relatively few schools were offering supervised and cooperative work-study programs, despite the promising potential of such programs in preventing dropouts and in linking school studies with gainful employment. Calling attention to the "social dynamite" being created in the growing army of out-of-school, unemployed youth, the panel stressed that lives and talents were being wasted and that the social, economic, and political structure of urban areas was being threatened. Finally, the report attacked the existing federal patchwork of legislation and called for the unification of federal legislation to provide a comprehensive and flexible foundation for vocational education.

Renewed Federal Efforts.   The Vocational Education Act of 1963 was hailed as the most significant piece of federal legislation on vocational education since 1917. Through the 1963 legislation and the amendments of 1968, most of the categorical restrictions in the earlier laws were eliminated. In effect, this legislation encompassed virtually any occupation or occupational cluster short of the professions and also removed the earlier restriction that had limited most programs to a level of less-than-college grade. Moreover, it allowed schools to develop integrated programs of vocational and general education so as to improve the learning opportunities of those with socioeconomic and educational handicaps.

Despite the significant increase in federal funds provided by this legislation, the appropriations were insufficient to the enormous task of reaching the majority of youth who might benefit from vocational education. Furthermore, exploding conditions in inner cities beginning in the mid-1960s led to a new patchwork of emergency, nonschool, educative programs reminiscent of the emergency measures taken by the federal government during the Great Depression.

Presage for a Dual System

There was also a dark side to the 1963 legislation, a side that raised the question of whether the provision for the construction of specialized vocational schools might lead to the beginnings of a dual system of secondary education. Although many cities, especially in the northeast, operated specialized vocational and academic high schools, the dominant American pattern consisted of high schools of the comprehensive type. Although the selective specialized vocational high school, such as New York City's High School of Aviation Trades, could boast outstanding records of gainful employment and college entrance on the part of graduates, America's unparalleled record of educational yield among the advanced nations of the world was to be attributed to the unitary school structure capped by the comprehensive high school.

Now the new federal legislation provided for the construction on a national scale of specialized area vocational schools with full-time enrollment and with shared-time enrollment. Under the shared-time arrangement students pursued their vocational coursework in the specialized school, continued their studies in their home high school in general education and exploratory and enrichment education, and participated in extraclass activities.

Initially, the availability of outstanding facilities and resources found instances when the specialized vocational schools were unable to meet the enrollment demands and were becoming selective, with the result that many students were being turned away. In other instances, the stigma of attending a vocational school resulted in severe enrollment shortfalls. Further, most adolescents were understandably unwilling to sever friendships and other ties with their home high school, such as participation in varsity sports and other extraclass programs. Although the shared-time pattern allowed for the continuance of these ties, at least theoretically, scheduling constraints arising from dual enrollment and transportation not only limited opportunities for participation in extraclass activities, but also found students being tracked in their academic classes in their home high school. At the same time, their elective options for exploratory and enrichment studies were limited by scheduling difficulties. Many college-bound students who might have elected certain vocational courses if offered in the comprehensive high school now found it singularly inconvenient and unappealing to pursue such courses in a separate school even on a shared-time basis.

Although these factors buttressed the case for the comprehensive high school and found the comprehensive high school continuing to represent the mainstream structure of American secondary education, there was no question that the investment in facilities and resources that went into the specialized schools would have gone a long way in making so many of the high schools truly comprehensive.

Perhaps the most striking lesson to be derived from these developments, aside from gaining a better appreciation of the powerful cultural roots of our unitary school structure, was that the federal legislation to create a nationwide system of separate specialized vocational schools at this juncture of history was met with virtually no opposition on the part of community leaders, school people, or the professorate. It should be remembered that the battle against the creation of a dual system of secondary schooling was won early in the twentieth century by progressive educators in opposition to the industrialists and vocationalists who favored a dual structure.

Half a century later, when the seeds were being sown for a dual system, academicians and others who were identified with the radical left and who presented themselves as champions of disadvantaged adolescents—such as Edgar Friedenberg (1967, pp. 250–252) and Paul Goodman (1970, pp. 86–89)—actually were making the case for a divided system. It seemed inexplicable that those on the radical left should join with the industrialists in seeking a dual school structure. Perhaps the academic left was revealing a masked elitism. Friedenberg, Goodman, and others were proposing that the high school be limited to serving exclusively the academically oriented, whereas the others would find other means of making their way into society. As was the case early in the century, leaders in the field of vocational education joined the industrialists in supporting proposed federal legislation to fund specialized vocational schools on the ground that it would provide added support for their field. They failed to realize that by removing vocational education from the comprehensive high school it was being removed from the mainstream of the public school system.

Further, with the notable exception of Conant, educational leaders in the United States seemed oblivious of the march of events in Britain, Sweden, and other leading European democracies in establishing the comprehensive high school in place of the traditional divided structure of secondary schooling.

The War on Poverty

Outbreaks of civil disorder in major cities beginning in the early 1960s resulted in the Economic Opportunity Act of 1964. In signing this act into law, President Lyndon B. Johnson declared a War on Poverty that was strangely reminiscent of Franklin D. Roosevelt's 1933 call to Congress "to wage a war against the emergency." The 1960s were different times in that mainstream America was in relative affluence and the nation was engaged in a real war in Southeast Asia.

Emergency Programs. With the establishment of the Office of Economic Opportunity (OEO), a variety of education programs for disadvantaged youth appeared. As in the case of the Great Depression, these emergency programs were administered largely outside the school system and by a new federal agency independent of the permanent education agency (U.S. Office of Education).

One of the most widely heralded programs was the Job Corps, established by the OEO in 1965. Job Corps centers were established throughout the United States under contracts with private industry to train out-of-school youth for skilled employment and to provide remedial education. The reasoning of OEO officials was that the schools had failed to provide disadvantaged youth with the skills necessary for gainful employment and that industry, with its know-how, would accomplish the task. It soon became apparent that many private corporations were engaging in Job Corps contracts solely for their own profit. Bidding companies were described in a national news magazine as acting "like blindfolded bulldogs in a butcher shop" (*Newsweek*, May 5, 1965, p. 75). The sponsoring corporations assumed no responsibility for employing youngsters who had completed the program, nor did they guarantee job placement elsewhere. No provisions were made for cooperative, supervised on-the-job training. Many of the centers for boys were located at abandoned military bases hundreds of miles from the youngsters' homes, and these centers tended to acquire a quasimilitary climate. The centers were assembled hastily, and difficulties were encountered in engaging qualified professional staffs. A study ordered by Congress to review the War on Poverty reported in 1969 that corps trainees did little better in the labor market than poor youths without such training (U.S. Senate Committee on Labor and U.S. House Committee on Education). During the ensuing years, many centers were relocated, and the program was virtually phased out.

In many respects, the OEO assumed a negative stance toward public schools, as evidenced by its education voucher plan for making federal funds available for alternative schools. Instead of seeking to identify the shortcomings of the public schools and to remedy the deficiencies, the federal policy under OEO was to set up separate educational programs at great expense and of questionable effectiveness.

Seething Social Problems

The president's National Advisory Commission on Civil Disorders, in its report of 1968, found from its survey data and arrest records in 20 cities that most of the rioters were unemployed and out-of-school late teenagers and young adults. The report called attention to the fact that only a small fraction of high school youth were enrolled in vocational education programs (pp. 74, 251). The commission recommended that these programs be greatly expanded and strengthened, to reach both in-school youth and dropouts, with emphasis being given to the development of part-time cooperative arrangements coupling formal education with supervised work experience. The commission also called for intensive efforts to develop programs in fields where critical shortages exist, such as in certain technical and health occupations.

In accordance with the vocational education amendments of 1968, the National Advisory Council on Vocational Education was created by Congress and, in 1969, issued the first of a series of reports. On the opening page of its first report, the council linked the rising racial unrest in cities with the continuing problem of youth unemployment and made a scathing indictment of a national attitude that looks with disfavor on vocational education and regards good education as purely academic—capped by a college degree.

> Our nation seethes. Racial unrest, violence and the unemployment of youth have their roots in inadequate education. Each year the ranks of the school dropouts increase by three-quarters of a million young men and women. They enter the job market without the skills and attitudes employers require. . . .
>
> At the very heart of the problem is a national attitude that says that vocational education is designed for somebody else's children. . . . We are all guilty. We have promoted the idea that the only good education is an education capped by four years of college. This idea, transmitted by our

values, our aspirations and our silent support, is snobbish, undemocratic, and a revelation of why schools fail so many students. (pp. 1–2)

The council pointed out that the opportunities in skilled occupations were expanding far more rapidly than were the opportunities for liberal arts graduates of U.S. colleges.

The growing army of unemployed and unskilled youth at a time of critical shortage of skilled workers impelled the editor of the journal of the American Association for the Advancement of Science to make vocational education the topic of an editorial.

> As a nation we have been preoccupied with fostering excellence of a limited group while neglecting the overwhelming majority of our youth . . . . Moreover, there have been many curriculum reform efforts benefiting college-bound students while vocational curricula have been little improved. One of our greatest mistakes has been to accord special prestige to a college degree while displaying indifference toward quality in craftsmanship. We reward verbal skill and abstract reasoning and deny dignity to manual workers. . . . In our society there is little place for the man or woman who has no special skill. If our increasingly technological society is not to deteriorate, we must find means of helping the young find useful roles whatever their particular aptitudes (Abelson, 1968, p. 635).

The editorial pointed out that despite technological advances, it was often necessary to wait weeks for the services of a skilled worker in the trades. Noting that federal funds for higher education were running almost 18 times the allocations for vocational education, the editorial recommended that a far greater investment be made in vocational education. In view of the leadership role played by the American Association for the Advancement of Science in the disciplinary curriculum reforms of the 1950s and 1960s, the editorial criticizing the one-sidedness of these curriculum efforts acquired a special significance. The main body of university intellectuals was far from recognizing the critical need for vocational education in the high schools. This situation pervades academia to this day.

Splitting Up the School System

Conant's fears for the survival of the American comprehensive high school seemed well founded from the course of events (1970a, pp. 73, 80). Most far-reaching educational reforms in leading democratic nations of Europe were being focused on the comprehensive school model in place of the traditional dualistic structure of selective schooling and its attendant social bias. This movement was conceived as a significant means toward social justice through the improvement of educational and social opportunity. It had become increasingly evident in these nations that it is not enough to restructure the school system administratively, but that the reconstruction of the curriculum is essential to the success of the comprehensive school (Husén, 1983; Benn & Chitty, 1997). The problem of developing a coherent curriculum in general education and a systematic curriculum in vocational education in the setting of the comprehensive high school demands concerted attention and support. In the past there had been the tendency in the United States to favor the college preparatory population and the academic side of the curriculum. Instead of moving to right the balance, American educational policy makers have embraced a set of alternatives that would split up the school system (Tanner, D., 1979, 2000).

New Agendas and Contravening Forces

Career Education

Havighurst had noted that studies of the interests of adolescents reveal that occupational planning and preparation are the principal interests of youth in the age group from 15 to 20, and he identified preparation for a career as one of he key developmental tasks of adolescence (1972, p. 64). A stigma has come to be attached to such terms as *vocational* and *occupational education*. Even many educators look on vocational preparation as mere job training, and they see the mechanic, for example, as being engaged in a mere job, whereas they ascribe the term *career* to such occupational fields as medicine, law, science, business, and the arts. It is not surprising, then, that people seek to measure themselves not according to their interest in their work, or in the value of their work to society, but according to the superior social status of their particular occupation over other callings. For example, in response to a newspaper article that classified nurses as service workers along with automotive mechanics, a registered nurse wrote the following in a letter of protest addressed to the editor:

> I had to train for three strenuous years. In order to receive my registration, I had to pass a long and complicated state board which included questions on anatomy, physiology, pharmacology, surgical and medical diseases, obstetrics, pediatrics, psychiatry, etc. I must constantly keep up with innovations in medical technique.

She noted that in classifying her as a "service worker" the author of the article had "caused me distress," and she ended her letter by stating that the author "owes an apology to nurses" (*New York Times Magazine*, 1973, p. 64). The writer of the letter failed to understand that obstetricians, pharmacists, lawyers, social workers, and orthodontists also are engaged in service occupations, and that society could not hold together without service. Moreover, she ignored the fact that the automotive and aircraft mechanic also must go through a strenuous program of preparation and must constantly keep up with innovations. The attitude that service is servile and that only the "higher" occupations are worthy is socially unconstructive. It pervades not only society at large but also educational institutions.

"Academic Snobbery."   In an address before the 1971 convention of the National Association of Secondary School Principals, the newly appointed U.S. commissioner of Education, Sidney P. Marland, admonished school administrators for being concerned mainly with college-entrance expectations and neglecting vocational-technical education. "We must purge ourselves of academic snobbery," declared Marland, and he proposed that "we dispose of the term *vocational education* and adopt the term *career education*" (in Goldhammer & Taylor, 1972, p. 35). He also proposed that a universal goal of education should be to equip every high school graduate to enter higher education or to enter useful and rewarding employment. Marland pointed out that each year 1.5 million youngsters either drop out of high school or end their formal education on graduation from high school and seek employment without any preparation for skilled occupations. Anyone who looks down on the skilled trades apparently has never had to engage an electrician, plumber, mason, or carpenter to make an emergency home repair.

Under Marland's leadership the concept of career education was promoted at virtually every level of schooling. As every teacher of young children knows full well, children develop their rudimentary understanding of human interdependence and society through their fascination with occupations. Clearly, the promotion of career education was implemented successfully for general education, especially at the elementary and middle school levels, whereas the focus and funding for specialized education at the high school level was lacking. The possibilities for career education to bridge the vocational and college preparatory programs of the high school are legion.

For example, in close coordination with the high school, summer programs could be instituted to provide for observational and participatory experiences to enable youth to explore, critically and constructively, all kinds of career opportunities in a wide variety of institutional settings. The youngster who is thinking about a career in law might be assigned courtroom observation; the adolescent interested in a career in nursing might be employed as a hospital aide; and the youth who is contemplating a career in merchandising might be employed in a department store. Such experiences would be conducted under the supervision of the school. Thus, the learning environment would be extended far beyond the school setting and, at the same time, the school would be impelled to make its curriculum more meaningful to adolescents by examining social problems and issues in realistic settings. Career education could be so developed as to have significant educative value in helping youth to continue their education in the community college and to make a successful transition to adulthood. Such a program requires significant changes in social institutions, for the school cannot do it alone. At the same time, career education might be implemented to create a fuller understanding of the interdependence of all members of a free society and to eliminate the divisive attitude that renders the academic studies a higher status than the vocational studies in the curriculum.

Myrdal referred to the United States as still a comparatively backward nation with regard to the failure not only to reduce poverty but also to provide programs of vocational education and employment opportunities for youth. Until this is accomplished, a large proportion of our adolescent population will continue to be "pressed down into an alien underclass" (1971). The situation described by Myrdal has continued as a critical national problem into the twenty-first century.

As discussed in detail in chapter 12, most of the proposals for the reform of secondary education during the 1980s called for reducing the curriculum to academic subjects and appropriating the function of vocational training to business and industry. However, contrary to myth, business and industry lacked the programs and interest in providing high school graduates with the training required for the skilled trades and other skilled occupations. A heavily documented report of a national commission, *The Forgotten Half: Non-College Youth in America* (1988), addressed the problem of school-to-work transition in these words:

> Too often, any discussion of the problems of youth leads quickly to a bashing of the schools for failing to do their job. Most such attacks are unfair and unwarranted. Students may work hard through the 12 grades of schools, may compile adequate records and may graduate in good standing, and their teachers may have effectively taught them the basic skills. Nevertheless, they are still likely to encounter problems in getting started in a productive career. (Commission on Work, p. 3)

The report went on to recommend a variety of school-to-work programs through the revitalization of vocational education and monitored work experience with schools in the vanguard so as to ensure the educative function of work experience. The reference to "school bashing" in this quotation was clearly directed at a certain report, *A Nation at Risk* (1983).

Curriculum Retrenchment

Whereas the National Commission on Excellence in Education (*A Nation at Risk*, 1983) had attacked the public schools for the nation's decline in the global industrial economy, it did not call for investment in vocational-technical education. Instead it demanded a curriculum focused on the "new basics" (the traditional academic subjects, with increased emphasis on math and science plus computer literacy), along with increased "standards" for high school graduation. Within 2 years after *A Nation at Risk*, most of the states had responded by mandating increased units in academic subjects for high school graduation. A report by a commission to study these developments for the Association for Supervision and Curriculum Development (1985), *With Consequences for All*, warned that there already were indications that the increased requirements would affect the curriculum in vocational studies and elective options and would neglect the need for a balanced and coherent program of general education. The report warned that the new curriculum mandates would serve to exacerbate the dropout problem (1985). A survey sponsored by the National Association of Secondary School principals revealed that the newly mandated requirements clearly impacted student electives and curricular options (D. Tanner, 1996, pp. 103–104), while enrollments in vocational education programs dropped precipitously.

Over an extended period, the federal expenditure for vocational education underwent a sharp decline. This was a time when the schools were being blamed for the nation's decline in the global industrial economy and for the problems of youth disaffection and social disorganization.

Integrating Academic and Vocational Studies

In 1990 amendments were passed to the 1984 Perkins Vocational Education Act providing federal funds for the integration of vocational and academic education, especially in school districts serving disadvantaged populations, and for designing vocational instruction so as to relate to all aspects of an industry (as opposed to segmental aspects). As discussed previously, progressive educators throughout the twentieth century had recognized the educative powers of practical and vocational studies and sought to bring such studies into joint association with the curriculum in general education in the cosmopolitan, comprehensive high school. The practical arts were brought into the elementary and middle school also in recognition of the significance of hands-on activity for cognitive and social development in meeting the function of general education.

Even at the professional level of education, problems arise when there is a neglect of practical ideas and applications in the curriculum. This problem has arisen even in the age of computer graphics, when students in elite schools of engineering were not developing their capabilities for making things. Lacking in work with real objects and in the arts and crafts, engineering students were found to be more familiar with mathematics than machinery, relying on single-answer mathematical solutions to rigidly defined problems, rather than seeing the multiple possibilities of knowledge applications. In effect, these students were found to be lacking in development of the mind's eye—the ability to visualize and act on possibilities in practical situations because of their excessive reliance on computer-generated numbers and designs (Ferguson, 1992).

A variety of rudimentary models have been identified for developing the integration of academic and vocational studies in the high school, such as incorporating more academic material into vocational courses, making the academic studies more relevant to vocational applications, engaging vocational and academic teachers in teams for instruction and curriculum development, and improving the horizontal and vertical articulation of the curriculum by organizing programs according to occupational or career clusters, thereby treating occupations (and the subjects in the curriculum) more interdependently.

In view of the segmental approach generally taken in basic education and in education in the fundamental literacies, and the corresponding neglect of building an integrated curriculum in general education, the effort to integrate vocational and academic education remains an enormous challenge. At the least it requires the reeducation of teachers on both preservice and inservice levels. College departments of mathematics, for example, are not known for their interest and capabilities in providing their student majors with the practical applications of mathematics in the world of work. The entire effort to integrate vocational and academic education should not be limited to enabling students to develop technical proficiency for entry-level employment, but to grow in the power of intelligence so as to open up the possibilities for advancing in their work, for meeting changing conditions, and for enriching their lives. In effect, the goals and functions of education, whether vocational or professional, must have common bearings in a free society.

"Tech/Prep" or "Two-Plus-Two"

Recall that the genesis of the idea of incorporating the upper two years of high school with the two-year community college so as to provide for an articulated four-year curriculum in vocational-technical education arose in the 1944 proposal by the Educational Policies Commission in *Education for ALL American Youth*. It is puzzling that it took almost half a century for this idea to take root through federal support and, typically, when it did take root no recognition was given to its origins. It was another instance of "rediscovering the wheel" in educational policy and program. In fact the idea of breaking down the barrier between vocational education in high school and

liberal or vocational education in college was advanced by the Commission on the Reorganization of Secondary Education in the *Cardinal Principles* report of 1918. It is no cliché to say that the experimentalist-progressivists through the first half of the twentieth century truly had a vision of possibilities that was ahead of the times.

Early in his administration, President Clinton and his secretary of Labor promoted an apprenticeship program patterned after the German system, apparently failing to realize that such a proposal, although promoted by American industrialists, was soundly rejected after World War I as alien to the American experience.

With the scrapping of the apprenticeship proposal, the Clinton administration embraced the tech/prep or two-plus-two design, in which the upper two years of high school are articulated with the two-year curriculum of the community college, as provided in the 1990 federal vocational education legislation. In cooperation with community colleges, this design has been developed in both comprehensive high schools and area vocational schools. In the latter, it has revitalized the school by making it more comprehensive in enrollment and curriculum. However, in other instances, it has resulted in a selective-type school serving students whose interests and talents are focused on the sciences, mathematics, and engineering. In the comprehensive high schools, it is incumbent on the administration and faculty not to construe the program segmentally as academic preparation for the community college, but to provide for an articulated curriculum in general education, vocational education, and advanced academic studies—and to articulate the upper-division high school curriculum with that of the community college.

The tech/prep or two-plus-two design was met with great enthusiasm on the part of school and community college leaders. However, the succeeding federal administration gave renewed priority to the academic side of the curriculum, coupled with national achievement testing for world-class standards and adult literacy, as called for in *America 2000*. As for vocational education, federal funds were increased to support for-profit schools in the private sector.

Private for-Profit Vocational Schools

Private for-profit vocational schools have had a long existence, and some have garnered good reputations for successful programs and job placement, particularly in the area of office occupations. After World War II, thousands of private for-profit vocational schools of less than college grade were established to take advantage of the lucrative funding possibilities of the GI Bill of Rights (Servicemen's Readjustment Act of 1944), which provided funds for veterans to pursue higher education and education of less than college grade. Similar benefits for veterans have been extended to this day. Many of these schools, established after World War II, engaged in questionable practices to maximize their income from federal funds to the extent that federal regulations were imposed to ensure ethical practices, leading to the closure of marginal institutions.

In recent years, federal financial aid to students has led to a resurgence of tuition driven for-profit proprietary schools and "colleges." One of the largest and rapidly expanding operations includes a chain of two-year online trade schools called "colleges," enrolling tens of thousands of students nationally (Golden & Rose, 2003, pp. A1, A3). Hundreds of telemarketers called "admissions advisors" must meet quotas in selling the program, and almost all applicants are admitted. Despite high dropout rates, the operation is so profitable that it exceeds the annual income of the national newspaper that owns the chain. Although regulations prohibit colleges or schools receiving federal aid from offering more than half their courses via distance learning rather than in the classroom, these institutions have lobbied successfully for waivers.

The dramatic growth of for-profit vocational schools is testimony to an enormous need that is not being served by the high schools and community colleges. The tech/prep or two-plus-two design seems ideally suited to this need.

Biases and Myths

As discussed earlier in this chapter, the long struggle to give vocational education a recognized place in the curriculum of the high school is rooted in no small measure in the historic bias against vocational education on the part of university intellectuals, particularly literary intellectuals. They appear not to recognize the vocational aspects of their own education that prepared them for their chosen callings, and they deny to others the educational possibilities of preparation for careers in the working world.

The split between the two cultures of academia, which C. P. Snow was so concerned about, is related to the split between the literary intellectuals and the working men and women of a technological society. That such a division and opposition take roots from the aristocratic notions of the past seems to be of little concern to those who see the literary studies as truly educational and who debase vocational preparation as mere training. In taking this stance, they fail to differentiate between a narrowly conceived training that is designed to fit a person to the existing industrial machinery, whatever its faults may be, and the kind of vocational education that aims at developing the individual's power and insight to bring about an improved social situation in the postindustrial society.

The Comprehensive Curriculum and Tracking

It has been pointed out that contemporary writers on education commonly confuse program options in the high school curriculum with tracking. They overlook the fact that the original conception of the comprehensive high school, explicated in the *Cardinal Principles* report, was to provide a common core of studies (with heterogeneously grouped students), coupled with program options for specialized, exploratory, enrichment and special-interest studies. In effect, the comprehensive high school was conceived as having a rich and diversified curriculum without tracks. Over the years, most colleges and universities have come to accept students whose pattern of high school coursework included vocational studies.

As cited earlier, many writers on education portray the comprehensive high school as inherently a school with curriculum tracks, thereby promoting inequality, and they advance the notion that a one-track (academic) curriculum promotes educational equality. They fail to recognize that the one-track academic curriculum will find students undergoing self-selection or externally determined selection for such courses as advanced algebra, trigonometry, calculus, physics, and the advanced placement courses. At the same time students, including the most academically talented, are denied the opportunities for enriched learnings that accrue from a diversified curriculum in a comprehensive high school. Students have been known to engage in organized protests when the curriculum is reduced. Students commonly exceed the number of credits required for high school graduation not only to enhance their chances for admission to the college of their choice, but also to take courses in the studio arts and vocational areas of interest and need.

An American Dilemma

Many educators, including the proponents of vocational education, fail to recognize that vocational education, in the setting of the school, offers unique opportunities for realizing the intellectual and cultural possibilities of vocations, inasmuch as the schools are protected from the narrow exigencies of direct profit pursuits. In other words, the schools can provide insight into ways of improving existing industrial conditions. To ignore vocational education entirely, or to conceive of it in the narrowest of terms, is to leave youth at the mercy of these conditions.

In regarding vocational education or the preparation for useful work in society as inferior education, intellectuals are wittingly or unwittingly perpetuating the historic aristocratic divisions in society. Perhaps the longshoreman-philosopher Eric Hoffer exaggerated the situation when he wrote, "Scratch an intellectual and you find a would-be aristocrat who loathes the sight, the sound and the smell of common folk" (1970, p. 120). During the latter 1960s the term *hardhat* entered the lexicon of college students as a derisive descriptor of the working person of industrial society and, at the same time, these college students attired themselves in the blue denims of the laborer. Hoffer pointed out that although many university intellectuals and radical college students presented themselves as champions of the poor, they showed little concern for equipping the poor with the skills and resources necessary for power in the world of work—by means of which they would be able to gain political and social power (p. 122). In the meantime, organized labor had gained unprecedented political and social power. Few politicians from urban areas could ignore the voice of organized labor.

Crisis in Black and White.   Many university educators who have focused their careers on the problems of the disadvantaged, particularly the problems of African-American youth, have portrayed vocational education as a kind of training for the exploitation of African Americans, whereas they see the arts and sciences as the liberating studies. In sharing this view, some scholars have pointed to the issue of vocational training versus liberal arts education for African Americans after Reconstruction. They have sided with William E. B. DuBois in his criticism against Booker T. Washington and the curriculum at Tuskegee, which favored technical and vocational education rather than the intellectual education of the liberal arts as DuBois would have it (Greene, 1965, p. 129; Curti, 1935; Myrdal, 1902; Generals, 1998).

In his classic study, *An American Dilemma* (1962), Gunnar Myrdal presented quite a different picture of this issue. According to Myrdal, the expensive vocational education needed by African Americans was never provided and that even at such leading African-American educational centers as Hampton and Tuskegee, the curriculum was less attuned to modern technical-industrial education than to academic studies for the preparation of school teachers. Further, even in the North, African American youngsters were not encouraged to enroll in the vocational programs in recognition that they would only encounter discrimination by employers and unions.

This problem is of rapidly increasing significance since formal vocational training is more and more becoming a prerequisite for entering skilled occupations," observed Myrdal, and "to avoid such training means to accept and fortify the exclusionist system, since no Negroes will ever be equipped to challenge it" (Myrdal, pp. 390–391).

Almost a quarter of a century after Myrdal's study was published, critics were describing the history and function of vocational education in highly contradictory terms. Vocational education was attacked as having served largely as the monopoly of "a working-class elite" and at the same time it was being condemned as a "middle-class prescription for the poor" (Smiley, 1967, pp. 123, 140; Carnoy & Levin, 1976, p. 264). Although African Americans had now gained virtually open access to higher education, their access to skilled vocations in trades and industries remained limited. The overwhelming majority of youth enrolled in full-time day classes in vocational education were whites, and organized labor in the skilled trades also continued to have only a very small representation of African Americans. The civil-rights legislation and court decisions of the 1960s had made it possible for the first time for African Americans to crack the barriers of the skilled trades so that large numbers of blacks might enter. Relatively few African Americans were qualified to gain such entry or to challenge any continuing discriminatory restrictions.

To this day, despite the gains made by African Americans in higher education, their population representation in the precision-production and technical areas of vocational education in trades and industries in high school has remained significantly below that of whites (see current data from the National Center for Educational Statistics).

Today there is much cogitation in academia about a utopian world of automation and leisure, and correspondingly little consideration of how we must come to grips with the grim realities of psychosocial destruction that derives from youth unemployment. In posing such questions, academicians were ignoring the fact that an increasingly technological society requires ever greater working skills and at the same time the increasingly leisured world is open mainly to those who can enjoy the fruits of their labors, not to those who are left unequipped for the world of work.

The Myth of Mental Discipline

In making their case against vocational education, many academicians view vocational education as antithetical to the academic side of the curriculum. They portray the traditional academic studies as intellectually and culturally generative, whereas vocational education is seen as narrowly manipulative and geared to conformity. "The preference for vocationalism is linked to a preference for character—or personality—over mind, and for conformity and manipulative facility over individuality and talent," wrote Hofstadter (1963, p. 264). Such assertions reveal a conception of mind as being separate from character, personality, and hand. The necessary organic unity between mind and character, between thinking and doing, is denied. A dichotomy and conflict is created between the thinking individual and the working individual. Vocational education is portrayed in its narrowest conception rather than in terms of its wide cultural possibilities.

Ravitch has cited Hofstadter in contending that the research findings on mental discipline and learning transfer were never decisively established. She fails to identify any replicative experimental studies that would support the doctrine of mental discipline and transfer, and she fails to show how the massive research that demolished the doctrine was faulty (1983, p. 49; 2000, p. 67). "For centuries, concerned scholars have asked what knowledge is most worthy, what schools should provide for the discipline and furniture of the student's mind," writes Sizer (1984) in borrowing the expression of "discipline and furniture of the mind" from Yale President Jeremiah Day in the nineteenth century (p. 89). To Sizer and other essentialist-perennialists, the answer resides simply in the fundamental academic disciplines.

Despite the long-standing evidence refuting the doctrine that the standard academic curriculum (composed of the traditional academic disciplines) is the only suitable preparation for college, the doctrine persists in many quarters. This doctrine also is centered on the myth that abstract knowledge is superior to practical knowledge for the "discipline and furniture of the mind." The history of human progress reveals repeated lessons of how abstract knowledge is derived from the real world of experience and is tested in the real world of experience (Bernal, 1971).

In upholding their belief in the superiority of academic knowledge, university academicians promulgate the fallacy that the so-called nonacademic studies are detrimental to college success. Ironically, this academically biased ideology is imposed on the secondary schools by many colleges that have broadened their own curriculum patterns in response to the demand for curriculum relevance on the part of students. Moreover, when college-bound students are led to believe that it is detrimental for them to take nonacademic courses, not only are they denied the enrichment possibilities of such studies but also the school fosters a social dichotomy between the "high" and the "servile" in the student body.

The Myth of Obsolescence

A common criticism of vocational education is that the accelerating changes in technology make preparation for skilled occupations obsolete. Perennialists and essentialists contend that the liberal arts and professional education equip one for further change, but they deny such possibilities to vocational education. The liberal arts graduate has encountered severe difficulties in finding suitable employment without occupational preparation, but the graduate in accounting, dietetics, nursing, or machine tool design remains in great demand. The argument that vocational education readily becomes obsolete as a result of advances in technology simply has not been borne out by experience. (Consider that the development of manned flight is credited to two bicycle mechanics.)

There is a continuity of adaptation and transformation not only in technological change, but also in the adaptability of the people who do the work of the world. Whether we are looking to technological changes in the workplace or in leisure, "we might take heed of the predictions of the demise of the theatre with the invention of the talking motion picture, the demise of the concert hall with the invention of the phonograph, the demise of the motion picture with the invention of television, and the demise of handwriting with the invention of the typewriter" (Tanner, D., 1983, p. A22). In the same vein, photography was expected to bring about the demise of the visual arts. Predictions that the computer would lead to the end of paper not only were misguided but failed to anticipate that it would create an insurmountable need for paper. Contemporary predictions that the print age is ending as the result of the electronic revolution have proved to be far off the mark. The demand for books is greater than ever, and people continue to read newspapers, magazines, and TV guides.

In looking back on technological change, we find that the sweeping contentions of skilled workers becoming obsolete and incapable of transferring and transforming their technical skills have been vastly exaggerated and misdirected. Contrary to such contentions, the aircraft mechanic who worked on piston engines did not become technologically outmoded with the development of the jet engine any more than did the engineer. The mechanics who had worked on horse-drawn coaches became the mechanics for the automotive industry. The aircraft industry grew out of the automotive industry. In each case of technological change, there were mechanics and engineers who made such changes possible by transferring and updating their knowledge and abilities. Just as the physician, the physicist, and the linguist must keep abreast of their fields, so must the computer technician, the farmer, and the automotive mechanic. Instead of setting up oppositions between the liberal arts (or general education) and vocational or professional education, or between theoretical and practical knowledge, they must be conceived as interdependent functions of the whole of education.

Work and Workmanship. When the world of work is regarded as menial, the outcome is a decline in the quality of workmanship with the end result that the whole society suffers. In looking to the future, academicians tend to portray work as becoming ever less meaningful to the individual and increasingly geared to serving the system. In *The Real World of the Public Schools*, Broudy predicted "although work will continue to be important in the society of the future, its importance will be greater to the system than to the individual—except for a small minority of high-level professionals and creative workers" (1972, pp. 158–159). However, in the real world of the young adult and adolescent, success in work is one of the most important life goals, and pursuit of a college education is closely connected to career goals. The skilled trades have not become obsolete, nor are they appropriately stereotyped as routine and unstimulating. The fallacy that work in the skilled trades is necessarily routine, boring, and devoid of problem solving can be illustrated by the following actual dialogue between the carpenter and client (co-author of this text) when encountering an unanticipated problem:

Mr. Schmidt: "What shall we do about this?"

Mr. Tanner (jokingly): "How should I know? You're the 'doctor.'"

Mr. Schmidt (smiling): "We use our imagination!"

Needless to say, a creative solution to the problem was found by the carpenter after evaluating the pros and cons of several possibilities. The point is that unpredictable problems arise in ordinary work and require imaginative and creative solutions. It is simply fallacious to assume that problem solving and creative thinking are the exclusive province of a professional class or a leisure class exempted from boring routines and practical work by virtue of a superior education or birthright.

Finally, if work is not important to the individual, as Broudy contends, then how can it be important to a democratic society? Advanced democratic nations are increasingly recognizing that industrial life must be democratized and that there must be pride and personal fulfillment in work if there is to be workmanship. Otherwise, the fabric of democratic society will deteriorate. Futurists tend to give far more attention to leisure than to work, as though work will become obsolete, as though there cannot be pleasure in work, and as though leisure is to be mainly an escape from work rather than a product of work (Toffler, 1974, pp. 76, 258).

The Myth of the Postindustrial Service Society

It has been contended for more than two decades that the United States is in the vanguard of a transformation from a production economy to a service economy in the information age. A tenet of the information age and service economy is that the focus on education must be directed at the basic literacies and computer literacy and that it is fruitless to continue to provide for vocational education in the production occupations.

In typical contradictory style of the reckless assaults on the public schools, *A Nation at Risk* (1983) blamed the schools on the one hand for the "steady 15-year decline in industrial productivity, as one great American industry after another falls to world competition," and on the other hand blamed the schools for putting the nation at risk by not preparing students for the "'information age' we are entering" (pp. 7, 18). In looking to the twenty-first century, Robert Reich has seen the future transformed as an "informating" economy, requiring that the training of workers be redirected from production skills to symbolic-analytic skills (1992).

The fact that the electronic age has generated a sea of information cannot be disputed. Indeed, we may already be drowning in it. The most prosperous nations in the global economy are those built on production. Although there has been a great increase in the service sector of the economy, this has been associated with lower paying jobs. Contrary to *A Nation at* Risk, compelling evidence revealed that the United States remains the world's leading industrial production economy and is not becoming a service economy (Baily, Bator, Hall, & Solow, 1993). If the United States has slipped in certain sectors of industrial productivity, this must be at least partly a reflection of the weapons-based sector of the economy from decades of Cold War and continuing hot wars.

The Myth of Industrial Know-How

Critics of vocational education commonly hold that preparation for skilled employment should be provided by industry and should have no place in the school curriculum. As pointed out, academicians on both the radical left and far right have taken this position, as did Robert Hutchins, in offering that youngsters who do not measure up to the traditional academic curriculum and who seek vocational preparation would be better off if "allowed to drop out of school and go to work, because they would have been trained on the job and not deluded into thinking the school had prepared them" (1972, p. 210). Such a stance naively ignores the fact that the industrial sector has not had a tradition of welcoming school dropouts for employment, let alone investing in their training in skilled occupations for career advancement. Further, there is a failure to recognize the implications of separating preparation for work from education.

As Veblen pointed out, the chief concern of industry is to employ its devices for pecuniary ends (1969, p. 92). The school, however, can provide a kind of vocational education that is attuned to personal-social growth rather than merely to fit the individual to a particular slot in the industrial machinery.

Effective programs of vocational education provide for carefully supervised work experience. There is a vast difference between work experience and educative work experience. The role of the school is to ensure that such experience is educative. Supervised work experience can be designed to keep the vocational curriculum up to date and also enable youth to gain insight into the problems of the business and industrial world.

When the federal government turned to industrial know-how to develop programs of job training for adolescents independently of the schools, such as through the Job Corps, it soon was evident that industry was unsuited to the task. The school's responsibility is to see to it that preparation for the world of work takes place in an educational environment. Moreover, as Myrdal pointed out, business and industry have concentrated their training programs mainly on those who are already employed and who already have a relatively high level of educational and work skills. The role of business and industry, notes Myrdal, should be regarded as essentially a supplement to, and not a replacement for, the vocational and general education that should be provided by public educational institutions (1965, p. 34).

Contemporary proposals for vocational education call for the school to focus on the new basics or literacies through grade 10 followed by workplace education and training in the private sector through apprenticeships and other arrangements. Aside from the dangers inherent in creating a dual educational system there remains the question of whether business and industry would be willing to provide the levels of investment required for entry-level, frontline employment training toward a career ladder. Contrary to the myth that such training is well provided by the private sector, the evidence reveals that formal training on the job for frontline workers is limited largely to orientation for new employees or short courses on safety and environmental regulation; and most of the upgrade training is directed on those employees who are already technically skilled, such as craftspeople and technicians. Then there is the question of industry's commitment to offer employment to those who complete an apprenticeship program (Carson, Huelskamp, & Woodall, 1993, pp. 293–297).

The education strategy of *America 2000* claims that the business community "will jump start the Design Teams that will design the New American Schools [and] will provide people and resources to help catalyze needed changes in local schools" (1991, pp. 21–22). The historic record of the influence of business and industry on education has not been flattering (Callahan, 1962; Weiss, 1989). When confronted with the proposal that industry should help remedy the defects of the educational system and other social institutions, Henry Ford II put the matter bluntly: "The business of business is business" (*New York Times*, 1972, p. 55). If the nation is vastly underinvested in vocational education at the high school and community college levels, it seems that the need is to invest more adequately in these institutions, rather than in shifting the allocation of public funds to business and industry for youth training.

The Myth of Adolescent Negativism Toward Schooling

The bias against vocational education and the attacks leveled at the schools by university academicians and politicians contrast sharply against the belief that adolescents share in the significance of schooling in their lives. Past efforts to shorten the years to the high school diploma have not been successful, even for the academically talented, as adolescents prefer to complete their high school studies with their classmates. The long-term decline in high school dropouts, and the preference of adolescents to enroll in their home high school and to reject shared-time arrangements, reflect a strong positive belief in mainstream schooling and the value of education. Strained by massive youth unemployment and alienation, the United States has begun to undertake renewed efforts to reconstruct vocational education through integration with academic studies, tech/prep programs, supervised work internships, and increased federal and state funding. At the same time, proposals for the schools to develop mechanisms for the certification of literacy skills through examinations, with transcripts of results to be presented to prospective employers for entrance to work apprenticeships at age 16, raise ominous dangers of creating a dual system. Certified literacy skills do not add up to a general education. Work apprenticeships do not add up to a comprehensive high school education.

Reality of the Human Community

Although since the mid-1960s there has been notable progress in making higher education more accessible to the disadvantaged populations, efforts to meet the educational needs of youth who were seeking to enter the world of work continued to lag. Gunnar Myrdal, a great admirer of the American commitment to education, observed in 1965 that "America needs very much greater efforts in the field of vocational training" and that "training for work has never been made a regular part of the American educational system" (p. 33). The major thrust of the War on Poverty of the 1960s had been focused on programs that were largely independent of the school system, and the ranks of the unemployed and socially disaffected youth continued to grow.

Recent years have witnessed federal and state support for programs, after decades of neglect, aimed at integrating academic and vocational studies in the schools. In too many instances, however, the efforts toward curriculum integration were more concerned with basic academic skills than with general education and, at the same time, vocational education in the high school needed new levels of support and vitalization.

The Lost Adolescent. Erik Erikson has described the pitiful and dangerous plight of youth who are left with crippling self-doubt and social destructiveness when denied a sense of "apprenticeship" or "work identity" necessary to partaking in the stream of social progress (1968, p. 185). Dewey wrote: "Nothing is more tragic than the failure to discover one's true business in life, or to find that one has drifted or been forced by circumstance into an uncongenial calling" (1916, p. 360).

In *Civilization and Its Discontents*, Freud observed:

> After primal man had discovered that it lay in his own hands, literally, to improve his lot on earth by working, it cannot have been a matter of indifference to him whether another man worked with or against him. The other man acquired the value for him of a fellow-worker, with whom it was useful to live together. (1962, p. 46)

Freud stressed that no activity in modern society can match that of work in giving the conduct of life roots to reality and in giving the individual roots to the human community.

No other technique for the conduct of life attaches the individual so firmly to reality as laying emphasis on work; for his work at least gives him a secure place in a portion of reality, in the human community. The possibility it offers of displacing a large amount of libidinal components, whether narcissistic, aggressive or even erotic, on to professional work and on to the human relations connected with it lends it a value by no means second to what it enjoys as something indispensable to the preservation and justification of existence in society. (1962, p. 27)

With the huge population of disadvantaged youth being denied roots to the reality of the human community, it is no wonder that the result is corrosive social disaffection and conflict. Yet, during the late 1960s and early 1970s, some academicians and antipoverty workers were advising unemployed youth and young adults that they are better off unemployed than working in so-called dead-end jobs—with the result that people employed in such jobs publicly defended their work as worthy and expressed resentment against those who would deprecate such work (*New York Times*, 1970, pp. 1, 25).

Eric Hoffer pointed out that youngsters from comparatively well-to-do families, as well as children of the poor, "are prevented from having a share in the world's work and of proving their manhood by doing a man's work and getting a man's pay," with the result that youth engage in sick forms of self-assertion: "crime in the streets and insolence on the campus" (1970, p. 30). Hoffer attributed the pathology of campus violence during the 1960s to the lack of social usefulness felt by college youth. He has expressed the view that the concern for the disadvantaged shown by university intellectuals and students and their corresponding antagonism toward the worker are symptoms reflecting their own feelings of questionable social usefulness.

The Emerging Curriculum in Career Education

The traditional oppositions between elite and mass education, cultural and practical education, and literary and scientific education are untenable in a modern, democratic, technological society where knowledge is not a monopolized commodity but grows out of interaction with the environment and enables individuals to improve the physical and social environment. Such a society requires that these traditional oppositions be eliminated and that the curriculum be developed as a unity of interdependent elements and functions.

The literary intellectual may not find any common interests with the agriculturist until he or she realizes that amidst the world population explosion most of humanity lives in hunger. The liberal arts graduate in the Peace Corps discovers that good intentions are insufficient to the task of combating poverty, and that the farmer with knowledge of scientific agriculture, the skilled worker in the machine and construction trades, and the nurse and medical technician all are equipped to apply their talents in attacking the most direct problems of humanity. Vocational education, no less than a literary education, can illumine social intelligence and bring knowledge to bear on the common problems of humanity, whether poverty, disease, ignorance, or injustice. In a democracy, social consciousness is not a monopoly for the intellectual elite but permeates the whole fabric of society. This requires a reconstruction of the curriculum so that cultural pursuits are not isolated from the real world and so that vocational pursuits are not separated from their cultural bearings.

Curriculum Unity and Interdependence

The ecological crisis has illustrated dramatically that social and intellectual interests cannot be separated from work in science, industry, agriculture, transportation, health, government, and so on. Insofar as the curriculum is concerned, although vocational education provides for specialized competencies and pursuits, it needs to be sufficiently broad so as to share with general education the cultivation of those understandings and sympathies that are common to all citizens of a free society.

Figure 13.1 is a schematic representation of how the various studies in general education, specialized education, and exploratory and enrichment education might be distributed throughout the phases of schooling and into college. The classification of a particular course is not determined solely by its subject-matter content but also by treatment of the subject matter and the functions it serves for the learners. Thus, eighth-graders may be studying industrial arts for purposes of general education, to gain an understanding of the evolution of craftsmanship, to learn how to translate concepts and schematic plans into the shaping of actual materials through the use of various tools, and to gain an appreciation

Figure 13.1 Apportionment of the Macrocurriculum, K–14.

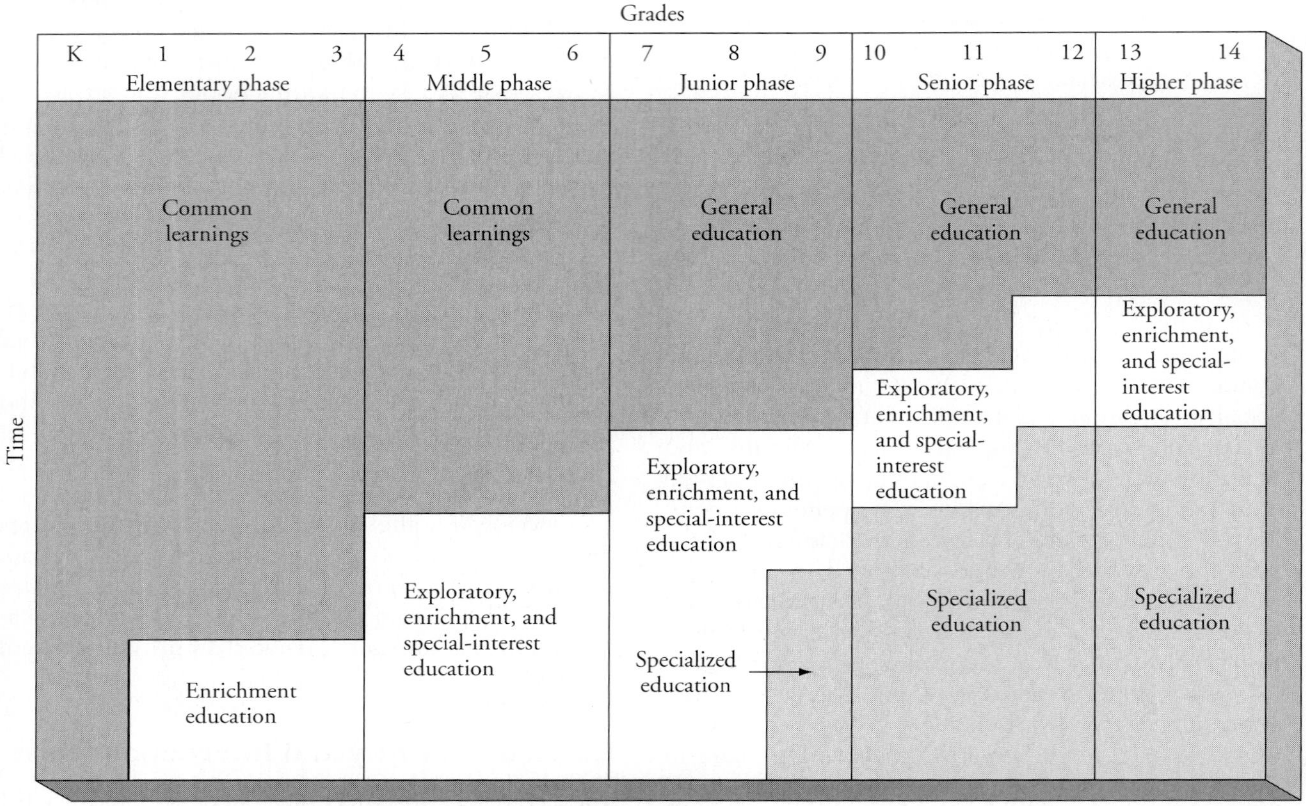

Grades

K 1 2 3	4 5 6	7 8 9	10 11 12	13 14
Elementary phase	Middle phase	Junior phase	Senior phase	Higher phase

Time

Common learnings

Common learnings

General education

General education

General education

Exploratory, enrichment, and special-interest education

Exploratory, enrichment, and special-interest education

Exploratory, enrichment, and special-interest education

Exploratory, enrichment, and special-interest education

Enrichment education

Specialized education

Specialized education

Specialized education

of the industrial processes and the influences of technology in modern society. The ninth-grader may elect a course in mechanical drawing for exploratory and enrichment purposes, whereas a classmate may enroll in the same course with the goal of becoming an architect or engineer. The 10-grader may take a course in electronics because he or she seeks to become an electrician, whereas a fellow student who plans on a career as an electronics technician or an engineer also enrolls in the course. Thus, the traditional separation between the academic and vocational divisions of the curriculum becomes less distinct, and students are not segregated according to curriculum tracks.

Vocational education shares with general education the goal of developing the learner's abilities to cope intelligently with environing conditions and to contribute to the improvement of these conditions. Curriculum tracking is avoided as the course work in general education and exploratory and enrichment education includes students who are in vocational and

college preparatory programs. Broadly conceived, vocational education should enable the learner to find roots in the reality of the human community, as Freud pointed out in his discussion of the significance of work in the conduct of life.

The Comprehensive Vocational Curriculum

"Vocational training, like education in general, must never lead to dead ends, but must help young people to move horizontally to other occupations, and vertically to higher responsibilities, as future opportunities may occur," stressed Myrdal (1965, p. 33).

The career-cluster concept embraces Myrdal's idea that vocational education should provide for the opening up of occupational opportunities. Figure 13.2 illustrates various occupational clusters, and Table 13.1 shows how the various federally supported programs of vocational education can be represented in the high school curriculum and at the

Figure 13.2 Career Clusters.

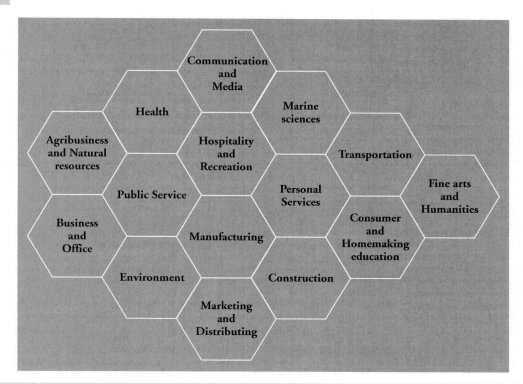

postsecondary level according to the career-cluster concept. For example, agriculture encompasses not only production farming but also agribusiness, agricultural technology, food processing, ornamental horticulture, and other careers. The urbanization of society not only has required specialized education at increasingly higher levels in production agriculture, as farmers must produce more food for more

Table 13.1   Selected Vocational Fields and Occupational Clusters.

Field	Occupational Categories (examples)
Agricultural education	Production agriculture, agribusiness, agricultural technology, food processing, ornamental horticulture
Distributive education	Distribution and marketing (apparel, general merchandise, and foods)
Health occupations education	Practical nursing, nursing aides, medical office assistants, dental assistants, medical record technicians
Home economics education	Child care, institutional services, clothing services, nutrition, home management
Office occupations education	Business data processing, office machines, stenographic-secretarial services, bookkeeping
Trade and industrial education	Construction, manufacturing, machine trades (maintenance and repair specialities)
Pretechnical and technical education	Electronics, computer programming, machine-tool design, medical technology

people on less and less acreage, but also has created an enormous need to develop a more attractive urban environment. This need has created a demand for specialists in ornamental horticulture and landscape architecture. An increasing number of urban high schools and community colleges have instituted programs to prepare students for these careers.

The expansion of industry and technology has been accompanied by a dramatic increase in the proportion of people engaged in distributive or service occupations. Almost one fifth of the total labor force is engaged in such occupations. Programs in distributive education prepare students for careers in distribution and marketing of apparel, general merchandise, and foods, and in various other areas of service. Many of these programs employ the project method, case analysis, directed observation and cooperative work experience. Cross-cluster or multiple-field programs combine distributive education with home economics, agribusiness, or trades and industrial technologies. Postsecondary programs in distributive education are offered through the high schools, community colleges, and four-year colleges.

Although most of the health occupations require postsecondary preparation, practical nursing programs have been instituted beginning in grade 12 and extending into a postgraduate year leading to a certificate in practical nursing as well as a high school diploma. In response to the rapidly growing demand for health services, an increasing number of community colleges have instituted programs to prepare registered nurses, medical technicians, and other health personnel. These programs typically include cooperative work experience.

Home economics has been extended beyond homemaking to include careers in child care, institutional services, clothing services, interior decoration, and other occupational categories. Work experience programs have been expanded through cooperative arrangements with child-care centers, nursing homes, and other institutions.

The traditional commercial subjects in high school have given way to systematized programs in office occupations including not only secretarial skills, bookkeeping, and the use of office machines but also business data processing and management. Increasing emphasis is also being given to instructional arrangements involving simulated office experience and cooperative work experience.

Programs in business data processing and computing occupations are widely offered in community colleges.

Trade and industrial education encompasses not only the construction and machine trades but also a wide variety of maintenance and repair specialties and technologies ranging from automotive mechanics to electronics. Although skilled craftsmen have been in short supply for many years, selection practices have made it difficult for schools to expand and improve their programs of cooperative work experience and their arrangements for apprenticeship entry. The high school enrollment in trade and industrial technologies has grown markedly, but more effective agreements are needed between the school and the unions and industry to provide for the necessary transition from school to apprenticeship and the world of work.

For a number of years, the demand for technicians has exceeded that for engineers. Career opportunities for technicians have expanded into many fields, from electronics to computer programming and machine-tool design. Pretechnical programs have been developed at some high schools, but mostly through the area vocational schools and community colleges. The community colleges have made notable progress in instituting and expanding the programs in technical education in recent years. Because the preparation required for many technical occupations is no less demanding than it is for baccalaureate programs, the community colleges have encountered difficulty in recruiting students who have the necessary preparation and aptitude for technical education.

Perspective

The ancient schism between thinking people and working people continues to be reflected in the attitudes of many educators toward vocational education. Many academicians portray the academic studies as generating intellective power, and the vocational studies are regarded as servile. These academicians regard the traditional academic studies as peculiarly cultural, and they deny the cultural possibilities of vocational education and the world of work. This oppositional concept of curriculum is untenable in a democracy where thinking people and working people must be one and the same. The inertia of educational traditions continues to perpetuate such opposition.

Contemporary revisionists of educational history and others on the radical academic left tend to portray vocational-technical education as a kind of training of the masses to perpetuate the corporate society. They fail to recognize that vocational-technical education has been made available only to a relatively small proportion of high school youth. They fail to recognize the strong vocational orientation of colleges and universities, and they rarely portray these higher institutions as perpetuating the corporate society. They deny to vocational education the possibilities for illuminating social intelligence and contributing to the solution of pervading social problems. The issue is not whether there should be a place for vocational education in the curriculum but how vocational education should be fashioned so as to reveal the fullest intellectual and social meaning of work in a free society. This requires that vocational and general education be conceived and designed as interrelated aspects of the curriculum and social meaning of work in a free society. This requires that vocational and general education be conceived and designed as interrelated aspects of the curriculum and not as independent or oppositional entities. It requires that vocational education be designed not to reflect existing industrial conditions but to provide insight into the improvement of these conditions. For this reason, the school and community college have an indispensable role in vocational education and such education cannot be given over entirely to industry, even if industry should seek to assume this total function. Effective programs of vocational education require larger social reforms so that the world of work is made more accessible to the rising generation. Moreover, the paths to continuing education must always remain open to all who can profit from further education. The development and expansion of specialized vocational schools raise the question as to whether the United States will allow its unitary educational structure to be split, thereby perpetuating social-class divisions as characteristic of the historic dual educational structure of the European nations. Unless high schools are made truly comprehensive, the danger of such a split is real.

Attacks on vocational-technical education by educators who regard themselves as representing the best interests of at-risk youth have been highly contradictory. These critics have contended, on the one hand, that vocational-technical education has been a monopoly of a working-class elite, but, on the other hand, they condemn it as a middle-class prescription for the poor. In reality, vocational education has been made accessible only to a small proportion of the disadvantaged populations. Access to higher education has far outstripped access to vocational education and access to the skilled occupations on the part of disadvantaged youth.

Educational futurists tend to view vocational education as being particularly vulnerable to technological obsolescence. They envision the twenty-first century as an era of leisure, as though work itself will become obsolete. But technology has opened up far more occupational opportunities than it has closed down. Moreover, the educational futurists deny to the skilled worker the capacity to keep up with changing conditions, and they see only the professional as having such capability. The automotive mechanic, the farmer, the electrician, and the nurse must be capable of meeting the challenge of change in their respective fields, just as the lawyer, the physician, the engineer, and the teacher must keep abreast of changing knowledge and conditions.

Modern programs of vocational or career education can be designed to provide broad preparation according to occupational clusters and, as Myrdal recommended, to enable youth to move horizontally to various occupations and vertically to higher responsibilities as opportunities develop. This will require not only curriculum reconstruction but also a concerted program on the part of business, industry, labor unions, and governmental agencies—all in cooperation with the schools.

In a democratic, technological society, leisure is a product of work and not an exemption from work. Moreover, without meaning in work, there can be no workmanship. Industrial democracies are increasingly recognizing that people are not something to be harnessed to technology but that they must have a voice in operating decisions and in the uses to which technology is put.

A democracy cannot hold together unless the dignity of work gains recognition in all walks of life.

PROBLEMS FOR STUDY AND DISCUSSION

1. The following statement was made by Dewey in 1917:

   The movement for vocational education conceals within itself two mighty and opposing forces, one which would utilize the public schools primarily to turn out more efficient laborers in the present economic regime, with certain incidental advantages to themselves, the other which would utilize all of the resources of public education to equip individuals to control their own future economic careers, and thus help on such a reorganization of industry as will change it from a feudalistic to a democratic order. [John Dewey, "Learning to Earn," *School and Society, 5* (March 24, 1917), pp. 334–335.]

   Do you see this as a pervading contemporary issue? Why or why not?

2. Academicians who oppose vocational education in high school tend to overlook the vocational education function of the college. How do you account for this?

3. Do you see a parallel between C. P. Snow's two cultures (discussed in chapter 10) and the divisions and oppositions that have marked the two sides of the curriculum: the academic and the vocational? Explain. What steps might be taken to develop the needed curriculum interdependence?

4. Some educators contend that vocational preparation should be provided only at the postsecondary level and, for those not continuing their formal education beyond high school, vocational training should be left to business and industry. Do you see any limitations and dangers in such a prescription? Explain.

5. "No other technique for the conduct of life attaches the individual so firmly to reality as laying emphasis on work," wrote Freud, "for his work at least gives him a secure place in a portion of reality, in the human community." [Sigmund Freud, *Civilization and Its Discontents* (New York: W. W. Norton, 1962), p. 27.]

   What are the personal-social implications of this statement in connection with society's denial of a place in the world of work for large proportions of youth?

6. Television and other mass media have been criticized for denigrating and stereotyping the blue-collar worker as an ignoramus hardhat (a racist-authoritarian type). Eric Hoffer maintained that university intellectuals share this antagonism toward the worker. Do you believe that this bias is prevalent in the media and in higher academia? Explain.

7. Many academicians have portrayed the ordinary worker as being engaged in meaningless work and being highly disaffected with his or her work role. Surveys and polls reveal a different picture. A Harris poll revealed that most Americans would rather keep working than take early or full retirement. How do you account for the picture of the ordinary worker drawn by many academicians, as contrasted with the findings of actual surveys and polls?

8. Intellectuals often associate the term *career* with the professions, and they regard other kinds of work as mere *jobs*. Is such a distinction justified? Explain.

9. Do specialized vocational schools pose a danger that the unitary school system will become a dual system reflecting the social class differences that mark the dual educational structure of most European nations? Explain.

10. As discussed in this chapter, *America 2000/Goals 2000* (endorsed by three American presidents) and the U.S. Department of Labor's report for *America 2000 (Learning a Living)* held that the most critical skills for the twenty-first century will be in the academic basics and computer literacy. These reports blamed the schools for failure to prepare students in the needed academic skills. The Sandia report (1993) and other research studies have found that the most critical skills in the workplace aside from technical skills are attitudinal and behavioral: responsibility, dependability, punctuality, and so on. Do these findings support the significance of vocational studies in the high school coupled with student-initiated projects in all areas of the curriculum, student clubs, and cooperative supervised work experience? Explain.

PART IV

IMPROVING THE CURRICULUM

> And where this progress will stop, no one can say.
>
> —Thomas Jefferson

CHAPTER 14

INTERPRETING RESEARCH FOR CURRICULUM IMPROVEMENT

"As social scientists we are deceiving ourselves if we naïvely believe that we are not as human as the people around us and that we do not tend to aim opportunistically for conclusions that fit prejudices," wrote Gunnar Myrdal. He pointed out that knowledge, as well as ignorance, can be used opportunistically to support biases. "We are not automatons like the electronic machines we use increasingly to master large masses of data," continued Myrdal. "The result is systematic biases in our work—even in our man-made programming of computing machines" (1969, pp. 43–44).

This book has stressed that educational practice and the nature, direction, and interpretation of educational research have been influenced by the larger sociopolitical scene. A key problem in educational research and practice is to understand the sources of bias, to subject the biases to scrutiny, and to protect ourselves, as much as possible, against these biases. Although this may seem to be another platitude that is not likely to elicit any debate, Myrdal noted that there is an irrational taboo on the part of social scientists against discussing the general lack of awareness of the sources and influences of bias in social science. "It is astonishing that this taboo is commonly respected," observed Myrdal, "leaving the social scientist in naiveté about what he is doing" (p. 4).

The focus of this chapter is on evaluating certain major contemporary directions in the curriculum field, assessing the research bases for these directions, and identifying possible ways of overcoming various biases that have influenced curriculum research, development, policy and practice. Rather than presenting a systematic, analytical treatment of the problem, the text examines certain major research projects, curriculum-reform efforts, and innovative practices to illustrate how educators can become aware of opportunistic and biased influences with a view toward overcoming these influences.

Curriculum Research, Development, and Practice: Protection Against Bias

What has been discussed thus far is not to be interpreted as a plea to build knowledge in educational and social science that is independent of valuations, for the substantive theory of educational and social science is based on valuation. To eliminate valuation is to reduce a field to narrow empiricism. Yet much research in educational and social science is cloaked in a methodological empiricism as though to convey an image of hard data and scientific neutrality that either masks the valuations underlying the research or conceals the conceptual emptiness of the research.

Alvin Gouldner warns of the emergence in social science of "a kind of methodological empiricism in which there is a neglect of *substantive* concepts and assumptions concerning specifically human behavior and social relations, and a corresponding emphasis on seemingly neutral methods, mathematical models, investigational techniques, and research technologies of all kinds, [leading to] a conceptually uncommitted and empty methodological empiricism" (1970, p. 445). Myrdal observed that seeking to establish the facts and factual relationships and ignoring valuation is to leave an essential equation missing that opens the door to arbitrariness and biases (1969, p. 8). Because no substantive questions can be asked in educational and social science independent of valuation, the task is to develop a keen awareness of the sources of valuation and their influences on research and practice—and, thereby, to protect against biases (Tanner, D., 1998).

Valuation Sources and Influences

The assumption that educational and social science can best be advanced by building a body of objective scientific knowledge of facts independent of valuation, and that one can then simply infer policy conclusions and solve practical problems through such "neutral" data, has been criticized by Myrdal as "naïve empiricism."

> This implicit belief in the existence of a body of scientific knowledge acquired independently of all valuations I soon found to be naïve empiricism. Facts do not organize themselves into concepts and theories just by being looked at; indeed except within the framework of concepts and theories, there are not scientific facts but only chaos. There is an inescapable *a priori* element in all scientific work. Questions must be asked before answers can be given. The questions are all expressions of our interest in the world; they are at bottom valuations. Valuations are thus necessarily involved already at the stage when we observe facts and carry on theoretical analysis, and not only at the stage when we draw political inferences from facts and valuations (p. 9).

According to Dewey, scientific method would be advanced much further if educators focused on organizing qualitative processes and results into significant intellectual connections rather than devoting their energies to the measurement of relatively unimportant quantitative by-products (1929a, p. 27; 1928c, p. 200). Significant problems for investigation are essentially qualitatively based, contended Dewey, and quantitative measures are instrumental or secondary to the qualitative conceptual scheme. This problem prevails to this day in educational research.

In seeking to avoid bias, according to Myrdal, the investigator must be aware of

> (1) the powerful heritage of earlier writings in his field of inquiry. . . ; (2) the influences of the entire cultural, social, economic, and political milieu of the society where he lives, works, and earns his living and his status, and (3) the influence stemming from his own personality.
> . . . [and] the logical means available for protecting ourselves from biases are broadly these: to raise the valuations actually determining our theoretical as well as practical research to full awareness, to scrutinize them from the point of view of relevance, significance, and feasibility in the society under study, to transform them into specific value premises for research, and, to determine approach and define concepts in terms of a set of value premises which have been explicitly stated. (pp. 3–5)

In this way, the sources of bias not only are understood and their influences minimized but also the search for knowledge and the solving of practical problems can be related effectively to ideals. Although this may appear to some to be an almost insurmountable task, it has been pointed out in earlier chapters how biases have influenced the direction and nature of curriculum research, development, and practice—and how such biases are eventually identified and countered by both theorists and practitioners. For example, as noted in chapter 11 and as discussed in some detail in this chapter, scientists themselves have not been immune from using data and facts opportunistically to support their own handiwork and biased notions in the curriculum field. As Myrdal observed, "facts kick" and, in so doing, provide a power for self-healing in social science (p. 40). The problem in education and in the curriculum field is that when data and facts are misused and abused in order to support sweeping changes in policy and practice so as to conform to narrow sociopolitical demands or to meet the dominant fashions of the times, it may be a long while before the facts kick and before self-healing can occur. In the meantime, a generation of young learners may be affected by such opportunistic influences.

"Generally speaking," writes Myrdal, "we can observe that the scientists in any particular institutional and political setting move as a flock, reserving their controversies and particular originalities for matters that do not call into question the fundamental system of biases they share" (p. 53). The key task, then, is to guard against the flock mentality and against narrow influences by being aware of the sources of bias, by taking measures to protect against biases, by bringing valuations out in the open, and by consciously and explicitly ascertaining how these valuations, together with the data, form the premises for theory, policy, and practice. In this way, the search for knowledge and the shaping of policy and practice can be directed at social betterment in accord with the higher ideals of a free society.

The Need to Look to Possibilities, Not Limitations

"Education has always been the great hope for both individual and society," observed Myrdal in *An American Dilemma*. He pointed out that "In the American Creed it [education] has been the main ground upon which 'equality of opportunity for the individual' and 'free outlet for ability' could be based" (1962, p. 882).

Yet Myrdal detected an intellectual defeatism on the part of social scientists, particularly the sociologists, with regard to the possibilities of using social science to induce social change (1962, pp. 19–20). This defeatism became openly evident during the early 1970s as social scientists sought to show that the effects of schooling were negligible in reducing the economic disparities between the advantaged and disadvantaged in society. Paradoxically, in reaching their pessimistic conclusions regarding the importance of education in combating inequality, these social scientists used much of the same hard data derived from earlier studies—data that previously had been used to point the way for educational reform as a key means of social reform. How can it be possible that essentially the same set of social science data should be interpreted so differently at different times? It appears the different times had called for different value premises, which, in turn, led to differences in the analysis and interpretation of the data.

As shown in the following discussion, research on the effects of schooling has profoundly influenced social policy and vice versa. Unfortunately, sweeping conclusions have been drawn from some of the research to justify a policy of education retrenchment. As discussed in earlier chapters, nationalizing influences (political agendas) are used to shape the direction and interpretation of educational research. This does not mean that teachers and school administrators should ignore research or even to view all research with suspicion, but rather that they must be aware of hidden agendas that may drive research opportunistically so as to serve a particular interest. Previous chapters cited a number of examples of how large-scale research studies have been used to prove the project (e.g., the national discipline-centered curriculum projects), or to justify a policy of back to basics, or to convey to the public a sense of massive failure of the public school system.

It cannot be overemphasized that in using research to guide practices, the teacher, curriculum coordinator, supervisor, and administrator must keep in mind the qualitative ideas underlying the research and the practical significance of the research for school and society. No amount of elaborate and intricate statistical treatments can compensate for poor qualitative ideas or for findings that are totally impractical. The point is that the education practitioner must

be a keen judge of qualitative ideas concerning the curriculum. The research specialist whose background is educational measurement and statistics or psychometrics quite typically is not highly knowledgeable of the curriculum field, nor of the rich heritage of research in the curriculum field. We need to ask whether a particular piece of research builds on the vast body of research and experience, and whether it looks to the possibilities rather than the limitations of the schools. We need to keep in mind that in much of the large-scale research on school effects, or on student achievement nationally or internationally, most of the variance cannot be accounted for simply because of the limitations of the testing instruments, not to mention problems in sampling, research design, and interpretation.

As discussed in chapters 5, 6, and 7 in connection with the curriculum paradigm, any research or curriculum reform measure that runs counter to social ideals, to the nature of the learner, or to the needs of the learner in a free society is destined to fail in the long run. To treat these elements as antagonistic or in isolation only fragments and isolates the curriculum and defeats the educative cause in a free society. One of the great beliefs shared by Americans is the belief in education. Research that sets out to attack this belief may serve a political agenda for education retrenchment, but will fail eventually when tested on the anvil of the American experience.

Statistics Are Not Factual or Objective Knowledge

It has been emphasized that researchers need to identify their value premises as a protection against bias. This enables the researcher and the consumer of the research to interpret the findings in the light of the stated value premises. Thus, the consumer of the research is better able to interpret the data more perceptively and critically. The researcher, in turn, is more likely to advance knowledge and improve practice in the field of study. By explicitly stating value premises, the researcher is protecting the study and the consumer of the research against hidden valuations. This does not mean that so-called qualitative research is less pervious to bias than quantitative research.

But many people tend to look on statistical data in the social sciences as though the data are hard facts representing objective knowledge. They are unaware that such data may have been derived from a single set of value premises and that another set of value premises might produce quite different data leading to very different interpretations and conclusions. Thus, it is most desirable to propose alternative value premises and working hypotheses. If one's value premise and hypothesis is that "schools do not make a difference," one is more likely to obtain data that point to limitations, whereas an opposite value premise and hypothesis are likely to lead the researcher to find possibilities.

If researchers look for limitations in humans and in the school as a learning environment, they will be able to find the limitations they are seeking. If they look for potentialities, the possibilities for improving existing conditions in the school as a learning environment are practically without limit. This is the great challenge for curriculum development.

Moreover, the value premises should be attuned to the culture under study. American culture has such a strong belief in education that some researchers, particularly revisionist historians and critical theorists, have made their reputations by attacking this belief. In so doing they have allowed their own opportunistic biases to shape their interpretations and conclusions.

Reason rather than bias should guide controversy. Myrdal puts the whole matter of value premises in research in these words:

> Values do not emerge automatically from the attempt to establish and collect the facts. Neither can we allow the individual investigator to choose his value premises arbitrarily. *The value premises should be selected by the criterion of relevance and significance to the culture under study.* (1962, p. 1045)

Myrdal emphasizes that if only one set of value premises is used, the researcher must understand and make it clear to others that both the direction and the practical conclusions of the research have only hypothetical validity, because another set of value premises might well have changed both. Thus, the formulation and utilization of value premises as instrumental norms in research places an enormous moral responsibility on the investigator.

Education and the American Creed

As mentioned early in this chapter, Gunnar Myrdal observed that Americans share a compelling faith in education, and this faith is a principal conclusion from the American Creed. Because this faith is so pervasive, no political leader can ignore it. Hence, high on the political agenda, almost invariably, are the

public schools. Unfortunately, the schools are often used opportunistically for negative attack rather than constructive redirection. Whereas American social science once had a long tradition of supporting the advancement of the public schools, the trend has been toward abandoning this tradition (1969, p. 41). Many social scientists, revisionist historians, critical theorists, and others identified with the academic left have built their reputations by challenging the educational ideal of the American Creed. They have sought evidence showing the limitations rather than the potentialities of education in American culture. However, their negativistic data and rhetoric have not been directed at the university—the source of their livelihood—but at the elementary and secondary schools. From the vantage point of the European, the American common school system was uncommon, indeed unique, in its comprehensiveness, relatively low social bias, and open access to higher education. For example, a widely read book throughout Europe during the late 1960s and early 1970s emphasized that America's power to create is attributable in no small measure to its open-access educational system. The author noted that in the United States, from three to five times as many children of workers and farmers have access to higher education as in the Common Market nations (Servan-Schreiber, 1967, p. 74). In England and Scandinavia it was discovered that it is not enough to expand the capacity for student places in the universities, but that accessibility to higher education required fundamental reforms in the structure of the school system, particularly in the direction of the comprehensive school.

"Other People's Children." Although many American social scientists and revisionist historians have generated negativistic research and rhetoric regarding the impact of schooling on the rising generation, it is doubtful that they have invested less in the education of their own children. Their negativistic message was for public consumption. Like most university professors, who had managed to gain for themselves the highest credential of academia, namely, the Ph.D., and like most college graduates, they likely sought to endow their own children with the greatest amount and highest quality of education possible. Their negativistic message clearly was directed at other people's children. In 1899, Dewey wrote: "What the best and wisest parent wants for his own child, that must the community want for all of its children. Any other ideal for our schools is narrow and unlovely; acted upon, it destroys our democracy" (1915, p. 7).

Thus, the social scientists who were manipulating data to show factually that schools make no difference for other people's children, and they themselves wanted the best and most education for their own children, were in effect undermining a principal conclusion from the American Creed. The belief in education in American thought and life is traced by Myrdal in these words:

> Research in, and discussion of, education is prolific. In America, pedagogy anticipated by several generations the recent trend to environmentalism in the social sciences and the belief in the changeability of human beings. It gave a basis for the belief in democratic values and expressed the social optimism of American liberalism.
>
> . . . The marriage between philosophy and pedagogy in Dewey and his followers has given America the most perfected educational theory in modern times. . . . America has, therefore, seen more of enterprising and experimental progressive redirection of schools than has any other country. (1962, p. 883)

Although the contemporary statistical attacks on education by social scientists have garnered a considerable following on the part of many of their colleagues and on the part of the media and education policy makers, the American public was not about to abandon its belief in education.

As discussed throughout this text, and more specifically in this chapter, some of the most influential policy decisions affecting the curriculum have been based on faulty or biased research, as well as on sound research. But all too often the research methodology and findings are fashioned on value premises to justify a negative outlook on the public schools. Fortunately, the American public has a profound belief in education despite the media bias favoring negative news on the public schools. As reported in a Gallup Poll on the public's attitudes toward the public schools over the course of 36 years, the closer one is to the local schools, the more favorable the attitude toward the schools. And despite the movement for alternative schools and charter schools, the 2004 poll reported that,

> The public is persistent in its belief that improvement should come through the existing public schools. That belief is grounded in the high levels of satisfaction that people express for schools in their own community, levels that rise the closer people are to those schools. This suggests to

policy makers at all levels that efforts at improving schooling should start with and build on the foundation that community schools provide. (Rose & Gallup, 2004, p. 51)

Over the years of polling the public has favored a balanced curriculum and equity in educational opportunity. That the American public has embraced such a strong belief in education was seen by Gunnar Myrdal as the principal element in the American Creed. This has been the most powerful antidote to the school blamers and to the negativistic valuations that lead researchers to look to the limits of schooling instead of looking to possibilities.

Research and Valuation: Equality of Educational Opportunity

Looking back on the Coleman report, *Equality of Educational Opportunity*, issued in 1966 as mandated by the Civil Rights Act of 1964, Daniel Bell referred to it as "the center of the most extensive discussion of social policy in the history of American sociological debate" (1972, p. 45). This massive cross-sectional study of 4,000 schools and 600,000 students clearly supported the need for school desegregation by linking school integration with higher achievement.

The Coleman report also revealed that although more favorable school resources—"higher per pupil expenditure, a curriculum that offers greater challenges, more laboratories, and more (cocurricular) activities"—are positively related to higher achievement, the most powerful relationship derives from "the attributes of a child's fellow students in school." The report cautioned that the possible stronger effects of variations in school resources and curriculum on achievement may well have been masked by the overwhelming variations in pupil characteristics (p. 316).

Moreover, methodology, instruments, and statistical measures connected with a large-scale survey present serious limitations in assessing complex qualitative phenomena. For example, in the Coleman study, no assessment was made of the quality of teaching or of the quality and uses of curriculum materials. Because the school characteristics were identified through questionnaires completed by school officials and teachers, with no independent assessment made of the accuracy of the reporting or of the qualitative differences in the school characteristics reported, it is not surprising that these characteristics did not account for large proportions of the total variance. Thus, for example, the fact that a school may report the presence of a full-time librarian or the number of volumes in the school library reveals nothing about the pupil usage of the library (circulation of books), the extent to which teachers assign pupils to library work, and the quality of such library assignments. In the words of the Coleman report, "It is clear that other variations among the schools in this survey have almost overwhelmed any effects of variations in the curriculum. A more intensive study, more fully focused on these curricular variables alone, would be necessary to discover their effects" (p. 316). However, no such study was undertaken. Instead, as discussed later, the Coleman document came to be used by school critics as evidence that investment in schooling is of negligible consequence for the disadvantaged.

The Nation's Mandate. Soon after the release of his report, Coleman called for a reduction of social and racial homogeneity of the school, and he singled out the neighborhood school for perpetuating this homogeneity. His chief proposal regarding schooling was framed in these words:

> For those children whose family and neighborhood are educationally disadvantaged, it is important to replace this family environment as much as possible with an educational environment—by starting school at an earlier age, and by having a school which begins very early in the day and ends very late. (Coleman, 1966, p. 74)

He called for curriculum changes to allow teachers to work with a wider range of pupils within the same classroom and to capitalize on the positive influences exerted by advantaged pupils on their disadvantaged compeers, along with vast increases in educational expenditures.

The national mandate for school desegregation seemed clear. Efforts in this direction were frustrated, particularly in the North, by the accelerating flight to the suburbs on the part of the advantaged whites, leaving inner-city schools with predominantly disadvantaged nonwhite enrollments, and by growing resistance against busing on the part of the remaining whites residing in white neighborhoods. As African Americans also demanded control over neighborhood schools, the national policy shifted from one of integration and equality to neighborhood control and compensatory education for the disadvantaged.

Under these radically shifting conditions, Coleman, as chair of the Panel on Youth of the President's Science Advisory Council, and the panel explored a variety of alternatives to school integration and curriculum reconstruction (1974). Four years later, concerned with the mounting data on youth alienation, Coleman once again prescribed a considerably extended role of the school in correcting certain growing deficiencies of the home and the wider society. "This qualitative change in the social-psychological environment provided by many families indicates to me that schools must begin to shoulder a broader set of responsibilities than they have in the past" (1978, p. 319).

It will be recalled that although Coleman's monumental study (1966) had pointed to heterogeneous schools and classrooms as the most powerfully positive influence on achievement of the disadvantaged, he had also pointed to the positive powers of a rich curriculum, improved curriculum resources, school facilities, and expenditures. However, Coleman's main focus of his research was on the powerful socialization factor in education, as mandated by the Civil Rights Act of 1964. The nation's failure to desegregate the inner-city schools, the failure of compensatory education and the so-called War on Poverty, coupled with the wave of attacks on the public schools in the popular literature from both the radical left and conservative right, gave cause for a policy of education retrenchment under the Nixon administration.

Social scientists opportunistically began to look for the limits of schooling rather than to the potentials. The leading and most influential research of the times was conducted by Christopher Jencks and his associates, who drew selectively from the Coleman report and U.S. Census data. In social research it is always easier not to find something. But as Myrdal commented, "there is truth in the biblical saying that 'he that seeketh, findeth'" (1969, p. 41). In the same sense, he who seeks not to find can find that it isn't there. From elaborate statistical techniques and massive data, Jencks and his associates reported that "the evidence suggests that equalizing educational opportunity would do little to make adults more equal," that "the character of a school's output depends largely on a single input, namely the characteristics of the entering children," that "everything else" regarding the characteristics of the school "is either secondary or completely irrelevant," and that "progress will remain glacial" if we "proceed by ingenious manipulations of marginal institutions like the schools" (1972, pp. 255, 256, 265).

In reaching these conclusions, Jencks did not focus on the curriculum variables, which, according to Coleman, would be necessary—for without an intensive investigation of such variables, they become submerged by other effects.

Many social scientists quickly accepted Jencks's conclusions as valid. The chairman of the sociology department of the University of California at Berkeley declared that Jencks's assessment of the data "agrees almost exactly with my own" and that "the book represents the best we know about the causes of individual success and about how far inequality in the causes accounts for inequality of success" (Stinchcombe, 1972, p. 6). Referring to the Jencks study, Seymour Lipset of Harvard's government department declared, "Schools make no difference; families make the difference" (Hodgson, p. 35).

Education Retrenchment. Jencks's conclusions were accepted all too readily not only by academicians and contractors for federal research such as the RAND Corporation, but also by influential political leaders. Daniel Patrick Moynihan, who at the time was a professor of education and urban politics at the Kennedy School of Government at Harvard and was serving as consultant to President Nixon, cited the RAND Corporation report for the President's Commission on School Finance in holding "that with respect to school finance there is a strong possibility that we may be already spending too much." Moynihan concluded: "A final fact is that at a point school expenditure does not seem to have any notable influence on school achievement," and "This 'discovery' was one of the major events in large-scale social science" (Moynihan, 1972, pp. 71, 73).

Double Standard. Jencks and the other social researchers, critics, and policy makers taking the position that the schools are marginal institutions in the lives and life chances of children were, of course, referring to "other people's children" and not their own (Tanner, D., 1974, pp. 222–225). And, as discussed earlier in this text, we need to ask how it is possible for most of the research on the effects of a college education to reveal highly positive results (Astin, 1983), whereas so much of the research on elementary and secondary schooling has been so negative. From all that is known about human development it is clear that childhood and adolescence are critical periods for cognitive growth, the shaping of personality, and the evolvement of enduring attitudes and values. Drawing from Myrdal's warnings, it is incumbent on social scientists to look to the possibilities of schooling and not the limitations if the research is to have validity and utility for constructive improvement. One cannot imagine the social scientists in institutions of higher education moving as a flock in generating research data devaluing higher education and supporting reductions in state and federal expenditures for higher education.

Jencks's anti-public school bias was revealed clearly in his earlier work for the U.S. Office of Economic Opportunity in which he proposed an alternative system of schooling by using public funds for education vouchers for the disadvantaged (Center for the Study of Public Policy, 1970). Apparently, Jencks's value premises against the system of public education had affected his treatment and interpretation of data.

Fortunately, as Myrdal observed, a more complete and valid picture of the phenomena under study eventually emerges as research biases and limitations are exposed when tested in the real world and against the belief in education by the American people. Hence it was only a matter of time before the facts were to kick. Unfortunately, the nation underwent an extended period of education retrenchment and back to basics.

Over the ensuing years, Jencks's facts from allegedly hard data began to backfire as research studies in the United States and other nations were revealing convincing evidence in support of what Americans already know: namely, that schooling does make a significant difference in people's lives. These studies revealed not only serious limitations and flaws in Jencks's research, but also that schooling has enduring effects into adulthood. In a large-scale analysis of data involving a population of 80,000 individuals, Hyman, Wright, and Reed found that "education produces large, pervasive, and enduring effects on knowledge and receptivity to knowledge." With respect to the attacks commonly leveled at the school regarding noncognitive influences, they stressed that much of this criticism is polemic and is refuted by the evidence.

Surely the image of the school as stultifying the student, as destroying the natural passion for learning and the love of intellectual discovery, is not compatible with our finding that with more education there is more information seeking and more receptivity to new knowledge, implanted so well that they survive old age and other circumstances of life. (1975, pp. 109–111)

Unlike Jencks's analysis of Coleman's data on the achievement of children at a given point of their schooling, the study by Hyman, Wright, and Reed traced achievement according to differences in the amount of formal education and the cumulative effects into adulthood. Reports of other studies pointed to limitations of the data used by Jencks and revealed that time spent in school is crucial to achievement, that econometric models for research in education are of questionable value because schools cannot be compared with industrial firms in input–output measures of production, and that contrary to much of the polemical literature in education and social science, schools help overcome rather than perpetuate social-class bias (Sewell, Hauser, & Featherman, 1976; Rehberg & Rosenthal, 1978). Jencks's data even impelled the British to undertake a large-scale study of secondary schools serving a high proportion of disadvantaged youth in inner-city London. From the British study it was concluded that "schools indeed have an important impact on children's development and it does matter which school a child attends." The researchers also found that various qualitative factors, such as "good conditions for pupils, and the extent to which children were able to take responsibility were all significantly associated with outcome differences between schools" and that "all of these factors were open to modification by the staff, rather than fixed by external constraints" (Rutter et al., 1979, pp. 252–254).

Despite the discrediting of Jencks's research, his conclusion that allocating increased funds for schooling to advance the knowledge and cognitive skills of the disadvantaged can yield only inconsequential results, continued to be advanced by social scientists and tax conservatives into the 1990s and beyond (Purnick, 2001, p. B1). Nevertheless, today the relationship between school conditions including expenditures, curriculum resources, facilities, teacher qualifications and school services is so universally recognized that appropriate data are reported annually or regularly in publications of the Organization for Economic Cooperation and Development (OECD), United Nations Educational, Scientific, and Cultural Organization (UNESCO), National Center for Education Statistics (NCES), International Association for the Evaluation of Educational Achievement (IEA), and other international and U.S. agencies. Unfortunately, instruments for assessing achievement (multiple-choice tests) measure only a small part of the learning outcomes or what is deemed important in the curriculum, such as patterns of inquiry, expanding interests in learning, social growth, and the cumulative effects of schooling. Multiple-choice tests cannot measure teacher enthusiasm and hands-on learning, factors that are highly influential for generative and enduring learning outcomes.

In effect, it is not enough for large-scale research to be directed at identifying the availability of curricular resources. The critical factor is the effectiveness in the uses of the resources that must be measured if connections to learning outcomes are to be made and if the research is to contribute to the improvement of the curriculum.

The inability to connect particular schooling variables with what is measured on standardized achievement tests is inadequate justification for concluding that no connection actually exists. In the words of the American humorist, Robert Benchley, "You can't prove that platypuses don't lay eggs by photographing platypuses not laying eggs." Scientific inquiry must be guided by powerful qualitative ideas and connections. The piling up of multiple-choice statistical data on tests to prove the case is scientism, not science.

The Politics of Education Reform

International Comparisons of Educational Yield

The importance of selecting and identifying value premises by the criterion of relevance and significance to the culture under study is illustrated vividly in the concept of educational yield. A traditional notion held by elitist educators is that more means worse; that is, mass education means a decline in the quality of education. This notion became a slogan that was widely echoed in attacks leveled against the comprehensive high school during the Cold War and space race. Conservative educators were joined by scientists, militarists, and politicians who advocated the adoption of an academically selective school system patterned after the dual European model. Most of the criticisms leveled at the curriculum of American schools centered on the priority subjects of mathematics and science, the two fields deemed most essential in meeting the crisis of the times.

From the inception of the first of a series of international studies of educational achievement (IEA) following Sputnik I to the present day, the findings have revealed that the United States has led all other nations in educational yield (the proportion of the school-age population that completes schooling and advances to higher education), and reflects the least social-class bias in educational access. As Torsten Husén, chairman of the first IEA study pointed out, the United States and other nations with comprehensive secondary schools have the highest educational yield. Husén stressed repeatedly that the average student achievement score in a comprehensive school system with a high retentivity of students cannot be compared fairly against the average score obtained from a selective school system. Fair comparisons could be made only by comparing the achievement of elite students in both types of systems and by assessing the educational yield of both systems in terms of how many are brought how far. When comparisons are made of equivalent student populations, it becomes clear that the most academically talented students in the comprehensive system compare favorably with those in a selective system—the chief difference being that more youngsters advance further in the comprehensive system. Such findings take on added significance when it is recognized that specialized academic high schools are endowed with facilities and resources superior to comprehensive high schools, and that nonacademic students in the comprehensive schools outperform their compeers who are in dual school systems (Husén, 1983, pp. 455–464; Husén, 1986; Rotberg, 1991, pp. 3–7; Benn & Chitty, 1997).

Media Bias and Negativism. The publication of the first IEA study (on mathematics achievement) was treated sensationally in the American press. A front-page story in the *New York Times* by that newspaper's education editor, Fred M. Hechinger, was headlined "U.S. Ranks Low in Math Teaching," and the Sunday edition of the *Times* featured a story by Hechinger under the headline "U.S. Gets Low Marks in Math." Similar articles appeared in other newspapers, and news magazines, along with reports and commentary on TV news. Despite the repeated warnings in the study against such misinterpretation and against treating the study as an international contest, the American press proceeded to do just that. Obviously, such news reached a high proportion of the American public, but relatively few laypeople and educators outside the field of mathematics read the actual IEA report. Near the end of 1968, the *New York Times* ran an article on page 74 concerning the findings of a report of the National Academy of Sciences showing that the

United States "is universally recognized as the leading producer of mathematics and mathematical talent in the world." This is evidenced by the high representation of international awards in mathematics won by Americans and the high proportion of research by Americans at international congresses and articles in the world's leading mathematics journals (1991, pp. C6, 6).

Looking back on the findings of the IEA study of mathematics achievement, Husén characterized the United States as having suffered from a "Sputnik psychosis" and a "spell of masochism" with an "eagerness to look for remedies in Europe" and a compulsion to embrace a national trust for "talent hunting." Husén summed up the major findings of the IEA study in these words:

> We have shown that an elite comparable in size and quality to that of an "elite system" can be cultivated within a retentive and often comprehensive system. In the selective system, however, the high standard of the elite is often bought at the price of low accomplishments of the mass. (1971, pp. 77, 79, 88)

He criticized the tendency to regard the term *standard* as "a metaphysically anchored concept" and to level the accusation of "lowering standards" whenever efforts are made to change the educational structure in order to broaden opportunities. Husén then reviewed the education reforms taken in Sweden to replace the selective academic secondary schools with comprehensive schools after authorities in that nation had subjected the latter to all kinds of comparisons to ensure that the change would not result in lowered standards.

The extension of education opportunity invariably has been accompanied by the contention that standards will be lowered. However, history has shown that an inclusive system of education provides for the greatest release of talents and aspirations. An inclusive system honors merit; an exclusive system tends toward privilege.

The slogan of raising standards has been used for exclusion, or for curriculum retrenchment with the accompanying slogan of back to basics and minimum-competency testing or mastery of the minima (after Sizer). Again, experience has shown that such efforts have lowered the educational yield by giving emphasis to educational limitations rather than possibilities (Tanner, D., 1997, pp. 115–120). It should also be realized that whatever the case may be, half of the schools will find that they test below standard and half will be above standard.

Misuses of Data.   The misuses of the IEA data have been reflected widely in political documents alleging massive school failure and calling for wholesale reform of the school system. Few such documents received the extensive media attention than did the report of the National Commission on Excellence in Education, which bore the alarmist title *A Nation at Risk: The Imperative for Educational Reform* (1983). The opening section of the report carried a list of 13 indicators of risk as to why schools were "sabotaging" the nation in its competition with Japan and Germany in the global industrial economy. The first indicator was the allegedly low test-score rankings of U.S. students against those of other industrialized nations. Near the end of the report it was acknowledged that U.S. students did compare favorably after all.

The introductory words of *America 2000*, President George H. W. Bush's education strategy issued in 1991, stated: "Eight years after the National Commission on Excellence in Education declared us a 'Nation at Risk,' we haven't turned things around in education." The president's message in *America 2000* contended that it was time to hold schools accountable for results and that new world-class standards must be set for the schools through new achievement tests. The president portrayed the situation as one of massive failure of public schools. Accordingly, nothing less than a "revolution" was required to "reinvent—literally start from scratch and reinvent the American school." Illogically, he declared the nation's system of American colleges and universities to be "the finest in the entire world," as he failed to explain how this was possible if the schools were failing (pp. 9, 51, 53, 55). Surely the excellence of colleges and universities is built on the quality of the students from the nation's schools. (If we may draw an analogy with big-time NCAA football, the colleges depend on the high schools for talent, and the pros depend on the colleges.)

The Sandia Study: Perspectives on Education in America

In earlier chapters, considerable discussion was given to the national syndrome of school blaming and of the widespread misuses of data in attacking the public schools. It was emphasized that educators need to draw on the fullest array of data sources to develop the most accurate picture of the education situation if constructive action is to be taken. One of the unanticipated developments in this direction was to occur from a study that had been authorized with the political expectation that the findings would lend support to the sweeping school-reform measures promoted in *America 2000*. Joining the Cabinet-level groundswell in support of *America 2000*, the U.S. secretary of Energy, Admiral James Watkins, announced in 1990 that his department was supporting a study of American education as a part of its new education mission. The U.S. Department of Energy, dating back to its predecessor agency, the Atomic Energy Commission, had been responsible for supporting research and development in nuclear energy and weaponry and other scientific work bearing on the military-industrial complex. The contractor for the study of American education was Sandia National Laboratories, a key research contractor for the Department of Energy. Earlier in his career, Watkins had served as head of submarine nuclear power distribution control under Admiral Hyman Rickover at a time when Rickover was launching his attacks against American schools, particularly against the comprehensive high school. However, the Sandia researchers, unlike researchers engaged in policy-driven research, were allowed to conduct their study of American education with no a priori premises to prove.

The outcome was a report, *Perspectives on Education in America*, that gave evidence refuting the allegations of massive school failure by the U.S. Department of Education and the president. Some discussion of the Sandia Study was presented in chapter 12, but further treatment is warranted here because of its significance for public education and as a case of how research findings favorable to the public schools can be suppressed when they controvene public policy.

Drawing from existing data banks of a host of federal agencies, the Sandia study found that, contrary to the allegations of massive failure of the school system, there was indeed powerful and pervasive evidence of success, and that many of the priorities set for education reform by the nation's leaders were clearly misdirected. Some of the principal findings were as follows:

1. When the SAT population is adjusted to match the test-taking population of the late 1970s, aggregate SAT scores are actually rising, and since the late 1970s, every minority group has maintained or improved on SAT scores.

2. Performance on the tests for the National Assessment of Educational Progress has been improving.

3. High school dropout rates are declining for all ethnic populations and community types with the exception of Hispanics, but up to half of all Hispanic dropouts are immigrants, and adult immigrants who did not complete high school in their native countries are counted as U.S. dropouts even though they had never dropped into U.S. schools.

4. Up to 5 million non-English-speaking children of immigrant parents will be entering public schools in the 1990s.

5. Dramatic and accelerating demographic changes are occurring in public schools as a result of immigration, so that today almost one third of the pupils are minorities, mainly from Latin America and Asia; these accelerating changes are concentrated primarily in central cities.

6. Despite declines in the college-age population, the cumulative number of bachelor's degrees in engineering, computer science, physical science, and mathematics has increased by more than 75 percent during the past 20 years, and the number of doctorates in these fields is at or near an all-time high.

7. Despite the dramatic increase in the proportion of college graduates in the tested population, scores on the Graduate Record Examination have risen significantly since the late 1970s.

8. The United States is the world leader in degrees earned by the nation's population in science and engineering as well as in all fields.

9. The alleged increase in K–12 per pupil expenditures is the result of the high cost of special education and the increasing proportion of pupils so classified, whereas the expenditures for "regular" pupils have remained almost constant during the past 20 years (adjusted for inflation).

10. A majority of American families with children under 6 years of age have both parents in the workforce, and over 40 percent of children are being reared by a single parent (Carson, Huelskamp, & Woodall, 1993, p. 261–310).

"Crisis Rhetoric" and Misplaced Priorities. In effect, the Sandia study refuted the allegations and prescriptions for the wholesale reform of the public school system as proposed in *America 2000* and *Goals 2000.* Unfortunately, the Sandia study was seen as politically embarrassing so that officials at the U.S. Department of Education sought to discredit the Sandia study and hold it from publication. It was never published as a federal document, but it was released belatedly for publication in an education journal of modest circulation. By the time it was released for publication it had virtually no impact on the media. Some of the principal conclusions of the Sandia researchers were as follows:

1. Much of the "crisis" rhetoric claiming systemwide failure in education is misinformed and only hinders constructive reform; the Sandia research shows that these allegations are based on improper uses of data.

2. The system of public education is being used as a scapegoat by many agencies for the perceived lack of U.S. competitiveness in global industrial markets.

3. The scientific community has been a party to distracting the nation from its real education problems; like the economic competitiveness argument, the contention that there is a continuing shortage of Ph.D.s in technical fields portrays the United States as losing ground to other nations whereas, in actuality, this is not the case.

4. Many current metrics are ill defined, flawed, misdirected, and provide no justifiable basis for the kinds of national education reforms that have been proposed (e.g., the improper claim of "declining SAT scores").

5. Much of the blame for problems in education (real or imagined) has been dropped at the feet of local teachers and administrators with demoralizing effects.

The Sandia report went on to point out that many of the reform prescriptions are mutually conflicting, such as supporting local empowerment and at the same time promoting a national curriculum, national testing of student achievement, and state-by-state comparisons of test results. The Sandia study also stressed that the call for revolutionary change in the education system sets the current reform cycle apart from others. The U.S. education system was built on a foundation of local control, state function, and federal interest, as shown by the nearly 16,000 independent school districts nationwide. Consequently, not only is it difficult to draw a reform consensus, but it may even be undesirable (Carson,

Huelskamp, & Woodall, 1991, pp. 170, 172; 1992, pp. 99–100, 105; 1993, pp. 259–310).

Turning to *America 2000/Goals 2000* it will be recalled that one of the announced goals was that U.S. students will be "first in the world in science and math achievement." Drawing on *A Nation at Risk*, the allegation is made in *America 2000* that U.S. students are "at or near the back of the pack in international comparisons" (p. 9). Again, this a gross distortion in that in many nations the student populations submitting to tests are selective, whereas the U.S. students represent an actual sampling of the total student population and age grouping. Nevertheless, the U.S. Department of Education and the Educational Testing Service, which constructs the tests, have certified the validity of the results, and the media continue to convey a grossly distorted picture of the results to the public.

We must also question how it is possible for science and mathematics education to be so deficient when the United States maintains overwhelming dominance over other advanced nations in scientific productivity.

National priorities for school reform invariably carry corresponding priorities for the curriculum. When reform measures are called for and initiated under an air of crisis, and when they are advanced to serve narrow interests, they divert us from the most significant problems in education. The strength of American democracy derives not from a narrow nationalism, but from cosmopolitanism.

The National Adult Literacy Survey

The Sandia Study appropriately criticized the wide use of flawed data to support improper claims with regard to the alleged failure of American public education. The release in 1993 of the findings of the National Adult Literacy Study (Kirsch, Jungeblut, Jenkins, & Kolstad) conducted by Educational Testing Service for the U.S. Department of Education, garnered sensational media copy. Although the survey was directed at the adult population, it was the K–12 public education system that took the brunt of the assault. A front-page article in the *New York Times* was headlined, "Study Says Half of Adults in U.S. Can't Read or Handle Arithmetic" (Celis, September 9, 1993). Reporters drew this sweeping indictment directly from the press release issued by the U.S. secretary of Education, who used the indictment to buttress President Clinton's *Goals 2000*. The press

release was carefully choreographed for the opening of the new school year and was featured that evening on the news telecasts for the three national networks.

Bias in Research. Even a cursory review of the premises and research methodology of the study by Educational Testing Service reveals serious flaws that raise questions as to the underlying intent of the researchers (Tanner, D., 1998, pp. 344–349). To begin, the definition of literacy formulated for the study was different from any that had been used previously by the U.S. Census Bureau or any other national or international agency. For the study, literacy was defined as "using printed and written information to function in society, to achieve one's goals, and to develop one's knowledge potential" (p. 2). Aside from the vagueness of the definition, it is doubtful that very many people in society will claim that they have achieved their goals and developed their knowledge potential, let alone voluntarily agreeing to a written test to demonstrate this proficiency.

The report of the National Adult Literacy Survey (NALS) claimed that it was based on a nationally representative sample of 13,600 adults (16 years of age and older) who submitted to a written test, coupled with interviews and tests conducted in 27,000 households. However, the proportion of immigrants in the national sample exceeded their proportional representation in the national population, and most of these immigrants had never attended U.S. schools. Also overrepresented in the study were Blacks and Hispanics whose years of schooling, test scores, and economic conditions are below those of Whites. For example, although Blacks constitute 11% of the U.S. population, they accounted for 19% of the sample. Moreover, almost 1 out of 10 males in the study were inmates of federal and state penitentiaries—hardly being in a position to meet the study's literacy definition: "to function in society, to achieve one's goals, and to develop one's knowledge potential." The proportion of the national population of males incarcerated in federal and state prisons is less than eight tenths of 1%. In effect, the number of male penitentiary inmates was overrepresented in the "scientific" sampling by almost 12 times or 1,200%. The proportion of female inmates also was grossly overrepresented in the sample.

Many of the test items seemed to raise questions of face validity. For example, in assessing the ability to "use printed information to function in society," test items required the extrapolation of information from bus schedules under such hypothetical situations as determining waiting time after having missed a connection. One might ask how many of us use a bus schedule in daily life. The test items were graduated to far more complex tasks, such as synthesizing information from complex and lengthy texts and documents, drawing information from lengthy and dense texts that contain distractors, and making high-level inferences or using specialized background knowledge.

As expected, the test scores were positively and strongly correlated with years of schooling completed in the United States. It was acknowledged in the study that of the 25% of those testing at the lowest level, almost one out of five had visual difficulties to the extent that reading print presented a problem under ordinary circumstances, let alone under the conditions of taking a timed test under supervision. More than one out of four were found to have physical, mental, or health debilities that prevented them from participating in regular work, school attendance, housework, or other activities.

It must be acknowledged that one surely needs the know-how of taking a multiple-choice test to get through school or college, and indeed the student gets plenty of practice on such tests. One hardly encounters the multiple-choice test in real life. Consequently, there is reason to question whether such a test is a fair simulation of life conditions.

Finally, the report of the National Adult Literacy Survey by Educational Testing Service failed to report the percentages of the population that declined to participate in the tests and submit to questionnaires and interviews requiring more than an hour under direct supervision. One might well infer that busy people were less likely to make themselves available for such a test. Considering the circumstances, there appeared to be good reason to recognize the positive findings that one out of five of the total population in the study actually performed at the highest test levels in their demonstrated capability of integrating information from long and dense documents or texts, making high-level inferences, using specialized background knowledge, and processing quantitative data in performing more complex operations.

The Facts Kick. Only two months after the announcement by the secretary of Education that half of the adult population does not have the literacy skills to function in society, when it became politically expedient to recognize the high competence of U.S. workers in order to promote the North American Free Trade Agreement, aides who had served both Presidents George H. W. Bush and Bill Clinton joined in declaring that "we have the world's most productive workers" (Snow & Carville, *New York Times*, November 2, 1993, op-ed page). Indeed, there was compelling evidence to support the high level of education in the U.S. workforce. As cited in chapter 11, the United Nations *Human Development Report* (1992) ranked the United States first among the world's nations on the index of educational attainment and tied for first in rate of adult literacy, whereas the United States failed to make the top 10 in life expectancy (p. 127). In other words, one of the most successful institutions is the public school.

Also, only a few weeks after the release of the National Adult Literacy Survey, a comprehensive study for the McKinsey Global Institute, with the assistance of Robert Solow, Nobel laureate in economics, and other economists concluded that U.S. manufacturing productivity is actually higher than that of Japan and Germany and that U.S. workers are not lacking in the necessary basic skills. The critical factors for workers in all three nations "are attitudinal—flexibility, dependability, and commitment (Baily, Bator, Hall, & Solow, 1993).

Within three months after the release of the National Adult Literacy Survey, an international study by the Organization for Economic Cooperation and Development (OECD) found that among the OECD member nations (industrialized), the United States has the highest proportion of adults with college degrees.

National Survey on Reading

In 2004 the National Endowment for the Arts released a report, *Reading at Risk: A Survey of Reading in America*, drawn from survey data from the U.S. Census Bureau over the course of twenty years. As with *A Nation at Risk*, the report of the survey opens with a condemnatory declaration:

> The comprehensive survey of American literary reading presents a detailed but bleak assessment of the decline of reading's role in the nation's culture. For the first time in modern history, less than half of the adult population now reads literature, and these trends reflect a larger decline in other sorts of reading. Anyone who loves literature or values the cultural, intellectual, and political importance of active and engaged literacy in American society will respond to this report with grave concern. (p. viii)

"Twenty years ago," concludes the report, "the landmark study, *A Nation at Risk* warned that 'a rising tide of mediocrity' had overtaken the school system and threatened a generation of students. . . . *Reading at Risk* reveals an equally dire situation, a culture at risk" (p. xiii).

Although the news media provided wide coverage stressing the negative findings of the *Reading at Risk* report by the National Endowment for the Arts, the study itself should have raised some puzzling questions as to methodology and possible bias that might well challenge the validity of the study. The report defined literature as "novels or short stories, plays, or poetry" (p. 1), arbitrarily omitting nonfiction (history, biography, politics, current affairs, and so on).

As expected, the survey found that the most important factor influencing the extent of literary reading is educational attainment, although the report gives no credit to the nation's public school system. Family income also was strongly related to the extent of reading. Geographically, the highest rate of literacy reading was in the West and the lowest in the South. It was also found that women were more heavily engaged in literary reading than men.

Not until the closing comments of the study was it reported, "Over the 20-year span of this analysis, Hispanics doubled their share of the total U.S. population, rising from 6.4 percent of the total in 1980 to 12.5 percent in 2003" and that "the literary reading rate for Hispanics was only half that of non-Hispanic whites" with the acknowledgment that "the dramatic population growth of Hispanics may have contributed to the lower literary reading rates for the adult population as a whole" (p. 30).

Data released by the Association of American Publishers reveal that the sales for adult books have not been in decline, but that there has been a marked increase in the sales of religious books (Weber, 2004, p. E4).

Clearly, the valuations held by the National Endowment for the Arts influenced the methodology and conclusions of the survey. This points to the importance of school teachers, supervisors, and administrators becoming intelligent consumers of research so that their work is built upon the best available evidence. More is said about this need later in this chapter.

Some Implications for the Curriculum. Teachers are continually selecting curriculum materials and, in the process, are engaged in their evaluation whether implicitly or systematically. The significance of readability formulas (number of words per sentence, paragraph and page; length of words, etc.) has been vastly overemphasized in the development and promotion of curriculum materials. When driven by interesting ideas, youngsters reveal a capability of extending their reading levels and gaining fluency in written and oral expression.

Teachers are often surprised when they find colleagues who are using college-level reading materials with great success with heterogeneous classes of ninth-graders. The passages in Figure 14.1, extracted from an article in *The American Scholar*, the journal of Phi Beta Kappa, illustrates how reading materials targeted for college graduates of exceptional academic ability can also be used appropriately for high school students in mixed-ability classes. The material is powerfully idea oriented, clearly written, and focused on the history of a provocative social problem, and it does not talk down to the reader. The macrocurricular function of the material is general education. In contrast, basic education, being focused on mechanical skills and drills, drives out interest, and defeats the cause of education. Specialized education, unlike general education, requires the uses of technical materials requiring technical competence, but this does not necessarily mean that the students are more likely engaged in higher-order thinking than in the case of general education. Hypothetical thinking, problem solving, and practical action can occur in general education and specialized education.

The account in Figure 14.1 goes on to describe the impact of such diseases as smallpox, typhus, and cholera on the course of history before the author moves on to venereal diseases and the prospects for AIDS. The author relates how Napoleon's army of a half million in the invasion of Russia in June 1812 was left with only 3,000 to complete the retreat by June 1813, and that the catastrophic losses occurred not from battle or cold, but from typhus and dysentery. Moving to the twentieth century, the author points out how the pedagogical problem with venereal disease in health-education classes was how to teach students about sex without their recognizing the subject.

Many of the textbooks in ecology or environmental science used for general education in science at colleges and universities are fully appropriate for 9th- and 10th-graders. These texts are not at all watered-down treatments, but deal authentically with problems that interconnect science and technology

Figure 14.1 Plagues, History, and AIDS.

Plagues, History, and AIDS

. . . This worldwide outbreak of a new infectious disease (AIDS) has engendered much fear and apprehension. As a result, there have been frequent references to previous epidemics. Perhaps most frequent are references to the Black Death, the epidemic of bubonic plague that swept through Europe in the middle of the fourteenth century. Despite current fears there has been little attempt to reexamine previous epidemics for comparisons and insights to the AIDS epidemic. . . .

First, one can look at previous epidemics and the ways in which they affected nations, politics, and even the course of history. Second, one can describe the internal "sociobiological anatomy" of an epidemic, the series of social and political responses that occur during the course of an epidemic. These reactions tend to be somewhat similar in all epidemics and are already occurring during the current outbreak of AIDS. Lastly, since AIDS is a sexually transmitted disease, it is illuminating to compare the response to AIDS with society's responses to other sexually transmitted diseases early in this century. . . .

Bubonic plague struck Europe in 1347 but events of the previous two hundred years had set the stage for the great epidemic. . . . The epidemic arrived in Marseilles in 1348, and by 1351 all of Europe was afflicted. The immediate effects of the epidemic were devastating. The most accurate estimate for total deaths during this first wave of the epidemic is 25 million or one-third of the population of Europe. No segment of society was spared. Following this epidemic, recurrent waves of plague kept the population at this level for another 150 years. . . .

The most recent worldwide epidemic was an outbreak of influenza A that swept the world in 1918–19. The first cases of influenza were recognized at Camp Funston, Kansas. Two months later massive epidemics began in Spain, France, and England. . . . Despite massive public health measures, influenza spread rapidly throughout the world. By the time the pandemic ended in 1919, there had been one million deaths in the United States, 10 million in India, and an estimated 30 million deaths throughout the world. . . .

Source: Robert M. Swenson, *The American Scholar, 57* (Spring 1988), pp. 183–185, 187.

with social problems and issues. Texts and curriculum materials need not be watered down or dumbed down when they deal authentically with problems and issues that connect the life of the learner with the life of society in meeting the function of general education.

The use of original source materials can lend power and authenticity to the curriculum in many ways. Figures 14.2 and 14.3 illustrate this with excerpts from Darwin's five-year journey around the world as chronicled in *Voyage of the Beagle* (1845), in which he repeatedly attacked the institution of slavery in his scientific belief that Blacks are human beings and in his convictions for social justice. Darwin's writings reveal vividly and eloquently a work that unifies the natural sciences, social sciences, and humanities—a work that is a literary masterpiece. The book might well be read in conjunction with the BBC television series that dramatized Darwin's account of the voyage. The student learns that scientific hypotheses and investigations are driven by the profound ideas, convictions, and emotions of the scientist. The sense of wonder is never pure thought apart from emotion.

Teachers may find it useful to make up sets of criteria for evaluating curriculum materials. In so

Figure 14.2 Excerpts from Charles Darwin, *The Voyage of the Beagle*.

Rio de Janeiro

April 4th to July 5th, 1832—. . . . As it was growing dark we passed under one of the massive, bare, and steep hills of granite which are so common in this country. This spot is notorious from having been, for a long time, the residence of some runaway slaves, who, by cultivating a little ground near the top, contrived to eke out a subsistence. At length they were discovered, and a party of soldiers being sent, the whole were seized with the exception of one old woman, who, sooner than again be led into slavery, dashed herself to pieces from the summit of the mountain. In a Roman matron this would have been called the noble love of freedom: in a poor negress it is mere brutal obstinacy. We continued riding for some hours. For the few last miles the road was intricate, and it passed through a desert waste of marshes and lagoons. The scene by the dimmed light of the moon was most desolate. A few fireflies flitted by us; and the solitary snipe, as it rose, uttered its plaintive cry. The distant and sullen roar of the sea scarcely broke the stillness of the night. . . .

On the 19th of August (1836) we finally left the shores of Brazil. I thank God, I shall never again visit a slave country. . . . It is often attempted to palliate slavery by comparing the state of slaves with our poorer countrymen: if the misery of our poor be caused not by the laws of nature, but by our institutions, great is our sin; but how this bears on slavery, I cannot see; as well might the use of the thumb-screw be defended in one land, by showing that men in another land suffered from some dreadful disease. Those who look tenderly at the slave owner, and with a cold heart at the slave, never seem to put themselves into the position of the latter; what a cheerless prospect, with not even a hope of change! Picture to yourself the chance, ever hanging over you, of your wife and your little children—those objects which urges even the slave to call his own—being torn from you and sold like beasts to the first bidder! And these deeds are done and palliated by men, who profess to love their neighbors as themselves, who believe in God, and pray that his Will be done on earth! It makes one's blood boil, yet heart tremble, to think that we Englishmen and our American descendants, with their boastful cry of liberty, have been and are so guilty: but it is a consolation to reflect, that we at least have made a greater sacrifice, than ever made by any nation, to expiate our sin.

---

doing, they will discover that materials that evoke higher-order thinking can indeed be appropriate for students of a range of academic abilities and grade levels when the materials are personally and socially relevant in meeting the function of general education.

Students readily forget the factual information memorized for the examination, but they have a life-long memory of field trips and action-oriented projects. In recognition that the traditional course in civics or government fails to stir the interest of students in participatory democracy, Katherine Isaac's *Civics for Democracy: A Journey for Students and Teachers* is a notable sourcebook for this purpose by presenting documented materials on student action projects in schools and communities around the nation (1992). By examining such materials and evaluating the efficacy of using them in their own schools, teachers can derive new insights into their own beliefs and those of their colleagues.

The Conceptual and the Experiential. This has been a long-term debate in the methodology of teaching reading, namely on phonics versus whole language. The No Child Left Behind Act of 2001 called for

Figure 14.3   Excerpts from Charles Darwin, *The Voyage of the Beagle*.

Return to England—Retrospect

On the 2nd of October (1837) we made the shores of England; and at Falmouth I left the Beagle, having lived on board the good little vessel nearly five years.

Our voyage having come to an end, I will take a short retrospect of the advantages and disadvantages, the pains and pleasures, of our circumnavigation of the world. . . . No doubt it is a high satisfaction to behold the many races of mankind, but the pleasures gained at the time do not counterbalance the evils. . . .

Many of the losses which must be experienced are obvious; such as that of the society of every old friend, and of the sight of those places with which every dearest remembrance is so intimately connected. These losses, however, are at the time partly relived by the exhaustless delight of anticipating the long wished-for day of return. If, as the poets say, life is a dream, I am sure in a voyage these are the visions which best serve to pass away the long night. Other losses, although not at first felt, tell heavily after a period: these are the want of room, of seclusion, of rest, the jading feeling of constant hurry; the privation of small luxuries, the loss of domestic society and even of music and the other pleasures of imagination. . . .

---

schools to follow "scientifically based" approaches reading instruction, a mandate widely interpreted as systematic phonics (Schemo, 2002, p. A16).

An analysis from the Early Childhood Longitudinal Study, Kindergarten Class of 1998–1999 (Xue & Meisels, 2004) found that children from families of higher socioeconomic levels learn more through whole language or integrated language instruction (p. 220). Those children enter school with higher literacy skills, obviously related to the home environment. Children from families of lower socioeconomic levels enter schools with lower entering literacy skills and do not benefit greatly from integrated language arts instruction (p. 220). This might lead some to conclude that whole language instruction should be employed for the more advantaged children, and phonics instruction should be followed for the less advantaged. Indeed the employment of segmental drill-skill methods with at-risk children, and aggregate or holistic methods focused on more conceptual learning for the more advantaged children, has been a fundamental dichotomy marking educational inequality. Xue and Meisels conclude that "early literacy instruction is best conceived as a continuum rather than a dichotomy" (p. 198). They called for the middle road: a balance between phonics and whole language (p. 197).

However, in seeing the solution as one of co-existence, here the researchers miss the most significant finding of their study, namely that of complementarity. Further, a school environment that is richly conceptual *and* experiential will result in higher achievement on all fronts and with all children. Historically, the experimentalists beginning with Francis Parker, who championed whole language over a century ago, did not ignore the mechanics of reading, but they recognized that *meaningful* (conceptual and experiential) learning strengthens the mechanics. Recent research is leading to this same conclusion (Xue & Meisels, p. 198).

The whole issue adds up to the following formula:

The Conceptual + The Experiential = The Consequential

Proving the Project Proves Counterproductive

The history of education/curriculum reform is replete with curriculum projects and innovations that have been promoted as panaceas. Supporters of the project often acquire a sense of ownership to the extent that they seek to prove the project, as opposed to engaging in systematic evaluation with a view toward the formative improvement of the project. In neglecting or avoiding research and evaluation during the formative stages of the project or innovation, supporters are prone to become increasingly susceptible to proving the project at the final or summative stage. This may serve a promotional purpose in the short run, but over the long run it may prove costly to the consumers not only in monetary measures but also in the lives of the learners.

Why Innovations and Reforms Have Failed

The failure of curriculum innovation and reform may be attributed less to technical shortcomings than to the following:

1. The biases in seeking to prove the project/product

2. The segmental approach taken in treating the subject or discipline as independent of other subjects or studies in the curriculum

3. The neglect of the rich body of research and experience that can provide a powerful base of successful practices on which to build

4. The tendency to undertake and support a singular or unilateral approach when more than one approach may be called for

5. The avoidance of formative evaluation and field trials under the most practical conditions

6. The avoidance of controlled research when such research is called for, and the tendency to claim as an experiment almost any departure from conventional practice

7. The neglect or distortion of the nature of the learner

8. The neglect of linking the subject matter to the practical and social life of the learner (e.g., the critical abilities required for productive citizenship in a free society)

9. The lack of teacher involvement in the development and evaluation of the project or innovation

10. Reliance on authoritative endorsement as opposed to the best available evidence

The national discipline-centered curriculum reforms under the direction of university scholars during the Cold War and space race was by far the most ambitious, far-reaching, and well-financed effort to reconstruct the academic side of the school curriculum

in the history of American education. The effort went awry for the most part because it failed to take into account most if not all of the considerations enumerated above. Or, to put it briefly, the national discipline-centered projects failed to take account of the curriculum paradigm that requires that the curriculum be so organized and treated as to take fullest possible account of the nature of the learner and the demands of a free society. Instead, the discipline-centered projects were focused on specialized, puristic knowledge to the neglect of general education and applied knowledge. At the same time, although the university scholars claimed that their curriculum projects were centered on methods of scholarly or scientific inquiry, they made sweeping claims for their efforts without submitting to research controls. In the rare instances when experimental controls were used, the control populations were set up as wooden-legged competitors.

Professional education associations in each of the academic fields are almost continually formulating sets of curriculum standards (K–12) for evaluating the quality of the curriculum and of student achievement. The success or failure of these contemporary efforts will depend in no small measure on the lessons to be learned from the adventures and misadventures of the national discipline-centered curriculum projects. There has always been a tendency for these professional associations to treat their particular academic fields as separate from the other fields that comprise the school curriculum, with the consequence that the subject matter is treated departmentally and in isolation.

Then there is the penchant for these associations and institutions of teacher education to get carried away by pervading reform sweeps, as when they endorsed the national disciplinary projects, such as the "new math" in the wake of the Cold War and space race. Or take, for example, the standard formulated at the English Coalition Conference and issued by the National Council of Teachers of English and the Modern Language Association holding that, by 2000, fourth-graders in science will "write and speak eloquently about observations and experiments" (Council for Basic Education, 1991). How many scientists or teachers of English can write and speak eloquently? The point is that professional educators have a responsibility to question any claim or demand that defies credibility, and this includes the number one goal declared in *America 2000* to be attained by 2000: "All children will start school ready to learn" (p. 19, *Sourcebook*). All policy demands and research affecting education must be tested by the criteria of credibility, practicality, and generalizability as well as validity (Tanner, D., 1998, p. 345).

One-Sided Value Premises

Many of the national curriculum reform projects suffered from one-sided value premises. For example, one of the key value premises underlying the discipline-centered projects was that subject matter should be selected and organized in terms of its purity as opposed to application and interdisciplinary treatments.

Early in this chapter, Myrdal was quoted to the effect that scientists in any particular institution or setting tend to move as a flock and resist calling into question the fundamental biases that they share. This situation appeared to prevail in connection with the discipline-centered curriculum reforms. The commitment to disciplinarity resulted in a long period when virtually no effort was made on the part of the leading curriculum-reform centers to develop interdisciplinary curricula that were focused on applications to pervading social problems and to test such alternative approaches against the disciplinary approaches. Instead, the superiority of the disciplinary premise was promoted and accepted as fact rather than as a hypothesis to be tested.

When systematic research was conducted under the auspices of the disciplinary projects, the research typically was designed to prove the project (curriculum package). Instead of evaluating the discipline-centered project in terms of equally well-supported interdisciplinary approaches, it was contrasted with so-called conventional practice. Instead of funding projects with the mandate to *find* the best curriculum approaches possible and to test the disciplinary premise against the interdisciplinary approach, the National Science Foundation (NSF) and the U.S. Office of Education simply funded the projects with the mandate to *produce* the best disciplinary curriculum packages. In other words, because these projects were committed to the disciplinary premise, virtually no systematic effort could be made to evaluate, either formatively or summatively, these curriculum packages against alternative interdisciplinary approaches. Instead of providing research funds for the independent summative evaluation of the projects, the NSF and the Office of Education allocated funds directly to the projects so that they could evaluate their own handiwork. Moreover, the funds allocated for such research and evaluation were relatively meager in comparison to the total budgets of the projects.

Avoidance of Controlled Research

The national discipline-centered curriculum reform program can be traced back to the leadership of Jerrold Zacharias, an MIT physicist who organized the Physical Science Study Committee (PSSC), which developed the high school physics course described by Jerome Bruner on the opening pages of *The Process of Education* as "the most highly developed curriculum of its kind" in representing "the profound scientific revolution of our times" and in meeting the "long-range crisis in national security" (1960, pp. 1–2). Zacharias established the Education Development Center, which served as an organizational locus for a number of the projects and which later became a Regional Educational Laboratory.

It turned out that the very scientists who had sought to develop curricula modeled so as to teach students the principles and practices of scientific inquiry violated these very same principles and practices. In most cases they avoided controlled research. Zacharias claimed that the materials for the PSSC course were developed "experimentally" and that "the entire program must be looked upon as an experiment." Yet the PSSC group failed to employ controlled research in evaluating their course. Instead, they resorted to testimonials and unsubstantiated claims. Although they indicated that the claims must be looked on as "hypotheses," they avoided the testing of their hypotheses and, instead, concluded that "it will be students and teachers who must decide upon the soundness of those hypotheses" (Zacharias & White, 1964, pp. 77, 79).

Unscientific Claims.   Not only did the university scientists fail to test their hypotheses and substantiate their claims in the light of scientific evidence, but they also grossly exaggerated that magnitude of impact of their projects. In reporting to the NSF on school enrollments in the new courses, the project directors submitted vastly exaggerated figures, approximately double those derived through independent surveys conducted by the U.S. Office of Education. For example, when the PSSC reported 200,000 pupils enrolled in its course, the Office of Education found the enrollment to be less than 100,000. Similar discrepancies were found in the enrollment data reported for the biology (BSCS) and the chemistry projects (Welch, 1968, pp. 225–234).

In effect the magnitude of error committed by the scientists was on the order of 100% (in favor of their biased premises). At the request of the embarrassed project administrators, the U.S. Office of Education ceased making any surveys on the enrollments in the discipline-centered courses.

Proving the Project

When those engaged in the development of new curriculum projects or innovations embrace from the beginning a singular one-best approach, they find themselves in the position of proving and promoting the project. However, when multiple approaches are undertaken from the beginning, along with systematic and formative evaluation throughout the development stages of the project, the dangers of bias are reduced and the possibilities for developing significant improvements are greatly enhanced. To this day, we find curriculum innovations being promoted and adopted without adequate evaluation and pilot study during the development stages. The story of the national discipline-centered curriculum projects offers invaluable lessons for educators because no other effort at curriculum reform in the academic subjects was so well supported financially at the federal level, so authoritatively promoted by the universities, so powerfully promoted by the media, and so readily adopted by the schools. It has been pointed out repeatedly in various chapters of this text that one of the key criteria for the success of a curriculum or course of study lies in the test of practical knowledge applications in the life of the learner and society. A common claim made by the developers of the disciplinary curriculum projects was that practical applications are (appropriately) excised in favor of puristic/abstract knowledge. Inexplicably, although the Physical Science Study Committee claimed that their physics course provided real knowledge of science and less technology, the committee also claimed that it provided the best background for terminal students as well as those going on to college, appealed to girls as well as boys, and stimulated class discussion and creative thinking (Education Development Center, 1967, pp. 75–76).

In stating that the PSSC course gives "real knowledge of science, less technology," the implication is that applied knowledge is not "real" knowledge. Moreover, the PSSC staff never made any effort to test these claims through controlled research. In fact, as educators not connected with the PSSC project found evidence that challenged each of these claims, the PSSC leaders responded by asserting that

"the committee's own evaluations are directed toward the improvement of the course, not comparisons with other courses" (Finlay, 1962, pp. 75–76). This antiscientific attitude seeking to justify an avoidance of controlled research was characteristic of the leading disciplinary projects in the sciences and other subjects.

It will be recalled that the PSSC course failed to serve not only the so-called terminal students, but also the academically talented. In fact, the sharp declines in college physics and chemistry majors at a time of record increases in the college population were traced to the experiences adolescents had with the new high school physics and chemistry (Ellis, S. D., 1967, p. 77; King, 1967, p. 44). The adolescent learner is vitally interested in the relevance of the curriculum to his or her life. To ignore this is to court curriculum failure.

Experimental Bias.   Among the major national curriculum projects, the Biological Sciences Curriculum Study (BSCS) stood virtually alone in supporting systematic evaluation and in developing multiple course versions, namely, three that differed in thematic orientation. However, extensive experimental comparisons were not made until after the three versions had gone commercial and, further, the three versions were not tested against each other but against a wooden-legged competitor called the conventional course. The BSCS leaders made sweeping claims for the superiority of the BSCS courses over the conventional biology course. In seeking to prove these claims, the BSCS conducted a large-scale study to compare the differences in achievement and attitudes between the BSCS students and those taking conventional courses.

The need for independent summative evaluation becomes readily apparent when one identifies the gross disparities in the treatment favoring the BSCS population over the control population in this experimental research (*BSCS Newsletter*, 1963). The teachers responsible for the BSCS group were paid an additional 10% of their annual salary to participate in the experiment. The control teachers were given no such bonus. The BSCS teachers participated in a special training program prior to the experiment and were provided the services of university biologists who served as resource persons during the course of the experiment. No such inservice training program or consultative resource personnel were provided the control teachers. All of the BSCS students were given new textbooks and laboratory books free of charge to keep permanently, whereas the control students had to use the used textbooks available in their schools on a loan basis. The BSCS teachers were given special supplementary guides for the experiment that were not part of the regular BSCS teacher materials. No comparable provisions were made for the control teachers. The schools with the BSCS classes were required to have good laboratory facilities and equipment, and when such equipment or materials were lacking they were provided for these schools on a permanent basis. No effort was made to ensure that the laboratory facilities, equipment, and resources of the control schools were generally on a par with those of the BSCS schools.

The BSCS students were given a practice sample version of the BSCS achievement test early in the school year, followed by the BSCS quarterly achievement tests, whereas the control students did not receive the benefit of such practice and exposure. Both student populations took the BSCS final examination at the end of the school year. Obviously, the benefit of practice and familiarity with the BSCS tests on the part of the BSCS students could be expected to improve the scores of these students on the final examination. Both student groups were tested at the end of the year on the Cooperative Biology Test of the College Entrance Examination Board as well as on the BSCS Comprehensive Final Examination. The former test was supposed to represent the conventional biology course, even though it was 13 years old and was not truly representative of conventional high-school biology circa the 1960s. The control group was not provided with any practice on the Cooperative Biology Test to counter the practice and exposure provided the BSCS group on the BSCS achievement tests. The BSCS Impact Test (designed to measure understanding of scientific principles and reasoning) and the BSCS Test of Understanding of Science (later renamed the Processes of Science Test) were administered to both populations at the end of the school year. Obviously, these tests were attuned to the subject matter of the BSCS course and, consequently, must be presumed to favor the BSCS group. Thus, all of the tests, with the exception of the Cooperative Biology Test, were produced by the BSCS project and were attuned specifically to the subject matter represented in the BSCS course, whereas the Cooperative Biology Test did not represent any given conventional course. The control population had been composed of students taking various non-BSCS

courses who were lumped together for comparison against the BSCS students.

Although efforts were made to match both populations according to aptitude and school and community characteristics, the disparities in the treatment were so obviously biased in favor of the BSCS group as to violate the basic scientific principles of controlled research. As expected, the BSCS group obtained higher scores than the control group on the BSCS Comprehensive Final. However, the control students outperformed the BSCS group on the Cooperative Biology Test. Although the BSCS group was expected to clearly outperform the control students on the BSCS Impact Test and on the BSCS Test of Understanding of Science, the control students made somewhat higher scores (at a statistically significant level) than the BSCS group on the Impact Test, whereas their performance on the other BSCS test matched that of the BSCS group. Subsequent studies of achievement in the first course in college biology revealed that the BSCS and non-BSCS groups performed at equal levels (Mayer, M., 1971, p. 2).

Protection Against Bias.   Not only is it essential that every effort be made to guard against bias in research, but the value premises underlying curriculum reform also must be carefully identified and tested before sweeping claims are made. When the continued funding of a multimillion-dollar project is dependent on favorable results, bias in the research and evaluation program is bound to become manifest. The evaluation goal, then, is to prove the superiority of the product and not to solve problems in curriculum development. If these projects had been funded in the first place to develop and assess alternative curricula based on alternative value premises, with the goal of developing the best courses possible, there would have been far less likelihood of bias in the research and evaluation. Although the formative evaluation would be conducted largely under the auspices of the particular project, it appears desirable to have the summative evaluation conducted by an independent agency.

All too often in proving the project, comparison populations or control groups are set up as wooden-legged competitors. When the wooden leg unexpectedly kicks, all kinds of rationalizations are proposed. Alternative approaches and value premises should help protect against such bias. Fortunately, over the ensuing years the BSCS group proceeded to undertake renewed efforts toward reconstructing the different curriculum versions and developing additional approaches for students at various school levels. As a consequence, the project has undergone continual renewal by connecting the curriculum materials to the nature of the learner and to the significance of biology in society so as to meet the function of general education.

Need for Alternative Approaches and Formative Evaluation.   The label *new math* readily captured media attention in carrying a sense of revolution and mystique during the late 1950s and early 1960s. This was aided in no small measure by the sweeping promotional claims for the new projects. Among the several projects embracing the new wave claim, the School Mathematics Study Group (SMSG) led the way both in funding by the National Science Foundation and in the extent of adoption in the schools. When questions began to arise about the need for systematic experimental comparisons, the SMSG group announced that "[i]nformation gathering rather than hypothesis testing should be stressed" (Begle & Wilson, 1970, p. 388)—anathema to the principles of scientific inquiry. When an extensive study was undertaken by SMSG to assess the impact of the new mathematics on pupil achievement, with the findings reported over a decade after its implementation, it was concluded by the SMSG director that "there are not many clear generalizations that can be made" (p. 388). Unfortunately, no assessment was made of pupil attitudes toward mathematics and the practical uses of mathematics. The SMSG project was disbanded, subsequently, in the wake of rising criticisms that the new mathematics was abstract and devoid of life applications.

Curricular Interrelationships

The nuclear physicist Alvin M. Weinberg contends that a valid measure of the merit of a field is its relevance to neighboring fields and its relevance to human welfare and values (1967, pp. 74–76). Consequently, efforts to improve the curriculum of a given field or discipline can be enhanced immeasurably by involving those whose work is in neighboring fields or disciplines. Unfortunately, the disciplinary curriculum-reform projects deliberately avoided the vantage points of scholars outside the target discipline, with the result that the applications and interrelationships of knowledge were neglected.

The curriculum in general education is conceived and constructed on the premise of revealing the vital interdependence of knowledge. But even in the fields of specialized knowledge today, work at the leading edge has become increasingly interdisciplinary. In an editorial in *Science*, the chief officer of the American Association for the Advancement of Science wrote, "no field stands alone." However, he pointed out that in our academic institutions, faculty are organized and rewarded according to discrete fields of learning in disciplinary "silos," with the consequence that departmentalized structures breed separation and mitigate the advancement of knowledge (Leshner, 2004, p. 729). As secondary school teachers are prepared according to departmental majors in the universities, they carry this culture of knowledge isolation and specialism to their schools, with the failure to recognize and address the need for curriculum articulation and integration. Their orientation to the curriculum is segmental as they lack a conceptual awareness, commitment, and capability for building the macrocurriculum in general education.

The Outside Vantage Point.   When the Nobel laureate in theoretical physics Richard P. Feynman examined the textbooks representing the new mathematics for grades one through eight, he found that much of the material was "an abstraction from the real world" and was loaded with technical terms— "carefully and precisely defined special words that are used by pure mathematicians in their most subtle and difficult analyses, and are used by nobody else." Feynman then observed that many of the books representing the new mathematics curriculum are "full of such nonsense," and he stressed that such material was so concerned with precise, technical language that clarity of ideas was being sacrificed along with the relevance of the subject to the real world.

> It is really quite impossible to say anything with absolute precision, unless that thing is so abstracted from the real world as to not represent any real thing.
>
> Pure mathematics is just such an abstraction from the real world, and pure mathematics does have a special precise language for dealing with its own special and technical subjects. But this precise language is not precise in any sense if you deal with the real objects of the world, and it is overly pedantic and quite confusing to use. . . .
>
> I believe that every subject which is presented in the textbook should be presented in such a way that the purpose of the presentation is made evident. The reason why the subject is there should be made clear; the utility of the subject and its relevance to the world must be made clear to the pupil. (1965, pp. 13, 14–15)

Had the projects in the new mathematics sought the vantage points of applied mathematicians and of scholars from other fields, such as Feynman, for purposes of curriculum development and formative evaluation, many problems could have been avoided and a more unified curriculum would more likely have resulted.

For obvious reasons, it is necessary to have such vantage points be integral to the project rather than be an afterthought in summative evaluation. Otherwise, the project staff is impelled to assume a defensive posture of justifying its product rather than taking measures to develop the best possible materials. The vantage points of persons outside a particular curriculum field or discipline not only can serve as a constructive basis for summative and formative research and evaluation, but when made integral to the input of the curriculum project such vantage points also can prevent the project from becoming narrowly wedded to a single set of value premises.

Scientists, no less than other people, find it difficult to change value premises once they are formed and become a basis for commitment. Instead of positing the single set of value premises that guided the scientists in their earlier curriculum-reform efforts as tentative and as hypotheses to be tested, the premises were promoted as valid principles and conclusions. Thus, when subsequent evaluations gave cause for serious questioning of their curriculum products, these scientists assumed a defensive posture. Criticisms such as those raised by Weinberg and Feynman cannot be dismissed. Based on well-informed and well-grounded value premises that challenged the validity of those embraced by the major curriculum-reform projects, such criticisms deserved serious study. Had they been part of the formative input of these projects, the results most likely would have been far different, and a generation of children and youth would have been better served by the national curriculum-reform movement.

Toward Curriculum Renewal

The contemporary scene is marked by the rediscovery of the need to link mathematics with other subjects and to hands-on applications.

A continuing problem in teacher education resides in the puristic orientation of university mathematics departments. The work of the National Council of Teachers of Mathematics (NCTM) in developing curriculum and evaluation standards for school mathematics reveals some encouraging efforts toward making these linkages to enable students to see the applicability of mathematics to real problems. However, many of the implementation examples in the NCTM standards seem forced and artificial, and they appear to reflect the problem of mathematics specialists and teachers working on the school mathematics curriculum apart from professionals in other fields. In fact, the current thrust in formulating curriculum and evaluation standards has been undertaken by professional teacher organizations representing each of the separate academic fields. The opportunity, for example, of integrating mathematics with social studies, ecology, and health science through social statistics presents enormous possibilities. Rich sources of data are available from various international and federal agencies. Students could learn to create graphs from base data to reveal trends and needs on problems of health, poverty, population, global hunger, resource management, and so on. They could learn about the uses and misuses of statistics in conducting experiments, in opinion polling, and in evaluating the effects of advertising in American culture.

As impressive beginning has been made in Project 2061 by the American Association for the Advancement of Science (AAAS) to formulate benchmarks to guide teachers in developing a more unified curriculum in science, mathematics, and technology. The benchmarks are sets of generalizations to be developed from the core studies in science revealing connections with mathematics and technology, and extending into the arts, humanities, and vocational studies. The approach is intended to reduce the sheer amount of material to be covered for short-term recall and the knowledge isolation that derives from organizing the curriculum into separate disciplines. An example of a benchmark of understanding for an eighth-grader might be the following: "Engineers, architects, and others who engage in design and technology use scientific knowledge to solve practical problems. But they usually have to take human values and limitations into account" (AAAS, 1993, p. 46). Unfortunately, Project 2061 has characterized the entire program as designed to promote scientific literacy. The multitude of different literacies being promoted for the different subject matters has resulted in increased fragmentation of the curriculum. From the historic experience on the idea and practice of general education in the school and college, it appears that the prospects for interfacing and integrating the different literacies for the benefit of the learner would be enhanced considerably under the rubric of general education as opposed to literacies. Project 2061 would do well to connect science and society.

Without a concerted effort at actually building alternative models of a coherent curriculum, there is also the danger that the curriculum standards and benchmarks for literacy will deteriorate into segmental items for achievement testing within each of the standard academic subjects in the school curriculum.

Curriculum Controversy

It is widely believed that the collapse of the national discipline-centered curriculum reforms came about as a result of a storm of controversy arising from one of the projects, namely Man: A Course of Study (MACOS), developed as an anthropology course for 5th- and 6th-graders. From its study of the MACOS controversy, the National Institute of Education attributed the collapse of these projects largely to value conflicts and censorship influences (Schaffarzick & Sykes, 1979). However, the national discipline-centered projects were in a state of collapse before the controversy over MACOS erupted. Historically, the school curriculum has come under censorship pressure whenever controversies arise such as the teaching of evolution in the biology course or *Huckleberry Finn* in American literature. In the end, an enlightened profession and public seeking the best available evidence are the best antidotes to censorship.

Following the discipline-centered rationale that guided the national curriculum reform projects supported by the National Science Foundation, MACOS was designed not as an integrated program in the social studies but as anthropology. In effect, the fifth- and sixth-graders were to learn how the anthropologist studies social behavior and institutions. The population targeted for study in a portion of MACOS was a subculture of the small group of Netsilik Eskimos in a small region of Canada. Although the Netsiliks had long abandoned their primitive tribal practices, the MACOS course used the study of those practices as the vehicle for teaching the fifth-graders how the anthropologist thinks (objectively, presumably). The multimedia mix of ethnographic films, filmstrips, role-playing games, and reading materials was indeed impressive. Problems arose because the course included references to such practices as cannibalism, bestiality, female infanticide, incest, the sharing of the favors of one's wife, the disposal of the elderly, and other behaviors. MACOS was also attacked for inculcating in youngsters the relativism of anthropological inquiry through which the target population is not to be judged by the cultural orientations, preferences, and biases of the investigator.

To some critics, such an approach smacked of indoctrination. Unlike other censorship efforts, the attacks on MACOS reached broader implications, some of which were hardly touched in the study by the National Institute of Education. For example, had the MACOS project been designed as integrated social studies for general education, rather than the discipline of anthropology, any intercultural comparisons would require the study of problems in the treatment of the elderly in American society (e.g., the high proportion of elderly in nursing homes, which is considered inhumane and illegal in some other societies, such as Denmark). Such treatment might well raise the hackles of the censors, but the point is that the function of general education requires that the subject matter be so organized and treated as to have the fullest possible bearings on the life and nature of the learner in a free society. This is far different from treating the fifth- or sixth-grader as a budding anthropologist or scholar-specialist.

The Cliché of *Experiment*

Young children like to put things together or break them apart just to see what happens. All too often when educators try something out to see what happens it is called an *experiment*. Resistance against systematic formative and summative evaluation not only has been characteristic of national curriculum projects, but also permeates educational innovation generally. The term *experimental* has become a fashionable label for almost any innovation or marked deviation from existing practice.

Many of the alternative schools of the late 1960s and early 1970s grew out of protest and embraced deviation from conventional practice along with a romanticized child-centered pedagogy and a laissez-faire approach to curriculum. It was common for these short-lived schools to dub themselves experimental schools, despite the fact that they were never guided by anything remotely resembling a program of systematic evaluation. Perhaps these short-lived efforts can be forgiven considering the conditions of social protest and naive enthusiasm that marked that period. However, it is not uncommon for college and university faculties to initiate new curriculum patterns and programs that are called *experiment* without any conceptual research base. In some cases the efforts represent truly promising ventures through which systematic evaluation might produce a substantive contribution to curriculum knowledge and practice. In other cases the so-called experimental program might be something that had been done before, but the faculty responsible for the program fails to recognize this and misses the opportunity to build on the knowledge base of previous experience. Today, many colleges are rediscovering the idea and practice of general education and have engaged in efforts to develop a coherent core curriculum. In instances where they lay claim to instituting the label of experiment, they might do well to examine the case of the Experimental Program instituted at the University of California at Berkeley in 1965 as an alternative curriculum for lower-division students. Actually, a traditional curriculum modeled after the Experimental College founded by Meiklejohn at the University of Wisconsin in the 1920s, the curriculum of the Experimental Program at Berkeley was focused on selected Great Books of Western civilization beginning with ancient Greece and culminating with readings from Marx, Freud, and Malcolm X. A report on the program titled *Experiment at Berkeley* not only is devoid of any evaluation program but also actually dismisses any need for systematic evaluation.

> We are skeptical about evaluation procedures and reluctant to get heavily involved in them. . . . A case for the program will have to be made, but apart from giving its rationale and reporting the experience, we do not really know what to do or what will be required.
>
> Moreover, the problems of continuity or institutionalization are so complex that, unless we can see the way to their solution, there is not much point in worrying about evaluation. (Tussman, 1969, p. 121)

Thus, we have a leading seat of higher-learning and research embarking on a curriculum labeled Experimental Program, deliberately avoiding any responsibility for conceptual research in evaluating its curriculum, and asking the academic community to accept its claims as theological revelations. One of the great paradoxes in higher education is that these very institutions that profess commitment to research so often tend to avoid research in instituting new curriculums that are labeled experimental. "Is experimentation a process of trying anything at least once, of putting into immediate effect any 'happy thought' that comes to mind, or does it rest upon

principles which are adopted at least as a working hypothesis?" asked Dewey in 1928, as he warned that without principles to guide hypothetical testing, the schools will allow improvisation to dictate their course and no contributions will be made in advancing education intellectually (1928c, pp. 197, 201).

The Best Available Evidence as Guide to Practice

Best Practices

Professional groups concerned with the various areas of the curriculum have developed a body of recommended practices, from research and practical field operations, although these practices are rarely presented in any single source of professional literature. Of course, such approved practices must undergo continuous assessment and reformulation to keep them attuned to changing knowledge and conditions. A few brief examples will illustrate what is meant by approved practice.

Holistic Approaches. Effective teachers know that students are more likely to generate interest and engagement in productive learning when the teaching process and curricular materials are idea oriented rather than error oriented, and when students have a shared responsibility for the curriculum such as through planning and conducting projects, panel discussions, demonstrations, and community activities that draw from and feed back into the school curriculum. If teacher-made tests are focused on interpretation and application of knowledge, as opposed to rote, such tests will serve as useful instruments in helping the teacher evaluate his or her own work and will help stimulate students toward higher-level thinking. When student assignments in the school resource center or library allow for exploratory work and the pursuit of special interests and enrichment, students will be more likely to engage in self-impelled learning such as reading for enjoyment. When teachers have a shared commitment for curriculum improvement and when they are provided with the time, resources, and expertise for engaging in systematic efforts toward curriculum correlation and integration, they not only contribute to the improvement of student learning, but they also grow professionally.

Obviously, the faculty that insists on pilot-testing an innovation is well ahead professionally of a faculty that simply adopts the innovation based on testimonial promotion or trendiness. In the case of the new math, one must ask why the schools so readily moved toward the wholesale adoption of the curriculum packages rather than engaging in pilot studies. A faculty conducting pilot studies of new curriculum materials is indeed engaging in best practices. This does not mean that every newly proposed practice or curriculum innovation must be pilot-tested, but it is important for a faculty to ascertain whether there is a sound research base for the innovation and, as discussed later, to examine the innovation at least for face validity.

Turning to another example: Teachers and school administrators tend to regard discipline as an entirely negative and destructive element in the classroom and school. A bulletin issued by the National Association of Secondary School Principals bears the title *Preventive Discipline* in black letters on a red background that seems to warn the prospective reader that he or she is treading on dangerous territory (Grossnickle & Cesko, 1990). Discipline is also a powerfully constructive force for learning responsible self-direction in school and society. When the classroom and school environment is designed to evoke in students the power for self-impelled learning and collaboration, and when there is engagement in teacher-pupil planning, students are more likely to become self-disciplined and to develop a sense of mutual responsibility. Such learnings have powerful payoffs for life success as well as academic success.

Need for Sound Qualitative Ideas to Guide Research

Mention has been made of the need for teachers to ascertain whether a proposed curriculum innovation has a sound research base. Through advances in statistical treatments (meta-analysis), researchers in education have sought to amass a knowledge base for educational policy and practice by analyzing the directions of many smaller-scale studies taken together. However, in the absence of powerful qualitative ideas to connect the best available evidence with the most significant curriculum problems and to separate the good research from the bad, the meta-analysis generates a sea of quantified data without much fish in the sea.

Teachers need not be intimidated by elaborate statistical treatments if they base their professional work on powerful qualitative ideas and if they evaluate the conclusions of the researcher in the light of

their professional experience. For example, as cited earlier, sweeping allegations have been made by national panels on education reform, by research officials in the U.S. Department of Education, and in national best-sellers that students of today are not as well educated as earlier generations of students. However, when a researcher simply set out to test this allegation by using earlier large-scale examinations on U.S. history and comparing the results past and present, he was able to draw the following clear and succinct conclusion:

> Indeed, given the reduced dropout rate and less elitist composition of the 17-year-old student body today, one could argue that students today know more American history than did their age peers of the past.
>
> Advocates for reform of education and excellence in public schooling should refrain from harkening to a halcyon past (or allowing the perception of a halcyon past) to garner support for their views. Such action, or inaction, is dishonest and unnecessary. (Whittington, 1991, p. 778)

The findings and conclusions from this study are fully consistent with those of similar studies undertaken in the past when the schools were under the assault of school blamers.

Segmentation and Dualism. As intelligent consumers of research, teachers can use their knowledge base of practical experience in detecting research that defies common sense. For example, the lead article in an issue of the *American Educational Research Journal* addressed the problem of the imbalance in curriculum in which excessive emphasis is given to basic skills, but problem solving and higher-order thinking are neglected. Now, this is indeed one of the most significant and pervasive curriculum problems. However, the researcher, as a specialist in organizational behavior in education, attacked the problem from the literature on behavioral decision theory and economics of organization. The researcher proposed the solution of having two types of teachers in the school. One type would specialize in teaching the basic skills to ensure that students will at a minimum develop these lower-order skills, whereas the second type would specialize in higher-order thinking and problem solving. "We argue that such a division would result not only in higher quality education, but also in a more equitable delivery of services from classroom to classroom," concluded the researcher (Hannaway, 1992, p. 20).

This proposal in a leading education research journal is made without any review of the body of research and professional literature on the curriculum over many decades revealing that, aside from the deleterious effects of splitting the faculty, it is counterproductive to separate basic skills from the ideas that generate the intelligent uses of these skills. Skills are not separate entities, but working tools in the development of concepts, ideas, appreciations, and problem-solving processes. The program, for example, of writing across the curriculum cannot succeed under a segmental and dualistic treatment that separates skills from higher-order thinking.

The segmentation of the subject curriculum finds teachers of chemistry, physics, the industrial arts, the trades and industries, and other subjects having to teach algebra and other higher mathematics—not to mention basic mathematics—because the separate subject of mathematics is devoid of practical applications with the consequence that students are unable to carry their mathematics from the math class into other classes.

We might also ask whether youngsters are to separate their basic-skill studies from ideas that govern thinking, or whether they are to postpone any work involving higher-order thinking until they have mastered the basics. Such a dualism between basic skills and higher-order thinking not only is educationally unsound, but it also engenders a schism dividing the faculty between high and low thinkers.

Quantification as Distortion. As a professional practitioner, the teacher must be able to draw on the best available evidence as a guide to improved practice. As an intelligent consumer of research, the teacher will bring his or her experience to the research reports and evaluate the research in the light of the best available evidence. No amount of statistics can compensate for faculty research ideas. The knowledgeable professional practitioner is able to evaluate the efficacy of research as a guide toward the improvement of practice and is able to point the way toward avenues for needed investigation.

Earlier we discussed the common problem in social research, including education, of bias that is masked by mounds of statistical data to convey a sense of objectivity and scientific authority. In more recent times, it has become fashionable in some circles of the social sciences to embrace revisionism and to use elaborate mathematical and statistical techniques to overthrow the conventional wisdom. The revisionist applying such techniques to history has been able to garner quick recognition and repute when other colleagues allow themselves to be intimidated by such techniques and computer-generated models and analyses. Not uncommonly, this has been the case even when the thesis borders on the outrageous. For example, two noted economists, Robert Fogel and Stanley Engerman, set out to examine the economics of American slavery through advanced mathematical and statistical techniques being used by other scholars who call themselves the "new economic historians," "econometric historians," and "cliometricians." They pointed out that the findings and methods of the new economic history had gained a solid foothold at Harvard, Yale, University of Chicago, University of California at Berkeley, "and other leading universities which together produce most of the Ph.D.'s in the field" (1974, p. 7).

Through the application of these advanced quantitative techniques, Fogel and Engerman amassed data showing that "[t]he material conditions of the lives of slaves compared favorably with those of free industrial workers," and further, that "[o]ver the course of his lifetime, the typical slave field hand received about 90 percent of the income he produced." They presented data to support their finding that "the average daily diet of slaves was quite substantial. The energy value of their diet exceeded that of free men in 1879 by more than 10 percent." And they concluded, "[t]he slave diet was not only adequate, it actually exceeded modern recommended daily levels of the chief nutrients." Among their other findings was that "[t]he slave mortality rate in childbearing was not only low on an absolute scale, it was also lower than the maternal death rate experienced by southern white women" (pp. 5–6).

In employing such quantitative analytical techniques to support a set of theses that are faulty to begin with, one could easily prove that a herd of milk cows on modern farms enjoys a better level of care and nutrition and a lower mortality rate in calf bearing than the general human population in childbearing, and that the cows receive in the care given them the equivalent of 90 % of the income produced. (This allows the farmer a net profit of 10%.) Of course, this defies all sense and sensibility, but it illustrates how statistical data can be used to validate assumptions that are invalid to begin with. Further, such research serves no social purpose other than that of embellishing reputations in the citadels of academia.

Freedom to Learn

In addressing the need to draw from the best available evidence as a guide to practice, teachers must think not only of such evidence stemming from research, but also have the freedom to use the best available curriculum materials. Growth in critical thinking requires that students learn to investigate issues using all pertinent evidence, to suspend judgment until all of the pertinent evidence is brought to bear on the issues, to test hypotheses, to discriminate fact from opinion, and so on. A free society requires this.

Ordinarily, teachers tend to think of censorship as external imposition, whereas much of the problem stems from self-censorship. This needs to be understood and addressed by faculty individually and collectively. For example, a given school faculty might make an intensive study of the extent to which they are ignoring pupil reading preferences and avoiding important controversial works and thereby engaging in a kind of self-censorship. The faculty may then want to establish certain procedures for attacking the problem of self-censorship by organizing inservice workshops, by convincing administrators to establish a standing budget for supplementary reading materials (such as paperbacks) dealing with important controversial works of interest to the pupils, and so on.

In case there should be a real problem of administratively imposed censorship on the teachers, the faculty might take measures to convince the school administration to place such matters under the jurisdiction of a permanent faculty curriculum committee. This makes the selection of materials a professional responsibility and counters political influences at the school board and administrative levels. For example, when the selection of certain reading materials that had been approved by a faculty committee became a subject of controversy at a school board meeting, the school board decided that the decision is a professional one and that the board is "not qualified to pass judgment on English textbooks or literature any more than it is qualified to judge the shorthand text." It was pointed out that to expect the board to pass judgment on reading materials would require it to review 250 textbooks each year, not to mention supplementary reading sources. "No one intends that we read these books and put ourselves up against the professional opinion of our teachers," concluded the board (in Tanner & Tanner, 1973, p. 89). "Controversy is

education in itself," wrote George Bernard Shaw, as he pointed out that to avoid controversial studies is to promote popular ignorance over science and knowledge (1950, pp. 310, 314).

Similarly, the faculty may assess the extent to which the curriculum is focused on rote learning and the regurgitation of information to the neglect of reasoning and the study of issues. From the results of such developmental evaluation, the faculty may take steps to change existing practices where they are found to be deficient. The common practice has been to implement or even to impose curriculum change on an ad hoc and piecemeal basis instead of viewing curriculum development in its totality and as an all-faculty responsibility.

Segmental Versus Aggregate Approaches to Curriculum Renewal

At times of national sweeps for curriculum renewal or reform, the practice has been to favor one side of the curriculum at the expense of another. Not only does this result in curriculum imbalance and the neglect of studies that should be recognized as vitally significant, but the synergy of the school curriculum also is defeated. Realms of knowledge are interdependent if they are to have bearings on the real world. Under segmental approaches to curriculum renewal, the sum of the parts fail to add up to a coherent total school curriculum and the learning outcomes invariably fail to measure up to the promotional rhetoric that attaches to the innovation.

When following the segmental-specialization approach to curriculum renewal, we find that the macrocurricular function of general education is neglected along with the nature of the learner and the wider social implications of the subject matter. In turn, the schools adopt and discard the packaged innovation on an ad hoc basis. The sociologist Morris Janowitz described the segmental-specialization model as "an *ad hoc* adaptation by introducing, on a piecemeal basis, new techniques, new programs, new specialists, and even new specific administrative procedures." With this model, Janowitz continued, "[t]he increased level of substantive knowledge and the importance of specific teaching techniques are offered as the rationale for the teachers' subordination to curriculum specialists" (Janowitz, 1969, pp. 42–43). In contrast, Janowitz pointed to the aggregate model as focused on the totality of the educational function with all important curricular elements and goals being treated in their interdependence. (1969, pp. 42–43; 1991, p. 295).

With school and society opting for the segmental-specialized model over the aggregate model, the Law of the Minimum, as described later, has been allowed to take its toll particularly with regard to the disadvantaged. The school has not been endowed with the necessary means for assuming a holistic personal-social-growth function. At various times it has been impelled to subvert its socialization function to the narrow skill-drill function with a focus on low-level cognitive goals; at other times the school is expected to fulfill a total socialization function in the absence of concomitant commitment to this function on the part of society. Then the school is blamed for not single-handedly regenerating the lives of children and youth. Under the segmental-specialized model, the personal-social-growth function of school and society is subverted in favor of narrow interests.

Shifting Expectations and Demands and Priorities

Throughout this text it has been shown how the school has been pressed to shift its priorities in response to shifting sociopolitical demands. The consequence has been that the school has tended to assume a segmental approach to educational change. Shifting expectations and demands come not only from radical school critics but also from such sources as the U.S. presidency on down to university scholars, business groups, and various private interests.

Again, it should be noted that the buffeting of the curriculum by shifting sociopolitical tides invariably is accompanied by a ceremony of school blaming, and all too often university scholars become a part of the ceremony by shifting their own grounds so as to be in synchrony with the dominant tide of the times. Thus in 1950 the eminent historian Henry Steele Commager wrote, "No other people ever demanded so much of education as have the Americans. None other was ever served so well by its schools and educators" (p. 46). Commager described how the American faith in education has imposed great tasks on the schools, tasks the schools have met. He identified these tasks as (1) providing for an enlightened citizenry, (2) creating a national unity out of diversity, (3) Americanizing the vast populations of immigrants, and (4) rendering the cause of American democracy.

Within a year following Sputnik I, Commager declared that we were entering a new era, that the Americanization function of the schools had been virtually accomplished, and the schools must no longer bear responsibilities in the nonacademic realm but should focus their efforts on traditional academic functions. Nonacademic functions should be left to the home and other agencies of society, contended Commager. In concentrating on its academic functions, the high school may be expected to speed up its work and accomplish in three years what it was taking four years to accomplish (1958, pp. 1–18). (In a telephone interview with one of the authors of this text a few years later, Commager admitted he had been taken away by the sweep of events of the Cold War.)

In 1968, amidst a rising national concern for the disadvantaged, Commager declared that "education is the beginning of social reform and regeneration." He admonished educators to "start by abandoning many of our preconceptions about the relation of the home and education" and advocated that we face up to "the sharing of responsibility between the two, and recognize that for many children in our society there are no homes, and no sharing of responsibilities" (1968b, p. 107).

In each instance of shifting demands and expectations, the schools have been impelled to respond in a segmental way, whether in embarking on a return to the fundamentals, adopting disciplinary curriculum packages, employing specialized educational innovations, instituting ad hoc compensatory programs for the disadvantaged, or implementing accountability machinery through the use of narrow testing measures. When these piecemeal efforts are shown to be inadequate to the task, instead of developing an aggregate model for curriculum improvement, the schools are criticized for making no difference, and they are pressed into adopting new piecemeal measures in search of miracle cures.

The Law of the Minimum

Earlier in this chapter certain methodological limitations were identified in connection with various studies that failed to identify specific school factors showing a powerful relationship to achievement. It was also noted that this failure led some researchers and educational policy makers to the conclusion that any further investment in schooling or implementation of curriculum improvements would make no difference. Aside from the methodological limitations of such research is the failure to take into account the vital interactive and cumulative elements between the school and the wider social environment of the learner.

A nineteenth-century agricultural chemist, Justus von Liebig, developed from his research the Law of the Minimum, a principle that holds valid to this day. According to the Law of the Minimum, "The amount of plant growth is regulated by the factor present in minimum amount" (in Russell, 1973, pp. 49–50). Thus, if an essential constituent is lacking or is insufficiently available, the full potential of a living organism cannot be realized by compensating for the deficient element by providing the organism with an extra abundance of other constituents. Extra water cannot make up for insufficient sunlight, nor can extra nitrogen compensate for insufficient potassium.

The full potential of the child as a growing organism requires the advantages of a rich and powerful learning environment provided by the school and by the larger society. Taken together in concert, the potential of the learner will be more fully realized. Until this is accomplished, it is totally unproductive to seek genetic explanations for educational failure and cognitive deficiencies, as some educators attempted to do (Jensen, 1973). Until the necessary educational and social conditions are optimized, the social ideal of human equality and human capacity to shape its fate will be an empty one.

In the same vein, educators and policy makers cannot assume that by addressing the problem of cognitive and social deficits of disadvantaged or at-risk children at the preschool and primary levels the need for attending to the adolescent is considerably reduced. Unfortunately, this policy can be traced back to the early years of the War on Poverty of the Johnson administration when data on human development were twisted to support a short-cut strategy (Bloom, B., 1964, pp. 88–89, 128–129). Schools of education formed new departments of early childhood education in response to infusions of federal funds for that target population, and the focus on adolescence was severely diminished. No less an authority than Bruno Bettelheim asked whether we will "continue to fool ourselves by thinking that we can change the lives of underprivileged children in school, when it is much too late for everything that really counts," and popular magazines were featuring cover articles under such titles as "Kindergarten Is Too Late" (Bettelheim, 1964, p. 4; Edwards, 1968, p. 69).

Middle and late childhood and adolescence are recognized periods of qualitative changes in cognitive, social, and physical development. Seeking to minimize the educational and social deficits during infancy and early childhood cannot serve as immunization against the deleterious effects of deficits that occur during later childhood and adolescence. Nor is there any scientific basis for assuming that older populations, including adults, can be written off because it is too late.

The Law of the Minimum has profound implications for the curriculum and the school as a living learning environment. It is easy to contend that the school curriculum be limited to the academic basics or to development of the intellect, but the development of intelligence is dependent on interests, attitudes, and emotions as well as good nutrition and health. Essentialist-perennialists such as Theodore Sizer may see the mission of the school as appropriately and exclusively focused on mastery of the minima—with most youngsters accomplishing this before high school, when compulsory school attendance would end. The high school then would be able to devote its work to the academically oriented students (1984, pp. 87–88). However, mastery of the minima fails to take account of all the essential nutrients in the Law of the Minimum. The power of socialization and maturation in the development of intelligence during the high school years cannot be overlooked without great cost to the individual and society. Sizer and others may choose to see education into the high school as an opportunity and privilege, rather than a right. In its wisdom, the U.S. Supreme Court ruled unanimously with reference to both elementary and high schools that education is "a right which must be made available to all on equal terms" (*Brown v. Board of Education*, 1954).

Knowledge/Ability Level

A fallacious assumption in educational policy, research, and practice is that given inputs will yield equivalent effects in all school systems. However, different school systems are characterized by vastly different knowledge/ability levels. When many of the most capable teachers and administrators leave inner-city schools for the suburbs, the result is that the knowledge/ability level of inner-city schools is diminished. Thus, these schools become less capable of maximizing or optimizing the resources that are made available in comparison to those schools that have a higher knowledge/ability level.

In terms of the Law of the Minimum, the amount of (educational) growth is regulated by the (knowledge/ability) factor present in minimum amount. Consequently, compensatory programs and efforts to improve the curriculum in inner-city schools are limited by the level of the knowledge/ability factor. Unfortunately, the Coleman research and Jencks's studies failed to take into account this vital factor. Limitations in the knowledge/ability factor of schools serving a high proportion of at-risk children and youth have concealed the potential benefits derived from curriculum improvement and other investments to improve the educational program. This does not mean, contrary to Jencks's contentions, that it is fruitless to increase investments in education because increases in input are not followed automatically by corresponding increases in output. Rather, it means that greater efforts must be made in improving the knowledge/ability level of such schools if they are to capitalize on such investments.

In a study designed to identify the knowledge/ability factor as developed by the authors in the first edition of this text, Celso found that elementary teachers in the same school vary greatly in their use of curricular resources and, in effect, provide vastly different learning environments for their pupils. For example, some teachers were observed to have drawn from their personal resources, along with whatever school resources were available, to develop an extensive classroom library, with pupils using the collection in their daily work; however, many of their fellow teachers' classrooms were devoid of such resources and activities (1978, pp. 189–193). Much of the research on the effects of schooling has suffered from the failure to account for qualitative variables and the tendency to deal with only those variables that are most amenable to quantitative treatment. Celso hypothesizes that the knowledge/ability factor can be demonstrated by categorizing teachers according to high and low knowledge/ability levels, based on a number of qualitative differences in their use of curricular resources, and then assessing a wide range of possible learning outcomes in their pupils.

In more recent years, the power of the school—more specifically, the curriculum—in influencing cognitive-affective development is receiving increasing recognition. Contrary to the distorted interpretation of Bloom's research, Bloom's findings and proposals for curriculum improvement are based on the alterability of human characteristics, as Bloom expressed belief that

> changes in the school environment can relatively quickly (in a single decade) make great changes in the learning of students. In contrast, attempts to makes changes in the home and the larger social environment, which are believed to be related to education and learning, are likely to take many decades before major effects would be felt in the schools. (1976, p. 17)

The significance of a powerful and continuous program of inservice teacher education and teacher support by providing the needed expertise, time, and resources is clearly indicated by the knowledge/ability factor.

The Deficiency of Efficiency

In his study of the historical influences of business values and practices on education, Raymond Callahan reported that although he had expected to find evidence of such influences,

> What was unexpected was the extent, not only of the power of the business-industrial groups, but of the strength of the business ideology in the American culture on the one hand and the extreme weakness and vulnerability of schoolmen, especially school administrators, on the other. (1962 Preface)

Callahan went on to state that he had expected more professional autonomy on the part of educators, but found instead that many education decisions are made not on educational grounds but in capitulation to whatever demands are placed on the schools (n.p.).

The influences examined historically by Callahan have not waned. Despite the considerable rhetoric calling for humanizing the schools, efforts to make the schools more efficient managerially and more accountable, as assessed by the quantifiable input-output measures, seem more powerful today than ever before (Weiss, 1989).

Pressures to improve educational efficiency through technological and managerial innovations, along with assessment and accountability measures, appear to augur a mechanical-segmental-skills model of the learner as opposed to a personal-social-growth model. As emphasized in earlier chapters, this opposition has profound implications for the curriculum, the learner, and society.

This has been manifested in the enormous growth of the testing industry and the support of testing by the states and federal government as measures of production efficiency and accountability. The business-industrial model is seen in *America 2000* leading the way to school restructuring and reform for excellence (1991, pp. 19–20, 27). The education research literature has come to use the term *process-product research* to denote the outcomes of classroom variables in quantitative measures—as though the ends of education are end products (Darling-Hammond & Snyder, 1992, pp. 63, 64–67). As emphasized throughout this text, education must be treated as an emergent or growth process rather than a production process.

Education as an Emergent Process

Robert Boguslaw, a systems design engineer, pointed to the need to differentiate between established and emergent situations. In the established situation, all action-relevant environmental variables are specifiable and predictable, whereas the emergent situation involves problems for which the conditions and solutions are not perfectly specifiable and predictable (1965, pp 7–9).

The established situation or established-convergent situation can be easily understood when we are dealing with products and services under the most uniformly reliable and routine conditions. The plant manager of a factory producing Wonder Bread must see to it that the product is as uniform as possible. Indeed, the machinery and mechanisms for quality control are designed to ensure uniformity of product. It is only when something goes wrong that the situation becomes an emergent one.

In education, even the most routine situations have a way of becoming emergent because we are always dealing with people problems and not products. The term *recipe* is often used to denote a direct and simple process. Follow the directions and the results will be predictable—so it is thought. In cooking as well as in other human enterprises, the results may be surprising. A recipe for coq au vin or French pastry, whether given to novices or master chefs, will likely produce surprises. The results will reflect differences in experience, taste preferences, and creativity, for even a recipe is often regarded as an opportunity for the expression of the individual's creative talents. Indeed, differences make improvement possible.

It might be contended that in following a blueprint in the industrial-arts class, or in conducting an experiment in the chemistry laboratory, the student is engaged in an established-convergent situation. This may indeed be the case, but it should be noted that the situation itself typically involves collaboration and even error through which the situation becomes emergent. Successful teachers know full well how student mistakes can provide opportunities for fruitful learning.

Even at the highest levels of technical professionalism, such as musicianship, no two symphony orchestras will perform a composer's work identically, for the art of music, like the art of teaching, resides not in technical skills alone, but in the art of interpretation.

Assessment and Accountability

"If we can construct a kind of Gross *Educational* Product, we will know a lot more than we do now about how we are conducting the nation's most important business," stated a 1966 report in *Carnegie Quarterly* in announcing that the foundation had initiated steps two years earlier for the national assessment of education. The Carnegie report noted that the construction of the national economic index, the gross national product (GNP), had made possible great refinements in the analysis and understanding of the economy. Drawing an analogy of questionable validity, the report contended that the construction of a gross educational product through a national assessment of education should enable us to determine "with greater certainty that investing so much—in terms of money or materials or teachers or time—to attack a particular problem will produce a given result" (pp. 2, 4). The report gave assurance that the assessment program would not influence the curriculum because the sampling methods in the testing program would make it impossible for teachers to teach to the test.

Influence on the Curriculum. In a publication for the American Association of School Administrators, Harold Hand warned that "the parties who determine what goes into the tests would control the public school curriculum (1966, pp. 5, 25). In 1973 the report of the National Commission on the Reform of Secondary Education made the following recommendation regarding national assessment:

The National Assessment of Educational Progress should become the bulwark of educational accountability. Local educators should be equipped to compare realistically the achievement of their students with regional and national results. The findings of National Assessment should lead to various [curriculum] content revisions, curriculum reform, in-service efforts, and improved competency-based instruction. (p. 44)

As the first results of the National Assessment of Educational Progress (NAEP) were being reported, the individual states were rapidly instituting their own statewide assessment programs through massive testing. By 1980, assessment programs were in operation or on the drawing boards in almost every state. At the same time the schools were gearing their curricula to specific performance objectives. Curriculum development appeared to be on its way toward becoming a matter of managerial and engineering technique designed to maximize the ratio of quantifiable outputs to inputs. Administrators of the project continued to draw parallels between efficiency in business and efficiency in education, as illustrated by the following statement, which appeared in a publication of the project:

> Possibly for the first time the public, the legislators, the educators and other interest groups are asking what business schools are in?. . . If education is in the business of helping children achieve, and of determining and teaching what's worth knowing, then assessment is a way of measuring that objective. It is no different than in business, where a successful corporation must achieve its goals on schedule. If not, they run the risk of cash flow problems which could lead to bankruptcy.
>
> As farsighted educational managers, we must provide ourselves with the needed measures for knowing when and to what extent we have achieved our objectives. Large-scale assessment is such a way. (*NAEP Newsletter*, July–August 1973, p. 3)

The history of NAEP and its influence on educational policy and the curriculum is well documented (Epstein, 1996). From the beginning, assurance was given to educators that NAEP would not come under federal auspices. Before long, however, it became a fully federally financed project. Since 1983 NAEP has been administered by Educational Testing Service under contract with the U.S. Department of Education. The influence of NAEP on the school curriculum has been pervasive and perverse. Although the national assessment had been likened to census data collecting, a census is directed at the gathering of descriptive-quantitative data, whereas the very testing instruments and data in NAEP are loaded with both explicit and hidden value premises. Indeed, the word *assessment* means to set a value on something. This has been borne out by the periodic issuance of the NAEP test results by ETS in publications under the series title, *The Nation's Report Card*, with each publication bearing a title appropriate for the specific subject field, such as *The U.S. History Report Card*, *The Mathematics Report Card*, *The Science Report Card*, and so on. These report cards have been used opportunistically by federal officials and the media in attacking the public schools for alleged deficiencies, but studies questioning the validity of the data have been virtually ignored (Carson, Huelskamp, & Woodall, 1993). The NAEP report card collection not only received the strongest endorsement in *America 2000*, but it was also recommended that the NAEP data be used for comparisons at district and school levels. Ironically, the originators of NAEP had recognized such comparisons as a misuse of the NAEP tests and had assured the education community that this would never happen. With regard to the uses and misuses of a national testing program, the issue was put bluntly by George Madaus in these words:

> The idea that any testing technique, be it a new test design or a national test system, can reform schools and restore America's competitiveness is the height of technological arrogance and conceals many of the negative possibilities of such a move under the guise of a seemingly neat technological fix. . . . [I]t is the teachers, not tests or assessments, that must be the cornerstones of reform efforts. (1993, p. 23)

Myrdal could well have been describing the NAEP and state assessment programs when he offered this observation:

> The chaos of possible data for research does not organize itself into systematic knowledge by mere observation. Hypotheses are necessary. We must raise questions before we can expect answers from the facts, and the questions must be significant. . . . Even apparently simple concepts presume elaborate theories. These theories—or systems of hypotheses—contain, of necessity, no matter how scrupulously the statements of them are presented, elements of *a priori* speculation. When, in an attempt to be factual, the statements of theory are reduced to a minimum, biases are left a freer leeway. . . . (1962, p. 1041)

Myrdal emphasized that social science becomes no better protected against bias when it assumes the entirely negative stance, under the guise of objectivity, of avoiding any responsibility for arranging its findings for practical use. Such a negative posture actually opens the way to further bias because the value premises are kept hidden in the data, rather than being explicitly treated in terms of practical implications and practical problem solving. The myriad specializations in social science also distance social scientists from the tests of practicality. Unfortunately, the National Assessment of Educational Progress had avoided questions and hypotheses, and therefore the facts contained no answers to educational problems. In avoiding significant questions and hypotheses, the data were left open to bias, speculation, and opportunistic exploitation.

Assessment of Charter Schools. The underlying assumption of the No Child Left Behind Act of 2002 is that public charter schools would serve as an appropriate alternative to public schools that fail to meet the testing standards as measured by the National Assessment of Educational Progress (NAEP). In this connection the NAEP governing board authorized the testing of a national representative sampling of test performance in reading and mathematics of fourth- and eighth-graders in charter schools. However, the report of the results were never issued as scheduled by the NAEP governing board. Instead the findings were buried in mountains of data without announcement, as compiled by the National Center of Educational Statistics of the U.S. Department of Education.

Researchers at the American Federation of Teachers (AFT) combed through the mountains of data and uncovered the results, which revealed that charter school students produced lower scores in both grades four and eight, statistically significant except for the grade eight reading. This translated to a half-year of schooling (Nelson, Rosenberg, & Van Meter, 2004, p. iii).

As a commonly used proxy for economic background in order to make a fair comparison between the charter school and regular school populations, the AFT researchers analyzed the test scores of students eligible for free or reduced-price lunch. Again, the scores were higher for the students in regular schools. With regard to central-city schools, the researchers found, "Both in terms of average scores and achievement levels for math and reading alike, regular public schools in central cities outperformed charter schools (p. iii). The findings of the AFT study, which had been unearthed from massive unrelated data in reports by the U.S. Department of Education, were of sufficient public interest to warrant extensive front-page coverage in the *New York Times* (August 17, 2004, pp. A1, 19), which viewed the findings as a blow to the federal administration, which supported charter schools. Once again, it seemed that, eventually, "the facts will kick."

But the most significant danger to democracy posed by the charter school movement was that of splitting up the school system. The battle for a unitary school system seemed to have been waged and won in the twentieth century, yet it has continued erupting to this day.

Authentic Assessment

The concept of authentic assessment has appeared in the education literature in connection with efforts to evaluate achievement through tasks in which students are actually engaged. The performance tasks are presumably set in contextualized situations (Wiggins, 1993). Although this promising movement has been heralded as new, it can be traced back to the comprehensive evaluation techniques and instruments developed for the Eight-Year Study and in the studies on the goals of general education (Smith & Tyler, 1942; French, 1957). For example, given a problem situation, is the student able to map out a procedural plan for solving the problem, starting with the formulation of the problem and hypotheses, along with the identification of information, data, and resources needed for solving the problem? Is the student able to test the hypotheses and formulate valid conclusions? Other forms of authentic assessment might be in student-initiated projects requiring systematic investigation, or through student portfolios, simulations, and various kinds of context-situated projects. Paper-and-pencil tests can indeed be related to authentic situational contexts, such as in demonstrating the ability to interpret social statistics by identifying trends, formulating hypotheses, and drawing inferences, implications, and conclusions. Given a problem or issue, is the student able to identify the sources that would be useful in gaining the fullest possible picture of the problem or issue? Such approaches contrast vividly against conventional tests with prefabricated answers, and they provide a more comprehensive and powerful connection between the curriculum and reality. In the real world, accomplishment is not so much a measure of speed but of motivation, application, or working power in the use of intelligence.

The irony of the term *authentic* assessment resides in the implication that the standard means of assessment are inauthentic. This may well be the case, for much can be done to improve the assessment process through the use of multiple criteria and means that are more relevant to the life and growth of the learner (Herman & Haertel, 2005).

The New Technology

The 1960s and the early years of the 1970s were called an era of innovation in education (Ford Foundation, 1961, Preface). Successful efforts were made with team teaching at various grade levels and, in the high school, modular-flexible scheduling (variable time allocations for courses and learning activities as opposed to the traditional lock-step schedule) (Bush & Allen, 1964). The new electronic technology was expected to usher in a veritable revolutionary transformation of education. Through televised instruction, programmed instruction, computer-assisted instruction, and language laboratories, the teaching-learning process was to extend to new dimensions. Initial financial support in promoting the adoption of the new technology was provided by the Ford Foundation, the Carnegie Corporation, and the Kettering Foundation until federal funding was made available through the National Defense Education Act of 1958 and the Elementary and Secondary Education Act of 1965. Through electronic language laboratories, it was held that almost everyone would have fluency in at least two languages in addition to English (Report of the Disciplines Seminar, 1962, p. 15). The installation of electronic language laboratories became commonplace in the schools, accompanied by overblown commercial exploitation. The entire effort was a dismal failure as educators had overlooked language learning as a social process.

Utopian Visions.   Visions of the wonders to come from the new electronic technology were exemplified in an official publication commemorating the centennial of the U.S. Office of Education in 1966. Acknowledging that "few schools and colleges have begun to utilize the technological concepts and products whose value has been demonstrated in industry, space exploration, and national defense," the report predicted that "computer-assisted instruction, teaching machines of various sorts, increasingly sophisticated communications systems, and other forms of

technology will alter the school more in the next century than it has changed in the last 2,000 years" (U.S. Office of Education, 1967). The report then presented a Utopian vision of education in the year 1997 in which Johnny does not go to school. Instead, in this deschooled society, Johnny receives his formal instruction from a computer console in his home, with the computerized instructional program being controlled from a concenter or central station. No mention was made of the place of the book in this vision of the future, as the book is obviously replaced by the computer. In a similar vein, Postman and Weingartner contended that, in the future, print will play only a secondary role in the classroom as the electronic media will take on the major role of educating the young (1973, pp. 88–89). (Those who make this case invariably resort to the medium of print to get their message across.)

In a feature article in *Fortune* magazine, Charles E. Silberman wrote in 1966 that in harnessing the new technology, "the new business-government thrust is likely to transform both the organization and the content of education, and through it, the character and shape of American society itself." He continued, "we may be on the verge of a quantum jump in learning and in man's creative use of intellect" (p. 122). In anticipation of the new business-government thrust, Francis Keppel left his post as U.S. commissioner of Education to become head of General Learning Corporation—a joint venture of Time, Inc., and General Electric—to develop and market materials for the technological revolution in education. Within a few years, the corporation was dissolved. In his 1970 report for the Carnegie Corporation, Silberman did an about-face and criticized the "advocates and prophets" of computer-assisted instruction for having made "extravagant predictions of wonders to come" (p. 186).

In 1966, Patrick Suppes of Stanford University stated, "One can predict that in a few more years millions of school children will have access to what Philip of Macedon's son Alexander enjoyed as a royal prerogative: the personal services of a tutor as well-informed and responsive as Aristotle" (p. 207). Eight years later, in reviewing the research on the effectiveness of learning via computer, Suppes and his associates acknowledged that "findings of no significant difference dominate the research literature in this area," but that it may be useful in small doses as a supplement to regular instruction with regard to elementary skill-drill practices (Jamison, Suppes,

& Wells, 1974, p. 56). Similarly, the great promise that television and programmed instruction would usher in a new educational age failed to materialize, as the research results failed to show that such media produce an improvement in learning.

Unrealized Potentials. The contemporary education literature is directed at computer literacy, information networks, and hypertext (a system that allows the user to jump from the primary text to related multiple sources and commentary with a keystroke). Despite the impressive technological advances, the changes in the school and college classroom have been that of accommodation, not revolution. The failure of computer-assisted instruction, television, and other technological media in effecting the promised revolution can be traced to several factors. The new technology was initially supported and promoted on the premise that it would effect a dramatic improvement in the quality of education. However, in reality the hidden agenda was the improvement of managerial efficiency in the educational enterprise: to educate more students in less time, with fewer teachers, with greater efficiency of space utilization, and at lower cost. In efforts to make television more economically feasible, the medium was used largely to convey to learners the messages of conventional instruction with the result that, instead of being used as a classroom window to the world, television was used to convey the talking face. Eventually, students at the school and college levels rebelled against the uses of television as an automation device for large-group instruction (Murphy & Gross, 1966, pp. 44–46).

Proponents of change contended that by opening the schools to innovation, the prospects for improvement are enhanced, and that the evaluation of results or consequences can come later. Indeed, the entire national Comprehensive School Improvement Program of the Ford Foundation, promoting the uses of the new technology, followed this premise only to admit belatedly in failure that "the projects were designed to demonstrate actual changes in school systems [and] on the assumption that changes, per se, would produce better education." Looking back, it was conceded that evaluation was needed if problems were to be solved (Ford Foundation, 1972, pp. 11–12).

Although the great technological-media advances of the twentieth century—from the motion picture and radio, to television and the computer—were heralded as ushering in a revolution in the conduct of schooling, the promised revolution has failed to materialize. There is no question that we have failed to capitalize on the educative potentials of television in the school and home. Instead of using school television to do what the teacher is unable to do, it has been used for extending conventional forms of teaching to larger groups of students. Although the computer has attained a presence in the schools, the software used for instruction remains geared largely to established-convergent repertoires, word processing, and information retrieval. To a considerable extent, the computer is used narrow mindedly as an electronic workbook. Over the years, computer laboratories have been installed in space previously allocated for the school library collection, to the detriment of student learning. Books, including textbooks but not workbooks, have been favorite targets for censorship, whereas computer programs have not, apparently because the computer programming has been geared mainly to established-convergent information (Tanner, D., 1999, pp. 133, 144).

The use of the Internet has served as an open source of information for students, although it also is a source of gross misinformation. Learning to discriminate reliable and valid sources of data is vital to the process of critical thinking. Here the Internet can serve as a significant medium for emergent learning, but it cannot replace the educational powers of print and socialization. Fabos and Young point out that overly optimistic claims have been made about technology-based projects and caution that the Internet "operates with private interests, not specific educational skills or pedagogical democracy in mind (1999, pp. 217, 249).

Over the years, computer advocates have concentrated their efforts at integrating computers into the curriculum, instead of using the computer to help integrate the curriculum. Computer advocates are still puzzling over and debating why the new technology is not more widely and intensively used in the schools (Zhao & Frank, 2003, pp. 807–840). They do not seem to recognize that education is predominantly a social process.

The high-tech prospects for virtual reality and the great information highway have been widely heralded. Experience has shown that the new technology cannot substitute for the social process in education. Like the great advances in knowledge during the twentieth century, the technological advances must be used to extend humanity, not to replace it. The technologists would do well to heed the words of Norbert Wiener (1964, p. 73), one of the pioneers in the field of technological control and communication (cybernetics): "Render unto men the things which are man's and unto the computer the things which are the computer's."

Perspective

Much research in education, as in social science, is cloaked in a methodological empiricism as though to convey an image of scientific neutrality through hard data, thereby masking the valuations underlying the research, or concealing the conceptual emptiness of the research. In seeking to establish the facts and ignoring valuation, investigators have opened the door to considerable bias, for the data to be derived from research is determined by the value premises underlying the research. Thus, it is necessary to have research guided by alternative value premises and hypotheses, rather than by a single set of value premises. By bringing valuations out in the open, and by seeking to ascertain how they influence the research data, the sources of bias can be minimized and research can be more effectively related to the solving of practical problems in accord with educational ideals.

In much of the large-scale education research, the influences of variations in the curriculum and of other school characteristics have been concealed by variations in the pupil populations and a host of qualitative variables. Because many qualitative factors in education cannot be readily quantified, researchers have tended to focus on those factors that lend themselves most easily to quantification. Important qualitative factors have been submerged by relatively unimportant quantitative by-products, with the result that misleading and biased conclusions regarding educational policy and practice have been drawn from the so-called objective data. More intensive and longitudinal studies are needed to shed light on the influences of qualitative factors in the complex process of education.

Most of the efforts to improve education have been based on a segmental curriculum model, with innovations being adopted ad hoc. If the schools are to fulfill a personal-social-growth function, an aggregate model of curriculum must be assumed. Through an aggregate model, the necessary interrelationships and cumulative interactions of the various elements can be taken into account. Segmental, short-term, and unarticulated innovations and compensatory programs in education have failed to fulfill the promises made for them because vital cumulative interactions

within the school, and between the school and society, have been overlooked or ignored.

A fallacious assumption in educational research, policy, and practice is that given inputs should yield equivalent effects in all school systems. Because different school systems are characterized by vastly different knowledge/ability levels, the relationship between investments in education and the outcomes of such investments has been concealed. Thus, the fallacious assumption has led to fallacious conclusions on the part of education researchers and policymakers who hold that it is fruitless to increase the investments in education. Efforts to improve the curriculum and educational conditions must be matched by corresponding efforts to improve the knowledge/ability levels of administrators, teachers, and parents, particularly in disadvantaged schools. Otherwise, such schools will be unable to capitalize on such investments.

The move for educational accountability has been marked by national and statewide testing programs and narrow performance objectives. These accountability and assessment programs have been premised on the notion that the amassing of data will provide answers to vital educational problems. Intelligent questions must be asked before intelligent answers can be obtained. Without such questions and hypotheses, the data derived from these massive assessment programs defy intelligent interpretation and intelligent application in solving problems in educational practice. As a consequence, the negative device, on the part of the assessors, of avoiding responsibility for arranging the findings for intelligent practical use has opened the way for every conceivable bias on the part of special-interest groups.

Many educational innovations have been promoted and adopted as though these innovations per se will automatically result in educational improvement. The evaluation of these innovations has been designed largely to prove their success rather than to find solutions to educational problems. In the absence of practices founded on theory to be tested through working hypotheses, these programs are energized by a spirit of improvisation and deviation. However energetic this spirit may be, improvisation and deviation are not substitutes for theory and experimentation. The result is that innovations and reforms are short lived, as each era of societal crisis calls for either a return to traditional practice (e.g., back to basics) or yet another reform in a direction counter to the preceding reform. Movement is then mistaken for progress. In neglecting to apply innovations to educational problem solving, many innovations have been turned to the narrow purpose of managerial efficiency. As a result, the premises and promises that the adoption of innovations will result in improving the quality of education have not been realized. Educators have been urged to adopt innovations and later to evaluate their effects. Intelligent evaluation requires intelligent questions and hypotheses to be formulated before a new practice is allowed to become operational, and, at the same time, evaluation must be continuous. Otherwise, there can be no intelligent problem solving in education.

The demand to humanize the schools is a healthy reaction to the drive for managerial efficiency in education through mechanical assessment and quantifiable accountability. In seeking to impose only quantifiable objectives on the educative process, the efficiency experts overlook not only the qualitative aspects of education but also the most important source of educational objectives, namely the democratic ideals that empower individuals to continue their education and find for themselves the values that need to be pursued as objectives. (Refer to the Best Practices Checklist on pages 481–499.)

PROBLEMS FOR STUDY AND DISCUSSION

1. Why is it so important for teachers, supervisors, curriculum coordinators, and school administrators to be intelligent consumers of research?

2. In this chapter, Gunnar Myrdal was cited for his observation that social scientists tend to "move as a flock" in their valuations and research pursuits. Would you say that school administrators tend to move as a flock in adopting and discarding policies, practices, and innovations? Explain.

3. Examine any of the highly influential national reports on education reform (e.g., *A Nation at Risk, America 2000*). Can you identify any unsubstantiated valuations? Do you take issue with any of these valuations? Explain.

4. Richard Feynman, Nobel laureate in physics, was cited in this chapter as contending that the value of any subject matter should be determined by what it contributes to other subjects in the curriculum, and that it must be developed so as to reveal to the learner the utility of the material and its relevance to the real world. What prompted Feynman to offer these criteria? Would you say that the curriculum today generally meets Feynman's criteria? Why or why not? Are these criteria relevant to the curriculum paradigm? Explain. (See chapter 6.)

5. Quoted in this chapter was Myrdal's contention that "biases in social science cannot be erased by keeping to the facts and by refined methods of statistical treatment of data." What examples can you give of the biases uses (or misuses) of

data taken from the National Assessment of Educational Progress (NAEP) or the International Study of Educational Achievement? How have these uses of data affected the school curriculum? Myrdal was also cited for contending that "[t]he chaos of possible data for research does not organize itself into systematic knowledge by mere observation. Hypotheses are necessary. We must raise questions before we can expect answers from the facts, and the questions must be 'significant.'" [Gunnar Myrdal, *An American Dilemma* (New York: Harper & Row, 1962), p. 1041.]

How do you account for the failure of national assessment and statewide assessment programs to be guided by hypotheses for investigation? What are the implications of such a failure insofar as educational policy and practice are concerned?

6. In discussing the limitations of quantitative data for educational practice, Dewey maintained that "[t]he intelligence of the teacher is dependent upon the extent in which he takes into account the variables that are not obviously involved in his immediate special task. Judgment in such matter is of qualitative situations and must itself be qualitative." [John Dewey, *The Sources of a Science of Education* (New York: Liveright, 1929a), pp. 64–65].

What are the implications of this statement with regard to the determination of educational accountability through the gathering of quantitative data, such as in the national assessment and statewide assessment programs?

7. The periodic clamor of back to basics invariably is accompanied by a corresponding emphasis on standardized testing as the key to raising standards. Why did educators fail to foresee the neglect of writing (one of the three Rs) as an inevitable outcome of standardized testing during the extended period of curriculum retrenchment (back to basics) from the latter 1970s through the 1980s? From the experiences in your own school, would you say that the recent rediscovery of the value of writing across the curriculum has been accompanied by adequate attention to the expression of ideas as well as to mechanics? Explain.

8. In *America 2000* the public schools were blamed for virtual systemwide failure, but the colleges and universities were hailed by the president as "the finest in the entire world." Do you find any inherent contradictions in this claim? How do you account for the tendency of education researchers in our universities to look so negatively at the schools and so positively at higher education in terms of measured outcomes? Do you see any inherent contradictions here?

9. In a report of the National Council on Education Standards and Testing, it is acknowledged that "[e]ducation in the United States is test happy." The report goes on to recommend a national examination system. [*Raising Standards for American Education* (Washington, DC: U.S. Government Printing Office, 1992), pp. F-6, 20.] Would you describe your school as test obsessed? In your opinion, to what extent do state or national tests drive the curriculum? Do you see any dangers of neglecting important curricular experiences because they are not amenable to large-scale testing? Explain.

10. How do you account for the failure of the new electronic technology to usher in the promised revolution in the schools?

11. What were the sources of bias in the design and conduct of the National Adult Literacy Survey (NALS) conducted by the Educational Testing Service? How do you account for the blind acceptance and sensationalistic treatment of the findings by the U.S. secretary of Education and the mass media in the face of compelling contravening evidence from studies sponsored by highly reputable national and international agencies? Do the NALS findings support the testing industry? Explain.

CHAPTER 15

WHO MAKES THE CURRICULUM?

Charm is a quality rarely found in papers delivered at professional meetings but the following statement by John Goodlad manages to be beguiling while dealing with a common misconception about the curriculum. (It may strike a chord of recognition for the reader.)

> Coming fresh out of Canada, where I'd been a teacher and director of education in a school for delinquent boys, I knew absolutely nothing about curriculum development. In fact, so far as I knew, the curriculum which I'd been involved with came down full blown from the head of Zeus. In no way could human beings interfere with this process. (Goodlad, 1981)

Goodlad, who studied curriculum development with Ralph Tyler, became a renowned expert in curriculum development and has made many contributions to curriculum knowledge. All too often the curriculum is seen as a mystical blend of knowledge and mandates handed down from above. In many cases the perception that curriculum decisions are made at a higher level is grounded in reality. However, there is no doubt that some teachers and principals perceive more constraints on their curriculum improvement efforts than actually exist. The intent of this chapter is to demystify the curriculum. By drawing away the dark curtains we can throw light on roles and reality, thereby helping professionals optimize their opportunities for curriculum improvement.

Demystifying the Curriculum

Myths abound about who makes the curriculum. For example, some would hold that textbook publishers control the content of instruction, whereas others would contend that the curriculum is controlled by some other dominant influence: state educational policy, federal policy, local school boards, the colleges, professional educational associations, and so on.

The Textbook Publisher Myth

It is often argued that textbook publishers determine the curriculum, and that they are primarily interested in profits, not in what students should learn. In the words of one critic, textbooks are "books without formal authors . . . ghost-written under conditions of stringent cost controls, geared to what will sell and not necessarily to what is most important to know" (Apple, 1986, p. 96).

This statement is misleading because it implies that textbook publishers are in control of the topics addressed in the texts that they produce. This is simply not the case, except by default. Authority for determining whether to buy the textbooks that publishers produce is vested in state and local education agencies. They decide whether the books contain what is most important to know and may either reject the books outright or make recommendations for changes, postponing acceptance until the changes are made. Publishers are concerned primarily with meeting market demands. The Association of American Publishers reports that 22 states have state-adoption policies (Manzo, 2003). It is clearly impossible to deal with these policies adequately in a short space but one problem—the censorship of ideas—is important for curriculum workers and will be mentioned. During the first decade of the twentieth century, southern states started to take control of the purchase of textbooks away from school districts, in part, to censor ideas they saw as a threat to the culture of the South. One cannot overestimate the importance of this reason, which stood in opposition to southern progress. However, it stands in sharp contrast to more recent policies of state education agencies.

In 1990, the Texas State Board of Education approved science textbooks with extensive coverage of evolution for grades 1 through 12. The decision was important for students in every state because Texas, like California, is one of the largest buyers of textbooks in the United States. Thus, Texas influences what publishers include in books that are sold to schools throughout the country. According to the director of a textbook review group in Houston, the decision marked "the end of the Dark Ages and the beginning of an enlightenment for science in Texas" (*New York Times*, 1990, A13).

However, as one of the authors of this text pointed out, "publishers also respond to the narrow-minded influences of special-interest groups when such influences are dominant" (Tanner, D., 1999, pp. 130–131). Texas was once notorious for such influences. However, publishers abhor censorship and have a long-standing record of exposing and opposing textbook censorship.

Since the early 1980s, states and local school systems representing a large proportion of the textbook market have become increasingly critical of the textbooks that publishers produce, and publishers have acted to make changes based on quality criteria. In 1982, New York City rejected three biology textbooks for use in the city's high schools. The reason was that the books did not give adequate treatment to Darwinian evolution as fundamental to biological science. Two of the three publishers were told that their books also were unacceptable because they endorsed creationism theory. In communicating with one publisher explaining why the book was rejected, the director of the district's division of curriculum and instruction wrote: "This book does not state that evolution is accepted by most scientists today, and presents special creation without characterizing it as a supernatural explanation that is outside the domain of science" (Maeroff, 1982, pp. 1, 23).

In New York, all new books and revised editions of older books require approval by a three-member committee for use in the schools. Also entering into consideration are state curriculum requirements and city curriculum guidelines. Publishers request the reviews. The committee is composed of the subject field director for the school district and teachers or supervisors in the subject field. New York City was one of the first large school systems to take a stand against national pressure to promote the creationist viewpoint, now termed *intelligent design*. (At the time legislators in several states had introduced bills that would make mandatory the teaching of creationism or creation theory as a viable alternative theory to be studied in biology along with evolutionary theory.)

In 1985, the California Board of Education, on the recommendation of the State Curriculum Development and Supplemental Materials Commission, unanimously rejected every science textbook submitted for use in seventh- and eighth-grade classes, stating that the textbooks are watered down so as to avoid controversy. The publishers were criticized by the board and the state superintendent for producing textbooks that fail to address adequately such controversial topics as evolution, human reproduction, and environmental problems. Within a matter of months the publishers produced revised editions of their textbooks. One publisher, who had not even listed the topic of evolution in the index, soon produced a revised edition with a whole chapter on evolution. The state superintendent also announced that textbooks for all other subject areas would be similarly scrutinized (Tanner, D., 1999, pp. 130–131).

Educators have the professional responsibility to scrutinize textbooks to determine whether the textbooks meet quality criteria. (The word *profession* comes from the Latin meaning a public vow.) The State Curriculum Development and Supplemental Curriculum Commission in California based its recommendations on the evaluation of a panel of experts consisting of university professors in the discipline and in education, curriculum directors and specialists from various school districts, and teachers. In making the evaluations, a framework of criteria drawn from the research literature in science education was used.

Education agencies are (should be) concerned that textbooks include topics that are idea-oriented, stressing more than the mastery of mechanical skills. Gilbert T. Sewell, the president of the American Textbook Council, a nonprofit association that reviews history and social studies textbooks, points out that in the early 1990s California exercised its powerful influence over publishers in requiring that textbooks mirror higher academic standards. The result was materials that "closely followed the state's widely acclaimed curriculum framework for history and social studies" (Manzo, 2003, p. 21).

State Controls: Pros and Cons. According to Sewell, the state controls have "forced improvements to textbooks" (Manzo, 2003, p. 21). Education agencies have been concerned with the accuracy of textbooks content. In 1991 the Texas Board of Education rejected five history textbooks for grades 8 through 12 because the books contained numerous errors. Jimmy Carter, in one text for instance, was called the first Democratic president since Harry Truman, overlooking Lyndon B. Johnson and John F. Kennedy. More than 300 such errors were found ("Errors Found," 1992). The publishers were given two weeks by the Texas Education Agency to identify and correct the errors. An ad hoc committee of board members was entrusted with determining whether the errors had been corrected. Publishers seek to avoid such situations by having the manuscript professionally reviewed before it is readied for production. State-level scrutiny of textbooks is not only a quality control but can free local school staffs from a truly tiresome task. That is an oft-cited argument in favor of state adoption policies. Economy is a clear advantage. Textbooks bought in volume can save a great deal of money. Publishers like state adoption systems because they can revise textbooks on a regular schedule. The advantages for teachers and students when publishers are able to put their resources into making quality texts in just one or two subjects at a given time are clear.

But as Sewell points out, state adoption systems have also made it possible for interest groups "to demand content that will not offend anyone regardless of its accuracy" (Manzo, 2003, p. 21). Moreover, state policies often limit teachers' latitude in textbook selection. For example, a teacher may have to choose between only two reading series. Some states, however, have extensive lists, and other states suggest only that districts use the lists as guides for purchasing textbooks. State money in Kentucky and Virginia is available for purchase of books not on the list (Manzo, 2003). In the early 2000s, legislators in some states were proposing changes in adoption policies that would give teachers more freedom to choose materials.

The Single-Factor Myth

A number of forces interact to produce the curriculum for a school at any given point. In the United States, each state prescribes what must be included in the curriculum. Teachers and building principals participating in local curriculum development projects will find that they must work within the boundaries of state regulations. There are other forces as well, including demands of influential persons that often seem to have the same result as laws (and may lead to the enactment of laws to support those demands).

At times, one or another of the forces will seem to be the supreme curriculum determinant. Take, for example, the political influence of the president. The education reform policy of President George W. Bush illustrates this influence vividly. Bush called for annual testing of all students in grades 3 through 8 in reading and mathematics. As Jennings points out, the No Child Left Behind Act, signed by Bush in 2002, "makes unprecedented demands on states and local school districts" (2003, p. 299). State testing programs had to be adjusted to Bush's requirement for annual testing. A central feature of Bush's standards-based reform is a requirement that states provide individual student test scores. The federal law imposes penalties on schools whose students do poorly. The effect on curriculum balance has not been unexpected. As Rosemary Coyle, president of the Connecticut Teachers Association observed, because teachers have to "focus so much time on preparing for the tests, they are forced to neglect subjects such as science and social studies that aren't covered on the tests" (Galley, 2001, p. 5).

More about political influences shortly. The point here is that the school curriculum is influenced by many sources and forces, often in conflict and contradiction, from the classroom teacher and local school board, right up to the state house, the White House, and the Supreme Court. These forces work in interaction, and the more they are understood by teachers and administrators, the better the chances are for curriculum improvement.

The Decision Makers

With respect to the question of who makes the decisions regarding the objectives and means of instruction, Richard Clark (1988) identifies the following categories of decision makers: the public, political leaders, test publishers, the media, higher education personnel, professional organizations, school boards and central administration within school districts, teacher groups, and individual teachers. The members of the public who seek to influence the curriculum fall into two subgroups: members of special interest groups (for example, religious groups who attempt to bar consideration of ideas they disagree with) and

Figure 15.1 Who Makes the Curriculum? Sources and Influences.

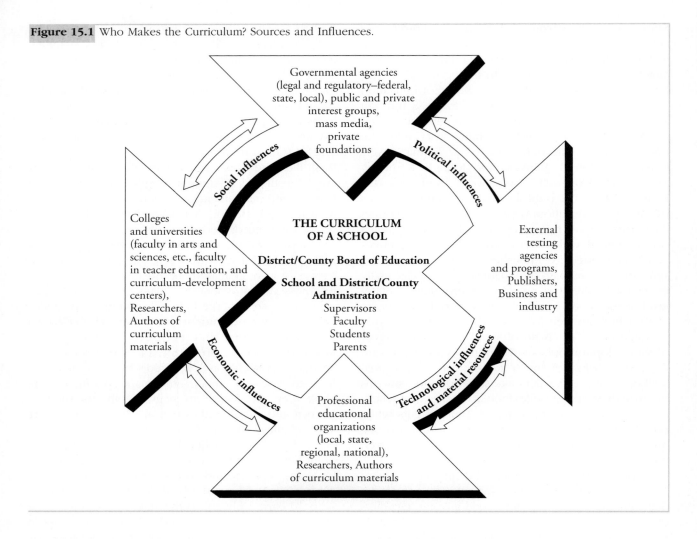

nonaffiliated individuals who usually interact directly with principals and teachers at the local school, usually where their children are enrolled.

Clark points out that "[d]ecisions are made with varying levels of specificity, depending on how far from the student the decisions are made," and, further (as in the example above of the president), "most of those who speak from the national and state level make statements of broad priorities" (p. 176). The actual events in the act of teaching, including what the student is expected to learn, are ultimately determined by the teacher. Teaching remains an individual experience.

The decisions at each level are of course important. Curriculum development, as Caswell once pointed out, is a process of synthesizing the forces that influence the experiences that learners have

under the guidance of teachers (Caswell & Campbell, 1935, pp. 74–75). We add that it is also a process of maximizing the favorable influences and countering the negative. The interactive influences on the curriculum are represented in Figure 15.1. Each will be considered separately.

Influence of the Public

Most members of the public do not devote their energies to influencing the school curriculum. Far from it. Although seemingly obvious, the point is important because it is easy to mistake public policy for the public will. In theory, enlightened public opinion should be represented in enactments by national, state, and school district officials. In actuality, public policy does not always represent enlightened public opinion; in fact, it may be in direct opposition. For example, one who reads about the legislative mandates and school board decisions concerning the curriculum in recent years might gain the impression that most people favor eliminating everything from the school curriculum except the basic three Rs and academic subjects in the elementary school and secondary school. However, the actual evidence contradicts this. Studies by John Goodlad (1984, 2003), Clark (1988), and the annual Gallup/Phi Delta Kappa polls of the public's attitude toward the public schools published in the September issue of the *Phi Delta Kappan* indicate that parents constantly want the curriculum to include more, in the areas of social and personal development as well as in academic and vocational development.

It is clear that the broader interests of parents concerning the curriculum have not been represented in school legislation. Eternal vigilance is required by parents, professionals (teachers and administrators), and all citizens if the schools are not to become the pawns of politically motivated legislators and powerfully organized pressure groups. The best theory recognizes that all citizens have a voice in the control—including the improvement—of public education. Most often this voice is exercised indirectly by voting. Parent groups should be involved in exploring curriculum problems.

In discussing the influence of members of the public who seek to influence the curriculum it is clear that they fall into two categories: organized members of the public and those attempting to make curriculum decisions as individuals.

Efforts by Organized Groups

A publishing house rejects a manuscript because of the fear that it may engender controversy and organized opposition. A large corporation sends executives to inner-city vocational high schools with the message that while a college education is nice "it is not necessary for a good career" (Corporation executives visit, 1991). (This corporation like many others views the schools as potential sources of trained workers, and even proceeded to make personnel available to develop high school curriculums for training students for jobs on its own assembly lines.) A Bible History class in 14 school systems uses Sunday school religious training materials to indoctrinate students (Gehring, 2000). A national gun-violence prevention

organization and lobbying group introduces a curriculum for grades prekindergarten through 12 and announces its implementation in five large school systems. A religious group develops a home schooling program so that children can be insulated and isolated from ideas with which the group disagrees. As Clark observes, in taking such children from the school, the group also affects the schooling of the children who remain. Although home schooling programs involve only a minuscule fraction of the nation's school-age children, they represent a decision made by an affiliated group (or an individual) concerning curriculum. Any number of special-interest groups have sought to influence the curriculum with more or less success, and according to Clark, "are active in influencing broad goals as well as in seeking to modify the implementation activities of classroom teachers" (1988, p. 180).

Generally, individuals and groups who concentrate their efforts at the local level are the most effective. Clark tells us from his own experience as a school superintendent that "individuals interacting directly with the principal and teachers at the school may have profound effects on the curriculum as students experience it," and "individuals who seek to have such influence most generally direct it at the school where their own children are enrolled" (pp. 180–181).

Parents. Organized groups of parents who are aggressive in their criticisms of the curriculum have made curriculum decisions. A group of parents in Princeton, New Jersey, for example, founded Princeton Parents for Curriculum Reform. The group, which was composed mainly of professionals in the fields of mathematics and science, complained about what they saw as weaknesses in the mathematics curriculum. District officials responded quickly. As described by a national newspaper: "District officials pointed out that in response to parents' concerns about the teaching of mathematics, they have speeded up their review of the curriculum and expect to have a revised course of study in place by the start of the school year next fall" (Viadero, 1992, p. 13). The Princeton parents also complained about "the underrepresentation of black and Hispanic students in advanced classes" (p. 1).

At times, parents have followed up on their curriculum decisions by paying for extra programs. A group of elementary school parents who have strong convictions about the need for Latin language instruction embark on a large fund-raising project that pays for the teacher of Latin. In so doing, they influence the curriculum in the school where their own children are taught. Not surprisingly, some school districts (Los Angeles, for instance) do not permit the above practice. The reason given is that disparities in curricular offerings deny equal access to the curriculum.

Parents, working through their networks and organizations, have contested various curricular decisions, with varying degrees of success. An example recounted by Horvat, Weininger, and Lareau (2003) concerns a mother whose daughter's school has decided to have an AIDS Awareness Week.

> Mrs. Hopewell . . . brought the matter before the PTA, arguing that it was inappropriate for young children and instigating a wide-ranging discussion. Although no consensus emerged among the parents, the school decided to send home formal notification of the program, offering parents the opportunity to hold their child out if they wished. (p. 339)

Parents vary in their interest in and impact on what is taught at the school district level. Some parents have worked tirelessly with professionals to generate support for bond issues that ensure the continuation of a balanced curriculum in their public school system.

Efforts by Individuals

An age-old story that we can retell in many contexts can be summed up in these words: One person can make a difference. Margaret Sanger's defense of contraception against opposition by religious conservatives contributed greatly to women's rights. Adolf Hitler's unique ability to exploit and maneuver events to his own purposes unleashed an unparalleled era of destruction in human history. Eugene Lang's offer to graduates of Public School 121 in New York to pay their college tuition if they stayed in school encouraged them to do well enough to qualify for college. For better or worse, one person's decisions carried to the point of action can affect the lives of others.

The point can be generalized to the curriculum. When carried out to the point of decision, one parent's perceptions about curriculum materials can influence the educational experiences of many children for good or ill. As Ken Donelson emphasizes, "it may take no more than one complaint mixed with a bit of doublespeak to get a book booted" (1990, p. 4). Thus,

a minority of one can influence the curriculum. (And that individual is not necessarily a member of the professional staff.) Donelson adds, "Too often the library board removes a book while it determines a book's guilt or innocence. . . . After that the temporary ban may ease quietly into permanence" (p. 4).

The curriculum-shaping activity of some individuals is inspired by what they have read in popular magazines about influencing the school to help their child. Individuals can also influence the curriculum through classroom involvement. A parent may feel strongly about the necessity for multicultural education. As Clark observes, "That individual, working with the teacher, may shape curricular experiences in the classroom with which he or she is working so that the general education for that classroom is considerably different from the general education in the classroom next door" (1988, p. 180).

Political Influences

Political influences include regulations that stem from the legitimate role of state and national political institutions. For example, states have the authority to set minimum essentials of the curriculum, which they sometimes do in great detail. Since the 1980s governors have attended four "education summits," where they promised to raise achievement and set agendas for improving testing programs and accountability systems. There has been attrition. In 1989, 49 governors attended the first summit with President George H. W. Bush; they promised to set goals to be met by the turn of the twenty-first century. A National Education Goals Panel was established and set six goals, as discussed in part III of this volume. In 1996, the second summit was held by the governors and the International Business Machines Corporation. The 43 governors who attended promised to adopt standards for educational achievement and tests to determine students' progress in meeting them. More importantly, perhaps, at this meeting an organization—Achieve, Inc.—was formed by corporate CEOs to put pressure on public school systems. Achieve, Inc. "is a constant driving force behind the accountability movement, stressing high academic standards and accountability for performance" (Goldring & Greenfield, 2002, p. 10).

In 1999, some half the governors attended the summit to set an agenda for improving teaching and developing accountability programs based on test results. Only 15 governors attended the fourth summit in 2001 (Hoff, 2001). The meeting came only a few weeks after the terrorist attacks on the World Trade Center and the Pentagon and the economy was in difficulty, which undoubtedly contributed to the dearth of governors. But one also notes that by 2000 there was a backlash in the making against tests, of which governors could not have been unaware.

Public concern about education is a remarkable opportunity to bring about real curriculum improvement. There is much that state officials can do as will be discussed shortly.

The Federal Level

When the U.S. president prescribes national curriculum standards for American schools (as with the six national goals in the 1990s), he is using his political office to put pressure on schools in a matter that is outside his specific authority.

Earlier, the influence of the president was brought to bear on the states by Ronald Reagan's administration. Responding to the report of the National Commission on Excellence in Education titled *A Nation at Risk* (1983), states increased the requirements for high school graduation in the so-called new basics: English, mathematics, science, social studies, and computer science. The changes were, for the most part, regulatory rather than changes in curriculum content. As Cremin (1990) put it, the report "assigned" (p. 31) the main responsibility of carrying out the recommendations to state and local authorities. Reagan was bringing the power of his office to bear on state and local officials (as well as parents, who were asked to make their children study harder). The Tenth Amendment to the U.S. Constitution (the reserved powers clause) specifies that those powers not listed for the federal government are reserved to the states. Education is not enumerated as a federal power and is, therefore, a state power. Nevertheless, the federal role in education has a long and powerful history of recognizing that education is necessary to "promote the general welfare," as declared in the opening sentence of the Constitution.

The federal government has provided aid to education, beginning with the land-grant colleges, created in Lincoln's administration and given its present contours a century later during the Johnson administration. The aid envisioned by Johnson was targeted to poor and educationally disadvantaged

elementary, secondary, and college students. Federal aid undertaken for such purposes has improved access to the curriculum for many such students.

The Curriculum Caste System. As discussed in part III of this volume, Congress, the legislative branch of the federal government, has directed pressures to improve teaching in certain curriculum areas through infusions of funds. The National Defense Education Act (NDEA) of 1958 provided federal funds in science, mathematics, and modern foreign languages. The NDEA provisions indicated that it was in these three fields that the nation's security and supremacy lay. This was during the Cold War with the Soviet Union. The attention to these curriculum areas was new for the federal government. Funds were provided to stimulate state efforts to improve instruction in the newly favored curriculum areas. NDEA summer and academic-year institutes and other programs were supported that school systems could not have afforded otherwise. The effects of the new curriculum hierarchy were psychological as well as fiscal, as the teachers in these fields rose in importance and those in other fields fell.

In the 1980s and 1990s, national policies continued to stress the importance of scientists and mathematicians and curriculum reform in these areas. But the climate of international insecurity now revolved principally on economic issues rather than national defense. For whatever reason, the effect of national policy on the curriculum was the same. In an era of economic retrenchment it was perhaps even more pronounced. Many school districts could afford to add new staff only in fields favored with federal funds and reduced staff in the industrial arts, studio arts, and other so-called nonacademic subjects. For all intents and purposes, a new curriculum hierarchy or caste system was emerging. The federal government has continued to formulate policies that favor some school subjects. What one policy expert calls "the modern federal role" (Jennings, 2003, p. 294) is today heavy on testing and accountability systems. There is virtually no concern with social and personal development (and pleasure in learning and living). It can be said without fear of controversy that federal policies are in direct opposition to a balanced curriculum.

The Supreme Court. According to Reutter (1980), "The Supreme Court of the United States has had a far greater influence on the course of public education than is generally realized" (pp. 6–7). This is especially so for the curriculum. Cases dealing with Bible reading in the public schools involve church-state separation, which is protected by the Constitution. The court has rendered decisions invalidating such exercises as part of the school program, thus influencing the curriculum. A decision of great significance for the curriculum was made by the Supreme Court in 1968 when it ruled invalid an Arkansas statute prohibiting the teaching of evolution. The court held that the statute was unconstitutional because it was enacted to promote a certain religious view (p. 37).

The Supreme Court has influenced the how of teaching as well as the what. A very important Supreme Court decision in 1974 provided the legal basis for instruction in a pupil's native language. In *Lau v. Nichols,* the court found that non-English-speaking children were not being provided with equal access to education because they did not understand instruction in English. As pointed out by McGroarty (1992), "Remedies were left to local discretion, with bilingual education and English-as-a-second-language instruction as two options and with the court recognizing that other options may have existed." Further, "Related federal regulations promoted bilingual education as the option of choice where there were large numbers of elementary school children from the same language background who did not know English" (p. 17). Ironically, the (Chinese-speaking) parents in *Lau v. Nichols* had petitioned for more English, not bilingualism; they proceeded to reject bilingual classes.

Whatever the remedies decided on by school systems, the proportion of non-English-speaking children is expected to grow in America's schools, thus influencing the curriculum. Today, bilingual classes enroll mostly children of Spanish-speaking families.

The State Level

State legislatures have almost absolute power concerning the what of the curriculum. Some states have passed highly detailed laws concerning the subjects to be taught. Texas, for example, prescribes in the Texas Administrative Code detailed curriculum standards (goals) to be met for each grade. The Texas Essential Knowledge and Skills (TEKS) are listed in every subject for each grade. Before each legislative session the State Board of Education reviews the appropriateness of the standards,

making recommendations for legislative changes as necessary. Documents such as *Texas Language Arts Standards* (1998) are made available to superintendents and school boards. State achievement tests are geared to the standards. Students who fail the tests could be held back and schools could be penalized under the federal No Child Left Behind Act. It is not surprising, therefore, that Texas and other states lowered their testing standards in order to avoid expensive sanctions. For example, in a field test for third-grade reading, the Texas State Board of Education voted to lower the number of questions that must be answered correctly to pass the new test, from 24 out of 36 to 20 out of 36 (Dillon, 2003, May 22).

In the early 2000s, there was no doubt about the driving influence of Achieve, Inc., on states. In New Jersey, for example, a revision of the language arts standards tells the tale.

> Achieve, Inc., reviewed New Jersey's 1996 standards in language arts literacy and provided recommendations for improvement. They suggested that the standards provide more clarity and specificity by including benchmarking at more grade levels. In addition, New Jersey standards should reflect sufficient rigor and complexity from grade level to grade level. . . . Achieve's recommendations are reflected in the revised standards. (New Jersey Department of Education, 2002)

Conflicting Decision Makers.   Earlier, we mentioned that sometimes there are conflicts between decision makers. The relaxation of education standards in order to avoid federal sanctions is a striking example. Regarding states lowering passing scores, a spokesman for the U.S. Department of Education stated, "The law includes safeguards to hold states accountable . . . there are enough checks in place to make sure they cannot game the system" (Dillon, 2003). But some legislatures were considering proposals for their states to opt out of the No Child Left Behind Act.

The real concern, however, is the effect of sanctions on curricula. Robert Linn, a past president of the American Educational Research Association, put it this way: "The severe standards may hinder educational excellence because they implicitly encourage states to water down their content and performance standards in order to reduce the risk of sanctions" (Dillon, 2003). Thus sanctions may well accomplish the opposite of what was intended.

State Policy and Curriculum Development. Since the early 1980s, state legislative activity in education has increased enormously. In 1986, a survey by the Education Commission of the States reported that since 1980, 45 states and the District of Columbia had increased their high school graduation requirements. Although the increases involved a number of subjects, more states increased requirements in mathematics and science than in any other subjects; mathematics requirements for graduation were increased in 42 states and science requirements in 34 states (Association for Supervision and Curriculum Development, 1985; Pipho, 1986).

As Pipho observed, in many states the movement toward more stringent control did not include implementation of reform. "It is fair to say that many legislators and other policymakers in many states did not have implementation of reform on their minds when they wrote the laws, rules and regulations" (p. K7). This is hardly surprising because some had a political agenda rather than an educational agenda (Hanson, 1991).

Actually states had sought greater accountability from teachers and local administrators since the early 1970s. The reform movement of the early 1980s was an outgrowth of the earlier movement. It had been given new energy by the education agenda of the Reagan administration as embodied in *A Nation at Risk* (1983), the report of the National Commission on Excellence in Education. The banner of this report was more stringent academic standards to meet the Japanese challenge for world industrial markets.

Even the most fleeting glance at the education literature of the 1980s, 1990s, and early 2000s reveals the existence of three state reform movements. None provided any real momentum toward curriculum improvement. They are well described by Firestone, Fuhrman, and Kirst (1991), Elmore and Fuhrman (1994), and Fuhrman (2001). The first movement took place in the period from about 1982 until 1986, receiving impetus from *A Nation at Risk*. The second began in 1986 and continued until the early 1990s. The approaches to reform in these first two movements, or "waves," were very different: centralization of decision making at the state capitol and local decision making at the school site. The third movement—standards-based reform—began in the mid-1990s.

In the first movement, the focus was on achieving excellence through increased course requirements in selected academic studies (especially science and mathematics), increased student testing, the establishment of achievement standards, and the alignment of curriculum to national standardized tests. This movement was virtually launched by *A Nation at Risk*.

Thus, the approach to reform in the first movement was centralized control from the state capitol in response to a national report that captured wide media attention. The reform measures taken by most states grew out of the conception that quality was synonymous with quantitative measures. Frequently, the newly required courses were quite similar to courses already being taught. The point of importance here is that the Reagan administration argued that the quality of American education had sunk precipitously, and the states followed suit by mandating increased academic course requirements and standardized achievement testing. Virtually no support was provided to finance curriculum reconstruction.

The Teacher as Problem. In the first reform movement, the teacher was identified as the villain behind the nation's education ills. According to a researcher who analyzed the reform movements of the 1980s, one assumption behind states' standardizing and regulatory approaches to reform was that "standardized programs and policies would almost naturally lead to higher levels of quality because their prescriptive nature would resist tampering by teachers" (Hanson, 1991, p. 31). A second assumption of state governments was that schools are more alike than different; therefore, reforms are to be made across the board or "one size fits all" (p. 31).

The Teacher as Solution. A number of education leaders reacted vigorously against the view of teaching implicit in the wave of state mandates. They criticized the prescribed content and standardized system of learning and argued that teachers must have autonomy if they are to help learners synthesize knowledge and develop a critical intelligence. For teachers to do anything less was to fail in their professional responsibility. Teachers must therefore be empowered to make curriculum decisions at the school level. As Hanson (1991) points out, "If the first wave of educational reforms identified teachers as the problem, the second wave identified them as the solution."

The second wave, "restructuring," followed the movement in U.S. business and industry. The school site was the focus and the emphasis was on instruction. According to Firestone, Fuhrman, and Kirst (1991), the wave was supposed "to reorganize instruction to improve teaching and learning for understanding, more depth of content as compared to coverage and more emphasis on higher-order thinking" (p. 240).

It had become clear once again that the teacher was the key to curriculum improvement. Or had it? States were sending out mixed signals. Some states passed laws requiring more local involvement and at the same time enacting curricular mandates that were more like the first movement. According to Hanson (1991), the two movements were alike where money was concerned; both "adopted the view that more education is possible for the same amount of money." In the first movement states rarely provided budgetary or staff assistance to local school authorities for implementation of the mandated reforms. In the second movement, states had found a convenient rationale for not providing consultants to help schools in their restructuring efforts, presumably under the premise that schools should have a greater responsibility in making curriculum decisions on their own. The rationale is, of course, faulty. Because schools should have this responsibility does not mean that they ought to be denied professional assistance and material resources for solving curriculum problems. As E. Edmund Reutter points out, "Frequently local school districts are not in a position to hire expert help in these matters and would not have the advantage of it were it not provided through the state department of education" (1980, p. 13). This idea seems to have gone with the winds of policy change, but its time may possibly come again, as will be discussed.

The Third Wave: Standards as Solution.

According to Fuhrman (2001), standards reforms seemed to be a combination of the features of the two earlier movements: Clear central direction and mandates for teachers to plan and put into effect more efficient instruction. But the greatly enlarged federal role and mandated annual testing made it more like the first wave than the second. The pressure for productivity borrowed from the practices of large corporations was even stronger in the third wave than the first. There was one real difference: Supervision would not just be from the state capitol via assessments as in the first wave. As Fuhrman tells us: "It was imagined that states and districts, having set clear directions, would also have to provide support for schools to achieve the directions" (p. 4). However, the support that schools need has not been provided. Recent

studies point to resulting problems of teacher morale. In an interesting study of a California school district's efforts to develop a standards-based curriculum, Ogawa, Sandholtz, Martinez-Flores, and Scribner (2003) report: "The teachers were frustrated by the expectation that they teach to the standards without accompanying support in the form of materials, textbooks, and professional development" (p. 167).

Inattention to implementation has been an unfortunate feature of a movement largely confined to specifying instructional outcomes. One teacher from the above school district related:

> We had numerous SIP (school improvement plan) days, and we spent a lot of time on revisions and filling out revision papers on standards that needed to be fixed. We spent a lot of time with that. None of it was really spent on implementation, on how we would teach them. (p. 167)

State Leadership in Curriculum Development.

Before the wave of rigid state mandates on the curriculum in the 1980s, Reutter could report that "[c]onsultants employed on the state level are increasing in number in most states as state-level educational agencies evolve from essentially a regulatory role to a true leadership role in improving the quality of education within their borders" (1980, p. 407).

Undoubtedly, this evolution came to a virtual halt in the early 1980s when politically inspired state regulations led to a deadening uniformity in many states. The detailed new regulations provided little if any scope for local districts for originality and curriculum experimentation. However, although the policies stifled local initiative many state officials honestly saw themselves as engaging in the unfinished tasks of raising standards and equalizing educational opportunity. Since the advent of the state school systems, far more progress has been made on these tasks by the state as a whole than could have been accomplished under the differing conditions of autonomous school districts. Whatever the motivations of state policy makers during the early 1980s, however, the restrictive requirements were not a stimulation to curriculum improvement in individual schools, nor was the lack of professional support for schools in the early 2000s (Herman & Haertel, 2005).

State Programs: The Integral Relation of Curriculum and Instruction.

There are models for a state's leadership role in curriculum development that are very different from current approaches.

One of the most interesting because of the large-scale involvement of teachers was the Virginia Curriculum Revision Plan in the early 1930s. The Virginia Plan was designed by Hollis L. Caswell of Columbia's Teachers College, who served as the general curriculum consultant, and Sydney B. Hall, Virginia's state superintendent of instruction. Caswell's earlier experience with state programs in Alabama and Florida had convinced him that the concept of curriculum must go beyond the course of study. "Courses of study gathered dust on shelves," recalled Caswell. "It became increasingly clear that revision of the curriculum should have as its central purpose the improvement of instruction, and that curriculum programs must utilize many means to achieve this end in addition to writing courses of study" (1966, pp. 2–3).

The state curriculum programs left their imprint on curriculum theory and practice. In the 1930s and 1940s the concept of curriculum development shifted from writing courses of study to the improvement of learning experiences for students. The reforms of the early 2000s were a giant step backward to writing objectives (standards).

The Need for Teacher Involvement. Caswell reported that the Virginia program and those that followed "led to the general acceptance of the idea that classroom teachers generally must take a major part in curriculum programs since change in practice depends on their ability and willingness to modify existing teaching procedures" (p. 10). This idea was rediscovered a half-century later when states mandated reforms but gave scant attention to implementation. States could establish macropolicies but could not control what went on behind classroom doors. State authorities in Virginia in the 1930s had to address the same problem. Caswell's approach to getting teachers to implement curriculum reforms is of interest and importance. From his research on the Virginia plan, Burlbaw (1991) reports that Caswell's curriculum revision plan for Virginia was a radically different approach to influencing teacher practice, based not on externally imposed mandates, but on invitation and cooperation aimed at improving instruction and learning.

All Virginia teachers were invited to participate in a curriculum study program in preparation for curriculum development work. Caswell's course syllabus included seven topics ranging from "What Is the Curriculum?" to "Measuring Outcomes of Instruction"

(Burlbaw, p. 237). The courses were conducted by trained leaders throughout Virginia, with 10,000 of the more than 16,000 teachers in Virginia participating. While the teachers were engaging in the study program, a committee of principals and teachers developed a tentative statement of the aims of education for Virginia's schools. The next step was crucial: One hundred laypersons, representing various groups, were asked to study the aims critically and make suggestions. The responses were used by the committee in making a revised report. The aims were also submitted to the editors of various newspapers in the state with a request for suggestions. The support of parents and others had made it more possible to use the new course of study effectively (Caswell & Campbell, 1935).

When the list of aims had been approved, teachers were invited to identify lessons and classroom activities to help students develop the skills and understandings embodied in the aims. For the interested reader, Burlbaw (1991) presents a detailed account of organization of county and school district production committees and their relation to the state production committee (pp. 233–254). Significantly, in the resulting *Tentative Course of Study for Virginia Elementary Schools*, teachers were encouraged to adapt the suggested activities to local conditions. Indeed, the choice of lessons was to be based on the availability of materials and resources locally.

The model was not perfect. Missing was the demonstration of teaching strategies and funds were not available for the intervisitation of teachers. Nevertheless, the program met with success. The Virginia Plan continued—with revisions—from 1932 until 1952. As Burlbaw concludes, its longevity "indicates that some of its aspects might be useful to curricular reformers today" (p. 249). Of particular interest is the view of state curriculum leadership on which the model was based, namely that mandated change is not as effective as is the statewide voluntary participation of teachers in developing and testing new programs. Democratic educational leadership is cooperative and participatory.

What States Can Do. State efforts to help teachers improve professional practice date from the beginning of our public school system. The problem of professional development was faced by Henry Barnard, and he came up with the idea of teachers institutes, which were held throughout Connecticut. They were conducted, as early as 1839, on a professional level. (See chapter 1.) Throughout history great leaders in education such as Dewey and Caswell had confidence in the teacher. The confidence paid off with challenging curricula that throbbed with life and led to improved student learning. Following Caswell, state departments of education provided consultants for curriculum problems. Today, that such policies ever existed seems to have gone out of memory. They are deemed "policy arenas where they [states] traditionally haven't played a big role" (Hoff, 2001). To think that all the support that all those state consultants gave to so many teachers has been forgotten.

Today, states still have important roles to play in professional support for teachers. Our experience at the state level has much to teach us about today. According to Sandra Feldman, a former president of the American Federation of Teachers, teachers "feel like they're under siege and without support," and, further, "you've got to have curriculum, and you've got to have professional development, or it's not going to work" (Hoff, 2001, p. 22). The "it," of course, is standards-based instruction. State officials need to accommodate themselves to the reality that they are today, as they always have been, part of the curriculum development infrastructure. This means a physical presence, not just supervision from some capitol via test scores. Today, there is no indication that state officials actually visit the schools that they criticize.

There are examples that they can learn from. For example, Helen Heffernan, the famous early childhood expert, worked out of her state department office in Sacramento, consulting with teachers in school districts across California.

The School District Level

Reutter makes these two points concerning curriculum development at the local level: The local board of education must follow state-level curriculum prescriptions, and the history of curriculum innovations in American public schools "is largely a history of local actions" (1980, p. 41). These ideas may seem in conflict to the reader but they are not, for three reasons. The first reason is that the local board of education is most closely involved with what children are taught; thus, it has tremendous powers for determining the curriculum in use.

Another reason is that many curricular offerings have simply been initiated by local school boards on their own, not because of a mandate—such as coursework in environmental science, family life, journalism, orchestral music, humanities, and so on. School boards can also drop and modify subjects and activities that are not state required (pp. 41–42). When a school board conceives a curriculum change such as a diversified secondary curriculum without tracking, and it proves successful, it is copied by other school systems. Any number of interesting developments in the curriculum began in this fashion.

A third reason has to do with the relation between curriculum and instruction. How instruction is carried on influences content. As we have seen in the earlier chapters of this book, by changing the ways of conducting the formal studies we can improve the curriculum. We can make it have greater significance in the student's own life. One could not tell by looking at the list of subjects taught in Dewey's laboratory school, for example, that children were engaged in investigating and creating. They were learning that knowledge is not ready made, but comes through inquiry. And they were pursuing their studies under conditions that fostered the realization of social goals. By changing the processes of teaching, Dewey and the teachers changed the curriculum.

"Generally speaking," says Reutter, "methods of instruction are chiefly within the province of local school authorities and individual teachers" (p. 43). By improving the way mandated elements in the school curriculum are taught, school districts change curriculum. This is why the two points with which this section began are not in conflict.

There is no doubt that states can control the curriculum (and to some extent, method) by prescribing textbooks, but textbooks should not determine the curriculum. They should be used with a rich variety of curricular materials, resources, and activities. The responsibility for designing and developing the curriculum resides with the professional staff of the school district and school. State curricular prescriptions are not an excuse for avoiding this responsibility. For instance, the state may mandate certain subjects for high school graduation, but it does not mandate how the subjects are to be organized or treated.

The point made about the relation between a state and school district also holds true here. Because local schools should be engaged in curriculum improvement does not mean that help from the central office should be lacking.

Test Agencies and Publishers

"The longer I teach, the more standardized tests are being given," observes a teacher in Texas. Her impression is on target. There are more standardized tests than ever. As shown in a recent study by Rhoades and Madaus (2003), the growth of school testing has been remarkable. For example, one of the largest testing companies saw its revenues rise more than tenfold from 1976 to 2002. In just the years from 2000 to 2003, Pearson Educational Measurement, which regards itself as the largest school testing company, increased its scanning equipment for answer sheets by two thirds (Henriques, 2003).

The tests are not being used to improve teachers' professional judgments. Test results are used, as the president of Educational Testing Service once acknowledged, "to rank students, schools and districts" (Anrig, 1992, p. 40).

Anachronisms. Self-defeating, counterproductive, anachronistic. These are terms that a curriculum worker might well use to describe sanctions-based assessment. Why anachronistic? Teachers' test-related instructional activities are often at odds with standards. Take, for instance, the standards promoted by the National Council of Teachers of Mathematics (NCTM). In their most interesting study of standards-based mathematics teaching, Fairman and Firestone (2001) report: "Teachers were conducting isolated, test-like activities that included a greater emphasis on mathematics topics or content that had formerly been ignored," but, "teachers continued to conduct lessons in ways that emphasized procedural skills . . . rather than creating opportunities for students to engage in reasoning, complex problem solving and connecting important concepts in mathematics" (pp. 142–143). Why was this the case? Certainly, in part, because professional development for teachers tended to focus on what district staff believed would be on state assessments rather than on helping teachers to use instructional approaches in accord with NCTM standards. A sanctions-based state policy can be expected to work against standards-based instruction because teachers' efforts are concentrated on high-stakes test performance rather than higher-level objectives (Smith, 1996).

When tests are used as an instrument of public accountability, they sap time and energy from the curriculum. That is what has happened in many American classrooms. A number of studies employing observations of classrooms and interviews with teachers and pupils have found that testing programs considerably reduce learning time, narrow the curriculum, and discourage teachers from attempting to meet goals or use materials that are not compatible with formats used by test makers (Smith, 1991). As Smith puts it, "multiple choice testing leads to multiple choice teaching" (p. 10). The proliferation of worksheets is symptomatic of the testing syndrome.

Teaching the Test

Textbooks and curriculum guides serve as key sources from which test objectives are drawn by test manufacturers. According to Mehrens and Green (1989), who analyzed the validity of nationally normed tests, the publishers of the tests argue that the content is quite representative of the areas taught by schools. It is obvious, however, that with such a vast number of objectives, no two test manufacturers will select the same objectives. Despite the fact that there are similarities in the curriculum across the United States, the tests as well as the textbooks selected by school districts differ. Moreover, the tests lack curricular validity, that is, they may not reflect the content of the district's curriculum. This is why so many teachers teach the test. The focus of instruction is on the test items selected by a particular testmaker. Teachers use the old tests to drill students in preparation for the high-stakes tests.

Effects of Assessment on Student Performance. The idea that testing and accountability systems will improve student performance lies at the heart of statewide assessments. However, the evidence to support this is lacking. Two states, Florida and Texas, are particularly interesting in this regard. According to Herrington and MacDonald (2001), a review of 30 years of Florida's reliance on accountability as a major reform approach generated scant evidence that accountability was enough to produce improvements in student performance. The performance of Florida's students, which has a history of being weak, did not improve relative to the performance of other states over this period.

Similarly, while governor of Texas, President George W. Bush developed the concept of using standardized tests to hold schools accountable for achievement. Ostensibly, this was a success story, but experts believe that the test used during Bush's governorship was much too easy (Dillon, 2003). There are also conflicting conclusions as to whether the Texas accountability system led to improvement (compared with other states) or whether it had, as advertised during the 2000 presidential campaign, "closed the gap between white students and students of color" (Herrington & Fowler, 2003, p. 281). In sum, not only have assessment and accountability had unplanned for, and certainly unhoped for, effects on curriculum and classroom practice, but there is also little evidence that they have improved student performance. Accountability assessment has also decreased teachers' potential for creativity and has made it less likely that teachers will seek to adapt the curriculum to the needs of their students. Teachers know much more about teaching than they can put into practice under these limiting conditions (Hlebowitsch, 2005, p.16).

The Merging of Politics and Testing

Despite the fact that the high-stakes testing epidemic in schools has not improved instruction and learning, states continue to eagerly accept tests as the answer to school improvement. Tests are still being asked to do what they cannot do. The question we must ask ourselves is why.

One reason is the symbiotic relationship between test producers and state legislators. Because of the political use to which test scores are put, testing has become a runaway business enterprise. "No other country in the world has as much achievement testing as the USA nor allows such commercial profiteering," note four educational psychologists (Paris, Lawton, Turner, & Roth, 1991, p. 13). Not only do test publishers and agencies reap enormous revenues from selling achievement tests and scoring them, but they also profit from the sale of curriculum materials that they produce to match the tests. Even Educational Testing Service, a so-called nonprofit agency, reveals such continued revenue growth in its annual reports that it compares favorably with many a commercial corporation in a growth industry.

Of profound importance in the merger of political and commercial interests is the way that legislators use the test data. As the same four educators observe, "scores are reported in the newspapers with inadequate explanations, and they invite comparisons among teachers, buildings and districts exclusively on the basis of test scores" (p. 13).

We would not be writing about the bigness and influence of the testing industry if some legislators (and other elected public officials) did not, themselves, personally benefit from the ensuing public concern about test scores. Improving mediocre achievement is a good plank in any politician's platform. Usually the remedy proposed is greater public accountability and more tests.

Public concern is also sustained by the test publishers. In scoring the tests, test publishers have to renorm them constantly because the very nature of standardized testing requires that half the population will score below standard. This means that continuous progress in raising test scores is made more difficult for some school districts, particularly those districts serving large numbers of educationally disadvantaged students.

Instructional Assessment: Building on Past Learning

"If learning is to improve," argued Anrig, "we desperately need reforms that support teachers and students" (1992, p. 40). Accountability testing undermines teachers and students and affects the curriculum negatively. Of profound importance is the difference between instructional assessment and traditional accountability testing. According to Anrig, instructional assessment "builds on past learning and leads toward future learning *in the classroom*. It is not a single activity, or test, conducted in isolation for external reporting."

The purpose of testing where teachers are concerned is to provide information that will help improve day-to-day teaching. Tests must be regarded as only one of a host of instruments and processes in tracing and improving students' progress. At present, accountability testing has become a powerful political vehicle with enormous media appeal. In addition to the direct cost to taxpayers, which is enormous, there is another cost: students' time for learning. According to the National Commission on Testing and Public Policy (1990), American children spend the equivalent of 20 million school days taking tests, and up to 20 times that number of days are spent preparing to take the tests.

According to Harold Howe, former U.S. commissioner of education, the most promising starting place for improving instruction and learning is not assessments. Rather, it is "to help teachers rethink their classroom strategies" (1992, p. 520).

University Professors

As shown in Figure 15.1, educators at all levels influence the curriculum. However, college professors seek to influence the education of children in different ways than do supervisors and teachers in schools. As Clark (1988) points out, for example, "they have been influential in attempting to set direction in much the same way as affiliated members of the public and politicians have been" (p. 184). Because their efforts to influence the curriculum are not the same as those of supervisors and teachers, we will deal with university professors separately here. This should not be taken to mean that the separation that has traditionally existed between the school and university is desirable. On the contrary, a necessary condition for curriculum improvement is free-flowing interaction between schools and universities. Unfortunately, much of the interaction has been top-down—from university to school.

Influence of Subject-Matter Specialists

Beginning with the Committee of Ten on Secondary School Studies and the Committee of Fifteen on Elementary Education in the 1890s (and even earlier), subject matter specialists in the universities have been highly influential curriculum makers. The national discipline-centered curriculum reforms of the 1950s and 1960s were a spectacular episode in the continuing effort of college and university specialists to subordinate the schools to their own narrow interests. University scholar-specialists also were involved during that period in developing teacher-proof materials. These were designed under the arrogant premise that teachers should not tamper with or modify the curriculum packages developed by university knowledge specialists regardless of local school or classroom conditions.

Despite the massive failures in the national discipline-centered curriculum reforms during the Cold War and space race, the federal government has continued to place great faith in university scholar-specialists as curriculum decision makers for the schools. (Charitable foundations tend to do the same in their funded projects.) Implied in such programs is that the professors know best. What Clark calls the "coalition of the political realm and higher education" (p. 184) has often resulted in narrow curricular priorities. More importantly, teachers are left out of the decision-making process.

A major way in which higher education has influenced the curriculum in elementary and secondary schools is, of course, teacher education.

Influence of Individual Professors. Thus far we have spoken of the influence of affiliated groups, but the ideas of individual scholar-specialists also find their way into some individual classrooms. For example, E. D. Hirsch, a University of Virginia English professor, specified in inventory format what every American should know in his widely read *Cultural Literacy* (1987). One elementary school principal committed her entire school faculty to teaching Hirsch's information. "I like the idea, from the accountability standpoint, of having specific information that we should . . . teach children," she said about Hirsch's work, and added, "The curriculum is also a very clearly sequenced set of content" (Core knowledge, 1992, p. A19).

Professors of Education

Curriculum professors in colleges of education have influenced the curriculum through their work as consultants to school districts. This work, in turn, has influenced their own teaching and writing and, thereby, the curriculum development specialists whom they train. Hilda Taba, a professor at San Francisco State University, was an outstanding example of this kind of reciprocal influence. An authority on curriculum design, she was particularly interested in the development of children's thinking about important social studies ideas. According to Fraenkel (1992), "many of Hilda's ideas influenced social studies educators considerably" (p. 172). For the interested reader, these ideas are well described by Fraenkel.

Obviously, space limitations prevent an adequate discussion of the efforts of individual professors of education to influence the curriculum. Two more strikingly different examples will be provided briefly. The first is the Accelerated Schools Project, developed by Henry Levin in 1986. According to Levin (1992), a Stanford professor of education economics, the premise underlying the project is that educationally disadvantaged students "must learn at a faster rate than more privileged students—not at a slower rate that drags them farther and farther behind" (p. 12). However, the emphasis actually is not so much on speed as on enriched and idea-oriented learning experiences. The schools in Levin's project introduce children early to meaningful reading and writing; indeed, the teaching methods are intensely concerned with gaining meaning through language in all subjects, including mathematics. This calls to mind Francis Parker's work with the children in Quincy, Massachusetts, during the 1870s (see chapter 2). There is nothing new either about the other reform approaches followed in accelerated schools that provide opportunities for children to learn through problem solving and independent projects. These are, of course, best practices for all children. The point of importance here is that Levin has influenced the curriculum in a number of schools by engaging the resources (funding) to influence teachers' classroom decisions.

Some professors of education have been active in setting curriculum policy in ways similar to the activities of politicians. In fact, some have worked collaboratively with governmental officials in efforts to set direction. The second example is Diane Ravitch, a former professor at Columbia's Teachers College, who argued for a narrow academic doctrine for curriculum. Her conception of the curriculum as a catalog of fixed subject matters is reflected in the report, *What Do Our 17-Year-Olds Know?* (1987), an assessment of students' knowledge of history and literature. Her co-author was Chester E. Finn, Jr., who at the time the book was published was serving with Ravitch in the federal Education Department. The book is strikingly reminiscent of Hirsch's *Cultural Literacy*, which is not too surprising. Hirsch was involved in developing the test items for the literature assessment. The assessment was based on students' recall of facts. Ravitch and Finn state that they "do not suggest that these facts (or any others) should be taught in isolation" (p. 256). However, assessment, including the methods of assessment, should stem from a curriculum's objectives. It is hard to imagine that teachers and other curriculum decision makers who read Ravitch and Finn's book could gain any impression other than that a curriculum based on the recall of facts through multiple-choice test items is the best way to teach literature and history. A more recent book by Ravitch (2000), along the same lines, was discussed in part III. As discussed in detail in part III, university faculty members actually have been engaged in the making of curriculum on a national scale with federal funding, which also provides for the support of teacher institutes in schools of education so as to ensure implementation.

Professional Influences

Like higher education personnel, classroom teachers and supervisors influence the curriculum both as individuals and professional groups.

Professional Associations

Professional organizations seek to provide their members with practical knowledge about recent trends in education that affect curriculum. In their brochures and publications, professional organizations promote points of view concerning effective learning. Some organizations are highly specialized, conceived to promote better teaching in a single subject area, as for example the National Council of Teachers of Mathematics. Others cut across subject lines, directing their efforts at the general problem of improving curriculum and instruction in the elementary and secondary schools.

The Association for Supervision and Curriculum Development (ASCD) is the leading example of an organization focusing on general goals and procedures for curriculum development. One of the largest organizations of American educators, ASCD has attempted to influence curriculum decisions through its publications and programs, as well as resolutions adopted at its annual conventions. For example, in 1992 the ASCD Resolutions Committee endorsed the following critical priority resolution concerning the integration of academic and vocational education:

> Academic and vocational programs are unconnected too often, leaving students in the vocational track without necessary academic skills and students in the academic track unaware of how their learning relates to the real world. Hence, many students are entering the work-force ill-prepared to accept and fulfill basic required responsibilities because they do not possess adequate academic skills and workplace ethics.
>
> It is imperative that students be provided with and have access to educational programs that will prepare them to meet the challenging, technological employment demands of the 21st century.
>
> ASCD strongly urges the development and revision of curriculum to integrate academic and vocational education in order to develop competent, skilled and technologically prepared students. (p. 1)

An implementation plan was also adopted by the resolutions committee. More important, perhaps, each member of the association received a copy of the resolution.

Central Administrators

Superintendents and school boards are obviously influencers of the curriculum. The superintendent makes crucial judgments about districtwide curriculum policies and takes them to the board for approval. In the early 1990s a number of city superintendents proposed additional requirements for high school graduation. And in the early 2000s, low-achieving Chicago schools were required to select from "a set menu of curricula" (Johnson, 2001, p. 3) including "scripted" lessons such as direct instruction, which leave scant room for innovation. As Campbell, Cunningham, McPhee, and Nystrand (1980) have pointed out, "The superintendent can by the allocation of resources determine which areas of the curriculum and which student activities will be promoted and which deemphasized" (p. 242).

Some superintendents provide outstanding leadership for curriculum development. They spend the major portion of their time in the schools and generate an atmosphere of intellectual vitality and experimentation. They keep up with the education literature themselves, cite the results in everyday meetings and, thus, encourage others to keep up with the literature. These strategies favorably influence the decisions made by the professional staff. They have been identified in studies of effective superintendents, that is, superintendents of large urban school systems that managed to reverse the trend toward decline (Hill, Wise, & Shapiro, 1989). They served as models for the entire professional staff. Recent history bears out the challenges facing the urban superintendency. In the words of Cronin and Usdan (2003):

> The urban superintendent, as the millennium approached and passed, was expected to become a curriculum reformer, an engineer of teacher reeducation, and a guarantor of academic standards substantially higher than had hitherto been expected of urban schools. (p. 185)

Not all central administrators seek to engage teachers in decision making on the curriculum. Some represent a vastly different picture, such as the scripted lessons mentioned earlier. Even superintendents who consider themselves business managers rather than educational leaders influence the curriculum. They do so by default; in their concern for cost effectiveness and production efficiency as measured by test results, they convey to school staffs the feeling that efforts to solve curriculum problems are a waste of time. Their focus is on established concerns.

Teachers

Teachers make curriculum decisions at the classroom, team, department, grade, and school levels. Each teacher is, in a sense, a choreographer of teaching events and that choreography consists of moment-to-moment decisions. Whatever the broad mandate from afar, students are individuals, requiring individual decisions (Jackson, 1968). These decisions comprise the actual curriculum. Teachers may not recognize that they are making curriculum decisions, but they are.

The actual events decided by the classroom teacher may be different from what was decided at another level. There is a good reason for this: Teachers are closer to the conditions under which the decision must be carried out. They must adapt it to the conditions in any case, but sometimes the decision itself (from another level) is simply unreasonable. The following is an actual situation. The new superintendent announces that the thematic guides for integrating the curriculum, which were developed by teachers in collaboration with central office personnel, will not be reprinted. Furthermore, there will be no more curriculum improvement projects guided by the central administration of the district, and no curriculum guides will be made available from the central office. Local schools will be expected to develop curriculum on their own with their limited resources. Teachers then decide to use the thematic guides and copy them for colleagues.

The teachers in the foregoing illustration were graduate students in a course given by one of the authors of this book. Some reported that they continued to use the guides because an integrated curriculum matched their vision of good teaching; others, because they were simply at a loss without a course of study. In the name of reform—setting high goals and letting teachers figure out how to reach them—the superintendent's decision added complexity to the teachers' ability to do their jobs by withdrawing the support of the central office for curriculum improvement. As pointed out in chapter 4, the central administration of every school system should include persons who are trained in curriculum development and who work with teachers and principals in systemwide programs of curriculum improvement. Without assistance from the central administration, coherent programs are an impossibility. The curriculum should be articulated throughout the district as well as within the school.

In another illustration, this time from Britain, teachers were required to give performance-based tests to determine whether the standards of the national curriculum were being met. The tests were time-consuming, involving science and mathematics experiments. For example, 7-year-olds were given two magnets and asked to explain how to determine which was stronger. "By all accounts," wrote an observer, "teachers found the experience a nightmare. They reported working an average of fifty-eight hours a week giving the tests and struggling to figure out how to grade them" (Chira, 1992, p. B9). Some teachers decided that rather than going through the painstaking testing process, they would use their own judgment as to whether children had reached levels of achievement.

In a third illustration, high school teachers in one California district resisted a standards-based curriculum because of its breadth. They reported being unable to explore concepts in depth because of the need to cover all of the topics on which students might be tested. Rather than teach what they considered to be an inadequate curriculum, many secondary teachers simply did not teach to the standards (Ogawa, Sandholtz, Martinez-Flores, & Scribner, 2003, p. 168).

In all three illustrations, teachers' decisions were guided by the circumstances in which they found themselves. They were by no means being unprofessional. In the second illustration, even those teachers who complained about the time-consuming performance tests actually voiced support for the tests, which they felt were more realistic and valid than traditional multiple-choice tests. Teachers felt that they were not given enough professional preparation, time, or aides to help supervise the class while the teacher administered the test to small groups.

Perspective

The answer to who makes the curriculum cannot be found in education law. The influence exercised at each governmental level interacts with decisions at other levels. At times, one or another of these influences will seem to be the supreme determinant. Concepts and contradictions may rule the day. The late 1990s and early 2000s saw federal power over the nation's education system expand—and not always in constructive ways. In the early 2000s the federal No

Child Left Behind Act imposed expensive sanctions on states whose students do not do well on standardized tests. Unreasonable progress targets led some states to lower their testing standards in order to avoid sanctions.

Oddly enough, the situation that led to such decisions can be traced to the states themselves, namely the governors. In four "education summits," hosted by IBM, the governors agreed to implement reforms that tie challenging standards to accountability systems. Executives from IBM formed an organization to evaluate and make suggestions on each state's standards. The goal of raising students' scores to 100 percent proficiency by 2014 is much like the production target of a large corporation (treating children as commodities). The influence of business on education seemed even more powerful in the early 2000s than a century earlier.

Actually, standards are nothing more or less than goals. Goals should be realistically achievable. Progress is achieved through support, not sanctions. The supportive role of states has been allowed to wither away in recent decades. The past has much to teach us about this role.

Although teachers often complain that other groups make all the important decisions, teachers make decisions at the most detailed level of specificity, for they are closest to the student. Teachers ultimately decide the actual events concerning what is to be taught, how it is to be taught, and why it is to be taught. This is clear from how some teachers responded to standards, as discussed in this chapter. Granted that the textbook determines the curriculum in many classrooms, textbook publishers do not control the curriculum, nor the topics addressed in the texts. Authority for textbook adoption is vested in state and local education agencies, and teacher committees also have an important say in most schools. In recent years states and local school systems that represent a large percent of the textbook market have become increasingly critical and have rejected books that fail to adequately address such significant topics as evolution, human reproduction, and environmental problems. The publishers have promptly produced revised and new editions.

In recent years, state legislation concerning the curriculum has increased enormously, much of it regulatory. Following the lead of federal policies established in successive administrations, most states increased high school graduation requirements. This interconnection between state and federal policies shows clearly that few of the attempts to shape the curriculum by any group of actors are made in isolation. Similarly, the bigness and influence of the test makers on the curriculum is attributable, in no small way, to the political uses and misuses of test scores. Elected government officials frequently call for more achievement tests as the means for achieving excellence (playing on the public's belief in quantitative comparisons). The amount of testing has increased enormously since 2000. The tests are not being used to inform teachers' judgments.

Even a minority of one can influence the curriculum. One parent's objections about curriculum materials can influence the educational experiences of many children. Generally, those individuals and special-interest groups who concentrate their efforts at the local school are the most effective. The further from the student, the broader and more general the decision.

There is no doubt that some influences on the curriculum are harmful. The growing national obsession with testing, fed by the media and opportunistic political leaders, is an illustration. There are also positive influences. Proposed changes in state textbook adoption policies that would give teachers more freedom to choose materials are an example. They signal that some legislators have come to recognize that the progress of students is bound up with teachers' curriculum decisions. (Refer to the Best Practices Checklist on pages 481–499.)

PROBLEMS FOR STUDY AND DISCUSSION

1. Are you in favor of laws imposing sanctions on schools whose students do poorly on standardized tests? Why or why not?
2. In connection with problem 1, if your answer was "no," what approach should state-level leaders follow to improve student learning?
3. Who decides what textbooks are used in your school and school district? Is the selection based on the best professional evidence that the books contain what is important for students to learn? Explain. If not, how would you improve the process?
4. As discussed in this chapter, some states that have state-adoption policies are considering proposals that would give teachers freedom to select their own textbooks. In your view, should a teacher be free to select the textbooks and other curricular materials for his or her classroom? Why or why not?
5. Draw up a list of quality criteria that could be used in selecting textbooks and other curricular materials for your classroom, team, grade, department, or school. Which, if any, are now being used? Explain.
6. Some large cities have appointed noneducators as school superintendents. According to Cronin and Usdan (2003), the employment of former military leaders, corporate executives, lawyers, and political leaders is based "on the assumption that running large school systems requires a set of financial, organizational, and management skills and political experience that traditional educators often lack . . . and that such leadership skills can be transferred to the urban superintendent. However," (p. 190), they add,

   there are those who do not accept this assessment, and who contend that experience and leadership in the core mission areas of teaching and learning are prerequisites for top-level school executives. (p. 190)

   In your opinion, are experience in teaching and instructional leadership prerequisites for appointment as a school superintendent, whatever the size of the school district? Explain.
7. Do you agree with the following statement by a middle school teacher? Why or why not?

   Teaching to the test is not bad, especially if what the test measures is what we want our students to know and able to do. [L. Williams (1992, June 17). Other voices, *Education Week, 11*, p. S13.]

8. Examine the laws in your state concerning the subjects to be taught. How much discretion is left to local authorities concerning the content of the curriculum? Explain.
9. In this chapter it was pointed out that how instruction is carried on influences content. What illustrations can you give?

10. It was noted in this chapter that parents seeking to determine what the curriculum will be for their own children (for example, the demand that Latin should be offered) have gone so far in some schools as to contribute money for extra teachers to teach the additional subjects. Thus, they have added programs that are not offered in other schools that do not contribute money. What are your views on this practice?

11. Hollis Caswell's concept of state-level curriculum leadership is a study in contrast to present-day regulatory approaches to curriculum improvement. In your opinion, does Caswell's model have lessons for educational policy makers at the state level today? Why?

CHAPTER 16

CURRICULUM IMPROVEMENT
ROLE OF THE TEACHER

Curriculum development is something that all teachers do. In the classroom they do it behind closed doors. No one can control all the decisions that teachers make even during a highly specified ("scripted") lesson. A series of research studies over a quarter century have found that teachers choose between alternative courses of action many times during a lesson, such as when a student gives an unexpected response to the teacher's question (Shavelson, 1983; Solas, 1992; Herbst, 2003).

Every teacher knows this, of course, but it helps to know that one's own experience is supported by research. More important is the consistency of the findings across policy eras. From the so-called teacher-proof curriculum era, which aimed to prevent teachers' decisions, to the standards-based curriculums, which depend on teachers' being thoughtful about their work, teachers have made and will continue to make decisions. (The idea here is for teachers to make increasingly better ones.)

What we are discussing here is nothing more or less than teachers being professionals. As Darling-Hammond and Snyder (1992) point out, to be professional is to make decisions based on the principles in one's field. This chapter is concerned with how teachers can be helped to base their decisions on educational principles and thus, it is hoped, improve the curriculum. This requires that (1) teacher education programs prepare teachers who are able to apply the principles relevant to particular situations as well as general professional practice, (2) teachers learn from changing conditions, and (3) teachers are provided with the support to participate in curriculum development. These conditions provide the organizing framework for this chapter and the chapter that follows on the administrator's role.

Teachers' Preparedness for Curriculum Improvement

If teachers are expected to make knowledge-based decisions, they must be prepared to do so. And they should feel that they are well prepared to implement new teaching methods.

Teachers' Feelings About Preparedness

Do teachers feel well prepared to meet present expectations for practice? It would be pleasant to record that most do, but this is just not the case. According to a study by the U.S. Department of Education's National Center for Education Statistics (1999) on how well prepared teachers feel, 41% felt very well prepared to implement new teaching approaches. Only 36% felt that they were very well prepared to implement state or district curriculum standards.

Teachers' feelings are but a single indicator of the extent to which their preservice teacher education programs and staff development sessions prepare them to improve the curriculum. There are other indicators but teachers' feelings are probably the most powerful one. For if one does not *feel* well prepared, how can one function well professionally? (An illustration of feeling unprepared to implement a standards-based curriculum was discussed in chapter 14.) This is a staff development issue, but it also relates to teachers' initial professional preparation. Since it may not have prepared teachers to meet present expectations, continual professional development, including how instruction occurs, is important.

Teacher Education and Curriculum Development

The need to develop teachers who can conceptualize, evaluate, and modify their procedures has been emphasized by educational theorists for centuries. Today it is also increasingly important for teachers to collaborate. As Gary Griffin (1999) observes, "Teachers are increasingly involved with one another in curriculum development work, school-based decision making, peer evaluation and mentoring, team teaching, and other schoolwide activities that have become familiar practices during the past twenty or so years" (p. 15). Many teachers, particularly those who obtained their preparation in the 1970s and early 1980s, were not provided with these experiences in their preservice programs. Teacher education was dominated by competency-based approaches. The emphasis was on training teachers as technicians. The objective was to program the teacher to perform explicitly specified behaviors. Competency-based teacher education is mechanical efficiency applied to teaching. According to Darling-Hammond and Snyder (1992), it is based on "the hope of finding the 'one best system,' codified by law and specified by regulations, by which all students may be educated," and, further, on the assumption "that students are standardized so that they will respond in identical and predictable ways to the 'treatments' devised by policymakers and their principal agents [schools]" (p. 16).

The assumption that students are uniform and uniformly predictable—or can be made so—is, of course, fallacious and ought to have been obvious at the time. Children have always had individual experiences, talents, and interests. Teachers have always had to treat children differently in order to provide them with optimal learning opportunities. Not surprisingly, the competency-based teacher education movement of modern times proved to be a disappointment. As pointed out in chapter 14, there was a striking change in the conception of the teacher in the mid-1980s. Some policy makers at the district and state levels began to recognize that there are no treatments that can be prescribed from afar for all students and that the emphasis on standardized operating procedures had probably impaired teachers' ability to meet the needs of their students. Indeed, a decline in students' reasoning abilities was widely attributed to the students' being treated in standardized ways.

A Crushing Blow to the Teacher's Role. Under competency-based teacher education, the teacher's role in curriculum development just shriveled. There was no provision made for decision making by the teachers. Competency-based teacher education conceived of the teacher as a technician who deals only with established-convergent decisions. The competency movement denied the obvious: namely, that teachers are inevitably involved in the curriculum development and that this function of teaching does not lend itself to a behavioristic, top-down, competency approach. Teacher education has had its dark side, but many policy makers are now concerned—forced to be concerned—with helping teachers grow in personal insight and initiative.

The Laboratory Ideal. If teachers are to relate their decisions to educational principles, they must be provided with opportunities to do so in their professional preparation. As early as 1904, Dewey conceived of a teacher education that was "calculated to develop a thoughtful and intelligent teacher" (p. 28). In such a program, theory and practice "grow together out of and into the teacher's personal experience" (p. 15). What was at stake, argued Dewey, was the laboratory ideal versus the apprentice idea. Here the focus of student teaching and the method of supervising and criticizing it were crucial. In a laboratory, the student teacher's intellectual growth and responsibility are given attention. In Dewey's words, "the practical work is pursued primarily with reference to its reaction upon the professional pupil in making him a thoughtful and alert student of education, rather than to help him get immediate proficiency" (p. 15).

When the apprentice idea dominates, however, the objective is "turning out at once masters of the craft" (p. 11). The most interesting part of Dewey's analysis is his comparison of teacher education with the preparation of other professionals. The history of other professions shows a preprofessional time when the idea was that students should from the beginning "be made as proficient as possible in practical skill." However, "professional schools have traveled steadily away from this position" and toward the laboratory ideal, in which the practice work is conducted under the student's "own initiative and reflective criticism" (p. 11).

In the apprentice situation, the student teacher is primarily concerned with maintaining the external attention of the class. The apprentice teacher gears actual methods of teaching not to the principles of professional practice but to what seems to work or fail from one moment to the next, to what he or she sees done by more experienced teachers who are more successful in maintaining order, and in conformance with the directions given by others. In this way, contended Dewey, the habits of teachers are fixed, with relatively little reference to principles in educational psychology and curriculum development (p. 14).

Dewey held that the apprentice situation had this antiprofessional effect: an unconscious duplicity in teaching. "There is," he said, "an enthusiastic devotion to certain principles of lofty theory in the abstract—principles of self-control, intellectual and moral—and there is school practice taking little heed of the official pedagogic creed." This was one of the "chief evils of the teaching profession" (p. 15).

New (Old) Directions for Reform. In the closing years of the twentieth century many teacher-education programs began to embrace the laboratory ideal, moving in a direction that Dewey would have applauded. In these programs student teachers and interns are expected to make explicit the reasons for their various pedagogical decisions. They are given experiences in making curriculum decisions collaboratively with school faculty and principals. Notable among these reform efforts in teacher education has been the professional development school, which links pedagogical theory and practice by bringing together school and university faculty in the professional preparation of teachers (Griffin, 1999). Such programs typically bring together university faculty, teachers, and principals, who share in the responsibility for the student teaching or internship experience, coupled with a seminar concerned with connecting the field experience and university courses. At the University of Louisville, for example, the seminar is team taught by teachers and university faculty (Whitford & Metcalf-Turner, 1999).

School-University Partnerships: Problems and Possibilities. The professional development school is based on the idea that professional development is lifelong. Thus teachers serving as cooperating teachers are also "learners who are engaged in ongoing inquiry into their practice," notes Grossman (1992, p. 182). "Engagement in the preparation of the next generation of teachers provides rich opportunities for teacher learning" (p. 179). The idea, then, is that learning is a two-way street, as cooperating teachers

can also learn from student teachers. According to Grossman, "Serving as a cooperating teacher holds the possibility for acquiring new knowledge about teaching, including new methods of instruction, alternative approaches to curriculum, or different perspectives in classroom management." Perhaps more importantly, it "can provide opportunities for reflection about one's own practice" (p. 185).

In theory, cooperating teachers should be open to new perspectives and incorporate them in their practices. Not all cooperating teachers, however, even all those who are looking for new ideas concerning curriculum and instruction, view student teachers as a source of new practices. For many, being a cooperating teacher is a reward for previous performance. Rather than a stimulus for further professional development, having a student teacher is viewed as an on-site sabbatical, an opportunity to do other things, as the student teacher takes on increasing responsibility for the classroom (p. 186). Others, who view themselves as experts, become somewhat defensive about their approaches to teaching instead of being open to new ideas. Still others are aware of new ideas concerning curriculum from their student teachers but do not attempt to implement these new approaches. As Grossman observes, new methods "may threaten the delicately balanced routines that manifest the teacher's expertise in the first place" (p. 189).

At issue here is whether the role of cooperating teacher should be recast at all. As Joyce and Clift point out (1984), the purpose of preservice teacher education is to prepare teacher candidates as professional teachers who are engaged in "the lifelong study of the theory and practice of teaching," and for participation in school renewal efforts, including curriculum improvement (p. 6). As Tyler (1975) informed us, "The primary function of teacher education is to help individuals develop a rough cognitive map of the phenomena of learning, teaching and professional ethics so that they can get the feel of professionalism" (p. 139). These views recall Dewey's laboratory ideal. More to the point, however, is that preservice candidates should not be expected to provide new ideas for cooperating teachers. This is not the purpose of their field experience, which is to help student teachers and interns "learn how to work out appropriate answers for individual situations" (p. 135). Some of these situations are at the classroom level, some at the school level. Teacher candidates should have opportunities to participate in curriculum problem-solving groups at the school level if we expect them to do so as inservice teachers.

Complaints and Conflicts.   In attempting to apply their views of learning and use the methods they were taught in university methods courses, student teachers frequently find that schools and universities have different views of teaching and learning. Thus, many cooperating teachers model their work on, and may even insist on, traditional methods emphasizing drill-skill techniques and rote learning. (This happens even in professional development schools.) Student teachers who expect children to learn through active experiences usually try to conform to the cooperating teacher's expectations. Experts in teacher education suggest that this problem can be overcome through staff development over a long period of time by providing inservice teachers with opportunities "to see new strategies modeled repeatedly" and to try them out, "receiving professional support while they are learning" (Winitsky, Stoddart, & O'Keefe, 1992, p. 7). The problems with this approach are manifold. First, it assumes a deficit view of inservice education instead of treating teachers as professionals. Second, cooperating teachers should have the skills, knowledge, and attitudes that will make them the best possible role models. This means that they should be competent to begin with. Placing student teachers with teachers who can help novices apply the relevant principles to a given situation because they do so themselves on their own initiative is crucial to the success of the student-teaching experience.

Finding good field placements for student teachers and interns is an old problem but such placements do exist. The solution still seems to be for universities (and schools) to be more selective in their placements.

Need for Curriculum Development.   Although interest in curriculum reform has continued to rise, a number of teacher-preparation programs that once required that prospective teachers study curriculum development no longer do so. This is residue from the narrowness of the competency-based teacher education movement. Because teachers were viewed as technicians, the study of curriculum development could not be defended as contributing to their abilities in the classroom. Curriculum development was now seen as a policy matter residing at higher levels of the administrative structure. Certainly an adequate education of teachers must include curriculum development

(both theory and the work of curriculum development) if teaching is to be a profession and if educational opportunities for learners are really to be improved.

It is not sufficient for teachers to take methods coursework in the subject(s) they teach. Teachers need to teach across the curriculum in meeting the macrocurricular function of general education.

The Enduring Idea of Professionalism.   The idea of professionalism was well expressed by Foshay (1967), a leader in the quest for professionalism. Foshay made the following observation concerning the term *professional* in education: "At the heart of its meaning is the idea of responsible action: the act of teaching, and the act of educational leadership. A professional is one who knows how to act," and the responsible act of teaching requires that the teacher "draw on what is known of educational practice [and] gather evidence in some coherent way" (p. 224). The ability to synthesize this knowledge in action is the hallmark of the professional teacher. Clearly, if teaching is to be professionalized, then knowledge of best practices in education (including the ability to implement such practices) and the ability to think experimentally should be required for entrance to the profession. Teachers should also be intelligent consumers of research. The preservice preparation program must help meet these aims.

Best practices and experimental thinking as approaches to curriculum improvement are discussed later. It should be noted here, however, that teachers' thinking experimentally ranges from everyday attempts to match the task to the learner to being an intelligent consumer of research to solve a classroom problem or to work effectively in redesigning the curriculum.

Professional Culture as Educator.   Whether or not a school has a professional culture matters for prospective and beginning teachers. In a school with a professional culture, many problems can be solved by consulting experienced colleagues. Often the new teacher gets the right answer. A good example concerns cooperative learning about which many new (and some experienced) teachers have misconceptions. They hear about the positive effects, but the difficulties in implementing this instructional approach are often skimmed over. A student of one of the authors was asked for suggestions by a new teacher down the hall who was experiencing little success in using cooperative learning. He was trying to implement it for every learning task. He was greatly relieved to hear that students do not have to work in groups all the time. This was the right answer. It is well supported in the literature (McCaslin & Good, 1996; Spencer, 2000). As Spencer suggests, "for the successful implementation of cooperative learning teachers must first recognize its limitations and understand that it is more useful for learning some tasks than others" (p. 72).

A professional culture, or "professional community" (Spillane & Louis, 2002), also may extend outside the school and include a network of teacher colleagues. Of particular interest and importance is that the ultimate effect of professional culture is on student learning. Researchers have found that schools with and without professional interaction (within the school) showed substantial variations in teaching and student achievement (Louis & Marks, 1998; Spillane & Louis, 2002). This literature shows that a democratic-participative professional culture can indeed impact positively on student learning.

The theme that runs through teacher education literature is the advance of professionalism. The tide of teacher education is running ever more strongly in the direction of professionalism. The reasons are its positive effects on student learning and its pleasant effects on teachers' personal and professional lives. What could be nicer for a young teacher than to know that the door of an experienced colleague is always open for consultation?

Resources for Problem Solving

It is hard to argue with the conception underlying the professional development of teachers. Preservice and inservice teacher education is an unbroken continuum. The difficulty is in providing the conditions and resources to help practicing teachers improve the curriculum. This is particularly critical in inner-city schools with high concentrations of at-risk students. Such schools typically suffer from overcrowded classes. These students also suffer from lack of individual attention. According to Hodgkinson (1991), a demographer, this is "particularly frustrating" because the evidence is clear that equity efforts "pay off in enabling of minority populations to gain opportunities for advancing educationally, economically, and socially" (pp. 12–13). Education is the key to life choices. In recent years a number of states and school districts have embarked on class-size reduction

programs in the elementary grades. Indeed, more than half of the states have done so (Finn, 2002). This is in response to research and reality. A summary of the research has found that "the benefits of small classes were *greater for minority students attending inner-city schools* than for white students in nonurban schools (p. 553). Teachers can speak to the reality factor. Their morale is improved and there are fewer interruptions and discipline problems (p. 555). A number of positive findings have emerged from studies on small classes. One finding from Finn's summary of studies (on the effects of small classes in early grades) is of particular interest here: "aspirations to attend college are increased, especially among African American students" (p. 556). (These students took SAT or ACT tests in high school.)

Changing Conditions. The conditions of teaching itself are always changing. The nonwhite percentage of the youth population will increase spectacularly by 2020. Indeed, in some states (Texas, California, and Florida, for example), the designation *minority* may no longer be accurate. "What do we call 'minorities' when they constitute a majority?" asks Hodgkinson. "It behooves us all to make sure that *every* child in America has a good education and access to a good job" (1991, p. 12). There is no need, of course, to call minorities (or majorities) anything, and that is a good thing. Children are children. Labels have always been dangerous. Despite the horrendous problems with the No Child Left Behind Act, discussed in chapter 14, the idea that all children will learn is basically democratic and lies at the heart of American education. This does not deny that some schools have special problems and need special help. The possibilities for a prosperous and unified society, enriched from the infusion of various cultures are "exciting," given adequate education, health, day care, and housing (Hodgkinson, 1991, p. 11; see also Carson, Huelskamp, & Woodall, 1993). The prospects convey a sense of great opportunity.

It has taken policy makers a long time to realize that an ongoing program for improving learning requires teacher professionalization. (Each of the four governors' summits highlighted that point.) One of the most promising changes in teaching as a profession is the emphasis on collaborative problem solving. Institutional change such as collegial time (different from formal staff development) are needed to support collaborative problem solving. In some schools such changes have occurred.

Three critically important resources for problem solving are time, expertise, and materials.

Time. Teachers must have time for shared deliberation to identify substantive problems and develop plans for attacking the problems. In her study on the conditions of school success, Little (1982) found that successful and unsuccessful schools can be distinguished based on the frequency of teachers' interactions for the purpose of solving curriculum problems and improving instruction. Schools were classified as successful or unsuccessful based on standardized achievement test scores and nomination by district administrators and staff developers. Successful schools supported and encouraged teachers' shared work. Teacher evaluation was linked with collegial participation in problem analysis and experimentation, with teacher access to resources, including released time. Teacher interactions in successful schools were found to be frequent and ongoing. In one high-success, high-involvement elementary school, faculty meetings were devoted to discussions of research and classroom practice. Teachers regularly worked together in grade-level teams to develop curriculum plans and materials. In a successful junior high school, formerly isolated departments reported that student performance and classroom discipline improved when teachers met more frequently to work on curriculum and instructional approaches (p. 333). Thus, as Kochan, Bredeson, and Riehl (2002) point out, it is especially important that principals be creative in finding time for doing so without losing students' instructional time. Examples are given in chapter 17.

Certainly one purpose of school faculty meetings should be to help teachers integrate theory and practice. Time in faculty meetings tends to be spent on clerical and routine matters rather than on ideas and their implementation. This is a problem of habit and tradition, an existing regularity that could be changed through democratic-participative educational leadership on the part of the principal and teachers. In almost every school, there are certain teachers who have interest and talent in this direction.

Expertise. Teachers must have the freedom to seek assistance in improving the curriculum. Outside experts, helping teachers, supervisors, and peers should be available to assist teachers on invitation, responding to the teachers' expressed needs. Although much can be accomplished by pooling a school's own resources—the strengths of its teachers and principal—schools must turn to outside resources in order to acquire new knowledge, new ideas, and new perspectives. Universities have a vital role to play in this regard. School-university cooperative programs for curriculum development can be enormously effective.

From the literature and professional organizations, principals and teachers can identify schools that are trying out new curriculum designs and materials. They should send task forces to explore the success and efficacy of using these approaches in the local school, and they should inform regional educational research laboratories and centers regarding the school's willingness to participate in the development and evaluation of curriculum materials.

Materials. Teachers must have materials to improve learning. When one considers that only a minute portion of the education budget goes to materials, doubling the amount would probably work wonders. One of the first places where school districts trim budgets is materials: textbooks, library books, curriculum materials, equipment, supplies and other instructional resources.

Although materials are an important resource, teachers should watch out for fads and fashions. Materials and methods must be contiguous with the philosophy of the school district and contribute to the improvement of learning. Goodlad (1978) articulated the problem in these words: "I wish we had some kind of Hippocratic oath to remind us always to keep solid principles of learning, teaching, and education at the center and to guide us in choosing what follows from them" (p. 332).

Professional Relationships

Of profound importance for teachers' involvement in curriculum development is the nature of their relationships with administrators and supervisors. A best practice in education is the active involvement of school faculty in making decisions about curriculum and instruction. Although not a new concept, it was given new life by policy makers at the state and local level in the restructuring movement of the early 1990s. As Fuhrman (2001) points out, among the restructuring reforms was "rearrangements of school schedules to promote teacher collaboration" (p. 2). It is up to school leaders to continue to support this democratic-participative process.

There are good reasons for doing so. As the findings of research indicate (and as we have pointed out elsewhere in this book), participative systems are more likely than autocratic systems to generate problem solutions. After the restructuring movement boosted participative decisions, some schools have given life to the concept. In fact, there is much that principals and teachers can do to make real progress. For example, faculty meetings should be devoted mainly to the improvement of the educational program. Teachers and principals should plan the agenda collaboratively. The meetings should not be dominated by the principal. None of these practices require additional resources. However, as Philip Jackson pointed out years ago, providing expert help for teachers (individual help and help in their collective curriculum pursuits) does cost money. "I see absolutely no hope for the future of inservice education," he wrote in 1971, "unless we are willing to pay for what we want" (p. 29). This requires a continuous and concerted program of collaborative work with teachers on problem solutions, with the provision of adequate released time, expertise, and material resources.

Supervisory Relationships. The supervisor-teacher relationship should be one of collegial collaboration, and the entire professional staff should function as a collegial team. In many schools supervision tends to be deficit oriented (fault finding). This inhibits curriculum improvement, because the teacher's own classroom concerns are ignored. Despite the fact that curriculum theorists have for decades advocated that curriculum improvement programs begin with problems identified by teachers, supervision continues to start—and often to end—by pointing out teachers' errors or shortcomings.

Formal Status and Right to Participate. One indication of successful schools is that the right to initiate and participate in curriculum work is not limited to administrators and supervisors. "In some schools," as Little (1982) has pointed out, "such rights are limited to principals, department chairs, and some influential teachers. In the more successful and adaptable schools, rights to initiate and participate are more widely distributed, rely less on formal position and are variable by situation" (p. 337).

Unfortunately, it is believed by many administrators and supervisors that most teachers lack the competence to make responsible curriculum decisions. Indeed, this view was reinforced in the 1986 Carnegie Forum on Education and the Economy report, *A Nation Prepared: Teachers for the 21st Century*. The report presented the concept of lead teachers: influential teachers in charge of identifying curriculum problems and the study and resolution of those problems. In the report, Mary Hatwood Futrell, a former president of the National Education Association, expressed "deep reservations" about this idea. "It suggests," she stated, "that some teachers are more equal than others. And it is not adequately differentiated from the flawed and failed merit pay and job ladder plans" (p. 117). She was right. This idea does not meet our needs in the 21st century—nor did it ever.

The notion that the rights of teachers to initiate collegial work be limited by their status is supported neither by research nor experience. A concrete illustration of the latter was the Denver Plan. The Denver curriculum program became the prototype for curriculum development in the 1920s. Although teacher participation in curriculum revision was not a new idea at the time, the Denver program had a new twist: substitute teachers were hired to free classroom teachers for curriculum development. A second new development, which was undoubtedly a factor in the success of the program, was that teachers had the ongoing help of many curriculum consultants.

These innovations are of superlative importance because they emerged from a new conception of the teacher as a professional. There can be little doubt that being treated as professionals by their administrative superiors had a positive impact on the Denver teachers who participated in curriculum revision and renewal. Hence, this treatment had a positive impact on curriculum improvement processes.

Levels of Curriculum Development

In most schools the teacher is presented with the curriculum as a fait accompli. What does it mean to improve the curriculum? How does the teacher proceed? Teachers need a guide to curriculum development that they can use to define their role. They need to see curriculum development as a total school enterprise and as a continual problem-solving process. It is with this need in mind that the levels of curriculum development are offered (see Table 16.1).

Table 16.1 Levels of Curriculum Development.

Level	Locus	Tasks and Activities	Principal Resources
Level I Imitative-maintenance	Microcurriculum Established conditions Segmental treatment Curriculum development as ad-hoc adoption of segmental practices (top-down)	Rudimentary Routine Adoptive Maintenance of established practice	Textbook, worksheets, workbook, syllabi (subject by subject), segmental adoption of curriculum packages, popular educational literature School principal
Level II Mediative	Microcurriculum Established conditions Segmental treatment Awareness of emergent conditions, aggregate treatment and macrocurriculum Curriculum development as adaptation (eclectic)	Interpretive Adaptive Adjustment of established practice	Textbook and resources beyond the textbook, courses of study (subject by subject with occasional correlation of subjects), multimedia, adaptation of segmental curriculum packages, professional literature on best practices Pupils, teacher colleagues, helping teacher, supervisor, curriculum coordinator, parents, community resources, school principal, inservice courses
Level III Generative-creative	Macrocurriculum Emergent conditions Aggregate treatment Curriculum development as problem-solving process (democratic-participative) Curriculum renewal Institutional renewal	Interpretive Adaptive Evaluative problem diagnosis problem solving Collaborative Improvement of established practice Search for best practices Renewal	Textbook and resources beyond the textbook, courses of study (across subjects and grade levels), alternative modes of curriculum design for knowledge synthesis and application, professional literature on research and best practices, multimedia, investigatory projects Pupils, teacher colleagues, helping teacher, supervisor, curriculum coordinator, parents, community resources, school principal, inservice courses, outside consultants, experimental programs, professional conferences and workshops

Teachers, administrators, schools, and school systems tend to function predominantly at one of three levels, as shown in Table 16.1: (I) imitative-maintenance, (II) mediative, and (III) generative-creative. Associated with each level are certain assumptions about what teaching is like and how teachers can best improve in their work. Teachers at Level I are concerned with curriculum maintenance, keeping the ship afloat, as it were. Principals are likewise concerned with maintaining a tight ship and maintaining the status quo. Teachers at Level II are aware that teaching should be more than routine management, but curriculum improvement tends to be viewed as refinement of established practice. Teachers at Level III have an imaginative vision of curriculum and are immersed in problem diagnosis and actions to meet emergent conditions. They use the best knowledge available as guides to action. The point of importance is that the levels do not constitute a sequence. It is not necessary to start at Level I to get to Level III. In fact, the very conditions for Level I will impede the possibilities; that is, one gets to Level III by instituting the conditions for Level III. Ends and means must be contiguous.

Level I: Imitative-Maintenance

Teachers operating at Level I rely on textbooks, worksheets, workbooks, and routine activities—subject by subject. Skills are treated as dead ends rather than as means of generating further learning. Ready-made materials are used without critical evaluation, resulting in a multiplicity of isolated skill-development activities. (The already segmental curriculum is further fragmented.) The imagination of the teacher does not go beyond maintaining the status quo. This teacher would like to think that one has less freedom than one may actually have for curriculum improvement. Teaching the test is common practice. In the secondary school, concern for curriculum development is largely confined to each departmental domain in isolation.

When change is made, it is made top down on the adoption level, without adaptation to local needs. As shown in Table 16.1, curriculum development at this level is plugging in the package to the existing situation without attention to the resulting interactions. Teachers at this level tend to be left alone to struggle with innovations that are handed to them or mandated from above. Schools are turned inward, with the principal as the sole resource for classroom assistance.

Level II: Mediative

Teachers at Level II are aware of the need to integrate the curriculum and deal with emergent conditions. (Societal problems such as the energy crisis and children's questions about the things that interest and concern them are examples of emergent conditions.) Although teachers at this level may have an aggregate conception of curriculum, implementation does not go beyond the occasional correlation of certain subjects. The locus of curriculum remains segmental; theory remains divorced from practice; curriculum improvement remains at the level of refining existing practice.

Teachers at Level II or mediative level of curriculum development do not blindly plug in an innovation or curriculum package to the existing situation. The necessary adaptations, accommodations, and adjustments are made (see Table 16.1). Teachers are aware of and capitalize on a range of resources for curriculum improvement, including pupils, parents, and peers, and they use resources beyond the local school. Teachers generally consume professional literature on best practices and tap the resources of the university through inservice courses. But the mediative level is a level of awareness and accommodation. Teachers are attracted to, and can articulate, new ideas, but their efforts to improve the curriculum fall short of the necessary reconstruction and commitment for substantive problem solving.

Level III: Creative-Generative

As shown in Table 16.1, teachers at Level III take an aggregate approach to curriculum development. Ideally, the curriculum is examined in its entirety by the teachers and the whole school staff, and questions of priority and relationship are asked. Although individual teachers should be at the generative-creative level, a macrocurricular approach requires democratic-participative planning for vertical and horizontal articulation.

Granted that teachers as individuals usually cannot create schoolwide curricula, an individual teacher can establish continuities and relationships in his or her own teaching and with other teachers. Teachers at Level III use generalizations and problems as centers of curriculum organization. They stress the broad concepts that specialized subjects share, and they use and develop courses of study that cross subject fields. These are aggregate treatments.

Teachers at Level III of curriculum development are problem solvers and try to find more effective ways of working, including the development of new best practices. They are able to diagnose emergent problems and formulate hypotheses for solutions. They experiment in emergent classrooms and communicate their insights to other teachers.

Teachers at this level consume research and seek greater responsibility for curriculum decisions at the school and classroom levels. They exercise independent judgment in selecting curriculum materials and transform them for local needs. They regard themselves as professionals and, as such, are continually involved in seeking problem solutions for the improvement of practice. To this end, their antennae are turned outward to a wide range of resources. Problems are seen as opportunities for curriculum renewal and school renewal.

Implications of the Levels

Although all teachers as professionals should be at Level III, most teachers and schools are probably at Levels I and II. However, one should not blame the teacher. As noted, in many schools teachers have been and continue to be treated as technicians. Equally distressing, many communities view teaching as managing on one's own with a closed door and minimal resources. The long hold of these old ideas is not yet broken. Relatively few school systems have ventured on the road to creating truly professional conditions for teachers. Most teachers are not provided with an office, secretarial help, or a place to meet except a classroom. "The old saying 'behind the classroom door' says it all," states Griffin, reminding us that beside the possible feeling of loneliness and isolation there is another problem: "What teachers do with their students . . . in fact, may be disconnected to what is happening behind other classroom doors in a school" (1999, p. 25).

Behind Closed Doors: Bane and Boon. The problem of resources has been discussed and will not be considered here, except to emphasize that superintendents must shift more central office resources to local schools. The decentralization of responsibility runs throughout most proposals for site-managed schools. As noted, such proposals are doomed to failure without accompanying resources. Closed doors can make teachers feel lonely, but they can be protectors of academic freedom. As mentioned, teachers have a greater degree of freedom than they often are willing

to acknowledge. Indeed, the public expects teachers to continually do a better job and be creative in their classrooms. What is important is that teachers capitalize on their autonomy to work more effectively and creatively behind the classroom door. In effect, teachers can transform their classroom isolation into conditions of professional autonomy and, at the same time, can work collaboratively and systematically on the improvement of schoolwide curriculum and instruction.

A Faulty Conception. Although inadequate resources is one reason for the large numbers of teachers at Level I, there is yet another more fundamental reason. Many teachers have an inadequate conception of what it means to improve the curriculum. Their stereotypical notion of curriculum improvement is producing courses of study. They do not understand that curriculum improvement necessitates much more than this. The levels of curriculum development in Table 16.1 provide a conceptual framework of the role of the teacher. Curriculum improvement rests on the ability of the teacher to make better decisions in diagnosing and solving problems and in implementing best practices.

Levels Not a Sequence. Students using previous editions of this book have asked the anthors why the levels of curriculum development are not a sequence. The question is not surprising, because students are often confronted with models of teacher growth that are stage theories. According to Kagan's model, for example, beginning teachers should focus on procedural routines, classroom management, and discipline. They should not be concerned with theoretical issues relating to curriculum improvement. These should be saved for later, "as novices' problem solving skills evolve" (1992, p. 155).

As Grossman (1992) points out, however, there is no evidence that beginning teachers are incapable of reflecting on issues related to curriculum and instruction. Indeed, they do so in good preservice teacher education programs. Then there is the developmental question itself. How can teachers reach Level III if they are expected to maintain the status quo? Grossman's insights about stage theories of teacher growth are very helpful here.

> An additional problem with stage theories is that they imply that earlier stages lead naturally to later stages. But there is no evidence that having developed classroom routines that work teachers will necessarily

begin to question those routines. In fact, there is evidence that suggests otherwise: As preservice teachers master the routines of teaching, many become satisfied with their teaching and less likely to question prevailing norms of teaching and learning. (p. 174)

If teachers are to improve the curriculum, they must be provided with opportunities to function at Level III from the very beginning. This is not a new idea, as pointed out earlier. John Dewey made the same observation in 1904, noting that teachers' ways of working without concern for educational principles become hardened into habit. From the beginning teachers should implement best practices. In this sense, teaching is no different from the practice of professions such as medicine, law, and engineering.

Best Practices

As shown in Table 16.1, a principal resource for teachers is the body of best practices in education. Best practices—those practices on which recognized authorities agree—are found in the literature of the field. Best practices may be research based or based on demonstrations of what works in the field. In effect, best practices are those that are powerfully and consistently supported in the professional literature (based on the best available evidence from research and practice over time). As an example, authorities in curriculum generally agree that because learning occurs through a wide variety of experiences, teachers must provide a wide variety of ways to learn. In many classrooms the teacher's repertoire of learning approaches is confined primarily to having pupils read the textbook and write and recite answers to questions about the textbook. Enriching and expanding this limited and limiting repertoire to include observation, participation, analysis, research, experimentation, problem solving, dramatization, and construction would be adopting a best practice in education.

A Generic (and Challenging) Concept

"I doubt whether we as educators keep in mind with sufficient constancy," wrote Dewey in 1904, "the fact that the problem of training teachers is one species of a more generic affair—that of training for professions" (p. 10). Our quest for professionalism, Dewey insisted, "is akin to that of training architects, engineers, doctors, lawyers, etc." Dewey suggested that teachers

try to determine "what they may learn from the more extensive and matured experience of other callings" (p. 10).

Taking Dewey's advice, we turn to what is happening in medicine. Medicine is a superb example of a field based on practices with evidence of effectiveness. A newspaper report is most interesting in this regard. Many hospitals inform their own doctors about guidelines for what are called best practices. One group of teaching hospitals—Mount Sinai NYU, Duke, Vanderbilt, Emory, Washington University, and Oregon Health Sciences—jointly owns a company, EBS Solutions of Nashville, that sells medical guidelines for health-plan doctors and members (Freudenheim, 2003, p. C3). The medical field is thus "presumably" moving toward "medical practices with clear evidence of effectiveness" (p. C3). Best practices are always in development and are a part of the development of practitioners. It is of interest that one of the largest health maintenance organizations published on its Web site guidelines developed and used by its doctors for treatment of many diseases "from asthma to visual impairment" (p. C3).

In education it is probably most important for parents and other members of the community to know that teachers are continually searching for and using better methods—those based on evidence. One best practice concerns motivation. Learning theorists tend to agree that the learner will persevere through obstacles and difficulties to the extent that he or she believes that the objectives and activities are worthwhile. Learning is dependent in no small way on whether the learner sees meaning and value in what he or she is doing. Thus, making certain that pupils understand why they are performing a given task and the practical significance of what they will learn from the school over a given period of time is a best practice.

The potential of best practices for curriculum improvement cannot be overestimated. Best practices are not necessarily new ideas on the educational scene. When a best practice, old or new, is adopted for the first time, it becomes in the truest sense an innovation. The best practices discussed here are merely illustrative. Teachers who want to follow the best-practices approach to curriculum improvement can feel hopeful; there is a surprising number of practices in the literature on which recognized authorities agree. Taken in context, best practices can be the seeds for school renewal.

The Application of Skills

One enormously important best practice concerns the application of skills. Experts in curriculum emphasize that the learner must be given a variety of opportunities to apply his or her skills. There is no mastery without intelligent application. In some elementary classrooms, reading consists of repetitive practice of word recognition skills followed by filling in blanks in workbooks or on worksheets. There is no opportunity for children to apply their skills in reading for pleasure or for information. Oddly, it is most often the poor reader (particularly in inner-city schools) who is taught reading as drill and skill and who rarely, if ever, gets a chance to apply skills in realistic situations. It is this learner who is least likely to be provided at home with opportunities to read for enjoyment. If the goal is children who are readers rather than children who can read, we must allow children to read. This seems almost too obvious to mention, but in many instances children are learning the mechanics of reading without reading for meaning. Little wonder that some children do not see the objective of learning to read as being enjoyable.

Being able to use the skill as a thinking process is the real objective. There is no reasonable expectation that learners will be able to use their skills unless they are provided with opportunities to apply them meaningfully in both established and new situations.

As Laura Zirbes, one of the pioneering women in the curriculum field, said: "When children ask, 'Why write?' it is not enough to say, 'You write to learn how to write'" (1959, p. 140). Nor is it enough to explain the value of writing or of any skill as something learners will find useful. Although verbal explanations are important for helping children to make sense out of the work of the school, they must be accompanied by real experience. Writing and reading are processes for thinking and communicating thought, and they must serve real purposes that are recognized by learners. The same applies to specific skills. Theorists have long pointed out also that a skill is learned when it is used. Moreover, the objective of having learners apply their skills is not to perfect the skill for its own sake. It cannot be overstated that the objective is to enable learners to use the skill for generative learning and to derive meaning and even to take pleasure in its use. Hence, reading and writing become processes for productive thinking.

The increasing press of standardized testing (particularly in reading) has caused a curriculum regression where the application of skills is concerned. Many teachers have been led (if not forced) to gear classroom events to the tests. In these classrooms, the functions of skills have become distorted; teachers and learners see skills as something to be mastered for testing purposes and not for learners' purposes.

Remember that Parker's methods in Quincy, Massachusetts, were based on the idea that skills must be applied to be mastered. Learning skills by using them has been a best practice in education since the infancy of the new education. From time to time, various influences have served to challenge this conception of skill development but it still remains a practice on which recognized authorities agree.

Idea-Oriented Teaching

Earlier it was mentioned that supervision of teachers tends to be error oriented rather than help oriented. Similarly, teachers tend to focus on pupils' errors rather than on ideas or concepts. One might say that teaching is error-skill oriented rather than constructive-idea oriented. Recognized authorities agree that teaching should be idea oriented rather than error oriented. As an illustration, teachers should read students' writing for ideas. What we examine when we read students' papers is students' thinking; the act of writing is the act of thought. What usually happens, however, is that the emphasis of evaluation is on students' grammatical errors and not on the quality of their thinking. It is small wonder that children and youth so often get the impression that their ideas are of secondary importance to their errors (or of no importance at all). Moreover, when evaluation is error oriented, students will restrict the style and substance of their writing to rudimentary safety. The opportunity to help students learn to examine their ideas critically is lost. (This does not mean that errors are to be ignored, but rather that they should be dealt with constructively and should not eclipse idea-oriented teaching.)

Inasmuch as the emphasis on errors does not improve and extend thinking processes, error-oriented teaching does not meet the demands of a democratic society. Furthermore, the negative emphasis of evaluation is likely to have negative results for motivation and perseverance. For these reasons, constructive-idea-oriented teaching has long been viewed by education theorists as a best practice in education.

Yet there are those who maintain that "[a]n idea-oriented curriculum places more of a burden on teachers" (Prawat, 1992, p. 388). This is true only if one regards professional responsibility as a burden. Moreover, idea-oriented teaching is more of a pleasure for the teacher. It is the teacher's pleasure in the excitement of ideas that arouses the interest of students. This interest in turn spurs the teacher on. Error-oriented teaching, however, makes students apathetic and has a depressing effect on the teacher. It is then that teaching becomes a burden.

Ecological Interaction

The curriculum must be dealt with in its ecological interaction. In designing curricula, we must take into account the interaction of the elements instead of the elements in isolation. What needs to be considered in curriculum improvement is the relationship of the parts to the whole. This is an enormously important best practice in education. Unfortunately, it is recommended rather than practiced. Education tends to be focused on the microcurriculum rather than the macrocurriculum.

Operationally, what this best practice means is that in revising one element of the curriculum, we need to take into consideration the effects on other elements of the curriculum. There must be an ecological relationship among the elements. What, for example, is the relationship of a new social studies program to literature and other elements of the curriculum? What is the relation of a new physics program to the mathematics program? The ecological relationship of the curriculum reforms in physics to the mathematics program was virtually ignored by educators in the 1960s, and with calamitous results. Many physics students did not have the mathematical skills and concepts that the new course in physics required.

Obviously, little or no interaction of the elements of the curricular ecosystem is evidence of curriculum fragmentation. What is even worse, there may be conflict between or among elements as in the foregoing case of physics and mathematics. The point is that the ecological relationship of curricular elements must be subjected to continual reappraisal.

The interaction of the elements of the curriculum with one another and the macrocurriculum is, in a sense, analogous to the interaction of organisms with one another and with the environment. However, there is a crucial difference. Growth and change is a law of nature but not of the curriculum as it is treated in the traditional school. Growth (improvement) in the curriculum requires an organic interaction of elements in a context of a coherent design. The design or structure of the curriculum determines its function. Consequently, curriculum integration requires a holistic design and structure as opposed to the traditionally segmental-compartmental subjects.

Involving Learners in Curriculum Planning

In a proposal for the middle school curriculum, Beane (1991) writes of a "new vision" that "begins with two kinds of questions and concerns: those that early adolescents have about themselves and their world and those that are widely shared by people in the larger world" (p. 11). The practice of students and their teacher cooperatively formulating problem areas to be studied during a semester or school year is deeply rooted in progressivist philosophy. The progressives argued that the problems identified by adolescents are of universal significance and, further, that adolescents must be given opportunities to examine societal problems with a view toward their constructive solution while they are still in school.

The progressives also insisted that social attitudes and personal development are inseparable from cognitive development. They stressed that learning is most effective when students are interested in what they are doing and when they understand the significance of what they are supposed to be learning. These ideas formed the basis for one type of core curriculum (see chapter 10). Moreover, as Beane points out, students' concerns about the environment, interdependence, poverty, war, racism, and other world problems offer enormous opportunities for curriculum integration.

Elementary school teachers have long been vigorous proponents of student participation in planning. The fact that they have remained so despite conservative criticism attests to their conviction that the practice is well founded. Obviously students can participate in goal setting (planning activities, projects, and schedules) even when curriculum content is prescribed and courses are required. Such participation is important for all students. Everyone needs to feel that they are part of the classroom community and that their thoughts matter.

For Hispanic students, a group with the lowest achievement and highest dropout rate, this may be crucial. According to Padrón, Waxman, and Rivera

(2002), it is important to give Hispanic students "the opportunity to participate in the development of classroom activities" (p. 77). For one thing, they need assurance "that they are important and that they can make important contributions to society," and, for another, conversation for these students is "an important principle of second language learning" (p. 77). What Padrón, Waxman, and Rivera argue really makes sense. When students get the impression that teachers are not interested in their thoughts, they lose the opportunity for the kind of classroom discussion that helps them to learn new concepts.

Access to the Curriculum

A tradition in American society is the seeking of equal opportunities to achieve. Nothing in the history of education is more impressive than the enthusiasm with which educators have taken up this challenge. Unfortunately, however, some curricular arrangements in the name of equalizing opportunity have had just the opposite effect. Schools in economically and socially disadvantaged communities tend to teach children mechanistically via a drill-skill-rote repertoire. On the other hand, children from more advantaged sectors of society often work on tasks and problems of genuine interest. Brookover and colleagues said it all: "The maximization of individual differences and the differentiation of educational programs are commonly advocated without regard to the effect of such education on the social structure or the opportunities for social mobility," and "[t]hese programs and policies do not recognize that equality of opportunity is not facilitated by highly differentiated programs based upon the presumed differences between lower-class and middle-class children" (Brookover, Gigliotti, Henderson, Niles, & Schneider, 1974, p. 162).

Creating Opportunities.   Integrated public schools and heterogeneously grouped classrooms are crucial in creating opportunities for poor children and others at risk for school failure. As a general rule, children with special needs should not leave their classroom for remedial help. As teachers can well testify, pull-out programs fragment children's learning experiences. This, plus the fact that pull-out programs are no more effective than providing such help in the classroom, is a good reason for eliminating such programs. A best practice for helping special-needs children is described as follows in the words of two teachers: The remediation specialist "moves from class to class assisting individuals

and working with small groups of students on skills within the classroom context" (Boles & Troen, 1992, p. 54). Teachers should, of course, also offer extra help to a student having difficulties and enlist students to help one another so as to create a cooperative classroom learning environment.

The Extra-Help Puzzle.   All sorts of ways have been thought of to provide students who fall behind the class with special help. Saturday sessions and after-school programs can help students make up work and settle some misunderstandings about assignments. But, as Balfanz, Ruby, and MacIver (2002) point out, they are not a total answer to the special-help problem. Some of the teachers may not know the students well, and some programs cannot accommodate all of the students who would attend. Nor is summer school an answer. It may help students meet requirements but "tends to be organized around a 'one-size-fits-all' model" (p. 138).

Help given students needs to be tied to the student's ongoing classroom work. Thus as Balfanz, Ruby, and MacIver state: "The missing piece in the extra help puzzle is finding a way to offer sustained, systematic, and differentiated high quality extra help to students *during the school day*" (p. 139). Schools need to find creative ways to do so. Smaller classes are one way, as discussed earlier. The idea always to keep in mind is that the extra help must be "linked to the student's regular classroom instruction" (p. 139). We would simply call it part of the student's classroom experience. (It is simply a means of personalizing or individualizing the learning experience.)

The Importance of Appropriate Interventions. In recent years the media have portrayed some children as doomed to school failure (and life failure), no matter how schools might try to intervene. Included in this group are children with prenatal exposure to cocaine and other drugs. According to Stevens and Price, "These children have been described as a biological underclass, a lost generation. Yet many children exposed prenatally to cocaine who receive appropriate interventions can score as well on measures of global development as their nonexposed peers" (1992, p. 19). Like all children, youngsters exposed to potentially damaging conditions vary in abilities and needs.

Curricular implications go well beyond the immediate problems of affected and abused children. As Stevens and Price point out, generations to come must be protected from the damaging effects of prenatal exposure to drugs (including alcohol). Given the increase in teenage pregnancy, in combination with drug use and heavy drinking, this challenge is enormous. According to Stevens and Price, these conditions "suggest that instruction on the effects of prenatal exposure to drugs and alcohol should be included in existing drug and alcohol curricula and in sex education and family life education" (p. 20). The curriculum is both a potential path to opportunity for all and a key to the solution of many of society's most critical problems.

Curriculum Improvement as Inquiry

The findings of research are a source for curriculum improvement. The teacher may be involved in classroom research or as consumer of research. Awareness of a classroom problem and application of research findings for the solution is a form of inquiry. What is being discussed here is the involvement of teachers in the diagnosis of problems and in classroom research to bring about curriculum improvement. Although the purpose of such involvement is to help teachers improve their own practices, research findings from classroom experimentation can contribute to theoretical knowledge about the curriculum. Taba (1962) was an unflagging exponent of this position.

Teacher Research

Recently there has been much interest in teachers contributing to the body of knowledge on teaching. This is not a new idea. The action-research movement of the 1950s was based on the idea that teachers should conduct their own investigations into their own problems. Like many pedagogical fads, the action-research movement swept various practical considerations aside in its all-encompassing fervor. The democratic ideal of equality was applied to conducting research under the premise that every member of the school faculty should be involved in classroom experimentation. Moreover, frequently the research was conducted without the help of consultants and statisticians. Understandably, action research in education became identified with research of poor quality. But the idea that teachers can improve the curriculum by investigating their classroom problems never left the literature. Good staff-development programs sought to provide teachers with opportunities to do so.

Recent interest in the teacher as a researcher began in the late 1980s. One can trace its roots to the restructuring movement, which involved teachers as decision makers, and to the idea of teacher leadership in school change. The name is different from the 1950s movement: "teacher research" instead of "action research." More importantly, the concept is broader than the 1950s movement. According to Cochran-Smith and Lytle (1999), "the concept of teacher research carries with it an enlarged view of the teacher's role—as decision-maker, consultant, curriculum developer, analyst, activist, school leader—as well as understanding the contexts of educational change" (p. 19).

In the 1990s, the teacher research movement saw itself as a kind of social-change movement. Among some leaders of the teacher research movement, "doing education" took a back seat to "critiquing school and societal contexts of education" (Hollingsworth & Sockett, 1994, p. 9). Its effectiveness was diluted. In their retrospective of the movement a decade after its inception, Cochran-Smith and Lytle wrote, "it is in danger of becoming anything and everything. As we know, however, anything and everything often lead in the end to nothing of consequence or power" (p. 17).

Our concern here is with the original and powerful idea behind the teacher as a researcher: curriculum improvement in one's own school or classroom. The requirements for teacher research are no different from those for any reputable research. Teachers can find the steps and methods in any educational research textbook. One point is of the essence: Unless research is done rigorously, it is useless.

Teacher Research as an Individual Activity. According to Smylie, Conley, and Marks (2002), teacher research has been mainly viewed as an individual endeavor directed toward teachers' professional improvement. How much of it is actually happening? As Richardson (1994b) points out, since it is not usually published or presented at scholarly meetings we do not know. Yet, along with Richardson, we do not doubt for a moment that it is going on. Occasionally, one reads about a teacher's work in an article or hears about it at a conference.

To view teacher research as simply a professional improvement activity is to sell it short. Teachers' practical investigations into their classroom work can provide new questions for university researchers (who, we might add, can inform their students on the best that is known).

Teacher Research as a Collaborative Activity. The individual teacher may seek to solve a problem or to improve practice by searching the research literature and even by conducting an individual inquiry, such as surveying pupil attitudes toward reading materials. The school faculty or the school system may undertake research on a wider scale, such as pilot testing a new curriculum project. In each of these instances, the function of the research is curriculum development in a contextual setting, in contrast to other kinds of educational research, which may be removed from action or application. Although it may be argued that the purpose of theoretical educational research is the improvement of classroom and school practices, prescriptive theories and models derived from educational research need to be tested in the practical setting. Educational research has, on the whole, failed to concern itself with teachers' classroom concerns. In studying the literature of educational research, it quickly becomes clear that researchers have not been concerned with problems relating to curriculum reconstruction. Where research on curriculum design is concerned, the literature is as dry as the Sahara. Since the Eight-Year Study and the research on activity schools, stemming back to the 1930s, there have been virtually no landmark studies on curriculum reconstruction.

Certainly, as some university researchers pointed out decades ago, there is a need to redirect education research so that the problems identified by practitioners are investigated (Dunkel, Gowin, & Thomas, 1972). Conditions have changed. Teachers are no longer waiting for Godot and are beginning to inquire into their own problems. Even should such a redirection occur, teachers would still need to be involved in putting theoretical principles to the test and in finding solutions to their own practical problems. University researchers are beginning to realize that effective teachers are engaged in practical inquiry and that such inquiry is indeed powerful in effecting improved classroom practice and school improvement, as compared with university-based research that is removed from the practical world of the school (Richardson, 1994a).

The involvement of both worlds would be ideal. Such a model is available and has been tested, with promising results. Two examples are given here. In the first example, five schools collaborated with a team of university researchers. Teachers and administrators together identified problems in their schools and the university researchers collected and analyzed the data. Clift, Veal, Holland, Johnson, and McCarthy (1995), who conducted the study of this collaborative school improvement project, found that the evidence that was collected resulted in new plans for school improvement. The larger effect of this project was probably more important: Clift and her colleagues found that the project contributed to teachers' strong sense of ability to deal effectively with problems in their schools.

In the second example a researcher, a staff developer, and a group of teachers in one school collaboratively identified a school problem, conducted research on the problem, and carried out a staff development program to address it. According to Tikunoff, Ward, and Griffin (1979), this process eventuated in substantial change in teachers' practices schoolwide. Both models point to the importance of involving university researchers in teacher research, not just from the standpoint of research design and data collection but, as noted above, because such studies can lead to new problems to investigate, and both models, particularly the first one, point to the need for university researchers to concern themselves with teachers' classroom concerns.

Supporting Teachers' Research Efforts. Having established the need for teacher research we turn our attention to how teachers can be supported in their research efforts. Research cannot simply be added to teachers' responsibilities. The importance of this problem goes without saying. Some school districts have created positions that include both teaching and research responsibilities, such as teacher-consultants, lead teachers, and peer supervisors. Some other proposals to make it more possible for teachers to conduct systematic inquiry are financial support for research projects, load reduction, released time, research teams, and summer workshops. In truth, one of the most important factors of all is whether school systems view teacher research as valuable. In 1990 Cochran-Smith and Lytle wrote: "This new approach will come about if schools and school systems realize that there is a direct connection between supporting the systematic inquiries of teacher-researchers and improving the quality of teaching and learning" (p. 9). Today, the connection is becoming increasingly clear.

Local Curriculum Development Programs

In the early 2000s, curriculum development at the school district level was, to put it mildly, in a quiescent stage. The emphasis was on testing as a means of raising achievement. The need to keep all parts of the curriculum vibrantly in balance was forgotten as personnel scrambled to meet federal requirements and avoid sanctions. But it was becoming increasingly clear, as revealed in the foregoing section, that addressing classroom problems is more likely to improve student achievement than the dominant policy of testing to raise achievement.

The teacher's role is pivotal in problem identification and solution at the classroom and school levels. But teachers also have a role in local curriculum development projects. By *local* is meant the school district level. However, many of the ideas that follow are applicable to curriculum development in individual schools.

The Gold Standard for Involvement: The Denver Plan

Teacher participation in curriculum development represents one of the oldest principles in curriculum theory. As mentioned earlier, an example from the 1920s that simply sparkles has much to teach us about today. The so-called Denver Plan for involving teachers in curriculum making was the brainchild of superintendent Jesse Newlon. It is of interest that Newlon's plan was initiated in 1922, and in 1925 he was elected president of the National Education Association. A year or so later teacher participation was a key feature in the model developed by the Rugg committee (see chapter 14).

Not only was Newlon's plan an advance in his time, but in many respects it would be in our own. To begin with, it is a systematic approach. As Weingarten (2003) points out, today many districts lack a systematic approach. According to Weingarten, who as president of a large local teachers' union has spent much time in schools, teachers at every level report an abundance of mandates and consequences for failure. "Over and over again these same teachers complained of what wasn't there—a curriculum," Weingarten concluded (p. 28). External testing and mandates had taken their toll.

Certainly, many districts have had a plan for curriculum development. It may have been put on hold, or even forgotten, in the rush to meet mandates. Meanwhile, teachers lack guides in a form that they can use or suggestions for instructional approaches. Actually, this has been a problem since the early 1990s. Before the standards-based reforms of the early 2000s, there was a predecessor movement, known as

the restructuring movement. The emphasis was on curriculum review and administrative reorganization at the local school level. In many districts publication of guides ceased and schools were denied professional assistance and material resources under the convenient rationale that each local school should have autonomy: be its own ship on its own bottom. Thus district-level curriculum development has had a setback from two successive movements—restructuring and standards-based education—each with a quite different rationale.

Of considerable interest in this regard is a recent Phi Delta Kappa/Gallup Poll of the attitudes of the public toward the public schools (Rose & Gallup, 2003). When asked who should have the most influence in deciding what is taught in the public schools: the federal government, the state government, or the local school board, a clear majority (61%) selected the local school board. (Twenty-two percent chose the state level.) The district's responsibility for developing a systematic procedure is clear.

In the same poll, 77% of public school parents were concerned that depending on testing in English and math to judge a school "will mean less emphasis on art, music, history, and other subjects" (p. 46). As Goodlad found in his research (see chapter 3), parents want more, not less in the way of curriculum and they want it in balance.

A master plan for curriculum development should embody the principle of curriculum balance and articulation. Newlon's plan met these criteria. The Denver Plan was based on the organization of two types of committees, subject matter committees and central organization committees. There were three sets of subject matter committees, one for the elementary schools, one for the junior high schools, and one for the senior high schools. Subject matter committees were composed of classroom teachers only. Central organization committees were composed of administrators and were concerned with such problems as graduation requirements, organization of curricula into major and minors, experimentation, and innovation.

The subject matter committees developed not only courses of study but also the macrocurriculum in general education. The course guides were published as part of the Denver Research Monograph Series. Not surprisingly, thousands of these course guides were sold to school systems throughout the United States. (This also happened to the teacher-developed syllabi published by the Winnetka Public Schools in the 1920s. They were snapped up as soon as they were available.)

Experimentation.   Curriculum experimentation was an important part of the Denver curriculum program. Proposed courses of study were tested experimentally, and one elementary school was designated "the curriculum school." This was consistent with Newlon's conviction that there should be centers of experimentation in every school system.

The Teacher as a Professional.   Newlon had a deep and abiding faith in the teacher as a professional. Because of this confidence and because he believed that the study of curriculum problems was the best kind of staff development, Newlon put teachers at the heart of the curriculum development process. This was revolutionary at a time when teachers usually were not looked upon as being well versed in teaching, not to mention the writing of courses of study. In most city systems prior to 1920, the staff development programs consisted largely of demonstrations of teaching conducted by supervisors. Teachers were expected to follow the course of study to the letter, not to write it. (This is similar to the scripted lessons in some urban school systems today, as revealed in an earlier discussion in this book.) Newlon's high regard for teachers, as shown by the professional responsibilities he delegated to them, did much to improve the image of the teacher in school systems throughout the nation.

Released Time.   Newlon's curriculum program was well funded by his board, and teachers were freed from their classroom responsibilities, sometimes for days at a time, while they were so engaged. Other school systems, caught by the contagion of Newlon's enthusiasm for the program, tried curriculum revision by teacher committees. Often, the results were disappointing. Puzzled and disappointed, the other superintendents failed to realize that there was at least one significant difference between their program and Newlon's. They either expected teachers to do the work after school or freed only one committee member, and only then for writing the course of study.

Extent of Teacher Involvement: Newlon's Proviso.   It is all too easy to overstate the extent of teacher involvement in curriculum making in Denver. In instances where field-tested textbooks and syllabi already were available, teachers did not write another course of study. (However, in some cities teachers wrote courses of study that did not even begin to measure up to existing textbooks and syllabi.) Having teachers write a course of study for every subject was as senseless

as keeping them entirely out of the process of course development. The problem was summed up this way by Newlon and assistant superintendent Archie Threlkeld:

> The policy of delegating entirely to teachers the making of curricula would be as fallacious as was the policy of leaving the teachers entirely out of this process, and would likewise fail to take account of the indispensable contribution that must be made by research and by specialists who, by devoting their lives to the study of teaching in particular subjects, become authorities in their fields. (1927, p. 240)

A Modern Prototype: Teacher-Instigated Curriculum Development in New York City

"By defining these educational results as clearly as possible," wrote Ralph Tyler in 1949, "the curriculum-maker has the most useful set of criteria for selecting content, for suggesting learning activities, for deciding on the kind of teaching procedures to follow, in fact to carry on all the further steps of curriculum planning" (p. 6). In the late 1990s and early 2000s school districts developed standards for student performance. This is the first area of Tyler's rationale for curriculum and instruction: the formulation of goals and objectives. Much less attention has been paid to curriculum content and the organization of learning activities. Schools have jumped from the first area of the rationale to the fourth: evaluation. Improving student learning is dependent not just on standards for student performance, not just on tests, but equally on the content, learning activities, and instructional procedures suggested by the standards. Objectives and tests do not a curriculum make.

By the early 2000s this had become apparent. The lack of a curriculum has serious implications for teacher retention as has become clear in New York City and other districts. An American Federation of Teachers report, *Making Standards Matter 2001*, concluded that the curriculum problem was general—in all 50 states. Summing up the findings, Randi Weingarten, president of the United Federation of Teachers in New York City, wrote that there was

> no comprehensive curriculum aligned with the standards and assessments in. . . . English language arts, math, science, and social studies . . . no grade by grade continuum of knowledge. . . . There were no guides organized in a format that teachers could

use, with information about specific content, instructional strategies, texts and additional resources. There were no collections of model lesson plans or units. (2003, p. 28)

As she noted, teachers should have models which they can adapt and modify to meet students' individual needs.

In 1999, the United Federation of Teachers (UFT), in collaboration with the school district, embarked on curriculum development. They began by talking with teachers who said that in addition to grade-by-grade knowledge, the curriculum ought to include sample lessons, suggested resources, and "a guide on how to teach the material, especially to diverse groups of students" (p. 30). Of crucial importance was the following:

> The curriculum should allow teachers to use their *professional judgment* regarding *instructional choices* and be linked to meaningful, embedded professional development. And it should be widely available. (p. 30)

Unlike the Denver Plan, curriculum development in the UFT project is on a K–12 basis to foster continuity and, unlike the Denver Plan, curriculum development was instigated by teachers rather than an enlightened, forward-looking superintendent. The New York City school system has been strongly supportive of teachers stepping in to develop the curriculum. As in Denver so many years ago, teachers do the curriculum writing.

The Curriculum. By 2003, teacher curriculum-developers in the UFT project had completed a K–12 curriculum in English language arts and one was nearing completion in mathematics. Other curriculum areas including science, social studies, the arts and foreign languages, "and even physical education" (p. 30) will follow. If done right, curriculum development is extremely arduous work. Each unit of study went through many drafts (10 on average), exacting peer review, and field testing. The union's idea was to provide guidance—to identify what should be taught, not to script teachers in teacher-proof fashion. Teachers need ideas and suggestions. Professional autonomy can never substitute for ideas. Both are needed. In the course of developing the curriculum, the name underwent a transformation from core curriculum to resource curriculum, which makes this point exactly. The resource curriculum consists of daily lessons which, of course, may take more than

one day depending on the teacher's judgment. The writers discuss teaching strategies that they and other teachers have found effective.

Daily lessons are combined to form a unit. Included in the curriculum guides are resources for three model units for each grade, sufficient to provide teachers with a good foundation for developing additional successive units by themselves or with colleagues. Each unit has a section where the teacher-writers offer their reflections and a rationale for how the lesson was presented. These sections, as Weingarten points out, "should inspire deep professional conversations" (p. 31) about ways to teach for effective learning. Thus teaching becomes the intellectual adventure it should be.

Just as with the Winnetka and Denver curricula, the New York curriculum has been in demand. Copies have been requested by teachers and principals across the nation and in England. At this writing it was available in print and CD-ROM.

The foregoing discussion allows us to see the value of teachers' involvement in curriculum making, both for themselves as well as students and other teachers. It is a resource that has been too long ignored by too many school systems.

Perspective

To function adequately as a professional, one must feel prepared to do so. Unfortunately, as revealed by a U.S. Department of Education study, American teachers do not feel very well prepared to improve the curriculum. One does not have to look far to find reasons for this lack of self-confidence, starting with the school district level. Before the mid-1990s most school districts had a master plan for curriculum development that involved the production of guides by teacher committees and consultants. Under the mantra of school restructuring, many school districts abruptly ceased this activity, leaving it to the local school. Then came standards-based reform in the late 1990s and early 2000s. The push to raise student achievement focused on two of the areas in curriculum development: objectives (standards) and evaluation (tests). Standards and tests do not a curriculum make.

Curriculum development should be carried out by the professional staff (including teachers) under the leadership of the superintendent. An early and excellent model, described in this chapter, was the brainchild of Denver's school superintendent, Jesse Newlon.

An issue with standards-based reform is that it has mitigated curriculum synthesis. It has made it less possible to address the macrocurriculum to "see the curriculum whole," which as Cremin pointed out is absolutely essential. Standards-based reforms rivet attention on one subject field at a time. Curriculum integration is not a concern in standards-based reform. Yet the connections must be made because they are real and a part of learning and life.

Achievement is higher in schools with a strong professional community, where teachers collaborate and learn from each other. Professional relationships in the school and the sharing of ideas about practice support individual efforts to improve the curriculum.

Feeling prepared begins, of course, with preservice teacher education. According to Dewey, the focus of student teaching should be on developing thoughtful and alert teachers who make decisions based on educational principles, rather than on turning out teachers who are as proficient as possible in immediate, practical skill. When student teachers and beginning teachers make explicit the reasons (based on the best available evidence) for their various pedagogical decisions, they are establishing habits of referring to educational principles. Whether one is a teacher or a physician, one must make decisions based on the principles in one's field from the start. Early habits become the behaviors of a professional lifetime. A good cooperating teacher functioning at Level III can help novices engage in reflective self-criticism without feeling threatened.

Teachers and administrators tend to function predominantly at one of three levels of curriculum development. At Level I (imitative-maintenance), the teacher or administrator mechanically performs established procedures and the objective is maintenance—keeping the ship afloat. Change (when it occurs) is a matter of plugging in the curriculum package to the existing situation. The curriculum is treated as segments and fragments. Teachers at Level II (meditative) are aware that teaching should be more than routine management and that there is a macrocurriculum, but improvement tends to be a matter of refining existing practice. Innovations are adapted rather than merely adopted. The teacher at Level III (generative-creative) conceives of the curriculum as an articulated whole and acts on this conception. Improvement of practice is actively sought by drawing on resources beyond the local school and school system. Imagination, artistry, awareness, and the testing of ideas are some qualities of the generative-creative level. All teachers and

schools should be functioning at this level for school renewal. But the levels of curriculum development are not a sequence; that is, one does not become creative by first being imitative.

The findings of the best available research are a source for curriculum development. A teacher may be involved in classroom research, but all teachers must be an intelligent consumer of research. In practical inquiry, the teacher is aware of a classroom problem, draws from the research literature, or even conducts an investigation to solve the problem. Thoughtful teachers are continually engaged in the diagnosis of problems and in classroom inquiry to bring about curriculum improvement. Important theoretical ideas grow out of and feed into practical problem situations. It behooves university researchers to recognize this and to connect their work to curriculum improvement.

Teachers should draw from research as they choose their methods and practices. Knowing how to engage in systematic inquiry can help teachers be knowledgeable consumers of research. By undertaking practical inquiry, teachers can improve individual practice. Good school systems support teachers' research efforts through grants, load reduction, released time, and the like.

Teachers who want to improve the curriculum will find a wide range of best practices in the education literature; there is a surprising number of practices on which recognized authorities agree. Providing learners with opportunity to apply skills in a variety of meaningful situations is one best practice. Another is involving learners in curriculum planning. For example, adolescents and their teacher can cooperatively formulate societal problem areas to be studied, and learning activities for engagement during a semester.

Best practices help teachers make informed decisions about instructional strategies. (A body of best practices is the hallmark of a profession.)

Mandates and test upon test—and the fear of sanctions—have caused many school systems to forget their master plans for curriculum development. But curriculum development is, as it always has been, a problem-solving process in which all school subjects are seen and treated in vital interdependence. A recent Phi Delta Kappa/Gallup Poll revealed the public's concern that the present emphasis on one or two subjects will result in neglect of other areas. The concern is well placed. One cannot compensate for a poor curriculum in science by having a strong curriculum in mathematics, or for a poor curriculum in literature by having a strong curriculum in social studies. School systems and individual schools must provide for continuity in curriculum-improvement efforts. Records must be kept and be readily accessible so that they may be drawn on in inquiry into current problems. Those who went before us taught us these things: The process of curriculum improvement must be inclusive—involving the concerted work of administrators, teachers, supervisors, students, and community members. It must be based on the best available knowledge. And it must be continuously building on previous work. (Refer to the Best Practices Checklist on pages 481–499.)

PROBLEMS FOR STUDY AND DISCUSSION

1. Two models of teacher involvement at the district level were discussed in this chapter. Which is the most promising road to curriculum improvement? Why?

2. Describe the curriculum development process in your own school district. To what extent are teachers involved? Does the plan reflect concern for curriculum balance? Explain.

3. Based on your study and experience, what changes would you propose in preservice teacher education to increase teachers' feelings of preparedness to implement state or district curriculum standards?

4. Some educators contend that preservice teachers should be concerned only with establishing the routines of teaching; that connecting educational principles to one's practice can be left for later professional development. [Kagan, D. M. (1992). Professional growth among preservice and beginning teachers. *Review of Educational Research, 62,* 129–169.] What is your assessment of this position?

5. According to Dewey, student teachers should connect their practices with theoretical principles in education. [Dewey, J. (1904). The relation of theory to practice in education. In C. A. McMurry (Ed.), *The relation of theory to practice in the education of teachers* (Third Yearbook of the National Society for the Scientific Study of Education, Part I, pp. 9–30). Chicago: University of Chicago Press.] How does Dewey's conception of professional growth contrast with that of Kagan's model cited in problem 4? What are the implications of these contrasting views for the teacher's curriculum improvement role?

6. In your opinion, what is the role of the cooperating teacher in helping student teachers operate at the generative-creative level?

7. In this chapter it was pointed out that teachers must have the resources they need if they are to function at the generative-creative level of curriculum development. Survey the teachers in a local school to ascertain what resources they have for curriculum development. Are their resources adequate? Explain. Use the teachers' responses and Table 16.1 in framing your answer.

8. Examine the curriculum development efforts of a school district or school. What strategies are used in curriculum development? To what extent is curriculum development being treated merely as the writing of courses of study? What changes would you make to improve the process? (Frame your responses with reference to the levels of curriculum development in Table 16.1.) At which level of curriculum development is the district or school functioning? Explain.

9. As discussed in this chapter, doctors are told by teaching hospitals about best practices, thus learning about what is the best care. Similarly, preservice teachers and school staffs discuss best practices in education. But some teacher educators see best practices as limiting teacher autonomy. According to Cochran-Smith and Lytle, for example, "the concept of best practice . . . de-emphasizes the role of the teacher as a decision maker" (1999, p. 22). Do you agree? Support your answer.

CHAPTER 17

CURRICULUM IMPROVEMENT
ADMINISTRATIVE LEADERSHIP

Teaching and learning are the core of the administrator's work. By administrator we are including the principal, who is close to the school; the general superintendent, who has the responsibility for the entire school district; and the supervisor, who moves around from school to school. Not one of these individuals works alone. Each works with and through others. The principal, for example, shares the tasks involved in curriculum improvement with other leaders in the school (department heads in the secondary school, for instance). Today, models of distributive leadership tend to view leadership in terms of performing key functions rather than the work of individuals who hold formal positions in the organization (Smylie, Conley & Marks, 2002). The best organizational theory holds that one does not begin with the formal administrative position; one begins with the work to be done. What is called for is an *ecologized* or *organic*—as opposed to a *mechanistic*—form of organization (Tanner & Tanner, 1987, pp. 121–161). As Smylie, Conley, and Marks put it, "it is more important that the work be done well than that it be performed by a particular individual" (2002, p. 172). The team perspective is characteristic of organic forms of organization, which lend themselves more readily to solving curriculum problems (including the effective implementation of best practices) than do mechanistic forms. As shown in Figure 17.1, the professional team model is focused holistically on the major function of the school: the education of students.

Leadership at the School and District Levels

In recent years, many teachers have become the equals of their principals where curriculum knowledge is concerned. Some teachers may be even more knowledgeable with regard to the curriculum. Leadership responsibilities involving curriculum development are often performed by teachers. Indeed, researchers have found that they are well performed (Heller & Firestone, 1995).

That said, it is the principal's job to lead. In order to meet the school's leadership needs, the principal has to know curriculum: the principles and practices of curriculum improvement. In addition to coursework in curriculum development, educational administration preservice programs should provide an internship where preservice students can apply the understandings from their coursework in addressing real problems. Such problems may result from state and national policies and issues (Pounder, Reitzug & Young, 2002). An example is the identification of successful strategies for curriculum design, evaluation, and renewal.

There have been changes—welcome, we might add—in the view of the superintendent's position. As Brunner, Grogan, and Björk (2002) note, the words in the literature on leadership tell the story. "Leadership in the superintendency, in particular, is now associated with words such as collaboration, community, cooperation, teams, and relationship-building," whereas leadership previously was expressed with words such as "control, power, authority and management" (p. 226). The reason for the switch, as Brunner, Grogan, and Björk point out, is a "renewed focus on instruction" (p. 226). Improving instruction is once again at the top of the superintendent's to-do list.

But historical comparisons are fraught with pitfalls. Granted that instruction is once again the focus, it is a different kind of focus from past efforts by superintendents to improve the educational program. Superintendents in earlier times were concerned with the total balanced curriculum, including such fields as

Figure 17.1 The Professional Team in the School System: An Organic Model.

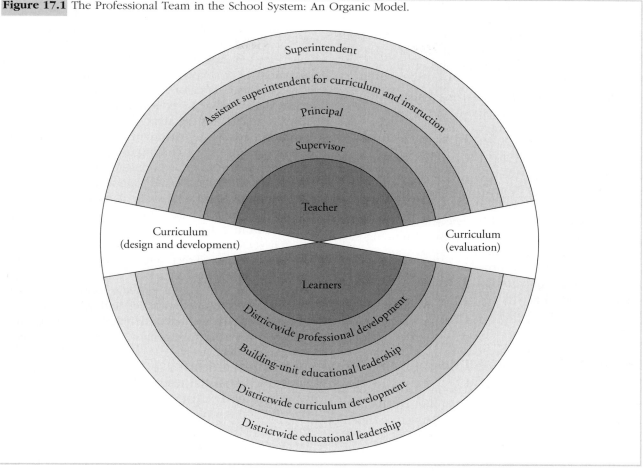

Source: Daniel Tanner and Laurel Tanner. *Supervision in Education: Problems and Practices.* New York: Macmillan, 1987, p. 74.

art, music, and vocational education. This was due in no small way to the fact that states gave aid and supervision to those fields. State policies fostered a balanced curriculum. In recent years political-minded state policies and federal priorities have worked against a balanced comprehensive curriculum. Today, many local school districts lack the stimulus to experiment with new curriculum ventures, confined as they are (perhaps more psychologically than in reality) by the fear of sanctions by state and federal government, should students not fare well on high-stakes tests.

Thus there are inadequacies in the present focus on instruction. The next step is attention to building the entire educational program, which is what the public wants (see chapter 15), is in accord with curriculum principles, and—last, but not least—which is the best way to achieve the loyalty and support of the community.

The Need for Expertise

As superintendents found out long ago, the distribution of leadership is not an option; it is a necessity. As populations burgeoned in the cities, superintendents were often responsible for thousands of children and hundreds of teachers. Curriculum development was placed in the hands of specialists. Titles such as curriculum director, assistant superintendent for instruction, director of elementary education, director of secondary education appeared on doors in the district office. But distributing leadership did not diminish the superintendent's instructional leadership role. In the words of Brunner, Grogan, and Björk, "instruction was uppermost in the mind of the superintendent, whose energies went into the support and facilitation of others' work" (2002, p. 234).

An outcome of the need for leadership at the district level was the development of curriculum as a field of study. According to the historian Lawrence A. Cremin (1971), this development can be traced to the famous program of curriculum revision that superintendent Jesse Newlon introduced in Denver in 1922. "Once the Denver program caught on," he explained, "it was obvious that specialists other than the superintendent would be needed to manage the process, and it was for the purpose of training such specialists that the curriculum field was created. Beginning initially as a subfield of educational administration in some universities, of elementary education in others, and of secondary education in still others, the study of curriculum gradually came into its own (p. 213).

Leadership Responsibilities

Leadership can improve instruction—that is, a certain kind of leadership. Team building and collaboration are often used to describe the role of school leaders. But these terms actually tell us very little. Collaboration could conceivably take place in the most authoritarian and closed organizations, ones that do not permit experimentation for improving learning. Fortunately, school systems in the United States have developed historically as decentralized entities (as opposed to systems with centralized control of curriculum and teaching methods), thereby fostering flexibility and originality. Local administrators and teachers play important roles in conducting schools, including engaging in the continued search for better methods. In the realm of professional leadership, there is ample scope for curriculum improvement. Behind those efforts is the feeling of responsibility. As Butts and Cremin pointed out many years ago: "It also contrasts sharply with those private systems of schools in lands where the professional administrators, teachers, and sponsoring agencies do not feel so responsible to the public, the parents, or the children" (1953, p. 564). (Responsibility is not the same thing as accountability, although they are often confused.)

The Superintendent

The superintendent is foremost an educational leader. He or she should be able to analyze the problems that face education and make sound professional judgments. Put simply, the superintendent should be a professional educator. The idea of a chief administrator who is also an educator comes straight from Horace Mann. As secretary of the Massachusetts Board of Education, Mann was an early shaper of educational policy. According to Paul Hill, "He urged that boards hire an expert educator who would serve as chief administrator of all schools in a community" (2003, p. 68). Mann strongly believed that the interest of public schools could best be served by expertise and vision in a democratic-participative system.

It is clear that this expertise and vision must be manifest with a direct interest in curriculum and teaching. Mann's policy, which was in the interest of raising standards and improving opportunity, was followed in many communities and states. In fact, it became the pattern. It was definitely in the direction of professionalism and when followed has served American society well.

As revealed in Table 17.1, the superintendent has many leadership responsibilities that bear directly on the quality of the educational program. Indeed, the role of the superintendent is nothing more or less than an attempt to provide a curriculum that is increasingly effective in meeting the needs of all children and youth. This is not to say that the responsibilities are all being performed effectively—or performed at all. Attention to the curriculum is all too frequently derailed.

Putting Teaching and Learning First.   As Paul Hill, notes, there are a growing number of "things that are controlled by rules and higher authorities" which are squeaky wheels that divert attention from curriculum improvement (2003, p. 62). One example is the need to comply with labor contracts, which "leaves to chance" amalgamation of the best faculty for the schools (p. 64). Another is the need to comply with federal and state requirements and court orders which limit flexibility in using funds for curriculum innovation and development, leaving such matters to chance. This, as Hill suggests, is a pessimistic view of public education governance. Not everyone, as he indicates, leaves curriculum improvement to chance. Some "superintendents, central office administrators, union

Table 17.1 Educational Leadership Functions.

Position	Leadership Responsibilities (Examples)
Superintendent	Amalgamating the best available teachers for the schools; selecting administrators and supervisors who see problems as opportunities for improvement; within guidelines provided by the state, establishing graduation requirements and approving goals for courses of study for students; providing for professional development; providing for a coordinated program for dealing with districtwide and local school problems; promoting a balanced curriculum; communicating with the school board concerning implementation of new programs and how problems are being solved; putting teaching and learning first.
Assistant superintendent for curriculum and instruction (or curriculum director)	Planning and conducting professional development programs; making guidelines for best practices available to teachers; providing learning resources (including sample lessons and units, for example); promoting horizontal and vertical curriculum articulation; working with principals on curriculum development and evaluation; interpreting the professional literature for application to local conditions; working with other supervisors on the total educational program.
Supervisor	Providing for a continuous program of curriculum development and evaluation; helping school staffs develop processes that will lead to the adoption of good textbooks; helping school staffs clearly describe the kinds of learning activities they want in their school; working with principals in solving problems; extending successful programs throughout the district; providing for professional development; coordinating school accreditation processes; interpreting the professional literature for application to local conditions.
Principal	Maintaining a positive school climate; identifying and allocating educational resources; filling open positions with the best available teachers; providing for a continuous program of curriculum development and evaluation; promoting horizontal and vertical curriculum articulation; structuring time for faculty to work together with faculty, parents and the community, addressing the kind of learning that matters and how it will be evaluated; working with the assistant superintendent (curriculum director), supervisors, and other principals on problems of common concern; providing for professional development; promoting and supporting collaborative research with universities; creating a culture of learning (modeling learning).
Department head (secondary school)	Working with principal, supervisors, and teachers on curriculum development across subject fields; diagnosing problems; providing leadership in problem solutions; working with other department heads and teachers on horizontal and vertical curriculum articulation; selecting curricular resources with supervisors and teachers; assisting teachers with professional improvement; scheduling course offerings and teaching assignments; interpreting the professional and research literature for application to local conditions.

leaders, principals and teachers . . . ignore the demands of other governors of the systems" (p. 64). Hill states:

These individuals are loved and lionized, because what they do is so risky and improbable. The fact that educators say it takes moral courage to put teaching and learning first is a powerful criticism of a governance system that puts so many other considerations at the head of the line. (p. 64)

By refusing to let anything stand in the way of improving the curriculum, these individuals are simply meeting their professional responsibility. Would a surgeon who followed best practices be "lionized"? The point hardly needs explication. Whatever the size of the school system, the superintendent is the one person who can ensure the conditions necessary for improving the educational program. Superintendents should have a clear vision of a balanced educational program and their own responsibility for keeping it in balance. As Cremin (1965) observed, "They have too often been managers, facilitators, politicians in the narrowest sense" (p. 111). The hope for the future is improved professional preparation and recruitment of superintendents. The tide is running in that direction, with the rediscovery of the superintendent as educational leader.

The Assistant Superintendent for Curriculum and Instruction

The assistant superintendent is the member of the superintendent's team who is concerned with the key function of improving curriculum and teaching. As shown in Table 17.1, an important responsibility of the assistant superintendent is articulation of the educational program from kindergarten through 12th grade. (This is all too often neglected.) The effectiveness of the assistant superintendent depends on the ability to provide leadership to many people as a team and to use their talents in developing ever improving school programs.

Curriculum Development and Professional Development. Does curriculum development involve professional development? A resounding, yes. As Hilda Taba (1962) told us, curriculum development and teachers' professional development are an integral process. As discussed in chapter 16, no matter how rich, plentiful, and available, instructional resources are ineffective unless teachers have a way to improve their competencies, knowledge, and abilities. And how resources are used reflects whether teachers view teaching as routine management or have an imaginative view of teaching (see Table 17.1).

Taba's insights came from experience in the field: her work with teachers in the San Francisco Bay area. Today, the concept that curriculum development is so intimately related to professional development that neither can exist without the other is the modus operandi of every good school system. Indeed it may be reflected in the title of the person who is concerned with these functions. For example, the classified advertising section of *Education Week* has featured vacancy announcements for the position of director of curriculum and professional development (pp. 22, 36, 41).

Professional Development Programs and Student Learning. In the 1980s and early 1990s, many districts shifted the responsibility for teachers'

professional development to schools. The reform proposal that each low-performing school develop its own curriculum improvement program and be held accountable for performance was irresistibly appealing to many superintendents. By that time central office professional development programs had already been severely reduced through budgetary cutbacks in supervisory staff. Still, the situation where absolutely no assistance or curriculum guides were available to schools was simply intolerable. Thus, as described in the previous chapter, some teachers associations embarked on curriculum development (with the blessing, in some cases) from superintendents. Until recently, district-level professional development has had a very long dry spell. The lost opportunities for teachers and students can never be recaptured. As Fuhrman (2001) points out, studies have found that professional development linked directly to the curriculum influences teaching practices and student achievement. Reconceptualizing and regenerating professional development programs depends on the leadership of the assistant superintendent for curriculum and instruction.

The Supervisor

The city's Education Department has hired 198 people—most of them currently superintendents or school principals—to serve as local instructional supervisors, a new administrative position. (Herszenhorn, 2003, p. B7)

A new administrative position? Teachers around the country who saw this item in the *New York Times* must have found themselves quite puzzled. There is nothing new at all about the administrative position of supervisor. What is new is that after decades of retrenchment in urban districts their absence is being felt. Thus the position is being reinvented, unfortunately in this case by "pulling outstanding principals from their schools" (p. B7).

But the reinvention leaves much to be desired. It would be pleasant to record that in the early 2000s districts were moving toward balanced supervisory staffing (generalists and specialists in various curriculum areas). But this has not been the case. Districts have continued to focus major attention on reading and mathematics to assure that students measured to new standards. For example, the instructional supervisors in New York were hired to supervise the implementation of a new reading and math program.

Since the 1960s, supervisory staffing in urban school systems has been vulnerable to the twists, turns, and abrupt reversals of educational policy. Court orders and funding show where the supervisors are. In the late 1960s, an outcome of federal aid to meet the special needs of disadvantaged children was the saturation of supervisory services for teachers in disadvantaged areas. Federal funding for the categorical purpose of reading instruction was a key factor. Many large districts severely retrenched supervisory programs in other curriculum areas, such as music and art. These programs have never really come back. "Squeaky wheels" (Hill, 2003), not best practices in educational administration, have governed the development of supervisory programs.

This approach to supervisory staffing is out of touch with reality. It is not reflective of the important place that music and art hold in our everyday lives, for example, and the need that teachers and students have for improving teaching and learning in these areas. It is a skewed system of priorities that good schools and the parents of children who attend them would not countenance.

Sharing Effective Programs. Many larger school systems have developed means for schools to share effective programs and practices through the district's central office. As shown in Table 17.1, this is a leadership responsibility of the supervisory staff. It may also be the responsibility of the assistant superintendent. In accord with the best administrative theory, one does not begin by stressing division of labor, but begins with the problem to be solved. The supervisor, deputy superintendent, director of elementary education, or director of secondary education may all be involved in helping schools to share an effective program. Overlap can be a good thing. In a small system, the responsibilities carried out in larger districts by the director of curriculum (sometimes called the assistant superintendent for instruction) must be performed personally by the superintendent.

Leadership at the Local School Level

The levels of curriculum development provide a perspective for viewing leadership responsibilities and activities; individual teachers and school staff need resources and expertise (the help of consultants) if they are to function at the mediative and generative-creative levels (see Table 17.1). The objective of leadership is to help teachers function at the top level of professionalism—the generative-creative level.

The Successful School Principal

A successful school thrives rather than simply survives, and the principal plays the key role. Crow, Hausman, and Scribner (2002) call it "an indispensable role" (p. 198). The role is dynamic; perhaps generative is a better word. Thus instead of attempting to control teacher behavior in classrooms (a useless endeavor in any event), principals provide teachers with opportunities to collaborate on curriculum development. Smylie and Hart (2000) describe the "interactional principal" who "constantly works within the school's social network to broker information and promote relationships among disconnected groups" (p. 429).

This is true enough—as far as it goes. But the principal has to assume other leadership aspects (see Table 17.1) and to put the ideas and ideals involved into harmonious action. A useful analogy is that of an orchestra conductor. The orchestral principal provides intellectual leadership to individuals and groups of teachers and brings the entire school staff together to improve the school in ways that are good for children and the society.

The orchestral principal attends to the conditions that are needed for curriculum improvement. Thus, as Wagner (2001) notes, the leader creates opportunities for teachers to learn about and use best practices. But an overall objective here is all too often ignored in discussions about best practices. Like all conductors the leader is concerned with harmony. The grand objective is to bring the curriculum into a harmonious whole.

Setting the Stage for Curriculum Improvement

Effective principals see that individual teachers and school staff are made aware of the resources available for curriculum improvement. These include human resources such as curriculum specialists and other teachers who are on the generative-creative level. They also include materials and time for meetings with colleagues to plan and coordinate curriculum.

Human Resources

Many if not most teachers have never had access to a curriculum consultant; most assistance in curriculum improvement comes from colleagues. Certainly, when curriculum specialists are available they should be used. Supervisors and administrators know all too well that underused personnel cannot justify their professional existence and soon disappear. When resources such as a helping teacher or a resource teacher are not handily available, curriculum improvement is almost discouraged because of the routines that are already established in the school system.

It seems clear that principals need to expand their idea of what resources are possible in their own school and district. They must look again at the needs of teachers and find the professional assistance for teachers that is beyond principals' own competence. Some districts have well-staffed departments of instructional support. When professional help for teachers is inadequate or nonexistent, principals, teachers, and other supervisors must play their legitimate role in seeking district and public support for additional professional development providers. Adequate professional assistance for teachers costs money. There is no way of avoiding this fact.

And teachers should be given opportunities to see for themselves what successful schools are like. As Wagner (2001) points out in a discussion of what today's effective leaders do and understand, such leaders provide teams of two or more experienced teachers—"the building leaders" (p. 382)—with opportunities to visit schools that use best practices and to discuss with their colleagues what they have learned. Along with the assistance of supervisors and other central office professional development providers "this general understanding of best practice evolves into a more specific set of skills that the teachers in every building can master" (p. 382).

However, a caveat is in order: Best practices can indeed gradually radiate out to the whole system. But the effective leader will give other teachers besides the building leaders opportunities to visit schools and see actual demonstrations of best practices. They are more likely to view the ideas with enthusiasm and understanding than if they merely hear about them second hand. Teachers should be provided with opportunities to attend conferences concerning the problems they encounter in their classrooms. Other human resources include university professors who offer courses in curriculum and pedagogical strategies.

Material Resources

Actually, the separation of human from material resources is specious; a role of the curriculum specialist is to find materials that are appropriate for a given teacher's needs, which translates to the needs of the learners. Professional development programs can help connect teachers with the best available materials. Moreover, teachers must have another, precious resource—time—to evaluate textbooks and curricular materials. Obviously, curriculum improvement depends on treating resources interrelatedly.

Nevertheless, there are wide differences from district to district in access to curriculum materials. In some districts, school staff clearly enjoy the availability of any materials that might be needed for the classroom for curriculum development. Teachers are given virtually an open-ended budget every year to order needed materials. However, the teachers and students in many school systems suffer from serious shortages of even the most basic resources. To provide the conditions for curriculum improvement the principal should have support from the district level. Hill (2003) proposes that every school be guaranteed "a minimum set-aside for purchasing materials, advice and assistance" (p. 74). As Hill writes, "This guarantees that no school will be unable to work on improving its instructional program" (p. 74).

What Hill is proposing is investment by school systems in the continuing improvement of educational programs. The proposal makes good sense. Where materials and professional development providers are in short supply, superintendents, principals, and teachers must play their proper role in seeking public support for such an investment.

Finally, a word about decisions concerning learning materials. No leader today can consider herself or himself adequate if she or he imposes resource decisions on the professional staff. This is not a matter of being philosophically committed to teacher empowerment. It is a matter of freeing the staff to function at the generative-creative level. No principal is able to unilaterally assess the resource needs of professional teachers. Effective leaders view this as an individualized as well as facultywide process (Mitchell & Tucker, 1992).

The criterion for budgetary allocations for resources is this: The entire professional staff collaborates fully on budgetary allocations for learning resources. The principal and teachers are provided discretionary funds for the purchase of special learning materials needed for improving the curriculum. Obviously, the availability of materials is no guarantee that they will be properly used. Curriculum specialists must be available to answer teachers' questions, particularly when the school district adopts a new curriculum. All too often teachers are left on their own to interpret the curriculum as though it is simply a matter of plugging in the new prepackaged materials.

Media Center. Professional books and journals are important resources for curriculum improvement. In addition, the school media center should maintain a rich collection of teaching resource units (for teachers) and learning resource units (for students). The professional staff should strive to have the media center meet the recommended standards of the American Library Association, as set in the latest edition of the association's publication, *Media Programs: District and School*. The media center should be attractive, functional, and serve as a true center for responsible, self-directed learning activities. Moreover, students should be encouraged to use the media center for recreational reading and browsing and to use the equipment for viewing and listening.

The school library now goes by the name of media center in many schools, but the function as a curriculum resource and a place to whet children's appetite for reading remains. The following commentary, made in the early 1990s, describes the unique function of school libraries—and the unfortunate condition of some school libraries:

> School libraries are an on-site resource, a curriculum adjunct, a place of wonderful treasures that can make kids want to read. The school library is tailored to the needs and wants of a particular school community. Often it is a refuge, an oasis for children who have little quiet, space, cheerfulness in their lives. Many children cannot get to public libraries by themselves; many need the close neighborhood richness of their own school library. These days, too many school libraries are nonexistent, eliminated in budget cuts. Those still in working order are lacking adequate book collections, and are too often staffed by nonprofessionals working with outdated resources with grim, decrepit spaces for students. (Lewis, 1991, p. A10)

If anything, the condition of many school libraries was made more dire in the early 2000s by deeper budget cuts.

The media center should be open after school hours. It should never be used as a "study hall" or place for student detention. It should be an attractive and stimulating environment for self-impelled learning.

Time. As has been indicated previously, time for curriculum improvement is one of the most critical problems with which principals must concern themselves. Lack of time is simply unacceptable as a reason for failing to improve the curriculum. The key indication of what is deemed most important in terms of function or need is the amount of time being devoted to that function or need. If improving the curriculum is considered sufficiently important, it will be done. Like any resource, time should not be considered independently of needed material and personnel resources. It is what happens in that time that counts—whether teachers receive the assistance that they may need to make changes, and whether they have access to needed materials. When an activity is valued, time will be made for it. Indeed, many principals have found a way (or ways) to provide time for the entire staff to learn together and work together on curriculum improvement.

Principals, according to Kochan, Bredeson, and Riehl (2002), have found a number of useful ideas to provide professional development time without losing students' instructional time. One idea is "learning lunches" (p. 302) in which faculty eat together in a quiet room, sharing ideas, readings, and teaching approaches. Another is "community learning times" in which outside groups give theatrical presentations or teach special skills "so that faculty can engage in their own learning activities" (p. 302).

The value of such activities depends on the context—whether they are part of a well-planned professional development program. But one can raise other questions. Having community members come into classrooms to give presentations to free teachers for professional development sounds like attempting to have one's instructional cake and eat it too. In no way can this be justified as instructional time for students. One should not expect to conduct professional development (and curriculum development) on the cheap. As discussed in chapter 16, some school systems have made appropriations for substitutes so that teachers can be released from teaching to work on professional problems.

There are other ways, of course, of structuring time for school-based faculty development. Regular faculty meetings can be turned to this purpose.

(Everyone knows stories of faculty meetings that are used to read announcements.) Time is a very precious resource; teachers' time, principals' time, and children's time.

Teacher Organizations

Teachers unions are frequently blamed for blocking the course of professional development by refusing to stay after the school day for professional development activities. The after-school approach to curriculum development has always failed. Actually, the position of the two major teachers unions (the National Education Association and the American Federation of Teachers) on professional development concurs strikingly with the literature on the conditions for successful professional development programs. According to unionists, if inservice professional development is viewed as something separate from the school's real business it will fail to be effective. Because successful programs are site based, "the school day must provide the core of inservice time," and, "helping teachers and other resource personnel must always be available at the site for follow-up and consultation" (Leiter & Cooper, 1978, p. 122).

According to McClure (1992), not only are teachers unions committed to school improvement, but their leaders and staffs also have competencies in curriculum improvement. McClure points out that both organizations are trusted by their members. Thus they are potentially effective resources for curriculum improvement.

Wilms (2003) describes a most interesting and apparently very successful professional development program for teachers run by the United Teachers Los Angeles (UTLA). Participants learned how to collaborate to develop a series of lessons based on a clear objective. According to an evaluation of the teachers in the program: "Ninety-six percent agreed that the model enabled them to improve the curriculum while they taught, and 92 percent reported that it enabled them to use their creativity and feel confident" (p. 611). Some of the lessons were published and "provide a library of high-quality lessons on which other teachers could draw" (p. 611). A curriculum development program that was run by the teachers union in New York was discussed in chapter 15.

Certainly the position of teacher unionists on professional development is supportive of possibilities for improvement. Supervisors should be encouraged by this knowledge and seek union support in creating conditions for professional development.

Together teachers, administrators, and supervisors can be overwhelmingly powerful.

Teacher Contentment and Resource Adequacy

In some schools, teachers seem satisfied with the resources that are available for curriculum improvement, even where the resources are clearly inadequate. At least there seem to be no complaints. Teacher contentment may be a poor indicator of resource adequacy, for these teachers tend not to have had other experiences with which to make comparisons. Teachers who have enjoyed more substantial resources in another school system are usually quite aware of an insufficiency. Just because teachers do not complain about inadequate resources does not mean that the resources provided by the school and the district are adequate.

Someone must assist teachers in finding resources, for example, resources to interrelate subjects in the curriculum (horizontal curriculum articulation). This is a responsibility of supervision. Curriculum leaders must be sources of ideas and materials, and organizers of opportunities that will help teachers stay abreast of promising innovations and grow professionally (Poplin, 1992).

Although curriculum articulation and integration can hardly be termed an *innovation,* it is a best practice. Teachers need to be made aware of what is available to help them implement best practices. When material resources are not readily available, leaders—the human resources—can help teachers find them and use them effectively.

Collaborative Approaches for Curriculum Improvement

The democratic-participative process is indigenous to teachers functioning at Level III, the generative-creative level. (See chapter 16.) At this level teachers are immersed in efforts to solve curriculum problems, improve established practice, evaluate promising new practices, and implement needed changes.

Recently, interest in site-based management has led many schools to embark on programs of participatory decision making. These programs may or may not be directly concerned with the solution of curriculum and instructional problems. For example, in some schools, teachers are now included on search committees for new teachers. This is a striking departure from traditional practice, and not long ago it would have been unheard of. Administrators alone were involved in staffing. In some schools, the teachers and principal collaboratively decide on-time allocation for various student learning activities, course scheduling, team teaching, and so on.

Needless to say, some state legislators and many school administrators have been concerned with distinguishing between the decisions that teachers should make and those that are administrative. What is often forgotten in such considerations is the purpose of giving teachers more authority in making decisions—namely, to allow them more flexibility in dealing with students' educational needs. Teachers at Level III are continually involved in making decisions concerning learning experiences. When teachers have wide latitude and support in diagnosing the problems of their school, the solutions can result in an improved curriculum. The problem of student apathy comes to mind. A faculty committed to dealing with the problem of apathetic students will (it is hoped) look to the curriculum.

An assumption on which site-based management is based is that professionals who work with and know the student have the best basis for making curriculum decisions and occasionally personnel decisions (Leithwood & Prestine, 2002; Hess, 1991). Although teachers and principals have greater decision-making power in such plans, district officials still bear the responsibility of supplying resources, including professional assistance, to teachers. According to Herrington and Fowler (2003), however, where states mandate site-based management, the building administration is strengthened "at the expense of the school board, superintendent and district office staff" (p. 289). In some states, local schools' professional development plans had to be approved by state departments of education, not by the local school board. The inevitable effect was a decline in district support for principals and teachers. "There is little evidence," write Herrington and Fowler, that such policies "translated into improved student learning" (p. 285). This should come as no surprise.

Setting a Common Vision

A popular approach to school improvement has been to have the school staff share a common vision for the school. Collaboratively the whole staff (or school council, created by law in some states) describes the tone and sets goals for their school. As Hargreaves and Fink (2003) point out, setting a vision can do more than establish goals for the school. It creates an open atmosphere in which staff feel they are included in decisions. This is absolutely essential for involving the faculty in solving practical curriculum problems. The principal should have a personal vision.

The idea of setting goals certainly has its merits. Organizational goals provide a framework within which principals and supervisors can help teachers realize their potential for curriculum improvement. An example is the goal of helping students become lifelong learners. Although stated in sweeping terms, no vision of the school is more powerful than motivating students for continued learning. Principals and supervisors can help teachers determine whether the curriculum and their instructional procedures are consonant with the goal of motivating students to go on learning.

Alice Miel (1946), who greatly enlarged the understanding of curriculum change as a social process, offered many suggestions for working with faculty groups. Lessons learned from experiences with curriculum development led Miel to offer this counsel: There is a need for goals "that give broad direction to individual and group efforts without limiting opportunity to be creative and individual," goals should be "within the present capabilities of individuals and groups [and] should be flexibly held so that they can be reexamined frequently and revised if need be" (p. 190).

Bringing the Vision to Earth. The articulation of a common vision by the school faculty can be a first step in launching a program of curriculum improvement, and visions that are vague and airy must not be allowed to remain so. Goals must be connected to vision. Immediate and clear steps should be delineated by the faculty toward the goals. The transformation of ideals into concrete actions requires leadership skills that are sensitive and decisive.

A common vision is akin to a school philosophy. Whether one begins with a statement of philosophy or a vision, the problem where curriculum development is concerned remains the same. Ralph Tyler (1949) put it this way: "For a statement of philosophy to serve most helpfully as a set of standards or a screen in selecting objectives it needs to be stated clearly and for the main points the implications for educational objectives may need to be spelled out" (p. 37). As stressed in chapter 9, we prefer to conceive of philosophy as a compass rather than a screen, but this does not diminish the significance of Tyler's point, for the test of philosophy is action in the formulation of educational objectives, the implementation of appropriate means, and the evaluation of outcomes.

District Levels Goals. Leithwood and Prestine (2002) provide an example of an Illinois district (hypothetically called Fairview), having five goals, each with a vision statement and an "action strategy" (p. 53) for achieving the goal. Each school in the district develops a school improvement plan in accord with the district's plan. The school-improvement plans guide instructional improvement and professional development in each individual school. The system seemed to be working well. However, when new state standards were published with benchmarks and tests, the district faced an apparent problem. The decision was made to integrate them into the curriculum. This was done by translating the standards into objectives for each grade level. District leadership provided professional-development opportunities. Strong emphasis was put on higher-order thinking and on developing students' problem-solving skills. Thus the district responded to these sensible state standards in constructive ways. According to one district administrator they were faced with "finding some way to use them to reach the goals of the district" (p. 53). The need to comply with the state policy was turned to an opportunity for curriculum improvement. Wise leadership can turn a problem into an advantage or opportunity.

Leaders as Filters. Many principals encounter policies that are simply inconsonant with the goals of their school. We would echo the counsel of Hargreaves and Fink (2003) that principals and other staff with sophisticated curriculum knowledge "learn to be critical filters for government mandates rather than mere pipelines for implementing them" (p. 697). As shown in the Illinois example, by focusing on aspects of policies that can be *made* consonant with school district goals, policies can be turned to a positive advantage— some policies at least.

We have had a spate of reforms that are initiated externally. Some aspects of these reforms may be quite consistent with the goals of the school and district. An idea that has begun to emerge in the literature can be very helpful to leadership. Principals and district leaders, teachers, and parents need to find and adopt aspects of external policies (such as standards-based reforms) that are sound from the standpoint of the schools' own goals and objectives (Leithwood & Prestine, 2002; Forsyth & Tallerico, 1998).

A Principal's Dilemma. There are some mandates that do not make sense because they are supported by neither research nor past experience. An example is New York City's 1981 mandatory retention program. Forty percent of seventh-graders who were held back eventually became dropouts, compared with 25 percent of low achievers who were not held back. In the words of one observer, "New York's 1981 mandatory retention program violated the most basic rule of medicine: first do no harm" (Winerip, 2004, p. B9). In 2004 in New York, there was a new mandatory retention policy holding back all children who failed the city's third-grade reading test. "Big mistake" (p. B9) were the words that ran through one principal's mind. Since 1978 he had been principal of a school on New York's lower East Side, one of New York's poorest schools, and when children fail the reading test he has managed to get them help without holding them back. And most have "bloomed" into fourth grade (p. B9). However, after consulting with teachers and parents, this principal will hold back some children. For example, in the case of Samantha T. in grade three, he explained, "She is an only child. Chinese was spoken at home, we felt she was young for her age and needed a year to grow" (p. B9). She did grow. "You have to make the decision based on best interest of the child," he maintains.

The question that concerns us here is what can the leader and professional staff do when externally imposed policies differ with what the school believes is in the best interest of children? (Especially, when what the school has been doing seems to work.) In this instance the policy was imposed by the mayor. A mayor can be judged for reelection by his or her approach to educational governance. An ideal model, in our view, is that of Boston. Like New York, the concern has been with improving educational performance, but the approach taken has been the professional route. Rather than appointing an education outsider as superintendent, as did New York, Boston's mayor opted for a professional educator as superintendent. As policy expert Michael Kirst (2003) tells us about this Boston superintendent: "His focus on teaching and learning tended to rely on professional norms, rather than sanctions, as a means of improving performance" (p. 212).

Although the mayors of New York and Boston were both concerned about school improvement, one chose an experienced educator to lead the schools. The choices were reflected in strikingly different educational policies and practices.

Problem Solving

Goal setting can inspire teachers to inspire students. Nevertheless, there is a danger that school problems will be bypassed in the goal-setting process. Goals are fairly general statements about what schools hope to do. Even when translated into school-improvement plans, they are not the same as teachers' concerns or problems. The curriculum-improvement function of leadership can best be approached by starting with addressing specific problem situations, from those of an individual teacher to problems of a whole school. In essence, curriculum development should be treated as a problem-solving process involving the entire professional staff of the school and school system.

Openness Versus Isolation. Most teachers have been brought up with the notion that disclosing one's problems is not a good idea. As children, they were socialized into keeping silent when they did not understand the teacher's directions. As teachers, they quickly grew to accept the common belief (justified or not) that having problems is bad. Disclosing problems could only create a poor impression and jeopardize merit-pay increases. (Sad to say, many principals have bought the myth that good teachers never have problems.) All of the advances that have been made in any field or profession were made because problems were openly identified and dealt with. As Fullan and Miles (1992) put it: "Problems are our friends because only through immersing ourselves in problems can we come up with creative solutions" (p. 750).

As discussed, involving teachers in identifying and solving curriculum problems serves as an antidote to the problem of teacher isolation and has long been a best practice in curriculum development. From time to time, in episodic efforts at reform, schools have followed the practice. Working collaboratively in search of continuous improvement became established practice in those schools that provided time for doing so in the teacher's schedule. Along with the time went the expectations and the support. In other schools, lacking in full commitment, the democratic-participative approach to problems quickly faded from interest and from practice—that is, until it was rediscovered and again came into fashion. Meanwhile, it never left the literature as a best practice.

Reaching Far Enough. Why do reforms take in some schools but not in others? In his study of why some reforms fail, Cuban (1990) found that schools in which reforms do not last make only superficial attempts to change. They have not reached far enough. His idea supports Sarason's (1982) conclusion that substantive and long-lasting improvement is attainable, but it requires organizational as well as interpersonal change. The importance of these ideas in the 2000s has already been indicated.

These ideas and experiences with repetitive reform cycles deliver a potent message for principals: Teachers are not likely to come forward with problems concerning the curriculum unless productive problem identification meetings are the norm (regularly held) in their school. Moreover, when curriculum problems are concealed or ignored, they are likely to fester into more serious problems and become problems of teacher morale. Thus local school leaders (and district administrators) should make problem solving one of what Sarason called "the existing regularities" (p. 63).

Basic Principles. Figure 17.2 presents a process for collaborative problem solving (Level III). Of great importance are the guiding principles underlying the process, and three stand out as most essential. First, the problem must be genuine, and there must be no predetermined solution. This seems obvious, and yet there is a risk for the leader being tempted to manipulate evidence in the interest of a predetermined solution. Second, all decisions should be based on the best available evidence. This requires that the principal and faculty have a strong commitment to the scientific methods or the method of intelligence of solving problems, as opposed to authoritative dictate, external pressure, bureaucratic regularities, concealment, or mere expediency. The importance of this commitment cannot be overemphasized. Third, whatever the size of the school system, the superintendent and members of the superintendent's team must provide for a coordinated approach to problem solving, and they must be aware that problems of an individual school often interface with the whole system. As shown in Figure 17.2, problems can be identified at any level of the school system.

An excellent example of the coordinated approach is provided by the principal of an inner-city high school in Phoenix facing low academic achievement, a high dropout rate, and poor attendance. The principal recounts: "The assistant superintendent asked for a list of needs and potential solutions. I could have given him my own wish list, but at South Mountain we are committed to a process of shared decision making"

Figure 17.2 Problem-solving—A Collaborative Process.

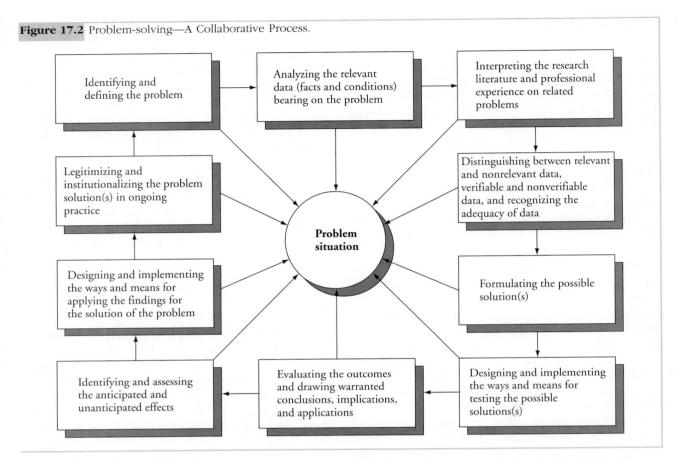

Source: Daniel Tanner and Laurel Tanner. *Supervision in Education: Problems and Practices.* New York: Macmillan, 1987, p. 96.

(Lebowitz, 1992, p. 12). By meeting formally and informally with the school staff, the principal developed a short-term list including telephones for teachers to contact students and parents and funds for learning materials. More importantly, the school improvement team, consisting of members of the school staff, administrators, parents, and students, developed long-term solutions and met with district-level administrators and supervisors. The collaborative plan fostered the development of interdisciplinary curriculum designs and initiated a system of social-service collaboration. Moreover, class loads were reduced to meet these priorities. Over a few years the dropout rate was cut in half, absenteeism decreased significantly, and achievement in mathematics and English increased on statewide tests, with the greatest improvement occurring in written expression. "The ultimate plan," advised the principal, "becomes the 'property' of neither one

person nor one school nor the district office, but is a joint resolution to a shared problem. This process occurs regularly at South Mountain" (p. 12).

In the early 1990s, much of the literature on factors critical to a school's improvement stressed school autonomy. District leaders were portrayed as being inherently resistant to having a school's problems solved in that they were seen as seeking to conceal rather than reveal problems. Or the principal was pitted against the district and portrayed as a superperson who creatively used subordination in dealing with frustrating problems. The real-life illustration we have presented, however, points to a coordinated approach as crucial in problem solving. The principal and professional staff of the school should have full access to the resources of the entire school district as needed in seeking problem solutions. In the words of Hill (2003), "Superintendent helps schools find the best providers of help" (p. 77).

Initiating the Procedure. Whatever the size of the school, the principal has the responsibility of providing for a continuous program of curriculum development and for assisting teachers in solving problems. Whatever the school's size or level, the steps in initiating collaborative procedures are similar. Secondary schools are organized departmentally, and the collaborative process concerning problems in the subject fields will be entrusted to department heads. Thus, the principal must gain the full support of department heads as well as assistant principals. Based on his experience in launching a program, a former principal in New York City stresses the importance of introducing to department heads the new goals, theoretical background, and ways of involving teachers. He chose a retreat as the setting for this crucial first step (Tewel, 1989). The next step is to prepare the department heads to conduct collaborative problem solving meetings with staff members. Recounting his experience, the principal reported that some department heads found it difficult to depart from the traditional supervisory role of setting goals for subordinates. They could not seem to accept the idea of participating with faculty members in problem solving and goal setting. For example, one department chairperson acknowledged that he considered teacher involvement in decision making about instructional matters a valueless activity. "The question-and-answer approach he used in his department meetings was not suitable for identifying teaching-related problems and his lack of understanding was obvious in such questions as 'Are there any more gripes?'" (p. 75). The principal continued to work with small groups of department chairpeople regularly in leadership training, but he found that he met with more success when he worked informally with them as individuals. In his words, "they did not respond well to being formal 'learners'" (p. 78). This was not surprising. Professionals learn new procedures best by using them in problem situations.

Although department heads will be leaders of the collaborative process in their own department, the principal should open the first meeting. There are at least three reasons why the principal's initial involvement is important: (1) the principal should pave the way for the department head, (2) the commitment of the administration to improving teaching and learning by involving teachers in real decision making must be communicated to the teachers, and (3) the involvement of the principal (a generalist)

is crucial if the faculty is to develop a coherent interdepartmental program of general education and other all-school programs. However important the problems of a given department concerning a given subject field, a problem of common concern to all of faculty is the need to reveal the relationships of studies along with their significance for the life of the learner and that of a democratic society. Indeed, this is one of the leading curriculum problems. As everyone knows, it is particularly pronounced at the secondary school level, where adolescents are undergoing profound changes physically, psychologically, and socially.

A problem-solving program in a school should not make the walls between departments higher. It should, rather, seek to bring them down by providing for collaboration among departments in dealing with their common problems. The school-improvement team described earlier by the Phoenix principal is a means of doing so; the team encouraged the development of interdisciplinary approaches as a means of dealing with dropouts. Although a combination of social services, curriculum changes, and reduced teaching loads probably accounted for the sharp reduction in absenteeism and dropouts, the new curriculum designs were an essential part of the strategy.

Identifying Problems. The principal or department head should assist the group in identifying problems. The focus of the meetings should be on practical problems connected with the curriculum. As shown in Figure 17.2, the cycle of problem solving is continuous. A school where a continuous program of curriculum development is already a regularity will be concerned with problem solving as a matter of course. The important point is to have a procedure in which teachers, who are closest to the instructional scene, can identify and deal with problems. Although the emphasis is on practical problems, solving them is an intellectual as well as practical process. Dewey (1910) pointed out that "the origin of thinking is some perplexity, confusion or doubt" (p. 12). Put another way, the origin lies in recognizing a problem situation.

The Critical Importance of Suspending Judgment. The next step is to find and test possible solutions to the problem. Dewey warned that although it is a temptation to accept any seemingly plausible solution and get on with other things, a sound decision must be based on sound knowledge. Interpreting the research literature and professional experience on the problem is crucial (see Figure 17.2). "To maintain the state of doubt and to carry on systematic and protracted inquiry—these are the essentials of thinking," said Dewey (p. 12). The leader's most difficult problem is twofold: to refrain from pressuring for a premature solution and to keep the process moving. Teachers will have responsibilities in the problem-solving process and principals or department heads should offer support where needed. According to a principal, providing teachers with assistance in fact finding is important or "some groups come to the second meeting to raise additional problems without first clarifying those identified in the first" (Tewel, 1989, p. 79). There are no short cuts in the problem-solving process and the process is arduous, but there is a reason why it is carried on in a growing number of schools: Their achievements in solving problems provide the professional staff with a sense of direction, pride, responsibility, and accomplishment. Moreover, being involved in systematic inquiry can be a source of great pleasure for teachers.

Generating Staff Support. There have been so many sudden policy shifts in response to alleged crises in education, with each crisis followed by a panacea, that it should be no small wonder when teachers become passive participants. Or they may respond to the latest reform shift with overt compliance and covert resistance. Therefore, it is not difficult to see why many teachers would be skeptical about administrators' newly announced commitment to improving teaching and learning through teacher involvement in real problem solving. As a principal himself suggests, it is important to counter skepticism in the first meeting, and principals should be open in talking to faculty. According to this principal, a principal might say to the faculty that although they "have seen school improvement programs come and go over the years . . . this time we're really serious about a new approach and we want to see it work. We're going to devote ourselves to it. But you're the ones who have to give it a chance to work" (p. 78).

How are the faculty to know that this time things are different? What should be emphasized in describing the approach in that the word *new* really does not apply to these procedures? The idea of a school faculty working together to diagnose and solve problems was developed by educators in the first half of the twentieth century and is a best practice in education. A basic idea undergirding teacher involvement in solving curriculum problems is that teachers are closest to

the scene—the classroom. Their insights are critical to the problem-solving process. Moreover, many heads are better than just one. Involving the faculty is a way to draw on the collective knowledge of professionals and use it in the solution of problems. In introducing a procedure to professionals and asking for their support, a principal should provide the knowledge base for the procedure. Collaborative decision making has a knowledge base. Support should come from the soundness of the procedure and not merely declarations to convince staff that this time we really mean it.

Reluctant Principals. If collaborative decision making is to enhance faculty motivation and capacity for problem solving, it is clear that the principal's commitment is absolutely essential. This commitment is by no means general. Even though recent policy supports the principle that teachers should work on problem solutions, principals in many schools remain reluctant to abandon a system in which they are (they think) in complete control. According to Nobel prize winner Herbert Simon (1976), control by sheer authority as a way of supervision cannot work because the elements involved in all but the most minor and routine decisions are too complex and it is impossible to control them all. Because teachers will make these decisions anyhow (their autonomy is a fact of life), they should make them on the best possible evidence (see Figure 17.2).

According to Elaine Fink, a superintendent, and Lauren Resnick, whose expertise is learning, many principals have quite another reason for their reluctance to develop decisions collaboratively (Fink & Resnick, 2001). They feel that they lack the competence to be a leader in a democratic group setting. Interestingly enough, writers on general education—that part of the curriculum concerned with developing socially responsible citizens in a free society—have long urged that the skills of working cooperatively be "part of the general education of our people" (Benne, 1952). Fink and Resnick (2001) and Fullan and Miles (1992) report that principals commonly lack these skills. Principals and supervisors who did not learn the skills of cooperative work as pupils in school or in their professional preparation for supervision are doubly disadvantaged.

All this adds up to the fact that their own professional development as it relates to ability for leadership in curriculum improvement is of enormous concern to principals. Indeed, in a survey of Chicago principals conducted by a consortium of area universities and the Chicago Public Schools, principals identified "leadership for instructional improvement (and enhancing their own capacities to lead)" as their most critical concern (Consortium on Chicago School Research, 1992).

There is no doubt that the qualities involved in cooperative work, including being a group leader, can be learned by principals and by most adults, for that matter. "Both casual and systematic observation," writes Robert A. Dahl (1989), a prominent political theorist, "provide good grounds for believing that many, perhaps most, human beings at birth possess the potentiality for developing these qualities," and whether they really develop them "depends primarily on the circumstances into which they are born and in which their development—or lack of it—takes place" (pp. 92–93). The circumstances, of course, include the nature of the society in which one lives. Only democratic political systems can provide the conditions under which the capacity to "engage in free and open discussion is encouraged in a search for the best decision." Indeed, "all other regimes reduce, often drastically, the scope within which adults can act," (Dahl, 1989, p. 93). Moreover, according to Dahl, this is the direction in which democracy must move if the United States and other advanced democratic nations are to continue to exist.

Teachers must model these behaviors as well as provide all students with the opportunity to participate fully in problem solving situations in the classroom and school.

What Good Leaders Do

"Like most people," write Fink and Resnick about principals, "they also tend to gravitate toward doing what they know how to do" (2001, p. 599). Some principals back away from leadership because they feel that their subject matter knowledge is lacking. The leader or prospective leader ought not to feel insecure about a specific subject. As Fink and Resnick point out, the focus is on leadership. Principals do not have to be specialists in the various school subjects (p. 600). What good leaders should be able to do is "to figure out what to do for a teacher—what kind of professional development would be appropriate for a given person at a given time" (p. 600). They remind us of what is all too often forgotten and causes many principals to shy away from the notion of curriculum leadership: "But the principal actually does not have to deliver the

professional development; staff development specialists can do that" (p. 600).

An important function of leadership is to find materials for teachers so that they can be more effective. (Some principals are even wizards at finding funds to pay for before-school programs and Saturday programs for students who need extra help.) The important word here is *help.* "How can I help you get the job done?" is what savvy leaders ask or convey to teachers. It is an atmosphere of expectancy and support, a feeling that the principal is openly available for consultation and support. As a consequence, problems are readily diagnosed and constructively addressed.

There are principals who are not involved in any collaborative effort because they are afraid of losing control of the faculty (and the decision). The best way of conquering that fear is this: When working with groups or teams, the principal should concentrate on providing service to the group. Thus the principal need not be concerned with maintaining or showing authority. The principal can profit from the counsel of curriculum pioneer Alice Miel (1946). (It still makes real sense.) As she pointed out, the leader's example in dealing with group members will influence the entire group: "Confidence, ease, poise, kindness and thoroughness are just as contagious as are fear, insecurity, excitability, irritability and callousness. Teachers are quick to sense these qualities in their leaders" (p. 160).

The following six practices have been identified by local school leaders and supervisors as important—indeed, essential—to sound collaborative action for curriculum improvement:

1. Clarify procedures. Progress in solving problems depends on a common understanding of the phases of collaborative decision making. Begin by analyzing the problem-solving procedures in Figure 17.2, which also provide a common vocabulary. Ground rules should be established early concerning how decisions are to be made.

2. Identify indigenous leaders and those with potentials for leadership, and provide them with opportunities to exercise leadership at the generative-creative level. Members of the professional staff, parents, and other adult citizens also have the potential to be leaders in problem solving. The principal or supervisor should assign particular responsibilities connected with the problem-solving process to group members. As reported

by a principal in our earlier illustration, it was useful to form mini-teams to carry out various aspects of the problem-solving procedure. As Miel pointed out, "Every committee chair created, every assignment of special responsibility means more chances for more persons to exercise leadership and test their effectiveness in actual group situations" (p. 179). In giving teachers opportunities for curriculum change, we are helping them to function at the generative-creative level. Moreover, the chances that the problem-solving process will lead to curriculum improvement will be enhanced. As Miel put it, "the greater the amount of effective leadership developed on the part of all members of the professional staff, the greater the probability that the experiences of learners in their charge will be educative" (p. 179).

3. Provide concrete assistance. The principal or supervisor provides information and locates information sources, and finds ways of providing material resources as needed. When the school staff needs the help of experts on the problem, the principal finds the person or agency best able to provide that assistance. The staff or team may also need to look outside to see how the problem has been dealt with elsewhere, and opportunities should be given to observe similar programs or projects in other school systems (Wagner, 2001).

4. Increase commitment. High and realistic expectations should be set for each member of the professional staff or team concerning their particular responsibilities for garnering the best available evidence bearing on the problem. Each individual should be asked to evaluate his or her progress in communicating what they have found.

5. Provide opportunities for constructive disagreement. Individuals should never be made to feel compelled to yield to consensus when they really have a valid basis for constructive disagreement. The principal or supervisor should seek to provide for the fullest expression of both initiative and constructive disagreement. As we have pointed out elsewhere, although the consensus model should be used in democratic-participative approaches, "group process, taken superficially, sometimes exerts its own tyranny of group pressure" (Tanner & Tanner, 1987, p. 133). We have all experienced situations in which someone with useful insights or a creative idea was made to feel compelled to keep silent rather than contributing

the suggestion. As a result the constructive insight was lost.

6. Deal constructively with team or faculty split on an issue. A decision may not be so easy to achieve. Even after a process of deliberation and discussion, the team or faculty may still be far from consensus concerning the best plan of action. A decision now would be premature, for this reason: A wise decision is based not only on the best available knowledge but also on the uncoerced consensus of all concerned, and so the decision should be delayed pending further study (by the team or faculty). In some situations an immediate decision of some kind must be made. Miel's counsel is pertinent here: The leader should "have it understood that the decision is a trial one" (p. 140). The idea of testing an action plan is, of course, integral to the problem-solving paradigm (see Figure 17.2).

Leadership for Curriculum Design, Development, and Evaluation

Collaboration is the route to improvement. Granted this, skillful leadership is needed if curriculum improvements are to be made in light of a grand design. Decisions concerning microcurricular problems must be made with regard to this macro design. A balanced and coherent curriculum depends on it. Here is evidence for the soundness of Cremin's assertion that someone must be responsible for seeing the curriculum as a coherent whole and raise questions of relationship (1965, p. 58). This is the job of curriculum leadership, both by the local school administrator and the school faculty. District-level supervisors and administrators have this responsibility at the school-system level.

Transforming Theory into Practice

Parts II and III of this book discussed the elements in design and the sources from which criteria for curriculum decisions are drawn. We pointed out that the elements of curriculum design are interrelated, as are the sources for and influences on the curriculum. It is the role of the curriculum leader to translate these ideas into practice and to contribute to the body of knowledge on curriculum. As discussed in chapter 15, Hilda Taba was this kind of leader and contributed influential ideas. Other curriculum theorists, including the present authors, have views of the curriculum development process that differ from Taba's in significant ways. As discussed in chapter 6, in her classic 1962 book on curriculum development, Taba identified the following seven-step sequence in the process: (1) diagnosis of needs, (2) formulation of objectives, (3) selection of content, (4) organization of content, (5) selection of learning experiences, (6) organization of learning experiences, and (7) determination of what to evaluate and of the ways and means of doing it (pp. 12–13). Taba conceived of these steps as a linear sequence; the authors of this textbook hold that the steps or functions are interdependent rather than rigidly sequential. For example, the diagnosis of needs and the formulation of objectives involve evaluation, which is integral to every step, including those concerned with the selection and treatment of subject matter. (See chapter 6 for an extended discussion of the interdependence of the various functions in curriculum development.)

The four questions that Ralph Tyler (1949) asks early in his monograph, and the discussion stemming from them, are intended to provide an orderly guide to curriculum development as a problem-solving process. It is noteworthy, in this regard, that the monograph was originally published as a syllabus for Tyler's curriculum course at the University of Chicago. It has already been pointed out that Tyler's formulation has been criticized for its linearity. Goodlad, who was one of Tyler's students, has a different view of the syllabus:

> One does not necessarily have to treat the four questions in the syllabus in linear fashion. One can begin almost anywhere with any one of the four questions. If you begin with question four, "How can we determine whether the purposes are being attained in the setting," then you clearly go back to question one. But one can begin with question three, "How can these experiences be effectively organized," and talk a good deal about the organizational questions before one necessarily has to get back to the first question of "What educational purposes should one seek to attain." (Goodlad, 1984)

Anyone who takes the time to read Tyler's monograph to the very end will, doubtless, arrive at the same conclusion, for Tyler states that where one begins with the questions depends on the school and the concerns of the staff. In one school,

the results of a follow-up study of graduates may focus attention upon identifiable inadequacies in the present program which will lead easily to systematic study. In another situation, the deliberations over a school philosophy may provide an initial step to an improvement of objectives, and then to a study of the learning experiences. The purpose of the rationale is to give a view of the elements that are involved in a program of instruction and their necessary interrelations." (p. 128)

In our model, unlike Tyler's, philosophy is incorporated as a regulator or compass for the curriculum-development process. (The reader may find it helpful at this point to refer to the discussion in chapter 7.)

Neglected Elements. All too often curriculum development is a segmental and haphazard (and even chaotic) process with decisions made by impulse or by whatever happens to be in vogue at a given time, rather than by systematically following theoretical principles. For example, even when Taba's steps are followed, there is a tendency to emphasize one or two sources for curriculum and neglect others. The needs of learners may be stressed and the needs of society ignored or vice versa. Generally, this is the result of the overriding influence of special interests or social forces at a particular point in time. It cannot be overemphasized that it is the responsibility of a professional staff to reflect *on* social forces and not mindlessly reflect social forces.

Just as there is a tendency to emphasize one source for curriculum and neglect the others, so there is a tendency to focus attention on one or two of Tyler's four questions and give the others little, if any, attention. According to Goodlad, the impact of Tyler's formulation has been greatest in the fourth question of the rationale, evaluation, and the first question, the development of goals and objectives. There has been far less attention to what learning experiences will be most suitable for attaining the objectives and even less to how shall the learning experiences be organized.

Although Tyler states that any of the four questions can serve as an entry point for curriculum improvement, he makes a condition: "providing the resulting modifications are followed through the related elements until eventually all aspects of the curriculum have been studied and revised" (p. 128). One can cite many gross violations of this proviso over many decades of curriculum reform and counterreform.

The point of entry for the national commissions on educational reform (see chapter 12) was Tyler's fourth question: evaluation. Because the purposes of the commissions tended to be political, the approach was based on a priori premises of systemwide school failure (Tanner, D., 2000a). The commissions were temporary bodies that proceeded to hit and run. They issued recommendations but were not responsible for their implementation. More importantly, there were problems with their treatment of Tyler's fourth question. Evaluation was based on invalid premises and invalid data to support the premises. According to Peterson, a policy expert, "[i]nstead of digging deep," the commissions made "exaggerated claims on flimsy evidence," and "they failed to find the real problems" (Hechinger, 1984, p. 6).

The Principal as Buffer. Considerable attention has been given in this chapter to the development of goals by a professional staff. The point of importance here is that it is the principal's responsibility to help the faculty move through the related elements in improving the curriculum.

In the 1990s and early 2000s, seeing the curriculum whole was perhaps more difficult than ever before for many leaders. They were focused on implementing policies that focused on one or two subjects, namely, reading and mathematics and on the "benchmarks" or progress areas to be assessed. A shadow hanging over leaders and teachers across America was the fear of sanctions (see chapter 15) if students' achievement fell below the benchmarks. The standards were published, and all administrators and many teachers and school board members received copies. Superficial compliance seemed out of the question. The point of importance, however, is that nothing could have been further from the thoughts of many leaders than the curriculum in its coherence and balance.

Nevertheless, in some districts and schools the idea of a balanced curriculum never left the minds of leaders and teachers. Perhaps that should be amended somewhat. In actuality, it was so deeply entrenched in the practices of the district that they never really thought about it; they just did it. In those districts, leadership functioned as a buffer. There is a leadership lesson here. In the words of Leithwood and Prestine (2002), "Effective leadership will always, for example, buffer staffs from their tendency to feel that they must respond comprehensively to demands for policy implementation from governments" (p. 50).

A selective response is called for when demands are sweeping and ill conceived. Such a response need not throw the curriculum design off track. Seeing the curriculum whole goes on and the effective leader will not be thrown off balance nor will the professional staff.

Forgotten Words. A curriculum design problem all too widespread is that schools conduct their curriculum improvement efforts without regard for continuity and integration of learning activities. The ways of developing vertical and horizontal curriculum articulation (other names for continuity and integration) are discussed in chapters 10 and 11. The point of emphasis here is that school staffs need to deal with curriculum continuity and integration. According to Goodlad,

> if there is anything that the curriculum field suffers from today, it is that words like "continuity" and "sequence" have practically disappeared from popular usage. . . . If there is anything that I would like to call out loudly for it is consideration of the basic questions of organizing a curriculum so that it might have continuity, sequence, and scope. (1984, April, p. 92)

Although made in the 1980s, the statement is right on the mark in the 2000s. It might have been made today. Of course, problems of continuity and integration do not end at the school door; systemwide curriculum planning is absolutely necessary for articulation, particularly in larger school systems. Teachers and supervisors, under the leadership of the director of curriculum, should be engaged in continuous and systematic curriculum development to articulate the curriculum throughout the district as well as within the school.

Curriculum Design, Development, and Evaluation: A Way of Thinking

The curriculum is never complete—nor should it be. Indeed, curriculum development may be profitably viewed as an endless problem-solving process. The problem of the curriculum requires definition, data gathering, formulating alternative and tentative approaches and hypotheses, and the testing of hypotheses to see which approach best solves the problem. As Ralph Tyler (1949) suggested, this process is never ending.

What is implied in all of this is that curriculum planning is a continuous process and that as materials and procedures are developed, they are tried out, their results appraised, their inadequacies identified, suggested improvements indicated; there is replanning, redevelopment and then reappraisal; and in this kind of continuing cycle, it is possible for the curriculum and instructional program to be continually improved over the years. In this way we may hope to have an increasingly more effective educational program rather than depending so much upon hit and miss judgment as a basis for curriculum development. (p. 123)

That curriculum development must be a continuous process is one reason for institutionalizing in the school a set of procedures and criteria for curriculum development, along with needed professional expertise and support services. There is a second reason: Curriculum reforms are constantly being pressed on the schools by external panels, commissions, and special-interest groups, and some of these reforms are not in the best interests of students and society. Take for example the premise embraced by the White House and statehouse—namely, that high-stakes standardized tests will improve public education. The consequence has been the test-driven curriculum and the widespread misuses of such high-stakes tests for student placement and promotion, teacher evaluation, and school and school-district evaluation.

When a curriculum proposal is urged on the school (or school system), the machinery should be already in motion for acting on that proposal. A way of thinking and behaving about the curriculum (founded on professionally validated principles) should be inextricably woven into the fabric of the school. Not incidentally, this is what happens when a new drug is developed by a pharmaceutical concern. Before the drug can be put on the market, it is submitted to rigorous tests required by the Federal Drug Administration. The machinery for appraisal is already in existence and in motion. Obviously, if no machinery were available, serious problems would result at the expense of the public welfare. Different criteria (or no criteria at all) would be applied, depending on the power of commercial and selfish interests. It cannot be overstressed that as long as a school system lacks a conceptual professional framework and machinery (procedures and criteria) for curriculum design, it is vulnerable to special interests, misguided political turns, and the exigencies of the moment.

Searching for (and Finding) a Compass for Curriculum Design, Development, and Evaluation. As discussed in detail in part II, curriculum theorists repeatedly point to three main sources for and influences on curriculum: (1) the ideals and needs of a free society, (2) the nature and needs of learners, and (3) the changing nature of knowledge. Theorists may disagree about the relative importance of these sources, but they seem to be of one mind on one thing: Criteria for curriculum development should be drawn from these sources in their interactions.

The curriculum leader who follows this guideline immediately encounters formidable problems. Each of the sources is characterized by conflict and controversy. Wandering through the maze of studies on the nature of the learner, one is struck by the conflicting views about learners on which these studies are based. As discussed elsewhere in this book, the principal psychological orientations—behaviorism and cognitive-field psychology—are divided on their view of the learner. Turning to the needs of society as a source for criteria, one runs into similar difficulties; there are many conflicting views on how the school can best meet societal needs. These views have led to conflicting curricular emphases in the past (witness Bobbitt's criterion of social utility and Dewey's social problem solving). One is not appreciably better off when turning to the nature of knowledge. There are many ways of organizing knowledge, depending on one's special interests, purposes and goals.

It is strikingly apparent that in and of themselves, the aforementioned sources cannot provide criteria for curricula. Indeed, without a compass of sorts to find one's way, the sources are virtually useless. There is, however, a compass available to curriculum leaders: philosophy. The content and methods of education are unremittingly related to concepts of the individual and his or her relationship to the society in which he or she seeks self-fulfillment and to social ideals. Hence, as we discussed in detail in part II, the development of a philosophy is critical in determining criteria for the curriculum. Conceptions of human nature, the individual, and his or her relation to society will point to the role of knowledge in education. Philosophy is fundamental in determining the very structure and function of the curriculum.

Design and Synthesis. According to Taba (1962), "the central problems of a curriculum design are to determine the scope of expected learning, to establish a continuity of learning and proper sequence of content, and to unify ideas from diverse areas (of organized knowledge)" (p. 13). Few theorists would disagree; this is the dominant conception of the work of curriculum development. The problem confronting the curriculum leader is, How does the work proceed?

With the work of curriculum development taking place at the district level, the building level, and the classroom level, scope, sequence, balance, and continuity are determined by decisions made at all three levels. A crucial task of supervision is that of coordination so that there is harmony in the overall design.

There are those who believe that starting at the grass-roots or teacher level is the most fruitful approach to curriculum design. Taba was an active proponent of this position. She believed that objectives developed at the district level were simply too broad and too vague to guide teachers in the selection of learning experiences. She argued:

> Because it is difficult to develop a new concept of scope and sequence apart from experimenting with the various centers of organization in the specific areas of a curriculum, it seems more efficient to explore first the new possibilities closer to the grass roots. . . .
>
> Many problems involved in formulating the framework cannot be realistically explored on the general level at all. The problem of effective integration can be explored with a reasonable functionality and precision only at the point of developing specific units for specific grade levels. One cannot decide flatly that these two or three subjects should be "unified." It is necessary to experiment with relating specific ideas, knowledge, and skills to ascertain what can be integrated. (pp. 439–440)

Much of the work of curriculum development must take place at the teacher level, if for no other reason than this is where it *does* take place. The classroom is a fertile field for theory development, and it is practically a virgin field for that matter. Taba believed in the potential of classroom experimentation for revealing valuable information about educational problems. This was decades ago. Recall from the discussion in chapter 16 that the concept of teacher research has again attracted the interest of some educational theorists. Such work should be supported at the building level and throughout the school district. Moreover, school districts have responsibility for systemwide curriculum development. Many problems can be most effectively approached at the school district level. Hypotheses (possible solutions) for solving curriculum problems can be developed at the district or school level and tested by teachers in their classrooms. The point is that a unidimensional approach to curriculum making is not enough. Curriculum design, development, and evaluation require both the development of broad hypotheses subject to verification and correction by individual teachers, and the development of solutions to problems that may lead to fundamental generalizations about the curriculum. It also requires that decisions based on best practices be made at the district level, building level, and teacher level. One best practice on which we have made little contemporary progress is curriculum synthesis or integration.

From the literature and experience, it is clear that the professional approach to curriculum improvement is a problem-solving process. A school can begin by developing its own vision and identifying its own problems as rooted in actual educational situations. What is important is that teachers have their creative energies unleashed by principals and supervisors whom they see as genuine educational leaders.

Perspective

Educational leadership is back. Administrators once again see their major task as the improvement of the educational program. Not that it ever really left the literature but there were certain digressions that obscured it and led to neglect. For example, a principal was viewed as first and foremost a manager. More recently, he or she was a salesperson, getting teachers to buy into something. There was the whip-cracker, a portrayal of the strong principal in some misbegotten plans for school improvement in a bygone era. Today, a very strong principal was described this way by a teacher in his school: "Any help that you need, any assistance that you need, he will provide it for you. We have the materials and support. So that kind of strong leadership allows us to do the things that we're doing in the classroom" (Merrow, 2004, p. 459).

The founding purpose of educational administration was the improvement of teaching and learning. As we discussed in the first chapter, that was the reason that drove American education's founding fathers and led to the creation of our inclusive public school system. But in the course of the twentieth century those concerns became secondary (at best) in many school systems as the field of school administration became attracted to a conception of leadership based on business management. In the twenty-first century we have come back to our roots, back to the role of administrative leadership originally conceived by Mann and further developed along with the field of curriculum. In a sense we have come full circle. Yet the circle is not complete. Early superintendents were concerned with the continued and balanced improvement of the curriculum. The balance has been upset in many districts by the scramble to meet external mandates and avoid sanctions if students fail to reach "benchmarks." In some districts nothing could be further from leaders' and school board members' thoughts than maintaining a balanced curriculum. Yet to do so is a leadership responsibility, insisted upon by parents—who, when able to do so, move away from districts that do not offer music, art and other opportunities in a rich, well-balanced curriculum.

For Horace Mann the goal of the principalship was curricular: upgrading the quality of instruction. Principals often and unhesitatingly demonstrated the practice themselves. One does not see too much of this these days. For one thing, most teachers are more skilled instructors than their administrators. For another, the leadership role is to provide help. This may mean determining the right kind of professional development opportunities for teachers. The idea of curriculum development and professional development as an integral process goes back to Hilda Taba. Today, studies show that professional development that is linked directly to curriculum development has positive outcomes for student learning.

Nevertheless, the principal is still responsible for curriculum improvement and as such has to know curriculum: the principles and practices. Effective principals and district leaders with their supervisory staff will find and adopt aspects of external reforms that are consistent with the best available evidence as relevant to school and district priorities. Effective leaders both filter and buffer the staff from their inclination to feel they have to implement uncritically governmental policies that may be ill conceived. Districts that respond to state mandates in critically constructive ways will be more successful in their mission than those that react with blind conformance.

Every school should have a vision that is collaboratively developed and serves as a starting point for problem identification and problem solution. The principal's leadership responsibility is to help teachers function at the highest level of curriculum development: the generative-creative level. Problem identification and problem solving are indigenous to schools at this level.

As principals use the democratic-collaborative style, the character of their relationships with teachers changes markedly; segmental relationships and efforts are replaced by sustained interaction involving the principal and groups of teachers. This chapter examined two collaborative strategies for curriculum improvement: forging a common vision, and involving the faculty in solving practical curriculum problems. Visions can inspire teachers to inspire students. Principals and teachers can seek to work with a broad vision by translating it into curriculum goals. Curriculum improvement can best be approached by starting with problems identified by the school faculty. However, if substantive and continual progress is to be made, problem solving must become one of the existing regularities in schools. Enhancing their own abilities for democratic leadership must be a critical concern of principals.

Although there has been much recent interest in working collaboratively with faculty, the two-dimensional character of supervision remains: evaluation of teachers and helping teachers. Principals still have the responsibility of providing their expertise (or enlisting outside consultants) to help individual teachers and faculty in their curriculum improvement efforts. Principals still make visits to classrooms, and they must play a key role in any effort to develop a coherent, schoolwide program to improve the curriculum. The difference between these visits and the visits made by authoritarian principals is that the purpose is collaboration rather than control.

Although *collaboration* has become a popular term in discussions of school improvement, the principal's concern is leadership: his or her own and that of other professionals. The kind of leadership provided by the principal should generate leadership opportunities among the professional staff. Principals should seek out opportunities for teachers to attend conferences concerning the problems that teachers encounter in their classrooms. Collaboration is the process of searching with others for problem solutions.

Principals must be alert to an insufficiency of teaching resources; teacher contentment may be a poor indicator of resource adequacy. The lack of resources and focus to articulate the curriculum is one reason why schools have made so little progress with curriculum synthesis. Promoting horizontal and vertical curriculum articulation is a leadership responsibility of principals and supervisors. When teachers have been given wide latitude in diagnosing school problems, the solutions are most likely to result in an improved curriculum. This is not surprising; the purpose in providing teachers with more decision-making authority is to allow them the flexibility to deal with students' motivational and learning needs. This may well involve creating an interdisciplinary curriculum so that students can see their own relationship to the world of knowledge and to a democratic society.

Teachers are more likely to function at the mediative and generative-creative levels, and not at the imitative level, if what they do is known and supported by the principal. Wholeness should pervade curriculum improvement efforts. Principals, district leaders, and teachers at all levels of the school system should (but seldom do) come together to examine the total curriculum for children and youth.

Although goal setting has been the entry point for curriculum improvement in many schools, it is the principal's responsibility to help the faculty move through the entire curriculum development process—including identifying problems and selecting and organizing learning experiences. This has been grievously neglected over the many years since Tyler's monograph was published.

Without a compass or guiding philosophy to find one's way, the sources from which to draw in curriculum development are inevitably conflicting. The development of a philosophy is fundamental in determining criteria for curriculum design, development, and evaluation. When a curriculum proposal is urged on the school, a procedure should already be in place for acting on that proposal. The principal, supervisor, and other members of the professional staff (as well as district-level administrator) have the responsibility for testing the proposal against the philosophy and ensuring that potentially harmful proposals are rejected. External proposals come along with surprising frequency.

The hypothesis-testing-correction cycle in curriculum is, as Tyler pointed out, never ending. Moreover, best practices in education are always evolving. Hence, a curriculum design is a vital living, changing thing. Curriculum development, like science, is an endless frontier. Principals and teachers must be leaders in a continuing process of investigation and application.

The superintendent, like the principal, has to make the right call when it comes to a curricular issue or problem. An example in the chapter contrasted an approach based on curriculum knowledge with one based on sanctions. The outcome points to the wisdom of Mann's idea of choosing a professional educator as superintendent. (Refer to the Best Practices Checklist on pages 481–499.)

PROBLEMS FOR STUDY AND DISCUSSION

1. The twentieth century was marked by a movement away from the original educational leadership focus of the profession of educational administration toward a concept of leadership based on business management. As a leader in the field put it, the profession's pedagogical roots "atrophied" [J. Murphy, 2002. Reculturing the profession of educational leadership: New blueprints. In J. Murphy (Ed.), *The Educational Leadership Challenge: Redefining Leadership for the 21st Century* (One hundred first Yearbook of the National Society for the Study of Education, Part 1, p. 76). Chicago: University of Chicago Press.] How do you account for the rediscovery of the idea that "Instructional and curricular leadership must be at the forefront of leadership skills [P. Hallinger, cited in Murphy, p. 80]? Why is it that a management focus inevitably fails to meet the needs of teachers and students?

2. Principals report that school-based management has increased their workloads, limiting the time that they can devote to curriculum improvement. Yet much curriculum development activity has occurred in many schools. Interview a principal whom you believe to be a curriculum leader to determine how the principal spends most of his or her time and the extent to which teachers are involved in decisions that affect the curriculum.

3. In your view, what are some of the ways that district leaders can support the curriculum improvement efforts of local school leaders?

4. Examine the supervisory staffing in your local school district. Does it represent a balanced view of the curriculum? Why or why not?

5. In connection with problem 4, if your answer was negative and you were a curriculum consultant what suggestions would you make to improve the staffing?

6. This chapter noted an advertisement for the position of director of curriculum and professional development. Is there support in the literature for such a combination? Explain.

7. The authors of this text take the position that superintendents should be professional educators (rather than from the field of business, for example). Based on your reading of this chapter and the functions in Table 17.1, do you agree? Why or why not?

8. Lawrence Cremin held that someone must be responsible for seeing the curriculum as a coherent whole. At the local school level is this someone the principal? Why or why not? If your answer is affirmative, should the principal raise questions about the interrelationship of subject areas as problems for the faculty to deal with, or should the principal wait until the problem is raised by the faculty? Justify your answer.

9. As discussed in this chapter, some principals balk at working with faculty in a democratic-participatory mode because they are afraid of losing control. Drawing from this chapter, what suggestions might be offered a principal who is reluctant to work in a collaborative setting for fear of losing administrative authority? From your experience, what additional suggestions can you offer for helping reluctant principals?

10. At which level of curriculum development would you say your school is functioning? Draw from the criteria in Table 16.1 in framing your answer.

11. Using the levels of curriculum development in Table 16.1, study a classroom or teacher to determine the level at which the teacher is functioning. As pointed out, teachers as professionals should be at Level III. If the teacher is at Level I or II, how would you as a curriculum leader make it more possible for this teacher to function at Level III?

CHAPTER 18

SCHOOL RENEWAL
WAYS AND MEANS

handwritten annotation: "lingo is biased / negative connotations"

"I like to quote the president: 'There's not a school in this country that doesn't need improvement'" (Dillon, 2004, p. A24). The comment by an education official in the second Bush administration dropped a shroud of gloom over an already ill-humored audience of parents and teachers. He was traveling the country to explain the president's new education law, or to put it differently, to put out fires. Their school, long considered excellent by the state, had been put on a watch list. A small group of fifth-graders who were special education students had missed proficiency targets and the school had been labeled "needing improvement." The label could result in removal of school staff or, at the least, would require the school to put into effect expensive remedial processes. Experts were predicting that ultimately the majority of American schools would be so labeled (p. A24).

This chapter is about school improvement. We begin by talking about language—the language of school improvement. The language used in discussions of how to improve the schools reflects a way of thinking about the nature of education and the people in schools. From this mind-set or way of thinking emerges a process for school improvement.

Reform and Renewal

John Goodlad (1999) identifies two contemporary school improvement movements: school reform and school renewal. As he points out, each has its own lingo. In the language of reform, "As with the familiar corporate litany, 'restructuring' and 'system' are favorite words" (p. 574). One might also add "innovation." (Table 18.1 examines various processes for school improvement.)

Goodlad, who has written incisively on this matter, reminds us of something of which we may already be uncomfortably aware but seldom articulate.

handwritten annotation: "good point"

> The language of reform carries with it the traditional connotations of things gone wrong that need to be corrected, as with delinquent boys and girls incarcerated in reform schools. This language is not uplifting. It says little or nothing about the nature of education . . . or the human community. (p. 574)

We turn now to renewal, the term itself. Renewal is positive, conjuring images of new life and constructive change (and maybe, even, springtime). Renewal is vital for life and growth. This is just as true for schools as for living things. The curriculum itself is a growth force. A high school senior wins a national science contest with a cancer study (Hoffman, 2004). His study concerns how cancer cells could be stopped from growing. His laboratory work was done at a biotechnology company in a summer internship. An obstacle that he had encountered is of interest here: His high school in North Attleboro, Massachusetts, "had only a small budget for science supplies" (p. B10). Today many school districts are trying to hold the line on school budgets, and teachers are focusing on teaching to the test. This situation is not favorable for students who want to do work out of a true love for a field. It is, of course, detrimental for all students.

Today, some subjects may be "squeezed" in the elementary school curriculum. Educators are finding it exceedingly difficult to maintain curriculum balance including hands-on lessons under federal policies that give priority to reading and mathematics over other studies. Children need hands-on learning experiences to meet their biosocial needs for constructing things, investigating, collaborating, and engaging in artistic projects. Educators engulfed by

Table 18.1 Processes for School Improvement.

Process	Organization	Function
Change	Segmental/micro	Efficiency/production Established learning
Innovation	Segmental/micro	Efficiency/production Established learning
Restructuring	Segmental/micro	Restructure/reorganize* Established learning
Reform	Composite(not integrated)	Remediate Established learning
Renewal/problem solving	Holistic/integrated/macro	Growth/development/synthesis Emergent learning

*Alternative schools, schools of choice, magnet schools

such policies need a compass to find their way and take some leadership. The key orientation or compass needed is that of renewal.

Dewey writes about renewal in the biological sense in the opening paragraphs of his classic book, *Democracy and Education* (1916). Living things use environmental energies—light and moisture, for example—to further their own existence. The return they get for their effort is growth. "Life is a self-renewing process through action upon the environment," says Dewey (p. 2).

Dewey's book is about school renewal. Democracy is irrevocably connected with growth and renewal through education. Realization of the democratic ideal requires a curriculum that is humanized through its connection with the interests and common concerns of all human beings. In Dewey's words:

> The scheme of a curriculum must take account of the adaptation of studies to the needs of existing community life; it must select with the intention of improving the life we live in common so that the future shall be better than the past. Moreover, the curriculum must be planned with placing essentials first, and refinements second. The things which are socially most fundamental, that is, which have to do with experiences which the widest groups share, are the essentials. The things which represent the needs of specialized groups and technical pursuits are secondary. (p. 225)

Teaching Democratic Citizenship

Overshadowed and in some cases buried by federal requirements to score higher on standardized tests, the principle of adapting subjects "to the needs of existing community life" was in decline in many schools over a period extending from the discipline-centered curriculum reforms of the 1960s to the current wave of high-stakes testing. A notable company of educators and political scientists (Barber, 1993; Goodlad, 2003/2004; Lipka, 1997; Pajak & McAfee, 1992; Tyler, 1988) have reminded administrators and teachers of the schools' central charge: To prepare students for democratic participation in civic life. Some teachers did not need reminding at all but continued, as always, to act on their vision of students as involved citizens.

Democratic citizenship is a practical goal and, as such, requires experience in democratic relationships. As one educator put it, "Its essence is transfer" (Parker, 1990, p. 17). In some schools students are engaging in the practice. No better example can be found than a sixth-grade classroom in Ohio. Investigating a real problem—a local creek contaminated by a chemical spill—the students became experts in testing water quality. After meeting with environmental experts and purchasing a chemical testing kit, they embarked on the task of sampling the tributaries to the area watershed. Quite appropriately, their class became a trusted source for testing local wells. Moreover, the class produced radio announcements on how to keep water supplies safe (Wood, 1990). Such activities are a continuation of the emphasis on democratic citizenship that is so much a part of the Deweyan view of education. Although alive and well in the education literature, education for citizenship—as part of the curriculum, not as a community service add-on for graduation—has been neglected. It is a responsibility to be shared by are teacher (Hlebowitsh, 2005, p.44). Principals have a crucial role in remedying the neglect by supporting and encouraging projects that help students see from their own experience that what they do as citizens makes a difference.

Service Learning. Interest in community service from national leaders has provided an opportunity for curriculum improvement. The National and Community Service Act of 1990, signed into law by President George H. W. Bush, and the National Community Service Trust Act of 1993, President Bill Clinton's initiative, may be so regarded. Both provided funding for community service programs in schools. In the 1990s many school systems added community service requirements. The problem then became one of how to integrate service projects into the curriculum. Often the project came first and the why of doing it came later if at all. Such an approach can hardly be expected to stimulate student interest and lead to participation, which was the intent of the legislation.

Nevertheless the legislation lent support for curricula that focus on problem solving and foster student participation in experiences that address real needs in their communities (Bohnenberger & Terry, 2002). The idea was hardly new. Good schools had been doing this for years, since the 1930s and earlier, as Conrad and Hedin (1991) point out in their review of research on the impact of service on student learning and development.

Best practices underscore the importance of beginning with the curriculum, not with the service. In one school students planted trees along the riverfront. Only afterward did they "reflect" on the project, learning that the original trees had died because of pollution. Thus an opportunity for teaching problem solving was missed.

Service-learning projects have a greater chance of success when the objectives are clear. Lipka (1997) suggests that the school staff help students select a variety of the following objectives.

To develop and apply participation skills such as planning and cooperation which are a part of effective citizenship.

To come aware of community problems and needs.

To develop a sense of self-worth through personal contributions to community life.

To develop a sense of personal responsibility for the quality of life.

To gain insight into other people's lives through interactions with citizens from various walks of life and of different age and diverse backgrounds.

To develop predispositions toward active community participation and service which will carry over into adult life. (pp. 58–59)

According to Lipka, well-organized projects have two elements: Direct experience via real community improvement projects and reflective thinking about what the experiences mean through journal writing, discussions, and other school activities. Thought and action "bring together the cognitive and affective dimensions which result in authentic learning" (p. 59). Dewey's—and our—concern is with the curriculum. We are particularly interested in how service-learning projects can be initiated from the curriculum itself. As Lipka points out, this readily happens when the curriculum is organized around compelling societal problems. As students study units based on such issues as "World Peace," "Living in Our Community" or "How Technology Influences Our Lives," they have an opportunity to study problems and how they might be resolved. And the development of service projects increases student interest—because what they are doing is real. (See chapter 10 for a discussion of integrated problem-focused curricula and the *Building America* series, edited by Paul R. Hanna, 1925–1948.)

Today there is no shortage of examples of curriculum-based projects in the literature—ideas where students have experienced democracy as a process in which citizens can really shape things to their higher purposes. In another example, 12th grade students in a government class in Indiana worked with transportation officials in their city to study ways of reducing traffic congestion. The outcome was a proposal to the transportation officials of a monorail system. In formulating the proposal, the students were engaged in conducting research, attending community meetings, undertaking surveys, and using skills in budgeting, mapping and design. "I learned that citizens do have a voice in what goes on," said a student who participated in the project. "It is important to make time to share your ideas and have officials take account of them" (Allen, 2003, p. 52). Schools can use community problems to an educational advantage and, in so doing, renew themselves.

Providing Shared Experiences. The environmental energies that Dewey talked about are social changes that act on the schools. Today, the most profound changes are environmental in the real sense; that is, the environments in which schools find themselves are rapidly changing, and cultural differences in school populations continue to grow. This is opportunity knocking at the door of democracy. Dewey's position that "emphasis must be put upon whatever binds people together in cooperative human pursuits and results" (1916, p. 114) retains its currency. Human experience is an interactive process. As the school helps each student to participate with others in finding the best knowledge to make a decision, a common experience is achieved. Such experiences are connected to the democratic ideal. The more diverse the school population, the greater is the need to provide shared experiences for developing mutual understanding and respect. Indeed, such experiences are clearly in evidence in many of the schools we have visited where the students represent an astonishing variety of cultural backgrounds.

Forces Impelling Renewal

Changing populations are just one influence impelling schools to renew themselves. Others include (1) progress in teacher professionalism, (2) the continuing study of what students should gain from the curriculum, (3) new ideas about how students learn, (4) equity concerns (increasing access to curriculum), (5) ideas about how organizations can function more effectively, (6) problems in the larger society—including those that students bring with them to schools, and (7) the perceived failure of previous reform efforts.

A good school is in a constant state of renewal, which is to say it is always improving. How is an administrator or supervisor to wend through the maze of often conflicting proposals for school improvement and provide leadership in the right direction? We examine the paths and prescriptions in light of their promise for school renewal and make suggestions for administrators and supervisors.

Processes for School Improvement

The Magic Bullet Approach

Proponents of school improvement tend to promulgate a single idea or approach to give the schools a new lease on life. Collegiality among school faculty

(with the hope of sparking innovation), intercultural education, new organizational structures, national education standards (penalties on schools that fail to comply was a new feature of this idea in the early 2000s), and gender-equity proposals (intended to offer the same opportunities to girls as boys) are examples. Those who promote a singular approach are likely to be impatient with other approaches and to convey the notion that there is only one road to improvement: theirs. In 1991 Joyce noted, "There is a tendency to suggest that those who follow any other approach to school improvement are off-track" (p. 61). Today, it can be stated that the tendency has not diminished.

Proponents of what might be called a single-factor path to reform see their proposal as a complete answer (Desimone, 2002). Reformers tend to use their own field of interest as a lens for viewing schools. Thus, those with an interest in organizational change may focus on administrative structure as the route to improvement. Those whose interest is instruction propose that school faculties study generic instructional skills and the styles of outstanding teachers. Those who believe that the application of research findings is the answer to school improvement propose that school leaders familiarize themselves with research on effective schools. Those whose specialty is computer-based instruction will see the computer program as the answer to curriculum problems. Each approach is treated as a magic bullet: a total prescription for school improvement by advocates. That there is a continuous barrage of segmental approaches may come as a shock to the new principal or supervisor. Segmental approaches often have conflicting effects or lead to distorted priorities. There are no magic bullets. Some approaches such as the foregoing can be synthesized as principals and teachers work together to solve problems. Teachers study *relevant* research in efforts to improve the curriculum. The emphasis is on relevance because not all of the research on effective schools is relevant to a given situation. To study research in absence of a problem can have two detrimental effects: teachers' time is wasted, which all too frequently happens with professional development programs, and more important, perhaps, teachers are encouraged to put findings into practice that may not be applicable to their own situation. As Joyce points out, approaches to school improvement are both connected and synthesized in the course of solving school problems:

Many specialists in organizational development have found that a faculty can best develop their collegiality in combination with solving actual school problems in an area of agreed-on need such as the curriculum. Keeping a real problem in mind ensures that practical problem solving is kept prominent and that group process doesn't become an end in itself. (1991, p. 60)

New Organizational Structures

As shown in Table 18.1, making structural changes in a school or school system is one approach to school improvement. Indeed, it was a very popular idea for improving schools in the 1990s. Whatever the stated principles that justify new changes in the governance of schools (curriculum decisions at the school site, for instance), the educational restructuring movement of the 1990s had its origins in business and industry. In business and industry, *restructuring* was a code word meaning reorganization for the purpose of slimming down the size of the organization and, presumably, making it more efficient. But downsizing had its down side, often leaving companies without experienced people who had solved various kinds of problems and who helped contribute to the organization's success (Rowland, 1993).

It has already been pointed out how some structural innovations in education had similar effects—how financially strapped school systems justified the downsizing of their central office staffs on the alleged ground that leaders should be granted independence to develop their own curricula based on the needs of their own students. This left teachers without supervisory support and model demonstration lessons. In education, restructuring has a broader meaning than in the business world (although one might be wise to keep the roots in mind). In education, the issue in restructuring is school improvement. Many of the allegedly new strategies proposed in the restructuring movement of the 1990s were not new; interdisciplinary curriculums and opportunities for teachers to work together are examples. In this sense, the restructuring movement was simply recalling educators to their best practices in the field of curriculum development. However, the focus of change was on new organizational structures, without making the needed connections with curriculum development and school improvement (Newmann, 1993). The idea (really an old mistake in school reform) is that if we just change the way schools are organized, substantive curriculum change will follow. Restructuring has generally stopped with organizational change. Take, for example, team teaching, in which teachers work on curricular themes. The objective of the team structure is curriculum improvement. As Newmann observes, generally curriculum is discussed "no more deeply than choosing a general theme for study (the environment, culture, estimation)" (p. 5). Newmann views the situation with a compelling sense that teachers need more time together to plan, and they need greater access to resources. We add that the resources should include actual examples and models of interdisciplinary units. Teachers need models to follow.

Strategies for restructuring include smaller schools, school choice, charter schools, local autonomy, national curriculum standards in subject areas, and interagency collaboration (coordinating community social services with school programs). In a critique of restructuring, Newmann points out that the proposed structural changes are not part of a coherent plan, and he points to the need for linking changes together (pp. 8–9). The reason they are not connected is that they were never intended to be. (See Table 18.1.) Each proposal is viewed by its advocates as the way to renew schools. Hence, instructional improvement is seen and treated as entirely separate from curriculum improvement. Not only is there the pervading problem of segmental and disjointed programs, but many of the ideas and strategies conflict. For example, there is a simultaneous effort to institute national standards in subject fields and to promote interdisciplinary curriculums. According to Kirst (1993), such standards are likely to have a detrimental effect on curriculum synthesis. (By the early 2000s it was clear that this had happened. The likelihood had become a reality.)

How are such conflicts to be avoided in school improvement efforts? As Newmann (1993) points out, the answer lies in focusing on curriculum development, improving learning opportunities for all students. It is inevitable that educators will run up against proposals that never touch the curriculum, but they must wage a constant battle to keep the curriculum—what is taught, why, and how—as the focus. Moreover, structural changes should stem from an educational problem, not from the purported answer to someone else's problem. Restructuring seemed desirable and efficient because business was doing it (Segal, 1996).

School Size and Curricular Gain. New educational structures have made it possible to solve the problem of a school that is too small—and one that is too large as well. School consolidation proved to be a successful solution to the inability of poor districts to support their small rural schools. Bus transportation made it possible for fewer schools of better quality to serve larger numbers of students. The larger schools had more competent teachers, more cosmopolitan school populations, an expanded and balanced curriculum, and better facilities and resources. It is true of course that some communities opposed (and continue to oppose) consolidation and district reorganization. The stressful conditions associated with inadequate tax resources and consequent inequality of educational opportunity have caused a continuing trend toward this kind of centralization in the United States.

In the larger cities the story was vastly different. Populations increased—indeed, burgeoned—concurrently with the development of public education, which had its greatest momentum in urban sections. From the start, urban centers demanded larger education facilities than did rural areas. Much has been written about the huge size and factorylike atmosphere of urban junior and senior high schools and the need for smaller schools that will give students more personal attention.

Providing Supportive Learning Environments: Schools Within Schools. The problem confronting educators is how to reorganize schools so that they are smaller and yet preserve the curricular advantages of large schools. For decades, there has been a solution: schools within schools. The story of this idea is a most interesting one. It involves a remarkable educational leader, a high school principal who would later become U.S. commissioner of Education under Lyndon Johnson. Back we go into the 1950s. We see Harold Howe II, who has become principal at Newton High School in Massachusetts. He has come from a principalship at Walnut Hills High School in Cincinnati, a selective high school similar to Stuyvesant High in New York City. At Newton High he finds an impersonal environment. There are 3,200 students, and the "average" student receives little attention. In an interview in 2000, he recounted how this principalship gave him the opportunity to experience "the inventiveness that could be brought to the factory-system school" (Goldberg, 2000, p. 161). With the cooperation of the faculty, community and school board, Howe introduces the house plan, which involves creating small houses within the school.

Here was an educational invention that would be followed in some large high schools. Two major principles were involved in Howe's structural change. One was that it stemmed from an educational problem. The other was that success in school improvement "is best achieved through working closely with teachers—and not by orders from above" (p. 160).

In the 1960s Evanston Township High School in Illinois adopted the house plan, which, as Goodlad (1984) points out, is "a term that is commonly used by private colleges" (p. 310). Whether or not the term was appropriated in order to ensure the support of parents for the reorganization is not known, and is left for historians of Evanston Township High School to determine. The school of several thousand students was divided into smaller schools, housed within the existing buildings. The houses were organized vertically so that students were connected with one house during their high school years. Each house has its own faculty and counselors, and it provides a curriculum of general education or unified studies—those learnings that all educated members of a society hold in common. Specialized studies are taken throughout the school.

In general, one can identify three advantages to the school-within-a-school plan. The first is more opportunity for faculty to get to know students and give them individual attention. This is important for all students but particularly for inner-city schools, which may have as many as 5,000 students, many of whom are considered at risk (McPartland, Balfanz, Jordan, & Legters, 2002). A second advantage is that the houses can share the library, laboratories, studios, shops, and other central resources that schools must have if they are to offer educational services of high quality. A third advantage is that teachers have a greater opportunity to work together with a given population of heterogeneous students throughout the high school years.

Today, national discomfiture with large impersonal high schools continues to grow, and this is reflected in recent local efforts to create small high schools or subdivide large ones. Chicago, New York City, and Philadelphia are examples of districts that are attempting to personalize the learning environment via smaller units. McPartland, Balfanz, Jordan, and Legters (2002) cite examples as well as grant programs to support such efforts. Of particular interest for educational leaders is that, "A federal competitive grant program, begun in 1998 to support schools-within-a school for high schools, has given added impetus to these reforms" (p. 154).

How does one establish a small school of high quality in a disadvantaged area? Deborah Meier, a secondary school administrator in Harlem, provides insights from her experience in her book, *The Power of Their Ideas: Lessons for America from a Small School in Harlem* (1995). According to McPartland, Balfanz, Jordan, and Legters, Meier's school "is a model of how a small school serving 450 students in grades 7 through 12 can provide an intellectually rigorous and creative education" (p. 154).

In the 1990s and early 2000s, some school districts, New York, for example, were establishing small alternative schools within existing school buildings and in separate sites (Dillon, 1993; Gootman, 2004). Curricular gain—or loss—must be the dominant and overriding consideration in any plan to develop smaller high schools. This means that careful consideration must be given to the possible danger of narrowing the curriculum in alternative schools to meet a special-interest function for a special (isolated) pupil population, and without the critical mass required for faculty specializations and a rich curriculum.

Forgetting About the Old School. "People kind of forget about the old school and focus on the new schools," said a senior at Bushwick High School in New York City. "It's like they're getting all the attention" (Gootman, 2004, p. B9). He was right. Today, many small alternative schools have been planted in large high schools in New York City and other districts. There are instances where careful consideration has not been given by school officials to the effects on the curriculum of host schools. Teachers, students, and parents who are devoted to their school are deeply concerned about what they see as draining its resources and curricular strengths.

Two recent instances will be mentioned here, both in New York City, which is a leader in the small school movement. Creating small schools in New York has been funding impelled. Small schools get private start-up money, much of it from the largesse of the Bill and Melinda Gates Foundation. At John F. Kennedy High School in the Bronx, some teachers actively opposed a plan to create a small school that could turn Kennedy's auto shop into classrooms. A number of teachers expressed their concern by holding a protest one evening. Their placards read "'Save Our Auto Shop'" and "'Mini Schools, Maximum Harm'" (p. B9). At DeWitt Clinton High School in the Bronx, the alumni association asked the city's

department of education to remove a small school that had been planted there: the Celia Cruz Bronx High School of Music. According to a Clinton alumnus, a former New York City deputy mayor, "What they were doing was taking one of the strengths of Clinton, the music department, and they wanted to break it out of the school." He added, "In my view there is nothing wrong with big schools, if it's done right" (p. B9). The alumni association's lobbying was successful. Celia Cruz would move.

Certainly, supporters of small schools tend to overlook the curricular advantage of large schools, one of which is a variety of elective courses, which small schools cannot offer for exploratory, enrichment, and specialized courses.

All this adds up to the fact that the house plan is still a sound strategy for renewing large high schools because all students have an opportunity to be in small units with access to total school resources.

Distinctive versus Cosmopolitan Schools. Schools, like individuals, have their own personalities. In the 1990s, however, some reformers carried this idea considerably further, arguing that by developing distinctive characters and functions schools would renew themselves. The idea that schools should be different from one another was promoted in particular by advocates of public school choice as a means of school improvement. A choice-based system is market based. As Hess (2003) points out in a detailed examination of choice systems, choice advocates maintain "that this approach permits a wide variety of schools and approaches to emerge, and that parents searching for quality options will ensure that effective schools flourish and will force ineffective schools to improve or eventually shut their doors" (p. 117). In a policy brief issued by the RAND Corporation's Institute on Education and Training (1992), this question was raised: "Does the school define and maintain an appropriate, distinctive character?" According to RAND, designing schools with distinctive character is the key to educational improvement: "the basic premise is variety, not uniformity." The focus on difference blurs the fact that good schools are alike in many ways. As Henry Levin pointed out in an interview in 1992, all good schools expose all youngsters to the richest possible experiences, and they also connect the school "Dewey-style" with the children's own experiences (Brandt, 1992, p. 20). Levin is noted for a program to accelerate and enrich the learning of at-risk children. His program has brought the children into the mainstream. Levin's program and underlying theses are not new, of course. The field of education has generated a core of best practices from research that good schools follow. There is a universal quality rather than a limited scope that characterizes good schools. This was borne out in the 1990s and early 2000s by what happened in some school districts with open enrollment, where students were allowed to transfer to other public schools in their district. Two New York City districts (Districts 2 and 4), Montgomery County, Maryland, and Cambridge, Massachusetts, are examples (Hess, 2003). Here it was found that parents seeking transfers for their children were looking for good schools, not different schools. It is this universal quality that Dewey's "best and wisest parent wants" (1900a, p. 7) and should be available to all children in our society. The cosmopolitan school, not the special-interest school, is required for renewal. Dewey goes further, of course, saying that "any other ideal for our schools" if "acted upon destroys our democracy" (p. 7).

Innovation

School choice advocates often cite innovative approaches for increasing achievement as the anticipated outcome. Generally, those who urge school choice argue that bureaucratic regulation has stifled innovation in the public system. As Lubienski (2003) points out, choice advocates have observed competition and choice in the consumer marketplace. They expect the same dynamics to lead to improved achievement, more parental options, and new pedagogical inventions, especially for "those groups traditionally marginalized in the current public system" (p. 396). Lubienski examined in detail how charter schools reflect such expectations. Interestingly, policy makers seemed literally in love with the word *innovation*. Indeed, the word was stated as a policy goal in about three quarters of the state laws authorizing charter schools. "No other goal—including academic achievement and the diversification of programmatic options—was mentioned more frequently" (p. 399).

Lubienski found that charter schools are "not offering innovations in the manner anticipated by reformers" (p. 397). Charters are an organizational innovation, it is true, but that is it. Charters are not innovative at the classroom level. Generally the approaches in charter schools are those widely available in public schools.

Puzzled and disappointed, some policy makers began to look more closely at the definition of innovation. Does an innovation have to be a strictly new invention? For example, integrated curricula and hands-on learning would be "innovative" in some schools. But then, these are already practiced in good public schools, as Lubienski observes, "thereby undercutting a critical R&D assumption of market-based reform" (p. 416). Innovations may be ideas already practiced in progressive schools. However, Lubienski notes, the appeal for parents of practices such as those in place in conservative private schools pulls the charter schools back toward a more standard or traditional model.

The mistake of many choice advocates has been to begin with market approaches. As Dewey suggested, one starts with the problem in the educational situation. The solution may be an "innovative approach." To begin with the idea that solutions (many of which already exist) will be marketable is at best a dead end, and at worst delusory and dangerous. In many cases it has led to a lower standard than that typically held in public schools. Our concern is with curriculum improvement as a way to generate and perpetuate school renewal. We hope policy makers will reject the idea that a market regime will lead to curriculum improvement. "Across charter schools in various states, research demonstrates virtually no innovation in curriculum or instructional strategies" (Lubienski, p. 419).

The Comprehensive-Connected Approach

In the previous section we examined some segmental approaches to school improvement. Although one still hears talk of magic bullets (testing is a favorite of policy makers), there has been a growing recognition that school improvement requires a comprehensive approach. How might this be done? We have seen a number of designs or programs, some of which have become very well known. Success for All, for example, is a "name-brand" whole-school reform model (Schmoker, 2004, p. 428). The recognition that a comprehensive approach is needed is a giant leap forward. The reform models, however, tend to be complex and prescriptive. Although all packaged reform models include important practices they have at least two shortcomings. First, there is little thought of staff collaboration. Models are promoted as a complete package; problems and solutions are already identified. According to Schmoker, an educational consultant, "They tend on the whole to slight or supplant the collaborative structures necessary for instructional improvement" (p. 428). Second, the plans are complex and often confusing, and implementation may add up to being simply another burden for teachers. With an inarticulate program, improvement becomes "disjointed and incoherent" (Fullan & Stiegelbauer, 1991, p. 97).

There is another approach. As indicated in the previous section, single-factor paths to reform are connected in the course of solving a curriculum problem. Curriculum frameworks, for example, require a coherent strategy for their implementation. The strategy includes providing improved programs of teacher education, staff development to help teachers understand and implement the new procedures, peer teaching, and the creation of networks to link teachers and scholars, such as the Foxfire Teachers Outreach Network, the (San Francisco) Bay Area Writing Project, and the Urban Mathematics Collaborative. If solutions are to be sustained, problem solving involves multifaceted strategies deriving from an ecological or environmental perspective. The education environment should be conjoint and supportive, not segmental and contradictory.

In chapter 15 it was pointed out that many teachers are working in an environment of contradictory policies. There has been a national policy shift from reforms focused on lower-level mechanical skills for disadvantaged children to higher-level skills and idea-oriented teaching for everyone. Meanwhile, standardized testing is often still geared to the old policy. In the 1990s, some reformers were seeking systemic change, an attempt to tightly align state policies—especially those concerning curriculum, textbooks, and assessment—with goals for student learning. That policies should promote a coherent environment for teachers rather than one of conflicting policies is inarguable. However, as Linda Darling-Hammond noted, there is danger in confusing linear approaches with coherence. "It is important for us to be connecting the right ideas to make the environment more coherent for school people," she said, going on to give this warning: "In a rush to get things lined up, there is always a danger that we will do something not very thoughtful" (Olson & Rothman, 1993, p. 13). We add that by starting with a curriculum problem rather than a series of disconnected ideas, policy makers at the state and local levels have

the best assurance of creating a coherent and supporting environment for teachers. Linear approaches tend to fit a factorylike production model of schooling, a model ill suited to the educative process that is concerned with human growth.

Another point of importance is that new ideas about teaching and learning may influence state and district policies, rather than the other way around. This may be difficult to believe in the 2000s in a field such as reading. Today, high-stakes tests have had a profound effect on the curriculum. Easily measured literacy tasks have in many schools become the curriculum. The direction of influence has been from the federal and state governments to the schools.

In the late 1980s, however, the direction of influence was from ideas about how children could be invited "into a world of books and reading" (Pearson, 2000, p. 178) to state policy makers. The role of literature in elementary reading programs had ascended like a rocket. "In terms of policy and curriculum," writes Pearson, "the most significant event in promoting literature based reading was the 1988 California Reading Framework" (p. 178). Pearson's chapter in the 2000 National Society for the Study of Education Yearbook, *American Education: Yesterday, Today, and Tomorrow*, explains this development in detail. The point of importance here is that teachers who believe in a new practice will often follow it despite the fact that policy has not caught up. As one of our students recounted:

Four years ago, I eagerly and enthusiastically began my teaching career in Spring Branch Independent School District. I was fulfilling my student-teaching requirement in the district in which I am employed. Student teaching provided many opportunities for administering language arts to the assigned first-grade class. As modeled by the supervising teacher, I strictly followed the curriculum guide page by page as composed by the district. Following these guides offered a sense of routine and structure that most new professionals find comforting. Of course, in reflecting, the curriculum at this particular school or School X was functioning at Level I (imitative-maintenance level) of the levels of curriculum development. The student teaching experience was not conducive for teacher creativity or imagination.

A year later I was officially hired by the school district to serve as a first-grade teacher at School Y. Now the setting was completely different from the prior year. Literature-based language arts was strongly supported and utilized by the first-grade teachers even though it contradicted the present curriculum in language arts. One should note that the actual curriculum guide called for the teaching of isolated skills or "clusters." Cluster tests were administered before progressing to the next set of skills or clusters. Obviously what was being promoted, supported and implemented at School Y did not have a place in the existing curriculum. Thus many teachers were forced to create their own unofficial, unwritten curriculums.

One can only imagine my anxiety. I was now to follow a curriculum of my own making, as was the case of all other teachers on that grade level. I survived my first year of teaching simply due to the total support of my fellow team members. The team (the other seven teachers on the grade level) "carried" me through my first year by modeling, sharing and most of all communicating effectively.

Ironically the following year the whole district made a 360 degree turnabout by adopting a brand new language-arts curriculum. This curriculum was totally a literature-base approach to teaching language arts. It provided the missing link that many teachers were looking for; it officially validated the implementation of literature-base language arts. School Y, which was already promoting literature-base language arts totally embraced this new curriculum with open arms.

Things changed again in the late 1990s. Advocates of whole language and literature-based reading were unable to respond to criticisms from the public policy arena that phonics must come first. According to Pearson, one problem was that those who supported the whole language movement never had the complete support of educators who were in accord with many of its principles and practices but who felt that the whole-language approach neglected systematic instruction in reading programs. They did not believe that skills are always "caught" by a child during a real reading activity and were concerned that teaching reading in content areas was being ignored—indeed, banned in some cases. But another problem was the lack of a program for professional development. Teachers had to know how to tailor reading activities to the needs and interests of individual learners. In many cases the teacher knowledge simply was not there.

In 1992 California fourth-grade children scored last in the nation in the fourth-grade National Assessment of Educational Progress (NAEP) in reading. It was the first time that scores were shown by

the state. According to Stephen Krashen (2002), a story circulating in California—and unsubstantiated by evidence—alleged that reading scores had fallen since 1987 when whole-language advocates took control over the Language Arts Framework Committee. Whole language was introduced; phonics, along with other forms of direct instruction, was banned; and reading scores fell. But California is now beginning to recover from the devastation, "thanks to a rational, sensible phonics-based approach to reading" (p. 749).

It made a good story. But according to Krashen, a professor emeritus at the University of California who had served on the Language Arts Framework Committee, that was not what happened. "Phonics was not banned. We simply proposed that language arts should be 'literature-based.' This is hardly controversial. In fact, I regarded it as part of the definition of language arts" (p. 749). According to Krashen, an examination of reading comprehension scores on state tests (California Achievement Program) from 1984 to 1990 shows no pattern of increases or decreases. But there is an explanation for the low scores. They are related to California's "print-poor environment." According to a recent analysis of school library data and public library data, California is last in the nation of the quality of its school libraries and ranks close to the bottom in the quality of its public libraries (McQuillan, 1998). Moreover, many of California's children live in poverty, and their homes have little reading material.

How does all this relate to reading scores, and what is its importance for school improvement? McQuillan found a strong correlation between access to print (books and other kinds of print available in the home, school, and community) and 1994 NAEP reading scores. "California's problem is not whole language but a lack of reading material," Krashen tells us (2002, p. 749). "There is excellent evidence that children with more access to books read more and that children who read more make excellent gains in literary development" (p. 749). Furthermore, libraries with more books and better staffing are associated with higher reading scores. Perhaps most important of all for teachers and supervisors is that when whole language is properly defined—that is, as including a lot of real reading—children in such classes perform as well or better than students in skills-based classes on tests of so-called skills (reading nonsense words, for instance). More importantly, children in the classes that include a great deal of authentic reading have more positive attitudes toward reading and do more reading on their own (Krashen, 1999).

Today the federal government thinks otherwise. The main stream of thought bearing on policy is that there is no evidence supporting the benefit of reading itself and teachers and supervisors should focus on intensive phonics and requiring children to read aloud in order that their errors can be corrected (Garan, 2001). But this story has just started, and it is within the power of policy makers (including teachers) to change the policy. Will more children have more access to real books? Crucial in this regard is whether policy makers base their policies on research. This in itself is a real problem (Pearson, 2000).

Finally, teachers should be encouraged by their supervisors to base their teaching on the body of best practices in the curriculum field whether or not those practices happen to support present policies.

The Ecology of Curriculum Renewal

Clearly the way to reform is not with a linear top-down approach. As a noted social scientist, Harlan Cleveland, observed, "the world of work consists mostly of horizontal relationships" (1985, p. 9). A number of educational theorists (who have also been deeply involved with practice) have given school renewal a biological turn by viewing those involved as part of an ecosystem (Tanner & Tanner, 1987, pp. 121–169). John Goodlad (1987) uses an ecological model in which policy makers at state and local levels, teachers, administrators, and others are concerned with an array of broad educational goals and the application of best practices for reaching them. Relationships among the individuals and groups in the ecology of schooling are multiple rather than linear, and the main concern of policy makers is to provide teachers with what they need for reaching the goals rather than with a punitive, intimidating atmosphere. For example, policy makers at the state and local levels must provide a supportive environment at the school level. From experience, we know that this is the only way that continuous, effective curriculum development activities at the school level will take place. As everyone knows, however, the support often fails to materialize. Goodlad provides us with some helpful ideas on why and how linkages so often fail to happen. According to Goodlad, the way people are now linked is ineffective for two closely related reasons: (1) top-down, one-way directives are the

approach to "improvement" and (2) there has been a "pathological emphasis on accountability"; each individual is concerned with the adequacy of the behavior of those at some other level or unit (pp. 4, 12). The model that has been followed for so long in the world of schooling is the established-convergent factory-production model; top-down directives are concerned with the production of high test scores. As Goodlad points out, a healthy school is concerned with more than test scores because society wants schools to meet personal-social growth and vocational goals as well as academic goals. High test scores can never be an indicator of school health. A healthy school is a renewing school, continually checking what it does in connection with knowledge about how students learn and teachers teach and in relation to changes in the larger society—the wider environment.

Toward an Organic System.   Recent education policies reflect the recognition that top-down strategies for curriculum improvement are ineffective. There has been a discernible movement in many school systems toward an organic system of organization, which is a concept similar to Goodlad's ecological model. There has been much interest in involving teachers in a collaborative effort to improve the curriculum. For the first time in many years, this critically important best practice in the literature has, in many sections, become formulated into a policy.

But there is usually a rider to the policy of collaborative curriculum improvement: Teachers must be held accountable for the decisions they make. Indeed, there is an emphasis on teacher (and principal) accountability in most school decentralization plans, and this is typically determined by pupil test results. Central administrators thus have not effectively detached themselves from the production model. There are, of course, stunning exceptions, and these superintendents have achieved marked success in renewing their school system (see chapter 16).

Goodlad suggests that the concept of accountability be changed to responsibility with each unit concerned with its own behavior. "Legislators, for example, should be concerned with whether they are providing what schools and those in them need to function effectively" (p. 12). The emphasis, Goodlad argues, should be on providing teachers with the time and resources they must have for curriculum renewal. What Goodlad is saying is that a different paradigm or view of the world must guide school renewal efforts. His own words concerning this paradigm shift are worth quoting: "One-way directives are replaced by multiple interactions; leadership by authority is replaced by leadership by knowledge; following rules and regulations is replaced by inquiring behavior; accountability is replaced by high expectations, responsibility, and a level of trust that includes freedom to make mistakes; and much more" (p. 4). Goodlad is not alone in proposing a holistic approach to school renewal.

Janowitz's Model. Morris Janowitz, a sociologist, emphasized the importance of following an aggregation model in transforming urban schools, as opposed to the specialization or segmental model and piecemeal change. In the aggregation model, the focus is on "the totality of the situation in which the teacher finds herself" (1969, p. 42). In Janowitz's model, teachers as professionals use curriculum specialists and other resource personnel, bringing them into the classroom as needed. According to Janowitz, the public school system's effectiveness in reaching its academic and social goals depends primarily on increasing teachers' authority and professional expertise. Like Goodlad, Janowitz argued that holistic conceptual models must guide policy makers.

In Janowitz's model, the concept of holism extends to curriculum. Janowitz believed that integrated curriculum approaches are important for renewing urban schools, particularly plans relating knowledge and the skills of democratic living. As a guiding principle, the curriculum should reflect "interdependence of academic and socialization goals" (p. 44). In a sense, observed Janowitz, educational psychologists have contributed to the rationale for a segmental rather than complete approach to curriculum. They have focused attention so completely on articulating curriculum content with the cognitive development of the child that it began to be viewed by many educators as a complete curriculum theory. The child's social needs and those of the larger society were forgotten or pushed far into the background. When thought of at all, social needs were treated as unrelated to and of less importance than academic goals. Janowitz's observations were made in the late 1960s. They are, if anything, even more relevant in the 2000s.

Piaget and Curriculum Improvement. Janowitz pointed out that Jean Piaget himself questioned the American adaptation of Piaget's process of intellectual development to curriculum reform (see chapter 8). According to Janowitz, Piaget's work and its interpretations have meaning for classroom teachers "not because they supply engineering-type guides for curriculum development, but because, directly or indirectly, they increase the interpersonal capacity of the teacher" (p. 47). Many streams flow into the teacher's professional knowledge and they interact continuously. School renewal requires an aggregate rather than segmental approach and making subject matter meaningful through synthesis is the way to curriculum reform.

The idea that social and academic goals must be dealt with as interdependent is, of course, not new; Dewey pioneered in melding these goals in his laboratory school (L. Tanner, 1997). Janowitz believed that educators in difficult schools could use the idea as the basis for teaching children social responsibility and concern for others. Social responsibility needs to have a more established place in the curriculum for all children but has an immediately functional purpose in schools where teachers have to struggle to keep order and where older children victimize the younger ones. From a practical standpoint, social goals are essential and one vitally connected with enabling students to do well in school. Or, in Janowitz's words, "any system of improved academic effectiveness must rest on the creation of a classroom climate based on mutual respect or value sharing" (p. 39).

Segmental Approaches Impede Renewal

A problem with segmental approaches is that they tend to deal with specific techniques, procedures, practices, or programs targeted for one population group or level of schooling, making curriculum articulation more difficult. Even more serious, the specialized-segmental changes not only work in isolation, but also often work in opposition and contradiction. Moreover, preoccupation with one group may cause the problems of other groups to remain neglected. This is shortsightedness in its most virulent form. The problems of one group do not remain their own, but affect other youngsters as well as us all. Kindergartners through twelfth-graders are part of an ecological community, in interaction with the environment of the school and with each other and the wider ecosystem outside schools.

The federal government's focus on early education well illustrates the segmental approach. The year 1965 saw the creation of Project Head Start, a program intended to compensate for the education handicaps of disadvantaged preschool children and give them a good start in school. Policy makers had been profoundly influenced by research on child development, especially Benjamin Bloom's (1964) conclusion that the major portion of brain development takes place very early in life. Although Bloom never said that high school was too late for intervention, many policy makers, seeking a shortcut, drew that conclusion from his book. As a consequence, the adolescent was largely neglected or written off. The idea that early childhood is a crucial period for countering adverse intellectual and social environments was supported by other authorities on child development. Early education as the means of ensuring a child's success in school—and a successful adult life—became national policy.

The next four decades were a record of continuing focus on young children. According to Schorr (1989), "Head Start was so deeply embedded in the American landscape that no administration could uproot it or even significantly cut it back" (p. 190). This surely cannot be debated. Schorr goes on to observe that preschool programs are "now widely recognized as the most successful large-scale attempts in the last quarter century to improve the prospects of high-risk children" (p. 190). She might have pointed out that although a part of the landscape, such programs have not been part of the school. (Granted that some Head Start programs are school based, they are administered separately.) The point of importance is that the effort to improve opportunities was targeted to young children, and the idea that they are the group most likely to be salvaged from lives of poverty has continued to affect present policies. Nevertheless, if preschool programs such as Head Start are to have long-term benefits, as opposed to short-term successes that wear out, then these programs will need to be integrated into a holistic and coordinated effort, from preschool through adolescence. Intense projects emphasizing college preparation for at-risk high school youth have been highly successful. The emphasis is on comprehensiveness and intensity. Schorr notes that when resources are diluted and spread to other schools after a project has been found successful, the program loses its impact. The point remains: There has been no attempt to meet the needs of older at-risk students on the scale of Head Start. The dropout rate continues to be high, especially among Hispanic and African American students.

It has long been argued that Head Start has not been maximally effective because children who are in the program enter traditionally organized schools. The overriding reason, however, is probably that reformers have failed to use an ecological model in planning their interventions with at-risk youngsters. They failed to consider the interaction of students in the ecosystem of a school (as well as outside school), and the direction of influence, which is from older to younger children. In inner-city poverty areas, teenagers have the most impact on the school's social environment and on the attitudes of children of all ages toward the school's goals. In view of this, Janowitz saw the early education movement as "at best a partial strategy. At worst a basic error in priorities." At-risk 14- to 18-year-olds generally "develop a sense of frustration and a group life in opposition to the goals of the school [and i]n this group are opinion leaders in the slum youth culture and the effective bearers of the culture of the slum from one generation to the next." Thus, he argued, a case could be made that this group should have the highest priority if comprehensive changes are to be made in the curriculum and school culture (p. 41).

Nearly 30 years later, Janowitz's observations on the tragic pathologies of urban ghettos would be echoed by another University of Chicago sociologist, William Julius Wilson (1996). Wilson proposed an aggregate approach to the problems. One of his solutions is to provide support to teachers for curriculum development.

Janowitz's observation about the impact of high school students on younger children seems even more valid today. Troubled adolescents still drop out and hang out on street corners; they still influence younger children, who also fail to make it to their own high school graduation. (The school environment is more violent in some inner-city neighborhoods than it was when Janowitz drew his conclusions in the late 1960s.) Curriculum improvement and school renewal are attainable, but only if a comprehensive approach is developed.

The Problem of Professional Isolation

The rationale behind school decentralization in the late 1980s and 1990s was that decision making in large school systems was overly centralized; individual principals had insufficient operational discretion to improve the curriculum and obtain the necessary resources. (Interestingly, this was also a rationale for decentralization in the 1960s; the two movements are probably best viewed by curriculum workers as continuous.) Janowitz had a different perspective on the principal's problem. The principal, he argued, actually has a great deal of power, and successful principals have mobilized considerable resources through the system itself and in the community. Moreover, the principal has a major role in shaping the school's social climate and the attitude of the school staff toward curriculum improvement. The principal's main problem, he contended, is isolation. "Each school is a comparatively isolated institution [and t]here is a relative absence of lateral communication among principals in the large urban school system" (1969, p. 28). (Suburban principals, however, are more deeply involved in professional and community organizations and are not as isolated as their urban counterparts.)

Janowitz made his diagnosis of isolation in the late 1960s. Since that time, with systems increasingly decentralized, the principal in an inner-city school has become even more professionally isolated. And, as noted, teachers have even less central-office support, which never existed to any great extent to begin with. Centralization was never the real problem for teachers either; central offices lacked the information and resources for controlling teachers' every move. As Janowitz saw it, rather than control through surveillance from the top, the teacher's problem is extreme professional isolation, even worse than the principal's.

The problem of extreme professional isolation has implications for curriculum; without the support of professional cohorts, programs for curriculum innovation and renewal are unlikely to be sustained or even initiated. Such support is needed if teachers are to function at Level III—the generative-creative level of curriculum development.

Fostering Interaction: Networks and Curriculum

Implementation. Studies on comprehensive approaches to school improvement have found that teacher networks and collaboration within a school or among schools are important for the success of such designs (Desimone, 2002; Stringfield & Datnow, 1998). Larry Cuban (1993) has noted that "the overall mortality for classroom reforms is high" (p. 4). But there is hope. Professional networks that foster interaction among teachers concerning

problems of practice have led to strong implementation of new curricula (Desimone, 2002). A study by Adams (2000) examined how a teacher network helped teachers implement a challenging new mathematics curriculum. The network contributed to teachers' determination and ability for curriculum implementation, while a traditional staff development strategy did not. In Adams's study, the network model linked not only teachers within schools and among schools but also "to professional expertise and practice beyond the school district's borders" (p. 144). As Ann Lieberman writes in a foreword to Adams's book, "Issues of implementation will continue to be inescapable and to dominate the process of school improvement" (2000, p. x). As she notes, how well these issues are understood will determine whether implementation is successful. Today it is clearly understood that the stronger a professional community of teachers, the more successful the implementation.

Many principals and teachers lack the formal and informal professional support networks that physicians, lawyers, and architects have. Urban principals feel particularly isolated, as noted in chapter 17. District administrators and supervisors must initiate informal networks for principals where they do not exist, in smaller school systems as well as the larger ones. Although it has been recently highlighted in the literature, the problem of the isolation of the classroom teacher has long been of concern to thoughtful education leaders. In 1900 Ella Flagg Young, who was Dewey's student at Chicago and a supervisor in his laboratory school, wrote her doctoral dissertation on the problem of isolation in the schools. Isolation in a social organization means more than being separated in space, she wrote. It means being deprived of one's opportunity to develop and use one's creative intelligence; teachers should build on one another's constructive ideas (Young, 1906, p. 44).

There were other kinds of isolation in schools, as well, that need to be dealt with by administrators, found Young. Among them are the isolation of the school and the curriculum from the real social world. Knowledge acquired because someone decides that certain facts are important "is mere information which is rarely at command when called for" (p. 82). The progressive ideas of Ella Flagg Young are part of the body of best educational practices. Today schools engaged in renewal continue in various ways to deal with the problem of isolation in all its various forms.

In 1909 Young became superintendent of schools in Chicago, the first woman to hold a superintendency in a major city.

The Curriculum Development Infrastructure

In the 1990s big cities (New York is a monumental example) found their physical infrastructures crumbling. Bridges, highways, and sewer pipes had been neglected over many years and had fallen into disrepair. Without an infrastructure a city cannot function. Similarly, today large school districts are finding themselves in the position of having to remedy years of neglect—in this case of support for curriculum improvement. A popular reform initiative in the 1980s and 1990s was to abolish central office staff concerned with curriculum development. This was, in part, a well-intentioned attempt to correct for micromanagement of instruction. The problem was stated by Karen Zumwalt as follows: Teachers "are increasingly burdened by petty rules and regulations that undermine their sense of professionalism and detract from the satisfaction of teaching" (1988, p. 148).

Doing away with central staff concerned with curriculum development was also a response to the portrayal of individual schools in the literature as self-contained entities for curriculum improvement. The picture of school improvement was this: Each school steers its own course, needing only to avoid the shoals of central office interference. The assumption is not supported by research and experience. As a matter of fact, research points to just the opposite. Based on a large-scale study of districts around the country conducted by the Consortium for Policy Research in Education (CPRE), Goertz (2001) states, "Districts are often the primary source of assistance to schools as they develop more effective curriculum and instruction" (p. 65). Unfortunately, as she notes, the role of the school district in curriculum improvement "is often overlooked in the current reform movement which focuses on schools as the primary unit of change" (p. 65).

According to Guskey (2003), the literature of many influential organizations purveys the notion that professional development should be site based. Guskey analyzed lists of attributes of effective professional development drawn from recent publications. As he points out, collaboration between school-based educators and central office staff "who have broader perspectives on problems" (p. 749) is necessary for effective professional development. A glance at the literature, however, makes clear that much of the literature is still steeped in the mythology that curriculum improvement does not require an infrastructure of support.

Role of the Central Office

Studies of schools where the quality of instruction is continually improving and student achievement is sustained have found that "the superintendent and central office supervisors are key figures in stimulating and facilitating efforts to maintain and improve the quality of instruction" (Pajak & Glickman, 1989, p. 62). In a study of three school districts, selected because they demonstrated continued improvement on state achievement tests for three years, Pajak and Glickman found that central-office supervisors worked closely with teachers and principals on curriculum improvement. This was the norm for these districts. What teachers had was "an infrastructure of support" through an aggregate approach involving the conjoint efforts of central-office supervisors, principals, instructional lead teachers, and peers (p. 62). The infrastructure depended heavily on the leadership of the superintendent. In each of the three districts the superintendent had established a collaborative organizational structure with staff in various leadership positions whose responsibility it was to promote communication for curriculum improvement.

Today, professional development in many districts is concerned with aligning instruction to state standards. The CPRE study found that although all districts in the study provided some kind of support for professional development the nature of that support varied considerably "ranging from traditional menu-driven workshops to school-based support to building learning communities" (Goertz, 2001, p. 65). One district did not establish district-level standards "in order to give schools greater flexibility and discretion over curriculum and instruction" (p. 65). However rationalized as providing "flexibility," weak guidance is a minus not a plus.

On the whole, standards-based reform has set forth goals without the means to achieve them. Many teachers and principals lack the infrastructure of support that they enjoyed in earlier times—from state departments of education, for instance (see chapter 15). An infrastructure of support begins at the state level.

Before examining what district-level supervisors do in successful schools (where the curriculum and student achievement are continually improving), we shall turn our attention to the myth that curriculum improvement does not require direct assistance to teachers and principals from central offices. How the myth got started is of interest and importance.

The Impact of Effective Schools Research

As discussed in chapter 1, we live with the ever-present danger that someone will propose a limited curriculum for poor children and it will become policy. The saving grace has been the mechanism of democracy. As indicated, the curriculum story has been ever more access to the curriculum for previously excluded groups. (At times it seems that the wheels of democracy turn very slowly.)

The 1970s are an instructive case. In 1972, a study by Christopher Jencks (see chapter 14) concluded that "the character of school's output depends largely on a single input, namely the characteristics of the entering children," and that "everything else" (concerning the characteristics of the school) is "either secondary or completely irrelevant" (pp. 255, 256, 265). The study provided a convenient justification for abandoning the school as a means of improving the opportunities of the inner-city poor and reducing the investment in schooling. It enhanced the belief among many that whatever schools in poverty areas do, they are bound to fail.

The story of the 1970s had not ended. In 1979, a large-scale study on inner-city secondary schools in London found great differences in student achievement depending on which school they happened to attend. The study concluded that student behavior, attitudes, and achievement are appreciably influenced by their school experiences and by the quality of the school as a social institution. Furthermore, the differences in the outcomes of schools in the study were related to specific school characteristics, such as the availability and use of curriculum resources, instructional strategies, and faculty collaboration on schoolwide problems (Rutter, Maugham, Mortimore, & Ouston, 1972).

The British study pointed the way to similar efforts in the United States to identify the "correlates of effective schools" (Edmonds, 1979). Effectiveness was defined more narrowly in the United States—in terms of scores on basic-skills tests. Researchers

investigating schools with high achievement levels found that these schools had a strong principal who supported a climate of achievement. This was fine, on the face of it. Achievement for these children meant something different than for other people's children (D. Tanner, 1974). It meant lower-level skills rather than critical-thinking skills. The policy of the federal government's school-aid program, as stipulated in chapter 1 of the Elementary and Secondary Education Act of 1965 (ESEA), was to improve the basic skills of at-risk children. A good principal was by implication someone who could raise pupils' basic skills levels (help them answer questions at a low cognitive level and pass the external examinations). Because the tests were narrowly focused, curriculum improvement was not an issue. Principals and teachers could help children to pass the tests by means of drill, and this could be done most economically and efficiently with worksheets and without the help of central-office staff.

In the 1980s and 1990s there was increasing criticism of basic-skills tests for creating a curriculum polarity between poor children and children from families of higher socioeconomic status. Subsequent evaluations of Title I of ESEA have recommended that all students be taught higher-order thinking skills and that Title I adopt new ways of measuring achievement. According to Borman (2002), since the reauthorization of Title I in 1994 the emphasis has been on "'world class' standards for *all* students" (p. 236).

The notion that all that is required for student achievement is a strong principal grew out of effective-schools research in the late 1970s and early 1980s. The studies were based on poor children's performance on tests of lower-level skills. In the words of the state superintendent of schools in South Carolina, whose state adopted a basic-skills curriculum, "the minimum became the ceiling" (Viadero, 1993, p. 12). A rich and stimulating curriculum, however, requires an infrastructure of support for teachers.

Finally, and perhaps most important, it was not unusual for schools serving advantaged students to reject effective-schools research as inapplicable to their situation (Joyce, 1991, p. 60). Such school districts went right on doing what good districts have always done—providing the assistance of central-office staff to teachers and principals. Just as the need for a rich curriculum for all students has become public policy, so should the need for an infrastructure of support for teachers.

Improving the Curriculum

The curriculum is what schools are all about. How could it be forgotten in proposals for school improvement? One wonders, but that is what has happened. Some proponents of choice-based reform, whole-school models, site-managed schools, and the like have concentrated so exclusively on organizational factors that they forgot the curriculum. In a discussion of California's outstanding curriculum framework, Bill Honig, who took the lead in developing the frameworks when he was California's superintendent of public instruction, argued for a curriculum focus instead. "The whole reform effort needs to be driven by what you want to teach and how you want to teach it," he said (Viadero, 1993, p. 11). "Some of the other reforms never get to that" (p. 11). The point cannot be overemphasized that if schools are to renew themselves, renewal must begin with the curriculum.

The Ecology of Curriculum Renewal.   Educational leaders must be willing to see curriculum development as an ecosystem and act on that recognition. As discussed, in the 1980s and 1990s proponents of decentralization were so concerned with each school developing its own unique character that they neglected and even argued against a role for the central office in curriculum improvement. Much has already been said about how readily school districts went along with the idea and the void it left in curriculum leadership. As Paul Houston (2001), a former superintendent and director of the American Association of School Administrators, reminds us, education is an ecosystem and its parts are interdependent. "The slightest change in one affects all the others" (p. 43). School improvement will depend on shifting the locus of improvement from the concept of the school as an independent entity to the need for an organic solution to problems. Leadership from the central office is of critical importance for a coherent curriculum districtwide.

Standards-Based Reform: The Curriculum Frameworks Approach.   In the 1980s and early 1990s the tendency among the most progressive states and school systems was to establish curriculum frameworks to provide focus for the improvement of teaching and learning in classrooms. The subject-field curriculum frameworks in California emphasize student understanding and engagement. The idea of the frameworks is to provide schools with a comprehensive and integrative view of what teaching should look like in a particular subject (Viadero, 1993). The frameworks are strikingly different from the fragmental subject matter of a generation earlier (Thomas, 1992). The science curriculum, for instance, suggests three to five big ideas for each grade level, or about 50 in all, in contrast to the more than 600 objectives called for in the early 1980s (Thomas, p. 9).

Curriculum frameworks—sometimes called content standards—define high-level, idea-oriented content for all students. For instance, the National Council of Teachers of Mathematics (NCTM) created K–12 mathematics standards and also suggested teaching strategies to support student learning (NCTM, 1989). A standard was defined "as a statement about what is valued" (Grouws & Cebulla, 2000, p. 222). According to Grouws and Cebulla, "the standards emphasized that knowing mathematics means doing mathematics, and mathematics instruction should allow students to experience real-life problem situations" (p. 222).

The standards recommended certain concepts and skills for increased attention and others for decreased attention. The document advocated that meaning behind operations, use of real-world problems, and statistics should receive increased attention while computational skills like long division, complex paper-and-pencil computations, and drill be de-emphasized. "Thus, it has been argued that the skills traditionally known as 'basic' were de-emphasized in the recommended curriculum" in favor of real problems and ideas (p. 222).

Indeed, although California "embraced" standards-based mathematics in the 1980s and 1990s, "In 1995 and 1996, the California State Board of Education listened to emotional parents who complained bitterly that their children were not learning rudimentary computational skills" (p. 224). What happened then is not surprising. In 1998, the board revised the state curriculum guide and went back to a curriculum that heavily emphasized computational skills as well as detailed tests of segmental competencies to be mastered by students.

This change nicely supported educational policies under the second Bush administration, which required testing of third-grade students in traditional basic skills. Moreover, today's assessment systems lend themselves to a basic-skills emphasis. In the words of Lorrie Sheppard (2004), an expert in assessment, "Most commercial tests cover only basic skills

frightening!

because including special topics or complex problem solving would risk misalignment between test content and the needs of local test selection committees" (p. 240). Thus the tests are what she calls "curriculum free" (p. 240). They are "as generic and detached from curriculum as possible" (p. 240). Small wonder, then, that teachers teach to the test. The curriculum plays second fiddle at best.

Returning to California's curriculum frameworks, although they were subject centered, the material is organized by broad fields. Moreover, the various broad fields are treated so as to reflect common qualities, including an emphasis on solving real-life problems, connections between what students are expected to learn and their own interests and experiences, extensive opportunities for students to work collaboratively, a view of instructional materials as instructional resources rather than serving narrowly to define the curriculum, and assessment that emphasizes students' application of knowledge and problem-solving skills (Thomas, 1992). The intention of the California framework approach is to provide students with something of a unitary experience within a broad-field subject curriculum.

Although California (and the federal government) view the curriculum in terms of content areas, some states view learning as interdisciplinary by nature. The policy in those states is to foster interdisciplinary learning. In Maine, for example, the state's curriculum-improvement document, *Maine's Common Core of Learning* (1992), is organized into four broad themes: The Human Record (history and the developing of creativity), Reasoning and Problem Solving (the ability to use knowledge), Communication (the ability to use media), and Personal and Global Stewardship (the development of social responsibility). Maine is an example of wide community participation. For well over a decade, teachers and community members have been engaging in a discussion of the aims of Maine schools. This process led to the creation of the 1992 document and to Maine's *Learning Results*, adopted by the legislature in 1997. According to Nave, Miech, and Mosteller (2000), "communities across the state continue to engage in local discussions about how to bring their curricula and teaching into connection with the high expectations outlined in *Learning Results*" (p. 131).

As has been indicated, high-stakes testing is usually expected to work in opposition to standards-based teaching. Maine districts seem not to be derailed from their curriculum efforts by such

pressures (Fairman & Firestone, 2001). Many teachers in other states with curriculum frameworks, however, stopped using integrated curricula in grades being tested. In Kentucky, for example, a state with a curriculum framework that included procedures for local curriculum development, statewide surveys of teachers found that "teachers at the testing grades de-emphasized nontested areas in favor of tested ones" (Kannapel, Aagaard, Coe, & Reeves, 2001, p. 247).

So are we to assume that curriculum frameworks are a lost cause? Far from it. They still represent an excellent model for curriculum development based on best practices. Research on higher level learning and constructivist views of knowledge conclude that students learn best when given an opportunity to incorporate what they are studying into their own experiences (Resnick, 1987; Howe & Berv, 2000). This principle is hardly new. As we have noted repeatedly, it appeared in the work of John Dewey. And the principle continues to be supported by research on cognitive learning. Integrative curriculum frameworks can have great influence in the implementation of the principle of connecting the curriculum to life experience.

Frameworks as Opportunities. Curriculum frameworks provide opportunities for teachers to function as professionals and for a curriculum appropriate to today's world. In the case of mathematics, for example, "A basic skills curriculum oriented to computational procedures alone is inappropriate in this technological age for any student" (Grouws & Cebulla, 2000, p. 249). In California, teachers who were regarded as knowledgeable about the broad subject field worked with the state's Curriculum Commission in the development of the frameworks. Indeed, a majority of the members were K–12 teachers. In Philadelphia teachers worked on the standards-based curriculum framework documents, which included model lessons, suggested instructional processes, suggestions for classroom assessments, and teacher resources (Nave, Miech, & Mosteller, 2000, p. 131).

Curriculum frameworks provide the flexibility that teachers must have if they are to meet the needs of the students in their school. The needs are changing as the student population changes. In Los Angeles County, for example, a majority of the children in public schools converse at home in a language other than English. Even if every child spoke English at home, all teachers would need the flexibility and guidance of frameworks in order to function as curriculum makers.

Teachers who are knowledgeable about a curriculum area should have a major responsibility in developing the frameworks and in fitting the parts into the whole curriculum. However, the education agency (state or school district) is responsible for establishing criteria, coordinating the work of committee members, bringing them into contact with the best sources of knowledge and material in each curriculum area, and assisting them in obtaining the needed expertise and resources. The responsibility for putting the framework in the hands of teachers and principals and helping them with implementation resides with the central office. Frameworks should be revised at scheduled intervals, but looking for better methods of implementing the frameworks should be a continuous process.

Realizing the Opportunities (Making the Vision Happen).   A curriculum framework is an opportunity for curriculum renewal but only an opportunity. What happened in California may be regarded as an early lesson in implementing standards-based teaching. In the beginning, the California State Department of Education staff who wrote the frameworks saw their work as vision making, not implementation. Some leading teacher educators who met with the writers of the mathematics framework in 1988 recount: "When we asked about the implementation of the framework we were chided, for the state department policy makers saw their work as 'transforming mathematics education,' not as implementing the framework" (Wilson, Peterson, Ball, & Cohen, 1996, p. 470). One staff member "spoke of creating circumstances, not attempting to control" (p. 470).

This was 1988, an era of "a big backlash against the teacher-proof curriculum movement," as Deborah Ball noted (1996, p. 506). There was much talk of teacher improvement, of allowing teachers to function as professionals. As indicated, this was all too easily translated into letting teachers alone. Yet as Ball observes, "carefully designed curriculum materials can offer teachers access to mathematical ideas and ways to represent them" (p. 506). This is not just true of mathematics. Teachers need ideas for teaching. As Ball puts it, a teacher needs to "develop a relationship with the curriculum material" (p. 506). Successful professional development projects are based on this premise.

A Lesson Learned by Some Policy Makers.   In California, State Department of Education staff learned through a process of trial and error that teachers need support. First they tried textbooks. Although some submissions were finally deemed acceptable, the books did not relate completely with the ideas of teaching and learning envisioned by the writers of the frameworks. Then they tried "replacement units"—small curriculum packages concerned with a single idea—for instance, measurement, consisting of activities, and investigations (Wilson, Peterson, Ball, & Cohen, p. 470). However, as policy makers (some of whom were former teachers) knew, materials—although necessary—were not enough. Teachers, they concluded, required time for evaluating the materials and for discussing them. "And so," as Wilson et al. relate, "the 'replacement strategy' employed materials *and* professional development" (p. 470). Teachers are recruited to attend summer workshops to learn about curriculum and professional development. Upon returning to their schools, they teach the new units and meet with other workers in the project to discuss their experiences. "These experiences, in turn, shape what future groups of teachers learn about the curricula" (p. 470).

On the whole, the idea is a good one. As Ralph Tyler once told the authors of this text, teachers adopt new curricula when they find it credible and consequential in the teaching-learning process. According to Wilson et al., they are more likely to adopt new curricula through the "development of communities of teachers, teacher educators, and policy makers who are working together" to solve a curriculum problem. One of the most important features of this notion of educational community is the addition of policy makers to the mix. In this case, they, too, became transformed. "Over time," write Wilson et al., "we have seen significant changes in their language, organizing principles, assumptions, knowledge and beliefs" (p. 470).

In the early 2000s, as we have seen in chapters 15 and 16, state departments of education tended to see their work as implementing federal policies. Hopefully, states will see themselves once again as a crucial part of the curriculum development infrastructure. In the early 2000s, many educators became frustrated by the approach of the federal government to standards-based education. They were particularly frustrated by the unwillingness of policy makers to address the need for curriculum development. Curriculum frameworks are standards-based education, albeit a different form (not even a distant cousin) from the standards-based reforms in the George W. Bush administration, which was obsessed with tests and sanctions. Schools need curriculum frameworks. Teachers who are knowledgeable about a curriculum area should have a major responsibility in developing the frameworks and in fitting the parts into the whole curriculum (e.g., the macrocurriculum in general education). However, the education agency (state or school district) is responsible for establishing criteria, coordinating the work of committee members, bringing them into contact with the best sources of knowledge and material in each curriculum area, and assisting them in obtaining expertise and resources for articulating the curriculum horizontally and vertically. The responsibility for putting the framework in the hands of teachers and principals and helping them with implementation resides with the district office. Frameworks should be revised at scheduled intervals. But looking for better ways of implementing the frameworks should be a continuous process.

Support for Teachers. The implementation of frameworks in classrooms requires that school systems provide support for teachers to help them implement the integrative ideas and new methods. The assistance must be sustained. Providing time for teachers to attend inservice education sessions is not enough. In a study on how schools are dealing with the issue of time for school renewal, Purnell and Hill (1992) found that most administrators support formal staff development activities by providing teachers with released time to attend a special course. However, school systems generally balk at offering teachers follow-up time for observing other teachers who practice and use the new approaches. Principals prefer the less expensive means of having teachers use their own preparation or lunch time to observe other teachers. Purnell and Hill point out that this is poor economy, because the school system has already made a considerable investment in employing outside experts and paying for teachers' released time and expenses to participate in the course.

Research on professional development indicates that teachers need to feel successful in using a new or best practice or they will not use it (Guskey, 1986). Success is simply this: seeing positive effects with one's own students. Teachers, like anyone else, tend to do things in which they are successful and avoid the other things. They become easily discouraged when a new practice seems not to work. School

systems can ensure that their investment will have optimal influence when they (1) provide professional development courses that include follow-up sessions and/or continuing school visits by the course instructors, (2) prepare teachers as facilitators to provide more immediate help for colleagues as problems develop, and (3) provide teachers with released time to observe and confer with other teachers who have demonstrated success with the new approaches.

Assessment for Curriculum Development

Obviously, a state or school district's tests of student progress should encompass the curriculum. Madaus and his coworkers put the matter this way: "The question, does this test cover the domain I am really interested in? is central to proper test use" (Madaus, Haney, & Kreitzer, 1992, p. 31). Madaus, Haney, and Kreitzer provide the illustration of using a standardized third-grade science test, covering mere facts concerning rock formations and machines, to evaluate an innovative hands-on science curriculum emphasizing skill development in such areas as observing, making generalizations, and formulating ideas for testing (p. 30). Obviously, the narrow-minded facts test fails to measure the higher order thinking that is the essence of the curriculum. Thus, in addition to the narrowing effect on the curriculum of high-stakes tests we have an additional problem: a disconnect between test questions and the focus of instruction, in this case developing students' ability to use science in applied situations. As indicated, test makers strive to develop generic, "curriculum-free," rather than "curriculum-specific," tests (Shepard, 2004, pp. 240–241).

There is, however, no necessary contradiction between assessments and classroom activities, including teachers' assessments of classroom work (Frederiksen & White, 2004). In California, for example, the objective of the Department of Education was to have the new assessment program "reinforce the vision in the curriculum framework" (Alexander, 1994). States and school districts can influence the curriculum in positive ways through the assessment program. Frederiksen and White (2004) furnish as an example California's scientific inquiry standard, which states that "students should develop their own questions and perform investigations" (p. 77; California State Board of Education, 2000). According to Frederiksen and White, such assessment activities can "serve an important instructional purpose, acting as culminating challenges for students along with providing information about students' performance that can be used for instructional and accountability purposes" (p. 77).

Interpreting and Using Test Results. In today's "accountability-oriented educational culture" (Airasian, 1994, p. 96), it is hard to think of testing in the spirit in which it was originally envisioned by Tyler (1949) and Bloom et al. (1956): to serve curriculum and instruction, not for curriculum and instruction to serve the test. And it was to be school and district based, not centralized at the state and national levels. Today, many teachers feel personally threatened by standardized tests for assessing student progress. As Hlebowitsh points out, when standards are reduced to test items on high-stakes tests, the result is producing a teaching-to-the-test mentality at the expense of liberating the teacher intelligence, not to mention pupil intelligence (2005, p. 16). Such teachers do not know that a major purpose of testing is to provide them with information about students that they can use in instructional planning. According to a former director of curriculum in a central office, the central office has a responsibility to provide teachers with information about students' strengths and learning needs "in a format that they perceive as helpful and useful in instructional planning." She points out:

> Individual schools rarely have the necessary
> resources of manpower and time that are needed
> to do the job thoroughly and consistently.
> Information about performance can be collected and
> summarized at the district level. Disaggregating data
> in a variety of ways and using sophisticated methods
> of test analysis will assist the individual school in
> identifying and bringing about necessary change,
> (Libler, 1992, pp. 123–124)

It must be remembered that standardized tests provide only a very limited perspective of what is learned in school, and even the most sophisticated analyses will not compensate for the inadequacies of standardized tests. There are, of course, other indicators of curriculum effectiveness in addition to test data, including high school retention/graduation rate, student projects, self-impelled learning activities beyond what is required in the curriculum (such as reading for pleasure), ability of graduates to gain employment success in the work world, percentage of graduates who go on to and succeed in college, and growth in intellectual curiosity and social responsibility. Obviously, such

information must be accessible to a school staff if they are to target their curriculum improvement efforts to real problems and if curriculum change is to result in improved opportunities for learners.

Unfortunately, too many district officers measure program success only on the basis of student performance on standardized tests and college entrance. One might well ponder the reasons for this narrow-minded approach. District officers may believe (rightly or wrongly) that this is how the school board, community, and the media judge their effectiveness as administrators. They may honestly think that standardized test scores are the only real determinant of program effectiveness. There seems little doubt also that in many school systems around the country the primary function of testing is accountability in education. Teachers are treated as employees whose productivity is assessed by outputs (standardized achievement test scores), and the curriculum-improvement function of test data is ignored. This is a far cry from enlightened school administration. Central office staff must make real the important relationship between program evaluation and changes in curriculum. Those at the top of the district organization must use a variety of indicators comprehensively to measure the district's success. Only as school staffs are informed about the aggregate effects of programs on students do they have a solid foundation for their curriculum-improvement efforts. The more information they have, the less likely they are to be working in the dark.

The Crucial Importance of Support for Curriculum Development

Schools where good things are happening—where there are integrated and thematic curricula and schoolwide writing programs, for example—are no accident. Studies of such schools have found that teachers talk to one another about problems and work together to develop teaching approaches. In organizational terms, as indicated in chapter 17, these schools have an organic form of organization, in which members view themselves as working toward a common goal and continually adjust their work through interaction with others in solving problems facing the organization. In a mechanistic system of organization, by contrast, the goals of the organization are broken down into abstract individual tasks and members pursue their own tasks in isolation. In schools that have this mechanistic form of organization, teachers' work is broken down and distributed automatically. According to Darling-Hammond (1993), the mechanistic form "fits with a behavioristic view of learning as the management of stimulus and response, easily controlled from outside the classroom by identifying exactly what is to be learned and breaking it up into small, sequential bits." However, as she points out, this model directly conflicts with the way students learn, which is "in a much more holistic and experiential fashion" (p. 754).

From Without or Within? Two Perspectives on Learning. What Darling-Hammond is describing here are two quite different perspectives on learning, which lead to differing approaches to school improvement. One holds that learning is externally imposed and tied to fear and sanctions. As Houston (2001) writes, "The accountability and competition movements are based on this belief system" (p. 432). However, those holding this viewpoint forget something:

> . . . that education and learning are essentially internal and tied directly to motivation. . . . Fear has never been a particularly effective motivational tool, particularly when complex thought processes are required. That means that reforms built on a foundation of fear are doomed. (p. 432)

excellent

How does this relate to school improvement? Houston, a former superintendent, argues that superintendents have to be leaders "who focus on the organic and wholistic qualities of learning and who structure learning that speaks to the hearts and minds of learners" (p. 432). He suggests that this is extremely difficult in an atmosphere of accountability. Certainly, it does not happen single-handedly. At least two changes are required where the superintendency is concerned. Superintendents must be team leaders and team builders, and course work for licensure must teach collaborative skills required in today's "connected environment" (p. 432).

An organic system fits with teachers' efforts to devise problems and units of work that interconnect the various studies and that engage students in the development of skills and concepts that cross through the entire curriculum. An organic system is a realistic reflection of the reality that students are not uniform and have special as well as common needs and interests. These reasons would be enough to make the organic model appropriate for schools. There is another reason as well: Improving teachers' knowledge and skills requires continual participation by individual teachers with others in trying to find better ideas and methods. Central offices have a responsibility to encourage communication and collaboration among professional staffs and others who can help teachers learn new practices. The importance of this function is underscored by research.

Learning Communities. A Stanford University study of secondary school teachers found that "not one of the teachers studied who was able to develop sustained and challenging learning opportunities for students was in isolation" and "[e]ach belonged to a professional learning community" (Rothman, 1993, pp. 1, 25). The learning communities were groups of professionals who addressed problems and developed solutions together. These networks included subject-matter departments, entire school faculties, and outside groups, in one case, the Urban Mathematics Collaborative. Central offices can foster the kinds of learning communities that create support for teachers. Without such support, teachers are likely to go back to their old methods. According to Pajak (2003), an important function of supervision is building a community of learners.

School principals create learning communities when they engage teachers in solving curriculum problems. However, central office staff can help teachers reach beyond the local school to find professionals with similar concerns. By doing so, central offices are moving toward an organic form of organization. The study by Pajak and Glickman mentioned earlier found that teachers in schools with sustained improvements in the quality of instruction "were professionally engaged with one another and were focused on improving instruction beyond their own classrooms" (1989, p. 62). The central office has a role to play in this engagement. In the three particularly effective school systems identified by Pajak and Glickman, central office staff and lead teachers had two main problems: first to get teachers close to one another for planning and then to provide teachers with direct assistance for implementing their plans. Pajak and Glickman report, "Time was built into the normal work schedule of staff whose primary responsibility was engaging teachers to talk about their classrooms, students' progress, lesson plans, and curriculum."

Bringing teachers together under democratic-participative curriculum leadership is a role of the central office. Some central offices have been very active in the effort. All need to be. The entire school system should be an organic system. Such systems do not happen of their own accord but require energetic leaders who are well aware of what is happening in the wide professional community and put teachers in touch. There must be free flow of communication upward and laterally as well as from the top throughout the system.

Carrying Out District Responsibilities

Curriculum leadership from the central office is not only authorized by law, but it is also a best practice. Currently, a number of developments impede central offices from carrying out their important role. Curriculum development at the district level has been hampered by three major developments: (1) the school restructuring movement, a feature of which is decentralized decision making; (2) the elimination of supervisory positions, particularly in large districts (as described in chapters 16 and 17); and (3) the accountability movement with its emphasis on high-stakes testing and, most recently, high-stakes sanctions. All of these developments have interfered with the responsibility of central office staff members to be curriculum leaders. In the early 1990s much attention was given in the literature to active teacher participation in improving the curriculum of their own school. As noted, many school districts all but abandoned curriculum development programs at the district level. And as discussed earlier, some districts, particularly large urban districts (Philadelphia, for example) even dissolved their departments of curriculum and instruction. It was argued that the departments were bureaucratic, rather than professional, and that teachers alone must face the learning problems of students and seek better methods and goals for the students in their own classroom and schools. The idea that central offices must be bureaucratic flies in the face of history. Extensive and intensive teacher participation in curriculum revision at the district level has been a best practice in educational leadership since the 1920s (see chapter 16).

To eliminate departments of curriculum and instruction in school systems is to deprive teachers of their infrastructure of support. Teachers are part of the infrastructure, but teachers cannot be the whole structure. It is unfortunate that central office reform is seen (by some, at least) as a matter of providing teachers with less support rather than more support. Moreover, someone must attend to vertical and horizontal curriculum articulation across the district, and no one has yet invented a substitute for central office staff.

District leaders have a job to do. Has it really changed that much? If by change one means being more difficult, the answer is "yes." But the role has not changed and is still essential. The legitimate role of districts, for example, is to meet teachers' needs for curriculum frameworks or guides. This, as discussed in chapter 16, is simply not being done in many districts. Teachers unions have picked up the slack in a few large urban districts, and the districts have been all too willing to let them. What we have is a patchwork of new curricula with plenty of gaps rather than comprehensive curriculum development. This is what happens when the legitimate role of the professional staff is ignored by policy makers.

Problems Faced by Central Office Staff

Our readers who plan on working at the district level, or may be already doing so, need to know about the problems. Central office members have always encountered problems in carrying out their responsibilities, as have all professionals, but now there are new complexities and perplexities. A study by the Consortium for Policy Research in Education (CPRE) of the roles being carried out by central office staff in three large urban districts throws a great deal of light on the problems. According to Corcoran, Fuhrman, and Belcher (2001), in a report of the study's findings, recent policies have made it more difficult for central office members to shape and support curriculum improvements. Restructuring reforms intended to give more authority to individual schools have promoted teacher collaboration and energized school staff to deal with problems. But increasing the decision-making power of individual schools has also spawned policies that pose problems for curriculum improvement.

Competing Whole-School Designs.   One problem is indicated by the proliferation of competing whole-school reform models and their marketers. Developers not infrequently made claims about their model without research evidence. Central office members were faced with a dilemma.

> Should schools be left to figure it out for themselves, or should the central office point them in the right direction and limit their options? Should the role of the central office be limited to providing schools with good information about designs, including what the research evidence shows? District staff members agonized about these and related questions. (Corcoran, Fuhrman, and Belcher, 2001, p. 79)

One of the districts in the study established a screening process that assessed the alignment between local standards and various whole-school designs and then examined the supporting evidence from the developers. Schools were allowed to select only the approved designs. Initially schools were limited to four whole-school models. Corcoran, Fuhrman and Belcher report that subsequently "the committee became more demanding and ruled out designs that could not present strong evidence of positive effects," and further, "school staff indicated that they appreciated the effort by the central office to rule out programs that might prove ineffective" (p. 80). Another district, however, did not use a screening process because staff members felt it was too prescriptive. A third district required schools with low-performing students to adopt a locally developed whole-school design. Although the schools made significant achievement gains, the district was unable to attract more adopters because the design was considered "remedial" and appropriate only for schools serving low-income students. This is not so surprising. Federal funding has been made available via a competitive procedure for schools that adopt "research-based, schoolwide" reform models (McPartland, Balfanz, Jordan, & Leiters, 2002, p. 157). The program is targeted to low-performing, high-poverty elementary and secondary schools—a fact of which school leaders cannot be unaware, so they steer clear.

As noted earlier, externally designed models cut school staffs out of the problem-solving process. They can be highly prescriptive, down to the last detail, including curriculum materials. Schools serving more advantaged students routinely use collaborative procedures to deal with problems. The best whole-school design is simply a school staff working on its own problems, drawing on the resources of the central office, the best available research, and the wider educational community as needed.

Creating an Evidence-Based Culture. Decision making is a part of any educational leader's professional preparation. The CPRE found district staff members well schooled in this respect. District staff members were committed to basing decisions on evidence, although they were often frustrated by contradictory findings on issues. (More about this shortly.) However, the study cited examples of instances in which opportunism and fads led the central staff to ignore evidence. One district, for example, mandated that smaller units be created in its schools, ignoring the evidence that the plan was creating a new tracking system (p. 80). All of the districts used the findings of evaluation to make changes in their programs (whether to continue or expand the program, for example). Local school staff, in contrast, gave homage to using research but were more confident in other teachers' recommendations than research and found research difficult to access and interpret. "So," the study concludes, "decentralization appeared to be undermining the use of knowledge rather than promoting it" (p. 81).

District leaders in the study held that they want the central office staff to make decisions based on evidence and that they support effective programs and practices. "Nevertheless," write Corcoran, Fuhrman, and Belcher, "district and school staff members were reluctant to put aside old patterns of decision making that focused on philosophy or on the 'goodness' of an option rather than its effects" (p. 84).

Immediately a problem about philosophy is posed. How can educational leaders, whether central office members or school staffs, make decisions without considering philosophy? One should be guided by philosophy. Philosophy undergirds the school's vision. Indeed, research itself is never value-free (see chapter 14). The philosophy is in accord with the goals of a democratic society. The principle of basing decisions on the best available evidence does not exclude philosophy. Nor does it exclude the recommendations of other teachers which are based on demonstrated effectiveness in the field. In sum, an evidence-based culture does not exclude philosophy because it cannot. What teachers as professionals think is part of the evidence.

Finally, there is no reason whatsoever why local school staffs cannot be members of an evidence-based culture. Such cultures can be built by using the problem-solving procedure (see chapter 17).

District or Local School?

The level at which curriculum development takes place depends on the purpose or problem. As pointed out, the creation of curriculum frameworks at the district (and/or state) level should involve teachers. As Oliva observes, "if a problem and its solution will affect teachers and pupils in more than one school, curriculum development must proceed on a districtwide rather than on a schoolwide basis."

Further, "Teachers group and regroup depending on the nature of the curriculum problem under study" (1989, p. 265). One example of a district-level curriculum development activity is the periodic revision of curriculum frameworks. The questions of what learning experiences should be taught at primary, middle school, and high school levels, and how teachers can be helped to take advantage of and build on the experiences that youngsters have had in previous years, are surely the province of all elementary school faculty and secondary school faculty. Decisions on these questions should be made in consultation with the assistant superintendent for curriculum and instruction, department heads, supervisors, and grade-level coordinators. According to Usiskin (1993), "A teacher, acting more or less alone, can change a single year's experience, but for multi-year curricular change, administrators, guidance counselors, parents and school boards need to be involved" (p. 18). There are questions about the sequence of experiences in all areas of the curriculum and how the various studies interconnect as a total curriculum. Such questions are rightfully the domain of all faculty working together regardless of specialization.

Professional Development.   The question of how teachers can be helped to build on students' previous experiences (with applications of knowledge, for example) is a professional development issue. Requests may be initiated by the local school, but to say that answering requests is where the responsibility of the central office begins and ends is simply not being realistic. As Usiskin (1993) observed, based on experience with his own mathematics project, curriculum change "cannot occur solely top-down or bottom-up. It must occur both ways at once" (p. 18). Actually, it must occur laterally across subject fields. Teachers have to understand and accept the reasons for curriculum improvement, and this does not happen by handing them a guide and saying, "Go to it." Curriculum improvement is an educational process, in the sense of professional development.

A finding of the CPRE study was that district-sponsored professional development activities lacked focus. One reason, points out Corcoran et al. (2001), was that although professional development specialists were intended to respond to the problems and needs of local schools they were most often used to communicate district initiatives. Another reason is that the districts had multiple initiatives going on in a "noisy reform environment" (p. 84). Something was needed to provide focus. The researchers suggest setting "a few priorities" (p. 83). Today, in the words of Corcoran et al., professional development in many districts is a "potpourri of workshops and events rather than a coherent program" (p. 83). Curriculum frameworks and guides give focus and coherence.

Curriculum Development: An Interactive Process. If change is to bring about improvement, it must be an interactive affair and tap teachers' ideas about curriculum. Information concerning teachers' reasons for teaching or not teaching certain material should be sought and used in any curriculum-improvement effort. Usiskin (1993) calls this "rethinking the curriculum" (p. 17.) Moreover, teachers' ideas on how curriculum improvement can be accomplished systematically are absolutely essential, particularly where a multiyear, sequential curriculum is concerned. It cannot be overemphasized that this is a districtwide problem and requires district-level leadership.

Continuous and Cumulative Curriculum Development

A fundamental principle of curriculum improvement is that it is both continuous and cumulative. The idea is to build on, not demolish, the gains of preceding eras. According to Goodlad (1987), one characteristic of a renewing school is that it has an agenda of cumulative curriculum improvement. The professional staff should generate, strengthen, and update the agenda as needed. As indicated, a record should be kept about the successes and failures of curriculum-improvement efforts. Efforts can be vastly enlightened and constructively directed if school staff know what happened in previous efforts to deal with a curriculum or instructional problem. The record should be kept in a place where it is readily accessible to teachers and administrators. The school library is one suggestion where a professional collection might be maintained.

Avoiding Curriculum Stagnation

In recent years, various reform movements have held the center of the curriculum stage, each for a brief moment in educational time. Writing across the curriculum, cooperative learning, idea-oriented teaching and higher-order thinking, performance assessments, whole-language reading programs, and standards-based reforms are but a few examples. Reform movements become the focal points for curriculum energies, and it is all too easy for the school staff to neglect or ignore the persistent curriculum problems that confront their school. Responding to each new development segmentally has led many teachers and administrators to feel that they are on the cutting edge of curriculum reform when, in fact, their curriculum may be stagnant. Real progress in curriculum improvement requires that the school staff continually ask questions on problems about their school's curriculum. Decisions based on the answers determine the curriculum at any given time.

Persistent Questions. The questions that keep a curriculum improving and vigorous are based on curriculum principles. An adequate approach to curriculum development bridges theory and practice. For example, a function of the macrocurriculum is exploratory education. Teachers are involved in continuous curriculum improvement when they seek answers to the question, "What exploratory options should we make available to middle school youngsters?" Another function of the macrocurriculum is general education and the school's democratizing function. Teachers are concerned with this function when they address the question, "What experiences for reducing racial prejudice and polarization in the life of the school are missing from the curriculum?" Since 1918, when the Commission on the Reorganization of Secondary Education named health as one of seven principal objectives of education, identifying and meeting students' health needs has been in the American curriculum legacy. Teachers and administrators are true to the legacy when they try to answer this question: "What are the health needs of our students and how can they be met in the curriculum?"

The questions may be persistent but the answers to the same question may change, depending on the moment in time. Conditions change and so, as Oliva (1989) points out, "The answer to a curriculum question at one time may not suffice at another time" (p. 269). Some questions may have to be asked constantly such as, "What broad career clusters should be included in the vocational program?"

Segmental and specialized curriculum movements and trends have not been a good thing for curriculum balance and articulation. During an extended period through the Cold War and into the 2000s,

although educational opportunity has been extended in many schools in some subject fields (mathematics and the sciences, in particular), art and music studios have been closed and studies in the industrial arts almost eliminated. The problem of curriculum balance and articulation is a difficult and important one and is closely tied to the democratic ideal of all individuals having the fullest education possible. All too often children have been deprived of experiences in music, sculpture, painting, dramatics, and the industrial arts that delight them. Schools are concerned with the principle of curriculum balance when they ask, "What kinds of experiences in the fine and practical arts are appropriate for children and adolescents?"

Societal problems (particularly but not exclusively in urban districts) have a way of spilling over into the school, causing faculty to ask neglected questions. For example, in the 1990s and early 2000s many schools were asking, "What experiences vital for developing social responsibility and concern for others are missing from the curriculum?" There are those who will simply bemoan a situation but, like it or not, the schools cannot ignore the problems youngsters bring with them. Certainly, the schools should not have to work alone in solving student problems stemming from family and social deficiencies. A true ecological model for school renewal includes the wider ecosystem; collaboration between the schools and social agencies is required. As a superintendent in a large urban district has noted, the services that schools and other agencies provide to assist families with problems are often uncoordinated and inconsistent (Payzant, 1992). Some school systems have developed an interagency approach in which social workers are placed in schools to work with families on specific problems identified collaboratively with district officials. Such programs, along with health and nutrition programs, need to be widely expanded. In the meantime, there is much that schools have yet to do to provide improved life chances for children and youth in the form of a rich curriculum.

Correlates of Effective Curriculum Improvement

The body of research and experience in curriculum point decisively to five correlates of an effective (and continual) curriculum improvement program:

1. **Design and Function.** The curriculum is more than the sum of the parts. The structure of a curriculum

determines its function. Consequently, structural connections need to be made among all of the various studies so as to build a truly interrelated curriculum that reveals the interdependence of knowledge. This requires a macro approach to curriculum development.

2. **School Climate.** There is a healthy and supportive school climate for teachers and children. Adequate funds are provided for released time and resources for planning, and teachers have an infrastructure of support. As Linda Darling-Hammond (1997) noted, the emphasis is on developing capacity rather than on designing controls. (Today, most states and the federal government focus on developing systems for control, rather than investing in teachers' expertise.) In renewing schools, teachers and principals continually and critically seek ways to transform their schools into more attractive and stimulating learning environments.

3. **Opportunity.** All students, whether gifted or at risk of school failure, are provided with optimal opportunities to learn and with access to a stimulating curriculum. The faculty of renewing schools are, at heart, environmentalists. That is, they believe that talent emerges through opportunity and cultivation by teachers and parents. This is not a new idea. More than a century ago Lester Ward (1886), a social scientist whose original field was botany, argued that many high-caliber minds remained undeveloped through lack of stimulation. Successful people are nurtured by parents and teachers. Ward's major point has been discussed earlier but bears restatement: There is no shortage of ability, only of opportunity.

   Contemporary school renewal efforts continue to confirm Ward's thesis. By using a gifted and talented strategy with disadvantaged children (enrichment, exploration and acceleration rather than dulling remedial work), teachers following Henry Levin's accelerated-schools model have found that the youngsters at risk can be brought into the educational mainstream. Moreover, many of the at-risk students have turned out to be gifted and talented. Again, the focus is on "building school capacity," in this case to accelerate the education of the students (Chasin & Levin, 1995, p. 136).

4. **World View.** School staff are outward looking; they are continually looking for better teaching strategies and ways of organizing the curriculum. For professionals, the search is endless. There is a sense that no matter how satisfactory things may seem, improvements are always possible. School staff are effective consumers of the professional literature and they get around. They visit other schools and attend conferences, sharing newly acquired ideas and strategies with colleagues. Faculty meetings are concerned with what is going on in the education field and implications for improving the school program.

5. **Problem Solving.** Curriculum development is seen by the entire school staff as an ongoing process of problem solving. Problems are seen as opportunities and not as obstacles to progress.

   These correlates are criteria of evaluation that a school faculty can and should apply to their school.

Perspective

Living things continually renew themselves, if they are healthy. And so do schools, if they are thriving environments. For such schools it is eternal spring. Renewal occurs if schools can take advantage of changing conditions and, in addressing emerging problems, recognize them for the opportunities that they are. Some of the influences enabling schools to renew themselves are new ideas about how students learn, progress in teacher professionalism, changing populations, equity and gender concerns (curricular access), curriculum articulation, and ideas about how organizations can function more effectively. The opportunities are surely there if renewal efforts begin with the curriculum and if the curriculum improvement setting is treated as an ecosystem.

Increasing the decision-making power of individual schools has hampered curriculum leadership from the central office staff. Local school "autonomy" has led to a proliferation of competing whole-school reform models and their developers, who are not always forthcoming with research evidence. Some districts screen models for alignment with local standards. Some whole-school models or designs are specific down to every detail, including curriculum materials. The research evidence on such models is uneven, and school staffs are excluded from the problem-solving process. Some schools continue to participate in some whole-school models although they have not made gains after a number of years (Corcoran, Fuhrman, & Belcher, 2001). The best whole-school model is a school staff working on its own problems, drawing on the resources of the district, the best available research and the wider educational community as needed. This requires a democratic-participative organization, and not a top-down structure.

Hard to believe but true: Some proposals for school reform never get around to the curriculum. The most effective way to renewal is the direct way, by starting with what is taught and how it is taught, which after all is what schools are about. Curriculum frameworks are an excellent example of a direct and coherent approach. They can counter the fragmentation and lack of coordination that characterize professional development programs in large systems. Frameworks bring things together. Rather than being treated as magic bullets, collaboration, teaching for understanding, connecting the curriculum with real life, performance assessments, and professional support networks are all woven into a single comprehensive approach for curriculum renewal. Curriculum frameworks (developed at the state or system levels) are infinitely preferable to detailed lists of competencies. If teachers are to function at Level III or the generative-creative level of curriculum development, central office supervisors must work closely with teachers and principals on curriculum improvement.

As sources for innovation and competition, schools of choice have been a disappointment. Superimposing ideas from business on schools has had a long and not so very successful history. The concept of accountability, for example, has not been a productive one for school renewal, nor is there reason to expect that it ever could be as long as it is rooted in the top-down, factory-production model of schooling. Individuals and groups external to the schools are concerned with imposing their own ideas of standards on teachers and schools without providing the needed support. The authors stand with Goodlad (1987) and others who believe that the concept of professional responsibility should replace that of accountability. School superintendents, for example, should be concerned with whether they are providing teachers with the support that teachers need to improve the curriculum. The best theory of supervision and curriculum development prefers the concept of professional responsibility as most likely to lead to school improvement. Best theory also prefers an aggregate, ecological, or comprehensive approach to school renewal over a segmental-specialized approach. What is needed is to consider the material resources and the interaction of the various individuals and agencies that comprise the ecosystem—teachers, administrators and supervisors, students, state departments of education, and so on—in their interaction and how they can be most effectively linked. If policy makers concerned with renewing urban schools had given adequate consideration to the influence of teenagers on younger children in inner cities, for example, it seems likely that they would have provided more support for adolescent education, rather than favoring preschool or early-childhood programs at the expense of adolescent education. An ecological perspective can prevent possible mistakes in priorities and promote the kind of efforts that will allocate and use resources most effectively for all the children of all the people.

School officials may feel that they are on the cutting edge of curriculum when they adopt whatever segmental innovation is in vogue. However, their curriculum may be suffering from stagnation. They fail to recognize that the segmental innovations may work in conflict as well as in isolation. Some schools are so caught up in efforts to apply new guidelines to the separate subject areas that they neglect the macrocurriculum and its functions. The high-stakes testing and accountability movement led to further neglect of the macrocurriculum in the early 2000s. The way to continued improvement lies in curriculum development as an ongoing process of problem solving. (Refer to the Best Practices Checklist on pages 481–499.)

PROBLEMS FOR STUDY AND DISCUSSION

1. In the late 1990s and early 2000s, some school districts established screening procedures for externally developed whole-school designs, ruling out the designs that lacked supporting evidence. Some districts left school staffs to obtain and examine research evidence on their own and did not limit options. Which, in your view, is the more promising course for school improvement? Explain.

2. Do you believe with the authors of this book that the best whole-school improvement design

is a school staff working on its own problems? Why or why not?

3. Identify some promising practices in school systems other than your own for teaching democratic citizenship. Which might interest teachers in your school or district? Explain.

4. Should the term *responsibility* replace the term *accountability*? Why or why not?

5. Examine some projects for creating small school units or houses within large urban high schools, or creating small alternative schools in urban districts, with each alternative school organized around a special theme or special interest. Do you see any curricular shortcomings in such alternative schools? Is there a likelihood of social isolation in these schools? Explain.

6. In your view, do California's curriculum frameworks have a holistic conception of curriculum? Explain.

7. A recent study of professional development activities in a large school district found "a potpourri of workshops and events rather than a coherent program of professional development" [Corcoran, T., Fuhrman, S., & Belcher, C.L. (2001), The district role in instructional improvement, *Phi Delta Kappan, 83*, p. 83.] Based on your reading of this chapter and your own experience, how might professional development programs be made more focused and coherent?

8. It is held that an important function of district wide testing is to provide teachers with information about students in a way that teachers see as helpful for their instructional planning. Why has this so often failed to be the case? What

implications does this function hold for the role of central offices?

9. Recently there has been much interest in service activities as a means of teaching democratic citizenship. According to Richard Lipka (1997), what are known as "service learning" projects can be initiated from the curriculum. Such projects emerge from various curriculum areas and interdisciplinary programs and involve direct experience via real improvement projects in the community. Lipka notes: "They bring together the cognitive and affective dimensions of authentic learning" (p. 59). Are curriculum-based service projects a part of your school program? Are they successful? Explain.

10. The following statement was made by Dewey in 1902: "The unity and wholeness of the child's development can be reached only in a corresponding unity and continuity of school conditions" [Dewey, J., (1902), *The educational situation*. Chicago: University of Chicago Press, pp. 25–26.] Do you see this as pertinent to contemporary school renewal efforts? Explain.

11. What recent trends can you identify in curriculum change in the elementary and middle school? In the high school? Do they look very different from what good teachers have always done? Consult earlier chapters of this book in framing your answer.

12. What have been the consequences of the federal policy of prioritizing early-childhood education over adolescent education?

13. In what ways are good schools alike?

BEST PRACTICES FOR CURRICULUM IMPROVEMENT AND SCHOOL RENEWAL

Throughout this text, emphasis has been given to the concept of curriculum development as a problem-solving process, with the school as the fundamental unit for educational improvement in conjunction with districtwide educational improvement. But practices for curriculum renewal and school improvement are documented throughout the text, most of which are research based or advocated in the professional literature as needed means or criteria for guiding our work.

The best practices in the instrument in this section of the text are not complete in any sense, but are intended to illustrate the scope or comprehensiveness of practices encompassed in a school self-study. The professional staff of a school will need to modify and add to the practices presented in this section to fit local conditions and needs. In this process they will need to draw from the work of the various professional education associations in identifying the more specific practices and recommended conditions pertaining to specialized concerns. Reference is made to a number of these organizations in connection with some of the practices in the following Best Practices Checklist. The items are organized according to the following categories: (A) Philosophy of the School; (B) Administrative Policy and Practice; (C) Proposals for Curriculum Reform/Renewal: Policy and Practice; (D) Climate for Curriculum Renewal; (E) Administrative Leadership: Roles and Functions; (F) Teacher Effectiveness and Classroom Climate; (G) Curriculum Development; (H) Professional Development; and (I) Teaching-Learning Resources, Facilities, and Services.

Using the Best Practices Checklist, the professional staff will be able to identify areas that need improvement in their school and school system. By comparing the responses on the Checklist rating scale by administrators, supervisors, and teachers, discrepancies can be identified so as to enhance communication, resolve conflict, and marshal the constructive energies of the entire professional staff through democratic-participative decision making. There can be no better basis for a professional-development program than working cooperatively on the identified problems and areas of need in the school as a whole.

Efforts to improve school effectiveness have tended to focus on inducing segmental changes confined within only one or two of the nine categories encompassed in the Best Practices Checklist. There is a common failure to recognize and treat the school as an ecological system. The consequence is that not only do segmental changes fail to deliver the promised results, but they also give rise to unanticipated problems. The Checklist is designed to enable the professional staff to see the curriculum and school as an ecological system and to identify possibilities for renewal through problem solving.

When school administrators and supervisors seek merely to "satisfice" rather than to optimize, they tend to meet external attacks and mandates by adopting slogans, fads, or currently popular innovations while failing to bring about the claimed improvements in conditions and practice. In this vein, they are likely to formulate or seize upon recommended practice segmentally and superficially. Incessant forays of conflicting demands and prescriptions for reform leveled at our schools from external sources impel many school administrators to demonstrate that their schools conform with whatever tide for reform is dominant. Such a response is largely political and results in great educational waste as the tides of reform shift in a countervening direction. At the same time, the expertise of the professional staff of the school and school district is allowed to go untapped, or is even curtailed or diverted to demonstrate compliance with external demands or mandates. Problem solutions require commitment and expertise on the part of the professional staff, along with time and supporting resources. The problem-solving capabilities of the professional staff remain a virtually untapped mine of talent and energy.

The Checklist enables the professional staff of the school and school system to function at the generative-creative level of knowledge/ability (Level III) rather than at the imitative-maintenance level (Level I) or the mediative-adaptive level (Level II) of knowledge/ability. When the Checklist is used as an instrument for the cooperative and continuous evaluation of the school and school system (involving all members of the professional staff), substantive problems will be revealed rather than concealed, and problems will be seen as opportunities for improvement. Through the cooperative engagement of the professional staff in self-study, administrators and supervisors can avoid the problem that plagues most ineffective schools—namely, overt compliance and covert resistance by the staff. Effective schools are marked by a commitment on the part of the professional staff to renewal.

The entire process of self-study, using the Checklist, should be seen as an educative process for the professional staff in which individual and collective energies and talents are marshaled for continued growth and renewal.

Best Practices Checklist for Curriculum Improvement and School Renewal

Circle the number that best expresses your evaluation of the extent to which each criterion, condition, or practice is in evidence in your school/district.

1 – Strongly in evidence
2 – Some evidence
3 – Little or no evidence
4 – Evidence to the contrary

A. PHILOSOPHY OF THE SCHOOL

1. The philosophy of the school is a working document, not a filed document, developed by the entire professional staff. It is used as a compass and regulator to identify possibilities, to make comparisons with actualities, and to actualize the professional staff toward the attainment of possibilities. The curriculum is the test of the philosophy in operation.   1 2 3 4

2. The professional staff shares a sense of vision and a commitment to the needs and mission of the school in a free society, and is actualized to meet these needs and fulfill this mission. This is reflected in the protection of the academic freedom of teachers and students, and in the curriculum, which fosters the development of independent thinking and democratic social responsibility.   1 2 3 4

3. The professional staff share a vision of future possibilities for the school and is working toward the attainment of longer-range goals, as well as meeting immediate needs. Immediate needs are consonant with long-range goals.   1 2 3 4

B. ADMINISTRATIVE POLICY AND PRACTICE

1. The local school board sees broad educational policies through full consultation with the administration, which, in turn, engages in full consultation with the professional staff.   1 2 3 4

2. The board of education relies on the expertise of the professional staff for the design, development, and evaluation of the educational program. The superintendent serves to "educate" the board on these matters and exercises the leadership needed for districtwide educational improvement.   1 2 3 4

3. The school board has a written policy that protects the academic freedom of teachers and students. The statement clearly places the responsibility for the selection and use of curricular materials with the professional staff. The statement meets the guidelines developed by the American Library Association, National Council of Teachers of English, National Council for the Social Studies, and National Science Teachers Association.   1 2 3 4

4. The principal and supervisory staff support the faculty against unfounded criticism.   1 2 3 4

5. A standing curriculum committee is in operation in the school, devoting its efforts to curriculum articulation and to the development of promising programs   1 2 3 4

for educational improvement. The committee is provided with the needed time and resources to perform its functions effectively.

6. External complaints concerning curricular materials or instructional practices, or any efforts to censor curricular materials, are referred to the standing curriculum committee for review and action.   1 2 3 4

7. A districtwide curriculum council works on districtwide curriculum articulation. Membership includes district supervisors and faculty representatives from the curriculum committee of each school. The council is chaired by the associate superintendent of curriculum/instruction or the director of curriculum.   1 2 3 4

8. Communication is maintained with other schools in the district and in other districts to share ideas and practices relating to common concerns through formal and informal contacts, jointly sponsored workshops and projects, and interschool faculty visitation. The schools in the district function as a network, not in isolation.   1 2 3 4

9. The school network facilitates the extension of successful programs and practices throughout the district. Care is taken to transform the programs and practices to meet the conditions of each individual school unit.   1 2 3 4

10. It is recognized that successful programs and practices in one school cannot simply be transplanted to or superimposed on another school, but that they require transformation through inservice education and commitment on the part of the faculty of each school.   1 2 3 4

11. Teachers are free to initiate requests for assistance from supervisors without first having to go through the principal for permission.   1 2 3 4

12. The administrative structure of the school district and school is democratic participative, and is reviewed periodically to ensure that it is fully functional.   1 2 3 4

13. The organizational structure of the educational program of the school is reviewed periodically to ensure that it is fully functional. Alternative designs— such as the school-within-a-school, nongraded classes/continuous progress, modular-flexible scheduling, and so on—are evaluated carefully.   1 2 3 4

14. The home is recognized and treated as a potentially powerful ally of the school, and systematic efforts are made by the professional staff to foster home-school cooperation. Parents are informed by the professional staff (teachers, counselors) on how they can contribute to the success of their children in school. Group conferences for parents are conducted on a regular basis by the professional staff.   1 2 3 4

15. Educational problems as well as accomplishments are communicated to parents and the wider community to enlist support toward the solution of problems.   1 2 3 4

16. The effectiveness of the school is determined not by any single measure, or narrow set of measures, but by the capacity and commitment of the professional staff (teachers, supervisors, administrators) to identify, diagnose, and solve emergent problems. The evaluation program is comprehensive and continuous.   1 2 3 4

C. PROPOSALS FOR CURRICULUM RENEWAL: POLICY AND PRACTICE

1. Proposals for reform—whether generated at national, state, or local levels— are evaluated carefully by examining the research literature and reviewing previous experiences with similar reform measures. (It is recognized that reform measures have a way of being reinvented and discarded at periodic intervals without educators seeking to learn from the lessons of the past.)   **1   2   3   4**

2. Reform measures are not adopted segmentally, but are instituted in organic relationship to the total educational program. The process is not one of adoption, but of adaptation and transformation to meet local conditions and needs. The improvement of curriculum and instruction is seen as originating in efforts to solve a problem, not in conforming to an external reform or adopting an innovation.   **1   2   3   4**

3. Reforms or innovations are implemented to benefit the entire learning community of the school, not to benefit one group at the expense of another (e.g., the gifted and talented over the disadvantaged), or one area of the curriculum at the expense of another (e.g., the sciences and mathematics at the expense of the arts and humanities).   **1   2   3   4**

4. Externally promoted curriculum reforms are evaluated critically by the professional staff in the light of the best available research evidence for effecting educational improvement, taking into account the philosophy of the school, the unique conditions of the local school, and the possible interactions of the reform measures with existing practices.   **1   2   3   4**

5. Reforms or innovations are adopted to improve the curriculum, rather than to demonstrate acquiescence to external pressures or eagerness to follow the latest tide of fashion.   **1   2   3   4**

6. Those who are most affected by reform proposals (e.g., the teachers) are directly involved in their evaluation (determining the efficacy of the proposals for improving the curriculum of the school) and in the decision making (adoption, adaptation, transformation, or rejection).   **1   2   3   4**

7. Reform measures or innovations are not adopted segmentally, but are transformed by the professional staff to meet local conditions, and the transformation is effected through a sense of commitment rather than compliance or imposition.   **1   2   3   4**

8. Reform measures and innovations are treated as hypotheses for testing through formative evaluation (in progress) and summative evaluation (at the end of a given time period), before they become institutionalized.   **1   2   3   4**

9. Pilot programs are developed for evaluating the reform measures or innovations. The expertise of the university is tapped as needed in the evaluation process.   **1   2   3   4**

10. Sufficient favorable evidence is available before reform measures or innovations are implemented on a wide scale.   **1   2   3   4**

11. Reform measures and innovations are adequately financed, but not at the expense of another ongoing program that is operating successfully or that is in equal need of attention.   **1   2   3   4**

D. CLIMATE FOR CURRICULUM RENEWAL

1. The school functions as a democratic-participative organizational system in which decisions are collaboratively developed by the entire professional staff and with the students.   1   2   3   4

2. The school climate is that of a community of belongingness, service, mutual respect, and support; responsibility for productive learning is shared by the administration, faculty, and student body.   1   2   3   4

3. Communication is open and free flowing rather than hierarchically downward.   1   2   3   4

4. The talents and motives for responsibility and self-direction on the part of the professional staff and students are fully tapped.   1   2   3   4

5. Support is provided for individual initiative by teachers as a means of catalyzing the spread of fresh ideas and practices.   1   2   3   4

6. Constructive ideas and suggestions are highly valued, widely shared, constantly elicited, and continuously implemented wherever practicable.   1   2   3   4

7. The motivational needs of teachers and students are productively expressed (belonging, self-esteem, competence, self-actualization, enlightenment, and creative engagement).   1   2   3   4

8. Education is seen as a developmental-emergent process, rather than an established-production process. The emphasis is on growth and optimizing human potentials, rather than on setting limits on students and teachers.   1   2   3   4

9. Concerted efforts are made to create optimal conditions for the school as a productive learning environment, rather than aiming at meeting minimal conditions.   1   2   3   4

10. Teachers readily communicate their problems and needs to the principal and supervisors.   1   2   3   4

11. Teachers and students are seen as the key sources for effecting educational improvement. They are not treated by the administration and supervisory staff as mere "channels for reception, transmission, or imposition" of policy and practice.   1   2   3   4

12. Student discipline is developed through responsible self-control, self-direction, and respect for others, rather than being a matter of authoritarian rule and imposition.   1   2   3   4

13. Teachers have professional autonomy to exercise initiative and responsible self-direction in the context of full collaboration with fellow faculty and other members of the professional staff of the school and school district. It is recognized that teacher isolation is not synonymous with teacher autonomy, and that decision making in the individual classroom does not add up to the decision making required for schoolwide and districtwide problem solving.   1   2   3   4

E. ADMINISTRATIVE LEADERSHIP: ROLES AND FUNCTIONS

1. The supervisory process is developmental (educative) rather than deficit-oriented (fault-finding).   1   2   3   4

2. The professional staff functions at Level III of knowledge/ability (the generative-creative level, rather than Level II (the mediative-adaptive level), or Level I (the imitative-maintenance level).   1 2 3 4

3. The administration supports supervisors and teachers in effecting improvement in the educational program, rather than seeking the maintenance of established practice ("running a tight ship").   1 2 3 4

4. The supervisor is an educational leader charged with the responsibility of working with the faculty, individually and collectively, on a collaborative basis in identifying, diagnosing, and solving classroom, schoolwide, and districtwide curriculum-instruction problems.   1 2 3 4

5. The principal functions as an expert generalist who sees the school as a whole and gives such direction to the school that it is consonant with the needs of the community and the wider society.   1 2 3 4

6. The expertise of the supervisor extends beyond a specialized subject field and encompasses the relationship of his or her specialty to the school curriculum as a whole.   1 2 3 4

7. A key qualification in the selection of supervisors is that they have expertise in curriculum development as a schoolwide and districtwide process, providing not only for curriculum articulation vertically (within a given subject field, grade level by grade level), but horizontally (between and among the various fields that comprise the total school curriculum).   1 2 3 4

8. A key qualification in the selection of teachers is that they are able to see the interdependence of the various studies, regardless of their particular specializations or levels of assignment, and are committed to the full articulation of the school curriculum.   1 2 3 4

9. The supervisor-teacher relationship is best described as one of collegial collaboration, and the entire professional staff functions as a collegial team.   1 2 3 4

10. The district is well staffed with qualified supervisors.   1 2 3 4

11. The principal and supervisors are highly knowledgeable concerning teachers' problems and assist teachers in solving problems.   1 2 3 4

12. The supervisory process is focused on the growth in the ability of teachers to identify, diagnose, and solve emergent problems in the classroom and school.   1 2 3 4

13. The faculty exhibits a strong collaborative commitment to problem solving as the key to school improvement.   1 2 3 4

14. Teachers, supervisors, and administrators seek to reveal problems, rather than to conceal them, so that action may be taken toward their solution.   1 2 3 4

15. The problems to be solved are derived from the educational situation, not from an external special-interest group or from individual promoters of special remedies.   1 2 3 4

16. The key focus of the supervisory program is on improving the curriculum, teaching, and learning.   1 2 3 4

17. The faculty together with the supervisory staff seek to identify (1) the qualities that make for the best school possible, (2) the strengths of the school and areas in need of improvement, (3) the ways and means of creating the kind of school that is envisioned, and (4) the ways and means of gauging the progress toward creating the best school possible.   1 2 3 4

18. The principal delegates routine detail work effectively so that the principal's time, talent, and energies can be devoted to the improvement of the educational program.   1 2 3 4

19. The principal works collaboratively with the professional staff on budgetary allocation for educational improvement.   1 2 3 4

20. Teachers are provided with the needed supportive technical assistance and material resources for problem solving.   1 2 3 4

21. The professional staff identifies short-term needs in consonance with long-term needs. It is recognized that when problems are masked by treating symptoms for the short term, the result is the compounding of problems in the long term (e.g., teaching-to-the-test may raise test scores in the short run, but this is done at the expense of important educational goals).   1 2 3 4

22. Working for student success (and the prevention of student failure) is a function of the entire professional staff. The approach is developmental in orientation (focused on student potentials, rather than deficiency oriented (focused on student limitations).   1 2 3 4

23. The principal and supervisors make frequent visits to classrooms to see the educational program in action and to elicit from teachers the kinds of help needed in solving problems.   1 2 3 4

24. Teachers freely initiate contacts with the principal and supervisors in seeking help with educational problems.   1 2 3 4

25. The principal and supervisors provide continual assistance to teachers in response to problems identified by teachers, while helping teachers to identify problems for diagnosis and treatment.   1 2 3 4

26. The principal's role is that of an educational leader, rather than a school manager, whose major function is to marshal all of the resources of the school and school district to improve the educational program.   1 2 3 4

27. Teachers receive written periodic evaluations from supervisors. The evaluations are developed cooperatively between the teacher and supervisor.   1 2 3 4

F. TEACHER EFFECTIVENESS AND CLASSROOM CLIMATE

1. The classroom functions as a participative-group system revealing a spirit of cooperation and mutual respect between teacher and students and among students.   1 2 3 4

2. The ways of teaching are congruent with the goal of developing the powers of students for independent thinking and democratic social responsibility.   1 2 3 4

3. Students share with the teacher the responsibility for the success of the class as a whole. More advanced students help others. The success of one student is not gained at the expense of another student.　　1　2　3　4

4. The teacher works for student success and the prevention of failure. The teacher's approach is developmental in orientation (focused on student potentials) rather than deficiency oriented (focused on student limitations). The curriculum focus is on the development of optimal competencies rather than minimal competencies.　　1　2　3　4

5. Communication is open—upward from student to teacher and laterally from student to student(s), as well as downward from teacher to student(s).　　1　2　3　4

6. Students are learning to assume the responsibility for initiating and directing many of their learning activities, rather than depending on the teacher to tell them what they must do.　　1　2　3　4

7. The social motive for productive learning is developed along with individual autonomy. Assignments include group projects and individual projects to enable students to learn how to work together for the common good, as well as how to work independently.　　1　2　3　4

8. Learning activities are appropriately varied to meet individual differences without creating student isolation. The work of subgroups is shared by the entire class; such work is not limited to mechanical exercises but involves collaborative investigation.　　1　2　3　4

9. The teacher is genuinely enthusiastic about the classroom work, and students share the enthusiasm and exhibit a genuine sense of interest and commitment to the learning activities.　　1　2　3　4

10. The teacher gives explanations or rationales for his or her decisions or actions to students. The decisions or actions by teachers are not seen by students as arbitrary because explanations and rationales are provided and, insofar as possible, students are involved in the decision making that affects them directly.　　1　2　3　4

11. Learning activities are designed to foster cognitive growth in conjunction with affective and social growth. Efforts are made to foster desirable attitudes toward learning in recognition that such attitudes are fundamental to cognitive growth and development.　　1　2　3　4

12. The teaching-learning process is idea oriented rather than error oriented. Facts and skills are not treated as ends but as the means and resources for the development of higher-ordered thinking abilities and the intelligent application of knowledge in the life of the learner.　　1　2　3　4

13. Class discussion is catalyzed by thought questions initiated by students as well as teachers.　　1　2　3　4

14. There is full class participation. Students are not reluctant to participate for fear of revealing their lack of knowledge or understanding. The classroom is not dominated by teacher "telling" or didactic instruction.　　1　2　3　4

15. Teachers give explanations and stimulate explanations from students in connection with classroom work. Teachers do not merely seek to elicit　　1　2　3　4

correct answers from students, but engage students in explaining how they derived their answers. When errors are made, teachers engage students in open inquiry in diagnosing the source of the error.

16. Students are not reluctant to reveal their need for assistance and are not embarrassed or penalized for revealing such need. Their willingness and capability in reporting their need for explanation or assistance is regarded positively rather than negatively by the teacher. Mistakes are treated as opportunities for improvement and for collateral learning.   1 2 3 4

17. Constructive and instructive suggestions, rather than negative criticisms, are offered by the teacher to students and by students to their peers. Such suggestions encourage and help students succeed in their work. This also applies to the teacher's evaluation of students' written work.   1 2 3 4

18. Individual variation in the classroom is recognized by providing sufficient time for the completion of given individual learning activities, and by selecting and assigning activities in recognition of individual differences without isolating individuals.   1 2 3 4

19. The teacher recognizes opportunities for collateral learning and capitalizes on such opportunities so as to motivate learners to go beyond what is required in the classroom (e.g., in studying about disease and health, the student becomes interested in the life of a particular scientist, and the teacher helps the student locate a biography of that scientist).   1 2 3 4

20. Time allocation for classroom activities is flexible, so that when students are productively engaged in an unanticipated emergent learning situation, the teacher will not terminate the event in order to shift to another activity that may be less productive.   1 2 3 4

21. Students are allowed sufficient time to gather their thoughts and to express them vocally and in writing.   1 2 3 4

22. Discipline is seen as integral to the educative process—as growth in purposive self-control and self-direction on the part of each student in the context of social responsibility, rather than a matter of external imposition or authoritarian control by the teacher.   1 2 3 4

23. Motivation is seen as a key factor in preventing discipline problems, and concerted and continuous efforts are made to stimulate genuine student motivation for learning.   1 2 3 4

24. Where problems of student motivation and discipline are in evidence, they are treated as curricular problems, rather than being treated in isolation. Growth in self-discipline is seen as an educational function, in contrast to the treatment of discipline as a matter of external, authoritarian imposition.   1 2 3 4

25. Students are grouped in classrooms not for the purpose of exacting uniformity, but to capitalize on the powerful educative learnings of a cosmopolitan group. Classroom learning activities are designed to enable students to learn from one another. Individual variation is seen as essential to the growth and vitality of the group, not as a negative factor.   1 2 3 4

26. The physical environment of the classroom and school is attractive and conducive to a productive psychosocial climate for learning.   1 2 3 4

G. CURRICULUM DEVELOPMENT

1. The school is recognized outside the district for its successful programs and practices, and it attracts educators from neighboring districts who seek to gain new ideas for school improvement.   1   2   3   4

2. Curriculum development is treated as a problem-solving process involving the entire professional staff of the school and school district.   1   2   3   4

3. The responsibility for the curriculum, including the selection and use of curricular materials, resides with the professional staff, not with any external source or special-interest group.   1   2   3   4

4. Teachers and supervisors, under the leadership of the director of curriculum, are engaged in continuous and systematic curriculum development to articulate the curriculum throughout the district as well as within the school. Curriculum articulation is developed horizontally (between and among subject fields) and vertically (from grade level to grade level and from school to school within the district).   1   2   3   4

5. The curriculum is treated as an ecological system rather than as an amalgamation of separate parts. Efforts to improve the teaching of a subject matter are undertaken in relation to its interdependence with all subjects in the curriculum and with the wider functions of the curriculum (the macrocurriculum), such as the function of general education. The professional staff gives concerted attention to the "grand design" of the school curriculum.   1   2   3   4

6. The curriculum is conceived and developed as a whole, with the various studies treated as interdependent through correlation and synthesis.   1   2   3   4

7. Transdisciplinary approaches enable students to become engaged in the study of problems of personal and social significance. (For example, the social studies, literature, and composition are treated interrelatedly; mathematics is related to the sciences and social studies; the relationships between science and society, and between the arts and society, are revealed; and so on.)   1   2   3   4

8. Teachers and supervisors are engaged in continuous and systematic curriculum development across the entire curriculum as well as within the subject fields. Supervisors do not work in isolation according to their fields of specialization.   1   2   3   4

9. Students work with the professional staff on curriculum improvement.   1   2   3   4

10. The curriculum is attuned to the nature of the learner (e.g., developmental stages and motivational needs) and to the qualities that make for democratic citizenship (individual autonomy in the context of social responsibility).   1   2   3   4

11. Instructional improvement is seen as integral to curriculum improvement and to the improvement of learning. The supervisory program treats curriculum, instruction, and learning as interdependent.   1   2   3   4

12. Statements of educational objectives emphasize the development of higher thinking abilities, in which facts and skills are put to meaningful use, rather than being treated as ends in themselves.   1   2   3   4

13. The units of study are organized according to concepts, ideas, themes, problems, and projects of personal-social significance that stimulate inquiry, rather than being organized according to topics.   1 2 3 4

14. The units of study are interconnected, rather than being treated in isolation, so that students can derive deeper and wider understandings, appreciations, and capabilities as they progress from unit to unit.   1 2 3 4

15. Learning skills are developed through growth in the use of concepts, ideas, and understandings that give rise to the meaning of experience, rather than being treated as isolated ends in themselves.   1 2 3 4

16. Skills are developed through the curriculum rather than being treated as separate subjects. (It is recognized that although general education encompasses basic education and much more, basic education is not a substitute for general education.)   1 2 3 4

17. Classroom activities and assignments are designed to stimulate students to seek and interpret relevant knowledge from a wide variety of subjects and sources, revealing the interdependence of knowledge.   1 2 3 4

18. The balance and coherence of the curriculum is maintained in the face of any special priorities that may be established for the school (e.g., priority given to science and math is not at the expense of the arts and humanities).   1 2 3 4

19. The responsibility for the actual design and development of the curriculum resides with the professional staff of the school district and school. State curricular mandates are not seen as an excuse for avoiding this responsibility. (For example, the state may mandate specific subjects for high school graduation, but it does not mandate how the subjects are to be organized and treated in the curriculum.)   1 2 3 4

20. Individualized learning provides for student self-direction and responsibility and derives from systematic teacher-student planning. Individualized learning is not regarded as synonymous with the convergent-mechanical exercises characteristic of workbooks, programmed instruction, and photocopy sheets.   1 2 3 4

21. The secondary school curriculum is not dominated by the college-preparatory function, but is comprehensive to meet the diversified needs of a cosmopolitan student population through vocational, college preparatory, enrichment, exploratory studies, and general education.   1 2 3 4

22. Students are not segregated into program tracks in the high school.   1 2 3 4

23. In the secondary school, there is a coherent curriculum in general education, rather than distribution-elective requirements.   1 2 3 4

24. A coherent program of general education provides for those learnings that all citizens in a free society share with opportunities to examine pervasive problems and issues of personal-social significance.   1 2 3 4

25. Teachers are free from external constraints and pressures that may lead to the censorship of the curriculum or of curricular materials, or to self-imposed censorship.   1 2 3 4

26. At the secondary level, the curriculum in general education is designed to meet the needs of a heterogeneous student population and to capitalize on the positive attributes of a cosmopolitan class group.   1 2 3 4

27. Elective options for exploratory, enrichment, and special-interest studies allow for multiage/multigrade groupings of students.   1 2 3 4

28. Block-time classes are offered in the middle school and junior high school to enable students to identify with a core teacher and to foster curriculum correlation and synthesis, especially in English language arts and social studies. Team-teaching arrangements may be provided. Social concerns and problems are examined through the reading of literary works and historical documents, the writing of themes, participation in panel discussions, and work on a variety of individual and group projects and community service.   1 2 3 4

29. Interdependent cooperation and planning are in evidence in the middle, junior, and senior high school to provide for horizontal curriculum articulation and for a coherent program of general education.   1 2 3 4

30. Standardized tests are used appropriately and do not mitigate a balanced and rich curriculum (e.g., students engage in writing across the curriculum, in working on projects in the fine arts and industrial arts, and so on—despite the fact that the learning outcomes from such activities are not evaluated vis-à-vis standard tests).   1 2 3 4

31. Standardized tests are used for diagnostic purposes, not for purposes of determining student grades or for segregating students into different classes. (It is recognized that standardized aptitude tests are not valid as sole predictors of student achievement and that ability grouping into separate classes does not, in itself, produce higher achievement.)   1 2 3 4

32. Teacher-made tests are focused on student growth in higher-order thinking through comprehension, analysis, application, and problem solving.   1 2 3 4

33. Teacher-made tests are used by the teacher to evaluate the teacher's success in effecting student growth in achievement.   1 2 3 4

34. The evaluation of student achievement is based on comprehensive criteria, rather than primarily on test results.   1 2 3 4

35. The school schedule is designed to facilitate the educational program, rather than to constrain it. (For example, classes in physical education recreation are scheduled block-time two or three days per week, rather than as a single period daily, to allow a greater proportion of time devoted to productive activity in relation to the time taken in the locker room and for warm-up routines.)   1 2 3 4

36. Scheduling considerations do not result in the tracking of students in their course work in the secondary school.   1 2 3 4

37. The schedule is designed to provide students with opportunity to pursue a full and rich program of studies and to participate in student activities.   1 2 3 4

38. The curriculum is not treated as a schedule of segmental subjects.   1 2 3 4

39. The fullest opportunity is provided for coeducational learning activities throughout the curriculum.   1 2 3 4

40. Teachers have the deciding voice in the selection of textbooks and other curricular materials, with care taken to ensure that adequate attention is given to the scope and sequence of the total school curriculum.   1 2 3 4

41. The textbook does not determine the course of study, but is used along with a rich variety of curricular materials, resources, and activities for productive learning.   1 2 3 4

42. Students are free to take their books and other curricular materials home with them.   1 2 3 4

43. Textbooks and other curricular materials are plentiful and up to date.   1 2 3 4

44. In the secondary school, the homeroom is heterogeneously grouped and functions as a significant social unit, rather than serving as a routine daily session for attendance and announcements.   1 2 3 4

45. The homeroom teacher functions in a guidance capacity and arranges for special help for those students whose achievement is below capacity.   1 2 3 4

46. Homework is meaningfully directed through assignments that enhance school achievement and stimulate student interest in the subject matter. It is not mechanical drudgery.   1 2 3 4

47. Teachers read and comment on all homework from a proficiency rather than a deficiency orientation.   1 2 3 4

48. A full range of advanced-placement courses is offered in the high school. Teachers do not seek to imitate the college professor in lecture methods, but use a wide variety of approaches appropriate for adolescents in stimulating their interest in advanced study (e.g., through panel discussions, theme writing, projects, and so on).   1 2 3 4

49. A comprehensive program of extraclass activities is provided, enabling students to assume responsibilities through self-directed learning. All students have opportunities for wide participation. Emphasis is given to the development of wholesome, lifelong, recreational interests.   1 2 3 4

50. Extraclass activities are recognized by the professional staff as integral to, not apart from, the total school curriculum.   1 2 3 4

51. Extraclass activities provide for multigrade/multiage grouping of students.   1 2 3 4

52. The student council is actively engaged in identifying and addressing schoolwide student concerns and problems, and works collaboratively with the faculty and administration on school improvement. The range and nature of student concerns and problems to be addressed are not limited by the administration and faculty.   1 2 3 4

53. Students are widely engaged in community-service activities of an educative nature, and these activities grow out of and feed back into the curriculum (e.g., children at the primary level may be planting seeds to beautify the school grounds; adolescents may be engaged in a reading project for the blind; and so on).   1 2 3 4

54. A full-time kindergarten is an integral part of the total educational program of the elementary school.

    1   2   3   4

55. The summer school program encompasses a comprehensive range of course offerings and activities for enrichment, acceleration, and recreation, rather than being confined mainly to remedial or makeup work.

    1   2   3   4

56. Periodic student surveys are conducted to elicit suggestions for curriculum improvement. The students are informed of the findings and are enlisted to work with the professional staff on curriculum improvement.

    1   2   3   4

57. The school district conducts a diversified program of adult classes and activities to meet community needs.

    1   2   3   4

58. Evaluation of student achievement and progress is diagnostic and constructive, not deficit oriented.

    1   2   3   4

H. PROFESSIONAL DEVELOPMENT

1. Teacher development is a districtwide responsibility, as well as a responsibility of the principal and faculty in the individual school.

    1   2   3   4

2. The entire professional staff of the school and district is engaged in a systematic program of inservice education to enhance continuous professional growth. The program is planned, conducted, and evaluated cooperatively.

    1   2   3   4

3. The principal, director of curriculum, and supervisors exercise leadership in coordinating the inservice program in full collaboration with the faculty, and ensure that adequate material resources are provided to help teachers grow professionally.

    1   2   3   4

4. Inservice education is an ongoing program for school improvement, guided by well-understood and agreed-upon goals. The program is developmental in orientation rather than deficit oriented.

    1   2   3   4

5. Inservice education is integral to the overall program of curriculum development.

    1   2   3   4

6. The needs of the school, the teachers, and the students are treated as mutually interdependent.

7. The inservice program is designed to enhance teacher motivation and capability for problem solving, to stimulate deeper insights and wider perspectives for educational improvement. The program is not concentrated on narrow convergent training, such as in the adoption and implementation of a prepackaged, segmental instructional program.

    1   2   3   4

8. Teachers are major decision makers in planning the inservice programs and in identifying and diagnosing the needs and problems to be addressed.

    1   2   3   4

9. The inservice education program provides teachers with sufficient time to reflect on their work and to develop the means for improving their effectiveness.

10. The inservice education program provides for (1) a regular schedule for classroom visitation with each teacher by the principal and supervisors, (2) a conference with the teacher following each visit for collaborative evaluation and planning, and (3) a sufficient number of visits with each teacher to observe a variety of teaching-learning situations.

    1   2   3   4

11. The goals and functions of the inservice program are consonant with the goals of the educational program of the school.　　1　2　3　4

12. Full opportunity is provided for "grass-roots" initiation to ensure that the inservice program is directed at problems and concerns of greatest significance to teachers.　　1　2　3　4

13. The functions of teacher evaluation and inservice education (professional development) are seen as mutually enhancing, rather than conflicting, because teachers are evaluated on their awareness of problems, willingness to expose problems, and efforts in seeking help in solving problems.　　1　2　3　4

14. Strong incentives are provided supervisors and teachers for working on problem solutions.　　1　2　3　4

15. The reward system favors the revealing rather than the concealing of problems.　　1　2　3　4

16. The teacher sees classroom problems as being within his or her capability of control and solution.　　1　2　3　4

17. When problems are beyond the teacher's capability, rather than resting the blame with some external causation, the teacher seeks and receives the needed help from the supervisors, and/or from the administrator, and from fellow teachers.　　1　2　3　4

18. The evaluation of teaching effectiveness is based on comprehensive criteria, rather than being narrowly focused on those classroom activities and student outcomes that are most easily amenable to quantifiable measurement. Teaching is understood as a complex process, and it is recognized that there are many ways of teaching effectively, just as there are many ways of learning effectively.　　1　2　3　4

19. Faculty morale is high as the result of a democratic-participation system of organization in which full support is provided by the administration for faculty development and educational improvement.　　1　2　3　4

20. Teachers seek help from supervisors in solving substantive educational problems, rather than looking for ready recipes.　　1　2　3　4

21. The faculty is actualized to seek educational improvement on a continuing basis, and the efforts yield demonstrable results.　　1　2　3　4

22. Teachers eagerly share their successful ideas and materials through faculty meetings, inservice education projects, teacher centers, scheduled interclass visitation-observation, and informal contacts.　　1　2　3　4

23. Recognition is given to individual and joint achievements of teachers in improving the educational program, and the successful practices are widely disseminated throughout the school, district, and the schools of neighboring districts.　　1　2　3　4

24. Outstanding teachers are enlisted in helping other teachers.　　1　2　3　4

25. Faculty meetings are devoted mainly to the improvement of the educational program; teachers, supervisors, and administrators cooperatively plan the agenda. The meetings are not dominated by the principal.　　1　2　3　4

26. The inservice program is well supported and sufficient provisions are made for released time for teachers, outside expertise, and material resources.　　1　2　3　4

27. Inservice workshops are planned cooperatively with the faculty and are focused on problem solutions. The workshops are evaluated in terms of the progress made in solving problems. The entire professional staff is involved in the evaluation process.　1　2　3　4

28. Inservice workshops are followed up with the needed support services and material resources to enable teachers to bring about the targeted improvements in the educational program.　1　2　3　4

29. Workshops, institutes, and other service sessions sponsored by the school and school district are not treated as substitutes for advanced university study.　1　2　3　4

30. Teachers participate widely in advanced university study to improve their professional capabilities and to develop collegial relationships with teachers from widely differing schools and school systems.　1　2　3　4

31. All teachers are fully certified and most have completed the master's degree or are actively engaged in pursuing the master's degree.　1　2　3　4

32. An interschool visitation program provides for wide faculty participation in observing promising programs and practices in other schools in the district, areas, and state.　1　2　3　4

33. Major aspects of the inservice program are evaluated formatively and summatively.　1　2　3　4

34. The orientation of new teachers is an integral function of the inservice program. The orientation takes account of the differences among beginning teachers and among experienced teachers from other schools in the same system as well as those from other systems. Special assistance is provided for teachers who have been transferred to meet school desegregation guidelines or changes in enrollment patterns.　1　2　3　4

35. A yearlong inservice program is conducted for beginning teachers in which their problems and concerns are shared openly, and through which appropriate support is provided, including the supply of material resources.　1　2　3　4

36. Special supervisory assistance is provided beginning teachers to help them in the successful transition from preservice education to professional teaching, and to ensure their professional growth (through appropriate assignments, plentiful resource materials, adequate facilities, and measures to prevent teacher isolation).　1　2　3　4

37. Beginning teachers are not assigned to courses (or students) "rejected" by veteran teachers or to facilities that are regarded as less desirable by veteran teachers.　1　2　3　4

38. The support system for new teachers encourages them to seek assistance with problems, and the help is readily provided.　1　2　3　4

39. New teachers participate in the selection of curricular materials that they will be using in their classes.　1　2　3　4

40. The working climate not only provides opportunities for beginning teachers and newly transferred teachers to express their ideas for improving the educational program, but their ideas are openly solicited and valued by the entire professional staff.　1　2　3　4

41. Experienced teachers who are new to the school are viewed as potential sources of ideas and suggestions and are enlisted in working on existing problems with their new colleagues. The principal works to involve all new teachers immediately in the total life of the school.

    1   2   3   4

42. In focusing on problem solving, the continuing inservice education program stimulates teachers to grow professionally, rather than to settle into established routines.

    1   2   3   4

43. Consultants are engaged regularly to work with the professional staff on problem solutions on both a short-term and a long-term basis. The consultants are responsible for the follow-up of their own work.

    1   2   3   4

44. The professional staff works with the university in seeking to solve school and school-district problems. A cooperative, ongoing school-university program is in operation for this purpose.

    1   2   3   4

45. The number of teacher preparations is never excessive, and teachers are provided with at least one period daily for preparation, individual conferences with colleagues, and for occasional visitation-observation in other classes.

    1   2   3   4

46. Alternative patterns of staffing are explored and implemented to reduce teacher load and to improve the educational program.

    1   2   3   4

47. If the school is located within reasonable proximity to a college or university, the school serves as a center for student teaching or internship. A core of cooperating teachers works conjointly with the college supervisor in designing and evaluating the program.

    1   2   3   4

48. A problem-solving approach is followed by the cooperating teacher and student teacher/intern to ensure that the experience is directed at professional growth rather than adjustment and compliance.

    1   2   3   4

49. The cooperating teacher shares with the student teacher/intern all of the available material resources, without requiring that they be used. The student/intern is encouraged to develop his or her own resources and repertoire.

    1   2   3   4

50. The supervisory staff and most members of the faculty hold membership in one or more of the leading professional educational associations noted for work on curriculum development (e.g., American Vocational Association, Association for Supervision and Curriculum Development, International Reading Association, National Art Education Association, National Council of Teachers of English, National Council of Teachers of Mathematics, National Council for the Social Studies, National Science Teachers Association, and so on).

    1   2   3   4

51. Supervisors and teachers are effective consumers of research and are engaged concertedly and continually in applying the best available evidence to the improvement of practice in the school and classroom. Where the evidence is incomplete, practices are treated as hypotheses for further testing.

    1   2   3   4

52. A high proportion of the faculty answer this question affirmatively: "If you were to begin your career over again, would you become a teacher?"

    1   2   3   4

I. TEACHING-LEARNING RESOURCES, FACILITIES, AND SERVICES

1. The school plant is physically attractive, functional, in harmony with community development patterns and needs, and is located with ready access to community recreational resources. (Ideally, the school site is adjacent to parkland.) The site is adequate for possible future expansion/modification of buildings and facilities. The outdoor recreational facilities are ample not only for student use, but also for community use.   1 2 3 4

2. The school site and physical facilities are so arranged that learning activities are not impeded by outside noise, or by inside noise from the gym, shops, music studios, and so on.   1 2 3 4

3. The school is of sufficient size to provide the professional staff, facilities, and resources required for a rich curriculum to meet the needs of a cosmopolitan pupil population. Yet the school is organized so that students and the professional staff are engaged in close working relationships.   1 2 3 4

4. In the case of the high school where a large enrollment is required in order to warrant the investment in the required specialized facilities and resources for a diversified curriculum, the school is organized under a "house plan" so that students are able to identify with a core professional staff affiliated with the "house." The house faculty is responsible for general education.   1 2 3 4

5. The facilities, equipment, and resources in all areas of the curriculum meet the standards set by the appropriate professional organization (libraries, laboratories, shops, studios, resource centers, gymnasium, athletic fields, auditorium).   1 2 3 4

6. There is a districtwide media program that is well coordinated, staffed, and financed. (See the current edition of *Media Programs*, published by the American Library Association.)   1 2 3 4

7. The school has a media program under the direction of a media professional who participates in curriculum development. The media program is integrated to the curriculum, not merely an ancillary service.   1 2 3 4

8. The facilities, staffing, and resources of the school media centers meet the guidelines of the American Association of School Libraries. (See the current edition of *Media Programs*, [the basic collection for a school with 500 or fewer users includes at least 8,000 to 12,000 books, or 16 to 24 books per user, with access to 60,000 titles to ensure satisfaction of 90 percent of initial requests, and 50 to 175 periodical/newspaper titles]. See also the standards for other media resources, including those for the computer-learning laboratory.)   1 2 3 4

9. The school media center is attractive, functional, and a true center for responsible, self-directed, learning activity.   1 2 3 4

10. The school media center is open to students for individual and group use throughout the school day, including the lunch period, and before and after regular school hours.   1 2 3 4

11. Class assignments engage each student in the use of the media center for investigative work and for the preparation of reports.   1 2 3 4

12. Students are encouraged to use the media center for recreational reading and browsing, and to use the equipment for viewing and listening.   1 2 3 4

13. The media center is never used as a study hall or for purposes other than for which it is intended.   1 2 3 4

14. Teachers receive help in preparing multimedia learning resources and are encouraged to draw upon the staff of the media center for assistance.   1 2 3 4

15. The entire professional staff collaborates fully on budgetary allocations for learning resources; the principal and teachers are provided with discretionary funds to buy special learning materials that are needed to improve the curriculum.   1 2 3 4

16. Students are surveyed periodically to ascertain their needs for learning resources and to elicit their suggestions for improving the facilities, resources, and services.   1 2 3 4

17. Students and teachers in the secondary school have ready access to word processors and other equipment.   1 2 3 4

18. A rich collection of teaching resource units (for teachers) and learning resource units (for students) is maintained in the school media center and is used extensively by teachers and students.   1 2 3 4

19. Teachers are assigned rooms of their own in which they conduct most of their classes, have their own desks and files, can store their instructional materials, and have shelf space for classroom libraries.   1 2 3 4

20. Students are provided with adequate work space. The classroom furniture is functional and movable for varied teaching-learning activities. Classroom storage space meets instructional needs. Students are provided with adequate locker space for their books and private belongings.   1 2 3 4

21. Teachers are provided with needed clerical-technical assistance and resources for the preparation of curriculum materials through the school media center, and avail themselves of such services and resources.   1 2 3 4

22. The district maintains an extensive professional library that is widely used by the professional staff.   1 2 3 4

23. The ratio of professional staff to students is no greater than 1:20. Class size is adjusted appropriately to age/grade level and to the nature of the learning activity. There are no overcrowded classrooms.   1 2 3 4

24. In the secondary school, each teacher has no more than 140 students in all classes combined on a daily basis.   1 2 3 4

25. The guidance and counseling program is well articulated districtwide from the elementary school through the high school. Each counselor is responsible for no more than 250 to 300 students in the secondary school. The facilities are attractive and afford privacy.   1 2 3 4

26. Students in the secondary school feel free to initiate contacts with their counselor for help with personal, social, and academic problems. An ongoing   1 2 3 4

program is in place to assist students with employment, and to provide for career counseling.

27. The guidance staff works closely with parents and with the faculty to improve the work of the teacher as a guidance person in the classroom.   1 2 3 4

28. An effective dropout-prevention program is maintained by the high school.   1 2 3 4

29. The high school operates a continuation program to enable students to earn their diplomas on a part-time basis.   1 2 3 4

30. Annual follow-up studies are conducted of graduates, transferees, and dropouts, the findings are widely shared by the professional staff for curriculum improvement and the improvement of the guidance and counseling program.   1 2 3 4

31. Transfer students receive special assistance to ensure successful adjustment: academically, psychologically, and socially.   1 2 3 4

32. In the secondary school, the physical facilities and the organization of the schedule allow each student free time to work independently in the school library, resource center, shop, laboratory, or studio. There are no study halls.   1 2 3 4

33. The schedule of courses is sufficiently flexible so that students do not have to make forced choices because of schedule constraints.   1 2 3 4

34. Remedial programs are provided without isolating and stigmatizing students. The programs are designed to correct any inadequacies in the ongoing instructional program of the school, as well as to provide individual remediation.   1 2 3 4

35. Handicapped students and students with special needs are provided with special support services without being isolated from other students.   1 2 3 4

36. Health facilities and services are fully adequate. Provisions are made for regular medical examination, referral, and follow-up.   1 2 3 4

37. The school serves as a center for community activities, including adult evening classes.   1 2 3 4

Abelson, P. H. (1967). Excessive educational pressure. *Science, 156*, p. 741.

Abelson, P. H. (1968, August 16). Toward better vocational education. Editorial. *Science, 161*.

Accelerated schools show progress with at-risk students. (1992). *Illinois School Journal, 60*, 12.

Adams, J. E., Jr. (2000). *Taking charge of curriculum: Teacher networks and curriculum implementation*. New York: Teachers College Press.

Adler, M. J. (1939). The crisis in contemporary education. *The Social Frontier, 5*, 62–63.

Adler, M. J. (1982). *The paideia proposal: An educational manifesto*. New York: Macmillan.

Adler, M. J. (1983). *Paideia problems and possibilities*. New York: Macmillan.

Adolescence isn't a terminal disease. *New York Times*, December 21, 1993, p. C12.

Ahlvors, L. V. (1962). Mathematics curriculum of the high school. *American Mathematical Monthly, 69*, 189–193.

Aikin, W. M. (1942a). *The story of the eight-year study*. New York: Harper.

Aikin, W. M. (1942b). *Thirty schools tell their story*. New York: Harper.

Aikin, W. M. (1953). The eight-year study: If we were to do it again. *Progressive Education, 31*, 11–14.

Airasian, P. W. (1994). The impact of the taxonomy on testing and evaluation. In L. W. Anderson & L. A. Sosniak (Eds.), *Bloom's taxonomy: A forty year retrospective*. 93rd Yearbook, National Society for the Study of Education, Part 2, pp. 82–102. Chicago: University of Chicago Press.

Alberty, H. B., & Alberty, E. J. (1962). *Reorganizing the high school curriculum* (3rd ed.). New York: Macmillan.

Alexander, F. (1994). What I saw at the education revolution. In H. Walberg (Ed.), *Radical reform in education*. Berkeley, CA: McCutchan.

Alexander, W. M., & McEwin, C. K. (1989). *Schools in the middle: Status and progress*. Chicago: National Middle School Association.

Allen, R. (2003). The democratic aims of service learning. *Educational Leadership, 60*(6), 51–54.

Alt, M. N., & Choy, S. P. (2000). *In the middle: Characteristics of public schools with a focus on middle schools*. Washington, DC: National Center for Education Statistics, U.S. Department of Education.

American Association for the Advancement of Science. (1989). *Science for ALL Americans*. Washington, DC: Author.

American Association for the Advancement of Science. (1993). *Benchmarks for science literacy*. New York: Oxford University Press.

American Association of School Administrators. (1966). *National education assessment: Pro and con*. Washington, DC: National Education Association.

Anderson, G. L., & Gates, A. I. (1950). The general nature of learning. In N. B. Henry (Ed.), *Learning and instruction*. 49th Yearbook, National Society for the Study of Education, Part 1, pp. 12–34. Chicago: University of Chicago Press.

Anderson, L. W., & Krathwohl, D. R. (Eds.) (2001). *A taxonomy for learning, teaching, and assessing: A revision of Bloom's taxonomy of educational objectives*. New York: Longman.

Anderson, R. H. (1988). Political pressures on supervisors. In L. Tanner (Ed.), *Critical issues in curriculum*. 87th Yearbook, National Society for the Study of Education, Part 1, pp. 60–82. Chicago: University of Chicago Press.

Anrig, G. R. (1992, April 1). Can tests lead the way to excellence? *Education Week, 11*, 40.

Apple, M. W. (1986). *Teachers and tests: A political economy of class and gender relations in education*. New York: Routledge & Kegan Paul.

Apple, M. W. (1990). *Ideology and curriculum* (2nd ed.). New York: Routledge & Kegan Paul.

Archambault, R. D. (Ed.). (1964). John *Dewey on education, selected writings*. New York: Modern Library.

Arias, M. B., & Casanova, U. (1993). (Eds.). *Bilingual education: Politics, practice, and research*. 92nd Yearbook, National Society for the Study of Education, Part 2. Chicago: University of Chicago Press.

Aristotle. (1952). *Politics. Great books of the modern world*. Chicago: *Encyclopedia Britannica, 9*, 544.

Aronowitz, S., & Giroux, H. A. (1983). *Education under siege*. South Hadley, MA: Bergin & Garvey.

Association for Supervision and Curriculum Development (ASCD). (1985). *With consequences for*

ALL. Alexandria, VA: The Association.

Association for Supervision and Curriculum Development (ASCD). (1992). *Association for Supervision and Curriculum Development resolutions 1992*. Alexandria, VA: The Association.

Astin, A. W. (1993). What *matters most in college?* San Francisco: Jossey-Bass.

Ayala, F. (1982). The evolutionary concept of biology. In G. A. Almond, M. Chodorow, & R. H. Pearce (Eds.), *Progress and its discontents* (pp. 113–124). Berkeley: University of California Press.

Ayers, L. P. (1912). Measuring educational processes through educational results. *The School Review, 20*, 300–309.

Bagley, M. B. (1907). *Classroom management*. New York: Macmillan.

Bagley, W. C. (1934). *Education and emergent man*. New York: Nelson.

Bailey, S. K. (1970). *Disruption in urban public secondary schools*. Reston, VA: National Association of Secondary School Principals.

Bailey, T. P. (1900). Some difficulties of child study. *National Education Association Proceedings*. Chicago: University of Chicago Press.

Baily, M., Bator, F., Hall, T., & Solow, R. (1989). *Manufacturing productivity*. Washington, DC: McKinsey Global Institute.

Baily, M., Bator, F., Hall, T., & Solow, R. (1993). *Manufacturing productivity*. Washington, DC: McKinsey Global Institute.

Bailyn, B. (2003). *To begin the world anew*. New York: Knopf.

Baker, G. D. (1938). An eleventh-grade field study: The coal industry. *Educational Research Bulletin, 17*, 173–188.

Balfanz, R., Ruby, S., & MacIver, D. (2002). Essential components and next steps for comprehensive whole school reform in high poverty middle schools. In S. Springfield & D. Land (Eds.), *Educating at-risk students*. 101st Yearbook, National Society for the Study of Education, Part 2, pp. 128–147. Chicago: University of Chicago Press.

Ball, D. L. (1996). Teacher learning and the mathematics reforms: What we think we know and what we need to learn. *Phi Delta Kappan, 77* (7), 500–508.

Bandura, A. (1969). *Principles of behavior modification*. New York: Holt.

Barber, B. R. (1992). *An aristocracy of everyone: The politics of education and the future of America*. New York: Ballantine.

Barber, B. R. (1993). America skips school. *Harper's Magazine, 287* (1722), 39–46.

Barnes, E. A., & Young, B. M. (1932). *Children and architecture*. New York: Teachers College Press.

Barrow, R. (1983). Does the question "What is education?" make sense? *Educational Theory, 33* (3), 191–194.

Barrow, R. (1988). Over the top: A misuse of philosophical techniques. *Interchange, 19* (2), 59–63.

Barzun, J. (1971). Where the educational nonsense comes from. In *Papers on educational reform*, Vol. II. Chicago: Open Court, 1–13.

Barzun, J., & Saunders, R. J. (1979). *Art in basic education*. Washington, DC: Council for Basic Education.

Baxter, T., & Young, B. M. (1933). *Ships and navigation*. New York: Teachers College Press.

Beane, J. (1991). The middle school: The natural home of the integrated curriculum. *Educational Leadership, 49*, 9–13.

Beard, C. A. (1932). *A charter for the social studies in the schools*. New York: Scribner's, 1932.

Beauchamp, G. A. (1975). *Curriculum theory*. Wilmette, IL: Kagg.

Becker, H. J. (1990). Curriculum and instruction in middle-grade schools. *Phi Delta Kappan, 71*, 450–456.

Begle, E. C., & Wilson, J. W. (1970). Evaluation of mathematics programs. In National Society for the Study of Education, *Mathematics education*. 69th Yearbook, Part I. Chapter 10. Chicago: University of Chicago Press.

Bell, D. (1968). *The reforming of general education*. New York: Doubleday/Anchor.

Bell, D. (1972). On meritocracy and equality. *The Public Interest* (3), 45.

Belth, M. (1965). *Education as a discipline*. Boston: Allyn & Bacon.

Bemis, E. W. (1894–1895). Relation of labor organizations to the American boy and to trade instruction. *Annals of the American Academy of Political and Social Science, 5*, 209–241.

Benn, C., & Chitty, C. (1997). *Thirty years on. Is comprehensive education alive and well or struggling to survive?* London: Penguin Press.

Benne, K. J. (1952). Theory of cooperative planning. *Teachers College Record, 53*, 429–435.

Bennett denounced by presidents of Harvard and Stanfords (1987, February 11). *Chronicle of Higher Education, 34*, 17, 21.

Bennett, W. J. (1987). *James Madison high school.* Washington, DC: U.S. Department of Education.

Bennett, W. J. (1988). *James Madison elementary school.* Washington, DC: U.S. Department of Education.

Bereiter, C., & Englemann, S. (1966). *Teaching disadvantaged children in the preschool.* Englewood Cliffs, NJ: Prentice Hall.

Berger, J. (1991, June 21). Arguing about America. *New York Times,* 1.

Berk, L. E. (1992). The extracurriculum. In P. W. Jackson (Ed.), *Handbook of research on curriculum* (pp. 1002–1043). New York: Macmillan.

Bernal, J. D. (1971). *Science in history* (Vol. 4). Cambridge, MA: MIT Press.

Berner, E. A., & Young, B. M. (1932). *Children and architecture.* New York: Teachers College Bureau of Publications.

Bestor, A. (1956). The *restoration of learning.* New York: Knopf.

Bettleheim, B. (1964, September 10). How much can man change? *New York Review of Books,* 4.

Bierce, A. (1875). *The devil's dictionary.* Garden City, NY: Doubleday (1967 edition).

Blatchford, P., Moriarity, V., Edmonds, S., & Martin C. (2002). Relationships between class size and teaching. *American Educational Research Journal, 39*(1), pp. 101–132.

Bloom, A. (1987). The *closing of the American mind.* New York: Simon & Schuster.

Bloom, B. S. (Ed.). (1956). *Taxonomy of educational objectives, Handbook I: Cognitive domain.* New York: McKay.

Bloom, B. S. (1964). *Stability and change in human characteristics.* New York: John Wiley.

Bloom, B. S. (1976). *Human characteristics and school learning.* New York: McGraw-Hill.

Bloom, B. S. (1980). The new direction in educational research: Alterable variables. *Phi Delta Kappan, 61*, 382–385.

Bloor, D. (1976). *Knowledge and social imagery.* London: Routledge & Kegan Paul.

Bobbitt, F. (1913). *The supervision of city schools: Some general principles of management applied to the problems of city-school systems.* 12th Yearbook, National Society for the Study of Education, Part 1. Bloomington, IL: Public School Publishing.

Bobbitt, F. (1918). *The curriculum.* Boston: Houghton Mifflin.

Bobbitt, F. (1924). *How to make a curriculum.* Boston: Houghton Mifflin.

Bobbitt, F. (1924). The new technique of curriculum making. *The Elementary School Journal, 25*, 45–54.

Bochner, S. (1969). *Eclosion and synthesis: Perspectives on the history of knowledge.* New York: W. A. Benjamin.

Bode, B. H. (1927). *Modern educational theories.* New York: Macmillan.

Bode, B. H. (1931). Education at the crossroads. *Progressive Education, 8*(7), 543–549.

Bode, B. H. (1935, January). Education and social reconstruction. *The Social Frontier, 1*, 20.

Boguslaw, R. (1965). *The new utopians: A study of system design and social change.* Englewood Cliffs, NJ: Prentice Hall.

Bohm, D. (1971). Fragmentation. *The Science Teacher, 38*, 10–15.

Bohnenberger, J. E., & Terry, A. W. (2002). Community problem solving works for middle level students. *Middle School Journal, 34*(1), 5–12.

Bok, D. (1978). The president's report. *Harvard Magazine,* May–June, n.p.

Boles, K., & Troen, V. (1992). How teachers make restructuring happen. *Educational Leadership, 49*, 53–56.

Bonser, F. G. (1920). *The elementary curriculum.* New York: Macmillan.

Bonser, F. G. (1927). Curriculum-making in laboratory or experimental schools. In G. M. Whipple (Ed.), *Curriculum-making: Past and present.* 26th Yearbook, National Society for the Study of Education, Part 1, pp. 353–362. Bloomington, IL: Public School Publishing.

Boorstin, D. J. (1958). *The Americans: The colonial experience.* New York: Vintage.

Boorstin, D. J. (1965). *The Americans: The national experience.* New York: Vintage.

Borman, G. D. (2002). Title I: The evolution and effectiveness of compensatory education. In S. Stringfield & D. Land (Eds.), *Educating at-risk students.* 101st Yearbook, National Society for the Study of Education, Part 2, pp. 231–245. Chicago: University of Chicago Press.

Born, M. (1964, April). What is left to hope for. *Bulletin of the Atomic Scientists, 20*, 2.

Boruch, R. F. (1991). The president's mandate: Discovering what works and what works better. In M. W. McLaughlin & C. D. Phillips (Eds.), *Evaluation and education: At quarter century.* 90th Yearbook, National Society for the Study of Education, Part 2, pp. 147–167. Chicago: University of Chicago Press.

Bowles, S., & Gintis, H. (1976). *Schooling in capitalist America.* New York: Basic Books.

Boyer, E. L. (1983). *High school: A report on secondary education in America.* Carnegie Foundation for the Advancement of Teaching. New York: Harper.

Boyer, E. L. (1987). *College: The undergraduate experience in America.* New York: Harper.

Bracey, G. (2003). Ever "at risk"? *Phi Delta Kappan, 84,* 562.

Bradley, A. (1998, April 15). Muddle in the middle. *Education Week, 17* (31), 38–42.

Brameld, T. (1935, November). Karl Marx and the American teacher. *The Social Frontier, 2.*

Brameld, T. (1971). *Patterns of education philosophy.* New York: Holt, Rinehart and Winston.

Brandt, R. (1992). On building learning communities: A conversation with Hank Levin. *Educational Leadership, 50* (1), 19–23.

Bredo, E. (2002). The Darwinian center to the vision of William James. In J. Garrison, P. Podeschi, & E. Bredo (Eds.), *William James & education.* New York: Teachers College Press.

Briggs, T. H. (1920). *The junior high school.* Boston: Houghton Mifflin.

Bronowski, J. (1956). *Science and human values.* New York: Harper.

Bronowski, J. (1958, September). The creative process. *Scientific American, 199,* 59.

Brookover, W. B., Gigliotti, R. J., Henderson, R. D., Niles, B. E., & Schneider, J. (1974). Quality of educational attainment, standardized testing, assessment, and accountability. In C. W. Gordon (Ed.), *Uses of the sociology of education.* 73rd Yearbook, National Society for the Study of Education, Part 2, pp. 161–191. Chicago: University of Chicago Press.

Broudy, H. S. (1972). *The real world of the public schools.* New York: Harcourt.

Broudy, H. S., Smith, B. O., & Burnett, J. R. (1964). *Democracy and excellence in America* (2nd ed.). Chicago: Rand McNally.

Brown, B. B., & Theobald, W. (1998). Learning contexts beyond the classroom: Extracurricular activities, community organizations, and peer groups. In K. Borman & B. Schneider (Eds.), *The adolescent years: Social influences and educational challenges.* 97th Yearbook, National Society for the Study of Education, Part 1, pp. 109–141. Chicago: University of Chicago Press.

Broyler, C. R., Thorndike, E. L., & Woodward, E. (1927). A second study of mental discipline in high school studies. *Journal of Educational Psychology, 18.*

Brubacher, J. S. (1966). *A history of the problems of education* (2nd ed.). New York: McGraw-Hill.

Bruer, J. T. (1999). In search of brain-based education. *Phi Delta Kappan, 80* (9), 648–654.

Bruer, J. T. (1999). *The myth of the first three years.* New York: Free Press.

Bruner, J. S. (1960). *The process of education.* Cambridge, MA: Harvard University Press.

Bruner, J. S., Chair. (1963). *Goals on school mathematics,* Cambridge Conference. Boston: Houghton Mifflin.

Bruner, J. S. (1966). *Toward a theory of instruction.* Cambridge, MA: Howard University Press.

Bruner, J. S. In Hall, E. (1970). Bad education—A connection with Jerome Bruner. *Psychology Today, 4,* 51.

Bruner, J. S. (1971). The process of education revisited. *Phi Delta Kappan, 53,* 18–31.

Brunner, C. C., Grogan, M., & Björk, L. (2002). Shifts in the discourse defining the superintendency: Historical and current foundations of the position. In J. Murphy (Ed.), *The educational leadership challenge: Redefining leadership for the 21st century.* 101st Yearbook, National Society for the Study of Education, Part 1, pp. 211–238. Chicago: University of Chicago Press.

BSCS Newsletter. (1963, September), *19.*

Burlbaw, L. M. (1991). More than 10,000 teachers: Hollis L. Caswell and the Virginia curriculum revision program. *Journal of Curriculum and Supervision, 6,* 233–254.

Burton, W. (1833). *The district school as it was.* Boston: Carter, Hendee.

Bush, R. N., & Allen, D. W. (1964). *A new design for high school education.* New York: McGraw-Hill.

Buttenweiser, P. L. (1969). The *Lincoln School and its times.* Unpublished doctoral dissertation, Columbia University, New York.

Butts, R. F. (1978). *Public education in the United States.* New York: Holt.

Butts, R. F., & Cremin, L. A. (1953). *A history of education in American culture.* New York: Holt, Rinehart and Winston.

Caldwell, O. W. (1927). The Lincoln experimental school. In H. O. Rugg (Ed.), *Curriculum-making: Past and present*. 26th Yearbook, National Society for the Study of Education, Part 1, pp. 271–289. Bloomington, IL: Public School Publishing.

California State Board of Education. (2000). *Science content standards for California public schools: Kindergarten through grade twelve*. Sacramento, CA: CDE Press.

Callahan, R. E. (1962). *Education and the cult of efficiency*. Chicago: University of Chicago Press.

Campbell, J. K. (1967). *Colonel Parker: The children's crusader*. New York: Teachers College Press.

Campbell, R. F., Cunningham, L. L., McPhee, R. F., & Nystrand, R. O. (1980). *The organization and control of American schools*. Columbus, OH: Merrill/Macmillan.

Carnegie Council on Policy Studies in Higher Education. (1979). *Giving youth a better chance*. San Francisco: Jossey-Bass.

Carnegie Forum on Education and the Economy. (1986). *A nation prepared: Teachers for the 21st century*. New York: Author.

Carnegie Quarterly. (1966, Spring), *14* (1), 1–4.

Carnegie Quarterly. (Fall, 1970), *18*, 5–6.

Carnoy, M., & Levin, H. M. (1976). *The limits of educational reform*. New York: McKay.

Carson, C. C., Huelskamp, R. M., & Woodall, T. D. (1993). Perspectives on education in America. *Journal of Educational Research, 86* (5), 259–310.

Carter, J. G. (1824a) *Letters to the hon. William Prescott, L.L.D. on the free schools of New England, with remarks upon the principles of instruction*. Boston: Cummings Hilliard.

Carter, J. G. (1824b). *The schools of Massachusetts in 1824*. Old South Leaflet, No. 135.

Carter, J. G. (1826). *Essays upon popular education, containing a particular examination of the schools of Massachusetts and an outline of an instruction for the education of teachers*. Boston: Bowles and Dearborn.

Caswell, H. L. (1950). Research in the curriculum. *Educational Leadership, 7*, 438–445.

Caswell, H. L. (1962). Difficulties in defining the structure of curriculum. In A. H. Passow (Ed.), *Curriculum crossroads* (pp. 103–111). New York: Teachers College Press.

Caswell, H. L. (1966). Emergence of the curriculum as a field of professional work and study. In H. F. Robinson (Ed.), *Precedents and promises in the curriculum field*. New York: Teachers College Press.

Caswell, H. L., & Campbell, D. S. (1935). *Curriculum development*. New York: American Book.

Celis, W. (1993, September 9). *New York Times*. Study says half of adults in U.S. can't read or handle arithmetic, pp. A1, 22.

Celso, N. (1978). *The knowledge-ability factor and school effectiveness*. Unpublished doctoral dissertation, Rutgers University, New Brunswick, NJ.

Center for Educational Research and Innovation. (1993). *Education at a glance: OECD indicators*. Paris: Organization for Economic Cooperation and Development.

Center for the Study of Public Policy. (1970). *Education vouchers*. Cambridge, MA: Author.

Central Advisory Council for Education (England). (1967). *Children and their primary schools*. London: Her Majesty's Stationery Office.

Chall, J., & Conrad, S. S. (1984). Resources and their use for reading instruction. In A. C. Purves & O. Niles (Eds.), *Becoming readers in a complex society*. 83rd Yearbook, National Society for the Study of Education, Part 1, pp. 209–232. Chicago: University of Chicago Press.

Chamberlin, D., Chamberlin, E. S., Drought, N. E., & Scott, W. E. (1942). *Did they succeed in college?* New York: Harper.

Charters, W. W. (1922). Activity analysis and curriculum construction. *Journal of Educational Research, 5* (5), 357–399.

Charters, W. W. (1923). *Curriculum construction*. New York: Macmillan.

Charters, W. (1924). Functional analysis as the basis for curriculum construction. *Journal of Educational Research, 10*, 214–221.

Charters, W. (1927). *Teaching of ideals*. New York: Macmillan.

Chasin, G., & Levin, H. M. (1995). Thomas Edison accelerated elementary school. In J. Oakes & K. H. Quartz (Eds.), *Creating new educational communities*. 94th Yearbook, National Society for the Study of Education, Part 1, pp. 130–146. Chicago: University of Chicago Press.

Cheney, L. V. (n.d.). *American memory*. Washington, DC: National Endowment for the Humanities.

Childs, J. L. (1931). *Education and the philosophy of experimentalism*. New York: Century.

Chira, S. (1992, January 8). A national curriculum: Fairness in uniformity. *New York Times,* p. B9.

Chomsky, N. (1968). *Language and mind.* New York: Harcourt.

Clark, R. W. (1988). Who decides? The basic policy issue. In L. Tanner (Ed.), *Critical issues in curriculum.* 87th Yearbook, National Society for the Study of Education, Part 1, pp. 175–204. Chicago: University of Chicago Press.

Clegg, A. In Maclure, J. S. (1968). *Curriculum innovation in practice.* Report of the Third International Curriculum Conference. London: Her Majesty's Stationery Office.

Cleveland, H. (1985). *The knowledge executive.* New York: E. P. Dutton.

Clifford, G. J. (1978). Words for the schools: The applications in education of the vocabulary researches of Edward L. Thorndike. In P. Suppes (Ed.), *Impact of research on education: Some case studies.* Washington, DC: National Academy of Education.

Clift, R. T., Veal, M. L., Holland, P., Johnson, M., & McCarthy, J. (1995). *Collaborative leadership and shared decision making: Teachers, principals, and university professors.* New York: Teachers College Press.

Coalition of Essential Schools. (1988). *Prospectus.* Providence, RI: Brown University.

Cochran-Smith, M., & Lytle, S. L. (1990). Research on teaching and teacher research: The issues that divide. *Educational Researcher, 19* (2), 2–11.

Cochran-Smith, M., & Lytle, S. L. (1999). The teacher research movement: A decade later.

Educational Researcher, 28 (7), 15–25.

Coleman, J. S. (1966, Summer). Equal schools or equal students? *The Public Interest,* 74.

Coleman, J. S., et al. (1966). *Equality of educational opportunity.* Washington, DC: U.S. Office of Education.

Coleman, J. S., Chair. (1976). *Youth: Transition to adulthood.* Panel on Youth of the President's Science Advisory Committee. Chicago: University of Chicago Press.

Coleman, J. S. (1978). Changing the environment for youth. *Phi Delta Kappan, 59,* 319.

Collings, E. (1923). *An experiment with a project curriculum.* New York: Macmillan.

Commager, H. S. (1950, October 16). Our schools have kept us free. *Life Magazine, 29,* 46.

Commager, H. S. (1958). A historian looks at the American high school. *The School Review, 66* (1), 1–18.

Commager, H. S. (1960). *The era of reform 1830–1860.* Princeton, NJ: D. Van Nostrand.

Commager, H. S. (1967a). *Lester Ward and the welfare state.* Indianapolis: Bobbs-Merrill.

Commager, H. S. (1967b). *The search for a usable past.* New York: Knopf.

Commager, H. S. (1968a). *Documents of American history* (8th ed.). New York: Appleton.

Commager, H. S. (1968b, Spring). A historian looks at the American high school. *The School Review, 66* (1), 1–18.

Commager, H. S. (1969). *The commonwealth of learning.* New York: Harper.

Commission on Achieving Necessary Skills. (1992). *Learning a living.* Washington, DC: U.S. Department of Labor.

Commissioner of Education. (1893). *Report for the year 1889–90* (Vol. 2). Washington, DC: Bureau of Education.

Commission on MIT Education (1970). *Creative renewal in times of crisis.* Cambridge, MA: MIT.

Commission on the Reorganization of Secondary Education. (1918). *Cardinal principles of secondary education.* Washington, DC: National Education Association.

Commission on Undergraduate Education in the Biological Sciences. (1967). *Content of core curricula in biology.* Washington, DC: American Institute of Biological Sciences.

Commission on Work, Family, and Citizenship. (1988). *The forgotten half: Non-college youth in America.* Washington, DC: Grant Foundation.

Committee of Ten. (1893). *Report of the committee of ten on secondary school studies.* Washington, DC: National Education Association.

Commons, J. R., et al. (1910). *A documentary history of American industrial society.* Cleveland: A. H. Clark.

Conant, J. B. (1945). *Public education and the structure of American Society.* Cambridge, MA: Harvard University Press.

Conant, J. B. (1949). *Education in a divided world: The function of the public schools in a unique society.* Cambridge, MA: Harvard University Press.

Conant, J. B. (1959a). *The child, the parent and the state.* Cambridge, MA: Harvard University Press.

Conant, J. B. (1959b). *The American high school today: A first report to interested citizens.* New York: McGraw-Hill.

Conant, J. B. (1960). *Education in the junior high school years.* Princeton, NJ: Educational Testing Service.

Conant, J. B. (1961). *Slums and suburbs.* New York: McGraw-Hill.

Conant, J. B. (1964a). *Two modes of thought.* New York: Trident.

Conant, J. B. (1964b). *Shaping educational policy.* New York: McGraw-Hill.

Conant, J. B. (1967). *The comprehensive high school.* New York: McGraw-Hill.

Conant, J. B. (1970a). The comprehensive high school. In A. C. Eurich (Ed.), *High school 1980.* New York: Pitman.

Conant, J. B. (1970b). *My several lives.* New York: Harper.

Conant, J. B., & Spaulding, F. (1940). *Education for a classless society.* Cambridge, MA: Harvard University Press.

Conrad, D., & Hedin, D. (1991). School-based community service: What we know from research and theory. *Phi Delta Kappan, 72* (10), 743–749.

Consortium on Chicago School Research. (1992). *Charting reform: The principals' perspective.* Chicago: Author.

Corcoran, T., Fuhrman, S., & Belcher, C. L. (2001). The district role in instructional improvement. *Phi Delta Kappan, 83* (1), 78–84.

Core knowledge curriculum project. (1992). *American School Board Journal, 179,* A19.

Cornbleth, C. (1982). Critical thinking and cognitive process. In W. R. Stanley (Ed.), *Review of research in social studies education,* 11–15. Boulder, CO: Social Science Education Consortium.

Cornog, W. H. (1963). What are the priorities for the public schools in the 1960s? *Occasional Papers, 5.* Washington, DC: Council for Basic Education, p. 3.

Corporation executives visit vocational high schools. (1991, July 21). *New York Times,* p. F21.

Council for Basic Education. (1991). *English Coalition Conference and Modern Language Association Standards,* n.p. Washington, DC: Author.

Council on Middle Level Education. (n.d.). *An agenda for excellence.* Reston, VA: National Association of Secondary School Principals.

Counts, G. S. (1927). Curriculum-making in public high schools. In G. M. Whipple (Ed.), *Curriculum-making: Past and present.* 26th Yearbook, National Society for the Study of Education, Part 1, pp. 135–162. Bloomington, IL: Public School Publishing.

Counts, G. S. (1932). *Dare the school build a new social order?* New York: John Day; Carbondale, IL: Southern Illinois Press, 1978.

Courant, R. In Carrier, G. F., et al. (1962). Applied mathematics: What is needed in research and education. *SIAM Review, 4,* 297–320.

Court upholds closing of Horace Mann-Lincoln School (1947). *Teachers College Record,* 48, 533.

Cox, C. B., & Boyson, R. (Eds.). (1977). *Black paper 1977.* London: Temple Smith.

Cremin, L. A. (1951). *The American common school.* New York: Teachers College Press.

Cremin, L. A. (1955, March). The revolution in American secondary education, 1893–1918. *Teachers College Record, 56,* 295–308.

Cremin, L. A. (Ed.). (1957). *The republic and the school: On the education of free men.* New York: Teachers College Press.

Cremin, L. A. (1961). *The transformation of the school.* New York: Knopf.

Cremin, L. A. (1965). *The genius of American education.* New York: Vintage.

Cremin, L. A. (1971). Curriculum making in the United States. *Teachers College Record, 73* (2), 207–220.

Cremin, L. A. (1973). The free school movement: A perspective. *Notes on Education,* October, 5.

Cremin, L. A. (1990). *Popular education and its discontents.* New York: Harper & Row.

Cronbach, L. J. (1977). *Educational psychology* (3rd ed.). New York: Harcourt.

Cronbach, L. (1986). Tyler's contribution to measurement and evaluation. *Journal of Thought, 21* (1), 47–52.

Cronin, J. M., & Usdan, M. D. (2003). Rethinking the urban superintendency: Nontraditional leaders and new models of leadership. In W. L. Boyd & D. Miretzky (Eds.), *American educational governance on trial: Change and challenges.* 102nd Yearbook, National Society for the Study of Education, Part 1, pp. 177–195. Chicago: University of Chicago Press.

Crow, G. M., Hausman, C. S., & Scribner, J. P. (2002). Reshaping the role of the school principal. In J. Murphy (Ed.), *The educational leadership challenge: Redefining leadership for the 21st century.* 101st Yearbook, National Society for the Study of Education, Part 1, pp. 189–210.

Chicago: University of Chicago Press.

Cuban, L. (1984). *How teachers taught*. New York: Longman.

Cuban, L. (1990). Reforming again, again and again. *Educational Researcher, 19* (3), 3–13.

Cuban, L. (1993). *How teachers taught: Constancy and change in American classrooms 1880–1900* (2nd ed.). New York: Teachers College Press.

Cubberley, E. P. (1909). *Changing conceptions of education*. Boston: Hougton Mifflin.

Cubberley, E. P. (1947). *Public education in the United States* (Rev. ed.). Boston: Houghton Mifflin.

Curti, M. (1935). *The social ideas of American educators*. New York: Scribner.

D'Agostino, J. V. (2000). Achievement testing in American schools. In T. L. Good (Ed.), *American education: Yesterday, today, and tomorrow*. 99th Yearbook, National Society for the Study of Education, Part 2, pp. 313–337. Chicago: University of Chicago Press.

Dahl, R. (1989). *Democracy and its critics*. New Haven, CT: Yale University Press.

Darling-Hammond, L. (1993). Reframing the school reform agenda: Developing capacity for school transformation. *Phi Delta Kappan, 74* (10), 752–761.

Darling-Hammond, L. (1997). *The right to learn*. San Francisco: Jossey-Bass.

Darling-Hammond, L., Ancess, J., & Ort, S. W. (2002). Reinventing high school: Outcome of the coalition campus schools project. *American Educational Research Journal, 39* (3), 639–673.

Darling-Hammond, L., & Snyder, J. (1992). Reframing accountability: Creating learner-centered schools. In A. Lieberman (Ed.), *The changing contexts of teaching*. 91st Yearbook, National Society for the Study of Education, Part 1, pp. 11–16. Chicago: University of Chicago Press.

Davis, Calvin O. (1917). *Public secondary education*. New York: Rand McNally.

Day, J. (1829). Original papers in relation to a course of liberal education. *American Journal of Science and Arts, 15*, 300–301.

DeGarmo, Charles. (1912). *Herbart and the Herbartians*. New York: Scribner's.

Dennison, G. (1969). The *lives of children*. New York: Random House.

Desimone, L. (2002). How can comprehensive school reform models be successfully implemented? *Review of Educational Research, 72* (3), 433–479.

Dewey, J. (1895). *Plan of organization of the university primary school*. Privately printed (University of Chicago Archives, Regenstein Library).

Dewey, J. (1897a). The psychological aspect of the school curriculum. *Educational Review, 13*, 356–369.

Dewey, J. (1897b). The university elementary school, history and character. *University Record* (University of Chicago), *3*, 72–75.

Dewey, J. (1897c). *My pedagogic creed*. New York: E. L. Kellogg.

Dewey, J. (1900a). *The school and society*. Chicago: University of Chicago. Originally published in 1899.

Dewey, J. (1900b). Froebel's educational principles. *Elementary School Record, 1*(3), 82–83.

Dewey, J. (1900c). The psychology of the elementary curriculum. *Elementary School Record, 1* (9), 221–232.

Dewey, J. (1902a). The educational situation. Chicago: University of Chicago Press.

Dewey, J. (1902b). *The child and the curriculum*. Chicago: University of Chicago Press.

Dewey, J. (1902c). Current problems in secondary education. *The School Review, 10*, 13–28.

Dewey, J. (1904). The relation of theory to practice in education. In C. A. McMurry (Ed.), *The relation of theory to practice in the education of teachers*. 3rd Yearbook, National Society for the Scientific Study of Education, Part 1, pp. 9–30. Chicago: University of Chicago Press.

Dewey, J. (1910, 1933). *How we think*. Lexington, MA: Heath.

Dewey, J. (1910, January). Science as subject matter and as method. *Science, 31*, 127.

Dewey, J. (1913). An undemocratic proposal. *Vocational Education, 2*, 374–377.

Dewey, J. (1915a). *The school and society* (Rev. ed.). Chicago: University of Chicago Press. Originally published in 1899.

Dewey, J. (1915b, April 17). Splitting up the school system. *The New Republic, 11*, 283–284.

Dewey, J. (1916). *Democracy and education*. New York: Macmillan.

Dewey, J. (1917, March 24). Learning to earn. *School and Society, 5*, 331–335.

Dewey, J. (1922). *Human nature and conduct*. New York: Holt.

Dewey, J. (1927). *The public and its problems*. Chicago: Swallow Press.

Dewey, J. (1928a). Progressive education and the science

of education. *Progressive Education, 5,* 196–204.

Dewey, J. (1928b, July–September). Progressive education and the science of education. *Progressive Education, 5,* 200.

Dewey, J. (1928c). *The sources of a science of education.* New York: Liveright.

Dewey, J. (1929a). The *sources of a science of education.* New York: Liveright.

Dewey, J. (1929b). *Individualism old and new.* New York: Capricorn (1962 edition).

Dewey, J. (1933). *How we think* (2nd ed.). Lexington, MA: D. C. Heath. Originally published in 1910.

Dewey, J. (1934, Nov.). Need for a philosophy of education. *The New Era in Home and School* (England), *15,* 212.

Dewey, J. (1934a). Education for a changing social order. *National Education Association Proceedings.* Washington, DC: National Education Association.

Dewey, J. (1937, May). Education and social change. *The Social Frontier, 1,* 22.

Dewey, J. (1938). *Experience and education.* New York: Macmillan.

Dewey, J. (1939). *Freedom and culture.* New York: G. P. Putnam's Sons.

Dewey, J. (1940). Presenting Thomas Jefferson. In A. O. Mendel (Ed.), *The living thoughts of Thomas Jefferson* (pp. 1–30). New York: Longmans.

Dewey, J. (1941). *The school and society.* Chicago: University of Chicago Press. Originally published 1899.

Dewey, J. (1946). *Problems of men.* New York: Philosophical Library.

Dewey, J. (1946). Individuality and experience. In *Art and education,* 2nd ed. Merion, PA: Barnes Foundation.

Dewey, J. (1948). *Reconstruction in philosophy.* Boston: Enlarged edition; original edition, 1920. Holt.

Dewey, J. (1958), *Experience and nature.* New York: Dover. Originally published 1925.

Dewey, J. (1962). *Individualism old and new.* New York: Capricorn. Originally published 1929.

Dickens, C. (1854). *Hard times.* Oxford, England: Oxford University Press (1955 edition).

Diggins, J. P. (1992). *The rise and fall of the American left.* New York: W. W. Norton.

Dillman, C. M., & Rahmlow, H. F. (1972). *Writing instructional objectives.* Belmont, CA: Fearson.

Dillon, S. (1993, April 5). New York City readies 37 specialized schools in big revision. *New York Times,* p. B10.

Dillon, S. (2003, May 22). States are relaxing education standards. *New York Times,* p. A29.

Dillon, S. (2004, February 22). Bush education officials find new law a tough sell to states. *New York Times,* pp. A1, A24.

Doll, R. C. (1992). *Curriculum improvement: Decision making and process* (8th ed.). Boston: Allyn & Bacon.

Donelson, K. (1990). You can't have that book in my kid's school library: Books under attack in the *Newsletter on Intellectual Freedom, 1952–1989. The High School Journal, 74,* 4.

Dreeben, R. (1968). *On what is learned in school.* Reading, MA: Addison-Wesley.

Dressel, P. L., and Mayhew, L. B. (1954). *General education:*

Explorations in evaluation. Washington, DC: American Council on Education.

Duke, D. L. (1978). *The retransformation of the school.* Chicago: Nelson-Hall.

Dunkel, H. B., Gowin, D. B., & Thomas, L. G. (1972). Introduction. In L. G. Thomas (Ed.), *Philosophical redirection of educational research.* 71st Yearbook, National Society for the Study of Education, Part 1, pp. 1–8. Chicago: University of Chicago Press.

Dunkin, M. J., & Biddle, B. J. (1974). *The study of teaching.* New York: Holt.

Edmonds, R. (1979). Effective schools for the urban poor. *Educational Leadership, 37* (2), 15–18.

Education Commission of the States. (1983). *Action for excellence.* Task Force on Education for Economic Growth. Denver: Author.

Education Development Center. (1967). *Annual report.* Newton, MA: Author.

Educational Policies Commission. (1938). *The structure and administration of education in American democracy.* Washington, DC: National Education Association.

Educational Policies Commission. (1941). *The civilian conservation corps, the national youth administration, and the public schools.* Washington, DC: National Education Association.

Educational Policies Commission. (1944, 1952). *Education for ALL American youth.* Washington, DC: National Education Association.

Educational Policies Commission. (1948). *Education for ALL American children.* Washington,

DC: National Education Association.

Educational Policies Commission. (1952). *Education for ALL American youth—a further look.* Washington, DC: National Education Association.

Edwards, E. F. (1968, June 15). Kindergarten is too late. *Saturday Review,* 69.

Egan, K. (1978). What is curriculum? *Curriculum Inquiry, 8* (1), 65–72.

Eggebrecht, J., Dagenais, R., Dosch, D., Merczak, N. J., Park, M. N., Styer, S. C., & Workman, D. (1996). Reconnecting the sciences. *Educational Leadership, 53,* 4–8.

Einstein, A. (1934). *The world as I see it.* New York: Covici-Friede.

Einstein, A. (1950). *Out of my later years.* New York: Philosophical Library.

Eisner, E. (1985). (Ed.). *Learning and teaching the ways of knowing.* 84th Yearbook, National Society for the Study of Education, Part 2. Chicago: University of Chicago Press.

Eisner, E. W. (1994). The *educational imagination: On the design and evaluation of school programs* (3rd ed.). New York: Macmillan.

Eisner, E. W., & Vallance, E. (Eds.). (1974). *Conflicting conceptions of curriculum.* Berkeley, CA: McCutchen.

Eliot, C. W. (1869). The new education. *Atlantic Monthly, 23,* 203–220, 356–367.

Eliot, C. W. (1893). Can school programs be shortened and enriched? In *Proceedings of the National Education Association* (617–625). Washington, DC: National Education Association.

Eliot, C. W. (1900). Discussion. In National Education Association, *Proceedings* (pp. 197–198). Chicago: University of Chicago Press.

Eliot, C. W. (1905). The fundamental assumptions of the Committee of Ten. *Educational Review,* 30.

Ellis, S. D. (1967). Enrollment trends. *Physics Today, 20,* 77–78.

Elmore, R. (2000). Leadership for effective middle school practice. *Phi Delta Kappan, 82,* 269, 291–292.

Elmore, R., & Fuhrman, S. (1994). *Governing curriculum: Changing patterns in policy, politics and practice.* In R. Elmore & S. Fuhrman (Eds.), *The governance of curriculum.* Yearbook, Association for Supervision and Curriculum Development, pp. 1–10. Alexandria, VA: The Association.

Elmore, R., & Sykes, G. (1992). Curriculum policy. In R. W. Jackson (Ed.), *Handbook of research on curriculum* (pp. 201–203). New York: Macmillan.

Elmore, R., & Wisenbaker, J. (2000). The crabapple experience: Insights from program evaluations. *Phi Delta Kappan, 82,* 280–283.

Elsbree, W. S. (1938). *The American teacher.* New York: American Book.

Englemann, S. (1999). The benefits of direct instruction: Affirmative action for at-risk students. *Educational Leadership, 57* (1), 77–78.

Engler, W. H. (1973). *Radical school reforms of the 1960s.* Unpublished doctoral dissertation, Rutgers University, New Brunswick, NJ.

Epstein, J. (1990). What matters in the middle grades—grade span or practices? *Phi Delta Kappan, 71,* 436–444.

Epstein, J. (1996). The national assessment of educational progress and educational policy making. In P. S. Hlebowitch & W. G. Wraga (Eds.), *Annual review of research for school leaders.* New York: Scholastic.

Erickson, F., & Shutz, J. (1992). Students' experience of the curriculum. In R. W. Jackson (Ed.), *Handbook of research on curriculum* (pp. 465–485). New York: Macmillan.

Erikson, E. H. (1950). *Childhood and society* (2nd ed.). New York: W. W. Norton.

Erikson, E. H. (1968). *Identity: Youth in crisis.* New York: Norton.

Errors found in textbooks: Publishers put on notice. (1992, January 11). *Houston Post,* p. A–19.

Eurich, A. C. (Ed.). (1970). *High school 1980: The shape of the future in American secondary education.* New York: Pitman.

Evangelof, J. (1989, April 19). Education reform seen hinging on truce between researchers, school officials. *Chronicle of Higher Education,* p. A18.

Eyler, J., & Giles, D. E. (1999). *Where's the learning in service-learning?* San Francisco: Jossey-Bass.

Fabos, B., & Young, M. (1999, Fall). Telecommunications in the classroom: Rhetoric versus reality. *Review of Educational Research, 69* (3), 217–259.

Fairman, J. C., & Firestone, W. A. (2001). The district role in state assessment policy: An exploratory study. In S. H. Fuhrman (Ed.), *From the capital to the classroom: Standards-based reform in the states.* 100th Yearbook, National Society for the Study of Education, Part 2, pp. 124–147.

510   REFERENCES

Chicago: University of Chicago Press.

Fass, P. S. (1989). *Outside in: Minorities and the transformation of American education.* New York: Oxford University Press.

Faunce, R. C., & Bossing, N. L. (1958). *Developing the core curriculum* (2nd ed.). Englewood Cliffs, NJ: Prentice Hall.

Ferguson, E. S. (1992). *Engineering and the mind's eye.* Cambridge, MA: M.I.T. Press.

Feynman, R. P. (1965, March). New textbooks for the new mathematics. *Engineering and Science, 28,* 13–15.

Fillmore, L. W., & Meyer, L. M. (1992). The curriculum and linguistic minorities. In P. W. Jackson (Ed.), *Handbook of research on curriculum.* New York: Macmillan.

Fink, E., & Resnick, L. B. (2001). Developing principals as instructional leaders. *Phi Delta Kappan, 82,* 598–606.

Finlay, G. C. (1962, Spring). The physical science study committee. *School Review, 70* (1), 63–81.

Finn, J. D. (2002). Small classes in American schools: Research, practice, and politics. *Phi Delta Kappan, 83,* 551–560.

Firestone, W. A., Fuhrman, S. H., & Kirst, M. W. (1991). State educational reform since 1983: Appraisal and the future. *Educational Policy, 5,* 238–240.

Fiske, E. B. (1978, February 26). Harvard is debating curriculum to replace general education. *New York Times,* p. 1.

Fitzpatrick, K. A. (1991). Restructuring to achieve outcomes of significance for all students. *Educational Leadership, 48,* 18–22.

Fitzpatrick, K. A. (2002). *Indicators of schools of quality.*

Schaumburg, IL: National Study of School Evaluation.

Flathmann, J. H. (1987). The *general education function of curriculum for democratic citizenship.* Unpublished doctoral dissertation, Rutgers University, New Brunswick, NJ.

Flexner, A. (1923). *A modern college and a modern school.* New York: Doubleday. Originally published in 1916 in *American Review of Reviews, 8,* 465–474.

Fogel, R. W., & Engerman, S. L. (1974). *Time on the cross: The economics of negro slavery.* Boston: Little, Brown.

Ford Foundation. (1957). *They went to college early.* New York: Author.

Ford Foundation. (1961). *Teaching by television.* New York: Author.

Ford Foundation. (1972). *A foundation goes to school.* New York: Author.

Forsyth, P., & Tallerico, M. (1998). Accountability and city school leadership. *Educational and Urban Society, 30,* 546–555.

Foshay, A. W. (1967). Professional education: The discipline of the act. *Theory Into Practice, 6,* 220–226.

Foshay, A. W. (1969). Curriculum. In R. L. Ebel (Ed.), *Encyclopedia of educational research* (4th ed.), (pp. 275–280). New York: Macmillan.

Fraenkel, J. R. (1992). Hilda Taba's contributions to social studies education. *Social Education, 56,* 172–178.

Frederiksen, J. R., & White, B. Y. (2004). Designing assessments for instruction and accountability: An application of validity theory to assessing scientific inquiry. In M. Wilson (Ed.), *Toward*

coherence between classroom assessment and accountability. 103rd Yearbook, National Society for the Study of Education, Part 2, pp. 74–104. Chicago: University of Chicago Press.

French, W., & associates. (1957). *Behavioral goals of general education in high school.* New York: Russell Sage Foundation.

Freud, S. (1962). *Civilization and its discontents.* New York: Norton. Originally published in 1930.

Freudenheim, M. (2003, January 24). Large H.M.O. to make treatment guidelines public. *New York Times,* p. C3.

Frey, K. (1982). *Curriculum conference: An approach for curriculum development in groups.* Kiel, Germany: Institute for Science Education.

Friedenberg, E. Z. (1967). *Coming of age in America.* New York: Vintage.

Fuhrman, S. H. (2001). Introduction. In S. H. Fuhrman (Ed.), *From the capitol to the classroom: Standards-based reform.* 100th Yearbook, National Society for the Study of Education, Part 2, pp. 1–12. Chicago: University of Chicago Press.

Fullan, M. G. (2001). *The new meaning of educational change* (2nd ed.). New York: Teachers College Press.

Fullan, M. G., & Miles, M. B. (1992). Getting reform right: What works and what doesn't. *Phi Delta Kappan, 73,* 745–752.

Galasso, B. J. (1986). *Attitudes of youth toward issues of democracy.* Unpublished doctoral dissertation, Rutgers University, New Brunswick, NJ.

Gallagher, J. J. (1967). Teacher variation in concept presentation. *BSCS Newsletter, 30* (17), 17–20.

Galley, M. (2001, October 21). State tests don't support good instruction, panel says. *Education Week, 21* (9), 5.

Garan, E. M. (2001). Beyond the smoke and mirrors: A critique of the National Reading Panel report on phonics. *Phi Delta Kappan, 82* (7), 500–506.

Gardner, H. (1987). Developing the spectrum of human intelligence. *Harvard Educational Review, 57*, 190–192.

Gardner, H. (1991). *The unschooled mind*. New York: Basic Books.

Gardner, J. W. (1959). In J. B. Conant, *The American high school today*. New York: McGraw-Hill.

Gardner, J. W. (1962). *Excellence*. New York: Harper.

Garrison, J., Podeschi, R., and Bredo, E. (Eds.). (2002). *William James and Education*. New York: Teachers College Press.

Gehring, J. (2000, January 19). Schools' bible courses "taught wrong," report says. *Education Week, 19* (19), 10.

Gehrke, N. J. (1991). Explorations of teachers' development of integrative curriculums. *Journal of Curriculum and Supervision, 6*, 107–117.

Generals, D. (1998). *The American creed: The educational philosophy and practices of Booker T. Washington*. Doctoral dissertation, Rutgers University, New Brunswick, NJ.

Giles, H., McCutchen, S. P., & Zechiel, A. N. (1942). *Exploring the curriculum*. New York: Harper.

Giroux, H. A. (1983). *Theory and resistance in education*. Boston: Bergui & Garvey.

Giroux, H. A. (1988). *Schooling and the struggle for public life.*

Minneapolis: University of Minnesota Press.

Glass, B. (1970). *The timely and the timeless*. New York: Basic Books.

Goertz, M. E. (2001). Redefining government roles in an era of standards-based reform. *Phi Delta Kappan, 83*(1), 62–663.

Goffin, S. G. (2001). Whither early childhood care and education in the next century? In L. Corno (Ed.), *Education across a century: The centennial volume*. 100th Yearbook, National Society for the Study of Education, Part 1, pp. 140–163. Chicago: University of Chicago Press.

Goldberg, M. F. (2000). 'Stirring the pot': An interview with Harold 'Doc' Howe II. *Phi Delta Kappan, 82*(2), 160–164.

Golden, D., & Rose, M. (2003, November 7). Kaplan transforms into big operator of trade schools. *Wall Street Journal*, pp. 1, A8.

Goldring, E., & Greenfield, W. (2002). Understanding the evolving concept of leadership in education: Roles, expectations, and dilemmas. In J. Murphy (Ed.), *The educational leadership challenge: Redefining leadership for the 21st century*. 101st Yearbook, National Society for the Study of Education, Part 1, pp. 1–19. Chicago: University of Chicago Press.

Good, C. V. (1959, 1973). *Dictionary of education*. New York: McGraw-Hill.

Goodlad, J. I. (1966). *The changing school curriculum*. New York: Fund for the Advancement of Education.

Goodlad, J. I. (1978). Educational leadership: Toward the third era. *Educational Leadership, 35*, 322–324.

Goodlad, J. I. (1979). *What Schools are for*. Bloomington,

IN: Phi Delta Kappan Foundation.

Goodlad, J. I. (1984, April). *The impact of basic principles of curriculum and instruction*. Paper presented at the meeting of the Society for the Study of Curriculum History, Los Angeles.

Goodlad, J. I. (1984). *A place called school*. New York: McGraw-Hill.

Goodlad, J. I. (1987). Structure, process, and an agenda. In J. I. Goodlad (Ed.), *The ecology of school renewal*. 86th Yearbook, National Society for the Study of Education, Part 1, pp. 1–19. Chicago: University of Chicago Press.

Goodlad, J. I. (1999). Flow, eros, and ethos in educational renewal. *Phi Delta Kappan, 80* (8), 571–578.

Goodlad, J. I. (2002). Kudzu, rabbits, and school reform. *Phi Delta Kappan, 84*, 17–23.

Goodlad, J. I. (2003, April 23). A nation in wait. *Education Week, 22*, 24, 25, 26, 32, 36.

Goodlad, J. I. (2003/2004). Teaching what we hold sacred. *Educational Leadership, 61* (4), 18–21.

Goodman, P. (1964). *Compulsory mis-education*. New York: Horizon.

Goodman, P. (1970). *New reformation*. New York: Random House.

Goodnough, A. (2003, April 11). Little change in dropout rate and many graduate late. *New York Times*, p. D4.

Gootman, E. (2004, April 14). City's small schools uneasy inside the big ones. *New York Times*, pp. A1, B9.

Gouldner, A. W. (1970). *The coming crisis in western sociology*. New York: Basic Books.

Graves, F. P. (1914). *A history of education in modern times.* New York: Macmillan.

Gray, K. (1991). Vocational education in high school: A modern Phoenix. *Phi Delta Kappan, 72,* 437–445.

Greene, M. (1965). *The public school and the private vision.* New York: Random House.

Greene, M. (1973). *Teacher as stranger.* Belmont, CA: Wadsworth.

Griffin, G. A. (1999). Changes in teacher education: Looking to the future. In G. A. Griffin (Ed.), *The education of teachers.* 98th Yearbook, National Society for the Study of Education, Part 1, pp. 1–28. Chicago: University of Chicago Press.

Grizzell, E. D. (1923). *Origin and development of the high school in New England before 1865.* New York: Macmillan.

Gross, P. R., & Levitt, N. (1994). *Higher superstition: The academic left and its quarrels with science.* Baltimore: Johns Hopkins University Press.

Grossman, P. L. (1992). Teaching to learn. In A. Lieberman (Ed.), *The changing contexts of teaching.* 91st Yearbook, National Society for the Study of Education, Part 1, pp. 179–196. Chicago: University of Chicago Press.

Grossman, P. L. (1992). Why models matter: An alternate view on professional growth in teaching. *Review of Educational Research, 62,* 171–179.

Grossnickle, D. R., & Cesko, F. P. (1990). *Preventive discipline.* Reston, VA: National Association of Secondary School Principals.

Grouws, D. A., & Cebulla, K. J. (2000). Elementary and middle school mathematics at the crossroads. In T. L. Good (Ed.), *American education: Yesterday,* today, and tomorrow. 99th Yearbook, National Society for the Study of Education, Part 2, pp. 209–255. Chicago: University of Chicago Press.

Gruhn, W. T., & Douglass, H. R. (1956). *The modern junior high school.* New York: Ronald Press.

Guskey, T. R. (1986). Staff development and the process of teacher change. *Educational Researcher, 15* (4), 5–12.

Guskey, T. R. (2003). What makes professional development effective? *Phi Delta Kappan, 84* (10), 748–750.

Guttman, A. (1999). *Democratic education.* Princeton, NJ: Princeton University Press.

Hall, G. S. (1891). The contents of children's minds entering school. *Pedagogical Seminary, 1,* 139–173.

Hall, G. S. (1905). *The psychology of adolesence,* Vols. I, II. New York: Appleton.

Hallinan, M. T. (2001). Today's youth: Ambitious but aimless? *Educational Researcher, 30*(6), 24–26.

Hand, H. (1966). *National Educational Assessment: Pro and con.* Washington, DC: American Association of School Administrators.

Hanna, P. R. (Ed.). (1925–1948). *Building America: Illustrated studies on modern problems.* Vols. I–XIII. New York: Americana.

Hannaway, J. (1992, Spring). Higher order skills, job design, and incentives: An analysis and proposal. *American Educational Research Journal, 29* (1), 20.

Hanson, E. M. (1991). Educational restructuring in the USA: Movements of the 1980s. *Journal of Educational Administration, 29,* 30–38.

Harap, H. (1937). *The changing curriculum.* New York: D. Appleton-Century.

Hargreaves, A., & Fink, D. (2003). Sustaining leadership. *Phi Delta Kappan, 84,* 693–700.

Harris, W. T. (1898). My pedagogical creed. In O. H. Lang (Ed.), *Educational creeds of the century* (pp. 36–46). New York: Kellogg.

Hartmann, G. H. (1937). The social attitudes and information of American teachers. In W. H. Kilpatrick (Ed.), *The teacher and society.* First Yearbook of the John Dewey Society. New York: D. Appleton-Century.

Hartwell, E. M. (1912). Discussion. *The School Review, 20,* 313–317.

Harvard Committee on General Education in a Free Society. (1945). *General education in a free society.* Cambridge, MA: Harvard University Press.

Harvard Committee Report. (1945). *General education in a free society.* Cambridge, MA: Harvard University Press.

Havighurst, R. J. (1972). *Developmental tasks and education* (3rd ed.). New York: McKay.

Hayden, J. C. (1992). *The council for basic education: From fringe to mainstream.* Doctoral dissertation, Rutgers University, New Brunswick, NJ.

Hechinger, F. (1967, March 7). U.S. gets low marks in math. *New York Times,* p. 11E.

Hechinger, F. (1984, February 28). Critical commission is criticized. *New York Times,* p. 6.

Heller, M. F., & Firestone, W. A. (1995). Who's in charge here? Sources of leadership for change. *Elementary School Journal, 96,* 65–86.

Hemming, R. W. (1965). Numerical analysis versus mathematics. *Science, 148,* p. 474.

Henriques, D. B. (2003, September 2). Rising demands for testing push limits of its accuracy. *New York Times*, pp. A1, A20.

Herbst, P. G. (2003). Using novel tasks in teaching mathematics: Three tensions affecting the work of the teacher. *American Educational Research Journal, 40*, 197–238.

Herman, J. L. & Haertel, E. H. (Eds.). (2005). *Uses and misuses of data for educational accountability and improvement.* 104th Yearbook, National Society for the Study of Education, Part 1. Chicago: University of Chicago Press

Herrington, C., & Fowler, F. (2003). Rethinking the role of states and educational governance. In W. L. Boyd & D. Miretzky (Eds.), *American educational governance on trial: Change and challenges.* 102nd Yearbook, National Society for the Study of Education, Part 1, pp. 271–290. Chicago: University of Chicago Press.

Herrington, C., & MacDonald, V. (2001). A thirty-year history of accountability legislation in Florida. In C. Herrington & K. Kasten (Eds.), *Educational policy alternatives: 2001*, pp. 7–34. Jacksonville: Florida Institute of Education, University of North Florida.

Herszenhorn, D. M. (2003, April 29). Education dept. hires 108 local supervisors. *New York Times*, p. B7.

Hess, F. M. (2003). Breaking the mold: Charter schools, contract schools, and voucher plans. In W. L. Boyd & D. Miretzky (Eds.), *American educational governance on trial: Change and challenges.* 102nd Yearbook, National Society for the Study of Education, Part 1,

pp. 114–135. Chicago: University of Chicago Press.

Hess, G. A. (1991). *School restructuring Chicago style.* Newbury Park, CA: Corwin.

Highlights of Dewey's life. (1949, October 22). *The New Leader,* p. 5–2.

Hill, P. T. (2003). What's wrong with public education governance in big cities and how should it be fixed? In W. L. Boyd & D. Miretzky (Eds.), *American educational governance on trial: Change and challenges.* 102nd Yearbook, National Society for the Study of Education, Part 1, pp. 57–81. Chicago: University of Chicago Press.

Hill, P. T., Wise, A. E., & Shapiro, L. (1989). *Educational progress: Cities mobilize to improve their schools.* Santa Monica, CA: RAND Corporation.

Hinsdale, Burke A. (1898). *Horace Mann and the Common School Revival.* New York: Scribner's.

Hirsch, E. D., Jr. (1987). *Cultural literacy: What every American needs to know.* Boston: Houghton Mifflin.

Hirst, P. H. (1974). *Knowledge and the curriculum.* London: Routledge.

Hlebowitsh, P. S. (1987). *Purpose and change in American educational policymaking and practice.* Unpublished doctoral dissertation. New Brunswick, NJ: Rutgers University.

Hlebowitsh, P. S. (1992). *Radical curriculum theory reconsidered.* New York: Teachers College Press.

Hlebowitsh, P. S. (2005). *Designing the school curriculum.* Boston: Allyn & Bacon.

Hodgkinson, H. (1991). Reform versus reality. *Phi Delta Kappan, 73*, 8–16.

Hoff, D. (2001, October 17). States urged to keep eyes on education. *Education Week, 21* (7), 1, 22.

Hoffer, E. (1970, November 23). Whose country is America? *New York Times*, p. 120.

Hoffman, C. (2004, March 17). Massachusetts student wins Intel science prize with cancer study. *New York Times*, p. B10.

Hofstadter, R. (1963). *Anti-intellectualism in American life.* New York: Knopf.

Hollingsworth, S., & Sockett, H. (1994). Positioning teacher research in educational reform: An introduction. In S. Hollingsworth & H. Sockett (Eds.), *Teacher research and educational reform.* 93rd Yearbook, National Society for the Study of Education, Part 1, pp. 1–20. Chicago: University of Chicago Press.

Holt, J. (1964). *How children fail.* New York: Dell.

Holt, J. (1967). *How children learn.* New York: Pitman.

Holt, J. (1972). *Freedom and beyond.* New York: Dutton.

Hook, S. (1973). John Dewey and his betrayers. In *Papers on Educational Reform*, Vol. II. LaSalle, IL: Open Court, pp. 111–133.

Hopkins, L. T., & Mendenhall, J. E. (1934). *Achievement at the Lincoln School.* New York: Teachers College Press.

Horvat, E. M., Weininger, E. B., & Lareau, A. (2003). From social ties to social capital: Class differences in the relations between schools and parent networks. *American Educational Research Journal, 40*, 319–351.

Houston, P. (2001). Superintendents for the 21st century: It's not just a job, it's a calling. *Phi Delta Kappan, 82* (6), 428–433.

Howe, H., II. (1992, June 17). Rethink classroom strategies. *Education Week, 11,* S20.

Howe, K. R., & Berv, J. (2000). Constructing constructivism, epistemological and pedagogical. In D. C. Phillips (Ed.), *Constructivism in education.* 99th Yearbook, National Society for the Study of Education, Part 1, pp. 19–40. Chicago: University of Chicago Press.

Husén, T. (1971). Does broader educational opportunity mean lower standards? *International Review of Education, 17,* 77–88.

Husén, T. (1983). Are standards in U.S. schools really lagging behind those in other countries? *Phi Delta Kappan, 64,* 456.

Husén, T. (1986). Why did Sweden go comprehensive? *Oxford Review of Education, 12* (2), 153–163.

Husén, T. (1989). The Swedish school reform—Exemplary both ways. *Comparative Education, 25* (3), 345–355.

Husén, T., & Boalt, G. (1968). *Educational research and educational change: The case of Sweden.* New York: John Wiley.

Hutchins, R. M. (1936). *The higher learning in America.* New Haven, CT: Yale University Press.

Hutchins, R. M. (1963). *On education.* Santa Barbara, CA: Center for the Study of Democratic Institutions, p. 18.

Hutchins, R. M. (1968). *The learning society.* New York: Praeger.

Hutchins, R. M. (1972). The great anti-school campaign. In Hutchins, R. M., & Adler, M. J. (Eds.), *The great ideas today.* Chicago: *Encyclopedia Britannica,* 155–227.

Hutchins, R. M. (1973). The schools must stay. *The Center Magazine, 6,* January–February, 12–13.

Hyman, H. H., Wright, C. R., & Reed, J. S. (1975). *The enduring effects of education.* Chicago: University of Chicago Press.

Illich, I. (1971). *Deschooling society.* New York: Harper.

Inglis, A. (1918). *Principles of secondary education.* Cambridge, MA: Houghton Mifflin.

Isaac, K. (1992). *Civics for democracy: A journey for teachers and students.* Washington, DC: Essential Books.

Jacobson, L. (2004, April 7). Schools enlist specialists to teach science lessons. *Education Week, 30* (23), 1, 15.

Jackson, P. W. (1968). *Life in classrooms.* New York: Holt.

Jackson, P. W. (1971). Old dogs and New Tricks: Observations on the continuing education of teachers. In L. J. Rubin (Ed.), *Improving in-service education: Proposals and procedures for change.* Boston: Allyn & Bacon.

Jackson, P. W. (Ed.). (1992). *Handbook of research on curriculum.* New York: Macmillan.

Jackson, P. W. (1998). *John Dewey and the lessons of art.* New York: Teachers College Press.

James, W. (1890). *The principles of psychology.* New York: Henry Holt.

James, W. (1958). *Talks to teachers.* New York: W. W. Norton. Lectures delivered in 1892.

Jamison, D., Suppes, P., & Wells, S. (1974, Winter). The effectiveness of alternative instructional media. *Review of Educational Research, 44* (1), 1–67.

Janowitz, M. (1969). *Institution building in urban education.* Chicago: University of Chicago Press.

Janowitz, M. (1991). *On social organization and social control.* Chicago: University of Chicago Press.

Jencks, C. (1972). *Inequality.* New York: Basic Books.

Jenkins, R. C., & Warner, G. C. (1937). *Henry Barnard.* Hartford: Connecticut State Teachers Association.

Jennings, J. (2003). From the White House to the schoolhouse: Greater demands and new roles. In W. L. Boyd & D. Miretzky (Eds.), *American educational governance on trial: Change and challenges.* 102nd Yearbook, National Society for the Study of Education, Part 1, pp. 291–308. Chicago: University of Chicago Press.

Jensen, A. R. (1973). *Educability and group differences.* New York: Harper.

Jensen, J. M., & Roser, N. L. (1990). Are there really three R's? *Educational Leadership, 47* (2), 7–12.

Jersild, A. T., Thorndike, R. L., & Goldman, B. (1939). An evaluation of aspects of the activity program in the New York City elementary schools. *Journal of Experimental Education, 8,* 166–207.

Jersild, A. T., Thorndike, R. L., & Goldman, B. (1941). A further comparison of pupils in "activity" and "non-activity" schools. *Journal of Experimental Education, 9,* 307–309.

Jessup, W. A. (1915). Current practices and standards in arithmetic. In S. C. Parker (Ed.), *Minimum essentials in elementary-school subjects—standards and current practices.* 14th Yearbook,

National Society for the Study of Education, Part 1, pp. 116–130. Chicago: University of Chicago Press.

Jickling, B. (1988). Paradigms in curriculum development. Critical comments on the work of Tanner and Tanner. *Interchange, 19* (2), 41–48.

Johnson, D. W., & Johnson, R. T. (1999). The three C's of school and classroom management. In H. J. Freiberg (Ed.), *Beyond behaviorism: Changing the classroom management paradigm* (pp. 119–143). Boston: Allyn & Bacon.

Johnson, M. (1980). *Toward adolescence: The middle school years.* 79th Yearbook, National Society for the Study of Education, Part I. Chicago: University of Chicago Press.

Johnson, M., Jr. (1967). Definitions and models in curriculum theory. *Educational Theory, 17* (2), 127–140.

Johnson, R. C. (2001, February 28). Chicago to add thousands more to summer rosters. *Education Week, 20*(24), 3.

Johnson, V. M. (1986). *Antidemocratic attitudes of high school students.* Unpublished doctoral dissertation, Rutgers University, New Brunswick, NJ.

Jones, H. M., Keppel, F., & Ulich, R. (1954). Committee on the teaching profession of the American Academy of Arts and Sciences, V, No. 2. New York: Author.

Jones, S. (2000). *Darwin's Ghost: The Origin of Species Updated.* New York: Ballantine.

Jowett, B. (1921). *The works of Aristotle, Politica* (Book VII, Cr. 2, Vol. X). Oxford, England: Clarindon.

Joyce, B. R. (1991). The doors to school improvement. *Educational Leadership, 48*(8), 59–62.

Joyce, B., & Clift, R. (1984). The Phoenix agenda: Essential reform in teacher education. *Educational Researcher, 13* (4), 5–17.

Judt, F. (1992). *Past imperfect: French intellectuals, 1944–1956.* Berkeley: University of California Press.

Kadushin, C. (1974). *The American intellectual elite.* Boston: Little, Brown.

Kaestle, C. F. (1973). *Joseph Lancaster and the monitorial school movement.* New York: Teachers College Press.

Kaestle, C. F. (1983). *Pillars of the republic: Common schools of American society.* New York: Hill and Wang.

Kagan, D. M. (1992). Professional growth among preservice and beginning teachers. *Review of Educational Research, 62,* 129–169.

Kandel, I. L. (1930). *History of secondary education.* Boston: Houghton.

Kannapel, P. J., Aagaard, L., Coe, P., & Reeves, C. A. (2001). The impact of standards and accountability on teaching and learning in Kentucky. In S. H. Fuhrman (Ed.), *From the capitol to the classroom: Standards-based reform in the states.* 100th Yearbook, National Society for the Study of Education, Part 2, pp. 242–262. Chicago: University of Chicago Press.

Keller, B. (2002, May 8). A delicate balance. *Education Week, 21,* 24–29.

Kilpatrick. W. H. (1918). The project method. *Teachers College Record, 19,* 319–335.

Kilpatrick, W. H. (1925). An effort at appraisal. In C. W. Washburne (Ed.), *Adapting the schools to individual differences.* 24th Yearbook, National Society for the Study of Education, Part 2, pp. 273–286. Bloomington, IL: Public School Publishing.

Kilpatrick, W. H. (Ed.) (1937). *The teacher and society.* First Yearbook of the John Dewey Society. New York: D. Appleton-Century.

Kilpatrick, W. H., & Van Til, W. (Eds.). (1947). *Intercultural attitudes in the making.* Yearbook of the John Dewey Society. New York: Harper.

Kimball, R. (1991). *Tenured radicals: How politics has corrupted our higher education.* New York: Harper.

Kindred, L. W. (Ed.). (1968). *The intermediate schools.* Englewood Cliffs, NJ: Prentice Hall.

King, L. C. (1967). High school failure rate serious problem. *Chemical and Engineering News, 45,* 741.

Kirkpatrick, E., & Kirkpatrick J. (1962). What is political science? In E. M. Hunt et al., *High school social studies perspectives.* Boston: Houghton Mifflin, pp. 103–125.

Kirsch, I. S., Jungblut, A., Jenkins, L., & Kolstad, A. (1993). *Adult literacy in America,* National Adult Literacy Survey, Educational Testing Service. Washington, DC: U.S. Department of Education.

Kirst, M. (1993, April). *The impact of federal policies on state and local reform initiatives.* Lecture before the Department of Education, University of Chicago.

Kirst, M. W. (2003). Mayoral influence, new regimes, and public school governance. In W. L. Boyd & D. Miretzky

(Eds.), *American educational governance on trial: Change and challenges.* 102nd Yearbook, National Society for the Study of Education, Part 1, pp. 196–218. Chicago: University of Chicago Press.

Kliebard, H. M. (1969). Reappraisal: The Tyler rationale. *School Review, 3,* 259–272.

Kliebard, H. M. (1977). Curriculum theory: Give me a "for instance." *Curriculum Inquiry, 6*(4), 257–269.

Kliebard H. M. (1986). *The struggle for the American curriculum 1893–1958.* Boston: Routledge & Kegan Paul.

Kline, M. (1973). *Why Johnny can't add: The failure of the new math.* New York: St. Martin's.

Kneller, G. F. (Ed.) (1971). *Foundations of American education,* 3rd ed. New York: Wiley.

Kochan, F. K., Bredeson, P., & Riehl, C. (2002). Rethinking the development of professional leaders. In J. Murphy (Ed.), *The educational leadership challenge: Redefining leadership for the 21st century.* 101st Yearbook, National Society for the Study of Education, Part 1, pp. 289–306. Chicago: University of Chicago Press.

Kohl, H. R. (1969). *The open classroom.* New York: Random House.

Kohlberg, L. (1970). Education for justice. In J. M. Gustafson (Ed.), *Moral education.* Cambridge, MA: Harvard University Press, 1970.

Koos, L. V., & Woody, C. (1919). The training of teachers in the accredited high schools of the State of Washington. In G. M. Whipple & H. L. Miller (Eds.), *The professional preparation of high-school teachers.* 18th Yearbook, National Society for the Study of Education, Part 1, pp. 213–257. Bloomington, IL: Public School Publishing.

Kozol, J. (1975). *The night is dark and I am far from home.* Boston: Houghton Mifflin.

Kozol, J. (1978). *Children of the revolution.* New York: Delacorte.

Kozol, J. (1985). *Illiterate America.* Garden City, NY: Anchor/ Doubleday.

Kozol, J. (1991). *Savage inequalities: Children in America's schools.* New York: Crown.

Krajcik, J., Mamlok, R., & Hug, B. (2001). Modern content and the enterprise of science: Science education in the twentieth century. In L. Corno (Ed.), *Education across a century: The centennial volume.* 100th Yearbook, National Society for the Study of Education, Part 1, pp. 205–238. Chicago: University of Chicago Press.

Krashen, S. (1999). *Three arguments against whole language and why they are wrong.* Portsmouth, NH: Heinemann.

Krashen, S. (2002). Whole language and the great plummet of 1981–92: An urban legend from California. *Phi Delta Kappan, 83,* 748–753.

Krug, E. A. (1964). *The shaping of the American high school.* New York: Harper.

Kuhn, T. S. (1970, 1996). *The structure of scientific revolutions.* Chicago: University of Chicago Press.

LaParo, K. M., & Planta, R. C. (2000). Predicting children's competence in the early school years: A meta-analytic review. *Review of Educational Research, 70*(4), 443–484.

Lawton, D. (1975). *Class, culture and the curriculum.* London: Routledge.

Lawton, D. (Ed.). (1978). *Theory and practice of curriculum studies.* London: Routledge.

Lawton, D., & Gordon, P. (1996). *Dictionary of education* (2nd ed.). London: Hodder & Stoughton.

Lazerson, M., & Grub, W. N. (1974). *American education and vocationalism.* New York: Teachers College Press.

Lee, G. C. (Ed.). (1961). *Crusade against ignorance: Thomas Jefferson on education.* New York: Teachers College Press.

Lebowitz, A. J. (1992). Staff buys in through shared decision-making. *The School Administrator, 49* (January), 12–13.

Leiter, M., & Cooper, M. (1978). How teacher unionists view in-service education. *Teachers College Record, 80,* 107–139.

Leithwood, K., & Prestine, N. (2002). Unpacking the challenges of leadership at the school and district level. In J. Murphy (Ed.), *The educational leadership challenge: Redefining leadership for the 21st century.* 101st Yearbook, National Society for the Study of Education, Part 1, pp. 42–64. Chicago: University of Chicago Press.

Leland, J. (2003, June 29). Pursuing happiness. *New York Times,* Sec. 4, p. 1.

Leonard, J. P. (1947). *Developing the secondary school curriculum.* New York: Holt, Rinehart and Winston.

Leonardo, Z. (2004). Disciplinary knowledge and quality education. *Educational Researcher, 33*(5), pp. 3–5.

Leshner, A. I. (2004, February 6). Science at the leading edge. *Science, 303* (5659), 729.

Lessinger, L. M. (1971). Accountability for results. In L. M. Lessinger & R. W. Tyler (Eds.), *Accountability in education* (pp. 1–15). Worthington, OH: Jones.

LeTendre, G. K., Hofer, B. K., & Shimizu, H. (2003). What is tracking? Cultural expectations in the United States, Germany, and Japan. *American Educational Research Journal, 40* (1), 43–89.

Levin, H. (1990). *Accelerated schools: A new strategy for at-risk students.* Palo Alto, CA: Accelerated Schools Project, Stanford University.

Lewis, H. (1991, February 16). CUNY's high school plan looks backward. *New York Times,* p. 18.

Lewis, M. (1991, April 1). School libraries, too, require our attention. *New York Times,* p. A10.

Lewis, W. D. (1914). *Democracy's high school.* Boston: Houghton Mifflin.

Libler, R. W. (1992). Effective schools: The role of the central office. *Contemporary Education, 63* (2), 122–123.

Lilla, M. (2001). *The reckless mind: Intellectuals in politics.* New York: Review Books.

Lincoln School Staff (1927). *Curriculum making in an elementary school.* Boston: Ginn.

Lipka, R. K. (1997). Research and evaluation in service learning: What do we need to know? In J. Schine (Ed.), *Service learning.* 96th Yearbook, National Society for the Study of Education, Part 1, pp. 56–68. Chicago: University of Chicago Press.

Little, J. W. (1982). Norms of collegiality and experimentation: Workplace conditions of school success. *American Educational Research Journal, 19,* 325–340.

Lottman, H. R. (1982). *The left bank.* Boston: Houghton Mifflin.

Louis, K. S., & Marks, H. (1998). Does professional community affect the classroom?: Teachers' work and student work in restructuring schools. *American Journal of Education, 106,* 532–575.

Lubienski, C. (2003). Innovation in education markets: Theory and evidence on the impact of competition and choice in charter schools. *American Educational Research Journal, 40,* 395–446.

Lucas, S. (1999). *Tracking inequality: Stratification and mobility in American high schools.* New York: Teachers College Press.

Macdonald, J. B. (1965). Educational models for instruction. In J. B. Macdonald & R. R. Leeper (Eds.), *Theories of instruction* (pp. 1–7). Alexandria, VA: Association for Supervision and Curriculum Development.

Macdonald, J. B. (1971). Responsible curriculum development. In E. W. Eisner (Ed.), *Confronting curriculum reform* (pp. 120–134). Boston: Little, Brown.

Macdonald, J. B., & Leeper, R. R. (Eds.) (1965). *Theories of instruction.* Alexandria, VA: Association for Supervision and Curriculum Development.

Macdonald, J. B., Wolfson, B. J., & Zaret, E. (1973). *Reschooling society: A conceptual model.* Washington, DC: Association for Supervision and Curriculum Development.

MacGinitie, W. H. (1991). Reading instruction: Plus ça change. *Educational Leadership, 48* (6), 56.

MacIver, D. J. (1990). Meeting the needs of young adolescents: Advisory groups, interdisciplinary teaching teams and school transition programs. *Phi Delta Kappan, 71,* 458–464.

Mackenzie, G. N. (1942). Emerging curriculums (Ch. 3). In *General education in the high school.* North Central Association of Colleges and Secondary Schools. Glenview, IL: Scott Foresman.

Madaus, G. F. (1992). The influence of testing on teaching math and science in grades 4–12. Chestnut Hill, MA: Center for the Study of Testing. *Educational Assessment, 1* (4), 23.

Madaus, G. F. (1993, Winter). A national testing system. *Educational Assessment, 1,* 25.

Madaus, G. F. (1999). The influence of testing on the curriculum (Ch. 4). In M. J. Early & K. J. Rehage (Eds.), *Issues in curriculum.* 98th Yearbook, National Society for the Study of Education, Part 2. Chicago: University of Chicago Press.

Madaus, G. F., Haney, W., & Kreitzer, A. (1992). *Testing and evaluation: Learning from the projects we fund.* New York: Council for Aid to Education.

Madaus, G. F., & Kellaghan, T. (1992). Curriculum evaluation and assessment. In P. W. Jackson (Ed.), *Handbook of research on curriculum.* New York: Macmillan.

Maeroff, G. I. (1982, June 24). City schools bar 3 textbooks said to endorse creationism. *New York Times,* pp. 1, 23.

Maine State Department of Education. (1992). *Maine's common core of learning.* Augusta: Maine State Department of Education.

Manzo, K. K. (2003, May 21). Lawmakers pursue flexible text selection. *Education Week, 22* (37), 17, 21.

Marcel, G. (1949). *The philosophy of existence*. (M. Harai, Trans.) New York: Philosophical Library.

Marland, S. P., Jr. (1971, January). *Career education now*. Paper presented at the convention of the National Association of Secondary Principals, Houston, Texas.

Marland, S. P., Jr. (1972). Career education now. In Goldhammer & Taylor (Eds.), *Career education*. Columbus, OH: Merrill/Macmillan.

Marsh, H. W. (1991). Failure of high-ability schools to deliver academic benefits commensurate with their students' ability levels. *American Educational Research Journal, 28*, 445–480.

Maslow, A. (1970). *Motivation and personality* (2nd ed.). New York: Harper.

Mayer, R. E. (2001). Changing conceptions of learning: A century of progress in the scientific study of education. In L. Corno (Ed.), *Education across a century: The centennial volume*. 100th Yearbook, National Society for the Study of Education, Part 1, pp. 34–75. Chicago: University of Chicago Press.

Mayer, M. V. (1971, January). The impact of BSCS biology on college curricula. *BSCS Newsletter, 42*.

Mayer, W. V. (1974). The unreal school in the real world. *BSCS Newsletter, 54* (1), 5.

Mayhew, K. C., & Edwards, A. C. (1936). *The Dewey school*. New York: D. Appleton-Century.

McCaslin, H., & Good, T. L. (1996). *Listening in classrooms*. New York: HarperCollins.

McClure, R. M. (1992). A teachers' union revisits its professional past. In A. Lieberman (Ed.), *The changing contexts of teaching*.

91st Yearbook, National Society for the Study of Education, Part 1, pp. 79–89. Chicago: University of Chicago Press.

McDill, E. L., McDill, M. S., & Sprehe, T. (1969). *Strategies for success in compensatory education*. Baltimore: Johns Hopkins University Press.

McDonald, F. J. (1964). The influence of learning theories on education (1900–1950). In E. R. Hilgard (Ed.), *Theories of learning and instruction*. 63rd Yearbook, National Society for the Study of Education, Part 1, pp. 1–26. Chicago: University of Chicago Press.

McGroarty, M. (1992). The societal context of bilingual education. *Educational Researcher, 21*, 7–9, 24.

McMurrin, S. M. (1967). What tasks for schools? *Saturday Review, 49* (1).

McPartland, J. M., Balfanz, R., Jordan, W. J., & Legters, N. (2002). Promising solutions for the least productive American high schools. In S. Springfield & D. Land (Eds.), *Educating at-risk students*. 101st Yearbook, National Society for the Study of Education, Part 2, pp. 148–170. Chicago: University of Chicago Press.

McQuillan, J. (1998). *The literacy crisis: False claims and real solutions*. Portsmouth, NH: Heinemann.

Meade, E. J., Jr. (1968). *Accountability and governance in public education*. New York: Ford Foundation.

Means, S. S. (1992). The interrelated curriculum. Chapter 2 in J. M. Jenkins & D. Tanner (Eds.), *Interdisciplinary curriculum*. Reston, VA: National Association of Secondary School Principals.

Mehrens, W. A., & Green, D. R. (1989). *Standardized tests and school curricula*. (ERIC Document no. ED322–150).

Meier, D. (1995). *The power of their ideas: Lessons for America from a small school in Harlem*. Boston: Beacon.

Menis, J. (1987). Students' ability to transfer basic mathematical concepts from mathematics to chemistry. *Studies in Educational Evaluation, 13*, 105–109.

Merrow, J. (2004). Meeting Superman. *Phi Delta Kappan, 85*, 455–460.

Miel, A. (1946). *Changing the curriculum: A social process*. New York: Appleton-Century-Crofts.

Miller, H. L. (1919). The University of Wisconsin plan for the preparation of high-school teachers. In G. M. Whipple & H. L. Miller (Eds.), *The professional preparation of high-school teachers*. 18th Yearbook, National Society for the Study of Education, Part 1, pp. 7–103. Bloomington, IL: Public School Publishing.

Mitchell, D. E., & Tucker, S. (1992). Leadership as a way of thinking. *Educational Leadership, 49* (5), 30–35.

Moehlman, A. B. (1925). *Public education in Detroit*. Bloomington, IL: Public School Publishing.

Monod, J. (1972). *Chance and necessity*. New York: Vintage.

Monroe, W. S. (1893). *The educational labors of Henry Barnard*. Syracuse, NY: C. W. Bardeen.

Monroe, W. S. (1907). *History of the Pestalozzian Movement in the United States*. Syracuse, NY: C. W. Bardeen.

Morris, V. C. (1970). Existentialism and the education of twentieth-century man. In S. Dropkin, H. Full, & E. Schwartz (Eds.), *Contemporary American education* (2nd ed.). New York: Macmillan, pp. 258–260.

Moss, S., & Fuller, M. (2000). Implementing effective practices: Teachers' perspective. *Phi Delta Kappan, 82* (4), 274–276.

Mossman, L. C. (Ed.). (1934). *The activity movement.* 33rd Yearbook, National Society for the Study of Education, Part 2. Bloomington, IL: Public School Publishing.

Moynihan, D. P. (1972, Fall). Equalizing education: In whose benefit? *The Public Interest, 29* (3).

Moynihan, D. P. (1973, March). In G. Hodgson, Do schools make a difference? *Atlantic Monthly, 231.*

Mulder, M., & Thijsen, A. (1990). Decision-making in curriculum conferences: A study of convergence of opinion. *Journal of Curriculum Studies,* 22 (4), 343–360.

Mumford, L. (1970). *The pentagon of power: The myth of the machine.* New York: Harcourt.

Murphy, J. (2002). Reculturing the profession of educational leadership: New blueprints. In J. Murphy (Ed.), *The educational leadership challenge: Redefining leadership for the 21st century.* 101st Yearbook, National Society for the Study of Education, Part 1, pp. 65–82. Chicago: University of Chicago Press.

Murphy, J., & Gross, R. (1966). *Learning by television.* New York: Ford Foundation.

Myrdal, G. (1962). *An American dilemma.* New York: Harper. Originally published in 1944.

Myrdal, G. (1965). *Challenge to affluence.* New York: Vintage.

Myrdal, G. (1969). *Objectivity in social research.* New York: Pantheon.

Myrdal, G. (1971, June 13). Address at Dartmouth College. Hanover, NH: Office of Information Services.

NAEP Newsletter. (1973, July–August). *6* (3), 1–4.

National Advisory Commission on Civil Disorders. (1968). *Report.* Washington, DC: U.S. Department of Health, Education, and Welfare.

National Advisory Council on Vocational Education. (1969, July 15). *First report.* (1969, November 5). *Second report.* Washington, DC: U.S. Department of Health, Education, and Welfare.

National Association of Scholars (2005). *An open letter to governors: Recommendations for reforming the high school.* Princeton, NJ: The Association.

National Association of Secondary School Principals. (1982). *Reducing the curriculum.* Reston, VA: Author.

National Association of Secondary School Principals. Council on Middle Level Education. (n.d.). *Agenda for excellence.* Reston, VA: Author.

National Association of Secondary School Principals. (1985). *Trends and practices in middle-level education.* Reston, VA: The Association.

National Association of Secondary School Principals. (1985, September). *Schools in the middle: A report on trends and practices.* Reston, VA: The Association.

National Association of Secondary School Principals. (n.d.). *Agenda for excellence.* Reston, VA: The Association.

National Center for Education Statistics. (1999). *The condition of education 1999.* Washington,

DC: U.S. Government Printing Office.

National Center for Education Statistics (2000). *In the middle.* Washington, DC: U.S. Department of Education.

National Center for Education Statistics. (2001). *Digest of education statistics, 2000.* Washington, DC: U.S. Department of Education.

National Center for Education Statistics. (2001). *The condition of education 2000 in brief.* Washington, DC: U.S. Department of Education.

National Commission on Civil Disorders. (1968). *Report.* Washington, DC: U.S. Government Printing Office.

National Commission on Excellence in Education, U.S. Department of Education. (1983). *A nation at risk: The imperative for educational reform.* Washington, DC: The Department.

National Commission on the Reform of Secondary Education. (1973). *The reform of secondary education.* New York: McGraw-Hill.

National Commission on Social Studies in the Schools. (1989). *Charting a course: Social studies for the 21st century.* Washington, DC: Author.

National Commission on Testing and Public Policy. (1990). *Reforming assessment: From gatekeepers to gateway to education.* Chestnut Hill, MA: Center for the Study of Testing, Evaluation, and Education Policy, Boston College.

National Council on Education Standards and Testing. (1992). *Raising standards for American education.* Washington, DC: U.S. Department of Education.

National Council of Teachers of Mathematics. (1989). *Curriculum and evaluation standards for school mathematics*. Reston, VA: Author.

National Education Association. (1893). *Report of the Committee of Ten on secondary school studies*. New York: American Book.

National Education Association. (1895). Report of the Committee of Fifteen. *Educational Review, 9*.

National Education Association. (1918). *Report of the committee on resolutions*. Washington, DC: Author.

National Education Goals Panel. (1992). *Building a nation of learners*. Washington, DC: U.S. Department of Education.

National Endowment for the Arts. (2004). *Reading at risk: A survey of literary reading in America*. Washington, DC: Author.

National Panel on High School and Adolescent Education. (1976). *The education of adolescents*. Washington, DC: U.S. Office of Education.

National Science Board. (1983). *Educating Americans for the 21st century*. Washington, DC: National Science Foundation.

National Science Teachers Association. (1992). *The core content, a guide for curriculum designers*. Washington, DC: Author.

National Society for the Study of Education. (1911). *The city school as a community center*, 10th Yearbook, Part 1. Bloomington, IL: Public School Publishing.

National Society for the Study of Education. (1953). *The community school*. 52nd Yearbook, Part 2. Chicago: University of Chicago Press.

National Society for the Study of Education. (1965). *Art education*. 64th Yearbook, Part 2. Chicago: University of Chicago Press.

National Society for the Study of Education. (1969). *The national Herbart Society yearbooks, 1–5, 1895–1899*. New York: Arno Press and *New York Times*.

National Society for the Study of Education. (1992). *The arts, education, and aesthetic knowing*. 91st Yearbook, Part 2. Chicago: University of Chicago Press.

National Society for the Study of Education (1994). *Bloom's taxonomy: A forty-year perspective*. 93rd Yearbook, Part 2. Chicago: University of Chicago Press.

National Study of School Evaluation. (1987). *Evaluative criteria* (6th ed.). Falls Church, VA: Author.

National Study of School Evaluation. (2002). *School improvement*. Schaumberg, IL: Author.

National Study of Secondary School Evaluation. (1969). *Evaluative criteria* (4th ed.). Schaumburg, IL: Author.

National Task Force on Citizenship Education. (1977). *Education for responsible citizenship*. New York: McGraw-Hill.

Nave, B., Miech, E., & Mosteller, F. (2000). A lapse in standards: Linking standards-based reform with student achievement. *Phi Delta Kappan, 82* (2), 128–132.

Neill, A. S. (1960). *Summerhill*. New York: Hart.

Nelson, F. H., Rosenberg, B., & Van Meter, N. (2004a). *Charter school achievement*. Washington, DC: American Federation of Teachers.

Nelson, M. R. (1978). Rugg on Rugg: His theories and his curriculum. *Curriculum Inquiry, 8*, 119–132.

Nelson, M. R. (1988). Issues of access to knowledge: Dropping out of school. In L. N. Tanner (Ed.), *Critical issues in curriculum*. 87th Yearbook, National Society for the Study of Education, Part 1, pp. 226–243. Chicago: University of Chicago Press.

Nelson, N., & Calfee, R. C. (1998). The reading-writing connection viewed historically. In N. Nelson & R. C. Calfee (Eds.), *The reading-writing connection*. 97th Yearbook, National Society for the Study of Education, Part 2, pp. 1–52. Chicago: University of Chicago Press.

New Jersey Department of Education. (2002). *Core curriculum content standards*. Trenton, NJ: The Department.

New York Times. (1968, November 24). p. 74.

New York Times. (1970, August 30). pp. 1, 25.

New York Times. (1972, May 12). p. 55.

New York Times. (1978, February 26). p. 1.

New York Times. (1991, December 24). p. C1, 6.

New York Times. (1999, December 4). p. A22.

New York Times. (2003, September 20). p. D5.

New York Times. (2004, May 8). p. A15.

New York Times. (2004, August 17). p. A1, 19.

New York Times Magazine. (1973, August 26). p. 64.

Newlon, J. H., & Threlkeld, A. L. (1927). The Denver curriculum-revision program. In G. M. Whipple (Ed.), *Curriculum-making: Past and present*. 26th Yearbook, National Society for the Study of Education, Part 1, pp. 229–240. Bloomington, IL: Public School Publishing.

Newman, R. E., Jr. (1960). *History of a civic education project implementing the social-problems technique of instruction.* Unpublished doctoral dissertation, Stanford University.

Newmann, F. M. (1988). *High school choice.* Newsletter. Madison, WI: National Center for Effective Secondary Schools.

Newmann, F. M. (1993). Beyond common sense in educational restructuring: The issues of content and linkage. *Educational Researcher, 22* (2), 4–11.

Newsweek. (1965, May 5). p. 75.

Nisbet, R. (1980). *History of the idea of progress.* New York: Basic Books.

Northrup, B. G. (1880). The Quincy methods. *Education, 1*(3), 131.

Nuland, S. B. (1988). *Doctors: The biography of medicine.* New York: Knopf.

Nye, B., Hedges, L. V., & Konstantanopoulos, S. (2000). The effects of small classes on academic achievement: The results of the Tennessee class experiment. *American Educational Research Journal, 37*(1), 124–151.

Oakes, J. (1985). *Keeping track: How schools structure inequality.* New Haven, CT: Yale University Press.

Oberholtzer, E. E. (1937). *An integrated curriculum in practice.* New York: Bureau of Publications, Teachers College Press.

Ogawa, R. T., Sandholtz, J. H., Martinez-Flores, M., & Scribner, S. P. (2003). The substantive and symbolic consequences of a district's standards-based curriculum. *American Educational Research Journal, 40,* 147–176.

Oliva, P. F. (1989). *Supervision for today's schools* (3rd ed.). New York: Longman.

Oliva, P. F. (2001). *Developing the curriculum* (5th ed.). New York: Longman.

Oliver, A. I. (1969). *Curriculum improvement: A guide to problems, principles and procedures.* New York: Dodd, Mead.

Oliver, A. I. (1977). *Curriculum improvement: A guide to problems, principles and process,* 2nd ed. New York: Harper & Row.

Olson, L., & Rothman, R. (1993, April 21). Road to reform. *Education Week, 12,* 13.

Oppenheimer, J. R. (1971). *Science and synthesis.* New York: Springer-Verlag.

Padrón, Y. N., Waxman, H. C., & Rivera, H. H. (2002). Resiliency among students at risk of academic failure. In S. Stringfield & B. Land (Eds.), *Educating at-risk students.* 101st Yearbook, National Society for the Study of Education, Part 2, pp. 29–48. Chicago: University Chicago Press.

Pajak, E. (2003). *Honoring diverse teaching styles: A guide for supervision.* Alexandria, VA: ASCD Association for Supervision and Curriculum Development.

Pajak, E., & McAfee, L. (1992). The principal as school leader, curriculum leader. *NASSP Bulletin, 76* (547), 21–30.

Pajak, E. F., & Glickman, C. D. (1989). Dimensions of school improvement. *Educational Leadership, 46*(8), 61–64.

Panel of Consultants in Vocational Education. (1963). *Education for a changing world of work.* Washington, DC: U.S. Office of Education.

Panel on Youth of the President's Science Advisory Committee. (1974). *Youth: Transition to adulthood.* Chicago: University of Chicago Press.

Paris, S. G., Lawton, T. A., Turner, J. C., & Roth, J. L. (1991). A developmental perspective on standardized achievement testing. *Educational Researcher, 20* (5), 12–20, 40.

Parker, F. W. (1894). *Talks on pedagogics.* New York: E. L. Kellogg.

Parker, W. C. (1990). Assessing citizenship. *Educational Leadership, 48* (3), 17–22.

Pascarella, E. T., & Terenzini, P. T. (1991). *How college affects students.* San Francisco: Jossey-Bass.

Payzant, T. W. (1992). New beginnings in San Diego: Developing a strategy for interagency collaboration. *Phi Delta Kappan, 74* (2), 139–146.

Pear, R. (2003, May 18). Smaller percentage of poor live in high-poverty areas. *New York Times,* p. 26.

Pearson, P. D. (2000). Reading in the twentieth century. In T. Good (Ed.), *American education: Yesterday, today, and tomorrow.* 99th Yearbook, National Society for the Study of Education, Part 2, pp. 142–208. Chicago: University of Chicago Press.

Perkins, D. N., & Salomon, G. (1988). Teaching for transfer. *Educational Leadership, 46,* 22–31.

Perry, N. E., & Winne, P. H. (2001). Individual differences and diversity in twentieth-century classrooms. In L. Corno (Ed.), *Education across a century: The centennial volume.* 100th Yearbook, National Society for the Study of Education, Part 1, pp. 100–139. Chicago: University of Chicago Press.

Peters, C. C. (1930). *Foundations of educational sociology.* New York: Macmillan.

Phenix, P. H. (1962). In A. H. Passow (Ed.), *Curriculum crossroads* (pp. 57–65). New York: Teachers College Press.

Phenix, P. H. (1964). *Realms of meaning*. New York: McGraw-Hill.

Phillips, D. C. (Ed.). (2000). *Constructivism in education*. 99th Yearbook, National Society for the Study of Education, Part 1. Chicago: University of Chicago Press.

Piaget, J. (1950). *The psychology of intelligence*. New York: Harcourt.

Piaget, J. (1970). *Science of education and the psychology of the child*. New York: Orion.

Pipho, C. (1986). States move reform closer to reality. *Phi Delta Kappan, 66*, K3.

Popham, W. J., Eisner, E. W., Sullivan, H. J., & Tyler, L. L. (1969). *Instructional objectives*. Chicago: Rand McNally.

Poplin, M. S. (1992). The leader's new role: Looking to the growth of teachers. *Educational Leadership, 49* (5), 10–11.

Posner, P. S. (1992, October 9). Data, crises, and a controversial report. *Education Week, 11*, 25.

Posner, R. A. (2001). *Public intellectuals: A study of decline*. Cambridge, MA: Harvard University Press.

Postman, N., & Weingartner, C. (1973). *The school book*. New York: Delacorte.

Pounder, D., Reitzug, U., & Young, M. (2002). Rethinking the professional development of school leaders. In J. Murphy (Ed.), *The educational leadership challenge: Redefining leadership for the 21st century*. 101st Yearbook, National Society for the Study of Education, Part 1, pp. 261–288. Chicago: University of Chicago Press.

Powell, A. G., Farrar, E., & Cohen, D. K. (1985). *The shopping mall high school*. Boston: Houghton Mifflin.

Prawat, R. S. (1989). Promoting access to knowledge, strategy, and disposition in students. *Review of Educational Research, 59*, 1–41.

Prawat, R. S. (1992). Teachers' beliefs about teaching: A constructivist perspective. *American Journal of Education, 100*, 354–395.

Prawat, R. S. (1993). The value of ideas: Problems versus possibilities in learning. *Educational Researcher, 22* (6), 5–14.

Presseisen, B. Z. (1985). *Unlearned lessons: Current and past reforms for school improvement*. Philadelphia: Falmer Press.

Purnell, S., & Hill, P. (1992). *Time for reform*. Santa Monica, CA: RAND Corporation.

Purnick, J. (2001, January 18). School dollars can expand young minds. *New York Times*, B1.

RAND Institute on Education and Training. (1992, October). Getting better schools. *Policy Brief*.

Raths, L. (1938). Some evaluations of the trip. *Educational Research Bulletin, 17*, 189–208.

Ravitch, D. (1983). *The troubled crusade*. New York: Basic Books.

Ravitch, D. (1987). *The revisionists revised*. New York: Basic Books.

Ravitch, D. (2000). *Left back: A century of failed school reforms*. New York: Simon & Schuster.

Ravitch, D. (2003). The language police: How pressure groups restrict what children learn. New York: Knopf.

Ravitch, D., & Finn, C. E., Jr. (1987). *What do our 17-year-olds know?* New York: Harper.

Ray, H. W. (1972). *The office of economic opportunity experiment in educational performance contracting*. Columbus, OH: Battelle Memorial Institute.

Redefer, F. L. (1949). Resolution, reactions, and reminiscences. *Progressive Education, 26*, 189.

Redefer, F. L. (1950). The Eight-Year Study... after eight years. *Progressive Education, 28*, 33–36.

Reese, W. J. (2001). The origins of progressive education. *History of Education Quarterly, 41* (1), 1–24.

Rehberg, R. A., & Rosenthal, E. R. (1978). *Class and merit in the American high school*. New York: Longman.

Reich, R. (1992). *The work of nations*. New York: Knopf.

Reid, W. A. (1988). The technological society and the concept of general education. In I. Westbury & A. Purvis (Eds.), *Cultural literacy and the idea of general education*. 87th Yearbook, National Society for the Study of Education, Part 2, pp. 115–131. Chicago: University of Chicago Press.

Remmers, H. H. (Ed.). (1963). *Antidemocratic attitudes in American schools*. Evanston, IL: Northwestern University Press.

Resnick, L. B. (1987). *Education and learning to think*. Washington, DC: National Research Council, National Academy Press.

Reutter, E. E., Jr. (1980). *The schools and the law*, 4th ed. Dobbs Ferry, NY: Oceana Publications.

Rhoades, K., & Madaus, G. (2003). *Errors in standardized tests: A systematic problem*. Chestnut Hill, MA: Center for the Study of Testing, Evaluation and Educational Policy, Boston College.

Rice, J. M. (1893). *The Public School System of the United States.* New York: Century.

Richardson, V. (Ed.). (2001). *Handbook of research on teaching* (4th ed.). Washington, DC: American Educational Research Association.

Richardson, V. (1994a). Conducting research on practice. *Educational Researcher, 23* (5), 5–10.

Richardson, V. (1994b). Teacher inquiry as professional staff development. In S. Hollingsworth & H. Sockett (Eds.), *Teacher research and educational reform.* 93rd Yearbook, National Society for the Study of Education, Part 1, pp. 186–203. Chicago: University of Chicago Press.

Richmond, W. K. (1971). *The school curriculum.* London: Methuen.

Rickover, H. G. (1958, November). European vs. American secondary schools. *Phi Delta Kappan, 40,* 61.

Rickover, H. S. (1959). *Education and freedom.* New York: Dutton.

Rickover, H. B. (1963). *American education—A national failure.* New York: Dutton.

Robinson, D. W. (1983). *Patriotism and economic control: The censure of Harold Rugg.* Unpublished doctoral dissertation, Rutgers University, New Brunswich, NJ.

Rogers, M. F. (1987). Confessions of a reformed textbook junkie. *Chronicle of Higher Education, 33,* 36–37.

Rose, L. C., & Gallup, A. M. (2003). The 35th annual Phi Delta Kappa/Gallup poll of the public's attitudes toward the public schools. *Phi Delta Kappan, 85,* 41–52.

Rose, L. C., & Gallup, A. M. (2004). The 36th annual Phi Delta Kappa/Gallup poll of the public's attitude toward public schools. *Phi Delta Kappan, 86*(1), 41–56.

Rosenberg, A. J. (1973, February). Educational existentialism and the Sudbury Valley School. *Educational Leadership. 30,* 479–480.

Ross, E. A. (1901). *Social control.* New York: Macmillan.

Roszak, T. (1969). *The making of a counter culture.* New York: Doubleday.

Roszak, T. (1972). *Where the wasteland ends.* New York: Doubleday.

Rothberg, I. (1991). Myths in international comparisons of science and mathematics achievement. *The Bridge, 3–10.*

Rothman, R. (1993, March 17). Study urges 'learning communities' to address isolation of teachers. *Education Week, 12,* 1, 25.

Rousseau, J. J. (1911). *Émile.* London: Dent. (Originally published 1762.)

Rowland, M. (1993, April 25). A spurt in new jobs for 'old pros.' *New York Times*, p. F18.

Rugg, H. O. (1927a). An adventure in understanding. In G. M. Whipple (Ed.), *The foundations of curriculum-making.* 26th Yearbook, National Society for the Study of Education, Part 2, pp. 1–8. Bloomington, IL: Public School Publishing.

Rugg, H. O. (1927b). Foreword. In G. M. Whipple (Ed.), *Curriculum-making: Past and present.* 26th Yearbook, National Society for the Study of Education, Part 1, pp. x–xiv. Bloomington, IL: Public School Publishing.

Rugg, H. O. (1947). *Foundations for American education.* New York: World Book.

Rugg, H. O., & Counts, G. S. (1927). A critical appraisal of current methods of curriculum-making. In G. M. Whipple (Ed.), *Curriculum-making: Past and present.* 26th Yearbook, National Society for the Study of Education, Part 1, pp. 425–447. Bloomington, IL: Public School Publishing.

Rugg, H. O., & Shumaker, A. (1969). *The child-centered school.* New York: Arno Press and *The New York Times.* (Originally published by World Books in 1928.)

Rury, J. L. (2002). Democracy's high school? Social change and American education in the post-Conant era. *American Educational Research Journal, 39,* 307–336.

Russell, E. W. (1973). *Soil conditions and plant growth* (10th ed.). London: Longman.

Rutter, M., Maugham, B., Mortimore, P., & Ouston, J. (1979). *Fifteen thousand hours: Secondary schools and their effects on children.* Cambridge, MA: Harvard University Press.

Ryan, K. (1978). An interview with Lawrence A. Cremin. *Phi Delta Kappan, 60,* 112–116.

Samuelson, P. (1983). In E. C. Brown and R. M. Solow (Eds.), *Paul Samuelson and modern economic theory.* New York: McGraw-Hill, pp. 1–14.

Sarason, S. B. (1982). *The culture of the school and the problem of change,* 2nd ed. Boston: Allyn & Bacon.

Saylor, B. G., & Alexander, W. (1974). *Planning curriculum for schools.* New York: Holt.

Schaffarzick J., & Sykes, G. (Eds.). (1979). *Value conflicts and curriculum issues.* Berkeley, CA: McCutchan.

Schemo, D. J. (2002, January 9). Education bill urges emphasis on phonics as method for teaching reading. *New York Times*, p. A16.

Schemo, D. J. (2003, July 11). Questions on data cloud luster of Houston schools. *New York Times*, pp. A1, 12.

Schiefelbein, S. (1978, April 1). Confusion at Harvard: What makes an educated man? *Saturday Review, 5*, 12.

Schlesinger, A. M., Jr. (1998 rev.). *The disuniting of America: Reflections on a multicultural society*. New York: W. W. Norton.

Schmoker, M. (2004). Tipping point: From feckless reform to substantive instructional improvement. *Phi Delta Kappan, 85* (6), 424–433.

Schoenfeld, G. (2004). The American opening. *New York Times Book Review*, March 28, p. 15.

School financing formula revised in New Jersey. (1990, June 23). *New York Times*, p. 30.

Schoonmaker, F. (2001). Curriculum making, models, practices and issues: A knowledge fetish? In L. Corno (Ed.), *Education across a century: The centennial volume*. 100th Yearbook, National Society for the Study of Education, Part 1, pp. 1–33. Chicago: University Chicago Press.

Schorr, L. B. (1989). *Within our reach: Breaking the cycle of disadvantage*. New York: Anchor Books.

Schorling, R. (1938). Editorial comment. *Phi Delta Kappan, 21*, 114–116.

Schwab, J. J. (1962). The concept of the structure of a discipline. *The Educational Record, 43*(8), 197–205.

Schwab, J. J. (1964). In S. Elam (Ed.), *Education and the structure of knowledge*. Chicago: Rand McNally, pp. 4–43.

Schwab, J. J. (1969). *College curriculum and student protest*. Chicago: University of Chicago Press.

Schwab, J. J. (1970). *The practical: A language for curriculum*. Washington, DC: National Education Association.

Schwab, J. J. (1974). The concept of the structure of a discipline. In E. W. Eisner & E. Vallance (Eds.), *Conflicting conceptions of curriculum* (pp. 162–175). Berkeley, CA: McCutchan.

Scriven, M. (1964). The structure of social studies. In G. W. Ford & L. A. Pugno (Eds.), *The structure of knowledge and the curriculum*. Chicago: Rand McNally.

Segal, H. P. (1996). The American ideology of technological progress: Historical perspectives. In S. T. Kerr (Ed.), *Technology and the future of schooling*. 95th Yearbook, National Society for the Study of Education, Part 2, pp. 28–48. Chicago: University of Chicago Press.

Senesh, L. (1971). Orchestration of social sciences in the curriculum. In I. Morrisett & W. W. Stevens, Jr. (Eds.), *Social science in the schools*. New York: Holt.

Servan-Schreiber, J. J. (1967). *The American challenge*. New York: Athenium.

Sewell, W. H., Hauser, R. M., & Featherman, D. I. (Eds.). (1976). *Schooling and achievement in American society*. New York: Academic.

Shavelson, R. J. (1983). Review of research on teachers' pedagogical judgments, plans, and decisions. *Elementary School Journal, 83*, 392–413.

Shaw, G. B. (1950). *Sham education*. London: Constable.

Shepard, L. A. (2004). Curricular coherence in assessment design. In M. Wilson (Ed.), *Toward coherence between classroom assessment and accountability*. 103rd Yearbook, National Society for Study of Education, Part 2, pp. 239–249. Chicago: University of Chicago Press.

Shepard, L. A., & Graue, M. E. (1993). The morass of school readiness screening: Reserch on test use and test validity. In B. Spodek (Ed.), *Handbook of Research on the Education of Young Children*, pp. 293–305. New York: Macmillan.

Short, E. C. (1991). Setting priorities in curriculum research. *Journal of Curriculum and Supervision, 6*, 358–365.

Silberman, C. E. (1961, April 6). The remaking of American education. *Fortune, 63*, 125–131.

Silberman, C. E. (1966, August). Technology is knocking on the schoolhouse door. *Fortune, 74*, 120–122.

Silberman, C. E. (1970). *Crisis in the classroom: The remaking of American education*. New York: Random House.

Simon, H. A. (1976). *Administrative behavior*, 3rd ed. New York: Free Press.

Sizer, T. R. (1964). *Secondary schools at the turn of the century*. New Haven, CT: Yale University Press.

Sizer, T. R. (1983). High school reform: The need for inquiring. *Phi Delta Kappan, 64*(8), 679–683.

Sizer, T. R. (1984). *Horace's compromise: The dilemma of the American high school*. Boston: Houghton Mifflin.

Skinner, B. F. (1968). *The technology of teaching*. New York: Appleton.

Skinner, B. F. (1971). *Beyond freedom and dignity*. New York: Alfred A. Knopf.

Sleeter, C. E. (1995). Curriculum controversies in multicultural education. In E. Flaxman & A. H. Passow (Eds.), *Changing populations/changing schools*. 94th Yearbook, National Study for the Study of Education, Part 2, pp. 162–185. Chicago: University of Chicago Press.

Smiley, M. B. (1967). Chapter 6 in National Society for the Study of Education. *The educationally retarded and disadvantaged*. 66th Yearbook, National Study for the Study of Education, Part 1. Chicago: University of Chicago Press.

Smith, B. O., Stanley, W. O., & Shores, J. H. (1957). *Fundamentals of curriculum development* (Rev. ed.). New York: Harcourt.

Smith, E. R., & Tyler, R. W., & Evaluation Staff. (1942). *Appraising and recording student progress*. New York: Harcourt.

Smith, M. (1970). Divergent paths to educational change. In *Papers on Educational Reform*. LaSalle, IL: Open Court.

Smith, M. L. (1991). Put to the test: The effects of external testing on teachers. *Educational Researcher, 20* (5), 8–12.

Smith, M. L. (1996). *Reforming schools by reforming assessment: Consequences of the Arizona student assessment program*. Tempe: Southwest Educational Policy Studies, Arizona State University.

Smylie, M. A., Conley, S., & Marks, H. (2002). Building leadership into the roles of teachers. In J. Murphy (Ed.), *The educational leadership challenge: Redefining leadership for the 21st century*. 101st Yearbook, National Society for the Study of Education, Part 1, pp. 162–188. Chicago: University of Chicago Press.

Smylie, M. A., & Hart, A. W. (2000). School leadership for school learning and change: A human and social capital perspective. In J. Murphy & K. S. Louis (Eds.), *Handbook of Research on Educational Administration* (pp. 421–441). San Francisco: Jossey-Bass.

Snedden, D. (1920). *Vocational education*. New York: Macmillan.

Snedden, D. (1921). *Sociological determination of objectives in education*. Philadelphia: Lippincott.

Snow, C. P. (1959). *Two cultures and the scientific revolution*. New York: Cambridge University Press.

Snow, T., & Carville, J. (1993, November 2). Victory made (sort-of) easy. *New York Times*, op-ed page.

Snyder, J., Bolin, F., & Zumwalt, K. (1992). Curriculum implementation. In P. W. Jackson (Ed.), *Handbook of Research on Curriculum*, pp. 402–435. New York: Macmillan.

Sokal, A., & Bricmont, J. (1997). *Intellectual imposters*. London: Profile Books.

Solas, J. (1992). Investigating student and teacher thinking. *Review of Educational Research, 62*, 205–225.

Spady, W. G. (1971). Status, achievement, and motivation in the American high school. *School Review, 79*(5), 380–385.

Spears, H. (1946). The changing curriculum. In H. L. Caswell (Ed.), *The American high school: Its responsibility and opportunity*. Eighth Yearbook of the John Dewey Society. New York: Harper.

Spencer, D. A. (2000). Teachers' work: Yesterday, today, and tomorrow. In T. L. Good (Ed.), *American education: Yesterday, today, and tomorrow*. 99th Yearbook, National Society for the Study of Education, Part 2, pp. 53–83. Chicago: University of Chicago Press.

Spencer, H. (1860). *Education: Intellectual, moral, and physical*. New York: Appleton.

Spencer, H. (1883). *What knowledge is of most worth?* (Originally published in 1859.) In *Education: Intellectual, moral, and physical*, Ch. 1, pp. 1–96. New York: Appleton.

Spillane, J. P., & Louis, K. S. (2002). School improvement processes and practices: Professional learning for building instructional capacity. In J. Murphy (Ed.), *The educational leadership challenge: Redefining leadership for the 21st century*. 101st Yearbook, National Society for the Study of Education, Part 1, pp. 83–104. Chicago: University of Chicago Press.

Spring, J. H. (1972). *Education and the rise of the corporate state*. Boston: Beacon.

Stahl, S. A., & Miller, P. D. (1989). Whole language and language experience approaches for beginning reading: A quantitative research synthesis. *Review of Educational Research, 59* (1), 87–116.

Stake, R. E. (1991). Retrospective on the countenance of educational evaluation. In M. W. McLaughlin & D. C. Phillips (Eds.), *Evaluation and education: At quarter century*. 90th Yearbook, National Society for the Study of Education, Part 2, pp. 67–88. Chicago: University of Chicago Press.

Stanley, A. (2001, October 27). Women in authority. *New York Times*, p. B9.

Steele, W. L. (1911). *Galesburg public schools: 1861–1911*. Galesburg, IL: Cadmus Press.

Stevens, L. J., & Price, M. (1992). Meeting the challenge of educating children at risk. *Phi Delta Kappan, 74*, 18–23.

Stevenson, D. L., Kochanek, J., & Schneider, B. (1998). Making the transition from high school: Recent trends and policies. In K. Borman & B. Schneider (Eds.), *The adolescent years*. 90th Yearbook, National Society for the Study of Education, Part 1, pp. 207–225. Chicago: University of Chicago Press.

Stinchcombe, A. L. (1972, Nov. 10). The social determinants of success. *Science, 178*.

Stoddard, A. J. (1957). *Schools for tomorrow: An educator's blueprint*. New York: Fund for the Advancement of Education, Ford Foundation.

Stratemeyer, F. B., Forkner, H. L., McKim, M. G., & Passow, A. H. (1957). *Developing a curriculum for modern living*. New York: Teachers College Press.

Strickland, D. S. (1990). Emergent literacy: How children learn to read and write. *Educational Leadership, 47*(2), pp. 18–23.

Stringfield, S., & Datnow, A. (1998). Scaling up school restructuring designs in urban schools. *Education and Urban Society, 30*(3), 269–276.

Suppes, P. (1966, September). The uses of computers in education. *Scientific American, 215*, 207.

Swenson, R. M. (1988). Plagues, history and AIDS. *The American Scholar, 57*(1).

Swett, J. (1876). *History of the Public School System in California*. San Francisco: A. L. Bancroft.

Szent-Gyorgi, A. (1970). Interdisciplinary science education: A position paper. *The Science Teacher*, Supplement, *37*.

Taba, H. (1945). General techniques of curriculum planning. Ch. 5 in R. W. Tyler, Chair, *American education in the postwar period* 44th Yearbook, National Society for the Study of Education, Part 1. Chicago: University of Chicago Press.

Taba, H. (1955). *With perspective on human relations*. Washington, DC: American Council on Education.

Taba, H. (1962). *Curriculum development: Theory and practice*. New York: Harcourt.

Tanner, D. (1971). *Secondary curriculum: Theory and development*. New York: Macmillan.

Tanner, D. (1973). Performance contracting: Contrivance of the industrial-government-education complex. *Intellect, 101*, 361–365.

Tanner, D. (1974, January). The retreat from education—For other people's children. *Intellect, 102*(2354), 222–225.

Tanner, D. (1979, September). Splitting up the school system. *Phi Delta Kappan, 61*(2), 92–97.

Tanner, D. (1983a). Knowledge divided against itself. *Bulletin of the Atomic Scientists, 39*(3), 34–38.

Tanner, D. (1983b, February 12). An educational speedup appropriate for some. *New York Times*, 21.

Tanner, D. (1983c, August 17). What a book can do that a computer can't. *New York Times*, p. A22.

Tanner, D. (1986). Are reforms like swinging pendulums? In H. J. Walberg & J. W. Keefe (Eds.), *Rethinking reform* (pp. 5–17). Reston, VA: National Association of Secondary School Principals.

Tanner, D. (1989). A brief historical perspective of the struggle for an integrative curriculum. *Educational Horizons, 68*, 6–11.

Tanner, D. (1990). The curriculum frontier. In W. G. Wraga & P. S. Hlebowitsh (Eds.), Science, technology, and the social studies, section, *Social Education, 54*, 195–197.

Tanner, D. (1991). *Crusade for democracy: Progressive education at the crossroads*. Albany: State University of New York Press.

Tanner, D. (1993a). A nation "truly" at risk. *Phi Delta Kappan, 75*, 288–297.

Tanner, D. (1993b). Dewey decimated, Dewey rehabilitated. Paper presented at the 1993 Annual Meeting of the American Educational Research Association, Atlanta, GA.

Tanner, D. (1996). The structure and function of the American secondary school: A national survey. In P. S. Hlebowitsh & W. G. Wraga, *Annual review of research for school leaders*. National Association of Secondary School Principals. New York: Scholastic.

Tanner, D. (1997, Spring). Standards, standards: High and low. *Educational Horizons, 75*, 115–120.

Tanner, D. (1998, January). The social consequences of bad research. *Phi Delta Kappan, 79*(5), 344–349.

Tanner, D. (1999). The textbook controversies. In M. Early & K. J. Rehage (Eds.), *Issues in curriculum*. 98th Yearbook, National Society for the Study of Education, Part 2, pp. 115–140. Chicago: University of Chicago Press.

Tanner, D. (2000a). The 'scold war': Persistent attacks on America's schools. *Phi Delta Kappan, 81* (1), 188–202.

Tanner, D. (2000b). Manufacturing problems and selling solutions: How to succeed in the education business without really educating. *Phi Delta Kappan, 82* (5), 188–202.

Tanner, D. (2002). *Crusade for democracy: Progressive education at the crossroads.* Albany: State University of New York Press.

Tanner, D. (2005). The mind's eye. In P. B. Uhrmacher & J. Mathews (Eds.). *Intricate Palette.* Upper Saddle River NJ: Merrill/Prentice Hall.

Tanner, D., & Lachica, T. (1967). *Discovering and developing the college potential of high school youth.* New York: Office of Research and Evaluation, City University of New York.

Tanner, D., & Tanner, L. (1987). *Supervision in education: Problems and practices.* New York: Macmillan.

Tanner, D., & Tanner, L. N. (1990). *History of the school curriculum.* New York: Macmillan.

Tanner, L. N. (1986). Contributions of the eight-year study. *Journal of Thought, 21,* 33–35.

Tanner, L. N. (1988). The path not taken: Dewey's model of inquiry. *Curriculum inquiry, 18,* 471–479.

Tanner, L. N. (1997). *Dewey's laboratory school: Lessons for today.* New York: Teachers College Press.

Tanner, L. N. (2000). Critical issues in curriculum revisited. *The Educational Forum, 65,* 16–21.

Tanner, L., & Tanner, D. (1973, October). News notes. *Educational Leadership, 31* (1), 87–95.

Tanner, L. N., & Tanner, D. (1987). Environmentalism in American pedagogy: The legacy of Lester Ward. *Teachers College Record, 88,* 537–547.

Task Force on Education for Economic Growth. (1983). *Action for excellence.* Denver: Education Commission of the States.

Taylor, H. E. (Ed.). (1968). *The humanities and the schools.* New York: Citation.

Tewel, K. J. (1989). Collaborative supervision Theory into practice. *NASSP Bulletin, 73,* 74–83.

Thomas, G. (1992). Learning for the 21st century. *Thrust for Educational Leadership, 22,* 8–9.

Thomson, V. (1938). In R. Weeks (Ed.), *A correlated curriculum.* Report of the National Council of Teachers of English. New York: Appleton.

Thorndike, E. L. (1906). *The principles of teaching.* New York: Seiler.

Thorndike, E. L. (1924). Mental discipline in high school studies. *Journal of Educational Psychology, 15,* 1–22, 98.

Thorndike, E. L., & Woodworth, R. S. (1901). The influence of improvement in one mental function upon efficiency of other functions. *Psychological Review, 8,* 247–261, 384–395, 553–564.

Thornton, S. J. (2001). Legitimacy in the social studies curriculum. In L. Corno (Ed.), *Education across a century: The centennial volume.* 100th Yearbook, National Society for the Study of Education, Part 1, pp. 185–204. Chicago: University of Chicago Press.

Tikunoff, W. J., Ward, B., & Griffin, G. A. (1979). *Interactive research and development on teaching study: Final report.* San Francisco: Far West Laboratory for Educational Research and Development.

Toffler, A. (Ed.). (1974). *Learning for tomorrow. Role of the future in education.* New York: Random House.

Tompkins, R. B. (2003, March 26). Leaving rural children behind. *Education Week, 22,* 44, 30.

Trump, J. L., & Vars, G. F. (1976). How is school learning organized?. In W. Van Til (Chapter 9), *Issues in secondary education.* 75th Yearbook, National Society for the Study of Education, Part 2. Chicago: University of Chicago Press.

Tussman, J. (1969). *Experiment at Berkeley.* New York: Oxford University Press.

Tyler, R. W. (1949). *Basic principles of curriculum and instruction.* Chicago: University of Chicago Press.

Tyler, R. W. (1957). *The Curriculum—then and now.* Proceedings of the 1956 Conference on Testing Problems. Princeton, NJ: Educational Testing Service.

Tyler, R. W. (1971). Curriculum development in the twenties and thirties. In R. M. McClure (Ed.), *The curriculum: Retrospect and prospect.* 70th Yearbook, National Society for the Study of Education, Part 1, pp. 26–44. Chicago: University of Chicago Press.

Tyler, R. W. (1973). The father of behavioral objectives criticizes them: An interview. *Phi Delta Kappan, 55* (1), 55–57.

Tyler, R. W. (1975). Accountability and teacher performance: Self-directed and external-directed professional improvement. In L. Rubin (Ed.), *The in-service education of teachers.* Boston: Allyn & Bacon.

Tyler, R. W. (1986). Recollections of fifty years of work in curriculum. *Journal of Thought, 21* (1), 70–74.

Tyler, R. W. (1987). Book reviews. *Teachers College Record, 88,* 604–608.

Tyler, R. W. (1988). Progress in dealing with curriculum problems. In L. Tanner (Ed.), *Critical issues in curriculum.* 87th Yearbook, National Society for the Study of Education, Part 1, pp. 267–276. Chicago: University of Chicago Press.

Tyler, R. W. (1991). General statement on program evaluation. In M. W. McLaughlin & D. C. Phillips (Eds.), *Evaluation and education: At quarter century.* 90th Yearbook, National Society for the Study of Education, Part 2, pp. 3–17. Chicago: University of Chicago Press.

United Nations Development Program. (1992). *Human development report.* New York: Oxford University Press.

U.S. Department of Education. (1991). *America 2000: An education strategy. Sourcebook.* Washington, DC: The Department.

U.S. Office of Education Mission. (1959). *Soviet commitment to education.* Report of First Official Mission. Washington, DC: Author.

U.S. Office of Education. (1967). *O101—Highlighting the progress of American education.* Washington, DC: Author.

U.S. Senate Committee on Labor and Public Welfare, 85th Congress. (1958). *Science and education for national defense.* Washington, DC: U.S. Government Printing Office.

U.S. Senate Committee on Labor and Public Welfare and U.S. House Committee on Education and Labor. (1969). *Review of economic opportunity programs.* Washington, DC: Superintendent of Documents.

U.S. Statutes at Large. (2002). No Child Left Behind Act of 2001. Public Labor 107–110, Vol. 115.

Usiskin, Z. (1993). Lessons from the Chicago mathematics project. *Educational Leadership, 50* (8), 14–18.

Vacca, R. T., & Vacca, J. L. (2002). *Content area reading* (7th ed.). Boston: Allyn & Bacon.

Vaihinger, H. (1924). *The philosophy of "as if": A system of the theoretical, practical and religious fictions of mankind.* London: Routledge & Kegan Paul.

Van Doren, Mark. (1959). *Liberal education.* Boston: Beacon.

Vars, G. F. (1991). Integrated curriculum in historical perspective. *Educational Leadership, 49,* 14–15.

Veblen, T. (1969; originally published 1919). *The vested interests and the common man.* New York: Capricorn.

Verhovek, S. H. (1991, June 20). A New York panel urges emphasizing minority cultures. *New York Times,* p. A14.

Viadero, D. (1992, April 28). Parent discontent fuels spirited school board races in Princeton. *Education Week, 11,* 1, 13.

Viadero, D. (1993, March 10). The coherent curriculum. *Education Week, 12,* 12.

von Glaserfeld, E. (1995). *Radical constructivism: A way of knowing and learning.* Washington, DC: Falmer Press.

von Neumann, J. (1947*).* In Heyward, R. B. (Ed.), *The works of the mind.* Chicago: University of Chicago Press.

Vygotsky, L. S. (1978). *Mind in society: The development of higher psychological processes.* Cambridge, MA: Harvard University Press.

Wagner, T. (2001). Leadership for learning: An action theory of school change. *Phi Delta Kappan, 82,* 378–383.

Walker, D. (1975). The curriculum field in formation: A review of the twenty-sixth yearbook, National Society for the Study of Education. *Curriculum Theory Network, 4,* 263–280.

Walsh, J. (1973). A conversation with Eugene Wigner. *Science, 181,* 533.

Walsh, M. (2002, May 22). Edison reels amid flurry of bad news. *Education Week, 21,* 1, 16.

Ward, F. C., et al. (1950). *The idea and practice of general education.* Chicago: University of Chicago Press.

Ward, L. F. (1883). *Dynamic sociology or applied social science.* New York: D. Appleton.

Ward, L. F. (1886). Broadening the way to success. *The Forum, 2,* 340–350.

Ward, L. F. (1909). Education and progress. *The "Plebs" Magazine, 1,* 218–221, 241–244.

Ward, L. F. (1911). *Dynamic sociology or applied social science.* New York: D. Appleton. Originally published 1883.

Washburne, C. W. (1927). The philosophy of the Winnetka curriculum. In G. M. Whipple (Ed.), *Curriculum-making: Past and present.* 26th Yearbook, National Society for the Study of Education, Part 1, pp. 219–228. Bloomington, IL: Public School Publishing.

Washburne, C. W., & Marland, S. P., Jr. (1963). *Winnetka: The history and significance of an educational experiment.* Englewood Cliffs, NJ: Prentice Hall.

Watley, D. J., & Nichols, R. C. (1969). *Career decisions of talented youth: Trends over the past decade.* Evanston, IL: National Merit Scholarship Corporation.

Watson, J. D. (1969). *The double helix.* New York: Atheneum.

Webb, N., Nemer, K., Chizhik, A., & Segrue, B. (1998). Equity issues in collaborative group assessment: Group composition and performance. *American Educational Research Journal, 35,* 607–651.

Weber, B. (2004, July 8). Fewer noses stuck in books in America, survey finds. *New York Times,* E1, 4.

Weinberg, A. M. (1967). *Reflections on big science.* Cambridge, MA: M.I.T. Press.

Weingarten, R. (2003, January 15). Writing a curriculum—It's union work. *Education Week, 22,* 30–31.

Weiss, J. O. (1989). *Education and the cult of efficiency revisited.* Unpublished doctoral dissertation. Rutgers University, New Brunswick, NJ.

Welch, W. W. (1968). The impact of national curriculum projects: The need for accurate assessment. *School Science and Mathematics, 68,* 225–234.

Wesley, E. B. (1957). *NEA: The first hundred years.* New York: Harper.

Wesman, A. (1945). A study of transfer of training from high school subjects to intelligence. *Teachers College Record, 46,* 391–393.

Westbrook, R. B. (1991). *John Dewey and American democracy.* Ithaca, NY: Cornell University Press.

Westheimer, J., & Kahne, J. (Eds.). (2003). Democracy and civic engagement. Special section. *Phi Delta Kappan, 85,* 9–40, 57–67.

Whipple, G. M., and Miller, H. L. (Eds.). (1919). *The Professional Preparation of High-School Teachers.* 18th Yearbook, National Society for the Study of Education, Part 1. Bloomington, IL: Public School Publishing.

Whitehead, A. N. (1925). *Science in the modern world.* Lowell Lectures. New York: Free Press.

Whitehead, A. N. (1929a). *The aims of education and other essays.* New York: Macmillan.

Whitehead, A. N. (1929b). *The function of reason.* Princeton, NJ: Princeton University Press.

Whitehead, A. N. (1947). *Essays in Science.* New York: Philosophical Library.

Whitehead, A. N. (1968). Dangers of specialization. In U.S. Senate Committee on Government Operations, *Specialists and generalists.* Washington, DC: U.S. Government Printing Office.

Whitener, S. (1974). *Patterns of high school studies and college achievement.* Unpublished doctoral dissertation, Rutgers University, Brunswick, NJ.

Whitford, B. L., & Metcalf-Turner, P. (1999). Of promises and unresolved puzzles: Reforming teacher education with professional development schools. In G. A. Griffin (Ed.), *The education of teachers.* 98th Yearbook, National Society for the Study of Education, Part 1, pp. 257–278. Chicago: University of Chicago Press.

Whittington, D. (1991, Winter). What have 17-year-olds known in the past? *American Educational Research Journal, 28* (4), 778.

Wickersham, J. P. (1886). *A history of education in Pennsylvania.* Lancaster, PA: Inquirer.

Wickersham, J. P. (1969). *A history of education in Pennsylvania.* New York: Arno Press and *The New York Times.* Originally published by Inquirer in 1886.

Wiener, N. (1964). *God & Golem, Inc.* Cambridge, MA: M.I.T. Press.

Wiggins, G. (1993, November). Assessment: Authenticity, context, and validity. *Phi Delta Kappan, 75* (3), 200–214.

Williams. G. (1980). *Western Reserve's experiment in medical education and its outcome.* New York: Oxford University Press.

Williams, L. (1992, June 17). Other voices. *Education Week, 11,* 13.

Willig, A. C., & Ramirez, J. D. (1993). Ch. 3 in M. B. Arias & U. Casanova (Eds.), *Bilingual education: Politics, practice, and research.* 92nd Yearbook, National Society for the Study of Education, Part 2, pp. 65–87. Chicago: University of Chicago Press.

Wilms, W. W. (2003). Altering the structure and culture of American public schools. *Phi Delta Kappan, 84,* 606–615.

Wilson, E. O. (1998, March). Back from chaos. *Atlantic Monthly, 281* (3), 58–62.

Wilson, E. O. (1999). *The diversity of life* (2nd ed.). New York: W. W. Norton.

Wilson, E. O. (2000). *Sociobiology: The new synthesis* (2nd ed.). Cambridge, MA: Harvard University Press.

Wilson, S. M., Peterson, P. L., Ball, D. L., & Cohen, D. K. (1996). Learning by all. *Phi Delta Kappan, 77* (7), 468–477.

Wilson, W. J. (1996). *When work disappears: The world of the new urban poor.* New York: Knopf.

Winerip, M. (2003, April 9). When a student prefers learning of the hands-on variety. *New York Times,* p. D9.

Winerip, M. (2004, February 4). Principal sees mistake in plan to hold back 3rd graders. *New York Times*, p. B9.

Wirt, J. G. (1991). A new federal law on vocational education: Will reform follow? *Phi Delta Kappan, 72*, 425–433.

Wirth, A. G. (1966). John Dewey as educator: His design for work in education 1894–1904. New York Wiley.

Wirth, A. G. (1972). *Education in the technological society*. Scranton, AP: Intext.

Witnitsky, N., Stoddard, T., & O'Keefe, P. (1992). Great expectations: Emergent professional development schools. *Journal of Teacher Education, 43*, 3–18.

Wittrock, M. C. (Ed.). (1986). *Handbook of research on teaching* (3rd ed.). New York: Macmillan.

"Wizard of quiz." (1957, February 11). *Time, 69*, 46.

Wood, G. H. (1990). Teaching for democracy. *Educational Leadership, 48* (4), 32–37.

Woodring, P. (1964). Introduction. In R. W. Heath (Ed.), *New curricula* (pp. 1–8). New York: Harper.

Worth, R. F., & Hartocollis, A. (2002, June 30). Johnny can read, but well enough to vote? *New York Times*, pp. B1, 24.

Wraga, W. (1994). *Democracy's high school: The comprehensive high school and educational reform in the United States*. Lanham, MD: University Press of America.

Wraga, W. G. (1996). A century of interdisciplinary curricula in American schools. In P. S. Hlebowitsh & W. G. Wraga (Eds.), *Annual review of research for school leaders* (pp. 117–145). New York: Scholastic.

Wraga, W. G. (2001). Left out: The villainization of progressive education in the United States. *Educational Researcher, 30*, 34–39.

Wright, G. S. (1949). *Core curriculum in public high schools: An inquiry into practices*. Washington, DC: U.S. Office of Education.

Wright, G. S. (1950). *Core curriculum in public high schools*. Washington, DC: U.S. Office of Education.

Wright, G. S. (1952). *Core curriculum development: Problems and practices*. Washington, DC: U.S. Office of Education.

Wright, G. S. (1958, 1962). *Block-time classes and the core program in the junior high school*. Washington, DC: U.S. Office of Education.

Wright, G. S. (1963). *The core program: Unpublished research*. Washington, DC: U.S. Office of Education.

Wright, G. S., & Greer, E. S. (1963). *The junior high school*. Washington, DC: U.S. Office of Education.

Wrightstone, J. W. (1935). *Appraisal of newer practices in selected public schools*. New York: Teachers College Press.

Wurman, R. S., Levy, A., & Katz, J. (1972). *The nature of recreation: A handbook in honor of Frederick Law Olmsted, using examples of his work*. Cambridge, MA: M.I.T. Press.

Xue, Y., & Meisels, S. J. (2004, Spring). *American Educational Research Journal, 41* (1), 191–229.

Yocum, A. D. (1913). *Culture, discipline and democracy*. Philadelphia: Sower.

Young, E. F. (1906). *Isolation in the school*. Chicago: University of Chicago Press.

Young, R. W. (1966). *Relationship between business and industrial courses in high school with academic achievement in college*. Unpublished doctoral dissertation, University of Michigan, Lansing, MI.

Zacharias, J. R., & White, S. (1964). The requirements for major curriculum revision. In R. W. Heath (Ed.), *New curricula*. New York: Harper, 1964, 68–81.

Zhao, Y., & Frank, K. A. (2003, Winter). Factors affecting technology use in schools: An ecological perspective. *American Educational Research Journal, 40* (4), 807–840.

Zilversmit, A. (1993). *Changing schools: Progressive education theory and practice, 1930–1960*. Chicago: University of Chicago Press.

Zirbes, L. (1925). *Practice exercises and checks on silent reading in the primary grades*. New York: Lincoln School of Teachers College.

Zirbes, L. (1959). *Spurs to creative teaching*. New York: Putnam.

Zumwalt, K. (1988). Are we improving or undermining teaching? In L. Tanner (Ed.), *Critical issues in curriculum*. 87th Yearbook, National Society for the Study of Education, Part 1, pp. 148–174. Chicago: University of Chicago Press.

ISBN 0-13-086473-0

90000>

9 780130 864734